The Cunning Man's Handbook
The Practice of English Folk Magic, 1550-1900

The Cunning Man's Handbook

Jim Baker

Dedicated to

Alex and Maxine

Francis and Isabel

Peg, Lucie, Jon and Phinneas

Published by *Avalonia*
BM Avalonia
London
WC1N 3XX
England, UK
www.avaloniabooks.co.uk

The Cunning Man's Handbook
Copyright © 2013 Jim Baker
All rights reserved.

First Edition, July 2014
ISBN 978-1-905297-68-9

Cover image from Sloane MS 3851. With the kind permission of the British Library in London.

Design by *Satori*, for Avalonia.

British Library Cataloguing in Publication Data. A catalogue record for this book is available from the British Library.

All rights reserved. No part of this publication may be reproduced or utilised in any form or by any means, electronic or mechanical, including photocopying, microfilm, recording, or by any information storage and retrieval system, or used in another book, without written permission from the authors.

Acknowledgements

I would like to thank the following persons for their support and encouragement in the composition of this book: Bernie and Lisa Sampson, Bob and Lyn Murphy, Patrice Hatcher, Chas Clifton, Jimahl, Karagan, Morven, Aud, and in particular, David Rankine, all of whom read parts of the work-in-progress and made favourable comments; Joseph H. Peterson, who graciously allowed me to use some of his digital transcriptions from the Esoteric Archives (www.esotericarchives.com) and saved me from a lot of redundant typing, and again, David Rankine for permission to include extensive quotes from *The Grimoire of Arthur Gauntlet* (Avalonia, 2011) and *The Book of Treasure Spirits* (Avalonia, 2009).

Finally I want to thank Sorita d'Este for accepting the (lengthy) manuscript for publication by Avalonia, and my wife Peg, who although she has no interest in the subject area, actively encouraged me in the composition of *The Cunning Man's Handbook*.

The Cunning Man's Handbook

The Practice of English Folk Magic, 1550-1900

Jim Baker

PUBLISHED BY AVALONIA
WWW.AVALONIABOOKS.CO.UK

Table of Contents

A TREASURE TROVE OF CUNNING, FOREWORD BY DAVID RANKINE 10
A WARNING TO THE CURIOUS, BY JIM BAKER 12

INTRODUCTION 15
ROMANCING THE SPIRITUS MUNDI – PRACTICAL MAGIC IN ENGLISH CULTURE 27
    SECTION ONE: HOW COULD MAGIC BE SUPPOSED TO WORK? 27
    MAGIC IN THE COSMIC PLAN 34
    THE FUNCTION OF ASTRAL IMPELLATIONS 39
    THE MAGICAL ACT 42
    SECTION TWO: ON SOULS, SPIRITS ND PHANTASMS 44
    SECTION THREE: MAGICAL EVOLUTION – HOW MAGNETISM CHALLENGED THE WORLD SOUL ... 47
UNDERSTANDING THE CUNNING FOLK 52
    THE CUNNING FOLK AND THEIR WORLD 52
    WHO WERE THE CUNNING FOLK? 54
    VISITING THE CUNNING FOLK. 56
DIVINATION, PART I 94
DIVINATION, PART II 134
GEOMANCY 161
DREAMS NATURAL, DEMONIC AND DIVINE 196
CHARMS I — CHARMS, SPELLS, AND CURSES 231
CHARMS II - PROTECTION, COUNTER-WITCHERY, THEFT AND LOVE 276
FOLK OR NON-COMPUTATIONAL ASTROLOGY 316
ASTROLOGY IN MAGIC AND THEORY 339
JUDICIAL ASTROLOGY 364
CONJURATION, PART I 412
CONJURATION, PART II 457
TREASURE HUNTING 497
CONCLUSION 517

APPENDICES
DEFINING ILLICIT MAGIC (FACULTY OF PARIS 1398) 526
"WHITE WITCHES: AN APOLOGY TO LOUISE HUEBNER" 533

BIBLIOGRAPHY 545
INDEX 550

FOREWORD BY DAVID RANKINE

A Treasure Trove of Cunning

As an author and researcher I always find immense pleasure in reading another author's work when it has been finely crafted with love and attention to detail, and all the more so when it is on a topic dear to my heart. *The Cunning Man's Handbook* is such a book, a superb study which goes further into the exploration of the practices and world-view of Cunning Folk than any previous work in the field.

When Jim Baker first contacted me to ask for permission to use extracts from some of the manuscripts I have worked on and published (*The Grimoire of Arthur Gauntlet* and *The Book of Treasure Spirits*), I was intrigued. I knew such a work would require an immense amount of research to do it justice. During the correspondence between us that developed on the topic, Jim asked me if I would critique his finished manuscript, an offer I was delighted to accept.

Circumstances were clearly in our favour, as he was due to visit London from his home in the United States at this time. We arranged to meet up at Atlantis Bookshop in Bloomsbury, the birthplace of numerous significant esoteric books and events since its opening in 1922, and retired to a nearby café to spend several hours talking about his work, and the many years of research and study that it had entailed. This most enjoyable meeting ended with Jim handing me an electronic copy of the draft of his book to read.

As I read *The Cunning Man's Handbook*, I found myself in the enviable position of struggling to find anything I disagreed with or felt could be improved. Reading through the chapters it was clear that here was a masterpiece of the art, not only bringing the Cunning Folk and their practices to life, but also contextualising them by exploring the social and cultural milieu of the time, as well as all the relevant theological and religious issues which pervaded. His conclusions might upset some people, emphatically demonstrating the entirely Christian worldview of Cunning practices, which nevertheless remained liminal due to their often unsanctified interpretation and presentation of Christian magic.

This book is a very large tome, of necessity, to include so much source material from so many period sources to illustrate the range of Cunning practices. Divination was one of the main functions performed by Cunning Folk, and as such the techniques used are covered in detail, including geomancy, dream interpretation, astrology and various forms of written oracle. In some respects what is absent from the practices of the Cunning Folk is as interesting as what is present, and the author explores the reasons for this as he systematically works through the centuries of source material and practices.

The other main practices of Cunning Folk, those of conjuration, charms, healing and treasure-hunting, are studied with the same thorough attention and contextualisation. Although most of the book is focused on practices in England, there are numerous digressions into American sources and practices as well, appropriately expanding the scope of the material to what was then the other main English-speaking part of the world.

In setting out to present a comprehensive elucidation of what is known about the actual practices of English-speaking Cunning Folk during the period from 1550-1900, Jim Baker set himself a momentous task. He succeeded admirably, and as a result the reader, working through this book will gain many new insights into not just Cunning practices, but also the theory, theology and practice of Christian magic over a period of centuries. The book dispels notions that have arisen through popular romantic views not based in historical fact, concentrating rather on what can be proved and demonstrated. Prepare to enter the world of the Cunning Folk, and be amazed, educated and illuminated!

David Rankine

Glastonbury, 17 April 2014

PREFACE

A Warning to the Curious

Having laboured in a career in historical scholarship, it was my intent to have fun with the subject of this book – a survey of the documented magical resources of English-speaking Cunning Folk – and while maintaining historical accuracy, throw off the shackles of academic composition such as compulsive footnoting, overtly technical language and submissive attention to the accepted opinions of experts in the field (scholarly or occult). I found this was harder that I had thought. Habits of a lifetime become pretty ingrained, and while endeavouring to keep the tone light and personal, I found I wasn't ready to skip supporting quotes, detailed source notes and abstruse terminology where it conveyed the meaning I had in mind better than any simplification could. The result isn't quite the popularly accessible book I once had in mind, therefore, and for that reason, I've included this cautionary preface.

The basis of this book are selections taken from the magical resources – primarily those that appeared in print – that were available to average (or advanced) Cunning Folk between 1550 and 1900. I have gone to some pains to emulate the context, style and format of the publications in which they appeared, as I believe it is important to present the selections as far as possible as they were originally presented. This includes most original spellings and typographical idiosyncrasies – except the long "s" (ſ), which has not been used because of the extreme number of substitutions that would have called for, and also contractions indicated by a macron over a letter (as "ā") indicating a contraction that omits an "m" or "n" are omitted where it is another "m" or "n" with a micron – there not being digital characters generally available for those letters. Page breaks within selections are indicated by forward slashes (/) except where slashes are found in the original text. Words divided between pages are usually given as whole words on the second page. My comments, omissions and clarifications within quotations are enclosed in square brackets ([]), except where curly brackets ({}) are used when square brackets were used in the original text. I have omitted spaces between the end of words and colons or semi-colons, and also paragraph indentations, which don't work with tabs in tables. Some original typographical elements could not be reproduced at all (like David Rankine's use of bold lettering to represent the original rubrics – red-coloured lettering – in his edition of the Arthur Gauntlet manuscript), but in general what you'll see reflects impression made by the typefaces (except for entire segments originally in black letter) and styles of the original text. I have also used a hybrid citation approach that combines in-text citations for sources with more than a single reference, with footnotes for single references, to avoid the need for a more cumbersome bibliography.

I have tried to ensure that each selection be as complete as possible so that the action involved can be fully understood. In certain cases involving very lengthy and complex systems such as astrology or conjuration, this was not always practical but there should still be enough information to understand the particular example if not the entire theoretical context. Similarly, in other instances, there are so many different possible examples – of charms in particular – that only a small if carefully chosen representative number could be included. Also, the source of each entry needed to be clearly identified so that readers could consult the originals if they wanted to examine the context or additional subject matter.

This isn't just a compilation of primary sources, however. Part of my interest in the subject lies in how its (usually unspoken or even never considered) theoretical constructs could be explained, and how – and why – they changed over time. I couldn't find any satisfactory existing analysis that answered the questions I posed, so I have constructed my own. As this analysis is both derivative and speculative, I cannot claim any particular historical authority for it, although I do believe it does offer a plausible description of the magical subculture and its evolution. As some readers are likely to find this contentious, I should also mention a few of the other potentially controversial premises on which the study is based.

The theoretical basis (or perhaps bases) for magic today is considerably different from that of the past, so to understand the Cunning Folk, I believe we need to approach the subject from their point of reference, not our own. This necessitates the setting aside of certain modern opinions about magic, and calls for awareness of the fact that the Cunning Folk didn't share our cultural opinions and judgments but inhabited an essentially foreign culture, albeit one out of which we today have evolved. For example, the modern view of "nature" as an essentially benign and cherished context for living stands in stark contrast to the anxiety with which our ancestors viewed the wilderness and the potential dangers outside of the tenuous safety of home and hearth. I realize that even suggesting such a thing will outrage many readers, for whom the conviction that country folk in historical times lived in comfortable harmony with and even worshiped the natural world is sacrosanct, but it cannot be avoided if historical accuracy is to be maintained. How the cultural changes alluded to above came about is discussed in the following chapter, but I must first identify certain anachronistic elements common to modern occultism that did not exist as concepts or practices under the old world view.

Firstly, we must discard some historical assumptions implicit in Wicca – and "Trad Witchcraft" as well – as accurately defining what "white witches" were doing before the 20th century. It will be objected by some that English magical practice wasn't limited to the essentially Christian system described here, but that a parallel underground inheritance of pagan magic existed as well and employed in secret (so secret that its very existence wasn't recognized until the 20th century) by certain bands of pagan "witches" or ritually-oriented Cunning Folk. I need to say that I found no support for this in the fairly extensive research I have done. The Cunning Folk are the only documented "white witches" in the (1500-1800) period under discussion. There is no *available* evidence of any underground survival of conscious paganism at work between 16th century England and about 1900, so I must disregard speculations concerning the worship of pagan gods and goddesses, organized covens, "initiations" of white witches, and any cycle of rituals and holiday observances apart from those embodied in Christian tradition. Although one cannot prove a negative, even an authority as sympathetic as Carlo Ginzburg categorically states that there were never actual earthly gatherings of "covens" or something like them – all the activity of the witch-fighters he found were carried out on the spiritual plane, not in local woods and fields (Ginzburg 1991: 10). The beliefs of the quasi-shamanistic *benandanti* did contribute to the conceptualization of the witches' sabbat, but no one has found any equivalent in English sources, at least before the concept of the sabbat began percolating in from continental circles. Atypical testimonies such as Isobel Gowdie's that are sometimes cited as a revelation of an otherwise hidden witch culture are not the tip of a cultural iceberg but simple anomalies.

Similarly, Free Masonry, which in its speculative form had so great an influence on occult organization in the 18th century and after, was in 1550 for the most part still a practical trade and its initiatory practices (deriving from trade guilds and medieval tradition) largely limited by its operative roots. The elaborate symbolic systems and initiatory "orders" that arose from it began to appear in the 17th century, but would not assume their modern importance until the following century. In their thoughtful survey of the origins of modern witchcraft, *Wicca Magical Beginnings* (2008), Sorita d'Este and David Rankine conclude that modern witchcraft derives primarily from the traditions of the medieval grimoires with contributions from the late Victorian ceremonial systems. Although I would suggest that the *institutional framework* of Free Masonry is equally important, I believe this to be essentially correct.

Secondly, while it is absolutely true that a lot of what constituted "Christian" magic had in fact been carried over from earlier pagan theory and practice, it does not appear to have been maintained by self-conscious alternative or transgressive cults. I think the real story is best expressed in an architectural metaphor developed by Ioan Couliano, illustrating the danger of assuming a cultural product can be defined by the sum of its origins, by *Quellenforshung* (German: *Quelle*, source + *Forschung*, research):

Let us suppose there is a scholar who, engaged in emphasizing the artistic influence upon a monument of Christian architecture, and knowing it was built on the ruins of an old Mithras temple, should undertake to establish an exhaustive inventory of the stones of the pagan temple used to construct the new basilica. Having stated, for instance, that 60 percent of the stones of the Christian structure come from the pagan monument, he would have to conclude—according to the principles of *Quellenforshung* (The study of the sources of, or influences upon, a [cultural] work)—that the basilica is 60 percent a Mithraic temple, which the reality would contradict all too quickly, the two buildings having nothing in common except the raw material, a minor factor. As soon as it came to establishing the difference of style and function between the two works, the *Quellenforshung* would prove entirely unable to serve our purpose, since, by a strange optical illusion, it is incapable of perceiving the two in their unity. (Couliano 1987: 119)

Thirdly, there appears to have been no significant influence of Cabalism on the Cunning Folk. Cabalism had entered into the speculations of educated magi during the Renaissance and was a significant influence on the philosophy and "high magic" of the period in the writings of Marsilio Ficino, Pico della Mirandola, Cornelius Agrippa, John Dee, and Robert Fludd, but it didn't trickle down to the popular level until the 18th century. The cosmic "chain of being" and astral spheres discussed below derived from the older Hermetic and Neoplatonic traditions, not from the Cabala, and remained firmly embedded in Christian theology.

Fourthly, many esoteric elements that are assumed to be ancient traditions today were not in the Cunning Folk's repertoire of traditional folk magic. For example, mediumship, clairvoyance, precognition and the other fruits of Mesmerism and Spiritualism after that, were unknown. Similarly, the Cunning Folk didn't use tarot cards. The use of ordinary playing cards—like that of tea leaves—for fortune-telling appeared over time (there are few mentions of fortune-telling by cards in the 16th and early 17th centuries and tea was not available to ordinary people until later) and became very popular, while the elaborate symbolism of the fortune-telling Tarot was a 19th century occult innovation.

Fifthly, while ceremonial magic and professional astrology existed in forms similar to those we know today, these rigorous systems were, like alchemy, beyond the capability of many Cunning Folk. Some more educated practitioners did use grimoires to summon spirits and undertook the complex mathematics and interpretation of serious astrology, but most relied on far simpler magical conjurations and the quasi-astrological predictions of geomancy, the *Wheel of Pythagoras*, and perpetual almanacs such as the *Arcandum* or the *Kalendar of Shepherds*.

Finally, personal "spirit guides" in the manner that Spiritualism or "channelling" conceive of them, as opposed to conjured spirits, "familiars", guardian angels and imps, did not exist. Cunning Folk might coercively enslave demons or obtain independent spirits as helpers, and communicate with them in dreams or crystals, but voluntary possession was not part of the picture. In addition, there wasn't anything much like New Age "shamanism" in the recorded activities of the Cunning Folk involved here. The late 20th century, having developed a fascination with "altered states of consciousness" in the 1960s and hence shamanism, embraced the idea that all magic can be characterised from this particular perspective. Although shamanism and its congeners may have been dominant in pre-Christian Europe, there isn't any real evidence that such states of "altered consciousness" were a regular factor in English magic in the period covered in this book – just the opposite, if anything. Just as intellectual fashion argued that magnetism was the basis of everything arcane in the late 18th century and the same claim was made for spiritualism and theosophy in the 19th, so in the late 20th century, there has been a effort (drawing on Michael Harner, Carlos Castenada, and assorted New Age gurus) to impose a broad-brush model of "shamanism" across occult history. Whatever the pre-Christian inhabitants of Britain may have done, their descendants in the early modern period were not working within any recognizable "shamanic" system.

So, gentle reader, if you are looking for the perky prose and cozy platitudes that characterise best-selling works on white witchcraft and kitchen magic, you are likely to be disappointed by the "dry" style of this book. If you find the historical assessments of Ronald Hutton and similar authors infuriating, you may expect to have that same reaction to what I have written. You have been cautioned! If, however, you are interested in the magical resources actually available to English-speaking folk magicians – the Cunning Folk – between 1550 and 1900, you may find the selections compiled here useful. You may even discover that my theories and conclusions about English folk magic as it was historically practiced are, if speculative, instructive. With these caveats in mind, we will now dig deeper into the activities of the Cunning Folk and their clients.

CHAPTER 1:

Introduction

> "People do not usually think logically about magic, especially if they believe in it". Daniel Pickering Walker, *Spiritual and Demonic Magic from Ficino to Campanella*, p. 47

This book is about the practices of the so-called "white witches" of England and America between 1550 and 1900 whom are most commonly referred to today as "Cunning Folk". It is the result of a long-term interest in the historical practice of folk magic in English culture, occasioned originally by the realization that popular assumptions about English witchcraft in contemporary Wicca and its antecedents could not be supported by documentary or archaeological evidence. My curiosity was first aroused in the early 1970s when I tried to find historical continuity behind the claim that a pagan "witch cult", which had ostensibly flourished in pre-Christian times, had survived in a decayed but recognizable form into modern times, as asserted by authorities such as Margaret Murray and Gerald Gardner.

I began by searching for physical rather than documentary evidence (I wanted something *tangible* to back up the innumerable claims and assertions) – in particular, examples of the pentagram, Wicca's primary symbol, in British archaeological or antiquarian collections and reports. Had the witch religion originally been as pervasive and important as its adherents claimed, it seemed there should have been surviving examples on Pictish stones or something of that sort. Although the symbol turned up in ritual magic manuscripts and occasionally as a non-religious decoration, there was simply no indication that it had ever been a *significant* and *widely used* religious symbol. I couldn't find more than one or two possible candidates, nor were there instances of the other ideograms in the *Book of Shadows* outside of the very narrow sphere of Judeo-Christian ritual magic.

More significantly, there was no indication that, whatever had been the case before or during the Middle Ages, there was any *demonstrable* cultural continuity of a pre-Christian religion that reflected Wiccan belief in Britain between the 16th century and the rise of neopaganism in the late 19th century. There were plenty of plausible if unrelated and usually foreign examples of mother goddesses and horned gods (predominately pre-historic), magical rituals or coven gatherings as imagined by witch hunters, but there was nothing that in any way reflected the singular *synthesis* of concepts that characterised modern witchcraft. After reading Francis King's *Ritual Magic in England* (1970) and his comments on Gardner and Wicca, I concluded the witch historical "party line" simply wasn't true. Although this has now been widely recognized, at the time it was still a novel – and bitterly contested – viewpoint. My analysis of the problem was eventually published in 1996 in James Lewis's *Magical Religion and Modern Witchcraft*.

If both the imaginary diabolic "witchcraft" of the trials and the ahistorical Wiccan alternative were false depictions of the past, then what had been the magical practices of the British populace? Setting aside the "learnèd magic" of Ficino, Agrippa and Dee as a separate problem, I pursued this question in a random manner; primarily following up footnotes from Thomas's *Religion and the Decline of Magic* (1971) and Kittredge's *Witchcraft in Old and New England* (1929) with the vague idea of writing a history of English folk magic. As my job included research (on quite different topics) in Widener Library, the British Museum, the Bodleian, the Warburg Institute and other fruitful locations, I accumulated a number of references – and no challenges to my suspicions about Wiccan history. Once Ronald Hutton and Owen Davies published studies I would like to have written, I decided to address a different historical gap and concentrate on the documented resources and practices of English-speaking folk magic in Britain and the U. S. from the early modern period to the end of the 19th century, or slightly beyond.

One shortcoming of otherwise excellent histories on the Cunning Folk is that complex magical and divinatory operations – the actual functioning of folk magic – are extensively cited but not presented in any detail, leaving the reader who is unfamiliar with such activities in the dark about what was actually being done. This is not a fault on the authors' part, as detailed illustrative examples after the manner of Victorian footnotes would break up the narrative and inordinately extend the length of already long books. However, as the average reader is unlikely to have access to the referenced sources (many are now online, but one often comes up against requests to subscribe to a journal or pay $30 for a five page article), my aim here is to compile a sourcebook of such selections, providing the omitted details and examples at some length so as to give the reader a background in the resources used by the Cunning Folk.

My intent is to provide extensive samples illustrating what was actually done in "folk magic", using the term broadly to indicate any use of preternatural means to foretell the future, cure the ill, detect and repel black witchcraft, identify thieves, consult with spirits, locate treasure and all the other services the Cunning Folk offered their clients. The key point – and limitation – here is documentary evidence. Although historians necessarily depend on written records, the tradition of "low magic" involved considerable oral transmission and shared experience that we will never be able to document. I do not in any way underestimate oral sources of magical knowledge and training, but much of what once existed is now unfortunately lost beyond recovery. Existing "oral tradition" is real and vitally important, but as Jan Vansina (*Oral Tradition as History*, 1985) so well demonstrates, it cannot be relied on nor is it dependable more than three or four generations for certain matters, especially in cultures where "iconotropy" ("the accidental or deliberate misinterpretation by one culture of the icons or myths of an earlier one, especially so as to bring them into accord with those of the later one") serves to obscure and mislead, as is evident in contemporary neopaganism, for example. To avoid unwarrantable assumptions and the projection of modern opinions on to the past, I limit my sources and examples to surviving *written* documents and publications, presented as closely as possible as they appeared in the original sources.

In addition to providing examples and selections, I have tried to examine some of the cultural contexts from which they derive. Collecting information is great fun; arranging and writing about it rather less so, but the real challenge comes in trying to define and explain it. The desire to *understand* magic in any specific cultural context is an intellectual puzzle not only for scholars but believers. As Mary Douglas recreates the thinking behind confronting inexplicable misfortune in the context of the supernatural, "There is a demand to be satisfied. Why? Why? Why? At each level there is a plausible answer. Why was I ill? Because I ate forbidden foods. Why do I have a chronic illness? Because I keep disregarding the rules. Why did she die? Because a jealous sorcerer got her. What is a sorcerer? One who is inherently immoral … someone who has brought occult power to transcend the moral rules, to vent his spite."[1] Modified for post-Reformation Christian belief, this pretty well describes the common view concerning the results of sin and the threat of witchcraft in the early modern era. Yet trying to pin down exactly what the beliefs were and how they determined actual practice is quite difficult.

There was not one single body of opinion concerning the preternatural in the 16th and 17th centuries but several; all overlapping and conflicting despite the efforts of theologians to prescribe how everyone should think about magic. Formally there was the official Christian position(s) on magic and the supernatural. In early modern England this had been considerably influenced by Protestant doctrine, yet it was also intersected by folk tradition, surviving beliefs inherited from pre-Reformation Catholicism, and medieval Aristotelian philosophy, as well as intellectual theories from Ficino to Agrippa and Dee. Together with the philosophical understanding concerning the Macrocosm and the Microcosm (the theories and principles governing the cosmos and the human condition), this body of concepts constituted a "*habitus*", a range of beliefs so embedded in the culture that it is both omnipresent and cognitively invisible, and which every individual unconsciously adopts to one extent or another. Although such things as astrology and divination were not technically "magical" in expert opinion in the past, they were both part of the contemporary *habitus* and important elements of the Cunning Folk's practice, and so have been included here. A *habitus* provides not only the existing "structure" of a system of belief, restricting what can be thought possible and correct, but it also conditions or shapes emerging

---

[1] Mary Douglas. *Implicit Meanings*. New York: Routledge, 1999, p. 95.

choices and opinions, channeling adaptation and change to conform to accepted principles. Through upbringing and education (and temperament), some people were better positioned to exploit the orthodox structures than others, either in elite culture or in the highly conservative sphere of village life. It is only when we encounter a genuine "paradigm shift" (to jump to another prominent explanatory principle) and the old *habitus* loses its strength, does it become visible and subject to criticism and real change.

The foremost characteristic of the early modern European *habitus* was that it was a Christian, or rather, an "Abrahamic" filter embodying the assumptions of Christianity, Judaism, and Islam through which earthly reality was defined. "A Christian of that time lived out his entire life – private, professional and public – within the embrace of Christianity. 'Today,' said Febvre, 'we make a choice to be Christian or not. There was no choice in the sixteenth century.'"[2] There was no independent or consciously alternative "pagan" social component in England by 1550, at least. Influences and adaptations from either pre-Christian Britain or Greco-Roman culture (which were numerous) either remained intellectually incoherent or, more generally, had been modified to fit the Abrahamic pattern. Like the rest of Christendom, the British shared a specific "ritual instinct" that convinced them that there was one effective and proper way to approach the supernatural. This was through the Christian world view, to the extent that they were knowledgeable of any doctrine at all. For example, the use of Latin in religion privileged the use of Latin in magic – even the spells in the Harry Potter series appear Latinate, as this still seems appropriate today. Yet the lack of Latin literacy was not necessarily a barrier to lay understanding, as Eamon Duffy explains in *The Stripping of the Altars* (1992). Popular magic generally followed the same premises that characterised religious ritual, which made sense in the Abrahamic *habitus*.

The important elements of the orthodox or official perspective were roughly these:

- God was not only the creator of the universe but also the sole omnipotent and eternal ruler thereof.
- Only God could work *supernatural* miracles (*miracula*, i.e., temporary suspensions of His own law); the most the Devil or any other being could do were "wonders" (*mira*), *preternatural* works that depended on unusual or hidden forces yet were still consistent with God's inescapable cosmic law.
- The Devil – a being with both an individual and sometimes a collective identity as the sum of all demons – was entirely under God's control, who employed him as tempter, tester and punisher of sinful human beings. The Devil was like Santa Claus – no matter how many lesser versions might be seen on street corners, he was still a single personality.
- The Devil could do nothing without God's permission, but with that, he could cause preternatural harm (*maleficium*) and perform wonders.
- The Devil was responsible for the evil in the world. He was a malicious trickster, deceiver, seducer, and generally all-round enemy of everything good in creation – mankind in particular.
- Part of the Devil's function was to entrap people in sin. God gave him latitude to test mortals' faith and moral steadfastness, and to seize their souls if they failed the test. This was done out of hatred and jealousy towards mankind, not to cooperate with God. Generally, only the sinful could be afflicted – but then sin was universal.
- One of the Devil's ploys was to play on peoples' desperation, fears, desires, hatreds and greed to lure them into sin through the temptation of using magic, either through witchcraft or sorcery.

---

[2] Stanley Tambiah. *Magic, Science, Religion and the Scope of Rationality.* Cambridge: Cambridge University Press, 1990, p. 88.

- Rigid Calvinists rejected the idea of intermediaries (such as the stars or angels) between God and the management of earthly affairs. God micromanaged the entire show, employing the Devil for the dirty work.
- Magic was real, but illicit, dangerous and to be avoided. Some critics said practically all magic was in fact clever illusions or misleading "wonders" orchestrated by the Devil.
- Many thought that magic harnessing the influence of the heavenly bodies by which God perhaps managed the affairs of the world was natural and legitimate. Others disagreed.
- Any magic beyond "natural magic" (i.e., inexplicable but still natural effects) was forbidden by God. All magic was suspect and shunned by the strictly religious.
- Unnatural magic was by default, demonic and possibly idolatrous, although there was a fairly extensive community of opinion that asserted that astral or angelic magic might be acceptable.
- No human had any innate magical power. It was always derived from God or the Devil, and through knowledge of how to achieve preternatural effects.
- Divination was also prohibited as heretical and impinging on God's Providence, which was beyond mankind's "need to know" – and deplored as *curiositas* or seeking after secret and forbidden knowledge.
- Witches became agents of the Devil through voluntary and explicit "pacts" or contracts, and caused great harm. Sorcerers were drawn into involuntary or implicit pacts, although they might not think this was so.
- Both thought, erroneously, that they were in control of the situation when in fact they were just dupes of the Devil.
- Charms were only signals to the Devil to perform some wonder – the words and objects had no innate magical efficacy.

The worst thing about witchcraft was that it was idolatry; devil worship, consorting with God's enemy – the worst sort of religious treason. If a community did not clean up its act and censure these terrible traitors, then He would punish it for failing to do so.

Where medieval Christianity had an assortment of official remedies against witchcraft and magic including miracles channeled though saints and church officials, exorcisms and consecrated materials, these were rejected by Protestants. The only defence they allowed against evil was fasting, prayer, faith and fortitude. People should also consider why God had allowed the Devil to bother them, as He would only do so (normally) if they were already sinful.

The use of counter-magic, either self-employed or by means of an agent (the "Cunning Folk", "Wise Men or Wise Women", "white witches", "charmers" &c.) was forbidden. Calvinists even asserted that all such agents were in fact a species of witch, and even worse than "black witches" in that, despite of what benefits they might offer, their actions lured their clients into sin – all the more reprehensible because it delivered their clients or victims into the Devil's hands under the cover of positive results.

It was the responsibility of ecclesiastical and civil authorities to enforce God's ordinances, to identify and punish anyone who consorted with the Devil (witches and sorcerers) or claimed preternatural skills (folk healers and fortune tellers).

But there was plenty of latitude for disagreement. Not only did the strictly orthodox position conflict with centuries of opinion about the possibility of legitimate defences such as the Christian "sacramentals" against Satan and his minions, there was among the educated widespread interest in occult or hidden knowledge that was preternatural in character, but still justifiable as an objective for human learning. The break between science as we understand it (which included functional examples of "natural magic") and the devout Christian view of the world was just beginning to appear. It would be generations before all but a few unusual individuals would be able to see beyond the religious *habitus*, and many who were called "atheists" (as being immoral persons or nonconformists) accepted God's existence and authority – what they disagreed with were the official details.

One indication of how difficult this separation was can be found in the very concept of "natural laws" – a phrase we still use today. In pre-materialist cultures, the reigning assumption was that the universe was created and managed by some divine authority whose reputed "laws" governed everything just as a king's laws did on earth. This was a basic confusion between "natural" (scientific) and "nominative" (human) law[3]. Whereas the former are in fact simply natural processes that function automatically without the necessity of a deity having established them, the latter are arbitrary social constructs. However, people sincerely believed man-made Christian "laws" to be as natural and mechanical as those of physics, and were unaware there was any difference between the two. Science as we know it could not be divorced from religion until the difference between truly natural functions and culturally determined prescriptions and moral standards could be understood (and we are evidently still working on that separation, as "creationism" demonstrates). Until then, unquestioned belief in a divine lawgiver who had "decreed" social rules that were as real as those of physics was dominant. The Christian view of the world – the Abrahamic filter – was firmly in place even with rationalists such as Reginald Scot in *The Discoverie of Witchcraft* (1584) or George Gifford in *A Discourse of the Subtill Practices of Deuilles by Witches* (1587) who tiptoed to the edge of logical observation, but still accepted God's rule and word (the Bible) unequivocally.

As a result of this confusion, it followed that "natural laws" might be abrogated by God (or evaded by magicians) just as earthly laws were by kings (or criminals), hence the plausibility of spiritual magic. We know now that the "laws" of gravity or thermodynamics can't be "broken" like a law against shoplifting, but that was not evident then. Before the Reformation, the Church and the saints were supposed to be able to employ preternatural and even supernatural forces under God's dispensation and strict regulation, but if they could do so, it was logical that others could also – illicitly. Since Christianity was indubitably true and the Bible presented magic, angels, demons, and witches as real, magic was officially verified. Protestantism rejected the official use of preternatural remedies and stricter theologians regarded magic as predominately spurious, but they couldn't dispute its existence altogether. If magic was real but just illegal, then wicked people could and did break God's law in using preternatural forces for their own selfish ends.

Educated magicians used these theoretical conflicts to defend their alternative views, but this probably had little influence on the general populace, who generally thought of magic as a natural and mechanical process. Exactly how magic worked and what role the Devil played in it, which so agitated preachers and theologians, was largely irrelevant. To many people, since witches were both real and dangerously effective, the use of counter magic officially sanctioned or otherwise, seemed an obvious recourse. Witches could inflict *maleficium* by a kind of evil eye ("fascination" or "overlooking") or by touch, curses (where someone was "forespoken"), or sorcery (by image magic in particular, but also via familiars or ritual action). This evil was detected and combated by the witches' primary opponents, the Cunning Folk, as it had been by priests before the Reformation.[4]

Ironically, the group that came closest to rejecting the actuality of witchcraft and sorcery, concentrating instead on the felonious act of *attempting* either and thus consorting with the Devil (which in itself warranted the death penalty), were the strict Calvinists. Although the Church of England was Calvinist, albeit of a rather moderate variety, the Puritan faction carried John Calvin's ideas closer towards their logical conclusion. Puritan theologians concluded that witches and magicians were deluded

---

[3] Normative statements affirm how things should or ought to be, how to value them, which things are good or bad, and whether actions are right or wrong. They are cultural constructs, not objective reality – although their social impact is real enough.

[4] I have chosen to use the preferred term "Cunning Folk" (with capitals) rather than "white witches" because the latter term was apparently not common in the earlier period (though often used by their theological opponents to strengthen the "witch" association), and to avoid confusion with modern Wicca, which is quite another thing.

in their belief that they could personally achieve preternatural effects, and that it was all a snare and delusion by the Devil.

In essence, what was supposed to occur was that the Devil would seduce some susceptible old woman to believe that, through witchcraft, she could have revenge on someone and pretended that he or his minions would obey her commands to do this. He then brings about some actual injury, under license from God. The victims were often convinced to fight fire with fire, and went to a "white witch" to identify the guilty witch so that she could be neutralized by being blooded or prosecuted, or provide some expedient whereby the damage is traced to the witch, so that she is exposed, usually by a spell that causes her bodily agony. If this succeeded as the Devil intended, he not only secured the damnation of the witch, but because of their meddling with defensive magic, the original victims and their agents (the Cunning Folk) were drawn into sin and possible legal prosecution as well – a triple header as it were – and yet it was all a (divinely-sanctioned) plot by the Devil from beginning to end.

Even innocent people, it was admitted, could be condemned as witches through Satan's lies, and what people thought was magical was actually "cosinage" or fraudulent illusion – except for the harm it caused. The Devil was equally ready to take credit for natural illnesses or losses if they could then be blamed on someone as witchcraft. If, as Puritans implied, God's "physical" laws were almost impossible for humans to manipulate, the sin involved was the wicked presumption of trying to do evil rather than in actually succeeding. Here we are very near rejecting magic altogether. They of course couldn't make that leap, but it got people thinking. By the end of the 17th century, a rising tide of skepticism ("Sadducism") alarmed some of the devout who recognized that if, against tradition, witches were personally powerless dupes (and ghosts an impossibility), the whole supernatural edifice of Christianity was being challenged.

Having attempted to outline an official view, I shall now try to survey the popular view. Unlike the official view, for which there are numerous if conflicting sources, the popular view wasn't written down or argued out in detail, so it can only be inferred by interpreting what we know people did or said when confronted by the authorities.

- God is real but awesome, mysterious and remote, rather like a monarch on a distant throne, and beyond the understanding of ordinary people. He might respond, arbitrarily, to prayers and devotion, if He so chose.

- Like other monarchs, while He can be the source of great benefit, He is also demanding, imperious and judgmental. But the real trouble usually comes from His earthly representatives; bishops, priests, and civil as well as church courts.

- Satan, too is real, and out to do whatever he could to vex and harm the innocent as well as the wicked.

- Witches are real and present dangers. Becoming a witch changed the individual's intrinsic identity to something inhuman (like a former human who became a vampire), in contrast to sorcerers (and Cunning Folk) who were still human but who possessed unusual knowledge and skills.

- Witches could automatically summon the Devil or send imps (familiars) to harm anyone they choose.

- Witches are almost everywhere, and one must be wary of offending one as he or she would then destroy, sicken or damage people, livestock, bees, crops and other goods.

- Witches can steal crops, milk, and foodstuffs by magic. They can also do other evil things by sorcery, such as poisoning, preventing beer from fermenting or butter from coming. The division between witchcraft, in which individuals achieved their ends largely through malicious imagination, and sorcery, which involved tools and ritual practices, is never clear or absolute.

- Witches use malevolent magic, and employ imps as familiars or spirits to be emissaries of malice. They have special marks or protuberances on their bodies to feed their imps. In England, they weren't believed to gather in covens but worked alone (except where family connections might exist).

- Religious authorities insisted on witchcraft being devil worship and idolatry, but although that might be true, the worst thing about witchcraft was the actual damage (*maleficia*) it caused. English civil prosecutions focused on *maleficium* rather than the satanic aspect.

- Generally, one expected to have to live with witches as with other instances of ill-fortune. However, if the harm caused by a witch becomes unbearable, the way to deal with witchcraft is to identify the witch and placate, neutralize or prosecute her.

- Magic is real and effective, and a crucial if illegal tool in countering witchcraft or other misfortune.

- Magic employs supernatural power directly from God, or from angels, the stars, the Devil, his demons, and even natural objects (the supernatural-preternatural classification being more an intellectual and theological concern).

- Magic simply works if you do it correctly, just as bread rises or grain ferments to make beer. In other cases, magic is accomplished by spiritual beings such as Angels, demons or elves – no one knows how. The spirits' powers and techniques are intrinsic to them and beyond human understanding.

- Humans can use magic, and if some have the power to do so innately (such as seventh sons of seventh sons or people born with cauls on their heads); it is most generally a learned skill.

- The "Old Religion" (i.e., Catholicism, not paganism) had pious remedies (sacramentals) that cured illness, brought good fortune and hindered witches. The parish priest may have "left off charming" (though not all did so) after the Reformation, but as practical weapons drawing on divine power, such things are still valid and necessary.

- "White witches" (more commonly referred to as "cunning" or "wise" men and women) are positive if sometimes intimidating benefactors in the community.

- A common belief is that Cunning Folk also dealt with the Devil (they heard this from the authorities often enough), which was frightening but could also perversely guarantee their effectiveness.

- Action against witchcraft was an important element in the Cunning Folk's repertoire, but they also provide many more magical services, including healing, theft-detection, divination, charming, love magic, simple fortune-telling and treasure hunting.

Up to this point, we have been considering the situation primarily from the perspective of the first century of the survey, from 1550 to 1650. Two important shifts occurred between 1650 and 1700. The first occurred during the Interregnum (1649-1660) when state censorship broke down and a number of magical texts previously available only in Latin were translated into English. Titles such as Cornelius Agrippa's *Three Books of Occult Philosophy* (1651); the *Fourth Book of Occult Philosophy* (1665) which also included the *Heptameron: or Magical Elements*, the *Isagoge (Of the Nature of Spirits)*, Cremonensis' *Astronomical Geomancy* and the *Arbatel of Magick*; the *Ars Notoria: The Notory Art of Solomon* (1657), and Della Porta's *Natural Magick* (1658) opened the wider world of "high" or intellectual magic to English-speaking readers. It is instructive to note that material from these same books regularly turned up in magical manuscripts circulating among the more accomplished Cunning Folk. At the same time, advances in empiric or experimental scientific thought hastened the shift away from dependence on traditional belief. This contributed to the swift decline in prestige of intellectual magic, and at the same time, civil authority lost its enthusiasm for persecuting witches. High magic was concerned with spiritual knowledge, enlightenment and experiential theology; low magic with practical results. The Cunning Folk were consequently primarily interested in the latter, although some might study alchemy, professional astrology and high magic out of curiosity or to give a gloss to their patter. Some individuals even mastered Latin (always the basis of a grammar school education) for the same reasons.

The second was the increasing availability of simplified and inexpensive published sources of information, such as almanacs, chapbooks, "Books of Knowledge" and similar compilations combining esoteric lore with more mundane subjects. After the Stationers' Company lost the authority to control publishing by licensing books (and limiting printers) in 1695, a veritable flood of cheap publications flowed forth, including many of an occult nature. Old titles were revived, often by multiple publishers, and new collections were cobbled together to meet what was evidently a steady demand. Increased literacy and the age-old esteem of book-learning may have lead to a greater dependence on written sources – even the illiterate had used books all along as props in their work.

After 1700, high magic "went underground" and the authorities ceased to credit low magic with either danger or efficacy. Studies in alchemy, astrology and hermeticism were quite out of fashion during the Enlightenment, and the consequent loss of intellectual respectability and public derision relegated these subjects to private obscurity. Official disbelief also resulted in the *Act against Conjuration, Witchcraft, and dealing with evil and wicked Spirits* of 1736 that repealed the earlier witchcraft laws: "That from and after the said Twenty-fourth Day of June, no Prosecution, Suit, or Proceeding, shall be commenced or carried on against any Person or Persons for Witchcraft, Sorcery, Inchantment, or Conjuration, or for charging another with any such Offence, in any Court whatsoever in Great Britain." Instead, the act redefined the offences as fraud. Anyone who might "pretend to exercise or use any kind of Witchcraft, Sorcery, Inchantment, or Conjuration, or undertake to tell Fortunes, or pretend, from his or her Skill or Knowledge in any occult or crafty Science, to discover where or in what manner any Goods or Chattels, supposed to have been stolen or lost, may be found" could be imprisoned for a year, with quarterly appearances in a public pillory for an hour each time. It was not often invoked, and Cunning Folk's work continued largely as it had before. Although contemporary skepticism was influential among the elite, it apparently had a lesser effect on the lower orders.[5]

Low magic continued to flourish (as Owen Davies has so thoroughly demonstrated), despite the ridicule heaped on it by rationalists and religious leaders of all sorts. As scholars have recently discovered, there also remained a lively interest in the arcane among a scattering of educated 18th century individuals and groups as well, from Sir Isaac Newton's fascination with alchemy, the Freemasons' delight in ritual and symbolism, and theosophical studies by the Philadelphians and Behmenists such as John Pordage, Jane Lead, Dionysius, Andreas Freher and William Law down to the occasional eccentric occultist.

The pendulum of intellectual fashion swung away from such extreme rationalism at the end of the 18th century, which resulted in England's first "occult revival" under the auspices of the Romantic Movement. The fad for the "Gothic" in architecture and literature was part of a reaction against the cerebral austerity of the Age of Reason, while the antiquarian pursuit of folklore that led to a renewed interest in the arcane soon followed. However, the Enlightenment break in the esoteric heritage, which had been sustained from ancient times to the 17th century, made it impossible to fully resurrect the old esoteric culture in its traditional form. For one thing, the fears educated people had once had about witchcraft or becoming involved with magic and sorcery, had dissipated to the extent they no longer worried much about potential spiritual danger, and felt freer to explore any avenue that intrigued them. The loss of the tradition's authority also meant they had less compunction about modifying it in the light of contemporary preconceptions. New concepts such as "animal magnetism" introduced changes in the way magic was perceived, and old material was refigured and modified to suit. The old problem of how natural magic and medicine actually worked was thought to have been discovered in electricity and magnetism, as "… an ethereal fluid pervading the world which – when properly understood – would

---

[5] *Statutes at Large from the Third Year of the Reign of King George the Second to the Twentieth Year of the Reign of King George the Second*, vol. 6, London, 1769, pp. 206-207.

explain universal phenomena such as magnetism, light, heat, electricity, and gravity. This was also to be the basis of medical reform since health was to be defined in terms of the proper flow of this fluid in the human body ... animal magnetism was the long-sought cause of sympathy and antipathy in nature." [6] The first generation of revivalists, such as Ebenezer Sibley (*A New and Complete Illustration of the Celestial Science of Astrology*, 1784-88) or Francis Barrett (*The Magus*, 1801) tended to respect their sources and transcribe the details fairly accurately, but they also tried to explain them in terms of the science of their day, which often resulted in a rather complicated tension between traditional cosmology and the emerging natural sciences.

Other revivalists, in particular "Raphael" (Robert Cross Smith, author of *The Astrologer of the Nineteenth Century* (1825), *Royal Book of Fate*, (1829); *Royal Book of Dreams*, (1830); *Raphael's Witch*, (1831); and *The Familiar Astrologer*, (1831), &c.) but also Henry Lemoine, editor of *The Conjurors Magazine* (1791-1793), "H. Kirchenhoffer", the pseudonymous author of *The Book of Fate, formerly in the possession of Napoleon* (1822), or John Parkins (*The Universal Fortune-Teller*, (1810); *The Cabinet of Wealth*, (1812)), were as interested in making a living out of the occult as restoring ancient traditions. These authors took liberties with the material they presented, inventing new products by cannibalising old practices. This resulted in bowdlerized methods of conjuration or divination that resembled traditional geomancy or *sortes* (fortune telling by lots), but which were more like parlour games suited for a genteel middle class market. Raphael did publish a fascinating miscellany of traditional magic and astrology in his collections (*Astrologer of the Nineteenth Century* and *Familiar Astrologer*) that could be useful grist for a Cunning Man's practice, but his books were also larded with lurid illustrations, occult fiction and sensational anecdotes aimed at amusing a casual audience.

However, the first occult revival did stay within the general bounds of the heritage of European esotericism and did not threaten the Cunning tradition. It was the second "revival", which began with the Spiritualist movement in the 1850s that changed the course of European occultism and contributed to the decline of traditional home-grown low magic. This revival involved the wholesale importation of miscellaneous baggage from Masonic and Rosicrucian ritual, Theosophical cosmology, "Secret Chiefs" and cabalistic terminology as well as a variety of reputedly Asian – generally Indian – concepts, which revolutionized the European occult "*habitus*". Coinciding with a new middle class interest in the esoteric inspired by mesmerism and spiritualism, the second revival embraced contemporary confidence in scientific discovery and "progress" and blithely went ahead to construct a "modern" occultism. The older systems were now not faulted as blasphemous or irrational – but rather as ignorant, quaint and obsolete – modern society's most damning form of rejection. Oral traditions assiduously sought out and recorded by folklore collectors were regarded as quaint, endangered examples of popular credulity and cultural backwardness rather than satanic threats. The condescension of some educated collectors stemmed from what they thought was the long-overdue disappearance of superstition (or, alternately, the regrettable death of an aspect of "Merrie England"). I suspect they would be surprised to discover that in time their labours would become fodder for new invented traditions.

The new intellectualised occultism of the second revival became a socially acceptable pastime for dilettantes, who viewed it more as a kind of self-actualisation or means of chatting with deceased friends and "spirit guides" than a practical solution to immediate problems and consulting with angels and demons. Nouveau occultism also had a strong social component, in contrast to the solitary activity of Cunning Folk and traditional magical adepts. Whether gathered around a séance table, organized as a society or working in a ritual order, the new occultists were great joiners and organisers. These "improvements" redefined the subject and undermined the old *habitus* to the extent that, with the exception of some gypsies and a few charmers here and there, the old fashioned Cunning Folk's trade withered. Why seek out some dubious back-street astrologer or village wise woman when you could consult someone with fashionable "Mysterious East" credentials or even do the magic or divination

---

[6] Allen G. Debus. "Scientific Truth and Occult Tradition: The Medical World of Ebenezer Sibley (1751-1799). *Medical History*, 1982, 26: pp. 275-76.

yourself? Magic not only survived but prospered, but in a modified "new age" form that overshadowed traditional occult problem solving and anti-witch defences.

It is often noted that increased literacy, improved communications, the materialism of Victorian science, religious liberalism, improved medicine, the insurance industry and the breakdown of isolated village communities all contributed to the decline of both the demand for and belief in traditional folk magic, but I am of the opinion that occult "progress" played an important role as well. As Patrick Curry observes concerning astrology, esoteric beliefs and practices had been vehemently attacked, ridiculed and rejected by "polite and educated society" from the late 17th through the 18th century, relegating them to a "popular" or "plebeian" status in which they were stubbornly retained by the lower classes.[7] Ridicule and rejection folk tradition could deal with, more or less, but direct competition with shiny new occult belief systems was something else again. It wasn't long before the new fashions were adopted by professional magical practitioners, and we begin to see "scientific" astrologers, mediums with benevolent spirit guides instead of conjurors conversant with dangerous demons and ghosts, and "psychic healers" and "clairvoyants" instead of Wise Women and Cunning Men. Even the belief that someone might have an innate ability at occult intuition in reading character and foretelling the future as opposed to having learned skills, was, despite echoes from "second sight" and ill-defined "seventh son" attributes, a major departure from tradition.

The end of the old tradition wasn't the death of "superstition and credulity" as commonly expected, but rather the modern transfiguration of western esotericism. Modern occultism shows the uninterrupted credence in and appeal of the esoteric, but it is *new* occultism, that over time gradually shifted from an Abrahamic foundation to a multicultural, even quasi-scientific perspective; a necessary adaptation to society's evolving world view. Even the expectations of everyday clients of magical services were influenced by the new ideas, and those in the business either moved with the times or faded away as the older, more conservative generation of customers died off. The Cunning Folk were in their own way, professionals. Theirs was a specialised vocation, whether for prestige or profit, and if "re-branding" was the way to increase trade, those who could adapt did so.

The scope of this survey therefore stops short of the second revival, despite the chronological overlap in the last half-century or so. It also avoids where possible, the traditions of "high magic" as represented by Hermeticism, Alchemy, Rosicrucianism, Cabalism, Theurgy and Theosophy and focuses on the pragmatic results-oriented interests of the Cunning Folk. Having said that, it must be stressed that there were no clear divisions between the intellectual and folk traditions, but rather a continuum of practices, mirroring the earlier borrowing by Neoplatonic theurgists of the methods – if not the aims – of goetic folk magic, or the adaptation by medieval ritual magicians of the rites of orthodox exorcists to raise and control spirits rather than banish them. Cunning Folk readily adopted the concepts and practices that trickled down from medieval Christianity and the intellectual magic of the Renaissance, and some of their traditional ideas made their way up the social scale as in the case of Paracelsus and other innovators. Similarly, folk magic covered a wide range of activity from simple single charms possessed by husbandmen and local healers to the sophisticated application of astrology, divination and conjuration by the most accomplished professionals in those arts, such as John Evans, Dr. John Lambe, Simon Forman, Joseph Blagrave, Richard "Dick Spot" Walton, John Parkins, Timothy Crowther or John and Henry Harries of Cwrt-y-Cadno.

The focus here is on the practice of folk magic and divination for access to the preternatural. For the historic and cultural role of the Cunning Folk, the reader should consult the excellent accounts by Owen Davies (*Witchcraft, Magic and Culture 1736-1951*, *Cunning-Folk: Popular Magic in English History*), Keith Thomas (*Religion and the Decline of Magic*), Ronald Hutton (*The Triumph of the Moon*), Alan Macfarlane (*Witchcraft in Tudor and Stuart England*), George Lyman Kittredge (*Witchcraft in Old and New England*), Eric Maple (*The Dark World of Witches* which, because the author was popular rather than academic, is usually overlooked even though he was a perspicacious pioneer in the study of Cunning Folk) and Stephen Wilson (*The Magical Universe: Everyday Ritual and Magic in Pre-Modern Europe*), as well as relevant articles in

---

[7] Patrick Curry. *Prophecy and Power*. Princeton: Princeton University Press, 1989, p. 113.

Folklore and other journals. Good introductions to the world view that supported their trade can be found in E. M. W. Tillyard's *The Elizabethan World Picture*, C. S. Lewis' *The Discarded Image*, and in greater detail, James Winny's *The Frame of Order*.

I begin with a preface that outlines what I was trying to accomplish in writing this book, what it says about traditional magical practice, and what it omits, as well as the peculiarities of my approach, followed by this introduction.

The first chapter explores the theoretical basis of Western magic during the period surveyed. As this is an area that is difficult to recreate adequately, the beliefs of the past being conflicted and lacking any single universally agreed-upon system, my perspective on the subject may conflict with both academic and contemporary occult conventions on the topic. It should nevertheless clarify the manner in which the preternatural was conceived by both the Cunning Folk and their more sophisticated contemporaries. It also includes a capsulated account of the "world view" concerning humanity's relationship with the physics and cosmology of early modern Europe, upon which many "occult" concepts depend.

The second chapter takes a look at who the Cunning Folk were, and the services they provided through a series of seven extended examples – partially fictionalized except for the last, to provide a detailed look at them at work. There are many more shorter examples given in the histories provided by Keith Thomas, Ronald Hutton and Owen Davies, but these extended narratives better illuminate the manner in which the Cunning Folk were perceived (usually by unsympathetic witnesses) and how they established their credentials and carried out the functions of folk magic.

The fourth, fifth and sixth chapters cover methods of divination; geomancy and the oracles of chance, *sortes* or lots, and dream interpretation respectively. I have selected a few specific applications that were significant in the Cunning Folk's repertoire to exemplify the rest. The chapters on geomancy and oracles are more complete, and illustrate how some important tools of the trade were used. In each case, selections from different historical periods demonstrate both the continuity and change these arts underwent.

The seventh chapter covers charms, spells, and curses – mostly verbal but also some material – an essential part of folk magic. As many of these were never revealed or existed only at an oral level, the examples are not as thorough as we might desire. Nevertheless, the selection should adequately illustrate the forms and aims of these magical actions. For early examples, I have in some cases gone outside my chronological and geographical parameters to include examples from medieval times and from Gaelic Scotland to show what might be missing through want of contemporary evidence. Examples from Wales and Cornwall are not included for the most part, for although these regions were rich in Cunning craft, they are less typical of English practice as a whole. Later examples from published sources, similarly, are so numerous and varied that I have had to limit them for the practical consideration of space.

The eighth chapter considers the particularly magical services most in demand by the Cunning Folk's clients: occult defence against witchcraft, the retrieval of stolen goods, personal safety and good fortune, treasure-hunting and wealth, love and marriage, and revenge. Here I consider both the social context of the requests and the methods by which these needs were addressed.

The ninth chapter deals with the use of astrological concepts, which I classify as "non-computational" astrology apart from the actual practice of astrology itself. It was by these methods that the Cunning Folk employ the art as provided to them by widely-popular inexpensive and ephemeral publications that served as guides before serious works on astrology became available in English, and allowed them to upgrade their practice and use astrology in a more professional manner.

The tenth chapter covers the important area of Astrology and healing. I have combined these two subjects, for while astrology is too complex to be adequately covered in a short chapter – there are a number of book-length studies that do this effectively – the importance of the art and its universal influence requires some discussion. It also ties in with my basic contention that astral influence is central to any period consideration of magical practice. At a time when orthodox medicine was either unavailable, too expensive or generally little more effective than the remedies offered by the Cunning Folk, the healing of both humans and livestock was a vital part of the folk magician's repertoire. Here the work of our professionals and amateurs such as the clergy and housewives responsible for their family's well-being overlap, as they all drew on the same traditions. Calling in a wise woman when home remedies failed and the local physician or surgeon was too expensive testified to confidence in the Cunning Folk's greater knowledge about such matters.

The eleventh chapter deals with the actual practice of astrology in the two forms most useful to the Cunning Folk – electional and horary. The more advanced folk practitioners took over the art of judicial astrology after it was rejected by the English elite, and preserved it while other European nations forgot the ancient art, and made possible its popular revival in the 19th and 20th centuries.

The twelfth and thirteenth chapters cover the most imposing of the Cunning Folk's skills – the conjuration of and consultation with spirits and demons. Although the more elaborate forms of conjuration involving comprehensive (and unpublished) traditional grimoires were beyond the scope of the majority of the Cunning Folk, the invocation of spirits in crystal-scrying, or as magical aids (as imps or "flies") and consultants in this arcane pursuit were common even into the last century of the survey.

The fourteenth chapter deals with one particular practice – combining conjuration with astrology to discover hidden treasure. Unlike many of the other arcane arts, treasure hunting enjoyed a wide appeal among even the highest levels of society – it was possible for Cunning Folk to actually be given official permission and encouragement to recover treasures (which were not just gold and jewels but also books, household items and veins of metal), despite the almost inevitable failure of their efforts.

The concluding chapter sums up the survey and also examines the well-documented subject of African-American "conjure and root work" as an analogous practice from which missing elements in our study might be deduced, and as an example of how a folk tradition can be commodified by the forces of modernity.

CHAPTER 2:

Romancing the Spiritus Mundi – Practical Magic in English Culture

"Unsatisfactory as it might be to those who would make history an exact science, the best that can be achieved in this area is an essay in the Burckhardtian sense, a possible interpretation of the known facts that does not claim to preclude the legitimacy of alternative interpretations."
B. J. Gibbons, *Gender in Mystical and Occult Thought* (2002), p. 21.

SECTION ONE: HOW COULD MAGIC BE SUPPOSED TO WORK?

This chapter is speculative as well as historical, for although there are innumerable scholarly and less-than-scholarly works dealing with European magic, I found that none of them answered the question posed – "how did magic work?" – to my satisfaction. Therefore I offer here a possible solution, although as the quote that heads the chapter says, it is merely one opinion among alternatives, framed in the speculative mode of Jacob Burckhardt (1818–1897), the great cultural historian of the Renaissance.

Since Sir James Frazer's time, the standard explanation of magic has involved three principles to describe the unconscious hypothetical premises that "primitive" people presumably employ in crafting the formulas they used: sympathy, imitation and contagion. The first refers to the assumption of a hidden ("occult") yet effective connection between the materials and rites chosen for the work and the person or event that the magician wants to affect. The second refers to analogical factors involved in those choices, as where physical and/or symbolic characteristics of the materials suggest a categorical connection. The leaf of the liverwort plant, shaped like a human liver, suggested that it could be used to heal that organ. A ritual that mimicked the thunder and energy of a rain storm would in fact manipulate natural meteorological forces to provide rain on demand. The third refers to a specific variety of sympathy where objects that were once associated with a person or thing could continue to exert their influence even after being physically separated from the original subject.

There is nothing wrong with these concepts for explaining magic from an outsider's "rational" point of view, but they are inadequate for explaining the complex assumptions and beliefs that underlay the magic – and religion – of Western Europe during the period under review. Rather than trying to force Frazer's procrustean "etic" (outsider's view) framework on the concepts involved, I have attempted an alternative hypothesis about "how magic was supposed to work" that I hope better reflects the point of view embodied in the works of the time. This cannot be a true "emic" (insider's view) depiction of a belief system, as the vanished culture involved cannot be analysed directly, but I hope it will help clarify the cultural suppositions that informed the magic of the Cunning Folk and their educated contemporaries. In my opinion, a better key to the "sympathies" and "antipathies" (and "imitative" categorizations) of traditional western magic is found in astrology rather than in physical appearance, while "contagion" is best illustrated in the beliefs associated with and derived from religious relics. This is magic viewed from a different theoretical perspective, from the inside-out.

Sources from early modern times tell us a great deal about how educated people thought magic worked, but little about the concepts of the average individual. Ordinary people's opinions about magic were unlikely to be quite the same as those of the experts, although there must have been a cultural correspondence between the two. In general, it seems probable that the continuum of opinion that extended from university-educated philosophers and theologians to illiterate rural labourers and their wives would parallel that in contemporary medicine. At one extreme, the educated physician who had mastered the teachings of Galen and Aristotle (which, to complicate the matter, did not agree on a number of points), based his opinions on the abstract theoretical system of the four humours inherited from the classical era. At the other end of the spectrum, the average citizen probably had little concern with theory, but simply took the remedies and procedures made available through folk tradition, local healers and popular publications on trust. This division between a structured view of how things worked versus the simple assumption of efficacy by appeal to analogical tradition characterised both magic and medicine until modern times.

As in ancient Greece where traditional practitioners were referred to pejoratively as "root-cutters", herbal folk medicine was not fashionable among the cultured in early modern England. On the other hand, the scarce, expensive and sometimes painfully invasive Galenic treatment might prove less appealing than more familiar remedies and charms. "The issue [was] whether one should look for hidden causes of disease, deduced by logical assumptions drawn from symptoms, or be content with manifest causes which one can easily identify from external factors …; this was a major point of contention between conflicting schools of thought. As Pseudo-Galen points out, 'Empiricists … declare that the apprehension of hidden things is useless; for nothing useful is discovered from hidden things'". [8] In magic, the same held true – some people were anxious or curious about how magic worked while others simply followed the directions in manuscripts, popular publications or local tradition without concern over the "hidden factors" by which they worked.

The evidence of the surviving spells, charms and invocations indicates that the fundamental motive power for all magic in English-speaking regions was the authority of Christianity, which was universally called upon to sanction and empower magical operations.

> "…within medieval culture, magical words were seen as effective not per se but rather as means for evoking the effective presence of the archetypal powers to which they refer. Magical language is not in a simple sense the *cause* of efficacy but rather its *occasion*; the cause is a network of forces released and coordinated by the magician's verbal cue. The situation is analogous to that of the Eucharist: the priest's utterance of the words of consecration is not the cause of transubstantiation but rather the divinely ordained occasion for divine intervention. One might suppose that this distinction is too subtle to have been clear to the common necromancer, but in fact the point is clearly articulated in the conjurations themselves, which not only acknowledge but insist that the source of their power is the archetypal forces they bring to bear on the situation at hand." (Kieckheffer 1997: 17)

Divine authority had not only created the world, but it also continued to providentially energize the cosmos through the movement of the primum mobile and the stars. The following explanation (defining God's providence and supernatural miracles as analogous to lesser cosmic forces) is undoubtedly theologically unacceptable from a Christian perspective, but I think it can logically account for the function of Western magic in general.

In practice, the collective instrumentality of magic may be characterised as a category of supernatural or preternatural force that I will call "*virtus*".[9] As we will see, this is not the same sort of cosmic force commonly referred to in magical operations today, which is analogous to the scientific forces of electricity or magnetism, but rather a completely spiritual sort of power more closely analogous to the Will of God – the ultimate motive source of the cosmos and all that it contained. Although all *virtus* ultimately came from God, there were two or perhaps three different kinds at work. Divine *Virtus*, which gave holy relics their potency in healing through separated spiritual substance and allowed saints to perform miracles that transcended cosmic laws, came directly from God. This same potency could even be transferred to artifacts called "brandia" through simple contact (or "contagion"). Astral *virtus*, by which the stars and heavenly intelligences were able to influence earthly things, originated from God as well, but had been refracted into a number of particular "virtues" divided among the zodiacal constellations and planets. This was the basis of "natural" magic. In addition to these legitimate sources

---

[8] M. J. Geller. "Look to the Stars: Babylonian medicine, magic, astrology and melothesia." Max Planck Institute, 2010, p. 24. http://www.mpiwg-berlin.mpg.de/Preprints/P401.PDF (accessed 7/20/2011)
[9] Or "*virtus caelestis*" – celestial force. Possible alternative terms such as psykhē, pneuma, spiritus, rays, currents, energy, vibrations and the like, are too apt to import the conceptual baggage from other occult systems.

of *virtus*, there may have been a kind of illicit but still efficacious preternatural *virtus* controlled by demons and the Devil by reason of their role in the cosmic plan (this is seldom made explicit – perhaps demonic *virtus* was also essentially astral in origin?). One of the great missing elements in the traditional definitions of magic – usually divided into defensible "natural" magic and suspect "spiritual" or demonic magic – is an answer to how, if astral *spiritus* channeled by sympathies and focused by the magus' imagination empowered natural magic, did spiritual beings work *their* magic? My solution is to suggest both were implemented through *spiritus*, if in different ways.

Although I have chosen to characterise the underlying mechanism of magic as purely astrological, it might be objected that "animism" or the pervasive influence of individualised spirits in nature, is a reasonable alternative to astral mechanism. I don't think that would answer the case for natural magic as well as ritual or spiritual magic, however. It might be argued that the concept of independent spirits, in particular demons, might better reflect what many people assumed was the mechanism behind magical operations (or both astral and animistic functions occurring confusedly simultaneously), but I think the evidence supports impersonalised causation rather than personalised causation. The spirits may have had innate *virtus* (like the energised god-like power ceremonial magicians hoped to achieve), but the *virtus* itself drew on the same divine reservoir as that of the stars.

Getting ritual magic to work, for example, required harnessing sufficient *virtus* to convince angels or to coerce demons into delivering the desired results. This was accomplished by drawing on sources of divine *virtus*, which in the case of conjuration meant invoking the sanctity inherent in the Trinity and other divine names, the names of saints, the Virgin, various angels, Biblical passages, and even the names of principal demons. This accumulation of *virtus* from intangible sources parallels the accumulation of astral power from material sources in natural magic in the form of characters and symbols, herbs, metals, stones and other things linked to the cosmic division of astral influence. The key difference between this conception of the natural functioning of the cosmos with that of modern science as it began to appear in the 17th century was that *virtus* was something separate and distinct from the material substance of things, like a soul in a body, whereas modern physics derives all of its effects from their molecular and chemical constituents.

There was no credible rival source of supernatural power in early modern Christendom. Spiritual or ritual magic inevitably included an appeal to the Father, the Son and the Holy Ghost in order to draw on divine *virtus* above the influence of the stars. Natural magic, on the other hand, could operate without an explicit invocation of the Trinity because the innate (astral) virtues it depended on were already established in the cosmic plan. It was only with the Enlightenment that the possibility of divine power from a non-Abrahamic (i.e., not Judeo-Christian or Islamic) source was even debatable. Even the involvement of elves, fairies, or the Devil and his demons was in theory enabled by God's forbearance and the working of His providence.

Essentially, as St. Augustine opined, magic was the selfish private use of religious forces for personal ends through a demonic symbol system, in contradiction to the religious acts performed by the Church for public good and to the glory of God. Although the ultimate prototype for magical ritual was the formula of the Mass, another archetype was Christ's ability to cast out demons and heal the ill – the basis for Church-sanctioned exorcism – which is why exorcism became the model for ceremonial magic. This might transgress the official policy that only the Church could legitimately wield the power of *virtus*, but orthodox opinion was not the only prescriptive set of rules governing such things. Magicians had their own ideas about how magic could and did work within the greater theological structure.

Among the Cunning Folk, concern over theory was as far as we can tell often negligible – it was the practical result that mattered. Their approach was akin to the use of culinary recipes where one simply follows the directions or even modifies them to taste without worrying about the chemistry at work. Results in magic as in cookery, depend more on the skill and experience of the magician or cook, the quality of the ingredients and observation of prescribed timing, rather than an understanding of underlying technical details. Yet in the case of conjuring spirits, for example, the complexity of the rituals did necessitate a basic understanding of how magical power worked, and those Cunning Folk who happened to engage in this crossed the line between just following directions and the mastering of the theory behind contemporary magical practice as described in the grimoires and similar handbooks.

The "cookbook" magic of the Cunning Folk did not require knowledge of theoretical or theological principles, but if we wish to appreciate how magic was supposed to work, we too must look to the intellectual and theological underpinnings that enabled both magicians and their critics to assume that magic was in fact effective. I will temporarily set aside my primary emphasis on folk magic to explore the wider subject of traditional magic, which was quite rational in its own way, if in a manner that may seem puzzling to modern readers used to scientific materialism. It is the premise behind magic that we explore here, even though there was never one all-inclusive, unchanging theory in the past, which makes any simplified description inevitably incomplete. As Michael Bailey observes, "… even within a given society not all people who engage in magic will necessarily see their actions as part of a single coherent system, or accept all (or indeed any) other elements of that system".[10]

There are any number of definitions of magic in academic and popular works, but I have chosen a simple one – "Magic is the tapping into the spiritual mechanisms of the cosmos to achieve practical results." Unlike modern science, which limits itself to technological processes, magic sought to utilise both matter and spiritual *virtus* in its quest for results. Understanding how "it was supposed to work" therefore requires analysis of what these "spiritual mechanisms" were and how they functioned. The traditional Christian world view that produced these concepts had been sustained and tinkered with over a millennium and a half, seeking to accommodate conflicting theories from Plato, Aristotle, Galen, Christian theology and other sources by amalgamating them in a comprehensive system. This included the arrangement of the cosmos, the hierarchy of spiritual beings and forces, and the place of Man in this system, including the parallel inner hierarchy of the human being, as the human constitution (the microcosm) mirrored the cosmic system (the macrocosm).

There are two major if interrelated forms of magic to be considered: natural/astral magic and spiritual/demonic magic. Natural magic presupposed a universal network of spiritual influences ultimately originating with God that were transmitted from the highest levels of creation by way of the celestial spheres of the stars and planets to govern everything in the material world we live in. The divine motive power that was diffracted through the heavenly bodies was also embodied in natural and man-made objects. By learning the different homologous affinities, the laws they obeyed and the mechanisms through which they interacted, the magician could manipulate them for his own purposes. Spiritual magic was concerned with the same pattern of influences, but went a step beyond by presuming the additional influence of powerful, sentient and independent-acting planetary beings ("intelligences"). The magician placed himself in direct connection with not only the natural spiritual forces or nature spirits at work, but also with demons and angels in addition to planetary intelligences. Sorcerers worked with the former; ceremonial magicians of the school of Agrippa with the latter as well.

An analogy might be the difference between a layman and a priest, or, better, a motorist and an automobile mechanic. The former is simply interested in getting from here to there, and knows how to operate his vehicle to do this, as well as a few basic technological facts that allow him to make simple adjustments to his machine. He can change the oil, add wiper fluid, and fill the tires, but the modern complexity of a computerized engine is beyond his expertise, resources or interest. The mechanic, on the other hand, can make substantial repairs and mechanical modifications because of his practiced skill, greater knowledge of the technology, ownership of specialised tools, and professional connections to manufacturers, distributors, and claims adjustors. They both are working with the same technology, but the driver is primarily an operator, while the mechanic is embedded in the (unseen) system that makes driving possible. Natural magic was merely operative (one did what one could with what was immediately available), whereas spiritual magic was transformative, providing the magician with a new status that conferred the ability and more importantly, the authority, to not only to enlist the aid of high-powered experts (angels and demons) but also utilizing divine support for his aims in getting the job

---

[10] Bailey, Michael D. "The Meanings of Magic", in *Magic, Ritual, and Witchcraft (Vol. 1, No. 1,* summer 2006), p. 2.

done. Natural magic was the magic of the Cunning Folk, who had little truck with spiritual magic beyond some traditional necromancy, and not the wilder ambitions of the Renaissance Magus.

Before going into astral and spiritual details, let us cut to the chase and establish the basic principles of western magic. Magic essentially aimed at managing *change* at the behest of the operator, at influencing the unceasing and inevitable shifting in time of all earthy things from their present state to their future ones. Magic depended on the relationships between the soul of the universe (the Anima Mundi) and the cosmic spirit (the Spiritus Mundi), and for spiritual magic, the human spirit and the cosmic spirit. In traditional philosophy, change came about primarily through movement, and the Anima Mundi was what moved the "first mover" (the *Primum Mobile*), the outer or uppermost sphere in creation at the boundary beyond the stars between God and his creation. Christopher Lehrich corrects the confusion resulting from "J. F[rench].'s" translation of Agrippa's "spiritu mudi" in *De occulta philosophia* (1651): "I translate "spiritus mundi" as World-Spirit throughout the present text; J.F. uses "Soul of the World" which is more poetic but somewhat confusing." (Lehrich 2003: 50). Both the Platonic philosopher Proclus (412-487 CE) and, following him, the great magical theorist Marsilio Ficino (1433-1499) go so far as to say that the *Anima Mundi* and the *Primum Mobile* was one and the same thing.

The universe and human beings each had a spirit as well as a soul for very practical reasons. Soul permeated and vivified matter, but didn't – couldn't – move it directly. Being an immaterial spiritual entity, the soul wasn't able to connect directly with the gross physical body – they were just too different. Therefore "spirit" (*pneuma*), made of a very refined but still physical material (the same stuff as the stars were composed of, which was incidentally a source of human *pneuma* or spirit), was used as a medium or flux to unite the two and enable them to interact. In the greater cosmos, this was the *Spiritus Mundi*; in the human, it was the "vital spirits" (sometimes combined with an astral body) that acted as the medium between body and soul, allowing communication and hence movement or change to occur, through energy traditionally identified as "Eros" or in the present instance, *virtus*.

C. S. Lewis says succinctly, "The Primum Mobile is moved by its love of God, and, being moved, communicates motion to the rest of the universe." (Lewis 1964: 113) As the old saying goes, "love makes the world go round", and love – Eros – was the energy which powered all change and action. Eros in this sense should not be confused with the mere appetite for physical sex, but understood as the universal influence of attraction and desire. Eros also enabled ordinary physical activity as well as magic.

All magic required faith (confidence in its efficacy), knowledge, and the intent/will-power necessary to do the job correctly. Spiritual magic required even more, including personal purity, theoretical understanding, and the god-like elevation of the magician's personal essence:

> "But while faith and virtue are indispensable to success in the magical act, Trithemius emphasized, no less indispensible is knowledge of magic's underlying principles, since 'without knowledge through their numbers, degrees, and orders of the middle, end and origin, the magician cannot, without scandal or impiety, effect his images, nor can the alchemist imitate nature, nor can a man conjure spirits, nor can a prophet of nature predict the future, nor can any curious person grasp the meaning of his experiences.'" (Brann 1999: 120)

It was through the interaction of the cosmic spirit and the magician's (perfected) spirit that the latter could indirectly engage the *Anima Mundi* – the ultimate source of change and generation (birth or coming into being) – to impose his intent on the workings of the world, whether in nature or in himself and other beings.

> "The Arabs say that when we fashion images rightly, our spirit, if it has been intent upon the work and upon the stars through imagination and emotion, is joined together with the very spirit of the world and with the rays of the stars through which the world-spirit acts." (Ficino 2002: 351)

The cosmic spirit connected everything the material universe, acting as its nervous system as it were. It coordinated the many beings and elements, from the great astral "intelligences" of the stars and planets (the pagan gods), angels and demons to the lowest material objects such as plants and minerals. Each of these had its own particular sub-category of *virtus* or a "virtue" (characteristic properties or qualities) that linked them together in specific chains of influence descending from the highest in the stars to the lowest on earth. In most cases the magician simply used the existing connections within the cosmic spirit as tools to get what he wanted. By understanding the nature of the different chains of influence, he could manipulate the hidden yet innate virtues in words, signs and objects to direct change towards the results he desired. Superior types of magic, on the other hand, required the direct intervention of the magician in the working of the *Spiritus Mundi* and with higher individual spirits to help in this regard, as in divine elevation of the magician as magus (Christian theurgy) involving the astral intelligences within the stars and even God Himself, or through simple necromancy. "Necromancy" in this context denotes the conjuration of demons in addition to the literal meaning of evoking the dead.

The appeal of necromancy was that it could coerce a knowledgeable and powerful inhabitant of the spiritual world to do one's bidding. It promised far more effective results that those of a mere mortal working on his own. Understandably, demons (or fairies) were not likely to welcome a mere mortal trying to manipulate them, and tended to resist, sometimes avoiding the attempt to command them, and at other times, fighting back to punish or destroy the annoying and presumptive magician. Getting involved in the spiritual world was dangerous not just because of the peril of being prosecuted by the church or state that had declared such individual initiative illegal, but the risk of arousing the ire of powerful spiritual beings. It was safer to stick with natural magic (although that too had its own earthly and divine perils to body and soul), but the thrilling challenge and promise of great rewards in pitting one's will against the forces of the cosmos was irresistible for would-be magicians, from learned clerics and intellectuals to the more ambitious Cunning Folk.

In the enhanced system Agrippa and others developed, magic melded with mysticism to promote a transcendent connection for less-coercive cooperation with higher powers – less dangerous (if done effectively) than intimidating demons in the older medieval form of necromancy, but still precarious given the chance for error, not to mention arousing the antagonism of ecclesiastical and secular authorities. If Lehrich is correct (and I think he is), Agrippa's "demonic" magic aimed to reach as high as the Almighty: "…the highest ritual magic is that by which the magician directly enacts the divine will in the natural and celestial worlds" (Lehrich 2003: 200), through a personal assumption of divine *virtus*. The authorities certainly would not sanction the grander claim of Renaissance magi that a mere magician could legitimately communicate directly with God through magical illumination, as Agrippa seems to have proposed. As Michael Keffer observes, this got dangerously near to the example of the heretical presumption of the arch-magician, Simon Magus.[11] What saved most would-be theurgists, however, was not only the isolated secrecy in which they pursued their art, but the discouraging difficulty in figuring out exactly how the complex and obscure theoretical practices were supposed to be carried out. Such magic was beyond the capacity of all but a tiny minority of especially accomplished (and economically independent) adepts; hence it was most often only of intellectual interest to anyone else. I strongly suspect that this grand Christian theurgy seldom went beyond the theoretical or bookish stage until centuries after Agrippa proposed it, by which time religious and secular sanctions had considerably weakened. An important consideration is that the ideal of Renaissance magus and Christian cabalist quite quickly faded away in the 17th century, making ritual magic a rarity whereas traditional magic or sorcery declined at an altogether slower rate.

This may appear quite like what many magical theorists in the 19th century magical orders and Aleister Crowley have been saying all along, but as noted above there was one important difference. The modern conception often appears to be that magical power is analogous to magnetism or electricity (or that it is psychological and subjective), analogous to neutral forces of physics, that can be accumulated and directed through the will and personal strength of the trained magician. The human is supposed to be able to emulate the powers of higher beings in his ability to control things through his or her individual psychic strength, even eliminating the need for cooperation with demons through commandeering the power of God himself, after the model – with modifications – of the Renaissance

---

[11] Michael Keffer. "Agrippa's Dilemma: Hermetic 'Rebirth' and the Ambivalences of De vanitate and De occulta philosophia." *Renaissance Quarterly*, Vol. 41, No. 4, p. 620.

magus. It isn't so much the skill in performing verbose rituals or gathering the appropriate objects (as in Ficino or Agrippa), but more of an individual's ability to focus on a particular concept and exercise an intense act of will to spark the flow of energy. Alternately, it is conceived of as the sort of inner *virtus* of the sort assumed to be innate in magical beings such as angels or demons, which could be acquired by humans through rigorous exercises and initiations. The key here is that it is no longer so much a mystical emanation of the divine, but rather a naturally occurring energy like gravity or magnetism, and thus as much or more like a scientific principal rather than an ineffable metaphysical potency such as *virtus* was. On how this change may have occurred, see Section Three, below.

In contemporary books and movies, magicians and spiritual beings are able to build and draw on personal reservoirs of this energy and cause changes by a word, the wave of a wand, or shoot it out like a lightning bolt or psychic wind towards opponents and objects. This is not reflected in the traditional theories. Magicians had no *innate* ability to accumulate and disperse *virtus* according to mainstream philosophers and theologians (the magus concept not being officially countenanced outside of the magical subculture). Instead they used their knowledge and skill to harness and direct *external* sources of *virtus* and direct them via the *Spiritus Mundi* by established rules. Although Agrippa postulated the possibility of transcending this limitation whereby the magus would in fact become the personal bearer of *virtus*, this was not actually achieved by the vast majority of magical workers. Traditionally, magical *virtus* didn't emanate from within the individual as from a battery in a taser, nor could it be instantly brought to bear without long and complex rituals and accumulations of necessary materials (nor would magicians be psychically drained after their "charge" was used up as opposed to being fatigued from the strain of concentrating on getting their interminable rituals and preparations correct). Theoretically spiritual magic could involve an increase in a personal charge of numinous power (and in a way it did, as in the case of seventh sons of seventh sons) but I believe the more common assumption was that of an increase in *authority* over spiritual beings through channeled *virtus* rather than the acquisition of personal preternatural power.

Innate *virtus* is the magic of fairy tales and fantasy or "Jonathan Strange & Mr. Norrell" and Harry Potter rather than Ficino or Trithemius. It was an individual's knowledge and experience in utilizing existing channels and vehicles of magic that counted in traditional magical work, not subjective psychological experience or inherited/acquired arcane potency. Demons and fairies could use their long lives and preternatural abilities to master far more magic than short-lived and physically limited humans, but they too seemed to have depended on universal laws and external heaven-sent *virtus*. A partial theoretical exception to this was the alleged ability of witches to perform what amounted to "negative miracles" through mere malice, drawing on Satan's store of magical power, but even here it is a question of standard preternatural magic employed unconsciously or otherwise by the witch via the Devil – not her own personal power.

Another significant detail is that astral ("natural") *virtus* was not a unitary force on earth; i.e. in the sub-lunar realm where the celestial sphere of the moon marked a tangible division between the astral and earthly realms. By this point, movement from the *Anima Mundi* had been diffracted into the series of separate "chains of influence" (or "impellations", as we will call them to avoid metaphorical confusion) that projected the individual influences of the various heavenly bodies into the world. Operative magic, for the Cunning Folk, largely became a factor of manipulating natural astrological forces.

For most magical activity, therefore, the magician didn't need the spiritual contact necessary in higher level conjuration, communication with higher intelligences, acquiring knowledge through the *Ars Notoria*, gaining a spiritual assistant (a "familiar" or a *parhedros*) or certain kinds or divination. This was certainly true for most of the work done by the Cunning Folk. A Cunning Man or Wise Woman just had to follow tradition to learn the ways in which the astral impellations could be attracted and focused. At this point we shall back up and consider the details that underlay the practical application of magic.

I attempt here a synthetic analysis of traditional magic (without claiming that it represents any sort of historical consensus) so that the work of both the Cunning Folk and traditional intellectual magicians may be made understandable. This is not a general or universal analysis of magic such as scholars from Frazer to Mauss attempted, but one for a particular time and culture, i.e., that of English-speaking peoples from early modern times to the end of the nineteenth century. There will be, however, extensions both back to the classical era from which many of the concepts were inherited and forward into the twentieth century when traditional beliefs still lingered. As the Cunning Folk were largely excluded from the complex and rarified world of academic scholarship and theology and had only second-hand access to their culture's more recondite metaphysical theories and rationales for magic, it will reflect learned opinion largely as it was diffused through the larger culture rather than from its own recondite sources.

Although my analysis is artificial in that it conflates orthodox religious activity with those of magicians in a manner not conceptually possible before the Enlightenment, it should help clarify the wide variety of period "esoteric" or spiritual practices in healing, detection, bolstering good luck, prognostication, character assessment and controlling destiny, as opposed to "manifest" or material functions of science. This may involve a number of activities that either modern or period definitions might exclude. For example, Owen Davies, the indispensible historical authority on Cunning Folk, excludes charmers from the rest of the practitioners of magical healing for sufficient reasons – but I do not. Similarly, historical physicians would not consider the traditional healing virtues attributed to stones and herbs as "magical", whereas they are for our purpose. Many authorities on European magic focus on only one of the two separate medieval contributions to magical tradition; the profane inheritance from pre-Christian cultures. Following Valerie Flint (*The Rise of Magic in Early Medieval Europe*), I include the equally influential ecclesiastical "magic" that was so central an element in Christian culture and whose influence is clearly evident in the Cunning Folk's repertoire.

Folk magic was used for practical purposes and aimed at material results, not supplication, worship, or spiritual elevation, as was the case with the theurgic aims of "higher magic". That was the bailiwick of ceremonial magicians, hermeticists and cabalists rather than the village Wise Woman or Cunning Man. There were no ritual magic orders, no witch "covens", no shamans or cabalistic fellowships in early modern England as there were (ironically) after the Enlightenment. The Cunning Folk were essentially independent artisans rather than pagans, heretics, intellectuals or wealthy adventurers.

The spectrum of magical understanding extended, as noted above, from simple acceptance without regard for principles at one end to complex and sometimes conflicted rationales at the other. Our Cunning Folk were more often (but not always) found at the simpler end of the scale, but concepts proposed by the "experts" influenced the opinions of all sorts of people through common culture. What were the common principles and conceptual models accounting for magical effects? To a large extent, the principles of magic were the same as the principles of the "scientific" world view inherited from classical antiquity. Magic and science shared the same understanding of how the Christian cosmos functioned. Those who denied astral influence or considered the stars as signifiers rather than causes, offered no pertinent alternative explanation. Also, magic could be supernatural (divine), demonic or natural – or a combination of the last two.

MAGIC IN THE COSMIC PLAN

> "This kind of magic [spiritual and demonic] had many sources. Perhaps the most important, though Ficino does not avow it, and may not have been conscious of it, is the mass with its music, words of consecration, incense, lights, wine and supreme magical effect—transubstantiation. This, I would suggest, is a fundamental influence on all medieval and Renaissance magic, and a fundamental reason for the Church's condemnation of all magical practices. The Church had her own magic; there is no room for any other." (Walker 1958: 36)

There were two "magical" traditions in medieval Europe, the sacred and the profane. The Christian church, which earlier had waged a righteous campaign against both pagan religion and pagan magic, eventually accepted the pragmatic necessity of fighting fire with fire, and created a powerful system of orthodox "magic" to oppose secular competition and co-opt the services (and acquire the status) of traditional healers and pagan thaumaturgists or "wonder-workers". Magical reality was redefined into two competing spheres; the miraculous and admirable spiritual triumphs of the Church as opposed to the mad, bad and dangerous wonders – real as well as illusory – of the sordid magical underworld. The former was God's work as undertaken by His ordained agents (by saints and bishops in particular), which healed the unfortunate, rewarded the virtuous and freed Christians from the machinations of the Devil through holy *virtus*. The latter was ostensibly demonic in origin (although natural forces might be involved), whereby people might be cured of disease, given a glimpse of the future or enriched in worldly goods only to lose their birthright of salvation in Christ's name.

The "magic" of the Church was not called that, of course, nor was the pagan concept of Eros the same as Divine Grace. Like the divine power that could be channeled by saints (who were given a magical franchise, so to speak), Christian operative magic was the responsibility of properly ordained vicars of Christ. Miracles could be wrought by saints apparently directly from the divine source, but for the others, certain rites and materials needed to be employed. In form and function, the obvious correspondence with the magic of antiquity in the use of consecrated substances, relics, charms, invocations and amulets was evident to unbiased or hostile observers. This was made clear by the glee with which Protestant reformers pounced on such things as exorcism, the sign of the cross, holy water and "conception billets" (a conjuration and prayer written on consecrated paper and sold by Carmelite monks – see chapter 7) as evidence of Catholic "witchery".

In theory, the spiritual power of the Church was the gift of the Holy Spirit that could suspend natural law and achieve an actual supernatural effect, a "miracle" (*miracula*). The magic of the competition, on the other hand, had no ability in theory to do anything truly *supernatural*. Their effects were limited to the "preternatural" – things unusual and beyond ordinary phenomena, but not impossible, which were classed as "wonders" (*mira*). These might mimic miracles, but they were not supernatural and were fully subject to the laws of the cosmos. By definition only bonafide churchmen had access to God's true supernatural *virtus*, whereas traditional magic was restricted to the preternatural sphere. This official position was not necessarily accepted by everyone, and many unorthodox practitioners claimed and very well may have believed they had the same supernatural ability as saints and bishops with all of its heavenly legitimacy, despite the strict disapproval of the Christian establishment, both ecclesiastical and legal.

For the purpose of developing a theory of magic, however, God's incalculable force behind the miraculous leads us nowhere. Holy *virtus* simply IS, resembling the indefinable power found in Mana, Manitou, the Dao, modern occult systems, or the *Star Wars*' "Force". It was also often early on predicated on the innate status possessed by certain individuals, such as saints, kings who inherited their power by blood descent from supernatural ancestors, or heroes in ancient myths. On a more mundane level, the inborn ability attributed to seventh sons of a seventh son, or the unruly and often regretted capacity for "second sight" reflects a similar concept in later ages. In these cases, such power ultimately had a divine origin, but lacked any characteristic beyond that. In the age-old philosophical discussion about traditional western magic, there has been a great more deal thought given to the other, preternatural sort of magic, which is what we deal with here. Ostensible "orthodox" Christian magic will turn up from time to time in comparison and as a source of more mundane magical traditions, but it is the classical understanding of folk magic that will inform this analysis.

The key to preternatural magic (and traditional science as well) is astrological – the influence of the heavenly bodies on earthly, sub-lunar existence. Deriving ultimately from the Stoic philosophers and Aristotle, the traditional view of creation was that everything in the universe was derived from and dependent on what lay outside of material existence in God's realm (the "*Empyrean*" or "*Pleroma*", the totality of all that was regarded as "divine"). From this external spiritual reality, God's Divine Providence flowed into and throughout the universe, causing and regulating everything in temporal existence through the laws of celestial harmony (via the soul/spirit of the world). We need not be concerned here with how this unitary influence (characterised as the instrumentalities of astral "motion", "light" and "*influencia*") was subsequently diffracted into a pattern of differentiated astral effects, just as white light is in a rainbow; suffice it to say that it was. These subordinate influences, effectively channeled through the stars, zodiacal constellations and planets, provided the significance of natural astrology, which no one questioned or rejected in early times. The system of astral influence could explain all movement, growth, change and decay; everything that happened in the tangible world could ultimately be traced to this series of emanations.

Astral influence was transmitted from the divine realm to the cosmos through the *Primum Mobile*, the crystalline sphere or heavenly plane that lay just below the boundary between the *Empyrean* and the material universe, and rotated eternally from east to west like a cosmic flywheel. It was this perpetual motion that brought temporal change into the world. Change was an everlasting process that characterised earthly existence, whereby everything that came into being grew or altered, aged or decayed, and passed away. In the *Empyrean*, by contrast, all was unchanging and eternal. For instance, in the *Empyrean* there existed immutable universal models or "Substantial Forms" for all the plurality of individual things on Earth. The form of "Table", for example, contained all that was essential for something to be perceived as a table, even though imperfect worldly examples could differ widely in numbers of legs, sizes, shapes, and materials. The variations, however, were mere "accidents" that in no way detracted from any particular table's essential "tableness", which it derived from the ideal *Empyrean* "Table" form. The *Empyrean* Form never changed – but worldly tables always did. Whether change came quickly or extended over eons, nothing in the physical cosmos remained static and unaltered.

This process was entirely natural and, in itself, the accepted explanation of how the physical universe worked. Logically, if someone was to learn about the system to the extent that he or she could: a) predict what impellations would occur in the future, and b) discover how to manipulate them to achieve a desired effect, it would be a wonderful advantage. To understand and ultimately have power over the astral forces was the definitive aspiration of the magical practitioner. This unceasing natural modification of the physical character of things (or if you will, the endless parade of different "form ideas" or "specific forms" that successively configure things as they pass through time) was what magic sought to predict or control. Essentially, preternatural magic was analogous to forcing a flower to bloom in a hot house. It is entirely natural, but because of the artificially arranged conditions (coldness, heat, humidity and light), materials (plant bulb, container, water, soil, and fertilizer), activity (bringing everything together and employing it correctly and with care) and above all, the knowledge and skill needed to perform the operation, a flowering takes place that would not have *then* otherwise occurred.

More about the forms or cosmic *ideas*: it was accepted that each earthly thing received its characteristics from its universal prototype, which was the general model for each individual instance. For example, there might be an archetypical or substantial "form" for human hair – thin protein filaments growing out of the skin on the head and elsewhere. In Plato, Socrates disputes with Parmenides as to whether "undignified" things like hair could even have a form, but as hair existed, there should logically be a hair form. Something had to give hair its character, regardless of temporal irregularities or "accidents". The difficulty here is how the perfect archetypal or essential form of "hair" could relate to the myriad "accidental" variations in actual heads of hair. When a baby first grew hair, for instance, the archetypal "hair" form gave it characteristics, but specific details such as colour and texture of the individual baby's hair was also influenced by inherited potential (a human only grows hair, not fur or bristles, with the type determined by the parents) "sown" as "seminal principles" (which functioned like DNA in determining development and reproduction) by earlier emanations. The growth of the hair itself was just a variant "instantiated" or individualised from the primal "form".

However, as nothing remains static in the sub-lunar realm, the soft, short infant hair is soon succeeded by longer and then coarser hair, all from the original form (this vastly simplifies and probably distorts the official theory with its contraries &c., but no matter). In everything, a continual flow of astral influences from the universal form apparently accounted for growth and aging (or just wear in inanimate objects); with a new variation or "image" of the form being installed each time the object alters. We might liken the process to the series of cells in a movie film, with each different image projected from the form by way of the astral influence, one quickly succeeding another. The result was the continuously changing physical appearance of the thing being informed – in the case of hair, perhaps, eventually being superseded by the "form" of baldness, a change dictated again by the individual's seminal hair principal. To shift metaphors, innumerable forms were broadcasting images all the time, but only a particular seminal principle attuned to picking up a particular form received the correct signal so that people couldn't accidently tune into and receive feathers instead of hair.[12]

Before we investigate the workings of astral forces on earth, a succinct description of the traditional cosmos might help those unfamiliar with the traditional Western world view. For anyone interested in more detailed but understandable accounts of the traditional world view, I recommend A. O. Lovejoy's *The Great Chain of Being* (1936), E. M. W. Tillyard's *The Elizabethan World Picture* (1959), C. S. Lewis' *The Discarded Image* (1963) and James Winny's *The Frame of Order* (1957), as the following account is by necessity quite simplified and concentrated primarily on the question of magic. A word of warning – in all of this, very little was ever truly settled or firmly established. Contradictory statements on everything from the actual number of spheres (from eight to fifty-five, depending on who you listened to) to the purported function of particular components of the cosmic pattern makes it difficult to reduce the information to a single synthesis. For example, while many authorities accepted a unitary view of the magic that linked the heavens to earthly things, Agrippa disagreed and made distinct separations between natural earthly magic, astral or "celestial" magic and "divine magic". I have chosen to favor Al Kindi's and Ficino's more unitary views as being a better reflection of tradition than Agrippa's complex innovations. As there is no single master account, it is necessary to select appropriately coherent elements, recognizing that conflicting historical opinions may cause this analysis to differ from other equally valid surveys.

We will now recapitulate the cosmic system described in the introduction. The material universe, from the *Primum Mobile* to the lowest depths of the Earth (or Hell), was conceived to be a series of concentric spheres, like the layers of an onion. There were nine crystalline spheres that supposedly revolved around the Earth in perfectly circular movements – the circle being considered the perfect shape and perfection a characteristic of the higher spheres – with no loose ends, no irregularities. Regrettably, there were in fact problems with this ideal, as the orbits were not in fact perfect circles and the error concerning Earth's actual position led to confusion (Ptolemy used epicycles to correct for this), but this is a difficulty we need not be concerned with. Earth *appeared* to be the centre around which all the other layers revolved – although theologically (or paradoxically, if you will), Earth was actually on the periphery and the Empyrean at the centre. However, from a geocentric perspective, it didn't appear that way, and the standard accounts describe the universe as it looked from an earthly perspective.

The next sphere inside of or below the *Primum Mobile* was the "*Stellarum*", the sphere of the "fixed stars" in which all the stars and galaxies moved together in a regular motion. The *Stellarum* derived its motion from the previous sphere, but it revolved in two opposing directions. Daily, it revolved from east to west, as was obvious by the rising and setting of the sun and constellations, but this was because it was carried along by the direction of the *Primum Mobile*. Its own natural motion was from west to east, which was evident in the "procession of the equinoxes", but as it was caught up in the powerful flow of the higher sphere, it made contrary progress very slowly, against the current, as C. S. Lewis says. This sphere was studded with 48 identified constellations (or 88, if the southern hemisphere is included, which wasn't the case in the Middle Ages) including the significant dozen on the ecliptic that comprised the zodiac as well as innumerable individual stars. Although we might think of a hollow sphere as a relatively thin figure, the *Stellarum* was described as immensely deep, conceptually similar to our "outer space". It would take at least 8,700 years to even ascend through the smaller spheres of the planets – our solar system – (at 40 leagues a day, according to Maimonides or the late 13th century *South English Legendary*). That the resultant 125 million miles wasn't literally accurate is irrelevant – the concept was one of enormous distance, and little more truly conceivable than that of our more extended universe. The real difference is that our ancestors "knew" what lay beyond the bounds of the physical universe (the *Empyrean*) while we don't – a source of cosmic disquiet and existential collywobbles for moderns who lack the old security of a bounded cosmos.

---

[12] A shifting of shapes might logically be the basis for the transformation by magic of a man into a toad, as is popularly imagined in fairy tales and fiction. However, no traditional theorist allowed that so drastic a shift was indeed possible.

Beneath the fixed stars were the seven spheres of the "wanderers" or planets, moving independently of the fixed constellations and of each other: Saturn, Jupiter, Mars, the Sun, Venus, Mercury and the Moon. Each planet was embedded in a separate sphere that had its own particular motion and influence, and its own self-aware "mover" – the planetary intelligence or angel/god/demon. The lowest or Lunar sphere was also the boundary between the heavens and the earthly or terrestrial realm that was the recipient of the astral influences. Everything below the moon was compounded of four "elements" (fire, air, water, and earth) subject to cosmic influence through motion (but also light and less definable "*influentia*"), whereas the relatively flawless heavenly bodies were composed of a superior fifth element, "spirit" or "quintessence". It was the effect of the cosmic *virtus*, primarily through heat and cold, on the four elements that made things happen.

Al Kindi's *On the Stellar Rays* was a very influential source for the explanation of magic and occult forces. Written by the Arabic philosopher Ya´kûb ibn Ishâk ibn Sabbâh Alkindi (ca. 801–873), who worked in the House of Wisdom established in 762 CE by Caliph Al-Mansur in Baghdad for the study of Indian, Greek and Persian science, *On the Stellar Rays* provides a logically coherent and fairly mechanical account of magical action, concentrating on the ways in which people could manipulate the astral emanations through words, images, inscriptions, and sacrifices. For Al Kindi, the world is governed by an immense complex of astral "rays", which was collectively referred to as "celestial harmony". This celestial harmony encompassed what we understand today as physics, chemistry and biology – plus magic. Al Kindi's work became well known in the 12th century and along with corresponding concepts from Aristotle, Augustine and Aquinas, the ideas he expressed had become familiar throughout Western culture by the time we are dealing with. The related discourse developed in educated circles by Ficino, Pico della Mirandola, Agrippa &c., on the other hand, was more complex and largely restricted to intellectuals until the mid-17th century, or later.

Each of these heavenly bodies emanated a particular influence, which corporately as the "celestial harmony" (also known as the "World Soul" – the *Anima Mundi* – or more specifically, the related *Spiritus Mundi*) determined the mutable conditions on earth. In addition, the stars' particular souls or Intelligences each had an individual sentience that worked to distribute the specific impellations of their sphere. These zodiacal constellations and the planets were more influential than the rest and worthy of particular consideration, as the total pattern of influence from all the stars was simply too complex to conceive of in its entirety. The investigation and analysis of these influences was what astrology was all about, while the manipulation of their natural impellations was the aim of magic.

On earth, the astral forces not only caused change, but also determined the elemental composition of material things. Everything below the moon was compounded out of the four basic elements of fire, air, water and earth. The particular composition or structure of each object and creature was determined by the form it received from above, as well as by the seminal principles that were embodied in its creation. These dictated its particular qualities. Not only were the receptions of forms attributed to astral influence, but also the "virtues" (divisions of the larger *virtus*) or innate properties and potencies supplied by the seminal principles. Earthly things were not simply passive recipients of astral influence, however. They also radiated their own influences in a lesser but similar manner to that of the stars, further complicating the situation. The sum of this holistic and interwoven pattern determined the multifarious conditions and events across the globe – a truly bewildering convergence of influence! Then there was a cast of other spiritual characters such as angels and demons that we will get to later.

To summarize, the perpetual fluctuation of earthly existence was driven by divine influence (motion &c.) divided and redirected through intermediary heavenly bodies. This was accomplished through a series of "rays" or emanations, each carrying the individualised characteristics of its source—whether astral or earthly. Without such motion, the world would cease to exist. The emanations transmitted forms for physical change and also active instigating impulses – which we call "impellations" so as to not confuse them with other less distinct terms such as "rays" or "vibrations" – that activated events and interactions among discrete entities linked through the *Spiritus Mundi*. The diversity of earthly conditions, as Al Kindi notes, was the result of both the "rays" or emanations, and the way in which the innate natures of material things received them.

THE FUNCTION OF ASTRAL IMPELLATIONS

How these impellations enhanced or conflicted with one another was the result of the terrestrial location of the affected object and the immediate arrangement and motion of the stars, predicated on the projection of their emanations from above. It should be emphasized that this "natural astrology" was commonly accepted by the pious and the profane alike as true – debates over astrology mostly concerned the ability of humans to interpret or control this process, not whether the stars' influence was real or not. Given the initial premise, a map of the heavens (or horoscope) at the moment of influence – together with an understanding of each planet or constellation's influence to interpret it by – could logically allow someone to analyse the composite results of astral influence, and also predict what would happen next.

Heavenly influence might be equated with fate – the source of a fixed destiny, but it was generally accepted that the future was not absolutely predetermined. Classical philosophy allowed for latitude in this matter, arguing that chance was necessary for free will to exist – and free will was a Christian theological imperative – despite the conflict with divine omniscience and the workings of Providence. This was a matter of debate. It is human nature that people who desire certainty and order are inclined to believe in the security of a highly-determined view of existence such as that John Calvin offered his followers, while others who felt oppression in unyielding predetermination, preferred a philosophy that allowed for contingency in which they saw opportunity, not chaos. In practice, room was found for both God's Providence and the capricious whims of the goddess Fortuna. Mankind was not bound by cosmic fate, but could to some extent enhance or avoid the impellations of the stars – and adjust the results.

Admitting astral influence to be real, however, raised another question – how did the impellations achieve their results? People could understand mechanical causes through the evidence of their senses. If you hit something with a rock, it broke. If you set wood on fire, it burned. You could forge and shape iron with fire, cut wood with iron tools, and make a house with nails and wooden boards. Other causes were less clear, but cause and effect relationships were easily demonstrable through experience. If you ate food, it became part of your flesh, through what was analogous to a process of "cooking" within the body. If you planted an acorn, it grew into an oak tree, because of both the seminal principle (or "virtue") in the seed and the effect of heavenly forms. Emanations, on the other hand, were imperceptible, and evidence of their existence could only be inferred from the ostensible result. They were hidden from both sense perception and rational understanding alike.

There *were* various manifest effects that had no physical explanation, including the action of spirit on matter, astral impellations, and certain mundane effects such as magnetism. As Godfrid Storms says, "The magic effect is characterised by the insensorial, indirect and mysterious connection with its cause" (Storms 1948: 37) .This was referred to as being "occult" or hidden rather than "manifest" or apparent. Today we are used to thinking of "occult" as a synonym for anything metaphysical, supernatural or ineffable, but originally it referred to effects that could not be explained by contemporary knowledge, such as poison, magnetism or life itself. These things were quite evident, but their cause was "occluded" and experimentation at the time didn't reveal any answers. As many things were inexplicable in the pre-scientific era, there was a widespread acceptance of occult causation, which could be learned from historical sources, and was generally labeled as "natural magic". These principles determined all preternatural results, which, as Stuart Clark (*Thinking with Demons*, 1999) has exhaustively demonstrated, were the means, in which angels and demons were far more proficient than any mortal, by which both men and demons affected their magical workings.

The astral impellations produced effects in things (even inanimate ones) through their individual spiritual natures – a kind of homology of "like speaking to like". The traditional philosophical explanation of life and consciousness postulated three varieties of the metaphysical substance "soul" (or alternatively "spirit" – see Section Two, below) that gave life to the cosmos. The highest sort was "rational soul", the self-awareness that gave rational beings the ability to think intellectually, and use reason to observe, learn and work out problems. This ability was shared by angels, demons and humans. The second sort was "sensitive soul", the capacity for sensual impressions, instincts and emotions. Humans and animals shared this attribute. The third sort was "vegetative soul", the ability for gestation, nutrition, growth and propagation – and death. This was possessed by humans, animals and plants. Everything else on Earth simply existed, although inanimate things too received and emanated impellations.

One question that bothered earlier thinkers was how something as intangible as an astral ray or impellation could "move" (affect) an inert, soulless material object. Their solution was the impellations could act on the "seminal principle" and the elemental composition of each thing by affecting the constituent elements, as these had the same heavenly origin as the impellations themselves.

However, as I have said, it was thought that this soul-stuff was so rarified that it could have no direct effect on the gross physical bodies of living things. A secondary spiritual substance was therefore postulated to act as intermediary between souls and bodies. This "vital spirit" (sometimes refined into varieties that we need not go into here) was the conduit by which the immaterial astral impellations, thoughts, sensations and vitality could act upon the physical body. It travelled through the circulatory system like smoke and enabled the soul to interact with the body in different ways.

Also, because humans alone embodied each of the cosmic substances – a compound rational, sensitive and vegetative soul, vital spirits and a physical body – they were analogous to the universe itself, miniature models of creation or "microcosms" that mirrored the complexity of the entire cosmos or the "macrocosm". Angels had only rational souls, demons had these (if debased) together with aerial bodies, while animals had sensitive and vegetative souls and accompanying spirits in material bodies, and plants just had vegetative souls (and spirits) in material bodies. Inanimate nature such as gems and stones, on the other hand, only had material "body" or substance. As Ficino notes, although spirit encompasses these also (otherwise they would have no magical virtues), "the spirit in them is inhibited by the grosser material. When this spirit is rightly separated and, once separated, is conserved," it can be used to generate more of their substance – the basis of alchemy – as well as act as a conduit for astral impellations (Ficino 2002: 257).

The endless diversity in earthly events and the roles of all creatures and objects, as we have seen, was caused by the different impulses radiating from the constellations, stars, planets, and elements as they were received at any particular moment, as well as the innate seminal principles of the receiving party. The impellations of a particular star were thought to be strongest when received in a straight line in a location directly opposite, as when a star is rising, at its zenith or setting, whereas impellations received obliquely in relation to location, were less potent. The influence differed as well from the character of the receptor's elemental character, as the same heat that will liquefy (melt) a metal will solidify (harden) clay into a brick. The impellations were always multiple – each planet and zodiacal constellation sending a different signal as it were, from the sobering influence of Saturn, the magnanimous influence of Jupiter, the excitable influence of Mars, the powerfully vivifying influence of the Sun, the amorous influence of Venus, the volatile influence of Mercury to the mutable influence of the Moon. The end result of the blended influences depended on the relative strength of each impellation, plus the inherent characteristics of the recipient. The blend is also forever changing, and like the famously mutable New England weather, if we wait a moment, the results become something different.

In addition to these diverse external influences, individual beings and objects had their individual seminal principles. They received these particular qualities through the *Spiritus Mundi*, in which each took on the characteristics of the specific constellations and/or planets most directly involved at their gestation or creation. All earthly things therefore had a dominant particularity reflecting the heavenly impellation that most strongly marked them, giving them traits that they shared with other things influenced by the same heavenly force. This included physical characteristics such as colour, shape and other elemental properties that "signed" them as being related to certain astral categories (most often divided by planet or zodiacal sign), which were called "correspondences". Such "signatures" could also provide tangible clues to innate potencies. People's physical characteristics revealed their particular ruling impellations, so that by an informed observation of their faces (physiognomy), the location of moles on the body (moleosophy) or lines on the hand (palmistry), not only was their true character revealed, but also their future fortunes, through the foreshadowing of the impellations they had been formed by and were susceptible to, just as a horoscope might. Similarly, animals, plants and minerals could bear signatures, manifest or not, of their dominant principles that indicated how they might be of use in medicine or magic.

The impellations of the celestial harmony were mostly received passively on Earth so that change occurred in an automatic, fully *natural* fashion, just as the stars revolved in a regular manner. There could be exceptions, however. Rational beings; angels, demons and (some) humans, were able to understand the conditions they were subject to, and attempt to manipulate them to their own ends. Presumably most angels preferred the divine stability they enjoyed at the highest level of creation, but on occasion they could become involved in sub-lunar situations in their roles as divine messengers or guardians. Demons and men, however, having been relegated to a chaotic earthly existence, had a far greater interest in learning about and adjusting the effects of the impellations to benefit their welfare.

They could not change or deflect the astral "motions" (impellations) themselves, but they could modify the results through magical rites and by utilizing the occult properties of *virtus* and intangible signs, or naturally-occurring objects and "artifacts" (that is, man-made things). Al Kindi accounts for the use of animals, herbs and gems, as all things send out "rays" or impellations, but he concentrates on the magic of names, words, figures, sacrifices, observation of times (when the astral configuration was best) and the vital requirement of active desire and willful intent to produce magical results. Intent alone, like wishes and daydreams, could never achieve a magical effect – it had to be accompanied by the appropriate invocations, objects and rituals. Correspondingly, not only did invocations have to be joined with visualised intent, they would only work under very specific conditions of time, place and so forth. Errors in wording or actions also rendered the effort useless. Just as the wrong turn of phrase could anger an audience, regardless of the speaker's real intent, even small mistakes and miscalculations could spoil the most elaborate and painstaking magical operation. Nevertheless, by tapping into the natural action of the celestial harmony, magicians could expect wondrous results.

That magic depended on astral impellations, including the secondary emanations from earthly objects and artifacts, is quite clear. There is, however, one other element in traditional magic that has also to be taken into account – the role of spirits (intelligences, angels, demons, fairies and ghosts) in magical operations.

There was a significant division between the common belief in the function of demonic magic and that of orthodox Christian theology, as Stuart Clark has indicated. It seems apparent that most people simply accepted that planetary intelligences, angels, the Devil, demons and assorted spiritual beings (such as elves, fairies, hags, imps and other sub-lunar creatures, which C. S. Lewis has usefully grouped together as the "Longaevi" – that is, "long-lived" but not immortal beings) could work magic supernaturally through their innate *virtus*. This belief was rejected by philosophers and theologians who did not allow for any supernatural ability that might compete with God's holy *virtus* in this regard. Al Kindi even registers disbelief in the existence of independent spiritual beings altogether, though Christian theorists could not go so far, since the Bible attested to the existence of such creatures. The educated position, as we have seen, was that all magic was limited to the preternatural realm, that no being besides God could suspend natural law. Similarly, no creature (except perhaps the stars, higher angels and perhaps – illicitly – certain higher demons) could personally work preternatural magic through their *virtus* rather than that of God's that governed the cosmos.

To illustrate this, we might use a metaphor of computer software. God was the original and sole "programmer" who had written the code for the function of His creation, and was the only one capable of modifying the basic code of Nature itself, temporarily, at His discretion. Everyone else had to work with the program as it had been compiled. Some beings, especially immortals and the Longaevi, were able to better master the complex program of Nature through long experience, elevated skill and deeper knowledge as well as a limited ability to set parameters, whereas few humans could transcend the "newbie" level of Nature's basic operations. No one could hack into the code itself or modify any procedure (or perform "supernatural" functions) except the Great Programmer, so all scientific and magical operations were restricted to the program as it stood. Saints and other true "miracle workers" could only achieve supernatural effects by God's aid in the temporary modification of His program in a specific instance. They couldn't do these things themselves but were merely benefiting from the deity's willing contrivance for some larger benefit to the Christian faith.

Therefore, the traditional division of magic into natural and demonic actually broke down to operations that people could effect by the use of learned procedures that utilised the natural if hidden or obscure functions of Nature's "program", while for those they didn't known about (or couldn't master) they needed to employ the aid of far more expert and skilled spiritual "hackers", of whom the Devil – a highly sophisticated fallen angel – was the most proficient. While the most censorious religious authorities might want to forbid any and all magic, the use of simple natural magic did have widespread acceptance in early modern culture – and a lot of what passed for science and medicine before the late 19th century was hardly distinguishable from magic, anyway. Where almost everyone except for hardcore enthusiasts drew the line was getting help from non-human entities, whether they were marginally less-objectionable angels and fairies, or demons and the Devil himself, some did choose to venture into forbidden territory. Such magic might be more effective, but its very use endangered the human soul and involved a fundamental threat of eternal damnation. God was very jealous about any unauthorized hacking of his program, despite the fact that He allowed the Devil to go after susceptible humans, using magical benefits as bait.

THE MAGICAL ACT

To work traditional magic successfully, the magician had to know and observe a number of factors:

- **Personal purity.** For many magical operations, the practitioner had to basically "clean house" – make himself more like a spiritual being and less like an earthly one, through the same sort of ascetic preparation that a priest might undergo involving fasting, prayer, contemplation, receiving religious sacraments and the like. This could range from almost no preparation on the part of a backstreet diviner to the elaborate and lengthy purifications of a conjuror and even the assumption though ritual and actions of the god-like potency achieved by the Agrippaean Magus.

- **Astrological conditions.** As the natural impellations of the cosmos were the motive force that empowered magical acts, the calculation of their influence was of paramount importance. Knowing the astral signatures and correspondences that identified objects' virtues was the most common requirement, but an awareness of appropriate days and times played an increasing role as popular astrology became more widespread. The ever-changing diversity of astral impellations meant that certain configurations of the stars and planets would be beneficial or supportive to a magical operation, while others could hinder or even prevent its success. For those educated in electional astrology (where the astrologer constructs a horoscope to see what the most propitious time to begin any endeavour) and had the required charts and tables, this could be easily done. However, not every practitioner had the skill or equipment to do this, so there were simpler alternative methods for choosing a proper time (or more often, avoiding a bad one). Lists of favourable and unfavourable days and times existed to aid in the decision of the best time to commence an operation.

- **Spells, names, invocations, psalms and charms.** As authorities from Al Kindi to Agrippa said, the use of words and utterances were vitally important in achieving magical ends. It was thought that most of these were originally received through inspiration from higher beings, which could be learned from tradition and books. Spoken or written with focused intent (or will), the proper words or names became impellations in themselves, allowing access to sources of magical *virtus*.

- **Figures and images.** The inscription of particular characters (including graphic sigils, pictures, numbers, and letters on paper, gems and other objects) were further reinforcements that tapped into the power of astral impellations. Sigils and characters, being abstractions, connected directly to the intangible *virtus* of the star, being involved in a way physical objects could not. Alternately, three-dimensional images, such as effigies, talismans, and "poppets" (commonly known today as "voodoo dolls") were also effective enhancers of magical operations.

- **Natural objects**. Naturally-occurring objects and substances, including parts of animals (as well as their blood and excretions), drugs, plants, and stones chosen for their innate potencies that were representative of particular astral impellations could achieve desired effects, either by themselves (as in medicinal formulas) or in conjunction with the things listed above.

- **Tools**. Although less important (except as props) than they were for ceremonial magicians, such things as crystals, wands, "mosiacal rods", mirrors, and knives (and costumes of robes and hats) were also part of the operative Cunning Folk's equipment.

- **Books**. Even for illiterate practitioners who could only use them as props, magical books and manuscripts were crucially important, and became more so as time went on. As Owen Davies observes, "In popular culture where most information was transmitted orally, and only a minority were able to read and write, literacy meant power. It comes as no surprise, then, to find that cunning folk made a great show of the fact that they possessed and used books and manuscripts. Not just any books, however, but ones that would impress." (Davies 2003: 119). Written resources made it possible to employ not only reputable astrology, but also have reference to a wider assortment of complex practices than might come their way through oral tradition.

The last item is the most significant for investigating the practice of magic in English culture. The surviving *literate* resources of the Cunning Folk are the basis for this book. Oral tradition cannot be relied on farther back than about three generations for historical accuracy, as traditions are forever mutating to adapt to changing circumstances, and we long ago lost the perishable inheritance of our pre-literate ancestors. As Adam Fox observed, the interaction between oral and written sources is key to understanding our subject:

> "Memories of the past in early modern England reflect the nature of this society as one in which oral and written tradition overlapped and interacted in reciprocal and mutually reinforcing ways. Verbal communication remained the medium through which knowledge was most often transmitted. A powerful quasi-autonomous oral tradition thrived at a time in which literacy levels were limited and popular culture could be highly parochial. And yet the influence of the written word, and increasingly of print, lay behind so much of this repertoire, informing it, structuring it and sustaining it. In this period, as for many centuries before, writing had supplemented and complemented the vernacular repertoire rather than necessarily undermining it. What began with the pen of a learned author could very quickly pass into the oral tradition of the people and even more quickly be assumed to be ancient."[13]

Every major change in what are known as cultural paradigms wipes out past presumptions and practices, and if these have not been artificially preserved in the medium of the written word, they are gone beyond recall. As this book is based on documented sources, they must suffice as a theoretical basis for the magic of the Cunning Folk and the beliefs of their contemporaries, although an actual witness from the period could very likely greatly improve upon the picture.

---

[13] Adam Fox. "Remembering the Past in Early Modern England: Oral and Written Tradition", *Transactions of the Royal Historical Society*, Sixth Series, Vol. 9 (1999), p. 256.

SECTION TWO: ON SOULS, SPIRITS AND PHANTASMS

>**Note:** I've included even more quotes and references in the following sections than elsewhere simply because I mistrust my capacity to effectively simplify the complex and contradictory ideas involved – better to let them speak for themselves.

It is difficult to try to describe the distinction between the soul and the human spirit. The two are recognized as independent entities; the one immaterial or purely numinous[14] and of divine origin; the other material, but of a very fine, attenuated sort of matter derived from the stars or the body itself. When it comes to details, however, authorities disagree about which did what. They could even fuse them together, as Alcher of Clairvaux did in his *De Spiritu* (ca. 1160):

> "The soul is an intellectual, rational spirit, always living, always in motion, capable of good or evil will. … It is known by various names according to its works. It is called soul when it vivifies; spirit, when it contemplates; a sense, when it senses; consciousness (animus), when it knows; when it understands, mind; when it discerns, reason, when it remembers, memory; when it consents, will. These are not, however, differences of substance, but the names, for all these things are a single soul: diverse properties, but one essence." (Caciola 2003: 182-183)

Functions one author says are the work of the soul are by another claimed to be those of the spirit, the difficulty arising from the conflicting perspectives of Aristotle, Galen and Christian theology. For example, Galen said the spirit was the cause of life in a body, while the philosophers said it was the soul. Some said the human spirit was entirely the product of the body, whereas others added an astral component. As the latter is vital to magical theory, we will take that as a given, even if it adds to the confusion. As D. P. Walker notes,

> "When the concept of spirit is combined with astrology, … the difficulties become more acute; what transcendence there is in the system is put into the stars, and therefore, since the spirit derives from these, it becomes almost a double of the soul (or vice versa)—both have a celestial or divine origin …, both are the total form of the body, both perform psychological activities. There are two ways out of this difficulty, neither of them quite philosophically satisfactory or religiously orthodox. Either one can get rid of the soul by identifying it, or merging it, with the spirit, as Melanchthon and, later, Agostino Donio and Jean Bodin did; or, like Telesio, Campanella or Descartes, one can drastically restrict the functions of the soul, reducing them to purely abstract thought and religious contemplation (i.e. to those of the intellect, *mens*), and allow the spirit to perform all other psychological and vital functions."[15]

At the most basic, the spirit was simply the *means* by which the soul worked in the body, so that if the soul is ultimately the source of life, motion, growth and consciousness, its actual function was carried out by the spirit. Although there were three major and a number of minor divisions in both the soul and the spirit, each worked in a holistic manner with interaction between the parts, determining the entire inner functioning of the individual. This must be kept in mind when describing the three divisions, which can appear to be rather more independent than they actually were. "Always remember, though, that just as the power of our soul is brought to bear on our members through the spirit, so the force of the World-soul is spread under the World-soul through all things through the quintessence, which is active everywhere, as the spirit inside the World's Body…" (Ficino 2002: 247).

The human soul ultimately came from God, which is straightforward enough, although there were controversies over how this occurred in practice. The origin of the spirit is more problematical. We can begin with the relatively succinct description by Robert Burton in his *Anatomy of Melancholy* (1621):

---

[14] I use the term "numinous" here in an attempt not to confuse the human or cosmic spirit with the other uses of the word "spirit": "… the term *spiritus* … could signify a rarified form of fire or air, the soul, mind, imagination or fantasy, the world-soul, the Holy Spirit, and so forth." (Bono 1984: 98) A lot to demand of a single term.

[15] D. P. Walker. "The Astral Body in Renaissance Medicine". *Journal of the Warburg and Courtauld Institutes*, Vol. 21, No. 1/2 (Jan. - Jun., 1958), p. 126.

> "Spirit is a most subtile vapour, which is expressed from the blood, and the instrument of the soul, to perform all his actions; a common tie or medium between the body and the soul, as some will have it; or as Paracelsus, a fourth soul of itself. Melancthon holds the fountain of those spirits to be the heart, begotten there; and afterward conveyed to the brain, they take another nature to them. Of these spirits, there be three kinds, according to the three principal parts, brain, heart, liver; natural, vital, animal. The natural are begotten in the liver, and thence dispersed through the veins, to perform those natural actions. The vital spirits are made in the heart of the natural, which by the arteries are transported to all the other parts: if the spirits cease, then life ceaseth, as in a syncope or swooning. The animal spirits formed of the vital, brought up to the brain, and diffused by the nerves, to the subordinate members, give sense and motion to them all." (Burton 1850: 96)

The spirit, or that part which was not astrally acquired, was made in the heart from external spirit or *pneuma* drawn in through breathing. It was processed in the left side of the organ to become internal *pneuma* or human spirit, and dispersed through the arteries to the rest of the body. The soul was supposed to be located in the same part of the heart (the left ventricle), which separated it from the grosser parts of the body. As Burton observed, there were three main types of spirit – natural, vital and animal. The natural spirit, which was processed in the liver, maintained the physical body, governing the functions of nourishment, growth and reproduction and traveled through the veins. It was the vehicle for the "vegetative" soul, delivering that soul's effects to the body. The role of the natural spirit and vegetative soul is quite straightforward and is not involved in magic. Galen and other physicians asserted that the human spirit was made in the liver and ascended to the heart for processing and thence rose to the brain, but the tripartite functional division was the same.

Problems of consistency come at the next level – the "sensible" soul and its vehicle, the vital spirit. The vital spirit provided life-giving heat and moisture to the body, and as the vehicle of the "sensible" soul, governed the faculties of perception, the appetites, breathing, bodily movement, and the emotions or passions (we still credit the heart with love, for example). Perception involved the five outer senses or wits – sight, hearing, smell, taste, touch – and three inner senses of "phantasy", "memory" and "common sense", to which some authorities added "estimation" and "imagination". This "common sense" was not what we think of as the common sense that consists of socially accepted opinions, but was rather the faculty that processed all incoming sense perceptions. Phantasy (or cognition) was where the sense impressions were made readable to the intellect by being interrelated into mental images or thought-forms (*phantasms*). The intellect could also create its own synthesized *phantasms* though imagination or involuntarily in dreams. Imagination was sometimes considered as a separate inner wit, but it too is not the same as our conception of imagination, which is more like the phantasy in function. Traditionally imagination referred to the ability to abstractly conceive and invent things. Memory – which thankfully is simply that – was where the thoughts/*phantasms* were stored to be retrieved for consideration by intellect, phantasy, or imagination.

"Phantasms" can also refer to external forms such as ghosts or evil spirits; misleading or dangerous spirit-forms that could delude or threaten the individual. These phantasms were not created in the mind but existed independently. In the current context, however, it is only the internal thought-forms that are being considered. Even here, illusory phantasms could arise through mistaken conceptualizations or "fancies" that did not reflect reality but were simple errors or playful exercises of the imagination.

The "appetites" were shared by the natural and vital spirits, although their effects were governed by the latter. They included the physical hunger, thirst, and sex, or "concupiscence" – desire in general, about which the *Catholic Encyclopedia* notes, "In its widest acceptation, concupiscence is any yearning of the soul for good; in its strict and specific acceptation, a desire of the lower appetite contrary to reason."[16] As Burton defines it, the appetite

> "… is divided into two powers, or inclinations, concupiscible or irascible: or (as one translates it) coveting, anger invading, or impugning. Concupiscible covets always pleasant and delightsome things, and abhors that which is distasteful, harsh, and unpleasant. Irascible, quasi aversans per iram

---

[16] http://www.newadvent.org/cathen/04208a.htm (accessed 8/8/2011).

et odium, as avoiding it with anger and indignation. All affections and perturbations [of the mind] arise out of these two fountains, which, although the [S]toics make light of, we hold natural, and not to be resisted. The good affections are caused by some object of the same nature; and if present, they procure joy, which dilates the heart, and preserves the body: if absent, they cause hope, love, desire, and concupiscence.

The bad are simple or mixed: simple for some bad object present, as sorrow, which contracts the heart, macerates the soul, subverts the good estate of the body, hindering all the operations of it, causing melancholy, and many times death itself; or future, as fear. Out of these two arise those mixed affections and passions of anger, which is a desire of revenge; hatred, which is inveterate anger; [&c.]" (Burton 1850: 103)

This definition also involves the passions or emotions, which arise from the influence of the two sorts of appetite, the "concupiscent" and the "irascible". Like the four humours, there were supposed to be four basic passions or emotions (emotions "e-move" the soul to feeling and action) from which all other emotional states derive: love, hatred, joy and sorrow. Aroused by the appetites and sense perceptions, the passions were notorious for leading people into temptation and error. It was the responsibility of the highest attribute of the spirit/soul, the "animal" or "rational", to govern and restrain the lower appetites and passions.

The animal spirit ("animal" = consciousness, not beastliness) or rational soul was divided into two parts; "understanding" and "will". Understanding was the agent that allowed people to learn from knowledge and experience, and judge correctly what was true and false, or good and evil. It was also the seat of the conscience. Understanding too might be divided into "intellect" and "reason", where the former apprehended the value of things intuitively (as when we fall in love, or have an instant dislike for someone) while the latter worked them out logically. Burton credited a number of sub-attributes to understanding, including "sense, experience, intelligence, faith, suspicion, error, opinion, science [reason?]; to which are added art, prudency, wisdom [and] conscience". The rational soul was the link with higher levels of reality, and those who exercised it correctly could obtain enlightenment through the contemplation of divinity.

Will was the active side of the rational soul that determined the appropriate physical movement (by activating the sensitive soul) in seeking pleasure and avoiding pain, according to the judgment of the understanding. By its nature, the will sought to do and acquire good things and avoid the bad and evil. However, the will could easily be corrupted in individuals by base desires and temptations (even a few beers could upset the delicate balance of the wits; the effect of such indulgence on the spirit, and hence the soul, was quite evident) and thus not measure up to its original potential. In fact, such weakness, usually attributed to original sin as well as the imperfections of the physical body, was the universal default.

One might ask how all of this figured in the actual practice of magic? For folk magic, the fact that it was the human spirit rather than the soul that was influenced by the astral impellations or magic in healing, cursing, divination and character-reading was unimportant – how it occurred being of less concern than that it did. For intellectual magic, however, the action of the spirit and its connection with the soul was paramount. The magician used his rational soul to give him the necessary faith in the work and to learn the techniques of his art; his phantasy (imagination) to muster the vivified images and virtues needed in ritual, and his will to both carry out the rites and project his intent through the connection between his spirit and those in the cosmos. He also had to master his passions through the exercise of will-power to avoid the debilitating effects of spiritual impurity that would sabotage the effort. He had to bring about changes in himself – in his spirit – before he could achieve magical wonders. As an example, we have Agrippa's mystical magic: "… the techniques assist the soul's cleaving to God, purifying and elevating the magician towards the divine. Second, through such elevation, the magician gains power over the angels and ministering forces and can manipulate them to produce worldly effects." (Lehrich 2003: 185). It was all a matter of managing the internal spiritual economy of the human being to align it with the cosmic order and reap the benefits.

SECTION THREE: MAGICAL EVOLUTION – HOW MAGNETISM CHALLENGED THE WORLD SOUL.

As noted earlier, the justification for magic underwent a significant evolution between 1550 and the 19th century, in which, although many of the concepts I've described were retained, several new assumptions challenged older traditional beliefs and broke down the old spiritual versus material consensus in the name of science. Most important were those about man's ability to personally embody (rather than just access) *virtus* or spiritual power, and the nature of that power. It was part of the cultural evolution that ultimately rendered the Cunning Folk obsolete and brought about the demise of their traditional vocation. This historical sequence was once conceived as the triumph of science over magic and the victory of rationality over credulity and superstition, as in Keith Thomas' *Religion and the Decline of Magic*. However on closer inspection, this "whiggish" view of social progress (which many of us who are of an age once accepted without question) has now been cast in doubt. Rather than a linear progression from superstition to science and the "disenchantment" of western culture following the rise of modernity, it now seems evident that the evolution of the scientific world view didn't displace alternative occult patterns of thought but rather was paralleled by a similar evolution in magical theory. Magic never went away – it just continues under new auspices. In fact, it appears that new scientific theories (belatedly) made essential contributions to occult belief, a process that continues today with the metaphorical fascination among occultists with quantum mechanics and chaos theory rather than magnetism and electricity.

In the same way, the historical concept of "occult revivals" may mis-state the case. Evangelical religion had similar "revivals" or "awakenings" without the suggestion that experiential faith had faded away between them, but merely that it enjoyed periodic flowerings that were more evident to the wider culture. The earlier depiction of magic being thoroughly marginalized during the Enlightenment has been modified to show that, despite claims of victory by the rationalists, there were strong continuities in magic and the occult, not only among the Cunning Folk (whose activities continued relatively uninterrupted throughout the 18th century) but also in religious circles among the followers of Jacob Boehme and Emanuel Swedenborg, and in continental Freemasonry. The most significant difference was that where magic was once rejected as impious or dangerous, it was then viewed as an irrational atavism and a cultural embarrassment. The arcane may have been out of fashion amongst opinion leaders, but then it had never had more than a minority following among them in the first place.

Two factors – the concept of the Renaissance magus and the rise of scientific materialism – were particularly significant in the evolution of the way magic was perceived in western culture. Between the late 17th century and the 20th, Agrippa's glorification of the magician as a "perfect agent" – the magus who had so elevated his soul by celestial magic as to assume a role equivalent to that of the planetary intelligences and angels – even God Himself – as master of magical *virtus* – combined with the scientific community's confidence in their new-found capacity to unlock the secrets of the nature through reason made it credible that humanity could transcend its dependant position in the great chain of being. Man could now, it was believed, become the master of the universe. The authority of classical philosophy was freely challenged by experimental science just as medieval theology had been by the Protestant Reformation, leading to unprecedented optimism for human progress. Both the magus and the scientist hailed a new era in which the superior individual could potentially attain a level of control over life that freed him or her from astral control, fear of demonic attack and the malice of Satan's witches, as well as allowing for the discovery of the true secrets of the cosmos long obscured by the tyranny of erroneous tradition.

Fundamental assumptions about four classical elements and the soul came under attack, leading to a contentious reconsideration of the way the universe was composed. As D. P. Walker observed, the soul was shunted aside in favor of the spirit as the central motive force. Correspondingly, the world spirit (whether *Anima Mundi* or *Spritus Mundi*) was transformed from a semi-conscious agency into a natural elemental force. In the 16th century, Paracelsus found this principle in the *archaeus* (the "ancient" or primal spirit), an equivalent of *virtus*, and made it part of his idiosyncratic revamping of the elemental makeup of the world in which he replaced the former four elements of fire, air, water and earth with sulphur, mercury and salt (not the physical chemicals but – like the earlier elements – their higher principles). Introduced into mainstream science by van Helmont, the *archaeus* was combined with William Gilbert's theories on magnetism to become one of a variety of principles thought to explain the interaction of everything in nature, including the arcane. As Tambiah says, "…the will of God and laws of nature were brought into correspondence in the seventeenth century".[17] The 17th century's attempt to find the true working principle behind nature began the process by which not only orthodox science but magic as well broke away from the conceptions inherited from the distant past.

The move was unintentionally aided by the more uncompromising versions of Protestantism, which effectively swept away the multiple causality of medieval science and religion to insist on God's Providence as the sole direct force for change in the universe. "Calvin substituted for this chain of being the notion of a truly omnipotent and unimpeded God as designer of the universe who acted according to his Providence. Calvin's insistence on absolutist rule by a [single] cosmic ruler, a radical monotheistic stress, did of course allow for the occurrence of miracles that God might perform if he so wished, but the more important implication of his absolutist cosmology was that it subsequently accommodated the notion of a God who acted according to regular laws of nature, which were designed by him."[18] Independent spiritual wielders of astral *virtus* were now out of the picture. It was then only a short step to shifting omnipotence from God to the laws of nature themselves – the question being what *was* the nature of this primal force?

The modern scientific consensus about matter didn't begin to reach a settlement until the end of the 18th century, and even then the new materialism had to ward off more esoteric alternatives for years. "Until [and even after] Lavoisier laid the foundations of modern chemistry, scientists usually expected to explain all life processes by a few principles; and once they believed they had found the key to the code of nature, they often lapsed lyrically into fiction." (Darnton 1968: 12) A number of alternative theories were raised and rejected by scientists, some of which were enthusiastically borrowed by occultists as an explanatory basis for their own beliefs. The most significant of these was a direct descendant of the *archaeus* principle – "animal magnetism" – as developed by Franz Anton Mesmer and his followers. Mesmer's theories took advantage of the great enthusiasm for popular science in the late 18th century, and it was indeed viewed initially as a tremendous scientific breakthrough. There's no need to recapitulate the story of animal magnetism's splashy rise and precipitous decline in popular culture – that has been done exceptionally well in the first chapter of Robert Darnton's *Mesmerism and the End of the Enlightenment in France*. Instead we can return to the narrower scope of magic and the occult, and see how animal magnetism and similar "scientific" concepts influenced the evolution of the occult.

Even though animal magnetism was soon rejected by the scientific community, it was eagerly adopted by occultists as the long-envisioned *physical* key to the function of magic. Francis Barrett in *The Magus* (1801) said "Every magical virtue therefore stands in need of an excitement, by which a certain spiritual vapour is stirred up, by reason whereof the phantasy which profoundly sleeps is awakened, which is that of Magnetism, and is excited by a foregoing touch. There is a magical virtue, being as it were abstracted from the body, which is wrought by the stirring up of the power of the soul, from whence there are made most potent procreations, and most famous impressions, and strong effects, so that nature is on every side a magicianess, and acts by her own phantasy …" (Barrett 1967: book II, 24). Similarly in 1843, Joseph Ennermoser claimed "Magnetism introduces us to the mysteries of magic, and contains on one side a key to the most hidden secrets of nature, as on the other it is adapted to exhibit mysticism and the wonders of the creative spirit."[19]

Mesmerism's occult reaction against an overly-rational world view was greatly enhanced by the rise of Romanticism and German Idealism. "The science of the Aufklärung [Enlightenment] declared all

---

[17] Stanley Jeyaraja Tambiah. *Magic, Science, Religion, and the Scope of Rationality*. Cambridge: Cambridge University Press, 1990, p. 51.
[18] *Ibid*, p. 16.
[19] *The History of Magic by Joseph Ennermoser. Translated from the German by William Howitt*. London: Henry G. Bohn, 1854, vol. 1, p. xvi.

these charm-workings to be humbug, ghost-stories, old wives' tales and completely devoid of reality. But Romanticism took a new interest in them, set about collecting the materials, and to some extent revived beliefs in their actuality." (von Dobschütz 1913: 429). Mesmer had begun in an orthodox scientific manner, but as his theories expanded in ever more debatable ways, they were combined with older esoteric ideas resurrected by his followers from earlier sources, and reinterpreted to suit the intellectual trends of the day. In so doing, the Mesmerists changed the perception of what "hidden forces" were at work behind or above the perceptions of everyday reality. The action of the magnetic force soon slipped from its earlier scientific moorings to become a most wonderful power capable of all sorts of amazing effects. Animal Magnetism was *virtus*, reborn in a "scientific' capacity.

The result was the transformation of the esoteric tradition I've described above into what became known, as Eliphas Levi labeled it – "occultism" – an interpretation of spiritual reality that attempted to achieve a correspondence with modern science just as earlier traditions had with Neo-Platonism, Aristotelianism and Galenism. "Court de Gebélin, the highly esteemed author of *Le Monde Primitif* [and the innovator who recast tarot cards as divinatory hieroglyphs], described mesmerism and 'the supernatural sciences' as the natural products of recent scientific discoveries. One of his fellow mesmerists exulted that 'physics would take the place of magic everywhere'; and another explained, 'Above science is magic, because magic follows it, not as an effect but as its perfection.'" (Darnton 1968: 38) The movement sparked by Mesmer was not so much a *revival* of the old world view as a revolution in western esoteric cosmology. As Wouter Hanegraaff sums up this cultural sea-change, "Occultism, I suggest, is essentially an attempt to adapt esotericism to a disenchanted world: a world which no longer harbours a dimension of irreducible mystery … based upon an experience of the sacred as present in the daily world. To the extent that it makes such an attempt, it accepts the world (consciously or unconsciously; in a spirit of resignation or with enthusiasm). The irony is that, by so doing, it cannot but distance itself from the 'enchanted' world of traditional esotericism."[20]

Animal magnetism became the favored explanatory "occult force", not only in its potential for healing that Mesmer had concentrated on, but for more radical applications, the most influential of which (for later occultism) was "induced somnambulism" or hypnotic trance. It was discovered by some of Mesmer's disciples, including the Marquis de Puységur and Alexandre Bertrand, that if a person was put into a "magnetic trance", he or she could communicate with angels or people at a distance (shades of Trithemius!), but most influentially, with the spirits of the dead. In addition, occultists of all stripes were quick to assert that animal magnetism was the vital principle that empowered their magic and preternatural efforts.

Mesmerism, discovered in the United States by Andrew Jackson Davis and Phineas Quimby (as well as Emerson and Mrs. Nathaniel Hawthorne) following Charles Poyen's lectures in 1836, led to the famous Hydesville séances and the nouveau necromancy of the Fox sisters in 1848. The resultant public fascination with Spiritualism and clairvoyance – both fashionable innovations in popular occultism – were far more influential than the more traditional forms of magic that were made available in translation about the same time, such as Hohman's *Long Lost Friend* (1846) or the *Sixth and Seventh Books of Moses* (1880). The middle classes no longer felt much need for the magical remedies the poorer classes still relied on, but went on to seek the thrill of otherworldly communications. As Jocelyn Godwin observes,

> "The new religion [Spiritualism] could have been designed by Madison Avenue. It offered evidence of immortality, direct contact with the departed—even pets—and required nothing in the way of intelligence or moral effort, while providing a whole new field of activity for the growing number of women in search for emancipation."[21]

---

[20] Wouter J. Hannegraaff. *New Age Religion and Western Culture*. Albany: State University of New York Press, 1998, p. 493. Hannegraaff's coverage of the changes I've been describing is excellent and far more detailed, for those who wish to study the subject further.
[21] Jocelyn Godwin. *The Theosophical Enlightenment*. Albany: State University of New York Press, 1994, p. 188.

Other reasons for Spiritualism's greater appeal was that it was both novel and personal – it was something everyone could become involved in and allowed you to converse with your own lost loved ones rather than outré angels or demons, make inanimate things move and have objects magically materialize out of thin air. The Spiritualist séance was entertainingly experiential and involved the patron in an intimate way that earlier magic did not, or at least not as pleasantly. It was rather like the personal appeal of genealogy as opposed to a general interest in regular history.

The occult "revival" that followed the advent of spiritualism in the 1840s began in the U.S. and quickly spread back to England and Europe, in turn stimulating a third revival inspired primarily by the Theosophical Society and the interest in the uncanny among the Decadents (it also included various obscure Neo-Rosicrucian organizations and the Golden Dawn that sought to reintegrate the more intriguing elements of ceremonial magic) towards the end of the century. Theosophy also fostered a growing fascination with the "Mysterious Orient", reincarnation and quasi-human "secret masters" – a concept that originated in continental Freemasonry – as sources of wisdom, whose exotic novelty appears to have had greater appeal for the general public than time-worn western traditions. We soon see turban-wearing "adepts" and astrologers, "Egyptian" fortune tellers and Gypsies with crystal balls who basically took the old fashioned Cunning Folk's place in popular magic and occultism. The century-long effort to find a scientific basis for the occult, from animal magnetism to "psychical research", opened a chasm between modern occultism and pre-enlightenment esotericism, only to reunite the two in new exceedingly complex and verbose amalgamations embracing occidental interpretations of Hinduism and Buddhism in the late 19th century hermetic and theosophical movements. In addition, while psychic researchers in England gravitated towards a human-*virtus* position involving innate abilities such as telepathy, clairaudience, and clairvoyance, spiritualists and researchers in Catholic France were less inclined to entirely banish the world of independent spirits.

At the same time, rationalists revived the old theory of Phantasy to postulate that all alleged "supernatural" phenomena such as ghosts were in fact projections of the disordered human mind, or psychological effects arising from the imaginative processes of the phantasy. Mechanical shows by magic lanterns (invented in the 17th century by Athanasius Kircher and greatly improved by later mechanics) of "phantasmagoria" – public shows of gothic imagery focused impressively on gauze screens or smoke by magic lanterns and mirrors (hence "all smoke and mirrors") became popular at the end of the 18th century. As Terry Castle observes, "… here was now an alienating force within subjectivity itself—a kind of crypto-supernatural agency implicit in the very act of thinking. One could be 'possessed' by the phantoms of one's own thought—terrorized, entranced, *taken over* by mental images—just as in earlier centuries people had suffered the visitations of real spirits and demons".[22] Too much thinking and uncontrolled reverie could unleash imaginary spectres, which of course proved attractive to certain occultists. By extension, skeptics argued that all magical visions and spirits were merely phantasms of the mind or optical illusions that excited popular credulity, but had no objective existence. Yet this concept too was adopted by some occultists to indicate that magic itself was indeed a psychological process, but that it *did* in fact have some sort of intrinsic reality and power in the external world beyond the phantasy of the operator – a view that has become part of the theoretical armory of many ritual magicians today.

Intellectual and popular fashion has tended to lose interest in occult "revivals" each time the novelty wore off, only to be surprised to find them re-occurring again "out of nowhere". Actually, the underlying traditions had always remained strong among small self-perpetuating coteries of enthusiasts whose beliefs were enshrined in obscure publications, so that with each outbreak, new seekers were able to discover that there was in fact an actual underground – "hidden" – tradition that they could tap into. It obviously answers a very human need that neither mere materialism or nor traditional religion can provide. As Michael Saler has so cogently described in his essay "Modernism and Enchantment"[23], the academic tendency had been to dismiss magic and the occult as either atavistic survivals of primitive

---

[22] Terry Castle. "Spectral Politics: Apparition Belief and the Romantic Imagination", in *The Female Thermometer*. New York: Oxford University Press, 1995, pp. 175-176.
[23] Michael Saler. "Modernity and Enchantment: A Historiographic Review". *American Historical Review*, vol. 111, no. 3 (June 2006), pp. 692-716.

thought that modern scientism would eventually overcome or as a debilitating weakness in modernity itself regrettably perpetuated in mass culture through the public's capacity for delusion. Historians now question whether modernity is actually as monolithic and positivistic as was once assumed, or whether fact and fiction, science and magic, not only co-exist in culture but in individuals as well, who recognize that they need a little mystery and wonder in their lives, even if it isn't "real" in every sense of the word.

I've included this brief and oversimplified account of evolution of occultism to indicate what appears to have been the reason the traditional magic of the Cunning Folk faded from public notice. Their magic gave way to modern occultism, as tentative theories in psychology and modern science were adapted by occultists in an attempt to make esoteric ideas and practices acceptable in post-Enlightenment culture. Now psychic energy has had to share the stage with psychological alternatives as an explanation, as well as our contemporary fascination with "altered consciousness" and shamanism, at least since the most recent "revival" of the 1970s.

CHAPTER 3:

Understanding the Cunning Folk

"People consulted cunning folk because they provided explanations and solutions for the many misfortunes that occurred in their daily lives, as well as holding out the prospect through the attainment of love and money. People came to them with requests ranging from the obscure and the petty – one man asked Billy Brewer to reverse magically the yellowing of his best clothes – to matters of life and death, when cunning-folk were called in to cure the terminally ill or assassinate suspected witches. No job was too small and few jobs were too big, short of resurrecting the dead."
Owen Davies, *Cunning Folk*, (2003), p. 93.

"I should probably point out that technically and historically the term Cunning Man refers to a solitary practitioner who earns a living by working spells for the local community, for fertility, good fortune, healing, etc. Some were snakeoil salesmen, or con men, and some were genuine practitioners but none claimed to be Witches, and in fact most were church-going Christians."
Peter Padden, *A Grimoire for Modern Cunning Folk*, (2010), p. 14.

THE CUNNING FOLK AND THEIR WORLD

For my purposes, the classification of an individual as a cunning man or wise woman depends on the following criteria. First, they offer some service to other people, whether for remuneration, prestige or personal satisfaction (or all of these), that depends on *preternatural influence*, ranging from simple charms, amulets and fortune telling to full-fledged astrology or conjuration. Owen Davies makes a reasonable case for excluding charmers from the general run of Cunning Folk, but I do not follow him here – the service they offered was religio-magical, not natural. On the other hand, a great deal of traditional herbalism could easily be seen today as preternatural, as the innate chemical composition of the particular plants could not possibly accomplish the cures claimed for them. However, both the methods of application (as external salves or internal ingestion) and the assumptions governing their use are indistinguishable from standard pharmacology, so it seems appropriate to omit ordinary herbal formulas from the list. If, on the other hand, herbs and other things are not ingested but are hung in bags around the neck, this would indicate magical usage despite the fact that such a distinction is not a period one.

Secondly, they are in a sense professionals, depending on acquired knowledge for their practice, and their abilities are recognized as being beyond those of ordinary people. They may have shared common beliefs in the preternatural potency of things, but they also "possessed the most elaborate and structured knowledge regarding the supernatural" among their contemporaries. As Davies observes, the Cunning Folk's "[c]areer prospects depended heavily on access to knowledge", and alongside oral tradition, written materials play an increasingly important role through the centuries. [24]

Thirdly, they expected to be remunerated by clients for their work in some fashion. They are not housewives tending their own family members or individuals who experimented with traditional divination, charms or superstitious rituals for their personal benefit (even if the practices were often identical to those performed or prescribed by Cunning professionals). This also excludes amateurs who might read about some magical or divinatory practice, and then try it out with their friends.

---

[24] Laura Stack. "Narrative and the social dynamics of magical harm …Finland", in Willem de Blécourt & Owen Davies *Witchcraft Continued*. Manchester Univ. Press, 2004, p. 74; Davies 2003: 69.

Lastly, the Cunning Folk were entrepreneurial. They had to go out of their way to undertake their practice. A magical vocation was seldom successfully passed from parent to child, as in other trades, although many presumably learned their art from a family member or neighbor. They chose to step outside safe and accepted social roles and take up an illegal if often quite profitable sideline. Most Cunning Folk were identified with some legitimate trade, such as artisan, craftsman, tradesman or husbandman (but seldom simple labourers), just as Mafia bosses have some sort of legal business as a "front". The majority was male but women could and did compete at all levels of skill. It could marginalize them in their community, and in fact marginal status may have been a benefit – Jews, gypsies and in the U.S., blacks and Indians, were more readily credited with exotic abilities than some Joe Bloggs who grew up around the corner.

Success in magic took a certain amount of showmanship and psychological shrewdness, whether the candidate was a cheat or a sincere practitioner, and *that* dividing line was crossed and recrossed indefinitely. As in what is known as "outsider art" today, marginality and exoticness helps establish authenticity. The well-attested theatrical dress and properties of Cunning Folk's consulting rooms were a necessary adjunct to establishing the *bona fides* (good faith) of the practitioner. Even the mysterious airs of a simple country wise woman or a gypsy fortune teller made it easier for the client to credit what was revealed, and feel he or she had gotten their money's worth.

The very nature of the Cunning Folk's vocation, that it was illegal, furtive, confused with black witchcraft by both the Establishment and some clients, and yet almost universally practiced, brings up the question of social liability. There is a common impression that the witchcraft persecution swept up a large number of Cunning Folk in its fatal wake, but this was not actually the case. Folk magicians were threatened and prosecuted on several levels, in the ecclesiastical and criminal courts as well as the "court of popular opinion", yet by and large, they enjoyed considerable success and seldom shared the extreme penalties that were inflicted in cases of "black witchcraft".

> "Prosecutions of black witches suspected of doing harm to other people were numerous enough. But the records of assizes and quarter sessions suggest that their white counterparts were unlikely to find themselves in the courts unless their activities were fraudulent or otherwise harmful. Every kind of magic was prosecuted at one time or another; fortune-telling, divining for / lost goods, healing by charms, or conjuring for treasure. But the number of extant cases seems disproportionately small beside that of the prosecutions for maleficent witchcraft, especially in view of what can be inferred about the number of cunning men and the extent of their activities." (Thomas 1971: 245-246)

While the occasional Cunning Man or Wise Woman did fall afoul of the legal system, the penalties were generally milder, and far fewer were hung or burnt than is commonly believed. Many Cunning Folk not only survived by remaining beneath the attention of the authorities, but also by benefiting from the good opinion of their neighbors (and clients), by which the severity of the law could be avoided. One way in which this occurred was through the practice of compurgation. "The process of compurgation, called 'Wager of Law' in England, was a type of absolution from a criminal or civil charge that enabled the defendant to come forward and swear to his or her innocence or nonliability. Through compurgation, the person on trial was able to conclusively contradict the charges and reinforce his or her position through others who testified under oath that they believed the defendant's testimony."[25] If an accused Cunning Man could get a number of his peers to come forward and basically attest on oath to his good character and the falsity of the charge, he could escape prosecution. As much of what occurred in the practice of folk magic took place in secret and thus was not easily proven beyond doubt, compurgation not only absolved him but also testified to the value of his role within the community.

Before we go further, it might be advisable to address the sometimes contentious problem of "black" and "white" witchcraft. The Cunning Folk have long been described by modern writers as "white witches", with the assumption that this clearly differentiated them from the black witches of popular belief. It did and did not. The problem starts from the fact that religious and civic authorities often differed with the general populace as to what constituted illicit magic. While some political leaders

---

[25] http://legal-dictionary.thefreedictionary.com/compurgator (accessed 6/23/2012).

and members of the nobility might personally accept and privately encourage certain magical pursuits (especially in the rarified areas of alchemy, astrology and conjuration), others were emphatic and highly vocal in their opposition to any arcane activity, denouncing *all* magic as undifferentiated satanic "witchcraft". To them, black witches and white witches were indistinguishably wicked, and the white witches were actually the worst of the two, as the benefits they provided – there was no doubt about their ability – seduced people into sin, whereas the black witch was at least openly and repulsively evil. In period diatribes against Cunning Folk, such as in John Brinley's *A Discovery of the Impostures of Witches and Astrologers* (1680), when the author says "If the Cattel be sick, the white-witch is presently sent for to bless it," this is to condemn the person as a witch, not to excuse her.

From pre-Christian times to the Enlightenment, there had always been severe condemnation and legal sanctions against "maleficium", that is, harm done by magic, just as there had always been desperate, angry or bitter people who actually tried to injure their neighbors in this fashion. Black magic was real even if "black witchcraft", that imaginary burgeoning conspiracy of evil witches who singularly or in groups made allegiance to Satan, was not. Fighting maleficent magic was in fact as much a part of the traditional mission of the Cunning Folk as it was of the authorities. However, the contemporary obsession for persecuting black witches was seized upon by anti-magic fanatics as reason to fiercely condemn anything that transgressed their narrow definition of spiritual orthodoxy. The witch hunts and trials themselves need no description, but the distorting effect of the stereotypes established in the witch trials on historical research into the Cunning Folk should be considered.[26]

Over several centuries, theologians shifted the definition of magic from "sorcery", in which the operator was in control, to witchcraft, a heretical association – demonolatry or worship of the Devil – in which the individual was just an agent of Satan. They conflated traditional sorcery with elite ritual magic to arrive at a unified view of magic that, even if unintentionally, always involved some sort of forbidden veneration of demons and was thoroughly diabolic in nature. As Michael Bailey observes, this led to the conceptualization of the stereotypical black witch who was empowered through the satanic pact, rather than being an independent magician. Where an actual sorcerer or magician might employ spiritual beings to further his work while remaining in control of the situation, the imaginary sabbat-attending black witch was in theory just a submissive tool of the Devil, a mere pawn or conduit for satanic malice.[27]

Despite the best efforts of the authorities to convince people otherwise, however, black witches and Cunning Folk were commonly recognized as being opposites. It was their opponents, not their neighbors who wanted to brand them witches (white or otherwise). The term "witch" had an almost universally negative connotation, and anyone so identified was therefore defined as wicked. People might use "witchcraft" loosely when talking about magic (they heard this often enough from the parsons and magistrates), but when specifics about locally valued Cunning Folk came up, they tended to be more careful with their labels. Thus any *favourable* connotation of the term "white witchcraft" is misleading, as it was seldom intended when referring to the Cunning Folk until the 19th century. The term "white witch" is both anachronistic and misleading.

WHO WERE THE CUNNING FOLK?

As noted in the introduction, the history of the Cunning Folk has been so thoroughly delineated by Keith Thomas, Owen Davies, and Ronald Hutton that only a few clarifying points are sufficient for present purposes. The Cunning Folk were not a homogeneous subculture consisting mainly of poor illiterate "hedge witches" but rather represented an extended continuum ranging from simple village or backstreet practitioners to quite sophisticated experts who could match the achievements of highly educated Renaissance magi.

---

[26] For a cogent if now somewhat dated discussion of the problem, see de Blécourt (1994), pp. 285-303.
[27] Michael D. Bailey. "From Sorcery to Witchcraft: Clerical Conceptions of Magic in the Later Middle Ages". *Speculum*, Vol. 76, No. 4 (Oct., 2001), pp. 960-990.

How numerous were the Cunning Folk, and how widespread were they? Although no exact figures exist, there is no doubt that there were an impressive number of them in England throughout the period (1550-1900) we are dealing with. Keith Thomas cites several early estimates, from one in which a Cunning Man estimated that there were 500 other Cunning Men in England, to Reginald Scot's assertion that every village had its own Cunning Man (Thomas 1971: 245). Another opinion even suggested that they were roughly comparable in numbers to parish clergymen (some of whom practiced cunning arts as well). There were, however, 15,000 parishes in England and Wales, and Owen Davies points out that this had to be a considerable exaggeration. (Davies 2003: 67-68). Alan Macfarlane found that "nowhere in Essex was there a village more than ten miles from a *known* cunning man" (my emphasis – Macfarlane 1970: 120). In 1807, Robert Southey wrote, "A Cunning-Man or a Cunning Woman, as they are termed, is to be found near every town, and though the laws are occasionally put in force against them, still it is a gainful trade."[28] There were a number of Cunning Folk even in Puritan New England, which was certainly not a congenial society for them, while the number of otherwise undetected hoodoo workers uncovered by Rev. Harry Hyatt in Adams County, Illinois and the southeastern states in the 1930s testifies to the extensive and continued demand for magical services and suggests the possibility of comparable numbers elsewhere. As prosecutions of Cunning Folk were low compared with those of black witches, available court records (until all the ecclesiastical court proceedings have been surveyed) can't reveal the population accurately, and many avoided prosecution altogether. Being hidden to history was a good thing if you were a Wise Woman, and many were.

Although Cunning Folk are generally thought to be primarily country dwellers, there were numerous practitioners in towns and cities as well, as records for London and elsewhere testify. Even in the First World War period, folklorist Edward Lovett found a number of traditional folk practitioners for his *Magic in Modern London* (1925).

Literacy is another problematic issue, as it is commonly assumed that the vast majority of the Cunning Folk were illiterate and relied entirely on oral tradition. It is certainly true that, especially in the earlier period, oral tradition and teaching was predominant among folk practitioners, yet even then written sources were thought important. More significantly, book-learning was considered to be the mark of the truly accomplished fortune teller, wizard or Wise Woman. Cunning Folk even pretended the use of written sources whether they could make neither heads nor tales of them or not. Indications of some level of literacy appear frequently enough to suggest that many practitioners did make the effort to study the commonly available chapbooks and almanacs – or even fairly recondite published sources such as Agrippa's *Three Books* or Scot's *Discoverie* – to enhance their practice.

Perhaps the situation paralleled the desire for literacy among the Puritans for whom the ability to read the *Bible* was paramount, or the need for some level of numeracy among businessmen, which led to higher rates than were found among the general populace. Again, Hyatt's work shows how pervasive oral tradition could be, but even there, the popularity of cheap magical handbooks such as the *Sixth and Seventh Books of Moses, Marie Laveau*, or the ubiquitous "numbers" or dream books is evident. As Davies observes, after the wave of arcane books that appeared in English during and after the Interregnum, "We find abstruse, erudite knowledge of the occult sciences being held by autodidact working men, who carried on a rural tradition of solitary magical experimentation, largely divorced from the middle-class occultism of the time." (Davies 2003: 130). Add to this the sometimes impressive magical libraries accumulated by Cunning Folk, and Thomas' comment that, although folk magic was once largely oral and local, "… for some kinds of popular magic books were essential…" (Thomas 1971: 229). This indicates a tendency towards written sources that only increased as time went on.

A related problem to literacy is the matter of charging for services. Although it was common for charmers in particular but also some lower-level Cunning Folk to not formally charge their patrons for services rendered (perhaps to avoid prosecution or to prove their disinterested status), this has been exaggerated by overlooking an often implicit assumption of voluntary "contributions" from the client.

---

[28] Robert Southey. *Letters from England.* London: The Cresset Press, 1951, p. 295.

A rather different difficulty arises from the assumption that as many of the Cunning Folk (and their clients) were denounced as not "good Christians" or not Christians at all – they were therefore self-consciously "pagan". The truth is that like a lot of people today, some weren't much of anything, although they conformed as much as it seemed prudent to do so. However, most were loyal Christians in their own estimation, however short of that they might fall in the opinion of the authorities. The annual visitations by church authorities insured that some sort of pressure was applied every so often, even in backwaters such as the eastern fens, as it is from these remote areas that accusations of impiety often derived. This point of view has been bolstered by the bias of contemporary reports by religious authorities (especially Puritans) who complained bitterly that many country folk were not "Christian" – that is, Christian to their demanding standards. Just as fundamentalist Christians today are given to asserting that communicants of main-line Protestant churches, not to mention Catholics or Mormons, are not true Christians at all, so ecclesiastical writers of the past were quick to decry ignorance of scriptural details or theological niceties as indications of outright atheism or paganism.

VISITING THE CUNNING FOLK.

Perhaps the best way to become acquainted with the Cunning Folk is to see them through the eyes of their contemporaries. Although the surviving accounts are far from unbiased or judgment-free, they do give a glimpse of the practice of folk magic and divination not otherwise obtainable. Keith Thomas observed that "… if he were lucky the cunning man left no [official] records behind him, and his consultations were always more or less furtive affairs" (Thomas 1971: 245). The result is that even in trial transcripts, it is difficult to get a clear impression of what happened between the client and the Cunning Man. As noted earlier, it would be redundant to recapitulate the easily available historical surveys of the Cunning Folk made by Thomas, Davies, George Lyman Kittredge, Ronald Hutton and others such as Cecil L'Estrange Ewen. However, as they seldom provide more than brief references of the Cunning Folk's work, it may be useful to look at a few detailed contemporary accounts as examples of these interactions. The chief drawback is that not only are the authors skeptical and antagonistic towards folk magic, they have also obviously fictionalized their narratives to a greater or lesser extent. Notwithstanding their obvious weakness as historical documents, a careful reading does shed light on the profession of the Cunning Folk. The descriptions had to be sufficiently credible to convince their intended audiences, which had a general knowledge about these activities. They couldn't be entirely fantastic and still serve their purpose as warnings to the unwary and overly credulous. With these caveats in mind, here are eight extended accounts of Cunning Folk at work, with two interviews made by Rev. Harry Hyatt to provide a modern comparison.

The first example is from Henry Chettle's *Kind-Heart's Dream* (1592), concerning a cheating Cunning Man and his confederates who engineer "robberies" in order to impress his would-be clients, and an itinerant Wise Woman, who does healing and fortune-telling, but in this instance cheats a greedy farmer and his wife out of seven angels (angel - a gold coin worth 10 shillings) while promising to magically find them a hidden treasure.

> "My impe [a servant, not a familiar], your man, while mistrisse, men, and maids were busied about prouision for the justices that sate, slips into a priuate parlour, wherein stood good store of plate, and conueying a massy sault [a decorative salt-cellar] vnder his capouch, little lesse woorth than twentie marke, got secretely to the back-side, and cast it into a filthie pond; which done, he acquaints your knaueship with the deed.
> By then your diet was drest, the sault was mist, the good wife cryde out, the maydes were ready to runne madde.
> Your man (making the matter strange) inquired the cause: which when they tolde, O (quoth hee) that my maister would deale in this matter; I am sure he can do as much as any in the world.
> Well, to you they come pitifully complaining, when very wrathfully (your choler rising) you demaund reason why they should thinke yee bee able to deale in such cases. Your kind nature (bent alwaies to lenitie) yeelded at the last to their importuning; onely wisht them to stay till the nexte day, for that you would not deale while the justices were in the house.

They must do as your discretion appoints. Next day, calling the good-man and wife to your bedside, ye tell them the salte was stolne by one of their familiars [again, a human servant], whom he had forced by art to bring it backe againe to the house, and in such a pond to cast it; because he would not have the partie knowne, for feare of trouble.

As you direct them, they search and find. Then comes your name in rare admiration; the host giues / you foure angels for a reward, the hostesse two french crowns; the maydes are double diligent to doe you seruice, that they may learne their fortunes; the whole towne talks of the cunning man, that indeed had onely conny-catcht [cony catcher = con man] his host.

If that slip-string bee still in your seruice, I aduise you to make much of him; for, by that tricke, he prou'd himselfe a toward youth, necessary for such a maister. This iugling passes Cuckoes play. Well, I aduise you play least in sight in London; for I haue sette some to watch for your comming that will iustifie all this and more of your shifting life..../

Now I will draw to an end, concluding with a master iugler, that he may be well knowne if he be got into any obscure corner of the countrey. This shifter, forsooth, carried no lesse countenance than a gentleman's abilitie, with his two men in blue coates, that serued for shares, not wages. Hee, being properly seated in a shire of this realme, and by the report of his men bruted for a cunning man, grew into credit by this practise. /

His house beeing in a village through which was no thorough fare, his men, and sometime his mastershippe in their company, at midnight woulde goe into their neighbours seuerall grounds, being farre distant from their dwelling houses, and oftentimes driue from thence horses, mares, oxen, kine, calues, or sheepe, what euer came next to hande, a mile perchaunce, or more, out of the place wherein they were left.

Home would they return, and leaue the cattel straying. In the morning, sometime the milke-maids misse their kine, another day the plough-hinds their oxen, their horses another time; somewhat of some woorth once a weeke lightly. Whither can these poore people go but to the wise mans worship? Perchaunce, in a morning, two or three come to complaine and seeke remedie, who, welcommed by one of his men, are seuerally demaunded of their losses. If one come for sheepe, another for other cattell, they are all at first tolde that his maistership is a sleepe, and till hee himselfe call they dare not trouble him.

But very kindly he takes them into the hall, and when his worship stirs promises them they shall speake with him at liberty. Now, sir, behind a curtaine in the hall stands a shelfe garnisht with bookes, to which my mate goes vnder to take one downe, and, as he takes it down, pulleth certain strings which are fastened to seuerall small bels in his maisters chamber, and, as the bels strike, hee knowes what cattell his neighbors come to seeke; one bell being for oxen, another for kine, another for swine, &c. A while after he stamps / and makes a noyse aboue; the seruingman intreats the suters to go vp, and hee, hearing them comming himselfe, kindly opens them the dore, and ere euer they speake salutes them, protesting for their losse great sorrowe, as if he knew their griefes by reuelation, comforts them with hope of recouery, and such like wordes. They cry out, Jesu blesse your mastership, what a gift haue you to tel our mindes and neuer heare vs speake! I, neighbors, saith he, ye may thanke God, I trust, I am come among ye to doe ye all good. Then, knowing which way they were driuen, hee bids them goe either east-ward, or south-warde, to seeke neere such an oake, or rowe of elmes, or water, or such like marke neere the place where the cattell were left; and hee assures them that by his skill the theeues had no power to carry them farther than that place. They runne and seek their cattle, which when they find, O admirable wise man, the price of a cow we will not sticke with him for, happy is the shire where such a one dwels. Thus doe the pore cousoned [cozened = tricked] people proclaime, and so our shifter is sought too, far and neere. I thinke this be iugling in the highest degree: if it be not, Cuckoe is out of his compasse. Well, the world is full of holes, and more shiftes were neuer practised. But this is Cuckoes counsell, that yee leaue in time, lest being conuicted, like my hoast of the Anchor, ye pine yourselues in prison to saue your eares from the pillory; and end too good for jugling shifters and cosening periurers."

William Cuckoe. /

"... It happened, within these few yeeres, about Hampshire there wandered a walking mort [unmarried itinerant "wise woman"], that went about the countrey selling of tape; shee had a good voice, and would sing sometime to serue the turne: she would often be a leach, another time a fortune teller.

In this last occupation wee will now take her, for therefore was she taken, hauing first ouer-taken an honest simple farmer and his wife in this manner.

On a summer's evening by the edge of the forest, she chaunst to meete the forenamed farmer's wife: to whom when she had offered some of her tape, she began quickly with her to fall in talke. And, at the first staring her in the face, assures her shee shall have such fortune as neuer had any of her kinne: and, if her husband were no more vnlucky than she, they should be possest of so infinite a sum of hidden treasure as no man in England had ever seene the like.

The plain woman tickled with her soothing, intreated her to go home, which she, at first making somewhat strange, was at last content: there had she such cheare as farmer's houses afford, who fare not with the meanest.

Shortly the good man comes in, to whom his wife relates her rare fortune, and what a wise woman shee / had met with. Though the man were very simple, yet made he some question what learning she had, and how she came by knowledge of such things. O sir (said she) my father was the cunningst jugler in all the countrey, my mother a gipsie, and I haue more cunning than any of them both. Where lies the treasure thou talkst on? said the farmer: within this three myles (quoth she.) I wonder thou thy selfe getst it not (saide the man) but liuest (as it seemes) in so poore estate? My pouertie (answered this coosner) is my chiefest pride: for, such as we cannot our selues be rich, though wee make others rich. Beside, hidden treasure is by spirits possest, and they keepe it onely for them to whome it is destinied. And more (said shee) if I haue a seuerall [private] roome to my selfe, hangd round about with white linnen, with other instruments, I will, by morning, tell ye whether it be destined to you.

The goodman and wife, giuing credite to hir words, fetch foorth their finest sheets, and garnished a chamber as she appointed: seuen candles she must haue lighted, and an angell she would haue laide in every candlesticke. Thus furnisht, she locks her selfe into the roome, and appointes them two onely to watch, without making any of their servants privie. Where, vsing sundrie mumbling fallacies, at last shee cald the man vnto her, whome she sadled and brideled, and hauing seuen times rid him about the roome, causd him to arise and call his wife, for to her belongd the treasure.

Both man and wife being come, in verie sober manner / she tolde them, that they alone must attend in that place, while she forst the spirits to release the treasure and lay it in some convenient place for them to fetch: but in any wise they must not reueale about what shee went, neither touch bread nor drinke till her returne. So, taking vp the seuen angels, away shee went, laughing to her selfe how she had left them waiting.

All night sate the man and his wife attending her comming, but she was wise inough. Morning came, the seruants mused what their maister and dame meant, that were wont with the larke to be the earliest risers: yet, sith they heard them talke, they attempted not to disturbe them. Noone drawing on, the farmer feeling by the chimes in his belly twas time to dine, was by his wife counselled to stay till the wise woman's returne. Which he patiently intending, on a sodaine the sent of the plough-swaines meate so pierced his senses, that had all India beene the meede of his abstinence, eate he will, or die he must. His wife, more money wise, intended rather to starve than loose the treasure: till, about evening, one of their neighbors brought them news of a woman coosener that by a justice was sent to Winchester for many lewd pranks. The man would needes see if it were the same, and, comming thither, found it to be no other; where, thinking at least to have good words, she impudently derided him, specially before the bench: who, asking hir what reason she had to bridle and saddle him: faith (saide shee) onely to see how like an asse hee lookt.

A number of such there be, whom I wil narrowly search for in my next circuit, and if my dreame bee accepted, sette them out orderly." (Chettle 1841: 47-48, 51-53, 57-59)

The second selection is from John Melton's *Astrologaster, or the Figure-Caster* (1620), which depicts the patter of a fictional London Cunning Man, to whom the narrator is referred by an old man he meets on the street after his pocket was picked. The first three paragraphs are spoken by the old man. Please note the elaborate recital of the magician's intellectual heritage:

"Sonne, said he, (for so I may properly call thee, because Smoothnesse and Alacrity, the Characters of Youth, sit on thy vnwrinkled forehead) these women your eyes did lately take notice of, are Creatures so ignorantly obstinate, that neyther the mild entretie of a Friend can perswade them from their folleys, nor the bad report of an Enemie disswade them from their perversnesse. The Party to whom they come, is a Bird, of whose kinde I thinke there are few liuing, for he professeth himselfe to be a Wise-man, and the cause of their coming, is to be solued either of Money, Siluer-Spoones, Rings, Gownes, Plate, Linnen they haue lost: some, to know how many Children they shall haue, some, how many Husbands, and which shall loue them best: others, about other businesse: but in generall, all of them to know something, which indeed at last comes to nothing. And I my selfe (like a Holy-day foole) haue beene there at least halfe a score times, onely to giue my money away, to bee laught at. Yet I haue words ynough: for he will promise more than twentie Courtiers, talke more for halfe a Peece then halfe a score Lawyers, and lye more than twentie / Chronologers: yet with some tricke, or euasion, hee will come clearly off, without being suspected for an Impostor, especially if he hauth some man he thinkes he dare worke on, as he hath done me for example.

For going to the Crosse one Sunday morning to heare a Sermon, some *Mercurian* [Mercury being the god of thieves amongst other things] and nimble-finger'd Pick-pocket, that had more minde of my Purse then the Preacher, gelt it of sixteene pound; so that I went home lighter by two Stone then I went out after I had fretted much, and to no purpose, I vsed all the meanes I could to recouer my losse, as by seeing the Keepers of Newgate, who know which of the Law are appointed to filch in euery part of the Citie; yet still I came home a greater looser then I went out: for always being in hope to finde that which I had lost, I lost more, by bribing one Knaue, to discouer another. At the last, it was my bad fortune to meet with an old Woman, that put greater confidence in the *Iewes Caballa*, and the *Talmud*, and the *Shepheardes Kalender*, and *Bookes of Palmistry*, then any part of the Bible; who aduised me to repaire to Doctor *P. C.* in *More-fields*, at the vpper end of this Alley, and if Art could helpe me to it againe, I should be sure to heare of it. This draught of good newes this old Woman gaue me, to quench the thirst of my desire, which I dranke in at mine ears as greedily, as a man sicke of a burning Feauer will the coolest Iulips [juleps = medicine]: so giuing this old Piece of Superstition a Tester [2 ¼ pence coin] for her newes, I instantly went to Master Doctor. Who perceiuing me to be one that loued Gold well (because Age most commonly couetous) thought the better to worke vpon me, as he did: for his Doctorship had the Art to hold me in hand three weekes, in which time, he made the sixteene pound I lost, twentie: and when all came to a Period, hee told me, that he had laboured hard for me, and at the last, by his no small industrie and pains, had found out the Theefe that had my Money, but he was fled into the *Low-Countries*, because there were many Warrants out to apprehend / him for many Thefts and Burglaries hee had committed; and if it pleased me to take shipping, and sayle hither, I should be sure to find him at the *Labor in Vaine* in *Bredawe*. But this comfort went as cold to my heart, as the Sentence of Death to a Man that stands arraigned at the Barre: for I had rather goe fiue thousand mile by Land, then fiue mile by Sea; and if it had been a hundred pound I had lost, I would rather haue giuen as much more, then hazard my selfe by Water. Yet howsouer I may doubt [suspect], nay truly resolue my selfe, that he hath palpably cheated me: yet it was impossible to finde him a lyar, except I meant to take more paines about it, then it was worth. Therefore as patiently as I am able, I am going home againe, purposing hereafter to take heed of two Pick-pockets; the one, the Diuer that met with me in Pauls Church-yard ; the other the Doctor in *More-fields*, that rob'd me as well as the first, who in my mind hath deseured, for his artificiall Cheating, the Pillory, as well as the other did the Gallowes for Stealing.

Thus Sir, according to my weake abilitie, haue I discoursed to you the condition of him, to whom these Women and my selfe came, the cause of our coming, with his manner of deluding vs: for howsoeuer he professeth himselfe to Astronomy, Physike, Metaphysikes, the Mathematikes, and Astrology; yet if a Scholler had him in handling, he should find him as meere a Mountebanke, as euer sold Sophistications in *Italy* or the *Low-Countries*.

He no sooner had deliured me this Relation, but he hasted away from me: therefore seeing he was importunate to be gone, I only shew'd my selfe gratefull in thanking him for his kindnesse, so he went homewards, & I into my Garden. But now my minde was quite transported from the sweetnesse of that Place, and only fixt on the subtiltie of the Doctor, and his Politike answer to the old Man about the recourie of his Money, so I could not be at quiet with my selfe, while I was truly resolued of the Art of this Star-gazer. /

Therefore on a Morning which was as calme as I could with my thoughts now were, I put on a Sute of course Northerne Dozens [coarse cloth from Yorkshire], with all accoutrements that were most suitable to that homlinesse, and with all expedition went to Master Doctor, and hastily knocking at his Welsh doore, there came running downe the stayers with a nimble dexteritie (the little *Mephistophiles*) his Boy, demaunding with whom I would speake; to whom, in a broad Somersetshire language [traditionally used to indicate rustics or hicks], I answered, with Master Doctor, vpon an earnest businesse. Vpon the deliurie of this Message, this young Spirit, like exhaled dew, nimbly flew away from me, who vpon an instant, like a flash of Lightning, was in my bosome againe before I could perceiue him; and then without any more Interrogatories, marshalled me vp into his Masters Study, who sat in this manner following:

The Figure-Casters Oration.

Before a Square Table, couered with a green Carpet, on which lay a huge Booke in *Folio*, wide open, full of strange Characters, such as the Ægyptians and Chaldeans were neuer guiltie of; not farre from that, a siluer Wand, a Surplus [surplice], a Watering Pot, with all the superstitious or rather fayned Instruments of his cousening Art. And to put a fairer colour on his black and foule Science, on his head hee had a foure cornered Cap, on his backe a faire Gowne (but made in a strange fashion) in his right hand he held an Astrolabe, in his left a Mathematical Glasse [scrying glass]. At the first view, there was no man that came to him (if hee were of any fashion) could offer him for aduice less then a *Iacobus* [25 shilling coin], and the meanest halfe a Peece, although hee peraduenture (rather than haue nothing) would be content with a brace of Two-pences.

I no sooner came into his Study but I did him the reuerence belonging to his Doctorship, and stood as long bare to him, as a poore Countrey Client that sues in *Forma Pauperis*, will to his hungry Lawyer. At the last, with the expence of many a Legge [bowing] (and may it please your Worship /), I told him, that the cause of my coming was, that hauing lately lost at the Kings Bench Barre in Westminster Hall a Chayne of Gold of three hundred Links, therefore I came to his Doctorship, hauing beene informed, that his Art could bring it to light againe; so putting my hand into my Leather Pouch, I greased his euer-dry Palmes with an Angell [10 shilling coin], who no sooner had a feeling of my bountie, but hee began to be more liberall to mee of his Tongue, then I was to him of my Purse: And while I stood leaning on my Staffe, he deliured this Emperike-like Oration in this or not much vnlike this manner.

Honest Friend, the losse you haue sustayned, is so great, that I make no doubt, what you now haue giuen, or hereafter shall giue, will not come forced or wrackt from you, but voluntarie and free. For it is wisdome in a Man to aduenture small things to regayne greater, where there is a possibilitie of obtayning. He is not worthy of Money, that will not seeke after it, and he cannot truly iudge, how to value so precious a Metall as Gold, that is not stung with the losse of it. Therefore, Sir, your care deserues a redresse, and this Booke (meaning his Ephimerides) with my Art and Industrie, shall be the Instrumentall Causes to make you happie in the recourie of that which is worthie both of my Care and your Cost. And to put you in some hope, if that Man that had your Chayne, liues eyther within the Horizon of England, Fraunce, Spaine, Italy, or the Low-Countries, I will vndertake to shew you him, and in what place, and what companie hee is in. There is / not a Spirit, eyther of the Fire, Ayre, Earth, or Water, but I haue at my command as ready as any Gallant hath his Page or Foot-boy: I can coniure them all together, and make them trot vp and downe in the Citie, leauing not a Pick-pockets, Gilts, Lifts, Decoyes, or Dyuers Hose vnsurueyed.

Looke here Sir (with that, hee aduanced his Mathematicall Glasse) with this Instrument, first deuised by that learned Man in our Art, *Hermes Tresmegistus*, otherwise called *Mercurie*, I can see all things done in Christendome. If in the day time I looke in it, I will as easily see what is done in the Citie, as in the Sunne. There cannot be a withered-faced Lady paint her decayed Countenance at her Chamber-Window, and set a faire glosse on it with her *Fucusses* and *Italian* Tinctures, but I see her as perfectly as her shee secretarie her Chamber-maid. There cannot a Compter Booke-Keeper and a Constable share a poore Mans Fees, that the Night before was brought into Prison (because hee would not giue the blinking Beadle or begging Watch-man a Tester), but I see it as easily as their fellow, the Bawd-like doore-keeper. There cannot a Iustices Clarke, that it may be is more Iustice then his Master, take a Bribe of a noted Cut-purse, whose Name perdauenture stands at least twentie seuerall times vpon record in *Newgate* Booke, but I percieue it as well as the Doxie that brought him in.

In the Night time, if I stand with this Instrument in my hand, I can see what is done in the Citie as well as the Man in the Moone. There cannot a Drunkard come reeling out of a Tauerne at twelue a Clocke at Night, but hee is manifest before mee, as the Drawer that beat him out of doores after hee had spent all his Money. I can see the commaunding Constable and the drowsie Watch sit nodding on a Stall, while a companie of Roaring-boyes, *alias* Brothers of the Sword, come by / first swearing them awake, then out of their Authoritie, who in spight of their teeth will craue leaue to passe by them. There cannot a Trades-mans Puritanicall Wife rise early in a Morning, vnder the pretence of hearing a Lecture, but I know where shee goes as well as the Foreman of her Shoppe that vshers her. Nay Sir, I haue seene the Pope goe in his *Pontificalibus* with his whole Heard of Cardinalls to Saint Peters Church in *Rome*, as often as any Citizen hath seene the Right Honorable the Lord Maior goe to *Pauls-Crosse* in *London*. As for *Prester Iacke*, the Great *Mogul*, the Sophy of *Persia*, and the Great Turke, I see them as often as I doe my Boy, that is neuer from my elbow. And all this is done by Astrologie, by sacred Astrologie, Diuine Astrologie, the Art of Arts, the Science of Sciences, for it is the Ancient, the most Authentike, the most excellent Art in the World. For old Father *Adam* was both an Astronomer and Astrologer; *Abraham*, and all the Patriakes: Nay, I will assure you, the Students of our Art haue been famous in all Countries; for *Porphyrius* and *Apuleius* deriue the Originall of *Magike* from the *Persians*, although *Suidas* will haue it from the *Maguseans*, and from them hee calls them *Magi*; the *Latines* call vs Wise-men ; the *Grecians*, Philosophers; the *Indians*, *Gymnosophists* ; the *Ægyptians*, Priests; the *Cabalists*, Prophets; the *Babylonians* and *Assyrians*, *Chaldeans*; the *Frenchmen*, *Bards*: And many excellent and eminent Men haue flourished in this Knowledge; as *Zoroaster*, the sonne of *Aromasius*, who laughed when hee was borne, among the *Persians*; *Numa Pompilius*, among the *Romans*; *Thesbion*, among the *Gymnosophists*; *Hermes*, among the *Ægyptians*; *Euda* among the *Babylonians*; *Zamolxis* among the *Thracians*, and *Abbaris*, among the *Hyperboreans*. A thousand more beside these, were excellent Astrologers; as *Ptholomeus*, whom some (though very fooles in their Opinion /) held to be the first Astronomer that euer was: then *Messahla*, *Aboasar*, *Abenragel*, *Alchibichuis*, *Albumazar*, *Abraham*, *Auenezra*, *Algazoi*, *Hermes Tresmigestus*, *Aratus*, *Higinus*, and *Thebit*; after whom, did arise *Maternus*, that famous Mathematician; then, *Georgius Purbachius* ; after whom, followed *Iohannes de Monte Regio*, *Alphonsus*, King of *Castile*, as his Tables can testifie. Was not broad-shouldered *Atlas*, that was bigger then the great Porter, an admirable Astronomer and Astrologer? Was not *Erra Pater* (whom I had almost forgot) a rare fellow at Astronomie? Yes, as this his Table can testifie, which hee made I know not how many yeers since, in an vnknown Language; but now faithfully translated into the *English* Tongue by my selfe."

A Heauenly Operation.
"What thinke you Sir, was not this learned Artist deepley read in the large-leau'd Booke of Heauen? Doe not you thinke hee could learnedly discourse of the Poles, Spheres, Orbes, Circumferences, Circles, Centres, Diameters, the Zodiake, the Zenith, the Artike and Antartike Poles, Tropicus Capricorni, and Tropicus Cancerı? Hee was as well acquainted with the Twelue Signes in Heauen, as any Trades-man with those in Cheape-side, and runne ouer the Nature of the Seuen Planets as nimbly as the French Vaulter ouer the Ropes. And I my selfe, (but that I know this kind of Learning is out of your Element) could discourse to you what a sullen fellow Saturne is (on whom the permanent continuation of all things depend) what a iouiall fellow Iupeter (on whom the fecunditie of Agent Causes relye) what a quarrelling Swash-buckler Mars (on whom the swift expedition of any thing to the effect doth hang) what a hot fellow Sol (whom all Agent Causes follow) what a wanton Wench Venus (on whom the fecunditie of all materiall Causes looke after) what a merry fellow Mercury (in whom a manifold vertue doth flourish) and what a madde Lasse Luna (on whom the encrease and decrease of Humane things consist.) For know, that the rich and golden Haruest that I haue gathered out of the sweete and fruitfull Fields of many Learned Mens Workes, and carefully hoorded vp in the Garner of my brest, hath made me full and copious in my Knowledge; so that there is no Art and Science, but I am deeply and profoundly read in, as those that haue taken the Worshipfull Degree of Doctor. I am so good at Physike, that euery Morning I haue whole troupes of Mad-men, and others, sicke of Sarpegoes, Gouts, Epilepsies, Feuers, and many others labouring vnder as dangerous Diseases as these, send their Vrine to / me, so that neuer Doctor was so famous: for when Medicine will not preuayle, and that neyther Galen, Paracelsus, Auecin, Hippocrates, nor all the Heires of Æsculapius can cure them; I haue a Spirit that will fright any disease from the most dangerous and ouer-spent Patient. My skill in Alchymie is so great, that I can turne anything that is brought to me as perfect Gold as euer came out of the Indies. Frier Bacon was an Asse, Doctor Faustus a foole, Ripley an Empericke, and Kelly a Coxcombe to me; they were not worthy to blow my Bellowes, or looke to my Stylls, while I worke for the Philosophers Stone. But for *Astrologie*, I can doe that none of my Profession, besides my selfe, could euer reach vnto: for there is nothing lost, but I can finde againe; nothing in hazard of losing, but I can preserue safe and sure; I haue giuen Trades-men Spirits, that haue kept their Shops as faithfully, as if they had twentie Iourveymen continually in it. There is not a part of the Body, but I can giue a Spirit to keepe it safe and sound.
Therefore Sir, to conclude, assure your selfe, that if all my Spirits and mine owne endeauours can doe you a pleasure (as you need no doubt of mine Art) you shall not faile of your *Chayne*: so merrily returne to your Lodging againe, and repayre to mee to morrow Morning, thirtie Minutes after six; and alwayes remember to admire the wonderfull power of Sacred, Diuine, and Heauenly Astrologie.
When hee had made an end of almost his endlesse Discourse, wherewith he had so bejaded and tyred mine ears, I was as glad as any young Dottrell, that had made an escape from the clawes of the Puttock-like Catch-poles. A sicke Man, that is troubled with the tedius impertinent discourse of a prating Nurse, could not be more happy at her silence, then I at his; for I was in doubt, that his voluble / Tongue being once on Wheele, would neuer haue left running. The Mountebanks Drug Tongue, the Souldiers bumbasted Tongue, the Gypsies Canting Tongue, the Lawyers French Tongue, the Welch Tongue ; nay, all the Tongues that were at the fall of Babylon (when they were all confusedly mingled together) could as well be vnderstood as his strange Tongue: so that if I had beene but as ignorant as he tooke me to be (supposing, that I did not apprehend what did belong to his learned Art of Cousenage) he would haue made me beleeue, that his worth was correspondant to his words. At the last recouering my selfe (for hee had almost talk'd me out of my Wits) I heartily thanked him; for his learned Discourse; secondly, for his Comfort; and thirdly, and as speedily as I could, made him this answer, which I hope will proue as great a terror to all Figure-Casters, as Newgate to Cut-purses." (Melton 1975: 5-15)

Melton's narrator then proceeds to tell the Cunning Man how great a cheat he is and leaves in triumph. However, the foregoing patter is an excellent example of a contemporary magician's sales pitch, with what Cunning Men claimed to do and also how they could rattle off the alleged intellectual heritage they had "mastered".

The third selection describes the magical practice of the unfortunate Wise Woman Ann Bodenham, who was convicted of witchcraft and hung in 1653. It is an informative account as to how a woman might employ fairly sophisticated methods of scrying and conjuration as well as the presumable assistance of some small boys as "spirits". I have broken up what were originally some very long sentences into sections to make the reading easier.

"There lived in *Fisherton Anger*, adjacent to the City of new *Sarum*, in the County of *Wilts*, one *Ann Bodenham*, Wife to *Edward Bodenham* Clothyer, aged 80, years, who formerly was (as she confessed) a Servant to Doctor *Lamb* of *London* long since deceased, but in her later years, taught divers young Children to read, pretending to get her livelyhood by such an employment.

She was a woman much adicted to Popery, and to Papistical fancies that she commonly observed, and would declare to her neighbours; she would often tell those, that had converse with her of lucky and unlucky days, which she would have them observe in their employments; she was likewise addicted much to Gossipping (as the vulgar call it) to tell strange unheard-of tales and stories of transactions, and things that have been, and might be done, by cunning and wise people; she was one that would undertake to cure almost any diseases, which she did for the most part by charms and spels, but sometimes used physical ingredients, to cover her abominable practices; she would undertake to procure things that were lost, and to restore stoln goods, upon which employments she was made use of by many people, and amongst the very many that came to her, there came one *Anne Styles* (then a servant to *Richard Goddard* Esquire, of the Close in new *Sarum*) who had lost a silver Spoon of her Masters, and it was suspected by many servants of the house, that the Spoon was stollen, who amongst /themselves resolved to send this *Anne Styles* to *Ann Bodenham*, or the cunning woman, to discover the person that had stoln the spoon;

she whereupon having receiv'd from the Cook Maid Bread and Meat to give the Witch, went to the Witches house, where she was entertain'd very kindly, and at her comming the Witch shaked her by the hand, rubbed her Head and Temples, and told her she knew wherefore she came, but said the wind did not blow, nor the Sun shine, nor *Jupiter* appear, so that she could not help her to the spoon; withall told her, that she should shortly have occasion to come again to her about a greater matter;

And then the Witch took of the Maid 12. pence, and also bid the Maid give her a Jug of Beer, which she did; after which the Witch told the Maid the spoon should be brought again shortly, by a little Boy which did use to her Masters house; And when the Maid came home, she told the Cook Maid, and *Elizabeth Roswel* an other of the servants in the same house, what the Witch had told her; At which time then *Elizabeth Rosewel* told *Anne Styles*, that Master *Thomas Mason*, Son in Law to Master *Goddard*, had lost three pieces of gold, of 22. shillings a piece, and that Master *Mason* desired her to go to the Witch to know who had the same, and withal bid her give the Witch what mony she demanded, and he would repay her; whereupon the Maid went to the Witches house again, who bade her come in, and told her she was welcome, and asked her wherefore she came; to whom the Maid answered, for gold that was lost; and the Witch immediately replyed, it was Mr. *Masons* gold, and that Master *Goddards* Boy, *Robert Beckford*, had been twice before with her about it;

the Witch put on her Spectacles, and demanding seven shillings of the Maid which, she received, she opened three Books, in which there seemed to be severall pictures, and amongst the rest the picture of the Devill, to the Maids appearance, *with his Cloven feet and Claws*; after the Witch had looked over the book, she brought a round green glass, which glass she layd down on one of the books, upon some picture therein, and rubbed the glass, and then took up the book with the glass upon it, and held it up against the Sun, and bid the Maid come and see / who they were, that she could shew in that glass, and the Maid looking in the glass saw the shape of many persons, and what they were doing of in her Masters house, in particular shewed Mistriss *Elizabeth Rosewel* standing in her Mistriss Chamber, looking out of the Window with her hands in her sleeves, and another walking alone in her Masters Garden, one other standing in a room within the Kitchin, one other standing in a matted room of her Masters, against the Window, with her Apron in her hand, and shewed others drinking with glasses of Beer in their hands; after the Witches shewing this to the Maid, she then bad her go home, which when she came home, she asked the people (she so saw in the Witches glass) what they had been doing while she had been wanting, and by their answers to her she found that they had been doing what she saw they were in the glass, and the Maid relating this to *Elizabeth Rousewel*, she replyed, that Mistriss *Boddenham*, (meaning the said Witch) was either a Witch, or a woman of God.

This being about one of the Clock in the afternoon the maid went about her imploiment till 6. a Clock in the evening, about which time *Elizabeth Rosewel* acquainting the Maid, that her Mistriss going to borrow money of her Daughter in Law Mistriss *Sarah Goddard*, the money was stained black, and there-upon *Elizabeth Rosewel* told the Maid that her Mistriss was afraid of being poysoned by the said Mistriss *Sarah*, and by her Sister Mistriss *Anne Goddard*, for that she had been thrice before in danger of being poysoned, and therefore desired the Maid to go to the Witch, to know if there were any such things intended, and the Maid as it was almost dark went to the Witches house, and to her apprehension there was a little black Dog that ran before her over *Crane*-Bridge, in the way between her Masters and the Witches, and so brought her to the Witches house, where the doors flew open without her knocking, and the Witch met her at the second door, and told her, she knew wherefore she came, and that it was about poysoning, and told the Maid further that it was intended that her Mistriss should be poysoned, and that there was moneys found in Mistriss *Sarahs* Pocket, that was stained, but she would prevent it;

And further said to her, that it was Mistriss *Sarahs* intention to go a journy into *Summerset*-shire, but / she would shew her a trick, as she spoke the words, she should break her neck before she went out of the Gate; and then the Witch took five shillings of the Maid, (that she had received from Mistriss *Elizabeth Rosewel*) and so the Maid lest her and went home, and when the Maid came home, she went into Master *Masons* Chamber, where Master *Mason* and Mistriss *Elizabeth Rosewel* were, and acquainted them with what the Witch had told her, and upon that, one of them replyed, the Devill appeared in the faces of Mistriss *Sarah* and Mistriss *Anne*, and desired the maid to go again the next day, to know of the Witch what the time should be that her mistriss should be poysoned,

and the next morning about six or seaven of the Clock, the maid went to the Witches house, and carried five shillings along with her, and gave it the Witch, and told her she was come to know the time when her mistriss should be poysoned, and the Witch told her it should be on a Friday, but she would prevent it before that time, and bade the Maid come again in the afternoon; and when the Maid returned home, Master *Mason* spoke to her immediately to go again to the Witch, to know of her; if one Master *Rawley* did intend him any mischief, for winning his money from him at play, and gave the Maid two shillings to give the Witch,

And the Maid did accordingly go, and did ask of the Witch what Master *Mason* bid her, and the Witch told her that Master *Rawley* had intended some mischief against him two several times, and had way-layd him, but she had and would prevent it, and would send him a charm, and took a piece of paper and put therein yellow powder, and so made it up in a cross figure, and gave it to the Maid to deliver it to Master *Mason* to wear about his neck; and the Witch further told her, that if the Charm were about him he need not fear what mony he owed, for no Bayliff could take hold or meddle with him, and so the Maid returned home and gave him the Charm.

The next day Master *Mason* sent the Maid again to the Witch, to tell her that he intended some Law sutes with his Father in Law Master *Goddard*, and to know of her whether he should have the better of it, and gave the Maid three shillings to give the Witch, and when the Maid came to the Witches house and told her what she came for, the Witch took her staff, and / there drew him about the house, making a kind of a Circle, and then took a book, and carrying it over the Circle, with her hands, and taking a green Glass, did lay it upon the book, and placed in the Circle an earthen pan of Coles, wherein she threw something, which burning caused a very noysome stinck, and told the Maid she should not be afraid of what she should then see, for now they would come, they are the words she used, and so calling Belzebub, Tormentor, Satan, and Lucifer appear, there suddainly arose a very high wind, which made the house shake, and presently the back Door of the house flying open, there came five spirits, as the Maid supposed, in the likeness of ragged Boys, some bigger than others, and ran about the house, where she had drawn the Staff, and the Witch threw down upon the ground Crums of Bread, which the Spirits picked up, and leapt over the Pan of Coals oftentimes, which she set in the middest of the Circle, and a Dog and a Cat of the Witches danced with them; and after some time the Witch looked again in her book, and threw some great white seeds upon the ground, which the said Spirits picked up, and so in a short time the wind was layd, and the Witch going forth at her back Door the Spirits vanished, after which the Witch told the Maid, that Master *Mason* should demand fifteen hundred pound, and one hundred and fifty pound per annum of Master *Goddard*, and if he denyed it, he should prosecute the Law against him, and begone from his Father, and then he should gain it, with which message the Maid returned and acquainted Master *Mason*.

She was sent by Mistriss *Rosewel* divers times to enquire concerning sweet-hearts, when she should be marryed, and how she should disingage her self from her sweet-hearts that formerly had solicited her in a way of marriage, the one now in *France*, the other with whom she broke a piece of Gold to bind their contract, to which the Witch gave her directions, and told her what would be the result and issue of those passages, and of many more of the like nature, that she was sent to propound to the Witch.

And in a short time after, Mistriss *Rosewel* sent her again to the Witch, to know of her when the day should be, that Mistriss *Goddard* should be poysoned, and delivered her eight shillings to give the Witch, so / the Maid went again to the Witch accordingly, and gave her the eight shillings, and the Witch replyed she could not tell her then, but gave the Maid one shilling, and bid her go to an Apothecary, and buy some white *Arsenick*, and bring it to her to prevent it, which the Maid did, and carryed it to the Witch, who said to her she would take it and burn it, to prevent the poysoning, but she burnt it not as the Maid could see at all; then the Maid returned home, and told Master *Mason* and Mistriss *Rosewel* what she had done, who laughed at it.

The next day being Tuesday, she was again sent by Master *Mason*, to know where the poyson should be found that should be given her Mistriss, and when the Maid had proposed the question to the Witch, she took her stick (as formerly is related) and making therewith a Circle, the wind rose forthwith, then taking a Beesom she swept over the Circle, and made another, and looking in her Book and Glass, as formerly, and using some words softly to her self, she stood in the Circle and said, Belzebub, Tormentor, Lucifer, and Satan appear; there appeared first a Spirit in the shape of a little Boy as she conceiv'd, which then turned into another shape something like a Snake, and then into the shape of a shagged Dog with great eyes, which went about in the Circle;

And in the Circle she set an earthen pan of Coles, wherein she threw something which burned and stank, and then the Spirit vanished, after which the Witch took her Book and Glass again, and shewed the Maid in the Glass, Mistriss *Sarah Goddards* Chamber, the colour of the Curtains, and the Bed turned up the wrong way, and under that part of the Bed where the Bolster lay, she shewed the poyson in a white paper; The Maid afterward returned home, and acquainted Mistriss *Rosewel* with what the Witch had shewed her in a Glass, that the poyson it lay under Mistriss *Sarahs* Bed, and also spoke to her that they might go together and take it away; but Mistriss *Rosewel* replyed no, let it alone for Gods sake, and would not, neither did she take it or suffer it to be taken away.

And the Witch further told the Maid (when she was with her the Thursday) that the next day being Friday, about 7. or 8. of the Clock at night, there should be Sage Ale made for her Mistriss, And that there should be a white Pot set upon / the Dresser in the Kitchin wherein poyson should be put but Mistriss *Goddard* should not drink it, and that Mistriss *Rosewel* knew best what to do; And on the Friday Night, there was Ale set on the fire (as the Witch before related) the maid being that while sleeping in the Hall; Mistriss *Rosewel* a waked her and bid her go into the Kitchin, and see whether or no there was not poyson in the Cup; And the maid looked and found something there, and called to Mistriss *Rosewel*, and told her there was something in it, which swimmed on the top, and something in the bottom, as the Witch before had told the maid should be.

And then mistriss *Rosewel* took the same and carried it up to her mistriss, and shewed it her, and the maid afterward asking mistriss *Rosewel* if she had told her mistriss of it, the replyed, that her mistriss knew well enough of it by her looks. The next day following being Saturday the maid was sent again to the Witch, to get some example shewen upon the Gentlewoman that should procure the poyson, upon which the maid went again to the Witch, and told her for what she was sent.

Then the Witch made a Circle as formerly, and set her pan of Coles as formerly, and burnt something that stank extremely, and took her book and Glass as before is related, and said Belzebub, Tormentor, Lucifer, and Satan appear, and then appeared five Spirits, as she conceived, in the shapes of little ragged Boyes, which the Witch commanded to appear and go along with the maid to a meadow at *Wilton*, which the Witch shewed in the Glass, and there to gather Vervine and Dill, and forthwith the ragged Boys ran away before the maid, and she followed them to the said meadow, and when they came thither the ragged Boys looked about for the Herbs, and removed the Snow in two or three places, before they could find any, and at last they found some, and brought it away with them, and then the maid and the Boys returned back again to the Witch, and found her in the Circle paring her Nayls, and then she took the said Herbs, and dryed the same, and made powder of some, and dryed the leaves of other, and threw Bread to the Boys, and they eat and danced as formerly, and then the Witch reading in a book they vanished away;

And the Witch gave the maid in one paper the powder, in another the leaves, and in the / third the paring of the Nayls, all which the maid was to give to her Mistriss; the powder was to put in the young Gentle womens Mistriss *Sarah* and Mistriss *Anne Goddards* drink or broth, to rot their Guts in their Bellies; the leaves to rub about the brims of the Pot, to make their Teeth fall out of their Heads; and the paring of the Nayls to make them drunk and mad.

And the Witch likewise told the maid, that she must tell her Mistriss, and the rest, that when they did give it them, they must cross their Breasts, and then say, *In the name of our Lord Jesus Christ, grant that this may be*, and that they must say the Creed backward and forward.

And when the maid came home and delivered it to her mistriss, and told her the effects of the powder, and the other things, her mistriss laughed, and said that it is a very brave thing indeed.

And her mistriss sent her again the same day to the Witch, to desire her to send her some Charm, or writing under her own hand, that should keep her from ill, and preserve her from danger, And the Witch took Pen Ink and Paper, and wrote something, and put some yellow powder therein, and gave it to the maid to give it to her mistriss, and bad her tell her, that she must never look in it, and must carry it in her Bosom by Day, and lay it in a purse under her Head by Night; And the Monday following, the maids mistriss, master *Mason*, and mistriss *Rosewel* importuned her to go again to the Witch to know of her whether or no she could not make the young Gentlewomen exemplary some other ways, seeing that they could not give them the powder, and whether she could not send a Spirit to bring them upon their knees, to ask her mistris forgiveness; but the Witch told her she could not have any power of them unless she could get her the tayls of their Coats, or *of their smocks*, and if she had but that she could make the house fall about their ears, and could do more than master *Lilly* or any one whatsoever; which message the maid carryed to her mistriss, upon which her mistriss replyed, That would be pretty to be done, and mistriss *Rosewel* spoke to the maid to cut off the same when they should be a bed, but the maid refused to do it, the young Gentlewomen mistriss *Sarah* and mistriss *Anne*, hearing / of these transactions about poyson, and that it should be laid to their charge, that they had a designe, and provided poyson to poyson their Mother; being much moved at it, and to vindicate themselves, that no such aspersion might lie on them (in regard it was also reported, that they should buy one Ounce and halfe of poyson that cost 6 d. at an Apothecaries) they went about *Sarum* to enquire whether any such thing was bought, and by whom, that the truth might be discovered, and the aspersion might be removed; and having found where the poyson was bought, the Maids fellow-servant *Mirian* and Mris. *Rosewell* told the Maid, that her Mistris wished her to goe away and shift for her selfe, otherwise they supposed that she should be examined before some Justice, and so there might some trouble and disgrace come upon them in the businesse:

And the same night the Maid went out of her Masters house, and lay at one *Mattershawes* the Cookes: The next day in the morning Mris. *Rosewell* sene her word that she would speak with her at *Longmans* house, and the Maid went thither, where Mris. *Rosewell* brought her her Cloaths, and wishe her to goe to *London*, and brought her 9 s, which she laid out before for the Witch and 12 d. as a gift from Mr. *Mason*; and Mris. *Rosewell* sent to the Witch, before she went, to know whether she did approve of her Journey to *London*, and the Witch wished her to go, and told her that she would send a Paper by her to Mr. *Mason*, and did then write in the paper divers Crosses and Pictures, and other things, and put black and yellow powder therein, and told the Maid she should give the same to Mr. *Mason*, and bid him use it how he pleased; which Paper the Maid carryed along with her as far as *Sutton* towards *London*, and there burnt it:

But before the Maid went away from the Witch for *London*, the Witch asked the Maid whether she would goe to *London* High or Low, To which she replyed, What doe you mean by that? She answered, If you will goe on High, you shall be carryed to London in the Air, and be there in two hours; but if you goe a Low, you shall be taken at *Suttons* Towns end, and before, unlesse you have help:

But before she departed, / the Witch earnestly desired the Maid to live with her, and told her, that if she would do so, she would teach her to doe as she did, and that she should never be taken; then the Maid asked her what she could doe? she answered, You shal know presently, and forthwith she appeared in the shape of a great Black Cat, and lay along by the Chimny: at which the Maid being very much afrighted, she came into her own shape again, and told her, I see you are afraid, and I see you are willing to be gone, and told her, if she was, she should say so, and not speak against her conscience; and the Maid replyed, she was willing to goe, and not to dwell with the Witch; then the

Witch said, she must seal unto her body and blood not to discover her; which she promising to doe, she forthwith made a Circle as formerly she had done, and looking in her Book, and called *Beelzebub, Tormentor, Lucifer,* and *Satan* appear, then appeared two Spirits in the likenesse of great Boys, with long shagged black hair, and stood by her, looking over her shoulder, and the Witch took the Maids fore-finger of her right hand, in her hand, and pricked it with a pin, and squeesed out the blood, and put it into a Pen, and put the Pen into the Maids hand, and held her hand to write in a great Book, and one of the Spirits laid his Hand or Claw upon the Witches, whilest the Maid wrote, and when she had done writing, whilest their hands were together, the Witch said *Amen*, and made the Maid say *Amen*, and the Spirits said *Amen, Amen*; and the Spirits hand did feel cold to the Maid as it touched her hand, when the Witches hand and hers were together writing; and then the Spirit gave a peace of Silver (which he first bit) to the Witch, who gave it to the Maid, and also stuck two Pins in the Maids head-cloathes, and bid her keep them, and bid her be gone, and said also I will vex the Gentlewoman well enough, as I did the Man in *Clarington* Park, which I made walk about with a bundle of Pales on his back all night in a Pond of water, and could not lay them down till the next morning." (Bower 1653: 1-10)

Fourthly, Daniel Defoe gives an allegedly true account of two early 18th century Cunning Men's operations in the form of a dialogue between the author (*Au.*) and a "Countryman" (*Co.m.*) he had met while travelling, in which the latter tries desperately to confirm his strong suspicion that his wife has been unfaithful. It describes some rather elaborate stage management provided in the second instance to lend verisimilitude to the claims of the anonymous Cunning Man. The interesting thing here is that despite Defoe's obvious disdain for Cunning Folk, the first magician actually tries to give the obsessed man good advice that he is unwilling to hear and therefore seeks a second opinion. Defoe accurately depicts the Cunning Men as good psychologists, as most were, and also shows that the common assumption that the Devil was involved rather than discouraging the clients, lent credibility to the consultations. He also reveals that an ostensible refusal to charge money was in fact a clever subterfuge to disguise a payment, similar to that shown in the sixth example.

"I was not unwilling to hear the Result of the Story, but was particularly curious to hear what the Magician at *Oundle* could do; so I resolved to stay at *Northampton* that Night, and we kept Company together to the Town. When we came to the Town, I put up at the *George Inn*, and thought he would have gone in with me; but when we came to the Door, he bad me Good-by for the present, for the Cunning Man, he said, liv'd two Miles out of the Town, and he would talk with him, and come to me at Night. /

I went into my Inn and staid there all Night, but heard no more of my poor Cuckold the Countryman all that Evening. The next Morning I was indisposed, which made me stay longer at the Inn than I intended, and indeed was obliged to stay there all that Day and Night too, but still I had no News of my Countryman, which made me a little Chagreen [chagrined]; but at last he came back again, and comes to me, but not 'till the next Day about eleven a-Clock.

Then as I had been waiting before very patiently, I began, and spoke a little angrily; What's the Business now, says I, what's the matter with you, that you dodge about so ?

O Sir, says he, let me come in, and I'll tell you the strangest things.

Well, come in then, says /, and sit down; I thought you had been lost, or had forgot your Promise.

So he came in, and we begun another short Discourse, as follows:

Co.m, O Master, I have had a hard Night's Work on't.

Au, What do you mean of a Night's Work, where have you been?

Co. m. Why first, Master, I went to my cunning Man, and gave him a Shilling, which it seems he takes before he will speak a Word.

Au. Ay, ay, they are in the right, 'tis the only thing I can call them cunning Men for.

Co.m. Why are they cunning in that?

Au, Because they know if they did not take the Money before-hand, no body would give it them afterwards, because they can tell nothing, nor say any thing to the purpose.

Co. m. Well, I gave him the Shilling; he demanded Half a Crown [two shillings, six pence], but I told him I was a poor Man, and so he condescended in Charity to take a Shilling. /

Au. That is to say, he saw there was no more to be had, so he took what he could get; and so they all do. But come, what did he do for it, what did he tell thee?

Co.m. O he examined me very strictly, I assure you.

Au. Examine you, about what?

Co. m. Why, how long my Wife had been gone, what she carried with her, what a-Clock she went at, what she said at parting; and took every thing down in Figures.

Au. Very well, this was all Grimace, to put a Countenance upon things.

Co. m. Then he bid me hold my Tongue, and he fell to making Figures and mutt'ring to himselfe; and on a sudden he starts up; Well, says he, I find your Wife is gone away, and that you beat her very severely before she went. Now, I could not deny that Part, Master, because I knew it was true; but how should he know that, Master, if he wan't a cunning Man?

Au, Well enough: when he had examined you so strictly before in all the Particulars, he might easily guess you had used her hardly, by the Rage you were in, when you came to him, and when you talk'd of hanging your self and murthering her, he might easily judge that you had talked the same to her, which had frighted the Woman, and she was runaway for fear of you; there's no great cunning in all that. I was a going to say so to you myself once, for I really thought of it before.

Co.m. Why then you are as much a cunning Man as he.

Au. Well, what else did he say to you?

Co. m. Nothing to the purpose, only to vex me and make me mad.

Au. Nay that he could not do, for I verily think you were mad before; but what was it? come, tell me.

Co.m. Why, Master, he fell to scribbling and scrawling again upon a Piece of Paper, and then he rises and walks up and down, and round and round, as I thought, he made Circles three or four times, and talk'd to himself all the while.

Au. Well, and that frighted you, I warrant you; did not you think he was going to raise the Devil?

Co.m. Why you know every thing, Master, aforehand, I think you are as cunning as he; I was so frighted I trembled like an Aspen Leaf, Master.

Au. Why, didn't you say you wanted to see the Devil; to tell you all?

Co.m. Ay, that's true, Master, but I was deadly fraid for all that, especially when I thought he was just a coming.

Au. Well, and how then, what came of it?

Co. m. Came on it! why, Master, the Man's a Rogue, a meer Cheat; he had got my Money, and when all come to all, he told me nothing, at least nothing that signified any thing to me.

Au. Well, but what was it? for I find he told you something, tho' you don't like it: did he bid you go home and be quiet and easie, and not trouble your self about it?

Co. m, Hang him, Rogue; when he had made all his Turns, and his Circles, and said all his Witchcraft over to himself, he sits down and calls me to him, and very civilly bad me sit down, and begun his ugly Story.

Au, I find he has not pleased ye: I really fancy the Man has given thee good honest Advice, and bid thee go home and mind thy Business, and be easie; did not I say the same to thee?

Co. m. I'll tell it you all, Master, if you'll have Patience; he's a Rogue; a Rogue, Master. I told you he would have my Money beforehand, and so he had, or he should never ha' had a Farthing; and he knew that well enough. /

Au. No, no, he knew Folks never pay when they don't like the Story; but go on, what did he say?

Co.m. Why, as grave as a Judge, he takes me by the Hand, felt my Pulse, holding his conjuring Paper in t'other Hand, all the while; Heark thee. Friend, says he, I have calculated the Times and the Seasons, I have brought your Names in a direct Opposition, I have done every thing to satisfy you, that can be done, and all my Numbers and Accounts agree, and this is the Sum of your Case; You are a poor, honest, fretful, passionate Fellow that stands here on one Side; and then he shewed me his damned Figures, and Crosses and Circles, on one side; and here's your poor Wife a t'other side, says he; and then he shewed me his Figures again; she has anger'd you, and scolded at you for your ill Usage of her, and you have fallen upon her and beaten her unmercifully, and threaten'd to murther her, and she is run away for fear of it; and now you call her Whore, and come to me to tell you who has made a Cuckold of you.

Au. And did the Man say all this to you, Friend?

Co.m. Yes, Master, and a great deal more, like a Rogue as he is. He a cunning Man! he's a Blockhead; why, I knew all that before.
Au. Ay, and he might easily gather it from your Discourse.
Co.m. No, Master, that he could not, I'm sure.
Au. Well then, you'll make him a cunning Man indeed, at the same time that you call him a Blockhead and a Fool. I tell you I gather'd as much before from you, and you can't help it; you are too full of your own Story. But go on, what did he say then?
Co.m, Why, then he fell to preaching, and giving me Advice; Go home, Friend, says the Toad, and be easie and quiet, and tell your Friends you are / sorry you have been in such a Heat, and that you hope your Wife will come home again, for you won't do her any Hurt; and then your Neighbours will tell her, and she'll come lovingly again to you; For I tell thee Friend, says he, thou art in the Wrong, the poor Woman is no Whore, I can show it to you in black and white here; and then he pointed to his cursed Conjuring Paper; she's a very honest Woman, thou hast only a Whymsie come in thy Head because she is gone, I tell thee thou art no Cuckold, go home and be quiet.
Au. And did he say all this to thee?
Co. m. Yes, to be sure Master, and a great deal more such Stuff; what should I be in such a Passion with him for else?
Au. Upon my Word, Friend, whether he be a cunning Man or no, that I have nothing to say to; he may make thee believe so, that's for his Advantage; but o' my Conscience I think he's a wise Man, and an honest Man, and I would advise thee to follow his Counsel; for I do tell thee, I firmly believe 'tis thy Case to a Tittle, and I tell thee thy whole Discourse discover'd it; he might have said it all without his Figures and Circles; that was done to amuse you, but 'tis plain from all you have said, that's thy very Case.
Co. m. Ay, ay, Master, 'tis no matter for that, let him be as cunning and as wise as he will, I have had another guess Account of it, and better Advice since; for I have been at *Oundle*, Master, since that, and there I have met with a cunning Man indeed.
Au. Why, have you really been consulting with the Devil then?
Co. m. I believe I have indeed.
Au. Nay, then 'tis like you have had good Advice indeed; mayn't a body know what you have met with there too? /
Co. m. Truly Master, I don't know whether I can tell it you or no, for I have been frighted out of my Wits. I'm sure if my Hat had been on, my Hair would have lifted it off, tho' I had had a good Basket of Apples upon my Head.
Au. Come let me hear it however, as well as you can.
Co. m. Why Master, when I came to the Man's House, ('tis within two Mile of *Oundle* I think, or thereabout,) it was almost dark, and that made it the worse. I knock'd at the Door, and out came a tall black frightful old Man. I begun to be frighted at the very first Sight, for I thought it had been the Devil was come before I ask'd for him.
Au. And are you sure it was not?
Co. m. Yes, I think he was not the Devils for he spoke very civilly to me; and when I ask'd him if he was the cunning Man, he smil'd, and had me come in; so he carry'd me into a large Room, which had but one dim burning Candle in it, and I trembl'd every Inch of me, for I thought the Candle burnt blue as soon as I look'd at it.
Au. Very well, so you thought you were come into good Company, did not you?
Co. m. Indeed, I wish'd my self out of the House again, that I did; but the old Gentleman whistled, and in came a young Fellow that look'd like a Servant, and he bad him go snuff the Candle, and bring in another, and that comforted me a little; then he sat him down in a great Elbow-Chair, with a little Table before it, and upon the Table was a great many Books, and a Pen and Ink, and Paper. Come Friend, says he, let me know thy Business, for tho' I am none of those ignorant Fellows you call Cunning Men, yet perhaps I may tell you what you want to know, upon a better foot./
Au. Well, he begun pretty high: what could he pretend to?
Co. m. I reply'd. Sir, I was told you was one that dealt in secret things, that understood the *Black Art*, and those we call Cunning Men; if I am mistaken, I am very sorry: and so made as if I would go away again, but he stopp'd me, and said. Look you Friend, I am none of those Fellows you call cunning Men, I look upon them to be all Cheats; my Practice is all Divine, of a superior Nature, I

study things in a higher Sphere, I deal in the Mysteries of an invisible World, and converse with the World of Spirits unembody'd, who are beneficent and kind to us, who are Spirits embody'd, and not only converse with us below, but are helpful and serviceable to us on all Occasions. I can't remember all his hard Words, Master, but he said a deal more to that purpose.

Au. Well, did not he ask for your Money before hand too, as t'other did?

Co. m. No indeed, but when he bad me tell him my Case, I put my Hand in my Pocket, and pull'd out two half Crowns, and went to offer him the Money, for I found he was not an ordinary Fellow, and so I thought he would not be very lowpriz'd.

Au. But he took the Money, I suppose?

Co. m. No, he said he did not do these things for Money, as he found I believ'd he did; but he said, you may put what you please in there, pointing to a Box that stood upon the Table; I shall dispose of it charitably, and to better Uses, it may be, than you would do your self; so I put the Money into his Box, which had a slit like a Tradesman's Till.

Au. Very well, this look'd great indeed.

Co. m. Then he bad me tell him my Case; for, says he, I perceive you are a Man of a troubled / Countenance, your Mind is oppress'd, the Passions of your Soul have been in a Perturbation, your Spirits are fluttering still, and in a Storm, tho' something abated of what they have been; pray be very free, and tell me your whole Case, as fully and plainly as you can.

Au. Well, I assure you, he spoke in state with a great deal of Majesty.

Co. m. Yes, and yet he spoke very courteously too, and I began to like him mightily; so I began, and told him my Case at large, just as I did you, Master.

Au. That is to say, that you wanted to be reveng'd of your Wife, and to find out the Man that had cuckolded you, and the like; so you expected presently he should tell you who it was.

Co. m. Yes, so I did; but he brought me to understand things better, and I found he was in Earnest, and that he was not to be cheated. He examined me too as t'other had done, and ask'd me abundance of Questions.

Au. And, I doubt not, gathered your Case in every Part of it from the weak inconsistent Account you gave him of it.

Co. m. I don't know that; but after he had done asking me all his Questions, he took his Pen and Ink too, and wrote down a great many things upon his Paper, and made Lines with a short brass Rule and a Pencil, and then took out a pair of Compasses, and drew several Figures and Marks, but I understood nothing of them, neither could I see them distinctly by the Candle Light; then he ask'd me my Christian Name, which I told him was *Edward*, and he set it down in great Letters, but such as tho' I can read Master, I am sure that I never saw such Before. Then he ask'd my Wife's Christian Name too, which I told him was *Abigail* and he set that down in the same kind of Letters as before; / then he ask'd my Age, and my Wife's Age, and the Age of my two Children; of all which I gave him a full Account.

Au. I suppose you had told him that you had two Children; he did not conjure out that, did he?

Co. m. Yes, he had ask'd me that before, and I told him; so when he had done all, and I believe we had talk'd together above an Hour, he rose up, and offered to go away, and I rose up too, but he laid his Hand upon my Arm, Do you sit still, says he, and I'll come to you again; at which I was a little frighted to be left alone, and he perceiv'd it. Don't be afraid, says he, there shall nothing hurt you, nor speak to you; and if you hear any Noise don't you stir, but sit still here. So he took up one of the Candles, and went into another Room by a little Door like a Closet-Door, and when he shut the Door after him, I perceiv'd a little Window of one broad Square of Glass only, that look'd into the Room which he was gone into.

Au. I warrant ye, you wanted to peep, did not ye?

Co. m. Yes, I did, but I durst not stir for my Life, because he had charg'd me I should not.

Au. Well, but you was to hear some Noises, was you not?

Co. m. But I did not, except once that I heard a Noise like the drawing of a Chair upon the Floor, which being nothing but what was ordinary, did not disturb me.

Au. Well how long did he stay?

Co. m. About half an Hour, and came in again, looking very well pleas'd, and ask'd me how I did, and then sit down as before. Well, says he, I have been consulting on your Case, and I find things not so threatning to you as I expected; perhaps you may not be in so ill a Case as you imagine ; however, I am order'd to tell you, that some Days after your return, your Wife shall come to a House / near you, and send to know if you will receive her again kindly; if the Person she sends is a Woman, you may conclude your Wife has abus'd you; but if she sends a Man, then she is innocent, and you are mistaken.

Au. This was point-blank, I assure you.

Co. m. I did not like it however, and that he might see well enough; for I can't allow any if's or and's. Tell me of being mistaken! said I to him, I can't be mistaken. Well, says he, I'll go again and consult farther about you; and seeing me begin to get up too, he turns again ; You are not afraid, says he, are you ? No, not at all, said I ? Well, nor you won't be afraid, will you, if you see nothing frightful? No, not at all, said I again. But I ly'd, Master, for I was almost frighted to Death, when he spoke of my seeing something; but as I had said No twice, and spoke it pretty heartily too, he said. Well then, come along with me into the next Room.

Au. I doubt you were afraid then indeed.

Co. m. Ay, so I was heartily, and he perceiv'd it too again; Well, says he, if you are afraid to go into my Room of Practice, I'll stay here with you; only, whatever you see or hear sit you still, and neither speak or stir out of your Chair.

Au. Well, did you observe his Direction?

Co. m. No, indeed Master, my Heart fail'd me; I durst neither go nor stay, but I'll tell you what I did when he was gone into the next Room, I went to the Window and peep'd.

Au. And what did you see? 'tis odd peeping at the *Devil*, I must tell you.

Co. m. 1 saw my old Gentleman in a great Chair, and two more in Chairs at some Distance, and three great Candles, and a great Sheet of white Paper upon the Floor between them; every one of them had a long white Wand in their Hands, the lower end of which touch'd the Sheet of Paper. /

Au. And were the Candles upon the Ground too?

Co. m. Yes, all of them.

Au. There was a great deal of Ceremony about you, I assure you.

Co. m. I think so too, but it is not done yet; immediately I heard the little Door stir, as if it was opening, and away I skipp'd as softly as I could tread, and got into my Chair again, and sat there as gravely as if I had never stirr'd out of it. I was no sooner set but the Door open'd indeed, and the old Gentleman came out as before, and turning to me, said, Sit still, don't ye stir; and at that Word, the other two that were with him in the Room walk'd out after him, one after another cross the Room, as if to go out at the other Door where I came in; but at the farther end of the Room they stop'd, and turn'd their Faces to one another and talk'd; but it was some Devil's Language of their own, for I could understand nothing of it.

Au. And now I suppose you were frighted in earnest?

Co. m. Ay, so I was; but it was worse yet, for they had not stood long together, but the great Elbow-Chair which the old Gentleman sat in at the little Table just by me began to stir of it self; at which the old Gentleman knowing I should be afraid, came to me and said. Sit still, don't you stir, all will be well, you shall have no harm; at which he gave his Chair a kick with his Foot, and said, Go, with some other Words, and of other Language, and away went the obedient Chair sliding two of its Legs on the Ground, and the other two off, as if some body had dragg'd it by that Part.

Au. And so no doubt they did, tho' you could not see it.

Co. m. As soon as the Chair was dragg'd or mov'd to the end of the Room, where the three, I know / not what to call' em, were, two other Chairs did the like from the other side of the Room, and so they all sat down, and talk'd together a good while; at last the Door at that end of the Room opened too, and they all were gone in a Moment without rising out of their Chairs; for I am sure they did not rise to go out, as other Folks do.

Au. What did you think of your self, when you saw the Chair stir so near you?

Co. m. Think! nay, I did not think; I was dead, to be sure I was dead, with the Fright, and expected I should be carry'd away, Chair and all, the next Moment. Then it was, I say, that my Hair would have lifted off my Hat, if it had been on I am sure it would.

Au. Well, but when they were all gone, you came to your self again, I suppose?

Co. m. To tell you the truth Master, I am not come to my self yet.

Au. But go on, let me know how it ended.

Co. m. Why, after a little while my old Man came in again, call'd his Man to let the Chairs to rights, and then sat him down at the Table, spoke chearfully to me, and ask'd me if I would drink, which I refus'd, tho' I was a-dry indeed. I believe the fright had made me dry; but as I never had been us'd to drink with the *Devil*, I didn't know what to think of it, so I let it alone.

Au. But you might e'en have ventured, for the old Necromancer was but a Man, whatever Correspondence he might have, and his Ale would not have hurt you. But what else did he say about your Business?

Co. m. Why, he told me the invisible Agents were favourable in their Answers; that there appeared nothing but well; that he was assur'd by the Aspects which any way concerned me; that I was more concern'd about this Matter, than / there was reason for; that I should go home and wait, till by the Signals he had given me, I might judge for my self, and till I heard from my Wife as before; and that if I could make any plain Discovery, that there was real Guilt, I should come to him again, and he would endeavour to point out the Man. But if I could not, I should rest satisfy'd that I had been wrong inform'd of things in my Family, and might make my self easy.

Au. This is an odd Story, why this Man is only a Cheat like all the rest; he bids you go home, and if you can find out any real Guilt, then come to him and he will tell you what to do; that is to say, he knows nothing: Is this your Necromancer! pray where does he dwell?

Co. m. Nay, Master, the Man has done me no wrong. I was directed to the House, but I can't find it again, if I was to be hang'd for missing it; however I won't betray him neither, let him be what he will.

Au. Well, but it seems you are not fully satisfy'd yet, because he does not confirm your Notion that your Wife is a Whore; I fancy you have a Mind it should be so.

Co. m. I don't care what she is, so I could but find it out.

Au. But you see, neither the honest Man at *Northampton*, nor the *Devil* at *Oundle*, would give you any reason to think so. I would have you go home, as the first Man advis'd you, and be quiet. I verily believe there's nothing at all in it, but you have been a cruel Husband, have us'd your Wife like a Dog, and frighted her with worse, and she is fled from you, as a poor naked defenceless Sheep would from a Lion or a Wolf.

Co. m. And you would have me go home and submit to my Wife? no, I'll hang my self first. /

Au. I don't say submit to your Wife; tho' if you have wrong'd your Wife, as I doubt you have, I see no reason why you should not make a Wise Satisfaction for the Injury done her Character, as well as you would to a Man that was able to cudgel you into it. But I say go home, and mend your Wife's Husband, and that will in all probability mend your Wife, and you may live comfortably again together.

Co. m. I can't promise, Master, to take any of their Advices, or your's either.

This Story is not told so much to give an Account of the Man, who was nothing as I could understand by it all, but a base passionate Fellow to an honest Woman his Wife; but 'tis a kind of a History of modern Magick, or of the Craft which is at this time in Practice in the World. Nor is it a singular Example, for we have many more People among us, who are Pretenders to the sacred Sciences, as they call them; who yet do not level their Knowledge of them to such mean Uses, as to go Mountebanking with them, to get a Crown or two for petty Discoveries, and set up for what they call cunning Men; which is indeed the lowest Step of this kind that a Spirit of the invisible World could well be suppos'd to take.

It is true, 'tis something hard to describe what this thing we call Magick is, and how it is to be understood now; what it was formerly we know something of, and yet even then no great things were perform'd by it; something they did, whether by the thing it self as an Art, or by the *Devil* being present to assist them, we know not; that which would be call'd wonderful is, that they did then, as they pretend to do still, several things which the *Devil* really has no Power to do; and particularly that of foretelling things to come, which we do not, generally speaking, grant the *Devil* to have in his / Power; he can indeed make better Judgment of things than we can, but that the Knowledge of Futurity is given him, I deny." (Defoe 1973: 261- 276)

The fifth selection is of a rather different sort, dealing as it does with a notorious "cursing well":

A Welsh Conjurer, 1831.—The following cutting from the *Lincoln Herald*, of August 19, 1831, is worth a place in the columns of FOLKLORE:

"A WELSH CONJURER.—Denbighshire Assizes. Before Mr. Baron Bolland.—John Evans, a Welsh seer, who officiates as high priest of the far-famed and much-dreaded Ffynnon Elian (or St. Elian's Well), near Abergele, was indicted for obtaining *7s.*[seven shillings] from one Elizabeth Davies, by falsely pretending that he could cure her husband, Robert Davies, of a certain sickness with which he was afflicted by taking his name out of the well.

"This case affords a remarkable instance of the ignorance and simplicity of the Welsh peasantry even in these days of the march of intellect. Ffynnon Elian is celebrated in Cambrian history and song; and owing to the popular belief in the virtue and extraordinary property of its waters, the number and extent of the impositions practised upon the credulity of the people in past ages by a succession of impostors almost exceeds credibility. A few years ago the magistrates of the county prosecuted one of the high priests of the well, who, in consequence, was found guilty of cunning, cheatery, and fraud, put into prison, and his well of holy waters destroyed. For a time the celebrity of St. Elian and the *protégé* died away; their anathematisation ceased; and their memories were fast sinking into obscurity, when the prisoner revived them by laying in a stock-in-trade, and commencing business near the same spot as the high priest and favoured minister of the Saint.

"The following is the method pursued by the prisoner to gull the poor people. Into the Ffynnon Elian (a very shallow well) he put a large quantity of pebbles, slates, and stones, inscribed with numberless initials and names. No sooner did he hear of any poor person's ill-health, or of anyone being afflicted with misfortune or disease, than he contrived to let them know that their names were in the well, and that nothing could cure or benefit them unless they were taken out. Of course this could not be done without money; and many hundreds of ignorant people were known to travel on foot thirty and forty miles to seek relief, and that, too, in the most distracted state of mind. The frauds of the prisoner were not the only evils which his abominable practices produced, for, like his predecessors, he pretended he had power to put anyone into the well, afflict them with misfortune or bad luck, and take them out for money, when he pleased. The consequence was, that ignorant persons were frequently induced to charge their misfortunes to the malignity of their neighbours, and thereby engendered the most disgraceful quarrels; whilst hundreds of equally ignorant fools would expend their money on the prisoner in order to gratify, as they thought, a bit of spite.

"The facts of the case were proved by Elizabeth Davies, who said: My husband has been ill for many years. I had heard of the virtue of the well of St. Elian; I went twenty-two miles to consult the defendant, who had the charge of it. I asked if my husband's name was in the well; he said he did not know, but he would send to see; he sent a little girl, who came back with a dishful of pebbles and small slates, marked with different sets of initials; he looked at them, and said my husband's name was not among them; he sent the little girl again, who returned with a number more, which were strewed upon the table, and I found a stone marked with the letters R. D. and three crosses. I said, Is that my husband's name? He said it was. I said I was not satisfied, and asked if my husband's name was in a book? The prisoner said he did not put the name in the well, or else it would be in the book, but the water would tell whether it was his name or not. We went to the well, which was in the garden, near the prisoner's house. He took out some water, and said, 'The water changes colour; it is your husband, sure enough.' I asked what it would cost to take my husband's name out of the well. He said *10s.* was the lowest. I told him I had no money, but could bring him some. I asked him to let me take the stone home, and he said I might, but I must not show it to any one. I asked him what I should do with it. He said I must powder it, and put it, with salt, into the fire. I then went away. In about two months I came again with my brother-in-law, William Davies. The prisoner was cross, because I had mentioned what had passed to Mr. Clough, a magistrate, but he said, for the sake of my brother-in-law, he would do something. He said I must have a bottle of the water of the well, and give *9s.* for it. I bargained with him for *7s.*, which he said must be given to the well. The money was given to the well, but the prisoner took it out and put it into his pocket. He muttered some spells, which I thought were Latin, but all I could make out was the name of St. Elian. The prisoner said the water must be taken by my husband three nights successively, and he must repeat a portion of the 38th Psalm. I asked him who had put my husband into the well, and he did not tell me, but he said if I wished he would put that person in the well, and bring upon him any disease I liked. I paid him the *7s.*

"William Davies, a tailor at Hollywell, brother-in-law of the last witness, corroborated her testimony as to what took place at the latter interview with the prisoner.

"The prisoner in his defence said he never sent for anyone to come to the well, nor did he say there was any efficacy in the water; but if a person believed that there was, and chose to give him some money, he took all that they had a mind to give.

"The Jury returned a verdict of Guilty; and the learned Judge—after expressing his regret that any person could be found so lamentably ignorant and credulous as to believe that any man, by such ridiculous means, had the power of relieving or controlling the diseases and afflictions of another—sentenced the prisoner to six months' imprisonment with hard labour."

EDWARD PEACOCK. *Bottesford Manor, Brigg, January* 10, 1890. (Peacock 1890: 131-133)

The sixth selection from the very end of the 19th century describes an illiterate Cheshire Cunning Man named Big Johnny Bracken (b. 1836), "Old Redcap", who typifies the stereotype of the village fortune teller, and his shopkeeper wife "Toffee Ann". This gives a rare glimpse into the cunning craft during the time of its imminent decline.

"Barnton [Cheshire] had its wise-man-in-chief, whom some regarded as merely a wiseacre, which is both more common and not quite the same thing. In his earlier life, when he had first set up as a "fortin teller," the villagers had accepted his claims in good faith; indeed they had been rather proud than otherwise of his gifts, and regarded him as one of their natural curiosities. But the prophet, according to time-honoured custom, had gradually grown into disrepute in his own country, and he had to trust to the neighbouring villages for a supply of credulous clients. Like many a politician of conservative leanings, he was wont to bewail those "good old times," when reforms were few and credulity was large. ... /

Behind the Police Station, on a little knoll called Rose Hill, stood a number of long lines of sordid-looking red-brick houses, which had been built for the miners and their families. The hill itself had once been grassy and garlanded with wild briers, but the trampling of the clogs of the colliers and the pattering of the feet of the children had long given to it a partially bald appearance. Here lived a man of some interest to the police, though he was never disturbed by the officious attentions of any of those grim ministers of the law. The rows of houses had some pretence of comfort with considerable real shabbiness, and a long row at right angles to the rest had not even a pavement before its front doors. In the centre of this row lived John Bracken and Ann his wife. Though they were well known in Barnton he from his mystic occupation, she from the no less useful and important calling of a casual midwife. If a stranger had asked for them by their "patronymic appellations," he would have been met by stolid ignorance. ... /

The little shop was nothing more than the front-room of a somewhat dingy cottage. The walls were adorned with a florid sampler, a pair of badly-cleaned pewter candlesticks hung up, one or two faded pictures of the nature of family portraits, and a mysterious astrological diagram, which Johnnie did not himself understand, though he often talked about it. A chest of drawers with a brown American-cloth cover and a large Bible thereon, four rickety rush-bottomed chairs, two similarly seated arm-chairs, a three-legged round table with a sort of shelf underneath it, which served the double purpose of supporting the fabric and of affording the cat a quiet resting place, a corner cupboard, a bread-creel, a pot-rack and a "winter-hedge" [clothes horse] formed the furniture of the chamber. A few rough-hewn deal shelves warped by the sun and weighed down by their contents, ornamented with fly-blown and curiously cut pink paper, had been stretched across the window. On these were set, in order due, six meagre bottles clouded over with domestic vapours and containing respectively Pomfret cakes [licorice], mintdrops, pink and white, yellow and white sugar sticks, aniseed pipes and wondrously compounded cough drops. Beneath these scanty examples of the sweets of life stood two big / brown paper bags, containing Barcelona nuts [dried hazlenuts] and their oilier brethren from Brazil. In the space between them lay a dusty heap of wizened oranges, which never seemed to diminish, and which looked more like mummies than actual fruit. Once a week the mistress of these more or less succulent treasures made several tins of sallow-hued, dirty looking and impoverished sugar toffee, the delight of her younger customers and the origin of her nickname.

Tuffee Ann herself was a thin, upright, pinched old woman, with brown hair just lined with gray, with cheeks like streaky red apples, faded dark eyes, and a nose which betrayed a liking for cordials of another nature than the vigorous treacle-beer which she dispensed in its proper season. She said she "wur plagu't wi' wyind I' th' stummick." But eccentric habits are wont to be palliated by aerial excuses. She used her occasional midwifery and the products of her shop to add a few shillings weekly to the precarious earnings of her husband. She had plenty of customers for toffee, as the Sunday-bedabbled cheeks of the neighbouring urchins plainly showed. She looked half-starved, and she was subject to periodical fits of blues, a circumstance which may have accounted for the redness of her nose. She had implicit faith in the magical powers of "her mon," though that did not prevent her from giving him an occasional taste of her elocutionary rhetoric, and she was a useful decoy-duck to the more credulous.

Big Johnnie had not been nicknamed in vain. He was by nature a tall old man of fully six feet in height, who had lost several inches by an inveterate habit of stooping from his middle, as if he were perpetually on the point of sitting down. He was a noteworthy and conspicuous man in more ways than one. When he took his walks abroad, he wore on his always-wagging head an old fur / cap which kept a perpetual moulting season, with the ear-flaps hanging about his large red ears, and their strings hanging loosely over his shoulders. When he stayed in the house, his headpiece was a dusky red flannel skull cap, which from its infancy had been kept quite innocent of the wash tub, and consequently had attained a rich copper colour. His thin gray hair formed a fringe of elf-locks round the margin of the one or the other of these top coverings, and closely resembled the frayed edges of his coat sleeves. He was comparatively speaking clean shaven, though the ragged attempts of a draggled beard commonly bristled upon and under his strongly marked chin. His nose was thin and peaked, and of remarkable length, and every now and then his nostrils moved involuntarily like those of a rabbit. His cheeks, from infrequent soaping, were of an ashen gray colour. They were gaunt and sunken, and like his wide forehead, seamed and furrowed with many finely-cut wrinkles. His thin lips were tightly pressed across his almost toothless gums, and were usually drawn down into an expression of vast solemnity.

But his eyes compelled attention. They were so deeply set in their sockets that their object seemed to be the exact scrutiny of the inner lining of the back of his head. They were large and of a light and lustreless blue, almost the tint indeed of the edge of a slop of skim milk upon the kitchen dresser. Their expression was filled with far-off dreaminess, which was occasionally varied by a sharp glance of extreme cunning shot forth so suddenly as to be quite discomposing to its recipients. He looked out of the corners of these eyes like a cat, and he had the further feline habit of turning his eyes to save him the trouble of turning his head. His lashes were long and nearly white, which did not improve their appearance, / and his eyebrows were dusty gray and almost met over his nose. Altogether his was not an easily forgotten face. It had some resemblance to that of a corpse buried and dug up in a rather dirty condition, after having lain several years in the bare ground.

His garments exactly suited his face and figure. His trousers had some shreds left of the semblance of corduroy. There was a green patch on one knee, a blue patch on the other, and a red one of an ampler size in an appropriate place, where it was only rendered visible by the rude familiarity of the wind. This variety of colour was due to no artistic whim of his own, but to the decorative taste of his wife and to the exigencies of her stock of mending materials. He wore a long, drab, dirty overcoat, which may have been light brown on its birthday. Its collar had once been fashioned handsomely of brown velvet, but now its edges were frayed, its pile was gone, and its colour had changed into a delicate yellowish green. A wide open waistcoat lay beneath this upper garment in huge wrinkles, and a once blue check shirt might be seen both at its proper point of view and through each of its well worn button holes. Round his neck he wore a scarf not unlike a Minorca hen in colour, though what its original tints had been could not be divined. When he walked in his own shuffling gait and deliberate manner he leaned heavily on an ancient Æsculapius stick twined with two rudely carved and plump bellied snakes.

Remarkable as was the old man's general appearance, his feet literally forced themselves upon the notice of all who saw them by their magnificent proportions and their extraordinary angle of inclination one to the other. Not without reason did the villagers call him splay-footed. His monstrous shoes were alike wide and long. When they / were at rest they made almost a straight line, and when they were in motion their heels rubbed affectionately together. Johnnie never blacked these capacious shoes, nor did he require his wife to perform that humiliating office for him. They were brown with age, and tradition asserted that the shoemaker, who made them by contract, died from exhaustion. …

Old Johnnie complains to the schoolmaster about the behaviour of local school children:

"Th' shameless young gomerils [fools] keeps on poppin' their nasty little yeads ivery day o' th' wick an' ivery neet at that into our Ann's dur-hole, an' they shout'n, Owd redcap, owd redcap, though they known weel enoof as aw've noan too mich yure [hair] upo' th' top o' my yead, an' aw've gett'n t' wear a red neet-cap fur t' keep my yead warm i' th' house. A wise mon mun keep 'is yead warm, or 'e'll loise 'is wisdom." …/"

Another example of how "non-payment" for magical services was actually not always so in practice:

"Simple as he was in some respects, the old fortune teller was shrewd enough in his profession of seer. He was the proud possessor of an egg-shaped glass or crystal, which would have filled the soul of the more famous Dr. Dee with envy. How he had come by it was not known, and he kept the secret to himself. He carefully locked his treasure up away from the common eye, and only produced it to satisfy a genuine inquirer. Through or in this wonderful glass it was his habit to look on behalf of his numerous clients and according to his own story he could see strange, if not invisible, sights. Many people in the innocency of their hearts, came to consult him about missing children, who usually happened to find their way home during the interval of consultation, and so established the seer's credit upon a tolerably sure foundation.

Amongst the numerous inquirers into future possibilities were those young women who had not as yet secured lovers, and whose lonely hearts were looking longingly forward to a better state of things. Johnnie escaped from the clutches of the law by making no charge for his scientific pursuits; but he always expected a present from the gratitude of the truthseekers. However, one sad morning a young maiden, innocent enough in the ways of this world, but under the / influence of "a yearning after the ideal," came on foot from a distance of seven miles to consult the sage. What she expected to see was probably the wraith of her future lover; what she actually did see remains unknown, because she never breathed a syllable about the matter. Clearly she was satisfied; and when she was going away, she asked in a grateful tone, "Weel, Mester Johni, what mun aw pay yo?"

After his wont the reverend seer summoned up as much of a benevolent smile as his hard features could assume. "Aw mak no chairge," he said.

"Aw con but thank yo' kindly," she replied, with unaffected simplicity and unalloyed gratitude, and began her journey home.

Johnnie, for his part, cared little for gratitude; what he wanted was the more tangible offering of silver or gold. He stared for a few seconds at the retreating figure of the maiden. Then he pulled himself together, and before she was out of hearing, he shouted, "Dosto ye'r, no' luck'll follow thee, withersoiver thou gooas!" … /"

Big Johnnie is only one example of a number of seers of various kinds, who have survived to the very skirts of the twentieth century. Wherever there are people who are desirous of knowing the future before it comes to pass, there will continue to be men who will volunteer to give the requisite information. The information may content them; but, like the ancient oracles, it is apt to be so vague, that / it may possibly come to pass. By such flimsy deceptions are the curious contented, and the pockets of more or less undeserving sages lined with silver. The old fortune teller, whose character has been sketched, lived to a round age, and he passed away with the reputation of a man affecting wisdom in the affairs of others, but supremely silly in the conduct of his own. Though he made much money for a working man, little of it stuck to his fingers; and all that remains of him is the memory of a simple philosopher, who cheated others, but who in his own village was the sport of boys and rabble-wit. (Fox 1902: 35, 36, 37-41, 47-48, 55-56)

We now turn to the United States for the seventh and eighth examples, with selections from *The Witches of New York* (1859), by "Q. K. Philander Doesticks, P. B" (Mortimer Thompson, 1832-1875), a humourous journalist who published a series of investigations of the city's fortune-tellers in the *New York Daily Tribune* in 1857. His accounts are coloured by his need to entertain and denigrate the people he met, as well as an obsessive concern with the squalor of his informants and their places of residence. Where there is an omission, it is a description of the foulness of the neighborhood, or some other irrelevant commentary. Except for these shortcomings, the descriptions of the Cunning Folk in antebellum New York are apparently accurate and allow us rare insight into the urban magical underworld. The author usually refers to himself as "Johannes" or the "Cash Customer".

The first example is of a Dr. Wilson, an old astrologer who typifies the poorer end of the trade, but whom appears to have been conscientious in his reading of the prognostication – unlike the majority of Doesticks' cases in which astrology is of the "non-computational" variety and card-readings or palmistry are the common tools of the business.

DR. WILSON, No. 172 DELANCEY STREET.

THIS ignorant, half-imbecile old man is the only *wizard* in New York whose fame has become public. There are several other men who sometimes, as a matter of favor to a curious friend, exercise their astrological skill, but they do not profess witchcraft as a means of living; they do not advertise their gifts, but only dabble in necromancy in an amateur way, more as a means of amusement than for any other purpose. On the other hand Dr. Wilson freely uses the newspapers to announce to the public his star-reading ability, and his willingness, for a consideration, to tell all events, past and future, of a paying customer's life. He professes to do all his fortune-telling in a "strictly scientific" manner, and / it is but justice to him to say, that he alone, of all the witches of New York, drew a horoscope, consulted books of magic, made intricate mathematical calculations, and made a show of being scientific. In his case only was any attempt made to convince the seeker after hidden wisdom, that modern fortunetelling is aught else than very lame and shabby guesswork. The old Doctor has by no means so many customers as many of his female rivals; he is old and unprepossessing—were he young and handsome the case might be otherwise.

He has been a pretended "botanic physician," or what country people term a "root doctor;" but failing to earn a living by the practice of medicine, he took up "Demonology and Witchcraft" to aid him to eke out a scanty subsistence. He does but little in either branch of his business, the public appearing to have slight faith in his ability either to cure their maladies or foretell their future. ... /

"ASTROLOGY.—Dr. Wilson, 172 Delancey street, gives the / most scientific and reliable information to be found on all concerns of life, past, present, and future. Terms—ladies, 50 cents; gentlemen, $1. Birth required."

The last sentence is slightly obscure, and it was not quite clear to Johannes that he would not have to be "born again" on the premises. But at all events there was something refreshing in the novelty of consulting a "learned pundit" in pantaloons, after all the tough conjurers of the other sex that he had undergone of late.

So he repaired to Delancey street in a joyous mood, nothing daunted by the requirements of the advertisement.

Delancey street is not Paradise, quite the contrary. In fact it may be set down as unsavory, not to say dirty in the extreme. The man that can walk through the east end of this delicious thoroughfare without a constant sensation of sea-sickness, has a stomach that would be true to him in a dissecting-room. The individual that can explore with his unwilling boots its slimy depths without a feeling of / the most intense disgust for everything in the city and of the city, ought to live in Delancey street and buy his provisions at the corner grocery. He never ought to see the country, or even to smell the breath of a country cow. He should be exiled to the city; be banished to perpetual bricks and mortar; be condemned to a never-ending series of omnibus rides, and to innumerable varieties of short change.

The delegate picked his way gingerly enough, thinking all the while that if Leander had been compelled to wade through Delancey street, instead of taking a clean swim across the sea, Hero might have died a respectable old maid for all Leander. And yet Johannes says he doesn't believe that History will give *him* any credit for his valorous navigation of the said street.

He at last reached the designated spot, sound as to body, though wofully soiled as to garments, and approached the semi-subterranean abode of the great prophet, and immediately after his modest rap at the basement door, was met by the venerable sage in / person. He walked in, and then proceeded to take an observation of the cabalistic instruments and mysterious surroundings of the great philosopher.

The room was a small, low apartment, about ten feet by twelve, the floor uncarpeted and uneven; the walls were damp, and the whole place was like a vault. The furniture was very scanty, and all had unwholesome moisture about it, and a curious odor, as if it gathered unhealthy dews by being kept underground. Three feeble chairs were all the seats, and a table which leaned against the wall was too ill and rickety to do its intended duty; many of the books which had once probably covered it, were now thrown in a promiscuous heap on the floor, where they slowly mildewed and gave out a graveyard smell. A miniature stove in the middle of the room, sweated and sweltered, and in its struggles to warm the unhealthy atmosphere had succeeded in suffusing itself with a clammy perspiration; it was in the last stages of debility; old age and abuse had used it sadly, and it now stood helplessly upon its crippled / legs, and supported its nerveless elbow upon a sturdy whitewash brush. There were a few symptoms of medical pretensions in the shape of some vials, and bottles of drugs, and coloured liquids on the mantelpiece ; a great attempt at a display of scientific apparatus began and ended with an insulating stool, and an old-fashioned "cylinder and cushion" electrical machine [a hand-operated static electrical generator]; a number of highly-coloured prints of animals pasted on the wall, having evidently been scissored from the show-bill of a menagerie, had a look towards natural history, and a jar or two of acids suggested chemical researches. The books that still remained on the enervated table were an odd volume of Braithwaite's Retrospect, a treatise on human Physiology, and another on Materia Medica; a number of bound volumes of Zadkiel's Astronomical Ephemeris, Raphael's Prophetic Almanac, Raphael's Prophetic Messenger, and a file of Robert White's Celestial Atlas, running back to 1808.

The appearance of the venerable sage of Delancey / Street was not so imposing as to strike a stranger with awe—quite the contrary. He partook of the character of the room, and was a fitting occupant of such a place; he seemed some kind of unwholesome vegetable that had found that noisome atmosphere congenial, and had sprung indigenously from the slimy soil. One looked instinctively at his feet to see what kind of roots he had, and then glanced back at his head as if it were a huge bud, and about to blossom into some unhealthy flower. The traces of its earthy origin were plainly visible about this mouldy old plant; quantities of the rank soil still adhered to the face, filled up the wrinkles of the cheeks, found ample lodging in the ears and on the neck, and crowding under the horny and distorted nails, made them still more ugly; and streaks and ridges of dirt clung to every portion of the garments, which answered to the bark or rind of this perspiring herb.

To drop this botanic figure of speech, Dr. Wilson is a man of about fifty-eight years of age, rather stout and thick-set, with grey eyes, and hair which was / once brown, but is now grey, and with thin brown whiskers; the top of his head is nearly bald, except a few thin, furzy, short hairs, which made his skull look as if it had been kept in that damp room until mould had gathered on it. He was in his shirt sleeves, and was attired, for the most part, in a pair of sheep's grey pantaloons, which were made to cover that fraction of his body between his ankles and his armpits; the little patch of shirt that was visible above the waistband of that garment, was streaked with irregular lines of dirty black, as if it had gone into half mourning for the scarcity of water.

The man of science made a musty remark or two about the weather and the walking, and then, after carefully seating himself at the decrepit table, he said: "I suppose your business is of a fortun'-tellin' natur'; if so, my terms is one dollar." The affirmative answer to the question and the payment of the dollar put new energy into the mouldy old man, and he prepared to astonish the beholder.

He demanded the age of his visitor, and then / desired to be informed of the date of his birth, with particular reference to the exact time of day; Johannes drummed up his youthful recollections of that interesting event, and gave the day, the hour, and the minute, with his accustomed accuracy. The sage made an exact minute of these wet-nurse items on a cheap slate with a stub of a pencil; then taking another cheap slate, he proceeded to draw a horoscope thereon, pausing a little over the signs of the zodiac, as if he was a little out in his astronomy, and wasn't exactly certain whether there should be twelve or twenty. He settled this little matter by filling one half the slate as full as it would hold, and then carrying some to the other side, so as to have a few on hand in case of any emergency.

When the figure was drawn, and all the mysterious signs completed, the shirt-sleeve prophet became absorbed in an intricate calculation of such mysterious import that all his customer's mathematical proficiency was unable to make out what it was all about. First he set down a long row of figures, / which he added together with much difficulty, and then seemed to instantly conceive the most unrelenting hostility to the sum total. The mathematical tortures to which he put that unhappy amount; the arithmetical abuse which he heaped upon it, and the algebraic contumely with which he overwhelmed it, almost defy description. He first belaboured it with the four simple rules; he stretched it with Addition; he cut it in two with Subtraction; he made it top-heavy with Multiplication, and tore it to pieces with Division—then he extracted its square root; then extracted the cube root of that, which left nothing of the unfortunate sum total but a small fraction, which he then divided by ab, and made "equal to" an infinitesimal part of some unknown x. Having thus wreaked his vengeance on the unhappy number, he laid away the surviving fraction in a cold corner of the slate, where he left it, first, however, giving a parting token of his bitter malignity by writing the minus sign before it, which made it perpetually worse than nothing, / and reduced it to a state of irredeemable algebraic bankruptcy. This praiseworthy object being finally achieved, he proceeded to translate into intelligible English the result of his calculations, which he announced in the terms following:

"The testimonial is not the most sanguine. If the time of birth is given correct there is reason to apprehend that something of an affective nature occurred at about eight years and ten months—at 16x10 I think I may say, if the time of birth is given correct, there is from the figures reason to expect that there is a probability of a similar sitiwation of events. At 24 there was a favourable sitiwation of events, if there was not somebody or somethin' afflictive on the contrary, the which I am disposed to think might be possible. At 25, if the time of birth is given correct, there is reason to expect great likelihoods of some success in life; I may, it is true, be mistaken in my calculations, but as the significators are angular, I think there is indications that such will be the sitiwation of events. At 30, if the time / of birth is given correct, I think you are an individdyal as may look for some species of misfortin'— there will be some rather singular circumstances occur, which might denote loss of friends, or the fallin' to you of a fortin', or great travellin' by water or land, or losin' money at cards, or breakin' your leg, or makin' a great discovery, or inventin' somethin', or gettin' put into prison on suspicion of sorcery and witchcraft. You will see that there are indications to denote that you will certainly be accused of sorcery and witchcraft by some individdyals who are not your friends—the indications denote great likelihoods that this will make you uneasy in your mind, but I think there is nothin' of a very serious natur' to be feared at that time of life, if the time of birth is given correct. When any misfortin' is comin' upon you there is no doubt (though I am not goin' to state positively that such will be the case, still there is strong likelihoods that the indications give such a probability) that it will give you warnin' of its approach. At 36, if the time / of birth is given correct, there is indications of a likelihood that you will fall upon some other misfortin'; I am not prepared to state positively that such will be the case, but I think you will have a misfortin', though I don't think it would be of a very afflictive natur'. There is at that time a circumstance of an unfriendly natur', though it may not happen to yourself; it might denote that your brother will get sick. There is another evil condition about this time which I will examine still furder. I see that there is indications of a likelihood that there is a probability of your having somethin' amiss by a partner, if somethin' of a favourable natur' does not interpose, which is not unlikely, though I may be mistaken and will not say positively. You will be lucky, however, after that, and many of your evils will gradually begin to recline, as it were. There is reason to believe that the significators denote that in the course of your futur' life you will sometimes be thrown in with men who you will think is your friends, but who will prove to be your enemy. This / I will not say positively, for I may be mistaken, which I think I am not, but if the time of birth is correct, you are an individdyal as gives likelihoods that such might be the case."

For more than an hour had the Inquirer been edified and instructed by these "solid chunks of wisdom," which, it will be remembered, were not delivered off-hand, but were carefully ciphered out by elaborate calculations on the slate aforesaid. Lucid and elegant as was the language, and interesting as was the matter of these oracular communications, he felt it to be his duty to interrupt them for a time and change the subject to a theme in which he felt a nearer interest; accordingly he asked the musty Seer about his prospects of future wedded bliss. This was a subject of so great importance that all the other calculations had to be erased from the slate—this little operation was accomplished in the manner of the schoolboys who haint got any sponge, and the dirty hand plied briskly for a minute between the juicy mouth and the dingy slate, and / became a shade grimier by this cleanly process. Then a new horoscope was drawn with more signs of the zodiac than ever, and in due time the result was thus announced:

"I shall now endeavour to give you a description of the sort of person you might be most likeliest to marry. There is indications that your wife might be respectable. The significators do not denote that there is a likelihood that you might marry a very old woman. She would be as likely to have fair hair and blue eyes as anything else; nor would she be likely to be very much too tall, and I don't imagine you are an individdyal that might be likely to marry a woman who was very short. She may not be very old, but I do not think that the indications point her out as being likely to be a child; in fact, I think it possible that she may be of the ordinary age, though I do not wish to be understood as being positive on all these points, for I may be mistaken, though I think you will find that there is a likelihood that these things may be so. You will be married twice, / and I think you are an individdyal that would be likely to have children—six children I think there is indications that you may be likely to have. The significators point out one very evil condition, and I think I may say that I'm quite sure. I'm positive that you will separate from your first wife. No, I will not say that yours is a quarrelsome natur', but the significators look bad. Things is worse, in fact, than I told you of, and now I look again and am sure you are prepared, I will say that there cannot be a doubt that *you will pizon your first wife*. It cannot be any other way; there is no mistake; it is so; it must be true; the fact is this, and thus I tell you, *you will pizon your first wife*. And, my young friend, I will advise you, in case your married futur' is unhappy, and you do find it necessary to give pizon to your consort, do not tell anybody of your intentions; do not let it be known; and you must do it in such a way as not to be suspected, or people will think hard of you, and there may be trouble."

This was a touch of wisdom for which Johannes / was not prepared; so he snatched his hat and hastily left the sepulchral premises, conscious of his inability to receive another such a "chunk" without being completely floored.

He now expresses the opinion that Dr. Wilson wanted to get the job of "pizoning" that first wife, and that he would have done it with pleasure at less than the market price. ("Doesticks" 1859: 149-150, 153-168)

The second "Doesticks" example of Madam Lant is included because it has an unusual instance of a physical charm being made up in addition to a fairly standard "reading". It also offers some insight into the unfortunate condition of urban Wise Women.

MADAME LEANDER LENT, No. 163 MULBERRY STREET.
I HAVE before suggested, in as plain terms as the peculiar nature of the subject will allow, that these fortune-telling women, having most of them been prostitutes in their younger days, in their withered age become professional procuresses, and make a trade of the betrayal of innocence into the power of Lust and Lechery. This assertion is so eminently probable that few will be inclined to dispute it, but I wish to be understood that this is no matter of mere surmise with me—it is a proven fact. And the evidences of its truth have been gathered, not alone from the formal and hurried records of the police courts, but from the lips of certain inmates of various Magdalen Asylums who have been / reclaimed from their former homes of shame; and from the mouths of other repentant women, who, under circumstances where there was no object to deceive, and at times when their hearts were full of grateful love for those who had interposed to save them from utter despair, have in all simple truthfulness and honor, related their life-histories. It is impossible to give even a plausible guess at the aggregate number of young women, in this great city, who compromise their honorable reputations in the course of a single year; but of those whose shame becomes publicly known, and especially of those who eventually enter houses of ill-repute, the percentage whose fall was accomplished through the instrumentality, more or less direct, of the professional fortune-tellers, is astounding. And a curious fact connected with this subject is, that of these unfortunates who thus wander astray, not one in ten but has ever after the most superstitious and implicit faith in the supernatural powers of the witch. Each one sees in her own case certain things that have been foretold to her by the / fortune-teller with such circumstantiality of time and place, and which have afterwards "come to pass," so exactly in accordance with the prophecy, that she can only account for it by ascribing supernatural prescience to the prophetess.

The true solution of the matter is, of course, that the wonderful fulfillments are achieved by means of confederacy and collusion with parties with whom the dupe is never brought in contact; a common *modus operandi* of this sort is elsewhere described.

Nor are the fortune-tellers and the brothel-keepers by any means content with playing into each other's hands in a general sort of way; there are, in New York, several *firms,* consisting each of a fortune-teller and a mistress of a bawdy-house, who have entered into a perfectly organized business partnership, and who ply their fearful trade with as much zeal and enthusiasm as is ever exhibited in the active competition between rival commercial houses engaged in legitimate trade.

Although this fact is one that cannot be substantiated / by the production of any sworn documents, it is as well proven by the observations of keen-eyed detectives attached to the police department, and to some of the charitable institutions of this city, as though attested articles of co-partnership could be exhibited with the signatures of the contracting parties attached thereto. A gentleman of this city, in whose word I have the most perfect confidence, tells me that he once, by a curious accident, overheard a business consultation between the two members of such a firm; and that such partnerships *do* exist, and that by their means hundreds of ignorant young women, of the lower classes, are every year betrayed to their moral ruin, I no more doubt than I doubt the rotundity of the earth.

If the illustrious woman who is the subject of the present chapter should ever surmise that the foregoing observations are intended to have a personal application to herself, the author will give her much more credit for sagacity and discernment than he did for supernatural wisdom. /

Madame Leander Lent is one of the most shrewd, unscrupulous, and dirty of all the goodly sisterhood of New York witches. She has so great a run of customers that her doors are often besieged by anxious inquirers as early as eight o'clock in the morning, and the servant is frequently puzzled to find room and chairs to accommodate the shame-faced throng, till her ladyship sees fit to get out of bed and begin the labours of the day. She is then impartial in the distribution of her favors; the audiences are governed by barber-shop rules, and the visitors are admitted to the presence in the order of their coming, and any one going out forfeits his or her "turn" and on returning must take position at the tail end of the queue.

The Fates show no favoritism. ... /

In this [Mulberry Street] , one of the dirtiest streets in this dirty metropolis, directly opposite the English Lutheran Church of St. James, in one of the dirtiest tenant-houses in the street, abideth Madame Leander Lent, the prophetess. Why the mysterious powers didn't select an earthly representative with a more reputable dwelling-place is a mystery; but there seems to be an inseparable congeniality between prophetic knowledge and concentrated nastiness, utterly beyond all power of explanation. The Madame advises the public of her business in the terms following:

"ASTROLOGY.—Madame LEANDER LENT can be consulted about love, marriage, and absent friends; she tells all the events of life at No. 169 Mulberry-st, first floor, back room. Ladies 25 cents; gents 50 cents. She causes speedy marriage. Charge extra." /

Her customers are much more addicted to love than marriage, so that the wedlock clause cannot be relied on to bring many fish to the net, but it is supposed to give an air of respectability to the advertisement.

The Cash Customer was, perhaps, an exception to this general rule, and feeling that he would on the whole rather like a "speedy marriage," and wouldn't so much mind the "extra charge," he went, in cold blood, with this matrimonial intent to the street, found the number, and heroically entered the house in the very face of a threatened unclean baptism from the upper windows.

His timid knock at the door of the room was answered by a sturdy "Come in," from the inside; hat defe[r]entially in hand he modestly entered, and was received by a fat woman with a bust of proportions exceeding those of Mrs. Merdle in "Little Dorrit," and who was attired in a dress which may have been clean in the earlier years of its history, though the supposition is exceedingly apocryphal. / This lady pointed to a chair, and then composedly seated herself and resumed her explorations with a comb, in the hair of a vicious boy of about three years old, the eldest scion of Madame Leander.

Her enthusiasm in the cause of entomological science was too ardent to be quenched by the mere presence of an observer, and she continued to hunt her insect prey with all the ardor of a she-Nimrod, and with a zeal that was rewarded by a brilliant success. The youth, over whose fertile head the game seemed to rove and range in countless numbers, was somewhat restless under the operation, and oftentimes disturbed the eager sportswoman, by manifesting a desire to run into the street and carry the hunting-ground with him, and was as often recalled to a sense of the proprieties by a few judicious slaps, which he stoically endured without a whimper, being evidently used to it.

This feminine lover of the chase, this Diana of the fiery scalp, looked up from her occupations long enough to say to her visitor that Madame Lent / would soon be disengaged. Meantime, he made a careful survey of the premises.

Two chairs, an old lounge with its dingy red cover fastened on with pins, and a trunk covered with an old bit of carpet, were the accommodations for seating visitors. A cooking-stove, and a suspicious-looking wash-bowl which stood in the corner of the room, without a pitcher, were probably for the accommodation of the Madame and the lady with the comb. On the shabby lounge sat a stolid-looking Irish girl, who was waiting her turn to have her fortune told. Having fully comprehended the room and everything in it, the visitor turned his attention to literary pursuits, and thoroughly perused an odd copy of a newspaper that lay invitingly on the table.

Visitors kept dropping in, mostly servant-appearing girls, though there were three women attired in silk and laces, who would have appeared respectable had their faces been hidden and their conversation been suppressed. The lady with the comb and the boy presently departed to some unknown region, and / soon returned with a reinforcement of chairs and stools. The number of visitors increased, until, besides the original stranger, nine were waiting. Among others, there came, in a friendly way, but still with a sharp eye to business, a tall woman, attired in a red dress and a purple bonnet, who is the keeper of a well-known house in Sullivan street, and whose name is not strange to the police. An unrestrained business conversation ensued between her and the heroine of the comb, which must have been interesting to the female listeners.

One hour and eleven minutes did the Cash Customer patiently wait before he was admitted to the mysterious conference with the queen of magic. At last, after the man who was at first closeted with her had concluded his inquiries, and the stolid Irish girl had been disposed of, the woman with the suggestive bust beckoned the long-suffering and patient man to follow, and he fearfully entered the sanctum.

The room of conjuration was a closet, dark and dirty, and was lighted by one tallow candle, stuck in / a Scotch ale bottle. A number of shabby dresses, bony petticoats, and other mysterious articles of women's gear, hung upon the walls; two weak-kneed chairs, a tattered bit of carpet upon about two feet square of the floor, and a little table covered with a greasy oilcloth, composed the furniture of the mystic cell. The cabalistic paraphernalia was limited, there being nothing but a dirty pack of double-headed cards, a small pasteboard box with some scraps of paper in it, and two kinds of powder in little bottles, like hair-oil pots.

Madame Lent is a woman of medium height, about thirty-five years of age, with light-grey eyes, false teeth, a head nearly bald, and hair, what there is of it, of a bright red. Her manner is hurried and confused, and she has a trick of drawing her upper lip disagreeably up under the end of her nose, which labial distortion she doubtless intends for a smile.

She was robed in a bright-coloured plaid dress, a dirty lace collar, and a coarse woollen shawl over her shoulders. Motioning her visitor to one chair, she / instantly seated herself in the other, and, without demanding pay in advance, commenced operations. She handed the cards to be cut, and then laying them out in their piles, uttered the following sentences:

"I see that your fortune has been and is quite a curious one. Your cards run rather mixed up, you have been very much worried in your head, you were born under two planets, which means that you have seen a great deal of trouble in your younger days, but you are now getting over it and your cards ran to better luck, but it is rather mixed up, your cards run to a lady, she is light-haired and blue-eyed, but she is jealous of you, for sometimes you treat her more kinder and sometimes more harsher, and just now she is in trouble and very much mixed up about you. There is a man of black hair and eyes, a dark *complected* man who pretends to be your friend and is very fair to your face, but you must beware of him, for he is your secret enemy and will do you an injury if he can; he is trying to get the lady, but I don't think he'll do it, though I don't know, for the thing / is so much mixed up—he has deceived you, and the lady has deceived you, they have both deceived you, but now they have got mixed up, and she turns from him with scorn, and seems to like you the best—I don't exactly see how it all is, for it seems rather mixed up like—you must persevere, you must coax her more; you can coax her to do anything, but you can't drive her any more than you can drive that wall —always treat her more kinder and never more harsher, and she will soon be yours entirely—beware of the dark-complected man; you must not talk so much and be so open in your mind, and above all don't talk so much to the dark-complected man, for he seems to worry you, and your affairs and his are all mixed up like."

Here her auditor expressed a desire to know something definite and certain about his future wife, whereupon the red-haired prophetess shuffled the cards again with the following result:

"You will have but one more wife. She will be good and true, and will not be mixed up with any / dark-complected man. She will be rich and you will be rich, for your business cards run very smooth, but your marriage cards do not run very close to you, and you will not be married for six or eight months; you will have three children; you will see your future wife within nine hours, nine days, or nine weeks; do not blame me if it runs into the tens, but I tell you it will fall within the nines. Another man is trying to get her away from you, he is a light-complected man, he has had some influence over her, but she now turns from him with disdain, and she will be yours and yours only—things are a little worried and mixed up now, but she will be yours and yours only, the light-complected man can't hurt you. I have something that I can give you that will make her love you tender and true; it will force her to do it and she won't have no power to help herself, but you can do with her just what you please; I charge extra for that."

Here was a chance to procure a love-philtre at a reasonable rate, and unless the dark woman kept that / article ready made and done up in packages to suit customers, he could observe the terrible ceremonies with which it was prepared, listen to the spells and incantations with an attent eye, and take mental notes of all the mighty magic. The opportunity was too good to be lost, and he at once signified his desire to try a little of the extra witchcraft, and his willingness to draw on his purse for the requisite amount of ready cash to purchase this gratification of a laudable curiosity.

Madame Lent now assumed an air of the most intense gravity, and shook into a very dirty bit of paper a little white powder from one of the pomatum pots, and a corresponding quantity of grayish powder from pot No. 2, and stirred them carefully together with the tip of her finger. When she had mixed them to her liking she folded the diabolical compound in a small paper. Then she prepared another mixture in the same manner, and made a pretence of adding another ingredient from a little pasteboard box, which probably hadn't had anything in it for a / month. Folding this also in a paper she presented them both to her interested guest, with these directions:

"You must shake some of the first powder on your true-love's head, or neck, or arms, if you can, but if you can't manage this, put it on her dress—the other powder you must sprinkle about your room when you go to bed to-night—this will draw her to you, and she will love you and you alone and can't help herself; this will surely operate, if it don't, come and tell me."

One more cabalistic performance and the hocus-pocus was ended. She desired her customer to give her the first letter of his true love's name. He, unabashed by the unexpected demand, with great presence of mind promptly invented a sweetheart on the spot, and extemporized a name for her before the question was repeated. Then the mysterious Madame required his own initial, which, being obtained, she wrote the two on slips of paper with some mystic figures appended, in manner following. E., 17; M., 24. Then she shiveringly whispered: /

"You must do as I told you with the powders before eleven o'clock to-night, for between the hours of eleven and twelve I shall boil your name and hers in herbs which will draw her to you, and she can't help herself but will be tender and true, and will be yours and yours only. When she is drawed to you then you must marry her."

The anxious inquirer promised obedience, and agreed to give the powders as per prescription, before the midnight cookery should commence, paid his dollar (fifty cents for the consultation and a like sum for the love-powders), and made his exit with a comprehensive bow, which included the Madame, the bony petticoats, the beer-bottle, and the fast-vanishing remains of the single tallow-candle in one reverential farewell. ("Doesticks" 1859: 241-245, 248-259)

Another interesting piece of history found in *The Witches of New York* is the evidently recent influence of modern occultism, in the shape of up-to-date "clairvoyants" in effective competition with the traditional Wise Women. It would appear that medical advice, which was not strongly regulated at the time, was thought to be a better "front" than the more suspect fortune-telling.

> THERE are a dozen or more of these "Clairvoyants" in the city who profess to cure diseases, and to work other wonders by the aid of their so-called wonderful power. As their mode of proceeding is very much the same in all cases, a description of one or two will give an idea of the whole. Their principal business is to prescribe for bodily ills, and did they confine themselves to this alone, they would not be legitimate subjects of mention in this book. But in addition to their medical practice they also tell about "absent friends;" tell whether projected business undertakings will fall out well or ill; whether contemplated marriages will be prosperous or otherwise: whether a person will be "lucky" in life, whether his children will be happy, and, in short, they do pretty much the regular fortune-telling routine, whenever the questions of the customer lead that way.
> The theory as given by them, of a Clairvoyant diagnosis of a malady, is this: that the Clairvoyant, when thrown by mesmeric influence into the "trance" state, is enabled to *see into the body* of *the patient* and discern what organs, if any, are deranged, and in what manner; or to ascertain precisely the nature of the morbific condition of the body, and having thus discovered what part of the vital mechanism is out of order, they are able, they argue, to prescribe the best means for restoring the apparatus to a normal state.
> There are many thousands of persons who believe this stuff, and endanger their lives and health by trusting to these empirics. Several of the most popular of them have as many patients as they can attend to, and are rapidly amassing fortunes. Most of them have a superficial knowledge of Medicine, and are thus enabled to do, with a certain amount of impunity / many dark deeds. ...
> There is one breed of the modern witch that pretends to a sort of superiority in blood and manners, and those who practise this peculiar branch of the business put on certain aristocratic airs and utterly refuse to consort with those of another stamp. They / disdain the title of "Astrologers," or "Astrologists," as most of them phrase it, and in their advertisements utterly repudiate the idea that they are "Fortune Tellers."
> These are the "Clairvoyants," who do business by means of certain select mummeries of their own, and who make a great deal of money in their trade. There are a great number of these in the city, so many indeed that the business is over-done, and the price of retail clairvoyance has come materially down. The same dose of this article that formerly cost five dollars, may now be had for fifty cents, and the quality is not deteriorated, but is quite as good now as it ever was. ("Doesticks" 1859: 171-173, 176-177)

The ninth and final example, which falls outside my stated remit, is included here to show "what might have been" if there'd been a diligent researcher who investigated the Cunning Folk as Rev. Harry M. Hyatt (1898-1978) did with the conjurors and root doctors in the U.S. in the 1930s. Hyatt compiled a voluminous collection of interviews (recorded on old-fashioned wax cylinders and scrupulously transcribed to present the remarks just as they were spoken phonetically by hundreds of informants) in his *Hoodoo – Conjuration – Witchcraft – Rootwork*, published in five large volumes between 1970 and 1973. His compilation accurately preserved the oral traditions and first-hand narratives of the (mostly but by no means all African-American) magical workers, allowing us an unprecedented insight into an otherwise ephemeral and invisible magical subculture. I include it here as an example of the sort of historical information that has been lost for the vanished world of the Cunning Folk, and to compare their traditions with another magical culture that also straddled the oral/written dichotomy. What Hyatt found reflected a largely oral tradition in which his respondents compounded their own "hands" (charms) and washes from locally-available materials, the conjure trade was already evolving in America's increasingly commodified society to use prepared commercial products from "hoodoo drugstores" and mail order catalogs, and learn their trade from popular publications offered by entrepreneurs such as L. W. de Laurence, Morton Neumann of the King Novelty Company, Joe Kay of the Dorene Publishing and Fulton Religious Supply or the anonymous "Mr. Young" who wrote under the pseudonym "Lewis de Claremont", and "Henri Gamache"[29].

In Hyatt's work, descriptions of visits to hoodoo workers are not dramatized or fictionalized, but represent events as they were recalled by the informants. The narratives below concerning George Williams of Fairmount, Maryland took place in the late 1890s, and were recorded by Hyatt 35 years later. In transcribing Hyatt's text, I have omitted his frequent use of underlining to denote emphasis (although capitalization for the same purpose is retained) as it is not necessary to the information given, and some of his asides and cross-references are omitted as well. Where text is in square brackets, it represents Hyatt's editorial comments – not my own, which are in curly ones – and where parentheses are used, it indicates questions he asked during the interview. The four digit numbers indicate the individual recorded entries.

> 3092. [I heard about George Jackson and Zippy Tull of the Eastern Shore at the same time and from some of the same persons ... The first two stories describing Uncle George, as he was called, are by Mrs. Elijah Williams – widow of George's nephew – whom I interviewed while collecting in Baltimore. She was also the mother of Jerry Williams, my contact man on the Eastern Shore and in Baltimore, who tells me the third story. The fourth story, statement rather, comes from Joshua Wilson, who as a young man drove an occasional client out to George Jackson or Zippy Tull.]
> Pitt's Creek wharh [where] he was born at. Tha's in Worcester County [Maryland]. Well then, after he growed up to be a man – of course that wus years and years before I was born – why then he moved to the place they called Fairmount. It's in Somerset County. And he stayed there his life – he died in Fairmount.
> (How long ago did he die?)
> Well, he's been dead about 35 years (before 1936).
> (How old was he when he died?)
> I don't know his age but I'm sure he wus around 70. I'm sure he wus.
> (H had quite a reputation?)
> Yes indeed.
> (How did he learn this work?)
> Well, I suppose it must have been gifted 'cause he couldn't read – he could not read or write, so he must have been gifted. But he could read the Bible. He didn't no one to learn him anything.
> (Was he born in slavery?) (I wanted to double-check his age.)
> Born in slavery? Oh, yes, indeed! Now, he might have been older than that when he died, but he, you know, he kept youngified. You wouldn't know he was old – you knew he was old, that's all.
> (Did anyone ever try to carry on his work? Did he have a son or anyone?)
> He never had no children.
> (Has anyone a photograph of him?)
> No, I have no photograph of him.
> (Was a photograph ever taken of him?)
> Not as I know of. You know, in them times they didn't take much photographs. He was never married, and he had a housekeeper. Now, whether she tried to do anything or not I do not know.
> (Where is he buried?)
> He was buried in Fairmount but I don't know the graveyard because I didn't go, neither did his nephew [informant's husband] becus we didn't know he was dead until the day he was buried. That was the first time they sent word that his uncle was dead.
> (His name was) George Jackson, but you know in olden time de folks who wus born children then, they named George Jackson and Nathan Williams and Josiah and all that, and they give 'em that

---

[29] For a very complete and enlightening study of these companies and their personnel, see the work of Catherine Yronwode at the Lucky Mojo website (www.luckymojo.com) and her book, *Hoodoo Herb and Root Magic: A Materia Magica of African-American Conjure*. Forestville, CA: Lucky Mojo Curio Company, 2002. Also, see Jim Haskins, *Voodoo and Hoodoo: The Craft as Revealed by Traditional Practitioners*. Plainview, NY: Orignal Publications, 1978; Carolyn Morrow Long, *Spiritual Merchants: Religion, Magic, and Commerce*. Knoxville, TN: University of Tennesee Press, 2001 and Jeffrey E. Anderson. *Conjure in African American Society*. Baton Rouge, LA: Louisiana State University Press, 2005.

name. But his re'lly name would have been George Jackson Dennis, George Jackson Dennis. Old John Hugh Dennis they called him, a white man, you know he was his owner, he was his master.
(John Hugh Dennis?)
Yes sur. Well, do you know – no, you don't know becus joo don't belong here (in Baltimore). Why Samuel Dennis used to be the chief jurge here in Baltimore, it was his father. /
(Where did he have the farm?)
They had the farm on – they called it the Cedar Hall. That was near Pocomoke City [Maryland].
[Baltimore, Md. (Mrs. Williams)]
3093. My mother – well, she was about 40 I guess or maybe 40 odd. She wus 42 – my brother wus two years old. She taken sick. She went outdoors – I wus livin' in Pocomoke [City, Maryland] then – an' she went out de door. Well, these ole houses, country places, the chimleys, shoo know, aside yeh house – an' she went out there an' stopped de side de chimley [for chimney-corner toilet] an' she taken a pain in her right [big] toe an' it went up on her knee. An' when she got in the house she said, "Mama, I can't walk." That was my grandmother an' my grandma lived to be 85. She said, "Mama, I can't walk," she said, "my knee – I got a pain in my toe an' it's went up in my knee. I can't walk."
So my grandmother – she wus a mighty one fer rubbin', you know, an' she rub 'er. An' she went an' got some ole horehoun' an [or] yard marvel – de grass, dey call it yard marvel grass – an' she stews this stuff up an' she rubs zer in it. An' it didn't do 'er any good. She couldn't walk. So she put her in the baid. An' when she got in the baid she couldn't get out any more – taken paralize all the way from 'er shoulder clear down. She couldn't move dat foot, dat right foot. She couldn't move her right foot no way – had to take 'er 'bout de baid an' put 'er in. She jes' gotta wha' choo call a perilous [paralysis] stroke, we thought. So we sent – my grandmother doh [though], she sent fuh de doctor. An' de Doctor Quinn come, why he said 'twas a col' [cold] rheumatis, so she got worser an' worser. All he did to 'er – everything he give 'er would make 'er worse.
So my husband an' I – that wus his uncle, Uncle George Jackson, yus – I said, "I very mind dey's somepin wrong about her – she can't walk an' de doctor can't do 'er no good, she can't use her side." Well, I thought then in that time that de people didn't take perlious strokes, shoo know, offten, like they do now.
So I says, "I don't believe it's any perilous stroke."
He says, "All right, then, let's us go."
So we walked, we got out about nine o'clock at night, one night, an' walked down to Fairmount [Maryland], down where I told joo Uncle George wus. When we got there 'twas about daybreak – he was setten' up then, he had his clothes on – I guess about five a'clock in the morning [eight hours walk]. It wus in June when we went. I suppose it wus about five a'clock in de morning 'cus it wus light. An' we rahpped [rapped] on de door an' he opened de door,
You know, mah husband didn't go to see 'im as offten as he wanted it to see 'im, to go see him. An' he said, "Uh-huh!" he said, "I knowed somepin happen'," he said, "iss [else] you wouldn't of been here."
So we laffed an' tole 'im, "No, not much happened."
He said, "Yes it did," he said – to me, he said. He said, "Ya, your mother's layin' pint [point] of death, she can't walk."
I said to 'im – I wus always kin'a jokin' – I said, "How did joo know that?"
"Uh huh!" he said – he was a great big fellah, he'd filled this chair up – he said, "Uh huh! Your mother's down and can't walk."
I said, "Yes."
"An' why didn't choo come fer 'er before!" He said, "She's been down now ever since Apurl an' you jis' come here in June."
I said, "Yes, she did."
He said, "She started to a show."
Well, she did. She started to git ready to go to a show an' she taken dat / pain in de feet. De show was at Pocomoke City, an' she wus down in kin's about two miles from de show, from de city, out in de country part.
An' he said, "Well, why didn't zhah come here before?" An' he said, "She wus getting' ready to go to a show an' dat's de show she got to!"
I said, "Well, that's true."

"Uh huh!" he said.

So he jis' set back in de chair – he always set in a chair, somepin like this.

"Uh huh!" he said. "Well, a lady dat she thought dat wouldn't nevah do 'er no harm, a woman," he said, "an' she's a lttle short woman." He said, "she's jist about so high" – an' sure enough she was – "an' she's light [in colour]," he said. "An' she put dat [image there because] she an' her husband got mad with 'er, cus she wanted her to go to her house an' she wouldn't go," he said. "An' she come down there an' laffed an' talked with 'er, an' went out side de chimley at night an' put a piece of a tin," he said. "So when you go back," he said, "they'll be a piece of tin put right inside [in the corner] of de chimly," he said, "an' it's in de shape of her." He said, "It's in the shape of your mother," he said, "an' it's got one foot off." – had been cut out a piece of tin. "An'," he said, "It wus put down," he said, "an' the foot's cut off."

H said, "You go back, Elijay" – he called mah husband – of course he was his nephew. He said, "Elijay, you go back, you go an' look, feel down, take a trowel," he said, "don't take anything else, don't take no spade, no shovel," he said, "an' take a trowel, an' you dig down an' you dig your mother-in-law up," he said, "an' I'll do the balance." He said, "You bring dat piece of tin to me," he said, "an' I'll do the balance. Zhoo [the informant] walk with him."

He laffed.

An' we stayed there all day. We stayed an' visited. We stayed there about fo' a'clock. We wus gon'a stay till five but he told us not to. He said, "Now, don't choo stay here no longer." He set an' talked with us, first one thing an' then another. He said, "Now listen, an' git yerself ready an' go on back so you kin take that up," he said, "befo' morning." He said, "I want choo to git up out of here, I want choo to git back in time befo' fo' or five a'clock tonight [that is, before sunrise] an' take that up." He said, "You'll find it."

An' sure enough we did git it.

We went back home, an' Elijah went an' took his trowel like he told him an' lifted that up. An' there was that piece of tin. It had legs an' all, an' this piece [a foot] wus cut off. An' took it back there. Now, I don't know whut he [George Jackson] did, but he took it back to him.

Mah mother got well. She lived about ten years after that, [Baltimore, Md. (Mrs. Williams) ; happened about 1896]

3094. My grandmother – well, I'm speaking of my aunt – just as well say grandmother, she was born a slave. She [aunt] said one night she dreamt that this friend of hers was mixing up something that was green, yet it was supposed to be milk. And she said to her husband next day, "Purnell, don't you take dinner with Bettie on Sunday." But sure enough he would go and take dinner with this woman on Sunday – they were friends – and sure enough this woman *did poison* her [aunt's] husband in milk. So he called on a man by the name of George Jackson who lived out here near Girdletree [Maryland] at that time – he's dead now. [George Jackson never lived at Girdletree.] And he went to call on this old man George Jackson. And he went to get some roots out of the woods and boiled it up. And while he was boiling these up he was singing a song. And the more he'd sing, the more the stuff would boil. I suppose that was just [uncle's] imagination. But when he got it boiled as much as he wanted it, he gave my uncle to drink. And there had / been things crawling up and down – running up and down – inside of him. You could hear them. She [aunt] said this had happened about two weeks after he took this dinner. You could hear these things squealing as if though they were mice and rats. And finally, when he drank this up, an hour or so afterwards, why these things come from his – he discharged these things. And they were wood bitches – ground puppies {salamanders}.

This happened down here at St. James [a Negro community in which I was to work a few days later]. St. James is five miles on the other side of Pocomoke [City, Maryland] right on the border of Virginia.

[The speaker is Jerry Williams, George Jackson's grandnephew and my contact man…]

3095. Uncle George [Jackson] always called for wah choo called a *jack*. This *jack* is a magnet, a magnet *jack*. Magnets dey called *jacks* them days. This magnet, you know, [is] a piece of little steel in pickin' up pins. He'd tell you git him a magnet, and he'd take this hair [which client brought from woman]. An' this magnet, an' gits de – I'm sure he had other things put with it, you know. But anyhow, that was fixed up in a bag. An' when he'd give you that you wore that an' they'd always [be] success[ful] ever he'd fixed that for 'em. You couldn't fool with a woman. I don't care how many

tried to beat it, they could not git here away from him. [Ten dollars was charged for this protective device …] [Princess Anne, Md.]
(Hyatt 1970: vol. I, 912-915)

An example of oral tradition that isn't often represented in published accounts of the Cunning Folk – the Arthur Gauntlet manuscript being a rare exception – are the miscellaneous short charms and spells that were part of a folk magician's standard repertoire. We can only regret that no one was able to interview a Cunning Man with the same attention to detail that Hyatt had with his anonymous "doctors". The closing selection is one of the shorter of these, from "Informant 1332" of Florence, South Carolina. It shows what an obliging conjure man might bring to mind when asked about his trade. Note the repeated refrain "dey says" to establish the authority of tradition for the spells rather than claiming them as personal inventions. As Hyatt seems to indicate, this was a "doctor" (male practitioner), so where the informant mentions "my husband" this probably indicates a hypothetical quote from someone who used the "trick" or spell. The spells include theft magic and love spells similar to those of English folk magic, but also the particularly African form of necromancy involving graveyard dirt. Unlike published English spell collections but in common with some manuscript sources, there is no differentiation made between beneficial spells and potentially invasive or even fatal curses.

Dey had fo' pins an ' two li'le balls of hair in a bottle wit some perfume in it. Dey said dat wuz tuh make *sharp love*.
[The term *sharp luck* for pins or needles is common enough, but *sharp love* is rare.]
(Where did they put that?)
Dey had it put in a close cornah in dey room where dey stayin' at.
(Let it stay in the *chamber lye*. {in the urine in a chamber pot})
Dey say dey kin run yo' crazy wit dat.
(How would they do that?)
Well, some of 'em says dey would put nine pins an' nine needles an' put dat hair, an' dem needles an' dem pins, in a li'le gourd or sompin 'nothah, an' put it in de watah, dey say *goin' up* – where de stream *goin' up*. It'll run yo' crazy.
[Water going up is the incoming tide going up a tidewater river.]
Dere's a simple thing yo' kin do tuh bring 'im back. Yo' see, yo' work yo' tricks wit: de Fatah, de Son an' de Holy Ghost. Yo' takes three pinches of cheese, three pinches of flour, three of salt, an' yo' make a li'le ball an' yo' put it in de *three cornahs* of de bedroom. An' yo' call his name an' talk to him, "*In de Name of de Fathah, de Son an' de Holy Ghost*, ah want chew tuh res' contented nowhere. Ah want chew tuh be aggravated an' terrified till yo' bring evah piece back whut chew take away from me." An yo' put it back in de cornah an' yo 'sposed tuh hear from 'em in 24 hours, or nine days. He'll shore git home in nine days.
(You say you only put this in three corners of the room?)
Three cornahs of de bedroom, in yore room or his room where he wuz sleepin' at. He'll come back.
Yo' take nine pins an' nine needles, dis way, and' some of his watah, an' yo' turn dat bottle – turn it [point the neck of the bottle] intuh de house, an' yo' make so many wishes by it, bury it, dat'll stop 'im from runnin' aroun'.
(Where do you usually bury that?)
Bury it comin' intuh de house, tuh steps turnin' intuh de house.
Turn de shoe bottom upwards. Whatevah yo' want, yo' turn de shoe bottom upwards an' make yore wish. An' yo' kin nail it down wit ten-penny nails an' [or] whatevah yo' wanta do wit de shoe.
If anybody stole anythin' from yo', yo' could make 'em bring it back.
Well, if anybody stole sompin from yo', [you] could take three pinches of bread crumbs, three of salt, an' three of lard, an' yo' put dis on de fiah – LAK DAT FIAH DAT'S BLAZIN' [IN THE INTERVIEW ROOM]. … /
An' yo' know de person name, yo' would call dere name [while the fire blazes], an' yo' says, "Ah don' mean fo' yo' tuh res' contented, ah mean fo' yo' tuh be aggravated an' terrified, *In de Name of de Fathah, de Son an' de Holy Ghost*, till yo' returns sech-an'-sech a thing back whut chew stolen from

me." An' yo' say dat while de fire's burnin' hot. An' dat person will be aggravated an' will be upset in de brains an' mind, till dey returns dat back to yo'.

Weah it [hat bow] in de bottom of de shoe or weah it in her stockin'. Dey say dat will make a man come back, make him love yo'.

(That little bow on the back of his hat?)

Yes.

If a person is away from yo' an' yo' want 'em to come back, yo' wanta bring 'em back wit dat pitchure. Yo' put dat pitchure ovah a glass of watah undah yore baid an' let it set dere so many days an' nights, an' dat person will return back.

If yo' stan' it up on de haid, why dat person will be neah by crazy till dey git back tuh yo'.

Dey say yo' kin take a person hair, if yo' wan' dere love tuh grow. Yo' go tuh a tree, a growin' tree on de east side an' yo' bury dat thing dere. Nail it down so many days, wit twelve tacks or ten-penny nails, an' dat person love will grow fo' yo'.

Well, if yo' got any business yo' wanta 'tend tuh, or anythuin', yo' goes tuh de grave, yo' go tuh two women grave an' one man [3 graves] an' yo' take up dat haidbo'd. Yo' call de dead, an' tell 'em yo' come tuh dem fo' he'p, in ordah tuh he'p yo' git sech-an'-sech a person outa jail, or yo' want 'em tuh grant sech-an'-sech a thin'. An' yo' pays 'em fo' dat'. Put a penny about where dey breast is. Yo' take up de haidbo'd an' jes' lak it wuz settin' heah, lak [you] in front of it, yo' turn it roun' [demonstrates]. See, yo' change dere min's.

(And then you put that headboard {headstone or wooden marker} right back in the same hole.) [I am describing his action.]

Right back in de same hole. All yo' do is change it. an' den yo' goes – yo' go [went] tuh de man. now, yo' wan' he'p, [you go to] dese two [dead] wimmins tuh take care of whatevah yo' want tuh do, yo' see. An' yo' pay 'em all off wit pennies. An' yo' git some of de dirt from each grave [each of the three graves]. Den yo' carry dat dirt home an' DERE A WHOLE LOTTA WAYS YO' KIN *FIX* DAT DIRT.

(Tell me what you can do with the dirt.)

Well, if yo' wanta upset anybody, yo' put some peppah in dere an' salt. Dat will bring de frien' an' keep de evil spirit away from yo'.

Well, jes' lak dat's out way [out of the way or undesirable], throw it.

(Throw it out of the house?)

Out in front of de house.

If you wanta do evil, yo' use peppah; n' if yo' wanta do good, wouldn't use no peppah, but use salt and sugah.

Dere's a whole lotta ways tuh fix it.

Yo' kin fix it [graveyard dirt] an' git – yo' kin git some sulphur, powdah [it], an' salt, an' yo' kin roll it till it come tuh a dust. Den yo' kin stan' outside – an' if yo' wanta bring plenty frien's, plenty people – YO' STAN' OUTSIDE [YOUR HOUSE] AN' BLOW DAT [DUST] BACK IN DE HOUSE an' make yore wishes. An' evahthin' will come kinda lak yo' wan' it.

(You do that if you are bootlegging or something of that sort – selling something, you do that.)

Yo' do dat, yo' know, jes' lak if yo' doin' any kinda business – a restaurant or any kin's business.

(You take that graveyard dirt, sulphur and salt, an blow it into your place?) /

Yes, dat'll bring good luck tuh yo'.

Jes' lak if he kill a man an' he got away, an' yo' wanta make him come back, yo' kin go tuh de cemetery fo' dat, too. Yo' kin go tuh de cemetery an' dey says, if yo' don't know who did it, yo' would say – jes' lak if it wus mah brotah, yo' says, "Ah come, Daid, ah come tuh yo' fo' he'p. Mah brotah's been killed, mah brotah's been taken away from me an' ah don' know how he come away from me, an' whoevah done it. Ah don't mean fo' dem tuh rest contented. Ah mean fo' 'em, *In de Name of de Fathah, de Son an' de Holy Ghost*, tuh be aggravated an' terrified in dere min', till dey come back."

Dey'll come.

But ah tell yo' de bes' thin' dey says tuh make a person tell a thin' lak yo' want 'em, is tuh go to tuh woods an' GO TUH A ELM TREE. An' yo' would FIN' TWO LI'LE SWITCHES, an' yo' take dem an' *baid 'em tugethah* lak dat [demonstrates] , an' yo' go an' git a heavy rock.

(YOU GET THOSE ELM SWITCHES AND YOU TAKE THOSE STEMS AND YOU BEND THEM LIKE THAT, LIKE YOU ARE MAKING A FORK – LIKE A "Y".)
Yes.
Yo' git de rock – yo' pick out de twigs, yo' know, in de day, an' befo' sunrise de nex' mawnin', dat 'bout de time yo' have tuh go dere an' do dat. An' yo' go dere an' bind dese two tuhgethah, an' yo' say, "Whoevah killed dis person" – or anythin' yo' wan' 'em tuh do, yo' jes' make yore wishes, *In de Name of de Fathah, de Son an' de Holy Ghost*. An' bow dese trees [switches] tuhgeteh. An' den yo' say, "Ah don't mean fo' 'em tuh res' contented. Ah mean fo' dem tuh be aggravated." Dey gotta tell whut dey done, see. An' den yo' put a rock on it.
(A rock on these two twigs?)
A rock on dese two twigs an' weigh [weight] dem down, an' dat person will have tuh tell, – have tuh come up. IF HE DON'T, HIS HEART WILL BUST [a rare remark in hoodoo].
[FORTUNATELY I HAD FORESIGHT ENOUGH AT THE TIME OF RECORDING TO REDUCE THE PRECEDING WORDS TO MY FOLLOWING COMMENT:]
(YOU GO OUT TO THIS TREE BEFORE SUNRISE, AND THERE ARE TWO TWIGS THERE ON THAT TREE, AND YOU BEND THEM TOWARD EACH OTHER – YOU DON'T CUT THEM OFF OR ANYTHING. THEY ARE STILL ON THE TREE. AND YOU "BOW" THEM TO EACH OTHER, BEND THEM DOWN TOWARD EACH OTHER. THEN YOU TIE A ROCK ON THEM TO KEEP THEM BENT DOWN.)
Den yo' weigh it down an' dat person who done de crime, why on a certain day he'll go crazy or he'll tell or he'll bring dat person tuh sight. Jes' lak if dey had kill a person yo' know an' yo' didn't know who done it.
An' yo' take a bat – ketch a bull bat {goatsucker or whippoorwill} an' take his heart an' make a *hand*.[30] Yo' put it in a piece of cloth of sompin [of some kind of material] an' yo' wash it. Say as lon' as yo' keep dat dey can't ketch yo'.
(That is for luck in gambling.)
Dey say yo' kin measure a man [foot] track an' tie a knot at each end [of the measuring string], or yo' kin measure anythin' about a man an' tie a knot at each end, an' den weah it roun' yore laig for a stockin' garter or anythin' lak dat. He won' go off.
Well, she has connection wit a man, an' aftah she gits through, she ketch some of dat [semen] in cotton or sompin an' put it in a bottle an' stop it up. An' he can't go wit nobody but 'er. Evah time he'll come tuh her, she'll loose dat – de stoppah slightly. An' den when he goes she stop it up tight.
(Where do you keep the bottle?)
Eithah in 'er trunk or somewhere 'bout 'er laigs.
Yo' go somewhere an' git a red onion.
(This fellow that has lost his *nature*?) {virility}/
Yeah, if he's lost it by a *trick* {in this instance, a curse or charm} laid on 'im, or if he lost it by sompin bad [disease] or sompin he ketched in his laig [walked over]. But if he lost it on account of somebody *tricked* him im, he gits a red onion an' cut a slice out it lak yo's cuttin' one, an' rubs 'isself down wit dat an' throw dat one away. YO' RUB WIT IT EVAH DAY AN' YO' THROW IT A DIFF'REN CO'SE [course or direction] TILL YO' THROW IT TUH DE *FO' CORNAHS OF DE WORL'*, an' wash it wit sweet milk, an' dat brings yore *nature* back tuh yo'.
(You mean you slice this onion – you slice it in four quarters – just like you do a watermelon?)
Jes' lak yo' do a watahmelon.
(And each day he takes one of those slices and rubs himself down. And then he throws one in each direction to the *four corners of the world*.)
Dat'll bring it [*nature*] back, an' sweet milk, if he's *tricked*. BUT IF HE'S NOT TRICKED, yo' know, AN' IT'S COME FROM 'IS KIDNEYS OR SOMEPIN OTHAH lak dat co'se he'll have tuh take sompin else.
Well, dey says IF YO' WANTA BREAK UP ANYBODY, YO' WOULD RUN BACKWARDS NINE TIMES, and {sic} yo' would write dat person name an' whut chew want on dat aig, an' den yo' must run backward. An' den yo' must throw dat. Break it undah de cornah of yore house an' dat

---

[30] A "hand" or "mojo" is a flannel bag containing one or more magical items.

will drive 'em crazy. But dey didn't break it on de cornah of de house, dey break it on mah do' an' it shore done whut dey break it fo'.
(Caused confusion in the house?)
Caused confusion, lawsuits.
(Now before he writes your name on that egg, he takes nine steps backwards.)
Yes.
(What must you do to win a lawsuit?)
Yo' would read de 35th Psalm, "Leave mah fate unto God an' strive."
[The opening words are, "Plead my cause, O Lord, with them that strive with me." *King James Version*.]
Den yo' gits nine, nine'r [nine or] twelve sage leaves, an' yo' use de disciples. Yo' take dem twelve sage leaves, an' yo' git a cheap pair of stockin's an' yo' put six in each shoe wit de twelve disciple name on 'em, an' yo' go on tuh de trial. Yo' go on tuh de co'thouse. An' den yo' have a li'le thin' dey call de *lucky glass*. Yo' hold dat in yore hand, shet it up in yore han', an' yo' have in yore min' dat chaptah whut chew read about, "Deliver me," an' dose twelve disciples.
[The complete verse of the preceding "Deliver me," is: "Deliver me, O Lord, from the evil man." Psalm 140:1, *King James Version*.]
Dem twelve mens [on the jury], some of 'em won't agree. Jes' speak tuh 'em [silently] holdin' dat glass, an' den yo' come cleah.
(What about the *lucky glass*? WHERE DO YOU GET THAT?]
[There was no answer. I may have accidently turned off my recording machine or suddenly decided the question unimportant. The *lucky glass* came from a hoodoo store.]
Well, if yo's in love wit somebody, yo' pull out one of his [a rooster's] feathahs, an' run 'em in yore han's, yo' know, an' git 'em hot. [Heating something in your hands is fairly rare – a friction rite.] See, rub 'em in yore han's day way, an' git 'em hot an' git de grease, an' den yo' go an' rub it ovah dat fellah's haid. Dey say, he go crazy mos' about chew.
(You pull this feather out of a live rooster. Any kind of rooster?)
Any kin' of a roostah, jes' since it a year-ole roostah.
Yo' git bulldog manure an' dirt – an' some of dis same graveyard dirt an' red peppah, an' yo' kin break up anybody wit dat.
(How do you use it?) /
Well, yo' uses it all tugethah, an' den yo' go an' throw it undah dere house – any way yo' wanta deal wit dat person.
Well, jes' lak if ah wanted any business wit chew, well ah git dat wood from dat tree an' ah'd write chure name on it.
(On a piece of wood that has been struck by lightning?)
Yes. An' aftah puttin' yore name dere, ah'd turn it down an' ah would sharpen dat [one end of the piece of wood] an' ah would bury it on de east side – on de east side of somepin. An' whenevah ah want tuh be done, it would happen.
(You would drive that peg down into the ground some place – on the east side of some place.)
Sometimes people wants tuh break up a man from 'is job, wanta bring 'im off 'is job, dey would write down dat name on de *lightnin' wood*, den dey would turn it down – lay it down in de groun'. Long as dat stay dere he could nevah work no place.
Dey say yo' kin take a straw from a broom an' jes' lak it if anybody be's heah, an' yo' don't want 'em in heah, yo' take dem straws from dat broom an' yo' break off so many pieces, nine pieces. An' jes' walk through yore house breakin' off. An' den sweep dat straw out. Dat person will den leave dere, dere business will go down lak dat.
(You get nine straws from the broom and you walk through the house just keep breaking them up?)
Breakin' dem up.
Well, yo' ketch a snail, an' jes' lak if yo' wanta take somebody *nature* or sompin othah, yo' ketch dat snail an' den yo' rub it on yore han'. An' den when yo' go tuh bed or sompin othah wit dat person, yo' rub dat ovah dat person. It won't rise for 'im. He don' know whut *hurt* 'im.
Jes' lak yo' wanta carry somebody 'way, yo' would write dere name on a piece of papah an' yo' would grease it an' sprinkle a li'le sugah ovah it, an' dey would put molasses or sompin on it, an' dey [ants] would eat all dat off.

(What do you do with the paper after it is all finished?)
Yo' put it in de ants' nest, de red ants' nest, an' dey'd eat, an' eat, an' eat, till dey carried off all of dat, carried dat papah [away]. Dey would carry dat person away jes' like dat.
(What does it do to the person? Carry them away of kill them?)
Jes' whatevah yo' write on dere. If yo' want 'em to leave town, tuh move – if yo' write dat on dere. An' if yo' want it tuh kill 'em, yo' write dat on dere.
If yo' an' a man's in love an' yo' wanta fin' out sompin 'bout 'im, yo' git fo' lemons an' yo' paint de fo' postes of de baid.
(You paint the four posts of the bed.)
Wit de lemons, wit de fo' lemons, an' if he are to marry yo', or anythin', he'll jes' make yo' a present of de fo' lemons in yo' sleep. But if he not tuh marry yo', dere be mo' den one woman comin'. Mah husban' gave me a present of three lemons, but ah did marry 'im.
(What do you do with those lemons? Do you tie them on those posts or what?)
No, yo' jes' rub 'em. An' yo' jes' carry 'em – dere 'nuff hole in dere tuh put, fo' dat tuh stay on dat post.
(You stick them on top of each post? If they have a hole, then stick one down on each post?)
Yes.
[The preceding lemon rite belongs to general folklore …]
Some people take a wasp an' put live thin's in yo'; take a snake an' do se same thin'. Dey simply git de haid – cut de haid off an' dey put it in a powdah / box in some private place an' let it dry off. When it dry off dey make dat tuh a powdah, an' give tuh them to eat off. Den dere will become live thin's in 'em whut ah hear. …
Fo' any favors, yo' know, lak ah would come tuh yo' – lak ah would come tuh yo' an' say ah want so many dollahs. Any favors yo' wants from a person, gits de *five-finger grass*, an' would a – dis fingah heah [demonstrates].
(That's the finger next to the little finger on the right hand.)
Yeah, yo' use dat fingah lak dat [demonstrates].
(You put your thumb against that finger next to the little finger on the right hand.)
Yeah, an' den yo' put dat in yore right-han' pocket wit dat *five-fingah grass*, an' den yo' talk to dat person about a favor – ask 'em anthin' yo' want an' dey quick tuh oblige yo'.
(You do that when you want a job.)
Well, yo' git a five-cent package of blueing, an' five cents salt, and five cents soda, an' yo' take nine teaspoons of each. But yo' couldn't take nine of de blueing, but yo' jes' put some of de blueling in de watah [from here on voice too low to transcribe]. …
Well, yo' take a piece of lodestone, take one piece – of two pieces, if yo' wanta make a lucky charm. [Word *charm* rare in HOODOO.] If yo' gon'a make a lucky charm, yo' take two pieces of lodestone, an' yo' would take some of dat *magic sand* {magnetic iron filings} wit it. An' den yo' would put, if yo' wants money tuh come large, yo' put two quartahs in dere; if yo' want it tuh come small, yo' put a dime in dere. An' den yo' weah dat fo' a *badge*, lucky yo' know. Yo' use whiskey on it. [*Feed* it with whiskey.] Yo' use whiskey sometime an' yo' use perfume sometime on it. Whiskey is best, see, aftah yo' use dat chance [charm]. Puts whiskey on it ovanight an' den de nex' mawnin' when yo' git up, yo' drop a li'le perfume on dere an' make yore wishes an' put it [charm] on. An' anythin' yo' wants, it come yore way.
[The preceding *lucky charm* or *charm* is rare in hoodoo, *magic sand* is fairly common, but informant's use of word *badge* for *hand* is otherwise unknown.]
If yo' havin' bad luck, yo' ketch a fish an' yo' stick 'im – he's alive or sompin othah – an' turn 'im back, loose 'im, an' dat change yore luck. (Hyatt 1973: v. III, 2200-220

It is significant that African-American magical practices in what were former English colonies, that is, hoodoo and obeah, strongly resemble the client-oriented folk magic found in Protestant England, whereas the Vodou, Santeria or Macumba of the Spanish, French and Portuguese colonies are, like Catholicism, highly ceremonial and focused on various deities and religious rites. As Carolyn Morrow Long explains it, it is due in large part to weaker ties to African religious belief:

Because fewer among the slave population of the American South were African born, because blacks were more acculturated to white ways and were more closely supervised [than in South America, the Caribbean and Louisiana], and because African religious traditions were so denigrated by Anglo-Protestant Christians, conjure became distanced from its sacred origins and lacked the African religious element found in Vodou, Santería, and New Orleans Voodoo. The concern is not with the relationship of human beings to the universe, maintaining spiritual balance, and serving and honoring the deities and the ancestors. There were no priests and priestesses; no community of believers, no ceremonies involving music and drumming, sacrificial offerings, and spirit possession. Personal misfortune is thought to result from the ill will of one's fellow man, not neglect of the deities, the saints, or the dead. Conjure is strictly pragmatic. (Long 2001: 74)

However, as hoodoo or conjure, and obeah so closely parallel the Cunning Folk's trade in England (in aims if not specific practices and symbolism), it may not be so much a result of deprivation and separation as it is of the cross-cultural pollination of arcane ideas at the lower end of the social spectrum in the South, Jamaica and the Bahamas, in addition to the absence of African memory and the inspiring example of high Catholic ritualism. This severing of cultural ties occurs within a few generations – consider how much more potent the equivalent break with pre-Christian religion was in Britain.

CHAPTER 4:

Divination, Part I

Fortune telling was the most universal of the Cunning Folk's operations. Unlike conjuration or astrology, it could be done by anyone, literate or illiterate. Divination disclosed hidden influences at work and provided an orientation for remedial action. Simply foretelling some future outcome in answer to a particular inquiry was only the beginning, although this was the most common and widespread use of occult prediction. Humans have always worried about their life trajectory; whether good fortune will favor them or misfortune defeat their hopes and plans. The universal desire to anticipate – and thus prepare for or mitigate – future events was accommodated by several methods of divination (from *divinatus*, "inspired by a god") available to British Cunning Folk, including folk (non-computational) astrology, palmistry, *sortes* or divination by lots, geomancy, cartomancy, and various other "-mancies". The future was sought in clues registered in previous events, as fossils found in stone reveal evolution, or by capturing snapshots of moments in time that could be examined to discover ongoing patterns of influence at work. Divination was also used to investigate past events, as who stole what, or where treasure was hidden.

Cunning Folk also interpreted signs and omens presumably sent through God's Providence into the natural world, as in the flight of birds or unsought dreams. Passive inspiration of that sort was considered natural if suspect for being possibly of satanic origin by Christian authorities, whereas divination by systematic means was considered unnatural and condemned. Any purposeful attempt to discern effects dependent on chance (or on man's free will) was deemed impossible by acceptable means, as these could not be foretold from causes apart from God's will, and inquiry there was forbidden. Being forbidden by authorities, however, had about as much effect on actual practice as analogous prohibitions have had on drinking, drug-taking, gambling and the like.

The other area opened up by divination was character analysis. The stars in a natal chart, lines on the hand, moles on the body, or facial features gave clues about the personality of the individual, and revealed how external forces might affect a specific character type. In fact, as faith in straight-forward foretelling of the future waned, character analysis eventually became the major focus of divination, especially in astrology, which dropped the suspect judicial branch of the art for the less controversial "humanistic" or psychological focus of natal astrology that deals more with the internal ego than the external world. It is revealing to note that the simple "non-computational" astrology of the *Erra Pater* or *Compost of Ptolomy* tended to focus on character and the zodiacal signs rather than the planets, just as modern popular astrology does. Interest in character, whether one's own or that of someone else, is naturally powerful and universal. Not only do we adore hearing about our (inner) selves, but we also share a fascination in what lies behind the visages of others. Can we trust the stranger at our gate, or even more compelling, what are our friends and neighbors *really* like? So much depends on the secret motives of others that we desperately want to know their true character.

There were two basic approaches to divination – revelatory and analytical. The first is intuitive; the result of "second sight", prophetic insight into the past or future, what we now think of as psychic ability, or as in the Notory Art, obtaining angelic visions by magical means. The second is systematic, in which the results of a defined procedure for capturing "chance in a moment", such as astrology, geomancy or lots (*sortes*), was interpreted by the appropriate inductive procedure. The two methods overlap in many instances, as where interpretation is needed to fully explain the outcome of an intuitive vision.

Until recently, the fundamental presumption in Western culture was that everything that happened was ultimately due to God's divine plan. There was disagreement whether *every* little event was directly instigated by God's purposeful activity or "Providence", or whether some occurred because of an embedded system of divine causes. Those who supported the former concept (the Nominalists) believed everything that happened was due to God's direct volition. For them, there were no accidents. Everything that happened was part of God's inscrutable plan – including His occasional permission for the Devil to do his worst – and it was wrong to even try to avert unlucky occurrences at all, rather than stoically endure them. The other school of thought maintained that God had delegated much of the cosmic function to intermediaries and channels of *virtus*, such as spiritual beings or astral influences, and these could legitimately be manipulated to defend against or rectify misfortune. The austere nominalist or providentialist position was found among legal-minded theologians such as John Calvin, and his followers, whereas the general public was inclined to the more latitudinarian tradition inherited from the Middle Ages. Whichever perspective was embraced, however, there was no question but that God was behind it all. Similarly, what we think of as "science" was not just merely an automatic function of physical laws but the will of the deity, which was the engine of destiny. Christianity defined – indeed, *was* – the culture. Although some people might be skeptical about details (particularly once the "Age of Reason" dawned in the late 17th century), there were no alternative "pagan" or non-Abrahamic spiritual systems lurking in the British countryside.

Because everything was deemed to either be predestined – an eternal pattern unfolding in linear time – or the end result of divine laws, future events could be predicted by analyzing the forces at work that would eventually bring them about. In pre-Christian times, there was seldom any hesitation in interrogating the gods through oracles (Apollo and Hecate being popular "informed sources") or by other methods of divination, but Christianity was more restrictive. Presuming upon God's Providence (pretending insight into God's unknowable plan) was prohibited. Thus the Church's official saints and prophets had a monopoly on legitimate prophecy and foresight in service of the Church, which was not allowed for ordinary individuals.

Most divination was supposed by critics to involve preternatural beings, and any illicit communication with spirits was assumed to be with demons (all the pagan gods having been reclassified as "demons") and the Devil. This was not to say it couldn't be done, or that it was necessarily fraudulent or ineffective. While the Devil might lie, he could also provide information hidden to ordinary mortals. Rev. Richard Bernard lists the ways in which the Devil could know about the future and use this to entrap unwary sinners:

> "He can counterfeit the resemblance of an holy man, his person and his words, and relate truly things past, and also foretell some things to come, as they shall fall out, as here, and as often hath been found true: which he doth, 1. By his knowledge of divine prophecies, and his understanding of the drawing near of their accomplishment. 2. By his exquisite skill in natural things, not only by the general causes, but those subordinate to them, with the particular operations, what necessarily they must produce. 3. By his diligent observation of innumerable instances, from the world's beginning, of the periods of kingdoms, and families, of the causes of their changes, and ruin, and so conclude by experience of the like to come. 4. By his own, and his fellow Devils' diligence in all places, whereby they are acquainted with all secret plots, consultations, resolutions, and preparations, which they will relate to others, which know them not, as predictions, which are only that which they elsewhere see and hear. 5. By his own persuasions, and working through his suggestions in men's hearts, and his observing the effectual operations thereof, provoking to bring the same about, and so can foretell what such will do. Thus he could have told of Cain's murdering of Abel and of Judas his treason, because he had won them thereunto. 6. By his knowledge of God's will, to allow him to do this or that, as he did to Job, to Abimelech and the Sichemites, of which he could have foretold. Thus can he tell many things, as he did Saul's death, and the Israelites overthrow. " (Bernard 1617: 63)

To make use of this service was to consort with mankind's ultimate enemy and court eternal damnation. Some operators, fully accepting Dr. Bernard's theses that the Devil's minions were likely to be most effective source for what they wanted, knowingly sought out the illegal services of demons by invocation or forbidden techniques, just as their descendants consort with gangsters, bootleggers and drug dealers despite very real dangers. Necromancy (which was not just communicating with the dead but with any spiritual being) and sorcery were as popular among college undergraduates then as various fashionable and "daring" transgressions are among their successors today. Others skirted such blatantly illegal arts by ostensibly restricting their communications to "good spirits" such as angels.

Take the famous example of Dr. John Dee. Here was a highly educated man, a leading scientist and mathematician with connections as high as Queen Elizabeth and the Holy Roman Emperor Rudolph II, who is perhaps best remembered today for his efforts to communicate with angels. Modern readers are often bewildered by this seemingly futile and (legally) perilous activity by someone who had so many other more productive outlets for his superior abilities. However, in the cultural context of the time, Dee's quest, while over-ambitious, makes perfect sense. His greatest desire was practical knowledge. Having mastered most of the mundane sources to that end, the logical next step was to consult with beings who knew what no mere mortal could hope to discover on his own—the angels who were God's intermediaries between heaven and the earthly realm. If you wanted to find out more about cosmic reality, what better approach than to ask someone who had that higher knowledge? It fit perfectly into the Christian cosmology that someone like Bernard or leading Puritan William Perkins might accept, howsoever much they would deplore any presumptuous meddling in prohibited activities through "curiositas" (the vice of lusting after forbidden knowledge about the world). In the manner of most "revealed knowledge", Dee and Kelly's visions seldom seem to have resulted in clear, practical information, and they spent much of their time and effort working out the snags in their highly intricate system of angelic communication.

However, most people preferred the relative safety of analytical divinatory arts for which there was at least the legitimacy of tradition, ranging from the "sieve and shears" and the simple "Sphere of Pythagoras" to highly complex practices like astrology or geomancy. Despite generations of religious authorities' efforts to stamp out divinatory practices, they have always flourished, and doubts about their orthodoxy rationalized away by careful arguments that claimed the various practices as natural or at least non-demonic. Mechanical or automatic divinatory methods also seemed to guarantee that the Cunning Folk were neither cheating nor manipulating the responses, as they could more easily do when reporting the results of questioning spirits or interpreting omens. In some cases the process operated on a similar principle to the medieval "trial by ordeal", where guilt was determined through *"judicium Dei"* – an appeal to God, who would protect the innocent by miraculously suspending the usual effect of touching red-hot iron, reaching through boiling water or some other dangerous test. There was no danger of physical harm, however, in the "ordeal" of the most common methods such as the sieve and shears (coscinomancy) or key and book (bibliomancy), but the assumption that "truth will out" by divine aid through technical means was the same. These basic techniques could be as easily performed by ordinary people as by Cunning Folk but the cachet of having an expert do the job made them as useful to the professional as to the amateur.

Another example of the basic use of lots to identify a thief was "to wrap up the pieces of paper bearing [the suspects'] names inside little clay balls, and put them into a bucket of water to see which would unroll first", preceded by a ritual to insure the outcome was successful. (Thomas 1971: 215) Directions for this can be found in the notebook of Cunning Man Arthur Gauntlet (Sloane MS 3851):

For Theft

Write the names of all the Suspected in Paper severally and put every name written in a piece of Clay And put them into a basin of fair water saying as followeth.

I Conjure thee thou Earth and Clay + By the Father + the Son + and the Holy Ghost + Amen + And by all the Holy names of God + Messias + Sother + Emanuell + Sabaoth + Adonay + Panthon + Craton +Anefeto + Theos+ Otheas + Eley + Eloy And by all the virtues of God by Heaven and Earth and by the Sea and all that be in them And by our blessed virgin Mary The Mother of our Saviour Jesus Christ And by his humility And by the holy company of Heaven And by all that God created In Heaven In Earth and in the Sea or other places And by all the names of God And by the virtues and merits of all the Saints, That amongst those names hidden within the Clay his name or her name which hath stolen these things may be known by him that liveth and reigneth world without end + Amen +

Again I Conjure thee water wherein those names are by the true and living God And by the Virgin Mary mother of our Lord Jesus Christ and by her virginity and humility and by Saint Michael and Gabriel Raphael Cherubim and Seraphim and by all the Saints Angels and Archangels by Thrones Dominions Principates and Potestates And by the four Evangelists + Saint Matthew + Mark + Luke + and John + And by all the holy Martyrs Confessors and Holy virgins of God And by all powers virtues and Joys of Heaven Also I conjure thee water wherein those names are by the Sun the Moon and Stars And by John the Baptist the which Baptised our Saviour Jesus Christ In the flood Jordan And by him that did walk upon the Sea And by the virgins And by the Sepulchre of Jesus Christ And by the dreadful day of Judgment And by the great name of God + Tetragrammaton + Than we may have true knowledge of these things we desire And that the name of the Man or woman which hath stolen those things may rise up of the water. Per eum qui venturus est Judecare speculum per ignem amen {"By him who is to come and judge through the age of fire. Amen"}
Then say these Psalms following viz.
Psalm :58: Psalm :43: Psalm :77:
Concluding every Psalm with Glory be to the father &c
Also say Athanasius Creed &c /
Also Te Deum Laudamus &c
Also In Principio &c
Also the Lord's Prayer and the Creed. Say all this iii times and no doubt but it will be done. (Rankine 2010: 142-143)

Coscinomancy, or divination by sieve and shears was an ancient and widespread method of determining a question, used not only throughout Europe but as Kittredge notes, "[d]ivination of the sieve-and-shears variety or analogous thereto is in use in India, in Africa, among the Melanesians, among the Malays, and elsewhere." (Kittredge 1929: 200) The English sources are quite consistent in their descriptions. A pair of shears (which were like old sheep-shearing or grass shears) is spread open and the blades wedged into the wooden ring or "rind" of a sieve. Two people held the combination upright each by a single finger. There is some uncertainty whether a supporting cord was used as well, or perhaps the sieve was balanced on some surface – the weight of the objects and their need to pivot makes simply suspending it by two fingers problematic. The individual managing the operation then proceeded to invoke Sts. Peter and Paul, and/or utter a magical phrase before reciting a list of names of those who may or may not be guilty of theft (the most common application), of witchcraft or which will prevail in some competition. When the appropriate name is said, the sieve will rotate, just as a planchette moves on an Ouija board. Reginald Scot, who was incredulous about the practice, described it simply in 1584:

> "Sticke a paire of sheeres in the rind of a sive, and let two persons set the top of each of their forefingers upon the upper part of the sheeres, holding it with the sive up from the ground steddilie; and ask *Peter* and *Paule* whether A. B. or C. hath stolne the thing lost; and at the nomination of the guiltie person, the sive will turn round. This is a great practice in all countries, and indeed a verie babble." (Scot 1985: 212)

John Aubrey provides another account in his "Remaines of Gentilisme and Judaisme" (Lansdowne MS 231, 1686-87), although his citation of Virgil seems to be in error – he probably was thinking of Theocritus' Idyll III, "Amaryllis":

> "The Magick of the Sive and Sheers, (I think) is in Virgil's Eclogues: The Sheers are stuck in a Sieve, and two maydens hold up the Sieve with the top of their fingers by the handle of the shiers: then say, *By St. Peter and St. Paule such a one hath stoln* [such a thing] the others say, *By St. Peter and St. Paul, He hath not stoln it*. After many such adjurations, the Sieve will turne at the name of the Thiefe." (Aubrey 1972: 213)

Another version of the invocation was used in Yorkshire in 1667: "Dec. 10, 1667. Cumberland.

'Before Thos. Denton, Esq. [Justice of the Peace], Mary, wife of Stephen Johnson, of Carleton, saith, that, as shee was coming from Clifton, shee mett with Jo. Scott, whoe told her that his wife had cast the riddle and sheares for some cloathes of George Carre's that was stole; and one Jo. Webster, of Clifton, told them that they knew as much as he could tell them, and that it was a little bleare-eyed lasse that gott them, whoe lived neare them.' The formula used by the operator was as follows: "By St. Peter and by St. Paul, If – – has stolen – 's –, Turn about riddle and shears and all."[31]

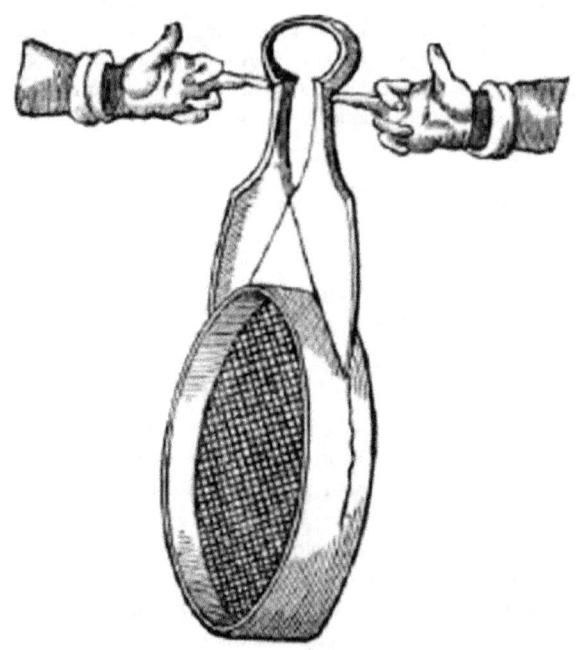

The magical invocation is mentioned by Sir Harry Ellis in *Brand's Antiquities*, which has the two persons holding the shears using their *middle* fingers rather than forefingers, as can be seen in a woodcut originally published in the 1567 edition of H. C. Agrippa's *De occulta philosophia libri tres*, and reciting "Dies Mies Jeschet Benedoftet, Dovvina Enitemaus" instead of invoking Saints Peter and Paul. (Brand 1900: 774) This phrase is given as "Dies, nues, ieschet, benedoefet, donuina, enitemaus" by Johann Weyer, in his *De praestigiis daemonum* (1563); as "Dies mies, Ieschet, bene doefet, Fowina, Enitemaus" by Barten Holyday in his play *The Marriage of the Seven Arts* (1618): "'Who shall have Astronomia? Shall Poetaa?' The sieve remains quiet. 'Shall Logicus?' No motion. 'Shall Geographus?' The sieve barely stirs. 'Shall Geometres?' The sieve turns round!'" and in the *Key of Solomon* as "Dies Mies Yes-Chet Bene Done Fet Donnima Metemauz" (and includes the saints' names as well). It seems to have been a more magical alternative or addition to Peter and Paul, and has no known meaning. Interestingly, H. P. Lovecraft, borrowing it from Waite's translation of Eliphas Levi's *Mysteries of Magic* to use as a powerful conjuration in "The Case of Charles Dexter Ward": "Then a voice of thunderous remoteness, differing greatly from Ward's voice, was heard to intone the phrase: DIES MIES JESCHET BOENE DOESEF DOUVEMA ENITEMAUS". Lovecraft wasn't referring to the sieve and shears, but he may have been familiar with that usage in colonial New England, as Cotton Mather tells us in the *Wonders of the Invisible World* (1693):

> "So 'tis to be feared, the Children *of New-England* have *secretly* done many things that have been pleasing to the Devil. They say, that in some Towns it has been an usual thing for People to cure Hurts with *Spells*, or to use detestable Conjurations, with *Sieves, Keys,* and *Pease,* and *Nails,* and *Horse-*

---

[31] Francis Andrews, ed., *Depositions from the Castle of York* Surtees Society, vol. 40, Durham, Yorks,, 1860, p. 82.

shoes, and I know not what other Implements, to learn the things for which they have a forbidden, and an impious *Curiosity*." (Mather 1862: 96)

Mather's list refers to other methods of sortilege as well. The mention of the key may refer to the similarly popular practice of the "key and book" or "cleidomancy", in which a large key is inserted in a book, usually the Bible, so as to touch an appropriate verse. The names of suspected thieves or candidates for something are written on slips of paper and inserted, one by one, into the hollow tube or barrel of the key (or wrapped around it). The book is then tied shut to keep the key in place. The book is suspended by two people's fingers as with the sieve and shears (and sometimes by a cord tied to the ring of the key as well) and the particular Bible verse is read out, causing the book to turn with the insertion of the appropriate name.

For example, one William Wicherly, a tailor and Cunning Man living on Charterhouse Lane in London, gave the following testimony at his trial before magistrate Sir Thomas Smith at his trial in 1549:

> "... about Easter last one of the grooms of the King's slaughter-house wife, whose name he knoweth not, had her purse picked of tenne shillinges, and the foresaid [John] Clereke [of Westminster] brought the said slaughterman's wife to this deponent, to lerne who had picked her purse. At which tyme she delivered to this deponent the names in writing of suche persons as she had in suspicion. Which names he put severally into the pipe of a kay, and laying the kay upon the verse of the spalter [psalter] in the spalter book, viz. *Si videbis furem*, &c. did say, *Si vedebis furem, correbas cum eo, et cum adulterem portionem tuam ponebas*. And when this verse was said over one of the names, which was a woman, the book and key tourned rounde, and thereupon this deponent said to the aforesaid Clerke, and the slaughterman's wife, that the same woman had the money whose name was on the kay, as farr as this deponent could judge, because the kay and boke did tourne at her name and at none others. And he saith that he hath used this practice so often that he cannot express how many the tymes; for people are so importune upon hym dayly for this purpose, that he is not able to avoyde them, but kepeth hymself within his doores." (Nichols 1859: 332)

A contemporary description is given by Reginald Scot (who cites an earlier numbering of the psalms, as the line cited – "When thou sawest a thief, then thou consentedst with him, and hast been partaker with adulterers" – is now the 18th verse of the 50th psalm in the King James version):

> "Popish preasts (saith [Hemingus]) as the *Chaldeans* used the divination by a sive and sheeres for the detection of theft, doo practice with a psalter and a keie fastend upon the 49. psalme, to discover a theefe. And when the names of the suspected persons are orderlie put into the pipe of the keie, at the reading of these words of the psalme (If thou sawesth a theefe thou diddest consent unto him) the booke will wagge and fall out of the fingers of them that hold it, and he whose name remaineth in the keie must be the theefe." (Scot 1985: 401)

A century later, an example turns up in the *Athenian Oracle*, a period newsheet later collected into one volume:

> "A Gentlewoman having lost several things out of her House, she suspected one of her Maids; whereupon she try'd this Experiment to find out the Truth, she call'd the suspected Person, and holding a Key upon her Finger, being put in a Bible, she repeated the following Words : Which are not thought fit to be printed, lest the Same ill use might be made of 'em by others; naming the Person's Christian and Sirname, whereupon the Bible immediately turn'd round, which makes the Lady believe the suspected Person guilty, pray your Thoughts upon it, whether any Certainty in it, or such a Prattice lawful?
> This is near a kin to the Trick of the Sieve and Scizzars, the Coskniomancy of the Ancients, as old as Theocritus ..."[32]

---

[32] *The Athenian Oracle*. London: Andrew Bell, at the Cross-Keys and Bible,1704, Vol II. p.309

By the 19th century, the need to discover thieves by book and key had lessened, and a then more pressing need was sought, to identify a future mate:

THE KEY AND BOOK CHARM

To find out the first two letters of a future wife's or husband's name, take a small Bible and the key to your front street-door, and having opened to Solomon's Songs, chap. viii., ver. 6 and 7, place the wards of the key on those two verses, and let the bow of the key be about an inch out of the top of the Bible; then shut the book, and tie it around with your garter, so as the key will not move, and the person who wishes to know his or her future husband or wife's signature, must suspend the Bible by putting the fore-finger of the right hand under the bow of the key, and the other person in like manner on the other side of the bow of the key, who must repeat the following verses, after saying the alphabet and letter to each time repeating them.

It must be observed that you mention to the person who repeats the verses, before you begin, which you intend try first, whether the surname or Christian name, and take care to hold the Bible steady; and when you arrive at the appointed letter, the book will turn round under your finger, and that you will find to be the first letter of your intended's name.

Solomon's Songs, chap. viii. ver. 6 and 7.

"Set me a seal upon thine heart, as a seal upon thine arm; for love is as strong as death, jealously as cruel as the grave; the coals thereof are coals of fire, which hath a most vehement flame. Many waters cannot quench love, neither can the flood drown it; if a man would give all substance of his house for love, it would be utterly contemned." (*Fontaine's Golden Wheel* 1862: 126-27)

Another example of the key and book used to discover a mate was recorded by Charlotte Latham at Fittleworth in West Sussex in 1868:

> "A spell less pardonable than these is sometimes resorted to in order to ascertain which of two persons will first be married. A key is fastened with a string within the pages of a small Bible, the ring of the key protruding from it, by which ring the book is to be suspended from a finger of each of the two young people who are trying their matrimonial fate. They stand as motionless as possible and repeat a verse from the Bible, usually the 16th of the first chapter of Ruth— "Intreat me not to leave thee," &c. After waiting a short time the fingers of course move imperceptibly, and the book turning slowly round presents a corner to one of the holders of the key, who is pronounced by the lookers-on to be the favoured one. I have heard even well-educated persons confess, not quite without a dash of superstitious belief, to having borne part in this strange ceremony." (Latham 1878: 31)

These simple but time-honoured methods survived from ancient time up to the end of our period of inquiry in the repertoire of the Cunning Folk.

A simpler alternative to the use of the key was the venerable *Sortes Sanctorum (or Bibliorum)*, in which the querent simply opened the Bible and without looking but with a specific question in mind, put his or her finger (or a pin) on the first passage found. This was then interpreted to reveal an answer or outcome to the problem. Historically, the Greeks had used Homer's *Iliad* (*Sortes Homericae*), while the

Romans preferred Virgil's *Aeneid* (*Sortes Virgilianae*). The *Aeneid* was even used in medieval times and after, as a famous anecdote (of which there are conflicting versions) about King Charles I illustrate:

> "... the Bodleian Library, Oxford, is the scene and Charles the First is the chief figure. Here the ill-fated king chanced upon that terrible passage in Aeneid 4 (615-620) which foretold so accurately his own tragic fate—loss of throne, children, friends, and life itself. The earliest authority in which the incident is discussed is Welwood's Memoirs, 105-107 (London, 1700). Dr. Welwood's vivid description follows:
>
> The King being at Oxford during the Civil Wars, went one day to see the Publick Library, where he was show'd among other Books, a Virgil nobly printed and exquisitely bound. The Lord Falkland, to divert the King, would have his Majesty make a trial of his fortunes by the Sortes Virgilianae, which everybody knows was an usual kind of augury some ages past. Whereupon the King opening the book, the period which happened to come up was ... part of Dido's imprecation against Aeneas (Aeneid 4.614-620)...
>
> It is said that K. Charles seem'd concerned at this accident, and that the Lord Falkland observing it, would likewise try his own fortune in the same manner; hoping he might fall upon some passage that could have no relation to his case, and thereby divert the King's thoughts from any impression the other might have upon him. But the place that Falkland stumbled upon was yet more suited to his destiny than the other had been to the King's, being the following expressions of Evander upon the untimely death of his son Pallas (Aeneid II. 150-157) ..."

Lord Falkland met his death on the field of the First Battle of Newbury, on September 20, 1643.[33]

The use of the Bible was more common, not only by Catholics but even austere Calvinist Puritans, seeking divine guidance through the *Sortes Sanctorum* in New England as well as the mother country. This oracle had been employed since ancient times as a Christian alternative to Virgil. As the procedure is self-evident, two examples will suffice. St. Augustine recorded in his *Confessions* (Book VIII, Chapter XII) how he resorted to the *Sortes Sanctorum* during his spiritual crisis while converting to Christianity in 32 CE:

> "So was I speaking and weeping in the most bitter contrition of my heart, when, lo! I heard from a neighbouring house a voice, as of boy or girl, I know not, chanting, and oft repeating, "Take up and read; Take up and read." Instantly, my countenance altered, I began to think most intently whether children were wont in any kind of play to sing such words: nor could I remember ever to have heard the like. So checking the torrent of my tears, I arose; interpreting it to be no other than a command from God to open the book, and read the first chapter I should find. For I had heard of Antony, that coming in during the reading of the Gospel, he received the admonition, as if what was being read was spoken to him: *Go, sell all that thou hast, and give to the poor, and thou shalt have treasure in heaven, and come and follow me:* and by such oracle he was forthwith converted unto Thee. Eagerly then I returned to the place where Alypius was sitting; for there had I laid the volume of the Apostle when I arose thence. I seized, opened, and in silence read that section on which my eyes first fell: *Not in rioting and drunkenness, not in chambering and wantonness, not in strife and envying; but put ye on the Lord Jesus Christ, and make not provision for the flesh, in concupiscence.* No further would I read; nor needed I: for instantly at the end of this sentence, by a light as it were of serenity infused into my heart, all the darkness of doubt vanished away.
>
> Saint Augustine, writing to Januarius in 400 CE, said that while it was an abuse of the oracles of God, it was preferable to having recourse to demons for the purpose of revealing the future." (Axton 1907: 33)

David Cressy, in *Books as Totems in Seventeenth-Century England and New England*, cites a revealing example of how a sophisticated man might still avail himself of this tradition, albeit with conflicted feelings:

---

[33] Helen A. Loane. "The Sortes Vergilianae" *The Classical Weekly*, Vol. 21, No. 24 (Apr. 30, 1928), p. 187.

In 1660 we find Lord George Berkeley, "being sick, and under some dejection of spirit, opening my Bible to see what place I could first light upon which might administer comfort." Berkeley's finger fell on the line in Hosea, "come, let us return unto the Lord," and at once he commenced a spiritual as well as medical recovery. Berkeley, a moralist of refinement and scholarship, felt sheepish in using such an unsophisticated practice, and so offers this apology: "I am willing to decline superstition upon all occasions, yet think myself obliged to make this use of such a providential place of scripture". Providence supplied the key. The book had power, which could be released and focused through blind stabbing at a randomly opened page. God would so work it that an appropriate message would come to the fore.[34]

There were other similarly mechanical and esteemed methods of divination that depended on a level of literacy and the ownership of manuals whose origins stretched back to pre-Christian times. One was the "Sphere of Pythagoras" (or "of Life and Death", "Democritus", "Petosiris", "Apuleius", &c.), a "wheel of fortune" system that determined positive or negative outcomes for a predetermined list of questions. Each version is accompanied by a diagram of a circle, usually divided into four sections, although the upper and lower division was the most significant. Each section contained a set of random numbers, with those in the upper half signifying a positive result, and those below, a negative one. The numbers on the left side of the vertical division sometimes indicated quicker results, while those on right side indicated a longer term. These "spheres" or "wheels" had existed in ancient times and turned up regularly in medieval manuscripts. A classic example from our period can be found in the 1725 *Original Book of Knowledge*. Small cheaply produced "books of fate" or "books of knowledge" of this sort, containing a curious miscellany of occult and mundane information, were an important resource for the Cunning Folk and are rather rare today. Although they were printed in large numbers, they (like early cook books and children's books) were also thumbed to death by their successive owners.

Of the Ancient Wheel of Fortune, approved and affirmed by the most eminent Philosophers; by which anything you desire to know, may readily and easily be resolved, according to the Rules of the Art.

Now that you may the more easily apprehend the Meaning of this Wheel of Fortune, and how such Questions as you propound may be resolved by it: First, pitch upon what number you like best, but let it not exceed 30: Then take the number of the day, as it is set down, and the Number of the Circle of the Wheel above the Letters; which must be the Letters that begin your Name. Then put

---

[34] David Cressy "Books as Totems in Seventeenth-Century England and New England" *The Journal of Library History*, Vol. 21, No. 1, (Winter, 1986), pp. 92-106.

the Number altogether, and divide them by 30, and look in the body of the Wheel for what remains; and if it happen in the upper Part of the Wheel, your answer will appear in the *Affirmative*, if in the lower Part, the *Negative*. In like manner, to know if the Party shall obtain their Love, take the number that stands over the first Letter of your Name, and of the Planet and Day of the Week; divide the Total of these by 30: If it be over, it will come to pass, if under, not.

QUESTIONS to be answered by the Wheel of Fortune.
1. *Whether any Fght [sic] shall happen in a Campaign, or not?*
2. *Which of the contending Parties that make War, shall have the Victory?*
3. *Whether a Town besieged, shall be taken or not?*
4. *Whether there shall be a Peace between two Princes at War?*
5. *Whether a Captain be courageous, or not?*
6. *The Favour you desire of a Person, shall you obtain it?*
7. *Preferment desir'd, shall a Man obtain it?*
8. *The Favour of a Prince, shall it be gain'd?*
9. *Shall a Captain be in Favour with his General.*
10. *Whether the Horse will win the Race he is to run?*
11. *In a suit of Law, who will overcome?*
12. *A Prisoner, shall he obtain his Liberty?*
13. *A sick Person, shall he recover?*
14. *Sickness, how long it shall continue?*
15. *Shall a Man obtain what he desires?*
16. *A Wife, shall her Husband have a child by her.*
17. *A Woman with Child, shall she have a Son or a Daughter.*
18. *A Child, shall it be happy or unhappy.*
19. *Things stolen, shall they be recovered.*
20. *Shall the Year be plentiful?*
21. *A Voyage at Sea, shall it be fortunate?*
22. *What Trade shall a Man thrive by?*
23. *Shall a Man gain by Marriage?*
24. *A Ship, shall it have a good Voyage?*
25. *A House, is it good to take it or not?*
26. *Shall a Man be rich or poor?*

These, or any other Questions of a like Nature may be resolved by this ancient Wheel of Fortune.

To proceed upon any Question by this Wheel, first chuse what Number you please: As 7, 8, 9, &c. Then take the Number you shall find in the Wheel, upon the first Letter of your Name: For example, if your Name be George, you may take G, and the Number which is over it; all which set down within the Wheel, and having added all into one sum, which divide by 30 and by the rest: As for Instance, if your total Number amount to 145, divide that by 30, and there will 25 remain; which Number you must look up on the Wheel, and if it be in the uppermost half, the Matter will succeed; if otherwise, miscarry.

And by the like Process you may find out anything you woul'd know; always observing, that the Numbers in the Wheel exceed not 30; as you see in the Wheel. (*Original Book of Knowledge* 1725: 52-54)

Interestingly, an almost identical text is found in *The Ancient Wheel of Fortune, Taken from the Book of Knowledge* [Glasgow] *1796* by private press printer Howard Coggeshall of Utica, New York. Three hundred and fifty copies of his little 16 page reprint were published in December 1940.

The diagrams of the wheels range in artistic complexity from the very simple to the impressively ornate. An example of the former can be found in the *Shepherd's Kalendar: or, The Citizen's and Country Man's Daily Companion* [ca. 1735], another example of the small quasi-astrological handbooks like the

Original Book of Knowledge. Here the "wheel" is nothing more than a standard square astrological figure with the four-fold division of numbers in the centre where the querent's name and dates are usually located. An unusually elaborate diagram, on the other hand, is found in a version of the *Book of Knowledge* by "Sam. Strangehopes", published in London in 1663. Here we have two circles or wheels, the upper one containing the favourable numbers within a foliated "wheel of fortune" with a fashionably-dressed gentleman rising on the left, a triumphant man with a sword and bag of money (and perhaps a crown) at the top, and an ordinary countryman descending upside-down on the right. The lower wheel is an winged dragon ouroborus surrounding the table of unfavourable numbers, with a cheerful little man upside down at the bottom. A more unusual divinatory wheel (that actually revolved, having a paper pointer affixed to the page) is found in "R. B's" *Choice emblems, divine and moral, antient and modern...* London (1732), which was a pirated edition of George Wither's emblem book turned by Nathaniel Crouch into a divinatory device.[35]

The continued popularity of the wheel or sphere resulted in a new version included by Robert Cross Smith ("Raphael") in his *The Familiar Astrologer* (1828) in two parts. As was typical of Smith's need to fill up the pages of his serial publication, there was a presumably fictional anecdote concerning Cagliostro sandwiched between the instructions for the use of the wheel:

ANCIENT DIVINATION
BY THE
WHEEL OF PYTHAGORAS;
Which is said to resolve all Questions, Past, Present, and Future,
PART I.
THE WHEEL.

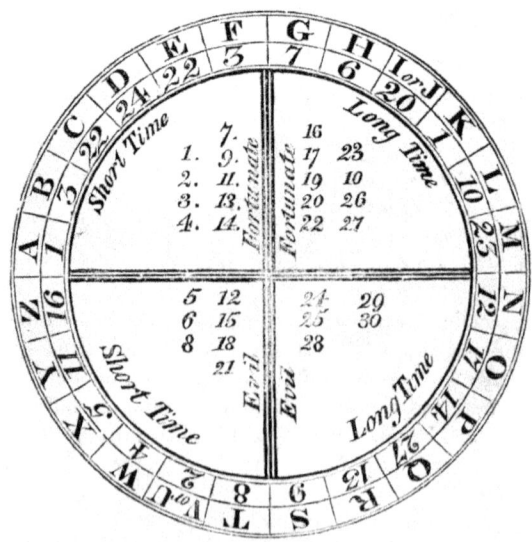

THE Ancients, who were extremely fond of divination, were wont to place great confidence in the "Wheel of Pythagoras," which resolves questions BY *Arithmancy*, or a species of sortilegy by numbers; wherein the result depends upon the unfettered agency of the mind and will, or intent to know "any difficult thing."

The Wheel of Pythagoras is said by former writers to resolve "all questions the asker may wish to be acquainted with, whether of the past time, the present time, or of the future." The following are said to be

---

[35] This wheel can be seen online at http://emblem.libraries.psu.edu/RB/rb206207.jpg (accessed 7/21/2012)

The Questions the Wheel answers.
1. If a horse shall win the race?
2. If a prisoner shall come out of prison?
3. If a sick person shall recover or die?
4. If an absent person shall return?
5. If the city besieged shall be taken?
6. Of two fighters, which shall prevail?
7. If the sickness shall be long or short?
8. If a suit at law shall be gained?
9. If thy wishes shall succeed?
10. If the day shall be fortunate?
11. If stolen or lost things shall be recovered
12. If it be good to buy or sell?
13. If the asker shall marry?
14. If the undertaking shall succeed?
15. If the asker is fortunate or unfortunate?
16. If any matter or thing whatever shall end good or ill?

Explanation of the Wheel.
The Wheel, it will be perceived, is divided into four compartments, the *upper* half of which contains in order the numbers which are termed propitious, good, and *fortunate;* the *lower* half contains those numbers of a contrary kind, or those which are termed evil, unpropitious, and *unfortunate.*
Round the Wheel are the letters of the Alphabet, to which are placed certain corresponding numbers which are required in the calculations: (these will be explained in Part 2). Besides which, the numbers in the right half of the wheel are said to denote "Long Time," or that the question which has these numbers in the working will be a length of time about; and those in the left half of the wheel are said to signify a short or brief space of time ere the affair is accomplished. Next follow the

TABLES USED IN WORKING THE WHEEL.
1. *The Mystical Numbers of each Day in the Week*

Sunday	106
Monday	52
Tuesday	52
Wednesday	102
Thursday	31
Friday	68
Saturday	45

2. *The Numbers of the Planets ruling the Days.*

Sunday	☉	34	Thursday	♃	78
Monday	☽	45	Friday	♀	45
Tuesday	♂	39	Saturday	♄	55
Wednesday	☿	114			

3. The Numbers to be chosen by Chance (as hereafter explained) in working the Questions.

1	11	22	28	29
6	2	12	23	30
15	7	3	13	24
19	16	8	4	14
25	20	17	9	5
27	26	21	18	10

The numbers attributed to the days of the week, and of the planet ruling the day, are of very ancient origin; and for which it would be difficult to assign a reason, or even account for in any way consonant with Astrological Science. They are, however, as well as the Wheel, a relic of former *traditional* foreknowledge by lots or numbers; probably invented, like Geomancy, in the monastic solitude of the Middle ages. The manuscript from whence this is compiled appears to have been written as early as the fifteenth century.—It was purchased at a high price at the sale of the late Mr. Cosway's library. But Christopher Cattan, a very old author, whose works are rare and expensive, makes some mention thereof; yet he fails in describing the manner of using the numbers, and in other parts of the process.

Arithmancy, or Divination by Numbers, on which the Wheel is founded, was variously practised. Many stupendous *"Tomes"* in the dead languages, now obsolete and forgotten, were to be found, explaining the "Arte and Manner" of these curious proceedings; in which the letters of the party's name were said to contain many hidden arcana, when decyphered by the "mysteries of numbers." The ancients went so far in these particulars, as to declare their belief that each individual may know the chief *secrets* of his destiny by the help of his name, or patronymical appellation; and also that there exists a peculiar sympathy between the name and the pursuits throughout life. These facts are here stated merely to apprise the reader of the unlimited fondness of the ancients for every kind of Aruspicy or Soothsaying, no matter how or where it was accomplished.

There have been several Italian writers of eminence who have treated of the power of numbers when chosen or combined by "lot;" amongst whom stands conspicuous Trithemius, the famous Abbot of Spanheim, whose work, entitled "Steganography," is exceedingly mystical, rare, and curious, but has never been translated into English.

ANCIENT DIVINATION,
BY THE
WHEEL OF PYTHAGORAS.
(PART II.)
TO RESOLVE THE QUESTIONS.

In the first place, the inquirer must refer to Table III. Page 60; and, while thinking earnestly upon the question he wishes resolved or answered, let him choose *a number* out of that table, without premeditation; or, what is said to be still better, let the inquirer take thirty pieces of card, and write thereon from No. 1 to 30; and these pieces being so numbered, and mixed together, *let one of them be chosen promiscuously,* and the number thereon taken notice of. This is the first step in the operation; but thereon depends the truth of the whole: therefore the inquirer must be particular in this part of the process.

Secondly. To this number, so chosen, either from the table or otherwise, let the inquirer *add the number answering to the first letter of his proper or Christian name;* which is seen in the Wheel itself, where the numbers stand in the inner circle, under the letters.

Thirdly. To this sum add *the number of the day of the week, and of the planet ruling the day;* which is plainly shown in Tables No. I. and II. page 64, of that day on which they ask the question. Then, add the whole together, and divide it by 30, or subtract 30 from it, as often as you can; and the remainder look for in the Wheel, observing in what part of the Wheel it falls; but if there be no remainder, then the number 30 itself must be looked for.

Now, to know whether the question or demand, which the inquirer or any one else propounds, shall succeed or not; take notice, if the number falls in the *upper half* of the Wheel, your fortune therein is GOOD, and the lot you have cast will cause your request to be fulfilled. But if it chance to be found in the *lower half* of the Wheel, your lot is evil and unfortunate; and the proposed question shall have an EVIL issue.

Note, also, if it be any question wherein time is concerned; as, how long or how short shall be the matter in hand before it be accomplished. Observe, that one half of the Wheel represents numbers of "long time," the other half of "short time;" and even so, in good or evil, shall the matter in hand fall out.

The whole of the questions *but one* in the list are answered thus; but, to No. 3, which is, "If a sick person shall recover or die?" to the above sums must be added, the "Moon's Age" on the day the question is asked; and the result proceeded with in the same manner.

Example 1.

Saturday, March 1, 1828—It was asked, If an undertaking should succeed? The number chosen was 14; and the first letter of the person's Christian name was R,

Number chosen	14
Number in the Wheel answering to R.	13
Number answering to Saturday	45
Number of the Planet ruling Saturday	55
Sum . .	127

This, divided by 30, leaves 7 for the remainder. Refer to the Wheel, and 7 is found in the upper half of the Wheel, and in the half marked "short time." This shows that the affair would be accomplished accordingly.

Example 2.

A person whose initial was S. asked, on Wednesday, If a sick friend should recover or die? and drew forth a card with the number 23 upon it, as his lot.

Number chosen	23
Number answering to S	9
Number answering to Wednesday. .	102
Number answering to the Planet	114
Number of the Age of the Moon	20
	268

> This, divided by 30, leaves 28 for the remainder, which is found to fall in the unfortunate half of the Wheel, and denotes long sickness, and dangerous, or of a doubtful issue.
> These examples will be sufficient to illustrate the method of resolving questions by the Wheel of Pythagoras, in which the only difficulty consists in choosing the first number. For which purpose, the manuscript from whence this is taken recommends the inquirer not to "ask but one question on the same day, and to refrain from all gibing, sporting, jesting, and unbelief, while divining," or making use of the Wheel, in order to know the truth.
> The reader will remember that this extract is put more for his amusement than for any avouching as to its actual certainty. Let him try it, and judge for himself. ("Raphael" 1828: 62-66, 157-160)

Comparing these versions of the wheel raises an interesting problem in that, although the format is the same in each case, the signifying numbers differ between the versions – not enough to be very different, but inconsistent all the same. Living as we do in a scientific age, we expect strict continuity in numerical tables, with inconsistency denoting fatal errors. There can be only one accurate or authentic version of a formula, and only one which will function correctly. This was not necessarily true in the case of traditional magic. While avoiding error in any particular operation is vital, contradiction between sources was evidently not a concern. Comparing the numbers in our examples, (or the lists of Unfortunate Days, below), we find marked discrepancies. Obviously later wheels were dependent on earlier examples, as the procedure remains essentially the same, but the location of individual numbers shows that absolute consistency was not necessary for the wheel to work. The model is more like that of culinary recipes where the directions in a specific recipe should be followed to get the desired result, but where there can also be a number of variant recipes, each capable of delivering an appropriate product. We might call this the "principle of acceptable variance", and it was a part of the world view of the Cunning Folk and their clientele. In many instances, there was no one correct version or method for effective divination or magical action, which may have been a hold-over from oral tradition where fixed texts have no existence. As with modern alternative medicine, effects could be achieved by a number of different approaches, rather than a single orthodox method or formula.

The principle of acceptable variance didn't just occur in the shadowy field of the preternatural. For example, consider the period approach to the serious problem of scurvy (i.e., vitamin C deficiency). The disease was common in cold weather when fresh fruit and vegetables were not available (our ancestors also had a bias against these foods for various reasons) but particularly at sea where fresh produce could neither be preserved nor obtained on long voyages. Every now and then someone would discover that citrus juice or scurvy grass (*Cochlearia officinalis*) was a good remedy for the disease, but this did not result in conscious adoption of these dietary supplements until the mid-18th century. It was just as likely some quite ineffectual remedy would be preferred as an alternative, despite an observable lack of effect. In 1614 John Woodall, Surgeon General of the East India Company, published *The Surgion's Mate* recommending citrus juices, and Edward Winslow, who came over on the *Mayflower* in 1620, wrote back to potential emigrants to suggest they "Bring juice of lemons and take it fasting; it is of good use," but suggestions like these had no universal influence. People were accustomed to accepting that any familiar remedy – or method – was as likely to be good as another.

While inauthentic alternatives have real consequences in the material world, it is not so clear that this was so in the realm of divination. Some might object that it was all nonsense anyhow, but there is another way of looking at it. The specific list of numbers (or dates) you happened to employ could be considered part of the overall working of the oracle. The first effect of fate or destiny encountered was therefore the selection of a particular array of numbers, making it the proper one for the individual user.

In the case of the wheels or spheres, the numbers in three upper or fortunate tables are:

Strangehopes 1663

1	7	4	0
2	9	6	2
3	1	7	3
4	3	9	0
	6	7	

Book of Knowledge 1725

1	7	5	10
2	9	7	26
3	11	8	27
4	13	9	
	14	1	
		4	

Familiar Astrologer 1828

1	7	16	23
2	9	17	10
3	11	19	26
4	13	20	27
	14	22	

The numbers in the lower unfortunate tables:

Strangehopes 1663

2	12	24	
6	15	28	30
8	18	25	
	21	29	

Book of Knowledge 1725

5	12	22	30
6	15	25	
8	19	28	
	23	29	

Familiar Astrologer 1828

5	12	24	29
6	15	25	30
8	18	28	
	21		

Another example of acceptable variance common to the Cunning Folks' trade was the various lists of "Egyptian" or "dismal" days (i.e., "dies mali" or "evil days"). The primary application of the list of these unpropitious days was deciding when it was safe to bleed patients to correct their imbalance of humours, but they were also consulted for planning weddings, travel, new projects and most significantly, days to avoid for divination and magic. It was strongly recommended that the "Sphere of Pythagoras" not be asked a question on one of the evil dates.

Unlike many occult elements misattributed to ancient Egypt, the "dismal days" have a historically valid connection. The Egyptians did have lists of days when it would be wrong to undertake any important project. These were adopted by the Greeks and Romans and maintained through the Middle Ages and down to our own time. One official "Egyptian" list, represented today on various websites (where uncritical borrowings across the internet encourages the opposite of old fashioned variance) includes an even number of 24 "unpropitious" days, or two to the month:

January 1 and 25
February 4 and 26
March 1 and 28
April 10 and 20
May 3 and 25
June 10 and 16
July 13 and 22
August 1 and 30
September 3 and 21
October 3 and 22
November 5 and 28
December 7 and 22

Not surprisingly, this is far too orderly to be historically representative. The Egyptians actually had about 36 unpropitious days, as well as 190 "good" days and 38 mixed ones.[36] In medieval times, lists ranged from a mere three unlucky days to several dozen. The implication among modern versions appears to be that there can be just one "authoritative" list, and that the best approach is to find the "original" version from ancient times. This is another example of our own hunger for scientific certainty in an area where none exists.

The observation of lucky and unlucky days was an important consideration in the operations of the Cunning Folk, and innumerable examples can be found in the sources they relied upon. Unlucky days were naturally rejected by the pious and the skeptical alike, who viewed them as a superstition observed by the "vulgar" sort of people (of whatever social status).

> "The Christian faith is violated, when so like a Pagan and Apostate any man doth observe those days which are called *Aegyptiaci*, or the Calends of *Ianuarie*, or any Moneth, or Day, or Time, or Yeere, eyther to travell, marry, or to doe any thing in: for whosoeuer beleeues thes things, hath erred from the Christain Faith and Baptisme." (Melton 1975: 56)

As they further illustrate the principle of acceptable variance, I include a number of these lists to illustrate both their long history and the diversity of their contents.

Bodleian MS Lat. liturg. e. 10, ca. 1440
Theys vnderwrytyn be þe perilous dayes for to take eny sekenes in, or to be huete in, or to be weddyd in, or to take eny journey vpon, or to begynne eny werke in þat he wold wele spedde. The noumbre of theys dayes be in the yere xxxij. þat be theys:
In Janivere beth vij: the j, þe ij, þe iiijth, þe v, the vij, the x and the xv. [1,2,4,5,7,10,15]
In Feverere beth iij: the vj, þe vij & the xviij. [6,7,18]
In March beth iij: the j, þe vj, the viij. [1,6,8]
In Aprill beth ij: the vj & the xj. [6,11]
In May beth iij: þe v, þe vj & þe vij. [5,6,7]
In June beth ij: þe vij & þe xv. [7,15]
In July beth ij: þe v & the xix. [5,19]
In August beth ij: þe xv & þe xix. [15,19]
In Septembre beth ij: þe vj and þe vij. [6,7]
In Octobre is j: the vj. [6]
In Nouembre beth ij: the xv & þe xvj. [15,16]
In decembre beth iij: þe xvj þe xvj & þe xvij. [16,16?,17]
Sed tamen In domino Confido.[37]

The Pronostycacion for euer of Erra Pater (1554)
January 1, 2, 4,5,10,15,17,19
February 7,10,17
March 12, 16,19
April 16,21
May 7,15,20
June 4,7
July 15,20
August 19,20

---

[36] Warren R. Dawson. "Some Observations on the Egyptian Calendars of Lucky and Unlucky Days". *The Journal of Egyptian Archaeology*, Vol. 12, No. 3/4 (Oct., 1926), pp. 263.
[37] John C. Hirsh. "Fate, faith and paradox: medieval unlucky days as a context for 'Wytte Hath Wondyr.'" *Medium Aevum*, vol. 66, no. 2, Fall, 1997.
http://findarticles.com/p/articles/mi_hb6408/is_n2_v66/ai_n28695647/?tag=content;col1

September 6,7
October 6
November 15,19
December 6,7,9, - 15,16

Richard Grafton. A Manual of the Chronicles of England (1565)
January 1, 2, 4, 5, 10, 15, 17, 29, very unlucky. February 26, 27, 28, unlucky; 8, 10, 17, very unlucky. March 16, 17, 20, very unlucky. April 7, 8, to, 20, unlucky; 16, 21, very unlucky. May 3, 6, unlucky; 7, 15, 20, very unlucky. June 10, 22, unlucky; 4, 8, very unlucky. July 15, 21, very unlucky. August 1, 29, 30, unlucky; 19, 20, very unlucky. September 3, 4, 21, 23, unlucky; 6, 7, very unlucky. October 4, 16, 24, unlucky; 6, very unlucky. November 5, 6, 29, 30, unlucky; 15, 20, very unlucky. December 15, 22, unlucky; 6, 7, 9, very unlucky. (Brand 1900: 319)

Book of Knowledge (1658)
In the change of every moon be two Dayes, in the which what thing soever is begun, late or never, it shall come to no good end, and the dayes be full perillous for many things. In January, when the moon is three or four dayes old. In February, 5 or 7. In March, 6 or 7. In April, 5 or 8. May, 8 or 9. June, 5 or 15. July, 3 or 13. August, 8 or 13. September, 8 or 13. October, 5 or 12. November, 5 or 9. In December, 3 or 13. (Brand 1900: 318)

The Original Book of Knowledge (1725)
XII. *Of the Evil or Perillous Days in every Month in the Year.*
There are certain Days in the Year, which concern all Persons to know, because they are so perillous and dangerous: For on these Days if any Man or Woman shall be let Blood, they shall die within twenty one Days following; or whoso falleth sick on any of these / Days, they shall certainly die: And whoso beginneth a Journey on any of these Days, he shall be in danger of Death before he return: Also he that marrieth a Wife on any of these Days, they shall either be quickly parted, or else live together with much Sorrow and Discontent. And lastly, whosoever on any of these Days beginneth any great Business, it will never prosper, nor come to its desired Perfection. Now since these Days are so Unfortunate, it highly concerns every one both to know and take Notice of them; which, that the Reader may do, I have set them down in the following Order.

In January are eight Days; that is to say, the 1st, 2d, 4th, 5th, 10th, 15th, 17th, and 19th.
In February are three Days, that is, the 8th, 17th, and 19th.
In March are three Days; that is, the 15th, 16th and 21st.
In April are two Days, the 15th and 21st.
In May are three Days, that is, the 15th, 17th, and 20th.
In June are two Days; the 4th and 7th.
In July are two Days, the 15th and 20th.
In August are two Days, the 20th and 25th.
In September are two Days, the 6th and 7th.
In October is one Day, the 6th.
In November are two Days, the 5th and 19th.
In December are three Days, the 6th, 7th, and 11th; and others say the 15th and 16th.
But besides these, there are also the Canicular or Dog-Days, which are Days of great Danger and Peril; and they begin on the 19th Day of July, / and end 27th Day of August, during which time it is very dangerous to fall sick, take Physick, or to be let Blood; but if necessity call for it, it is best to be done before the midst of the Day. (Original Book of Knowledge 1725: 39)

Raphael. The Familiar Astrologer (1828).
UNFORTUNATE AND EVIL DAYS, WHEEL OF PYTHAGORAS.
THE same manuscript also contains a tradition relating to the evil days, or days of misfortune, whereon no question should be asked; as follows:—

"There be evil and unfortunate days, so called by the ancient philosophers, in the which, if a man fall sick, he shall be in danger of death, or else to be long sick; or, if any person take upon him a journey, and set forward in any one of these days, he shall have ill luck in his doings: neither is it good to plant, to make bargains, or banquets, in any of them.

"JANUARY hath five ill days ; that is, the 3d, 4th, 5th, 9th, and 11th. FEBRUARY hath three; that is, the 13th, 17th, and 19th. MARCH hath three; that is, the 13th 15th, and 16th. APRIL hath two ; that is, the 5th and the 14th. MAY also hath two; the 8th and the 14th. JUNE hath but one ill day; and that is, the 6th. JULY hath two ill days; the 16th and 19th. AUGUST hath two; the 8th and the 16th. SEPTEMBER hath three; that is, the 1st, 15th, and 16th. OCTOBER hath but one ill day; and that is, the 16th. NOVEMBER hath two; that is, the 15th and 16th. DECEMBER hath three; that is, the 6th, 7th, and the 11th." (Familiar Astrologer 1828: 160/61)

Gypsy Dream Book (1882)
January 1, 2, 4,6,11,12,20
February 1,17,18
March 14, 16
April 10,17,18
May 7,8
June 17
July 17,21
August 20,21
September 10,18
October 6,
November 6,10
December 6,11,15 (Gypsy Dream Book 1882: 17)

Albertus Magnus; or Egyptian Secrets (n. d., edition ca. 1950)
January 1, 2, 4,6,11,17,18
February 8,16,17
March 1,12, 13,15
April 3,15,17,18
May 8,10,17,30
June 1,7,10
July 1,5,6
August 1,3,18,20
September 15,18,30
October 15,17
November 1,7,11
December 1,7,11 (Albertus Magnus ca. 1880: 132)

L. Lloyd Aldridge. The Secret Book of Black Arts. (1950)
Unlucky Days. A list of unlucky dates for any important event, translated from ancient Astrological writings. Figures in **bold-face** type are supposed to be the most disastrous.
January 1, 2, 4,5,10,**15**,17,**29**
February 8,**10**,**17**,26,27,28
March 16, 17, 20
April 7,8,10,**16**,20,**21**
May 3,6,7,15,20
June **4**,8,10,22
July **15**,**21**
August 1,**19**,**20**,29,30
September 2,4,6,7,21,22
October 4,6,16,24

November 5,6,**15**,20,29,**30**
December **6**,7,**9**,15,22[38]

There is obviously no one true set of dates. There were also lists of particularly lucky or propitious days, but those are less common (and just as varied).

One example of a "fortunate days" list will suffice. This list is from the mid-18th century chapbook, *The High German Fortune-Teller* (ca. 1745, with many reprints), which has short debased versions of a variety of divination techniques aimed at the popular penny pamphlet market.

> Happy Days of each Month, relating to Love and Business
> On January 6, 9, 25,
> The work you undertake will surely thrive,
> February 10, 19, 23,
> If love you take in hand it will agree.
> The first of March is lucky held by all,
> And April's 12th and 18th so we call.
> May's 4th, 14th, and 21st are sure
> To bring prosperity that will endure.
> June's 19th, and 21st, and 4,
> Do proper business, and secure your store.
> If that you love you quickly would obtain,
> Begin in July, in dog star's reign.
> August the 5th and 6th are likewise good,
> If then you court you will be understood.
> September's 4th, 18th, and 28th.
> October's 3d and 6th, and 10th create
> Such good beginnings as do give us bliss.
> November's 9th and 12th bring happiness.
> December's 4th, 8th, 13th, and the day
> Our Lord was born, reckon we may.
> The rest are most indifferent,
> and some we find to be malevolent. (High German fortune-teller 1810: 20)

A related system of divination by lot or *sortes* was the "Books of Fate". These books had answers to a prescribed series of questions, very much like those of the Sphere of Pythagoras but with a different method of arriving at an appropriate answer. The earliest surviving example of this divinatory system is the "Oracles of Astrampychus". A Christianized version written in Greek from the second century CE is available in a modern English translation by Randall Stewart and Kenneth Morrell. The author's name is apparently a pseudonym, and the other names of course had nothing to do with the work. This sort of pseudepigraphical or fictional attribution and authorship is common to most such books. Astrampsychus or Astrampsychos was also credited with a Byzantine "oneirocriticon" or book of dream interpretation.

> "The oracle is made up of an introduction, a list of ninety-two questions numbered 12 – 203, a table of correspondences, and 1,030 responses divided into decades, or groups of ten. The introduction takes the form of a letter allegedly written by Astrampychus of Egypt to King Ptolemy in which the former declares he is sending the book to the latter. The book, he declares, is the work of Pythagoras and was used by Alexander the Great, who owes to it his success as ruler of the world…
> The book is used in the following way. A customer selected one of the ninety-two questions from the list … The vendor then told the questioner to pick a number between 1 and 10, assuring him that god would put the number in his mouth. Let us suppose he chose 91 ("Have I been poisoned?") and god placed the number 3 in his mind. The vendor added these two numbers together and located the sum (94) in the table of correspondences. The number next to it (in this case 29)

---

[38] L. Lloyd Aldridge. *The Secret Book of Black Arts*. Toronto: Metropolitan Publishing Co., ca. 1950, p. 28.

indicated the decade of answers in which the responses should be sought. Locating decade 29 in the bookroll of responses, the oracle monger now looked down the list of responses until he reached the number the questioner had originally picked at random (in this case, 3). Response number 3 in decade number 29 read: "You have not been poisoned. Do not be distressed." The ninety-two questions deal with topics of a personal nature—romance, money, travel, health, and job—focusing generally upon themes of fortune-telling that remain familiar to us today."[39]

There were ten possible answers to each question, with a balance between positive and negative responses. An examination of the books revealed that, to baffle and impress the client, the responses were shuffled (which was corrected for by the correspondences even if that appeared to be another level of chance) and because of the numbering scheme, 110 answers were "dummies" that could not be accessed through the oracle. "The overall result was a book that was easy to use but difficult to fathom, and this must have been [the author's] intent."

Books of fate derived from Arabic sources appeared in the Middle Ages, but their kinship with Astrampychus is clear enough. A 12th century medieval example described by T. C. Skeat had 12 questions and 144 answers. The querent selected one of the questions to ask, and taking its number, for example 5, then threw dice to get a second number, say 10. He then referred to a table with twelve columns and twelve rows of short answer texts (rather like fortune cookie lines, but more serious), counted across the columns to the fifth column, and then counted off 10 more columns (inclusive of the fifth), and arriving at the twelfth or last column, goes back to the beginning and ends up at the second column. He then counts down eight rows to arrive at the cell containing the correct answer. As Skeat observes, "… the hall-mark of [the Book of Fate] is the apparently miraculous manner in which the inquirer, pursuing his way through a labyrinth of jumbled answers, finally arrives at one appropriate to the question asked".[40]

The best early published example of these books is "Jean de Meun's" *The Dodechedron of Fortune, translated from the 1556 French edition by "Sir W. B. Knight"* (both names being pseudonyms) in 1613 for revealing fortunes based on a roll of a twelve-sided die. The twelve sections (divided by the twelve celestial houses "according to Astrologie" and covering appropriate topics for each house) have twelve "demaundes" or questions, making 144 in all. Every question has a dozen possible answers in rhyming couplets, totaling 1728 in all. Directions are given for constructing the "dodechedron" die, with even numbers on one set of faces and odd ones on the other. The querent, on selecting one of the questions, notes the number of its "house" and then the number of the particular question. Consulting the 12x12 table of numbers, one locates the correct "house" number (in Roman numerals), which run diagonally from the upper left to the lower right on the table. The querent places a finger on the house number, then beginning with that cell, count towards the right as many cells as the number of the question indicates. If the end of the row is reached before the number, return to the beginning of the same row and continue until the correct number of cells have been covered, and place the finger there. The die is then thrown and the uppermost number on the die is used to count down the column (starting at the top of the same column if necessary) until the indicated cell is reached. The final cell number indicates which page (or leaf) of the particular series of "house" answers to consult, while the number on the die indicates which of the twelve answers is the correct result. Each page of text has an odd name at the top, about which the comment of the preface is: "And concerning the strange words which are at the top of euery leafe. I know not the meaning nor what langiage they are, hauing found them in the first originall from the Authour, so that I esteeme them inuented words, rather than to signifie any import."

The example the author uses selects the seventh house, "which pretendeth marriages" and the fifth question on that page, which is "Whether there be cause of Iealousie or no." On the table the seventh house row begins on the seventh cell (#79). Counting from this cell towards the right five places, one arrives at the next to last cell or #127. Pointing at this cell, the die is tossed, and comes up "eight".

---

[39] *Anthology of Ancient Greek Popular Literature*. William Hansen, ed. Bloomington, IN: Indiana University Press, 1998, pp 287-88.
[40] T. C. Skeat. "An Early Mediaeval 'Book of Fate'". *Mediaeval and Renaissance Studies*, Vol. III, 1954, p. 54.

Counting down the column eight cells (which requires going to the top and down two), one arrives at cell #122. The querent then refers to page number 122, on which the eight verse is "Be not Ielous nor misdoubt thy wife / For shee shall be true all daies of here life".

The relevant pages are shown below:

VII.	Hadigas.	The 7. House
1	Whether it be good for thee to marie or no.	
2	Whether shall be thy best to marie a maide or a widow.	
3	Whether being married thou shalt continue to loue, or no.	Of Marriages
4	Whether the married couple be loyal the one to the other, or no.	
5	Whether there be cause of ielousie, or no.	
6	Whether the child shal be adduicted to armes and warres, or no.	
7	Whether this yeere there shall be peace or warre.	Of War and combats.
8	Wither the warres begunne shall bee short or long, or cruell and bloodie.	
9	Whether of the two now in controuersie and to fight shall overcome.	
10	Whether it shall be good to buye or sell much now, or now.	}Of traffick.
11	Whether the thing wanting shall bee had againe, or no.	}Of things lost.
12	Whether the sport of hunting or hawking be best for thee.	}Of hunting.

THE TABLE OF THE TWELVE HOVSES

I Natus	I 1	13	25	37	49	61	73	85	97	109	121	133
II Vincit	2	II 14	26	38	50	62	74	86	98	110	122	134
III Fratrem	3	15	III 27	39	51	63	75	87	99	111	123	135
IIII Pater	4	16	28	IIII 40	52	64	76	88	100	112	124	136
V Filium	5	17	29	41	V 53	65	77	89	101	113	125	137
VI Infernus	6	18	30	42	54	VI 66	78	90	102	114	126	138
VII Vxorem	7	19	31	43	55	67	VII 79	91	103	115	127	139

VIII Mors	8	20	32	44	56	68	80	VIII 92	104	116	128	140
IX Ambulat	9	21	33	45	57	69	81	93	IX 105	117	129	141
X Regnat	10	22	34	46	58	70	82	94	106	X 118	130	142
XI Fortuna	11	23	35	47	59	71	83	95	107	119	XI 131	143
XII Incarceratur	12	24	36	48	60	72	84	96	108	120	132	XII 144

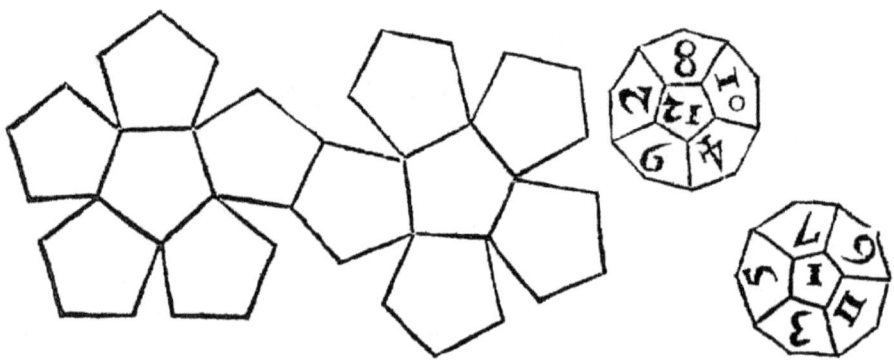

12-sided Dodechedron die.

122	Algarismaris
1	By his good wit, iudgement, and diligence, He shall in briefe get of you acquittance.
2	A better season cannot be had, To begin any thing that's good or bad.
3	If that thy life be religious and right, Thy end shall be honour, and death delight.
4	Be you not dismaide, but be of good cheere, Although it fall out a very ill yeare.
5	Take opportunitie, forstow no time, But follow thy businesse while it is prime.
6	He shall light on such an unluckie place, That he shall be made a slaue very base.
7	Death to all men is bitter and sower. But unto the wicked it is a worse hower.

8	Be not Jealous, nor misdoubt not thy wife,
	For she shall be true all daies of her life.
9	Take kitchin physicke for so he shall mend,
	For the Doctor his drugges are to no end.
10	For all your delights and sports whatsoeuer,
	Follow not the Church not preaching neuer.
11	This house is built strong and substantiall,
	You need not doubt that euer it will fall.
12	This noble prelate, of whom you inquire,
	Is worthy the best setae for his due hire. ("de Menu" 1613: unpaginated)

Another French example called *Pratique Curieuse Ou Les Oracles Des Sibylles* was published by Claude Commiers in 1693 and went through a number of editions in the 18th century. The book contains two systems of divination, each with its own list of questions and method of searching through a complicated maze of numbers numerologically derived from given names of the querent (and his mother), the planet of the day of the week, the age of the moon, and so forth – or by pointing with a finger or a pin (with eyes closed) at a number in a cell in a six by ten table. The answers for the first series of 48 questions are divided among the 12 Sybils, the answers to the second 60 questions among some 60 "gods, godesses, demi-gods and great men" (some of which were collective, such as harpies or muses) of the Roman era. It may have inspired a rather simpler English production called *The Temple of Cythnos* (London, 1778) purportedly "found in the ruins of Pompeji; and now consists in some of the Oracles delivered on the two first days of each Season, a short description, or introduction prefixed to each day, the account of the origin of these Oracles, as above-mentioned, and a story which illustrates the morals conveyed through the whole work."[41] A later edition is entitled *The oracles: or, the secrets of fortune and wisdom laid open. Adapted to the four seasons of life.* (London, 1790) and had the same text.

This book, somewhat more so than the *Pratique Curieuse*, was intended as much for idle entertainment as for serious fortune telling. There is little coverage of serious matters such as theft or success in battle and it was probably of less use to Cunning Folk, but it indicates the growing social acceptance of divination as an elite pastime, including seeking out gypsy "professionals" for palmistry. The questions are however presumably what someone might ask a gypsy or Cunning Man in the late 18th century – inquiries concerned with middle class anxieties about relationships and personal success – that had always been but part of the broader scope of earlier lists of questions. The first "day" in each season is intended for women, the second for men. There is no chart and the method is quite simple – the querent, on choosing a question, just picks a number from one to seven. He or she then turns to the pages of the particular question and reads the numbered "oracle" that consists of two sections, the "Fortune" and the "Wisdom". For example, the table of questions for the Second Day of the Summer (for men) is, with the page numbers for the oracles to consult:

```
FIRST QUESTION
Whether he is to be happy in wedlock?                          55, 56
SECOND QUESTION
Whether he is to preserve the affection of his wife?           57, 58
THIRD QUESTION
Whether his children will profit by their education?           59, 60
```

---

[41] *The Temple of Cythnos, or the oracles of fortune and wisdom, for the four seasons of life. Translated from the Greek* (London: N. Conant, 1778), p. v.

FOURTH QUESTION
What is that which interferes with his happiness?   61, 62
FIFTH QUESTION
Whether he can rely upon his friend?   63, 64
SIXTH QUESTION
Whether he shall get the better of his enemies?   65, 66
SEVENTH QUESTION
Whether he is to attain the end of his particular pursuit?   67, 68

The table of questions for the First Day of Winter (for women) is:
FIRST QUESTION
Whether she is to meet with any happy moment in her present stage of life?   106, 107
SECOND QUESTION
What passion is still alive in her heart?   108, 109
THIRD QUESTION
Whether she can rely on those who attend her?   110, 111
FOURTH QUESTION
Whether she has well settled her account with the world and herself?   112, 13
FIFTH QUESTION
Whether she is to surmount the terrors of death?   114, 115
SIXTH QUESTION
Whether she is to be regretted by her friends?   116, 117
SEVENTH QUESTION
Whether her memory shall be held in honour, or doomed to oblivion?   118, 119

From the first list, we might choose to ask the third question about the actual value of the education one's children received, which is still a concern today. Then we are directed to the responses on pages 59 and 60:

THIRD QUESTION
Whether his children will profit by their education?

The Oracles of FORTUNE and WISDOM.

ORACLE I.
FORTUNE.
As he over-rates their abilities, they will hardly repay his troubles, much less answer his expectations.
WISDOM.
The cultivation raises the tree, but it is Nature that gives the fruit its agreeable flavour.

ORACLE II.
FORTUNE.
His preponderous applause will spoil their good dispositions, by making them overbearing and proud.
WISDOM.
And ignorant too: for there is no making any progress in learning without a becoming modesty.

ORACLE III.
FORTUNE.
By neglecting to give them the varnish of politeness, he will render them unfit for society.
WISDOM.
Civility may be called a varnish, but true politeness is that benevolent disposition of the mind which attracts esteem and love.

ORACLE IV.
FORTUNE.
His ambition of seeing them rise in the world will be satisfied, but I cannot secure them against a fall.
WISDOM.
That fall is almost certain, if he has not minded their morals; for honest men are the only ones who stand upon firm ground.

ORACLE V.
FORTUNE.
His perpetual solicitude and extensive cares for their education will be fully rewarded.
WISDOM.
He will then deserve the name of father, and the glorious appellation of an excellent citizen.

ORACLE VI.
FORTUNE.
The giddiness of youth baffles all his cares, although they are not wanting in good dispositions.
WISDOM.
In that case, let him trust them to reason and experience, the two teachers that Nature has lighted to show man his paths.

ORACLE VII.
FORTUNE.
He runs a risk of seeing his hope disappointed, for not having considered that the mind of youths must not be turned contrary to its natural bent.
WISDOM.
Shall a father be less careful than a gardner, who so minutely adapts cultivation to Nature?

Most of the answers are cautionary and negative in tone. Only if the selected number was 5 will a happy outcome be seen as a sure thing. This illustrates the different tone of the oracles of the 18th century from their modern equivalents, where positive answers are more common and generally to be expected.

Let us now turn to the female side of the picture, and see what the Oracles provide for a woman who chooses the seventh question from the second list dealing with permanent reputation and public esteem, even celebrity status – a concern today more commonly felt about one's living reputation rather than posthumous fame. The unpredictability of early death made this a matter of greater concern than we are familiar with today:

SEVENTH QUESTION
Whether her memory shall be held in honour, or doomed to oblivion?

The Oracles of FORTUNE and WISDOM.
ORACLE I.
FORTUNE.
Her name will not be easily forgotten by the multitude who resort to places of dissipation and idleness; but hardly remembered in those assemblies where Wisdom presides.
WISDOM.
A no less precarious than inglorious fame is that which is acquired under the banner of Folly, whose whims are as mutable as the decrees of Wisdom are permanent.

ORACLE II.
FORTUNE.
Her excellent qualifications are not calculated for making a lasting impression on the mind of the unthinking men.
WISDOM.
There is a nobler reward for modest and amiable virtues than the weak breath of human praise.

ORACLE III.
FORTUNE.
Had she always kept in view that immortality for which she now seems so anxious, it would have been an easy matter for her to attain it.
WISDOM.
It cannot be a dull and groveling soul who wishes for an honourable fame; and therefore it is yet in her power to deserve it.

ORACLE IV.
FORTUNE.
As long as virtue and goodness shall be remembered among mankind, her name cannot be forgotten.
WISDOM.
She may, at least, rely on the interested rule of society which prescribes to stigmatize, the wicked and to exhalt the just.

ORACLE V.
FORTUNE.
Posterity will blush for the present inconsiderate generation, who has suffered her to live in obscurity notwithstanding her acknowledged merit.
WISDOM.
To enjoy solitude, and be certain of celebrity, are two of the shares of happiness, which so seldom go together, that the person favoured with both, is not to be pitied.

ORACLE VI.
FORTUNE.
Her faults and her virtues will be equally remembered and accurately weighed against each other; therefore with a little consideration she may unravel her fate.
WISDOM.
Let her disregard the world, who, at best, is but a severe judge; and turn to the gods, who are pleased to throw mercy into the unfavourable side of the scales.

ORACLE VII.
FORTUNE.
Through the simplicity of her life she has been so little noticed by the world, that she cannot expect that any one should remember her existence.
WISDOM.
The sweet violet is often disregarded by men as a mere weed, though its fragrance raises it to the honour of adorning the shrines of the gods. (*The Oracles* 1790: 54,105, 59-60,118-119)

The most influential and popular oracular book of fate in the 19th century was *The Book of Fate, formerly in the possession of Napoleon*, by "H. Kirchenhoffer", first published in 1822. This elaborate production was allegedly obtained from an ancient Egyptian manuscript discovered by Charles Sigisbert Sonnini (1751-1812) while on the Emperor Napoleon's service in Egypt in 1801, and translated from a German version by Herman Kirchenhoffer. However, no German editions of the book appear to exist before 1822 and nothing has ever been uncovered about its hypothetical translator, so it seems that this was yet another occult pseudepigrapha. A facsimile of the first edition was published in 1927 by the Personal Arts Co., and a modern edition by Richard Deacon (with a Victorian-like mass of quasi-historical filler) in 1976.

A large fold-out chart with a table of 32 by 32 cells with "hieroglyphs" or ideograms in each indicated which series of responses was appropriate for the 32 provided questions (below). In addition, each column is headed with a geomantic-like figure of stars or asterisks, but where ordinary geomantic figures are "tetragrams" with four rows of stars; these are "pentagrams", having five rows in order to have enough figures to accommodate 32 questions, with no geomantic values, although earlier five-line geomancy did exist, as found in commentaries about Dante. The ideograms in the table are also not actual Egyptian hieroglyphs, but the sort of images that had passed for hieroglyphs in European culture for centuries, especially following the rediscovery of Horapollo's *Hieroglyphica* in the early 15th century. Europeans believed that the hieroglyphs were images that spoke directly from the page to the mind of the informed reader, without the mediation of actual words or phrases; natural rather than conventional signs that transcended language altogether. This resulted in an imaginary (as far as real hieroglyphs were concerned) but highly creative fascination with pictographic signs that would in time produce wonderful emblem books and influence 19th century beliefs about tarot cards. In this context, however, the little pictures are just decorative markers as are the five-row pseudo-geometric figures, and have no signification in the results of the oracle. The method of consulting the oracle is also based loosely on geomancy, with a lot of ritual complications.

1. *Inform me of any or of all particulars of the Woman I shall **Marry**.*
2. *Will the **Prisoner** be released or continue Captive?*
3. *Shall I live to an **Old Age**?*
4. *Shall I have to **travel** by Sea or Land or to reside in foreign Climes.*
5. *Shall I be involved in **Litigation &** if so, shall I gain my Cause?*
6. *Shall I make, or mar, my Fortune by **Gambling**?*
7. *Shall I ever be able to retire from Business with a **Fortune**?*
8. *Shall I be eminent and meet with **Preferment** in my Pursuits?*
9. *Shall I be **Successful** in my present undertaking?*
10. *Shall I ever inherit **Testamentary** property?*
11. *Shall I spent this year **Happier** than the last?*
12. *Will my Name be **Immortalised** & will posterity applaud it?*
13. *Will the **Friend** I most reckon upon prove faithful or **treacherous**?*
14. *Will the stolen **Property** be **recovered** & will the **Thief** be detected?*
15. *What is the aspect of the **Seasons** & what **Political** changes are to take place*
16. *Will the **Stranger** return from abroad?*
17. *Will my **Beloved** prove true in my absence?*
18. *Will the **Marriage** about to take place be happy & prosperous?*
19. *After my Death will my **Children** be virtuous & happy?*
20. *Shall I ever recover from my present **Misfortune**?*
21. *Does my **Dream** portend good luck or Misfortune?*
22. *Will it be my lot to experience **Vicissitudes** in this Life?*
23. *Will my reputation be at all, or much affected by **Calumny**?*
24. *Inform me of all particulars relating to my future **Husband**?*
25. *Shall the **Patient** recover from the Illness?*
26. *Does the person I love, **Love** and regard me?*
27. *Shall my intended **Journey** be prosperous or unlucky?*
28. *Shall I ever find a **Treasure**?*
29. *What **Trade** or **Profession** ought I to follow?*
30. *Have I any or many **Enemies**?*
31. *Art **Absent Friends** in good health & what is their present employment*
32. *Shall my Wife have a **Son** or a **Daughter**? (Kirchenhoffer 1835: folding plate, frontispiece)*

There is a fair amount of filler in the book, including a fictional account of the alleged manuscript's discovery, its translation (with the help of an ancient Copt or Egyptian Christian who knew the secret behind the hieroglyphs in which the original papyrus was written) into German rather than French for some reason, the oracle's use by Napoleon and its eventual recovery after he lost it following the disastrous battle at Leipzig. This is followed by a potted history of ancient oracles and an account of the *Book of Fate's* ostensible authorship by one "Balaspis" at the command of Hermes Trismegistus, and finally, actual directions for its use. The original footnotes, indicated by numbered asterisks and dagger glyphs, are appended at the end of the selection:

HOW THE ENQUIRER SHALL OBTAIN A TRUE ANSWER TO THE QUESTION WHICH HE PUTTETH TO THE ORACLE.

When a man or woman doth come to enquire ought of you, O Priests! let the gifts be made and the sacrifices offered up; and let the invocations of the servants of the temple be chaunted.

When silence hath been restored, the DIVINER shall direct the stranger who hath come to enquire of the ORACLE, to trace, with a reed dipped in the blood of the sacrifice, in the midst of a circle containing the twelve SIGNS OF THE ZODIAC, * five rows of upright or inclined lines, in the manner following | | | | | | | | | | | | | | , taking care that each be readily seen to contain more than twelve lines, in respect of the number of the SIGNS OF THE ZODIAC, but he must by no means do this studiously, or count the number he hath marked, but guide the reed quickly, so that the number, while it be more than twelve, shall be entirely of chance, as far as he knoweth.

The DIVINER shall now reckon from the left unto the right hand line of each row, which the enquirer hath written, marking off twelve, thus : | | | | | | | | | | | | , | | | and keeping count of the remainder, so that he may know whether the remaining number of each be *odd* or *even*.

If the number of a row be odd, the DIVINER shall attach to the right hand side thereof one small star, and if it be even, he shall attach two stars; and in the same manner with the other rows, as herein set down;—

| | | | | | | | | | | | , | | | * (odd)
| | | | | | | | | | | | , | | ** (even)
| | | | | | | | | | | | , | | | | * (odd)
| | | | | | | | | | | | , | | ** (even)
| | | | | | | | | | | | , | | | | * (odd)

This double column of stars shall be, to the DIVINER, for a SIGN whereby he shall be enabled to discover the fate of the ENQUIRER.

Let the ENQUIRER now consult his own breast what he requireth to know; and whether the matter cometh within compass of the question herein writ, and set down in order, as followeth. *2—If it doth, the Enquirer shall straightway pronounce the question, audibly as it is written, without adding to, or diminishing therefrom, and shall while he uttereth the words, point to the number of the questions with the forefinger of his *left* hand.

The DIVINER, in his proper vestments, having invoked OSIRIS, shall now place the forefinger of his *right* hand on the spot whereon the ENQUIRER had previously placed the same finger of his left: he shall then search out among the SIGNS, or columns of stars, placed above the hieroglyphics, for that *individual* SIGN, or column, which shall answer in every respect to the one which hath been cast up, by the addition of the lines previously traced by the ENQUIRER.

When the DIVINER hath found the corresponding SIGN, or column of stars, he must place thereon the forefinger of his *left* hand; he shall now move this finger, and likewise the same finger of the right hand, from the points whereon they have been placed, so that they may approximate, or meet each other, at right angles.

The HIEROGLYPHIC whereat the fingers meet, must now be noted; and the DIVINER, having looked into the roll, is therein to search out the *counterpart* of the same HIEROGLYPHIC.

Having found it, he is to search further on the left hand side of the matter, or answers, appended unto this hieroglyphic for the counterpart of the SIGN, or column of stars, which, in the commencement of the consultation, had incidentally, OR BY THE ORDINATION OF FATE, been produced by the enumeration of the surplus over twelve, of the lines traced by the ENQUIRER within the circle.

The words attached to the SIGN, or column of stars, will be the just and true answer to the question put; which see no one do pervert to any false purpose of deceit, enmity or wickedness.

No further ceremony now remaineth, but that the PRIEST who hath acted in the divination, do write down the answer truly, and, with his finger placed upon his lips, hand it unto the PROPHET or PROPHETESS, who shall in a loud voice proclaim its contents unto the person who came to enquire.†

In conclusion, I am commanded to write unto you, that it is the duty of the PRIESTS to instruct all those who consult the ORACLE, that it behoveth them to be contented with whatever ANSWER, they may through FATE receive; and to follow implicitly, and without reservation, whatever the ORACLE, in its Answers, may happen to dictate. If the instructions of HERMES be not obeyed, what booteth it to enquire?—If the CONSULTER be herein disobedient to the will of OSIRIS, the evil be upon his own head.

Further, O PRIESTS! be warned to make no divination, nor to admit of any gift, sacrifice or consultation, save during the night season, and that too, only whilst Isis shineth in the fulness of her beauty. *3 Neither shall ye give Answers on those days or nights in which either OSIRIS who ruleth the heavens by day, or the Queen of his love, who ruleth by night, do veil the comeliness and majesty of their countenances from the eyes of mortals, and whilst they do retire from the labours of their celestial course, within the chambers of their sanctuary of rest. †2

These are the words which I, BALASPIS, have been commanded, by my great master HERMES TRISMEGISTUS, to write unto you, O PRIESTS OF THEBAIS.

* The translator feels it incumbent on him, here to notice (from the experience of himself and others in consulting the Oracle,) that he considers some of the above mentioned formalities may, on most occasions, be dispensed with. He has found that for all *ordinary* consultations the circle and signs may be omitted; and instead of a reed dipped in blood, he and his friends have, invariably and without the least detriment, used a *pen* dipped in *common ink*. As to the gifts, sacrifices, and invocations, he considers them in a Christian land to be entirely superfluous; but in their stead it is doubtless requisite that the consulter should have a firm reliance on the goodness and providence of the Creator of all things.
*(2) See the Frontispiece [the table of 32x32 ideograms], containing the questions, their hieroglyphics and signs.
† In order to make the English reader, as much as possible, acquainted with the proper mode of finding answers to the questions of those who consult the Oracle, it be will necessary here to state one example. I shall take the same rows of lines, and the same SIGN, or double column of stars, as are set down in the original instructions for consultation, as above. We shall suppose, then, that the QUESTION asked is No. 27, as marked in the Frontispiece or TABLE, viz: *Shall my intended journey be prosperous or unlucky?*
By looking at the column of stars, or SIGN, corresponding with that *cast up* we shall find it numbered 20, and the consequent HIEROGLYPHIC produced by the combination of this SIGN and the QUESTION asked, will be that of the CROSS BONES.
Now by reference to this HIEROGLYPHIC and its subservient SIGN, or column of stars, in the Book of Fate, (folio 14) we find that the ANSWER given by the Oracle is "When thou hast arrived at thy place of destination, lose no time in executing thy errand, and return without delay," which ANSWER, whilst it suggests a necessary caution, whereby evil or danger is avoided, perfectly corresponds with the QUESTION asked.

In a similar way, appropriate ANSWERS will be given to all the other QUESTIONS in the TABLE; that is, by paying attention to their particular HIEROGLYPHICS and SIGNS.

N. B. The Translator considers it proper to state, that in order to facilitate the search for the Hieroglyphic (resulting from the combination of the QUESTION and SIGN,) in the BOOK OF FATE, it will be necessary for the CONSULTER to cast his eye over the highest line of Hieroglyphics in the FRONTISPIECE, and to note the NUMBER which lies immediately *over it*. This number will be found to correspond with that folio of the BOOK OF FATE, over which presides the Hieroglyphic in question.

*(3) I presume that here the meaning of BALASPIS, is, that the Oracle should not be consulted but when the MOON is at the full. Among the ancient Egyptians ISIS typified the Moon, whilst the name of OSIRIS was always given to the Sun.

†(2) By this mode of expression, it is evident that eclipses of the SUN and MOON are meant; But it is necessary to notice, that, as far as the experience of the translator and his friends has enabled them to judge, there is no apparent reason or necessity for confining the consultation of the Oracle to any particular tune or season. One thing, however, the Consulter should be aware of, which is, that it would be improper for him to ask *two* questions on the same day; or even to ask the *same* questions, with reference to the same subject, twice within one calendar month. (Kirchenhoffer 1835: xxviii-xxxi)

In simpler terms, the enquirer or querent first draws five rows of perpendicular lines without conscious deliberation or counting, as is standard in geomancy, with a minimum of 13 for each. The diviner (or Cunning Man) checks to see how many lines *more* than 12 there are, and notes whether these totals are even and odd in number, thereby obtaining the correct pseudo-geomantic sign.

The diviner has the querent point with the left forefinger to the question on the printed table that he or she wants to ask. The diviner then puts his own right forefinger on that question, and locating the specific sign at the top of the columns, selects the column with his left forefinger. He moves both fingers to the cell where row and column meet, and notes its particular ideogram. He then turns to the pages of answers, finds the 32 answers headed by that ideogram and selects the answer indicated by the original pseudo-geomantic sign.

It would be interesting to know who the actual author of *Napoleon's Book of Fate* was, as it is impressively imaginative in its hieroglyphical table and historical inventions. The questions and answers, however, are standard "wheel of fortune" material, and one wonders how they could have been of much use to Napoleon, if he actually had owned it. The former emperor had conveniently died the previous year. Sonnini, like Napoleon, was a real person and had been in Egypt, but had no perceivable connection with the "Book of Fate" (which was recognized as a modern production at the time it was published). Bonaparte's notoriety had resulted in astrological publications featuring his supposed nativity and the fate of Europe. In 1822, astrologer Robert Cross Smith (Raphael) and professional "Aeronaut" or balloonist George W. Graham (G. W. G.) published a manual of geomancy and astrology called *The Philosophical Merlin*. Both *The Philosophical Merlin* and *The Book of Fate*, it was claimed, had been Napoleon's, and each was acquired by a German officer after the disastrous Battle of Leipzig in October 1813. By its style, Smith would seem a likely candidate for authorship of the *Book of Fate* if he hadn't published his own versions of the book of fate in *Raphael's Witch!!! or the Oracle of the Future*, (including a "Mystical Wheel of Pythagoras", London, 1831), and *The Royal Book of Fate. Queen Elizabeth's Oracle; From an Illuminated Manuscript, Found in the Library of the Unfortunate Earl of Essex...* (London, 1832), which has tables for 64 questions, using "geomantic" figures with *six* rows of asterisks. Smith was never shy about crediting himself, or rather his pseudonym with all of his productions, and it appears that he borrowed some ideas from "Kirchenhoffer" for his own titles. He was also prone to "discovering" ancient manuscripts (printed sources being equally likely), including some in the collections of miniature artist Richard Cosway and bookseller John Denley.

Under variations in title, such as *Napoleon's Oraculum, Napoleon's Book of Fate, &c.*, "Kirchenhoffer's" work went through a great many editions in English, Spanish and even a Welsh translation. A simplified version turns up in a number of cheap fortune telling books, such as *The Unerring Fortune-Teller, containing the celebrated Oracle of Human Destiny, or Book of Fate* (New York, 1866). The *Unerring Fortune-Teller* was a compilation of divinatory and occult resources, the urban descendant of the *Book of Knowledge* and the *Shepherd's Kalendar*. In the "Oraculum" section, there are only 16 questions, so it was possible to use the traditional four-row geomantic figures rather than the unusual five-row ones as in "Kirchenhoffer". There is nothing geomantic about the oracle, so the ancient figures simply add to its "mysterious" nature.

NAPOLEON'S ORACULUM; OR, THE BOOK OF FATE.
The Oraculum is gifted with every requisite variety of response to the following questions:

1. Shall I obtain my wish?
2. Shall I have success in my undertakings?
3. Shall I gain or lose in my cause?
4. Shall I have to live in foreign parts?
5. Will the stranger return?
6. Shall I recover my property?
7. Will my friend be true?
8. Shall I have to travel?
9. Does the person love and regard me?
10. Will the marriage be profitable?
11. What sort of a wife, or husband, shall I have?
12. Will she have a son or a daughter?
13. Will the patient recover?
14. Will the prisoner be released?
15. Shall I be lucky or unlucky?
16. What does my dream signify?

HOW TO WORK THE ORACULUM

Make marks in four lines, one under another, in the following manner; making more or less in each line, according to your fancy.

```
*   *   *   *   *   *   *   *   *
*   *   *   *   *   *   *   *   *   *
*   *   *   *   *   *   *   *   *   *   *
*   *   *   *   *   *   *   *   *   *   *   *
```

Then reckon the number of marks in each line, and, if it be odd, mark down one dot; if even, two dots. If there be more than nine marks, reckon the surplus over that number only, viz.:—
The number of marks in the first line of the foregoing is odd;

therefore make one mark, thus	*
In the second, even, so make two thus	**
In the third, odd again, make one mark only	*
In the fourth, even again two marks	**

TO OBTAIN THE ANSWER

You must refer to the Oraculum, at the top of which you will find a row of dots similar to those you have produced, and a column of figures corresponding with those prefixed to the questions: guide your eye down the column at the top of which you find the dots resembling your own, till you come to the letter on a line with the number of the question your are trying, then refer to the page having that letter at the top, and, on a line with the dots which are similar to your own, you will find your answer.

The following are unlucky days on which none of the questions should be worked, or any enterprise undertaken: Jan. 1, 2, 4, 6,10, 20, 22; Feb. 6, 17, 28; Mar. 24, 26; April 10, 27, 28; May 7, 8; June 27; July 20, 22; Aug. 20, 22; Sept. 5, 30; Oct. 6; Nov. 3, 29; Dec. 6, 10, 15.
*** It is not right to try a question twice in one day.

ORACULUM

QUESTIONS.	* * * *	** * ** *	* ** * *	** * * **	** ** ** *	** ** * **	** * * *	** ** ** *	* * * **	* * ** **	** ** * *	* ** ** **	* ** ** *	* * ** *	* ** * **	** ** ** **
1. Shall I obtain my wish?	A	B	C	D	E	F	G	H	I	K	L	M	N	O	P	Q
2. Shall I have success in my undertakings?	B	C	D	E	F	G	H	I	K	L	M	N	O	P	Q	A
3. Shall I gain or lose in my cause?	C	D	E	F	G	H	I	K	L	M	N	O	P	Q	A	B
4. Shall I have to live in foreign parts?	D	E	F	G	H	I	K	L	M	N	O	P	Q	A	B	C
5. Will the stranger return?	E	F	G	H	I	K	L	M	N	O	P	Q	A	B	C	D
6. Shall I recover my property?	F	G	H	I	K	L	M	N	O	P	Q	A	B	C	D	E
7. Will my friend be true?	G	H	I	K	L	M	N	O	P	Q	A	B	C	D	E	F
8. Shall I have to travel?	H	I	K	L	M	N	O	P	Q	A	B	C	D	E	F	G
9. Does the person love and regard me?	I	K	L	M	N	O	P	Q	A	B	C	D	E	F	G	H
10. Will the marriage be prosperous?	K	L	M	N	O	P	Q	A	B	C	D	E	F	G	H	I
11. What sort of a wife, or husband, shall I have?	L	M	N	O	P	Q	A	B	C	D	E	F	G	H	I	K
12. Will she have a son or a daughter?	M	N	O	P	Q	A	B	C	D	E	F	G	H	I	K	L
13. Will the patient recover?	N	O	P	Q	A	B	C	D	E	F	G	H	I	K	L	M
14. Will the prisoner be released?	O	P	Q	A	B	C	D	E	F	G	H	I	K	L	M	N
15. Shall I be lucky or unlucky?	P	Q	A	B	C	D	E	F	G	H	I	K	L	M	N	O
16. What does my dream signify?	Q	A	B	C	D	E	F	G	H	I	K	L	M	N	O	P

The answers are all simple and direct, and their location is fairly easily worked out. If the querent selected the sixth question, "Shall I recover my property?" and came up with the figure for the seventh column, the answer on page "M" is "You will find your property at a certain time". If the question was the ninth, "Does the person love and regard me?" and the figure in the tenth column, the answer on page "A" is "You had better decline this love, for it is neither constant nor true." This version also appears up in *The Gipsy Dream Book and Fortune Teller* (New York, 1882 and Philadelphia, n. d.) and *The Witches Dream Book and Fortune Teller* (Baltimore, 1909 and 1913), where although some of the questions are modified – "Does the person love me?, "Will the marriage be happy?" or "Have a son or a daughter?" – the rest of the contents are identical. Another version of the oracle can be found in *Napoleon's Lucky Dream Book: A Book of Fate* (Philadelphia, 1858) with the same 32 questions, although the five-row pseudo-geomantic figures are turned on their sides (probably for ease in printing).

Raphael's Witch!!! (the exclamation points are part of the actual title) deserves some mention. Accompanied with two elegant lithographed fold-out tables (Cross understood the attraction of illustrations in popular publications) and ten coloured plates by Robert Cruikshank, the book offered 30 questions and 900 answers divided into lists headed by the letters of the alphabet (26 in capitals and four in lower case), which were in turn identified by the symbols of the zodiac, the planets and astrological aspects. To arrive at an answer, the querent made a four-row geomantic type of figure, that added all of the strokes together to get a number (the example has lines of ten, nine, eight and eleven to a total of 37). The next step was to find a numerical value of the first letter of the querent's name ("G" in the example, with a value of 21) on the first table called the "Mystical Wheel of Pythagoras" although it is nothing more than an illustrated circle with numbers assigned to the letters of the alphabet (A 4, B 6, C 26, D 18, E 12, F 4, G 21, H 28, I or J 11, K 16, L 12, M 19, N 11, O 6, P 12, Q 17, R 12, S 4, T 6 [sic], U or V 9, W 18, X 13, Y 2, Z 3). The querent then finds the "age of the moon" for the day the question is asked from charts for the years 1831 and 1832 (presumably an almanac could be consulted for later years) which is 19 in the example (January 1st or 31st, March 2nd, &c. for 1831). The three numbers add up to 77. Taking away 30 twice, the remainder of 17 indicates the number of the oracle.

A pair of alphabetical tables are then consulted, using the number of one of the thirty questions to find the row (15 in the example: "What shall be the asker's *fortune in marriage*, if a male?"), and 17 to find the column. The appropriate cell has a capital "A" in it, and there is also the astrological sign for Mercury under the "17". The querent now turns to the pages of answers headed "A", and finds the answer denoted with Mercury's sign, for the answer: "The asker will marry a prudent and clever female, a stranger from the west, dark but comely, and a female thou will love." Raphael also provides a slightly simpler method of working the oracle with a 5x6 table of numbers instead of the drawn figure where the querent is to arbitrarily choose a number which is then added to the value for the querent's initial and the moon's age. The second folded table has the list of 30 questions and another table with numerical values for the "cabalistic alphabet" (A 1, B 2, C 3, D 4, E 5, F 6, G 7, H 8, I + J 9, K 10, L 20, M 30, N 40, O 50, P 60, Q 70, R 80, S 90, T 100, V 700, U 200, W 1400, X 300, Y 400, Z 500) which is used for numerological work later in the book. There is also a variety of other systems, formulas and stories to fill the pages. These various procedures could be used by the ordinary reader, but they were also useful for Cunning Folk in their work. Ronald Hutton notes that Clayton Chaffer, a 19th century fortune teller and herbalist of Duckinfield near Manchester, had "a paper entitled Raphael's Witch or Oracle of the Future surrounded by an engraved border representing warlocks and witches in a dance" pasted on his wall. This was probably the first folding table, although dancing witches only occupy the lower right hand corner of the lithograph. (Hutton 1999: 89)

The remaining method of divination by sortes to be considered in this chapter is a version of cartomancy or fortune telling by playing cards. Although there are possible references to this art in England as far back as the mid-16th century, though probably not in the modern way where each card has some ascribed meaning (Melton 1975: 42), I have not located a text explaining the modern process in English earlier than 1729 (with gratitude to Mary K. Greer's superb "Tarot Blog"[42]) and it is the one described as being a *new* method: Dr. Flamstead's and Mr. Patridge's *New Fortune-Book containing . . . Their new-invented method of knowing one's fortune by a pack of cards* (London, ca. 1730)[43] in which all of the answers deal with romance. However, a much older method of using cards as a tool for casting sortes or lots appeared in a book by Francesco Marcolini of Forli in 1540, with a second edition in 1550. Entitled *Le sorti intitolate giardino d'i pensier*, it was "a large and elaborately illustrated volume for consulting the oracle by using a pack of playing cards"[44]. Marcolini lists 50 questions, 13 for men, 13 for women and 24 for both genders. To each question he has 90 answers written in rhymed triplets, 4,500 in all. The method involves drawing cards three times (a pair is chosen to begin) between selecting the question and arriving at the answer. The querent uses a pack of cards consisting of only aces, deuces, 7s through 10s and the three court cards. After choosing the question, the querent went to the appropriate "Allegory of Human Quality or Defect" that corresponded to the question and drew a pair of cards. He or she then consulted an "Allegory of Abstract Principle" that the first "Allegory" assigned to that particular pair of cards

---

[42] http://marygreer.wordpress.com/2010/01/18/oldest-cartomancy-meanings-in-english/
[43] *Dr. Flamstead's and Mr. Patridge's New Fortune-Book containing . . . Their new-invented method of knowing one's fortune by a pack of cards*. London : printed for A. Bettesworth and C. Hitch; R. Ware; and J. Hodges, [1730?]
[44] M. G. Kendall. "Studies in the History of Probability and Statistics. XII. The Book of Fate", *Biometrika*, Vol. 48, No. 1/2, p. 221.

(order of the draw usually did not matter). These were shown in pictorial lists of all possibilities associated with the indicated principle. They then drew a third card and followed the instructions that the second "Allegory" had for *that* card, proceeding then to a "Philosopher" (Socrates, Zeno, Plato, Heraclitus &c.) assigned to the third card to draw a last specified type of card, taking note of a second "fixed" card assigned to it by the "Abstract Principle" The answer was the three-line verse associated to this last pair of cards on the appropriate "Philosopher's" page.

Although this book was never available in English, it may have influenced the first known pack of English playing cards especially published for divination (52 plus two with instructions) by Dormann Newman in 1690. The designs later became the property of John Lenthall, who published his first edition in 1711. A facsimile deck by Harry Margary of Lympne Castle, Kent was published from the 3rd Lenthall edition of 1714 in 1972, and it is from those we take our example:

The Use of the Cards

When any Person is desirous to try their Fortune, let them go to one of the four Kings and chuse what Question they please, and carry in their mind the Number and Word set down before the Question, and let them go to that Sphere marked with the same Word and Number, then let them draw a Card after they have been shuffled, and remember the Number drawn on the Knave standing for Eleven and the Queen for Twelve, and the King for Thirteen then look in the lower Ring of the Sphere for the same Number you have drawn and above that Number you will find a Word and Number, then go to the Queens and Knaves, for the Book under which you will find the same Word and Number set down look into that Book and it shall send you to that Card that hath the very same Word and Number, then look on the Line that answers that Number drawn, and you shall read your answer.

EXAMPLE

Suppose you take the Question which demands whether the party is beloved or / not : Over that Question You will find the Letter or Word A. and Figure 1, which signifies that you must go to that Sphere marked with the same Letter A and Figure 1. Then lay that Sphere on the Table. Then draw any Card out of the Pack after they are well shuffled, observe the Number which that Card bears. Let us suppose a nine of Clubs, then look for Figure in the lower Ring of the Sphere, and above that Number in the two other Rings you will find (falls 29.) then look among the Books supported by the Queen and Knave for that which is denoted by the same Word and Number, which you will find in Hens [hence?-] on the Knave of Clubs, look in that Book in which you will find Europea and Number 50, which shews that you must go to the Sybile Europea and Number 50, then read that Line marked with the same Number with the Card you draw, which as supposed was the 9 of Clubs, and there you will find your Answer, thus.

The Stars foretell, they love you so well.

Sold by John Lenthall, Stationer at the Talbot against St. Dunstans Church, Fleet street, London.

This is a little unclear. The question ("Whether party is belov'd or not") is found on the King of Clubs, "A 1 (y^e)". The 9 of Clubs (philosopher "Artemedorus") has 9 in the lower wheel and 29 in the outer wheel, but the word in between is "miss", not "'falls". The "9-falls-29" combination is actually on the 9 of *Hearts* ("Fryer Bacon"), which sends the querent to the Knave of Clubs, who holds a book with "Falls 29" above "S. Europea" and "50". This directs the search to the 8 of Diamonds (the Sybil "Europea"), on which the 9th answer is the one cited.

Dice were another randomizing device that like cards could be employed in divination. The Greeks and Romans used sheep anklebones as well as the more familiar cubic dice. In Latin, the four-sided anklebones were called *Tali* or *Astragali* and the standard six-sided dice, *Tesserae*. A simple version of divination by dice, using a single die, is found in *The High German Fortune-Teller* (ca. 1745):

How to know your Fortune, good or bad, by throwing Dice.
For Men to cast Fortunes.
KIND will she be to more than you,
Yet let not this your love undo;
You may succeed, and be well pleas'd,
And by her have your passion eas'd.
2. A pretty lass I vow she'll be,
And will much pleasure bring to thee,
By her three children and no more,
Yet to help thee there's riches store.
3. Be wise, and marry e're it's too late,
Else time will put you out of date,
Lose not the offer, if you're wise,
For of her you will have a prize.
4. Come cater, make the even lay,
Her Ace makes it join'd to a Tray,
So take her, and you win the game,
But she'll not always be the same.
5. You need not fear she will be kind,
If you to court her are inclin'd,
If you lose time and do delay,
Then without hope repent you may.
6. Now if you hit not I mistake,
She stay'd till this time for your sake.
A well-complexion'd lass is she,
And money'd too, then soon agree.

Thus when the Men have tried lots for the Women, it is reasonable the Women should try for the Men, in the same manner by Dice, according to the following verses.

For WOMEN.
He is a handsome man and tall,
Yet unto you his love is small,
But 'tis your fault because you frown,
And do with scorn on him look down.
2. Thou wilt be sure of your desire,
In time three husbands to acquire,
The first and second will be kind,
But in the third no comfort find.
3. Come listen to what he doth say,
He'll make you happy many a day,
But if you stand in doubt of it,
Consider but his parts and wit.
4. No, no, it must not be; you time
Is to stay longer – but your prime
You shall not pass e're you shall wed,
Or else part with your maidenhead.
5. Hoist up you sails, old widow now
The fellow's willing, and does vow
He will you and your money have,
Therefore be wise and act the brave.
6. The man is real and upright,
The stories fram'd on him are spite;
Then in a pet break not this tie,
Lest you repent it e're you die. (*High German fortune-teller* 1810: 4-6)

Two far more extensive examples appear in *The Combination Fortune-Teller and Dictionary of Dreams* (1866), which combines three individual fortune telling titles. The first, "Fortune-Telling with Dice" in *Le Marchand's Fortune-Teller and the Dreamer's Dictionary*, uses two dice to answer 32 questions from 21 possible combinations of the throw of the two dice. All of the questions and answers are concerned with romance and relationships, and for some unexplained reason, the lists of questions and answers are numbered from 5 to 36. The querent simply finds an image of the numbers shown on the dice, and then refers to the number of the question in the following list of 32 answers. In *Le Marchand's Fortune Teller and Dream Book*, "The Lady's Love Oracle" uses three dice to answer 80 questions, the first 60 of which also deal with relationships, but the last twenty also cover more general topics such as "64. Shall I obtain rank?", "68. Shall I lose my law-suit?", "70. What is wisdom?", "77. Where shall I find happiness?", or "80. Shall I prefer love to money?". In this system, the querent adds up the numbers shown on the three dice and refers to a table on which the numbers of the questions are listed next to a series of 18 random numbers indicating what the correct *page* in the following lists of answers is, with the appropriate answer indicated by an image of the three dice resulting from the throw. As neither of these systems is likely to have been of much interest to professional fortune tellers, I have not included the actual texts. They simply illustrate the possible use of dice, like cards or dominoes, as a medium for divination.

More subjective methods of divination did not depend on figures, numbers or movement, but on the interpretation of random patterns found or induced in nature. Augury of this sort involved the flight of birds, the movement of flames, or any of a number of other fluid formations including shapes created by the action of the diviner, such as blobs of melted wax or lead dropped into cold water. There are long lists of such divinatory methods with fancy Latin names that were reputedly practiced, but few provide any rules or descriptions of their actual operation. There is one example of augury of shapes, however, that although it was not introduced into Europe before the 18th century, quickly achieved widespread popularity. Tasseomancy is the interpretation of the shapes and arrangement of shapes formed by coffee grounds or tea leaves, a method of divination employed by ladies at their leisure or by marginal individuals such as Gypsies and former slaves, as innumerable Victorian images and stories indicate.

By tradition, the first person in Europe to provide rules for tasseomancy was an 18th century Italian from Florence named Tomaso Tamponelli (or Tomponelli). Although his work is often described in secondary sources as having been published, it may have only existed in manuscript form. Quotes from this seminal work in an 1826 work by Collin de Plancy indicate that it closely resembles the published 19th century English sources for tea leaf reading, although it includes a short invocation not found in some versions. When pouring water into the coffee pot, the operator was supposed to intone: *"Aqua boraxit venias carajos"*. While stirring the residue with a spoon, he or she said, *"Fixatur et patricam explinabit tornare"*, and when depositing the residue into a saucer, *"Hax verticaline, pax Fantas marobum, max destinatus, veida porol"*. Among the figures described for example are the triangle, the crown and the bird:

- A single triangle promises an honorable vocation. Three triangles a short distance from one another indicate good fortune. In general, this figure is a good omen: if there are just a few, they indicate receiving an honor; if there are many, it indicates wealth.
- If you find the shape of a crown, it foretells your success in court.
- The figure of a bird is an omen of fortune and presages a stroke of good fortune. If the bird seems caught in a net, this indicates a suit that you will commence shortly.[45]

An early English example comes from *Mother Bunch's Golden Fortune-Teller*, a small penny chapbook of the sort favored by Cunning Folk in the mid-19th century intended for the lower end of the economic spectrum.

THE ART OF TELLING FORTUNES BY THE GROUNDS OF TEA OR COFFEE.
To pour out the Tea or Coffee Grounds.

Pour the grounds of tea or coffee into a white cup, shake them well about in it, so that their particles may cover the surface of the whole cup; then reverse it into the saucer, that all the superfluous parts may be drained, and the figures required for fortune-telling be formed. The person that acts the fortune-teller must always bend his thoughts upon him or her that wish to have their fortune told, and upon their rank and profession, in order to give plausibility to their predictions. It is not to be expected upon taking up the cup, that the figures will be accurately represented; but the more fertile the fancy shall be of the person inspecting the cup, the more he will discover in it. In this amusement, each must himself be a judge under the circumstances he is to make changes in point of time, speaking just as it suits, in the present, the past, and the future. /

The Roads, or superfluous lines, indicate ways; if they are covered with clouds, and in the thick, they are marks of the past or future reverses; but if they appear clear or serene, they denote some fortunate change near at hand; encompassed with many points, or dots, they signify an accidental gain of money, likewise long life.

The Ring signifies marriage; if a letter near it, it denotes to the person that has his fortune told the initial of the name of the person to be married. If the ring is in the clear, it portends happy and lucrative friendship. Surrounded with clouds, denotes that the party is to use precaution in the friendship he is about to contract, lest he should be insidiously deceived; but is most inauspicious if the ring appear at the bottom of the cup, as it forebodes the entire separation from a beloved object.

A Leaf of Clover is, as well here as in common life, a lucky sign; its position in the cup alone makes the difference; if it is on the top, it shows that good fortune is not far distant; but it is subject to delay if it is in the middle, or at the bottom. Should clouds surround it, many things disagreeable will attend the good fortune; in the clear, it prognosticates undisturbed happiness.

The Anchor, the emblem of hope and commerce, implies successful business carried out by water and land, if on the bottom of the cup; at the top, and in a clear part, it shows constant love, and unshaken fidelity. In thick and clouded parts it also denotes love, but tinctured with the inconsistency of the butterfly.

The Serpent, always the emblem of falsehood and enmity, is here a general sign of an enemy. On the top, or in the middle of the cup, it promises to the consulting party the triumph which he desires

---

[45] Collin de Plancy. *Dictionarie Infernal, ou, Bibliotheque Universelle*. Vol. 4. Paris: A La Librairie Universelle de P. Mongie, 1826, p. 64.

over his enemy; but he will not obtain it as / easily if the serpent be in the thick or cloudy part. By the letter which frequently appears near the emblem, the enemy may easily be guessed, as it marks the initial of his name.

The Letter,—by letters we communicate to our friends either pleasant or unpleasant news; such is the case here. If the emblem is in the clear part, it denotes the speedy arrival of welcome news; surrounded by dots, it announces the arrival of a considerable remittance in money; but hemmed in by clouds, it is quite the contrary, and forebodes some melancholy tidings. If it be in the clear and accompanied by a heart, lovers may expect a letter, which secures to the party the possession of the beloved object; but in the thick it denotes a refusal.

The Coffin, the emblem of death, prognosticates the same thing here, or long illness if it be in the thick. In the clear, it denotes long life; in the thick at the top of the cup, it signifies a considerable estate left to the party by some rich relation; in the same manner, at the bottom, it shows that the deceased is not so nearly related to the consulting party.

The Star denotes happiness if in the clear, and at the top of the cup; clouded, or in the thick, it signifies long life, though exposed to various troubles; if dots are about it, it foretells great fortune, harmony, &c. Several stars denote so many good and happy children; but surrounded by dots, show that your children will cause you grief and vexation.

The Dog, at all times an emblem of fidelity or envy, has a two-fold meaning here. At the top, in the clear, it signifies faithful friends; but surrounded by clouds and dashes, it shows these whom you take for your friends are not to be / depended on; but if at the bottom of the cup, you have to dread the effects of envy or jealously.

The Lily, at the top or in the middle of the cup, signifies the consulting party has, or will have, a virtuous spouse; if at the bottom, the reverse. In the clear, it denotes long and happy life; if clouded, or in the thick, it portends very great trouble or vexation.

The Cross, be there one or more, generally predicts adversity. As its position varies, so do the circumstances. At the top, in the clear, it denotes the party's misfortunes near at an end; but if in the middle, or at the bottom, in the thick, the party must expect many sever trials; if with dots, either in clear or thick, it promises a speedy change of sorrow.

The Clouds, if more light than dark, you may expect a good result from your hopes; but if black, you must give it up. Surrounded by dots, they imply success in all your undertakings.

The Sun is an emblem of great luck and happiness, if in the clear; but in the thick it denotes a great deal of sadness; if surrounded by dots or dashes, an alteration will speedily take place.

The Moon, if in the clear, denotes high honours, if in the thick parts, sadness without great prejudice; but if at the bottom of the cup, fortunate by land and sea.

Mountains,—If only one, it indicates the favour of people of high rank; but several of them, in the thick, are signs of powerful enemies; in the clear, the contrary.

Trees,—One tree only, if it be in the clear or thick part, points out lasting good health; several trees denote your wish will be accomplished; if they are encompassed with dashes, your fortune is in its blossom, and requires time to bring it / [to?] maturity. If accompanied by dots, you will make your fortune in the country where you reside.

The Child, in the clear part, bespeaks of some innocent intercourse with another person; in the thick part, excess in love matters, attended with great expense; at the bottom of the cup it denotes the consequences of libidinous amours.

The Woman signifies much joy in general; if in the clear more favourable; there it shows very great happiness; in the thick a great deal of jealousy. If dots surround the image, it explains the lady's fertility or wealth. The different positions in the cup show, at the top and in the middle, that you will be in love with a virgin; at the bottom, with a widow.

The Pedestrian denotes in general a merchant, good business, pleasant news, and recovery of lost things; also that the consulting party will soon enlist, or get some engagement.

The Rider denotes good news from abroad, in money matters, a good situation in a foreign country, or good prospects. Who doubts his fortune is promised a lasting one by this emblem.

The Mouse, living by stealth, is here an emblem of theft and robbery; if it be in the clear, it shows that you will get again in a wonderful manner what you have lost; but if in the thick, you may renounce the hope.

The Rod shows difference with relations about legacies; in the thick, illness.

Flowers.—If the party be married, he may expect children, who will be a blessing to him in his old age.

The Heart, if in the clear, signifies future pleasure; it promises recovery of money, if surrounded by dots. If in a ring, or two hearts, the party is about to be married or betrothed; if a letter be perceptible near it, it shows the initial of / the person's name; if the letter is in the clear, the party is a virgin; if in the thick, a widow.

The Garden, or Wood, signifies a large company[.] In the clear, it indicates good friends of which it will consist; in the thick, or encompassed with streaks, it warns the consulting party to be cautious, and not to take for his friends those who merely profess themselves such.

The Bird, if in the clear, signifies that you will have to combat with troubles, but of short duration; in the thick, good living, and a speedy successful voyage or journey, and to a great distance if there are dashes.

Fish imply lucky events by water, if in the clear; but if in the thick, the consulter will fish in troubled water, and rely upon that which others have already lost before him. Surrounded by dots, his destiny calls him to some distant place.

The Lion, or any other ferocious beast, at the top, in the clear, signifies prosperity; at the bottom, it warns you of persons who envy your fortune.

The Green Bush shows the benevolence of your patrons, and gives you hopes of the honours you wish for; without foliage, it is a token of the caprice of fortune; in the clear, it announces an unexpected remittance of money.

Worms at the top, or in the middle of the cup, denote good luck at play, and in matrimony; below, it warns you against rivals in your courtship, and enviers in your trade.

The House indicates, at the top of the cup, success in your enterprises, and that your situation will soon be better. In the middle or elbow, it cautions you to be vigilant over your servants.

The Scythe, if combined with an hour-glass, denotes imminent dangers; below, a long and happy life. (*Mother Bunch's Golden Fortune-Teller* 1850, p. 3-8)

This chapter has surveyed the availability and use of mechanical methods of discovering things by *sortes* or lots, an approach that continued in use from medieval times (and before) down to modern times. Most of these methods required the use of books and charts, which became more available as time went by, yet which were simple (if convoluted) in practice and open to anyone who was literate and possessed the necessary means. The "Mother Bunch" chapbook represents a transition between written and oral references; those in which books or manuscripts are required, and others where the information could be kept in the memory. The next chapter will consider methods of divination that did not require handbooks or lists, but could rely on memorized (and improvisational) interpretations that non-literate practitioners could excel at.

CHAPTER 5:

Divination, Part II

The previous chapter dealt with inductive fortune telling by sortilege and the active operation of chance. This chapter is concerned with naturally-occurring patterns by which character and fortune could be interpreted by the location of marks and signs embedded in the bodies (or bones) of living beings, through palmistry, moleosophy, and scapulimancy. The first two methods are part of the broader practice of divination of human physiognomy – the art of identifying a person's temperament and moral character (as well as their fate and fortune) from the outward appearance of the body. Physiognomy is most commonly concerned with the facial features, but as that does not play so large a role in divination as the interpretation of palms and moles, I will forego focusing on that part of the art.

It was universally believed that cosmic influences left indications of what was in store for people on their bodies in a manner similar to the astral "signatures" stamped on plants and minerals. The lines on the palm and location of moles on the body (in particular, those on the face) were a sort of microcosmic equivalent of the alignment of stars in the macrocosm. Although it might be debated whether the planets actually caused change or merely indicated deeper influences at work, there was no question but that moles were simple indicators. They were markers that could be read to determine an individual's character and how this could foretell his or her fate.

Not only were physiognomy and palmistry very ancient arts, they were also the particular fortune-telling practices cited in laws from 1530 to 1824 (a version of which is still in force today) as forbidden to "vagrants"; i.e., not just homeless wanderers but any suspicious marginal persons, including Cunning Folk. Vagrancy is an unusual legal status in that is not based on committing a criminal act (or failing to perform a prescribed legal obligation) but rather on a course of conduct. Living without a visible means of support, engaging in "dissolute" behaviour, illicit practice of magical divination and healing, prostitution, illegal gambling, unlicensed entertainment, drunkenness, and failing to support one's family were all possible determinants of the status of vagrancy, in addition to idle wandering and loitering, even today:

> 22 Hen. VIII., c 12 (1530-1) … All proctors and pardoners, and all other idle persons going about, some of them using divers and subtle crafty and unlawful games and plays, and some of them feigning themselves to have knowledge in physic, physiognomy, palmistry, or other crafty sciences, whereby they bear the people in hand, that they can tell their destinies, diseases, and fortunes, and such other like fantastical imaginations, to the great deceit of the King's subjects, are punishable by whipping for two days together.
>
> 9 Eliz., c. 4 (1597-8) … All persons calling themselves Schollers going about begging, all Seafaring men pretending losses of their Shippes or goods on the sea going about the Country begging, all idle persons going about in any Cuntry eyther begging or using any subtile Crafte or unlawfull Games and Playes, or fayning themselves to have knowledge in Phisiognomye Palmestry or other like crafty Scyence, or pretending that they can tell Destenyes Fortunes or such other like fantasticall Imagynacons…
>
> 13 Anne, c. 26 (1713) … That many parts of the kingdom are oppressed by the usual method of conveying vagabonds or beggars from county to county, by having such persons conveyed as vagrants who ought not so to be … All persons pretending themselves to be Patent Gatherers or Collectors for Prisons Gaols or Hospitals and wandring abroad for that purpose; all Fencers Bearwards Common Players of Interludes Minstrels Juglers all Persons pretending to be Gipsies or wandring in the Habit or Form of Counterfeit Egyptians or pretending to have skill in Physiognomy Palmestry or like crafty Science or pretending to tell Fortunes or like phantastical Imaginations or using any subtile Craft.

5 George IV. Cap. 83 (1824) IV. And be it further enacted, That every Person committing any of the Offences herein-before mentioned, after having been convicted as an idle and disorderly Person; every Person pretending or professing to tell Fortunes, or using any subtle Craft, Means, or Device, by Palmistry or otherwise, to deceive and impose on any of His Majesty's Subjects…

These statutes indicate that palmistry and other "crafty sciences" associated with physiognomy were among the most common magical practices thought to pose a threat to the commonwealth, aside from witchcraft and conjuration. As with astrology and geomancy, most period sources are too long for inclusion in full, but I hope to provide examples to sufficiently illustrate what the period interpretation of hands and moles was like. The earlier examples differ from modern versions in tone and content, having less of the "feel-good" aspect in the seriousness of possible negative results. By the end of our period, the emphasis had shifted to a greater focus on personal relationships intended to address the concerns of women, who had become the primary customers for such divination.

Palmistry

Although there were comprehensive works on palmistry available in English, such as Fabian Withers' translation of John Indagine's 1522 *Introductiones Apotelesmaticae* as *The Book of Palmestry and Physiognomy* (1651) and Royalist astrologer George Wharton's translation of John Rothmanne's *Keriomantia* (1651), the Cunning Folk would more likely have learned the art from the shorter synopses found in cheap handbooks such as Lilly's *New Erra Pater* or *The Book of Knowledge* that appeared at the end of the 17th century and went through innumerable editions after the Licensing Order for the censoring of printing in England lapsed in 1694, or even by mimicking the Gypsies who were already known for palmistry in the 16th century. The following selection, from *The Book of Knowledge; treating of the wisdom of the ancients*, by "Erra Pater [and] Made English by W. Lilley" (1731) is the second part of a three-part section on physiognomy that included directions for reading faces and moles as well:

> *Of Palmestry, shewing the various Judgment made from the Hand.*
> I shall next say something of *Palmestry*, which is a Judgment made of the Conditions, Inclinations, and Fortunes of Men and Women, from the various Lines and Characters, which Nature has imprinted in the Hand, which are almost as various as the Hands that have them. And to render what I shall say more plain, I will in the first place present the Scheme or Figure of a Hand, and explain the various lines therein.
> By this Figure the Reader will see one of the Lines, and which is indde is reckoned the Principal, is called the

> Line of Life; this line incloses the Thumb, separating it from the hollow of the Hand. The next to it, which is called the Natural Line, takes its Beginning from the rising of the Fore-finger, near the Line of Life, and reaches to the Table Line, and generally makes a Triangle thus, Δ. The Table Line, commonly called the Line of Fortune, begins under the little Finger, and ends near the middle Finger. The Girdle of *Venus*, which is another Line so called, begins near the Joint of the little

Finger, and ends between the fore Finger and the middle Finger. The Line of Death is that which plainly appears in Counter Line to that of Life, and is by some called the Sister line, ending usually at the other Ends: For when the Line of Life is ended, Death comes, and it can go no farther. There are also Lines in the fleshy Parts, / as in the Ball of the Thumb, which is called the mount of Venus; under each of the Fingers are called mounts, which are each one, governed by a several Planet, and the Hollow of the Hand is called the Plain of Mars.

I now proceed to give Judgment of these several Lines: And in the first place take Notice, that in *Palmestry* the Left hand is chiefly to be regarded; because therein the Lines are most visible, and have the strictest Communication with the Heart and Brains. Now having premised these, in the next Place observe the Line of Life, and if it be fair, extended to its full Length, and not broken with an Intermixture of cross Lines, it shews long Life and Health, and it is the same if a double Line of Life appears, as there sometimes does. When the Stars appear in this Line, it is a significator of greater Losses and Calamities: if on it there be the Figure of two *O's*, or a *Y*, it threatens the Person with Blindness If it wraps itself about the Table Line, then it does promise Wealth and Honour, to be attained by Prudence and Industry, if the Line be cut or jagged at the upper End, it denotes much Sickness. If this Line be cut by any Line coming from the mount of *Venus*, it declares the Person to be unfortunate in Love, and Business also, and threatens him with sudden Death. A Cross between the Line of Life and the Table Line, shews the Person to be very liberal and charitable, and of a noble Spirit. Let us now see the Signification of the Table Line.

The *Table-Line*, when broad, and of a lovely Colour, shews a healthful Constitution, and a quiet and contented Mind, and courageous Spirit. But if it have Crosses toward the Little finger, it threatens the Party with much Affliction by Sickness. If the Line be double, or divided in three Parts in any of the Extremities, it shews the Party to be of a generous Temper, and of a good Fortune to support it: But if this Line be fork'd at the End, it threatens the Person shall suffer by Jealousies, Fears and Doubts, and with the Loss of Riches got by Deceit. In three Points such as These . . . are found in it, they denote the Person prudent and liberal, a lover of Learning / , and of a good Temper. If it spreads it self towards the fore, and middle Fingers, and ends blunt, it denotes Preferment. Let us now see what is signified by

The *Middle Finger* [Girdle of Venus?]. This Line has in it oftentimes (for there is scarce one Hand in which it varies not) divers significant Characters: Many small lines between this and the Table-Line threatens the party with Sickness, but also give him Hope of Recovery. A half Cross branching into this Line, declare; the person shall have Honour, Riches, and good Success in all his Undertakings. A half Moon denotes cold and watry Distempers; but a Sun or Star upon this Line promiseth Prosperity and Riches. This Line double in a Woman shews she will have several Husbands, but without any Children by them.

The *Line of Venus*, if it happens to be cut or divided near the Fore-Finger, threatens Ruin to the Party, and that it shall befal him by means of lacivious women, and bad Company. Two Crosses upon this Line, one being on the Fore finger, shews the Party to be weak, and inclined to Modesty and Virtue, and therefore those who desire such Wives, usually chuse them by this Standard.

The *Liver Line*, that it be straight and crossed by other Lines, shew the Person to be of a sound Judgment, and a Piercing Understanding; But if it be winding, crooked, and bending outward, it shews Deceit and Flattery, and that the person is not to be. If it makes a Triangle ∆, or a Quadrangle ▢, it shews the person to be of a noble Descent, and ambitious of Honour and Promotion. If it happens that this Line and the middle Line begin near each other, it denotes a Person to be weak in his Judgment, if a Man, but if a Woman, Danger by hard Labour.

The Plain of *Mars* being in the Hollow of the Hand, most of the Lines pass through it, which render it very significant: This Plain, being hollow, and the Lines being crooked and distorted, thereat the Party to fall by his Enemies. When the Lines beginning at the Wrist / are long without the Plain, reaching the Brawn of the Hand, they shew the Person to be one given to quarrelling, often in Broils, and of a hot and fiery Spirit, by which he shall suffer much Damage. If deep large Crosses in the middle of the Plain, it shews the Party shall obtain Honour by Martial Exploits, but if it be a Woman, that she shall have several Husbands, and easy Labour with her Children.

The *Line of Death* is fatal, as when any Crosses or broken Lines appear in it, for they threaten the Person with Sickness and a short Life. A clouded Moon appearing therein, threatens a Child-bed Woman with Death. A bloody Spot in the Line, denotes a violent Death. A Star like a Comet, threatens Ruin by War, and Death by Pestilence. But if a bright Sun appears therein, it Promises long Life and Prosperity.

As for the Lines in the Wrist, being fair, they denote good Fortune, but if crossed and broken, the contrary.

Thus much with respect to the several Lines in the Hand. Now as to Judgment to be made from the Hand itself: if the Hand be soft and long, and lean withal, it denotes a Person of good Understanding, a lover of Peace and Honesty, discreet, serviceable, a good Neighbour, and a Lover of Learning. He whose Hands are very thick, and very short, is thereby signified to be faithful, strong, and labourious, and that cannot long retain Anger. He whose Hands are full of Hairs, and these Hairs thick, and great ones, if his Fingers withal be crooked he is thereby noted to be luxurious, vain, false, of a dull Understanding and Disposition, and more foolish than wise. He whose Hands and Fingers do bend upwards is commonly a Man liberal, serviceable, a Keeper of Secrecy, and apt, to his Power, (for he is seldom fortunate) to do any Man a Courtesy He whose whole Hand is stiff and will not bend at the upper Joint near his Finger, is always a wretched miserable Person, covetous, obstinate, incredulous, and one that will believe nothing that contradicts his own private Interest.

And thus much shall suffice to be said of the Judgment made by Palmestry.[46]

The second selection is from the *High German Fortune-teller* chapbook (no date, 19th century edition, originally ca. 1750) and an example of the most basic possible directions, and like many contemporary interpretations, weighted towards relationships:

Fortunes on the Lines of the Hand

THIS art is of high esteem in most nations, and is of great efficacy; and thus I give an insight into it.

If the lines that pass to the root of the little finger be clear, (which root is called the mount of Jupiter,) then richess and success in business may be expected.

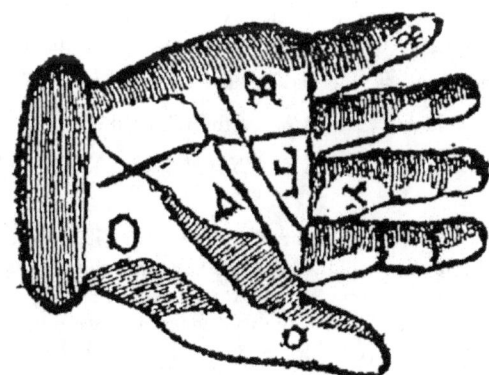

If a line runs across the line of life, it shews crosses, troubles, and sickness—perhaps untimely death.

If the plain of Mars be cut by two cross lines in the hollow of the hand of a woman, it shews she will marry a warlike person, but his rash adventurers will not give her leave to enjoy him long.

The wrinkles in the right wrist denotes as many husbands or wives.

The ball of the thumb is called the mount of the moon, and if there be a circle like to a moon, it promiseth riches by navigation, but the man to be unconstant in love, wavering and unstable.

There are many times certain letters in the hand, engraved by nature, as G, H, L, M, and the like; these generally denote the initials of the christian name of the party you shall marry, and sometimes the lines in the hands make these. The veins in the wrist likewise are figures or letter that answer the same purpose.

To show how these later simplifications differed from the original sources, I include the introduction and the subsequent chapter dealing with line of Life from John Indagine's original *Book of Palmestry*, which also illustrates the close association with astrology:

---

[46] Pp 59-62.

CHAP. I
Of the Distinctions of the Hand.

The ancient Greeks, who (as it may appear by the long and old use of the Word) did use this sort and kind of Divination which is gathered by the beholding of mans hand, called it by this proper name of *Chiromantia*. Wherefore, I intending to write the rules and observations thereof, do think it necessary, and meet, first of all to describe the hand of Man, and point out and set forth his parts; whereby such rules and precepts as shall be given upon this Manual Divination, may the more easily be understood and known. The hand therefore being extended or opened abroad, the plane within is call'd the Palm, in the midst thereof, there is a / certain place called the concave or hollow-ness, out of which the five fingers have their original and beginning.

Amongst which, the first being the strongest and most gross, is called the thumb; the next is called the *Index* or Forefinger, because in shewing or pointing to anything, we do commonly use that finger; the next that followeth, and is in the midst of the five, is by the same name called the middle finger; next after this is the Ring-finger; so-called, because it is commonly to wear a Ring of Gold upon it, and especially that on the left hand; or because, as learned men hold opinion, there doth pass a certain sinew from that finger to the heart of man, wherefore it seemed good, in time past to the Antiquity, to wear a Ring as a Crown upon that finger, or else as some do suppose, That gold by nature doth comfort the heart. The last finger, and least of all, is called the Ear-finger, because it is commonly used to make clean the ears.

And thus far concerning the fingers. Moreover, the Hand being closed or shut with the fingers turned in, we call the Fist; the nether part thereof (amongst such as use, this Art) is commonly called the percussion or stroke of the hand. Then the place where the hand is drawn and gathered in, and joyned to / the arm is called also the Wrist. Furthermore, every finger hath its proper rising or swelling of the flesh, which doth rise at the root or nether part of the five fingers, and of some are called hills, and are attributed unto the manes of the Planets: Among the which is reckoned the rising or the hill in the nether part of the fist, called the percussion of the hand, so that in the hand are limitted and appointed several places unto every of the Planets, whereby Judgment may be gathered. For the rising or hill of the Thumb is assigned to *Venus*, and marked with this Character ♀: the hill of the fore-finger to *Jupiter*, and is thus noted ♃: the middle finger is attributed to *Saturn*, with this note ♄: the Ring finger, to the *Sun*, with this Character ☉: the hill of the little or Ear finger is under *Mercury*, with this mark ☿: the rising or hill which is in the percussion, the *Moon* doth possess, and is thus figured ☽.

Now what place *Mars* shall have, we will shew you hereafter; but first: we will make description of the incisions and divisions of the hand, which we call the lines, amongst the which these be chief and principal: the wrist, which divideth the hand from the Arm, and is almost joyned to the line of life; or of the heart, the which beginneth under the hill of / the forefinger, as it were between the fore finger and the thumb, and doth divide the hand, stretching downward toward the wrist. In the same side of the hand, at the hill of the fore-finger, beginneth a line which passeth over-thwart the hand to the hill of the *Moon*, and is called the middle or mean natural line. And these two lines thus beginning and passing sundry ways make the form and shape of a triangle. To the which, if the line of the Liver or Stomach, which beginneth over against the wrist, and passeth under the hill of the thumb, to the hill of the *Moon*, by the end of the middle natural line do appear, as in some it doth not, it finisheth the triangle, And the space contained within these lines, is attributed and given unto *Mars*, and is called the Triangle of *Mars*, noted with this figure ♂. There is also another line, called the Table-line, beginning under the ear-finger, at the end of the hill of the *Moon*, and runneth to the fore-finger: and is so called, because the space between it and the middle or mean natural, doth argue or shew the fashion of a Table, and that space is always called the Table quadrangle of the hand, and the line is also called the line of fortune. And there be almost the chief divisions or lines of the hand, to the which / all other less and smaller incisions and lines are referred.

But now as near as we can, we will describe them all, and as far as apperteineth to this Art, shew their nature and signification. And first, I think meet to speak of those lines which take their denomination, or name, of the three principal members of mans body: that is, of the Heart, the Brain, and the liver. For as in those parts, whatsoever is in man, is altered and changed: so by those three incisions and lines, a man may fore-see and prognosticate whatsoever shall happen touching health or adversity, or any other things natural. The which if any man think to be vain and trifling; let him call to remembrance the ancient *Phylosophers* of *Pythagoras* Sect:, who chiefly by the proportion and lineaments of mans body, did declare and prognosticate the manners, state, and end of mans life. For what is said of *Socrates* when that a certain man professing the Art of *Physiognomy* or speculation, beholding *Socrates,* judged him by his outward habit to be a very evil man, of unclean life, libidinous, and given to all evil, was therefore wonderfully rebuked of his schollars, as though he had shamefully slandered him. Socrates answered, That indeed naturally he felt such motions and inclinations, / so that if he had not corrected his vices of this nature, by the rules of reason, he had been such a one as he had pronounced him to be; meaning thereby, all those vices which nature and destiny hath planted in us, may easily by reason and Custom be amended, if we will strive against destiny, And the Prince of the Peripateticks, *Aristotle*, said the hand of man to be made of nature the principal Organ and Instrument of mans body. For since it is his office to minister, and serve all other parts of the body; and that in humane generation, the vertues, powers, and strength of all members do come together. It is very consequent and agreeable; some certain signs and tokens of the quality and complexion of man to be known and perceived by the hand.

Such is the proportion of members among themselves, that they do partake one with another in all things. And further that this Art of *Chiromancy* was used in the time of *Pliny;* he himself doth affirm; notwithstanding I take it to be my duty to admonish you what you ought to attribute to this Art, and what it is else to be joyned with it lest any man should think to include or shut up the knowledge of so high and great things into so straight and narrow corners. /

Wherefore, what I judge herein, I think good to shew: As often as I must answer to any that inquireth, by and by, as is accustomed, I look upon the hand, and there-withall behold the whole body, with the Lineaments, and Proportions of the same which is called his *Physiognomy,* (whereof in the Book following I will Entreat:) then I cast my mind to the Hour of Nativity, Month, Day, or Year; the which known, I refer straight to the rules of Natural *Astrology,* hereafter by me written: then plainly judging none of these by themselves sufficient; and thinking it better to judge them Fools in giving light credit, than I to be counted rash, foolish, and hasty, in giving Sentence. So that when 1 have gathered all these things together, and taken hold of that which I think meet for my use, I utter my judgment; esteeming it the part of a Mad man, by looking only in the hand, to give Judgment of the life, and all the states of mans body. And now I return to the rules of *Chiromancy*. /

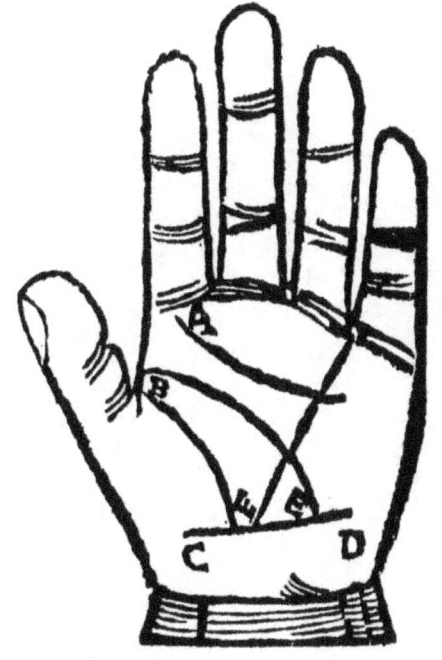

A The Table Line, or Line of Fortune,
B The Line of Life, or of the heart.
C The Wrist of a Woman.
D The Pomel of the Hand.
E The middle natural line.
F The Line of the Liver, or Stomach.

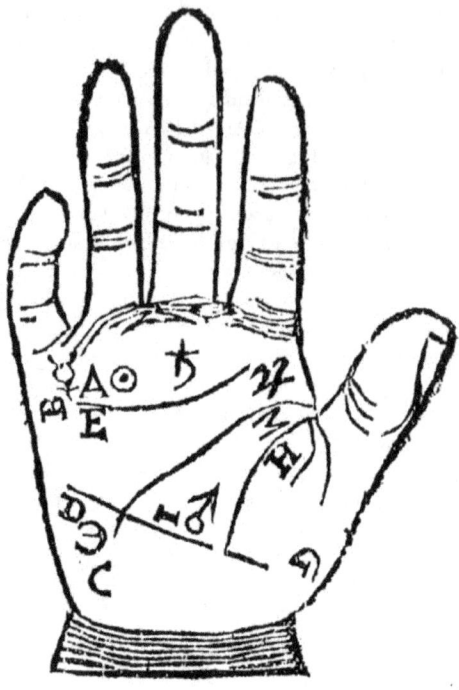

A The Table Line.
B The Pomel of the Hand.
C The Wrist of a Man.
D The Line of the Liver.
E The Table or Quadrangle.
G The Hill of the Thumb.
H The Line of Life, or of the Heart.
I The Triangle.
K The middle Natural Line.

The Names of the Fingers, after the PLANETS.

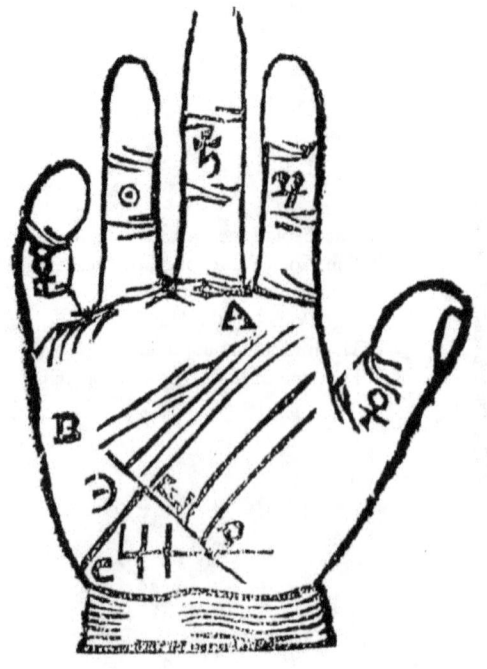

A The Imperfect Table-Line.
B The Sister to the Natural Line.
C The Line of the Liver or Stomach.
D The Sister to the Line of Life.
E The Line of Life.

CHAP. II.
Of the Line of Life, or of the Heart.

The Line of Life, called also the Line of the Heart, beginneth, as it is said before, at the hill of the fore-finger, passing by the midst of the palm, goeth to the wrist. The which if it be long, straight, lively coloured, bright and clear, it betokeneth long Life, undamaged with few diseases or sicknesses. *Pliny* affirming the same, saith that it is a token of long life to have upright shoulders, and two long incisions or lines in one hand, the which are to be understood of the line of life, and the middle natural Line. If that the natural powers be weak, and that the Line do appear short, and of divers colours, running in and out, thin or slender, and cut or parted in sunder, with many overthwart rivals or small crests, it doth declare shortness of life, much sickness, small strength, and that he in whom this is so noted, shall seldom or never bring any thing to a good end. So likewise, the line gross, long, and undivided, doth shew the contraries to the same. Wherefore if any man do require or ask a Reason of this thing? we answer, the blood which doth nourish / the heart, and is also thought to be the seat and resting place of the mind, is the cause efficient of this thing, for it is most certain, that as the blood is pure, or unpure, so the line shall be coloured, either clear or nark: so as long blood doth abound, it sheweth ruddy and bright; and contrariwise pale and swart, when the blood doth fail or wax scarce. Whereby as well the natural heat diminished in the weak body, as also the strong and lusty body, is shewed and declared. Then if this line be narrow, subtle, and well coloured, stretch'd forth toward the middle natural; it signifieth a man of good counsel, of subtle understanding, and of an high and princely mind and stomach; and if it be broad, ill coloured, and pale, it signifieth the contrary.

This is alwaies to be noted in all principal lines, that if they be straight, not divided, neither cut, and well couloured, it doth declare a good complexion: if they be contrariwise disposed or set, it sheweth the contrary. Also, if the line of life be gross, deep, and diverse coloured, that is to say, one place red, another pale, or swart, it is a sign of malice, craft, envy, and the man be a great talker, and boaster, and one that understandeth much in his own conceit. If the line be gross and very red, it betokeneth / a crafty, a filthy, and an unconstant man; but if it be pale, mixed with a certain redness, it signifieth an angry man, almost mad with anger. And if it be very red, mixed with paleness, or swartness, like lead, it sheweth an inconstant, unshamefac'd, wavering traiterous, and angry man, and delighting to stir up mischief, and sow discord. But if it be red in the part next the wrest, It signifieth cruelty: and often times it chanceth to be forked in the upper corner, which betokeneth an unstable man, a runner about Countries, and marvellous in all his doings, the which if it be crooked and writhen towards the middle natural line, it signifieth a crafty deceitful wanton, and a man of a perverse and froward mind. And if you happen to find in the hand of a woman, a cross with three small lines at the upper corner of the Line of Life, it signifieth an unshamefac'd and unhonest woman: but if that cross be found about the right corner in the line of life, and be deep in, it signifieth an ungodly, and mischievous Woman, that shall suffer great Punishment for her mischief: For such a cross in that line, doth always betoken evil, both in man and woman, if that there be found two lines in the end of the rising of the thumb, near the line of Life, as they were lying on the one side; by that token I judge the man to die shortly. And if the Line of Life have branches stretched out toward the middle natural in form as you see in the margin, it is sign of Riches, Honour, and perfection, But if the Branches run downwards toward the wrist in this manner, it signifieth poverty, and damage, by houshold servants, through their untruth. And if the said branches do pass strait through the Triangle to the middle natural, it signifieth a man after divers and sundry dangers and changes of fortune, to come to prosperity and riches. Moreover, many small lines, dividing the line of life, betokeneth much sickness. Further, if there be in the line of life certain points or grains, scattering, it declareth a man unshamefaced, a fornicator, and in jeopardy of his Life for Murther in a tumult; whereof he was author himself; and shall be divers times wounded.

When in the beginning of the line of Life there be three small crooked lines, dividing it in this manner, it is a token of a Leprosie to come; for it doth declare the ill disposition of the Liver. Whereupon that which is already said, may be gathered, that if the line of life be long and deep, well colloured, having a good proportion with the middle natural line, and the line of the Liver or stomach, and that the two be of due quantity at length, and well colloured; it is a good sign of long life, good nature, wit, disposition, and complexion, And oftentimes there be found in the line of life

(.) or)(.) of these notes which do signifie the loss of either of one or both eyes: the which although yet they be seldome found, in my self I have had the experience; for in the same place of my hand is the same mark, the which when I saw, I called to remembrance in what danger I was of one of my eyes: for sitting by the fire in Winter, I fell therein; and tumbling in the flame with my left eye I was vehemently tormented. Albeit, I find, that not only that did prognosticate that evil to me, but also the opposition of *Mars* and the *Moon* to my Nativity, For I find at the time of my birth, *Mars* to be in the eleventh house, in a manly sign, and the *Moon* likewise in the Fifth House; which Constellation is observed of the Astronomers to signifie some such thing. And in somuch as I find this true, it doth so much the more verifie that which I said before, that these *Aries* were joyned together, as it were by a certain alliance or affinity, and that one without the other could very little prevail: For it is most certain, that the inferiour bodies are governed by them above; and as / all strength and power hath its influence from those heavenly bodies; so likewise all lack and default cometh by them, it is most sure. Wherefore we may well consider that Nature was a carefull workman above the Creation of mans body, which hath given knowledge to man diversly and manifoldly, to judge by these three most Noble and principal parts.

In the other parts she hath not so done for she hath set in the hand of a man certain signs and tokens of the heart, brain, and Liver; because that in them the life of man chiefly consists. But she hath not so done of the eyes, Ears, Mouth, Hands, and Feet, because those parts and members of the body, seem rather to be more for comlieness or beauty to the body, than for any necessity. Therefore all hands have the three Lines aforesaid; but the other incisions or lines, many do want or lack; Husbandmen being also excluded from hence, for their continual labour. Wherefore, since there two Sciences need such a mutual help one of the other, I will declare unto you out of *Astrology,* the nature of the *Erratical* Signs, which the Greeks call *Planets. Saturn* maketh sad, circumspect, covetous, slow, and little speakers and self-lovers. *Jupiter* causeth, pleasant, / liberal, quiet, sober, and eloquent persons. Contariwise, *Mars* causeth cruel, fierce, and lyars. The *Sun* maketh Godly, witty, happy, fortunate, and couragious men. *Venus* causeth incontinent, libidinous comely and fair. *Mercury* causeth subtle, crafty, learned in Sciences, and nimble men. The *Moon* maketh quick Witted and comely, but unstable and slow.

Now I have spoken to the diversity of dispositions and wits; I will also shew somewhat of voice and speech, whereby the divers effects and workings of the *Planets* amongst themselves, may the better be understood and known. *Saturn* doth cause a slow and screeking voice for speech. *Mars* a crashing voyce, like the breaking of Metals, *Jupiter* a shrill sounding and a gentle voice. *Venus* maketh a weak, soft, pleasant and effeminate voice, And so likewise doth the *Sun* and *Mercury*. The *Signs* also have their proper voices: For *Virgo, Gemini, Libra, Aries, Taurus, Leo, Capricorn,* and the last part of *Sagittary,* cause mean voices, *Cancer, / Scorpio.,* and *Pisces,* are either altogether dumb and without sound, or else minister some great impediment in the speech, there be also certain signs called fertile, because they do increase, which are, *Cancer, Scorpio,* or *Pisces:* and others be called barren, as *Gemini, Leo, Capricorn.* So that whatsoever a man can do, may be applied to the Signs as furtherers of the same. The which thing in that it cannot be denyed, so much the more are they to be counted slanderers, which esteem and report *Astrology* not as Divine, but as vain frivolous Art, or knowledge: whom in their place we will set forth in their colours. But now to return to our purpose. /

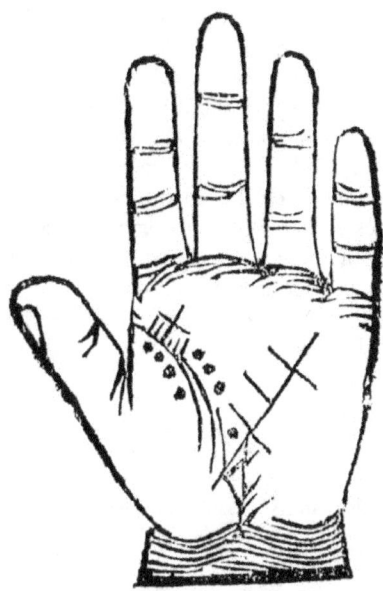

If you find a cross in this sort about the upper corner, proceeding out of the line of life, and on the other side three small lines, and on the upper side two, as you may see by this figure; it signifieth a libidinous and an unshamefac'd woman. But if the three lines be found in the nether end of the line of life toward the wrist, it betokeneth that the woman shall suffer grievous punishment for some mischeif or evil doing. /

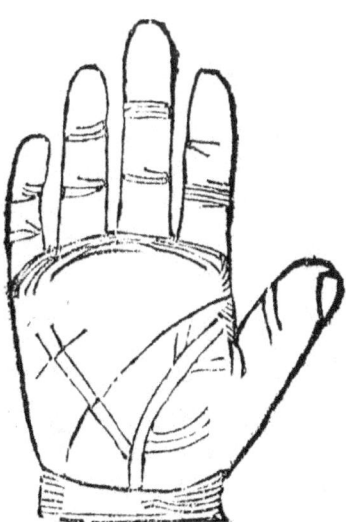

When that certain small lines do divide or touch the line of life in the upper end, in form prescribed; it doth declare the infirmity and sickness of the body. but if on the other part of the middle natural line, there be incisions in this manner, lying as it were directly from the nether part of the line, and rising upward, it betokeneth evil as pain in the head which cometh of exhalations / of the Stomach, or some such other disease. And these three lines on the end of the line, doth betoken evil, as shall appear hereafter.[47]

---

[47] *The Book of Palmestry and Physiognomy ... Written in Latine by John Indagine, Priest, and Translated into English by Fabian Withers, Seventh Edition, Corrected.* London: J. R. for T. Passengers, 1683. [no pagination].

Palmistry fell out of intellectual fashion during the 18th century, and was left almost entirely to the Gypsies and Cunning Folk. They were quite as willing to amuse the idle bourgeois as they were to perform a serious reading for their usual poorer customers – as long as they were paid. Palmistry was resurrected in 19th century in France by Casimir D'Arpentigny (*La Chirognomie*, 1839), and Adrien Adolphe Desbarolles (*Les Mysteres de la Main*, 1859) as part of Romanticism's fascination with, and revival of, everything occult. While D'Arpentigny concentrated on the form of the entire hand in an attempt to match the "scientific" approach accorded the head in phrenology, Desbarolles opted for a more traditional approach of lines and areas. The new palmistry reached England in the latter half of the 19th century, as demonstrated by the very influential work of "Chiero" (William John Warner, 1866-1936), but until then, the older tradition that lingered on in popular culture. An example of the latter can be seen in *Le Marchand's Fortune Teller and Ladies' Love Oracle* (1863), which like the *High German Fortune-teller*, reduces the explanation to a basic level:

PALMISTRY;
OR, TELLING FORTUNES BY THE LINES OF THE HAND

For this purpose, the left hand is always the one chosen, it being supposed that the heart and brain have more influence over it than its fellow. The art of palmistry is no guess-work, as many persons suppose—but is founded upon, and determined by simple rules and long observation.

The practical art of palmistry, is that which gathereth probable predictions from lines, the places of the planets in the hand, and from the notes and characters everywhere pointed and marked on in the hands and fingers. Our readers will therefore be careful to let the following rules be duly observed:—

(1) Forefinger: Jupiter   ♃

(2) Middle Finger: Saturn   ♄

(3) Ring Finger: The Sun   ☉

(4) Little Finger: Mercury   ☿

(5) Thumb: Venus   ♀

Each hand has five main lines.

(1) The Life Line: Vitalis.

(2) The Natural Line. Naturalis.

(3) The Table Line: Mensalis.

(4) The Liver Line: Hepatica.

(5) The Wrist Line: Rascetta.

(*See Engraving.*)

Life begins between ♃ and ♀ (the thumb and forefinger) and the length of life is in proportion to

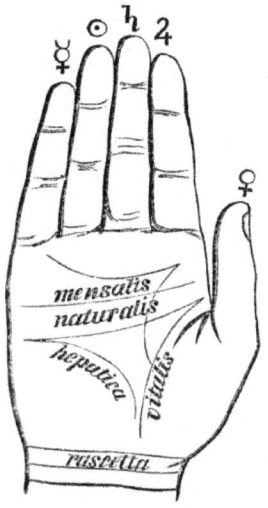

1. VITALIS; OR, THE LINE OF LIFE.

The principal line in the hand is called *Vitalis*, or the line of Life.

This being broad, of a lively colour, and decently drawn in its bounds, without intersections and points, shows the party long lived, and subject to few diseases.

If slender, short and dissected with obverse little lines; and deformed either by a pale or black colour, it presageth weakness of the body, sickness, and shortness of life.

If the line of Life is anywhere broken, it threatens extreme danger of life in that part of the age where the break in the line shows. The line of /

the length of the line of Life. If you wish to find out the dangerous years of your age, you must divide the line into seventy parts, and commence to count the number of divisions, beginning from Rascetta, or Wrist line, and the number falling where the line is broken, shows you your unlucky or unhealthy year.

In most cases, one or more lines run from the Natural line to the line of Life. This indicates the partner of one's life. The point where the junction takes place denotes the point of time of the marriage. If this occurs near the commencement of the line, of course the marriage will take place early in life. If two lines unite with the line of Life, it indicates two husbands (or two wives). If no line joins it, the person will remain unmarried.

NATURALIS; OR, NATURAL LINE.

The next line in importance is Naturalis, or the Natural Line. This line takes its beginning at ♃ and runs to ☿. If this line is straight and continued, and not dissected by lines, it denotes a strong constitution, excellent digestive organs, and an amiable disposition. Large crosses in this line signify imprudence, loss of property, and a fiery temper.

MENSALIS; OR, THE TABLE LINE.

Mensal is, or the Table line, commonly known as the line of Fortune, begins under ☿ and ends under ♃. If this line is broad and fair, without being broken, it is a sign that, with care and industry, the person will lead a happy life; but if broken, it shows that great prudence is needed to avert threatened misfortune. If well defined, this line indicates an amorous temperment, and signifies good fortune in love and wedlock.

Sometimes little lines sprout from this one and run between the fingers, or opposite the base of the fingers. If one of these lines terminates at the base of ♄, it denotes wealth and honors; if at ☉, it foretells success in love; if between ♄ and ☉, it is a sign of sorrow and disappointment; if between ♃ and ♄, you will some day lose a large sum of money, either by being cheated, or making a bad bargain.

From the ring finger (Solis ☉) there commonly runs one or more lines into the Table line. These denote the various inclinations of the heart. If but a single line is actually visible, and if it is deep and long, the person loves or will love faithfully and warmly. If a number of smaller lines are found in its place, the person is inconstancy itself, a butterfly roving from flower to flower. Add up all these little lines and the sum will give you the number of times the person will fall in love. /

HEPATICA; OR, THE LIVER LINE.

This line runs from the outside of the hand under ☿ to the base of ♃. If it is straight and strongly defined, it signifies a robust constitution, a merry disposition, and great intelligence. If it is short and broken, it foretells sickness and death. If it throws out branches near its commencement, it portends a mischievous inclination to play pranks; it also shows wit and acuteness, great determination, and presence of mind.

RASCETTA; OR, THE WRIST LINE.

When this line is perfect and unbroken, it signifies good fortune in all matters of importance. It portends health and strength, success in love and money matters, and a happy and long life. If the Rascetta line is broken and imperfect, it portends a long life, and final success, after enduring many hardships and trials.

OBSERVATIONS ON THE FINGERS

The structure if the hand itself is most admirable in respect to the proportion it beareth to the face, and certain parts thereof, which is this:—

The whole hand is of equal length with the face.

The greater joint of the forefinger equals the height of the forehead.

The other two (to the extremity of the nail) is just the length of the nose, viz., from the intercelis, or place between the eyebrows, to the tip of the nostrils.

The first and greater joint of the middle finger, is just as long as it is between the bottom of the chin and the top of the upper lip.

But the third joint of the same finger is of equal length, with the distance that is between the mouth and the lower part of the nostrils.

The largest joint of the thumb gives the width of the mouth.

The distance between the bottom of the chin and the top of the lower lip, the same.

The lesser joint of the thumb is equal to the distance between the top of the under lip and the lower part of the nostrils. The nails obtain just the half of their respective uppermost joints, which they call omychios.[48]

Moleoscopy

The interpretation of the moles or nevi found on the human body (Moleoscopy) was a perennial favorite in physiognomy, as the many published guides of the art would indicate. Moles are probably determined before a person is born, and most moles appear in the first 30 years of a person's life. Ten to forty moles are normal for an adult. Some moles may slowly disappear over time. Moles on the human body – the microcosm – were seen as analogous to stars in the macrocosm, and related to astrological signs. The first example is quite detailed, having been copied from some literate source (perhaps Richard Saunders?) for inclusion in a generic *Book of Knowledge*. There is an extensive emphasis on moles hidden from view and on those located in the "privy" or genital area that may have provided an excuse to examine these areas and opened the way for sexual exploitation. The relationship between the moles on the face and others on the lower body is unexplained – perhaps it was a sort of "check-sum" control where if the secondary moles were found, it testified to the accuracy of the reading.

---

[48] *Le Marchand's Fortune Teller and Ladies' Love Oracle* New York: Dick & Fitzgerald, 1863, pp. 111-113.

A Treatise of

MOLES,

And their Signification, &c.

MOLES are held by the Learned to be certain Marks imprinted as it were by Providence, Characters whereby Mankind is enabled to read himself, and know in many Cases what shall befall him; a brief Account of which, and their significations, take as followeth,

A Man or Woman having a Mole on the left side the Forehead, under the Line of *Saturn*, signifies another on the right side of the Breast answerable in Colour and Proportion, denoting good Success in affairs, and riches by Building, Tilling, Planting, &c. /

A man or woman having a mole on the right side of the Forehead, under the Line of *Jupiter*, not touching that of the Line of Mars he or she hath another in equality, promising to men good fortune in Marriage, long life, and Success in their undertakings; to a woman, signifies a happy contentment of life, many Children, and a healthful constitution.

A mole on the right side of the Forehead, beneath the line of *Mars*, denotes the like on the right Arm, promising the Party Riches, good Fortune, and many prosperous Days.

A mole on the right side of the Forehead, under the line of the *Sun*, signifies another on the Back, fore shewing the Parties sudden rise and promotion, the favour he shall receive from great Persons.

A mole on the right part of the Forehead, under the line of *Venus*, has another answerable on the right side of the Belly, which promises man a kind and loving wife through whose means he shall grow rich, and be in great esteem; and the like to a woman, in case such marks should be found.

A mole on the right side of the Forehead, under the line of *Mercury*, signifies another on the right Breast, declaring the party to be of prompt wit, industrious, and one that will attain riches and preferment, by his labour and diligence.

A mole appearing on the right side of the Forehead, under the line of the *Moon*, not cutting nor hindering it, shews another on the right side of the Belly, prognosticating the Party be prosperous and fortunate in marine affairs if on a man; but on a woman it denotes she will / be much sought for love, and in the end be a happy match.

A mole on the left side of the Forehead, beneath the line of *Saturn*, is a sure token of another on the left side of the Back, denoting to Man Imprisonment and Crosses; to Women difficult Labours, melancholy Thoughts, jealousies, and the like Anxieties.

A mole on the left side of the Forehead, under the line of *Mars*, promises another under the left Arm, betokening in Man rashness and fury, which shall occasion him much trouble and vexation, and to Women it signifies mischief and contention.

A mole on the left side of the Forehead, under the Sign of *Jupiter*, denoting another on the left side of the Stomach, declares the Party to be riotous and wasteful, prodigal of his Fortunes, and one whose extravagance will bring him to beggary; in a Woman it denotes boldness, impudence and much lavishness.

A mole on the left side of the Forehead, under the *Sun's* Line, signifies another on the left side of the Breast, threatening hard fortune to a Man, by falling under the displeasure of great ones, and to a Woman it promises Poverty and Discontent.

A mole on the left side of the Forehead, under the Line of *Venus*, intimates another one on the left Shoulder, signifying labour, crosses, and Captivity.

A mole on the left side of the Forehead, under the line of *Mercury*, promises the like on the left side, denoting the party quarrelsome, subject to brawls and contention, to which much strife arises; if so it happen in a woman, it declares lustful and insatiate. /

A mole on the left side of the Forehead, cutting the line of the *Moon*, signifies another on the left side of the Belly, near the Navel; threatening Men and Women with sickness and adversity.

A mole in the middle of the Forehead, under the Line of *Venus*, denotes another between the Breasts, which denotes the Party subject to Sickness and many other infirmities, by which the Party, either Man or Woman, shall be much afflicted.

A mole appearing on the middle of the Forehead, under the Line of *Mercury*, signifies another under the Breast, denoting Calamity to the Party, with many afflictions occasioned by such as profess themselves friends.

A mole on middle of the Forehead, under the line *Luna*, signifies another in the Privy-parts, denoting the party to be vicious, intemperent, and one given to many extravagancies.

A mole appearing in the middle of the Forehead, under the line of *Saturn*, signifies another on the right Thigh near the Huckle bone, denoting the party to be rich and fortunate, attaining it by the help and assistance of strangers.

A mole appearing in the right end of the line of *Jupiter*, denotes another on the right Huckle [hip] bone, which to a man promises unexpected riches, and to a woman it promises a good dowry and happy marriage.

A mole appearing on the Left side of the Forehead, at the end of the Line of *Mars*, denotes another under the Muscle of the right Arm, which denotes a Man to be fortunate in Gaming and War, whereby he shall much profit himself.

A mole on the right side of the Forehead, to the end of the Line of the *Sun*, denotes another / on the right side of the Reins, signifying a man to rise by the favour of great men, and to a woman that she shall be fortunate in all her undertakings.

A mole on the right side of the Forehead, at the end of the Line of *Venus*, denotes another on the middle of the Breast, signifying good fortune in Men, occasioned by Women, as by marriage and the like; and to Women in the same kind is predicted advancements.

A mole at the end of the Line of *Mercury*, promises another under the right Breast, towards the right side, denoting a Man to be successful in remote Regions, and greatly to advance himself by Travel; to a Woman it promises a pregnant Wit, good Foresight in domestick Affairs, and a comfortable residence.

A mole appearing on the upper side of the Temple, in either Sex, demonstrates another on the extremity of the Belly, signifying to a Man a steddy Fortune, and continuation of Riches; to a Woman happy Marriages, and a peaceable Life, &c.

A Man or a Woman having a mole near the Eye-brow, on the right Temple, it denotes another on the right Loyn, signifying the party, either man or woman, to gain much esteem, favour, love and advantage, and considerable riches, by Legacies, Doweries, and Reversions.

A mole on the right side behind the Eye, signifies another on the right side of the Buttock or Haunch, declaring much honour or preferment to befal a man, and to a woman much praise for her virtue, and a continuation of prosperity.

A mole appearing on the right side the Temple, in the lower part, inclining somewhat towards / the Neck, signifies another on the right Ribs, betokening a man to be of a natural promptness, industrious, and thereby obtaining riches; to a woman it promises the good Fortune, and a long life, modesty, charity, and a comely behaviour.

A mole on the right side the Temple, near the Eye, below, denotes another beneath the right Thigh, signifying to either Sex riches to be obtained by wisdom and industry.

A mole on the left side, towards the upper part of the corner of the Eye, signifies another under the left Loyn or Thigh, denotes to either Sex, perils in travel, and dangerous diseases, trouble, discontent, and sometimes a violent death.

A mole on the left side the Temple, near the Eye-lid, in a man or woman, signifies another on the left side the Buttock, betokening a rustick, harsh, and sordid temper, and that the party shall be in contempt and hatred of Men.

A mole appearing on the left side of the Face, near the corner of the Eye, denotes another on the left Buttock, signifying much Sickness and Trouble, many thwartings and unexpected Crosses.

A mole on the left side, near the corner of the Eye, and towards the Hair, inclining to the Ear, signifies another on the left side of the Huckle-bone, behind, denoting the Party, either Man or Woman, to be of a sullen, morose Temper, viciously inclined, insomuch, that Punishment is threatened; and ten to one a Woman having this Mark, if she does not defile her Marriage bed.

A mole on the left Cheek, inclining towards the left part of the Ear, signifies another on / the left Thigh, denoting to a Man, sorrow and anguish, crosses by Children, and losses in goods or estate; threatening a Woman with Death in Child bed.

A mole on the upper part of the right Ear, denotes another on the right side of the Belly, signifying the Party to commit such Crimes as will cause him to fall into the Hands of Justice, and endanger his Life; denoting a Woman false and inconstant.

A mole on the outward lower part, near the middle of the right Ear, signifies another on the right side, to a Man denoting, he will fall under the Power of his Enemies, and that they gaining advantage over him, will for some time oppress him, though in the end, it will redound to their Shame; to a Woman it betokens Loss and Imbezzlement.

A mole on the lower part or tip of the Ear, signifies another under the right side, predicting a Man or Woman subject to hurts and bruises, by falls or blows, with many other casualties indangering Life.

A mole appearing on the out side the upper part of the left Ear of a Man or Woman, signifies another on the left side of the Belly, threatening the former with great misfortune, and to the latter Infamy and Disgrace, tho' undeserved.

A mole appearing upon the middle of the left Ear, the like is to be found on the lower part of the left side, denoting a Man to be of an evil Nature, cruel and inhumane; and to a Woman it portends a short life.

A mole on the lower part of the left Ear, signifies the like on the lower part of the left side, denoting a Man to fall into great trouble through / occasion of women, as by quarrelling and fighting on their behalf, betokening a woman to be of a mischievous disposition, threatening her with the Commission of some Murther, either by Poison or otherwise.

A mole on the lower part of the Eye-lid, between the hollow of the Eye and the beginning of the Nose, in either Sex, signifies another on the right side of the Privy part; denoting a man to be much beloved by women, fortunate in Marriages; and a Woman to be ingenious, chaste and faithful.

A mole under the hollow of the right Eye, by the inward part of the Nose, will have another on the middle of the Body above Members, signifying a Man to be hasty, proud and furious; denoting a Woman to be self conceited, vain-glorious, and of a weak understanding tho' pretending to much knowledge.

A mole on the upper part of the right side the Nose of either Sex, signifies another on the Privy-member, threatening the Party with weakness and diseases, occasioned by too much venery, though it denotes him or her to be generally beloved.

A mole on the left side, in the hollow between the Eye-lid and the Nose, signifies another on the left side the Privy-member, betokening the Person to be envious and lustful, given to rapes and adulteries, &c.

A mole in the middle part of the left Eye-lid, denotes another on the left part of a man's Privities, near the root, which threatens him with causeless infamy and disgrace; a woman having this mark, being on the upper part of her Privities, denotes her to lose her Honour, / and be much subject to obloquy and disgrace, not without cause.

A mole under the left Eye, somewhat near the Nose of a Man, signifies another on the left side the Yard, denoting him to be an obscene Person, potent in venery, luxurious, and very lascivious; to a woman this mark, the latter being on the left side the Privities, shrewdly suspect her to be unchaste.

A mole between the beginning and middle of the upper right Eye-lid, towards the Temple, denotes another on the right side of the Belly, in a man signifying good fortune, the love of women, many Children; and in a woman health, easy Child-birth, peace, and a calmness of life.

A mole appearing in the white of the Eye, denotes another near the left Dug [nipple]; denoting to a man pains in the head, and to a woman danger of death in child-bed.

A mole on the Face near the right Nostril, in a man or woman, signifies another on the right side of the Shoulder, predicting to man good fortune in all his undertakings, and to a woman, riches, love, and charity.

A mole on the extremity of the Nose, between the Face and the Nose-end, on the right side, denotes another on the right side of the Hip, signifying a man to be lustful and much given to venery, whereby he shall weaken himself, and greatly impair his health; it declares a woman to be fortunate, much beloved, yet somewhat loose and wanton.

A mole appearing on the right Nostril, between the end of the Nose and the Face, near the middle, describes another on the right side the Privy-member, which betokens a man to be / a deceiver, and an intemperate Person; and to the same effect in its signification in women.

A mole on the left side the Nostril, just over it, near the end of the Nose, denotes another on the Breast, inclining to the left side, denoting the Party to be vicious, and one inclining to many debaucheries.

A man or a woman having a mole on the left side, on the lower part of the Nostril, in a manner between the Nostril and the Face, it signifies another at the bottom of the Belly, signifying the Parties will suffer by hapless marriages.

If a mole happen on the left side, between the top of the Nose and the Face, about the middle of the Nose, another is signified on the left side of the Privy-member, fore-shewing the man or woman to be given to much debauchery, and desirous of copulation, through which occasion they shall suffer much pain and trouble.

A mole appearing in a man or woman, under the very fore-point of the Nose, towards the middle, describes another on the fore-part of the Privy-member, denoting the party to suffer much in old Age, by pains and disorders, occasioned by excess and extravagencies in their youthful days.

A mole appearing on the left side, or in the very hollow of the Nostril, signifies another on the left side of the Genitals, threatening to a man untimely or sudden death, and to a woman hard labour and crosses.

A mole appearing on the top of the bridge of the Nose, either in a man or woman, denotes another in the extremity of the Privy-parts, promising Children and happiness in Wedlock, tho' but short enjoyment. /

A mole on the right-side of the corner of the Mouth, towards the jaw, denotes another on the right side the lower part of the Privy-member, promising good fortune and many happy Days to either Sex.

A mole on the left side of the Mouth, nearly touching it, signifies another on the left Arm, between the Elbow and the Wrist, denotes the Party adverse to wedlock state, but rather desirous to lawless copulation, which will endangers Body and Estate.

A mole on the middle of the upper Lip of a man or woman, signifies another on the Privy-member before, signifying the party to suffer much by crosses and afflictions, and much desirous of Preferment, but unable to obtain his or her wishes.

A mole happening on the middle of the Chin, in the hollow between the Lip and the Mouth, denotes another on the right Foot for the most part, the sometimes in such a case it happens on the left, according as it more or less inclines to the right or left, denoting the Party to be of a rambling inclination, much given to love and excess, especially to lawless love, whereby shame and disgrace will accrue.

A mole appearing in the middle of the Chin, on the fore-part, seeming as much below as above, signifies another on the shin-bone, right or left, according as it inclines, denoting a man to be of grat strength, given to quarrel, and run himself into danger by presuming thereon; to a woman it denotes labour and pain, and danger by water.

A mole appearing on the left edge of the Chin, signifies another on the left Huckle-bone, denoting / a man difficult to please, light and inconstant, yet fortunate and successful in his undertakings.

A mole appearing on the right side of the edge of the Chin, touching its under edge, signifies another on the right Hip, denoting a man capable of Learning, and studious in Arts and Sciences; and to a woman Wisdom, tho attended with care and infilicity.

A mole found naturally on the Gullet of the Throat, signifies another between the Navel and the Privy-members, denoting the party will die a violent death, or suffer much affliction.

A man or woman having a mole on the right side of the Throat or Gullet, it signifies another on the right side of the Thigh, denoting a man to be of a pregnant wit, one that shall procure great riches to himself, and be in good esteem with most men.

A mole on the Throat, on the left side the Wind-pipe, signifies another on the right side Hip, denoting the party to suffer much by falls and bruises, if on a man it happen, but if on a woman, it denotes to her danger by water, or blasted by lightning, &c. And thus much for Sympathy.

A mole on the upper part of the left Check of a man or woman, signifies danger by wounds, and that the party shall be exposed to much hazard and hardship.

A mole on the middle of the left Cheek, denotes diseases, uncertain abiding, and shortness of days.

A mole on the lower part of the left Cheek, signifies the same with the former. /

A mole on the right Cheek, either in the upper part or middle, denotes good fortune to man or woman, to be obtained by prudence or industry.

A mole on the lower part of the right Cheek, signifies the party shall overcome many misfortunes, and in the end live happy.

A man or woman having a mole on the hinder part of the Neck, inclining to the right side, gives a reasonable happy life, yet accompanied with some dangers, which the party may overcome.

A mole on the upper part of the middle of the Neck of a man or a woman, threatens the former with strangling, and the latter with danger in child-birth.

A mole on the left side of the Neck, somewhat near the middle, signifies the same with the forc-going.

Moles on both sides of the Neck of one Person, either man or woman, being opposite to each other, threatns the party with loss of life.

A mole appearing towards the right arm, on the lower part of the Neck, denotes servitude, fruitless love to a man, but to a woman honour and advancement.

A mole on the lower part of the Neck, towards the Shoulder, denotes a man evily affected, coverting things not lawful; and a woman inclining to lewdness, regardless of her honour, and one that is not studious of her fame and reputation.

A mole above a fingers breadth about the Mouth, on the right side of the upper Lip signifies to a man or woman good fortune, happy marriages, and obedient children. /

Now I shall take leave of Moles appearing in the Face, &c. and proceed to say something of those in the Body, that all Parties having them any where may be satisfied, for likely it is that same People may have none on the Face, yet they may appear in the Body. As thus.

A mole on the right Arm denotes riches and good fortune for the party; if on a Man, to be Proficient in Arms, and gain Honour in Military Affairs; to a woman it portends a happy marriage, health and long subsistance.

A mole on the left Arm of a man, signifies him rash, malicious, and one apt to do violence to others, whereby he shall endanger himself to the Law; the like to a woman, denotes her to be of an untractable, harsh disposition, much given to study malice and revenge.

A mole under the right Arm, signifies a man prosperous by his ingenuity, much given to activity, a gaimster, or player at interludes; to a woman it promises inheritance from Parents, or other relations, whereby she shall be advanced in the World, and gain a good repute and esteem.

A mole on the left Arm, between the Elbow and the Wrist, denotes the Party to be crossed in his issue, but that she shall attain Riches, &c.

A mole on the right Arm, between the Elbow and the Shoulder, signifies good fortune to the party, that he or she is kind, and of a good nature, not inclinable to wrong or injury any person. /

A mole on the Arm-pit denotes Sickness, diseases, and many disorders of the Body, hardships in travail, and the like.

A mole under the left Arm-pit threatens the party with an untimely death, especially if they be not wary in tampering with themselves by extraordinary course of Physick.

A mole on the right side of the Breast, denotes the party to increase in Wealth by Tillage and other Rural Employments.

A mole on the Breast or in the Region of the Liver, on the right side, declares good fortune in marriages, happy undertakings and great Possessions.

A mole on the Back, inclining to the right side, denotes riches and honour to accrue by the favour of great men.

A mole on the right side of the upper part of the Belly, denotes to a man good fortune in marriages, riches and preferments insuing by means of his Wives Relations, and to a woman a love and regard from her Husband, and a comfortable continuance in this life.

A mole appearing on the right side of the Belly, near the middle part, denotes a man to be fortunate in Merchandize, Traffick, and bartering of wares, also a happy marriage; to a woman it denotes her chiefest Blessing on Earth will consist in her happy Nuptials.

A mole on the upper part the left side the Back, signifies to a man long Journey, losses, crosses, and imprisonments, upon light and frivolous occasions; to a woman it signifies that she will travel into distant lands. /

A mole on the left side the Breast threatens bad fortune to a man, occasioned by falling into the dislike of his Superiors; and to a woman, poverty, by neglect and disregard of her affairs.

A mole on the middle of the Breast, denotes a man to be of a flegmatick constitution, an uneven temper, uncapable of business requiring great ingenuity.

A mole on the left side of the Belly denotes in indifferent good fortune to a man or woman, through signifying the latter to be weak in capacity, and not over-studious in affairs to her advantage.

A mole in the midst of the Belly, denotes a man to have a good utterance, and eloquent in speech, fit to manage affairs, wherein the use of the Tongue is most required, but in a woman it is not good.

A mole near the middle of the Breast, towards the lower part, threatens a man with indisposition of Body, and many other grievances, crosses and afflictions; and to a woman weakness in child-bearing, and many other natural infirmities.

A mole under the Breast threatens the party with calamity, vexation and trouble, yet denotes him industrious, and promises he shall overcome his afflictions.

A mole on the midst of the Breast inclining to the right side, promises the man good fortune to accrue to him by means of his friends and relations, or by advantagious wedlock, and the same to a woman.

A mole under the Breast on the right side denotes a man to be fortunate in distant Lands, advanced thereto by his own ingenuity, which / shall be taking with great Person; and to a woman it promises pregant wit, and such conduct in her affairs, as shall render her much loved and esteemed.

A mole on the left side of the Back, signifies to a man poverty and crosses through his own neglect and unadvisedness; and to a woman the like.

A mole on the lower part of the left Breast denotes a man shall be reduced to poverty, by his extravagancy in drinking and gluttony; and renders a woman vain and conceited, over loquatious to no purpose.

A mole on left side of the Back declares a man to be contentious, given to quarrels and brangling, inclinable to Martial Enterprises and Feats of Arms; denoting a woman to be regardless of her Fame, bold and resolute in attempting things above her sphere.

A mole on the left side of the Belly denotes to a man strife and affliction by sickness, and to a woman bad success in marriage.

A mole under the left Breast on the Ribs, denotes a man to be of a sordid temper, full of malice and hatred; and to a woman it signifies that she shall calumniated, but find those that shall vindicate her, and take off the asperson.

A mole on the left side of the Belly, between the Navel and the Side, it denotes to a man flight, and absconding through trouble, occasioned by some great Misdemeanour; and to a woman and crosses and afflictions by reason of a bad Husband. /

A mole on the upper side of the Buttocks, signifies the party is subject to cold infirmities, contracted by extravagencies and debaucheries; and to a woman it denotes lasciviousness.

A mole on the left Buttock threatens a man with Sickness and Poverty; and a woman with dishonour and disgrace.

A mole on the Shin-bone either right or left, denotes a man to be rash, sturdy, bold, and one much given to quarrel by presuming upon his own Strength, whereby he shall fall into tribulation; and the like portends to a woman.

A mole near the right Dug, denotes a man exceeding amorous of the Female Sex, proceeding therein so far that he impoverish and disgrace himself; to a woman it signifies ill fortune, extravagent enterprizes and a great desire of copulation.

A mole on or near the left Dug in a man, signifies he shall indanger himself by rash actions, and may happen to die an untimely death; and much to the same purpose is its signification to a woman.

A mole on the Foot, either right or left, denotes to the party an unhappy off-spring, yet he shall obtain riches, though not without vexation and trouble.

One observation of the Feet which seldom fails, is worthy here to be noted, *viz*. If on either Foot the Toe next the great Toe, extend it self beyond the great Toe, or be longer than it, let him or her whom it belongs, know that riches one time or other will fall to his or her lot, if not by inheritance, yet unexpectedly. /

A mole on the Groin, inclining to the right side of the Loyn, denotes prosperity and good fortune to man or woman by marriage or otherwise.

A mole on the Groin the left side, denotes the party to be lacivious, much given to debauchery.

A mole appearing on the right or left Knee, denotes a Person desirous of travel, and by visiting strange Countries, advantage himself both in learning and fortune.

A mole on the right Loin, promises a man the goods of fortune, and that he shall continue happy and prosperous; to a woman it signifies the like, and that she is chaste and virtuous.

A mole under a man's right Loin, denotes him thrifty and industrious, that he shall attain to some dignity; and to a woman it likewise signifies good fortune.

A mole on the Calf of a man's leg, denotes him exceeding lustful, and desirous of other mens Wives, indangering himself thereby, and a woman much affliction.

A mole on the Calf of the right Leg, denotes a man to be provident and industrious, whereby he shall not only procure to himself wealth, but a good name; to a woman it denotes advancement in happy marriage, which shall fall to her share under the age of twenty, if not hindered by the obstinacy of her Parents.

A mole in the midst of the body, denotes a man to be cholerick, rough, and untractable, one that for his disquietude procures himself hatred and contempt; to a woman it denotes a conceit of her own perfections, a levity of mind yet she shall be fortunate. /

A mole on the middle of the Privy-member, often denotes great infirmity, a continuation of troubles to a Man; but to a Woman it denotes that altho' she be of a weak Constitution, yet she shall be much beloved.

A mole on the right side of the Privy-member, near the extremity or end, signifies a Man unfortunate in Love, and the like; at the bottom of the Privy member of a Woman, betokens loss of good Name.

A mole on the right side, somewhat above the lower part of the Member, concludes a Man fortunate, especially in Marriage; and a Woman in her Friends and Relations.

A mole on the left side of the Belly, near the Navel, denotes divers Infirmities to Man, attended with outward Crosses, and perhaps shortness of Life; threatening a Woman with danger in Child-birth, and diseases of the Womb.

On the right side, near the Navel in the upper part a mole happening, denotes good fortune to a Man, occasioned by Women; and to a Woman the like, through the occasion of a Man.

A Man or Woman having a Mole on the hinder part the Neck, inclining to the right side, it promises a reasonable felicity, yet threatens him or her with danger of drowning, or the like Casualty.

A mole on the lower part the Neck, near the shoulder on the right side, denotes a Man to be an extraordinary lover, but he shall find crosses and delays therein; but to a Woman it signifies success. /

A mole on the lower part of the Neck, near the Shoulder on the left side, signifies a Man much Trouble and anxiety, as also publick Punishment; and to a Woman much the same.

A mole appearing in the midst of the Privy-member, denotes a Man honest and virtuous, yet subject to reproach undeserved, and to a Woman an impotent Honour, though nevertheless subject to the malice and calumny of evil Tongues.

A mole on the right side of the Ribs, denotes a Man to be very industrious, a great admirer of Arts and Sciences, by which he shall attain to Riches and Honour; to a Woman it denotes advancement to be obtained by her virtuous and modest Behaviour.

A mole on the left Ribs declares a Man to be rough, of an untractable Disposition, one that is much addicted to quarrels and disorders; and a woman to be proud, vain-glorious, unquiet, &c.

A mole on the left side of the Stomach, denotes the party to suffer much through the means of women, by giving way to their alurements.

A mole on the lower part of the Shoulder-blade, denotes a man, if on the right side stable, firm in his resolves, and of a healthful constitution; to a woman it signifies a continued success of fortune.

A mole on the right Thigh, near the Huckle-bone, denotes the party to grow rich by rural affairs; and a woman to get wealth and esteem by good houswifry. /

A mole on the right Thigh, betokens a man descended of a noble and generous stock, one of admirable wit, whereby he shall attain to riches and promotion; and much the same does it signify to a woman.

A mole under the left Thigh, threatens the party with perils, sickness, and very many diseases.

Two moles answering equally on either side the Gullet or Neck, threatens the party with untimely death.

And thus much for moles and their signification, as far as Art and Experience has gathered, in relation to either Sex, though in these and the like cases, notwithstanding second causes, we must submit to over-ruling Providence, by which the ways and actions of men are guided and disposed, as the all-wise Creator sees proper. (*Original Book of Knowledge* 1725: 92-118)

The second example from the 19th century in *Mother Shipton's Gipsy Fortune Teller and Dream Book* (1890) illustrates the simpler versions found in later popular divinatory manuals.

MOLES.

Time-honoured predictions of a person's disposition and future lot by the aid of Moles.

Though moles are, in their substance, nothing else than excrescences, or ebullitions, which proceed from the state of the blood whilst the foetus is confined in the womb, yet they are not given in vain, as they are generally characteristic of the disposition and temper of those that bear them; and it is also proved by daily experience that from the shape, situation, and circumstances they bear a strong analogy to the events which are to happen to a person in future life. But before I presume to give any directions to those who are to form the prognostic, who are desirous to be duly enabled to pronounce an infallible judgment, I shall, in the first place, teach you now to tell and duly inform any person whom you never saw in your life, even at a hundred or ten thousand miles distance, on what particular parts of the body they have any.

MARKS, SCARS, OR MOLES.
FROM AND BY THE FIGURE OF THE HEAVENS AT THE TIME OF THEIR BIRTH, WITHOUT ANY OTHER COMMUNICATION OR REFERENCE WHATEVER.

In the first place, you must observe what sign that is which is upon the cusp of the ascendent, and in that part of the native's body which that signs governs there will be a mole. For instance, if Aries be the sign ascending at birth, the mole will be on the head or face; if Taurus, on neck or throat; if Gemini, on the arms or shoulders; if Cancer, on the breast; and upon any other part of the body which the sign ascending shall govern. Observe next in which of the houses the lord of the ascendent is posited, and in that part of the body the sign governs which happens to fall upon the cusp of that house, the native will have another mole. Next observe the sign descending on the cusp of the sixth house, and in whatever part of the body that sign governs the native will find another mole; and upon that member also which is signified by the sign wherein the lord of the sixth house is posited will be found another. Observe also what sign the moon is posited in, and in that part of the body which is governed by it shall the native or querent find another mole. If the planet Saturn be the significator, the mole is either black or of a dark colour. If Mars be the significator, and in a fiery sign, it then resembles a scar, cut, or dent in the flesh, but in any other sign it is a red mole. If Jupiter be the significator, the mole is of a purple or bluish cast. If the sun, it is of an olive or chestnut colour. If Venus, it is yellow; if Mercury, of a pale lead colour; if the Moon, it is whitish, or participates of the colour of that planet which she happens to be in aspect. And if the planet which gives the mole be much impeded or afflicted, the mark or mole will then be larger or more visible to the eye of the beholder.

If the sign and planet which gives the mark or mole be masculine, it is then situated on the right side of the body; but, if feminine, on the left side. If the significator or planet which gives the mole be found above the horizon—that is, from the cusp of the ascendent to the cusp of the seventh, either in the twelfth, eleventh, tenth, ninth, eighth, or seventh house—the mark or mole will be on the forepart of the body; but if the significator be under the earth—that is, in either the first, second, third, fourth, fifth, or sixth house— it will be situated on the back or hinder part of the body. If only a few degrees of the sign ascend upon the horoscope, or descend on the sixth, or if the lord of the ascendent, lord of the sixth, or the moon, be posited in the beginning of any sign, the said mole or mark will be found upon the member those signs govern. If half the degrees of a sign ascend, or the significators are posited in the middle of any sign, the mole or mark will be in the middle of the member; but if the last degrees of a sign ascend, or the significators are in the latter degrees of a sign, the said mark or mole will then be situated on the lower part of the member such sign governs.

These observations are of excellent use, in order to know whether a question be logical, fit, and proper to be judged; for if the question be found thus radical, the time rightly taken, and the querent of sufficient age, this rule will never be found to fail.

1. I shall now proceed to give you herein the common prognostications by moles found in all the various parts of the body, according to the doctrine of the ancients. And first, it is essentially necessary to know the size of the mole, its colour, whether it be perfectly round, oblong, or angular; because each of these will add to or diminish the force of the indication. The larger the mole, the greater the prosperity or adversity of the person; the smaller the mole, the less will be his good or evil fate. If the mole is round, it indicates good; if oblong) a moderate share of fortunate events; if angular, it gives a mixture of good and evil; the deeper the colour, the more it announces favor or disgrace; the lighter, the less of either.

If it is very hairy, much misfortune may be expected; if but few long hairs grow upon it, it denotes that your undertakings will be prosperous.

2. A mole that stands on the right side of the forehead or right temple signifies that the person will arrive to sudden wealth; and honor, according to their birth and situation in life; which must always be attended to with due consideration.

3. A mole on the right eyebrow announces speedy marriage, and that the person to whom you will he married will possess many amiable qualities and a good fortune.

4. A mole on the left of either of those three places announces unexpected disappointment in your most sanguine wishes.

5. A mole on the outside corner of either eye denotes the person to be of a steady, sober, and sedate disposition; but will be liable to a violent death.

6. A mole on either cheek signifies that the person never shall rise above mediocrity in point of fortune, though, at the same time, he never will fall into real poverty.

7. A mole on the nose shows that the person will have good success in most of his or her undertakings.

8. A mole on the lip, either upper or lower, proves the person to be fond of delicate things, and much given to the pleasures of love, in which he or she will most commonly be successful.

9. A mole on the chin foreshows that the person will be attended with great prosperity, and be highly esteemed.

10. A mole on the side of the neck shows that the person will narrowly escape suffocation; but will afterwards rise to great consideration by an unexpected legacy or inheritance.

11. A mole on the throat denotes that the person shall become rich by marriage.

12. A mole on the right breast declares the person to be exposed to a sudden reverse from comfort to distress by unavoidable accidents. Most of his children will be girls.

13. A mole on the left breast signifies success in undertakings, and an amorous disposition. Most of his children will be boys.

14. A mole on the bosom portends mediocrity of health and fortune.

15. A mole under the left breast, over the heart, foreshows that a man will be of a warm disposition, unsettled in mind, fond of rambling, and light in his conduct. In a lady it shows sincerity in love, quick conception, and easy travail in child-birth.

16. A mole on the right side, over any part of the ribs, denotes the person to be pusillanimous, and slow in understanding anything that may be attended with difficulty.
17. A mole on the belly denotes the person to be addicted to sloth and gluttony, selfish in almost everything, and seldom inclined to be nice or careful in point of dress.
18. A mole on either hip shows that the person will have many children, and that such of them as survive will be healthful, lusty, and patient in all hardships.
19. A mole on the right thigh shows that the person will become rich, and also fortunate in marriage.
20. A mole on the left thigh denotes that the person suffers much by poverty and want of friends, as also by the enmity and injustice of others.
21. A mole on the right knee signifies that the person will be fortunate in the choice of a partner for life, and meet with few disappointments in the world.
22. A mole on the left knee portends that the person will be rash, inconsiderate and hasty, but modest when in cool blood, modest, and inclined to good behaviour.
28. A mole on either leg shows that the person is indolent, thoughtless, and indifferent us to whatever may happen.
24. A mole on either ankle denotes, a man to inclined to effeminacy and elegancy of dress; a lady, to be courageous, active, and industrious, with some spice of the termagant.
Various are the opinions of authors respecting this art of divination by moles, but the above-mentioned definitions appear to me to come as near the truth as possible. However, the best way of giving judgment upon the fate of any native is first to duly examine the face of the heavens at the time of their birth; then, secondly, judge the same by their whole assemblage of features, contained in the never failing and well-established rules of physiognomy; then, thirdly, by comparing your said judgment in all the above-mentioned sciences with this said prognostication of moles; you will then see how they agree in respect to their several accounts, which are thus to be derived from them, always remembering that the major number of testimonies and the most votes will always carry the day. (*Mother Shipton's* 1890: 37-39)

Scapulimancy

As a correlation to marks on human bodies, marks or shapes found in other natural objects could also be read to discover the workings of providence or fate. An example of this sort of divination, found in Britain (largely in Celtic areas) as well as in the Near East, Mongolia and among the Native Americans of North America, was scapulimancy – the interpretation of the bumps, pits and cracks found on the scapular or shoulder bone of a sheep or some other herbivore. Asian and American scapulimancers exposed the bones to a fire, and made their determinations by the cracks that resulted, but Europeans boiled the shoulder meat off before searching the bared bone for signification.

Despite the long lists of divinatory methods found in reference sources such as hydromancy, pyromancy, or the like, there is seldom any actual information available describing the traditional interpretation. In the case of scapulimancy, however, Charles Burnett, Professor of the History of Islamic Influences in Europe at the Warburg Institute in London, has published a number of articles on the subject that makes it possible to understand this ancient art. Of particular interest is the description of how scapulimancy was supposed to work, as translated from the Latin of Hugh of Santalla (the theoretical part of which is attributed to Al-Kindi):

> "God has placed all the secrets of the universe in the upper world. These secrets are brought down from the upper world with the rain, and rain provides the nourishment of grass. Therefore there is a certain hidden force in grass which is transferred to those animals that eat grass and is lodged in their shoulder-blades. It is in fact the sheep that is chosen as the herbivorous animal with the most suitable blade. A sheep is either taken from the fold of the 'master of the shoulder-blade' (or 'master of the sheep') or bought from an honest merchant. It is tethered for three nights in the house where it is to be slaughtered. One then takes the animal out very early in the morning, placing one hand on the shoulder and saying, 'Provide everything for me'. The animal is decapitated in a clean place, in such a way as it does not see the sword by which it is slain. After the carcassse is boiled in water without salt until the meat falls from the bone. The shoulder-blade is extracted, wrapped in an

unused cloth and placed under the head of the person who will 'read' it, so that he may sleep on top of it. The following day this man takes the shoulder-bone and wipes it with the cloth it is wrapped in, and he sees many wonderful things in it." (Burnett 1996: 35)

The idea that cosmic "secrets" might be introduced on to the earth by rain seems a bit odd, but it does align with the larger concept of the transmission of signs from the heavens into the mundane world by whatever medium. Burnett cites accounts from Giraldus Cambrensis (c. 1146 – c. 1223), Robert Kirk (*The Secret Commonwealth of Elves, Fauns, and Fairies*, 1692), and other authors on the use of sheep scapulars in popular divination up through the 19th century, for which two later examples from Inverness-shire and the Isle of Lewis can be cited:

> "[Shoulder-blade divination] was called *Slinnairachd*, from *Slinnig*, the shoulder. In Badenach, a central and isolated, though large, district of Inverness-shire, until lately there were men skilled in this sort of divination. I mention the custom here because the sacrifices offered on *Nollig* and *Callaiwn*, i.e. Christmas Eve and New Year's Eve, were those from which the knowledge of future events could properly be drawn. The last man in the parish of Laggan who was skilled in *Slinnaireachd* died about 70 years ago. His name was MacTavish, and he had been many years *Aireach* to Mr. MacDonald, of Gallovie."[49]
>
> In Lewis divination by means of the blade-bone of a sheep was practiced in the following manner. The shoulder-blade of a black sheep was procured by the inquirer into future events, and with this he went to some reputed seer, who held the bone lengthwise before him and in the direction of the greatest length of the island. In this position the seer began to read the bone from some marks he saw in it, and then oracularly declared what events to individuals and families were to happen. It is not very far distant [in time] that there were a host of believers in this method of prophecy.[50]

The following description of the method and meanings associated with scapulimancy draws mainly from Prof. Burnett's work. Although perhaps there had been some sort of earlier indigenous practice – the method having been so widespread in early times – which encouraged its adoption, scapulimancy was apparently introduced into Europe from Islamic sources during the Middle Ages. It was brought to Britain, according to Gerald of Wales (c. 1146 – c. 1223), by Flemings who had been encouraged to settle in Pembrokeshire by King Henry I in the mid-12th century, about the time when the Arabic sources were being translated into Latin.

> "A strange habit of these Flemings is that they boil the right shoulder-blade of rams, but not roast them, strip off all the meat and, by examining them, foretell the future and reveal the secret of events long past. Using these shoulder-blades, they have the extraordinary power of being able to divine what is happening far away at this very moment. By looking carefully at the little indents and protuberances, they profesy with complete confidence periods of peace and outbreaks of war, murders and conflagrations, the infidelities of married people and the welfare of the reigning king, especially his life and death."[51]

The left side of the bone (the right shoulder bone was selected for use) was concerned with private affairs, while the other larger section dealt with political and public affairs, such as the fate of the king. Archdeacon Gerald describes several usages of the art (in which the detection of adultery seems to have been important), including its use for theft detection:

> "In our own days, and this is well worthy of report, it happened that a man who was inspecting one of these bones not only gave notice of a theft, the manner of the theft, the name of the thief and all the attendant circumstances, just by looking at it, but even said he could hear a bell ringing and a trumpet sounding, just as had happened when the crime was being committed, although this was

---

[49] William J. Thoms. "Divination by the Blade-Bone". *The Folk-Lore Record*, Vol. 1 (1878), pp. 177.
[50] John Abercromby. "Traditions, Customs, and Superstitions of the Lewis". *Folklore*, Vol. 6, No. 2 (June 1895), p. 167.
[51] Gerald of Wales. *The Journey Through Wales / The Description of Wales*. Translated by Lewis Thorpe. London: Penguin Books, 1978, p. 145.

some little time before. It is really quite remarkable that occult prognostications of this sort seem to be able to reproduce events with the same imagined verisimilitude to the eyes and also to the eyes."[52]

Evidence for the continued use of scapulimancy in 17th century Scotland four hundred years later can be found in Andrew Lang's 1893 edition of Kirk's *Secret Commonwealth*:

> "13. THE Minor Sort of Seers prognosticat many future Events, only for a Month's Space, from the Shoulder-bone of a Sheep on which a Knife never came, (for as before is said, and the Nazarits of old had something of it) Iron hinders all the Opperations of those that travell in the Intrigues of these hidden Dominions [this Science is called *silinnenath*]. By looking into the Bone, they will tell if Whoredom be committed in the Owner's House; what Money the Master of the Sheep had; if any will die out of that House for that Moneth; and if any Cattell there will take a Trake, as if Planet-struck, [called *earchal*]. Then will they prescribe a Preservative and Prevention."[53]

Lang omitted the phrases here supplied by Prof. Burnett of the original Gaelic terms for scapulimancy ("silinnenath") and misfortune ("earchal"). A contemporary reference is found in Rev. James Kirkwood's *A Collection of Highland Rites and Customs* (Bodleian Library MS Carte 269, ca. 1685) that also mentions the use of scapulimancy in Scotland at the end of the 17th century:

> "They foretell Events by looking on the Shoulderbone of a Sheep. They have a care not to toutch it with the Teeth or a Knife. They by it foretell Deaths, Commotions, and Tumultuary Conventions within the bounds."[54]

Proper preparation of the bones required that the boiled meat be removed by hand – "with neither teeth nor knife" – following the requirements mentioned by Hugh of Santalla. Although we do not have details as to how the bone was interpreted in Scotland, it was presumably similar to the practice described in the Arabic and Latin manuscripts.

A sheep's scapular bone forms a rough narrow triangle, rather like the blade of a mattock or adz. There is a projection at the narrow or distal end where it is jointed to the humerus, from which it flares out to the wider dorsal end, with a spine or ridge running on the inner side dividing it into two unequal parts. Sometimes it is so thin on the broader part as to be translucent. Diviners mapped the bone in some detail (there were some 60 or 70 separate locations for signifying marks in Arabic tradition), with each identified location revealing a separate fact depending on the indications found there.

The scapular, as divided by the spine, was separated into "the Muslims' (the wider right side) and "the polytheists" (the narrow left or dark side), in which the Arabs included Christians on the strength of the Christian Trinity, or "the Saracens" and "the Christians" in the Latin version. Private affairs were revealed on the spine and the left side where the household affairs of the "master of the sheep" were indicated. Presumably it was personal rather than public events that most interested the average British "reader" of the bone. Burnett's Latin text specifies that "only close members of the family were allowed to read this 'private side'". The spine represents the property of the master, divided into three parts: his marital relationship, his demesne or property, and his family. The area between the neck of the bone and the spine is also divided in three parts, dealing with the females in the household, the "child-bearing maid", his daughters and sisters, and his wife, which is where sexual matters are revealed, and whether the man is ruled by his wife or vice-versa. The household economy can be examined at the point where the spine rises from the flat blade, such as the loss of livestock and the potential death of the master.

Burnett provides an English version of the earliest Latin manual on scapulimancy as translated from Arabic sources in Spain (Bodleian MS Canon, Misc 396, fols. 108r-112r), from which I include some examples of the interpretations dealing with personal matters. The entire document has 236 numbered lines:

---

[52] *Ibid,*, p. 147.
[53] Andrew Lang. *The Secret Commonwealth of Elves, Fauns, and Fairies*. London: David Nutt, 1893, p. 31-32
[54] From Rev. James Kirkwood "A Collection of Highland Rites and Customs", in Michael Hunter. *The Occult Laboratory: Magic, Science and Second Sight in Late Seventeenth-Century Scotland*. Rochester, NY: Boydell Press, 2001, p. 59.

77 The sixth part.
100 And when you see in the middle of the shoulder-blade — i.e. in the white part — something like a hollow white cloud, silver and money will be stolen from the master of the shoulder-blade 101 And if you find it in the place of the soul, it is severe suffering or money is taken from him. 102 And if you want to know what kind of money, if it is a very small black point, they are coins. 103 And if it is a very large point, they are clothes. 104 And if you see round the tomb [a standard kind of mark, not defined – perhaps a hole?] a white point, they are flaxen cloths …
111 The seventh part.
112 If you see a path in the areas of the face of the shoulder-blade and you see in the pit of the money-box something like a face of a triangle, if it turns to the blackness, then the husband will be against the wife. 113 And if it does not arrive so far as the bed, there is a thief entering the house by night. 114 And if you see a red or yellow point by the bed, and it turns persistently (?) towards to it and turns away from the bed, it indicates a girl in the house who will get married to an old man. 115 And if you see whiteness in the money-box, it signifies joy. 116 And if you see blackness, it portends sadness and grieving. 117 And if you see whiteness and redness and yellowness on the top of the head of the money-box heading outwards towards the face of the shoulder-blade, it portends a man having clothes in his house and money removed from place to place. 118 And if you see the pit of the money-box now turned outwards, then the master of the shoulder-blade is in debt, and there happens to him a loss in his money. 119 And if you see something (?) going out from the top of the money-box, it hints strongly at suffering and mental stress for the master of the shoulder-blade. 120 And if you see it straight, not twisted, it portends happiness about to come to the master of the shoulder-blade. 121 And if you see redness in it, then the female cook of the shoulder-blade is red, having eyes of different colours. 122 And if you see a very small red point in it, the female cook of the shoulder-blade has smallpox or there are on her face moles or scars. 123 And if you see under the pit of the money-box in the part which is next to the summit a black point, it signifies that the meat has been stolen from the pot, and the number of pieces stolen is according to the number of points. 124 And if you see in that place something going out, then the master of the shoulder-blade or his brother or his sister or his son or his relative will be pierced. 125 And if you see a round opening in it, it indicates construction …
162 the eight part
163 And if you see in the lower part of the shoulder-blade in the place of the seat of the king blackness, then the sheep was black. 164 And if there is redness or whiteness, it is according to that colour. 165 And when you see the shoulder-blade now completely blackened, then the person who cut the throat of the sheep was polluted. 166 And if the left-hand side is blackened and the right-hand pure, then it denotes that the sheep had its throat cut in a dirty place.167 And when you see the shoulder-blade yellow verging on red, the female cook of the shoulder-blade has a bad smell. 168 And when you see it covered with protuberances, it signifies that a great profit come to the master of the shoulder-blade. 169 And when you see the top of the shoulder-blade in the area of the neck very twisted, it portends great hardship for the master of the shoulder-blade. 170 And if you see that it is straight, it signifies joy for the master of the shoulder-blade. 171 And when you see whiteness dominating the shoulder-blade, it denotes a great amount of snow and cold weather in that year. 172 And when you see the shoulder-blade white with its surface scraped off, if you know the master of the shoulder-blade will be from the company of the house, judge that the meat of the shoulder-blade has been sent as a present … 178 And when you see the nose of the shoulder-blade rise above the money-box, it signifies grieving in the house. 179 And when you see it bent against the neck, then it denotes a woman having large buttocks. 180 And when you see the nose of the shoulder-blade twisted on <one> side, it portends that the sheep will have been captured by force and will have had its throat cut. 181 And when you see under that nose great twistedness, the female cook of the shoulder-blade will have a pain in her back or has an old illness in her womb or is pregnant. 182 And when you see at the root or the tip something like a tooth rising up, the female cook lies with a black servant. 183 And if you see that the nose is very sharp, she fornicates with a white servant. 184 And when you see in the place of the bed something long, then the cook of the shoulder-blade is a man and not a woman. 185 And when you see that nose shattered, it is a woman pregnant with a female child. 186 And when you see the middle of the tip turned back, the husband is ill. 187 And if the tip is curved in, the male cook of the shoulder-blade is a fool or lies at home as a cripple, or the man

who cut the throat of the sheep is club-footed or left-handed. 188 And when you see the last part of the top not white, then someone has approached his wife. 189 And when you see in the breadth of the top a black path verging on red and going to the bed <of the man>, it signifies that someone is approaching his wife. 190 And if you see a red path in the house, <he is?> going out to the house of the other one, and, if you see two or more paths going it, it signifies a thief. 191 And if you see that there is on the inside of the rising footsteps (?) a red or a black point, it signifies the recovery of the stolen goods. 192 And if you do not see a point in its more elevated place, the thief will enter the house and the goods will not be recalled. (Burnett 1996: 128-129, 131-133)

It is quite likely that the art practiced in Britain in early modern times was simpler than in this original source, but the *manner* in which the bone was "read" in the interpretation of colours, marks and locations was probably approximately the same. It should also be noted that the language of denotation and signification, as well as the surprisingly random nature of the revelations (ranging from the serious problems of theft or adultery to quite trivial facts that the cook had body odor or the sheep was killed in a dirty place) shows continuity with the language and revelations found in the instructions for interpreting moles and the lines on a palm.

The appeal of divination is universal. Divination provides a culturally confirmed (if often illicit) source of credible information about matters hidden to normal human perception.

CHAPTER 6:

Geomancy

Astrology was a philosophical foundation for both magic and science in Western culture. However, despite its preeminent cultural position, astrology had one tremendous drawback as a practical application at the beginning of our period – it was necessary to not only compute the correct celestial alignment but also master an extensive and bewildering amount of interpretive data to gauge the heavenly influence on earthly affairs. Drawing up a horoscope required astronomical observations and written resources, even before the complex art of prognosis came into play. As Christopher Cattan said in support of the superior practicality of geomancy, "… by Astrologie things can not be knowen and understoode, but with great paine, difficulty, and long space of time, as well for the instruments which be requisite thereunto, as the Astrolabe, the Quadrant, or Diall, and a great number of books," to which we can add Keith Thomas's observation, "In the age of Edward VI the bulk of astrological learning was locked up in the obscurity of a learned language, whereas by the time of Charles II there was no branch of the subject which could not be studied by the English reader."[55]

Professional astrology was not a viable option in Britain during the early Middle Ages, and even after the recovery of classical texts by the 13th century, it was long limited to an elite few. At the same time, the compelling desire to identify the astral influences at work called for alternative methods, of which geomancy was the most impressive. As Wim van Binsbergen observes in *The astrological origin of geomancy* (1996):

> "Ibn Khaldun's Muqaddima, written by the end of the 13th century CE, explains the emergence of geomancy as resulting from a situation when would-be astrologers, typically poor, under-educated and urban, had no longer access to the astronomical tables and the complex techniques necessary for calculating a proper professional horoscope, and therefore replaced the empirical input (the actual, astronomically absolutely correct, position – in most cases simplified to a mere longitude – of the heavenly bodies at the particular moment which the horoscope seeks to interpret) by the mock-astrology of geomancy: a series of chance outcomes of simple manipulations with a stick on sand, with pebbles, beans, shells or with pen on paper, but subsequently interpreted in the light of a conventionalized or better ossified astrological idiom deprived from all spatio-temporally specific astronomical input." (van Binsbergen 1996: 36)

European Geomancy originated in North African Islamic culture where it was known as "cilm al-raml" or "sand science". Writing in sand was a traditional way to perform mathematical calculations just as chalk and blackboards were later, and was used in ancient Greece, but its adaptation for divination was Arabic. In geomancy, the operator (in a state of pious abstraction – he was not to consciously observe or count the results) began by making 16 rows of marks or dots in the sand (or in some other medium), running from right to left, as Arabic is written, rather than from left to right as in English. Each row was then checked to see if it contained an even or odd number of marks. The object was to "project" or compose the four primary tetragrams ("the Mothers") upon which all else depended. If a row was made up of an even number of marks, the operator recorded a pair of stars (or a single line); if it was an odd number, he recorded a single star. Each set of four rows was then represented in a stack of four double or single stars, of which there were 16 possible combinations. The following table from "Of Geomancie" in "Henry Cornelius Agrippa's" *Fourth Book of Occult Philosophy* (1559, English translation 1655), giving the Latin names of the 16 geomantic figures and their planetary rulers:

---

[55] Cattan 1591: 2, (Thomas 1971:. 288).

The greater Fortune. * * * * * *	The lesser Fortune. * * * * * *	Solis. ☉
Via. * * * *	Populus. * * * * * * * *	Luna. ☽
Acquisitio. * * * * * *	Laetitia. * * * * * * *	Jovis. ♃
Puella. * * * * *	Amissio. * * * * * *	Veneris. ♀
Conjunctio. * * * * * *	Albus. * * * * * * *	Mercurii ☿
Puer. * * * * *	Rubeus. * * * * * * *	Martis. ♂
Carcer. * * * * * *	Tristitia. * * * * * * *	Saturni. ♄
☊ Dragons head. * * * * *	☋ Dragons taile. * * * * *	

The following is a brief overview of the mechanical production of the geomantic chart, using the example given by Agrippa in *Of Geomancy*. The marks from his 16 lines are recorded thusly, with pairs indicated as an "H" and singles as an "I". I have added the row totals:

* *	H H H H H H H H H	18
* *	H H H H H H	12
*	I H H H H H H	13
* *	H H H H H	10
*	I H H H H H	11
*	I H H H H	9
* *	H H H H H	10
*	I H H H H	9
* *	H H H H H H	12
* *	H H H H H H	12
* *	H H H H H H	12
*	I H H H H H	11
*	I H H H H H	11
*	I H H H H	9
*	I H H H H	9
*	[I H H H H]*	9

* This row is missing in the 1655 edition.

The figures in the left-hand column become the four "Mothers", concluding the role of chance in the process. Henceforth, the other 11 figures are derived by transposing and combining these first four tetragrams. The full working out of the chart results in 15 figures in all, always running from right to left. The four Mothers are arranged thus: ⁝ ⁖ ⁘ ⁙ . The next four figures are derived by taking a segment from each of the four stacks to make new combinations. The four segments of each stack are known as the "heads", "necks", "bodies" and "feet". In order to make the fifth figure, for example, you take each of the "heads" and recombine them in descending order, thus forming this figure: ⁖ , and then do the same with the other segments. The fifth, sixth, seventh and eighth figures are consequently, ⁝ ⁖ ⁘ and ⁖ . These are called the "Daughters", and this completes the top row of the chart. The next row contains four figures called the "Nephews" that are derived from combining or conjugating two of the preceding figures into "odd" or "even" segments. As an example, Mothers I and II (⁝ & ⁖) combined – being all odd totals – yields the figure ⁝ . The Nephews row is accordingly ⁖ ⁘ ⁖ and ⁝ . The next row derived from combining the Nephews in the same manner creates two "Witnesses", which are ⁖ and ⁘ . Finally, a single "Judge" is produced by combining the Witnesses: ⁝ , which is the ultimate figure that provides the answer to the original questions.

The sixteen geomantic figures are not particularly important individually, although they have varying connotations from the favourable through indifference to the unfavourable, intrinsically as well as conditionally. They stand more as markers for the multi-referential influence of the constellations, planets, elements and other astral influences in interpretation. Their chance allocation as the one of the two "Witnesses" in determining the inclination of the resultant "Judge", or their presence in one or more of the 12 zodiacal houses could be significant. Unfavourable Witnesses can render the Judge (ment) less positive, with the opposite being true for favourable ones (see "Of the two witnesses", below). Although the first four figures are received through independent input in the randomizing process, the remaining eight are just secondary conjugations of the first four. Their extension into a zodiacal chart is also arbitrary – there is disagreement over how this should be done as there is no obvious connection between the "shield" of 15 geomantic figures and the 12 astrological houses. Some authorities simply put the figures in order starting with the first astrological house, while others complicate the process by placing the four Mothers in the "angular" houses (first, fourth, seventh and tenth), the Daughters in the "succedent" houses (second, fifth, eighth and eleventh), and the Nephews in the "cadent" houses (third, sixth, ninth and twelfth), omitting the Witnesses and the Judge.

Actually, geomancy (despite the fact that it had been "…saturated, like almost all divinatory and occult sciences in Late Antiquity, with astrology" (van Binsbergen 1996: 33)) could function quite effectively without the astral apparatus, as can be seen in C. W. Roback's simplified tables – reproduced below – or in the derivative "books of fate". However, as geomancy was supposed to deliver the same insight into cosmic patterns as orthodox astrology, the need to frame the information in the same manner was inescapable. The extra layer of signification also provided both intellectual legitimacy and contextual aid in interpretation. Most of the complex interpretive tables and connotative lists found in Cattan's *Geomancie* (1558, English translation 1591) or Thomas Heydon's idiosyncratic *Theomagia or the Temple of Wisdom* (1662-1664) are simply traditional astrological correspondences with the geomantic figures substituted for astronomical positions in this alternative "earthly" system. Geomancy may appear to be an inductive or rule-determined art dependent on the results of the outcome of the initial random derivation of the Mothers, but in practice it allowed for a largely intuitive interpretation, given the broad scope of astrological associations.

The underlying rational for the art is that geomancers could discover the astral influences directing change on Earth by examining terrestrial indicators, just as astrologers did by heavenly ones. Robert Fludd (1574-1637) used the Renaissance Neo-Platonic terminology that characterised the combined astral influences as the "World Soul" or Anima Mundi to explain how geomancy worked. Considerably simplifying his explanation, the geomancer, (having achieved the proper receptive frame of mind) enabled his internal "anima intellectualis" to unconsciously tune into the cosmic Anima. Through this correlation, the four series of four lines of dots (four being the number of "earth") that he projected truly reflected the cosmic forces at work, and legitimated the analysis that followed.

However, while there was no sophisticated mathematics or astronomical data involved, geomancy did require knowledge of the signification of the 16 geomantic figures and their individual significations, and optionally, zodiacal, planetary, and elementary correspondences if they wanted to advance to the quasi-horoscopic extension of the art, the geomantic "theme" in which twelve of the figures are inserted into a standard twelve-house horoscopic chart or "theme". This presumably limited many Cunning Folk to the basic 15-figure geomantic "shield" chart, leaving the more complex interpretation to better-educated practitioners such as Robert Fludd, Simon Forman and John Heydon.

For an example of the traditional explanation of the process, plus samples of the interpretive material, I include the first seven sections from Cattan (1591) and two of his house interpretations. [NB: the formatting of the Cattan excerpts departs from my usual rule, in that I felt that putting the bulk of the text into black letter would have made it even more tedious to read, so the normal font here represents black letter type and bold font, roman type.]

**The Geomancie of Maister
Christopher Cattan,
Gentleman.**
The first Booke.
What Geomancie is, and wherefore it is so called.
Chap. 1.

Geomancie is a Science and Art which consisteth of points, prickes, and lines, made in steade of the foure Elementes, and of the Starres and Planets of Heauen called, the Science of the earth, because in times past it was made on it, as well will heareafter declare. And thus every pricke signifieth a Starre, and every line an Element, and every figure the foure quarters of the worlde, that is to say, the **East, West, South** and **North**. Wherefore it is easie to knowe that **Geomancie** is none other thing but **Astrologie**, and a third meane, that is to say, participating of two, which is **Alquemy**. **Geomancie** is called **Gy** a greeke worde, which signifieth earth and **Mancie**, which is to say knowledge. Or defining it more properly, it is deriued from **Gyos** & **Magos**, which signifieth knowledge of earthly things, by the power of the superior bodies, of the foure Elements, the seuen Planets, and the twelue Signes of Heauen. And this Arte may be made upon the Earth, or in white Paper, or uppon any other thing, whereon it may commodiously be done, so that the prickes and lines may be knowen. /

Of the being, essence, and nature of this Arte, and end thereof.
Chap. 2.

The nature of this Arte and his essence, is none other thing, but the cogitation of the heart of the person, and the will to knowe the thing uncertaine: or to tell more true, it is the proper and naturall mouing of the bodies superiall and celestial. As to the end and intention thereof, it is to take counsell and advise, aswel of things publike as priuate, and the profite which commeth thereof is to know, and haue understanding of things doubtfull and uncertaine. For of things certaine there is needth not any doubt, question, or demaund. This Arte is also (as we haue already touched) put and numbered amongst the parts of Philosophie: so Philosophie is none other thing but a knowledge and love of Science, and therefore is not to be despised or reiected as some ignorant dul headed and rash men wil say, and stand in it. For, as Aristotle saith, **Omnibus scientia est de genere bonorum**, that is, all knowledge is of the number of good things: and this was inuented to know upon a sodaine, all things past, present, and to come, because that by **Astrologie** things can not be knowen and understoode, but with great paine, difficulty, and long space of time, as well for the instruments which be requisite thereunto, as the Astrolabe, the Quadrant, or Diall, and a great number of books, which by the want and lacke of sunne many times darkened, and not casting his beames upon the earth, by reason of the exalations and vapors thereof which hinder his light, besides the difficultie and labour to reckon the houres, minutes, and points. But as for this Science it needs not so much paine, nor to search so many things on this wise, that at what time or houre a man will he may practise this Arte, whereof it is called, the daughter of **Astrologie**. The beginning and originall of this Art came from the **Indians**, which found it before the world was drowned, as ye may perceiue by a booke alleged here before which beginneth thus, **Estimauerunt Indij**. This Arte may be practised whensoeuer that a man will, according to the demaunde that is made, be it night or day, faire weather or fowle, raine or wind: and ye must note, that for the question or demaund that you worke this Arte, / the figure must be made but one time: but tearing the figure, and forgetting the iudgement which was first made (if any fault be found in the demaunde, or in the said figure) then make another in another sort and manner, and iudge the second time according as ye shall finde your figure.

Of the Instrument of this Arte, and of the manner
how to make it. Chap. 3.

The instrument of this Arte is a penne, inke, and paper, or a boarde wel shaven, and a little bodkin, or punchin, or else upon the ground in dust, or sand well purged and made cleane with a little sticke, which is the very manner which was used in the olde time, before incke and paper were invented by the **Chaldeans, Persians, Hebrews** and **Egyptians**, whereof that Arte unto this day holdeth the name, and is called (as we saide before) **Geomancie**. But now the best way to practice the same, is with penne, incke, and paper, for to worke it with fingers, Beanes or other graines is the maner of the curtizances [courtesans] of Bolognia, when they would knowe news of their friends absent, and as yet it is used throughout all **Italie**, which maner doth not please me, neither is that way so certaine as the other. Moreouer, ye must note, that when the workeman, to frame his figure doth make prickes, he must forme fours, the first line of prickes like unto foure fingers of the left hand, without counting the prickes, so that at the least there be to the number of fourteene prickes in every finger: the first line thereof must be sufficient large, line unto the first finger, called the **Index**: the seconde line the more larger, in fashion of the second finger called **Medius**: the third line more shorter, like unto the finger called **Medicus**: and the fourth line lesser then any of the other, like unto the little finger called **Auricularis**: and thus frame all your other lines of prickes unto a number of sixteene: and he must not lay his hand upon the paper, or table, earth, or sand (which of these soeuer it please him to worke by) till he hath made the sixteene lines, always pondering in his heart, moving his hand, the question wherfore he maketh the figure. Ye must further / understand, that the first line is attributed to the **Fire**, the second to the **Aire**, the third to the **Water**, and the fourth to the **Earth**.

And also, that all these prickes signifie one Starre in the firmament, and all these lines one Element: and the foure first lines the first Element, which is the **Fire**, the second foure the second Element, which is the **Aire**, the third foure lines the thirde Element, which is the **Water**, and the foure last lines the fourthe Element, which is the **Earth**. And furthermore, the said lines be attributed the one to the Orient, another to the South, another to the North, and another to the West, in maner and forme as followeth:

Fire
{
  Fire 1.line
  Aire 2.line
  Water 3.line
  Earth 4.line
} 1. figure

Aire
{
  Fire 1.line
  Aire 2.line
  Water 3.line
  Earth 4.line
} 2. figure

Water
{
  Fire 1.line
  Aire 2.line
  Water 3.line
  Earth 4.line
} 3. figure

Earth
{
  Fire 1.line
  Aire 2.line
  Water 3.line
  Earth 4.line
} 4. figure

/ By this example you must learne to frame them like vnto Starres if ye will, but it needs not.

Fire
{
  Fire 1.line
  Aire 2.line
  Water 3.line
  Earth 4.line
} 1. figure

Aire
{
  Fire 1.line
  Aire 2.line
  Water 3.line
  Earth 4.line
} 2. figure

Water
{
  Fire 1.line
  Aire 2.line
  Water 3.line
  Earth 4.line
} 3. figure

The manner how to ioine the prickes, and of them to forme the figures of the twelue lines, and howe they be appropriated vnto the foure partes of the world. Chap. 4.

After that the 16. lines of prickes haue been made, you must take the prickes from two vnto two, ioyning them together with a stroke of your penne. And when you come to the end of the line, if the last prick be even, so let them there remaine, and if there be but one, let it so stand one alone, without anie stroke of your penne between the two last in anie line, if they so remaine even, or else to the one that is fortuned to stand alone at the ende of any line, as appeareth by this example following. /

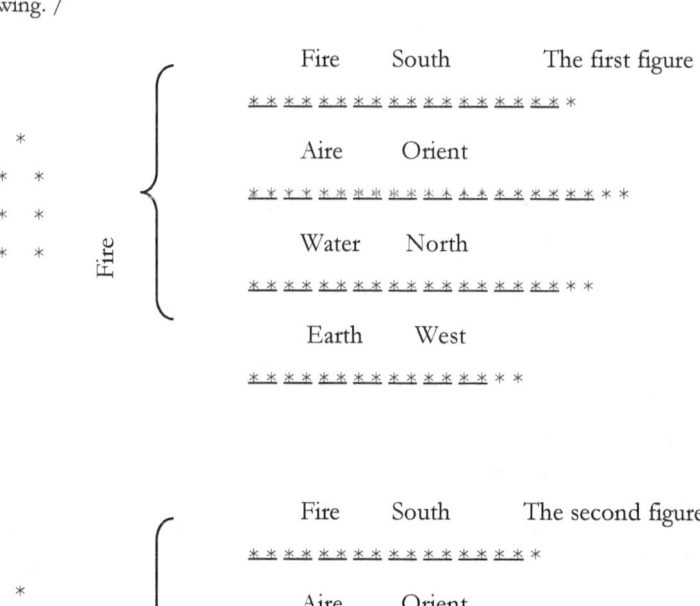

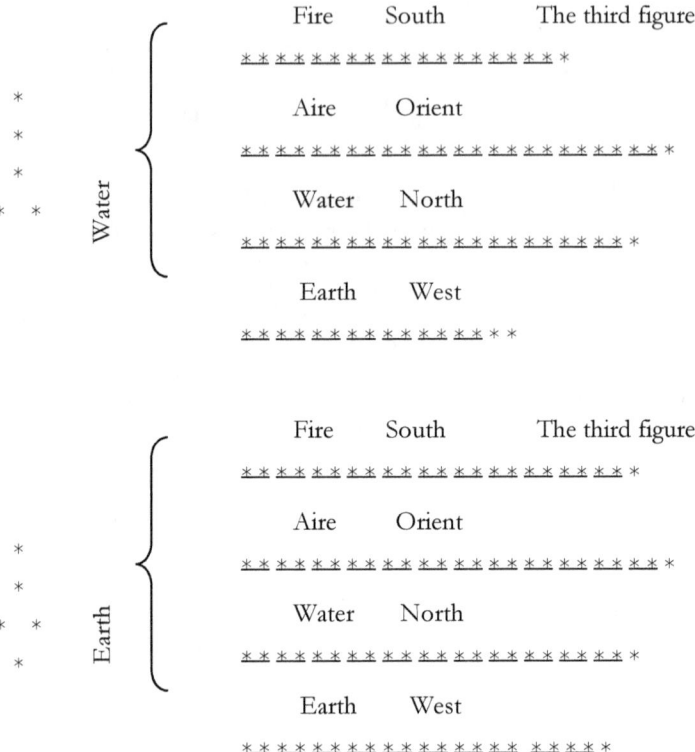

/ The Indians, Chaldeans, Hebrews, Arabians, Egyptians, with a parte of the Greekes, and Latines, do erect their figures in the maner here aboue shewed, because that those Nations do reade contrary unto us, although on that contrary wise they may erect and assemble the saide prickes, as ye may see by the example following, which is a new inuented manner to ivoke this Arte, and many at this day use it as the better and easier way, but yet the other is good, wherefore each man may make the figure as he listeth, either on the right hand or on the left hand, for all commeth unto one purpose, without any difficultie either of one or the other. Here followeth an example.

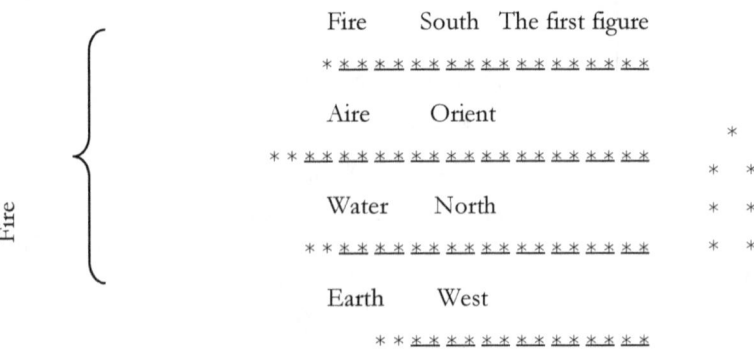

The manner to frame this Arte and giue eache his place his name.   Chap. 5.

After that you haue set your prickes into lines, and thereof drawn out and formed the figures as we haue shewed unto you: you must take and set the foure first lines of the first figure and set them aside, and this is called the first figure: and then you must take the second of the other foure lines, and set them by the first, and so haue ye there two figures, companions, and sisters: and then shall ye drawe the third figure of the other foure lines consequently following, and put that apart, and that is called the third figure: and finally, you shall take of the other foure last lines, the fourth figure which shallbe called the fourth mother, and set that by the other three, and so shall the third and fourth be companions and sisters, as ye shall hereafter see, but aboue all things take good respect to place the first wel, to make / the other to followe after, and you shall put it on the right hand, according to this example following.

	Earth	Water	Aire	Fire	
	4	3	2	1	
	*	*	*	*	
the left	*	*	* *	* *	the right
hand	* *	*	* *	* *	hand
	*	* *	* *	* *	
	West	North	Orient	South	

These foure figures be called the mothers, whereof the first is attributed to the Fire, the second to the Aire, the third to the Water, the fourth to the Earth. Of these foure mothers bee ingendered foure daughters, in taking the first pricke of the first line of the first figure, be it euen or odde, and if it be euen set it euen, and if it be odde set it odde. [the printer has omitted the second instruction] And after you must take the first pricke of the first line of the third figure, be it euen or odde, and set it under the two first. And likewise take the first pricke of the fourth figure, be it euen or odde, and set under the other three. And thus haue you formed one figure, which is the daughter ingendered of the four mothers, and shall be called the fift figure, as ye shall here under see by example. And in this manner and fashion ye shall doe of the other lines, taking of the second line of the first figure the second pricke, and so following, from the first, second, third, and fourth figures, you make the sixth figure, and from the third line of the saide foure figures, you shall make the seuenth figure, and from the fourth line the eighth figure. And so of the foure mothers, or from the first sign next you have made foure daughters, as ye shall see by this example: on the right hand whereof be the foure mothers, and on the left hand foure daughters, as hereafter followeth. /

		Daughters				Mothers			
	8	7	6	5	4	3	2	1	
	* *	* *	* *	*	*	*	*	*	
The left hand	* *	* *	* *	*	*	* *	* *	* *	The right hand
	* *	*	*	*	* *	*	* *	* *	
	*	* *	*	*	*	* *	* *	* *	
	Earth	Water	Aire	Fire	Earth	Water	Aire	Fire	
	West	North	East	South	West	North	East	South	

Of the significance of the Mothers and of the Daughters, and how Nephews be ingendered of them.
Chap. 6.

The figures, as well the Mothers as the Daughters, haue such signification as we haue already written: but yet when they be set in the twelve houses (as shall be declared in the second Booke), the haue other significations then we haue yet spoken of, but hereafter shall be treated thereof, on such wise, that the figure which is set for the South, or that which is set for the East, shall have another importance according unto the rule which I will place hereafter. And nowe therefore that I haue shewed you how to forme the Mothers and Daughters, and their qualities, nowe resteth it to declare the making of the Nephews with their qualities, Therefore to forme them, you must first take the first pricks of the first and second figures, and right under them, if their pricks be even, make two pricks, and if it be odde, make but one, and so consequently from the second line of the two figures, and of the third and fourth, you shall do as much for the third and fourth figures, to form the tenth figure, as ye did of the first and second to forme the ninth figure: and the like shall ye doe of the other lines and figures, to frame the eleventh and twelfth figures: and so the Mothers, Daughters, and Nephews will make such a figure, as you will see here by example. /

8	7	6	5	4	3	2	1
* *	* *	* *	*	*	*	*	*
* *	* *	* *	*	*	*	* *	* *
*	*	*	*	* *	*	* *	* *
*	* *	*	*	* *	* *	* *	* *

The left hand   *The right hand*

12	11	10	9
* *	*	* *	* *
* *	*	* *	* *
*	* *	*	* *
*	* *	*	* *

Earth	Water	Aire	Fire
West	North	Orient	South

How to frame the witnesses and the Iudge.
Chap. 7.

These twelve figures formed and made (as we haue here shewed to you) nowe comes the question how to make the two witnesses, & the Iudge out of them, to haue a certaine resolution, sentence and stay upon the question propounded, and of the difference thereof. Of the which two witnesses that on the right hand is engendered of the ninth and tenth figures, and that on the left hand commeth of the 11. And 12. figures, and they must be made and formed in the manner and form as the Nephews were: and if the last pricks be euen, you must put them euen, and if they be odde, you must put them odde. Of these two Witnesses by the same maner is made an other figure, the which is called the Iudge, unto whome appertaineth the iudgement and discussion of the whole figure, on such wise, that if he be good, the demaund shall like wise be good, and if he be euill or naught, the demaund shall like wise be found ill, as appeareth by this example. /

8	7	6	5	4	3	2	1
* *	* *	* *	*	*	*	*	*
* *	* *	* *	*	*	*	* *	* *
* *	*	*	*	* *	*	* *	* *
*	* *	*	*	*	* *	* *	* *

12	11	10	9
* *	*	* *	* *
* *	*	* *	* *
*	* *	*	* *
*	* *	*	* *

the left hand Witness	14	13	The right hand Witness
	*	* *	
	*	* *	
	*	*	
	*	*	

15
*
*
* *
* *

(Cattan 1591:1-11)

Catten then continues with the names of the figures (as shown in the table from Agrippa, above) and discussion of the four elements, the cosmic structure, the Zodiac, and the planets and their relationships in geomancy, before treating actual divinatory interpretation of the figures in the twelve astrological houses in the second and third books. His coverage of the signification of the seventh house from the second book and additional details from the third book will serve to illustrate the interpretive style:

Of the seuenth house, and of the demaundes [queries] therein contayned. Chap. 7.

1. The seuenth house, which is the Angle of the Occident, contayneth properly and naturally the signifycations of the questions and demaundes which may be mooued on the contrary of the demaund of any person.
2. Also vppon all debates, suites in lawe, theeues and fugitiues.
3. The demaundes also which may be made commonly vpon a friend, and vpon any accord of marriage, to know whether it shall take effect or not.
4. The ill will likewise which is betweene two persons, and which way he goeth that taketh his iourney.
5. Which of them which playeth at lots, cardes or dice, shall winne or loose.
6. Of the two battels ready to fight, which shall haue the victorie, and on which part it shall be.
7. If the mayde be a virgine or not, and whether shee haue any louer, and if she haue, then howe standeth the amitie betweene them.
8. This house also contayneth the demaundes which may be made touching marriages, whether there shall happen any / strife or debates amongst the doers thereof.
9. Whether a woman or friende lost, shall be recouered againe.
10. If the woman ye would marry be rich, and whether she shall haue a good marriage.

11. If the companion appointed to you be a good man or a badde.
12. If there shall be warre or peace, and whether the man shall goe foorth, and if the warre shall last long.
13. If the man be of a good esprit and vnderstanding.
14. If the friendshippe betweene two persons be good or ill, trustie or vntrustie.
15. Whether the thing stolen be in the house, and whether it shall be found, and who did the robberie be of that house, or be a stranger, and of what sort or clothing he is, and where he is.
16. If the agreement made betweene two persons shall continue.
17. As touching the members of man, this house containeth the demaundes which may be made vppon the buttockes and arse.

These be the principall demaundes and questions which bee proupounded in this house, the signifycations whereof shee contayneth in such order, as hereafter ye shall finde.

Finding in the seuenth house this figure *Aquisio*, it signifyeth to make accorde and amitie betweene enemies, the sute in lawe shall be on the plaintiues part, the thing is not stolen, but only scattered away: in the house suspected there are not many thieues, the fugitiue will returne againe, the person is of none ill will, it is good to marry and to make marriages, for there shall be no debate: the wife hath to doe with others then with her husbande, the mayde is no virgine, the woman lost will be found againe, the companion will be good to his wife, there will be no warres but all peace and quietnesse, the person is of a good esprite and entendement, the husbande is not in the house, the man shall not goe to warre, the agreement made betweene two parties shall continue long. For to knowe into what part the person is gone ye must looke to what qualitie, & vnto which / of the foure partes of the worlde the figure belongeth and is attributed: if it be Orientall, the person is in the East, if it be Meridionall, he is in the South, if it be Septentrionall, he is in the North, if it be Occidentall, he is towarde the West, and thus shall ye iudge all the other fygures.

Finding this fygure *Amissio* in the seuenth house, it signifyeth that the open enemie is ill, but he is no great power, and each thing that he doeth, he doeth with an anger and hastinesse, but his anger is soone past, the partie shall loose his sute, the partie suspected is the theefe and hath stolen the thing: the fugitiue will not be taken: the woman married will be a whoore: the man is of ill will, he shall loose at dice and cardes, the marriage will quickly take force, but to no great profite to the one part or vnto the other: for warre it is ill, the wife loueth not her husband well, but hath company of others then hee: the mayde is no virgine: the woman lost will not bee founde: the man shall goe to warre, but not profite much thereby: there shall be no great feate of armes doone, but onely assaultes and skyrmishes, the accord shall not long last, for because the person is not faithfull: the partie hath no witte but to doe harme, the theefe is not of the house but is runne away, and the thing lost shall not be had againe: there will be none accorde: in all the demaundes which ye make in this house this figure is ill, but for bauderie.

When in this house yee finde *Fortuna major*, it signifyeth that the enemie is strong, mightie and of good constitution, the plantiue shall winne his sute, there is no theefe in the house, it is good to contract marriage, and for a friend also, the fugitiue will returne home againe, the woman is honest and loueth none but her husband, the partie hath no ill minde, the gamester shall winne, there shall be peace and no warre, a woman or friende lost will be recoured againe, the woman is rich, and a great marriage, the companion is good, the person hath good forecast and vnderstanding, the aimtie shall endure long. And to bee short, this figure is good for each demaund in this house.

*
    *
* *

* *

If in this house ye finde this fygure *Fortuna minor*, it signifyeth that the enemie is wicked and of evill heart and affection, / strong & mightie, and entendeth much harme: the plantiue shall winne his sute, but not without great paine, trauayle and diligent soliciting: the thiefe is subtill and craftie, the fugitiue will not be found, neither returne againe: the woman is choloricke: the marriage will be for the small profite that commeth thereof: the man is ill minded: the gamester shall loose or haue but small winning: the warres will be great: the woman hath to doe with more then her husbande: the mayde is no virgine: the woman or friend lost will not returne againe: the woman is not of the richest: the man shall goe to warre & haue the victorie, he hath good knowledge in warres: the theefe will not be founde, neyther the thing lost: the accord made betweene two parties will not long continue. In all demaundes which ye may make in this house, this figure is ill, except it be for warres or actes venerall.

Finding this figure *Laticia* in the seuenth house, it signifyeth but small force in the enemie, and besides that he hath none ill minde: the plantiue shall obtaine his sute: the man is not robbed: the fugitiue will not retune home againe: it is good for a wife, marriage, and for a friend. If ye make a figure to knowe what your friend doth, and then finde his figure in this place, it signifyeth that he weepeth for the great affection he beareth to his friend which is now absent: the person hath no ill will or minde: the gamester shall not winne much: the marriage is sufficient good, so that the tenth [house] consent thereunto: there will bee no warre but peace: the mayde is a virgine: the wife or paramour loueth none but her husbande or friend, and them they loue heartely: the woman is not rich: the companion will vse him selfe well and faithfully: the thing stolen will be recouered, and he that keepeth it doth it but in iest and pastime: the agreement newly made will not long last. To be briefe, in all thinges which ye may demaunde in this house, this figure signifyeth a mediocratie.

When ye finde this figure *Tristicia* in this house, it doth signifie the enemy to be strong and mightie, and is ill minded, and will be auenged ouer all his enemies: the sute is in hazard to be lost on the plantiues part: the thiefe or fugitiue will no bee / found: the wife and leamon [lover] be good and vse themselues loyall: the marriage begunne shall be ended: the partie hath a very ciuill affection : the gamster shall win, but it shall be by cogging [cheating] : the mayde is no virgine : the wife loueth her husbande, and the leaman her friend: the man shall goe to warre and haue the victorie, and when he hath taken his enemie, will let him goe againe: the person hath good vnderstanding and is of great enterprise: the coopartner shall doe his part well: the theefe is in the house, and the thing is therein hidden. If that ye make a figure to knowe if that two persons do loue together, this figure signifyeth that the friendshippe is but fayned : the accorde made shall last long, so that the tenth consent thereunto, in all other thinges this figure is ill, but it is good to keepe a thing secrete which ye would not haue reuealed.

If by chance ye finde this figure *Puella* in this house, the enemie hath no more minde to worke his displeasure vnto the other: the sute shall haue good successe, the person is not robbed: the fugitiue will come home againe, it is good for a woman, a leaman, marriage, and play: there will be no warres, but firme peace: the married woman and the leaman fansie others then becometh them. If that a figure be made to knowe whether a friend doe loue faythfully, this figure signifyeth that the loue is feruent: the woman or leaman gone away will be found in the end: the person is of a good esprite and hath vnderstanding in musicke and to play on instrumentes, the thing lost will be found againe, the agreement shall be made and last long: in all the demaundes contayned in this house this figure is good but for warre: by this figure it signifieth that the woman that is married is with childe by others then by her husband.

Finding in this house this figure *Puer*, it signifieth that the enemy is strong and mightie, and mindeth to kill his enemie, the sute will be lost by negligence and lacke of paines taking of the soliciters, the theefe is crafty and malicious, the fugitiue will not come home againe: it is not good for the woman married for she accompanieth an other man besides her husband: it is ill for marriage, for they will neuer liue without brawling and discord, the man is ill minded: about the game will come / strife and quarrell, the mayde is no virgine, the wife is not loyall to her husband, the man is wise and inuentious, and especially about warres, we shall haue warre, the man that goeth to warre shall haue the victorie: the amitie betweene two persons cannot holte: the man suspected hath stolen the thing and is fled: the thing lost shall not be had againe: there shall be none agreement betweene the parties, but mallice shall encrease more and more betweene them. In all questions of this house this figure is ill, but for warre.

If in this house ye finde this figure *Rubeus*, the enemie is very angry, but he is but of small power, and mindeth to kill his enemie, or else to burne his substance with fire if hee may come by it hansomely. The plaintiue shall loose his sute, there were many theeues at that robbery, the fugitiue will neuer returne: it is ill for marriage, for the husband will runne away from the wife and forsake her, by occasion whereof the woman will deale with other men, there will be much debate and strife in the gameing, it is ill for warre, for there will be losse and no profite, and yet the beginning good and the end ill: the mayde is no virgine, and hath but small substance, the friend loueth not his friend, the companion is not good but doth evill entreate his wife, the man shall goe to warre, but it shall be to his losse, the partie is dull esprited, and hath but small vnderstanding or experience, but in things of the fire: the friendshippe is faigned, it will be none agreement. To be short, in all things that may be demaunded in this house, this figure is ill, but for things of warre, and fire.

When this figure *Albus* is in this house, the enemie is of no ill minde, neither seeketh to displease the other, or for his death: the partie shall haue a good end to his sute, there is no theef in the house. the fugitiue will returne, the marriage shall be with honour, and both parties pleased, the woman shall bee good and honest, and the man shall well entreat her, the friende is of good heart, the person hath no ill affection, the woman or friend will be found againe, the mayde is a virgine, the woman is rich, there will be no warre, the man is of good esprite and industry, the agreement shall be made, in all things that ye / may demaunde in this house this figure is good, but for warre: in case of loue, the querant is in loue with a rich woman and of great parentage.

* *   Finding this figure *Coniuntio* in this house, the ennemy is feeble in his
*   reines [kidneys], and seeketh to come to an agreement, the querant
*   shall obtaine his sute to his profite, so that the tenth do consent: it is
* *   good for marriage, and better then al the other, for it always doth signify the accomplishment thereof: the theef that is suspected hath imbezeled the thing lost, and he shall bee taken, and in danger to be hanged, the fugitiue wil not returne, the woman is honest. If the fygure be made to know whether a man lie with his leaman, this fygure is good, and signifieth, that he shall enioy his request, the gamester shall winne, the wife setteth little by her husband, or the leaman by her friend, the mayde is no virgine, the man is of great vnderstanding, the companion is good and loyall for his parte, the theefe is of the house, and the thing lost will scarcely be found, because it is out of the house, the vnitie shall be made, and long last: for al the things of this house this fygure is meetly, but for war, for which it is ill.

* *   Finding this Figure *Caput draconis* in the seauenth house, although the ennemy be
*   strong, yet will he come to reason without any more to doe: the querant shall winne
*   his sute, there be no theeues, the fugitiue will come againe: it is good for marriage,
*   for the woman is good and gentle, it is good for a friend, but the man shall not haue his company: it is good for the gamester, the person is of no great ill will, the maide is a virgine, the woman loueth here husband very well, the woman is rich, the man is of great vnderstanding, the fellowe is good and gentle to his wife, and vseth here wel: the thing lost will be found againe: in all demaundes which ye may deamunde in this house this figure is ill [?] but for warre, whereunto it is ill, for it signifyeth peace. If that ye make a fygure to knowe that a woman be with childe, and fynde this fygure in this seauenth house, say that it shall be a boy.

*   When ye finde this Figure *Cauda draconis* in this house, the ennemy is
*   wicked, and seeketh to kill the other by / treason or villanie: the
*   querant shall loose his sute, the theefe hath stolen much, the fugitiue
        will neuer come againe, it is ill for marriage, for the husband shall
* *   forsake his wife immediately as he is married, ye may thinke the like by a friend: and to be shorte, ye cannot demaunde the thing in this house but this fygure is ill for it, but for warres, and to worke treason, and to put fire in mines.

Finding this fygure *Carcer* in the seauenth house, the ennemy is strong and boisterous,   *
and is secrete, and dissembleth in his designs, so ye can knowe nothing of him: the   * *
querant shall haue good success in his sute: the theefe hath stolen much secretly, the   * *
fugitiue will neuer come againe: it is ill for marriage, for there will be some lightnes in   *
the woman, the woman is poore, the woman loueth not her husband: the gamester shall loose in the beginning, but winne in the ende: the man shal be taken in battle and haue no victorie: the fellow is ill and loueth not his wife, the maide is a virgine: in all the demaundes which ye can demaunde in this house this fygure is ill, except it be to take a prisoner.

When in this house ye fynde *Populus*, there is a great number of enemies assembled about mutterings, quarrelles and debates, it is ill for him that sueth by lawe, and also for the theefe, for he hath stolen, the fugitiues will not returne: it is indifferent in marriage, but iudge as ye fynde in the first, it is good for friendship and company, the maide is no virgine. In all other things which ye may demaunde in this house this fygure is meane [average] but for warre, to the which it is maruelous good, and dooth signifie victorie, for that the tenth doe agree thereunto.

If this fygure *Via* be in this house, the enemy is feeble and of small power, the plaintiue shall loose his suite: the theefe is craftie, the fugitiue will come no more, for marriage it is ill, for the man will put his wife away, and be separated from her: the gamester shall not winne much, the maide is no virgine. In all the demaundes which ye can put in this house this fygure is ill (except it be for voyages) especially by water ... (Cattan 1591: 102-109)

Of the good or ill house, and which they be, where the figures be in their places. Chap. 2.

The good houses, to be briefe, are the first, fift, tenth, and eleuenth: the meane houses be the second, third, fourth and ninth: the euill be the sixt, seuenth, eight and twelfth, houses.

The houses wherein the figures be found to be good.

Aquisitio is goode for profite, and amongst al other figures it is good in the first, second, and tenth house.

Amissio is good for losse of substance, and therefore is good in the eight house, and very ill in the second.

Fortuna major is good for gaine in things where a person hath hope to winne, and therefore it is very good in the fift, sixt, ninth and eleuenth houses.

Fortuna minor is good in any affaire, wherein a person / would goe quickely, and is therefore very good in the second house, and ill in the eight house.

Laetitia is good for ioy, as well present as to come, and for that cause is founde good almost in all the houses, where she is good: and specially in the first and second houses.

Tristitia is a very ill figure in all the houses, but in the eight and twelfth, where she is good: and meane in the first and second houses.

Albus is good for a man which hopeth to haue gaine or profite in any thing, and also to have entrie into any place, and in this respect is found good in the first and fourth houses.

Rubeus is ill in all good things, and good in all ill things, and many times signifyeth death, she is neuer found in the first house to make a iudgement as is tolde you before, she is ill in the second, fourth, seauenth, and tenth houses, and almost in all the other, sauing in certain demaundes.

Puella is very good in all things that ye may demaunde, and especially in things of women, and she is very good in the ninth and fift houses.

Puer is vey ill in all the questions and demaundes which may be made in all the houses, sauing in the second, and sixte where he is meane.

Carcer is a fygure likewise ill in all the houses, and especially in the sixt, eight, seuenth and twelfth houses, and signifyeth always to be stayed.

Coniunctio is good with good, and ill with ill, and signifyeth always recouerment and restitution of thinges scattered or lost. And she is found good in the seuenth, ninth and tenth houses, and ill in the eight, and signifieth death, & in the twelfth signifyeth to be kept in prison.

Caput draconis is good with good, and ill with ill, and is good in the seauenth and second houses, and sheweth to haue a good issue in the things where a man hopeth to haue gaine.

Cauda draconis is very good with the ill, and very ill with the good, in matter of losse she is good, and to passe out of an affaire: she is found good in the fourth, sixt, ninth and twelfth houses, and ill in the second: ye must note that in the ninth she / is good to learne Science, and ill to iourney, signifying spoiling and robbing, she is also ill in this place for other things.

Populus is sometimes good and sometimes bad, with good she is good, and with ill she is ill, she is good in the tenth, and ill in the eight house.

Via is a fygure which breaketh and spoileth al the goodnes of the others, sauing in demaundes of iourneys and voyages, and to goe from place to place to the which she is very good, she is good in the third, sixt, and seuenth houses, because she signifyeth that letters shall come which shall bring good newes: in the twelfth house she is common.

Of the two witnesses.   Chap. 3.

After that we haue sufficiently treated of the 12. houses and the fygures and of their translation and concorde, and which be had. Now resteth it to speake of the two witnesses and the Iudge, now must you know that the **Zodiacke**, whereof the one must be placed in the Figure forward to the right side, which is the thirteenth Figure, and is called the right witnes, the other must be placed on the left side of the Figure, and is the fourteenth Figure named the left witnes: the right witnes is put for the querant, and signifyeth all that which by the first Figure, and all the others which bee on the right side (that is to say the second, third, fourth, ninth, and tenth) is discerned, which is the motiue of the question before propounded. The left witnes containeth all that which the figures doe signifie which be on his side, that is to say, the fift, sixt, seuenth, eight, eleuenth and twelfth, on such wise that the right witnes signifyeth the querant, and the left witnes the thing demaunded, propounded and enquired. Besides this, the right witnes signifyeth ioy and happines of the thing lately passed to the person which propounded the question, and the left witnesse signifyeth heauinesse, unquietnesse and mishap of the thing to come, and put in question: you must further note, that these two witnesses be no houses, neither naturall Figures, but bee / onely aicidentalles, taken from the other to giue a iudgement certaine on the question propounded.

Of the Iudge.   Chap. 4.

The Iudge of the fifteenth figure is procreated of the two witnesses to iudge the ende of all the signification of the demaund, to know if it be good or bad. The which iudge ought always of neccessitie to be euen: for if it be not, the figure should be false: and so if the Iudge be good, the signification of the demaunde shall come to a good ende, and if he be ill, it shall come to an ill ende. If the Iudge doe agree with the first, and with the other fygures which be on the right side, it signifyeth good to the querant and in the thing demaunded. And if he agree wyth those of the left hand which be called the daughters, it signifyeth to the querant an ill issue of the thing demaunded. And so must ye say and esteeme of the accorde which he hath with the right or left witnesse, as ye shall see by the example following [omitted], according to the doctours in this Arte, as well Hebrewes as Chaldeans, and other which haue treated thereof. ... (Cattan 1591: 157-16)

Our second selection is from the *Fourth Book of Agrippa*, covering the same material with an example of interpretation of the signs as they fall in the astrological chart.

And now you have the whole Figure of true judgement constituted according the true and efficatious reasons, whereby I shal shew you how you shall compleat it: the Figure which shall bee in the first House shall give you the signe ascending, which the first Figure sheweth; which being done, you shall attribute their signes to the rest of their Houses, according to the order of the signes; then in every House you shall note the Planets according to the nature of the Figure & then from all these you shall build your judgement according to the signification of the Planets in the signes and Houses wherein they shall be found, and according to their aspects among themselves, and to the place of the querent and thing quesited; and you shall judge according to the natures of the signes ascending in their Houses, and according to the natures and proprieties of the Figures which have placed in the severall Houses, and according to the commisture of other Figures aspecting them: The Iudex [judge] of the Figure which the Geomancers for the most part have made, how it is found in the former Figure.

But here we shal give you the secret of the whole Art, to find out the Iudex in the subsequent Figure, which is thus: that you number all the points which are contained in the lines of the projections, and this you shall divide by twelve: and that which remaineth project from the

Ascendent by the several Houses, and upon which House there falleth a final unity, that Figure giveth you a competent Judgement of the thing quesited; and this together with the significations of the Judgements aforesaid. But if on either part they shall be equal, or ambiguous, then the Iudex alone shall certified you of the thing quesited. The Example of this Figure is here placed

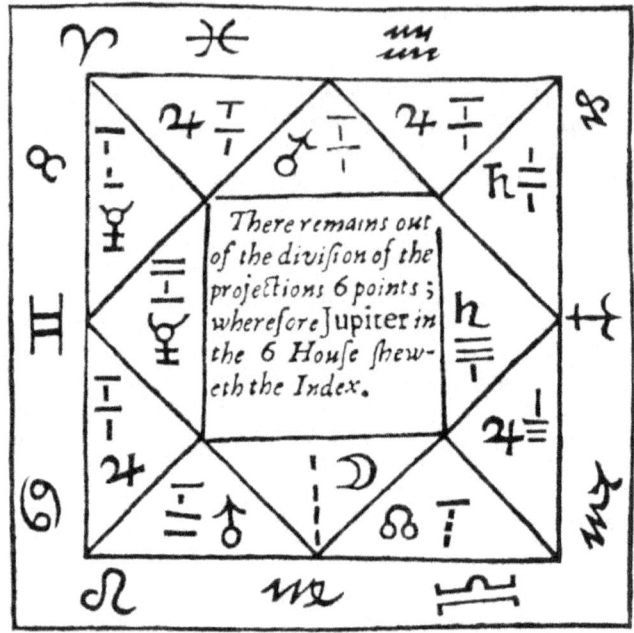

It remaineth now, that we declare, of what thing and to what House a Question doth appertain. Then, what every Figure doth shew or signifie concerning all Questions in every House.

First therefore we shall handle the significations of the Houses; which are these.

The first House sheweth the person of the Querent, as often as a question shall be proposed concerning himself of his own matters, or any thing appertaining to him. And this House declareth the Judgement of the life, form, state, condition, habit, disposition, form and figure, and of the colour of men. The second House containeth the Judgement of substance, riches, poverty, gain and loss, good fortune and evil fortune: and of accidents in substance, as theft, loss or negligence. The third House signifieth brethren, sisters, and Collaterals in blood: It judgeth of small journeys, and fidelities of men. The fourth House signifies fathers and grandfathers, patrimony and inheritance, possessions, buildings, fields, treasure, and things hidden: It giveth also the description of those who want any thing by theft, losing, or negligence. The fifth House giveth judgement of Legats, Messengers, Rumours, News; of Honour, and of accidents after death: and of Questions that may be propounded concerning women with childe, or creatures pregnant. The sixth House giveth Judgement of infirmities, and medicines; of familiars and servants; of cattel and domestick animals. The seventh House signifies wedlock, whoredom, and fornication; rendreth Judgement of friends, strifes, and controversies; and of matters acted before Judges. The eighth hath signification of death, and of those things which come by death of Legats, and hereditaments; of the dowry or portion of a wife. The ninth House sheweth journeys, faith, and constancie; dreams, divine sciences, and Religion. The tenth House hath signification of Honours, and of Magisterial Offices. The eleventh House signifies friends, and the substance of Princes. The twelfth House signifies enemies, servants, imprisonment, and misfortune, and whatsoever evil can happen besides death and sickness, the Judgements whereof are to be required in the sixth House, and in the eighth.

It rests now, that we shew you what every Figure before spoken of signifieth in these places; which we shall now unfold. (*Agrippa His Fourth Book* 1978: 8-10)

Then follows an analysis of the significance of each of the sixteen geomantic figures should it appear in any of the twelve astrological houses. As random examples, I have taken "Albus" ("white", 0 – ruled by Mercury) and "Rubeus" ("red", * – ruled by Mars) which some may note are the first names of Dumbledore and Hagrid in the *Harry Potter* books.

"*Albus* in the first House signifies a life vexed with continual sickness and greivous diseases; signifies a man of a short stature, broad brest, and gross arms, having curled or crisped hair, one of a broad full mouth, a great talker and babler, given much to use vain and unprofitable discourse, but one that is merry, joyous and jocond, and much pleasing to men. In the second House *Albus* enlargeth and augmenteth substance gained by sports, playes, vile and base arts and exercises, but such as are pleasing and delightful; as by playes, pastimes, dancings and laughters: he discovereth both the theef, and the theft or thing stollen, and hideth and concealeth treasure. In the third House *Albus* signifies very few brethren; giveth not many, but tedious and wearisom journyes, and signifies all deceivers. In the fourth House he sheweth very small or no Patrimony, and the Father to be a man much known; but declareth him to be a man of some base and inferiour Office and Imployment. In the fifth House *Albus* giveth no children, or if any, that they shall soon die; declareth a woman to be servile, and causeth such as are with young to miscarry, or else to bring forth Monsters; denoteth all rumours to be false, and raiseth to no honour. In the sixth House *Albus* causeth very tedious sicknesses and diseases; discovereth the fraud, deceit and wickedness of servants, and signifies diseases and infirmities of cattel to be mortal, and maketh the Physitian to be suspected of the sick Patient. *Albus* in the seventh House giveth a barren wife, but one that is fair and beautiful; few suits or controversies, but such as shall be of very long continuance. In the eighth House if a question be propounded of any one, *Albus* shews the party to be dead; giveth little portion or dowry with a wife, and causeth that to be much strived and contended for. In the ninth House *Albus* denoteth some journyes to be accomplished, but with mean profit; hindereth him that is absent, and signifies he shall not return; and declareth a man to be superstitious in Religion, and given to false and deceitful Sciences. In the tenth *Albus* causeth Princes and Judges to be malevolent; sheweth vile and base Offices and Magistracies; signifies a Mother to be a whore, or one much suspected for adultery. In the eleventh House *Albus* maketh dissembling and false friends; causeth love and favour to be inconstant. *Albus* in the twelfth House denoteth vile, impotent and rustical enemies; sheweth such as are in prison shall not escape, and signifies a great many and various troubles and discommodities of ones life. ... (*Agrippa* His *Fourth Book* 1978: 23-24)

Rubeus in the first House, signifies a short life, and an evil end; signifies a man to be filthy, unprofitable, and of an evil, cruel and malicious countenance, having some remarkable and notable signe or scar in some part of his body. In the second House *Rubeus* signifies poverty, and maketh theeves and robbers, and such persons as shall acquire and seek after their maintenance and livelihoods by using false, wicked, and evil, and unlawful Arts; preserveth theeves, and concealeth theft; and signifies no treasure to be hid nor found. In the third House *Rubeus* renders brethren and kinsmen to be full of hatred, and odious one to another, and sheweth them to be of evil manners, & ill disposition; causeth journeys to be very dangerous, and foresheweth false faith and treachery. In the fourth House he destroyeth and consumeth Patrimonies, and disperseth and wasteth inheritances, causeth them to come to nothing; destroyeth the fruits of the field by tempestuous seasons, and malignancy of the earth; and bringeth the Father to a quick and sudden death. *Rubeus* in the fifth House giveth many children, but either they shall be wicked and disobedient, or else shall afflict their Parents with grief, disgrace and infamy. In the sixth House *Rubeus* causeth mortal wounds, sicknesses and diseases; him that is sick shall die; the Physitian shall erre, servants prove false and treacherous, cattel and beasts shall produce hurt and danger. In the seventh House *Rubeus* signifies a wife to be infamous, publickly adulterate, and contentious; deceitful and treacherous adversaries, who shall endeavour to overcome you, by crafty and subtil wiles and circumventions of the Law. In the eighth House *Rubeus* signifies a violent death to be inflicted, by the execution of publike Justice; and signifies, if any one be enquired after, that he is certainly dead; and wife to have no portion or dowry. *Rubeus* in the ninth House sheweth journeys to be evil and dangerous, and that a man shall be in danger either to spoiled by theeves and robbers, or to be taken by plunderers and robbers; declareth men to be of most wicked opinions in Religion, and of evil faith, and such as will often easily be induced to deny and go from their faith for every small occasion; denoteth Sciences to be false and deceitful, and the professors thereof to be ignorant. In the tenth House *Rubeus* signifies Princes to be cruel and tyrannical, and that their power shall come to an evil end, as that either they shall be cruelly murdered and destroyed by their own Subjects, or that they shall be taken captive by their conquerers, and put to an ignominious and cruel death, or shall miserably end their lives in hard imprisonment; signifies Judges and Officers to be false, theevish, and such as shall be addicted to usury; sheweth that a mother shall soon die, and denoteth her to be blemisht with an evil fame and report. In the eleventh House *Rubeus* giveth no true, nor any faithful friends; sheweth men to be of wicked lives and conversations, and causeth a man to be rejected and cast out from all society and conversation with good and noble persons. *Rubeus* in the twelfth House maketh enemies to be cruel and traiterous, of whom we ought circumspectly to beware; signifies such as are in prison shall come to an evil end; and sheweth a great many inconveniences and mischiefs to happen in a mans life." (*Agrippa His Fourth Book* 1978: 26-27)

The last example is from C. W. Roback's *The Mysteries of Astrology and the Wonders of Magic* (1854), an unusual mid-19th century American book on divination and the occult aimed at the popular market that includes a straight-forward, simplified version of geomancy.

GEOMANCY.

GEOMANCY is the art of foreshowing future events by combinations of dots or points. The friars of the Middle Ages, who, notwithstanding their public fulminations against sorcery and magic, practised in the seclusion of their monasteries and abbeys all the methods of divination with which their black letter lore, and the traditions of former ages had made them familiar, especially affected this branch of occult science. Shut out from the ordinary pleasures and occupations of life by their monastic vows, they seem to have compensated themselves for the sacrifice of worldly indulgencies by seeking to penetrate the veil which hides from man the secrets of Destiny. That powerful clerico-military brotherhood, the Knights Templars, were at one time accused of practising Demonology, and many of the order were tried and sentenced to excommunication and death on this charge. Whether the accusations brought against them were true or false, we have now no means of ascertaining; but it is quite certain that many of the monks of that era were well-versed in celestial magic. The innocent and yet wonderful art of Geomancy, as well as the more abstruse science of Judicial and Horary Astrology, was studied and reduced to practice in cells and oratories, the inmates of which were supposed by the outside world to be solely employed in fasting, prayer, and holy meditation.

But human nature is pretty much the same in the cloister as it is elsewhere. Curiosity, which we all honestly inherit from our common mother, is sharpened rather than extinguished in retirement, and the good fathers finding little field for it in their gloomy present, were indefatigable in devising ways and means for obtaining a peep into futurity.

As the processes of Geomancy are interesting and amusing, the cowled tenants of the religious houses beguiled many a weary hour in endeavouring to wring from Fate her undeveloped mysteries by its aid. Nor were their efforts fruitless, for in all cases, where the inquirer is sincere and earnest in his or her questions though this medium, the sympathy which prevails throughout nature, and which cannot be accounted for except by referring it to something higher than material influences, will insure him a true and intelligent answer.

The art or science of Geomancy consists of two parts, *simple* and *compound*. *Simple Geomancy* is the art of ascertaining events to come, from the nature and properties of sixteen emblematic figures, without combination by house, place or aspect.

Compound Geomancy can scarcely be called an art: it is a science. It teaches the means of discovering not only the general answer to the question propounded, but all its contingent relations; and involves in its formula some of the operations of Astrology.

Strange to say this branch of magic although extensively practised has rarely been made the subject of explanatory treatises; and at this day it is almost impossible to obtain a book in relation to it at any price. The author of this work has in his possession a volume of illuminated manuscript, bearing date 1429, in which there is a tolerably full description of the Geomantic *modus operandi*, and from this and other data collected during his travels, as well as from the knowledge derived from practical experience, he will endeavour to give a concise sketch of the mode of proceeding.

The method of working questions in simple Geomancy consists in rapidly marking down with pen or pencil a series of dots or points, the precise number being left to chance. The mind of the querist, while doing this, must be earnestly fixed upon the matter upon which he desires information, and as free from doubt and skepticism as possible. The latter point is essential to a veracious and rational answer.

The ancients believed that when these conditions were observed, an invisible spirit or planetary angel controlled the hand of the questioner, causing him so to arrange the mystic dots as to obtain an authentic solution of his query.

The forms and names of the sixteen Geomantic signs or figures are as follows [only eight are shown in the book]:

0 0
  0
0 0
  0
	Acquistio.	0 0
		  0
		  0
		  0
			Caput.

0
0 0
  0
0 0
	Amissio.	0
		  0
		  0
		0 0
			Cauda.

0 0
  0
0 0
0 0
	Rubens.	0 0
		0 0
		  0
		  0
			Fortuna major.

0 0
0 0
  0
0 0
	Albus.	0
		  0
		0 0
		0 0
			Fortuna minor.

In the first place, as has been stated, the dots are casually marked down, without counting. The next proceeding is to join them into a scheme or figure, whence the answer is derived.

Such is the present formula; but an almost illegible black letter volume of the twelfth century, in the library of the British Museum, from which by permission extracts have been made for this book, contains the subjoined directions for divining by Geomancy, which cannot fail to be accounted impressive as well as quaint and curious. /

Divination by the Seven Planets.

"The seven planets are called the kings of the world; and every one of these may do in his hemisphere as an Imperator in his empire, or a prince in his kingdom. They are named by wise men, the seven candlesticks of light and life, and are as seven quick spirits whereunto all living things and all terrestrial affairs are subjective.

"To *divine* by their influences is the scope of our doctrine, even the art called Geomancy which is none other than the cogitations of the heart of the asker, joined to the earnest desire of the will to know the thing or matter uncertain or dark, which is, nevertheless, contained in the penetralium or hidden cabinet of nature, and governed by the secrets of fortune.

"This art, curious in its method, and of diverse efficacy, is attainable by him alone who will, amidst thorny paths and rugged journeys, guide his footsteps aright; for doubtless divers ways lead to the selfsame end. But know, O man! whoever thou art, that shall inquire into these hidden mysteries, that thou must forbear to consult the heavenly oracles, or to cast thy divining points, in a cloudy, windy, or rainy season; or when the heavens above thee are stricken with thunder; or when the lightnings glare amidst thy path; for thou art governed by an invisible demon who wills thy answer, and will guide thy trembling fingers to cast thy figure rightly. So that what to thee may seem the sport and pastime of every chance, is the work of an unseen power. Therefore, mark well, else the mighty spirits of the earth, who rule thy destiny, will be to thee as deceivers, and even as the false and lying spirits recorded in Holy Writ.

"Thou shalt therefore cast thy divining points in earth (thy fellow clay) tempered according to the high and hidden mysteries of the seven wandering tires of heaven, which the vulgar call planets, or stars. Thou shalt take clean earth, in the manner of sand, *mingled with the dews of the night, and the rain of the clouds that shall fall during the full of the moon, commixed in equal portions for the space of seven days,* under the celestial signs or reigning / constellations, or otherwise in the lordship of the hours of the presiding planets; and then shalt thou mingle the whole mass together, to the intent that, by their commixion, the universal effect may be the better known, and the end thereof prophesied.

"Choose, therefore, a clear and goodly season, bright and fair, and neither dark, windy, nor rainy—and fear not, but rest assured thou shalt be satisfied.

"Moreover, shouldest thou make use of the *magical* suffumigations of the heavenly orbs, thou shalt make glad (by sympathy) the spirits of the air. They are these,—viz. mastic, cinnamon, frankincense, musk, the wood of aloes, coriandrum, violets, saunders, and saffron. Commix and ignite these in due and just proportions; and then mayest thou proceed to consult thy future lot."

The following and more modern plan is, however, equally efficient and less complex and laborious.

THE FIRST PROCESS.

When the asker or inquirer has thought earnestly upon the subject or matter of which he inquires, let him mark down *sixteen* lines of dots, marks, or points, without counting them, so that at the least there be not less than twelve points in each line,—which done, let him join the points or marks in each line together, two and two; and if the number of points be *even*, which is, if they will all join together, let him mark down at the end of the line *two* dots, ciphers, or marks; but if the number of points in the line be *odd*, which is *when one remains, after they are joined by two and two,* then let him write down but one point. Every four lines form one Geomantic figure, as follows:—

```
                                                                        Figure 1.
0—0 0—0 0—0 0—0 0—0 0—0 0—0 0—0 0—0 0—0     .      .      ..    0  0
0—0 0—0 0—0 0—0 0—0 0—0 0—0 0 0  .           .      .      ..      0
0—0 0—0 0—0 0—0 0—0 0—0 0—0 0—0 0—0          .      .      ..    0  0
0—0 0—0 0—0 0—0 0 0—0 0                      .      .      ..      0
                                                                        Figure 2.
0—0 0—0 0—0 0—0 0—0 0—0 0—0 0—0 0—0          ..     .            0  0
0—0 0—0 0—0 0—0 0—0 0—0 0 0                  .      ..     .       0
0—0 0—0 0—0 0—0 0—0 0—0 0—0 0—0 0—0  0       ..     .              0
0—0 0—0 0—0 0—0 0—0 0—0 0 0                  .      ..     .       0
                                                                        Figure 3.
0—0 0—0 0—0 0—0 0—0 0—0 0—0 0 0 . .          .      ..     .       0
0—0 0—0 0—0 0—0 0—0 0—0 0—0 0 0              .      ..     .       0
0—0 0—0 0—0 0—0 0—0 0—0 0—0 0—0              .      ..     .     0  0
0—0 0—0 0—0 0—0 0—0 0—0 0—0 0—0 0            .      ..     .       0
                                                                        Figure 4.
0—0 0—0 0—0 0—0 0—0 0—0 0—0 0—0 0—0 0—0      .      ..     .     0  0
0—0 0—0 0—0 0—0 0—0 0—0 0—0 0—0 0 0—0        .      ..     .       0
0—0 0—0 0—0 0—0 0—0 0—0 0—0 0 0—0            .      ..     .     0  0
0—0 0—0 0—0 0—0 0—0 0—0 0—0 0 .              .      ..     .       0
```

These are called the four first steps of the figure; and in placing them they must be read from right to left, as underneath.

```
    4th            3d          2d          1st
    0  0           0           0  0        0  0
    0  0           0           0           0
    0  0           0  0        0           0  0
    0  0           0           0           0
```

The next process is to form *four* other figures from out of the first four, which is done by taking the number of points in the first lines of each figure: thus, in the figure

Figure 5.

No. 1, the points in the first line are *two*, placed thus   .   .   .   0 0

In No. 2, the points in the first line are also *two*, placed thus   .   .   0 0

In No. 3, there is but *one* point thus   .   0

In No. 4, there are again *two*, thus   .   .   0 0

Giving this figure,
No. 5.
$$\left\{ \begin{array}{l} 0 \ \ 0 \\ 0 \ \ 0 \\ 0 \\ 0 \ \ 0 \end{array} \right.$$

Figure the 6th is found the same way, by taking the odd or even points in the *second* line of the figures, thus:—

Figure 6.

In the second line of No. 1 is an odd point, thus .   0

In the second line of No. 2 is also an odd point .   0

In the second line of No. 3 is also an odd point .   0

In the second line of No. 4 are two points, thus .   0 0

Giving this figure,
No. 6.
$$\left\{ \begin{array}{l} 0 \\ 0 \\ 0 \\ 0 \ \ 0 \end{array} \right.$$

Figure the 7th is also found the same way; thus—

Figure 7.

In the *third* line of No. 1, there are two points, thus   0 0

In the third line of No. 2, one point, thus   .   .   0

In the third line of No. 3, two points, thus   .   .   0 0

In the third line of No. 4, also two points, thus   .   0 0

Giving this figure, No. 7.	$\left\{\begin{array}{l} 0\quad 0 \\ 0 \\ 0\quad 0 \\ 0\quad 0 \end{array}\right.$

Figure the 8th is formed thus, the same way.

Figure 8.

In the *fourth* line of No. 1, one point . . .	0
In the fourth line of No. 2, one point . . .	0
In the fourth line of No. 3, one point . . .	0
In the fourth line of No. 4, two points . . .	0 0

Giving this figure, No. 8.	$\left\{\begin{array}{l} 0 \\ 0 \\ 0 \\ 0\quad 0 \end{array}\right.$

The next step is to place the whole in order from right to left, as under.

8	7	6	5	4	3	2	1
0	0 0	0	0 0	0 0	0	0 0	0 0
0	0	0	0 0	0 0	0	0	0
0	0 0	0	0	0 0	0 0	0	0
0 0	0 0	0 0	0 0	0 0	0	0	0

Next, a figure is formed out of each pair of figures, by joining together the 1st and 2d, the 3d and 4th, the 5th and 6th, and the 7th and 8th figures, according as the points in each are odd or even,—thus:

0	0	0	0 0
0 0	0	0	0 0
0	0 0	0 0	0
0 0	0 0	0	0 0

By this means, an additional four figures, Nos. 9, 10, 11, and 12, are gained, which are again to be joined together,—thus:

12	11	10	9
0	0	0	0 0
0 0	0	0	0 0
0	0 0	0 0	0
0 0	0 0	0	0 0

```
           14                                    13
          0  0                                    0
           0                                      0
           0                                      0
          0  0                                    0
```

And lastly, Nos. 13 and 14 are joined in like manner together, thus; No. 13 has one mark and odd in the first line, and No. 14 two.

Figure 7.

The number *three* is *odd,* marked thus . .	0
In the second line of each, *two* points, *even* .	0 0
In the third line of each, *two,* also even . .	0
In the fourth line of each, *three,* odd . .	0

The whole process is exemplified in the complete figure which is here given.

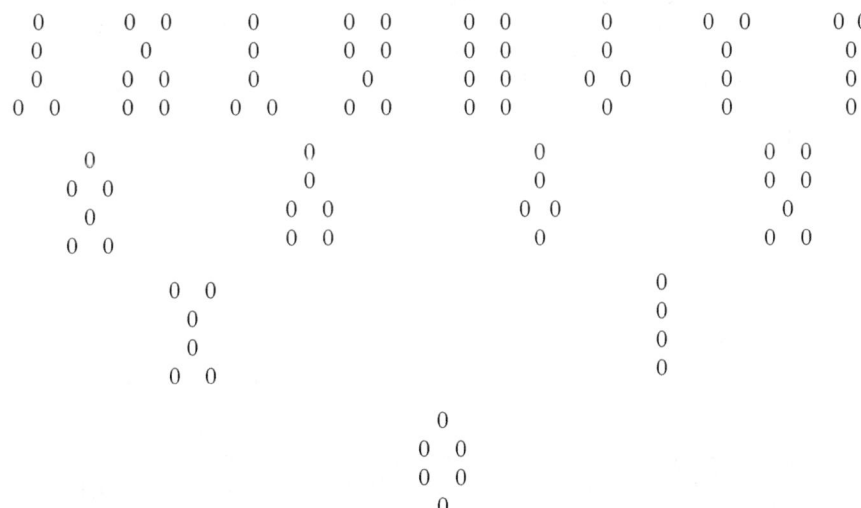

WITNESSES AND JUDGE IN THE POREGOING EXAMPLE.

```
        14                                              13
    Left Witness.                                  Right Witness.
         0                                               0
        0  0                                            0  0
        0  0                                             0
        0  0                                             0

                          15
                        Judge.
                         0  0
                         0  0
                          0
                          0
```

In resolving questions by *simple* Geomancy, it is tine *three last figures alone,* Nos. 13, 14, and 15, which are used in giving the answers. These are termed

A FIGURE OF TRIPLICITY.

Of these three figures, No. 13 is termed the *Right Witness,* and No. 14 the *Left Witness;* out of these two is drawn the JUDGE of the whole figure, to whom the sentence or answer of the whole question belongs, as will be hereafter shown.

There is a striking peculiarity, or *arithmetical* property, in a scheme of Geomancy thus cast; which is, that only eight out of the sixteen figures can ever be found in the place of the Judge; the latter, therefore, is always formed of *even* points. For it must be observed, that to the first four figures belong the groundwork of the whole; and these must be either odd or even :—if odd, the next four figures will be also odd; and, according to a geometrical axiom, out of two negative qualities comes an affirmative; and, therefore, the *Judge* will be even. Again, if the first four figures are even, the next four figures will be even also, and of course *the Judge will always be even.*

At first sight, the reader may discover many difficulties in the way of casting a figure; but a little practice will render the system familiar, plain, and easy, therefore let him not reject it without a trial.

The method of forming a figure of Geomancy, has been already shown; as also, what is termed, the "Figure of the Triplicities;" for the better judging of which, the old authors have left on record certain Tables, which contain the "*Sentence*" of the witnesses and judge; by which an answer, negative or affirmative may be found without trouble.

It has been also observed, that only eight out of the sixteen figures can ever be judge; yet, as there are two witnesses also to be taken into account, the *variations* to the answers are 8 multiplied by 16, and therefore equal to 128 in number. In these cases, however, it is of consequence to notice on which side the good or evil figures fall, as *that* gives the variations in the result. Thus, for instance, the Triplicities—

```
0 0        0                    0        0 0
0 0        0                    0        0 0
0 0        0                    0        0 0
0 0        0        and         0        0 0      although the judge
        0                            0
        0                            0
        0                            0
        0                            0
```

is the same in each, yet the answers corresponding are different; and so in all other cases whatever.

In order to work by the following Tables, the reader must cast the figure, and refer to the page for the answer to his question: thus, for instance, in the following figure:—

```
        0 0                         0
        0 0                         0
         0                         0 0
        0 0                         0
              0
              0
              0
              0
```

If the question were "of the Length of Life," the answer would be, "*Short Life.*"

If it were of an affair connected with "Money," the answer would be, "*Unfortunate.*"

If it were of "Sickness," it would denote "*Death*" to the Patient, and so on in all other cases; referring to that page of the work which has the required Triplicities.

The following Tables are compiled from an old and curious author, now out of print: the answers are concise, and the explanation simple; which is all that can be wished.

Jim Baker

```
•  •  •
•  •  •
•  •  •
•  •  •
```

THE SENTENCE OF THE JUDGE
IN THE QUESTIONS RELATING TO

1. 𝕷ength of 𝕷ife.   6. 𝕻regnancy.

2. 𝕸oney or 𝕲ain.   7. 𝕾ickness.

3. 𝕳onor or 𝕮redit.   8. 𝕴mprisonment.

4. 𝕭usiness.   9. 𝕵ourneys, and

5. 𝕸arriage.   10. 𝕿hings lost.

ACCORDING TO THE MOST FAMOUS AUTHORS OF FORMER TIMES.

```
0 0            0 0            0 0                  0
0 0            0 0            0 0                  0
0 0            0 0            0 0                  0
0 0            0 0            0 0                  0
        0 0                                0
        0 0                                0
        0 0                                0
        0 0                                0
```

QUESTIONS	ANSWERS	QUESTIONS	ANSWERS
Life,	Moderately long.	Life,	Moderate.
Money,	Meanly good.	Money,	Evil.
Honor,	Meanly good.	Honor,	Mean.
Business,	Fortunate.	Business,	Unfortunate.
Marriage,	Good.	Marriage,	Good.
Pregnancy,	A Daughter.	Pregnancy,	A Son.
Sickness,	Dangerous,	Sickness,	Health.
Imprisonment,	Delivery.	Imprisonment,	Quick Release.
Journey,	Good by Water.	Journey,	Good and Quick.
Things Lost,	Found.	Things Lost,	Not Found.

```
        0                    0                    0                    0   0
        0                    0                    0   0                0
        0                    0                    0   0                0
        0                    0                    0   0                0
                0   0                                          0
                0   0                                          0
                0   0                                          0
                0   0                                          0
```

QUESTIONS	ANSWERS
Life,	Evil.
Money,	Evil.
Honor,	Good.
Business,	Fortunate.
Marriage,	Good.
Pregnancy,	A Daughter.
Sickness,	Dangerous.
Imprisonment,	Long.
Journey,	Good by Sea.
Things Lost,	Not Found.

QUESTIONS	ANSWERS
Life,	Good and Long.
Money,	An Increase.
Honor,	Good.
Business,	Good.
Marriage,	Good.
Pregnancy,	A Son.
Sickness,	Health.
Imprisonment,	Late Out.
Journey,	Ends good.
Things Lost,	Found

```
        0   0                0   0                0   0                0
        0   0                0   0                0   0                0
        0                    0                    0                    0   0
        0                    0                    0                    0   0
                0   0                                          0
                0   0                                          0
                0   0                                          0
                0   0                                          0
```

QUESTIONS	ANSWERS
Life,	Favourable.
Money,	Fortunate.
Honor,	Mean.
Business,	Fortunate.
Marriage,	Good.
Pregnancy,	A Girl.
Sickness,	Health.
Imprisonment,	Come out.
Journey,	Good and Speedy
Things Lost,	Found.

QUESTIONS	ANSWERS
Life,	Mean.
Money,	Mean.
Honor,	Good.
Business,	MeanlyGood.
Marriage,	Good
Pregnancy,	A Son.
Sickness,	Health.
Imprisonment,	Deliverance.
Journey,	Soon Return.
Things Lost,	Found.

```
  0 0           0 0           0 0              0
  0 0           0 0           0 0              0
   0             0             0              0 0
  0 0           0 0           0 0              0
        0 0                          0
        0 0                          0
         0                           0
        0 0                          0
```

QUESTIONS	ANSWERS	QUESTIONS	ANSWERS
Life,	Moderate.	Life,	Short Life.
Money,	Mean.	Money,	Unfortunate.
Honor,	Mean.	Honor,	Ill.
Business,	Mean.	Business,	Evil.
Marriage,	Indifferent.	Marriage,	Unfortunate.
Pregnancy,	A Daughter.	Pregnancy,	A Daughter.
Sickness,	Perilous.	Sickness,	Death.
Imprisonment,	Deliverance.	Imprisonment,	Perilous.
Journey,	Very good by water.	Journey,	Mean.
Things Lost,	Part Found.	Things Lost,	Not Found.

```
  0 0           0 0           0 0              0
   0             0             0              0 0
  0 0           0 0           0 0              0
  0 0           0 0           0 0              0
        0 0                          0
        0 0                          0
        0 0                          0
        0 0                          0
```

QUESTIONS	ANSWERS	QUESTIONS	ANSWERS
Life,	Very evil.	Life,	Moderate.
Money,	Unlucky.	Money,	Meanly Good.
Honor,	Very ill.	Honor,	Mean.
Business,	Unfortunate.	Business,	Indifferent.
Marriage,	A bad one.	Marriage,	Prosperous.
Pregnancy,	A Girl.	Pregnancy,	A Daughter.
Sickness,	Perilous.	Sickness,	Long Sick.
Imprisonment,	Death.	Imprisonment,	Soon out.
Journey,	Robbed.	Journey,	Slow.
Things Lost,	Not Found.	Things Lost,	Found.

```
 0  0           0  0           0  0                   0
 0  0           0  0           0  0                   0
 0  0           0  0           0  0                   0
    0              0              0                0  0
        0  0                           0
        0  0                           0
        0  0                           0
        0  0                           0
```

QUESTIONS	ANSWERS	QUESTIONS	ANSWERS
Life,	Short.	Life,	Very Evil.
Money,	Unlucky.	Money,	Very Ill.
Honor,	Evil.	Honor,	Ill.
Business,	Evil.	Business,	Unlucky.
Marriage,	Jarring.	Marriage,	Evil.
Pregnancy,	Abortion.	Pregnancy,	Abortion.
Sickness,	Death.	Sickness,	Perilous.
Imprisonment,	Dangerous.	Imprisonment,	Long.
Journey,	Unlucky.	Journey,	Unlucky.
Things Lost,	Not Found.	Things Lost,	Not Found.

```
        0              0              0                  0
     0  0           0  0           0  0               0  0
     0  0           0  0           0                     0
     0  0           0  0           0                     0
        0  0                              0  0
        0  0                              0  0
        0  0                              0  0
        0  0                              0  0
```

QUESTIONS	ANSWERS	QUESTIONS	ANSWERS
Life,	Long.	Life,	Long.
Money,	Mean.	Money,	Fortunate.
Honor,	Mean.	Honor,	Good.
Business,	Unlucky.	Business,	Very Good.
Marriage,	Good.	Marriage,	Pleasant.
Pregnancy,	A Son.	Pregnancy,	A Son.
Sickness,	Danger.	Sickness,	Dangerous.
Imprisonment,	Come out.	Imprisonment,	Delivery.
Journey,	Good.	Journey,	Voyage Good.
Things Lost,	Not Found.	Things Lost,	Part Found.

```
        0                  0   0                 0                   0   0
    0   0                  0                     0                   0   0
        0                  0   0               0   0                 0   0
        0                  0   0                 0                   0   0

              0                                        0
              0                                        0
              0                                        0
              0                                        0
```

QUESTIONS	ANSWERS	QUESTIONS	ANSWERS
Life,	Moderate.	Life,	Short.
Money,	Mean.	Money,	Unlucky.
Honor,	Ill.	Honor,	Mean.
Business,	Ill.	Business,	Mean.
Marriage,	Ill.	Marriage,	Indifferent.
Pregnancy,	Child dies.	Pregnancy,	A Daughter.
Sickness,	Perilous.	Sickness,	Death.
Imprisonment,	Come out.	Imprisonment,	Soon out.
Journey,	Ill end.	Journey,	Mean.
Things Lost,	Not Found	Things Lost,	Part Found.

```
        0                  0                     0                   0   0
        0                  0                     0                   0   0
      0   0                0   0                0   0                   0
        0                  0   0                 0                   0   0

              0                                        0
              0                                        0
              0                                        0
              0                                        0
```

QUESTIONS	ANSWERS	QUESTIONS	ANSWERS
Life,	Short.	Life,	Long.
Money,	Unlucky.	Money,	Great Riches.
Honor,	Evil.	Honor,	Excellent.
Business,	Evil.	Business,	Very Good.
Marriage,	Unlucky.	Marriage,	Good.
Pregnancy,	Daughter.	Pregnancy,	A Son.
Sickness,	Soon die.	Sickness,	Dangerous.
Imprisonment,	Soon out.	Imprisonment,	Come out.
Journey,	Vexatious.	Journey,	Voyage Good.
Things Lost,	Not Found.	Things Lost,	Found.

```
  0 0              0              0              0 0
  0              0 0              0              0 0
  0              0 0              0              0 0
  0              0 0            0 0                0

       0                                 0
       0                                 0
       0                                 0
       0                                 0
```

QUESTIONS	ANSWERS	QUESTIONS	ANSWERS
Life,	Long.	Life,	Short.
Money,	Very Good.	Money,	Ill.
Honor,	Good.	Honor,	Ill.
Business,	Good.	Business,	Mean.
Marriage,	Mean.	Marriage,	Very bad.
Pregnancy,	A Son.	Pregnancy,	A Daughter.
Sickness,	Health.	Sickness,	Danger.
Imprisonment,	Come out.	Imprisonment,	Dangerous
Journey,	Good.	Journey,	Unlucky.
Things Lost,	Found.	Things Lost,	Not Found.

```
      0              0            0 0            0 0
      0              0              0              0
      0              0            0 0            0 0
    0 0            0 0              0              0

         0 0                             0 0
         0 0                             0 0
         0 0                             0 0
         0 0                             0 0
```

QUESTIONS	ANSWERS	QUESTIONS	ANSWERS
Life,	Short.	Life,	Long.
Money,	Unlucky.	Money,	Very Fortunate.
Honor,	Evil.	Honor,	Good.
Business,	Ill.	Business,	Fortunate.
Marriage,	Unlucky.	Marriage,	Fortunate.
Pregnancy,	Daughter.	Pregnancy,	Daughter.
Sickness,	Death.	Sickness,	Health.
Imprisonment,	Dangerous.	Imprisonment,	Delivery.
Journey,	Loss.	Journey,	Good.
Things Lost,	Not Found.	Things Lost,	Found.

```
  0 0              0              0              0 0
   0              0 0            0 0              0
  0 0              0              0              0 0
   0              0 0            0 0              0
       0 0                            0
       0 0                            0
       0 0                            0
       0 0                            0
```

QUESTIONS	ANSWERS		QUESTIONS	ANSWERS
Life,	Mean.		Life,	Good.
Money,	Bad.		Money,	Good.
Honor,	Ill.		Honor,	Mean.
Business,	Ill.		Business,	Mean.
Marriage,	Ill.		Marriage,	Mean.
Pregnancy,	A Daughter.		Pregnancy,	Abortion.
Sickness,	Health.		Sickness,	End, Health.
Imprisonment,	Come out.		Imprisonment,	Long.
Journey,	Mean.		Journey,	Good.
Things Lost,	Not Found.		Things Lost,	Not Found.

```
    0              0            0 0            0 0
   0 0            0 0            0              0
    0              0             0              0
   0 0            0 0           0 0            0 0
       0 0                            0 0
       0 0                            0 0
       0 0                            0 0
       0 0                            0 0
```

QUESTIONS	ANSWERS		QUESTIONS	ANSWERS
Life,	Short.		Life,	Mean.
Money,	Unlucky.		Money,	Mean.
Honor,	Ill.		Honor,	Indifferent.
Business,	Evil.		Business,	Mean.
Marriage,	Evil.		Marriage,	Mean.
Pregnancy,	Doubtful.		Pregnancy,	A Son.
Sickness,	Perilous.		Sickness,	Death.
Imprisonment,	Difficult.		Imprisonment,	Perilous.
Journey,	Unlucky.		Journey,	Good by water.
Things Lost,	Not Found		Things Lost,	Not Found.

The Cunning Man's Handbook

```
  0 0              0             0            0 0
   0              0 0           0 0            0
   0              0 0           0 0            0
  0 0              0             0            0 0
      0                                 0
      0                                 0
      0                                 0
      0                                 0
```

QUESTIONS	ANSWERS	QUESTIONS	ANSWERS
Life,	Moderate.	Life,	Mean.
Money,	Mean.	Money,	Mean.
Honor,	Bad.	Honor,	Mean.
Business,	Indifferent.	Business,	Good.
Marriage,	Mean.	Marriage,	Good.
Pregnancy,	A Daughter.	Pregnancy,	A Daughter.
Sickness,	Dangerous.	Sickness,	Dangerous.
Imprisonment,	Long.	Imprisonment,	Late out.
Journey,	Evil.	Journey,	Ill.
Things Lost,	Found.	Things Lost,	Found.

```
       0             0             0             0
      0 0           0 0            0             0
      0 0           0 0           0 0           0 0
       0             0             0             0
                                  0 0           0 0
         0 0         0 0          0 0           0 0
         0 0         0 0
         0 0         0 0
         0 0         0 0
```

QUESTIONS	ANSWERS	QUESTIONS	ANSWERS
Life,	Ill.	Life,	Moderate.
Money,	Evil.	Money,	Indifferent.
Honor,	Vexatious.	Honor,	Good.
Business,	Unlucky.	Business,	Mean.
Marriage,	Ill.	Marriage,	Mean.
Pregnancy,	A Daughter.	Pregnancy,	A Son.
Sickness,	Perilous.	Sickness,	Health.
Imprisonment,	Long.	Imprisonment,	Dangerous.
Journey,	Difficult.	Journey,	Good.
Things Lost,	Not Found.	Things Lost,	Part Found.

0	0 0	0	0 0
0	0 0	0	0 0
0 0	0	0	0 0
0 0	0	0	0 0

0	0
0	0
0	0
0	0

QUESTIONS	ANSWERS	QUESTIONS	ANSWERS
Life,	Good.	Life,	Moderate.
Money,	Lucky.	Money,	Ill.
Honor,	Powerful.	Honor,	Mean.
Business,	Good.	Business,	Ill.
Marriage,	Good.	Marriage,	Good.
Pregnancy,	A Son.	Pregnancy,	A Son.
Sickness,	Health.	Sickness,	Health.
Imprisonment,	Come out.	Imprisonment,	Soon out.
Journey,	Good.	Journey,	Voyage Good.
Things Lost,	Found.	Things Lost,	Not Found.

The rules, principles and clear examples of Simple Geomancy have now been given. The Compound branch of the science is far too abstruse to be comprehended by the general reader, and those who desire to learn concerning their fate, through this medium, should apply to a competent astrologer and professor of magic. (Roback 1854: 85-104)

It is unlikely that geomancy – especially the advanced sort involving the 12 houses – was ever widely practiced by the Cunning Folk. The complexity of both astrology and geomancy may have militated against their practice at the lower end of the magical profession, but some acquaintance with these systems was required for professional credibility, especially after the mid-17th century.

CHAPTER 7:

Dreams Natural, Demonic and Divine

"Pyrates dream of their spoyles and preyes, and what gain they have met with; Robbers, of Manslaughters; theeves, of theft; and fornicators, of their whores." Paracelsus. *The Archidoxes of Magic* (1656), p. 46.

The interpretation of dreams has always played an important role in the divinatory arts. Cultures fascinated by these spontaneous nightly visions have been almost universally convinced that some dreams were more than mere perturbations of the bodily humours or spirits; that some of these intriguing visualizations were messages from the spiritual world involving divine guidance or foretelling the future. The *Bible*, in particular, is filled with dreams sent by God to individuals, a precedent that went far in legitimating limited dream interpretation in Christian culture. Dream interpretation was an important aspect of ancient and classical cultures as well, most significantly for members of the social and political elite who solicited supernatural advice by sleeping in sacred spaces for dreams that were either explicit revelations or required symbolic interpretation by religious experts. A more democratic practice was that of medical *incubatio* – the "sleeping-in" of temples of Asclepius (following appropriate ceremonial preparation) to solicit dreams that would result in a cure or provide information for appropriate treatment based on the interpretation by temple officials.

The most famous and influential work of dream interpretation in the ancient world, and the ancestor of the majority of dream books since that time, was the *Oneirocritica* of Artemidorus Daldianus (2nd century CE). This pagan work, which was later expurgated and edited for a Christian audience, contains not only listings with the meaning of various things and actions found in dreams, but also a complex theoretical approach to their analysis. Dreams are divided into various types and sub-types, from a primary division between predictive and non-predictive dreams to the many possible meanings for different people depending on status, age, gender, wealth, occupation and so forth. The *Oneirocritica* formed the basis of the first important dream book published in English, Thomas Hill's *The Moste Pleasunte Arte of the Interpretacion of Dreames* (1576), and there were a number of editions of Robert Wood's 1606 translation of the *Oneirocritica* into English, which was reprinted well into the 18th century. Later dream books, however, generally omitted Artemidorus' theoretical framework and simply presented alphabetical lists of the interpretive meanings of symbolic objects and actions seen in any sort of dream.

It might be useful, nevertheless, to be aware of some of the traditional theories about dreams and dreaming. Firstly, as Artemidorus noted, not all dreams were of equal significance. It was recognized that many were the result of bodily indispositions such as illness or indigestion (when cold humours from the stomach rose to the brain and confused the soul in sleep), or from the anxieties and concerns of daily life. The late pagan philosopher Macrobius (4th century CE) developed a standard taxonomy of dreams accepted by medieval Christians that divided dreams into five types; three that had oracular content and two that did not (which later writers called "true" and "vain" dreams).

1. Enigmatic or allegorical (Greek – *onerios*; Latin – *somnium*).
2. Prophetic (*horama; visio*).
3. Oracular (*chremaismos; oraculum*).
4. Nightmare (*enypion; insomnium*).
5. Apparition (*phantasma; visum*).

Of the "vain" dreams, nightmares encompassed all uncomfortable, physically or demonically-induced dreams (including the witches' sabbat), while apparitions only occurred "in the moment between wakefulness and slumber" when the dozing dreamer was apt to see illusory ghostly intruders. Neither of these types signified anything. Among the "true" dreams, the prophetic dream involved a clear intimation of what would actually occur, usually the following day. In the oracular dream, a message was delivered by a wise or powerful being (God, angels, saints, deceased parents or demons), and except in the case of the latter, concerned what truly would or would not happen. It might as well be accompanied with divine advice. The danger was to mistake demonic illusions for the reliable messages of the good spirits.

The allegorical dream, the most common variety of "true" dream, was the subject of the common dream books in which occurrences or objects had symbolic meanings requiring interpretation. Macrobius divided these allegorical dreams into five sub-categories:

6. Personal; things that appear to happen to the person dreaming,
7. Alien; things that are seen to happen to someone else,
8. Social; things involving the dreamer and other people,
9. Public; events in public venues such as markets and cities,
10. Universal; events or visions of the heavens and the entire earth.

St. Thomas Aquinas outlined the basic Christian position on dreams, which minimized their predictive potential, but left room for true prophetic and oracular dreams:

> "Accordingly it is to be observed that the cause of dreams is sometimes in us and sometimes outside us. The inward cause of dreams is twofold: one regards the soul, in so far as those things which have occupied a man's thoughts and affections while awake recur to his imagination while asleep. A suchlike cause of dreams is not a cause of future occurrences, so that dreams of this kind are related accidentally to future occurrences and if at any time they concur it will be by chance. But sometimes the inward cause of dreams regards the body: because the inward disposition of the body leads to the formation of a movement in the imagination consistent with that disposition; thus a man in whom there is abundance of cold humours dreams that he is in the water or snow: and for this reason physicians say that we should take note of dreams in order to discover internal dispositions.
>
> In like manner the outward cause of dreams is twofold, corporal and spiritual. It is corporal in so far as the sleeper's imagination is affected either by the surrounding air, or through an impression of a heavenly body, so that certain images appear to the sleeper, in keeping with the disposition of the heavenly bodies. The spiritual cause is sometimes referable to God, Who reveals certain things to men in their dreams by the ministry of the angels, according to Num. xii. 6, *If there be among you a prophet of the Lord, I will appear to him in a vision, or I will speak to him in a dream*. Sometimes, however, it is due to the action of the demons that certain images appear to persons in their sleep, and by this means they, at times, reveal certain future things to those who have entered into an unlawful compact with them." (Aquinas 1920: vol. 9, pp. 204-205)

The subject of dream interpretation was potentially a serious and complex study in the early modern era, with many factors to be accounted for to assure reliable elucidation, such as the matter of worthy or unworthy recipients, a proper frame of mind, the time of day and season in which the dream was seen, the dreamer's social status, wealth, age and so forth. "Set and setting" – the necessary mental and environmental conditions for true dreams was equally important, as Cornelius Agrippa noted in his *Three Books of Occult Philosophy*:

> "Therefore it is necessary, that he who would receive true dreams, should keep a pure, undisturbed, and an undisquieted imaginative spirit, and so compose it, that it may be made worthy of the knowledge and government by the mind and understanding: for such a spirit is most fit for prophesying, and (as Sinesius saith) is a most clear glass of all the Images which flow everywhere from all things: when therefore we are sound in body, not disturbed in mind, not dulled by meat or drink, nor sad through poverty, nor provoked by any vice of lust or wrath, but chastly going to bed, fall asleep, then our pure and divine soul being loosed from all hurtfull thoughts, and now freed by dreaming, is endowed with this divine spirit as an instrument, and doth receive those beams and representations which are darted down, and shine forth from the divine minde into it self; and as it were in a deifying glass." (Agrippa 1651: Book III, Chapter 51, p. 512).

Thomas Hill, in *The Moste Pleasunte Arte of the Interpretacion of Dreames* (drawn largely from Artemidorus but also other authorities on sleep and dreaming), discussed a number of the important considerations for the interpreter of dreams:

> "Yet hovv Dreames may be known to him, whiche neuer had true dreame, in that they onlye happen to suche, whose spirites are occupyed with no irrationall imaginatio[n]s, nor ouercharged with the burthe[n] of meate or drinkes, or superfluous humours, nor giue[n] to any other bodelie pleasures. For those which are co[n]trary to this order, are not properly dreames, but to be named vain dreames, no true signifiers of matters to come but rather shewers of the present affections and desires of the body. and yet dreames seene by graue & sober persons, do signifie matters to come, and a spirite vndoubtedlie shewinge to them, whiche by her nature is a Prophetesse, that se[n]dth forth such a motion & workmanshippe, throughe whiche the bodye as in her proper dwellyng, may either be defended fro[m] the instant euils & perils, or moued to the attayinge of good things to come & that with diligence workinge the same, that as it were into loking Glasse of the body placed, it might so beholde and foreshewe matters imminent. Therefore this difference of true dreames from the vayn ought diligently to be noted. …
>
> And it shalbe necessarye for the interpretoure to consider and knowe what the persone tradeth or occupyeth, & of what birth hee is & what possessio[n]s he hath & what state he is in for the healthe of bodye & of what age he is also which seeth & dream. Also a dreame ought exactly to be told as eyther withoute anye addinge to of matter, or taking fro, For y^t these doo cause great error vnto the vnderstanding of a truth. …
>
> But well consideringe that the ayre is the outward cause of dreames, because in the first it receiueth the impressio[n] of the starres, and after touchethe the bodies of men and beastes, which are altered of it yea in the daye tyme, like as appearethe in the nighte Rauen and Owle, whiche (as moste men affirme) by his synginge ouer the chamber of the sicke, is prognosticated shortlye after deathe …"

The entries in Hill's and Artemidorus' books were generally given in narrative form and could be rather extensive, as the following example for "loss of teeth" indicates:

> "And the losse of teeth, or els fallinge or violently pluckinge out of them, doth for the most part signify, the losse or deathe of kinfolkes, or elles one of the same family or householde, or els the losse of substaunce: For the lyke is to be applied betweene the house, family, and substaunce therin, as betwene the mouth, and the teath. And besydes the ryght teeth signifye the men, and the lefte teethe the women excepte it so happe[n], that in on house be all women, and in another house all men: for then in those houses, the righte teeth signify the elder, and the lefte teeth the yonger persones. And further the foor teeth signify verye yonge persones, and the sharpe teeth lyke to dogges teth, signifye parsons of middle age: and the theke teeth, old persones.
>
> And therfore who that dreameth to leese any toohe, shall lose such a frende, as that tooth signifieth: but when not onely men, but also the losinge possessions bee signifyed: then it is thought or supposed, that the cheke teeth to signify treasures / or riches layd vp or els hid. And ye sharp teeth to signifie those thinges which bee of no great momente or value.
>
> And the foreteeth signifye simple householde stuffe, or els other mouables within the house. Therefore very lyke it is y^t some of them falling out, to signifye the losse of money, ryches, & facultyes: & further the teeth also signifye necessary matters to lyfe, and of these the cheeke teeth, signify secrete & privy matters. And the sharpe teethe signifye those thynges, whiche be not manifest to many, & open maters, and of these thinges which be compared by the talke & worde. And therfore the teeth fallinge out, be, or signifye the hynderaunce or losse of the lyke matters, to them belonginge, also all the teeth fallynge out together, signify a desert house lefte and forsayken by all the persons departing together from it. And further teathe fallinge oute to those that be sicke do signify a longe sicknes and the scabbes or blistrings: but yet the giue theim not to dye. For of the deade bodies, none after leaveth a tooth. Wherfore what so / euer happeneth not to deade folkes, is a notice of healthe to sicke persons yet better it is that sicke persons to lose all their tethe, for so the[y] y^t soner to healthe.
>
> And to a servaunte to lose his teethe, signifyeth after libertye & freedome. And to marchauntes this dreame signifyeth the spedy prouision a desposition of packes and other goods, & especially if they shalbe in that iourney wyth them. Also certayne of the teeth waxing aboue the others so that the on exceadeth the other in bygnes, or elles that be louse and fall not out, signifye sedicion or variaunce in his house whiche seeth the dreame. And who that thinketh in his dreame to haue blacke, rotten, worme eaten, or broken teath, and to loase theym, signifyeth the deliuerye frome al trouble, and misery: & yet some, as often tymes the elder men, haue lost by this dream: besydes he that thinkethe

in hys dreame to haue Iuorye teeth, signifyeth good to all persons: but hee that thinkethe in his dreame, to haue golden teeth, signifyeth especiallye good to eloque[n]ce & learned speakers: as it were of the golden teethe prono[u]cinge the talke / but to others this dreame after threatneth fyre and burning of the house which se this dream, and to certayne also this dreame signifye sicknesse, co[m]myng and beynge of the multitude of choler. And he y^t thinketh in his dreame to haue teeth of waxe, signifyeth that he shall come to a speedy death, for such cannot chew meate wyth them: and to haue teethe of leade or tynne sygnifyeth reproche or infamy & shame to ensue: And to haue teethe of glasse or woode, doothe portende violente death: and he that thinketh in his dreame to haue siluer teethe, signifyeth to hym that is learned, to get money by his talk, and eloquence; but to riche men this dreame porte[n]deth, the expence of money into foode, and meates. And if any thinkethe in his dreame that his foreteeth fal out & the other grow in their places doth portend the chau[n]ge of life, into a better state Also be the seconde teeth shalbee better & fayrer, then ye other afore: but into a worser state, if they shalbee worser & fouler." (Hill 1576: not paginated)

There had been other, simpler sorts of dream books in the Middle Ages, in some of which the actual content of the dream played no part. One was the "dream alphabet" or "chance book" in which the interpreter used a version of book sortilege. The interpreter began by saying "In the name of the Father and the Son and the Holy Spirit. Amen", then opened a particular book at random, noted the first letter on the page, and consulted a list of significations keyed to that particular letter. This method seems to have died out by the 16th century but was resurrected after a fashion by "Raphael" in his *Royal Book of Dreams* (London, 1830), where the author employs his favored quasi-geomantic process of five-line figures to interpret dreams – irrespective of their content – by means of a table keyed to lists of random interpretations, which he dubbed the "Sephromantic Art". Another "content-free" approach was used in the "dream lunar" book where the only significant factor was the phase of the moon when the dream was experienced, which pointed to a related meaning for any dream occurring at that time. A version of this turns up from time to time, even as late as in the *Witch Doctor's Dream Book and Fortune Teller* (1891), but it was not as popular as the standard "dream dictionary" for allegorical interpretations. In the "Influence of the Moon Upon Dreams", there is a list of significations for each of the 28 nights of the moon's age, from new moon through full to new moon again, which could be used to support or reject other dream book entries:

1. Are regarded as fortunate.
2. Can not be depended upon.
3. Are sure to prove true.
4. Will be without any effect.
5. They are apt to be successful.
6. Will not be realized at once.
7. Do not communicate your dream.
8. May be expected to come to pass.
9. Are favourable to the dreamer.
10. Should be accepted as warnings.
11. Must be taken in a contrary sense.
12. Are regarded as truthful.
13. Is sure to prove reliable.
14. Cannot be accepted as truthful.
15. Are of great importance.
16. Are prophetic of great issues.
17. Nothing of importance will follow.
18. May be regarded as cautionary.
19. They cannot be relied upon.
20. Will be followed by good results.
21. May be disregarded as false.
22. Study the meaning of this dream.
23. Depend on it, something will occur.

24. Not altogether to be relied upon.
25. These are accepted as truthful.
26. Invariably prove true.
27. Are regarded as quite favourable.
28. Are accepted as unfortunate. (*Witch Doctor's*: 94-95)

The majority (including we suppose the Cunning Folk) appear to have preferred the "allegorical" tradition of interpretation by symbol as represented by widely-popular alphabetical dream books that derived from classical and medieval precedents such as Artemidorus, the *Somniale Danielis* or the *Oneirocriticon* of Astrampsychus.

Here we encounter the sort of dream book that is still being published today in considerable numbers, although the lists of things seen and done in dreams, as well as the meanings attributed to them, have inevitably changed over time. As Roger Bastide (1898-1974) observed, dreaming "…takes place at the crossroads of nature and culture, because it arises both from the physiology of the nervous system and from the culture from which its images and meaning one gives them derives". Christian dream books omitted the examples of pagan gods (and graphic sexual circumstances) found in Artemidorus' original Greek text, while the monks or eunuchs found in the medieval texts were dropped from English post-Reformation books.

There were also suggestions from time to time about how true dreams might be encouraged. The *Fourth Book of Agrippa* offers an invocatory approach to gaining true dreams:

> "But natural things, and their commixtures, do also belong unto us, and are conducing to receive Oracles from any spirit by a dream: which are either Perfumes, Unctions, and Meats or Drinks: which you may understand in our first book of Occult Philosophy.
> But he that is willing always and readily to receive the Oracles of a Dream, let him make unto himself a Ring of the Sun or of Saturn for this purpose. There is also an Image to be made, of excellent efficacie and power to work this effect; which being put under his head when he goeth to sleep, doth effectually give true dreams of what things soever the minde hath before determined or consulted on. The Tables of Numbers do likewise confer to receive an Oracle, being duly formed under their own Constellations. And these things thou mayst know in the third book of Occult Philosophy. /
> Holy Tables and Papers do also serve to this effect, being specially composed and consecrated: such as is the Almadel of *Solomon*, and the Table of the Revolution of the name *Tetragrammaton*. And those things which are of this kinde, and written unto these things, out of divers figures, numbers, holy pictures, with the inscriptions of the holy names of God and of Angels; the composition whereof is taken out of divers places of the holy Scriptures, Psalms, and Versicles, and other certain promises of the divine Revelation and Prophecies.
> To the same effect do conduce holy prayers and inprecations, as well unto God, as to the holy Angels and Heroes: the imprecations of which prayers are to be composed as we have before shewn, according to some religious similitude of Miracles, Graces, and the like, making mention of those things which we intend to do: as, out of the Old Testament, of the dream of *Jacob, Joseph, Pharaoh, Daniel*, and *Nebuchadnezzar*: if out of the New Testament, of the dream of *Joseph* the husband of the blessed virgin *Mary*; of the dream of the three Wise-men; of *John* the Evangelist sleeping upon the brest of our Lord: and whatsoever of the like kinde can be found in Religion, Miracles, and Revelations; as, the revelation of the Cross to *Helen*, the revelations of *Constantine* and *Charles* the Great, the revelations of *Bridget, Cyril, Methodius, Mechtild, Joachim, Merhir*, and such-like. According to which, let the deprecations be composed, if when he goeth to sleep it be with a firm intention: and the rest well disposing themselves, let them pray devoutly, and without doubt they will afford a powerful effect.
> Now he that knoweth how to compose those things which we have now spoken of, he shall receive the most true Oracles of dreams. And this he shall do; observe those things which in the second book of Occult Philosophy are directed concerning this thing. He that is desirous therefore to receive an Oracle, let him abstain from supper and from drink, and be otherwise well disposed, his brain being free from turbulent vapours; let him also have his bed-chamber fair / and clean, exorcised and consecrated if he will; then let him perfume the same with some convenient

fumigation; and let him anoint his temples with some unguent efficacious hereunto, and put a ring upon his finger, of the things above spoken of: let him take either some image, or holy table, or holy paper, and place the same under his head: then having made a devout prayer, let him go unto his bed, and meditating upon that thing which he desireth to know, let him so sleep; for so shall he receive a most certain and undoubted oracle by a dream, when the Moon goeth through that signe which was in the ninth House of his nativity, and also when she goeth through the signe of the ninth House of the Revolution of his nativity; and when she is in the ninth signe from the sign of perfection. And this is the way and means whereby we may obtain all Sciences and Arts whatsoever, suddenly and perfectly, with a true Illumination of our understanding; although all inferiour familiar Spirits whatsoever do conduce to this effect; and sometimes also evil Spirits sensibly informing us Intrinsecally or Extrinsecally." (*Agrippa's Fourth Book*, 1978: 63-65)

For another far simpler example, in Wecker's *Eighteen Books of the Secrets of Art & Nature* (1661), we find how

That all things may be revealed in Sleep.
A fume to see when one sleep what good or evill shall befall. Take the congealed blood of an Ass, and the fat of a Wolf and Storax, mingle all these in equall weight, and make them up, and forme them into Pellets, and perfume a house with them, and then you shall see in your sleep one that shall tell you all things. *Albertus Magnus* (Wecker 1661: 21)

In Arthur Gauntlet's early 17th century manuscript book of magic (Sloane MS 3851), the 47th psalm is used to invoke a dream specifically to identify a thief:

47 Magnus dominus [Psalm 47:2 "Great is the Lord."]
Si furtum factum in domo tua scribe hunc Psalm cum deus et poni sub capite tuo cum vadis cubitum in lecto et videbis dormiendo furem uitrari. ["If theft is committed in your house, write this Psalm when the second {night begins} and put it under your head when you go to the bedroom in your bed and you will see while sleeping the thief entering."]

Mr Rich Nitt S: told me that verissimam formam videbat. ["...he had seen a true form."] (Rankine 2011: 267-268)

Similarly, the following charms for dreaming are provided in the *Sixth and Seventh Books of Moses*.

THE SIXTH SEAL

The most obedient Angels of Power, seu Potestates, with their Citatioriis Diviniis verbis hebraicis, are the following four elements: Schunmyel, Alymon, Mupiel, Symnay, Semanglaf, Taftyah, Melech, Seolam, Waed, Sezah, Safyn, Kyptip, Taftyarohel, Aeburatiel, Anyam, Bymnan. This is the mystery

or Seal of the Might-Angels. The peculiar Arcanum of this Seal of the Mighty is the following: ex Thora Vlta Arcanorum sacra scriptura. If a man wears this Seal in bed, he will learn what he desires to know through dreams and visions. (*Sixth and Seventh Books of Moses*:12)

THE NINTH TABLE OF THE SPIRITS OF VENUS.

Reta, Kijmah, Yamb, Yheloruvesopijhael, I call upon thee, Spirit Awal, through God Tetragrammaton, Uhal, by Pomamiach † that you will obey my commands and fulfill my desires: Thus truly in and through the name of Esercheije, which Moses named, and upon which followed hail, the like of which was not known since the beginning of the world, f. f. f.

The Ninth Table of the Spirits of Venus makes one beloved in all respects and makes known secrets through dreams. Its spirits also assist liberally in all kinds of business. (*Sixth and Seventh Books of Moses*: 22)

(It should be noted that these texts have been corrected by Joseph H. Peterson in his definitive edition in print and online, but I have chosen to give them as they appeared in the original 1880 English translation. The images of the seals, however, are taken from the clearer examples in the 1865 German version.)

A 19th century example:

TO CAUSE TRUE DREAMS.

The seeds of flax and flea-wort, finely powdered, and often smelt to, occasion prophetic and ominous dreams. The manuscript from whence this was taken deems it infallible. ("Raphael" 1832: 18)

Perhaps the most commonly sought-after dream revelations were those of eager adolescent girls anxious to identify their future mates. In addition to the examples in Chapter 8, the popular chapbook *Mother Bunch's Closet Newly Broke Open* (1685) has a number of marriage-dream "experiments", including these:

> I have another way for to teach thee how thou shalt come to know who must be thy husband, and I have approved it true ; for I tryed it myself, and now is the best time of the year to try it, therefore take notice of what I say: Take a St. Thomas onion, and peel it, and lay it in a clean handkerchief and lay it under your head; and put on a clean smock, and be sure the room be clean swept where you lye, and as soon as you be laid down, be sure lay thy arms abroad, and say these words:
>
> > Good St. Thomas do me right,
> > And bring my love to me this night,
> > That I may look him in the face,
> > And in my arms may him embrace.
>
> Then lying on thy back, with thy arms abroad, fall asleep as soon as thou can, and in thy first sleep thou shalt dream of him which shall be thy husband, and he will come and offer to kiss thee, but do not hinder him, but strive to catch him in thy arms, and if thou do get hold of him that is he which must be thy husband but if thou get not hold of him thou must try another night, and if thou do get hold of him hold him fast, for that is he. This I have try'd, and it has prov'd true. Yet I have another

pretty way for a maid to know her sweetheart, which is as followeth: Take a summer apple, of the best fruit you can get, and take three of the best pins you can get, and stick them into the apple close to the head, and as you stick them / in take notice which of them is in the middle, and what name thou fancies best give that middle pin and put it into thy left handed glove, and lay it under thy pillow on a Saturday at night, but thou must be in bed before thou lays it under thy head, and when thou hast done, clasp thy hands together, speaking these words :— :

>If thou be he that must have me
>To be thy wedded bride,
>Make no delay, but come away,
>This night to my bedside.

And in thy first sleep thou shalt see him come in his shirt and lie down by thee, and if he offer thee any abuse it will be a great sign he will prove one that will love other women as well as thee; but if he do put his hand over thee to imbrace thee be not afraid of him, for it is a great sign he will prove a good husband; and this is a good way for a young man to know his sweetheart, giving the middlemost pin the name he fancies best, putting an apple in his right handed glove, and lay it under his pillow, when he is in bed, saying,

>If thou be she that must have me
>In wedlock for to join,
>Make no delay but come away
>Unto this bed of mine.

And that night he shall see her come, and if she come in her smock and petticoat, which is a great sign she will prove a very civil woman ; but if she come without her petticoat there is / danger she will prove a ranter, and therefore better lost than won. And now, daughter, the time passeth away and I must be gone, and so I bid you farewel. Mother Bunch, I give you many thanks for your good counsel, and intend to take your advice, and so fare you well. (Gomme 1885: 7-9)

A "St. Thomas onion" is the "Dutch blood-red onion", whose colour and flattened mature shape may have suggested a heart.

The Dream book in Popular Culture

How active a role the Cunning Folk played in the interpretation of dreams in the earlier years of this survey is unclear – there aren't many references to dream interpretation in the sources I was able to consult, but Keith Thomas identifies it as a standard practice (Thomas 1971: 130). However, dreams did become an increasing important part of their trade later on, for as Owen Davies notes: "In London, … cunning-folk such as Sarah McDonald were, it seems, more recognized for their prowess at fortune-telling and fortune-making than for their unbewitching skills. With the decline of this aspect of their business, many cunning-folk were, to all intents and purposes, little more than common fortune-tellers." (Davies 1997: 611). The proliferation of cheap printed dream books in this same period indicates an increasing "self-help" movement in dream interpretation as well.

The great variety of popular dream dictionaries in the 19th century makes it impossible to identify any particular title as more characteristic than another. Rather than reproducing a specific and lengthy single dream book text, therefore, I have chosen a hundred sample entries to adequately represent the early genre, and followed these with particular items from the 16th to the 19th century. The first 74 entries are all taken from vernacular compilations that were not solely dream books, from the assumption that these entries were presumably thought by the editors to be of common interest and thus likely to reflect sources familiar to the Cunning Folk and their clients. To bring the list up to an even hundred examples, I also took 26 entries from a late-19th century English dream book of objects that might appear in the dreams of people today. The basic sources in chronological order (several are reprints of earlier works) are:

1. Thomas Lupton. *A Thousand Notable Things*. London : printed for Edward White, dwelling at the little North-doore of Paules, at the signe of the Gunne, 1586. (Lupton)
2. "E. P., Philomathem". *The Covntry-mans Covnsellor*. London: Printed by B. A. and T. Fawcet, for Leonard Brooks, 1627. (C-M C)

3. "Mr. Lilly". *A Groatsworth of Wit for a Penny, Or, the Interpretation of Dreams*. London W.T., ca. 1670. (Groats)
4. "Erra Pater". *The Book of Knowledge, Treating of the Wisdom of the Ancients*. Suffield [CT]: Edward Gray, 1799. (EP99)
5. *The High German Fortune-Teller*. Birmingham: S. & T. Martin, ca. 1810. (HG)
6. *A Thousand Notable Things on Various Subjects*. London: Walker, Edwards, and Reynolds, 1815. (1000NT)
7. *The Wide, Wide World and All The Year Round Dream Books*. London: "Published for the Booksellers", n. d. (ca. 1880; the first title being the one used). (WWW)

To these I've added parallel entries from other dream books (again, several are probably reprints of earlier works) in smaller type, including:

8. Daldianus Artemidorus. *The Interpretation of Dreams Digested into Five Books by that Ancient and Excellent Philosopher, Artemidorus ... The Tenth Edition*. London: Printed for B. G. and S. K. and are to be sold by Tho. Bever, at the Hand and Star in Fleetstreet, 1690.
9. "Peletiah Pettengill" *Pettengill's Fortune Teller and Dream book* (Dick & Francis, 1860) New York: Padell Book Co., 1944 (reprint).
10. *The Golden Wheel Dream Book*. New York: Dick & Fitzgerald, 1862. (Golden Wheel 1862:)
11. *Le Marchand's Fortune Teller and Dream Book*. New York: Dick & Fitzgerald, 1863.
12. *All The Year Round Dream Books*. London: "Published for the Booksellers", n. d. (ca. 1880)
13. *Old Gypsy Madge's Fortune Teller and the Witches Key to Lucky Dreams*. New York: M. Young, 1880.
14. *Aunt Sally's Policy Players Dream Book* (I. and M. Ottenheimer, 1889), Los Angeles : Indio Products, 2011 (reprint).
15. *Mother Shipton's Gypsy Fortune Teller and Dream Book with Napoleon's Oraculum*. I. & M. Ottenheimer Publishers, Baltimore, 1890.
16. *Witch Doctor's Dream Book and Fortune Teller*. New York: Wehman Bros, 1891.

For some entries, there are few later examples (those dealing with church attendance, for example), whereas more common items might have parallel examples in each later source. I've limited the secondary examples to six at a maximum in each case. An important addition to American dream book entries in the early 19th century was the "policy number". Playing the "policy" or "numbers" game was a form of gambling that originated as an adjunct to the many state and private lotteries that were conducted from colonial times until Victorian moralism did away with them in the antebellum era.

Poor people who could not afford a legitimate lottery ticket were able to bet a few pennies or a nickel on various number combinations made available through neighborhood "policy shops", which would pay winners holding numbers drawn in various ways at 600:1 or more for a winning three-number "gig" sequence. Bettors might try for a single "day" or "station" (drawings at various hours) number, a "saddle" of two numbers, the common "gig" of three numbers, or even a "horse" combination of four winning numbers. The symbols representing various numbers could be identified from daily experiences, but the promise of the truly adventitious dream revelation was especially popular, with numbers combinations associated from each dream symbol. "There were ... policemen's gigs, beer gigs, washer women's gigs, dead gigs, Irish gigs, money gigs, working gigs, 'Negro gigs', and gigs for various days of the week and for famous criminals."[56] Perhaps the most famous of these was the "washer woman's gig" – 4.11.44 – which was pictured on the covers of *Aunt Sally's Policy Players Dream Book* (ca. 1880s and still available) and *Old Aunt Dinah's Sure Guide to Lucky Numbers and Lucky Dreams* (1850s with reprints into the 1900s). Books listed above with an asterisk included policy numbers with their entries. Policy was particularly popular among blacks, whose adherence to dream book advice might on occasion cause considerable consternation among the policy agents when a popular

---

[56] Ann Fabian. *Card Sharps, Dream Books, & Bucket Shops*. Ithaca: Cornell University Press, 1990, p. 143.

combination such as the "dead gig" (9.19.49) actually came up (one wonders whether 2012 presidential candidate Herman Cain's 9-9-9 might suggest such a combination for contemporary lottery bettors).

Looking over the entries, there are several points that might deserve comment. Firstly, the preponderance of significations dealing with sex and marriage is notable – this was one area in which a single decision could have life-long ramifications, especially for women whose livelihood usually depended on their mate. The next most common concern is economic, with many significations pointing to success or failure in business. Secondly, the frequency of reversed meanings, where a negative dream experience foretold a positive life outcome, and vice versa, is noteworthy. This is a very old tradition, with similar reversals being common in classical sources. Another social defence occurs in the interpretation of "beer" in a dream. The English publications saw beer as a healthy alternative to hard liquor, but under the potent influence of the Temperance movement, American books saw beer drink as a bad sign. While most of the entries are of the "allegorical" variety with no specific time of occurrence indicated, the dreams listed in *A Groatsworth of Wit for a Penny* are pointedly "prophetic" in nature, implying immediate effect.

Perhaps the most salient consideration, however, is that most of the entries reflect a way of life no longer true for many of us. Bastide's comment about the importance of the cultural context of dream symbolism is particularly cogent here. If there were some changes in the objects and events listed in dream dictionaries between those of the 16th and 17th centuries and those in the second half of the 19th century, that shift pales in comparison with the changes between the latter time period and today. Technological advances and modern urban or suburban life makes it improbable that barns, bees, beheadings, and corn fields, or eagles, hares, hens and lice are part of our everyday experience, and therefore are far less likely to turn up in our dreams. Yet even so, the strength of tradition in dream books supports the continued and apparently profitable reprinting of classic titles such as *Aunt Sally's Policy Players Dream Book*, or the *Gypsy's Witch Dream Book of Numbers*. That published policy or rather lottery numbers have also retained their interest to patrons is clearly evident from the 40 different titles of "monthly lottery books" (bearing such titles as "Vibrations". "Dr. Fu", "Grandpa", "Hot Number", "Sneaky Pete" and "Fist Full of Dollars", as well as the 46 dated and undated almanacs ("Proff. Hitt's Secrets", "3 Wise Men Encyclopedia" "Billy Bing's Almanac" "Kansas City Kitty" and so forth) sold by the Double Red Company of Denville, NJ.

A final if obvious observation—these interpretive dream books, whose contents reflect the common cultural heritage of several millennia, do not share Sigmund Freud's psychological perspective that dreams are solely the product of the individual unconscious mind, and that said content is invariably of a sexual nature. The tremendous influence Freudian psychology had during most of the 20th century is much diminished today. Perhaps other ways of approaching the mysteries of the dream state may find some useful clues in the long-sustained way that dreaming was addressed in western culture as represented here.

Dream Book Symbols and Their Significance.

1. ARMED MEN
If you dream you see men with Bills & swords with writing in their hands, then beware, of being arrested the next day. (Groats: 5)
ARMED MEN. (*See Zouave*)
ZOUAVE. To dream you see Zouaves, as well as other soldiers and armed men, denotes, that, you will have quarrels and trouble in your family, if you have one, and if you have not, among your relatives: to a single man, this dream foreshadows that his sweetheart loves another better than himself; and to the maiden it signifies her lover will try and seduce her. 58, 1, 77. (*Golden Wheel*: 84)
Armed Men.—To see them in your dream is a good sign, and denotes one void of fear; to dream you see an armed man fly is a sign of victory; to see men in arms against you signifies sadness. (*Old Gypsy Madge's*: 59)

ARMED MEN – To see them in your dream is a good sign and / denotes one void of fear. To dream you see an armed man fly is a sign of victory; to see men come in arms against you signifies madness [sic]. 18, 25, 52. (*Aunt Sally's*: 8-9)

2. BANQUETS
To dream you are at banquits, but do not eat, betokens scarcity. (EP99: 64)
Neither to see, nor to eat such meat as on dreams is prepared for the feasts of the dead, is not good to dream. Neither in like sort to dream that you make such a feast for your Parents or Friends; for it signifieth and foretelleth to the sick his own death, and to him that is in health, the death of some familiar Friend of his. (Artemidorus 1690: 138)
BANQUETS. To dream of banquets is very good and prosperous, and promises great preferment. 11. (Le Marchand 1863: 91)
BANQUET. To dream you are at a banquet, is a caution to avoid pleasures which may cost you dear. 36. 60. (*Mother Shipton's*: 4), also (*Aunt Sally's*: 10-11, with same numbers)
Banquet.—To dream that you are at a banquet, is indicative of good and prosperous times for the dreamer, who will become a great favorite in the circle of acquaintances in which he or she is in the habit of moving. (*All The Year Round*: 18)

3. BARN, FULL
To dream of seeing a Barn well stored, signifies Marriage to a rich Wife. (1000NT: 117)
BARN. To dream you see a barn stored with corn, shows that you shall marry a rich wife, overthrow your adversary at law, i[n]herit land, or grow rich by trading. 4, 75. (Le Marchand 1863: 91)
BARN. If you dream that you are in a barn that is well stored with hay and grain, it predicts that you will marry rich; or else inherit land. If the barn be empty, it will be the reverse of this, or else you will meet with a loss. 4, 75. (*Golden Wheel*, 13), also (*Pettingill's*, 29)
Barn.—to dream of a barn, and that you see it well stored with corn, denotes much good; it foretells to a man that he will marry some rich woman; to a maid, that she will marry a man who will grow very rich by his industry, and he will be promoted in the state. If you dream you see an empty barn, the reverse will happen. (*Old Gypsy Madge's*, 60)
BARN – Filled with grain, a rich marriage; you will gain a lawsuit; it also signifies that you will live a happy life. 10, 44. (*Aunt Sally's*: 11)
BARN.—If you dream of one filled with grain, it signifies a rich marriage and also a happy life. if you have a lawsuit on hand you will be successful in gaining it. 23, 44, 32. (*Witch Doctor's*: 16)

4. BEES
To follow bees / betokens gaine or profyt. (Lupton 5:56 *Michael Scotus, et Artemidorus*: 122)
Bees are good to Plowmen, and to such as thereby get profit: to others they signifie trouble, by reason of the noise they make; and wounds, by reason of their sting; and sickness, by reason of their hony and wax. (Artemidorus 1690: 68)
BEES. It is good and lucky to dream of bees: to a farmer it predicts good crops: to a lover, excellent success with his sweetheart: to a maid it promises a good and wealthy husband: if you see bees at work and coming in under a roof where you are, it is a sure sign of thrift and opulence: to rich married people it foretells of the birth of a child that will be distinguished. (*Pettingill's*, 29)
BEES. To dream of bees is good and bad: good, if they sting not, but bad, if they sting the party dreaming, for then the bees do signify enemies; and therefore to dream that bees fly about your ears, shows your being beset with many enemies; but if you beat them off, without being stung by them, it is a sign of victory, and of your overcoming them. To dream of seeing bees, indicates profit to country people, and trouble to the rich; yet to dream that they make honey in any part of the house or tenement is a sign of dignity, eloquence, and good success in business. To take bees, shows profit and gain, by reason of their honey and wax. 17, 62, 4. (Le Marchand 1863: 91)
BEES. They signify wealth and success in business; if they sting you, a friend will betray you; if a dreamer kills a bee, he will have great losses; seeing bees leave their honey, is a sign of honor and fortune; if they fly into their hives, losses through enemies. 3. 4. 16. 55. (*Mother Shipton's*, 4), also (*Aunt Sally's*: 12)

Bee-hives.—For a young man to dream that sees a number of bee-hives, is a sign that his industry and close application to business has won the approbation of his employers, and they will promote him to the office of foreman in the department in which he is engaged. He will rise through his own effort into a position far above want, and he will find in his experience that the old adage is true, "God helps those who help themselves." For a young woman to have this dream means, prosperity in work, success in study, and contentment at home, where her attention to comfort and cleanliness will be seen to advantage by a young man who is love-sick upon her account. (*All The Year Round*, 23)

5. BEHEADING
to haue your head cutte off for a heynous offence, sygnifyes the death of friends: (Lupton 6:28 *Mizaldus* 141)
Of being Beheaded
To dream that he is beheaded, whether justly or otherwise, is ill to him which a Father, Mother, and Children; for he shall lose them. (Artemidorus 1690: 18)
BEHEADING. To dream that one is beheaded, and that the head is separated from the body, denotes liberty to prisoners, health to the sick, comfort to those in distress; to creditors, payment of debts. To princes, good fortune, and that their cares and fears will be turned into joy and confidence in their subjects. If one dreams that a person of his acquaintance beheads him, he will share with him in his pleasures and honors. If any one dreams that a young child, who has not yet attained the age of his youth, hath cut off his head, if the dreamer be sick, he will not live long; if in health, he will get honor. If a woman with child dream thus, she will bring forth a male child, and her husband will die suddenly; for he is her head. To dream that you see one beheaded, betokens sickness. 74, 19, 10. (Le Marchand 1863: 91)
BEHEADING. To dream you see a person that is going to be beheaded or if you see one beheaded, it is an excellent sign; in love you will be successful; in prison you will be released; and in any trouble you have will soon vanish; it is also a sign you will soon meet a long absent friend who will be glad to see you. 17, 19, 10. (*Golden Wheel*: 14), also (*Pettingill's*: 29-30)
BEHEADING – To see one beheaded denotes the rapid realization of / your wishes; to be beheaded, success in love; to the poor it denotes they shall become rich. 4, 7, 69. (*Aunt Sally's*: 12-13)
Beheading.—To dream you see any one beheaded, is a good omen—if you are in love, you will marry the object of your affections. If you are in prison, you will speedily gain your liberty. (*Old Gypsy Madge's*: 60)

6. BESHITTEN
If you dream you are beshitten and you are not, then you will have good fortune in your business the next day: (Groats: 6)
PISS-A-BED. To dream that you wet the bed in your sleep, is a sign you will lose something by fire: your house may not burn, but / some article will either fall in the fire or be damaged by it—perhaps your servant may spoil some clothing while ironing. 5, 11, 55. (*Golden Wheel*: 56-57), also (*Pettingill's*: 74)

7. BIRTH
31. If a Woman dreams of being delivered of a Child, yet is not big, it is a sign she shall at length be happily brought to bed. If a Maiden dreams the same dream, it signifies Banquet, Joy, and succeeding Nuptials. (1000NT: 117)
BIRTH. To dream of a birth is good for a poor man; to the sick it denotes death. 13, 42. (*Golden Wheel*: 14)
Birth—To dream of one's birth is good for him who is poor, but to him who is rich, this dream signifies that others shall rule over him against his will. (*Old Gypsy Madge's*: 61)

8. BREAD
It is bad to dream of Birds, or cackling Hens, but very good to dream of Bread and Corn: (Groats: 6)
BREAD. To dream of eating such bread as is usual, or as the person dreaming is accustomed to, is good: but to dream of eating unusual bread is bad: and therefore for the poor to dream they eat

white bread, denotes sickness, and for the rich to dream they eat brown bread, shows they shall meet with some obstructions in their affairs. To dream of barley-bread, is good for all, for it signifies health and content. 1, 15. (Le Marchand 1863: 93)

BREAD. To dream of bread is an excellent sign. If you see a good deal, the better the dream. It foretells good fortune to either man or woman. To lovers, it predicts that they will make a good match and will be well off, if not rich. To farmers it promises full and abundant crops. 1, 15. (*Golden Wheel*: 15)

Bread.—To dream you see a great quantity of loaves of bread, denotes success in life. to dream you are eating good bread, denotes that you will be shortly married. To dream the bread is musty and bad, denotes the loss of friends, and that some near relation will shortly die. (*Old Gypsy Madge's*: 60)

BREAD – To eat wheaten bread, gives great gain to the rich, but loss to the poor; to eat rye bread, is the reverse. 48. (*Aunt Sally's*: 15)

BREAD.—If of wheat, signifies gain to the rich and loss to the poor, but if the bread is made of rye flour, then the reverse may be accepted as the interpretation of the dream. 5, 19, 41. (*Witch Doctor's*: 19)

9. BRIDGE

To dreame that you go ouer a broken Brydge, betokens feare: (Lupton 6:28 *Mizaldus* 141)

BRIDGE. For one to dream that he goes over a broken bridge, betokens fear; and to dream you fall upon a bridge, is a sign of obstruction in business. 56, 2. (Le Marchand 1863: 93)

BRIDGE. To dream you are crossing over a bridge, denotes prosperity in life, and success in love; but to dream you are passing under a bridge, indicates difficulties in life, both in love and business; if you meet with obstructions, either on or under the bridge, it foretells illness. To dream a bridge breaks down with you sudden death. 56, 2. (*Golden Wheel*: 16), also (*Old Gypsy Madge's*: 60)

BRIDGE. To pass one, shoes success in life through industry; to fall from one, loss of business and disappointment in love. 2. 18. 19. 24. 56. (*Mother Shipton's*: 5), also (*Aunt Sally's*: 15)

BRIDGE.—To go over one, implies that industry will cause success in the life of the dreamer, but to fall from one signifies loss of business and disappointment in love. 18, 62. (*Witch Doctor's*: 19)

10. CANDLES

To dream you are making candles, denotes great rejoicing. (EP99: 65)

CANDLE. To dream one sees a candle extinguished, denotes sadness, sickness, and poverty. When one dreams he sees a shining lighted candle, it is a good sign to the sick, denoting recovery and health: and if he that dreams is unmarried, it shows he will speedily marry, have success, and prosper in his undertakings. To dream that you make candles, is a sign of rejoicing. To dream that you see candles not lighted, shows you shall have a reward for something you have done. 21, 67, 46. (Le Marchand 1863: 93)

CANDLES. To dream of lighted candles, is a sign that you will become religious, or will be soon visited by a minister who will tell you good news. To see a candle extinguished is a sign of a funeral. To light a candle, success in what you undertake. 21, 67, 46. (*Golden Wheel*: 17), also (*Pettingill's*: 32)

CANDLE. If it burns brightly, happiness; if the light be dim, misfortune; if you light it, success in what you undertake. 21. 66. 78. (*Mother Shipton's*: 5), also (*Aunt Sally's*: 17)

CANDLES.—Burning brightly portend a desirable religious condition. If burning dimly, suggest the leaving of some one who is dear to you. 24, 37, 56. (*Witch Doctor's*: 20)

11. CARDS

To dream that you are playing with cards is a very good sign. (EP99: 65)

CARDS. If you dream of winning money in playing cards, it is a sign of poverty and disgrace. If you are only handling the cards, or playing without a bet, it foretells that you will presently fall in some danger to your person. (*Pettingill's*: 32)

CARDS. Playing at cards, tables, or any other game in a dream, shows the party shall be very fortunate: and tables allude unto love, for love is the table, fancy the point that stands open; and he that dreams much of table playing, shall be a great gamester, as well with Joan as my lady. 76, 17. (Le Marchand 1863: 94)

CARDS. Playing at cards, dice, or any other game in a dream, shows the party will be fortunate in love affairs, for the tables and cards allude to love. 76. 17. (*Golden Wheel*: 17)

Cards—To dream that you are playing at cards, is a sure prognostic that you will be in love, and speedily married. If you hold a great many picture cards your marriage will be the means of making you rich and happy. If your cards are mostly diamonds, the person you marry will be of a sour and disagreeable temper. If they are mostly hearts, your marriage will cement love, and you will be very happy and have many children. If they are mostly clubs, you will get money by your marriage. If they are mostly spades, your marriage will turn out very unhappy, and your children will be unfaithful and subject to many hardships. If you are in expectation of a place [i.e., job], you will get it, and if you are in business, you will be successful. (*Old Gypsy Madge's*: 62)

CARDS – To dream of cards denotes great wealth; hearts, riches and honor; diamonds signifies that you will quarrel with your lover; clubs, happiness and money; spades, that you will meet with many hardships. 4, 12, 52. To dream of card playing is a bad omen. 2, 13, 52 Of a card-maker, good tidings. 2, 17, 76. (*Aunt Sally's*: 17)

12. CHICKENS

It is bad to dream of Birds, or cackling Hens, but very good to dream of Bread and Corn: (*Groats*: 6) to dreame of chickens and birds, ill luck, &c. (C-M C: 225)

HENS. To dream of seeing hens that appear happy, and are singing, is an excellent omen, as it foretells thrift, and a large number of children, and domestic enjoyment generally: if the hens are disturbed and cackling, it shows that something will occur to mar your happiness. If you dream of a hen with many young chickens around her, it is a sign that some one in the family will soon get married. If a young girl dreams this, she will probably get married before the chickens have time to grow to henhood. (*Pettingill's*: 50)

HEN. If you dream you hear hens cackle, or that you catch them, it denotes joy, and an increase of property, and success in business. Dreaming you see a hen with her chickens, means loss and damage. If you see a hen lay eggs, that denotes gain. 19. (*Le Marchand 1863*: 101)

CHICKEN. To dream of a hen or chicken, signifies loss in trade, and deceit in love. 19. (*Golden Wheel*: 19)

CHICKEN. Its cooking is a sign of coming good news. 2. (*Mother Shipton's*: 5), also (*Aunt Sally's*: 19)

Chickens.—To dream of a hen and chickens is the forerunner of ill luck; your sweetheart will betray you and marry another. If you are a farmer, you will have a bad crop and lose many of your poultry. If you are in trade, some sharper will defraud you. If you go to sea, you will lose your goods and narrowly escape shipwreck. (*Old Gypsy Madge's*: 63)

13. CHURCH, BUILDING

To dream you build a church or erect an altar, signifies, some of thy family will become a priest. (EP99: 65)

CHURCH. To dream of building a church, is a good sign to the dreamer; to enter one, you will receive a kindness from some one; to play in one, success and marriage. 2. 19. 88. (*Mother Shipton's*: 5), also (*Aunt Sally's*: 19)

14. CHURCH, PERSON IN

To dream you see a person sitting or lying in a church, signifies change of apparel. (EP99: 65)

15. CHURCH, WITH LOVER &C.

If a Maid love a Man, and dream she is going to Church with another man, and that she run from him, then she will assuredly have the man she desired; but if she dream she goeth into the Church with another man, then she will not have the man she loveth. (*Groats*: 2)

If the man dream anything like the aforesaid; it doth denote the like as is for the woman. (*Groats*: 2)

16. CHURCH SERVICE

To dream you are going to hear divine service, signifies consolation. (EP99: 65)

MASS. To dream of going to this religious celebration, is a sign that some one will either cheat you or rob your house. if a girl dreams this, let her look out that her lover does not prove to be a worthless scamp. 13. (*Golden Wheel*: 45)

Chapel.—To dream that you are at service in a chapel, or other place of worship, is a bad sign. There will be a continuance of annoyance in your family, from one of your children. He or she will be troubled with a desire to take other people's goods, for no other reason than that they have an accountable desire to possess them. They are troubled with that curious failing known as kleptomania, which will continually disturb your peace of mind. (*All The Year Round*: 35)

Church.—To dream of church is portentious of evil. If you are in a church during divine service, you will be engaged in a law-suit, or some other quarrel that will go very near to ruin you. If you are in love, your sweetheart is unfaithful, and prefers another. If you expect a place, it forebodes disappointment. If you are in trade, you will never thrive in your present situation. (*Old Gypsy Madge's*: 63)

17. COFFINS

If the man or woman dream of a black Coffin, it denotes that some kindred of theirs are dead: (Groats: 6)

To dream of black coffins & mourners / denotes the death of some loving friend or relation. (EP99: 63)

COFFIN. To dream of one, denotes the death of a friend, or some near relation. 74, 6. (*Golden Wheel*: 20), also (*Pettingill's*: 33)

COFFIN. To dream of a coffin, signifies that you will soon be married, and own a house of your own. 9. 49. 50 (*Mother Shipton's*: 6), also (*Aunt Sally's*: 20)

COFFIN.—Is interpreted to mean that you will soon have a house of your own in which you can live with your family and be very happy. 35, 45, 48. (*Witch Doctor's*: 23)

18. CORN DAMAGED

12:23 To dream you see a Stack of Corn burnt, signifies Famine and Mortality. (1000NT: 117)

GRAIN. To dream of regular fields of ripe grain, is a good omen, as it is a sign of thrift: if the grain is broken down or imperfect, it shows troubles with the thrift: if it is mouldy or mildewed, you will experience losses. An abundance of grain in bulk is likewise a sign of plenty; but scattered grain is the reverse of this. 69. (*Golden Wheel*: 32), also (*Pettingill's*: 44)

19. CORNFIELD

To dream you are in a field of standing corn, betokens prosperity and love. (EP99: 64)

Sheaves of Corn, or like grain, are also hindrance; for this is not ready meat. (Artemidorus 1690: 70)

GRAIN. If you dream of seeing and gathering grain, it denotes prosperity; if you dream of eating it in pottage, it is bad. 69. (Le Marchand 1863: 100)

CORN. To dream that you see corn eared, and gather it, signifies profit and riches; to dream you see stacks of corn, signifies wealth and abundance to the dreamer; and on the contrary, to see a small quantity, denotes poverty. 69. (*Golden Wheel*: 20), also (*Pettingill's*: 33)

CORN. To see it blooming, shows an increase in your family. 41. 46. (*Mother Shipton's*: 6), also (*Aunt Sally's*: 21)

WHEAT – To see a field of wheat growing is a sign of grief; 10, 20, 44. To dream you gather wheat denotes weakness of character. 1 to 70 combination. To dream of wheaten flour shows you will lose a lawsuit. 10, 51, 62. To dream of wheaten bread denotes success in business. 10, 15, 20. (*Aunt Sally's*: 84)

Corn.—To dream you see fields of corn, or that you are among unt[h]rashed corn, is a very favourable omen; it denotes success in business; to the lover it announces that you will marry, have many children, and become rich and happy. If you are a sailor, it denotes a lucrative voyage and fine weather, and that you will be near marrying in the next port you touch at. If you dream you are gathering ripe corn, it is the most favourable dream you can have. (*Old Gypsy Madge's*: 63)

20. COURTSHIP

To dream you are courting a beautiful woman betokens flattery. (EP99: 64)

21. DEAD SIBLINGS

To dream you see your deceased brothers or sisters, signifies long life. (EP99: 65)

RELATIONS DECEASED. To dream one sees and discourses with father, mother, wife, brother, sister, or some other of his relations and friends, though they are dead, is an advertisement for the party to mind his affairs, and to behave himself properly in the world. 70. (Le Marchand 1863: 109) also (*All The Year Round*: 128)

22. DOCTORS AND LAWYERS

To dream of physicians and attornies, it shows crosses in affairs. (HG:12)

Places of Pleading, Judges, Attorneys, and Proctors, are trouble, anger, expence, and revealing of secrets. ... Physicians seen in a dream to him which is in Law, signifies the same that Attorneys and Proctors. (Artemidorus 1690: 74)

ATTORNEYS. To dream you are speaking with them, shows hindrance in business, and that it requires much circumspection to insure success in your affairs. It also denotes loss of property. 16. (*Golden Wheel*: 12)

23. DRINKING

To dream of drinking unmercifully, denotes displeasure, crosses and sickness. (EP99: 65)

Of Drinks

To Drink cold water, is good to all, but hot, signifieth sickness and hinderance of affairs. To drink Wine with reason, and not to be drunk is good: but to drink much, and without reason, signifieth much evil: Also it makes you be in the company of drunkards. To drink sweet Wine, or to see fair women, or to sleep under shady trees, to him that would take a Wife, it betokeneth a good success in love. ... vessels of glass are evil, because they break easily; they also reveal secrets, by reason of / their transparence; otherwise these vessels may signifie our friends, which we embrace; when therefore the vessels are broken, it signifieth the death of some of our friends or affinity. (Artemidorus 1690: 37-38)

DRINKING. To dream you are drinking, when you are very dry, is an assured sign of sickness, especially if your dream be near the break of day, and the dreamer be of a sanguine complexion, and lying on the left side. 67. (Le Marchand 1863: 97)

DRINK. To dream you drink cold water, is good to all; hot, sickness and hinderance; wine is good; sweet wine success in love; oil, sickness; from vessels of gold, or silver, or earthenware, intends tranquility; of horn, implies good; glass, evil. 67.

> If maids do dream of drawing drink
> In cellars they may waking think,
> That their sweethearts without delay,
> Will leave them, and run away. (*Golden Wheel*: 23)

Drink.—To dream you drink cold water, is good, but hot signifies sickness and hinderance of affairs. To dream you drink wine with moderation, is good; to drink oil, signifies poison. To dream that you are drinking when you are dry from a stream or fountain, is a sign of sickness. If a man dreams he is drunk with sack, or some sweet pleasant drink, it is a sign he will be beloved by some lady and grow rich thereby. (*Old Gypsy Madge's*: 66)

24. EAGLES

To dreame that Eagles flyes ouer your head: doth betoken euil fortune. (Lupton 5:56 *Michael Scotus, et Artemidorus*: 122)

to dreame of Eagles flying ouer our heads, to dreame of mariages, dancing and banqueting, foretels some of our kinsfolkes are departed, (C-M C: 224)

To see an Eagle flying over a stone, or a tree, or in a high place, is good for those who would undertake business; but to those which are in fear, it is evil. ... An Eagle flying, and falling onto the head of him which dreameth, it signifies death. (Artemidorus 1690: 66)

EAGLE. To dream you see an eagle in some high place, is a good sign to those who undertake any weighty business, and especially to soldiers. If one dreams that an eagle lights upon his head, it betokens death to the dreamer. 48. (Le Marchand 1863: 97)

EAGLES. To dream you see an eagle soaring very high in the air, denotes prosperity, riches and honors; to the lover, it foretells success in love and marriage. 48. (*Golden Wheel*: 24)

EAGLES. To see one in your sleep, flying above you, is a good sign; if it lights upon your head, some accident will befall you; if it conveys you into the air, some friend or relative will die. 2. 8. 40. (*Mother Shipton's*: 7), also (*Aunt Sally's*: 27)

25. EGGS

If you dream of Eggs that are broken, there was much anger portending against you, but it is past and gone; (Groats: 6)

if a Woman dream of Eggs that are whole, she and her Neighbours will have a sad bout of scolding the next day; (Groats: 6)

Eggs to Physicians, Painters, and those which sell and trade with them, are good; To others it is good to have little store of them, and signifies gain; but plenty of them, is care, pain, noise, or Lawsuits. (Artemidorus 1690: 82)

EGGS. (*See Rotten.*) If married people dream of eggs it is a sign they will be prolific of children. If a newly married lady dreams of finding a nest full of eggs, it foretells that her first born will be twins or triplets. If a young girl dreams such a dream, it is a sign she will soon be married, or get in a condition that she ought to be a wife. 4, 47. (*Golden Wheel*: 25) … to imagine that you handle rotten eggs, foreshadows disgrace. 35. (*Golden Wheel*: 65)

EGGS. Mean happiness; to see many broken eggs is a sign of quarrelling and lawsuits; fresh eggs, good news. 8. 35. 65. 66. (*Mother Shipton's*: 7), also (*Aunt Sally's*: 28, with 8, 39, 65, 68)

Eggs.—To dream you are buying or selling eggs, is a very favourable omen; whatever you are then about will succeed, whether it be love, trade, or getting a place. To dream you are eating eggs, denotes that you will shortly have a child, and that all your affairs will go well. To dream your eggs are broken, denotes loss of goods, quarrels and poverty; if you are in love, it forebodes a separation between you and your sweetheart.

> To dream of eggs will profit give,
> And show that thou shalt thrive and live. (*Old Gypsy Madge's*: 66)

26. FIGHTING

To dream of contending and conquering, promises advantage; but to be overcome, the contrary. (HG:12)

To dream you fight and overcome, signifies you will get the better in lawsuits or other controversies. (EP99: 63)

Of Combating.

For to combat with any one, is ill to all men for besides shame, he shall have hurt. Likewise it signifieth much strife and contention and to be wounded in fight betokeneth shame and dishonour. Notwithstanding, it is good for such as live by bloodshed, as Chirurgions, Butchers, and Cooks. (Artemidorus 1690: 36)

FIGHTING. To dream of fighting, signifies opposition and contention; and if the party dreams he is wounded in fighting, it implies loss of reputation and disgrace. 44, 78. (Le Marchand 1863: 98)

FIGHT. To see women fighting, signifies jealousy; men, sorrow. 4. 9. 48. 57. (*Mother Shipton's*: 7), also (*Aunt Sally's*: 31)

Fighting.—To dream you are fighting, denotes to the lover, that you will lose the object of your affections through a silly quarrel. It also forebodes much opposition to your wishes, with loss of character and property, after such a dream, you are urgently recommended to quit your present situation, because such a dream indicates you will not prosper in it. to the sailor it denotes storm and shipwreck, with disappointment in love. (*Old Gypsy Madge's*: 68)

27. FIRE

if you dream much of fire, you shall hear of hasty news the next day; (Groats: 6)

To dream of fires denotes anger & loss. (EP99: 64)

To dream you cannot quench fire, denotes overcoming anger, and recovery from sickness. (EP99: 64)

12:23 If a Woman dreams she is kindling a Fire, it denotes she will be delivered of a Male Child. (1000NT: 17)

Of Household-Fire

To dream you see fire on the Hearth, clear and little, is good; but much is ill. Little and clear, is abundance of goods: Dead fire is poverty, and if there be any one sick in the house, it is death. (Artemidorus 1690: 57)

… To kindle the fire easily in the Oven or Hearth, is a sign of Generation; but for it to go out straight after, is hurt. (Artemidorus 1690: 58)

FIRE. When a man dreams of fire, or that he sees fire, it means the issue of his choler; and commonly they that dream of fire are active and furious; if a man dreams he is burnt by fire, a violent fever is prognosticated thereby. When a man dreams that his bed is on fire, and that he perished, it betokens damage, sickness, or death to his wife; and if the wife dream it, the same will happen to her husband. If one dream that the kitchen is on fire, that denotes death to his cook. 26. (Le Marchand 1863: 98)

FIRE. If in your dream, you see a house on fire other than your own, it foretells that some event will happen to make you melancholy and sorrowful, such as the death or ruin of some esteemed friend. If you dream your own house or place of business is burning, it is a sign of a quarrel in bed. For this dream, play your age first. 26. (also, *Pettingill's* without lucky number, 40)

> To dream of sitting by the fire,
> When it is late, doth show desire;
> But if you sit till the fire's out,
> Your love will prove false out of doubt. (*Golden Wheel*: 28)

FIRE. If it is blazing furiously, danger and separation of friends; if it is extinguished, poverty. If a female makes a fire without much trouble, she will / have fine healthy children; if she has much difficulty in kindling it, she will meet with shame and dishonor. If you burn yourself, you will have a fever. A sparkling fire denotes money in abundance. 6. 46. 69. (*Mother Shipton's*: 7-8), also (*Aunt Sally's*: 32)

28. FLIES

to take flyes, sygnifies wrong or iniury. (Lupton 6:28 *Mizaldus* 141)

FLIES. To dream of a swarm of flies, denotes that you have many enemies; it also denotes that your sweetheart is not sincere, and cares but little about you; to dream you kill them is a very good omen; it denotes success in love and trade. 21, 49. (*Golden Wheel*: 28)

Flies.—To dream of a swarm of flies, denotes that you have many enemies; it also denotes that your sweetheart is not sincere, and cares but little about you. To dream you kill them is a good omen. (*Old Gypsy Madge's*: 68)

FLIES – To dream of flies shows that you carry extreme hatred to your enemies and an addition to your fortune. 3, 5, 8. (*Aunt Sally's*: 33)

29. FLOWERS AND WOODS

To dream you are walking in a garden of flowers, and among groves of trees denotes much pleasure and delight to ensue from virtuous conversation. (EP99: 65)

GARDEN. To dream of walking in a garden, and gathering flowers, shows the person is given to pride and to have high thoughts of herself. If a man dream of seeing fair gardens, he will marry a chaste and beautiful wife. 31, 17. (Le Marchand 1863: 100)

GROVES. Dreaming you have land and groves adjoining, denotes you will marry well, and be blessed with children. 31. (Le Marchand 1863: 101)

LAND. If a man dream he has good lands, well enclosed, he shall have a handsome wife. If he dreams that the lands have gardens, fountains, pleasant groves, and orchards, he will marry a discreet, chaste, and beautiful wife, and have children. 34, 61,18. (Le Marchand 1863: 102)

GARDEN. Your fortune will be enlarged, to walk in one, joy. 15. 78. (*Mother Shipton's*: 8)

FLOWERS.—Are significant of happiness. By gathering them you become the possessor of that which will add greatly to your pleasure in life. 2, 16, 47.

FLOWERS.—Destroying, signifies that you will waste the powers that have been bestowed upon you. This may be accepted as a caution, and you will do well to change your habits. 18, 29, 46.

FLOWERS.—Planting, denote that you will be the author of some undertaking that will outlive you, and so hand your name down to posterity in honor and distinction. 3, 38, 57 (*Witch Doctor's*: 31 – this book occasionally includes several varying entries under the same heading and with separate numbers)

30. FLYING
To dream you fly in the air, and are fearful, denotes you stand ticklish in the favour of those you most trust in. (HG:12)
To dream to fly a little height from the Earth, being upright, is good; for as much as one is lifted higher than those that are about him, so much greater and more happy shall he be. … to fly with wings, is good generally for all; to Servants it is liberty, to the Poor riches, to the Rich office and dignity. To fly very high from the Earth, and without Wings, is fear and danger; as also to fly over the Houses, and through the Streets, and forlorn ways, is trouble and sedition. (Artemidorus 1690: 89)
FLYING. To dream you are flying is a very excellent omen; if you are in love, your sweetheart will be true to you; and if you marry, you will have many children, who will do very well and be happy. 35. (*Golden Wheel*: 29)
Flying.—To dream you are flying, is a very excellent omen. It foretells elevation of fortune. That you will arrive at dignity in the state and be happy. If you are in love, your sweetheart will be true to you, and if you marry, you will have many children., who will do well and be very happy. It indicates that you will take a long journey, which will turn out to be advantageous to you. (*Old Gypsy Madge's*: 69)
FLYING – Is a very excellent omen; it foretells elevation of fortune, that you will arrive at dignity in the State, and be happy. 10, 69, 70. (*Aunt Sally's*: 33)

31. FOREHEAD OF A LION
34. To dream of having or seeing the Forehead of a Lion, betokens the getting of a Male Child. (1000NT: 117)
FOREHEAD. To dream that you see yourself having a handsome forehead, shows that you possess great spirit; if it is very much rounded, it is a sign of good fortune. To dream you have a forehead of iron, steel or brass, shows you carry extreme hatred to your enemies. A large, fleshy forehead shows eloquence, courage and power. 46. 57. (*Mother Shipton's*: 8), also (*Aunt Sally's*: 34)

32. FRIEND IS DEAD
if you dream that your friend is dead, it signifies that they are well: (Groats: 6)
To dream you see a friend dead, denotes the person to be in good health. (EP99: 64)
DEAD. To dream of talking with dead folks, is a good auspicious dream; it shows great courage, and a very clear conscience. To dream a man is dead, who is alive and in health, denotes great trouble and being overthrown at law. 61, 4. (Le Marchand 1863: 96)

33. GLASS OF WATER
29. To dream he has a Glass full of Water given him, signifies a Marriage. (1000NT: 117)
GLASS. If one dreams that he hath a glass given him full of water, he shall be married speedily, and his wife shall have children [.] But if the glass is cracked, he must look sharp after his wife's chastity. 11, 64. (Le Marchand 1863: 100)
Glass.— … To dream you receive a glassfull of water, is indicative of a speedy marriage and that you will have many children, who will all do well. If the glass appears broken, the death of a sweetheart, or, if married, of your spouse, is predicted. For a woman with child, or a married man whilst his wife is with child, to dream of breaking a glass of wine or water, denotes that the child in the womb will be preserved, after much danger, and perhaps the death of the mother. If either of them dream that they spill wine or water, it is indicative that the mother will live but the child will die. (*Old Gypsy Madge's*: 70)
GLASS – To dream of receiving a glass of water, signifies that you will soon be married; if you break it your sweetheart will forsake you. 28, 42, 52. (*Aunt Sally's*: 36)

34. GLOVE

To dream you put on a new glove, & it remains so, betokens new friendship or marriage. (EP99: 64)

GLOVES. To dream of wearing good gloves, brings happiness; if the gloves are torn, many disappointments. To the lover this dream is a sign he will get the mitten from [be rejected by] his sweetheart. 25, 9. (*Golden Wheel*: 31)

GLOVES. To dream of wearing good gloves, brings happiness; if the gloves are torn, many disappointments. 4. 24. 57. (*Mother Shipton's*: 8), also (*Aunt Sally's*: 36, with 4, 24, 67)

GLOVES.—Bring happiness if you dream of wearing good ones, but on the other hand, if you see that the gloves are torn, then many disappointments will fall to your lot. 4, 59. (*Witch Doctor's*: 34)

35. HANDS, CLEANLINESS

to make cleane the hands, betokens troubles: to see hands fylthy or fowle, doth sygnify losse and daunger: (Lupton 6:28 *Mizaldus* 141)

HAND – ... Clean, ruddy hands, denote for the poor, friends who will assist; ... 5, 16, 45. (*Aunt Sally's*: 38)

36. HARE

to handle lead, to see a Hare, death; (C-M C: 225)

To dream you are hunting a hare, and she escapes, denotes disappointment in business. (EP99: 64)

HARE – To see a hare, denotes the dreamer will engage in some profitable enterprise. 65. (*Aunt Sally's*: 38)

HARE.—Signifies that the dreamer is soon to engage in some business enterprise that will yield a handsome return for his investment in a short space of time. 11, 17, 55. (*Witch Doctor's*: 35)

37. HILLS

if you dream you go up to the top of an Hill, then the next day you will put an end to some great Business, which you have long desired to finish, or else other good fortune will fall out; but if you dream that you fall down again before you get on the Hill top, then your Suit will be lost; (Groats: 5)

To dream you are failing against your will to descend from a pleasant hill betokens falling from promotion, and disappointment in preferment. (EP99: 64)

HILLS. To dream you are travelling over hills, and wading through great difficulties, and meet with assistance in the way, means that you shall have good counsel, and overcome all your troubles. 1, 46, 18. (Le Marchand 1863: 101)

HILL. To dream of going up a hill is a sign you will rise in the world, and of going down hill the reverse: if, in your dream, you seem to be approaching a smooth high hill, it shows that you will / shortly have a piece of good fortune; but if the hill be rugged and stony, it foretells difficulties in connection with the good fortune. 1, 46, 18

> To dream of mountains, hills or rocks,
> Does signify shouts, scoffs, and mocks;
> Their pains in passing over shew,
> That she whom you love, loves not you. (*Golden Wheel*: 36-36)

HILLS. To dream of travelling over steep hills, shows that you will experience much care and trouble, and meet with many disappointments; to the lover, it denotes rivalry. 9. 36. (*Mother Shipton's*: 9), also (*Aunt Sally's*: 40)

Climbing— ... To dream you are climbing up a very steep hill, or place, foretells many difficulties in life, and much sickness. If you reach the top, you will get over all your difficulties, and recover from your illness; but if you awake before you have attained the top, you will be disappointed in love and all other projects, and die in your next illness. (*Old Gypsy Madge's*: 63)

HILLS.—Are suggestive of good fortune. If they are green, a life without pain or trouble to the dreamer may be expected. 52, 64. (*Witch Doctor's*: 36)

38. HORSEBACK

If that you are on horseback, and seem to ride swift, shews some sudden journey you'll take:—and so of others. (HG:12)

To dream you are on horseback, and that he run away with you denotes you shall speedily be called away from some business contrary to your liking. (EP99: 64)
Of Riding
To Ride a Horse nimbly, is good for all; for the Horse signifies a Woman, or a Friend, the Ship, the Master and Guide to govern, and the good friend: So then as a finds his Horse well, so shall he do all this. (Artemidorus 1690: 34)
HORSES. If you dream of a horse, it is a good sign: or if one dreams he mounts a horse, it is a happy omen. To dream you are riding on a tired horse, shows one shall be desperately in love. 2, 11, 22. (Le Marchand 1863: 101)
HORSE. If you dream of riding well and easily on the back of this noble animal your fortune is sure to advance in the world: but if you imagine you are thrown from a horse, it is a sign of disgrace. To dream of swapping horses shows that some one will cheat you in a bargain; of selling a horse, it is a sign of loss; but buying one, predicts that you will make money by some speculation, or else by / selling property. Horses are excellent animals to dream about. 2, 11, 22. (*Golden Wheel*, 36-37), also (*Pettingill's*, 51)
RIDER – A good sign to one who never rides on horseback; to fall from a horse, signifies loss. 6, 27. (*Aunt Sally's*: 68)

39. JOY
To dream a sudden fit of joy at the sight of any thing, betokens the arrival of friends. (EP99: 64)
JOY. To dream that you are in an ecstasy of joy at anything that has happened, bodes pain and trouble: something will be sure to occur to make you unhappy. Great joy at a wedding denotes sorrow at a funeral: joy at having got a lot of money, promises that you will be in distress for some: an abundance of good things to eat, predicts hunger: beautiful new clothing for you, shows a loss of some either by theft or accident, &c. If a girl dreams that a young man has begun to pay her attention, and that the circumstance causes her much joy, it is a sign that he will either desert or seduce her. (*Pettingill's*, 51)
JOLLITY. Dreaming of jollity, feasts, and merrymakings, is a good and prosperous dream, and promiseth great preferment. 20. (Le Marchand 1863: 102)
JOY. To dream that you are in the ecstacy of joy at anything that has happened, bodes pain and trouble; something will be sure to occur to make you unhappy. 46. (*Golden Wheel*, 39)
JOY. To be joyful in sleep, is a forerunner of bad tidings. 14. (*Mother Shipton's*, 10), also (*Aunt Sally's*: 43)
Joy.—To dream of joy and festivity is a token of good for such as would marry, or it betokens enjoyment for those fond of society. To the sad and fearful it announces absence of heaviness and fear. (*Old Gypsy Madge's*, 73)

40. KEY
To dream you find a key, denotes admission into some place of trust. (HG:12)
A Key seen in a Dream, to him which would marry, signifieth a good and handsome wife, or a good Maid. It is cross to a Traveller; for it signifieth he shall be put back and hindered, and not received: It is good for such as would take in hand or effect other mens business. (Artemidorus 1690: 105)
KEYS. To dream you lose your keys, denotes anger. But to dream you have a bunch of keys, and that you give them to those that desire them of you, shows goodness to the poor. A key seen in a dream, to him that would marry, denotes he shall have a handsome wife and a maid. 41, 8. (Le Marchand 1863: 102)
KEY. If you dream of finding a key, or a bunch of keys, it is a sign that some one will tell you a secret; to dream of losing a key, or keys, is a bad omen, as it predicts that you will come to shame. Such a dream is particularly unfortunate for a young lady. 41, 8. (*Golden Wheel*, 40)
KEY. To lose it, signifies hate and anger; to find a key, brings fortune and love. 18. 49. 57. 70. (*Mother Shipton's*, 10), also (*Aunt Sally's*: 44)
Keys.—To dream of keys is favourable to a person in trade, and to a sailor, they denote some gift and that the dreamer will become rich. To dream of finding a key, denotes an addition to your estate. If you are married, it foretells the birth of a child. If you give another a key, you will be speedily married. In love, keys betokens faithfulness and a good tempered sweetheart.

To dream your keys are gone or lost,
Denotes that you'll be vexed or crossed. (*Old Gypsy Madge's*, 73)

41. KISSING
To dream one is kissing and embracing you, denotes you are beloved either in friendship or marriage. (HG:12)
A woman dreaming she kisses another woman denotes disappointment in love & barreness. (EP99: 64)
KISSING. Dreams of kissing work curiously: if a girl dreams that she is kissed by a young man in whom she takes no particular interest, it may be a good omen, and it may not; for if he happens to be a silly fellow who imagines that she is in love with him, it is a sign that she will be slandered in a way that will make her unhappy; but if he has no such sentiment, then the sign is exactly the reverse—that is, some one will speak well of her to those whom she esteems highly—perhaps to her lover. If a girl dreams she is kissed by her lover, it predicts that he will say something unpleasant to her at their next meeting; if a lover dreams that his sweetheart kisses him the sign is similar. 1. (*Golden Wheel*, 40), also (*Pettingill's*, 55)
KISS. To kiss the earth, shows sorrow and care; to kiss the hand of a lady, good luck; if you kiss her face, you will be successful in love and trade, through courage. To be kissed signifies disagreeable visitors. 13. 47. (*Mother Shipton's*, 10)
Kissing.—For a man to dream of kissing a young maid, and that she vanishes away before he can accomplish his desire, denotes that the next day he shall see a great store of good cheer. To dream you kiss a person deceased, signifies longlife. (*Old Gypsy Madge's*, 73)
KISSING.—Implies deceitfulness and intrigue among those by whom you are surrounded. Look among your friends and search out the traitor. 4, 23, 61. (*Witch Doctor's*: 39)

42. LAMBS
to feede Lambes, sygnifies griefe, or payne: (Lupton 6:28 *Mizaldus* 141)
LAMBS. To see young lambs frisking around their mother, is an excellent omen, as it denotes thrift, and also happiness in your family ties; if you see them sucking, it is a sign of an increase in your family by the birth of a child. For lovers to dream of young lambs, foretells a speedy and happy marriage. 24, 69. (*Golden Wheel*, 41)
LAMB – To lead or bring a lamb to slaughter signifies distress; to see one feeding upon grass denotes health and happiness. 4, 8, 44. (*Aunt Sally's*: 45)
LAMBS.—Signify that you will be sustained in your walks of life by a partner who will have more virtue and morality than intelligence. 11, 21, 63. (*Witch Doctor's*: 40)

43. LEAD (METAL)
to handle lead, to see a Hare, death; (C-M C: 225)
LEAD. TO dream of lead denotes sickness, but to dream of leaden bullets, good news. If you dream you are wounded by leaden bullet, it is a sign you will be successful in love. 49, 50. (Le Marchand 1863: 103); also (*Golden Wheel*, 46)
LEAD – You will have suits at law, or some other ill-business that will occasion the loss of your estate. 1, 10, 44, 51. (*Aunt Sally's*: 46)

44. LIGHTNING
33. To dream of being touched with Lightning, to the unmarried, signifies Marriage; but it breaks marriages made; and makes friends enemies. (1000NT: 117)
LIGHTNING. To dream of bright and vivid white lightning, denotes you will soon go on a pleasant trip or journey; blueish silver forked lightning foretells good crops and excellent success in business; red forked lightning the same, but attended with calamity, or the death of relatives by violence. 24. (*Golden Wheel*, 43)
Lightning.—To dream of lightning without tempest, and falling near, without touching the body, signifies change of place. If a man dreams he saw lightning fall below him, it will hinder his traveling. But if you dream that you are all burned and consumed with lightning / it is death to the dreamer. (*Old Gypsy Madge's*: 74-75)

LIGHTNING – If the dreamer sees lightning strike his house, or fall upon his head, it is the sign of a death of a relative. 39, 62, 78. (*Aunt Sally's*: 46)

45. LION
To dream a lion fawns upon you, denotes the favor of great persons. (EP99: 63)
To see a gentle, familiar, and fawning Lion, signifieth good and profit. ... To see or have the forehead of a Lyon, is good for all, and most often the begetting of a man-child. (Artemidorus 1690: 60)
LION. If you dream of seeing the king of beasts, and he is mild and gentle looking, it shows that you will easily rise to a better position than you now occupy; to dream of an angry and roaring lion, who tries to get at you, shows, that although you may rise in position, jealous people will annoy and try to injure you. 14.

> Dreams of lions, bears, bulls, bees,
> Nests of wasps or hornets, these
> Are emblems whereby are expressed
> Discord with those whom you love the best. (*Golden Wheel*: 43),
> also (*Pettingill's*: 59, without poem or number)

Lion—To dream of seeing this king of beasts, denotes that you will appear before your betters, and that you will be promoted to some lucrative office, accumulate riches, and marry a woman of great spirit. It argues success in trade, and prosperity from a voyage by sea. (*Old Gypsy Madge's*:74)
LION – To see one, denotes admittance to the society of distinguished persons. To fight with a lion, signifies a quarrel with a dangerous person. If you overthrow him, victory over trials and sorrows. To sit or ride on the back of a lion, denotes the protection of some powerful personage. To dream of eating the flesh of a lion, shows high office in store for you; the skin of a lion augurs great wealth. To see a lion run away, predicts great folly. To see a lioness, brings good luck to your family. 4, 44, 54, 60. (*Aunt Sally's*: 47)

46. LOOKING-GLASS
To looke in a glasse: doth portende some yssewe, or a chydle. (Lupton 5:56 *Michael Scotus, et Artemidorus*: 123)
LOOKING-GLASS. To dream of a looking-glass, is a bad omen, and signifies that you will be surrounded with false friends, who will rob you until your property dwindles down to a shadow. To dream you see your face in a looking-glass is a sign of sickness. To break a looking-glass, it is a sign he will desert or seduce her. 18, 61. (*Golden Wheel*: 44)
LOOKING-GLASS. The sign of treachery. 3. 21. 26. (*Mother Shipton's*: 11), also (*Aunt Sally's*: 47)
Looking-glass.—To dream of looking in a glass, denotes children to the married, and to the unmarried, it promises a lover speedily. (*Old Gypsy Madge's*: 74)
LOOKING-GLASS.—To dream of a broken looking-glass foretells the death of a member of your family. To simply see one dictates that your associates are not to be relied on. 14, 32, 45. (*Witch Doctor's*: 42)

47. LOUSE
To dream a louse falls from your neck, betokens a sign of friends. (EP99: 64)
To dream to have some little quantity of Lice, and to find them upon his body or gown, and kill them, signifies that one shall be delivered from care and heaviness. But to have a great quantity, is long sickness, captivity, or great poverty, for in such cases, Lice abound. (Artemidorus 1690: 95)
LICE. To dream of lice denotes sickness and poverty. 2. (*Golden Wheel*: 42), also (*Pettingill's*: 58)
Lice.—To dream that you are lousy and that you are killing a great number of them, is a very good omen. It denotes great riches to the dreamer. They also portend deliverance from enemies, and that you will overcome much slander and malice. (*Old Gypsy Madge's*: 75)
LICE – Signify wealth; abundance of gold and silver. 21, 41, 54. (*Aunt Sally's*: 46)
LICE—These insects are invariably to be regarded as money, and to see many of them indicates that you will have an abundance of wealth throughout your life. 18, 61. (*Witch Doctor's*: 42)

48. MARRIAGE
To be marryed: sygnifies that some of your kynfolkes is dead. (Lupton 5:56 *Michael Scotus, et Artemidorus*: 123)
Seeing that Marriage and Death have some Affinity, as the one signifying the other, I purpose in this place to speak thereof. To marry a Maid, to him that is sick, is death: It is good for him which would enterprise any good business, for he shall have good issue: And he which hopeth for any good, shall obtain it, for he which marrieth, gets some good dowry by his Wife: To others it is trouble or divulgation, for without this, men make no weddings. (Artemidorus 1690: 88)
MARRIAGE. To dream that you do the act of marriage, denotes danger. Marriage, or the wedding of a woman, is a token of the death of some friend; and for a man to dream that he is newly married, and that he hath had to do with his now wife, it denotes some evil accident will befall him. 2, 78, 42. (Le Marchand 1863: 103)
WEDDINGS. For a man that is sick, to dream that he is wedded to a maid, shows that he shall die quickly. If one dreams he is wedded to a deformed woman, it signifies discontent; if to a handsome woman, it denotes joy and profit. 42, 78, 2. (Le Marchand 1863: 110)
MARRIAGE. If any one should be so unfortunate as to dream that he or she was present at a happy and jolly wedding, it denotes that they will attend a funeral; it will not necessarily be at the burial of either of the persons you dreamed you saw married, but you will undoubtedly be called to mourn some friend or relative. To dream of being married yourself, foretells your death. 2, 78, 42. (*Golden Wheel*, 45), also (*Pettingill's*, 61)
MARRIAGE. If any one should be so unfortunate as to dream that he or she was present at a happy and jolly wedding, it denotes that they will attend a funeral; it will not necessarily be at the burial of either of the persons you dreamed you saw married, but you will undoubtedly be called to mourn some friend or relative. To go to weddings when one is wide awake is exceedingly pleasant, but we should be careful how we dream about them. To marry your sister, danger; a virgin, honor; a widow, losses. 4. 29. (*Mother Shipton's*, 11)

49. MONEY FOUND
To dream of finding money, denotes disappointment, but of receiving the same, promises advantage. (HG:12)
MONEY. To dream of finding money is an excellent omen, as it foretells that you will soon get some: if, in your dream, you see bank bills of a large denomination, or large gold pieces, the sign is similar: to see small pieces of money, is not so good, although it is a pretty fair dream. To dream of receiving money is a good omen; in love, it foretells marriage and children. To dream you lose money, is a proof you will be unsuccessful in some favorite pursuit. 18, 4. (*Golden Wheel*, 47)
MONEY – To find money, mourning and loss; to lose money, good business; to see it without taking it, anger and disappointment; to count it, gain. 45. (*Aunt Sally's*: 51)

50. MOON(S)
if a man is born under the Planet *Mars*, dream that he seeth two or three Moons at once, then let him look to hear strange news from the great ones; (Groats: 6)
To dream of moons contending in the firmament, denotes division among friends, and relations. (EP99: 65)
MOON. If any one dream that he sees the moon shine, it shows that his wife loves him extremely well; it also implies the getting of silver; for, as the sun represents gold, so the moon doth silver. Dreaming you see the moon darkened, denotes the death or sickness of your wife, mother, sister, or daughter; loss of money, or danger in a voyage or journey, especially if it be by water; or else it denotes a distemper in the brain or eyes. To dream you see the moon darkened, and grow clear and bright again, implies gain to the woman that dreams, and to the man joy and prosperity; but to dream that you see the moon clear, and afterward cloudy, presageth the contrary. To dream you see the moon in the form of a full white face, implies to the virgin, speedy marriage; to the married woman, that she will have a handsome daughter. If the husband dream it, it implies that his wife will have a son. To dream you see the moon at full, is a good sign to handsome women, of their being beloved by those who view them; but it is bad for such as conceal themselves, as thieves and murderers, for they will certainly be discovered: but it signifies death to those that are sick, and to

seafaring men. To dream the moon shines about your bed, implies grace, pardon, and deliverance by some woman. To dream you see the new moon, is a sign of expedition in business. Dreaming you see the moon decrease, betokens the death of some prince or great lord. To dream you see the moon pale, is joyfulness. To dream you see the moon dyed with blood, indicates travel or pilgrimage. Dreaming you see the moon fall from the firmament, is a sign of sickness. To dream you see two moons appear, betokens increase of sorrow. 19, 18. (Le Marchand 1863: 104)

MOON. To dream of a sharp new moon with horns pointing upwards is a sign you will be rich: if the horns point sideways or downward, it foretells poverty: seeing a full moon in your dream denotes a thrifty and happy marriage: a half moon shadows forth the loss of a wife or husband by death or desertion. Dreaming of seeing a half moon is fatal to the prospects of lovers. 19, 18. (*Golden Wheel*: 47), also (*Pettingill's*: 63)

MOON. To see the moon, foretells delay in receiving money, good business; if its light be dim and clouded, trouble; if it is dark, misfortune; bright, high honor. 13. 20. (*Mother Shipton's*: 11), also (*Aunt Sally's*: 54)

Rising of the Moon.—To dream you see the moon rise, is a sign you will lose some female friend, your mother, if she be living; you will experience great uneasiness on account of a woman; your sweetheart will be unfaithful; poverty will overtake you and misery end your days. (*All The Year Round*: 129)

51. NEIGHBOR'S WIFE
if a man dream that he is lying with his Neighbours Wife, & is not, the Devil is doing his best endeavour to rob him of that he ought not lose: (Groats: 6)

52. OIL POURED
To haue oyle powred vpon you sygnifies ioy. (Lupton 5:56 *Michael Scotus, et Artemidorus*: 123)

OIL. Dreaming that you are anointed with oil, is good for women; but for men it is ill, and implies shame. 1, 41. (Le Marchand 1863: 106)

Oil—Dreaming that you are anointed with oil is good for women, but for men, denotes shame. (*Old Gypsy Madge's*, 77)

OIL – To dream it is spilled on the floor, signifies damage; to spill it on yourself, profit. 6, 7, 17, 75. (*Aunt Sally's*: 59)

53. PIT
To dream you fall into a deep pit, denotes some sudden surprise or danger. (EP99: 64)

PIT. Dreaming you see a pit full of fair water in a field, where there is none at all, is a good dream; for he who dreams this is a thriving man, and will suddenly be married, if he be not so already, and will have good and obedient children. To dream you see a pit whose water overflows the banks, implies loss of substance, or the death of wife and children; and if the wife have the same dream, it shows her death, or the loss of her substance. To dream you see a friend fall into a pit, shows that such a person is then near his end; and if it be a parent, aunt, or child, that you dream falls, expect to see the death of such relation very suddenly. 54. (Le Marchand 1863: 107)

Pit.—To dream of falling into a deep pit shows that some very heavy misfortune is about to attend you. That your sweetheart is false, and prefers another. To a sailor it forebodes some sad disaster at the next port you touch at. To dream you are in a pit, and that you climb out of it, foreshows that you will hold many enemies and experience much trouble, but that you will overcome them, marry well, and become rich; to sailors it denotes that you will experience shipwreck, and will be cast on a foreign shore, where you will be hospitably received, and marry a rich and handsome wife, and live at ease. (*Old Gypsy Madge's*, 78)

PIT – If you dream you fall in a pit, you will fall heir to an estate; to dream you come out of one, disgrace. 11, 69, 70. (*Aunt Sally's*: 63)

PIT.—Signifies that some trouble is about to occur, which will involve you in much shame and mortification, but you will come out all right. 22, 31, 47. (*Witch Doctor's*: 50)

54. PREGNANCY
A woman to dream she is with child betokens sorrow and heaviness. (EP99: 64)

If any being poor, dream that he is great with child, he shall become rich, and shall gather a great deal of money: If he be rich, he shall be in pain and care. He which hath a Wife, shall lose her, having no more need that she shall bear children. He that hath no wife shall have a gentle one. (Artemidorus 1690: 3)
PREGNANCY – Augurs ill success in life. 11, 50, 52, 22. (*Aunt Sally's*: 65)

55. PORK, ROAST
35. To dream of Roasted Swine's Flesh, signifies speedy Profit. (1000NT: 117)
Of Flesh …
To eat flesh which one hath dressed himself, is good, except Beef and Mutton, which signifieth lamantation and loss, and anger. Swines flesh is good for all men, especially rosted, for it signifies speedy profit. (Artemidorus 1690: 39)
PORK – Is an unfavourable dream. 4, 28, 71. (*Aunt Sally's*: 64)

56. RAIN
33. To dream of little Rain and Drops of Water is good for Plowmen. (1000NT: 117)
RAIN. To dream of a gentle rain is a good omen, as it foretells success in any undertaking; if you dream of a violent rain-storm accompanied by wind and thunder and lightning, it predicts much trouble and misfortune, though ultimate success in your undertakings. 21, 72. (*Golden Wheel*, 62)
RAIN. If it rains lightly and unaccompanied by wind, it is a good dream for workingmen. To dream of a storm, is bad for men in business. For the poor man it is a sign for better fortune. 43. 45 (*Mother Shipton's*, 13), also (*Pettingill's*, 80), and (*Aunt Sally's*: 67)
Rain.—To dream of being in a shower of rain, is particularly favourable to lovers. It denotes constancy, affection and sweet temper. If it be a very heavy rain, accompanied by thunder and lightning, then expect to be assailed by thieves. (*Old Gypsy Madge's*, 80)

57. REFLECTION IN WATER
To dreame that you see your face in ye water: sygnifyes long lyfe. (Lupton 5:56 *Michael Scotus, et Artemidorus*: 122)
to see ones face in water, or to see the dead, long life; (C-M C: 225)

58. RING
To dream one puts a ring on your finger, is speedy marriage. (HG:12)
For a woman to dream a ring is put on her finger, denotes success in love and marriage; but if it be suddenly took off, or near off, it signifies disappointment in love, & the breaking off the match. (EP99: 64)
RINGS. To dream of rings, betokeneth weddings, because they are then required. 4, 20. (Le Marchand 1863: 109)
RING. For a lady to dream that a gentleman presents her with a ring, or that she has a ring belonging to a gentleman, is a sign of a wedding. If a young man dreams he has got a lady's ring, the omen is similar. To dream of finding a ring, foretells that the person finding it will marry within a year. 4, 20. (*Golden Wheel*, 65)
Ring.—To dream of a ring is favourable, if it be on your finger. If you are in love, expect to be speedily united to the person on whom you have placed your affections. To dream your ring falls off your finger betokens evil. Also the death of some dear friend. To a woman with child, it shows that the child with which she is pregnant will encounter many difficulties, and be far from happy. To a maiden, it is a warning to beware of her present lover. (*Old Gypsy Madge's*, 80)
RING – To receive one, friendship; to give one, confidence. 32, 42, 62. (*Aunt Sally's*: 68)

59. RUNNING
if you dream you ran swiftly, and like to out-run a Hare, then you will receive a Letter or Letters the next day: (Groats: 6)
RUN. To dream of running swift is a sign of good success in your undertakings; but if you stumble or fall, it denotes accidents or misfortune; if you imagine that you see people run, while you are still, foretells disappointment. (*Pettingill's*, 86)

RUN. It is a good sign to dream of running. To run naked, denotes infidelity in marriage; to run after an enemy, victory; to see many people running, signifies quarrels. 6. 15. 40. (*Mother Shipton's*, 14), also (*Aunt Sally's*: 69)

Running.—To dream that you are running, is a very excellent omen; it foretells elevation of fortune; that you will arrive at dignity in the state, and be happy. If you are in love, your sweetheart will be true to you, and if you marry, you will have many children, who will do well, and be very happy; it indicates that you will take a long journey, which will turn out advantageously to you. (*All The Year Round*, 135)

60. RUNNING WATER

If a Sick Person dreams of a River or Fountain of clear water, denotes a Recovery. (1000NT: 117)

Rivers having their water clear, and clean, gliding gently, are good for Servants, and those which have Law-suits, and such as would travel, for they signifie the Masters and Judges who will do as they will; and also to Travellers, because they run daily. (Artemidorus 1690: 72)

RIVER. To dream you see a river water clear and calm, presages good to all persons. To dream of swimming in a great river, signifies future peril and danger. 34, 20. (Le Marchand 1863: 109)

FOUNTAIN. To dream you are at a fountain, is a favourable omen; if the water is clear, it denotes riches and honors; and in love, it foretells happiness in marriage; but if muddy, it denotes vexation and trouble. 71, 20, 18. (*Golden Wheel*, 29)

River.—To dream you see a flowing river, and that the waters are smooth and clear, presages happiness and success in life. if the water appears disturbed and muddy, or has a yellow tinge, it denotes you will acquire considerable riches. (*Old Gypsy Madge's*, 81)

61. SAILING

To dream you are pleasantly sailing in calm water denotes a peaceable and quiet life; but in a storm denotes troubles. (EP99: 64)

SAILING. To dream of fair sailing on clear water, is an excellent omen, as it foretells abundance and success; heavy winds that endanger your boat, or muddy waters, point out difficulties which will probably be overcome. (*Pettingill's*, 86)

BOAT. To dream you are in a boat upon a river, lake, or pond of clear water, is very good, and indicates joy, prosperity, and good success in affairs. If a man dream that he is walking in a boat, and recreating himself without fear, he will have comfort mid success in his affairs: but if the water be rough and tempestuous, it falleth out contrary. 71, 10. (Le Marchand 1863: 92)

YACHT. To dream you are sailing a yacht or boat in rough or stormy weather, indicates that you will be very successful in business, and happy in love or domestic matters, providing the water looks clear and green. If the water looks black or muddy, it is a sign you will soon have some sort of trouble. If the water is smooth and clear, it portends that a rich relative will die aid leave you a fortune. 21, 1. (Le Marchand 1863: 110)

BOAT. To dream you are sailing in a boat in pleasant weather, and enjoying yourself, denotes good success in business; to lovers it foretells happiness; if the weather is boisterous, it predicts quarrels, which will be speedily settled; dreams of sailing smoothly in boats are emphatically good ones to all kinds of people. 71, 10. (*Golden Wheel*, 15), also (*Pettingill's*, 30-31)

Navigation.—If anyone dreams that he is sailing in a boat and recreating himself without fear, he will have comfort and success in his affairs, but if the water be tempestuous, it falleth out contrarily. To dream of being in a ship or boat, and in danger of oversetting or shipwreck, it is a sign of danger, unless the party be a prisoner or captive, and in that case it denotes liberty and freedom. (*Old Gypsy Madge's*, 76)

SAILING – To dream you sail pleasantly along denotes honor. 1, 10, 50, 69, 70. To see the sails of a ship denotes fortune. 4, 11, 48. To see a sail maker denotes unfavourable news. 38, 40, 50, 48. (*Aunt Sally's*: 69)

62. SHOOTING A BOW

To dream you are shooting in a bow, signifies honour and preferment. (EP99: 65)

Shooting.— ... To dream you are shooting with a bow and arrow is a very favourable dream, especially to lovers and tradesmen. (*Old Gypsy Madge's*, 82)

63. SILVER AND GOLD

to / dreame of siluer, if thou hast it giuen to thy selfe, sorrow; of gold, good fortune; (C-M C: 225)
Of Gold ...
For a man to dream he hath Gold, is not bad, because of the matter, as every one will say; but contrarywise, it is good, as I have known by experience ... (Artemidorus 1690: 52)
GOLD. To dream of gold is a good sign, providing you see enough of it: to see large pieces of gold, or bars of gold, predicts that you will shortly have a pretty good supply of it yourself. On the contrary, small bits of gold seen in your dream is a sign that you will want something that you can't get. To dream of digging large lumps of gold is a most excellent dream of getting money, but if you dig and don't find much, it shows that money will be scarce with you. (*Pettingill's*, 44)
GOLD. To dream of receiving gold is a good sign, and shows you will be successful in all your undertakings. To dream you pay gold, betokens increase of friends. 49, 7. (Le Marchand 1863: 103)
SILVER. TO dream that you are presented with spoons, or any silver plate for household use, foretells that you or some near relative, will shortly marry; if you dream of buying these articles, it is a sign of poverty. To dream of silver dollars, or bars of silver, used in commerce, is a sign that you will gain money either by a legacy or speculation. 49, 6. (Le Marchand 1863: 103)
GOLD. To dream of receiving gold, is a very good omen; it denotes success in your present undertakings, after experiencing some little difficulties. If you pay gold, it betokens increase of friends and business. 49, 7. (*Golden Wheel*, 31)
GOLD. The sign of ambition and avarice. 68. 74. (*Mother Shipton's*, 8), also (*Aunt Sally's*: 36, with 63, 74)
SILVER.—Is equivalent to some great disappointment, but if made into ware a fortune is coming to you from a source not expected. 4, 23, 37. (*Witch Doctor's*: 56)

64. SILVER COINS

It is good to dream of Gold but dangerous to dream of small pieces of Silver: (Groats: 6)
To dream of gathering up small pieces of money, betokens loss and disappointment, but receiving of money profit and advantage. (EP99: 64)
Some say, that to dream of Mony and all kind of Coyn, is ill. But I have tried that little mony of Brass and Bullion signifies heaviness and angry words; but mony of Silver, words, and talk of great Affairs; of Gold, far greater. It is also better to dream to have little Silver, than much; because that one cannot imploy great heaps without pain, and care. (Artemidorus 1690: 86)

65. SNAKES

If you dream of a Snake or Serpent, and that they come near to hurt you, then look well to your self for there are private Enemies seeking to destroy both you and yours: (Groats: 5)
To dream you are bit by a Serpent, signifies some danger will befal you by secret and subtile enemies. (EP99: 63)
SERPENTS. To dream you see a serpent turning and winding himself, signifies danger and imprisonment; it denotes, also, sickness and hatred. To dream you see many serpents, signifies you will be deceived by your wife. 27. (Le Marchand 1863: 109)
SNAKE. To dream of snakes is a sign of an enemy, or that some one is slandering you; it also denotes quarrels and angry disputes; if an engaged young lady dreams of them, she had better ascertain positively whether her lover is all right before she marries him. 47, 59. (*Golden Wheel*, 71), also (*Pettingill's*, 93)
SNAKE. A snake signifies an injury by the malice of a man, or the treachery of a woman. To kill one, victory. Sickness and ill-fortune, to dream of one twining around you. 16. 32. 49. 64. (*Mother Shipton's*, 15), also (*Aunt Sally's*: 73)

66. SOW & PIGS

To dream you see a sow with pigs, denotes fruitfulness. (EP99: 64)
SOW. To dream of a sow with a large litter of pigs, denotes abundance to a farmer, but is a sign of ill-health to a tradesman or mechanic: if a girl dreams this, it foretells that she will soon marry a man in bad health. 4, 12, 43. (*Golden Wheel*, 71)
PIGS. Signify there are sluggards who wish to live at your expense. 4. 50. 70. (*Mother Shipton's*, 13)

67. TEARS

to weepe in sleepe, joy; (C-M C: 225)

To weep and grieve, whether it before any Friend departed, of for any cause, it is joy and mirth for some good act. (Artemidorus 1690: 86)

TEARS. To dream of shedding tears of sympathy, is a sign that some one is in love with you; this applies to both sexes, but more particularly to girls who cry easy: if you imagine you cry from grief, some good fortune awaits you, and you will have riches in proportion to the tears shed: if you dream that you shed tears from vexation, it shows that you will experience a loss in proportion to the tears, or that some one will injure your prospects by circulating a scandal. 14. (*Golden Wheel*, 75), also (*Pettingill's*, 98)

68. TEETH, LOSS OF

to lose an axle-tooth or an eye[tooth], the death of some friend; (C-M C: 225)

To dream your teeth are drawn or drop out, denotes the loss of Children or other relations. (EP99: 65)

TEETH. If a person who has fine teeth dreams that any of them are rotten, it is a sign of sickness: for one who has decayed teeth to dream they are sound and handsome, it foretells uninterrupted good health, and excellent fortune: if those who have scraggy teeth imagine they are straight, it denotes success and good luck. (*Pettingill's*, 98)

TEETH. To dream you lose your teeth, denotes loss of friends, troubles, and misfortunes; to the lover it shows the loss of your sweetheart's affection: to dream you cut a new tooth, denotes the birth of a child who will make a figure in the world. 33, 11, 2. (*Golden Wheel*, 75)

Teeth.—To dream you lose a tooth, denotes the loss of some friend by death, and that troubles and misfortunes are about to attend you. To the lover, it shows the loss of your sweetheart's affection. To dream you cut new teeth denotes the birth of a child, who will make a great figure in the world. (*Old Gypsy Madge's*, 83)

TEETH – To lose a tooth, you will meet with success; to cut one denotes the birth of a child. 3, 10, 33. (*Aunt Sally's*: 78)

69. VOICE, UNSEEN

To dream you hear a voice but / see not what utters it, denotes you shall be deluded by feigned pretenders. (EP99: 64)

NIGHTMARE DREAMS – Are ominous to the dreamer. If you hear a voice be careful of your character. 8, 12, 50. (*Aunt Sally's*: 58)

70. WATER, FALLING INTO

if you dream of troubled waters, and that you fall into the water, then you may look to hear bad news the next / day: (Groats: 5)

NAVIGATION. To dream of being in a ship or boat, in danger of oversetting and shipwreck, is a sign of danger, unless the party be a prisoner or captive; and in that case it denotes liberty and freedom. He that dreams he falls into the water or the sea, and that he awakes starting, it signifies that he either doth or will enjoy a married woman, and spend his days, substance, and fortune with her. 22. (Le Marchand 1863: 105)

71. WATER FROM WELL

29. If a young Man dreams he draws Water out of a Well, it signifies he will be speedily married. (1000NT: 117)

WELL. ... if you imagine you draw clear water from a well, and drink it, you will surely have good fortune of some kind. 7, 14, 77. (*Golden Wheel*, 81)

Well.—if a young man dreams he draws water out of a well, it signifies a speedy marriage to a fair maid who will bring him a portion. If the water be troubled, he will be disturbed by her, and suddenly fall sick. If he seems to give to others clear well water to drink, it denotes that he will enrich them. But if the water be troubled, he will afflict them. If he dreams he sees a person fall into a well, it signifies that the person dreamed of shall die quickly. (*Old Gypsy Madge's*, 86)

72. WILD ANIMALS
To dream any furious beast assaults you, as a Bull, Bear, Lion, Wolf, Mastiff, &c. denotes open enemies, contriving mischief for you, but to be bitten by snakes or adders it is private treachery. (HG:12)
To dream you are pursued by furious wild beasts, but cannot avoid them, denotes danger from enemies. (EP99: 65)
WILD BEAST. Of any kind, signifies the protection and favor of persons of distinction. 3. 4. 28. (*Mother Shipton's*, 17), also (*Aunt Sally's*: 84-85)
WILD BEAST.—To dream of a wild beast pursuing you signifies that you are under the protection of some persons of distinction who will see that your fortune is not neglected. 16, 25, 71. (*Witch Doctor's*: 67)

73. WINE
35. To dream of drinking Sweet Wine, betokens success in Law. (1000NT: 117)
… sweet wine success in love; (*Golden Wheel*, 23 – see above. under DRINK.)
WINE. To dream of drinking wine is a sign of poverty: if a lover dreams that his sweetheart treats him to a glass of wine, it foretells that she will be an unthrifty wife. 39. (*Golden Wheel*, 82)
WINE. To dream of drinking good wine, shows power and fortune; wine and water, bad health; white wine, pleasure trips; if the wine is not clear it signifies wealth; to see it flow, the spilling of blood. To get drunk from good wine, indicates office and good fortune. 10, 29, 48. (*Mother Shipton's*, 17), also (*Aunt Sally's*: 85)

74. WORSHIP
To dreame that you worshyp God: sygnifies gladnes. (Lupton 5:56 *Michael Scotus, et Artemidorus*: 123)
GOD. Dreaming that we worship God, is good. To dream of receiving pure gifts from Him, shows good health. 1. (Le Marchand 1863: 100)
WORSHIP – To dream you are at worship shows contentment. 1, 6, 7. (*Aunt Sally's*: 85)

The following primary entries are from *The Wide Wide World Dream Book*, which is English, and shows somewhat different expectations from its American contemporaries.

75. ACCORDION
.—To dream you hear music from this reed instrument is good. It denotes pleasure and happiness in the house and family in which you reside. You will have much domestic felicity, and the pleasures of your home-life will be greatly increased. (WWW: 8)
Concertina.—for a young man to dream that he hears one of these instruments play, means that he will become fond of the art of dancing, in which he will be an adept by practice. (*All The Year Round*, 44)

76. AUTHOR
To see one or more, is a bad sign, you will lose money. To dream that you are an author signifies misery and disappointed hope. 1 (*Mother Shipton's*, 4) [– couldn't resist adding this one], also in (*Witch Doctor's*: 14), with numbers 16, 24.

77. BAFFLED
.—To dream you are baffled in your purposes, is a good dream. If you are in love, and baffled in your attempts to gain the ear of the woman your heart's affections are fixed upon, it is a sign of your ultimate success. Keep the motto in mind: "Faint heart never won fair lady." By persistent effort the dream will prove a prognosticator of the prosperity of your suite, you will win the prize you seek. If baffled in your business transactions, some change of plans will be / profitable. Keep the news of the first failure of your schemes secret from your business compeers, and persevere, by plodding, pushing tact, you will find out that you are only baffled for a time. (WWW: 16/17)
BEWILDERED – To be puzzled in a dream is a sign you will hear good news from abroad; to the rich it is rather unlucky, but to the poor success. 51, 54, 74. (*Aunt Sally's*: 13)

78. BANANA
.—To dream of this delicious fruit is a good omen; if you dream you are eating a banana, it is a sign you will be rich and happy. To dream you see banana growing denotes success in love matters. If a girl dreams that her lover presents her with a ripe banana it foretells she will soon be married, or ought to be. (WWW: 17)
BANANA. of this delicious fruit is a good omen; if you dream you are eating a banana, it is a sign you will be rich and happy. To dream you see banana growing denotes success in love matters. If a girl dreams that her lover presents her with a ripe banana it foretells she will soon be married, or ought to be. 4, 11, 14 (*Golden Wheel*, 13)

79. BEER
.—For a young man to dream that he is drinking beer, is a sign that domestic peace will be his lot, his father and mother will enjoy the pleasure of their son growing up abstemious, thoughtful and wise. He will detest the sensual indulgences of the fast young men of the day, and take pleasure in some of the sciences and more advanced studies of a theological character. If a / young woman has this dream, she will become quiet in her demeanour, chaste in her language, and upright in her character.   (WWW: 21/22)
BEER. To dream you are drinking beer, is a sure sign of domestic troubles. 6, 8. (*Golden Wheel*, 14)
BEER. To drink it, trouble. 42. (*Mother Shipton's*, 4), also (*Aunt Sally's*: 12, with 42, 70)
BEER.—Signifies trouble if you dream of drinking it, but if others are indulging in it, you may regard the dream as signifying that you will avoid some great trouble. 45 (*Witch Doctor's*: 17)

80. BREAKFAST
.—To dream that you are eating your breakfast shows you will do something of which you will be sorry. (WWW: 26)
BREAKFAST. To dream that you are eating breakfast shows you will do something of which you will be sorry. 21, 4. (*Golden Wheel*, 16)
BREAKFAST. To dream you are eating breakfast, shows that you will commit some folly. 36. 55. (*Mother Shipton's*, 5), also (*Aunt Sally's*: 15, with 30, 36, 59)
BREAKFAST.—If you dream that you are partaking of this meal, then beware, for it indicates that you are on the verge of committing some great act of folly. 7, 30. (*Witch Doctor's*: 19)

81. CELLAR
.—That you are in a cellar in any dream, is a sign that shortly some discoveries will be made by you of a startling nature. You will find out that you are the rightful heir to property that you have been deprived of because you had not the means wherewith to engage counsel to represent your claim in the court of law, at the time when the current owners got possession. It may be that you will be able to bring other things to light with regard to the pedigree of your family, that will be of service in obtaining the possession of other lands or money either in this country or the colonies. What you want is a friend to advance the cash for the purpose of properly establishing your claim. (WWW: 34)
CELLAR. To dream you are in a cellar, is sign of sickness and an unlucky law suit. 75, 2. (*Golden Wheel*, 18)
CELLAR. Signifies sickness and misery. 12. 27. 36. (*Mother Shipton's*, 5), also (*Aunt Sally's*: 18)
CELLAR.—Is regarded as foretelling either sickness or misery. If there is no way of getting out from the cellar, then a fatal ending of the trouble is indicated by the dream. 16, 70. (*Witch Doctor's*: 21)

82. CIGAR
.—To dream you are enjoying the luxury of a first-class cigar, is a significant dream. You have much to be thankful for, no carking care will annoy your breast, and, if sorrow and trouble should come, the fumes and flavour of you finest brands will help you lighten the load of trouble that would, if you would let it, sit like the night-mare upon your breast. You will find the following acrostic to be true:
C omfort in your home will dwell,
I ndustry will help to swell

G ratitude and joy supreme,
A s the fragrant pleasures gleam,
R ound your pathway like a stream. (WWW: 38)
SEGAR. To dream you are smoking a segar, is a sign you will have misfortunes and troubles with your business matters: if you imagine the fire of your segar goes out, it is a sign you will meet with losses; in love matters this dream is a bad omen. 49, 7, 9. (*Golden Wheel*, 68)
CIGAR. To the man who smokes it, success; if it be not lit, signifies misfortune; if he light it, he may hope. 1. 8. 20. (*Mother Shipton's*, 5), also (*Aunt Sally's*: 19)
CIGAR.—If not lit, signifies misfortune, but if the dreamer lights it the trouble will be averted, while if it is already lit, then some happy event is about to occur. 49, 63. (*Witch Doctor's*: 22)

83. COAT
.—To dream that you have torn the skirt of your coat, is a sign that in the down-hill of life, it will not be well with you. The children you have reared will desert you and leave you chargeable to the parish, and if you are not an inmate of the workhouse, you will be compelled to accept out-door relief. To dream you tear the sleeve of your coat, is a sign you will commence a new business, and strive to be successful, but you will not make it answer to expectations and desires. To dream that you are adorned in a beautiful dress-coat of the newest pattern, is a sign that pecuniary troubles will shortly overtake you. (WWW: 39)
Of the Apparel …
To have a delicate and sumptuous Gown, is good for rich and poor: For to the first, their present prosperity shall continue; / and to the other, their goods shall increase. Broken and torn Gowns, is hurt and hindrance of affairs … A Coat, a Jacket, or short Cloak, or Skirt of Woollen-Cloth, is anger, and loss of a Law-suit. Wherefore it is better to dream you lose them, than you have them. (Artemidorus 1690: 49/50)
CLOTHES. If a man dream he has a new suit of clothes, it is a sign of honor. To dream that you see your clothes burned, denotes loss and damage. To dream that you see yourself in black clothes, signifies joy. To dream that you take your clothes to put them on, denotes loss. If a man or woman dream they are meanly clothed, it betokens trouble aid sadness. If one dreams his clothes are dirty, that he hath bad clothes, tattered and much worn, it means shame. To dream your clothes are embroidered all over with gold, or any other kind of embroidery, signifies joy and honor. 24. (Le Marchand 1863: 95)
CLOTHING. Clothed in rags, signifies mourning and trouble; to wear good clothes, a happy life; dirty clothes, disgrace; to steal clothing, gives success in love and business. To wear clothing of many colours foretells disappointed hopes. 21. 69. (*Mother Shipton's*, 6)
COAT – Denotes much happiness. 4, 31, 44. (*Aunt Sally's*: 20)

84. DENTIST
.—to dream you visit a dentist is indicative of indigestion becoming a source of illness to you. You had better take care of your health. (WWW: 50)

85. FERRET
.—If you dream you see one of these little animals, it is a sign that you will have a desire to search out difficult things, explain problems, unravel mysteries, and understand puzzles. (WWW: 63)

86. GEM
.—To dream that you wear a costly gem, in the shape of some precious stone or jewel of some kind, is a sign of a falling off of your resources financially, your prosperity in business will not be so good in the future as it has been in the past; it will be better for you to husband your resources and prepare for the day of adversity. (WWW: 72)
JEWELS. Chains, pearls, or precious stones, etc., and all adornings upon the heads and necks of women, are good dreams for the fair sex; to widows and maids they signify marriage; and to those that are married, riches. If a man dreams of possessing jewels, it is a sure sign he will lose something of great value. 46, 75. (*Golden Wheel*: 39)

GEMS – Denotes that you will rise in the world. 2, 11, 12, 20, 22. To see much jewelry denotes riches. 16, 60, 64. (*Aunt Sally's*: 36)
JEWELS.—Indicate that you will be fortunate in your undertakings and that you are on the road to success, both in love and in business. 41, 58. (*Witch Doctor's*: 39)

87. GOWN
.—For a woman to dream that she sees a new gown brought home for her by her dressmaker, is a sign that some retrenchment will be needed in the expenses of the family, of which she is constantly reminded by her husband, who will get cross and sour-tempered about the large amount he will have to pay at the end of the current quarter. If a woman have this dream more than once, it proves her to be a person of vain desires and fashionable extravagance. For a woman to dream her gown is torn and mended in several places, is a good sign; her husband will make progress in business, and amass a pretty large fortune. (WWW: 76)
All those things which encompass us, or receive us, have the same consideration. … all such things may have reference to the Body. and therefore not without cause, one which dreamed that his Gown was broken and torn, was wounded in his Body, and in the same places where he dreamed his Gown was torn; and as the Gown shewed it self to be the case of the Soul. (Artemidorus 1690: 124)

88. GUITAR
.—To dream that you play on a guitar, signifies cheap pleasure. (WWW: 78)
GUITAR. This dream denotes luck in love affairs, if the dreamer sings and plays upon the instrument at the same time. 45, 24. (*Golden Wheel*, 33), also (*Aunt Sally's*: 37, with 4, 20, 45)

89. HELL
.—To dream that you are descending into hell, and return thence, signifies to those that are great and rich, misfortunes; but it is a good sign to the poor and weak. (WWW: 51)
DESCENDING INTO HELL. To dream that you are descending into hell, and return thence, signifies to those that are great and rich, misfortunes; but it is a good sign to the poor and weak. 17. (Le Marchand 1863: 96)
HELL. To dream of seeing Hell, denotes that the dreamer's life is a bad one, and intimation to him of reformation. 1. 57. 61. 78. (*Mother Shipton's*: 9), also (*Aunt Sally's*: 39)

90. HIPS
.—To dream that your hips are larger and stronger than usual, denotes joy, health, numerous posterity.
N.B.—The loins and spine have the same meaning as the hips, and presage, besides, that comfort and felicity will attend the dreamer and their children. Hips, backbone, or loins, to have them broken and unable to move, denotes affliction, sickness, loss of children. To have them bruised by the blow of a sword, stick, or any other weapon, speedy death, a couple about to be separated, or at the least a great embarrassment in the family, which will spring from husband or wife, according to the sex of the dreamer. To have them cut off by the middle, misplaced trust between husband and wife. (WWW: 84)
HIPS. Strong hips signify healthy and handsome children. 6. 8. 45. 55. (*Mother Shipton's*, 9), also (*Aunt Sally's*: 40)
HIPS.—To dream of large and strong hips on a woman signifies that you will have healthy and handsome children of whom you will be justly proud. 12. (*Witch Doctor's*: 36)

91. JUSTICE
.—To dream you are brought to justice, denotes happiness. To be punished by a justice, very intimate flirtation. To see an execution, unfaithfulness. (WWW: 92)
JUSTICE – Denotes poverty and wretchedness. 2, 21. (*Aunt Sally's*: 44)

92. MANSION
.—For a young unmarried woman to dream that she is seated in a very handsome mansion, all her own, and that she is married to her sweetheart, is a sign that she will become poorer by her marriage

union, her social standing will be lowered, and her respect in society will be lessened. Those who formally kept her company will leave her, and she will have none to look to but her husband, who will never amass a fortune, for he will be lazy, profligate, shiftless, vain and conceited in his notions. (WWW: 102)

COUNTRY HOUSE – To see one denotes that you will shortly receive some glad tidings. 1, 14. sides. To look at a countryseat denotes that your sweetheart is faithful 1, 14, 29 (*Aunt Sally's*: 22)

93. MUSICAL INSTRUMENTS

.—To dream you play upon, or hear another play upon an instrument, denotes a funeral, death of a parent. If in a concert, or where there are many instruments, consolation, recovery from illness. To play, or hear others play upon wind instruments, trouble, quarrel, loss of a law-suit. (WWW: 108)

94. NEGLIGEE[57]

.—For a young woman to dream that she loses her negligee, means that some of her good looks which have long been her pride and boast, will fade away, because she will become "love-sick," she will pine for the affections of a young man whom she has seen, but who has not had the courage or inclination to put himself into her company. She dearly wishes it was the fashion for young ladies to propose to gentlemen, for she is so much in love with him that she would soon dare do even that. but she must give up, for custom has denied her the privilege and opportunity of letting this gay and good looking youth know the state of her feelings in regard to him; there is no remedy for her, and her health will suffer in consequence. For a young woman to dream that her negligee is broken by a young man's arm being placed where this ornament hangs is a sign that she will fall out with her lover, and the rupture of their feelings will last for a great length of time; but by perseverance and wisdom on her part, the breach will be healed. (WWW: 110)

95. PARENTS

.—For a young person to dream of his parents, is a good or bad dream, according to circumstances. If you parents are dead and you dream you have a visit from them, it means, if you are about to undertake any new calling, or speculation, that you must be very careful or give up your new project. If you have been guilty of any act of indiscretion, or folly, and you see your parents in your dream, be sure that it is meant as a rebuke to you, and if your actions have made other people suffer, you must try to make some reparation to them for it. If a young woman is about to get married, and her parents appear to her in her dream, with smiling countenances, she may be sure that her marriage will be a happy one; but if they appear to have a frown upon their faces, it means that it will be best to break off the engagement, and annul the marriage contract, for nothing but evil will come of it. (WWW: 117)

PARENTS – Is good to the dreamer and signifies long life, 1, 22, 60 (*Aunt Sally's*: 61)

96. PIMPLES

.—For a young woman to dream that her beauty is very much marred by pimples coming upon her face, is a sign that she will be held up by a host of admirers, as one of the most beautiful of the fair sex that the neighborhood contains. She will be admired of by the male portion of the inhabitants, and envied by the female section. To see pimples on the nose in your dream, means prosperity in business, to see them on the cheeks means success in you love affairs; to see them on the eyelids, means you will have good judgment in the choice and selection of dress; and to dream that you have them upon the forehead, means that you will be much praised by your fellowmen or women for your sound judgment, love of honesty, and impartiality in giving an opinion on any subject that is a debatable one. (WWW: 121)

97. REFRIGERATOR

.—This dream denotes death, or at least sickness for one of the ladies in the house. (WWW: 128)

---

[57] Negligee: A flexible chain of beads, pearls, links of a precious metal or rope like strands, about 50cm to 75cm long and with two pendants of unequal length or a tassel-like pendant. Sometimes also called a sautoir. – http://www.harlings.com/glossary.html (accessed 9/27/2011).

98. STUMBLE

.—If you dream that, while walking or running, you stumble, but do not fall, it foretells luck and success in some undertaking; but if you fall down, the omen is one of misfortune; if a girl / dreams that she stumbles while walking with her intended, it is a sign that she will permit him to take liberties with her person which she would be ashamed to have known, but in this case it will turn out all right, as the incident denotes good fortune and a happy marriage. (WWW: 138/139), also (*Pettingill's*, 95)

99. UNDER-GROUND

.—To dream that you go down under ground, whether into all, a deep cellar or vault, or a cave, denotes your early death; but if you dream that you are digging in the ground and are in a hole which you have dug, the omen is different, for it denotes riches and long life. (WWW: 147), also (*Golden Wheel*: 78-79, and *Pettingill's*: 103)

DIGGING. To dream you are digging, is very good; but if you dream that your spades or digging tools seem to be lost, it portends loss of labour, dearth of corn, and ill harvest weather. 14, 71. (Le Marchand: 96)

GROTTO. To dream of being in a grotto, or cavern in the earth, shows that you will soon meet a near and dear relative: if you live away from home, something will occur to cause your return: such a dream always foretells meeting your absent friends. 49, 2 (*Golden Wheel*: 33), also (*Pettingill's*: 46)

100. WADING

.—If a girl dreams of wading in clear water, it is a sign that she will soon marry, and be delighted with her husband's embraces; if she imagines the water is rily or muddy, it foretells that she will enjoy the pleasures of illicit love. If a man dreams of wading, it denotes that he will be engaged in some intrigue with a female—the deeper the water the more difficult the realization of his wishes; muddy water denotes loose women. (WWW: 153), also (*Golden Wheel*: 80, and *Pettingill's*: 104)

CHAPTER 8:

Charms I - Charms, Spells, and Curses

"Let none be found among you, that is a Charmer". Deut. 18. 11.

Introduction

The English language allows a lot of leeway as to what may be considered a "charm" – it can be a short spoken or written evocation of magical power for a particular purpose, a physical object or collection of items (usually of small sizes) imbued with magical power, or the magical spoken act that exercises that power. Spells and curses are both verbal and more specific in intent; the former can be indifferently good or bad but is usually coercive, whereas the latter has a definitively harmful intent. A spell is a written or oral narrative, so that a "gospel" was originally a "god spel" or "good story" (not a "God spell"). Charms and spells often involve stories as well as formulas, in which by the recitation of some apocryphal "miracle event" involving Christ and/or popular saints, the magician drew on the power and authority of those involved. The narratives might be just a few lines (as spoken charms usually were), or longer and more complex texts for preternatural action. Curses are essentially negative spells, using the same procedure to damn or harm someone rather than bless, cure or control them.

They are also more open to modification and substitution by the operator than the strictly prescribed Christian rites and usages. Jan Veensta notes, "… magical texts are a malleable genre as opposed to canonical texts, that are less subject to variation. Since magical texts were written for practical use, they were subject to change and there may have been as many variants of a text as there were different audiences and groups of users", which is a characteristic of oral traditions in general.[58] The actions and objects that accompany charms are also simpler than the complicated rites and paraphernalia required by learnéd magic. As a genre, they are analogous to recipes rather than chemical formulae. It is instructive to observe how culinary recipes in the period shade imperceptibly into medicinal prescriptions (both are commonly included in early modern cookbooks) and prescriptions in turn employ astrological and humoural assumptions that approximate those found in magical charms. The main distinction is that in charms, materials (whether herbal, animal or mineral) are not usually consumed, but work through attribution or proximity. Although it may be evident to us today that they rely on astrological or sympathetic magic rather than physiological action for their effect, this qualification was not a significant factor, as classical Galenic medicine ratified these influences.

Charms might be performed by ordinary people as well as Cunning Folk, and there was a subdivision of otherwise non-occult magical healers who only used a particular charm or two they happened to possess. Owen Davies has made a good case for differentiating these "blessers" and "charmers" from the more versatile Cunning Folk, especially in the way they were regarded as non-controversial and legitimate by their neighbors. However, for my purposes, charmers, Cunning Folk and ceremonial magicians all occupy a single spectrum as manipulators of preternatural power. While healing charmers might operate apart from other Cunning Folk, medical charms are regularly found in collections containing a variety of magical applications, indicating that there may have been more flexibility in practice at one time.

When I began work on this book, my general assumption was that it would consist in large part of magical formulas, charms and spells with commentary – the earlier the better. As it turned out, there aren't that many different interesting early formulas and charms that survive. As Katherine Briggs

---

[58] Jan R. Veensta. "The Holy Almadal" in Jan N. Bremmer & Jan R. Veensta. *The Metamorphosis of Magic from Late Antiquity to the Early Modern Period.* Dudley, MA: Peeters, 2002, pp. 201-202.

observed, "Spoken spells are less common in the manuscripts than the charms and incantations that were meant to accompany ritual action. A quantity of them was used both by the witches and the ordinary countrymen, but only a few have found their way into magical manuscripts."[59]

The majority of the charms and spells are rather mundane and repetitive, and little different when substances are involved from contemporary medical remedies. The herbal concoctions that appear similar to pharmaceutical medicines yet are not consumed but hung around the neck, or objects that have no possible physiological effect (such as precious stones), blur the line between charms and medicine. Early modern charms are also as strictly Christian in content as the charms of the Anglo-Saxon period, and many are no more than standard prayers or religious excerpts in Latin, the language of traditional magic. The weight of tradition seems omnipresent in this respect, whether there is evidence of borrowing from either liturgical sources or traditional conjuration.

A survey of published "esoteric" resources that could be afforded by the average reader from Tudor to Georgian times turns up extensive material on divination, astrology, healing and "natural magic", but very little on spiritual magic or conjuration. As Owen Davies notes, an apparent caution or self-censorship existed among the publishers of English almanacs and chapbooks that prevented them from including more striking examples of folk magic, in contrast to popular compilations available in France, Germany and other continental countries. While some overtly magical material found its way into print in expensive books such as Scot's *Discoverie of Witchcraft* (1584) or Turner's translation of the *Fourth Book of Occult Philosophy* (1655), there were almost none in vernacular publications. It was only in the 19th century, once cultural authorities had abandoned their fear of magical heterodoxy and the Romantic Movement gave the occult renewed legitimacy, that publishers of chapbooks and cheap paperbacks followed the example of "Raphael" (Robert Cross Smith), the anonymous compiler of *Witchcraft Detected and Prevented* (1824) or Lauron William De Laurence in pillaging older magical sources for their own profit. At the same time, folklorists were busily preserving whatever fragments of the fading oral culture of magic they could uncover; so much of what we have to work with is from the very end of the Cunning tradition. Although innumerable charms, spells and curses were never recorded and are lost to us, it seems safe to assume that most were similar to those that survive.

Words of Power and Objects of Virtue

The content of charms, spells and curses were derived not only from traditional magical "sympathies" and astrological affinities, but also from medieval Christian liturgical models, which only makes sense since the source of supernatural power was universally assumed to be the same reservoir the Church employed for rituals and "sacramentals" (holy water, blessings, relics, the sign of the cross, consecrated bells &c.), which theologically were more like prayers asking for divine help than sacraments that operated directly. Although the latter were scorned and rejected during the Reformation as "papist sorcery", many people still trusted charms that employed the familiar forbidden elements offering protection and healing by illicit means. Tapping into spiritual power logically required the same devices the priests used for the sacraments or in the case of ceremonial magic, in exorcism.

The fundamental basis for wielding sacred power was "hallowing" or consecration, through which divine power could be infused into earthly matter such as salt, water or other artifacts. That same power could be wielded by authorized individuals to control spiritual entities, to banish them from possessed individuals in exorcism or force them to perform tasks in ritual magic. The Protestant clergy may have dismissed the Catholic belief that such forces could actually be manipulated by either priests or the laity, but they did not reject the agency of charms altogether. Instead, they asserted that charms did not draw on divine power at all but were the work of the Devil. The basic premise was that although a charm, spell or curse had no efficacy in itself, it was "a signe and watchword" for Satan to perform some sort of preternatural effect. William Perkins clarified the Protestant position when he said, "... the Devil is furnished for this purpose, is his own exquisite knowledge of all naturall things; as of the influences of

---

[59] Katherine M. Briggs. "Some Seventeenth-Century Books of Magic" *Folklore*, Vol. 64, No. 4 p. 452.

the stars, the constitutions of men, and other creatures, the kinds, virtues, and operations of plants, rootes, hearbs, stones, &c. which knowledge of his, goeth many degrees beyond the skill of all men, yea even of those that are most excellent in this kind, as Philosophers, and Physicians." (Perkins 1615: 617) It is instructive that Perkins credits the existence of hidden virtues in natural things and attests to the influence of the stars on earthly events, even though he insists that astral influences are general rather than specific, and discounts the ability of astrologers to predict particular events, or of magicians to manipulate these influences (he had studied arcane subjects in depth in his youth).

Even though Protestant orthodoxy rejected the entire system of consecration and exorcism, there was still a need for a practical protection against preternatural attack (given the fixed belief in the reality in magic and witchcraft) that resulted in an adaptation of accepted Calvinist procedures that mirrored the function of charms. As Keith Thomas observes, "... it seemed that the Protestant remedy of fasting and prayer might well be developed into a ritual claiming something very near mechanical efficacy" (Thomas 1971: 571) – and by all indications, the faithful did just that.

The Precedent of Consecration

The "conception billet" is a good example of a legitimate medieval sacramental that could act as a prototype for illicit charms. Conception billets, small documents (think billet doux – "sweet notes" or "love letters") sold by Carmelite monks, consisted of a religious formula on a consecrated paper. Buried in the corner of a field, they were supposed to give protection against bad weather and destructive insects.

> The Conception Billet
> "I conjure thee, paper (or parchment), thou which servest the needs of humanity, servest as the depository of God's wonderful deeds and holy laws, as also according to divine command the marriage contract between Tobias and Sarah was written upon thee, the Scriptures saying: They took paper and signed their marriage covenant. Through thee, O paper, hath also the devil been conquered by the angel. I adjure thee by God, the Lord of the universe (sign of the cross!), the Son (sign of the cross!), and the Holy Ghost (sign of the cross!), who spreads out the heavens as a parchment on which he describes; as with divine characters his magnificence. Bless (Sign of the cross!), O God, sanctify (sign of the cross!) this paper that so it may frustrate the work of the Devil!
> "Ye who upon his person carries this paper written with holy words, or affixes it to a house, shall he freed from the visitations of Satan through him who cometh to judge the quick and dead.
> "Let us pray.
> "Mighty and resistless God, the God of vengeance, God of our fathers, who hast revealed through Moses and the prophets the hooks of thy ancient covenant / and many secrets of thy kindness, and didst cause the Gospel of thy Son to be written by the evangelists and apostles, bless (sign of the cross!) and sanctify (sign of the cross!) this paper that thy mercy may be made known unto whatsoever soul shall bear with him this sacred thing and these holy letters; and that all persecutions against him from the devil and by the storms of satanic witchcraft may be frustrated through Christ our Lord. Amen. "(The paper to be sprinkled with holy water.)"[60]

Another sacramental that resembles a charm or amulet is the "Agnus Dei". These were very popular in pre-Reformation England, but the possession of one afterwards could result in seizure of property and imprisonment, under the statute of 27. Eliz., cap. 2 (1585). They only went "out of production" by the Catholic Church in 1964.

> The name "Agnus Dei" was given to special discs of wax impressed with the figure of a lamb, the "Lamb of God" which were blessed by the reigning Pope in a ceremony so solemn that the Pope was said to consecrate the sacramentals. Popes traditionally consecrated Agnus Deis only during the first year of their pontificate and again every seven years.
> In earlier times, on Holy Saturday, the Pope, with the assistance of the Archdeacon of Rome, prepared the wax from the previous year's paschal candles, adding both chrism and balsam to the

---

[60] Abraham Viktor Rydberg. *The Magic of the Middle Ages*. New York: Henry Holt, 1879, pp. 65-66.

wax. The Agnus Deis were subsequently consecrated on the Wednesday of Easter week and distributed on Saturday of the same week. In more recent times, the wax was prepared by monks and then consecrated by the Pope and distributed. When visiting Cardinals would visit the Holy Father, an Agnus Dei wax disc (or several of the discs) would be placed into his miter. The Cardinals then distributed the Agnus Deis as they saw fit.[61]

The verses recited with the Agnus Dei might appear, as well, "charm-like":

Tonitrua magna terret,	May loud thunders terrify,
Et peccata nostra delet;	And destroy our sins;
Ab incendio praeservat,	Save us from fiery destruction,
A submersione servat,	Save us from drowning
A morte cita liberat,	Free us from sudden violent death,
Et Cacodaemones fugat,	And put to flight the evil demons,
Inimicos nostras domat	Let us overcome our enemies,
Praegnantem cum partu salvat,	Save the woman with child during childbirth,
Dona dignis multa confert,	Grant great gifts to the worthy,
Utque malis mala defert.	And bring evil to the evil ones.
Portio, quamvis parva sit,	May a portion, however small,
Ut magna tamen proficit.[62]	Nevertheless be of great benefit.

A number of charms called for the recitation of standard Latin Catholic formulas, such as the Pater Noster, Ave, and the Creed. They also used the Sign of the Cross, and invoked the Trinity ("In the name of the Father, and of the Son, and of the Holy Ghost") just as the Church did. As these are more often simply referred to rather than included with the text of the charm, I add them here:

Pater Noster
Pater noster, qui es in caelis;
sanctificetur nomen tuum;
adveniat regnum tuum;
fiat voluntas tua, sicut in caelo et in terra.
Panem nostrum quotidianum da nobis hodie;
et dimitte nobis debita nostra,
sicut et nos dimittimus debitoribus nostris;
et ne nos inducas in tentationem;
sed libera nos a malo. Amen.

Ave Maria
Ave Maria, gratia plena; Dominus tecum:
benedicta tu in mulieribus, et benedictus
fructus ventris tui, Iesus.
Sancta Maria, Mater Dei, ora pro nobis peccatoribus,
nunc et in hora mortis nostrae. Amen.

The Creed
Credo in Deum, Patrem omnipotentem, Creatorem caeli et terrae.
Et in Iesum Christum, Filium eius unicum, Dominum nostrum:

---

[61] http://www.sacramentals.org/agnusdei.htm (accessed 4/21/2011)
[62] Andrew Dickson White. *A History of the Warfare of Science With Theology in Christendom.* Amherst, NY: Prometheus Books, 1993, vol I, p. 343.

qui conceptus de Spiritu Sancto, natus ex Maria Virgine,
passus sub Pontio Pilato, crucifixus, mortuus et sepultus:
descendit ad inferos; tertia die resurrexit a mortuis:
ascendit ad caelos; sedet ad dexteram Dei Patris omnipotentis:
inde venturus est iudicare vivos et mortuos.
Credo in Spiritum Sanctum, sanctam Ecclesiam catholicam,
Sanctorum communionem, remissionem peccatorum,
carnis resurrectionem, vitam aeternam. Amen.

Consecrated prayers could become rather garbled in the hands of the Cunning Folk, such as the widely-cited "White Paternoster" and vernacular versions of the Creed:

The "White Paster-noster"
White pater-noster, Saint peter's brother,
What hast I' th' t'one hand? white book leaves.
What hast I' th' t'other hand? heaven yates keyes.
Open heaven yates, and steike [shut] hell yates:
And let every crysome child creepe to its owne mother.
White Pater-nostyer, Amen. [63]

Another version:

God was my foster,
He fostered me
Under the book of Palm tree.
St. Michael was my dame,
He was born at Bethlehem.
He was made of flesh and blood,
God send me my right food;
My right food, and dyne too,
That I may too yon kirk go,
To read upon yon sweet book,
Which the mighty God of heaven shook.
Open, open, heaven's yaits,
Steik [fasten], steik, hell's yaits,
All saints be the better,
That hear the white prayer, Pater-noster.

There was also a "black paternoster":

The Black Pater-noster.
Four neuks [corners] in this house for holy angels,
A post in the midst, that Christ Jesus,
Lucas, Marcus, Mathew, Joannes,
God be unto this house, and all that belong us. (Forsyth 1827: 270)

The "Creed"
"Creezum zuum patrum onitentem creatorum ejus anicum, Dominum nostrum qui sum sops, virgini Mariae, crixus fixus, Ponchi Pilati audubitiers, morti by sonday. Faher a fernes, scelerest un judicarum, finis a mortibus. Creezum spirituum sanctum, ecli Catholi, remissurum, peccaturum, communiorum obliviorum, bitam et turnam again." (Choice Notes 1859: 111)

In other cases, particular Biblical passages were transcribed and made into amulets, such as this passage from the *Gospel of John*, just as they had been in pre-Reformation times. This example was found on a 17th century parchment roll (Brit. Mus. Addit. MS 25311.) of magical sigils and prayers. Note: In the

---

[63] John White. *The Way to the True Church*, London. 1624, cited in *Choice Notes from "Notes and Queries": Folklore*. London: Bell and Daldy, 1859, p. 111.

examples, I've used the "+" sign to indicate the action of making the sign of the cross, and (unless it is spelled out or occurs differently in the original citation) "☧" for the written sign of the cross.

☧ In Principio erat Verbum, et Verbum erat apud Deum, et Deus erat Verbum; hoc erat in principio apud Deum; omnia per ipsum facta sunt, et sine ipso facta [factum] est nihil, quod factum est. In ipso vita erat, et vita erat lux hominum; et lux in tenebris lucet, et tenebrae eam non comprehenderunt. Fuit homo missus a Deo, cui nomen erat Joannes; hic venit in testimonium, ut testimonium perhiberet de luniine, ut omnes crederent per illum. Non erat ille lux, sed ut testimonium perhiberet de lumine. Erat lux vera, quae illuminat omnem hominein venientem in hunc mundum. In mundo erat, et mundus per ipsum factus est, et mundus eum non cognovit. In propria venit, et sui eum non receperunt; quotquot autem receperunt eum, dedit eis potestatem filios Dei fieri, his, qui credunt in nomine ejus; qui non ex sanguiuibus, neque ex voluntate carnis, neque ex voluntate viri, sed ex Deo nati sunt. ET VERBUM CARO FACTUM EST, et habitavit in nobis, et vidimus gloriam ejus, gloriam quasi unigeniti a Patre, plenum gratiae et veritatis. Deo gratias. (These words will be recognised as the Gospel for Christmas Day – St. John, i, 1-14). (Simpson 1884: 327)

Other examples of straight *Bible* verses used by Cunning Folk are found in "Raphael's" *The Astrologer of the Nineteenth Century*:

A 𝕮𝖍𝖆𝖗𝖒 AGAINST FURIOUS BEASTS
REPEAT earnestly and with sincere faith these words:—
"At the destruction and famine thou shalt laugh, neither shalt thou be afraid of the beasts of the earth."
"For thou shalt be in league with the stones of the field, and the beasts of the field shall be at peace with thee."— JOB, chap, 5, v. 22, 23.
A 𝕮𝖍𝖆𝖗𝖒 AGAINST TROUBLE IN GENERAL.
"He shall deliver thee in six troubles, yea, in seven there shall be no evil touch thee."/
"In famine he shall redeem thee from death, and in war from the power of the sword.
"And thou shalt know that thy tabernacle shall be in peace, and thou shalt visit thy habitation and shalt nor sin."—Job, chap. 5, v. 19, 20, 24.
A 𝕮𝖍𝖆𝖗𝖒 AGAINST ENEMIES.
"Behold, God is thy salvation; I will trust, and not be afraid, for the Lord Jehovah is my strength and my song; he also is become my salvation.
"For the stars of heaven, and the constellations thereof, shall not give their light; the sun shall be darkened in his going forth, and the moon shall not cause her light to shine.
"And behold, at evening tide, trouble; and before the morning he is not; this is the portion of them that spoil us, and the lot of them that rob us."—ISAIAH, chap. 12 and 17.
A 𝕮𝖍𝖆𝖗𝖒 AGAINST PERIL BY FIRE OR WATER.
Thus, also, where we would avoid peril by fire or water, we make use of this passage:—"When thou passest through the waters, I will be with thee, and through the rivers they shall not overflow thee; when thou walkest through the fire, thou shalt not be burnt, neither shall the flame kindle upon thee."—ISAIAH, chap. 43, v.2. ("Raphael" Astrologer 1825: 197-98).

Additionally, quotes from the *Book of Psalms* were used aggressively rather than defensively. Lines from psalms that sounded suitably hostile could be used to invoke divine affliction through extempore curses on evil spirits or enemies. Psalm 109 in particular was used in attack mode, but there were many other "cursing Psalms" that contained appropriate lines for execration. For example, in Psalm 69 enemies are suitable damned in verses 23 and 24: "May their eyes be darkened so they cannot see, and their backs be bent forever. Pour out your wrath on them; let your fierce anger overtake them," or there is Psalm 137 (verses 8 and 9) – best known today as lyrics for the Melodians' Rivers of Babylon (1970) – which thunders, "O Daughter of Babylon, doomed to destruction, happy is he who repays you for what you have done to us – he who seizes your infants and dashes them against the rocks," or Psalm 35, verse 8: "Let destruction come on him; he will not know; and let his net which he concealed catch him; let him fall in it, into destruction."

Another source of magical psalmody can be found in the American translation of "… the Hebrew mystical text *Sepher Schimmush Tehillim*, or the magical uses of the Psalms. This was translated by Gottfried Selig (1722-1795), publisher of the German (Leipzig) periodical Jude, about Jewish customs and practices. This popular text is a medieval compilation, and was frequently printed in pamphlet form."[64] Joseph H. Peterson, who edited a critical version of this text in his *Sixth and Seventh Books of Moses* (Ibis Books, 2008), has also made the work available on his extremely valuable website, the "Twilit Grotto" at www.esotericarchives.com. I am very indebted to Mr. Peterson's website for both reference and as a means to avoid having to retype many textual selections. The *Sixth and Seventh Books* has long been an important source for the practice of folk magic in the United States, the Caribbean and elsewhere, and are part of the transatlantic contribution to English-speaking tradition of the Cunning Folk.

The cheap translated version omits the original Hebrew letters in the psalms, which rather negates their usefulness (Peterson has restored them in his edition). As an example of the transmission of this influential work, here is the information on the 13th psalm, first in the manner it appears in the English translation, secondly as corrected by Mr. Peterson, and thirdly an image of the original German version from the William Radde edition of 1865 (rather stained from heavy use, I'm afraid).

> ("Egyptian Publishing Company") **Psalm 13.**—Whoever prays this Psalm daily with devotion, together with the proper prayer belonging thereto, and thinks at the same time of the powerful name of Essiel, that is, My help is the mighty God, will be safe for the next twenty-four hours from an unnatural death and from all bodily sufferings and punishments. The prayer is as follows: Protect me according to thy good will and pleasure from violent, sudden and unnatural death, and from all other evil accidents and severe bodily afflictions, for thou art my help and my God, and thine is the power and the glory. Amen.—Selah.
>
> According to tradition this Psalm is also a good cure for dangerous and painful diseases of the eyes. The patient must procure a plant that is good for the eyes, and with this must pray this Psalm with a suitable prayer, trusting firmly in the certain help of the mighty Essiel, and then bind the plant upon his eyes. The letters composing this holy name are contained in the words: Ezoth, verse 3; Mismor, verse 1; Jarum, verse 3; Aneni, verse 4; Ojewi, verse 5, and Jagel, verse 6. (Sixth and Seventh Books of Moses, n. d.: 150)
>
> (Peterson – online edition) **Psalm 13.**— Whoever prays this Psalm daily with devotion, together with the proper prayer belonging thereto, and thinks at the same time of the powerful name of עזריאל **Esriel**,[19] that is, My help is the mighty God, will be safe for the next twenty-four hours from an unnatural death and from all bodily sufferings and punishments. The prayer is as follows: Protect me according to thy good will and pleasure from violent, sudden and unnatural death, and from all other evil accidents and severe bodily afflictions, for thou art my help and my God, and thine is the power and the glory. Amen — Selah.
>
> According to tradition this Psalm is also a good cure for dangerous and painful diseases of the eyes. The patient must procure a plant that is good for the eyes, and with this must pray this Psalm with a suitable prayer, trusting firmly in the certain help of the mighty Essiel, and then bind the plant upon his eyes. The letters composing this holy name are contained in the words: צעות **Ezoth**, verse 3; מזמור **Mismor**, verse 1; ירום **Jarum**, verse 3; ענני **Aneni**, verse 4; אדיבי **Ojewi**, verse 5, and יגל **Jagel**, verse 6.
>
> 19. EE: Essiel.

---

[64] Joseph H. Peterson. *The Sixth and Seventh Books of Moses*. Lake Worth, FL: Ibis Press, 2008. http://www.esotericarchives.com/moses/67moses.htm (accessed 5/27/2011)

Pfalm 13.

Wer diesen Psalm mit dem dazu gehörigen Gebet täglich andächtig betet, und stets an den kraftvollen Namen עזריאל Esriel, d. h. meine Hilfe ist der mächtige Gott, denket, der ist jedesmal 24 Stunden sicher vor einem unnatürlichen bösen Tod, und andern harten Leibesplagen und Strafen. Das Gebet heißt: Behüte mich nach Deinem heiligen Wohlgefallen und Willen vor einem bösen schnellen und unnatürlichen Tod; vor allen andern bösen Zufällen und harten Leibesstrafen, denn Du bist mein Helfer und mein Gott, und Dein ist die Macht und die Herrlichkeit. Amen. — Sela.

Eben so soll nach der Tradition dieser Psalm auch noch vor alle gefährliche und schmerzhafte Augenkrankheiten ein herrliches Hilfsmittel sein. Es soll sich nehmlich der Patient ein den Augen dienliches Kraut suchen, dabei aber den Pf. mit einem den Umständen gemäßen Gebet im völligen Vertrauen auf die gewisse Hilfe des mächtigen Esriel, andächtig beten, und es hernach über die Augen binden. Die Buchstaben des heiligen Namens sind genommen aus den Worten עצרה Ezoth V. 3. מזמור Mismor, V. 1 ירום Jarum, V. 3. עיני Aneni, V. 4. — אויבי Ojewi V. 5. — יגל Jagel, V. 6.

(*Das scheste und siebente Buch Mosis*. NY: Wm. Radde, 1865, pp. 281-82)

Magical Influences

Orthodox elements appropriated from the rejected Catholic religious heritage were only part of the story. Apocryphal narrative charms were an equally important resource in "Christian magic". These were short anecdotes ("historiole") in which Christ, the Virgin Mary, the Apostles or various saints wrought cures and other marvelous effects. The underlying concept was that by rehearsing the earlier miracle and adding an invocation, the same effect would take place again. This device was very ancient, and Anglo-Saxon examples often contain fragments from the earlier pagan versions that had been edited and adapted for Christian use. These narrative charms were largely medicinal in nature, as can be seen in the section dealing with healing, below.

Katherine Briggs gives an example an apotropaic (i. e., protection) charm from a 17th century manuscript that combines several religious usages, including a variety of the apocryphal narrative, an invocation or command, a curse and liturgical formulae:

> The Night Spell. (From Regulae Utilissimae. Brit. Mus.. Addit. MS 36674, p. 89.) This charme should be said at night or against night about the place or field or about beasts without field, and whosoever cometh in he goeth not out for certaine. "On 3 Crosses of a tree, 3 dead bodyes did hang, 2 were theeves, and 3rd was Xst [Christ] on whom our beleife is, Dismas and Gesmas, Xst amidst them was, Dismas to heaven went, Gesmas to hell was sent, Christ that died on that roode, for Maries love that by him stood, and through the virtue of his blood, Jesus save us and our good within and without and all this place about and through the virtue of his might let noe thief enter in this night : noe foot further in this place that I upon goe, but at my bidding there be bound, to do all things that I bid them do. Starke be their sineiues therewith & their lives mightles and their eyes sightles, dred and doubt them enclose about, as a wall wrought of stone so be thes crampt in the ton, crampe and crookeing and fault in thier footing, the might of the Trinity, save these goods for me. In the name of Jesus, holy benedicite all about our goods bee, within and without and all place about", then say 5 pr. nrs., 5 av. & i cred. etc. (Briggs 1953: 452).

Among other charms cited and condemned by Reginald Scot in *The Discoverie of Witchcraft* is this cure for dysentery, known then as "the flux" that shows a similar if simpler combination:

For a bloodie flux, or rather an issue of bloud.

TAke a cup of cold water, and let fall thereinto tree drops of the same bloud, and betweene each drop saie a Pater noster, and an Ave, then drinke to the patient, and saie ; Who shall helpe you ? The patient must answer S. Marie. Then saie you ; S. Marie stop the issue of bloud. ◊ Otherwise : Write upon the patients forhead with the same bloud ; Consummatum est. ◊ Otherwise : Saie to the patient ; Sanguis mane in te, sicut fecit Christus in se ; Sanguis mane in tua vena, sicut Christus in sua poena; Sanguis mane fixus, sicut Christus quando fuit crucifixus: ter. ["Blood remain in thee, as Christ made in himself; Blood remain in thy vein, just as Christ's did during His punishment; Blood remain fixed, just as Christ's did at the time of crucifixion: recite three times.] (Scot 1973: 222)

A charm against spiritual attack found in the 19th century *"Albertus Magnus ... Egyptian Secrets"* that was not included in the original *Book of Secrets* attributed to Albertus, which was strictly limited to the "natural magic" properties of herbs, minerals and animal parts. Here the appeal to the symbols of the Passion is expressed in a much more imperative, magical style, being a contribution from German folk magic:

> If a Human Being or Beast is attacked by Evil Spirits, how to restore Him and make Him well again. Thou arch-sorcerer, thou has attacked N. N.; let that witchcraft recede from him into thy marrow and into thy bone, let it be returned unto thee. I exorcise thee for the sake of the five wounds of Jesus, thou evil spirit, and conjure thee for the five wounds of Jesus of this flesh, marrow and bone; I exorcise thee for the sake of the five wounds of Jesus, at this very hour restore to health again N. N., in the name of God the Father, God the Son, and of God the Holy Spirit. [recite] Three times. (Albertus Magnus n d.: 51)

The inclusion of Christian elements in charms and spells attests to two concerns shared by practitioners of folk magic: credibility – in a society that believed in the ultimate reality of the Christian world view, the use of conventional empowering formulas was useful in establishing the client's trust; and legitimacy – framing the charm in terms and symbols indistinguishable (by the layman, at any rate) from those of the Church sought to avoid censure for dealing with demons or the practice of witchcraft.

The other determinative influence was of course traditional ritual magic, a corpus of magical methods and assumptions that stretched back through Judeo-Christian and Moslem cultures to Hellenistic times and the magical papyri. Like the religious formulas co-opted from medieval Christianity, established magical procedures provided credibility, if not legitimacy, to the work of the Cunning Folk. Magic was (until recently, at least) a profoundly conservative practice that depended on past authority and static custom for its claim to authenticity and agency (i.e., its ability to actually do things). Charms influenced by traditional conjuration might include such things as magical squares, the names of spirits rather than Biblical individuals, strange characters and "sigils" ("a sign or image supposedly having magical power", from the Latin *sigillum*, "a little sign", in turn from *signum*, "a sign" or image) and invocations. In the examples that follow, there are a) arbitrary characters (followed by a divisional marker with four dots), b) standard astrological signs, c) round magic sigils or seals, d) the names of spirits (possibly angels), e) words of power or names, f & g) seals with both magical characters and names, and h) a "magical square". Names, special characters, images and abstract symbols were all ways in which magical power could be invoked and fixed in material objects, as opposed to the inherent virtues found in natural objects, as in amulets and some fetishes. Spoken charms, spells and curses relied primarily on the power attributed to words, names and symbols, in which the vast repertoire of religious and magical tradition was channejled for a specific effect.

Write these words in uirgins wax and aske what thou wilt of anny one and it shalbee giuen thee.

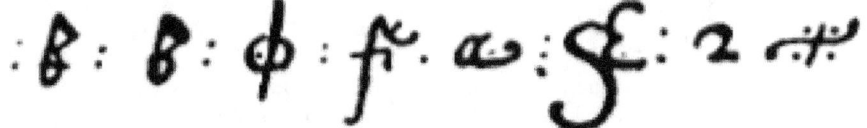

The holly ghost Bless us now and ever mor amen. I Bequeath thys place all about and all my goods within and without to the Blessed trinity that one god and three persons to all Christs Apostles to all Angells Archangells Chirubims and Seraphimes: I Bequeath this place all about and my goods to

Jesus Christ and to saint John the Euangelist that was that true deciple that noe theeues away take But keepe holy for our Blessed Ladyes St: maryes Sake that not from hence no theeues feet goe but keepe them hear still O Blessed trinity through the uertue of thy godhead that Created heaven and earth And all things Contained therin: and By the uertue of hys powerfull passion that hee suffered in his manhood for our Redeeption : and by his holly name Jesus and by all the holly names of god that are to be spoken and that are not to be spoken: and by the name that is aboue all names wherwith god Created all things: And by the uertue of his Body in forme of bread: And by uertue of euery mass that hath beene saide both more and less: And by the uertuouse worlds stones and grass: By all the names aboue rehersed: I charg youe euery one and the four Euangelists Mathew: mark: Luke: and John: By all the mightye powers of god by the gloryouse Ascention of our Lord Jesus Christ By all the names and miracles of the apostles martyrs / Confessours uirgins I Charge youe for to keepe him or them hear still: I Charge youe seauen plannets

I Charg the the twelfe Signes:

I Charg you all hear to keepe (him) or them still By the miracles of god and of hys apostles and of all holly martyres: by the uirginitie of our blessed Lady and uirginities of all other uirgins that they pass no foot untill they haue told euery stone in the way and euery watter drop that drops in the sea. I pray youe all that It bee soe and that you binde them hear as did St. Barthallamew the deuill with an haire of hys beard theeues. theeues. theeues. Stand by the uertue of the blessed trinity and by all the uertues before Rehersed: And by the uertue of the passion of Christ by his death and buryall and his upriseinge and Ascention and by his Comming at the dreadfull day of Judgement to Judge both the Quicke and the dead allso I bind youe by the dread- full name of god tetra gramation untill to morrow that I Com to speake with him or them hear or ther untill I Liscence them to goe their way: I Charg youe all aforesaid that it bee soe by the uertue of the Blessed trinity the Lord of might: Amen

 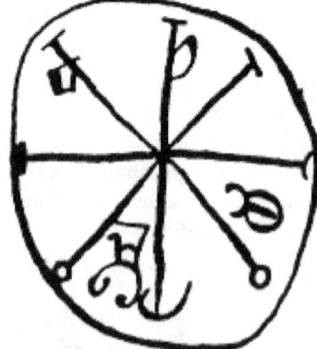

(left) Whoso hath this figure about him let him fear no foe but fear God. (right) Whoso hath this about him all spirits shall do him homage. (Gaster 1910: 377-378)

A Love Spell
Take an Apple in thy hande as it hangeth on the tree & wryte in yt these names followinge. Anaell, Satnell, Asiell & then saye I conjure thee Apple of Apples by the name of these devels, which

deceptfully deceaved Eve in paradyce, that what woman soever it be that doth eate or tast of this Apple that she may burne in love of me. Saye this 4 tymes upon the Apple & then geve the Apple to what woman you will. (Briggs 1953: 456)

A Charm to Protect Against Thieves

Whoso will protect himself against thieves by night or by day, let him wear this charm (written on virgin parchment) about him, and repeat the words thereof every morning, so shall no theft happen to annoy him. – Original manuscript, dated May, 8, 1577, in the posession of Mr. Graham, the Aeronaut.

The Charm

Deus autem transiens per medium illorum, ibat ✠ **Ihus xpus** ✠ benedictus Deus quotidie prosperus iter facit **Deus** salutaris noster ✠ **Ihus** obstinenter occuli eorum ne videant, et dorsum corum ni curva ✠ **Ihus** ✠ effundus supre eas ira tua, et furor ire tue comprehendat cos ✠ **Irrnat** ✠ supra inimicas meos formido et pavo in magnitudine brachii fiant eniobiles quasi Lapis, donec per transeat famulus tuus ✠ quem ✠ redemisti ✠ dextera tua magnificata est, in virtute **Domini** per crusist imimicus in multitudine virtutis tuæ deposuisti omnes adversarious meos ✠ **Ihesu** ✠ eripe me et ab in surgentibusque in me libera me ✠ **Ihesu** ✠ eripe me de opera tibis que iniquitate et a viris sanguine salva me ✠ gloria **Patri** ✠ **Anthos** ✠ **Anostro** ✠ **Moxio** ✠ **Bay** ✠ **Gloy** ✠ **Apen** ✠ **Agia** ✠ **Agais** ✠ Yskiros ✠. ("Raphael" 1825: 504)

Some other Figures to Preserve the Sight.

Make thee a round Lamen of the best lead in the hour of ♀, the ☽ being in the Signe ♈, and in the same hour: to wit, in the hour of ♀, engrave the Signes and letters which you see written in the following Figure: Afterwards in the hour of ♄, make a Copper Lamen of the same Quality and Form as the Leaden one; when ☽ is in the signe ♑, the Characters which you see in the Figure, are to be engraven. And then both Figures are to be kept and preserved so long until ♀ comes into Conjunction with ♄: and then in the point of the Conjunction both the figures are to be conjoyned together so, that the Characters and Signes may mutually touch one another; then close them fast with Wax, that they receive no moisture, and sew them up in a piece of Silk, and hang it about the Neck of the Patient on the day and hour of ♀. This is the best Remedy to recover the Sight of the Eyes, and to preserve the Eyes from Pain and Diseases. It preserveth the Sight in old Age, as perfect as it was in youth. (Archidoxes 1656: 504)

To Preserve the Sight.

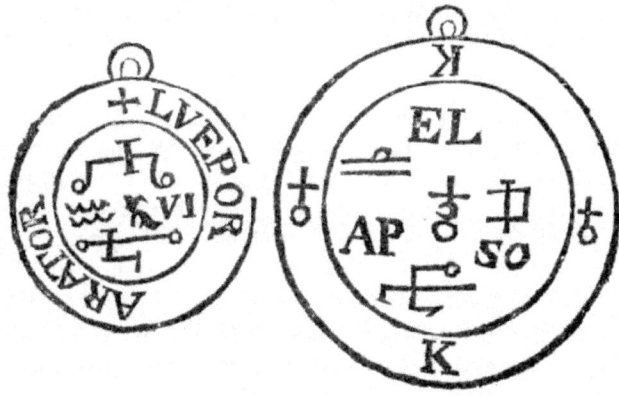

CHARM FOR PROTECTION FROM ENEMIES.

THIS talisman should be made of pure cast iron and engraven at the time of new moon. Before suspending it round the neck fumigate it with the smoke of burnt Spirits of Mars (a mixture of red saunders, frankincense, and red pepper,), or a ring of pure gold might be made, with the characters engraven on the inside. The size and form of this talisman is immaterial so long as the proper time for making it is observed and the prescribed incense is used before it is worn. In any form it will protect one from enemies, and counteract the power of the evil eye. (Hewett 1900: 72-73)

The Art of Extinguishing Fire without the aid of Water.

Inscribe the following letters upon each side of a plate, and throw it into the fire, and forthwith the fire will be extinguished: (Albertus Magnus n d.: 51)

S	A	T	O	R
A	R	E	P	O
T	E	N	E	T
O	P	E	R	A
R	O	T	A	S

The famous square is recommended in the same book for a number of other uses, such as identifying witches (p. 78), healing cows (p. 91), avoiding pestilence (p. 123), and against sorcery (p. 125). It is obviously considered to have an innate power unrelated with its perceptible content. It is also found in Arthur Gauntlet's collection (Sloane MS 3851) to insure luck in gambling:

> Write these words [the "sator" square] in virgin Parchment with the blood of a Turtledove and put the Parchment on a linen cloth sown round that it may go about thine arm that shall throw the dice. (Rankine 2011: 317)

Charms, spells and curses, like the rest of the Cunning Folk's repertoire, always aimed at practical results. The remainder of this chapter is comprised of examples of healing or blessing charms – the most common variety of the genre – and their polar opposite, curses (inverted charms) and transgressive or "black" magic, plus some miscellaneous charms that do not fit in any other context. The following chapter's examples are divided among the other most common charming goals: protection (including defences against witchcraft and demonic attack), love and marriage, treasure-hunting, and theft detection.

One further comment – I have chosen for the most part not to speculate the semantics of the charm; on how the motif or symbolism employed in any particular charm was perceived by the operator in achieving the desired result. I believe that we are too far removed from the mindset of the Cunning Folk to effectively do this. History cannot do what anthropology does in uncovering the opinions in detail from living cultures: "… it is precisely because Turner seeks the meanings of symbols in the verbal explanation (exegesis) of his informants that he has successfully pushed our understanding of ritual away from sympathetic magic to expressive symbolism." (Tambiah 1968: 206) Even then, the cultural biases of the observer can complicate things. Also, it does not appear that there was much conscious concern over the theoretical basis behind individual charms – reliance on tradition and trust in familiar forms worked against any need to explain or justify.

The modern imperative to analyse, dissect ("deconstruct") and rationalize cultural artifacts and to construct metanarratives to account for them, as scholars from Sir James Frazier to Godfrid Storms have done, seems to me to result more often in revealing the intellectual preconceptions of the author than in dependable explanations of what was actually thought in the past. Postmodernists go on about the impossibility of identifying authorial intent, and although I am not as dogmatic about this as they are, I do think the rationale behind most magical constructs are not easily retrievable. What we do need to recognize, however, is that what is said and done aren't simply irrational associations. They were meaningful and deliberate, even if their logic may escape us (and may not have been obvious to the individual practitioner, who might have garbled them anyhow), and that they were originally created within a specific, conscious cultural context of signification.

Healing

The most common function of charms and charming was medicinal. Before the Reformation, the use of magico-religious remedies had an established if contested role in Christian culture, with examples recorded in approved texts date back to Anglo-Saxon times. After Protestantism rejected the whole idea of religious consecration from the Mass on down to the simplest sacramental, this sudden divestiture of the Church's armory of charms, relics, images, medals, holy sites and official blessings for protection and healing, left the population that had depended on them for centuries psychologically adrift and all the more eager to receive the same services from Cunning Folk and individual charmers. At a time when the effectiveness of even the best professional medicine was at best dubious, the pressing need to relieve both men and beasts from disease spawned an immense number of charms.

The charms below are divided by the particular ill they were to cure and then chronologically. Before dealing with the charms of the 1550-1900 period, however, it might be useful to see some earlier precedents from the famous Anglo-Saxon "leechbooks" or medical manuscripts, as translated by Thomas O. Cockayne in *Leechdoms, Wortcunning, and Starcraft of Early England*. (1864-1866). The examples that have obvious pagan elements (such as the famous Æcerbot charm from vol. I, p. 399ff, or the "Nine Worts Lay", vol. III, p. 31) have been thoroughly publicized and need not be repeated here. Despite their attractiveness as (dubious) romantic examples of early "resistance" to Christian "hegemony", they constitute a very tiny subset among hundreds of Christian or neutral listings.

The first example is an herbal recipe from the *Herbarium of Apuleius* to cure a snake bite. The term "deer" was not then limited to our Cervidae animals, but to wild animals in general:

> WALL WORT, or ELDER WORT [Dwarf Elder Sambucus ebulus]
> 2. For rent by snake, take this same wort, which we named ebulurn, and ere thou carve it off, – hold it in thine hand, and say thrice nine times, "Omnes malas bestias canto," that is, in our language, "Enchant and overcome all evil wild deer" ; then carve it off with a very sharp knife, into three parts ; and the while that thou be doing this, think of the man whom thou thinkest therewith to leech, and when thou wend thence, look not about thee ; then take the wort and pound it, lay it to the cut; soon it will be whole. (vol. I, p. 203)

The next, taken from the *Lacnunga* ("Remedies") manuscript, is very like the charms in use five or six hundred years later:

> If the worm or the bleeding fig (haemorrhoid) turn downwards, delve round a plant of celandine root and take it with thy two hands turned upwards, and sing over it nine Pater Nosters, and at the ninth, at "Deliver us from evil," snap it up, and take from that plant and from others that may be there a little cupful (of juice) and let the man drink it; and let one rub him at a warm fire; it will soon be well with him. (vol. III, p. 39).

Some charms were limited to magical actions, with or without words:

The Medicina De Quadrupedius of Sextus Placitus (fl. 370 CE).
6. Ad mulieris fluxum ["To the woman that hath an issue", i.e., a problem with her menstrual flow]. Take the comb with which she alone combed her head, and with which no other man has combed nor shall comb. Under the tree morbeam [mulberry], there let her comb her hair; let her gather what is lost in the comb, and hang it on an upstanding twig of the morbeam, and again after a while, when clean, let her gather it from the twig and preserve it. That shall be a leechdom for her, for the one who there combeth her head. (vol. I, p. 333).

The hanging of hair on a tree rather resembles a 19th century cure for ringworm (see below, pages 256 and 260).

Others were more truly magical, as in this "ingestion" of the written words of the spell, from the ninth-century *Leechbook of Bald*:

Lxii (3) An exorcism of fever:
A man shall write this upon the sacramental paten, and wash it off into the drink with holy water, and sing over it +++Λ+++++CD+++++++++ In the beginning, etc. [John i.1] Then wash the writing with holy water off the dish into the drink, then sing the Credo, and the Paternoster, and this lay, Beati immaculati, the psalm [psalm cxix], with the twelve prayer psalms, I adjure you, etc. And let each of the two men [leech and patient] then sip thrice of the water so prepared.

There then follows three lines from the third part of the *Carmen Paschale*, a work by the fifth century poet Sedulius, as a sort of invocation:

Inde salutiferis incedens gressibus urbes,
Oppida, rura, casas, vicos, castella peragrans
Omnia depulsis sanabat corpora morbis.
[From thence they entered the city and came on healthful,
The towns, the country, houses in the villages, forts wandering through
All things have driven away all he had healed their bodies of disease.] (vol. 2, p. 137)

For difficulty in giving birth, a charm addresses the unborn child and orders it to come forth, using rather oddly the narrative of the resurrection of Lazarus from the dead as the impetus (translation from Joseph Frank Payne's *English Medicine in the Anglo-Saxon Times*, 1904, p. 137):

Maria virgo peperit Christum. Elisabet sterilis peperit Iohannem Baptistam.
Adiuro te infans si es masculus an femina per patrem et filium et spiritum sanctum ut exeas, et [non] recedas; et ultra, ei non noceas neque insipientiam illi facias. Amen.
Videns Dominus flentes sorores Lazari ad monumentum lacrimatus est coram Iudeis, et clamabat:
—Lazare, veni foras! et prodiit, ligatus manibus et pedibus, qui fuerat quatriduanus mortuus.
"The Virgin Mary gave birth to Christ. The barren Elizabeth [she was quite old] gave birth to John the Baptist. I conjure thee, infant, whether thou be male or female, by the Father, the Son, and the Holy Ghost, that thou come forth, and draw not back, and further that thou injure not the one nor commit any folly against the other. Amen." (Perhaps it merely means 'that thou do no harm to thy mother.')
"The Lord, seeing the sisters of Lazarus weeping by his tomb, himself wept in sight of the Jews, and cried out, Lazarus! come forth; and he came out, bound hand and foot, who had been four days dead."
Write this on wax which has never been applied to any work, and bind it under her right foot (vol. I, p. 392). Interestingly, this same charm was found written in a contemporary hand between the end-papers of a copy of Gaigny's *Scholia on the Epistles of St. Paul* (Paris, 1539). (Folk-Lore 1887: p. 265)

This charm against contagion doesn't explain how one should bloody the (probably extinguished) torch, but the charm itself is clear (Payne's translation, p. 135):

For flying venom (I. e. air-borne infection). Make four strokes with an oaken brand towards the four quarters of heaven. Make the brand bloody, throw it away and sing this three times:—
"+ Matheus me ducat + Marcus me

conservet, + Lucas me liberet +
Iohannes me adiuvet semper. Amen.
Contrive [contere] Deus omnem
malum et nequitiam per virtutem
patris et filii et spiritus sancti
sanctifica me Emanuhel ms xps
libera me ab omnibus invidiis inimici
benedictio domini super caput meum.
potens Deus in omni tempore. Amen" (vol. III, p. 53)
"Matthew, lead me! Mark, preserve me! Luke, deliver me! John, assist me! [Amen] Lord, crush all evil and wickedness by the power of the Father, the Son, and the Holy Ghost, &c. sanctify me Emmanuel IHS XPS free me from all envy of the enemy. The blessing of the Lord be upon my head. Mighty God, at all times. (vol. III, pp. 185-6). The "IHS" refers to the Greek initials of Christ IHΣ iota eta sigma and also "in hoc signo", Latin for "by this sign we conquer", referring to the cross. XPS is the alternative "chi-rho" (XP) symbol with a final sigma, for Iesous Christos – Χριστός.

These examples do not differ in any significant way from the examples from centuries later, testifying to the force of tradition, yet there is one major distinction – the Anglo-Saxon charms were largely acceptable to the cultural authorities of their time, whereas later examples were not. Even charms that retained some official sanction following the Reformation lost whatever institutional legitimacy they once had during the 19th century. But the loss of authoritative recognition had little effect on the faith people had – and still have – in this magic.

What has been lost is not the popular attraction of or belief in charms, spells and curses, but the traditional world view that underwrote their theoretical basis from antiquity until modern times. Once the Christian hegemony that defined western culture for those two millennia lost its grip over society in the face of Enlightenment rationalism, mechanistic science and exposure to other cultures, magical practice no longer needed to fit within an antagonistic religious construct. It could become "post-Christian" in the same way it slowly became "post-pagan" during the Middle Ages. Charming and magic today often no longer reflect Christian theology but rather a new, if inchoate, alternative "pagan" world view. Since the traditional practices of the Cunning Folk could not be easily separated from the old beliefs, their trade was superseded by our contemporary eclectic occultism that is loosely labeled "Pagan" or "New Age" today. There is no less "magic" now than there was four or five centuries ago, but it only dimly echoes, rather than reproduces, the magic of yesteryear.

The following charms of healing represent a cross section of the methods and usages of the traditional Cunning Folk. Not surprisingly, the most common charms reflect the categories Owen Davies uses in his survey of charms: 1) bleeding, 2) toothache, 3) ague and fever, 4) scalds and burns, 5) adder or snakebite, and 6) strains and sprains. (Davies 1998)

The ague (malaria or intermittent fever):

Although we associate malaria with the tropics, "… malaria was endemic along the coasts and estuaries of south-east England, the Fenlands, and estuarine and marshland coastal areas of northern England."[65]

> (4/46) Pare the nailes of one that hath the quarteyn ague, whych being put into a lynnen claoth, and so tyde about the neck of a quick Eele, and the same Eele put into the water: thereby that ague wyll be dryuen away. Geber et Alb[ategnius]. (Lupton 1579: 92-93)

This charm, from *Art and Nature Joyn Hand in Hand* (1697), is also found in Blagrave's *Astrological Practice of Physick* (1689). (Durant 1697: 11)

---

[65] Mary Dobson. *The history of malaria in England* 1/12/1999. .http://malaria.wellcome.ac.uk/doc_WTD023991.html (retreived 5/23/11)

For an Ague.
WHEN Jesus went up to the Cross to be Crucified, the Jews asked him, saying, Art thou affraid, or hast thou an Ague; Jesus answered and said, I am not affraid, either have I the Ague, but all those which beareth the Name of Jesus about them, shall not be affraid nor have the Ague, Amen, Sweet Jesus, Amen, Sweet Jehovia, Amen.
Another.

Write these characters in a piece of Parchment, and wear them about you, and they are the following,

```
        Abracadabra.
        Abracadabr.
        Abracadab.
        Abracada.
        Abracad.
        Abraca.
        Abrac.
        Abra.
        Abr.
        Ab.
        A
```
(Durant 1697: p. 11)

FOR AGUE.
"When our Saviour saw the cross, whereon he was to be crucified, his body did shake. The Jews said, 'Hast thou an ague!' Our Saviour said, 'He that keepeth this in mind, thought, or writing, shall neither be troubled with ague or fever.'" (Couch 1871: 148)

AGUE
It is customary for the eldest female of a family—a member of which suffers from ague—to speak the following charm up the chimney on the eve of St. Agnes—
"Tremble and go!
First day shiver and burn:
Tremble and quake!
Second day shiver and learn:
Tremble and die!
Third day never return."

A variant for personal use is—
"Ague, ague, I thee defy,
Three days shiver,
Three days shake,
Make me well for Jesus' sake."

To be written on a three-cornered piece of paper, and worn round the neck till it drops off. (Northall 1892: 125-26)

Charm, for the Ague.—Our Saviour Christ when he came in sight of the cross where he was to suffer his body did shake. The Jesus asked him if he had the agoe. he answered and said "All these that keep this in woord or writing shall never be troubled with an agoe or fever." So Lord help they servants that put their trust in thee through Jesus Christ. Amen. (Amery 1899: 112)

Anesthesia

The concept of preparing patients for operations with soporifics was well known before modern times but if it was to be effective it was also very dangerous, as Lupton's warning testifies:

4/1 Make Dwale as followeth, which makes one to sleepe, whyles he be cutte or burned by Cawterizing, as followeth. Take the gall of a barrowe swyne, the iuyce of Humlocks three spoonefull, of the iuyce of wylde Neppe [bryony], three spoonefull, of the iuice of Lettys, of iyuce of Poppie, or the iuyce of Henbane, and Asell [vinegar], of each thee spoonefull : myxe them all together, and boyl them well, and doo them in a glasen vessell well stopped, and put three spoonefulles thereof in a quart of good wine or Ale, and mixe them together: And let him that shalbe cut or Cawterized syt against a good fyre, and geve him drynke thereof tyll he fall asleepe. This I had also out of an olde wrytten booke. Use it warely, and proue [test] it advisiedly: if you begyn with a lytle quantitie, you maye encrease it when you wyll: but if you geue too much at once, you cannot dyminish it when you lyst [choose]. (Lupton 1579: 79)

Arrhythmia, or Heart Palpitations

For the trembling of the Heart.

The hearts of men do sometimes suffer trembling, especially of Nobles and great men; for seldom doth this Disease take poor and mean men or women. From whence may be seen how God Almighty hath so artificially / distributed passions to every state and Condition for their correction and admonition, without respect of persons. It is not to be numbered among easie Diseases: for when it begins to rule, it casts the Patient upon the earth, and bereaveth him of strength and sense, and sometimes of life. It riseth from the membranes and receptacles wherein the Heart is involved, it being compressed with corrupt and ill Flegm. Against this, make a Sigil as follows, observing the due times.

First, in the day and hour of ☽ , take of ☽ ℨ ß. [half-ounce] which put and keep in a melting-pot until the hour of the Sun, which is the 4 hour following in the order of unequal hours; then melt it with the fire, and the ☽ being melted, cast in two ounces of ☉ purely refined, as the ☽ ought to be : these two Metals being well melted and mixt together, leave them to cool in the Melting-pot by themselves, and keep them till the hour of Venus next following : then melt them again, and cast in two drams of pure ♀, and pour it out; then work it into a Lamen with a Hammer, & prepare it ready for the engraving of the Signes : then mark when the Moon and Venus behold one another with a good Aspect ; then engrave upon the Money these two Signes which you see here.

Afterwards in the point of the New Moon engrave these three Characters following under the other two.

Let it rest from that New Moon until the next Full Moon, and in the point of that Full Moon in the same face of the Money over all the Signes let these following words be written.
For the trembling of the Heart.

This being done, mark when the Sun enters Leo; and in the same hour of his ingression, inscribe the Characters and Words you see in the other figure, on the other-side of the Money; and let them all begun and ended the same hour.

This Sigil being thus prepared and finished, is to be hanged about the Patients Neck in the / hour and point of the Full Moon, that it may touch his naked flesh upon his Heart.

Against this trembling of the Heart, there is also a most excellent secret; our Aurum Potabile, and Quintessence of Pearl, of our description, also oyl of Coral prepared as followeth.

The manner of Preparing Oyl of Coral
against the trembling of the
Heart.

℞ of Coral, ℔ 1, Of Common Salt, manip. 3.

Let them be wrought into a most fine powder, and put it into a Glass strongly Luted according to the sequent description: Take common Clay, or Potters white Clay, ashes made of the bones of the heads of four-footed Beasts, filings of Iron, Glass in powder, common Salt, Ceruse, &c. which being wet, mingle them together, &c. Put the luted Glass with the matter into Ashes contained in an Iron Kettle, according to art; kindle first a gentle fire, and increase it by degrees until the Spirit and Fumes do pass into a Vessel below ; then increase the fire more vehemently, until there remaineth no more moisture. This Oyl is a most excellent Remedy for the trembling of the Heart, taken alone by it self, without any thing else added to it. (*Archidoxes* 1656: 131-34)

Charms to control bleeding and hemorrhage:

The first example against bleeding cites the "flem Jordan", i.e., the Jordan River, a usage common enough that narrative charms in general are sometimes referred to as "flem Jordan" charms.

A verbal spell of the same kind to stop bleeding is to be found in *A Book of Experiments out of dyvers authors*, dated 1622. (MS. Bod. E Mus. 243). It runs: "God that was borne in the borough of bethlehem & baptised in the water of flem Jordayne The water was both wylde and wode, the chylde was both meeke and goode. He blessed the floude, & still it stoode. With same blessinge that he blessed the floude I doe blesse the bloude By virtue of the childe so goud. & say 5 pater nosters, 5 avies & 2 creedes." (Briggs 1953: 454)

3. A Sure Means to Staunch Blood.

It is helpful, though the person is far absent, if the one who uses this means for him, pronounces his name right. Jesus Christus, precious Blood! Which soothes the pains and stops the Blood. Help thee (name) God the Father, God the son and God the Holy Ghost. Amen. (Brown 1904: 107)

FOR STANCHING BLOOD.

"Our Saviour was born of Bethleam of Judeah. As He passed by revoor of Jorden, the waters waid were all in one. The Lord ris up his holy hand, and bid the waters still to stan, and so shall the blood. Three times."

A CHARM FOR BLOOD. "Baptized in the river Jordan, when the water was wild, the water was good, the water stood, so shall thy blood In the name &c." (Couch 1871: 149)

For Wounds and Stopping of Blood.
Blessed is the day on which Jesus Christ was born; blessed is the day on which Jesus Christ died; blessed is the day on which Jesus Christ arose from the dead. These are holy three hours; by these, N. N., I stop thy blood. Thy sores shall neither swell nor fester; no more shall that happen, than that the Virgin Mary will bear another son. t t t [+ + +] (Albertus Magnus n d.: 11)

The Holy Vervain (Verbena officinalis)—Holy Herb—Simpler's joy, was formerly held in great esteem as a styptic, and healer of wounds. When gathering it, one said—

All hele, thou holy herb, Vervin,
Growing on the ground;
In the Mount of Calvary
There wast thou found;

Thou helpest many a grief,
And stanchest many a wound.
In the name of sweet Jesus,
I take thee from the ground,
O Lord, effect the same
That I do now go about.
Or—
In the name of God, on Mount Olivet
First I thee found;
In the name of Jesus
I pull thee from the ground. (Northall 1892: 125-26)

TO STAUNCH BLOOD.
As Christ was born in Bethlehem and baptized in the river Jordan, He said to the water, "Be still. 'So shall thy blood cease to flow. In the name of the Father, Son and Holy Ghost'.—Amen." (Hewett 1900: 68)

TO CURE BLEEDING OF THE NOSE. TAKE one or two fine old toads, place them in a cold oven, increase the heat until sufficiently fierce to cook the toads and reduce them to a brown crisp mass. Remove from the oven and beat them to powder in a stone mortar. Place the powder in a box and use as snuff! (Hewett 1900: 76)

A CHARM TO STOP BLEEDING AT THE NOSE.
SAY nine times with great faith these words:
Blood abide in this vein as Christ abideth in the church, and hide in thee as Christ hideth from himself. The bleeding will presently cease. (Hewett 1900: 80)

ANOTHER REMEDY FOR STAUNCHING BLOOD. TAKE a fine full-grown toad; kill him, then take three bricks and keep in a very hot oven until they are redhot. Take one out and place the toad upon it; when the brick is cold remove the toad; then take the other bricks and place the toad on them successively until he be reduced to powder. Then take the toadashes and sew them up carefully in a silk bag one and-a-half inch square. When one is bleeding place this bag on the heart of the sufferer, and it will instantly stay the bleeding of the nose or any wound. (Hewett 1900: 81)

Bruises:

TO CHARM A BRUISE.
Holy chicha ! Holy chicha !
This bruise will get well by-and-bye.
Up sun high! Down moon low!
This bruise will be quite well very soon!
In the Name of the Father, Son, and Holy Ghost. Amen. (Hewett 1900: 68)

Burns:

Another.
There came two Angels from the East, the one brought Fire, the other brought Frost, In the Name of the Father, Son, and Holy Ghost, out Frost, in Fire.(Durant 1697: 11)

44. For a Burn.
Burn, I blow on thee. It must be blown on, as the fire of the sun, three times in one breath. ✠✠✠ (Brown 1904: 113)

Burn. — To cure a burn, the following words are used: —
"Here I come to cure aburnt sore;

If the dead knew what the living endure,
The burnt sore would burn no more.
The operator, after having repeated the above, blows his breath three times on the burnt place. (Choice Notes 1859: 37-38)

FOR A BURN.
"As I passed over the river Jordan, I met with Christ, and he says unto me, 'Woman, what aileth thee?' 'Oh! Lord my flesh doth burn.' The Lord saith unto me, 'Two angels cometh from the west, one for fire, one for frost, out fire and in frost, in the name of, &c.'

FOR SCAL.
"There was three angels cam from the West
The wan brought fiar, and the other brought frost.
And the other brought the book of Jesus Christ
In the name of the Father &c." (Couch 1871: 149)

For Burns.
Away burns, undo the band; if cold or warm, cease the hand. God save thee, N. N.; thy flesh, thy blood, thy marrow, thy bone, and all thy veins. They all shall be saved, for warm and cold brands reign, t t t [+ + +] Three times spoken.

Another Remedy for the Same Ailment.
Our Lord Jesus Christ and St. Peter walked over the field.
They saw and smelt a wild, hot fiery brand. Christ, with his powerful hand quenched N. N. his wild, hot, fiery brand, so that no longer fire is sent, and friendly becomes that element, just like our dear matron's child again became well, t t t Three times. (Albertus Magnus n d.: 9-10)

TO HEAL BURNS.
THE witch repeats the following prayer while passing her hand three times over the burn :
Three wise men came from the east,
One brought fire, two carried frost.
Out fire ! In frost!
In the Name of the Father, Son, and Holy Ghost. (Hewett 1900: 66)

Cancer in the Mouth:

Blow the ashes of scarlet cloth into the mouth and throat. This seldom fails. JENKINS, p. 4 (Gutch 1901: 170)

Childbirth:

... Also, if a woman be in travell, laie this writing upo hir bellie, she shall have easie deliverance, and the child right shape and christendome, and the mother purification of holy church, and all through vertue of these holie names of Jesus Christ following:

✠ Jesus ✠ Christus ✠ Messias ✠ Soter ✠ Emmanuel ✠ Sabbaoth ✠ Adonai ✠ Unigenitus ✠ Majestas ✠ Paracletus ✠ Salvator noster ✠ Agiros iskiros ✠ Agios ✠ Adanatos ✠ Gasper ✠ Melchior ✠ & Balthasar ✠ Matthæus ✠ Marcus ✠ Lucas ✠ Johannes. (Scot 1973: 187)

A charme to release a woman in travell.
Throwe over the top of the house, where a woman in travell lieth, a stone, or any other thing that hath killed three living creatures; namelie, a man, a wild bore, and a she beare. (Scot 1973: 197)
For the day of Labor Pains. A certain Remedy.

First of all write the Following in one Line upon a Paper:
A b h z P O b L 9 h b m g n
Subratum nome nex gr.

After this the patient's name in the centre. Under this inscribe the following words, also † in one row: † Ecgitar † Circabato † Bessiabato † Argon † Vigaro Tanet . Put this into a bag of leather and sew the same up, but the seam must be on the right side.

N. B. This must be made without a knot, on thread or band, and hung up during an uneven hour. (Albertus Magnus n d.: 93)

Colic:

Toads (and moles) were important if unfortunate "participants" in English folk magic:

TO CURE THE COLIC.

Mix equal quantities of elixir of toads and powdered Turkey rhubarb. Dose—Half a teaspoonful fasting for three successive mornings. (Hewett 1900: 67)

Cramps:

FOR CRAMP.

"The cramp is keenless, Mary was sinless: when Mary bore Jesus, let the cramp go away in the name of Jesus." (Couch 1871: 148)

For Gangrene or Mortification [also "cramp, palsy or apparition"] .

Christ the Lord went through the field, and met a person who was sick of palsy. Christ the Lord spake: Whither art thou going, thou cold face? The face thus addressed replied: I will enter into that man. Christ the Lord said: What wilt thou do in the body of that man? I will shatter his bones to death, eat his flesh, and drink his blood. Christ the Lord sayeth: Thou palsied face, thou shalt not do so; pebble stones thou must devour, bitter herbs thou shalt pluck; from a well thou must drink, and therein shalt thou sink, t t t

On a Friday it was, when our Lord was tortured. As this is the case, so may Christ deliver me from Cramp, from palsy, and apparition. In the second place, thou shalt stand quietly, half of the back, shank or leg, or any other limb or member, I may possess on my body, be the same dull, blind, pliable or pliant; therefore, cramp, palsy or apparition, thou canst go no further, such commandeth unto thee the man who suffered death upon the cross as Jesus Christ; He who by His bitter tortures and by His death hath been sacrificed. All may move—foliage and grasses, all things which upon earth do grow, as also our dear Master Jesus Christ's water and blood; that he may do unto all believing Christian people, who bent themselves on account of His great nature, while the holy body hung on His Cross. Therefore, the Jews spake: Master, thou didst first comfort the cramp, the palsy and the apparition; but Jesus replied: Cramp, palsy and apparitions I do not have. Be it woman or man; so help me Christ, the joy and comfort of the sacred cross of Him who is arisen out of corruption's womb; burst ye the spell, break from your gloom! By the joy He caused unto His mother, Jesus of Nazareth, God be merciful to me, a poor sinner, t t t

Whoever carries this letter with him on his person, so as to be enabled to recite the same at will, will never more of cramp, palsy or apparition become ill. (Albertus Magnus n d.: 6)

Diarrhoea:

TO CURE DIARRHOEA. TAKE a stale Good-Friday cross-bun and place it in a hot oven to dry. By grating when hard into powder, and, when required, mixing it with cold water and taken as a medicine, it will cure diarrhoea.

"When Good-Friday comes, an old woman runs
With one, or two-a-penny hot-cross-buns.
Whose virtue is, if you'll believe what's said,
They'll not grow mouldy like the common bread." (Hewett 1900: 77)

Dropsy (edema):

For Dropsy

Three flowers stand upon the grave of the Saviour Jesus Christ. The one signifies goodness of God, the other, humility, the third, God's will. Water, stand still. t t t (Albertus Magnus n d.: 103)

TO CURE DROPSY. TAKE several large fully-grown toads, place them in a vessel in which they can be burned without their ashes becoming mixed with any foreign matter. When reduced to ashes, pound them in a stone mortar. Place the ashes in a wide-mouthed jar, cork closely and keep in a dry place.

Dose.—One teaspoonful of ashes in milk to be taken at the growing of the moon for nine mornings. (Hewett 1900: 76-77)

Epilepsy:

Against the falling evill.

Moreover, this insuing is another counterfet charme of theirs, whereby the falling evill is presentlie remedied.

Gaspar fert myrrham, thus Melchior, Balthasar aurum,
Hæc tria qui secum portabit nomina regum,
Solvitur à morbo Christi pietate caduco.
Gasper with his myrh beganne
/ these presents to unfold,
Then Melchior brought in frankincense,
/ and Balthasar brought in gold.
Now he that of these holie kings
the names about shall beare,
The falling yll by grace of Christ
/ shall never need to feare.

This is as true a copie of the holie writing, that was brought downe from heaven by an angell to S. Leo pope of Rome; & he did bid him take it to king Charles, when he went to the battell at Roncevall. And the angell said, that what man or woman beareth this writing about them with good devotion, and saith everie daie three Pater nosters, three Aves, and one Creede, shall not that daie be overcome of his enimies, either bodilie or ghostlie; neither shalbe robbed or slaine of theeves, pestilence, thunder, or lightning; neither shall be hurt with fier or water, nor combred with spirits, neither shall have displeasure of lords or ladies: he shall not be condemned with false witnesse, nor taken with fairies, or anie maner of axes, nor yet with the falling evill... (Scot 1973: 186-87)

For the falling evill.

Take the sicke man by the hand, and whisper these wordes softlie in his eare, I conjure thee by the sunne and moone, and by the gospell of this daie delivered by God to Rubert, Giles, Cornelius, and John, that thou rise and fall no more. ◊ Otherwise: Drinke in the night at a spring water out of a skull of one that hath beene slaine. ◊ Otherwise: Eate a pig killed with a knife that slew a man. ◊ Otherwise as followeth.

Ananizapta ferit mortem, dum lædere quærit,
Est mala mors capta, dum dicitur Ananizapta,
Ananizapta Dei nunc miserere mei.
Ananizapta smiteth death, whiles harme intendeth he,
This word Ananizapta say, and death shall captive be,
Ananizapta ô of God, have mercie now on me. (Scot 1973: 195-96)

For all manner of falling evils. Take the blood of his little finger that is sick, and write these three verses following, and hang it about his neck:
Jasper fert Mirrham. Thus Melchior, Balthazar Aurum,
Haec quicumque secum portat tria nomina regnum,
Solvitur a morbo, Dominipietate, caduca.
and it shall help the party so grieved. (Choice Notes 1859: 267)

Erysipelas:

28. A Good Remedy for St. Anthony's Fire (or Erysipelas) as well as for wounds: Also for Aching Limbs on which the Erysipelas appears.

St. Anthony's Fire and the Dragon's red, Together over the Brook they fled. St. Anthony's Fire is done; The Dragons they are gone. ††† (Brown 1904: 111)

Fever:

For Fever.

Nut tree, I come unto thee; take the seventy-seven fevers from me. I will persist therein, t t t

This must be written upon a scrap of paper, and, with the same, hie [go] to a nut tree ere the sun rises. Cut a piece of the bark, insert the paper under it, recite the above sentence three times, and put the bark in its place again, so that it may grow together. (Albertus Magnus n. d.: 7)

35. To Drive Away Fever.

With the following words on a scrap or billet of paper, wrap the billet in a broad plantain leaf and bind it on the navel of the one who has the fever:

Potmat Sineat,
Potmat Sineat,
Potmat Sineat. (Brown 1904: 112)

For the Fever.

Suspend, upon a Friday, a letter containing the names set forth below, between the hours of eight and nine, upon the patient's neck, in the following manner: Fold together, and tie it in grayish red cloth, which must he unbleached, and pierce through the cloth and the letter, three holes. Draw red thread through them, while calling the three holiest names. Suspend the same around the neck of the patient, and let it remain eleven days. After taking it off, burn it before the lapse of one hour [the repeated line is in the original]:

```
H B R H C H T H B R H
H B R H C H T H B R
H B R H C H T H B
H B R H C H T H
H B R H C H T
H B R H C H
H B R H C
H B R H
H B R
H B
H
```

(Albertus Magnus n. d.: 56)

TO CURE A FEVER. WRITE on parchment the following and bind it over the heart of the patient. "In the name of St. Exuperus and St. Honorius, fall-fever, spring-fever, quartian, quintain, ago, super ago, consummatum est." While fixing this charm to the patient, repeat three Paters and three Aves. The patient will recover after wearing the charm nine days. (Hewett 1900: 82)

Fits:

Fits.—That little animal the mole is the victim of an absurd and cruel practice arising from ignorant belief, as the following rustic prescription will show: – A Kentishman residing in 1865 on the border ground of Norfolk and Suffolk, was asked by an elderly dame to "catch a live moll" for her. "For what purpose?" said the Kentishman. "Why, sir, you see, my darter's little gal is got fits, and I'm told if I get a / live moll, cut the tip of his nose off, and let nine drops bleed onter a lump of sugar, and give that to the child, 'tis a sartin cure." (Glyde 1872: 87-88)

Goiter:

CURE FOR A LARGE NECK [goiter]

A common snake, held by its head and tail, is slowly drawn, by some one standing, nine times across the part of the neck of the person affected, the reptile being allowed, after every third time, to crawl about for a while. Afterwards the snake is put alive into a bottle, which is corked tightly and then buried in the ground. The tradition is, that as the snake decays the swelling vanishes.

The second mode of treatment is just the same as the above, with the exception of the snake's doom. In this case it is killed, and its skin, sewed in a piece of silk, is worn round the diseased neck. By degrees the swelling in this case also disappears. ROVERT. Withyam, Sussex. (Choice Notes 1859: 36)

Gout and related diseases:

For Burn-gout.—Three or four fair maidens came from divers lands crying for burn-gout—acheing, smarting, and all kinds of burn-gout—they went to the burrow toun— there they had brethren three—they went to the salt seas and they never more returned again—he or she shall have their health again in the name of the Father, and of the Son, and of the Holy Ghost. Amen. So be it.
(Mr. W, Marystowe.)

There was three brothers come from the North West going to the South, to kill and to cure (name person in full) for Ringworm — Wild Titters — Burn-gout — Itching Gout— Smarting gout— Water-gout—Chicken-pox—St. Tanterous Fire—Girdleing or whatever it may be, in the name of the Father, Son, and Holy Ghost. Amen.

In using this, the charmer hung a branch of white thorn on a wall, without allowing it to touch the ground. Then she took nine small pieces of different-coloured cloths tied in a bunch, and some raw cream. The patient sat under the thorn, the bits of cloth were dipped into the cream and "dapped" upon the ringworm, etc. It must be done 5, 7, 9, 11, 13, or any odd number of times before charmer or patient had broken their fast.
(Mrs. L , Launceston.)
(Amery 1899: 113-14)

Headache:

A charme for the headach.
Tie a halter about your head, wherewith one hath beene hanged. (Scot 1973: 197)

CHARM TO CURE THE HEADACHE.—If the pain be on the right side of the head, make a comb out of the right horn of a ram; and if the head be combed with it, it will take away the pain. But if the pain be on the left side of the head, then make a comb out of the left horn of a ram, and if the head be combed therewith, it will stop the pain. (Mother Shipton's 1880: 59)

The most certain cure of a violent head-ache, is to take any herb growing upon the top of the head of an image [statue]; the same being bound, or hung about one with a red thread, it will soon allay the violent pain thereof. (Barrett 1967: 47)

Heartburn:

To cure the 'water-springs,' an old name for acidity or heartburn, old people tell me the following is an infallible cure if taken in time—a very wise proviso—burnt oyster, cockle, and mussel shells ground to powder, equal parts, and mixed in worm-water. This latter was prepared by gathering a handful of worms from the churchyard and boiling them. The burnt shells might do good; ordinary water and chalk would have been equally efficacious, had they but known it. (Blakeborough 1898: 138)

Hernia:

To Heal the Hernia or Rupture.

Write the name of the patient upon paper, drill a hole in three prune trees, and prepare an oaken bolt, and put into every hole the three most sacred names, drive every one of these bolts in with three strokes, and pronounce the following sentence; N. N., I drive your rupture into this tree, God may thy physician be; Rupture forget thy growth and walk, like our Lord forget one man; hernia leave my flesh and bone. Rupture, rupture, rupture, depart hence in the name of the Lord, etc. I beseech thee in the name of the living God, that thou may heal upon the rod, that thou may become sound and straight, and growest stronger every day. Hepheta open thyself! † † † A. 0. B. Tibas. (Albertus Magnus n d.: 42)

Hydrophobia:

Against the biting of a mad dog.

Put a silver ring on the finger, within the which these words are graven + *Habay* + *habar* + *hebar* + & saie to the person bitten with a mad dog, I am thy saviour, loose not thy life: and then pricke him in the nose thrise, that at each time he bleed. ◊ Otherwise: Take pilles made of the skull of one that is hanged. ◊ Otherwise: Write upon a peece of bread, *Irioni, khiriora, esser, khuder, feres*, and let it be eaten by the partie bitten. ◊ Otherwise: *O rex gloriæ Jesu Christe, veni cum pace: In nomine patris max, in nomine filii max, in nomine spiritus sancti prax:* Gasper, Melchior, Balthasar + *prax* + *max* + Deus I *max* + (J. Bodinus. *lib. de dæmon* 3. cap. 5.) (Scot 1973: 196)

To prevent evil effects from the bite of a mad dog, write on an apple, or piece of fine white bread, the following charm, and swallow it three mornings, fasting—

O King of Glory, come in peace,

Pax, Max, and Max,

Hax, Max, Admax, opera chudar.—AS. 179.

(Northall 1892: 126)

CHARM TO HINDER FROM THE BITE OF A MAD DOG.—The tooth of a mad dog which has bitten any human being, tied in leather and hung at the shoulder, will preserve and keep the wearer from being bitten by any mad dog so long as he wears it. It may be worn next to the skin, or concealed in the clothing. (Mother Shipton's 1880: 59)

Inflammation:

The "Queen of Parest" has not been identified, but Owen Davies has offered a few possibilities: "The 'Queen of parest' may derive from the verb 'pare' meaning to injure or to impair, and so could be interpreted as 'Queen of harm or injury.' Two possible alternatives, kindly suggested by Jacqueline Simpson, are that it is a corruption of 'Paradise,' or of 'pharisees,' a dialect term for fairies." (Davies 1996: 30-31)

Receipt for a Inflamation.—Our Saviour Christ bless for an Inflamation or any other evil thing or any like evil. (bless.) The Queen of parest is gone into a far country to kill and destroy both men women and children, and then her meet our blessed Lord and Saviour Jesus Christ. He said "Where art thou going thou Queen of parest?" "I am going into a far country to kill and destroy both men women and children." "Thou Queen of parest turn again: thy evil shall never do no harm, in the name of the father and of the Son, and of the Holy Ghost. Amen."

Copy of a charm lately found at Marystowe among the papers of a former inhabitant of a neighbouring parish. (Amery 1899: 111)

For Inflammation.—As our Blessed Vergen Mary was walking over along leading her youngest son by the hand he hang down his hed. "Why dew you hang youre hed so low my son"? "My hed doth ake and all my bones." "I fear some ill things you have. I will bless you for ill things". (red ill, wite ill, black or blew or all other) down to the ground in the name of our Lord Jesus Christ.
I bless thee (you must mention the name of the person) in the name of our Lord Jesus Christ, Amen—of the Father, the Son, and Holy Gost. Amen.
In using this the charmer must pass the hand the same way as the sun goes, and pass it towards the ground. (Mrs. C, Marystowe.) (Amery 1899: 112-13)

For Inflammation.—Our Lord Jesus Christ came from the Mount's foot (&) saw Abraham asleep on the cold ground— Our Lord spoke and said "What liest thou here for"? Abraham spoke and said "It is good to know what I lie here for. (I am) taken, without blow, acheing, burning that I know not what to do." Our Lord Jesus Christ said "Rise up Abraham, rise up Abraham from the cold ground—I will make thee safe (&) sound. In the name of the Father and of the Son, and of the Holy Ghost. Amen." (Mr. W , Marystowe.) (Amery 1899: 113)

TO CURE INFLAMMATION. SCOUR the inflamed part with strong brine, afterwards wash with plenty of soap, plenty too of hot water. Eat much raw beef for nine days. (Hewett 1900: 72)

Itch:

The Itch or scabies (the result of an infestation of microscopic mites) was traditionally thought to be a common imbalance of the bodily humours and treated by bleeding if not charms.
TO CURE ITCHING.
To cure itching in the palm of the hand—
Rub it on the eye,
'Twill go by-and-bye;
Rub it on wood,
'Twill sure to come good. (Hewett 1900: 77)

Menstruation:

CHAP. XIII
For Womens Terms.

An inordinate Flux of this Disease, doth doth extremely grieve many Women, sometimes divers years : by so much the more healthy and strong such women are, by how much they have their Courses in their ordinary seasons, and are then delivered from them. From whence arises a twofold way of reducing them into due order. The first is to stay the Flux, and reduce into a due course : the latter is to be used in the defects thereof, to provoke them to an ordinary Flux : the defect of them bringeth death ; whereof to provoke them, let there be formed of pure Copper, without any mixture of any other metal, a Seal in the hour of ♀, as is in the following Figure : But if the same cannot be perfectly finished in that hour, let it then remain imperfect until the same hour of ♀ comes again, and then perfect it : The form whereof must be this. /
For the Menstruæ.

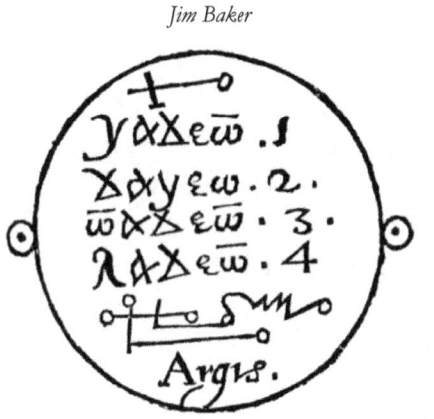

This Sigil ought to be formed with a File into one piece, and is to be bound with a string upon the Back of the woman through two Rings, applying it at the beginning of the Back-bone upon the Testes, laying the sculpture upon the flesh, and that in the hour of the ☽.

But if nature suffer through too much abundant Fluxes, let the Characters be engraven in pure Silver in the hour of the ☉, on both sides of the Money, as they are drawn in the following Figure. Then let them be wrapped and sewed up in silk, (for it must not be applied to the naked flesh) and let it be bound upon the Navel of the Woman, turning to face next her body which is marked with the number 10. And afterwards when the Flux begins to stay, let her / wear it 30 days, then take it off: for if she wear it any longer, there is danger lest they be quite driven away and stopped; and so cause greater harm than the first.

For the Menstruæ.

(Archidoxes 1656: 125-27)

Prognosis:

They say, also, that a tike [tick], if it be taken out of the left ear of a dog, and it be altogether black, if the sick person shall answer him that brought it in, and who, standing at his feet, shall ask him concerning his disease, there is certain hope of life; and that he shall die if he make him no answer. (Barrett 1967: 46)

Rheumatism:

The significance of the appropriate gender, either in the performance or the communication of charms, is frequently emphasized. One wonders how "ancient" a charm involving potatoes could be, and what earlier vegetable may have been used.

A CURE FOR RHEUMATISM. AN ancient Devonshire superstition is the potato-cure for rheumatism, which should be applied in this way.

Take a freshly dug early grown kidney potato, wash it free from soil, and ask a member of the opposite sex to yourself, to place it unobserved in a pocket of one of your garments. Having once worn the tuber you can change it yourself into another pocket at will, but it must be worn continuously, not intermittently, or its charm will be lost. It is believed that as the potato hardens the rheumatism will leave the system. A common practice among agricultural labourers, is to carry one in every waistcoat pocket until its looks like a small grey stone, and has become quite as hard. (Hewett 1900: 78-79)

Thomas Forbes describes a unique charm for rheumatism associated with Dr. Dee and Queen Elizabeth I:

Queen Elizabeth I, it is reported, suffered from rheumatism. Dr. John Dee, the court physician and a famous mathematician and astrologer, had an elaborate curative bracelet, inscribed with charms, made for the queen. She is said to have worn it, but we do not know whether her rheumatism improved. The bracelet passed into the hands of the Earls of Peterborough and then to other owners, among them Horace Walpole. Eventually it was acquired by Constance, Lady Russell, of Swallowfield, near Reading. Through the courtesy of Sir Arthur and Lady Russell, my wife and I were privileged to examine this curious ornament in the summer of 1961.

The bracelet proper consists of two wide semicircular silver straps joined by a hinge; the clasp is missing. Too small for any but a woman's or child's wrist, the bracelet has four pendant attachments. One is a basket of silver wire loops; we were told that the basket contains the dried remains of a nutmeg. The second pendant consists of three silver straps enclosing a polished, light-brown flint stone 13 inches in diameter. The third pendant consists of a / circular silver frame. A large, flat polished flint is set into one side of the frame, while three smaller flints are fastened in the other. The stones are a dull grayish brown. The fourth pendant is an empty silver setting with a serrated edge. The outer surface of each half of the bracelet proper bears an inscription in niello, a kind of black enamel. One side reads: † IONA † IHOAT † LONA † HELOI † YSSARAY † † MEPHENOIPHETON † AGLA † ACHEDION † YANA The other side reads: BACHIONODONAVALIZ [or 3] ILIOR † BACHIONODONAVALIZ [or 3] ACH †. Most of this is unintelligible, but we do recognize AGLA.[66]

112. For Rheumatism. — Very Good and Sure.

This recipe has been sold as high as $2; it is the best and surest remedy for the Rheumatism. The formula is written on a letter and sewed up in a piece of linen cloth with thread and hung to the neck by a band on the last Friday in the old of the moon. The cloth, band and thread must not have touched the water, and the thread have no knot in it. In folding the letter, 3 ends must be laid together at one side. You say the Lord's prayer and the Creed when you hang it on. The following is the formula:

God the Father, Son and Holy Ghost grant; Amen. Like sought / and sought; that God the Lord grant thee by the first man; so God on the Earth may be loved, like sought and sought: that God the Lord grant thee by the Evangelist Luke and the holy Apostle Paul. Like sought and sought; that grant thee God the Lord by the 12 Apostles. Like sought; that grant thee God the Lord by the first man, so God may be loved. Like sought and sought, that God the Lord grant thee by the loving, holy Father, so as it is done in the godly holy scriptures. Like sought and sought; that God the Lord grant them by the loving, holy angels, and fatherly, godly Almightiness and heavenly trust and faith, like sought and sought; that grant thee God the Lord by the fiery furnace which is supported by God's blessing. Like sought and confessed. That grant thee God the Lord, by all power and might, by the prophet Jonas who, for 3 days and nights is preserved in the whale's belly. Like sought and confessed. That grant thee God the Lord by all the power and might, out of godly humility to go even to eternity; therefore † N † be no evils to thy whole body, whether racking gout, or yellow, or white, or red, or black gout or torturing rheumatism, or pains or tortures known by any name, may

---

[66] Thomas R. Forbes. "Verbal Charms in British Folk Medicine". *Proceedings of the American Philosophical Society*, Vol. 115, No. 4 (Aug. 20, 1971), pp. 307-308

they do the † N † no harm in thy whole body, whether, head, neck, heart, belly, in thy veins, arms, legs, eyes, tongue; in all thy veins in thy whole body be no evil. This I write for thee † N † with these words: In the name of the Father and the Son and the Holy Ghost. Amen. God bless thee. Amen.

REMARK.—When one writes for another, where the letter N stands he must write the first name of the patient. (Brown 1904: 123-124)

Ringworm:

There are no worms involved in "ringworm" or "tinea", which is caused by a communicable fungus. Imaginary worms as a cause of disease (in toothache, for example) are a very ancient belief dating to pre-Christian times. Tinea is a skin disease characterised by a ring-like red rash.

> Ringworm. — The person afflicted with ringworm takes a little ashes between the forefinger and thumb, three successive mornings, and before taking any food, and holding the ashes to the afflicted part says —
> "Ringworm! Ringworm red!
> Never mayst thou spread or speed,
> But aye grow less and less,
> And die away among the ase (ashes)." (Choice Notes 1859: 38)

> TO CURE BARNGUN, OR RINGWORM.
> BARNGUN is cured by blessing, and the outward application of clotted cream, thus: Take three locks of wool—one white, one grey, one black—dip them into a basin of clotted cream, and when thoroughly saturated, take each lock and rub in succession each infected spot on the skin. Hang the wool on sprigs of white thorn against the wind to dry. Repeat this process five, seven, or nine times, as the case may require. While lubricating the sores chant in monotone the following: There were three angels come from the west, to cure Simon Fluke (or other) of the barngun, white barngun, red barngun, black barngun, aching, sticking, pricking, barngun, all sorts of barngun, barngun-bubee, ill will I prove 'e. I stick thee up on thees yer thorn, there thou shalt die, and never come near'n no more, in the name of the Father, Son and Holy Ghost.—Amen. (Hewett 1900: 78)

Scrofula:

Scrofula (from the Latin, scrofa "breeding sow") is tuberculosis of the neck, usually a result of an infection in the lymph nodes. It was long believed that "royal touch", the touch of the monarchs of England or France, could cure the disease through to the "divine right of kings" and henceforth was commonly known as the "King's Evil". As the ritual enhanced the belief in the divine sanction for royalty, the Stuart monarchs willingly practiced the old rite (it was discontinued in England by the first Hanoverian, George I, but survived into the 19th century in France) which included giving a special gold coin called a "touchpiece" to those who came to be stroked by the royal hand, which may have contributed to the second cure cited here.

> TO CURE KING'S EVIL. BAKE a toad and when dried sufficiently to roll into powder, beat up in a stone mortar, mix with powdered vervain. Sew in a silken bag and wear round the neck. (Hewett 1900: 76)

> THE HALF-CROWN CHARM FOR THE CURE OF KING'S EVIL.
> AFTER morning service in the parish church, the nearest male relative, in the case of a woman; or in the case of a man, the nearest female relative, stations him or her self, on the right-hand side of the porch, holding his or her hat, into which young men (or women), between the ages of sixteen and twenty-one, drop a penny to the number of thirty. The pennies so collected are changed for a silver half-crown. The centre of this coin is cut out, and the outer ring is suspended as a charm to the neck of the afflicted person. The centre piece is reserved until the next funeral takes place, when it is dropped into the grave just before the coffin is lowered into it. (Hewett 1900: 72)

Sciatica:

TO CURE SCIATICA OR BONESHAVE. TAKE a pail of clean river water, dipped from the down-flowing stream, a pair of shears, a large key, and a new table knife. Dip the knife into the pail of water, draw it back upwards, downwards and across the hip three times each way. Then dip the key into the water and proceed as before. Then dip the shears into water, shear the hip as though it were covered with wool. Return the water left in the bucket to the river and sing—
As this watter goeth to zay, So flow boneshave away. (Hewett 1900: 77-78)

Scurvy:

104. For Scurvey of the Gums and Foul Throat.
Job was jogging o'er the land: had his staff in his hand,
Blessed him God the Lord and said: Why, O Job, so very sad?
Ah Lord, he said, and why not sad? My mouth and throat are very bad.
Said God to Job, there in the vale; a fountain flows which thee will heal (n. n.).
The throat and mouth in the triune name; but say the names and say, Amen. Repeat three times, morning and evening, and at the words "thee will heal," breathe in the child's mouth. (Brown 1904: 122)

Shingles:

FOR WILDFIRE.
"Christ he walketh over the land, Carried the wildfire in his hand, He rebuked the fire and bid it stand; Stand, wildfire, stand, (three times repeated). In the name of the Father, Son, and Holy Ghost." (Couch 1871: 148)

TO CURE SKIN DISEASE.
PLACE the poison found in a toad's head in a leathern bag one inch square: enclose this in a white silk bag, tie it round the neck, allowing the bag to lie on the pit of the stomach. On the third day the patient will be sick. Remove and bury the bag. As it rots so will the patient get well. (Hewett 1900: 66)

Snakebite:

A CHARM FOR THE BIT OF AN ADDER. * "Bradgty, bradgty, bradgty, under the ashing leaf. To be repeated three times, and strike your hand with the growing of the hare. Bradgty, bradgty, bradgty to be repeated three times before eight, eight before seven, and seven before six, and six before five, and five before four, and four before three, and three before two, and two before one, and one before every one, three times for the bit of an adder." *Probably braggety, which means mottled or spotted, as the adder is. The adder has, it is supposed, an antipathy to the ash. (Couch 1871: 148)

ADDER-BITE.
A piece of hazelwood, fastened in the shape of a cross, should be laid softly on the wound, and the following lines twice repeated—
"Underneath this hazelin mote,
There's a bragotty worm with a speckled throat,
Nine double is he;
Now from eight double to seven double, And from seven double to six double." And so on to—
"And from one double to no double,
No double hath he."
(Northall 1892: 125)

66. For a Snake Bite.
God enacted everything, and everything was good,
But thou alone, viper, art accursed,
Accursed shalt thou be and thy poison.
††† tzing, tzing, tzing. (Brown 1904: 116)

Sore Throat:

TO CURE SORE THROAT. READ the eighth Psalm seven times for three successive mornings over the patient. (Hewett 1900: 76)

Sprains:

SHETLAND FOLK LORE

The Wresting Thread. — When a person has received a sprain, it is customary to apply to a person practiced in casting the "wresting thread." This is a thread spun from black wool, on which are cast nine knots, and tied round a sprained leg or arm. During the time the operator is putting the thread round the afflicted limb, he says, in a muttering tone, in such a manner as not to be understood by the bystanders, nor even the person operated upon. —
"The Lord rade (rode),
And the foal slade (slipped);
He lighted,
An she righted,
Set joint to joint,
Bone to bone,
And sinew to sinew,
Heal in the Holy Ghost's name !!!" (Choice Notes 1859: 37-38).

FOR A STRAIN.
"Christ rode over the bridge, Christ rode under the bridge; Vein to Vein; Strain to strain, I hope God will take it back againe." (Couch 1871: 148)

Teething:

TO ASSIST CHILDREN IN TEETHING. MAKE a necklace of beads cut from the root of henbane and place round the child's neck. (Hewett 1900: 76)

Thorns:

FOR A THORN.

"Jesus walked upon the earth, he pricked his foot with a thorn, his blood sprung up to heaven, his flesh never rankled nor perished, no more shall not thine. In the name, &c.
ALSO,
"When Christ was upon middle earth the Jews pricked him, his blood sprung up into heaven, his flesh never rotted nor fustered, no more I hope will not thine. In the name, &c.
ALSO,
"Our Saviour was fastened to the Cross with nails and thorns, which neither rats nor rankles, no more shan't thy finger. (For a thorn three times). (Couch 1871: 149)

THORN.
"Christ was of a Virgin born,
And crowned was with a crown of thorn,
He did neither swell nor rebel,
And I hope this never will."

At the same time the middle finger of the right hand must be kept in motion round the thorn, and at the end of the words, three times repeated, the thorn should be touched each time with the tip of the finger. Then, with God's blessing, it will give no further trouble. Suffolk Garland, New, p. 173: CB. 48. (Northall 1892: 133)

CHARM FOR A THORN IN THE FLESH.
OUR dear Lord Jesus Christ was pricked with thorns. His blood went back to Heaven again, His flesh neither cankered, rankled, nor festered, neither shall thine, M. or N. In the name of the Father, Son and Holy Ghost.—Amen, Amen, Amen. (Hewett 1900: 71)

Toothache:

Against the toothach.
Scarifie the gums in the greefe, with the tooth of one that hath beene slaine. ◊ Otherwise: *Galbes galbat, galdes galdat.* ◊ Otherwise: *A ab hur hus*, &c. ◊ Otherwise: At saccaring of masse hold your teeth togither, and say *Os non comminuetis ex eo* (That is, You shall not breake or diminish a bone of him).◊ Otherwise: *strigiles falcesq; dentatæ, dentium dolorem persanate*; O horssecombs and sickles that have so many teeth, come heale me now of my toothach. (Weyer 1991: 389; Scot 1973: 197)

A CHARME.
First, he must know your name, then your age, which in a little paper he sets downe. On the top are these words: *In verbis, et in herbis, et in lapidibus sunt virtutes*: vnderneath he writes in capitall letters, AAB ILLA, HYRS GIBELLA, which he sweares is pure Chalde, and the names of three spirites that enter into the bloud and cause rewmes, and so consequently the toothach. This paper must be likewise three times blest, and at last with a little frankincense burned, which being thrice vsed, is of power to expell the spirites, purifie the bloud, and ease the paine, or else he lyes, for he hath practised it long, but shall approue it neuer. (Chettle 1841: 28)

CHARMS FOR TOOTHACHE. (1)—Carry a dead person's tooth in the left waistcoat pocket.
(2)—Bite a tooth from the jaw of a disinterred skull.
(3)—"As Peter sat weeping on a stone our Saviour passed by and said, 'Peter, why weepest thou?' Peter said unto Him, 'I have got the toothache.' Our Saviour replied, 'Arise and be sound.'"
And whosoever keeps this in memory or in writing will never suffer from toothache.
(4)—Mix Two quarts of rat's broth.
One ounce of camphor.
One ounce essence of cloves.
Dose—Take one teaspoonful three times a day. (Hewett 1900: 68)

TO CURE TOOTHACHE. CUT your toe and finger nails, take these parings, wrap in tissue paper, and insert the packet into a slit made in the bark of an ash tree before sunrise. You will never have toothache again as long as you live. (Hewett 1900: 75)

FOR THE TOOTHACHE.
"Peter sat at the gate of the Temple, and Christ said unto him 'What aileth thee?' he said, 'Oh, my tooth!' Christ said unto Peter, follow me, and thou shalt not feel the tooth ache no more. To be hung round, or about the patient's neck." (Couch 1871: 149)

For Toothache and Neuralgia. Write down, with a goose-quill and ink, new made—but be careful that nothing is wasted from the quill but what belongs to shape the pen—on the outside of the cheek, where the pain is situated, the following signs: "MOT, TOT, Fot." After this being done, light a candle, and proceed therewith under the chimney. Burn the pen by the light under the hearth, until not a vestige thereof remains. All this must be done noiselessly, while a person who suffers the pain must at once put the head in a bandage, retire to bed, and remain quiet, and by no means, speak a word to anybody for twenty-four hours. (Albertus Magnus n d.: 19)

Typhus:

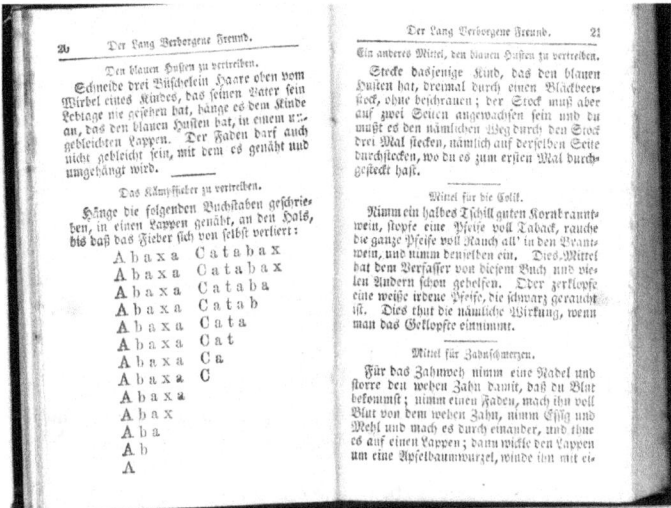

The "Camp Fever" charm in the original German.
Johann Georg Hohman. *Der Lange Verborgene Freund* (Scheffer edition, Harrisburg, ca. 1854)

33. To Drive Away the Camp Fever [typhus].
Write the following order of letters, sew them into a patch, hang it about the neck till the fever leaves:
A b a x a   C a t a b a x
A b a x a   C a t a b a x
A b a x a   C a t a b a
A b a x a   C a t a b
A b a x a   C a t a
A b a x a   C a t
A b a x a   C a
A b a x a   C
A b a x a
A b a x
A b a
A b
A (Brown 1904: 112)

Venereal Problems:

Certeine popish and magicall cures, for them that are bewitched in their privities.
For direct cure to such as are bewitched in the privie members, the first and speciall is confession: then follow in a row, holie water, and those ceremoniall trumperies, Ave Maries, and all maner of crossings; which are all said to be wholesome, except the witchcraft be perpetuall, and in that case the wife maie have a divorse of course.
Item, the eating of a haggister or [mag]pie helpeth one bewitched in that member.
Item, the smoke of the tooth of a dead man.
Item, to annoint a mans bodie over with the gall of a crow.
Item, to fill a quill with quicke silver, and laie the same under the cushine, where such a one sitteth, or else to put it under the threshold of the doore of the house or chamber where he dwelleth.

Item, to spet into your owne bosome, if you be so bewitched, is verie good.

Item, to pisse through a wedding ring. If you would know who is hurt in his privities by witchcraft; and who otherwise is therein diseased, Hostiensis answereth: but so, as I am ashamed to english it: and therefore have here set down his experiment in Latine; Quando virga nullatenùs movetur, & nunquam potuit cognoscere; hoc est signum frigiditatis: sed quando movetur & erigitur, perficere autem non potest, est signum maleficii. (Scot 1973: 65)

CHAP. VII
Of the Members of Generation.

The loss of strength and virtue in the Members of Generation is a certain Sympathy proceeding from gross Fatness, which as a certain Spasma impedites the power of the Members of that place. This happens by divers accidents; some whereof are natural, others against nature by Witchcraft. For the Remedy of the natural Passion, we use this remedy: Let these Words, with the Characters adjoyned, be written in new Parchment, which afterwards is to be bound about the nut of the yard.

A u g a l i r t o r σαλί χίοπομφιλ ובבא

A V G A L I R I O R   σαλιχιαλοιλ ובבא

This Writing in Parchment ought to be renewed every day by the space of 9 dayes, before Sun-rising every morning, by binding it, or rowling it with the Writing backwards about the Prepure, and there let it remain night and day; and as often as you renew the Parchment, or change it, let the old one which you take off, be burnt to ashes, and let the Patient drink it in a draught of warm wine. This is a most excellent / Remedy, to be had with the least cost. But if any one desires to be preserved from these evils, let him wear about his neck a Lamen of Silver, with the same Words and Signs engraven thereupon: Or if one make a Lamen of Gold, and engrave the same Words and Characters thereupon, it will be far better. But when it happens that this Disease is brought upon any one by Witchcraft, or some Diabolical Art, wrought by the malice of wicked people; let the Patient take a piece of a Horse-shooe found in the high-way, of which let there be made a Trident-Fork on the day of ♀, and hour of ♄, as you see in this Figure following.

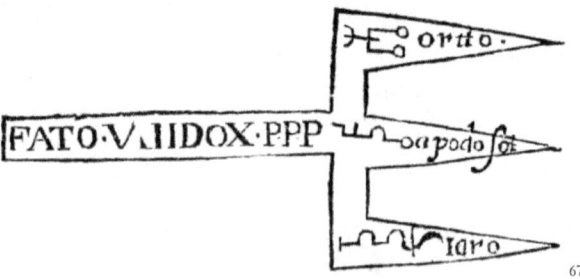

The Fork aforesaid being made, let those Words with their Characters be engraven upon the Three teeth, as you see in the Figure. And upon the Handle thereof, those Words and Signs which you see in the Figure, on Sunday before Sun-rising : which being done, let the Fork be fastened in the ground under a running Stream of Water, so deep, that the handle may not be seen, and that it cannot be found : by this means, thou / shalt be delivered in 9 dayes ; and the person that hath wrought this mischief upon thee, shall get something himself in that place, from which he shall not so easily be delivered : So we ought to resist Diabolicall Arts by Nature, as Christ by the holy Scripture proposed to the Devil in the Wilderness. (Archidoxes 1656: 113-115)

---

[67] The "L" in VLIDOX" has been engraved backeards.

Warts:

Charms for the removal of warts are among the most widespread and varied types of charms, due in part to the frequency of their mysterious disappearance after a few months.

The next curious charm comes from Cornwall.
Wash the hands in the moon's rays focussed in a dry metal basin, saying—
"I wash my hands in this thy dish,
O man in the moon do grant my wish,
And come and take away this."—AH. v. 200. (Northall 1892: 136)

TO REMOVE WARTS.
Take an eel and cut off the head.
Rub the warts with the blood of the head.
Then bury the head in the ground.
When the head is rotten the warts fall off. (Hewett 1900: 66)

ANOTHER CURE FOR WARTS. TAKE as many small stones from a running stream as you have warts, put them tightly into a clean white bag, and throw them into the highway or street. Then wash each wart in strong vinegar seven successive mornings. Whoever picks up the bag of stones will get a transfer of the warts. (Hewett 1900: 82)

Whooping Cough:

(W)HOOPING OR CHINCOUGH.
Find a briar growing in the ground at both ends, pass the child under and over it nine times, for three mornings, before sunrise, repeating—
"Under the briar, and over the briar,
I wish to leave the chincough here."
The briar must be cut, and made into the form of a cross, and worn on the breast. Staffordshire. CP. 37.

In Essex, the afflicted person must crawl under a similar bramble, or be passed through seven times from one side to the other. The spoken charm is—
"In bramble, out cough,
Here I leave the whooping cough."—AO. 70. (Northall 1892: 136-37)

A CHARM TO CURE WHOOPING COUGH. BRING an ass before the door of the house, into whose mouth thrust a slice of new bread, then pass the sick child three times over and under the animal's body, and the charm is completed. (Hewett 1900: 79)

Wounds:

50. To Cure Wounds and Pains.
Wound, thou must not (inflame) heat.
Wound, thou must not sweat.
Wound, thou must not water.
So conjure I thee by the Holy Virgin. ✠✠✠ (Brown 1904: 114)

To make the Sympathetic Powder, from Sir Kenelm Digby; for curing wounds at a distance, without seeing the party injured.
TAKE six ounces of Roman vitriol, pound it in a morter and searse it fine. Dr. Blagrave recommends this to be done when the ☉ is in ♌, which usually happens about the middle of July; then spread it fine upon an earthen glazed dish, and expose it for forty days to the diurnal heat of the sun, and be careful it gets no damp at nights. With this powder alone, great cures have been performed; and though it failed in the instance of the perfidious Count Konickmark, that failure

cannot be attributed to its want of efficacy, but to the unskilfulness of the preparer, or it was the will of the all disposer of things to set the sympathetic property aside for that time, for no cures whatever can be performed without divine auxilliarism. Dr. Butler relates various instances of its wonderful effect. A brother of his living at Southcote, near Reading, had a mastiff dog shot in the neck with a brace of bullets; the animal being very much swelled, lay pining away, and was in appearance near expiring. A gentleman doming by accidentally, having some of this powder about him, immediately made trial thereof upon this dog: and taking some of the running matter with blood from the wound, which was in his neck, applied a small quantity of the powder to it, keeping it warm, whereupon presently the dog seemed to revive, stood up and appeared very grateful for the ease procured him. (Witchcraft Detected 1824: 46)

Zweemy-headedness (dizziness):

TO CURE ZWEEMY-HEADEDNESS. WASH the head with plenty of old rum. The back and face with sour wine; wear flannel next the skin, and carry a packet of salt in the left-hand pocket. (Hewett 1900: 71)

Curses

A curse is an inverted blessing, a prayer against someone rather than for their benefit. Like charms for healing, curses were used by ordinary individuals as well as Cunning Folk. Curses were commonly cast for very personal reasons as emotionally-charged responses to a perceived injury or grievance, but they could also be motivated by a desire for revenge, enrichment or political advantage. While cursing for selfish and undeserved reasons was strongly discouraged and necessarily kept secret, a curse involving personal injustice was often a very public, socially justifiable act. The classic method was to kneel down in a public street or church on bare knees and loudly execrate (the reverse of "consecrate") the offending party by name, calling down God's divine vengeance on him or her. Specifically calling on God to send a judgment on an enemy, as Isabel Oxley did in 1634 – "Godes plague and Godes curse light of the[e] and thine beasts, and God lett never they or anie thing thou hast prosper or doe well" (*"Acts of the High Commission ... Durham"* 1858: 73) – rather than just mumbling "may your pigs all die", separated the conscious curse from simple angry swearing, and made it a mechanism of social redress. Cursing was the classic weapon of the powerless against the powerful (and women against men). The "Beggar's Curse" (for lack of charity) was supposed to be particularly potent, as was the curse of a parent on an erring child. Alternately, a parental blessing was supposed to protect the child from harm, while a blessing from the curser would negate the effect of a curse.

Cursing was also the foundation of "black witchcraft". The witch's sin and crime, beyond her allegiance to the Devil, was damaging or destroying lives and property through unjustified curses that drew their power from the Devil rather than God. Cursing was a dangerous activity for Cunning Folk, as it opened them to the charge of black witchcraft or sorcery, but it could also be profitable and enhance their underground reputation as powerful practitioners. Some people preferred having a willing professional perform a curse, assuming a greater potency or from the fear that a curse might rebound upon them, and there are many cases where it was a professional who made the fatal charm or wax poppet. A random example of this service, which can stand for the rest, occurred in the 1840s in Norfolk:

> They tell of a wonderful old man who lived at a sea-side town hard by in the forties; and how, if provoked, he could put a spell on the rat-catchers' dogs and ferrets, so they could catch no rats. He cursed professionally. One old woman tells how she went to consult him, because she knew she had enemies in the village, who had sought to do injury to herself and son. There was a copper bowl upside down on the table. "Would you like to see them as is done it?" he asked. She said yes. Then he lifted the bowl, and there lay three little dolls the exact likeness of the three men in the village whom she suspected. The wizard asked what he should do to them. She preferred leaving that to him; and so, only a few weeks afterwards, one went out of his mind, another hanged himself, and the

third died of a fistula. "Now, 'tis no use o' talking, said the tottering old dame as she thumped her stick on the floor, if that wasn't through old S—, what was it?" (Roper 1893: 795)

The efficacy of the non-satanic curse depended on the justification behind it. "An unprovoked malediction would only rebound against its author, but the more justified the curser's anger, the more likely that his imprecation would take effect." (Thomas 1971:505). Religious authorities maintained that legitimate cursing, like any other petition for God's supernatural power, was restricted to the officers of the Church (Catholic or Anglican), but this had little effect on popular practice. Cursing was rejected by Protestant theologians early on in the Reformation as a blasphemous imposition by presuming to command God to damn people, but it was never entirely eliminated, and in the 17th century, cursing was eagerly adopted by radical Puritans as a righteous weapon for the pious in a wicked world.

Cursing was based on the universal belief in divine vengeance, and the ability of religious authorities to call down a "plague of God" on the unregenerate. The Bible is full of examples of cursing and the Church made liberal use of curses and anathemas as sanctions against ungodly practices and to promote social control. A classic example cited by Johann Weyer (1583) is the famous "Curse of St. Adalbert" against theft (greatly influenced by *Deuteronomy*):

> On the authority of Almighty God, Father, Son and Holy Spirit, and of the Blessed Virgin Mary, mother of Our Lord Jesus Christ, and of the holy angels and archangels, and St. Michael, and St. John the Baptist, and in the name of blessed Peter the apostle, and the other apostles /and St. Stephen and all the Martyrs, St. Silvester and St. Adalbert and all the Confessors, and St. Augustine and the holy virgins and all the saints in heaven and on earth, to whom is given the power of binding and loosening, we excommunicate, damn, curse with the bond of anathema, and drive from the doorstep of the Holy Mother church those thieves, sacrilegious persons, or robbers (along with their henchmen, their advisers, their helpers male and female), who have committed this theft or this evil or who have profited from it at all. May their lot be with Dathan and Abiron (Num. 16) whom the earth swallowed up for their sins and their pride; may their lot be with Judas the betrayer who sold the Lord for a price, Amen. May their lot be with Pontius Pilate and with those who said to the Lord God "Depart from us, we do not wish a knowledge of your ways." May their children be made orphans. May they be cursed in the city, cursed in the field, cursed in the woods. May they be cursed in their homes, in their granaries, in their beds and their bedchambers. May they be cursed in the court, on the road, in the village, cursed in the fortress, in the river, cursed in the Church, in the cemetary, in the tribunal of law. May they be cursed in the marketplace, cursed in war, cursed in their tarrying, their speaking, their remaining silent, their waking, their sleeping, their eating, their drinking. May they be cursed in touching, in sitting, in lying, in standing, at rest, at every time. May they be cursed in their whole body, their whole soul, and their five bodily senses. May they be cursed in every place. Cursed be the fruit of their womb, cursed be the fruit of their land, cursed be all that is theirs. Cursed be their head, mouth, nostrils, nose, lips, jaws, teeth, eyes, pupils, brain, palate, tongue, throat, breast, heart, womb, liver, entrails, stomach, spleen, navel, bladder, legs and shins. Cursed be their feet and the shackles upon their feet. Cursed be their neck, shoulders, back, arms, elbows, hands, and fingers. Cursed be the nails of their hands and feet. Cursed be their ribs, their semen, their knees. Cursed be their flesh, their bones, their blood, the skin upon their bodies, the marrow in their bones. Cursed may they be from the top of their head to the soles of their feet and whatever is between – that is, the five senses of sight, hearing, taste, smell and touch. And may they be cursed in the Holy Cross and in Christ's passion, in the five wounds of Christ, the shedding of Christ's blood, and the milk of the Virgin Mary. I adjure you, Lucifer, and all your followers, by the Father, Son and Holy Spirit, and by the humanity and nativity of Christ, and by the power of all the saints, to take no rest day or night until you bring these men to destruction – whether they be drowned in rivers, or hanged, or devoured by wild beasts, or burned to death, or killed by their enemies as an object of hatred for all living creatures. And just as the Lord has / conferred upon blessed Peter the Apostle, and upon his successors (in whose place we stand), and upon us (however unworthy), such power that whatever we bind upon earth is bound also in heaven, and whatever we loose on earth is loosened in heaven, so do we close heaven to those men if they are unwilling to reform, and we refuse them the earth for burial – let them be buried in the grazing grounds of asses. And cursed be the earth in which they are buried. May they perish in the judgment to come, and may they have no

association with Christians nor receive the Lord's Body at the moment of death. May they be like dust before the face of the wind; and just as Lucifer was cast down from heaven, and just as Adam and Eve were driven out of Paradise, so may these be driven from the light of day. May thou also be joined with those to whom the Lord says on the day of judgement, "Depart, ye accursed into the everlasting fire which has been prepared for the Devil and his angels, where the worm will not die nor the fire extinguished." (Matt. 25-41) And as the candle cast from thy hands be extinguished, so may their works and their lives be extinguished in the foulness of the pit unless they return what they have stolen before the limit that has been set." Let us all say "Amen" and then sing. "In the midst of life we are in death." (Weyer 1991: 381-83)

In addition, a "General Sentence" was regularly proclaimed in individual churches against people who transgressed the laws of the Church. The Anglican Church abandoned the older practice of declaring such a curse on a quarterly basis in 1549[68], but kept the Ash Wednesday Commination Service in which a series of curses was read out by the priest, to each of which the congregation responded "Amen.":

> Cursed is the man that maketh any carved or molten [cast] image, to worship it. Cursed is he that curseth his father or mother. Cursed is he that removeth his neighbour's landmark. Cursed is he that maketh the blind to go out of his way. Cursed is he that perverteth the judgement of the stranger, the fatherless, and widow. Cursed is he that smiteth his neighbour secretly. Cursed is he that lieth with his neighbour's wife. Cursed is he that taketh reward to slay the innocent. Cursed is he that putteth his trust in man, and taketh man for his defence, and in his heart goeth from the Lord. Cursed are the unmerciful, fornicators, and adulterers, covetous persons, idolaters, slanderers, drunkards, and extortioners.

Another popular application was the "book curse" where a malediction was added in a manuscript against its potential theft. These examples are from the Litterascripta website:

> Thys boke is one
> And God's curse another;
> They that take the one
> God geve them the other.
> He who steals this book
> may he die the death
> may he be frizzled in a pan...
> This present book legible in scripture
> Here in this place thus tacched with a cheyn
> Purposed of entent for to endure
> And here perpetuelli stylle to remeyne
> Fro eyre to eyre wherfore appone peyn
> Of cryst is curs of faders and of moderes
> Non of hem hens atempt it to dereyne
> Whille ani leef may goodeli hange with oder.
> Steal not this Book my honest Friend

---

[68] This selection will give the tone of the General Sentence: "First Alle they ar accursed, that has presume to take awey, or to pryve any churche of the right that longeth therto, or elles ageyn right stryve to breke or trouble the libertees of the Churche. And also they that purchace any maner letres fro any temporal court, to lette any processe of spiritual juges in suche causes, as longeth unto spirituel court And all they that with peple and noyse come to spirituel courts and putte the juges, or the parties, that there plede, in feere; or elles, forasmuche as the parties serve in spirituel court suche causes as long unto spirituel court, make or procure any of the said parties here advocates, procuratours, or other ministres of spirituel court to be emlited, arrested, or any other wyse to be vexed.
Also, all they that presume to distourbe or trouble the peece and tranquillite of the kyng and his reaume of England; and they that wronggefully withhold any right, that longeth to the kyng.
"Also, alle that wetyngly here false witnesse, and procure false witnesse to be borne; or elles wytingly bryng forth in jugement false wittenesse, to lette rightfull matrimony, or procure disherityng of any person." [&c.] John Johnson. *A Collection of the Laws and Canons of the Church of England*, vol. 2. Oxford: John Henry Parker, 1851, p. 494.

For fear the Galows should be your hend,
And when you die the Lord will say
And wares the Book you stole away?[69]

There was no shortage of models and precedents for common people to follow in creating their own curses.

Unfortunately, as personal curses were generally composed ad-lib orally by the person involved, there were few instances where these were noted down in detail, and some were omitted on purpose. Weyer states (and Scot copies him) that it would be inadvisable to include the spell for an example of image magic, as it might well be used by people reading the book. "… with the rehearsall of certaine words, which for the avoiding of foolish superstition and credulitie in this behalfe is to be omitted." (Scot 1973: 208). This in fact was percipient if regrettable, as the use of Scot by Cunning Folk as a source for magical formulae – quite against his original purpose – is well known.

Most of the surviving examples appear in accounts of subsequent trials that can only be consulted by viewing the original records in English archives, which I am not in a position to do, but will have to rely more on partial examples from secondary sources and anecdotes. For example of cursing in practice, here are two 19th century instances:

P. F. S. A. *A Curse.*—A young yeoman, farming his own estate near Ashburton, received anonymously, in April, 1889, the following curse—names, however, of person and place are for obvious reasons fictitious.

> AN INJURED ONE'S CURSE.
> *Nickson*, repent, the time is near,
> When before thy God you shall appear;
> Thy life has been a wicked race,
> So pray to God to give thee grace.
> Thy bonnie bride, when she has borne
> A son, shall leave thy home forlorn;
> And when the first born son is won,
> And *Furzdon* goes to first born son;
> It's then my curse shall have its sway,
> From that time forth to judgment-day,
> Without some act of special brand,
> To a despised and suffering man,
> You wipe away by glorious deeds
> The act that makes my heart to bleed;
> When this is done my curse is o'er,
> No *Nicksan* its weight shall bear no more."

In May his wife presented him with a son and heir, which, however, died very suddenly in September following. The curse much troubled the poor man, who was very ill for some time, and evidently believed that more bereavement would follow. Happily time has treated him kindly, and the curse appears to have gone off if not home to roost.

26. WITCHCRAFT IN SOMERSET. (III. xvii. 1.)—It is hardly credible, but there exists, even in our day, a belief in Witchcraft in some parts of Somerset.

The following incidents happened during this year. A poor woman, the mother of a large family, had for a period of two years a series of misfortunes; her husband was ill, two children were injured accidentally, they were all laid up by a prevailing epidemic; the woman herself, no doubt tired and worn out, came to the conclusion that this long and bitter trial, being, as she considered, undeserved, must be the result of an evil agency at work, and she pronounced herself "overlooked." Once the idea took possession of her, it seemed to spread through the family, her husband and children testifying that they saw strange looking little black objects sitting on the boxes at night, and that these little things used to try to pull them by the feet out of bed.

---

[69] http://www.litterascripta.com/bibliomania/curses.shtml (accessed 5/30/2011).

She became so thoroughly convinced that she was bewitched, that she went to interview a wise man who lives at Wells; he took the same view of the case, and said that he would have to pray for her, the point at interest being, who had bewitched her? She had to go through a list of names, names of women; after mentioning many and not the right one amongst them, as she was turning away, remembering one more, she mentioned her, and that one the wise man pronounced to be the woman who had bewitched her. He told her that he could break the charm and take away the power of the witch, but it would take a lot of prayer and work. He then gave certain directions which the woman and her husband were to follow, in order to break the spell. About the hour of midnight she and her husband were directed to sit in front of their fire and burn salt, and for the space of one hour no conversation had to pass between them, only they had to repeat the following words:
"This is not the thing I wish to burn
But Mrs—'s heart of — Somerset to turn
Wishing thee neither to eat, drink, sleep nor rest
Until thou dost come to me and do my request
Or else the wrath of God may fall on thee
And cause thee to be consumed in a moment—Amen."
This accomplished, they were to retire backwards to the foot of the stairs, climb the stairs still backwards, repeating at the same time the Lord's Prayer also backwards, and then not speak a word to one another till they were in bed; in this way they would break the spell.
The man and his wife tried this, with implicit faith that the enchantment would be broken, or the evil eye averted.
[Our correspondent wishes to remain anonymous, but I can vouch for the truth of the story: in fact, I know the locality and some of the characters quite well. EDITOR FOR SOMERSET.] (*Notes and Queries for Somerset and Dorset 1895: 157-58*)

Reciting the Lord's Prayer backwards was frequently used for harmful magic, but here it was supposed to have a positive effect. Exactly how this was done is seldom explained, but here are two possible variations:

The Lord's Prayer Backwards (phonetically):
Nema! livee, morf su revilled tub noishaytpmet ootni ton suh deel sus tshaiga sapsert that yeth. Vigrawf eu za sesapsert rua suh vigrawf derb ilaid rua yed sith suh vig neveh ni si za thre ni nud eeb liw eyth muck modngik eyth main eyth eeb dwohlah nevah ni tra chioo. Retharf rua!
Or:
Amen.
for ever and ever.
the power, and the glory,
For thine is the kingdom,
but deliver us from evil.
and lead us not into temptation,
as we forgive those who trespass against us,
and forgive us our trespasses,
Give us this day our daily bread,
on earth as it is in heaven.
Thy will be done
Thy kingdom come.
hallowed be thy name.
Our Father who art in heaven,

Another method of cursing was the "black fast". The true black fast was an approved Catholic ritual for the devout, but the name apparently suggested negative magic and was also used to characterise the practice of a sort of supernatural hunger strike (also called St. Trinian's Fast) whereby an individual would pray against (curse) someone while strengthening their effort through fasting. An example of this is Mabel Brigg's fast against Henry VIII and the Duke of Norfolk in 1486:

#487 11 March. 1487. THE FASTING OF MABEL BRIGGE.
R. O. Confession of Agnes Lokkar, 28 Jan. 29 Henry VIII. before Thomas and James Ellerkar, John Goldewell, and Patrick Tomson. {Headed: Copy of the first examination or confession.}
1. That one Mabel Brigge came to the house of John Lokkar at Reysome Grange, a se'nnight before Cross Days last, with two children, and immediately afterwards one Nelsone, the farmer of Risome Garth, sent his maiden, one Margaret, to the foresaid Lokkar, desiring that the above named Mabel might remain and he would see her costs paid. John and Agnes Lokkar then perceiving that the said Mabel fasted the next Friday, Saturday, and Sunday till mass was done, asked her why she did so. She replied that it was a charitable fast, and said she had never so fasted before but once for a man, and he brake his neck or it were all fasted, and so she trusted that they should do that had made all this business and that was the King and this false Duke. John Lokkar asked her why she fasted it so, and she said she was hired by Isabel, William Bukke's wife, for the above intent, on which Lokkar put her out of the house and went to Isabel Bukke, who admitted that she had hired her so to fast and came with Lokkar to her own house, where she said Mabel was. Lokkar was angry and rebuked them, and Isabel went home and declared the matter to her husband, who went and entreated Lokkar to let the matter go no further. Isabel Bukke also said, she took this fast "at" her ghostly father, Sir Thomas Marshall, chantry priest at Hompton (Holmpton). Then old Bukke and his son sent for Lokkar and prayed him to be good and let (i.e., prevent) this matter to be opened abroad, and young Bukke's wife gave him 3s. and 2 yds. of linen cloth. Mabel then departed from John Lokkar and went to William Fletcher in Welwik, where she took another fast calling it the Black Fast, and said "Now I have ended this fast and all Holderness may pray for Bukke's wife and me."
(Letters and Papers of Henry VIII 1901: 177)
Further evidence revealed that "Mabel Brige did fast what was called Black Fast or St. Trynzan fast … she fasted six weeks together, every week one day on bread and water…" Mabel (who seems to have been a Wise Woman who also used fasting for divination) and three others were subsequently executed for treason.

In addition to verbal curses, there were physical charms used to curse people, such as the ancient lead cursing tablets that were well-known across pagan Europe, and the use of cursing stones in wells and on stone cairns such as the "altoirs" on Innishmurray island off the coast of County Sligo, Ireland or the Farc-y-Ceryg Sanctaidd ("The Field of the Holy Stones") near Llansadurnen in Wales. Pre-Christian curse tablets have been found in England, such as this example from Bath:

> 96. England, Bath … Lead alloy tablet measuring 10.5 x 6.0 cm., written on both sides but not folded. This tablet is notable for several reasons. First, it is the only one with a text (Side A) completely written in reverse order; the first letter inscribed in the first line is actually the last letter of the text and vice versa. Second, the standard formula for identifying the suspected thief ("whether man or woman …") is here supplemented in unique fashion by the addition of "whether pagan or Christian." The date is probably in the fourth century C. E. Bibl.: Tomlin, pp. 232-34 (no. 98).
> (**Side A**) Whether pagan or Christian, whether man or woman, whether boy or girl, whether slave or free, whoever has stolen from me, Annianus (son of) Matutina (?), six silver coins from my purse, you, Lady Goddess, are to exact (them) from him. If through some deceit he has given me …[corrosion] and do not give thus to him but reckon as (?) the blood who has invoked this upon me.
> (**Side B**) Postumianus, Pisso, Locinna, Alauna, Materna, Consula, Candidina, Eulicius, Latinus, Senicianus, Avitianus, Victor, Scotius, Aessicunia, Paltucca, Calliopis, Celerianus.
> The tablet is corroded at this point and impossible to read. The editor proposes that the sentence is meant to be apotropaic, designed to turn aside any counterspell invoked by the thief (Tomlin, p. 234). In this list, the names are written in proper order from top to bottom, but the letters of each name are reversed. (Gager 1992: 195)

Note the reversed names, used more than a millennium before the 19th century example. Professor Gager was puzzled by a 17th century curse tablet found at Lincoln's Inn in London (p. 29) that bore a strong resemblance to the classical examples, despite the fact that no other such tablets have been found later than the 8th century CE, and wondered if somehow the tradition had survived unrecorded over the intervening 1,200 years. However, the origin of the newer tablet was adequately explained in an article by W. Paley Baildon in 1900:

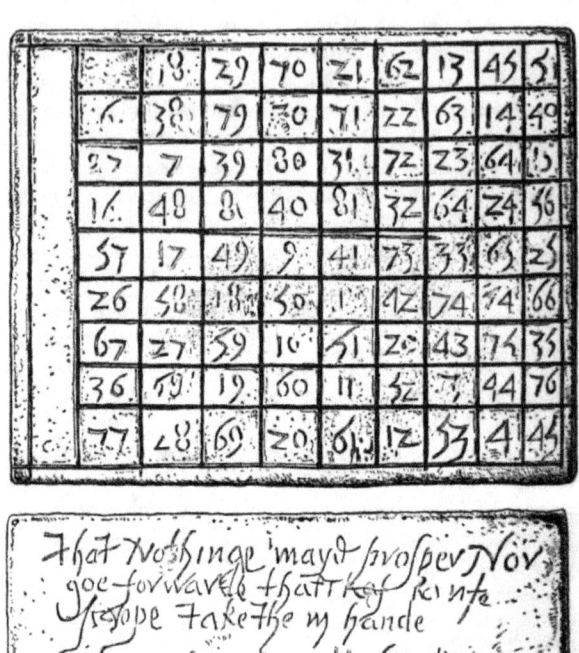

In the course of some extensive drainage operations carried out in Lincoln's Inn last autumn the customary lot of little things left behind by absent-minded people was found. Amongst these was the charm which, by the kindness of the Benchers of the Inn, I am able to exhibit here to-night. It consists of an oblong plate of lead, 4 3/16 inches by 3 ¼ inches and 1/8 inch thick. On one side is engraved or scratched a square of 81 small squares, each of which contains a number; on the other side is written 'That Nothinge maye prosper Nor goe forwarde that [Raf erased] Raufe Scrope take the in hande.' Underneath this pious wish are the names 'Hasmodai,' 'Schedbarschemoth,' and 'Schartatan,' with three astrological symbols.

The object is a charm invoking the spirits of the moon against Ralph Scrope.

The square with the numbers is one of the so-called 'magical squares' which were supposed to have occult virtues and powers. The horizontal and vertical rows of figures and the two diagonals should add up to the same total, in this case 369. This particular square has been wrongly constructed by the John Wellington Wells [the cunning man in Gilbert and Sullivan's "The Sorcerer", 1877] of the period, for two numbers are used twice, 45 and 64, and two are not used at all, 54 and 55. The result being that the first and third horizontal lines do not add up correctly.

A lot of curious information about these squares will be found in 'Three Books of Occult Philosophy, written by Henry Cornelius Agrippa …1651.'

> It is remarkable that this edition makes exactly the same mistake in the lunar square as is made on this charm, and has at least one other besides. My friend Mr. Eugene Street, who has made some study of these matters, suggests that this may have been done to account for want of success if the spell did not work satisfactorily. …
>
> The square on this charm is the square of nine, and 'the number nine belongs to the Moon, the utmost receptacle of all Celestiall influences, and vertues'. 'The seventh table,' as Agrippa tells us, 'is of the Moon, of a square of nine multiplied into it self, having eighty one numbers, in every side and Diameter nine, producing 369. and the sum of all is 3321. And there are over it divine names with an Intellegency to what is good, and a spirit to what is bad. And of it are drawn the Characters of the Moon, and of the spirits thereof. This fortunate Moon being engraven on Silver, renders the bearer thereof grateful, amiable, pleasant, cheerfull, honored, removing all malice, and ill-will. It causeth security in a journey, increase of riches, and health of body, drives away enemies and other evil things from what place thou pleasest; and if it be an unfortunate Moon engraven in a plate of Lead, where ever it shall be buried, it makes that place unfortunate, and the inhabitants thereabouts, as also Ships, Rivers, Fountains, Mills, and it makes every man unfortunate, against which it shall be directly done, making him fly from his Country, and that place of his abode where it shall be buried, and it hinders Physitians, and Orators, and all men whatsoever in their office, against whom it shall be made.' On turning to the table we find that the spirit of the moon is Hasmodai, and the 'spirit of the spirits of the Moon' is Schedbarschemoth Schartathan. These two, or three, names are accordingly written on the charm underneath the invocation that I have already mentioned, accompanied by their proper sigils, seals, or characters. …
>
> The Ralph Scrope, against whom this charm was directed, can be identified with tolerable certainty. He was the fourth son of John Scrope of Spennithorne, county Yorks, and Hambledon, county Bucks, and was admitted to Lincoln's Inn on July 4th, 1543. He was called to the Bar in 1548 … (Baildon 1901: 141-46)

Baildon also notes other Agrippa-influenced tablets; a similar lead one found in North Yorkshire and an iron Mars and a copper Venus tablet exhibited by S. Baring-Gould.

A notorious example of curse magic involved the "baleful well" of St. Elian, near Colwyn Bay in Wales. There are (or all too often, were) numerous holy or healing wells in Britain that had been "Christianized" with the attribution of saints, but the "Ffynnon Elian" in question had a dire reputation as a site where people's names written on stones and placed in the shallow water of the spring wrought a curse on them. St. Elian was an authentic 6th century religious worker in Cornwall, which doesn't explain how he became associated with this sort of thing. Although its magic was also used for other purposes, St. Elian's Well was foremost a cursing well in the 18th and 19th centuries until the well-head covered over in 1828. However, one John Evans opened another outlet to the spring on his own property and profitably managed the cursing well despite being prosecuted for fraud until he relented in 1854.

> Denbighshire Assizes. Before Mr. Baron Bolland [August 3, 1831].—John Evans, a Welsh seer, who officiates as high priest of the far-famed and much-dreaded Ffynnon Elian (or St. Elian's Well), near Abergele, was indicted for obtaining 7s. from one Elizabeth Davies, by falsely pretending that he could cure her husband, Robert Davies, of a certain sickness with which he was afflicted by taking his name out of the well. (Peacock 1890: 131-33)

For more details on the 1831 case, see in Chapter 3, "Understanding the Cunning Folk". An outlet from the well still exists today. There were other such wells such as Ffynnon Gybi and another Ffynnon Elian on Anglesey that were also used for curses.

The most common physical charm involved in cursing was the doll or poppet (the infamous "voodoo doll" was not limited to African religious offshoots) for which Scot gave several examples that he got from Weyer, although as in the original, only one included a spell used to activate it:

> To do more savage harm, a similar image is fashioned in the form of a man, and a specific name is written upon its head, and the following names are written upon the ribs: *"Alif cafiel zaza hit mel meltat leviatan leutatace"*. It is then buried in a grave. (Weyer 1991: 386). Scot modified the spell *"Ailif, casyl, zaze, hit, mel metat;"* and omits the detail about the grave. (Scot 1973: 209).

Another example of how such images might made comes from *The Examination of John Walsh or Welshe* (1566):

> ... he being farther demandyd to whate ende the Sprites yn the likenes of Todes and the pictures of man or woman made yn wax or claye to whate ende the[y] serve he saithe that theire temperature of pictures made yn wax, will cawse the ptie [party] to contynewe sicke ii hole yeres bycawse hit wilbe too hole yeres er[e] the wax wilbe consumed and as for the pictures of claye, their confection is after this manner [:] ye must take the yerthe of a newe made grave[,] the ribbe bone of a dedde mann or woman bornyd [burned] to asshes of a woman for a woman[,] and of a man for a man and a blacke athercobbe [spider] with also the Inner pithe of an ellder [tree] tempered all yn water [,] wherin the said Todes must first be wasshed [,] and after all cerymonyes endyd they put a pricke videlt ["that is"] a pynne or a thorne yn any member wherin they wold the ptie shuldbe greved [,] and yf the sayde pricke be put to the hartte, the ptie diethe wi[thi]n ix dayes ,] which Image they burye yn the moste moystie place they kan finde ... (Gibson 2003: 23)

"Temperature" in this instance doesn't refer to heat but rather the "temperament" or physical characteristics of the person cursed. Such figures or "pictures" as they were often called were made from wax, clay, grave earth, and metal. The standard method of activating them was to bury them in horse dung in a stable or in a dunghill.

Other curses were more simply done, based on the principle of magical artifacts wasting away. Burning candles against someone was documented in the London courts in 1480 (Kittredge 1929: 85) and in Norfolk in 1843:

> 15.—Arising out of an assault case, a curious story about witchcraft was told to the Norwich magistrates. Mr. and Mrs. Curtis alleged that a Mrs. Bell had bewitched them three days after Tombland Fair, and they had been bewitched ever since. "Mrs. Curtis saw Mrs. Bell light a candle and fill it with pins. She then put some red dragon's blood, with some water, into an oyster-shell, and having repeated a form of words over it, her (Mr. Curtis') husband's arms and legs were set fast, and when he lay down he could not get up again without somebody helping him." The man made a similar statement, and said that to the dragon's blood and water Mrs. Bell added some parings of her own nails, put the mixture over the fire, and muttered an incantation. (Mackie: 43-31)

Regrettably, the oral curse is missing as usual. Other curse/charms were very simple:

> THE HERRING-BONE CHARM TO CAUSE DEATH. SEW into a garment which is worn next to the skin a long thin herring-bone. As the bone dries up, or withers, so will the person wearing it gradually pine away and die. (Hewett 1900: 82)

I'll close the chapter with two examples illustrating the older "lyrical" style of curse that survived in Gaelic Scotland into modern times, which can be found in Carmichael's *Carmina Gadelica*:

A Malediction (vol. II, pp. 60-61)

THAINIG dithis a mach	THERE came two out
A Cathrach Neobh,	From the City of Heaven,
Fear agus bean,	A man and a woman,
A dheanadh nan ōisnean.	To make the 'ōisnean.'
Mallaich dha na beana bur-shuileach,	Curses on the blear-eyed women,
Mallaich dha na feara fur-shuileach,	Curses on the sharp-eyed men,
Mallaich dha na ceithir saighde, guineach, guid,	Curses on the four venomous arrows of disease,
Dh' fhaodadh a bhi 'n aorabh duine 's bruid.	That may be in the constitution of man and beast.

Another lyrical curse in the form of a "poem" is introduced by Carmichael:

> This and other poems were obtained from Isabella Chisholm, a travelling tinker. Though old, Isabella Chisholm was still tall and straight, fine-featured, and fresh-complexioned. She was endowed

with personal attraction, mental ability, and astute diplomacy of no common order. Her father, John Chisholm, is said to have been a 'pious, prayerful man'—terms not usually applied to his class. Isabella / Chisholm had none of the swarthy skin and far-away look of the ordinary gipsy. But she had the gipsy habits and the gipsy language, variously called 'Cant,' 'Shelta,' 'Romany,' with rich fluent Gaelic and English. She had many curious spells, runes, and hymns that would have enriched Gaelic literature, and many rare words and phrases and expressions that would have improved the Gaelic dictionary.

The Wicked Who Would Do Me Harm (vol. II, pp. 194-95)

ULC a dhean mo lochd Gun gabh e 'n galar gluc gloc, Guirneanach, gioirneanach, guairneach, Gaornanach, garnanach, gruam.	THE wicked who would do me harm May he take the [throat] disease, Globularly, spirally, circularly, Fluxy, pellety, horny-grim.
Gum bu cruaidhe c na chlach, Gum bu duibhe e na 'n gual, Gum bu luaithe e na 'n lach, Gum bu truime e na 'n luaidh.	Be it harder than the stone, Be it blacker than the coal, Be it swifter than the duck, Be it heavier than the lead.
Gum bu gointe, gointe, geuire, gairbhe, guiniche e, Na'n cuilionn cruaidh cnea-chridheach, Gum bu gairge e na'n salann sion, sionn, searbh, sailte, Seachd seachd uair.	Be it fiercer, fiercer, sharper, harsher, more malignant, Than the hard, wound-quivering holly, Be it sourer than the sained, lustrous, bitter, salt salt, Seven seven times.
A turabal a null, A tarabal a nall, A treosdail a sios, A dreochail a suas,	Oscillating thither, Undulating hither, Staggering downwards, Floundering upwards.
A breochail a muigh A geochail a staigh, Dol a mach minic, Tighinn a steach ainmic.	Drivelling outwards, Snivelling inwards, Oft hurrying out, Seldom coming in.
Sop an luib gach laimhe, Cas an cois gach cailbhe, Lurg am bun gach ursann, Sput ga chur 's ga chairbinn.	A wisp the portion of each hand, A foot in the base of each pillar, A leg the prop of each jamb, A flux driving and dragging him.
Gearrach fhala le cridhe, le crutha, le cnamha, Le gruthan, le sgumhan, le sgamha, Agus sgrudadh cuisil, ugan is arna, Dha mo luchd-tair agus tuaileis.	A dysentery of blood from heart, from form, from bones, From the liver, from the lobe, from the lungs, And a searching of veins, of throat, and of kidneys, To my contemners and traducers.
An ainm Dhia nam feart, A shiab uam gach olc, 'S a dhion mi le neart, Bho lion mo luchd-freachd Agus fuathachd.	In name of the God of might, Who warded from me every evil, And who shielded me in strength, From the net of my breakers And destroyers

CHAPTER 9:

Charms II - Protection, Counter-Witchery, Theft and Love

"…all such superstitious persons, men or women, as use Charmes and Inchantment for the effecting of any thing upon a superstitious and erroneous perswasion, that the Charmes have vertue in them to doe such things, not knowing that it is the action of the devil by those meanes; but thinking that God hath put vertue into them, as he hath done into herbes for Physicke. Of such persons we have (no doubt) abundance in this our Land, who though they deale wickedly, and sinne grievously in using Charmes, yet because they intend not to joyne league with the devil, either secretly, or formally, they are not to be counted Witches." (Perkins 1631: 637)

Although the healing charms of the previous chapter were the most common example of the genre, there were also a great many traditional charms for other problems and desires. The Cunning Folk served a society that lacked many of the safeguards and resources we take for granted. Christian belief in the existence of witchcraft, as demanded by Biblical example, was universal, even among those who thought the threat was minimal or (at a later date) no longer extant. However, the clergy had ceased to provide the supernatural defences against witchcraft and malice for those who believed they were attacked by witches (their advice was often "suck it up and have faith in God's unsearchable providence") as their Catholic predecessors had done. There were no police forces to protect the public or effectively root out and apprehend thieves and robbers. There wasn't insurance available (as there was for shipping and trade) to make up for losses due to the death of breadwinners, crop failures, loss of livestock, house fires or other misfortunes until the 18th century. Contemporary Galenic medicine was generally ineffectual in curing complaints of all sorts.

So much depended on God's providence – or chance, luck, fortune – that the craving for foreseeing the future through divination and seeking to influence it by magic was sometimes irresistible. For example, women, whose lifelong prosperity and happiness depended on acquiring a suitable husband (nor could ordinary men well manage the "little commonwealths" that were their households without a good woman at their sides), the temptation of identifying their future spouse spawned a seemingly endless variety of predictive charms and spells. Perpetual insecurity, the knowledge that disaster could strike at any moment as well as the anger and anguish that calamity brought in its wake, guaranteed that the Cunning Folk would flourish if not always prosper throughout our period. Also, it wasn't just ordinary country folk or townspeople that sought their services. Even members of the elite, intrigued by curiosity or in desperation when other alternatives failed, might also sneak off to consult the local Wise Woman.

The most important challenges charms were employed for were defence against witchcraft, theft detection, protection in general, and love. The examples in this chapter are arranged under these headings, followed by a selection of miscellaneous charms for other uses.

Witchcraft:

One of the most significant requests for the Cunning Folks' expertise was in defence against witchcraft. It perhaps needs to be noted here that the connotation of the term "witch" from time immemorial until the 20th century was, by default, negative. Even "white witch" – a term originally more often used by the Cunning Folk's enemies than by their clientele or they themselves – tended to imply the demonic nature of *any* magical practitioner rather than mildly mitigate some of them. It was applied to cunning men or wise women by theologians to indicate the seductive sinfulness of seeking good ends through evil means, whereby the client might avert worldly misfortune only to risk eternal damnation.

Adapting Éva Pócs classification of witch-types (*Between the Living and the Dead* 1999: 10-11), I suggest that there are four classes to be considered:

- The Neighborhood or "Social" Witch – a real person accused by reason of community conflict who may or may not actually practice magic; the common victim of local gossip, official persecution and the witch trials.
- The Cunning Folk – local or regional sorcerers, healers and fortune-tellers ("White Witches"); actual practitioners of folk magic.
- The Night Witch – the folkloric witch; the stereotypical evil menace of tradition as well as the purported demonic adversary of the witch persecution – non-existent but a status "ascribed" to real people.
- The Fairy Tale Witch – non-existent but influential fictional archetype.

Suspect "Neighborhood" and imaginary "Night" witches were widely feared and identified and defended against by the charms and spells of both ordinary people and professed "unwitchers", whether clerics or Cunning Folk. Sometimes the alleged assailant remained an imaginary generic "Night Witch", but more often her traits were ascribed or assigned through accusation to an actual individual, who when indentified was placated, or attacked and/or prosecuted.

Witches, Preservative against.—

> Mr. Brand transcribed from his physical MS. dated 1475, the following charm against witchcraft: "Here ys a charme for wyked Wych. In nomine Patris, et Filii, et Spiritus Sancti, Amen. Per Virtutem Domini sint Medicina mei pia Crux ✠ et passio Christi ✠. Vulnera quinque Domini sint Mediciua mei ✠. Virgo Maria mihi succurre, et defends ab omni maligno Demonio, et ab omni maligno Spiritu: Amen. ✠ a ✠ g ✠ l ✠ a ✠ Tetragrammaton. ✠Alpha. ✠ oo. ✠ primogenitus, ✠ vita, vita, ✠ sapiencia, ✠ Virtus, ✠ Jesus Nazarenus rex judeorum, ✠ fili Domini, miserere mei Amen. ✠ Marcus ✠ Matheus ✠ Lucas ✠ Johannes mihi succurrite et defendite Amen. ✠ Omnipotens sempiterne Deus, hunc N. famulum tuum hoc breve Scripturn super se portantem prospere salve dormiendo, vigilando, potando, et precipue sompniando ab omni maligno Demonio, eciam ab omni maligno spiritu ✠." (Brand 1900: 616)

Anti-Witch:
> Put five spanish needles into an egge through the shell & seethe it in the uryne of one that is bewytched, & whyle it is seethinge the witch will come without doubt. Prt est. prt est prt est. (Briggs 1953: 456)

> *To spoile a theefe, a witch, or anie other enimie, and to be delivered from the evill.*
> Upon the Sabboth daie, before sunrising, cut a hazell wand, saieng : I cut thee O bough of this summers growth, in the name of him whome I meane to beate or maime. Then cover the table, and saie + *in nomine patris* + *& filii* + *& spiritus sancti* + *ter*. And striking thereon saie as followeth (english it he that can) *Drochs myroch, esenaroth,* + *betu* + *baroch* + *ass* + *maaroth* +; and then saie; Holie trinitie punish him that hath wrought this mischiefe, & take it away by thy great justice, *Eson* + *elion* + *emaris, ales, age*: and strike the carpet [carpets were used as table coverings in Scot's day] with your wand. (Scot 1973: 219; from Weyer: 381)

The following charms were found among others in Bodl. e Mus. 173 (ca. 1600). I have not kept the editor's very careful editorial conventions in this example, as they are quite complex and conflict with those used elsewhere in this book.

> *To spoyle a theefe or witch or any other enemie and to be delyuered from the evell.*
> Q *Ante solis ortum* [Before the rising of the sun]. I gether the boughe of this sommers growth in the name of such a one **N.** when you haue gathered the wande then cover the table and say + In nomine patris + et filii + et spiritus sancti + Amen. [In the name of the Father and of the Son and of the Holy Spirit. Amen] thrice. And so strikinge vpon the carpet saye as followeth. *droche. myrocke.*

esenaroth. + betu + baroch + Ass + maaroth + and then say holy trinitie punnish him that hath wrought this mischeefe and tak yt away by thy great Iustice *Eson + Elyon + Emaris + Ales + Age +* and strike the carpitt with the wande

To make a witch confesse her evell before you
Take a lambe skyn made in parchment and make therin 2 images, one of a man and another of a woman and make them on the satturday morninge at the sonne rysinge and vse them in this manner, Take a bodkyn or a nayle and look in what place you would haue them hurt In that place prick them and doe so twyce or thrice a day and the partye that you shall vse so shall never take rest nor sleepe untill she hath seene you and requeired pardon at your hands. In prickinge say as heareafter followeth I compel and constrayne thee thou wicked person or you wicked persons which haue commytted and done this wicked and devilish act, by the true god, by the lyvinge god and by the holy god that thou nor you haue no power to withstand or resist any callinge but with all hast and speed possible without delay or tarrieng thou come vnto me and confesse thy naughtye and wicked deeds which thou hast done in the name of god. And also I coniure and constrayne thee to come by all the holy names of god and especiallye by thes *Semurhamephoras + Agla + Adonay + Anabona + panton + Craton + Agyos + Eskyros + Athanatos + messyas + Sother + Alpha + et Omega + Emanuel + Sabaoth + vnigenitus + Via + Vita + homo + Vsyon + principia + Cormogenitus + Sapentia + Consolator + Adiuvator + primus et novissimus + El + Elemay + on + Tetragramaton +* and by the holy name Ihesus at which name all things both in heaven in earth and also in hell doe bowe [*Philippians 2:10*] / And by the holy virgine marye mother of our lord Ihesus christ. And by St John Baptist which was the foreronnere of our lord Ihesus Christ and by the golden girdle which St John sawe gyrte about the loynes of our lord [*Revelation 1:13*] and by the two edged sword that proceeded out of the mouth of god, [*Revelation 2:16*] and by all that god is able to doe and by all the powers in heaven, in earth, and under the earth

I adiure you by the 7. planets and 12. sygnes, and by all that you be subiect vnto, and by all the names of Angels, and especially of thes *Michaell + Gabryell + Raphaell + Basquiel + Samael + Anael + Capael + Carafax + Wiel +* and by all things that god hath made to the honour and glory of his name that thou or you which haue done this wicked and develish deed haue no power to resist nor withstand my callinge but without all delaye or tarienge to come speedelye in all hast possible in payne or vnder payne of eternall damnation from worse payne to worse In the name of the father, the sonne, and the holy ghost Amen. (Klaassen 2011: 9-10)

Counter charmes against these and all other witchcrafts, in the saieng also whereof witches are vexed, &c.
ERuctavit cor meum verbum bonum, dicam cuncta opera mea regi. ◊ Otherwise: *Domine labia, mea aperies, & os meum annunciabit veritatem.* ◊ Otherwise: *Contere brachia iniqui rei, & lingua maligna subvertetur.* (Scot 1973: 211)

A prettie charme or conclusion for one possessed.
The possessed bodie must go upon his or hir knees to the church, how farre so ever it be off from their lodging; and so must creepe without going out of the waie, being the common high waie, in that sort, how fowle and durtie soever the same be; or whatsoever lie in the waie, not shunning anie thing whatsoever, / untill he come to the church, where he must heare masse devoutlie, and then followeth recoverie. (Memorandum that hearing of masse be in no case omitted, quoth Nota.) (Scot 1973: 199)

Another
There must be commended to some poore begger the saieng of five *Pater nosters*, and five *Aves*; the first to be said in the name of the partie possessed, or bewitched: for that Christ was led into the garden; secondlie, for that Christ did sweat both water and bloud; thirdlie, for that Christ was condemned; fourthlie, for that he was crucified guiltlesse; and fiftlie, for that he suffered to take awaie our sinnes. Then must the sicke bodie heare masse eight daies together, standing in the place where the gospell is said, and must mingle holie water with his meate and his drinke, and holie salt also must be a portion of the mixture. (Scot 1973: 199)

Another
The sicke man must fast three daies, and then he with his parents must come to church, upon an embering fridaie [the Ember Days – a Wednesday, Friday, and Saturday on a quarterly basis – were particular potent times for witchcraft], and must heare the masse for that daie appointed, and so likewise the saturdaie and sundaie following. And the preest must read upon the sicke mans head, that gospell which is read in September, and in grape harvest, after the feast of holie crosse *In diebus quatuor temporum*, in ember daies: then let him write it and carrie it aboute his necke, and he shall be cured. (Scot 1973: 199-200)

A charme to drive away spirits that haunt a house.
Hang in everie of the four corners of your house this sentence written upon virgin parchment; *Omnis Spiritus laudet Dominum: Mosen habent & prophetas:Exsurgat Deus et dissipentur inimicie jus.* (Scot 1973: 199).

The same charm was recommended in a later derivative source:

Charm to drive away Spirits that Haunt a house,
Hang on the four corners of the house, these sentences written upon virgin parchment.
Omnis Spiritus laudet Dominum.—PSALM 150V
Mosen habent & prophetas.—LUKE 16.
Exsurgat Deus,& dissipentur inimiciejus.—PSALM 64 [67]
N. B. This is called the PARACELSIAN Charm. (*Witchcraft Detected* 1824: 43)

Yf one be bewytched of any, put quycksyluer into a quyll and stoppe it, or els into a hollowe Nut shel, inclosed fast with waxe: and laye the same vnder the threshold of the doore where he enters into the house or Chamber. *Iohannes Weckerus* (Lupton 1586: 163)

This charm was originally from Johann Jacob Wecker's *De Secretis Libri XVII* (Basel: 1582), which was translated into English by Dr. Read in 1661 as *Eighteen Books of the Secrets of Art & Nature*. The charm was part of a section on bewitchment for love, and other cures such as the following were cited:

For those that are enchanted and bewitched by Women.
Put of the excrements of the womans belly in the morning, some part into the right sock of him that is bewitched, and so soon as he smels the stink of it, the witchcraft is ended. Alexius. (Wecker 1661: 35)

The charms and spells in Arthur Gauntlet's manuscript include several to protect a person from witchcraft:

90 Qui habitat in adiutori [Psalm 90:1 "He that dwelleth in the aid (of the most high)]
Scribe hunc Psalm in carta cum sanguine colombae, & suffumum cum ligno aloes et rosis siccis & conservabitor contra demonis et eoy potestates et ferras et Amabo visu et ab omni timori si in evis nocte et podest multum poter timorem si portantur super se: ["Write this psalm on papyrus/paper with the blood of a pigeon & fumigate with lignum aloes and dried rose & you will be protected against demons and their powers and their wild and evil appearance even if {they are}unavoidable at night and you will go forth more powerful against much that is feared if this is carried with one."] (Rankine 2011: 264)

Against witchcraft:~:
Take Oil of Pompilion [poplar bud oil] ii {2} d{rams} But first make the parties water Seeth in a pan Then put in the oil Then take an Iron Red hot and put it into the water Saying In the name of the Father and of the Son And of the Holy Ghost Avoid all witches and wicked persons from this party from this time forth forevermore. And say it iii {3} times. But in any case shut the doors and windows And let nobody come in while that you be about your business, And keep the party so

close that nothing may see her while you be about your business. And let her say her prayers. (Rankine 2011: 299)

William Lilly included a section of "remedies" against witchcraft in his *Christian Astrology* (1647), following instructions for determining astrologically "If one be Bewitched or not":

NATURALL *Remedies* FOR WITCHCRAFT.

Having by the Figure discovered and described the Party, either by the Planet who is Lord of the 12th, or posited in the 12th, and doth behold the Lord of the ascendant with a malicious aspect, you must let one / Watch the party suspected, when they goe home to their owne house, and presently after, before any body goe into the house after him or her, let one pull a handfull of the Thatch. Or a Tile that is over the Door: and if it be a Tile, make a good fire and heat it red hot therein, setting a Trevet over it, then take the parties water, if it be a man woman, or child, and poure it upon the red hot Tile in the fire, and make it extremely hot, turning it ever and anon, and let no body come into the house in the mean time.

If they be Cattle that are bewitched, take some of the Haire of every one of them, and mix the Haire in faire water, or wet it well, and then lay it under the Tile, the Trevet standing over the Tile: make a lusty fire, turne your Tile upon the Haire, and stir up the Haire ever and anon: after you have done this by the space of a quarter of an hour, let the fire alone, and when the ashes are cold, bury them in the ground towards that quarter of heaven where the suspected Witch lives.

If the Witch live where there is no Tile but Thatch, then take a great handfull thereof, and wet it with the parties water, or else in common water mixed with some salt, then lay it in the fire, so that it may molter and smother by degrees and in a long time, setting a Trevet over it.

Or else take two new Horse-shooes, heat them red hot, and naile one of them on the Threshold of the Door, but quench the other in Urine of the party so Bewitched; then set the Urine over the fire, and put the Horse-shooe in it, setting a Trevet over the Pipkin or Pan wherein the Urine is; make the Urine boyle, with a little salt put into it, and three Horse-nails untill it's almost consumed, viz. the Urine; what is not boyled fully away poure into the fire: keep your Horse-shooe and nails in a clean cloth or paper, and use the same manner three severall times; the operation would be farre more effectual, if you doe these things at the very change or full Moon, or at the very hour of the first or second quarter thereof. If they be Cattle bewitched, you must mix the Haire of their Tailes with the Thatch, and moysten them, being well bound together, and so let them be a long time in the fire consuming. These are naturall experiments, and work by sympathy, as I have found by severall experiments: I could prescribe many more, *Multa creduntur raitione experimentiæ, non quod vientur vere vi rationis. (Lilly 1985: 465-466).*

We must now jump forward in time for further anti-witch examples, as this particular danger is not as often addressed *in print* after the late 17th century, although the fear of witchcraft remained widespread among the general population, as folklorists would discover a century later. The first two examples, however, come from John George Hohman's *Long Lost Friend* (1863), which was a fully operational manual of healing and magic.

7. For Slander or Witchcraft.

Art thou slandered, or thy head, flesh, limb, send it back home to the false tongues, thus: ††† Take off the shirt, and put it on wrong side out, put the two thumbs at the pit of the stomach, and carry them around under the ribs as far as to the hips. Do this three times, carefully and devoutly. (Brown 1904: 108)

119. Against Witches — for Beasts Write it one Stall — for Human
Beings Write it on the Bedsteads.

Trotter head, I pray thee my house and my Court, I pray then my horse-and-cow-stall, I pray thee my bedstead, that thou shed not thy consolations on me; be they on another house till thou goest over all mountains, countest all the sticks in the hedges and goest over all waters. So come the happy day again to my house, in the name of the Father and of the Son and the Holy Ghost. Amen. (Brown 1904: 126)

To drive away Ghosts, or Spirits that haunt a house.
This is a curious secret, and I think never before made public, or privately practised but by a few. To do this, take the wool that grows between the two eyes of a black sheep, burnt to powder, and after it has been steeped a night and a day in man's urine, mix this with the powder of nightshade, or wake Robin, an herb so called, boil them in a quarter of a pint of Aqua Vitæ; sprinkle the walls of the chamber you fancy is haunted with it, and no disturbance will happen if you turn your face when you go to repose to the eastward, when in bed, and say your prayers. (*Witchcraft Detected* 1824: 50)

This to be carried about one for the prevention of Witchcraft, &c.
These misfortunes generally happen under the power of the moon, who (as ancients hold) is the favourer of magic, or enchantment, take the opposite planet to her in allaying her force this way, which is Jupiter, write his character thus ♃ on a piece of parchment, and add to it the following characters that are the signs of the Zodiack, viz. ♍ ♎ ♏ and this number, 1, 3, 2, 5, 7, 1—1, 1—7, 1—4th; after this, set down the number of the figurative letters in your name make, wrap it up in as small a compass as you can, and sowing it up in a piece of black silk that has been steeped in juice of vervine, hang it about your neck when the moon changes, and you will be sure from any danger of this nature if you lead a good life. (*Witchcraft Detected* 1824: 51)

To help a person under an ill tongue, and make the witch appear, or the ill effect cease.
Cut off some of the party's hair, just at the nape of the neck, clip it small and burn it to powder in salarmoniack, write the party's name you suspect backwards, and put the paper dipt in AquaVitæ into the other two, then set it over a gentle fire; let the party afflicted, sit by it, and diligently watch it, that it run not over to catch flame, speaking no word whatsoever noise is heard, but take notice of what voice or roaring is heard in the chimney, or any part of the room, and then write how often you hear it, and fix before each writing this character, ☽ and if the party who afflicts you appears not visible, tho' you may know the voice, repeat it again, and if she appear in no visible shape, it may make her charm important, and give relief to the afflicted party. (*Witchcraft Detected* 1824: 52)

To find out a Witch, and prevent and cure mischief wrought by charms or witchcraft.
One principal way is, to nail a horse-shoe at the inside of the outermost threshold of your house, and so you shall be sure no witch shall have power to enter thereinto. And if you mark it, you shall find that rule observed in many country houses. Otherwise, let this triumphant title be written crossways in every corner of the house thus: Jesus ✠ Nasarenus ✠ Rex ✠ Judreorum ✠. Memorandum. You may join herewithall the name of the Virgin Mary, or of the four Evangelists; or *Verbum caro factum est*. Otherwise, in some countries they nail a wolf's head to the door. Otherwise, they hang scilla (which is a root, or rather in this place garlic) in the roof of the house, for to keep away witches and spirits; and so they do Alicium [*alyssum*] also. Otherwise, a perfume made of the gall of a black dog, and his blood besmeared on the posts and walls of the house, driveth out of the doors both devils and witches. Otherwise, the house where herba betonica is sown, is free from all mischief. Otherwise, it is not unknown, that the Romish church allowed and used the smoke of sulphur to drive spirits out of their houses, as they did frankincense and water hallowed. Otherwise, Apuleius saith that Mercury gave to Ulysses, when he came near to the Inchantress Circe, an herb called verbascum, which, in English is called mullein, or tapsus barbatus, or longwort, and that preserved him from the enchantments. Otherwise, Pliny and Homer both do say, that the herb called moly, is excellent against enchantments. (*Witchcraft Detected* 1824: 62)

To cite a Witch. Take an earthen pot, not glazed, yarn spun by a girl not yet seven years old. Put the water of the bewitched animal into the pot, then take the egg of a black hen and some of the yarn and move the latter three times round the egg, and ejaculate in the three devils' name; after this put the egg into the water of the pot, seal the lid of the vessel tightly that no fumes may ooze therefrom, but observe that the head of the lid is below. "While setting the pot upon the fire, pronounce the following: Lucifer, devil summon the sorcerer before the witch or me, in the three devils' name. (*Albertus Magnus* n d.: 68)

For Sorcery. Take elmwood on a Good-Friday, cut the same while calling the holiest names. Cut chips of this wood from one to two inches in length. Cut upon them, in the three holiest names, three crosses, t t t Wherever such a slip is placed, all sorcery will be banished. (*Albertus Magnus n d.*: 69)

TO DESTROY THE POWER OF A WITCH. TAKE three small-necked stone jars: place in each the liver of a frog stuck full of new pins, and the heart of a toad stuck full of thorns from the holy thorn bush. Cork and seal each jar. Bury in three different churchyard paths seven inches from the surface and seven feet from the porch. While in the act of burying each jar repeat the Lord's prayer backwards.

As the hearts and livers decay so will the witch's power vanish. After performing this ceremony no witch can have any power over the operator. (Hewett 1900: 74)

TO FRUSTRATE THE POWER OF THE BLACK WITCH. TAKE a cast horse shoe, nail it over the front door, points upwards. While nailing it up chant in monotone the following:
So as the fire do melt the wax
And wind blows smoke away,
So in the presence of the Lord
The wicked shall decay,
The wicked shall decay. – Amen. (Hewett 1900: 68)

I Naphumphytor Tetragramatan ☉ ☽ ♂ ☿ ♃ ♀ ♄ and desire you all by your powers to Gard A.B. from all evil spirits and from all bad washers, faires, and night-mare, and from all desorders, fits, cramp, and all other desorders, and give him good elth and store of wealth all his days.—O Lord, Amen. Charm on a small piece of paper in a canvas bag to be worn, owned by a farmer from Pendle Gorest ca. 1830-40.

Another "for the house" "Omnes spiritu laudet domnum moson habent dusot prapheates exurgrat dispentur inimicus" [the end of psalm 68]. (Weeks 1910: 105-06)

Against Thieves and Theft:

Next to witchcraft, theft was a paramount concern and solving these crimes was an important part of the Cunning Folk's repertoire. The detection of thieves and the return of stolen property was then as now a serious problem (especially as most people had very few possessions compared with today, and most of those vital to their well-being). At a time when one's clothes and kitchen equipment might require the budgetary equivalent of an automobile or 60-inch TV, the loss of a shift, shirt or cooking pot could be economically devastating. Although some unscrupulous Cunning Folk were guilty of fraudulent attempts to milk the desperate victims of theft, in many cases others were able to solve the crime through their knowledge of local events and reputations, or by intimidating the thieves with the threat of preternatural retribution. At any rate, their success rate may have been as good or better than that of the local constable (or most police forces today).

> The eye of Abraham. The noble experiment of Troy. To knowe who they be that have stolen anything out of your house, and to make them confesse the same. Take argentum vivum and the white of an egge and mingle them together and make an eye upon a wall in this manner then call in all them that thou suspectest & tell them behold the eye, & his or her eye that stole the thing will water, if they will not confess take a copper key, & put it on the eye of the wall & strike upon it sayinge hare et jures vales, and the party that is guilty shall cry out myne eye myne eye. Probat: est. (Briggs 1953: 451)

A popish periapt or charme, which must never be said, but carried about one, against theeves.
I doo go, and I doo come unto you with the love of God, with the humilitie of Christ, with the holines of our blessed ladie, with the faith of Abraham, with the justice of Isaac, with the vertue of David, with the might of Peter, with the constancie of Paule, with the word of God, with the

authoritie of Gregorie, with the praier of Clement, with the floud of Jordan, _p _p p c g e g a q q est p t 1 ka b g 1 k 2 a x t g t b am g 2 4 2 1 q; p x c g k q a 9 9 p o q q r. Oh onelie Father + oh onlie lord + And Jesus + passing through the middest of them + went + In the name of the Father + and of the Sonne + and of the Holie-ghost +. (Scot 1973: 188)

Robert Allen's magical notes (1552) [Ms. Harl. 424, f.1]
No. 1 on parchment
Iu a mañ haue stolen any thyñg of thyne.
Take & wryte in pchment. ✠ Agios ✠ Agios ✠ Agios ✠ Crux Crux Crux Sptiritus s'cus Spritus s'cus spiritus be wt the suunt of God. & putt yt ouer thy hed, & in the same nyght thow shalt knowe wh yt ys.
No. 2. On another piece of parchment.
If any man of woman haue doñ the thefte.
Take & wryte the names in vyrgen waxe. ✠ Agios ✠ Agios ✠ Agios ✠. & holde yt in thy left hand vnder thy ryght eyre, & lay the to slepe, and thow shalt haue a vysyon & knowledge who hathe thy thyng. (Nichols 1859: 326)
No. 4. On paper.
And yff thow weylt wette wether a man tell ye a false talle or a trewe, take the letters of hes name & of hes surname & of that daye, & putto all the nowmbere xxx. & than depart alle that holle nowmbere be xxvti , & yf ther leve even nowmbere at the laste ende, yt ys falss that he tellett, and yff yt be oode yt ys trwe. (Nichols 1859: 327)

From MS. Bod. E Mus. 243:

f. 7. *To know yf one be bewitched or no*
Looke well in ther eyes & yf you can deserne your picture [reflection] in them, they are not bewitched, et contra.

f. 4. *Bewitched*
Yf any 3 byters have thee forbidden
Wth wicked tongue or with wicked thought
or wth wicked eyes all ye most, I praye /
god be thy boote. In ye name of the father, & of the Sonne & of ye holy ghost God yt set vertue betweene water and lande, be thy helpe & succour with this prayer yt I can, for Jesus sake & St Charitie Amen. Say this 9 tymes over, & at every third tyme say a pater noster, and Ave, & a creede. (Briggs 1962: 263)

For theft or **anything thou desirest**. Say the iiiith {4th} Psalm invocarem &c And when you come to the verse, be angry and sin not, Say it thrice Afterwards say Kyrilayson Christilayson Kyrilayson Our father &c Ave maria &c Credo &c Then write their Greek names in parchment + Alga + Cad + Iskiros + Mediator + Elyson + Panton + Craton + Cisas In the name of + Thou + In the name of + Jesus + Christ + the life eternal
Then roll them in virgin wax and put it under your head and Sleep and you shall see whatsoever you desire **+ finis + Amen + fiat** (Rankine 2011: 288)

The right Spell for thieves
In the name of the father and of the son and of the holy ghost Amen,
Defend this my house ground and goods this night and all other times from all thieves Witches also spirits Elves and all other evils and I charge thee thou spirit that hast the charge especial of open as of secret things and by the virtue of the omnipotent power of Almighty god maker of heaven & earth and Creator of all mortal flesh and of all other things visible and invisible and I charge thou spirit by all the holy names of God the most highest + Elo Ely Sabaoth Adona{y} Saday Tetragrammaton Alpha et Omega and by all the names of god that may be spoken or not spoken also I remind thee thou spirit Which are called Banalum by all the aforesaid naming & by the virtue and power of them that if any thief or thieves hitherwards to me within this place where I go with my goods belonging to me or else also I charge thee Banalo [sic] by the great virtue and power of

almighty God and of the Virgin mary Gods mother and by all the powers of St. Peter and St. Paul and by all the holy company in heaven and by the Angels and ArchAngels that if any thief or thieves hitherwards come they may be struck down both blind and that still stand to or they are kept as siff as any staff. (Rankine 2011: 298)

A Nightspell to catch Thieves
This following will drive away any Evil Spirit that use to haunt any house or place, and having it about one, no Thief can do you any harm; & being used as directed, it is a certain way, that if a Thief come to rob a Garden, Orchard, or House, he cannot go till the Sun riseth.
Having in every four corners of the House this sentence written upon Virgin Parchment.
Omnes Spiritus laudet Dominum, mosem habet &
prophitas exarget Deus dissipenter..................
Inimicus..
But if for a Garden or Orchard, it must be placed at the four corners thereof, and if to keep one from Thieves, when one rideth on the Road, let him have it always about him, and fear none but God only.
The Author saith it will do many more pretty knacks, as keeping a Thief till the Sun rising and the like. (*Groatsworth* 1670: 11-12)

How to find out a Thief.
PUT down the minute when the goods were stolen, and then planets ruling the day. This done, put down the following characters on a fair piece of parchment or paper, Σ (-) § || ├ ‡ ¶ Ǝ [note: the original has two capital serif "M" type pieces on their sides bracketing the other figures, as indicated here by the Σ and the Ǝ] —And if you hear no news of the thief in 24 hours, as ten to one you will, prick the parchment full of holes, and hang up the chimney that the fire may scorch it, and the Thief will be so restless that he will bring or send back the goods. (*High German* 1810: 22)

To prevent being robbed on the road.
CONSIDER under what planet you set out : the Moon ruling on Monday, shews inconstancy; Mars, Tuesday, Violence, Mercury Wednesday, Fraud, Saturn, Saturday Malice; but the Sun, Jupiter, and Venus ruling Sunday, Thursday, and Friday, being friendly planets, shews success. But any days are proper by the following caution
Gather Vertune [*Verbena officinalis*] in its proper season being before noon, hang it up to dry; then powder it, keeping it in Agnus Castus. [*Vitex agnus-castus*] /23 This temporized in proper manner, will powerfully influence over travellers at all seasons, and they may go safe and free from danger, keeping their minds stayed on good things. (*High German* 1810: 22-23)

78. To Hold a Thief Fixed, that He Cannot Move. It is the
Best Charm for this Purpose in the Book.
O Peter, O Peter! Take from God the power; may I find — what I would bind — with the band, of Jesus' hand — that robbers all, great and small — That none can go no step more, neither backwards nor before — till I then with my eyes perceive, till I then with my tongue releave — till first they count me every stone, twixt heaven and earth, and drop of rain — each leaf of tree and blade of grass; this pray I to my foe for Mass. †††
Say the Creed and the Paternoster. To compel him to stand, say this thrice. If the thief is to be permitted to win, the sun must not shine on him before you loose him. This loosing is done in two forms. The first is: bid him in the name of St. John to go forth. The second is this: with the words with which you (or *those*, if only *one*, or a woman) were stopt, you are loosed. (Brown 1904: 118)

137. To Curse a Thief to Make Him Stand.
This saw must be said on Thursday, early in the morning, before sunrise, under the open sky. So grant God the Father, Son and Holy Ghost. Amen. Full three and thirty angels by one another stand. They come with Mary to comfort her. Then said the dear, holy Daniel: Sad, dear, lady I see thieves, go which wish thy precious child to steal; that can I not from thee conceal. Then said our dear lady St. Peter: / Bind, St. Peter, bind. Then said St. Peter: I have bound with a band, with Christ his own

hand, as my thieves are bound with Christ's own hands, if they would steal anything of mine, in the house, in the chest, in the meadow and acre, in wood or field, in tree, and plant, and garden, or wherever they would steal anything of mine. Our dear lady then said: Steal who will, but if he steal, he shall stand as a bock [goat], and stand as a block; and count all the stones that on the earth lie, and count all the stars as they stand in the sky. So gave I thee praise and demanded of thee for every spirit, that every thief may know a master, by St. Daniel, to bring the goods of earth, to one's burden, to one's hearth; and thy face must not be towards the place, that my eyes may not see thee and my fleshly tongue may not praise thee. This demand I of thee holy Virgin Mary. Mother of God, by the power and might, when he created heaven and earth, by the angelic host and by all God's holy ones, in the name of God the Father, God the Son, and God the Holy Ghost. Amen. When you would lift the bann, bid him go in the name of St. John. (Brown 1904: 129-130)

138. Another Similar.

Ye thieves, I conjure you to obey, even to the cross, and stand with me, and go not from my sight, in the name of the holy Trinity, I command you by the power of God and the humanity of Jesus Christ, that ye go not from my sight, ††† as Jesus the Lord stood in Jordan, when St. John baptized him. After this, I command you, horse and man, that you stand to go not from my sight, as Christ the Lord stood when they nailed him to the cross, and he destroyed the power of the old-father of hell. Ye thieves, I bind you with bonds, as Christ the Lord has bound Hell, so are ye bound; ††† with the words with which they are fixed, they are also loosed. (Brown 1904: 130)

141. To Cause the Thief to Return Stolen Goods.

Early in the morning, before sunrise, go to a birch-tree, take with you three nails out of a hearse or three horse-shoe nails that have / never been used; hold up the nails towards the rising sun and say: Oh Thief, I bind thee by the first nail which I make to pierce thee in the brow and brain, that thou return the stolen goods to their former place; to the man and place whence thou stealest them, else it shall be as sad to thee as it was to the disciple Judas when he betrayed Jesus. The second nail which I make to pierce thy lungs and liver, that thou return the stolen goods to their former place; to the man and the place whence thou hast stolen them, else it shall be as sad to thee as it was to Pilate in the pains of hell. The third nail which I make to pierce thy foot, thou thief, that thou must return the stolen goods to their former place, whence thou hast stolen them. Oh thief, I bind thee and bring thee by the sacred three nails which pierced Christ through his hands and feet, that thou must return the stolen goods to their former place, whence thou hast stolen them. ††† (Brown 1904: 130-131)

185. To Cause the Return of Stolen Goods.

Go out early in the morning before sunrise, to a juniper-bush and bend it towards the sun with the left hand and say: Juniper-bush, I make you bow and stoop till thief puts the stolen goods of N. N. to their place. Then take a stone, lay it on the bush and under the stone on the bush, place the skull of a malefactor †††. You must take care when the thief has returned the stolen goods, to take the stone off the bush, and lay it where and as it was and release the bush. (Brown 1904: 141)

Charms to find out a Thief.
THE means how to find out a thief, are these. Turn your face to the east, and make a cross upon crystal with oil olive, and under the cross write two words, "SAINT HELEN."
Then a child that is innocent, and a chaste virgin, born in true wedlock, and not base begotten, of the age of ten years, must take the crystal in her hand ; and behind her back, kneeling on thy knees, you must devoutly and reverently say over this prayer thrice: "I beseech thee, my Lady St. Helen, mother of King Constantine, which didst find the cross whereupon Christ died ; by that holy devotion and invention of the cross, and by the same cross, and by the joy which thou conceivedst at the findng thereof, and by the love which thou bearest to thy son Constantine, and by the great goodness which thou dost always use; that thou shew me in this crystal (i. e. looking-glass) whatsoever I ask, or desire to know, Amen."
And when the child seeth the angel in the crystal, demand what you will, and the angel will make answer thereunto. Mem. That this be done just as the sun is rising, when the weather is fair and clear. / (*Witchcraft Detected* 1824: 41)

Another way to find out a Thief that hath stolen any thing from you.
Go to the sea side and gather as many peebles is you suspect persons for that matter; carry home the stones and throw them into the fire, and bury them under the threshold where the parties suspeced are likely to come over. There let them lie three days, and then before sun rising take them away. Then set a porringer full of water in a circle, wherein must be made crosses every way, as as [sic] many as can stand in it; upon the which must be written: Christ overcometh, Christ reigneth, Christ commandeth. The porringer also must be signed with a cross. Then each stone must be thrown into the water in the name of the suspected. And when you put in the stone of him that is guilty, the stone will make the water boil as though glowing iron were put thereinto. (*Witchcraft Detected* 1824: 41)

How to shew the Thief in a Glass that hath stolen any thing from you.
Take a glass vial full of holy-water, and set it upon a linen cloth, which hath been purified, both by washing and sacrifice, &c. On the mouth of the vial or urinal, two olive-leaves must be laid across, and these words pronounced over it, by a child; (to wit thus,) "*Angele bone, angele candide per tuam sanctitatem, meamq; virginitatem, ostend mihi furem:* now repeat three paternosters, three aves, and betwixt each of them make a cross with the nail of the thumb upon the mouth of the vial; and then shall be seen angels ascending and descending as it were motes in the sun beams. The thief all this while shall suffer great torment, and his face shall be seen plainly. (*Witchcraft Detected* 1824: 42)

To safeguard for an orchard, park, warran, or field, to take a Thief, &c.
The several places being guarded by one and the same planet, not to be too tedious to you, one and the same thing will indifferently serve to secure any / of them from thieves that come to make robbery or depredation, whether it be for the fruits of the earth or any kind of cattle, or to steal away timber in fields or woods; to make which, take the following direction, have a piece of curious clean parchment, made of a sleek skin, cut it with five points or corners in the form of a star, but so large, that you may write in the centre of it, what is to be written, viz. ♊ ♁ ♊♊, the characters of the celestial signs governing these affairs, add the character of the planet for the day, as before directed, and suppose it to be Tuesday, Mars that govern that day has this character, which set down thus ♂, and this number, 1, 7, 11, 12, 1—2, 1—8th, close it up with virgin's wax, as I should have told you, (you ought to have done with the former, and sprinkle it with the juice of fumitory, and place the same if in a garden in the hole of a wall;) if in a forest, park, or wood, in the hole of a tree, having laid it before in goose tansey; and so whatever any thief takes in these several grounds, he shall not be able to carry off till the sun-rising; but then if not watched he may do it. (*Witchcraft Detected* 1824: 49-50)

To prevent being robbed on the road, or meeting with any bad accident.
Consider in this case, what planet you set out under, ruling as to the day and its influence : the moon ruling Monday, denotes inconstancy in success: Mars Tuesday, violence: Mercury on Wednesday, deceit and fraud: Saturn on Saturday, envy and malignity: but the Sun, Jupiter and Venus, governing Sunday, Thursday, and Friday, are very friendly planets, promising success. However, either days are proper enough, with the cautions I shall give you hereafter; and this is as followeth, to prosper and prevent ill fortune in being robbed, falling from your horse, or sick, falling into any pit, water or the like.
Now note, that the malignant planets are friendly to others, and befriended of them again; Sol is friendly to Jupiter and Venus; Luna to Jupiter, / Venus and Saturn; Mars is friendly to Venus; Mercury is friendly to Jupiter, Venus, and Saturn; Jupiter is friendly to Sol, Luna, Mercury, Venus, Saturn; Venus is friendly to Sol, Luna, Mars, Mercury and Jupiter; Saturn is friendly to Jupiter, Sol, and Luna; and these are temporizing to hinder the malignity of each other, therefore the promises considered, now as to what you are to put in practice for your security.
Gather vervine, an herb so called, in the new of the moon, hang it up in the chimney to dry, then powder it, and steep it in the water of agnus custus, then dry it again, and reduce it to fine powder; these temporise with the planets Venus and Mercury which are so powerful in their influence for the protection of travellers: put this powder into a hollow ring, of any kind of mettle, and have these

characters engraved on the inside of it, ♀ ☿ ♄ then you may go or ride safe without danger of any violence keeping your mind on good things. (*Witchcraft Detected* 1824: 54-55)

To find, out a thief, and make him or her bring back the goods stolen.
You must set down the day, hour, and minute if you can, when the goods were stolen, and the name of the planet ruling the day, as I have before set down to direct you : this being done, set down the following characters, in a fair piece of parchment ☽ ☉ ♄ ✱ Λ Σ this done, turn round thrice, and if you hear no news in 44 hours of the thief, as ten to one you will, then prick the parchment full of holes, and hang it up in the chimney, where the heat / of the fire may a little scorch it, and the thief is held to be so restless in his mind, and tormented that he or she will discover the thief to be at ease, or bringing home your goods, throw them privately into your house, or some place appertaining to you. (*Witchcraft Detected* 1824: 55)

HERBS THAT ACT AS A CHARM AGAINST SPIRITS.
"There is an herb called corona regis (or rosemary); the house that is suffumigated therewith, noe devil nor spirit hath power over the same. *Piony* hath the same virtue."—(*Manuscript*.) ("Raphael" 1832:19)

To see Spirits.
"Take the juice of Dill, Vervaine, and St. John's gresse, (St. John's wart), and anoint your eyes for three days, and you shall see spirits visible'"—*Old MSS*. ("Raphael" 1832: 233)

A Spell against thieves, to be said three times while walking round the premises :—
In the name of the Father, Son, and Holy Ghost,
This house I bequeath round about,
And all my goods within and without,
In this yard or enclosed piece of land,
Unto Jesus Christ, that died on a tree,
The Father, Son, and Holy Ghost. All Three,
Thieves! Thieves! Thieves! By virtue of the Blessed Trinity.
That you stir not one foot from this place until the rising of the sun next morning with beams full clear. And this I charge you in the name of the Trinity; Jesus save me and mine from them and fetching. Amen. (Harland & Wilkinson 1867: 159).

A charm (unfortunately without the original "chart" or diagram) from the notebook of the celebrated Yorkshire cunning man, Timothy Crowther (1694-1761) who was the parish clerk for the town of Skipton, for "recovering things stolen by making a plate of wax."

"Take yᵉ Bigness of a man's hand in Wax & make thereof a Four-squar plate, & therein cut yᵉ names of them Four Spirits yᵗ yu will use in your operation with / thier carrecters, and within yᵉ midst this Name Sathan, & the other Four Spirits to be obedient, & within ye Names of the stoln goods and the owner's name and Sirname, and then say your conjuration Three times a day Three days togather, kneeling; and close ye carractures of yᵉ seven planits in yᵉ Wax {here comes the symbol for Mercury} Reigning at yᵉ time you begin your opperation, and Lay it in yᵉ ground and Kneel down and say your conjuration every Day till that yᵉ Thief or yᵉ goods do appear before you. Never Leave, for either one or yᵉ other will come unto that place. Yᵉ Figure of the plate must be made thus : {here comes a chart}. Then you may begin your conjuration, these sentences:—' In the name of God Almighty, maker of Heaven and earth: I conjure ye N : K: (Nameing ye Names of all the Spirits in yᵉ plate) wheresoever you be, that you come quickley and Fullfill my desire to bring this Thiefe or goods in this plate, with Posting speed, and hear confess his fault before he goe away, and that you bring them away with all Speed. And I hereby Conjure and Constraine you : N : R : by all the powers of Heaven and in the Name of the Father, Son, and of yᵉ Holy Ghost, and in ye Name of Jesus Christ the son of the Living God." (Dawson 1882: 392-393)

To compel a Thief to return the Stolen Property. Obtain a new earthen pot-with a cover, draw water from the under current of a stream while calling out the three holiest names. Fill the vessel one-third, take the same to your home, set it upon the fire, take a piece of bread from the lower crust of a loaf, stick three pins into the bread, boil all in the vessel, add a few dew nettles. Then say: Thief, male or female, bring my stolen articles back, whether thou art boy or girl; thief, if thou art woman or man, I compel thee, in the name. t t t (*Albertus Magnus n d.*: 20)

For Cunning Thieves, may they be ever so sly. Pronounce this grace every morning three times, over all thy possessions, with devotion.
Our dear mother in a garden came. Three angels comforted her there. The first is named St. Michael; the other, St. Gabriel; the third, St. Peter. Then spake Peter to our beloved Mary: I saw three thieves enter there. They intend to steal thy dear child and kill it. But the beloved mother Mary said: Peter, bind; St. Peter, bind; and Peter bound them with iron bands, with God's own hands, and with his holy five wounds, for this be with Gabriel, upon this day and night, and this entire year, and forever and all times, my possessions bound. Whoever attempts to steal therefrom, must stand still, like a stick, and see like a brick, and must stand quiet. He must go upward, that he cannot depart from hence until I permit him to proceed from thence. With my own tongue I must tell him this. This is my order and Gabriel's will, which now, by day and night, and all the year, for all times to come, will utter to every thief, for them to repent. For this may God his blessing lend. God the Father, God the Son, and God the Holy Spirit . Amen. (*Albertus Magnus n d.*: 31)

A particular Way to recover Stolen Goods.
Mark well whence the thief left and by which door; from it cut three pieces of wood while pronouncing the three most sacred names, take these scraps of wood to a wagon, but in a noiseless manner, take a wheel oft the wagon and insert the wood in the nave, again pronouncing the three holiest names, then drive the wheel backward and ejaculate: Thief, thief, return with the stolen article, thou shalt be compelled by the omniscience of God the Father, the Son and the Holy Spirit. God the Father calls thee back, God the Son turn thy footsteps that thou must return, God the Holy Spirit guide thee to retrace thy steps until thou again reachest this place. By dint of God's power thou must come back, by the wisdom of the Son of God thou shalt enjoy no peace nor rest till all the stolen things are returned to the rightful owner. By the grace of God the Holy Ghost, thou must run and leap, canst neither rest nor sleep till thou shalt arrive at that place where thou has committed the theft, God the Father bind thee, God the Son compel thee, God the Holy Ghost cause thee to return. The wheel, thou must not rapidly turn, or the soles of his feet may blister and burn, he will in pain and anguish cry, and ere you catch him, thus may die; Thou shalt come in the name of the Father, the Son and the Holy Spirit Thief, thou must come, t t t Thief thou must come. t t t If thou art mightier, thief, thief, thief, than God and the Holy Trinity, then stay where thou art. The ten commandments force thee to observe not to steal, hence thou must return, t t t Amen. (*Albertus Magnus n d.*: 37)

To Cause the Return of Stolen Property.
Take three pieces of bread, three pinches of salt and three pieces of hog's lard, make a strong flame, put all the articles upon this fire, and say the following words, while keeping alone:
I put bread, salt and lard for the thief upon the fire, for thy sin and temerity so dire. I place them upon thy lungs, liver and heart, that thou art troubled with terror and smart, a distress shall come over thee with dread as if thou wert to be smitten dead, all veins in thy body shall burst and break, and great havoc and trouble shall make, that thou shalt have no peace nor rest, till what thou hast stolen thou hast returned and brought all back from whence it were taken. Three times to recite and every time the three holiest names spoken. (*Albertus Magnus n d.*: 71)

A Spell against thieves, to be said three times while walking round the premises :—
In the name of the Father, Son, and Holy Ghost,
This house I bequeath round about,
And all my goods within and without,
In this yard or enclosed piece of land,

Unto Jesus Christ, that died on a tree,
The Father, Son, and Holy Ghost. All Three,
Thieves! Thieves! Thieves! By virtue of the Blessed Trinity.
That you stir not one foot from this place until the rising of the sun next morning with beams full clear. And this I charge you in the name of the Trinity; Jesus save me and mine from them and fetching. Amen.
Quoted from a note on "Spells" (by G.B.P. in the *Eastern Counties Collectanea*), by J. T. Varley, E. A. Handbook, 1885, p. 100. (Gurdon 1893: 159)

A CHARM WHICH PROTECTS FROM THIEVES AND ENEMIES.
SAY daily at sunrise:
In the power of God, I walk on my way
In the meekness of Christ, what thieves soe'er I meet
The Holy Ghost to-day shall me keep.
Whether I sit, or stand, walk or sleep,
The shining of the sun
Also the brightness of his beams, shall me help.
The faith of Isaac to-day shall me lead;
The sufferings of Jacob to-day be my speed.
The devotion of the holy Lamb thieves shall let,
The strength of Jesus's passion them beset,
The dread of death hold thieves low,
The wisdom of Solomon cause their overthrow.
The sufferings of Job set them in hold,
The chastity of Daniel let what they would.
The speech of Isaac their speech shall spill,
The languishing faith of Jerom let them of their will.
The flaming fires of hell to hit them, I bequeath,
The deepness of the deep sea, their hearts to grieve
The help of Heaven cause thieves to stand.
He that made the sun and moon bind them with his
hand So sure as St. Bartholomew bound the fiend,
With the hair of his beard. With these three sacred names of God known and unknown. Miser, Sue, Tetragrammaton, Christ Jesus! Amen. (Hewett 1900: 79-80)

General Apotropaic or Protective Charms:

The simplest sort of protection was a widely-popular combination of magical herbs – St. John's wort, dill, and vervain. These *fuga daemonum* (demon-repelling) plants might be carried in ligatures (little mojo-like bags) or hung in a house to deflect evil magic and misfortune. They were often picked at special times such as Midsummer's Day (the Feast of St. John – June 24, when St. John's wort is in bloom), or with a picking charm:

Hallowed be thou, Vervain,
For in the Mount of Calvary,
There thou wast first found.
Thou healedst our Saviour Jesus Christ,
And staunchedst his bleeding wound;
In the name of the Father, Son, and Holy Ghost,
I take thee from the ground.
"And so they pluck it up and wear it. Their prayers and traditions of this sort are infinite, and the ceremonies they use in their actions are nothing inferior to the Gentiles in number and strangeness. Which any man may easily observe that converseth with them." Quoted from John White. *The Way to the True Church*, London. 1624. (Harland & Wilkinson 1867: 113-114)

Many also use to weare vervein against blasts [evil strokes, including curses]; and when they gather it for this purpose, firste they crosse the herbe with their hand, and then they blesse it thus:
Hallowed be thou, Vervein,
As thou growest on the ground,
For in the Mount of Cavalry,
There thou wast first found,
Thou healest our Saviour Jesus Christ,
And staunchedest his bleeding wound;
In the name of the Father, the son, and the Holy Ghost,
I take thee from the ground. (*Choice Notes* 1859: 112)

Others were derived from classical sources, such as:

Herbarium from Dioskorides, etc.
The Croton oil plant. CLXXVI. [Castor Bean *Ricinus communis*]
For hail and rough weather, to turn them away, if thou havest in thy possession this wort, which is named ricinus, and which is not a native of England, or if thou hangest some seed of it in thine house, or have it or its seed in any place whatsoever, it turneth away the tempestuousness of hail, and if thou hangest its seed on a ship, to that degree wonderful it is, that it smootheth every tempest. This wort thou shalt take thus speaking, "Herba ricinus, precor uti adsis meis incantationibus, et avertas grandines, fulgora et omnes tempestates, per nomen omnipotentis dei qui te iussit nasci": that is, in our language, "Wort ricinus, I pray that thou be at mine songs, and that thou turn away hails and lightning bolts, and all tempests, through the name of Almighty God, who hight thee to be produced"; and thou shalt be clean when thou pluckest this herb. (*Leechdoms*, vol.I, p. 309-11)

PIMPERNEL.
According to a MS. on Magic, preserved in Chetham's Library, Manchester, "the herb pimpernel is good to prevent witchcraft, as Mother Bumby [from John Lyly's *Mother Bombie* (1694), a widely-popular image of a Wise Woman] doth affirm;" and the following lines must be used when it is gathered :—
Herb pimpernel I have thee found
Growing upon Christ Jesus' ground;
The same gift the Lord Jesus gave unto thee,
When He shed his blood upon the tree.
Arise up, pimpernel, and go with me,
And God bless me,
And all that shall wear thee. Amen.
Say this fifteen days together, twice a day; morning early fasting, and in the evening full.—*(MS. Ibid.)*
(Harland & Wilkinson 1867: 71-72)

A CHARM SUNG BY WITCHES WHILE GATHERING HERBS FOR MAGICAL PURPOSES.
Hail to thee, holy herb,
Growing on the ground,
All on Mount Calvary
First wast thou found.
Thou art good for many sores,
And healeth many a wound;
In the name of St. Jesu!
I take thee from the ground.
The muttering of this charm, while concocting
drugs or simples, balsams or elixirs, contributes
marvellously to their efficacy. (Hewett 1900: 81)

Other charms used when gathering herbs for protection in Scotland can be found in Carmichael's *Carmina Gadelica*:

AN EARR-THALMHAINN

BUAINIDH mi an earr reidh,
Gum bu treuinide mo bhas,
Gum bu bhlathaide mo bheuil,
Gum bu ceumaide mo chas;
Gum bu h-eilean mi air muir,
Gum bu carraig mi air tir,
Leonar liom gach duine,
    Cha leon duine mi.

THE YARROW

I WILL pluck the yarrow fair,
That more brave shall be my hand,
That more warm shall be my lips,
That more swift shall be my foot;
May I an island be at sea,
May I a rock be on land,
That I can afflict any man,
    No man can afflict me.
(Carmichael 1900: 94-95)

GARBHAG AN T-SLEIBH

GARBHAG an t-sleibh air mo shiubhal,
Chan eirich domh beud no pudhar;
Cha mharbh garmaisg, cha dearg iubhar mi,
Cha riab grianuisg no glaislig uidhir mi.

THE CLUB-MOSS

THE club-moss is on my person,
No harm nor mishap can me befall;
No sprite shall slay me, no arrow shall wound me,
No fay nor dun water-nymph shall tear me.
(Carmichael 1900: 116-117)

Other simple protections included "hol(e)y stones" (i.e., stones found with a natural hole through them), and horse shoes (which also had to be found by chance). The hole stones were threaded on a string and hung up around a house, while the horse shoe was nailed up over a doorway or fastened on the door sill. Iron, like silver, was reputed to be repugnant to spirits.

> "I have in my possession two witch stones, one of which was in actual use by an old woman, who gave it me from her door, by which it was hanging from a nail. She said it was her grandmother's, and that no witch could enter a house thus protected by a witch-stone. Such a stone must have a hole through it, and be found without being looked for, and, of course, the longer it is used the more esteemed it becomes. This stone is simply a three-cornered flint with a hole through it. The other is an oblong stone with a hole near one end, apparently bored out by some iron implement, much in shape like a bone label for a bunch of keys." J. A. Penny, Stixwould, Lincoln.[70]

> Then the rector [of Wispington, Lincolnshire] brought out a "witch-stone" from his treasure store to show us; this he found hanging on a cottage door and serving as a charm against all evil. It is merely a small flint with a / hole in the centre, through which hole was strung a piece of cord to hang it up with. A "witch-stone" hung up on, or over, the entrance door of a house is supposed to protect the inhabitants from all harm; in the same way do not some enlightened people nail a horse-shoe over their door "for good luck"? To ensure this "good-luck" I understand you must find a horse-shoe "accidentally on the road" without looking for it; to procure a "witch-stone" you must in like manner come upon a stone (of any kind) with a hole through the centre when you are not thinking about any such thing. (Hissey 1898: 397-398)

More elaborate protections involved both written charms and the use of magical materials.

The Epistle to Abgar

By tradition, Abgarus V of Edessa was supposed to have written a letter to Christ and received a reply, ca. 29 CE. This famous "pseudepigrapha" (mis-attributed text) was written rather later, and enjoyed a reputation as a protection against witchcraft and other threats. As von Dobschütz notes in his

---

[70] *Notes and Queries*, No. 125 May 19, 1894, p. 397.

article, "*Charms and Amulets (Christian)*", the custom of inscribing the "Epistle to Abgar" in houses survived in England even into the 18th century.

The Epistle to Abgar
"Abgar Ouchama to Jesus, the Good Physician Who has appeared in the country of Jerusalem, greeting:
"I have heard of Thee, and of Thy healing; that Thou dost not use medicines or roots, but by Thy word openest (the eyes) of the blind, makest the lame to walk, cleansest the lepers, makest the deaf to hear; how by Thy word (also) Thou healest (sick) spirits and those who are tormented with lunatic demons, and how, again, Thou raisest the dead to life. And, learning the wonders that Thou doest, it was borne in upon me that (of two things, one): either Thou hast come down from heaven, or else Thou art the Son of God, who bringest all these things to pass. Wherefore I write to Thee, and pray that thou wilt come to me, who adore Thee, and heal all the ill that I suffer, according to the faith I have in Thee. I also learn that the Jews murmur against Thee, and persecute Thee, that they seek to crucify Thee, and to destroy Thee. I possess but one small city, but it is beautiful, and large enough for us two to live in peace."

The *Doctrina* then continues:
When Jesus had received the letter, in the house of the high priest of the Jews, He said to Hannan, the secretary, "Go thou, and say to thy master, who hath sent thee to Me: 'Happy art thou who hast believed in Me, not having seen Me, for it is written of Me that those who shall see Me shall not believe in Me, and that those who shall not see Me shall believe in Me. As to that which thou hast written, that I should come to thee, (behold) all that for which I was sent here below is finished, and I ascend again to My Father who sent Me, and when I shall have ascended to Him I will send thee one of My disciples, who shall heal all thy sufferings, and shall give (thee) health again, and shall convert all who are with thee unto life eternal. And thy city shall be blessed forever, and the enemy shall never overcome it.'"
"Et salvus eris, sicut scriptuum: qui credit in me salvuserit, sive in domo tua sive in civitate tua sive in omni loco. Nemo inimicorum tuorum dominabit, et insidias diaboli ne timeas et carmina inimicorum tuorum distruenter et omnes inimici tui expellentur a te, sive a grandine sive a tontitruo non noceberis et ab omni periculo liberaberis. Sive in mare sive in terra sive in die sive in nocte sive in locis obscuris, si quis hanc epistolam secum habuerit securus ambulet in pace." (von Dobschütz 1913 v. III: 425)

The Powder of the Hermit Pelagius
Obtain as much as you might wish of the substances from the candles blessed at Candlemas, from Easter wax and incense, from herbs ground into powder on the feast of the Assumption, from pulverized Offertory bread blessed in the Lord's Supper, and from the powdered soil of the cemetery, adding to these holy water and salt! Put the powdery substances through a sieve until they are finely ground! Then place the mixture made from these powders and from the wax into warm water which has been blessed until all the constituents are combined as thoroughly as possible into a single mass! After this, standing above the result, proceed to utter the Lord's Prayer, the Ave Maria, and the Apostles' Creed.
The purpose of this complicated operation, we are told, is to obtain the crystallization of "tiny crosses" (*cruces parvulas*), which are then to be scattered, together with holy water, in the house, yard and stables.[71]

A General Protective Spell:
A charm found on a long strip of parchment inside the hollow 15th century enameled Ingleby Arncliffe Crucifix. Locations of the small "AGLA" square found at the end of the entry is indicated by asterisks:

---

[71] Brann 1999: 76, citing Trithemius' *Antipalus*, lib. II, cap. 3, pp. 326-27. Pelagius was Fernando of Cordova.

The ORIGINAL LATIN.

"✠* In nomne patris et filii et spiritus sancti. Amen. Conjuro vos elphes et demones et omnia genera fantasmatis, per patrem et filium et spiritum sanctum, et per sanctam Mariam matrem domini nostri Jesu Christi, et per omnes apostolos dei, et per omnes martires dei, et per omnes confessores dei, et per omnes virgines dei Jesu Christi, et viduas, et omnes electos dei, et per quatuor evangelista *(sic)* domini nostri Jesu Christi, Marcum, Matheum, Lucam, Joheannem *(sic)*, et per nacionem *(sic)* domini nostri Jesu Christi, et per passionem dei, et per mortem domini nostri Jesu Christi, et per descensionem dei ad inferos, et per resurrectionem domini nostri Jesu Christi, et per passionem *(sic, lege* ascensionem*)* domini nostri Jesu Christi ad celos, et per quatuor evangelistas domini nostri Jesu Christi, * *(sic)* Marcum, * Matheum * Lucam, * Johannem, * et per virtutem domini nostri Jesu Christi, et per magna nomina dei ✠A✠G✠L✠A✠ ON ✠ tetra ✠ Gromaton *(sic, lege* tetragrammaton*)* ✠ sabaoth ✠ adonai ✠ et omnia nomina,—ut non noceas *(sic, lege* noceatis*)* Huic famulo [famula *interlink* dei Adam osanna, nocte neque die, sed per misericordiam dei Jesu Christi maximam, adjuvante sancta Maria matrem *(sic)* domini nostri Jesu Christi, ab omnibus malis predictis et aliis requiescat in pace. Amen. ✠*. In nomine patris et filii et spiritus sancti. Amen, * et requiescunt in Domino suo [*requiescunt* interim.] requiescat iste isti *(sic)* famulus dei Jesu Christi Adam Osanna, adjuvante sancta Maria Matrem *(sic)* domini nostri Jesu Christi, ab omnibus malis predictis et aliis, Amen ✠ ***** Quinque [*supple* vulnera] domini nostri Jesu Christi, et sancte marie de osanna *(sic)*, sanctus dunstanus, sancte andrea *(sic)*, sanctus nicholaus, sancta Margareta, sancte petre, sancte paule, sancte mathea, sancte bartholomee, sancta [*supple* vulnera] domini nostri Jesu Christi, sancta brigida * Christus vincit * Christus regnat * et Christus inperat *(sic)** et Christus Adam Osanna ab omni malo defendat. Amen."

TRANSLATION.

"✠* In the name of the Father, and the Son, and the Holy Spirit. Amen. I conjure you, ye elves, and demons, and all kinds of apparition, by the Father, and the Son, and the Holy Spirit, and by Saint Mary, the mother of our Lord Jesus Christ, and by all the apostles of God, and by all the martyrs of God, and by all the confessors of God, and by all the virgins of God Jesus Christ, and the widows, and all the elect of God, and by the four evangelists of our Lord Jesus Christ, Mark, Matthew, Luke, John, and by the birth of our Lord Jesus Christ, and by the passion of God, and by the death of our Lord Jesus Christ, and by the descent of God to hell, and by the resurrection of our Lord Jesus Christ, and by the ascension of our Lord Jesus Christ to heaven, and by the four evangelists of our Lord Jesus Christ, * Mark, *Matthew, *Luke, **John, and by the virtue of our Lord Jesus Christ, and by the great names of God ✠A✠G✠L✠A✠ON ✠ tetra ✠ Gromaton (for *tetragrammatorn)*, ✠ Sabaoth, ✠Adonai, ✠ and all (his other) names, that you hurt not this servant of God, Adam Osanna, by night nor by day, but that, through the very great mercy of God Jesus Christ, by the help of Saint Mary, the mother of our Lord Jesus Christ, he may rest in peace from all the aforesaid and other evils. Amen.** ✠ In the name of the Father, and the Son, and the Holy Spirit, Amen, * and they rest in their Lord, that servant of God Jesus Christ, Adam Osanna, may rest, by the help of Saint Mary, the mother of our Lord Jesus Christ, from all the aforesaid and other evils. Amen. ✠ *****! The five (wounds) of our Lord Jesus Christ, and Saint Mary de Osanna, Saint Dunstan, Saint Andrew, Saint Nicholas, Saint Margaret, Saint Peter, Saint Paul, Saint Matthew, Saint Bartholomew, the holy five (wounds) of our Lord Jesus Christ, Saint Brigida. * Christ conquers, * Christ reigns, * and Christ commands, * and let Christ defend Adam Osanna from all evil. Amen."

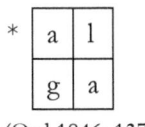

a	l
g	a

(Ord 1846: 137-38).

The Night Spell (Brit. Mus. Addit. 36674), p.89.
This charme shall be said at night or against night about ye place or field or about beasts without field, and whosoever cometh in, he goeth not out for certaine.
On 3 Crosses of a tree, 3 dead bodyes did hang, 2 were theeves, ye 3rd was xst on whom our beliefe is, Dismas and Gesmas, Xst amidst there was, Dismas to heaven went, Gesmas to heaven, was sent, Christ that died on yt roode, for Mries love that by him stood, and through the virtue of his blood, Jesus save us and our good within and wthout and all this place about and through the virtue of his might lett noe thief enter in this night; no foote further in this place that I upon goe, but at my bidding there be bound, to do all things that I bid them do. Starke be their sineiues therewith & their lives mightles and their eyes sightles, dred and doubt enclose them about, as a wall wrought of stone so be thes crampt in the ton [toes], crampe and crookeing and fault is their footing, the might of the Trinity, save these goods for me. In the name of Jesus, holy benedicite all about our goods bee, within and without and all place about, then say 5 pr. Nrs., 5 av. & I cred. etc.
Disparibus miseritis pendent tria copora varius
Dismas et Gesmas medio divina potestas.
Alta petis Dismas, infelix infima Gesmas,
His versis discas ne furta tu tua perdas. (Briggs 1962: 260)

Popish periapts, amulets and charmes, agnus Dei, a wastcote of proofe, ... &c.
These vertues under these verses (written by pope Urbane the fift to the emperour of the Græcians) are conteined in a periapt or tablet, to be continuallie worne about one, called Agnus Dei, which is a little cake, having the picture of a lambe carrieng of a flag on the one side; and Christs head on the other side, and is hollow: so as the gospell of S. John, written in fine paper, is placed in the concavitie thereof: and it is thus compounded or made, even as they themselves report.
Balsamus & munda cera, cum chrismatis unda
Conficiunt agnum, quod munus do tibi magnum,
Fonte velut natum, per mystica sanctificatum:
Fulgura desursum depellit, & omne malignum,
Peccatum frangit, ut Christi sanguis, & angit,
Prægnans servatur, simul & partus liberatur,
Dona refert dignis, virtutem destruit ignis,
Portatus mundè de fluctibus eripit undæ:
Balme, virgine wax, and holie water, an Agnus Dei make:
A gift than which none can be greater, I send thee for to take.
From founteine cleere the same hath issue, in secret sanctifide:
Gainst lightning it hath soveraigne vertue, and thunder crackes beside.
Ech hainous sinne it weares and wasteth, even as Christs precious blood,
And women, whiles their travell lasteth, it saves, it is so good.
It doth bestow great gifts and graces, on such as well deserve:
And borne about in noisome places, from perill doth preserve.
The force of fire, whose heat destroieth, it breaks and bringeth downe:
And he or she that this enjoieth, no water shall them drowne. (Scot 1973: 185-86)

Against Nightmare & Incubus
S. George, S. George, our ladies knight,
He walkt by daye, so did he by night;
Untill such time as he hir found,
He hir beat and he hir bound,
Untill hir troth she to him plight,
She would not come to hir [i. e., him] that night.
Whereas S. George our ladies knight,
Was named three times S. George.
Item, hang a stone over the afflicted persons bed, which stone hath naturallie a hole in it, as wherein a string may be put through it, and so be hanged over the diseased or bewitched partie; be it man, woman or horse. (Scot 1973: 68)

A charme against shot, or a wastcote of proofe.

Before the comming up of these *Agnus Deis*, a holie garment called a wastcote for necessitie was much used of our forefathers, as a holy relike, &c: as given by the pope, or some such archconjuror, who promised thereby all manner of immunitie to the wearer thereof; in somuch as he could not be hurt with anie shot or other violence. And otherwise, that woman that would weare it, should have quicke deliverance: the composition thereof was in this order following.

On Christmas daie at night, a threed must be sponne of flax, by a little virgine girle, in the name of the divell: and it must be by hir woven, and also wrought with the needle. In the brest or forepart thereof must be made with needle worke two heads; on the head at the right side must be a hat, and a long beard; the left head must have on a crowne, and it must be so horrible, that it maie resemble Belzebub, and on each side of the wastcote must be made a crosse. (Scot 1973: 186, from Weyer: 418)

Another amulet.

Joseph of Arimathea did find this writing upon the wounds of the side of Jesus Christ, written with Gods finger, when the bodie was taken away from the crosse. Whosoever shall carrie this writing about him, shall not die anie evill death, if he beleeve in Christ, and in all perplexities he shall soone be delivered, neither let him feare any danger at all.

Fons + alpha & omega +figa + figalis + Sabbaoth + Emmanuel + Adonai + o + Neray + Elay + Ihe + Rentone + Neger + Sahe + Pangeton + Commen + a + g + l + a + Matthæus + Marcus + Lucas + Johannes + + + titulus triumphalis + Jesus Nasærenus rex Judæorum + ecce dominicæ crucis signum + fugite partes adversæ, vicit leo de tribu Judæ, radix, David, aleluijah, Kyrie eleeson, Christe eleeson, pater noster, ave Maria, & ne nos, & veniat super nos salutare tuum: Oremus, &c. (Scot 1973: 188)

A papisticall charme.

Signum sanctæ crucis defendat me à malis præsentibus, præteritis, & futuris, interioribus & exterioribus: that is, The signe of the crosse defend me from evils present, past, and to come, inward and outward. (Scot 1973: 189)

A charme to drive awaie spirits that haunt anie house.

Hang in everie of the foure corners of your house this sentence written upon virgine parchment; *Omnis spiritus laudet Dominum: Mosen habent & prophetas: Exurgat Deus et dissipentur inimici ejus*. This is called and counted the Paracelsian charme. Psal. 150. Luk. 16. Psa. 64. (Scot 1973: 199)

117. A True and Approved Charm. Useful against a Conflagration and Pestilence.

Welcome thou fiery guest; seize no further than thou hast. This I reckon to thee, Fire, for a penance, in the name of the Father and the Son and the Holy Ghost.

I pray, thee, Fire, by God's power which does and creates all things, that thou stay and go no further, even as Christ stood on the Jordan and was baptized, by the holy man John. That I reckon to thee, Fire, as a penance, in the name of the holy Trinity.

I pray thee, Fire, by the power of God, that thou restrain thy flames; even as Mary restrains her virginity before all dames, chaste and pure; wherefore, stay thy rage, Fire. This I reckon to thee for a penance, Fire, in the name of the Almightiest Trinity.

I pray thee, thou wilt allay thy ardor, by Jesus Christ's precious blood, which he shed for us, our sins and misdeeds. That I reckon thee, Fire, for a penance, in the name of the Father and the Son and the Holy Ghost.

Jesus of Nazareth, King of the Jews, help us out of this stress of fire, and protect this land and country from all plague and pestilence.

REMARKS. —This charm was brought from Egypt by a christian Gipsy King. In the year 1714, the 1st day of June, six gipsys were brought into the Prussian Kingdom, condemned to be hung. A seventh, an old man of 80 years of age, and condemned to be / beheaded, was brought in on the 16th of the same month. Fortunately for him, a conflagration broke out; the old gipsy was loosed and brought to the fire to try his art, and to the wonder of all, he subdued the fire in a half a quarter of an hour; for which he was pardoned and set free. This was known in the royal palace of Prussia, and in the general Superintendency of Konigsburg, and has been openly put to the proof. It was first tested in Konigsberg by Alexander Banman, in 1715. Whoever has this formula written in the house, is safe from the danger of conflagration or thunderstorm; likewise, if a pregnant woman has it about her, magic cannot injure her or her child; it protects likewise against plague and pestilence. When one repeats the form he must go around the fire 3 times. It always helps. (Brown 1904: 125-126)

129. Protection of the House and Court from Sickness and Robbery.
Ito, Alo Massa Dandi Bando, III. Amen.
I. R. N. R. I.

Our Lord Jesus Christ went into the hall, there the Jews specially sought him. So also must my days be with those who revile me with their evil tongues falsely, and smite, and for praise of God must I bear the suffering, be silent, be dumb, faint, ashamed, ever and always. God thereby bestows praise. Help me I. I. I. ever and eternally. Amen. ["The 3 I's signify Jesus three times."] (Brown 1904: 128)

177. A Charm for Bad People.
It is said, that if you suspect a person for badness, and he sits down on a chair, and you take a shoemaker's wax-end, that has not been used, and stick one end of it on the under side of the chair, and you sit on the other end of it, he will immediately make water, and in a short time die. (Brown 1904: 138)

Against rape:
And it is said, if a woman takes a needle, and bewray it with dung, and put it into earth in which the carcass of a man has been buried, and carry it about her in a piece of cloth used at a funeral, no man can defile her as she carries that. (Barrett 1967: 34)

A RING FOR POWER, AND TO OVERCOME ENEMIES.
Let the character of Saturn (♄) be engraved upon a magnet, or piece of loadstone, in the time of the moon's increase; and being worn on the right hand, no enemy or foe shall overcome the wearer. ("Raphael" 1832: 18)

A safe way to secure a House.
If you suspect your house will be robbed, and would secure it from thieves, as no doubt but you are desirous, consider the night what planet reigns, and is lord of the ascendant; and these are the characters, the Sun ☉ on Sunday, the Moon ☽ on Monday, Mars ♂ on Tuesday, Mercury ☿ on Wednesday, Jupiter ♃ on Thursday, Venus ♀ on Friday, Saturn ♄ on Saturday. Now consider on what night you do this, as to these planets, and write on fair parchment these charactars, ♌ ♈ ♑, and, supposing it to be on a Sunday, add the planatary character ☉ with this number, 1, 3, 5, 1—4, 1—7, and at that night, lay this under the earth, or covered with a tile in the middle of the house, as near as may be, sprinkle it over with the juice of nightshade, and so go to sleep as soon as you have thrice repeated them over, and if the thieves have power to enter the house, they shall have no power / to get out again, or to carry any thing away till the Sun rises ; and if you be watchful, then you may easily apprehend them before they are able to depart.
And thus you may do any day in the week, adding the character of the planet that rules that day as I have set it down, to what is beside set down in order. (*Witchcraft Detected* 1824: 48)

To prevent affrightening dreams, and fear in the night.
You must take laudanum a dram, frankincence the like quantity, of bezoar-stone as much; beat these into powder, and write upon a piece of parchment these characters, ♄ ♃ ♉ ☿ , and under them your name; put the powder in the paper you write on, and when you repose, bind them on your forehead / and stomach, for you must have two papers ordered one and the same way, as directed, putting half the powder in the one, and other half in the other. (*Witchcraft Detected* 1824: 51-52)

A CHARM AGAINST NIGHTMARE.
If you wish to be secure against the nightmare in your sleep, place your shoes side by side upon the floor, at the foot of the bed, so that the toes will point not toward the bed, but in the contrary direction, as if they were going from it. (*Golden Wheel* 1862: 130)

Abracadabra Charm:
The word "Abracadabra" written on parchment was given by an Exeter white witch, to a person who desired to possess a talisman against the dominion of the grey witch, pixies, evil spirits and the powers of darkness! It cost a guinea, and was sewn up in a small black silk bag *one inch* square. This was hung round the neck and never removed. Should it by chance fall to the ground, all its properties for good would be lost and a new charm must be procured from the same white witch, or dire misfortune would overtake the owner. In "Reminiscences and Reflections," of an old West Country clergyman (the Rev. W. H. Thornton, rector of North Bovey), the word "Abracadabra" occurs on page 44, in connection with a meeting of spiritualists, held in London in 1848.

(Hewett 1900: 73)

A Scots Charm:
The Scotch appear to have held similar notions on these subjects with ourselves, for in Sinclair's *Satan's Invisible World Discovered* we find the following charm, "To preserve the house and those in it from danger at night:"—
Who sains the house the night?
They that sains it ilk a night,
Saint Bryde and her brate;
Saint Col me and his hat;
Saint Michael and his spear;
Keep this house from the weir—
From running thiefe—
And burning thiefe—
And from and ill Rea:—
That be the gate can gae :—
And from an ill wight:—
That be the gate can light.
Nine reeds about the house;
Keep it all the night.
What is that what I see,
So red, so bright, beyond the sea.
'Tis he was pierced through the hands,
Through the feet, through the throat,
Through the tongue,
Through the liver and the lung.
Well is them that well may
Fast on Good Friday. (Harland & Wilkinson 1867: 74)
CHARM AGAINST TROUBLE IN GENERAL.— Repeat reverently, and with sincere faith, the following words, and you shall be protected in the hour of danger: "He shall deliver thee in six troubles, yea, in seven there shall no evil touch thee; in famine he shall redeem thee from death, and

in war from the power of the sword; and thou shalt know that thy tabernacle shall be in peace, and thou shalt visit thy habitation and shall not err." Job 5:19, 20,24 (Mother Shipton's ca. 1880: 59)

A Spell as a protection from Assault. . .
"Whoever thou art that meanest me ill,
Stand thou still!
As the river Jordan did
When our Lord arid Saviour, Jesus,
Was baptised therein.
In the name of Father, Son, and Holy Ghost." Amen. /
It is not easy to get hold of spells . ... many people disown any knowledge of Spells, believing there is something "uncanny" in their use. (Gurdon 1893: 159)

CHARM FOR PROTECTION FROM ENEMIES.
THIS talisman should be made of pure cast iron and engrave at the time of new moon. Before suspending it round the neck fumigate it with the smoke of burnt Spirits of Mars (a mixture of red Saunders, frankincense, and red pepper), or a ring of pure gold might be made, with the characters engrave on the inside. The size and form of this talisman is immaterial so long as the proper time for making it is observed and the prescribed incense is used before it is worn. In any form it will protect one from enemies, and counteract the power of the evil eye.

(Hewett 1900: 73-74)

TO DISPEL VAPOURS AND DRIVE AWAY EVIL SPIRITS.
ST. John's Wort, or Devil's Flight, gathered on St. John's Day or on a Friday, dried and placed in a closely-covered jar and hung in a window, will protect the house from thunderbolts, storms, fire, and evil spirits.
If the flowers and leaves are dried and ground into powder and then placed in a silken bag and hung round the neck, the person will be successful in love, and be cured of the *vapours* and all mental afflictions. To insure perfect immunity from these ills, it is necessary to operate in July, on the evening of the full moon. (Hewett 1900: 75)

A man in one of the villages in East Norfolk bordering on the sea coast, was observed for a long time to drive a horse round whose neck something was tied, which he said would act as a preservative against every mishap, stumbling included. This, when stolen by a mischievous urchin at the instigation of Borne village wags, was found to be the thumb / of an old leather glove, containing a transcript of the Lord's Prayer. (Glyde 1872: 44-45)

"Overlooking" or the Evil Eye:

Being "overlooked" or cursed by the Evil Eye (which could occur on purpose through envy, or involuntarily by someone afflicted with this "gift") was an ancient source of misfortune. (Carmichael 1900: 52-53 – there are several others given as well)

UIBE RI SHUL

UIBE gheal chuir Muire mhin,
A nail air allt, air muir, 's air tir,
Air bhrig, 's air ghat fharmaid,
Air mhac armaid,
Air fiacaill coin-ghiorr,
Air siadhadh coin-ghearr,
Air tri chorracha-cri,
Air tri chorracha cnamh,
Air tri chorracha creothail,
'S air lion leothair lair. [? Leobhar]

Ge be co rinn dut an t-suil,
Gun laigh I air fein,
Gun laigh I air a thur,
Gun laigh I air a spreidh,
Gun laigh I air a shult,
Gun laigh I air a shaill,
Gun laigh I air a chuid,
Gun laigh I air a chlainn,
Gun laigh I air a bhean,
Gun laigh I air a loinn.

Clomhaidh mise an t-suil,
Somhaidh mise an t-suil,
Imirichidh mi 'n t-suil,
A thri feithean feiche,
'S teang eug an iomalain.
Tri maighdeana beaga caomh,

SPELL FOR EVIL EYE

THE fair spell that lovely Mary sent,
Over stream, over sea, over land,
Against incantations, against withering glance,
Against inimical power,
Against the teeth of wolf,
Against the testicles of wolf,
Against the three crooked cranes,
Against the three crooked bones,
Against the three crooked 'creothail,'
And against lint 'leothair' of the ground. [? Long]

Whoso made to thee the eye,
May it lie upon himself,
May it lie upon his house,
May it lie upon his flocks,
May it lie upon his substance,
May it lie upon his fatness,
May it lie upon his means,
May it lie upon his children,
May it lie upon his wife,
May it lie upon his descendants.

I will subdue the eye,
I will suppress the eye,
And I will banish the eye,
The three arteries inviting (?),
And the tongue of death completely.
Three lovely little maidens,
Born the same night with Christ,
If alive be these three to-night,
Life be anear thee, poor beast.

Charms.—*The* Evil Eye.— Going one day into a cottage in the village of Catterick, in Yorkshire, I observed hung up behind the door a ponderous necklace of "lucky stones," *i.e.* stones with a hole through them. On hinting an inquiry as to their use, I found the good lady of the house disposed to shuffle off any explanation; but by a little importunity I discovered that they had the credit of being able to preserve the house and its inhabitants from the baleful influence of the "evil eye." "Why, Nanny," said I, "you surely don't believe in witches now-a-days?" "No! I don't say 'at I do; but certainly I' former times there *was* wizzards an' buzzards, and them sort o' things." "Well," said I, laughing, "but you surely don't think there are any now?" "No . I don't say 'at ther' are; but I *do* believe in a *yevil* eye." After a little time I extracted from poor Nanny more particulars on the subject, as viz.: — how that there was a woman in the village whom she strongly suspected of being able to look with an evil eye; how, further, a neighbour's daughter, against whom the old lady in question had a grudge owing to some love affair, had suddenly fallen into a sort of pining sickness, of which the doctors could make nothing at all; and how the poor thing fell away without any accountable cause, and finally died, nobody knew why; but how it was her (Nanny's) strong belief that she had pined away in consequence of a glance from the evil eye. Finally, I got from her an account of how any one who chose could themselves obtain the power of the evil eye, and the receipt was, as nearly as I can recollect, as follows:—

"Ye gang out ov' a night—ivery night, while ye find nine toads—an' when ye've gitten t' nine toads, ye hang 'em up ov' a string, an' ye make a hole and buries t' toads i't hole—and as't toads pines away, so't person pines away 'at you've looked upon wiv a yevil eye, an' they pine and pine away while they die, without ony disease at all!"

I do not know if this is the orthodox creed respecting the mode of gaining the power of the evil eye, but it is at all events a genuine piece of Folk Lore.
MARGARET GATTY.
Ecclesfield, April 24. 1850.[72]

Love and Marriage:

Identifying the appropriate mate in marriage was so personally, socially and economically momentous a milestone in women's lives that an enormous number of charms and spells were dedicated to that particular problem. Love magic after the 17th century encompassed a larger and larger proportion of popular magical and divinatory practice, as books containing oracles and charms were increasingly aimed at a female audience. While some "love spells" were about compelling an indifferent sexual partner to cooperate (more commonly a masculine objective), the majority of the published spells and charms were intended for women with marriage in view. A large number of these are more properly a matter of divination than magic – there seems to have been a strong belief in the predestined "match made in heaven", but many were coercive and intended to snare a desired spouse, or compel a wandering lover to return.

Possibly the best example of the number and variety found in love charms is from the notebook of the 17th century practicing Cunning Man, Arthur Gauntlet (Sloane MS 3851 in the British Library manuscript collections). This singularly revealing and informative text, which has been expertly edited and published by occult scholar David Rankine, is a wonderful contribution to our knowledge about the practices of a professional magical worker. Towards the end of the manuscript, Gauntlet has gathered some 60 different attraction and related spells, 18 of which involve an apple. A sampling of these follows:

> **To gain the love of Man or woman** Go to the Herb vervain when it is flowered near the full of the Moon And say to it + The lords Prayer + Then say + In the name of the father + vervain I have sought thee In the name of the Son I have found thee + In the name of the Holy Ghost + I will gather thee + Then say + I charge thee vervain by the virtue of our Lord Jesus Christ And by the holy names of God + *Helion* + *Heloy* + *Adonay* + and by all the holy names of God That when I carry thee in my mouth that whosoever I shall love or touch that thou make them obedient unto me And to do my will in all things + fiat + fiat + fiat + Amen + (Rankine 2011: 303)
>
> **To know whether a Maid be virgin** Cause her to sit down upon the Herb [vervain] unwittingly. If She be not a Maid She will not nor cannot. (Rankine 2011: 304)
>
> **Write** in an Apple Raguell Lucifer Salthanus And say I conjure thee Apple by these three names written in thee That whosoever shall eat thee may burn in my love until such time she hath fulfilled my desire (Rankine 2011: 306)
>
> **Write** in an Apple before it fall from the Tree + *Aleo* + *Deleo* + *Delaton* + And say I Conjure thee Apple by these three names which are written in thee that what woman or virgin soever toucheth and tasteth thee may love me and burn in my love as fire melteth wax till my will be fulfilled. (Rankine 2011: 307)
>
> **Write** in an Apple your names And these three names *Gosmer Synady Heupide*, And give it to eat to any man that thou wouldst have after thy will and he shall do as thou wilt (Rankine 2011: 308)
>
> **Write** these letters in thy left Hand, *h l d p n a g u s t*, carry them in the morning before Sun rising and touch whom thou wilt and she shall follow thee, fiat.

---

[72] *Notes and Queries*, vol I. (1850) p. 429.

Write this sign in thy Left Hand and touch whom thou wilt before Sun rising and say unto them follow me. You may try it upon a Dog or Bitch.

 (Rankine 2011: 308)

Take iii {3} hairs of her head And a thread spun upon a Friday of a pure virgin and make a Candle therewith of virgin wax iiii {4} square And write with blood of a Cock Sparrow the name of the woman And light the Candle whereas it may not drop upon the Earth, And she will come to the Candle (Rankine 2011: 310)

Take a nutmeg and sweat it iii {3} or iiii {4} days under thy right Armhole. Grate it and mingle it with the ashes of a Green Frog and give it to a Maid, et amabit te ["And she will love you."] (Rankine 2011: 310)

Make an Image of her you love Of virgin wax And Christen it in Holy water Saying, I Baptise and Christen thee In the name of the Father and of the Son and of the Holy Ghost, And write the name of the woman In the forehead of the Image And thy name in her breast And write upon her head Venus. Then take iiii {4} new needles Prick one of them in the Back of the Image right against the Navel And in her Right side another In her left side And the other above the Navel And write in her left side *Sieate*, And on her Right side *gratuell* And at her Navel *Almederio* And at her back *Mammoye*. Then say. I Conjure you Spirits by the power of the Father which is divine And by the power of the Son which is human And by the power of the Holy Ghost which is Latitude of the world That you will come speedily and make no tarrying either in Hell or in the Sea Or in the world before you have fulfilled my will and pleasure, Come therefore from the East from the South from the west And from the North And rest not day nor night until I have my pleasure as I will with her And I conjure you again by the power of Lucifer Belsebub Astiroth and by him which hath any power in love or to love that you rest not in any place until AB be enforced to love me, I conjure you holy Angels of the East west North and South *Lathinos Imbroson Samabathon Samyn Anthreson vene fatha Thini Reanet unn tend Belissemd Monoy Tymon* and by all the names of the most high God And by all the powers and orders of the Heavens and Earth that you increase love between AB and me and that she may be obedient unto my will and accomplish my desire. Then make a fire in her name, The coals being kindled lay them abroad and write in the Ashes her Image and a little Mustard seed and a little Salt upon the picture. Then lay up the coals again, As the composition leapeth and swelleth so shall her Heart And she shall be kindled in thy love that she might be with thee. (Rankine 2011: 311)

Write these words with thine own blood And lay them in the bed of a woman, Badull arbrculus arbarculare, and say, I Conjure thee by the prince of Devils that thou neither sleep nor sit eat nor drink until thou hast fulfilled my desire. (Rankine 2011: 312)

Take the Heart of a Turtledove and seeth it in water then put it into a heap of salt until it be dry. The powder thereof will get the love of a woman Or if you rub it about your lips and Kiss her She will be enamoured. (Rankine 2011: 313)

Among the various examples that follow, I have included a satirical but comprehensive survey of popular love magic from a mid-18th century periodical (*The Connoisseur*, 1755) and one short Victorian collection (from *Le Marchand's Fortune Teller and Dream Book*, 1863) in their entirety. If it wasn't for their length, other publications such as *Mother Bunch's Closet Newly Broke Open* (1685) would serve as well. The fictional "Mother Bunch", by the way, enjoys a long career in the chapbook trade in works dealing with love magic. First appearing as an alewife in a book of humourous folktales in 1604, the character was borrowed by chapbook writers to become the wise old woman who advises girls on how to identify or entice a mate. *The History of Mother Bunch of The West* (1780) and *Mother Bunch's Golden Fortune-Teller* (ca.

1850) carried the tradition into modern times. The first two titles were reprinted by G. L. Gomme in 1885.

Love charm
Take an Apple in thy hande as it hangeth on the tree and wryte in it these names followinge: *Anaell, Satnell, Assiel* & then saye I coniure thee Appel of Apples by the neame of cheefe devels, which deceptfully deceaved Eve in padyce, that what woman soever it be that doe eate or tast of this Apple that she may burne in love of me. Saye this 4 tymes upon the Apple, & then geve the Apple to what woman you will. (e. Mus. 243) (Briggs 1962: 172)

f. 49 v. *for love. Another* (MS. Bod. E Mus. 243)
Lay an Egge in a pismyre bank [ant hill] ye 18 daye of March, & lett it lye ther 3 dayes then take it out & whosoever thou touchest with yt shall Love thee. (Briggs 1962: 262)

A Love Charm.
These are Charms of themselves; the brain of Murilegus [bat], and of a she Lizard; the menstrual blood of a whore, a Lizard called *Stincus* [sand fish or *Scincus scincus*], so is *Hippomanes* [a lumpy calculus found at horses' births]. All these things rather change the minde, than compell one to love them from whom they take them. But they are commonly made of excrements, or of creatures bred of putrefaction, or of the seed of Man; as is that made of it, and the matrix of a Bitch that is [preserved with] salt; if a Dog be kept long by her and not admitted to her, then he runs almost mad for lust. There are other Love-Charms which are not to be eaten, that are taken from dead mens cloaths, Candles, Measures, needles, and generally such things as are provided for Funerals [such as scarves, gloves and rings]. *Card[ano] de Subtilitat.* (Wecker 1660: 35)

Cockle Bread:

John Aubrey (1625-1697) has an extensive commentary of the practice of making "cockle bread", a practice that rather scandalized Victorian editors who seemed determined to bowdlerize the practice and claim it to be nothing more than a children's game. They noted that "cockle" was derived etymologically from the Latin conchylium "mussel, shellfish," and from the Greek konkhylion "little shellfish", and hence had nothing to do with the embarrassing usage. However, they neglected to consider the slang or "cant" use of the term for the vagina (anyone who has seen a cooked mussel can appreciate the simile), which as Aubrey indicates, renders it is a rare surviving example of obscene love magic.

Aubrey himself first though it was just a game or a joke, but having discovered a graphic description of the practice in the *Decretum* of Burchard of Worms (1012 CE.), realized that it was a real example of folk magic, even if it later became merely a game. In essence, the girls kneaded actual bread dough with their vulvas, and then served the baked result to their lovers. He also records a spell in which small live fish were inserted into a girl's vagina where it smothered, after which it was cooked and served with the same purpose in mind,

> Young wenches have a wanton sport, which they call *moulding of Cocklebread; viz.* they get upon a Table-board, and then gather-up their knees and their Coates with their hands as high as they can, and then they wabble to and fro with their Buttocks, as if the<y>. were kneading of Dough, with their Arses, and say thes words, viz. —
> "My Dame is sick and gonne to bed,
> "And I'le go mowld my Cockle-bread".
> I did imagine nothing to have been in this but meer Wantonnesse of Youth — (*rigidae pruringe vulvæ.* Juven. Sat 6) — But I found in <lib. XIX> c. <5.> Burchardus in his Methodus Confitendi on the VII Commandment, one of the articles of interrogating a young Woman is, if she did ever *subigere panem clunibus,* and did bake it, and give it to one that she loved to eate: *ut in majorem modum exardesceret amor?* So here I finde it to be a relique of Naturall Magick: an unlawful Philtrum.
> "Tis a poeticall expression, *to kisse like Cockles.*
> "The Sea-nymphes that see us shall envy our bliss,

"Wee'll teach them to love, and like Cockles to kiss.

I have some reason to believe, that the word Cockle is an old antiquated Norman word, which signifies *arse*: from a beastly Rustique kind of play, or abuse, which was used when I was a school-boy by a Norman Gardiner, that lived at Downton, neer me: so hot Cockles is as much as to say hott or heated buttocks, or arse.

An old filthy Rhyme used by base people, viz:

"When I was a young Maid, and wash't my Mothers Dishes,

"I putt my finger in my Cunt, and pluck't-out little Fishes.

See Burchardus, *ut antè*, where there is an interrogatory, if she / did ever *immittere pisculos in vulvam*, and let it die there, and they fry it, and give it to her Lover to eate, *ut majorem modum exardesceret amor?* The Lord Chancellor Bacon sayes — thus the fables of the Poets are the Mysteries of the Philosophers: and I allude here, that (out of fulsome Ribaldrie) I have picked-out the profoundest natural Magick that ever I met with in all my Life.

"The young Girls in and about Oxford have a Sport called *Leap-*

"*candle* for which they set a candle in the middle of the room in a

"candlestick, and then draw up their coats in the form of breeches,

"and dance over the candle back and forth, with these words

"The Taylor of Bisiter, he has but one eye,

"He cannot cut a pair of green Galagaskins if he were to die.

"This sport in other parts is called *Dancing the candle rush*.

<Dr.> W.K<ennett>. (Aubrey 1972: 254-255)

A compilation of "love magic" from *The Connoisseur*:
To Mr. T O W N.
DEAR SIR: *Feb 17, 1755.*

YOU must know I am in love with a very clever man, a Londoner; and as I want to know whether it is my fortune to have him, I have tried all the tricks I can hear of for that purpose. I have seen him several times in Coffee-grounds with a sword by his side; and he was once at the bottom of a Tea-cup in a coach and six with two footmen behind it. I got up last May morning, and went into the fields to hear the cuckow; and when I pulled off my left shoe, I found an hair in it exactly the / same colour with his. But I shall never forget what I did last Midsummer Eve. I and my two sisters tried the Dumb Cake together: you must know, two must make it, two bake it, two break it, and the third put it under each of their pillows, (but you must not speak a word all the time) and then you will dream of the man you are to have. This we did; and to be sure I did nothing all night, but dream of Mr. *Blossom*. The same night, exactly at twelve o'clock, I sowed Hempseed in our back yard, and said to myself, "Hempseed I sow, Hempseed I hoe, and he that is my true-love, come after me and mow." Will you believe me? I looked back, and saw him behind me, as plain as eyes could see him. After that, I took a clean shift, and turned it, and hung upon the back of a chair; and very likely my sweetheart would have come and turned it right again, (for I heard his step) but I was frightened, and could not help speaking, which broke the charm. I likewise stuck up two Midsummer Men [rose-root[73]], one for myself, and one for him. Now if his had died away, we should never have come together: but I assure you he blowed [bloomed] and turned to me. Our maid *Betty* tells me, that if I go backwards without speaking a word into the garden upon Midsummer Eve, and gather a Rose, and keep it in a clean sheet of paper, without looking at it, till *Christmas* day, it will be as fresh as in June; and if I then stick it in my bosom, he that is to be my husband will come and take it out. If I am not married before the time comes about again, I will certainly do it; and only mind if Mr. *Blossom* is not the man.

I HAVE tried a great many other fancies, and they have all turned out right. Whenever I go to lye in a strange bed, I always tye my garter nine times round the bed-post, and / knit nine knots in it, and say to myself, *This knot I knit this knot I tye, To see my love as he goes by, In his apparel and array, As he walks in every day.* I did so last holidays at my uncle's; and to be sure I saw Mr. *Blossom* draw my curtains and

---

[73] "Rose-root: any of certain perennial mountain plants, as *Sedum rosea, Sedum rhodiola,* or *Rhodiola rosea,* so called because the roots smell like roses".

tuck up the cloaths at my bed's feet. Cousin *Debby* was married a little while ago, and she sent me a piece of Bride-Cake to put under my pillow; and I had the sweetest dream – I thought we were going to be married together. I have, many is the time, taken great pains to pare an Apple Whole, and afterwards flung the Peel over my head; and it always falls in the shape of the first letter of his Sirname or Christian name. I am sure Mr. *Blossom* loves me, because I stuck two of the Kernels upon my forehead, while I thought upon him and the lubberly squire my pappa wants me to have: Mr. *Blossom's* Kernel stuck on, but the other dropt off directly.

LAST Friday, Mr. TOWN, was *Valentine's* Day; and I'll tell you what I did the night before. I got five bay-leaves, and pinned four of them to the four corners of my pillow, and the fifth to the middle; and then if I dreamt of my sweetheart, *Betty* said we should be married before the year was out. But to make it more sure, I boiled an egg hard, and took out the yolk, and filled it up with salt; and when I went to bed, eat it shell and all, without speaking or drinking after it: and this was to have the same effect with the bay-leaves. We also wrote our lovers names upon bits of paper, and rolled them up in clay, and put them into water; and the first that rose up, was to be our Valentine. Would you think it? Mr. *Blossom* was my man: and I lay a-bed and shut my eyes all the morning, till he came to our house; for I would not have seen another man before him for all the world. /

DEAR Mr. TOWN, if you know any other ways, to try our fortune by, do put them in your paper. My Mama laughs at us, and says there is nothing in them; but I am sure there is, for several Misses at our boarding school have tried them, and they have all happened true: and I am *sure* my own sister *Hetty,* who died just before *Christmas,* stood in the Church Porch last Midsummer Eve to see all that were to die that year in our parish; and she saw her own apparition.

Your humble servant ARABELLA WHIMSEY. (*Connoisseur* 1755: 333-336)

To make Love-Powder to cause Love.

OF mother of pearl take one dram, of crabs eyses as much, mix them up with the juice of parsley, then dry them again, and beat them to powder, then give half of it at a time in a glass of ale, or wine, or any other Liquor, and it will affect in a strange manner, as you will soon see by the motion of the eyes, words, toyings, &c. (*High German* 1810: 17)

Another Way.

GET bay berries, and gum of ivy, fern-root and claws of a crab; dry them to powder, and sift them through a sieve, and if you want to know any one's affection, put a dram of it into a Glass of wine or some other liquor, and it will work strange effects, without injuring the health of the party. (*High German* 1810: 17)

A CHARM
To make a young woman seem to be in love with a young man.
Take new wax and the powder of a dead man, make an image with the face downward and in the likeness of the person you wish to have: make it in the ouers of mars and in the new of the mone: under the left armpoke place a Swaler's hart and a liver under the rite: you must have a new needal and a new thread: the Sprits name must be menchened, his sine and his character.
I take this opportunity to inform my frinds that about 16 *years ago this Charm was put in practice by sum willains of witches at Needhammarkett, William Studd been one of them: and they have put me to much torment and lamed me many times, they own to me that they make use of part of the bones of Mrs. Wilkerson of Felixstow, she that suffered at Rushmere sum years ago; this is sartainly true, and I am ready to give it upon oth if required.—Tho. Colson.*
Acts the 9 & 5. "It is hard for the to kick against the pricks." "The Suffolk Garland," 1818. (Harland & Wilkinson 1867: 98)

How to make an enchanting Ring.
Get a hollow ring, and goat's hair, taken from the beard, steep it in the juice of Nightshade, or wake / robin, (an herb so called) put it through the ring and whoever wears it will fall in love with you. (*Witchcraft Detected* 1824: 57-58)

To make a true love powder.
Take elacampane, the seeds and flowers of vervine, and the berries of Misellto; dry them well in an oven, and beat them into fine powder: give the party you design upon a dram in a glass of wine, or other liquors and it will work wonderful effects to your advantage. (*Witchcraft Detected* 1824: 58)

To dissolve bewitched love, and to cause love.
The party bewitched must make a jakes [outhouse] of the lover's shoe. And to enforce a man to love an old hag, she giveth unto him among meat, her own dung. In this way an old witch made three Abbots of one house successively to die for her love. (*Witchcraft Detected* 1824: 58)

TO PREPARE A LOVE POTION
The following substances must be gathered in silence when the full moon is in the heavens: Three white rose leaves, three red rose leaves, three forget-me-nots, and five blossoms of Veronica.
All these things you must place in a vessel, then pour upon them five hundred and ninety-five drops of clear Easter water, and place the vessel over the fire, or what is better still, over a spirit-lamp. This mixture must be allowed to boil for exactly the sixteenth part of an hour.
When it has boiled for the requisite length of time, remove it from the fire, and pour it into a flask. Cork it tightly, and seal it, and it will keep for years without losing its virtue.
That this potion is certain in its effect I myself will guarantee, for I have gained more than thirty hearts by its help. Three drops swallowed by the person whose love you desire, will suffice. (*Golden Wheel* 1862: 124-125)

ANOTHER MEANS TO COMPEL LOVE.
Take a healthy, well-grown frog. Place it in a box which has been pierced all over with holes with a stout darning needle or gimlet. Then carry it in the evening twilight to a large ant-heap, place it in the midst of the heap, taking care to observe perfect silence.
After the lapse of a week, repair to the ant-heap, take out the box, and open it, when in place of the frog you will find nothing but a skeleton. Take this apart very carefully, and you will soon find among the delicate bones a scale shaped like that of a fish and a hook. You will need them both. The hook you must contrive to fasten in some way or other into the clothes of the person whose affections you wish to obtain, and if he or she has worn it, if it is only for a quarter of a minute, he will be constrained to love you, and will continue to do so until you give him or her a fillip with the scale.
This method is over three thousand years old, and it has been practised by thirty-thousand of our ancestors with the most complete success. (*Golden Wheel* 1862: 125)

EASTER WATER.
In speaking of a love potion, I made mention of Easter water; many of my readers have, I suppose, never heard of this singular kind of water, I will explain it to you. It is water which is drawn from the river upon Easter morning, before the sun has shone upon it. To obtain it, therefore, you must rise on Easter morning while it is still quite dark, take your way to the river in silence, fill your pitcher in silence, and then make your way home in silence, without looking behind you. You may then go to bed again and have your sleep out. This Easter water has this peculiarity: it will keep sweet throughout the whole year. You can, therefore, fill as many bottles with it as you please, cork them tightly, and lay them away.
Besides its use in the above-named love potion, it is beneficial in various maladies, especially in diseases of the eye, and, in addition to this, it is an approved cosmetic. (*Golden Wheel* 1862: 130)

From *Le Marchand's Fortune Teller and Dream Book*, 1863, pp. 130-133:
CHARMS AND CEREMONIES
THE CHARMS OF ST. CATHERINE.
THIS day falls on the 25th of November, and must be thus celebrated. Let any number of young women, not exceeding seven or less than three, assemble in a room, where they are sure to be safe from interlopers; just as the clock strikes eleven at night, take from your bosom a sprig of myrtle,

which you must have worn there all day, and fold it up in a bit of tissue paper, then light up a small chafing dish of charcoal, and on it let each maiden throw nine hairs from her head, and a paring of her toe and finger nails, then let each sprinkle a small quantity of myrtle and frankincense in the charcoal, and while the odoriferous vapor rises, fumigate your myrtle (this plant, or tree is consecrated to Venus) with it. Go to bed while the clock is striking twelve, and you will be sure to dream of your future husband, and place the myrtle exactly under your head. Observe, it is no manner of use trying this charm, if you are not a real virgin, and the myrtle hour of performance must be passed in strict silence.

HOW TO MAKE YOUR LOVER OR SWEETHEART COME.

If a maid wishes to see her lover, let her take the following method. Prick the third, or wedding finger of your lefthand with a sharp needle (beware a pin), and with the blood write your own and lover's name on a piece of clean writing paper, in as small a compass as you can, and encircle it with three round rings of the same crimson stream, fold it up, and exactly at the ninth hour of the evening, bury it with your own hand in the earth, and tell no one. Your lover will hasten to you as soon as possible, and he will not be able to rest until he sees you, and if you have quarrelled, to make it up. A young man may also try this charm, only instead of the wedding finger, let him pierce his left thumb.

APPLE PARINGS.

On the 28th of October, which is a double Saint's day, take an apple, pare it whole, and take the paring in your right band, and standing in the middle of the room say the following verse:
St. Simon and Jude,
On you I intrude,
By this paring I hold to discover,
Without any delay,
To tell me this day,
The first letter of my own true lover.
Turn round three times, and cast the paring over your left shoulder, and it will form the first letter of your future husband's surname; but if the paring breaks into many pieces, so that no letter is discernible, you will never marry; take the pips of the same apple, put them in spring water, and drink them.

TO KNOW HOW SOON A PERSON WILL BE MARRIED.

Get a green pea-pod, in which are exactly nine peas, hang it over the door, and then take notice of the next person who comes in, who is not of the family, and if it proves a bachelor, you will certainly be married within that year.
On any Friday throughout the year—Take rosemary flowers, bay leaves, thyme, and sweet marjoram, of each a handful; dry these, and make them into a fine powder; then take a tea-spoonful of each sort, mix the powders together; then take twice the quantity of barley flour and make the whole into cake with the milk of a red cow. This cake is not to be baked, but wrapped in clean writing paper, and laid under your head any Friday night. If the person dreams of music, she will wed those she desires, and that shortly; if of fire, she will be crossed in love; if of a church, she will die single. If any thing is written or the least spot of ink is on the paper, it will not do.

TO KNOW WHAT FORTUNE YOUR FUTURE HUSBAND WILL BE.

Take a walnut, a hazel-nut, and nutmeg; grate them together, and mix them with butter and sugar, and make them up into small pills, of which exactly nine must be taken on going to bed; and according to her dreams, so will be the state of the person she will marry. If a gentleman, of riches; if a clergyman, of white linen; if a lawyer, of darkness; if a tradesman, of odd noises and tumults; if a soldier or sailor, of thunder and lightning; if a servant, of rain.

TO KNOW IF A WOMAN WITH CHILD WILL HAVE A GIRL OR BOY.

Write the proper names of the father and the mother, and of the month she conceived with child, and likewise adding all the numbers of those letters together, divide them by seven; and then if the remainder be even, it will be a girl; if uneven, it will be a boy. /

TO KNOW IF A CHILD NEW-BORN SHALL LIVE OR NOT.

Write the proper names of the father and mother, and of the day the child was born, and put to each letter its number, as you did before, and unto the total sum, being collected together, put twenty-five, and then divide the whole by seven; and then, if it be even, the child shall die; but if it be uneven, the child shall live.

TO KNOW IF ANY ONE SHALL ENJOY THEIR LOVE OR NOT.

Take the number of the first letter of your name, the number of the planet, and the day of the week; put all these together, and divide them by thirty; if it be above, it will come to your mind, and if below, to the contrary; and mind that number which exceeds not thirty.

MIDSUMMER-DAY CHARM, TO KNOW YOUR HUSBAND'S TRADE.

Exactly at twelve, on Midsummer-day, place a bowl of water in the sun, pour in some boiling pewter as the clock is striking, saying thus:— /
Here I try a potent spell,
Queen of Love, and Juno tell,
In kind union unto me,
What my husband is to be,
This the day, and this the hour,
When it seems you have the power
For to be a maiden's friend,
So, good ladies, condescend.
A tobacco-pipe full is enough. When the pewter is cold, take it out of the water, and drain it dry in a cloth, and you will find the emblems of your future husband's trade quite plain. If more than one, you will marry twice; if confused and no emblems. You will never marry; a coach shows a gentleman for you.

A CHARM FOR DREAMING.

When you go to bed, place under your pillow a Common Prayer Book, open at the part of the Matrimonial service, in which is printed, "With this ring I thee wed," etc., place on it a key, a ring, a flower and a sprig of willow, a small heart cake, a crust of bread, and the following cards, the ten of clubs, nine of hearts, ace of spades, and the ace of diamonds; wrap all these round in a handkerchief of thin gauze or muslin, on getting into bed cross your hands and say: /
Luna ever woman's friend,
To me thy goodness condescend;
Let me this night in visions see,
Emblems of my destiny
If you dream of storms, trouble will betide you; if the storm ends in a fine calm, so will your fate; if of a ring, or of the ace of diamonds, marriage; bread, an industrious life; cake, a prosperous life; flowers, joy; willow, treachery in love; spades, death; diamonds, money; clubs, a foreign land; hearts, illegitimate children; keys, that you will rise to great trust and power, and never know want; birds, that you will have many children; geese, that you will marry more than once.

THE FLOWER AUGURY.

If a young man or woman receives a present of flowers, or a nosegay from their sweetheart, unsolicited, for if asked for, it destroys the influence of the spell; let them keep them in the usual manner in cold water four-and-twenty hours, then shift the water, and let them stand another twenty-four hours, then take them, and immerse the stalks in water nearly boiling, leave them to perish for three hours, then look at them ; if they are perished, or drooping, your lover is false; if revived and blooming, you will be happy in your choice.

HOW TO TELL BY A SCREW, WHETHER YOUR SWEETHEART LOVES YOU OR NOT.

Get a small screw, such as the carpenters use for hanging closet-doors, and after making a hole in a plank with a gimlet of a proper size, put the screw in, being careful to oil the end with a little sweet oil. After having done this, take a screw-driver and drive the screw home, but you must be sure and observe how many turns it takes to get the screw in so far that it will go no farther. If it requires an *odd* number of turns you can rest assured that your sweetheart does not love you yet, and perhaps is enamored of some other person; but if the number of turns is an *even* number, be happy, for your sweetheart adores you, and lives only in the sunshine of your presence. [end of *Le Marchand's* series]

A Lover's Summoning:
Over-anxious maidens sometimes try to *summon* their future husbands thus: A blade-bone of mutton is laid in a secret place, and taken out on three successive Friday' evenings and a slit cut in it and replaced, after which it is affirmed the future husband will cut his finger, and come to have it bound up.
It is interesting to compare the spells made use of in different districts. A young woman at Wakefield, in York / shire, not long ago, thus practised a variation of this mutton bone spell. She obtained the bladebone of a shoulder of mutton, and into its thinnest part drove a new penknife; then she went secretly into the garden and buried knife and bone together, firmly believing that so long as they were in the ground, her betrothed would be In a state of uneasiness, which would gradually increase till he would be compelled to visit her. (Glyde 1872: 11-12)
This spell is differently used in Buckinghamshire. There the damsel desirous of seeing her lover sticks two pins across through the candle she is burning, taking care that the pins pass through the wick, using the same rhyme adapted to the candle. [It's not this post alone I stick, But Will Marshall's heart I mean to prick, Whether be he asleep or awake, I'd have him come to me and speak]. By the time the candle burn down to the pins and go out the lover, it is believed, is certain to present himself. In the North of England a similar use of candles and pins prevails. A servant in the city of Durham peeped, out of curiosity, into the box of her fellow-servant and was astonished to find there the end of a tallow candle stuck through and through with pins. "What's that, Molly," said Bessie, "that I see'd i' thy box?" "Oh," said Molly, "it's to bring my sweetheart. Thou see'st sometimes he's slow a coming, and if I stick a candle full o' pins it always fetches him." (Glyde 1872: 12)

Love Presents and Witching Spells.
Take three hairs from your head, roll them up in a small compact form, and anoint them with three drops of blood from the left-hand fourth finger, choosing this because the anatomists say a vein goes from that finger to the heart; wear this in your bosom (taking care that none knows the secret) for nine days and nights; then enclose the hair in the secret cavity of a ring or a brooch, and present it to your lover. While it is in his possession, it will have the effect of preserving his love, and leading his mind to dwell on you. A chain or plait of your own hair, mixed with that of a goat, and anointed with nine drops of the essence of ambergris, will have a similar effect. Flowers prepared with your own blood will have an effect on your lover's mind; but the impression will be very transient, and fade with the flowers. If your love should be fortunate, and you are married to the object of your wishes, never reveal to him the nature of the present you made him, or it may have the fatal effect of turning love into hate. (*Mother Shipton's* ca. 1880: 35)

DRAGON'S BLOOD (Sanguis draconis).
Wrap in paper some of the drug called *dragon's blood*, and throw it into the fire with these words – "May he no pleasure or profit see, Till he come back to me." (Northall 1892: 157)

CHARM FOR OBTAINING LOVE AND FOR SUCCESS IN ALL UNDERTAKINGS.
WHOEVER wears this charm, written on virgin parchment, and sewn up in a small *round* silken bag continuously over the heart, will obtain all the love he or she may desire, and will be successful in every undertaking.

 (Hewett 1900: 74)

Miscellaneous Charms:

Charms were found for any number of needs and uses. These are just a few of the many surviving examples to illustrate the wide scope of folk magic. As Owen Davies notes, there is a puzzling dearth of published charms in England after Scot (in contrast to the situation on the Continent where quite explicit collections of traditional charms could be found in popular publications and cheap chapbooks), the anonymous 1824 *Witchcraft Detected and Prevented* being a notable exception. I have included some American examples (which did make their way to England) to cover these missing years.

The first ten are from Thomas Lupton's *A Thousand Notable Things*, a 16th century "book of secrets" with mundane, astrological, medical and magical "receipts" in ten "books" of a hundred items each. Books of secrets were common sources for supposedly esoteric cures and formulas, although they omitted suspiciously magical charms. Nevertheless, as these examples show even some of the "natural" formulas border on the overtly magical. Lupton also included bits of astrological and dream lore in his compilation, and borrowed heavily from a similar French publication *De Arcanis Naturae* (1558) by French astrologer and writer on medicine, Antonio Mizauld (1510-1578), an acquaintance of Dr. John Dee. Interestingly enough, a copy of Lupton's "useful" book apparently came to America on the *Mayflower* in 1620, as it was found in the probate inventories of Deacon (and surgeon) Samuel Fuller, and then in that of Elder William Brewster, the colony's religious leader. *A Thousand Notable Things* went through a number of editions, and the last in 1815 is notable in its own way in that all of the more arcane entries have been replaced with less controversial ones.

Book 2:21 When thou wilt driue away Flyes fro[m] from any place, that there shal none be seene there again, make the image of a Flye in the stone of a Ring: or as my booke sayth *Mizaldus*, in a plate of brasse or copper, or of Tyn, make the image of a Flye, of a Spyder, & of a serpent, the second face of *Pisces* then ascending. And whyles you are mayking or graiuing of them, saye: This is the image which doth cleane ryd all Flyes for euer. Then burie the same in the myds of the house, or hang it in any place in the house, (but if thou hast fowre such plates, and burie or hang them in fowre corners of the house, or hyde them within the walles, that no body take them awaye, it were farre better.) But this laying of them must be when the first face of *Taurus* doth ascend. And so no Flie wyl come in there, or tary there. *Ptolomie* sayeth, that he sawe the tryall hereof in the house of *King Adebarus*: who was verie wyse, and was marvelous expert in naturall Magicke, in whose Pallace or Place, there was neyther Flye, nor any other hurting worme. And that I might search it out, sayeth he: I brought to thyther lyve Flyes, which presently dyed. *Mizaldus*. (Lupton 1579: 29-30)

Book 5:52 A Lamen, or thyn plate of Gold, borne on the seame of the brayne, doth strengthen the brayne. The same hanged against the region or place of the harte doth helpe the beating of the harte, and encreaseth gladnes. And if it be put vpon the reynes of the back: it strengthens the reynes, and cooles the same, and easeth the paynes of the back. But *Mizaldus* wysheth that the same plate be beaten and made of pure / and fyne Golde, when the Sunne is in Leo, called the Lion: And *Iupiter* and the Moone beholding each other happly. *Hermes. Arnoldus Villa nounaus, &c. Alij*. (Lupton 1579: 121-122)

Book 5:59 IF you put a Tode in a new earthen potte, and the same be couered in the groundes in the myddes of a corne fyelde: it is sayde there wyll be no hurtfull tempestes or stormes there. As *Archibus* dyd wryte to *Antiochus* king of *Siria. Plinio Authore*. (Lupton 1579: 123)

Book 7:2 THe tongue of a Dogge layde vnder the great toe within the shoe : doth cease the barking of Dogs at the party that so weares the same. *Mizaldus*. (Lupton 1579: 168)

Book 7:31 IF you wyll knowe in what yeare Wheate wyll be deare or cheape, and what tyme of the yeare, and what month the same wyll chaunce: Elect or thuse [choose?] tweluе fayre cornes of Wheate, in the kalends of Ianuary, (which is y̓ first day of Ianuary,) then sweepe the fyre hath cleane, and make a fyre; then take a yoūg wench, or a boye of the house. or el son y̓ dwels nye you, and byd the same boye or wench laye one of the sayde Cornes on the same harth, being hotte and made cleane: and when that is done, marke dilligently, whether the sayde Corne abyde styll in the place, or leape: If it be styl, then saye that the price wyll contynew: If it leape a lytle, the pryce wyll abate a lytle: If it leape much, then perswade thyself, that it wyll ware very cheape: If it leape towards the fyre, it wyll be dearer in the fyrst month, and so more or lesse, for the greater of lesser accesse of the same to the fyre. Doo so with the second Corne, and it will presayge for the second month, that is, for February: And so you maye judge of all the rest. That is, the thyrde Corne for March: the fourth, for Aprill: and so of the other. *Mizaldus* hath heard that it hath bene proued of many. (Lupton 1579: 170)

Book 8:23 IF the scull of an aged man, be hanged in a Dooue-house [dovecote]: Pygions wyll be encreased there, and wyl lyue quietly. *Albertus*, as *Mizaldus* doth wryte. (Lupton 1579: 194)

Book 9:17 THe two hornes of a Snayle borne vppon a man: wyll plucke away carnall or fleshy lust from the bearer therof. I had this out an olde wrytten booke. But howe true it is I know not. (Lupton 1579: 224)

Book 9:36 YF the figure of a Lyon be graued in thyn plate of Golde, when the Sunne is in *Leone*, (that is the sygne called the Lyon) So that the Moone beholde not then the syxt house, nor the Lord of the Ascendent behold *Saturne* or *Mars*, and the Moone then I or rather free from them: it doth put away the intolerable paynes and tormentes of the backe, or touch the same. And if Trociskes [troches] be made of the powder of pure Olibanū and / Goates bloud, and after sealed with the same Lyon, and after dryed, and then being dyssolued in whyte Wyne and droonke fasting: it workes a marueious effect against the stone of the reynes & the blather. *Andreas Cordubensis* to *Gregory* y̓ Bishop of Rome. (Lupton 1579: 248-249)

Book 9:98 IF one make a lytle rope of the guts of Woolf, and then bury the same vnder sand or earth, there wyll neither Horse nor Sheepe go that way: though you beate them with a staffe. *Albertus*. (Lupton 1579: 253)

Book: 10:15 THe toothe of a man hanged at the necke of the partye that is tormented with toothe ache, doth take away the payne therof, especially: if a Beane be put / therto, wherin there is a hoale bored, and a lowse put therin, and ye same beane wrapt in a peece of sylk, and then hanged about the parties neck, as is before sayde. *Anthonius Mizaldus*. (Lupton 1579: 257-258)

Arthur Gauntlet's collection of charms includes a number of possible aids to gamblers, of which these two are examples:

Take the good stone called Solsequium {"...probably heliotrope..."} (Marigold or Turnsoll) for all gaming Before the Sun rising And kneeling towards the East Say as followeth.
I Conjure thee Solesquium by the virginity of our blessed Lady St Mary the Mother of God and by the Maidenhead of St John the Evangelist And by the Maidenhead of St Catherine **Also** I Conjure thee By all thee by all [sic] the Apostles And by the four Evangelists Matthew Mark Luke and John and by all the Martyrs and Confessors and by all virgins And by all the Joys of our Lady St Mary And by all the four Elements Fire Water Air and Earth, And by these holy names of God *Helli Helli Helli Lamasabacthani* {This is clearly derived from "Eloi Eloi lama sabacthani" ...} *uetu Adonay Eloy Semhamephoras* And by the name that Aaron bore on his forehead And by the Planet under which thou art And by the Character and Seal of the same And by all of the holy names of God whatsoever they be **I Conjure** thee Solesquium that thou let me not be overcome of by any Creature Neither that I lose at any kind of Game Or Games but that I may have the victory of all Mankind

whatsoever I desire to play with all while thou Solesquium art about me Or in my mouth Non veniet in mematitia superbi nec manus Proditoris moreat me finis Solesguii ["it will not come in (mematitia?) of the proud nor will the hand of the betrayer/traitor hinder me", perhaps a garbled paraphrase of Psalm 36:11: *Non veniat mihi pes superbiae et manus peccatoris non moveat me*: "Let not the foot of pride come against me, and let not the hand of the wicked remove me."]. (Rankine 2011: 315)

Take the longest feather in a Swallows wing And write with the blood of a Bat In virgin Parchment *Abat Abac Fala aio abac abasack* And hold it in thy left hand And touch the Dice Saying *Abac Ida adita abac abac abracala abasac*. (Rankine 2011: 315)

Gaster Ms. (Cod. Gaster, No. 1562), written mostly by a certain Thomas Parker in the years 1693-5

(4) How for to know a womans Councill. Take virgine wax and write theron these words ✠ lacus ✠ stratus ✠ Dromedus ✠ Frigius. And when shee sleppeth put it betweene her breasts and shee will shew thee all her meaneing. (Gaster 1910: 376)

(6) [unidentified herb] Uerum: Iff it bee put into watter all the fish will comen to it: Iff a man Bear yt about him hee shall not bee hurt of hys Enemy: Iff anny thing bee stolen let him that is suspected bee touched with it and Iff hee bee guilty he will say hould I haue it. It must bee gatherd in may may (sic) on munday befor the feast of holly Cross. (Gaster 1910: 377)

To Take fysh (Brit. Mus. Sloane 3850) f. 162
Take the roote of a daisy & franchesent & beat them small together & temper it with manisy it will be like a salve or gum & keepe it in a boxe & you will Anoynt your bayte when you fysh they will com to it (Briggs 1977: 260)

Here is one to have money always. "Take a mole in March and make a purse of the dryed skynne, and with a hawk's fether and the bloude of a batt wryte thes names Rosquilla dunstallum, & looke what summe you have in your purse, & so much you shal fynde al ways." (Briggs 1953: 456)

Prison to escape
Gather Celendyne, in ye morninge of St peeter ad vincula [August 1] saying 3 pater nosters & beare it about thee, & thou shalt fear no imprisonments. (Briggs 1977: 263)

Another
Ther is a tirrible name of God by ye which Joshua did overcome 22 Kinges wth ther Armies & made the sonne to stande while he fought with ye Gabeonites. + Achio + noya + he that carieth thes names about him cannot be holden in prison nor be overcome in warre, yt hath bine pved. (Briggs 1977: 263)

Official charm against fire:
+ *mentem santam spontaneum honorem Deo patrie liber,* (A holy mind and willing, honor to God and freedom for my county) known as "St. Agatha's letters," supposed to have been inscribed on St. Agatha's tomb by an angel accompanied by a 100 others.[74]

A charme to open locks.
As the hearbes called Aethiopides [Clary Sage? or Moth Mullein?] will open all locks (if all be true that inchanters saie) with the help of certeine words: so be there charmes also and periapts, which without any hearbs can doo as much: as for example. Take a peece of wax crossed in baptisme, and doo but print certeine floures therein, and tie them in the hinder skirt of your shirt; and when you would undoo the locke, blow thrise therin, saieng:

---

[74] *American Journal of Archaeology.* vol. 23, no. 2, p. 205.

Arato hoc partiko hoc maratarykin. I open this doore in thy name that I am forced to breake, as thou brakest hell gates, *In nomine patris, & filii, & spiritus sancti, Amen.* (Scot 1973: 199)

A charme against vineager.
That wine wax not eager, write on the vessell, *Gustate & videte, quoniam suavis est Dominus.* (Scot 1973: 201).

Spoilt wine was a problem before secure corkage and the understanding of hygienic conditions.

To know how any relation, absent friend, or acquaintance does, during their absence, or if travelling into any other country.
IT is well known nature has a secret communication within herself through all her works, and the occult principle is found in human nature, as well in animal and inanimate bodies. If you wish to know how it fares with an absent friend in respect to their health, you must possess yourself with some of their live blood, and while it is warm, infuse into it a small quantity of white vitriol or spirits of wine, and keep it close stopped up in a glass from the air; now if your friend is well, the blood will look lively fresh and florid; but on the contrary, if he is ill, or the least thing indisposed, you may perceive it by the changing colour of the blood, which will immediately happen according as he is diseased in his body. If the blood gains a redder hue, you may pronounce him in a fever, but if it grows paler and seems mixed with water, and to part in different colours, his sickness is dangerous, and he is reduced to the last stage of weakness. And after this indisposition if he recovers his health, the blood will again look fresh and lively as at first; but unfortunately, should death ensue, the blood will putrify and stink accordingly, just as the rest of the body decays. This has been proved several times, as Dr. Blagrave in his Astrological Physic reports, and the same effects have been produced with Sir Kenelm Digby's sympathetic powder, which will cure wounds at a distance, being applied to some fresh blood collected therefrom. (*Witchcraft Detected* 1824: 45)

So if any one shall swallow the heart of a lapwing, swallow, weasel, or a mole, while it is yet living and warm with natural heat, it improves his intellect, and helps him to remember, understand, and fortel things to come. (Barrett 1967: 37)

MYSTERIOUS PROPERTIES OF THE SUNFLOWER.
Albertus Magnus relates that the heliotropium, or sun-flower, is endued with wonderful virtues; for, if gathered when the sun is in the fifth sign of the zodiac (♍), and wrapped in a laurel leaf, thereto being added a wolf's tooth, the person who carries it about him shall find that nobody can have the power of using any other than mild language to him. Moreover, if anything has been taken from him by stealth, let him lay it under his head at night, and he shall see the thief, and all the circumstances of the theft. ("Raphael" 1832:19)

CHARM TO MAKE A TREE BEAR FRUIT.— The seeds of roses, with mustard Seed, and the foot of a weasel, tied together in something, and hung among the boughs or branches of a tree which bears but little fruit, will remedy the defect, and render the tree amazingly fruitful. (*Mother Shipton's* ca. 1880: 59)

20. To Obtain the Object of your Petition.
Let a little of the plant called Five-Finger be worn about one, when he seeks a favor from a lord or an officer, and he will surely succeed. The juice of this plant is good for the Dysentery. (Brown 1904: 110)

105. To Gain a Law Suit.
It is said, that if one has a law-suit, and will take of the largest sage, and will write the names of the 12 Apostles on a leaf and put them in his shoe before he goes to the Court House, he will gain his case. (Brown 1904: 122)

143. To Win in a Play.
Bind to the arm with which you throw the heart of a field mouse, with a red silk thread and you will always win. (Brown 1904: 131)

Hohman's *Long Forgotten* (or "Long-Lost") *Friend* (1820) also has an unusual number of charms to prevent being shot or injured by weapons, as well as one to improve one's marksmanship:

13. To make sure to Hit in Shooting.
Take the † heart of a † field-mouse, and put a little of it † between the ball and the powder, and you will hit what you wish. You must use the three highest names when you begin to load, and you must not finish the words till you finish loading. (Brown 1904: 109)

160. A Safeguard Against all Weapons.
Jesus, God and Man, protect me from every kind of firearms, weapons, long and short, sword of every kind of metal and, hold thy fire, as Mary retained her virginity before and after her parturition. Christ bound every weapon as he bound himself in humanity full of humility. Jesus stops every gun and sword, as Mary, spouse of the mother of God; therefore protect the three holy blood-drops which Jesus sweat on the Mt. of Olives: Jesus Christ protects me from the death-stroke and burning fire. Jesus permits me not to die, much less to be damned, without partaking of the holy supper. That helps me God the Father, Son and Holy Ghost. Amen. (Brown 1904: 134)

171. Another, Similar.
I conjure thee, sword, rapier, knife, whatever is injurious and destructive to me, by every prayer of the priest, and him who brought Jesus into the temple and said, a piercing sword shall go through thine soul, that thou suffer not me, as a child of God to suffer. J. J. J. ["Jesus" 3 times] (Brown 1904: 137)186.

A Warding off of Balls.
May the heavenly and holy sackbuts warm and ward off from me all balls and misfortune, — off from me instantly. I take refuge under the tree of life which bears twelve manner of fruit. I stand under the sacred altar of the christian church. I commend myself to the holy Trinity. I. N. N. entrench myself behind the sacred body of Jesus Christ. I commend myself to the wounds of Jesus Christ, that I may not be seized by the hand of any man, nor bound, nor cut, nor shot, nor stabbed, nor thrown down, nor slain, and especially may not be wounded; to this help me N. N. ☞ Whosoever carries this little book with him is safe from all his foes, visible or invisible, and so also he who carries this little book with him can never be killed without the entire sacred body of Jesus Christ, nor be drowned in water, nor burned in fire, and no unjust judgment can be pronounced against him. Thereto help me ††† (Brown 1904: 141)

If a Man or Beast is attacked by Wicked People, and how to banish them forever from the House so that they may never be able to do any Harm, Bedgoblin and all ye evil spirits, I forbid you my bedstead, my couch; I forbid you, in the name of God, my house and home; I forbid you, in the name of the Holy Trinity, my blood and flesh, my body and soul; I forbid you all the nail holes in my house and home, till you have traveled over every hillock, waded through every water, have counted all the leaflets of the trees, and counted all the starlets in the sky, until that beloved day arrives when the mother of God will bring forth her second Son. † † †

This formula, three times spoken in the house of the person whom we seek to aid, always adding, in the right place, both his baptismal and other names, has been found excellent in many hundred cases. (*Albertus Magnus* n. d.: 1)

A particular Performance by which it is caused that a Person will always obtain Right before a Court of Justice. Take the herb called suntull (skunk cabbage) gathered during the month of August, while the sun stands in the sign of the lion, wrap a little thereof in a bay leaf, add a dandelion to it, carry this talisman on your person, and you will have the best of everybody, and receive the greatest advantage from it. (*Albertus Magnus* n. d.: 17)

When a Man or Cattle is Plagued by Goblins, or Ill-disposed People. Go on Good Friday, or Golden Sunday, ere the sun rise in the East, to a hazelnut bush, cut a stick therefrom with a sympathetic weapon, by making three cuts above the hand toward the rise of the sun, in the name of the t t t Carry the stick noiselessly into the house, conceal it so that no one can get hold of it. When a man or beast is plagued by evil disposed people, walk three times around such a haunted person, while pronouncing the three holiest names; after this proceeding, take off thy hat and hit it with the stick and thus you smite the wicked being. (*Albertus Magnus n. d.*: 19)

To manufacture a Golden Ring, by which not only House and Home, but also Man and Beast are secured against all Misfortunes, Pestilential Epidemics and Diseases, and are secured against the Arts and Wiles of the Powers of the Devil. May God direct and rule, that this hour, day and year and all the time may be as good and blessed as our dear Lord Jesus Christ; that grant God, the Father, and God the Son, and God the Holy Spirit. Amen.

May God, the Father, make a golden ring around this house, around this stable, around all men and beasts that belongeth thereto and goeth in and out of it; also around my fields and forests, yea, this very ring encircles our beloved Mary with her dear infant, Jesus Christ they protect, watch over, maintain, shelter, cover and defend all mankind, both male and female, small and large, young and old, as likewise, all cattle, oxen, steers, cows and calves, horses and foals, sheep, goats, beef-cattle, and swine, geese, ducks, chickens, pigeons, large and small, whatever is contained in this house and these stables and all that cometh in and goeth out; for all misfortunes, evil, colic wild fire, losses, epidemics, and other diseases; for all bad and heated blood; for all bad and malicious enemies and storms; for all evil hours, day and night; for all magic power of witchcraft, and the designs and powers of the devil and his infernal hosts, to be visible or invisible, or for all wicked people who contemplate to rob me, that they may not be able to carry or spoil aught, anything that these people and animals, young and old, large and small, nothing excepted, whatsoever belongeth to these premises and their surroundings, and goeth out and cometh in, from whence and hence that no loss may occur, nor any evil be done at home or abroad, in the field or in the woods, in the meadows and on the plains, in grass, wood or heath, whether it works or rests, sits, lays, runs, or stands, they shall all now for all time to come be included in this ring, and be secure and protected from bullet and sword, by the very holy blood-drops of the dear beloved infant, Jesus Christ, which he hath suffered and shed for us by his circumcision and upon the cross and thereby vouchsafed and sealed his love everlasting, for such, they, the magicians will find no herb which may open, break or move or pervert, because our dear Lord Jesus Christ, protects and defendeth such with his ever holy hands, and his supremely sacred five wounds, at all times, by day and by night, and at all hours, forever and ever eternally. In the name of God the Father, the Son and the Holy Spirit.

Three Fridays in succession, in the morning, this should be repeated three times over house and all the estates, and all that lives and dwells therein will be protected from all evil and harm. (*Albertus Magnus n. d.*: 29-30)

To prevent that the Fire on the Hearth becomes extinguished.
When a new house is built, write upon three separate pieces of paper: Deus Pater, Deus Filius, Deus Spiritus Sanctus in Oleum Trinitatis Sun and Moon have their course over water and over land, that no fire and flame in this house shall cease, above inscriptions be placed, and on three corners under the For this, three tin boxes must be made, and in each one the threshold or stones be laid, so that they do not decay or moulder in the ground, and the fires in such a house will never go out. (*Albertus Magnus n. d.*: 42)

To Obtain Money. Take the eggs of a swallow, boll them, return them to the nest, and if the old swallow brings a root to the nest, take it, put it into your purse, and carry it in your pocket, and be happy. (*Albertus Magnus n. d.*: 74)

To Open Locks.
Kill a green frog, expose it to the sun for three days, powder or pulverize it. A little of this powder put into a lock will open the same. (*Albertus Magnus n. d.*: 74)

To Make a Mirror in which Everything may be Discerned.
Procure a looking glass, such as are commonly sold. Inscribe the characters noted below upon it. Inter it on the crossing of two pathways, during an uneven hour. On the third day thereafter, hie to the place at same hour, and take it out: but you must not be the first person to look into the glass. It is best to let a dog or a cat take the first look into the mirror: S. Solam S. Tattler S. Echogardner Gematar. (*Albertus Magnus n. d.*: 89)

Butter, to Come:

Due to atmospheric conditions, it was sometimes difficult to almost impossible to get butter out of suspension in milk or cream and collect on the dasher of a churn. This difficulty was very often attributed to witchcraft.

> Ady, in his *Candle in the Dark,* 1655, says "... an old woman in Essex came into a house at a time when as the maid was churning of butter and having laboured long and could not make her butter come, the old woman told the maid what was wont to be done when she was a maid, and also in her mother's young time, that if it happened then butter would not come readily, they used a charm to be said over it, whilst yet it was in beating, and it would come straightways, and that was this –
> 'Come, butter, come,
> Come, butter, come, /
> Peter stands at the gate
> Waiting for a butter'd cake;
> *Come,* butter, come !'
> (*A Candle in the Dark*, Ed. 4to. 1665, p. 58).
> "This, said the old woman, being said three times, will make your butter come, for it was taught my mother by a learned churchman in Queen Mary's days, when as churchmen had more cunning and could teach people many a trick, that our ministers nowadays know not." (Northall 1892:150-151)

For the following interesting information on this subject of minor superstitions I am indebted to Mr. C. Kille of Minehead.

If you are asked to a christening, and wish to carry luck to the house, and give the child a propitious start in life, you would do well to go to your cupboard and reach down a piece of bread and some of the best cheese you have got to put on the top of it. When you get out of your house, give the bread and cheese to the first child you meet. Take care, however, if you are going to assist at the baptism of a boy, you give your bread and cheese to one of the opposite sex, and observe a similar care also if it should be a girl, or your offering may not be propitious after all. (Hancock 1897: 251)

TO PREVENT FLEAS FROM ENTERING A HOUSE. WHEN you first hear the cuckoo in the Spring, take some of the earth from the place on which your right foot is standing, and sprinkle it on the threshold of your front door ; but speak of it to no one. Neither fleas, beetles, earwigs, or vermin of any sort will cross it. (Hewett 1900: 75)

This collection of charms, which is in no way exhaustive, exemplifies the diversity and character of the Cunning Folk's repertoire. They were selected to indicate the span of time and variety of this area of folk magic. I have omitted most of those aimed at protecting livestock – a vital economic resource – as they are presumably of less interest to modern readers. Charms were, of course, also known and used by ordinary people without professional guidance. Most of the examples here are from published sources available at the time the Cunning Folk were at work, but some are from early manuscripts that only appeared in print more recently. I have chosen to include the latter as an indication of the many that were in use in the past that otherwise would remain unknown.

CHAPTER 10:

Folk or Non-Computational Astrology

Geomancy was perhaps the most sophisticated example of what has been called "mock astrology" – the application of astrological concepts and symbolism independent of astronomy or astrology proper, although there were other sources for "non-computational" astral theory as well. Astrological information of a basic sort permeated the culture of the Cunning Folk and their clients, just as the concepts and terminology of psychology and physics does our own. Before increased literacy and vernacular manuals made actual astrology popular, it was often a matter of confusion for the less- or uneducated. For example, when Anne Baker of Bottesford, Leicestershire was accused of witchcraft in 1618, she claimed that "there are foure colours of Planets, Blacke, Yellow, Greene, and Blew: and that Blacke is always Death. and that shee saw the Blew Planet strike Thomas Fayrebarne, the eldest Sonne unto William Fayrebarne …"[75], apparently thinking of planets as individual spirits and confusing them with elves and fairies which were traditionally classified by colours. Similarly, Cunning Folk sometimes claimed to be "planet masters" able to overcome the effects of bad aspects, although whether they conceived of planets as stars or spirits, or both, is unclear.

Much of the astrological lore available to the ordinary wise man or woman was of the generic kind found in commonly available sources, a list of which was given by Gabriel Harvey in 1572:

> The A.B.C. of owr vulgar Astrologers, especially such, as ar commonly termed Cunning men or Arts-men. Some call them wissards. Erra Paters prognostication for euer. The Shepherds Kalendar. The Compost of Ptolemeus. Sure fewe add Arcandam: & a pamflet, intituled, The knowledg of things vnknowne. I haue heard sure of them name Jon de indagine. Theise be theire great masters: & in a manner theire whole librarie: with sum old parchment-roules, tables, & instruments. Erra Pater, their Hornebooke. The Shepherds Kalendar, their primer. The Compost of Ptolemeus, their Bible. Arcandam, their newe Testament. The rest, with Albertus secrets, & Aristotles problems Inglished, their great Doctours, & wonderfull Secreta secretorum.[76]

This is the essential Cunning Folk's "bibliography" for the 16th century, at the time when literate resources began their influential descent from the elite to the common level of the magical world. That these titles were well known even among the educated elite shows the importance of the written sources. A century later, these same rudimentary jumbles of esoteric and practical information were still going strong, even though more detailed and useful (and more expensive) works were then available in English. Most of these mock astrological publications went through dozens of editions, with a kaleidoscope of variable contents sharing familiar titles from the 16th through the 18th century before being supplanted by the syncretic products of the 19th century occult revival. The practical value of much of the information was questionable (as the examples below demonstrate), but it provided generations of professional magic workers with theoretical understanding, methodology and vocabulary for their practice.

The *Erra Pater* – *The pronostycacyon for euer of Erra Pater, Doctor in Astronomy and Physic, very profitable to keep the body in health* – (ostensibly written by a "Jew borne in Jewery" because Jews, as a marginal community, were supposed to be particularly knowledgeable in esoteric lore) was a basic introduction to astrological constructs. A "prognosticon" or "prognostication" was ordinarily a supplement to early almanacs with important dates, predictions about the weather and astrological matters for the specific

---

[75] *The Wonderful Discoverie of the Witchcrafts of Margaret and Phillip Flower, Daughters of Joan Flower neere Beuer castle: Executed at Lincolne, March 11.1618*. London: G. Eld for I. Barnes, dwelling in the long Walke neere Christ-Church, 1619, f

[76] C. G. Moore Smith. *Gabriel Harvey's Marginalia*. Stratford-Upon-Avon: Shakespeare Head Press, 1913, p.163.

year. The *Erra Pater*, on the other hand, was a "prognosticon forever" – the same subject matter unrelated to specific dates or places. It was useful in providing a grounding in astrological concepts that lent credibility to a cunning man's pronouncements, and could serve as a "primer" for those who wanted to learn more. The earliest versions, such as that published by Robert Wyer about 1540, were simple chapbooks instructing readers in the hypothetical relationship of personal health (the four humours or "coolers" – cholers) and the external cosmos, including the stars, planets, and cardinal directions, with a list of "dyssemall" days. There is a particular focus on weather prediction, a crucial concern for any agricultural community, and some on universally allowed astrological predictions. While there is no overtly magical information, the *Erra Pater* was an introduction to the system of invisible influences that lay behind what could be observed in nature. To give some idea of the style of this early source, I include examples dealing with humoural health and with weather. In addition to these sections, the Erra Pater contained information on the humours, the division of time (when clocks and calendars were still rare), the seasons (included below), the "dismal" or unlucky days, an outline of cosmology, the 12 astrological signs, cycles of the Moon, months for bloodletting, meteorology (included below), and the significance of thunder on different days. There is no pagination in this 32 page pamphlet and there are forward slashes in the text, so I have not used them to indicate page breaks in the examples following:

The Dysposycion of the
Fyrste Season of the yere.
Capricornus, Aquar[i]us, and Pisces.

THE Fyrste Season of the yere yt hath domynacion of the bodye on man, is iij. Monthes, and they be named these iij. Sygnes, Capricorne Aquarie, and Pisces. And these three sygnes haue power of all flumes [phlegms] of the body of man and woman, and they be colde and moyste, and they begyn to reygne the xxiiij. daye of Decembre, & dureth to the xxiiij day of Marche.

The Dysposycion of the .ij.
parte of the yeare.
Aries, Taurus, and Gemini.

THE .ii. parte of the yeare is other three monthes and these ben the sygnes. Aries Taurus and Gemini. And the haue power in the bodye of man of the breaste. And the be hote and moyste. And they begyn to reygne the .xxiiij. daye of Marche, and dureth vnto the .xxiiij. daye of Iune.

The dysposycion of the .iij. season of the yeare.
Cancer, Leo and Virgo.

THE .iij. season of the yeare ben other .iij. monthes, & these be the sygnes. Cancer, Leo and Virgo. And the haue power in the boyde of man, of the yelowe Coolers [cholers], & they be hote and drye, and they begyn to reygne on the .xxiiij. daye of Iune, and dureth vnto .xxiiij. daye of Septembre.

The dysposycion of the .iiij. parte of the yeare.
Libra, Scorpio, and Sagittarius.

THe .iiij. parte of the yeare be other three monthes, and these be the sygnes. Libra, Scorpio, and Sagitarius. And the be colde and drye, and they begyn to reygne the .xxiiij. daye of Septembre, and dureth to the .xxiiij. daye of Decembre.

And by the maner of there .iiij. seasons euery man maye kepe hym from all contraryes of Meates / Drinkes / and Clothynge / and from other contrayes. And yf a man wyll kepe hym after the maner whiche is rehersed in this Booke, he shall neuer haue infyrmities of body by the grace of God.
Take Phylter of Spayne [**Anthemis pyrethrum**], and chawe it in thy mouthe, for it is good to spourge the head and the body. Also to eate fenell seede, and Cōmen [cumin] seede, for eche of these Seedes dystroye the flumes that all those euviles in any mannes body come of. ...

For to Understande / and
knowe the yeares that shall be
plenteous and in great &
habundaunce of Goodes.

In die Dominica.
That is Sondaye.

IN the yeare that Ianyuere [January] shall enter vpon the sondaye, the wynter shall be colde, and moyst, and the sōmer shall be hote, and the tyme of harueste shalbe wyndy, and rayny, with great habundaunce of corne, of all gardyne fruyte and herbes. There shalbe lytell Oyle habundaunce shall be of all maner of fleshe. Some great newes shall men here spoken of kynges, of prelates of the churche and other erthly prynces. Great warres and robboryes shall be made, & many yonge people shall dye.

In die Luna.
That is Mondaye.

In the yeere that Ianyuere, shall enter on the mondaye, the wynter shall be pleasyble ynoughe, and the sommer shall be very temperate. Than shall be great flodes of water, that shall breke out of theyr lymytes and bondes, and many Shyppes vpon the see shall peryshe, and in this yeare shall raygne dyuers [divers] syckenesses and chaunges of great lordes shall be made, many women shal perysshe in trauvylyng [giving birth] with chylde, many great Lordes shall dye.
This yeare shalbe lytell grasse, and mustarde seede, but there shalbe plentye of corne, of wynes and good chepe fleshe and but lytell Oyle.

In die Martis.
That is Tuesdaye.

In the yeare that Ianyuere, shall enter on the Tuesday, the wynter shall be chaungeable and not stedfast, for in the Pryme tyme [spring time] of trueth it shall freese, & that shall hurte sore the Rye the vynes and the flowers, and the sommer shalbe drye, hote, and burynge, in so moche that the herbes in gardynes / shall haue no power to come out of the grounde. All thynges shall be deare saue onley corne, many men shall dye, of the blody flyxe, there shall be no no tydinges of thondre, lyghtnynge and tempeste, but all fleshe shall be dere, many wynes shall turne.

In die Marcurij.
That is Wednesdaye.

In the yeare that Ianyuere, shall enter on the Wednesdaye, the wynter shalbe temperate, but in the ende there shalbe Snowe, and Froste, the Pryme tyme shalbe raynye great habundaunce of all Corne, of wynes of fruytes, of haye, of grasse, and generally of all good thynges. The Sommer shall be a lytell clowdye, by whiche there of shall come great sycknes, poore labourers, as handercraftes, and artyfycers shall gayne metely well this yere many Theues shalbe, by whome the meane people shalbe sore pylled [pillaged]/ and dyscomfyted, great warres, battyle and slaughter shall be, towards the myds of the yere, by the whiche shall come great goodes to some men. In the ende of the yere shalbe dyuers pestylences botches [sores], and fallynge euylles and specyally next the see.

In die Iouis.
That is Thursdaye.

In the yeare that Iauyuere, shall enter on the Thursdaye, the wyntere shalbe longe and moste parte drye, and this yeare shalbe verye holsome. The Pryme tyme shall be very wyndye, the sōmer shalbe good and temperate, and Haruest shalbe moste parte raynye, by the whiche the waters shall sore brake out of theyr bondes, the Wheete and wynes shall be good chepe. There that be of Otes, of Haye / of Grasse, and of fruytes, competenlye ynoughe, greate warre and deuysyon [division] shall be, betwene the Churche, the Kynges, and the Princes and in the endethe pryncess shall haue the victorys of theyr enterpryses. ☞ Women shall set them seules moche to Lechery, the people shall be well eased of taxes and tallages.

In die Veneris.
That is Frydaye.

In the yeare that Ianyuere, shall enter on the Fryday, the wynter shall be longe and dyrke, and the sōmer unholsome, haruest shalbe drye, all corne shalbe deare, the vyntage shalbe good ynoughe, and habundaunce of oyle, of fruyte, of hay, of grasse, and of all gardyn herbes, the worlde shalbe sore persecuted with dyuers sycknesses, as soore Eyes and of all Etykes ["hectics" – consumptive diseases]. Many yonge chyldren shall dye, great thondre, lyghtnynge, and tempestes shalbe that shal greue sore all the grounde, there shal be earthquakes, and good chepe clothe, poore people shall gayne lytell nothynge, many beastes shall dye for hunger, for the dyuersytie and maladye of the tyme.

In die Sabbati.
That is Saturdaye.

In the yeare that Ianyuere, shall enter on the Saturdaye, the wynter shalbe temperate suffycentlye , and in the Pryme tyme shalbe Frostes / the whiche shall dystroye the Ryes / the Vines / the Oyles / and the fruytes / the sōmer shall be metelye temperate, the haruest tyme shalbe drye, the Otes and other Corne shall be good chepe. All gardyne herbes shall be chepe ynoughe, and flesche shalbe good chepe, many olde people shall dye. Feuers Tercians shall greue sore the worlde that shalbe sycke through euyll heet. |And many murmurations / Warres/ and murthers shalbe done, by the one agaynste the other, and neyghboures agaynste neyghboures. And manye other cases / shall be oftentymes comytted and done.[77]

The *Erra Pater* became so popular that it went through at least 12 editions before 1600 and dozens afterward, including some published in America around the time of the Revolution. The author's name was also borrowed for similar compilations like the *Book of Knowledge* and after 1708, combined with William Lilly's to exploit the reputations of England's most celebrated astrological experts – one mythical and the other deceased – in competing editions.

The *Shepherd's Kalendar* (not to be confused with Edmund Spenser's 1579 work of the same name) was originally quite a different production. The early editions are impressive quarto (about 12 inches tall) volumes of 192 or more pages with many high-quality woodcuts. The original 1493 *Le Compost et Kalendrier des bergiers* was translated into both Scots and English and printed in Paris in 1503. The first London edition was published in 1506 by Richard Pynson. Early *Kalendar of Shepherdes* included 1) a perpetual calendar, 2) a complex section on the seven deadly sins and related vices (presented in the form of branching boughs and twigs) with their punishments in Hell, 3) a shorter section on the contrasting "field of virtues", and 4) physical health and medicine, before dealing with 5) cosmology, astrology, physiognomy and related matters, parts of which were recycled in subsequent popular chapbooks. The selection below is taken from the fifth section of the *Shepherdes Kalendar*, "To knowe the fortunes and destenies on mā [man] borne vnder the .xii. sygnes after Ptholomeus prynce of astronomy". As with the previous selection, the backslash is punctuation (acting as a comma) rather than an indication of a page break, and the ocassional macron over a letter (as "ā") indicates a contraction omitting an "m" or "n".

To know vnder what planet a man is borne it is nedefull to wete that there is .vii. planettes on ye skye/ y^t is to say Sol. Venus. Mars. Mercurius. Iupyter. Luna/ and Saturnus. Of the seuē planettes is named the .vii. dayes of ye weke/ for euery day hath his name of ye planet reygnynge in ye begynnyng of it. The auncyent phylozophres sayth that Sol domyneth the sonday/ the cause is they say for the sonne amōge ye other planets is moost worthy/ wherfore it taketh ye worthiest day that is sonday. Luna domyneth the fyrst houre of mondaye. Mars the fyrst houre of Tuesday. Mercury of Wednesday. Iupyter for Thursday. Venus for fryday. And Saturnus for Saturday. The day naturell hath foure and twenty houres and in euery houre reygneth a planet. It is for to be noted y^t whā a man wyll begyn to rekē [reckon] at sonday he must reken thus Sol. Ven^9. Mercurius. Luna. Saturn^9.

---

[77] The *Pronostycacion Foreuer of Erra Pater: A Iewe boryne in Iewery, a Doctour in Astronomye and Physyke. Profytable to kepe the Bodye in helth. And also Ptholomeus sayth the same.*
[colophon] Imprinted by me Robert Wyer dwellynge at the Sygne of S. Iohn Evangelyste, in S. Martyns pareysche, in the Duke of Suffolkes rentes, besyde Charynge Crosse. (ca. 1530).

> Iupyter. Mars. And whan the nombre is fayled [failed/ended] he must begyn at the houre yᵗ he wold knowe what planet reygeneth. The mōnday he ought to begȳ at Luna. The Tuesday at Mars. The Wednesday at Mercury. The Thursday at Iupyter. The fryday at Venus. The saterday at Saturnus. And euer whan the nombers of the planettes is fayled he must begyn by odre as is sayd. It is to be noted also that the grekes begynneth theyr day in the mornyng/ the yewes at noone/ and the crysten men at mydnyght/ and there we ought to begyn to reken/ for at one of the clocke on sonday in the mornynge reygneth Sol/ at two reygneth Ven⁹/ at .iij. reygneth Mercury/ at .iiij. reygneth Luna at .v. reygneth Saturnus/ at .vi. reygneth Iupyter/ at .vij. Mars. And at .viiii. begyn agayne at sol/at .ix. venus/ at .x. Mercury/ and consequently of the other by ordre in euery houre. Whan a chylde is borne it is to be knowen at what houre/ & yf it be in the begynnynge of the houre/ in the myddes/ or at the ende. Yf it be in the begynnynge he shall holde of the same planet/ & of yᵉ other afore. If it be in the myddes/ it shall holde of that onely. Yf it be borne in the ende it shall holde of the same/ and & of that yᵗ cometh next after/ but neuertheles yᵉ planet that it is borne vnder ne shall not domyne the other/ & and that of the day shall be aboue it whiche is yᵉ cause that a chylde holdeth of dyuers planettes/ & hath dyuers condycyons. He that is borne vnder Sol shall be prudent and wyse/ a grete speker/ & that whiche he prayseth he holdeth vertues in hym selfe. Who that is borne vnder Venus is loued of euery man/ good to godwarde & reguler/ who yᵗ is borne vnder Mercury is well berded/ subtyll/ mylde/ verytable/ & is not moost prudēt. Who yᵗ is borne vnder Luna hath an hye forheed/ ruddy/ mery vsyage/ shamefast/ and relygyous. Who that is borne vnder Saturne is hardy/curteys/ of shorte lyuynge/ & is not auracyous. Who that is borne vnder Iupyter is hardy/ fayre vysaged & ruddy chast and vagabunde. Who yᵗ is borne vnder Mars is a grete speker/ a lyer/ a thefe/ a deceyuer/ bygge and of reed coloure. They that wyll knowe of this more euydently lett theym torne to the proprytees of the seuen planets afore reherced.[78]

Editions of this work were published up to 1656, but after that the title was borrowed for general "books of knowledge" such as the ca. 1735 edition whose lengthy title aptly sums up its contents:

> The Shepherd's Kalendar: or, The Citizen's and Country Man's Daily Companion: Treating of many Things that are Useful and Profitable to Man-kind, with above Two Hundred wonderful Curiosities, never before Published. Also, A Discourse of the Eclipses of the Sun and Moon, with Rules to know when they will happen, Infallible Signs of the Weather: To know when Wet or Dry, and when sudden Storms arises, Hot or Cold Weather, by living Creatures: A curious Observation never made Publicke before. An Account of the Lucky and Unlucky Days [t]hroughout the Year. The Mosiack Wand to find out Hidden Treasures. The Calculation of Nativities and to Resolve all Lawful Questions.
> To which is added: The Country Man's ALMANAC, Directions when to Bled, and Dyet the Body: A Treatise of Bees, Warrens, ordering of Cattle, Hawks, and how to Kill Vermine. The Measuring Land and Timber: the Art of Ringing: The true Value, or Worth of a Single Penny: Or, a Caution to keep Money.
> Being the above Forty Years Study and Experience of a Learned Shepherd. The Third Edition, with Additions.
> LONDON: Printed by and for Tho. Norris: and Sold by Edw. Midwinter, at the Looking Glass on London-Bridge.

The *Compost of Ptolemeus*, included in the *Shepherdes Kalendar* and issued later as a separate publication, was allegedly the work of the great Hellenistic geographer and astrologer Claudius Ptolemy (c. 90 – c. 168 CE). "Compost" in this case meant "compilation" and was not a comment on the veracity of the material. An early example was printed in 1530 by Robert Wyer, publisher of the *Erra Pater* and England's first "occult publisher". The *Compost* went through fewer editions than the *Erra Pater* (with which it might be combined) or the *Kalendar*, but maintained some measure of popularity over the centuries. The following selections are from a reprint of an undated, probably 17th century edition. The information is quite traditional in character and the chapter headings give a good idea of its scope and content. Most of the chapters are very short, no more than a few paragraphs:

---

[78] H. Oskar Sommer. *The Kalender of Shepherdes.* London: Kegan, Paul, Trench, Trubner, & Co., 1892, pp 156-158.

- The Prologue of Ptolemeus
- [image of the pre-Copernican concentric cosmos] A Figure of the Heavens, with the Four Elements, and Planets above the Earth.
- The Judgement and Opinions of other Astronomers, concerning the Authors Prologue before Rehearsed.
- Of the twelve Celestial Signs, showing how they rule and govern the twelve parts of the body of Man: and which be good, indifferent, evil for letting blood. [with an image of the Astrological Man found in all almanacs]
- Of the nature, quality and disposition of the twelve Signs.
- Of the Anatomy of the Bones in Mans body. And the number of them in all, two hundred forty eight.
- Of Phlebotomy, with the names of the Veins, and where they rest, and how they ought to be let blood.
- How to come to the knowledge whether a man be in health and well, or whether he be disposed to sickness.
- Of the sign to know when a Man is in health, and well disposed in his body.
- Of the Signs which are contrary to the former, showing when a man is disposed to sickness.
- Of other signs like to them aforesaid, showing the repletion of evil humours, and for purging of the same.
- Of the division and regiment of Time, which Ptolomeus use: with the time of the Year and Seasons requisite.
- Of the regiment or rules for the Spring time, which is, March, April and May.
- A rule for the time of Summer, that is june, July, and August.
- A rule for the time of Harvest, which is September, October, and November.
- A Rule for the time of Winter, which is December, January, and February.
- Of the four Elements, and the four complexions of Man.
- Of the Astronomy of Ptolomeus, showing a figure of the Heavens, the four Elements, and how the Planets are placed above the Earth, & etc. [same image as in second heading]
- Of the four Elements, and similitude of the Earth, and how each Planet is one above the other; also, which of them are Masculine, and which Feminine, & etc.
- Of the Equinoctial and Zodiack which are in the Skies, containing the Firmament under it.
- Of the motion and subtle variations of the Heavens and Skies.
- Of the two great circles, that is to say, the one the Meridian, the other the Horizon, which intersecteth one the other and doth cross directly. [with diagram of the same]
- Of two other great circles in the Skies and of four which are lesser.
- Of the rising and the setting of the twelve Signs in the Horizon.
- Of the rotundity, division, and the several regions contained in the same.
- Of the four parts of the World, with some particular Kingdoms, and countries of the same. [a very crude map of the hemispheres]
- The Countries, or Kingdoms. [a list keyed to the map, missing a few numbers]
- Of the variation that is for diverse habitations, and Regions of the Earth.
- Of the division and several Climates, and the parts that are inhabited. [with a diagram of the seven zones]
- Of the great and marvelous considerations and understanding of the Astronomers and the Astrologians.
- Of the Pomell of the Sky, being a Star called the Star of the North, near the which is the Pole Artic, called Septentrional.
- Of Andromeda, a Star Fixed.
- Of Perseus, a Star Fixed.
- Of Ozyron, a Star Fixed, and his follows.
- Of Alhabor, a Star Fixed.

- Of the Lions Heart, a Star Fixed.
- Of the Stars Fixed, called Nebuluae, and of the other called the Golden Cup.
- Of Pork Espike, a Star Fixed [porc despyne, or porcupine; i. e., *Spika*]
- Of the Crown Septentrional, a Star Fixed
- Of the Scorpions Heart, a Star Fixed
- Of the Eagle, a Star Fixed
- Of the Fish Meridional, a Star Fixed
- Of Pegasus, which signifieth the Horse of Honor, a Star Fixed
- Of the division of the twelve Houses, as well in the Earth as in the Heavens.
- How the Planets reigneth in every hour of the Day and Night.
- Of the nature of the seven Planets, after the saying of Ptolomeus.
- Of the fortunes and destinies of Man and Woman, born under the twelve Signs, after the saying of Ptolomeus.
- Ptolomeus upon the twelve Signs.
- Of the twelve Signs, and first Aries, which is good to let blood.
- Of the Science of Physiognomy, teaching to know the natural inclination of Man and Woman. [with two rough cuts of three men's faces each]
- Of Palmistry, with the judgment, distinction, and Lines of the Hand. [with six cuts]
- [a list of 32 similies comprehending the microcosm]
- [a cut of a dragon in the sky]

Having already excerpted the hidden astral characteristics of the days of the week and the seven planets, we now have the implications of birth under the twelve signs, as found in chapter 52 of the *Compost*:

CHAP. LII
Of the twelve Signs, and first Aries, which is good to let blood.

Those people which are born under the Sign of *Aries* (from the midst of March to the midst of April) shall be of good wit, and shall not either be rich nor poor; they shall have damage by his neighbors, they shall have power over dead folks goods, they shall be soon angry, and soon appeased, and shall have diverse fortunes and discords; the man will desire learning, and eloquent people, and shall be expert in many degrees ; he will be a liar, and boaster of courage, and shall take vengeance on his enemies, and he shall be better disposed in youth than in age; he shall be a fornicator, and shall be wedded at twenty five years, if he be not he shall not be chaste, and he shall be a mediator for some of his friends, and shall gladly be busy in the deeds of others, he shall have a mark on his shoulder, and on his head & body; yet he will be rich by the death of others, his first son shall not live long, he will be in great danger of four footed beasts, and shall have much sickness at three score and three years, and if he escape, he shall live fourscore years after nature.

The Woman.

The Woman that is born in this time, she shall be ireful, and suffer great wrongs from day to day, she will be a liar, and shall lose her husband, and recover a better, she will be sick at five years of age, and at twenty five be in great danger of death; and if she escape she will be in danger till forty years, & will suffer much pain in the head ; the days of Sol and Mars shall be good to them, but Jupiter contrary, they shall be like sheep to lose their fleece one year and get it in another.

Of the Sign of Taurus, evil for letting blood.

A Man which is born in this Sign of *Taurus*, from mid April to mid May, shall be very strong, hearty and full of strife, delit[er]ious, and shall possess goods given him by other men, and what he would have done must be sudden, and will enforce himself to finish it; in his youth he will despise every person, and will be ireful, he shall go on pilgrimage, leaving his friends to live amongst strangers, he shall be put in offices, and will exercise them well, he shall be rich by Women, and come to good estate, he will take vengeance on his enemies, and shall be bitten by a dog, he will be in danger at twenty three years, and in peril of water; at thirty years he will be rich and rise to great dignity, and shall live fourscore and five years after nature, and he shall see his fortune sorrowful.

The Woman.

The Woman that is born in this time will be a pains taker, a liar, and shall suffer much shame, she will enjoy the goods of her friends, and that which she conceiveth in her mind shall come to pass, she will have many husbands, and many children, and will be in her best estate at sixteen years, she will be sickly, and if she escape she will live threescore and sixteen years after nature, she ought to bear rings and precious stones about her: The days of Jupiter and Luna are good for them, and the days of Mars are contrary, as well as the Man as the Woman may be likened to the Bull that laboureth the land, for when the seed is sown he hath but a straw for his par ; they will keep their own well, and it shall not profit to them nor to other, and will be reputed unkind.

Of the Sign of Gemini, evil to let blood.

He that is born in the Sign of *Gemini*, from mid May to mid June, shall have many wounds, yet he will be merciful, he will lead an open and reasonable life, and he shall receive much money, he will go into unknown places, he will praise himself, and will not abide in the places of his Nativity, he will be wise and negligent in his works, he shall come to riches at twenty six years, his first wife will not live long, but he shall marry strange women, and he will be late married: he shall be bitten of a dog, and will have a mark of iron or fire, he will be fermented [?] in water, and shall pass the Sea, and will live a hundred years and ten months after nature.

The Women.

The Woman then born, shall come to honor, and be enriched by the goods of others, and be aggrieved of a false crime; she ought to be wedded at fourteen years (if she shall be chaste, and eschew all peril) and shall live threescore and ten years after nature, and will honor God: The days of Mercury and Sol are right good for them, the days of Luna and Venus are to them contrary, and as well the man as the woman shall augment the goods of their successors, but they shall hardly use their own goods, they shall be so covetous.

Of the Sign of Cancer, indifferent to let blood.

He that is born under *Cancer*, from mid June to mid July, will be very avaricious, and of equal stature, he shall love women, and shall be merry, humble, good and well renowned, he shall have hurt by envy, he shall have money of others in his guide, and will be full of strife and discord among his neighbors, and will revenge him on his enemy: by his stateliness many shall mock him, he will be fearful on the water, he will keep his courage secretly to himself, and shall suffer dolor of the womb [!], he shall find hidden money, and labour sore for his wife, he shall see peril in a certain year, the which shall be known to God; his goods will decrease thirty three years, he shall pass the sea, and shall live threescore and ten years after nature, and fortune shall be very favourable unto him.

The Women.

The Woman that shall be born in this time will be furious, incontinent, angry, and some appeased ; she is nimble, serviceable, wise, and she will suffer many perils, if any person do her any service, she will recompense them well, she will be laborious, and take great pains unto thirty years, and then have rest, she will have many sons, she must be wedded at fourteen years, honors and gifts will be bestowed on her, she will receive many wounds and be helped thereof, and be in peril of water ; she will be hurt in a secret place, and shall be bitten of a dog, yet live (after nature) threescore and ten years: The days of Jupiter, Venus, and Luna are very good for them, and the days of Mars very evil ; and as well the Man as the Woman will have good fortune, and have victory over his enemies.

Of the Sign of Leo, evil for bloodletting.

Certain it is, he that is born under the Sign of *Leo*, from the midst of July to the midst of August, will be very hardy, and he shall speak openly, yet very merciful, and he will weep with the weepers, and shall be stately in years shall he be in danger of some evil, but he shall escape it; his benefits shall be unkind, he will be honored of good people, and obtain his enterprise, he will be unkind to thieves.

And shall be great and powerful, and have charge of the community, and as much as he loseth he shall win; he will come to dignity, and shall be amiable, and he shall take the fortune of three wives, and shall go often on journeys, and he will be nimble of light, and have a fall from on high; he will be fearful of water, and shall find hidden money; at eighteen years of age, he will be sick, he will be in peril and doubt of some great Lord, and at thirty six years he shall be bitten of a dog, and be whole with great pain, and he will live fourscore years after nature.

The Women.

The Woman that is born in this time will be a great liar, fair, well spoken, merciful, pleasant, not abide to see men weep, she will be meek; her first husband will not live long, she shall have pain in her stomach, and be beloved of her neighbors, at seventeen years she will grow to great riches, and will have children by two men, and be subject to the bloody flux ; she will be bitten by a dog and will fall from on high, yet live threescore and seventeen years after nature the days of Mercury, Sol and Mars are to them very good, but the days of Saturn are contrary, and both the Man and the Woman will be great quarrelers, yet merciful.

Of the Sign of Virgo, indifferent to let blood.

Of the Sign of *Virgo*, I find that he which is born from mid August to mid September shall be a great householder, ingenious, and take delight in his work, he will be shamefast, and of great rage, and all that he seeth he shall covet in his understanding; he will soon be angry, and surmount his enemies. Scarcely shall he be with his first wife, he shall be fortunate at thirty one years; he will not hide that he hath, and shall be in peril of water; he shall have a wound with iron, and shall live threescore years after nature.

The Women.

She that then is born shall be shamefast, ingenious, and will take pain, and she ought to be wedded at twelve years, she shall not be long with her first husband. Her second husband shall be of a long life, and shall have much good of another woman, she shall fall from high, her life be in peril, and shall die shortly, she shall suffer dolor for ten years. If she escapes the dolors she shall live threescore years after nature.

She shall bring forth virtuous fruit, and everything shall favor her, she shall rejoice in divers fortunes. The days of Mercury, and of Sol, shall be right good for them, and the days of Mars shall be contrary. And as well the man as the woman shall suffer many temptations so that with great pain they may resist them they shall desire to live chaste, but they shall suffer much where ere they be.

Of the Sign of Libra, indifferent to let blood.

Amongst the Signs *Libra* ought to be remembered, for he that is born from mid September to mid October, shall be mightily praised and honored in the service of Captains ; he shall go in unknown places, and he shall get in strange Lands; he will keep well his own, if he not make revolution by drink, he will keep his promise, and be envied for silver and other goods, he shall be married, and go from his wife, he will speak quick, and have no damage amoungst his neighbours, he will have under his power the goods of dead folks, and he shall have some sign given unto him, he will suffer damages and hurt, he will be enriched by women, and experience evil fortunes, men shall ask counsel of him, and he will live threescore and ten years after nature.

The Women.

The Woman that is born at this time will be amiable, and of great courage, she will announce the death of her enemies, and shall go in places unknown, she will be debonaire and merry, and rejoice by her husband: If she be not married in thirteen years, she will not be chaste and shall have no sons in her first husband, she will go many journeys; after thirty years she will prosper, and have great honor and praise, then after that she will be very sick, at twelve years of age she will be burnt on the feet and will live three score years after nature. The days of Venus and Luna are right good for them, and the days of Mercury contrary; and as well the Man as the Woman shall be in doubt unto their death.

Of the Sign of Scorpio, good to let blood.

He that is born in the Sign of *Scorpio*, from mid October to mid November, will have good fortune, he shall be a great fornicator ; the first wife that he shall have will be religious, and he will worship Images, he shall suffer pain in his privy members at the age of fifteen years, he shall be hardy as a lion, and amiable of form; and he shall have many faculties, and be a great traveler, and visit divers countries for to know the customs and estates of cities, and will have victory over all his enemies, and they may not hinder him in no manner of wise; he shall have money of his wife, and shall suffer divers dolors of the stomach, he will be merry and love the company of merry folks; and in his right shoulder will be a mark, and by flattering words he shall be deceived; he will often say one thing and do another, and he shall have a wound with iron, he will be bitten of a dog, or some other beast; he will have divers enemies at the age of thirty three years, and if he escape, he will live fourscore and three years after nature.

The Women.

The Woman that is born at this time shall be amiable and fair, and shall not be long with her first husband, but will have joy with another; by her good and true service she will have honor and victory over her enemies, she will suffer pain in the stomach, she will be wise and have wounds in her shoulders, she ought to fear her latter days, which will be doubtful by poison: and she will live threescore and ten years after nature: The days of Mars and Saturn to them are very good, and the days of Jupiter to them are contrary; she will be sweet of words, a wanton, detracting other, and say otherwise then they would be said by.

Of the Sign Sagittarius, good to let blood.

He which is born under *Sagittarius*, from mid November to mid December, he will have mercy and every Man that he seeth, he will obtain, and have revelation, and he shall go far into desert places unknown and dangerous, and will return with great gains, he shall see his fortune increase from day to day, and will not hide what he hath, yet be fearful; at twenty two years of his age he will pass the sea and get riches, and he will live threescore and seventeen years and eight months by nature.

The Women.

The Woman which is born at this time will love to labour, and she will have divers thoughts, and loveth not to see one weep, she will have victory over her enemies, and will spend much silver by evil company; she will suffer many evils, taking great pains to have the goods of her kinsmen; she out to be married at thirteen years, and will have palsy in her eyes at fourteen years, and will have by envy joy at eighteen years, yet suffer valor by envy, and separated from joy, and will live after nature threescore and twelve years.

The days of Venus and Luna are for them very good, and the days of Mars and Saturn evil, and as well the Man as the Woman will be inconsistant, yet be of good conscience and merciful, better to strangers then to themselves, and they will fear God.

Of the Sign Capricorn, evil to bleed.

He which is born under *Capricorn*, from mid December to mid January, will be very forward, a fornicator and a liar, and nourished with strange things, and he will have many crimes, he will be a governor of beasts, and shall not be long with his wife: he will suffer much sorrow in his youth, and will lose much goods and riches; he will have great peril at sixteen years he will be of great courage and will use honest company, he will be rich by women, and be a conductor of maidens, his fear will make divers overlook him, and he will live threescore and ten years and four months after nature.

The Women.

The Woman that is born at this time will be honest, and surmount her enemies, and have children by three men, she will go many journeys in her youth, and after have great wit, she will be rich, but have great pains in her eyes, and be in her best estate at thirty years; she will live threescore and ten years and ten months after nature: The days of Saturn and Mars to them are good, but the days of Sol are contrary; and both the Man and the Woman will be reasonable, yet be jealous.

Of the Sign of Aquarius, indifferent for blood letting.

He that is born under this Sign of *Aquarius*, from mid January to mid February, will be lovely and ireful, he will not believe in vain things, he shall have silver, at twenty four he shall be in estate, he shall win where he goeth, or he will be sore sick, and be hurt with iron, yet he shall have good fortune, and will go to divers countries.

The Women.

The Woman which is born in this time she will be delicious, and be in great peril at the age of twenty four years, she will be happy, yet she will have hurt by beasts, she will live threescore years and seventeen years after nature: the days of Venus and Luna are very good for them, but the days of Saturn and Mars are contrary; both the Men and the Women will be reasonable, and yet they shall not be over rich.

Of the Sign of Pisces, indifferent to let blood.

The Man which is born under *Pisces*, from mid February to mid March, he will be a great goer, a fornicator, a mocker, covetous, and say one thing and do another; he will find money, and will trust in his wisdom, and have good fortune, and shall be a defender of orphans and widows, and will be fearful of the water, and he shall soon pass all his adversities, and will live threescore and thirteen years and five months after nature.

The Women.

The Woman that is born in this time she will be delicious, familiar in jests, pleasant of courage, fervent, and will have sickness in her eyes, and shall be sorrowful by shame; her husband will leave her, and she will have much pain with strangers, and shall not have her own, she will have pain in her stomach, and shall live threescore and eighteen years after nature: the days of Jupiter, Mercury and Venus are right good for them, but the days of Saturn to them are contrary ; and doth the Man and the Woman shall live faithfully. (*Compost* 2007: n. p.)

The *Arcandam* was a translation from the French of Richard Roussat's *De veritatibus et praedictionibus astrologiae* (1541). It enjoyed a steady popularity throughout the 1640s and the title was still being published though the 18th century. The *Arcandam* presented a curious numerological method to allegedly determine a person's astrological status that bypassed actual astrological practice entirely. This was undoubtedly an attractive alternative for people who had no knowledge of either astrology or their actual birth date and time. The two selections below are the directions as published in *The Most Excellent and Profitable and pleasant book,, of the famous Doctor and expert Astrologian Aracandam or Aleandrin ... Now newly turned out of French into our vulgar tongue by William Warde.* London: Thomas Orwin, 1592; and *Arcandam's astrology, or book of destiny ... ,* Translated from the French of J. Fr. Neveau, London: J. Bew, 1774; with examples of the interpretations for (at random) Gemini in each case.

A BRIEFE DECLARATION MOST
certain, and profitable for to find
out (as much as the Arte of Astrologie can
certifie) mans Fate, and constellation
indicatiue touching the natu-
rall inclination of Man.
Made by *Arcandam,*
the learned, and expert
Astrologian.

The maner to find out the destinie, & constellation is this. First yee will know the constellation of any man, take his naturall name, which is commonly called his proper name, & the proper name of his mother, in such sort, as neither of the two names, in any wise bee changed, or depraued from the vulgar or proper calling (as oftentimes it chaunceth by comon appellatiō of men's names) but that they be perfect, & not diminished. And for two causes yᵉ name of the mother is taken, & not of the father. First, because mothers side is more apparant than the fathers.

Secondly, although the father bee the originall of the conception and generation of the childe, yet the childe touching the body, hath more of the mothers matter and substance, then the fathers. Yea, and oftentimes it happeneth, some part of the fathers seede doth not enter nor serve, touching the materiall composition.

For Man is a very actiue, and of no means passiue, and touching himselfe can haue no action. Whereby it consequently appeareth, that the childe concerning the body, hath more of the mothers substance then the fathers. /

Whereunto a third cause may bee added, that forasmuch as the Childe is nourished of the mothers substance, and not of the fathers : that then the constellation enforcing his effect and signe in the childes body, do rather conuert the same with the mother, and the body of the mother, then the father, and the body of the father.

And therefore truly and determinateth / to know and learne, the childes fate and constellation, his proper name must bee taken, together with the naturall and proper name of his mother. Then diligently consider every letter of the sayde two names, and amongst the same, gather the numerall letters, such as signifie a number, which according to the ancient accompt, are seuen: as I signifieth one. V. five. X. tenne. L. fifty. C. a hundreth. D. five hundreth, M. signifieth a thousand.

Taking all and singular letters of the saide two names, as well the number, as such as signifie a number.

Then gather the whole sum, which summe so collected, deuide [divide] it if it be possible by xxix. because of the xxix. constellations of the Starres, or because of the particular signes celestiall, which after the auncient manner, is the first diuision of the signes.

And hereby it appeareth, that the principall parts of the particular Starres and signes celestiall, in number are, xxix. / as hereafter shall appear. So that the number signified by the numerall letters of the two proper names aforesayd ought to be deuided by reason of the sayd signes. And sometimes the sayde number dooth amount iust to that summe of *29.* & sometime exceedeth the same, wherin it is to be noted that either the number doth exceed or else is equall.

If it exceede, then the number ought to be applyed, and deuided by their unities to the sayde signes, adding to euery of the signes their unities, beginning at the first signe which is the head of *Aries,* and so the rest successiuely. And where so ever the last unitie shall fall, or be placed, there and in that signe, and in part of the signe, the infant (whose constellation you seeke to know) undoubtedly is borne, as thereby you shall giue iudgment and truely pronounce that in that signe the fate and constellation of the infant consisteth.

Notwithstanding, that peradventure, according to the same manner and course / of the Starres, times and monethes, some other signe should seeme to have dominion over that natiuitie. And because that the signe, wherein certainely the infant is borne, doeth not alone beare rule in the time of birth, but all the singular effectually doe concurre, according to the more or lesse in euery natiuitie. So that eftsoones it chaunceth that some signee distinct from that sign appropriate to the month, do more effectually rule, and more excellently expresse his effectes. Therefore to the intent you may perfectly beholde the fate and constellation of the partie that is borne, you must not onely looke upon the signe, allotted and appropriate to the moneth, wherein determinately any is borne: but chiefly you must haue respect to that signe, which especially hath dominion abouve others, in the time of the birth, notwithstanding the signe appropriate to the moneth, hath the principall effect.

And whether one signe is more excellent / or effectuall than another, you may most certainly, and truely know by this arte. Let us return then unto the former proposition, and say that either the summe of the number signified by the numerall letters, of the names aforesayd, doth not amount to xxix, or els that it doth principally attaine to that summe, or is equal or els exceedeth the same.

But nowe after the agreement and concord of the number, take also the convocation and assembly of the signes celestiall, which are touching their particular partes, xxix. as is aforesaid, or xxx. as shall bee sayd hereafter, beginning at the first particular signe, which is the head of the signe *Aries.* And wheresoeuer the last vnitie [unity, i. e., instance] of this number shall rest or remayne, that is the speciall signe as is of most force, of the time of the natiuitie.

But if this number doth not surpass the number of xxix. but thereunto is equal, then the last signe, which is the Tayle of *Pisces,* is the chiefest signe at the natiuitie. / Semblably [seemingly], if this number doth exceede the number of xxix. then this number is to be diuided so many times by xxix. till the number of xxix. bee founde out. And then for euery vnity one signe must bee accounted, yeelding to euery signe his vnitie: and then the last vnitie, which is xxix. is attributed to xxix. and to the last signe, which is the tayle of *Pisces*, as was sayde a little before. And that signe chiefly hath dominion in the natiuitie of infants. But if that number lastly remayning, bee within the number of xxix. then euery vnitie of this number ought to bee distributed to euery particular signe, beginning first at the head of *Aries*: and wheresoeuer the last vnitie of this number doth remaine, the same is the principall signe, and chiefly hath gouernment in the birth of the Infant.

Here also ought diligently to bee noted, that the celestiall signes may bee taken two wayes, that is to say, totally or touching the whole effects of the / same and are in the number but *12*. That is to witte: *Aries* (which is the first signe, at which you must beginne, and then follow successiuely, till you come to the signe of *Pisces*, which is the twelfth) *Taurus, Gemini, Cancer, Leo, Virgo, Libra, Scorpio, Sagittarius, Capricornus, Aquarius, Pisces*. Nowe each of these signes, in his whole effect doth especially beare rule in the moneth, which is appropriate to the same.

And euey signe entirely hath dominion ouer euery moneth, such as thereunto is appoynted. And for example, *Aries*, hath dominion in March, which is the first moneth, according to the computation of Astronomers.

Likewise *Taurus*, in Aprill, and so the rest consequently succeeding. And although the aforesaid Signs singularly, and appropriately have their months especially assigned, as is aforesayde. Yet all these *12* Signs in euery moneth, at all times, euery day, and hour, euery momente and minute of an houre, doe concurre / in the natiuitie of euery birth, although not equally, yet according to the more or lesse.

And that signe, which chiefly hath dominion of the natiuitie, the same is the constellation of the Infant. Moreouer the signe wherein the Infant is borne, although it bee not that which is appropriate to the moneth, but some other, yet it is easie to be knowen from the signe particularly appoynted to the sayd moneth. Likewise the sayde signes which bee taken two wayes, not entirely, but specially touching their partes, and by accepting the same, in such particular wise, (chiefly after the reckoning of the auncient Astronomers) they bee *29*. For fiue of them, that is to say: *Taurus, Gemini, Leo, Scorpio, Aquarius*, are euery one of them deuided into three principall parts. As the head, the belly, and the tayle, and is as much to say, into the beginning, the middle, and the ende.

Whereby it followeth, that these fiue / figures so deuided, doo include fifteene principall partes, for three times fiue, make fifteene. And the other seuen signes. That is to say: *Aries, Cancer, Virgo, Libra, Sagittarius, Capricornus, Pisces*, amongst whom three partes are contained in *Virgo*, for his tayle is divided into twayne, as shall be shewed hereafter, although here it hath but two partes. All which seuen are divided but into two principall parts, to wit, into the head and tayle, and so include foureteene particular signes, for twice seuen is foureteene. Whereby it manifestly appeareth by the premisses, that the signes particularly excepted are in number twentie nine, because fifteene and foureteene make twentie nine. Furthermore it is to bee noted that in all and euery the foresayde signes being wholly accoumpted, according to the manner before remembered, all these twelue are concurrents, eyther more or lesse in the natiuitie of euery Infant. / …

GEMINI, THE THIRD
Celestial and principle
Sign.

THE third treatise of this Booke, hath discourse over the third principall and entyre signe Celestiall called Gemini, and is deuided into six chapters like to the other, which immediately before proceedeth. Whereof the first entreateth of the head of Gemini, the second of the belly, and the third of the tayle: The fourth of the iudgement of Gemini touching the male. The fifth concerning the female, and the sixt treateth the generall fortune of Gemini.

The first chapter entreateth of the head of Gemini, being the sixt signe particular, and includeth fiue

starres disposed in this form. Whatsoeuer is born in this signe, touching the inclination of his body, and fyrst according to yͤ quality & quātity therof, he shal bee fair, mean of stature, beautiful in yͤ face, and hath his eyebrows comely, & all his mēbers well proportioned, his

```
  *
 * *
 * *
```

sight cleer and sharpe. But touching the qualitie, his hayre is black, his voice blacke [sic] and pleasant. / Hee hath a signe or a stripe in his body, that is to say, upon his head, in his eyes, hands or knees, and his mouth hurt. Hee is of great strength and force, hayry and naturally slowe. And after the disposition of his minde: he is giuen much to prayer, fearfull and not prone to anger. He is naturally ryotous, although with women he shall not be very fortunate. Concerning his living and manner thereof, he shall be troubled with payne in the backe, and shall be vexed with an euill spirite. Hee shall lose certayne of his teeth, and shall live till he be 7. or 12. yeares old 40. or 84. shal die in his bed. And after his good fortune hee shall haue much goods, and shall be greatly praysed of men. His honour shall with better successe happen in the age thē of youth. And touching his euill fortune, he shall have 2. wiues, but that directly hath not respect to the euill fortune, but indifferēt. Hee shall apply with diligence his own affayres, if hee be borne in the latter part of the night, he shall be a seller of flesh, and a marchaunt of cattayle, which are apt to be eaten and saleable in the shambles. And / so consequently shall be a sheader of blood.

The 2. Chapter intreateth the belly of Gemini, which is the seuenth particular signe, and hath foure starres disposed in this form, and is called Alaya. Where is to be noted that whosoeuer is borne in this signe, first touching the disposition of the body, hee is naturally black, hayry,   * *
       * *

of short stature, and strange. He hath fayre eyebrowes, and a black spot upon his elbow, or privy members. And after the disposition of his minde, hee shall be most happily given to prayer. He shall bee timerous and fearfull: His wordes sweet and pleasant, notwithstanding he shall be ryotous & unthrifty. He shall liue till he bee ten yeare olde, & if he escape his sicknes, then hee shall liue till hee bee thirty, and if his life be prolonged any further, then hee shall liue hee bee 44. and if he reuiue of his sicknes, then he shall liue 72. Hee shall bee troubled with the payne of the back, and vexed with an euill spirite. He shall haue much substance, & rule over his owne affayres. If hee bee borne in the / second houre of the naturall day, then after his bodyes disposition, he shall be hairy and haue a spot in his eyes, and shall leese many of his teeth. Likewise if he be borne in the third houre of the day, he shalbe happy, and of nature hot and moyst. But if hee be borne in the night, then he shall be a seller of flesh, or a sheader of blood, and shall liue of such substance as happeneth to him by marryage.

The third Chapter of this treatise, describeth the latter part of Gemini, and is the eyghth particular signe celestial, hauing two starres disposed in this forme,   * *
and is called Aladaman. Where is to be noted, yt whosoeuer is born in the sayde signe, touching the disposition of the body, is naturall cholerike and drye, his Gall ascending into the head by his fumosity. His eies seeming to threaten or disdayne, and his face chaunging colours, sometime both white and pale, and sometime reuerteth to his own naturall colour, that is to say, like to honie, and yet notwithstanding handsome and well made in his members and body, saving that his eyes are somewhat little: his voyce great, and vpon his forehead or face he hath a marke or stripe, or els ye like upon one of his hāds, his breast, his priuy parts, or yarde. And after the mindes inclination hath a good and honest heart, and benevolent will, a fine and pregnant witte, by reason whereof he shal learn many things, insomuch as through the viuacity of the same, he shall perceiue and thoroughly understand the things that he heareth, applying the same as before they touched himselfe. He is mery and pleasant, notwithstanding of a cholerick nature: & as he is soone angry, euen so is he soone reconciled. Hee is bolde of speech and words before the presence of his Prince, by reason whereof he will not spare to touch any man. Likewise he is very prone and apte to swearing : doing or speaking nothing without an oath. Hee is light of suspition, and thereby will utter words unseemly. Hee is a great dissembler and spreader abroade of fantasies, and trifles or joyes [joués]. Hee is a great dronkard and very ryotous, and so by reason of much / bibbing and swilling of wine, greatly given to lechery. His first sicknes shall be at 7. years of age, which if hee escape, then the second shall bee at 24. 80. or 90. and shall die of a disease in the throate. According to his good fortune, he shall finde money and treasure hidden in the earth. Hee shall have two children at one birth. And after his evill fortune, he shall liue vnquietly with his wife, who shall liue but a short

space. His parents shall not be rich, whome he shall bury, and shal haue no brother like vnto himself but one.

The fourth chapter determineth the iudgement of Gemini touching the male.
And whosoeuer is borne in Gemini, in whether part of the same soeuer hee bee borne, first touching the disposition of his body, he shall haue an indifferent & comely stature, beautifull and fayre of face, strong & of great force. He shall haue great authority & things of such value to be solde. His body shall be naturally marked. And after the disposition of the minde, he shall be an ingenious and cunning Artificer, & much giuen vnto excellent arts. He shall be naturally wise, and shall trust much therein, and by reason of the same, whatsoever hee intendeth to goe about and accomplish, he shall bring it the sooner vnto good effect. Likewise hee is pleasaunt and mercifull, easie to bee spoken vnto, and by vertue of his constellation shall be acceptable to all men. Hee shall not bee much curious ouer his own affayres, hee shall be sober and moderate in meat, and drynke, yet not withstanding luxurious and giuen to women. Hee shall bee contentious and vnquiet with his neighbours by reason of his prone disposition to anger and choler. And for his sayd promptitude to choler, hee shall sustayne much perill and blame, and yet notwithstanding a profitable man, and beloued of all men. Touching his life, and maner of his life, hee shall bee entangled in many troubles by reason of his wife. And concerning his euill fortune, hee shall suffer much payne in his backe, or guttes within and about the stomack. But then if it happen that he escape his first diseases, he shal liue to be one hundred and ten, and three moneths. /
Likewise as touching his good fortune, hee shall come to bee with cattel greatly enriched. He shall finde money that hath been hidden in the ground, and shall triumph ouer his enemies. His chiefest fortune shalbe towards the East, and therefore towardes the same let him dispose all his affayres. In the fiftieth yeare of his age towards the sayd East part he shall find money. And touching his euill fortune, he shall trauayle much vppon the Sea, and when he is two & thirty yeares old, he shal be in daunger of fire and sword, but yet delivered from that perill, and shall receiue hurt of some four-footed beast. The Tuesday is his vnfortunate day and therefore vpon that day let him attempt no enterprise, nor wash his head or feete, or put on any new apparell, or such like.

The 5. chapter entreateth of the iudgment of *Gemini* touching the female. Where is to be noted, that whatsoeuer mayd childe is borne in this signe, first touching her body, she shalbe very fayre and have a wound vpon her body. And touching her minde, she shall of nature be very wise and ingenious. She shall be merry and courtlike, diligent and ready to obey. She shall be very willful and hote of mind, and by reason of the sayd heat of wil, complexion, or nature, somewhat angry, which will not long continue: and because she is free of speech, she shall be much boasting of her selfe, and a great liar, speaking one thing and dooing the contrary. If this mayd or woman doo escape the force of her diseases, shee shall liue to 83. yeares of age. She shal sustayne many notable infirmities and diseases of her body within the time of her age of 33. and chiefly about 25. years the Phrensie or Lunatike passion by the space of forty dayes, which disease is commōly called the Moone age, or infirmity of the Moone, whereby the patient is called *Lunaticus*. Semblably until she be 38. shall passe ouer many sorrowes, but by reason of Phisicke which shall be ministered vnto her shee shal recouer. Likewise touching her good fortune, because of many troubles which she shall suffer, at length shee shall attayne to great honour, and much service / and obedience shalbe done vnto her, and through her husbands fortune shee shall very much rejoyce, and through him attayne to great promotion. And at 43. shee shal begin to wax rich. Shee shal see revengement ouer her enemies, and after 45. shalbe called a mother of Children. And first begotten shall be no male but a female, according to the force of her naturall constellation. And touching her euill fortune, she shalbe laborous and painfull, and till 35. years of age shee shalbe enwrapped with much payne and sorrowe. She shalbe hurte with hot water, and shall haue a fal from an high place. She shalbe bitten with a dogge. Tuesday is her contrary and vnfortunate day, therefore let her not wash her head vpon that day, or doo any new fact or enterprise

The sixth chapter mentioneth the common fortune of *Gemini*, where it is to be noted, that this signe hath singular fortune in learn[i]ng and knowledge, and specially in the seuen liberall Arts & Sciences, chiefly in philosophy, in the lawes, & in physick, the like exigation, and bestowing of things, also in all Beasts not meete to be ridden, in tillage, and in beasts for tillage, and shall diligently apply himself in the service of his elders. This signe to them that bee borne in the same, is a great occasion of the strangurie and stone, and of payne in the armes. He hath three good days, that is to say: Sonday, Tuesday, and Wednesday. His evil days: Thursday, Fryday, and Saturday, and yet Friday and Saturday be indifferēt. Likewise frō the midst of the moneth of March, untill the midst of September, they borne in this signe is fortunate. His chiefe fortune is toward the West, and therefore let him dispose his doings towards that part, and turne the doore of his house, and his bed that way. They borne in this signe is naturally sanguine, and therefore so soone as he shal obtain friends, even as soone he shall loose them agayne. (Ward 1592: n.p.)

The same information in the 1774 edition demonstrates a definite continuity over the intervening two centuries, even if the later version is considerably abbreviated – and made clearer for modern readers.

How to calculate the Nativity of any Person.

In order to shew the method of performing this, it is necessary previously to set down the following table, exhibiting the period of each sign's governance, and the number of parts it consists of.

Sign		Month	Day		Parts
Aries		March	21		2 parts
Taurus		April	21		3
Gemini		May	21		3
Cancer		June	21		2
Leo	begins to reign	July	21	is divided into consists of	3
Virgo		August	21		2
Libra		Sept.	21		2
Scorpio		October	21		3
Sagittarius		Nov.	21		2
Capricorn		Dec.	21		2
Aquarius		Jan.	21		3
Pisces		Feb.	21		**2**

In all 29 parts.

Now, to calculate the exact nativity of any particular person, or, in other words, to find the identical part of what sign he or she was born in, (which is necessary to enable you to form your judgment nicely) take his or her christian name, with the surname of the mother before her marriage, and / observe how many numerical letters they contain, that is, such as express a number, as

I,	which signifies	1
V or U,	--------	5
X,	--------	10
L,	--------	50
C,	--------	100
D,	--------	500
M,	--------	1000

In this the mother's name is preferred to the fathers's, because the most certain, and as every child partakes more of the mother than the father; besides, the child is nourished by the mother, not the father.

When the names are taken, and the amount of the numerical letters are cast up, then the number of all the letters is to be added, and the amount of the whole taken. This sum total is to be divided by 29, because of the 29 parts into which the signs are divided; then the remaining number after such division, is to be counted off on the parts of that sign in which the person was born, and that part of the sign on which the last units falls, has dominion over the nativity sought for, and the destiny is hereafter laid down in its proper place. What signs rule in every month of the year, with the several parts of each, is already exhibited in the foregoing table.

Indeed, the number may be reckoned totally, or in the whole, without the division, counting it off upon the parts of the sign as though it were the remainder after the division. —but this is very tedious. / …

REIGN *of the Third Sign*
GEMINI.

This Sign is divided into three parts, head, belly and tail. /
The head includes five stars in the following order:

*

* *

* *

Of the Man.

Whosoever is born in this part, in regard to his body, shall be fair, of a middling stature, comely in the face, with good eyebrows, and all his limbs well proportioned, his sight clear and sharp, his hair black, his voice shrill, but pleasant. He will have a wound on his body or head, with a mark on his hands, knees, or mouth, he shall be strong, and hardy, but naturally slow. As to his mind and inclination, he shall be given to prayer and devotion, be fearful, and not prone to anger. He shall be naturally libidinous, yet will not be very fortunate with women. As to the incidents of his life, he will be subject to pains in his back, he will lose some of his teeth, and his chief sicknesses will be at the age of 7, 12, 40 or 84, when he shall die in his bed. His good fortune will be to be possessed of riches, and to be greatly loved by all men. He will be honoured more in age than youth. He shall be married twice. He shall apply with diligence to his own affairs, and will not neglect others. If he be born in the night, he will be most prosperous by dealing in flesh, being a salesman in eatables, and consequently will be a shedder of blood. /

The second part of *Gemini* is the belly, which is called *Alraya*, and hath four stars disposed as follow,

* *

* *

Whoever is born in this sign, with regard to his person, shall be naturally black and of a short stature, with fair eyebrows, and a black mark near his elbows or privities. As to his disposition, he will be wavering, timorous, and inclinable to prayer and works of piety; his words mild, sweet, pleasant, notwithstanding which he shall be riotous and unthrifty. At the age of ten he shall have a sickness, which if he recovers, he shall enjoy a tolerable share of health till thirty, when he shall have a severe illness, but probably overcome it. At 44 he will again be in danger, but if he survives he will live to the age of seventy-two. He will be subject to pain of the back. He shall be possessed of affluence, and shall rule over his own affairs. If he be born in the second hour of the natural day, he will be very hairy, have a spot in his eyes, and shall lose several of his teeth, if he be born in the third hour, he shall be happy, and of nature hot and moist; but if he be born in the night, then he shall be a seller of flesh, or a shedder of blood, but shall live chiefly on what he obtains by marriage.

The third part of *Gemini* is the tail, which is called *Aldaman*, and consists of two stars disposed in the manner following,

* *

/ Whosoever is born in this sign will be naturally passionate, choleric, and dry, his eyes seeming to threaten distain, and his face changing colour frequently, his natural complexion inclinable to the yellow, yet pleasant, he will in general be well featured, but will have small eyes, a strong voice, and on his forehead or face a wound or natural mark, or upon one of his hands, his breast, or privities. His heart will be honest, and benevolent, and he will be endued with a pregnant wit, which will enable him to attain to knowledge. He will be merry and pleasant, notwithstanding his choleric temper, and as he will be soon angered, may be soon pleased. He will be bold of speech, and liable to boast of his qualifications before his superiors, to the prejudice of others, will be very subject to swear, suspicious, and subject in his heat to utter words unseemly, a great dissembler, and spreader of falsehoods for amusement ; a great drinker, and much given to letchery. He will have a sickness at seven years of age, another at 24, which if he escapes, he will have a return of it between 80 and 90, and will die of a complaint in his throat. According to his good fortune, he shall discover hidden riches, and shall have two children at a birth. According to his evil fortune, he shall be uncomfortable with his wife, who will not live long. His parents will not be able to leave him much property; but he shall live to bury them both.

GENERAL INFLUENCE *of* GEMINI.

Whosoever is born in any part of this sign, shall be of a middling stature, and strong. He shall be in authority, and have many things of value in his possession for sale. His body shall be naturally marked, he shall be ingenious, and much inclined to arts; he shall be naturally wise, shall confide in his own abilities, and generally succeed in whatever he attempts. He shall be pleasant, merciful, and easy of access, and will render himself respectable to the world, though he will get the ill will of some individuals. He shall not pay any regard to his own affairs, but shall be commonly sober and moderate in his diet, yet at times luxurious and given to women. He shall be entangled in several troubles through his wife; and will endure great pains in his back, breast or bowels. If she survives his first diseases, he will live to about 100. As to his good fortune, he shall be greatly enriched by cattle, and by riches in the ground; and shall triumph over his enemies. His fortunate point is the east, and therefore towards the same let him dispose of his affairs. He will discover riches about his 56th year of his age. As to his evil fortune, he will travel much on the sea; and, about his 32nd year, he will be in great danger both of fire and sword; but, being delivered of that, he shall suffer by four-footed beasts. Tuesday is his unfortunate day; therefore therefore, on that day, let him undertake / no great concern, neither wash his feet, nor put on any new garment.

Of the WOMAN.

Whosoever is born in this sign, shall be fair, but shall be wounded in the body. She shall be wise and ingenious, merry and courteous, diligent, and ready to oblige; yet she shall be passionate, subject to anger, but of no long continuance, she shall be free of speech, and full of her own praises, a great liar, speaking contrary to her own knowledge. If she escapes the diseases of her youth, at the age of 23 she will have a fit of sickness, again at 33 and 38, when she shall be subject to a lunacy, which, however, she will recover, and, in all probability, live to 83. As to her good fortune, notwithstanding much opposition, she will arrive at honour, and have much service and homage done unto her; and she shall be happy in her husband's success, thro' whom for the most part, she will attain her promotion. She shall become rich at the age of 40 or 50, and shall see her enemies downfall. At the age of 45, she shall be the mother of children, and her first-born will be a female. She shall be a pains-taking, careful woman, but shall have sorrow and trouble till her 35th year. She shall be hurt by hot water; shall have a fall from a high place, and shall be hurt by a four-footed beast. Tuesday is her unfortunate day; therefore, let her not undertake any thing of moment on that day, nor must she wash head or feet on that day, or put on any new garment.

Common to the MAN *and* WOMAN.

All persons born in this sign shall be fortunate in the liberal arts and sciences, especially in philosophy, law, and physic; also in beasts not to be rode on, and in tillage and beasts for tillage. They shall be subject to the stranguary and stone, and pains in the arms. They have two lucky days, viz, Sunday and Wednesday, their unlucky day is Tuesday. Their chief good fortune will come from the East ; therefore, let all those born in this sign dispose of their transactions towards that part, let the door of their house or chamber, as the situation of their bed, be there. (Neveau 1774: 11-12, 24-30)

The Knowledge of Things Unknown, attributed to "Godfridus super Palladium", is yet another compilation of astral and other lore published by Robert Wyer about 1540. Although there were only a few editions of this title, "Godfridus" continued to be credited in later versions of the "book of knowledge" genre alongside *Erra Pater*. Unlike the other pseudonymous collections, however, the origin of this particular example is known, and it illustrates how material might be extracted out of respectable books by exploitive publishers such as Wyer. As Mauro Ambrosoli explains, Gottfried Von Franken (fl. 1350) was the author of a book on the cultivation of fruit trees, grape vines and grafting based on Palladius' "De Re Rustica" (4th century CE), to which he added material from Galen and other sources. Gottfried divided the text by the 12 months, a common arrangement for agricultural handbooks as in Thomas Tusser's popular *Five Hundred Points of Good Husbandry* (1557), and naturally included some standard astrological information. However, "Godfridus was turned into the author of an almanac brought out in London, undated, by Robert Wyer – *Here begynneth the Boke of Knowledge unknown apperteyninge to Astronomye with certayne necessarye Rules, and certayne spheres contaynyng herein Compyled by Godfridus super Palladium de agricultura Anglicatum*. All the information on the cultivation of fruit trees and so on was suppressed, while the astrological part, the influence of the stars and planets on Man's life, were left and expanded. Godfridus and Palladius were reduced to a mere title …"[79] This was the equivalent of extracting all the naughty bits from a serious literary work and exploiting their erotic value in a cheap pamphlet.

The inclusion of "Jon de indagine" (John Indagine's 1522 *Introductiones Apotelesmaticae*, which wasn't available in print in English until Fabian Wither published his translation as *The Book of Palmestry and Physiognomy* in 1651) as a name to be reckoned with suggests that the Cunning Folk were aware of erudite and expensive esoteric sources – including those in Latin and of foreign publication – even if they did not possess them. This is true of *Aristotles problems Inglished* and the *Secreta secretorum* as well, although neither were likely to be as useful as Indagine. The original "Problems" (not written by Aristotle himself, but apparently collected by his followers in the Peripatetic school of philosophy) is a curiously unsystematic series of inquiries about almost everything people wonder about, from medicine and odors pleasant and unpleasant to sexual matters and human physiology, followed by possible answers. It was first translated into Latin in 1260, and most famously became the basis of a commentary by Peter of Abano (the *Expositio Problematum*, 1310) A few shorter examples will show the style:

> IV:24 Why is it that those who have sexual intercourse or are capable of it have an evil odour and what is called a hircine [goat-like] smell, whereas children do not? Is it because, as has already been said, in children the breath concocts [digests, processes] the moisture and perspiration, whereas the perspiration of grown men remains unconcocted?
> XVIII:7 Why is it that some persons, if they begin to read, are overcome by sleep, even against their will, whereas those who wish to go to sleep are made unable to do so if they take up a book? Is it because in those in whom movements of breath take place owing to the coldness of their nature or of melancholic humours, which by their coldness engender an unconcocted excretion of breath—in these when the intelligence is set in motion and does not think of anything with concentrated attention, the intellect is checked by the second movement, and so they undergo a great mental change and go to sleep (for the movement of breath is overcome)?
> XXV:17 Why is it that substances enclosed in inflated skins and closely covered vessels remain uncorrupted? Is it because things which are in motion become corrupt, and all things that are full are without motion, and such skins and vessels are full?
> XXXIII:16 Why do people shiver after sneezing and passing urine? Is it because by both actions the veins are emptied of the warm air which was previously in them, and, when they are empty, other air enters from without colder than that which was previously in the veins; and such air entering in causes shivering?
> XXXV:2 Why do we feel tickling in the armpits and on the soles of the feet? Is it owing to the thinness of the skin? And do we feel it most where we are unaccustomed to being touched, as in these parts and the ears? (Aristotle 1927: 879, 917. 939, 963, 964)

There was enough miscellaneous "scientific" information among the hundreds of queries and statements derived from classical cosmological and humoural orthodoxy to provide responses to questions posed to Cunning Folk or anyone else, although there wasn't much esoteric or magical content. However, Harvey's reference *may* not have been to the *Aristotle's Problems* that the Cunning Folk

---

[79] Mauro Ambrosoli. *TheWild and the Sown*. New York: Cambridge University Press, 1997, p. 34.

would be most familiar with. An entirely independent *Problems of Aristotle*, originally composed in Latin in the 13th or 14th century first published in an English translation in 1595 flourished alongside with the "real" *Problemata Aristotelis*. The format was similar to the learned version, both being examples of the classic "problemata" genre, but it was better organized and more concise (about 150 "questions" as opposed to the 286 of the original), and provided a fairly clear and detailed synopsis of traditional physiological and medical theory.

This text, which also included the "problemata" of Antonius Zimaras and Alexander Aphrodiseus, later appeared in 18th century and subsequent editions of *Aristotle's Master-Piece*, an underground classic of medical and sexual knowledge that originated in the 1680s and went through dozens of cheap editions even into the 20th century. It became a forbidden best-seller (banned in Britain from the 19th century to the 1960s), being almost the only available vernacular handbook on sexual and obstetrical matters for several centuries. It was equally prized by young people for its mildly salacious content, which only shows how hard up they were for such things. The entire *Master-Piece*, which was sometimes entitled *The Works of Aristotle*, began as a single book on "the Secrets of Nature, in the Generation of Man" but by the early 18th century had grown to be a four-part compilation including the original *Master-Piece*, *Aristotle's Experienced Midwife*, *His Book of Problems*, and *His Last Legacy*. The *Master-Piece* was made up of selections from *The Complete Midwives's Practice* (1680) and Lemnius' *The Secret Miracle of Nature* (1658), while the *Experienced Midwife* included material from Culpeper's *Directory for Midwives* (1651), Sadler's *The Sick Woman's Private Looking-glasse* (1636), and similar sources. As there are a great number of reprints of *Aristotle's Master-Piece* available today, I won't include extensive quotes, beyond the following selection just to give the flavour of the alternative *Problems*:

> Among all living creatures, why hath man only his countenance lifted up towards heaven? Unto this question there are divers answers.
> First, It proceeds from the will of the Creator. And although the answer be true, yet in this our purpose it seemeth not to be of force, because that so all question easily might be resolved.
> Secondly, I answer, that for the most part every workman doth make his first work worse, and then his second better ; so God, creating all other beasts before man, gave them their face looking down to the earth : And then, secondly, he created man, as it doth appear in Genesis, unto whom he gave an honest shape, lifted them unto heaven, because it is drawn from our divinity, and derogate from the goodness of God, who maketh all his works perfect and good.
> Thirdly, It is answered that man only among all living creatures is obtained to the kingdom of heaven, and therefore hath his face elevated and lifted up to heaven, because, that despising worldly and earthly things, he ought to contemplate on heavenly things.
> Fourthly, That the reasonable is like unto angels, and finally ordained towards God ; at it appears by Averrois, in the first de Anima ; and therefore he hat[h] a figure looking upward.
> Fifthly, That a man is a microcosm, that is a little world, as it pleaseth Aristotle to say in the eighth of his work, and therefore he doth command all other living creatures, and they obey him.
> Sixthly, It is answered, that naturally there is unto every thing and every work that form and figure given which is fit and proper for its motion; as unto the heavens roundness, to the fire a pyrimidical form, that is broad beneath, and sharp towards the top, which is most apt to ascend; and so man had his face up to heaven, to behold the wonders of God's works. …
>
> OF CARNAL COPULATION.
> Why do living creatures use carnal copulation?
> Because it is the most natural work that is in them to begat their like, for if copulation were not, all procreation had sunk ere now.
> What is carnal copulation?
> It is a mutual action of male and female, with instruments ordained for that purpose to propagate their kind; and therefore divines say, it is a sin to use that act for any other end.
> Why is this action good in those who use it lawfully and moderately?
> Because, say Avicen and Const, it eases and lightens the body, clears the mind, comforts the head and senses and expels the melancholy. Therefore, sometimes through the omission of this act,

dimness of sight doth ensue, and giddiness; besides the seed of man retained above its due time, is converted into some infectious humour.
Why is immoderate carnal copulation harmful?
Because it destroys the sight, drys the body, and impairs the brain; often causes fevers, as Avicen and experience shew; it shortens life too, as is evident in the sparrow, which, by reason of his often coupling, lives but three years.
Why doth carnal copulation injure melancholy or choleric men, especially thin men? Because it dries the bones much, which are naturally so. On the contrary, it is good for the phlegmatic and the sanguine, as Avicen says, because they abound with that substance which by nature is necessarily expelled. Though Aristotle affirms, that every fat creature has but little seed because the substance turns to fat.
Why do not female brute beasts covet carnal copulation, after they be great with young? Because then the womb or matrix is shut, and desire doth cease. ... (*Works of Aristotle* 1801: 217, 253)

The *Secreta secretorum* (which is primarily concerned with advice for monarchs, although it did have sections on "scientific" subjects such as health, physiology and meteorology) is another long-time popular book of worldly advice attributed to Aristotle. It takes the form of a letter supposedly from Aristotle to his former student Alexander the Great during his campaign in Persia. There were other manuscripts circulating under the name *Secreta secretorum* such as the one written by one "T. R." in 1570 quoted from by Reginald Scot in *The Discoverie of Witchcraft*, or one which Katherine Briggs consulted that were true magical handbooks: "To begin with one mentioned by William Stapleton [in 1528/29], there is a copy of *Secreta Secretorum* in the Bodleian Library. All books with this title may not be the same, but this particular copy is an example of theurgic magic. It deals almost entirely with the angels". (Briggs 1953: 449) As all of the other titles listed by Harvey are published books, it is unlikely that he did not have one of these in mind, nor would a manuscript of that sort be readily available to the ordinary "wise man".

Like the *Problems*, the *Secret of Secrets* has some information of possible interest to Cunning Folk, such as the classic example of physiognomy addressed to Alexander:

Of the physonomy of people.
Among all other thynges of this worlde I wyll that thou knowe a noble and mervaylous scyence that is called physonomy by the which thou shalt knowe the nature and condycyon of people. And it was founde by a phylosophre named Physonomyas, the whiche sought the qualytees of the nature of creatures. In the tyme of the sayde Physonomyas reygned the moost wyse physycyen Ypocras [Hippocrates]. And bycause the fame of Physonomyas and his wysdome was so gretely spredde, the dyscyples and servauntes of Ypocras toke his fygure secretly, and bare it to Physonomyas to here how he wolde Juge and say by the sayd fygure of Ypocras. And bade hym say and tell the qualyte therof. Whan Physonomyas had well beholden it, he sayd: 'This man is a wrangeler lecherous and rude.' This herynge the dyscyples of Ypocras they wolde have slayne Physonomyas, and sayd to hym: 'Aa fole this is the fygure of the best man of the worlde.' Whan Physonomyas saw them thus moeved, he appeased them the best waye that he coude with fayre wordes saynge. I knowe well that this is the fygure of the wyse man Ypocras. And I have shewed you by scyence as I knowe. Whan the dyscyples were come to Ypocras they tolde hym what Physonomyas had sayd. And Ypocras sayd, 'Truely Physonomyas hath tolde you the trouthe, and hath left nothyng of my complexyon in the whiche ben all my vyces. But reason in me overcometh and ruleth the vyces of my complexyon.'
Dere sone I have shortely abreged to the, the rules of this scyence of Physonomy, the whiche shall infourme the gretely. Yf thou se a man with salowe coloure, flee his company, for he is inclyned to the synne of lechery, and to many evylles. Yf thou seest a man that smyleth lyghtly, and whan thou beholdest hym he wyll loke shamfastly and wyl blusshe in his face and sygh, with teeres in his eyes yf thou blame hym for ony thynge, surely he feareth the and loveth thy persone. Beware of hym as thy enmy that is tokened in his face, and of hym also that is mysshapen. The best complexyon that is, is he that is of meane coloure with browne eyes and heere, and his vysage between whyte and reed, with an upryght body, with a heed of metely bygnesse, and that speketh not but of nede be, with a softe voyce, suche a complexyon is good, and suche men have about the. If the heeres be playne and

smothe the man is curteys and meke, and his brayne is colde. Harde heere and curled is a token of foly, & lewdnesse. Moche heere on the brest and on the bely betokeneth very yll or very good complexyon naturally and is very amerous, and kepeth in his herte the injuryes that hath ben done to hym. Blacke heere betokeneth to love reason & Justyce.

Duskysshe eyes betokeneth fooly, & lyghtly to be angry. Gray eyes betokeneth honeste, & lovynge peas. Bygge eyes betokeneth to be envyous, unshamefast, slowe & unobedyent. Eyes meane between blacke and yelowe is of good understanding, curteys, and trusty. Wyde retchynge eyes and a longe face betokeneth a man malycyous and yll. Eyes lyke an asse alway lokyng downe is of harde nature and nought. Waveryng eyes with a long face betokeneth gyle, rennynge mynde and untrusty. Reed eyes betokeneth to be stronge and of a grete courage. He that hath spekles about his eyes, whyte, blacke, or reed, is the worst of all other men. Thycke heered eye lyddes is an yll speker, he that hath them hangynge longe to his eyes, is neyther true nor clene. He that hath heere ynough betwene his two browes and be thynne and not to longe, is of a good and grete understandyng.

A sklendre nosed man is soone angry. A longe nose hawked to the mouthe, is a token of honeste and hardynesse. A snytted nose is a token of a token to be soone vexed. Wyde nosethrylles in a man is slouth and boystousnesse and soone angered. A brode nose in the myddes is a grete speaker, and a lyer. But the best is he that is meane neyther to wyde nor to close. The vysage that is ful & flat, and that is not swollen nor to bygge is a token of an yll persone, envyous, injuryous, and a wrangeler. But he that hath a meane vysage of fourme of chekes and eyes, neyther to fat nor to leane, he is trusty, lovynge, and of grete understandynge, wyse and full of servyce and wytte.

He that hath a wyde mouthe loveth batayle and is hardy. He that hath thycke lyppes is folysshe. And he that hath a wrynkled face is a lyer, and careth not of many debates. He that hath a sklender face is of grete reason. He that hath a lytell vysage and yelowe of colour is a deceyver, dronken, and evyll. Full eyes & smothe chekes is soon angry.

Small eeres betokeneth foly, and lechery.

He that hath a small voyce & speketh thycke loveth feyghtynge. He that hath a meane voyce, neyther to bygge, nor to lytell, is folysshe and unreasonable. And he that speketh to moche with a sklender voyce, is not over honest, and of smal care. He that hath a femynyne voyce is soone angry, and of yl nature. A softe voyced man is often angry and envyous. He that hath a fayre voyce, is folysshe, and of hyghe courage. He that speketh lyghtly, lyeth often, and is a deceyver. And he that speketh without moevynge his handes, is of grete wysdome and honeste.

He that hath a sklender necke, is hote, deceytfull, and folysshe. He that hath a grete bely is proude, lecherous, and unwyse.

He that hath a large brest, thycke sholdres, and bygge fyngers, is hardy, wyse, gentyll, and of good wytte. He with a sklender backe agreeth never with ony other. He that hath his brest and backe egall, is a token of honeste. Hye reysed sholdres, is a token of lytell tydelyte, nought, and sharpe. He that hath longe armes rechynge to the knee, is of grete boldenesse, sadnesse, & lyberalyte. Shorte armes betoken that he loveth socour, and is folysshe.

Longe palmed handes with longe fyngers, is ordeyned to lerne many scyences, and artes, and specyal handy craftes, and to be of good governaunce. Fyngers short and thycke, betoken foly.

Shorte thycke fete and flesshy, betokeneth to be folysshe, and full of injury. A lytell lyght fote, is a man of smal understandynge. A sklender fote sheweth a man to be symple, and of small knowlege. He that hath a thycke fote is hardy and folysshe.

The length of the legges, & the heles, betoken strength of the body. A thycke flesshy kne, is soft and weyke.

A man that gooth a grete pace, is wyllynge in all thynges, and to hasty.

He is of a good nature and complexyon, that hath softe flesshe and moyst, meanely smothe and rough, and that is kyndly between reed and whyte.

He that hath a smothe contenaunce, soft here & playne, with meane eyes of bygnesse, with a well proporcyoned heed, a good necke and suffycyent in length, with sholders somdele lowe, and his legges and knees metely flesshed, his voyce competent clere, the palmes of his handes and fyngers longe, and not thycke, and that he laughe but lytell, and that is no mocker, with a smylyng chere and mery, is of good complexyon. Howbeit dere sone I commaunde the not to Juge all upon one sygne, but consydre all the tokens of a man whiche moost habounde and sheweth the foly in hym, and holde the to the best and moost prouffytable party.[80]

The "Albertus secrets" in Harvey's list is *The boke of secretes of Albertus Magnus, of the vertues of Herbes, stones and certayne Beastes* (published by John King, 1560) or *The booke of secretes of Albertus Magnus of the vertues of Herbes, stones and certayne Beastes* (published by William Copland, ca. 1565). Again, modern editions of this work (including the scholarly edition edited by Best and Brightman and published by Oxford University Press in 1973) are widely available. I won't include examples in this chapter, but will use appropriate extracts in other chapters as they pertain to magical work. There was also an alternative version of *Albertus' Secrets* that first appeared in early 18th century Germany, which would eventually become an extremely influential magical source book in America. David Kriebel notes that "… the first American edition appeared in German in Pennsylvania in 1842, under the title *Albertus Magnus bewahrte und approbirte sympathetische und naturliche egyptische Geheimnisse fur Menschen und Vieh*, and the first English edition [*Albertus Magnus Being the Approved, Verified, Sympathetic and Natural Egyptian Secrets, or, White and Black Art for Man and Beast*] was published at Harrisburg in 1875."[81] This little compilation of occult lore, which is still available in a cheap paperback version that has been in print since the 19th century, can also be found online at Joseph H. Peterson's invaluable Esoteric Archives website (www.esotericarchives.com).

All of this miscellaneous information was "grist for the mill" for Cunning Folk – they could appear learned and knowledgeable by the use of these accepted "secrets", and weave them into their analysis of people's problems. However, the most suggestive item on Harvey's list might be the "old parchment-roules". Although we must rely almost entirely on printed sources in trying to assess Cunning Folk activities, there was an indeterminable number of manuscript resources used by our professional magic workers that can only guessed at. It was not uncommon for entire books of any sort to be copied by hand from either printed or manuscript originals – the period equivalent of photocopying and scanning – and these may even have included the magical version of the *Secreta Secretorum* or some other grimoire. Few surviving lists of Cunning Folk's collections of books seem to include the more seriously esoteric works, but then they did have had Scot's *Discoverie* to ransack, especially the augmented 1665 edition. Many examples of personal notebooks and collections of spells and formulas of Cunning Folk exist; some as elaborate as Arthur Gauntlet's manuscript notebook (Sloane MS 3851) in the British Library or MS D253 in Richard Rawlinson's (1690-1755) collection in the Bodleian Library at Oxford or Simon Forman's extensive manuscripts, but others as basic as the scraps found among Robert Allen's "magical notes" in 1552 (see Chapter 8). Few of the collections made by ordinary magical operators can be easily surveyed today – those that were not scattered or destroyed after their owner's death are usually in collections inaccessible to anyone who lacks the time and resources to examine them in person. We have therefore relied on examples that are available, with the assumption that they represent a reasonable sampling of the rest.

---

[80] Transcription of Robert Copland's edition of 1528, at http://www.colourcountry.net/secretum/node74.html (accessed 8/4/12)

[81] "Powwowing: A Persistent American Esoteric Tradition", David W Kriebel, Ph.D. http://www.esoteric.msu.edu/VolumeIV/Powwow.htm (retrieved 12.17.2010;)

CHAPTER 11:

Astrology in Magic and Theory

"The force behind faith in astrological predictions or in curing by spells lies not in the severity of danger in the situation, nor in an anxious need to believe in an illusory solution to it, but in a conviction of their truth. These practices are comprehensible within the framework of a historically particular view of the nature of reality, a culturally unique image of the way in which the universe works, that provides a hidden conceptual foundation for all of the specific diagnoses, prescriptions, and recipes that [Keith] Thomas describes. The common linking element is not a psychological attitude but an ontology. The particular beliefs continued to be immune to the skeptical or empiricist onslaught as long as the more general, unarticulated view of reality remained undisturbed." Hildred Geertz[82]

Astral magic has already been covered in some detail in "How Magic Was Supposed to Work" and the chapters on charms. The primary focus then, however, was on preternatural rather than natural magic. In this chapter, the emphasis will be on the employment of astral influence through the use of natural objects such as images, animal parts, herbs, stones, metals – and talismans – primarily for healing. That astral forces or impellations that gave earthly things their specific appearances ("signatures") and virtues, that is, their potency to harm or heal, was never in doubt. As Agrippa attested, "The Celestiall souls send forth their vertues to the Celestial bodies, which then transmit them to this sensible world. For the vertues of the terrene orb proceed from no other cause then Celestiall." (Agrippa 1651: 337) The question was which substance did what, and how – and when – were they best utilised. This was most often answered by the identification of the particular planet which "ruled" the thing in question. The influences associated with the planet were those shared by its sub-lunar dependents or receptors, and the best time for their use was when that planet was in a favourable aspect. There is, however, very little information about how astrological magic was used in England, if it was consciously used at all before the 19th century, outside of medicine.

Although the earlier discussion on astrological *virtus* presented the influence of the stars as a single quality, there were actually two separate though related ways in which celestial influence was imparted to earthy things; as "elemental qualities" and as "occult properties": "Wherefore, he that desires to enter upon this study must consider, that every thing moves, and turns it self to its like, and inclines that to it self with all its might, as well in property, *viz.* Occult vertue, as in quality, *viz.* Elementary vertue." (Agrippa 1651: 34) Earthly objects obtained their elemental qualities through the seminal reasons they received at the time of their gestation or creation, and which they maintained throughout their existence. However, they received in addition a continuous flow of occult potency or virtue from the same star's or planet's impellations over time.

The desired astral influence for a remedy or magical ritual dictated the choice of which series or species of planetary receptors to use, be they animals, herbs, stones or something man-made, to bring the right influence to bear. An object's particular virtue, while always the same, could be stronger or weaker depending on the alignment of its governing star among the other heavenly bodies. If a governing planet was in a bad aspect, its receptors' efficacy was diminished. The practitioner needed not only to know *which* objects were receptors for a particular star, but also determine *when* that virtue could be most effectively made use of. Although the subject is moving through time rather than space in the

---

[82] Hildred Geertz. "An Anthropology of Religion and Magic, I". *The Journal of Interdisciplinary History*, Vol. 6, No. 1 (Summer, 1975), p. 83.

case of astral influence, this might be analogous to mobile phone reception, where the signal waxes and wanes as one moves among high buildings in a city. Catching the right moment to prepare a remedy is like halting on the sidewalk where the signal is strongest. It was important to choose the best celestial configuration under which to gather the materials, prepare the remedy or fashion the talisman. As Ficino (see below) notes, "In consequence, just as a given thing is fortunately born and coalesces and is preserved not elsewhere than here nor at any other time but just then, so also such or such a material action, motion, or event does not obtain full or perfect efficacy except when the celestial harmony conduces to it from all sides." [Ficino 2002: 305]

This also suggests a possible sidelight in the evolution of magical belief. Astrology retained an uninterrupted influence in England, in contrast to the other European nations where it effectively disappeared during the Enlightenment. If we observe the divide in the theoretical basis for magic between the natural (and spiritual) influence of elemental qualities due to the seminal reasons, as opposed to the astrologically derived occult properties of celestial *virtus*, folk magic in Germany appears to have shifted almost entirely to the former, while magic in England and France (as shown in *Le Petit Albert*), continued to favor latter. This may explain why the magic found in 19th century manuals such as the *Romanus-Büchlein* and the derivative *Egyptian Secrets of Albertus Magnus* and Hohman's *Long Lost Friend* almost entirely omit astrological correspondences in favor of a more conservative collection of charms, prayers, psalms and the elemental qualities of earthly things using factors of *virtus*. Analogous English publications such as Hardick Warren's *Magick and Astrology Vindicated* (1651), the anonymous *Art and Nature Joyn Hand in Hand* (1697) and "Raphael's" astrologically-centreed serial publications avoid traditional magical use of prayers, psalms and overt conjurations in favor of astrological connections, while the unique *Witchcraft Detected and Prevented* (1824) has both. It was in part because of English magic's tendency to favor astrological properties that I chose to stress that factor in my analysis.

The relationship of the objects in any planet's species of earthly receptors are usually referred to as "correspondences," that is, all members of a planet's species are affiliated and have a corresponding connection to their ruling planet. They all carry the same sort of astral and magical virtue. Tradition and empirical experiment identified innumerable specifications as to which herb or other item would cure this or cause that, and for many of the Cunning Folk, simply learning these formulas was all that was needed to practice their art. However, as we have seen, it wasn't just arbitrary custom that established these connections; a theoretical basis of great antiquity had codified and legitimized the correspondences under their astrological headings, a pattern that may be familiar to readers from compilations such as Crowley's *777*, which has an analogous series of Cabalistic correspondences. As this sort of astral classification had been widely disseminated through medical texts, herbals, lapidaries and "books of secrets" since Anglo-Saxon times, Cunning Folk would inevitably be familiar with the concept.

The question is, to what extent did they take the theoretical side into consideration? At first glance, it would seem that their "cookbook" lists of charms and remedies (oral or written) needn't involve astral considerations at all. All they had to do was follow directions. However, the medical culture they shared with their clients and professional doctors was permeated with astrological concepts, and even home remedies were often more complex than what we today might assume was appropriate for housewives – or Wise Women – while astrological medicine in which both diagnosis and prognosis was derived from an astrological chart was very common. Beyond healing, the whole realm of natural magic was essentially founded on astrological principles.

We know that better educated Cunning Men were curious enough to search out rare and difficult source material, as is evident from their libraries and notebooks, but how far down the social spectrum did this extend? The problem is how widely dispersed was information found in published if rather recondite sources among the general populace, and the Cunning Folk in particular? Whether any simple village and back-street Cunning Folk ever made use of such information is unclear, although it is known that they were often familiar with Reginald Scot, Agrippa's *Three Books* and the misattributed *Fourth Book*. Those practitioners could have found similar information from Ficino and others in compilations such as *The Book of Secrets of Albertus Magnus*, Lupton's *Thousand Notable Things*, Dr. Read's English edition of Johann Jakob Wecker's *Eighteen Books of the Secrets of Art & Nature*, Lævinus Lemnius' *Secret Miracles of*

Nature in Four Books, or the massive and rather confusing "Rosicrucian" works of John Heydon. In the end, there isn't enough evidence to know for sure how concerned the lesser Cunning Folk were with what this chapter covers, but as classic astrological and humoural theory was the basis for the medicine and nutrition in English culture until modern times, it is a worthwhile subject for investigation.

The most significant contribution to the science of astral influence was made by Marsilio Ficino in his *De Vita Libri Tres* (*Three Books on Life*, 1489). He revived an impressive number of long-forgotten (in Europe) Neoplatonic and Hermetic sources by translating them in to Latin, and then codifying their content in the *De Vita*, most particularly in the third book that concentrated on the use of astrological correspondences in improving human life and healing. One of the most important (if unacknowledged) sources for his work was the notorious Arabic book on astrological magic, the *Picatrix*, which comprehensively surveyed the theory and practice of utilizing astral influence for a wide variety of human needs and desires. For example, Ficino describes the manner in which the gathering together of things in the solar species could be used to infuse the beneficial influence of the Sun in a person:

> If you want your body and spirit to receive power from some member of the cosmos, say from the Sun, seek the things which above all are most Solar among metals and gems, still more among plants, and more yet / among animals, especially human beings; for surely things which are more similar to you confer more of it. these must both be brought to bear externally and, so far as possible, taken internally, especially in the day and the hour of the Sun and while the Sun is dominant in a theme of the heavens. Solar things are: all those gems and flowers which are called heliotrope because they turn towards the Sun, likewise gold, orpiment, and golden colours, chrysolite, carbuncle, myrrh, frankincense, musk, amber, balsam, yellow honey, sweet calamus, saffron, spikenard, cinnamon, aloe-wood and the rest of the spices; the ram, the hawk, the cock, the swan, the lion, the scarab beetle, the crocodile, and people who are blond, curly-haired, prone to baldness, and magnanimous. The above-mentioned things can be adapted partly to foods, partly to ointments and fumigations, partly to usage and habits. You should frequently perceive and think about these things and love them above all; you should also get a lot of light. (Ficino 2002: 247,249)

He also mentions the theoretical basis for the reception of astral *virtus* through the *Spiritus Mundi*.

> "All these discussions are for this purpose, that the rays of the stars opportunely received, our spirit properly prepared and purged through natural things may receive the most from the very spirit of life of the world (i.e., the Spiritus Mundi). The life of the world, innate in everything, is clearly propagated into plants and trees, like the body-hair and tresses of its body. Moreover, the world is pregnant with stones and metals, like its bones and teeth. It sprouts also in shells which live clinging to the earth and its stones. For all of these things live not so much by their own life as by the common life of the universal whole itself. This universal life indeed flourishes much more above the earth in the subtler bodies, which are nearer to the Soul [the *Anima Mundi*]. Through its inward power, water, air and fire possess living things proper to them and partake of motion… / Likewise by a frequent use of plants and a similar use of living things, you can draw the most from the spirit of the world, especially if you nourish and foster yourself by things which are still living, fresh, and all but still clinging as it were to mother earth; and if you dwell as frequently as possible among plants which have a pleasant smell, or at least not a bad one. For all herbs, flowers, trees, and fruits have an odor, even though you often do not notice it. By this odor, they restore and invigorate you on all sides, as if by the breath and spirit of the life of the world. Your spirit, I say, is very similar by nature to odors of this sort; and through the spirit, a mediator between the body and the soul, the odors also easily refresh the body and are of wondrous advantage to the soul. [Ficino 2002: 289, 291] (Ficino could almost seem to have the Bach flower remedies in mind.)

It should also be noted that herbs were not necessarily tied to a single star or a single use. For example, in his description of the influences of the fixed stars, that is, individual stars in constellations of both the zodiac and otherwise, Ficino includes the herb mugwort (*Artemisia vulgaris*) as a receptor for the influences of Algol, the "Goat" (Capella in Gemini), one of the stars in Canis Major and one in Ursa Major, Spica, and Deneb Algedi (the Tail of Capricorn). Presumably, the seven planetary stars were the strongest and most significant influences at work, however.

Agrippa enlarges on this theme in his *Three Books of Occult Philosophy*. In the 34th and 35th chapters of the first book, which covers natural magic, he observes:

> *How by Naturall things, and their vertues we may draw forth,*
> *and attract the influencies, and vertues of Celestiall bodies.*
>
> Now if thou desirest to receive vertue from any part of the World, or from any Star, thou shalt (those things being used which belong to this Star) come under its peculiar influence, as Wood is fit to receive Flame, by reason of Sulphur, Pitch, and Oile. Nevertheless when thou dost to any one species of things, or individual, rightly apply many things, which are things of the same subject scattered amongst themselves, conformable to the same *Idea* [primary form], and Star, presently by this matter so opportunely fitted, a singular gift is infused by the *Idea*, by means of the soul of the world. I say opportunely fitted, *viz.* under a harmony like to the harmony, which did infuse a certain vertue into the matter. For although things have some vertues, such as we speak of, yet those vertues do so ly hid that there is seldom any effect produced by them: but as in a grain of Mustardseed, bruised, the sharpness which lay hid is stirred up: and as the heat of the fire doth make letters apparently seen, which before could not be read, that were writ with the juice of an Onion or milk: and letters wrote upon a stone with the fat of a Goat, and altogether unperceived, when the stone is put into Vinegar, appear and shew themselves. And as a blow with a stick stirs up the madness of a Dog, which before lay asleep, so doth the Celestiall harmony disclose vertues lying in the water, stirs them up, strengtheneth them, and makes them manifest, and as I may so say, produceth that into Act, which before was only in power, when things are rightly exposed to it in a Celestiall season. As for example; If thou dost desire to attract vertue from the Sun, and to seek those things that are Solary, amongst Vegetables, Plants, Metals, Stones, and Animals, these things are to be used, and taken chiefly, which in a Solary order are higher. For these are more / available: So thou shalt draw a singular gift from the Sun through the beams thereof, being seasonably received together, and through the spirit of the world. ... When therefore any one makes a mixtion of many matters under the Celestiall influences, then the variety of Celestiall actions on the one hand, and of naturall powers on the other hand, being joyned together doth indeed cause wonderfull thing, by ointments, by collyries [eye-washes], by fumes, and such like ... (Agrippa 1651: 69-70)

The importance of specific astral impellations, accumulated by gathering together various earthly receptors and used at the opportune time of their greatest strength, is obvious. The lists of the items that identify their particular planetary species were central to both magical work and for healing. A revealing example of this in magic, where such an accumulation of receptors was part of a ritual whereby the threatening influence of a particularly unfortunate astrological configuration, can be seen in the famous rite which Tommaso Campanella worked for Pope Urban VIII, as described by D. P. Walker.[83] The Pope had been in the habit of doing astrological predictions about the deaths of his associates. Some who were his rivals in the Spanish-French factions at the Papal court put together a prediction that it would be the Pope who would die in the wake of the comet predicted for that year. Urban took this seriously and, together with the Hermetically-inclined priest, Tommaso Campanella, took a room, sealed it up magically and proceeded to make a miniature magical zodiac on the floor with lamps and candles which would offset the effects of the real zodiac outside. They remained in the room for ten days; drinking wines specially imbued with the right astrologically selected herbs, and then safely emerged. Urban then issued a bull making it illegal for anyone to predict the death of a Pope.

Lists and identifications of astral correspondences are found throughout early books on medicine and astrology, from "reputable" ones such as Ficino and Albertus Magnus (the legitimate *Book of Secrets* which was translated into English in 1550, not Pseudo-Albertine works such as the *Egyptian Secrets, or White and Black Art for Man and Beast*) to John Fage's *Speculum Egrotorum: The Sick Man's Glass* (1606) and Nicholas Culpeper's *Complete Herbal* (1653). More thorough surveys were made available in astrological works such as (Joseph) Blagraves *Astrological Practice of Physick* (1671), Richard Saunders, *The Astrological Judgment and Practice of Physick* (1677), and of course Lilly's *Christian Astrology* (1647). Although the medical profession avoided the outright astrological attribution of medicinal herbs with the stars, their remedies

---

[83] D. P. Walker. *Spiritual Magic From Ficino to Campanella*. London: The Warburg Institute, 1958, 205-212

were still predicated on the elemental qualities derived from astrological tradition for their effect on the four bodily humours of blood (sanguine), yellow choler (choleric), phlegm (phlegmatic) and black choler (melancholic). Single herbs ("simples") and remedies compounded from a number of ingredients were classified by their elemental qualities as hot or cold, moist or dry – and not just by those four qualities but also by four "temperatures" or degrees of strength (note how some are assigned degrees of both heat and moisture):

"… [the qualities] are more easily apprehended by the effectual operations which they have to alter a Man's body, we will go to that work, for seeing that (in this sense) that is temperate, which hath no power eminent to Heat, Cool, Dry or Moisten the body of a man, that is accounted the first Degree which obscurely and but a little altereth it. The second degree is when the body is manifestly altered, yea without any hurt, offence, or trouble. The third degree is, when the Body is altered, not only apparently, but also vehemently, not without trouble, yet without Corruption. The fourth is, that which alters the Body most vehemently, and not without very grievous hurt… /

Temperate Plants and Fruits are,

Maidenhair, Asparagus, Licorice, PineNuts, Figs, Raisins, Dates, Woodruff, Bugle, Goat's Rue, Flaxweed, Cinquefoil, etc.

Hot in the first degree are,

Wormwood, Marsh-Mallows, Borage, Bugloss , Oxeye, Beets, Cabbage, Camomile, Agrimony, Fumitory, Wildflax, Melilot, Comfrey, Avens, Eyebright, Selfheal, Chervil, Basil, etc. Sweet Almonds, Chestnuts, Cypress Nuts, Green Walnuts, Ripe Grapes, Ripe Mulberries, Seeds of Coriander, Flax, Gromwell, etc.

Hot in the second degree are,

Brooklime, Green Anise, Angelica, Parsley, Mugwort, Betony, Groundpine, Fenugreek, St. Johns Wort, Ivy, Hops, Balm, Horehound, Rosemary, Savory, Sage, Maudlin, Ladies Mantle, Dill, Smallage, Marigolds, Carduus Benedictus, Scurvygrass, Alehoofe, Alexander, Archangel, Devilsbit, Sanicle, Capers, Nutmegs, Dry Figs, Dry Nuts; The Seeds of Dill, Parsley, Rocket, Basil, Nettle. The roots of Parsley, Fennel, Lovage, Mercury, Butterburr, Hog's Fennel, etc.

Hot in the third degree are,

Asarabacca, Agnus, Arum, Dry Anise, Germander, Bastard, Saffron, Centaury, Celandine, Calamint, Fleabane, Elecampane, / Hyssop, Bays, Marjoram, Pennyroyal, Rue, Savine, Bryony, Pilewort, Bankcresses, Clary, Lavender, Feverfew, Mint, Watercresses, Hellebore, etc.

Hot in the fourth degree are,

Selatica, Cress, Spurge, Pepper, Mustardseed, Garlic, Leeks, Onions, Stonecrop, Dittander or Pepperwort, Garden Cresses, Crowfoot, Ros Solis, and the root of Pellitory of Spain.

Cold in the first degree are,

Orage, Mallows, Myrtle, Pellitory of the Wall, Sorrel, Woodsorrel, Burdock, Shepherd's Purse, Hawkweed, Burnet, Coltsfoot, Quinces, Pears, Roses, Violets.

Cold in the second degree are,

Blites, Lettuce, Duckmeat, Endive, Hyacinth, Plantain, Fleawort, Nightshade, Cucumbers, Chickweed, Dandelion, Fumitory, Wildtansy, Knotgrass, etc. Oranges, Peaches, Damsons, etc.

Cold in the third degree are,

Purslane, Houseleek, Everlasting, Orpine, etc. Seeds of Henbane, Hemlock, Poppy.

Cold in the fourth degree are,

Henbane, Hemlock, Poppies, Mandrake, etc. /

Moist in the first degree are,

Bugloss, Borage, Mallows, their flowers and roots, Pellitory, Marigolds, Basil, the roots of Satyrion, etc.

Moist in the second degree are,

Violets, Waterlily, Orage, Blites, Lettuce, Ducksmeat, Purslane, Peaches, Damsons, Grapes, Chickweed, etc.

Dry in the first degree are,

Agrimony, Camomile, Eyebright, Selfheal, Fennel, Myrtle, Melilot, Chestnuts, Beans, Barley, etc.

Dry in the second degree are,
Pimpernel, Shepherd's Purse, Wormwood, Vervain, Mugwort, Betony, Horsetail, Mint, Scabious, Bugle, Carduus Benedictus.

Dry in the third degree are,
Southernwood, Ferns, Yarrow, Cinquefoil, Angelica, Pilewort, Marjoram, Rue, Savory, Tansy, Thyme, Hellebore.

Dry in the fourth degree.
Garden Cresses, Wild Rue, Leeks, Onions, Garlic, Crowfoot.[84]

The manner in which astrally charged objects had their affect, whether in healing a bodily illness or influencing events, was by elemental interaction. The three *instrumentalities* (the agencies by which the stars controlled things on earth) – motion, light and the mysterious *influentia* – acted on the elements in earthly things by heating or cooling, moistening or drying, thus affecting the physical bodies of everything through their elemental makeup. Motion was the primary force at work in providing heat, with light (especially from the sun and moon) as a secondary influence of the same sort, while *influentia* was an "explanation" for those effects not otherwise attributable to perceptible forces, such as the astral effect on metals "growing" too deep in the earth to be reached by motion or light. As the *virtus* involved had its effect through elemental interaction, the use of herbs and all the other receptors was merely the application of a suitable species of objects that would directly change the humoural balance in people, and restore their well-being. This, plus the universal practice of draining away of excess or corrupt humours through bleeding, purgatives and laxatives, comprised traditional medical practice. In magic, similar collections of effective objects were used to offset the elemental balance of normal astral influence, strengthening one specific virtue to obtain a specific balance of the elements or humours. Talismans were essentially astral "solar panels" or batteries that by attracting and storing a particular virtue through correspondences, sigils and images, allowed the operator to have a particular virtue continually emitted for whatever use, even when its planet's immediate impellations were weak.

Lilly includes lists of planetary significations in his *Christian Astrology* that were of importance in healing and magic as well as electional and horary work. Here is one full example of significations, that of the Moon, with lists of the corresponding items useful for magic and healing for the other six planets.

CHAP. XIIII.
Of the Moon *her properties and significations.*

Name.	THE Moon we find called by the Ancients, *Lucina, Cynthia, Diana, Phœbe, Latona, Noctiluca, Prosperpina*, she is neerest to the Earth of all the Planets; her colour in the Element is vulgarly knowne [i.e., everyone knew what the Moon looked like]; she finisheth her
Motion.	course through the whole twelve Signs in 27 days, 7 hours and 43 min. or thereabouts; her meane motion is 13 degr. 10 min. and 36 seconds, but she moveth sometimes lesse and sometimes more, never exceeding 15 degr. And two min. in 24 hours space.
Latitude.	Her greatest North latitude is 5 degr. and 17 min. *or there=*
	Her greatest South latitude is 5 degr, and 12 min. *abouts.*
House.	She is never Retrograde, but always direct; when she is slow in motion, and goes lesse in 24 hours then 13 degr. and 10 min, she is then equivalent to a Retrograde Planet.
Triplicity.	She hath the Signe ♋ for her house, and ♑ for her detriment; she is exalted in ♉, and hath her fall in grad. ♏ : she governeth the Earthly Triplicity by night, *viz.* ♉ ♍ ♑ ;
	The *Sun* and she have no Termes assigned to them.

---

[84] William Coles. *The Art of Simpling*. (London, 1656). St. Catherines, Ontario: 1968, pp. 79-82.

In the twelve Signes she hath these degrees for her Decante or Face.

In ♉, 11 12 13 14 15 16 17 18 19 20.

In ♋, 21 22 23 24 25 26 27 28 29 30. /

In ♎, 1 2 3 4 5 6 7 8 9 10.

In ♐, 11 12 13 14 15 16 17 18 19 20.

In ♒, 21 22 23 24 25 26 27 28 29 30.

Nature.

She is a Feminine, Nocturnall Planet, Cold, Moyst, and Flegmatique.

Matters or Actions when well placed dignified.

She signifieth one of composed Manners, a soft, tender creature, a Lover of al honest and ingenious Sciences, a Searcher of, and Delighter in Novelties, naturally propense to flit and shift in Habitation, unstedfast, wholly caring for the present Time, Timorous, Prodigal, and easily Frightened, however loving Peace, and to live free from the cares of this Life; if a Mechanick, the man learnes many Occupations, and frequently will be tampering with many wayes to trade in.

When ill.

A meer Vagabond, idle Person, hating Labour, a Drunkard, a Sot, one of no Spirit or Forecast, delighting to live beggarly and carelesly, one content in no condition of Life, either good or evil.

Corperature.

She generally presenteth a man of faire stature, whitely coloured, the Face round, gray Eyes, and a little louring; much Haire both on the Head, Face, and other parts; usually one Eye a little larger then the other; short Hands and fleshy, the whole Body inclining to be fleshy, plump, corpulent and flegmatique: if she be impedited of the ☉ in a Nativity or Question, she usually signifies some blemish in, or neer the Eye; a blemish neer the Eye if she be impedited in Succedant Houses; in the Sight, if she be unfortunate in Angles and with fixed Starre, called Nebulousæ.

She signifieth Queens, Countesses, Ladies, all manner of Women; as also, the common People, Travellers, Pilgrims, Sailors, Fishermen, Fish-mongers, Brewers, Tapsters, Vintners, Letter-carriers, Coachmen, Hunts-men, Messengers, (some say the Popes Legats) Marriners, Millers, Ale-wives, Maistors, Drunkards, Oister-wives, Fisher-women, Chare-women, Tripe-women, and generally such Women as carry Commodities in the Streets; as also, Midwives, Nurses, &c, Hackney-men, Water-men, Water-bearers.

Sicknesse

Apoplexies, Palsie, the Chollick, the Belly-ache, /

Colours and Savours.

Diseases in the left Side, Stones, the Bladder and members of Generation, the Men-strues and Liver: in Women, Dropsies, Fluxes of Belly, all cold rheumatick Diseases, cold Stomak, the Gout in the Rists and Feet, Sciatica, Chollick, Wormes in Children and men, Rheumes or Hurts in the Eyes, *viz,* in the Left of Men, and Right of Women: Surfets, rotten Coughs, Convulsion fits, the Falling sicknesse, Kings-evil, Apostems, smal Pox and Measels.

Hearbs, Plants

Of Colours the White, or pale Yellowish White, pale Green, or a little of the Silver colour. Of Savours, the Fresh,

and Trees.	or without any flavour, such as is in Hearbs before they be ripe, or such as doe moysten the Braine, &c. Those Hearbs which are subject to the Moon have soft and thick juicy leaves, of a waterish or a little sweetish taste, they love to grow in watry places, and grow quickly into a juicy magnitude; and are The Colwort, Cabbage, Melon, Gourd, Pompion, Onion, Mandrake, Poppy, Lettice, Rape, the Linden-tree, Mushromes, Endive, all Trees or Hearbs who have round, shady, great spreading Leaves, and are little Fruitfull.
Beasts or Birds.	All such Beasts, or the like, as live in the water; as Frogs, the Otter, Snailes, &c. the Weasel, the Cunny, all Sea Fowle, Coockoe, Geese and Duck, the Night-Owle.
Fishes.	The Oyster and Cockle, all Shel-fish, the Crab and Lobster, Tortoise, Eeles.
Places.	Fields, Fountains, Baths, Havens of the Sea, Highwayes and Desert places, Port Townes, Rivers, Fish-ponds, standing Pools, Boggy places, Common-shoars, little Brooks, Springs, Harbours for Ships or Docks.
Minerals.	Silver.
Stones.	The Selenite, all soft Stones, Christals.
Weather. *Winds.*	With ♄ cold Ayre; with ♃ Serene; with ♂ Winds red Clouds; with the ☉ according to the Season; with ♀ and ☿ Showres and Winds. In Hermetical operation, she delighteth towards the North, and usually when she is the strongest Planet in the Scheame, *viz.* in any Lunation, she stirs up Wind, according to the nature of the Planet she next applies unto.

Is 12. degrees before and after any Aspect.	*Orbe.*
Her greatest yeers are 320. greater 108. meane 66, least 25. in conceptions she ruleth the seventh moneth.	*Yeers.*
Holland, Zealand, Denmarke, Norimberge, Flanders, Gabriel.	*Countries.* *Angel.*
Her day is Monday the first hour and the eight, after the rise of the Sun are hers. Her Enemy is ♄ and also ♂.	*Day of the weeke.*

(Lilly 1985: 81-83)

Lilly's species of planetary correspondences listed below for Saturn, Jupiter, Mars, the Sun, Venus, and Mercury indicate their appropriate uses. As with the case of the herbs and the fixed stars, some items are found under more than one ruling planet. Weather, which was believed to be astrally caused, is also included:

[Saturnine] *Sicknesse*	[Book I, Chap. VIII.] All Impediments in the right Ears, Teeth, all quartan Agues proceeding of cold, dry and melancholly Distempers, Leprosies, Rheumes, Consumptions, black Jaundies, Palsies, Tremblings, vain Feares, Fantasies, Dropsie, the Hand and Foot-gout, Apoplexies, Dog hunger, too much flux of the Hemoroids, Ruptures if in *Scorpio* or *Leo*, in any ill aspect with *Venus*.
Savours. *Hearbs.*	Sower, Bitter, Sharp, in mans body he principally ruleth the Spleen.

Plants and Trees. *Beasts &c..*	He governeth Bearsfoot, Starwort, Woolf-bane, Hemlock, Ferne, Hellebor the white and black, Henbane, Ceterach or Fingerferne, Clotbur or Burdock, Parsnip, Dragon, Pulse, Vervine, Mandrake, Poppy, Mosse, Nightshade, Bythwind, Angelica, Sage, Box, Tutsan, Orage or golden Hearb, Spinach, Shepheards Purse, Cummin, Horstaile, Fumitory. Tamarisk, Savine, Sene, Capers, Rue or Hearbgrace, Polipody, Willow or Sallow Tree, Yew-tree, Cypress-tree, Hemp, Pine-tree. / The Asse, Cat, Hare, Mouse, Mole, Elephant, Beare, Dog, Wolfe, Basilisk, Crocodile, Scorpion, Toad, Serpent, Adder, Hog, all manner of creeping Creatures breeding of putrifaction, either in the Earth, Water or Ruines of Houses.
Fishes, Birds, &c..	The Eele, Tortoise, Shel-fishes.
Places.	The Bat or Blude-black, Crow, Lapwing, Owle, Gnat, Crane, Peacock, Grashopper, Thrush, Blackbird, Ostrich, Cuckoo. He delights in Deserts, Woods, obscure Vallies, Caves, Dens, Holes, Mountaines, or where men have been buried, Church- yards, &c. Ruinous Buildings, Cole-mines, Sinks, Dirty or Stinking Muddy Places, Wells and Houses of Offices [outhouses], &c.
Minerals.	
Stones.	He ruleth over Lead, the Load-stone, the Drosse of all Mettals, as also, the Dust and Rubbidge of every thing.
Weather.	Saphire, Lapis Lazuli, all black, ugly Country Stones not polishable, and of a sad, ashy or black colour.
Winds.	He causeth Cloudy, Dark, obscure Ayre, cold and hurtfull, thick, black and cadense Clouds: but of this more particularly in a Treatise by it selfe. He delighteth in the East quarter of Heaven, and causeth Easterne Winds, at the time of gathering any Plant belonging to him, the Ancients did observe to turn their faces towards the East in his hour, and he, if possible, in an Angle, either in the Ascendant, or tenth, or eleventh house, the ☽ applying by a △ or ✳ to him.
[Jovial] *Diseases.*	[Book I, Chap. IX.] Plurisies, all Infirmities in the Liver, left Eare, Apoplexies, Inflamation of the Lungs, Palpitation and Trembling of the Heart, Cramps, paine in the Back-bone, all Diseases lying in the Vaines or Ribs, and proceeding from corru[p]tion of Blood, Squinzies, Windinesse, all Putrification in the Blood, or Feavers proceeding from too great abundance thereof.
Savours.	He governeth the Sweet or well sented Odours; or that Odour which in smell is no way extream or offensive.
Colours. *Hearbs and Drugs.*	Sea-green or Blew, Purple, Ash-colour, a mixt Yellow and Green. / Cloves and Clove-Sugar, Mace, Nutmeg, Gilly-flower, the Straw- bury, the herb Balsam, Bettony, Centory, Flax, Ars smart, Fumitory, Lung-wort, Pimpernell, Walwort, Organy or Wild Majorane, Rubbarb, Self heale, Borage, Buglosse, Wheat, Willow- hearb, Thorough-Leafe, Violets, Laskwort, Liverwort, Bazil, Pomegranets, Pyony, Liquorish, Mynt, Mastix, the Dazy, Feversend, Saffron.
Plants, Trees.	Cherry-tree, Birch-tree, Mulbury-tree, Corall-tree, the Oae, Ba[r]buries, Olive, Goosburies, Almond tree, the Ivy, Manna, Mace, the Vine, the Fig-tree, the Ash, the Pear-tree, the Hazel, the Beech-tree, the Pyne, Raysons.
Beasts.	

The Cunning Man's Handbook

Birds.	The Sheep, the Hart or Stag, the Doe, the Oxe, Elephant, Dragon, Tygar, Unicorne, those Beasts which are Mild and Gentle, and yet of great benefit to Mankind, are appropriate to him.
Fishes.	
Places.	The Stork, the Snipe, the Lark, the Eagle, the Stock-dove, the Partridge, Bees, Pheasant, Peacock, the Hen.
	The Dolphin, the Whale, Serpent, Sheath-fish or River Whale.
Minerals, Precious Stones.	He delighteth in or neer Alters of Churches, in publick Conventions, Synods, Convocations, in Places neat, sweet, in Wardrobes, Courts of Justice, Oratorie.
	Tyn.
Weather.	Amethist, the Saphire, the Smarage or Emrald, Hyacinth, Topaz, Chrystall, Bezoar, Marble, and that which in *England* we call the Free-stone.
Winds.	He usually produceth serenity, pleasant and healthful North Winds, and by his gentle Beams allayes the ill weather of any former Malignant Planets.
	He governeth the North Wind, that part which tendeth to the East.
[Martial]	[Book I, Chap. X.]
Diseases.	The Gall, the left Eare, tertian Feavers, pestilent burning Feavers, Megrams in the Head, Carbunckles, the Plague and all Plague-sores, Burnings, Ring-wormes, Blisters Phrensies, mad sudden distempers in the Head, Yellow-jaundies, Bloody-flux, Fistulaes, all Wounds and Diseases in mens Genitories, the Stone both in the Reins and Bladder, Scars or smal Pocks in the Face, all hurts by Iron, the Shingles, and such other Diseases as arise by abundance of too much Choller, Anger or Passion.
Colour and Savours.	He delighteth in Red colour, or Yellow, fiery and shinning like Saffron; and in those Savours which are bitter, sharp and burn the Tongue; of Humours, Choller.
Hearbs.	The Hearbs which we attribute to ♂ are such as come near to rednesse, whose leaves are pointed and sharp, whose taste is costick and burning, love to grow on dry places, are corrosive and penetrating the Flesh and Bones with a most subtill heat: They are as followeth. The Nettle, all manner of Thistles, / Rest-harrow or Cammock, Devils-milk or Petty spurge, the white and red Brambles, the white called vulgarly by the Hearbalists Ramme, Lingwort, Onion, Scammony, Garlick, Mustard-seed, Pepper, Ginger, Leeks, Ditander, Hore-hound, Hemlock, red Sanders, Tamarindes, all Hearbs attracting or drawing choller by Sympathy, Raddish, Castoreum, Arsmart, Assarum, Carduus, Benedictus, Cantharides.
Trees.	All Trees which are prickly, as the Thorne, Chestnut.
Beasts and Animals.	Panther, Tyger, Mastiffe, Vulture, Fox; of living creatures, those that are Warlike, Ravenous and Bold, the Castor, Horse, Mule, Ostrich, the Goat, the Wolf, the Leopard, the wild Asse, the Gnats, Flyes, Lapwing, Cockatrice, the G[r]iffon, Bear.
Fishes.	The Pike, the Shark, the Barbel, the Fork-fish, all stinking Wormes, Scorpions.
Birds.	The Hawke, the Vultur, the Kite or Glead, (all ravenous Fowle) the Raven, Cormorant, the Owle, (some say the Eagle) the Crow, the Pye.
Places.	Smiths Shops, Furnaces, Slaughter-houses, places where Bricks or

Minerals.	Charcoales are burned, or have been burnes, Chimneys, Forges. Iron, Antimony, Arsenick, Brimston, Ocre.
Stones.	Adamant, Loadstone, Blood-stone, Jasper, the many coloured Amatheist, the Touch-stone, red Lead or Vermilion.
Weather.	Red Clouds, Thunders, Lightning, Fiery impressions, and pestilent Aires, which usually appear after a long time of drinesse and fair Weather, by improper and unwholesome Mysts.
Winds.	He stirreth up the Westerne Windes.

[Solar]

Sicknesse	[Book I, Chap. XI.] Pimples in the Face, Palpitation or Trembling, or any Diseases of the Braine or Heart, Timpanies Infirmities of the Eyes, Cramps, sudden swoonings, Diseases of the Mouth, and stinking Breaths, Catars, rotten Feavers; principally in man he governeth the Heart, the Braine and right Eye, and vitall Spirit, in Women the left Eye.
Colours and Savours.	Of Colours he ruleth the Yellow, the colour of Gold, the Scarlet or the cleer Red, some say Purple: In Savours, he liketh wel a mixture of Sower and Sweet together, or Aromatical flavour, being a little Bitter and Stiptical, but withal Confortative and a little sharp.
Hearbs and Plants.	Those Plants which are subject to the ☉ doe smell pleasantly, are of good flavour, their Flowers are yellow or reddish, are in growth of Majestical form, they love open and Sunshine places, their principal Vertue is to strengthen the Heart, and comfort the Vitals, to cleer the Eye-sight, resist Poyson, or to dissolve any Witchery, or Malignant Planetary Influences; and they are Saffron, the Lawrel, the Pomecitron, the Vine, Enula, Campana, Saint Johns-wort, Ambre, Musk, Ginger, Hearb-grace, Balm, Marigold, Rosemary, Rosasolis, Cinamon, Celendine, Eye-bright, Pyony, Barley, Cynqfoile, Spikenard, Lignum Aloes, Arsnick[!].
Trees.	Ash-tree, Palm, Lawrel-tree, the Myrrhe-tree, Frankinsence, the Cane-tree or plant, the Cedar, Heletropion, the Orange and Lemon-tree.
Beasts.	The Lyon, the Horse, the Ram, the Crocodile, the Bul, Goat, Night-wormes or Glow-wormes.
Fishes.	The Sea-Calf or Sea-Fox, the Crabfish, the Starfish. /
Birds.	The Eagle, the Cock, the Phoenix, Nightingale, Pecock, the Swan, the Buzzard, the flye Cantharis, the Goshawke.
Places.	Houses, Courts of Princes, Pallaces, Theators, all magnificent Structures being clear and decent, Hals, Dining-Rooms.
Minerals or Metals.	Amongst the Elements ☉ Hath domination of fire and cleere shining flames, over mettals he ruleth Gold.
Stones.	The Hyacinth, Chrisolite, Adamant, Carbuncle, the Etites stone found in Eagles nests, the Pantaure, if such a stone be the Ruby.
Weather.	He produceth weather according to the season; in the spring gentle moysting Showers; in the Summer heat in extremity if with ♂; in Autumn mists; in Winter small Raine.
Winds.	He loves the East part of the World; and that winde which proceeds from that quarter.

[Venereal]

Sicknesse	[Book I, Chap. XII.] Diseases by her signified, are principally in the Matrix and members of Generation; in the reines, belly, backe, navill and those parts; the Gonorrea or running of the Reines, French or

	Spanish Pox; any disease arising by inordinate lust. Priphisme, impotency in generation, Hernias, &c. the Diabetes or pissing disease.
Savours colours.	In colours she signifieth White, or milky Skie colour mixed with browne, or a little Greene. In Savours she delightes in that which is pleasant and toothsome; usually in moyst and sweet, or what is very delectable; in smels what is unctious and Aromaticall, and incites to wantonnesse.
Hearbs and Plants.	Myrtle always green; all hearbs which she governeth have a sweet savour, a pleasant smell; a white flower; of a gentle humour, whose leaves are smooth and not jagged. She governeth the Lilly white and yellow, and the Lilly of the valley, and of the water. The Satyrion or Cuckoe pintle, Maidenhaire, Violet; the white and yellow Daffadil.
Trees.	Sweet Apples, the white Rose, the Fig, the white Sycamore; wilde Ash, Turpentine-tree, Olive, Sweet Oranges, Mugwort, Ladies-mantle, Sanicle-Balme, Vervin, Walnuts, Almonds, Millet, Valerian, Thyme, Ambre, Ladanum, Civet or Musk, Coriander, French Wheat, Peaches, Apricocks, Plums, Raisons.
Beasts.	The Hart, the Panther, small cattle, Coney, the Calf, the Goat.
Birds.	Stockdove, Wagtayle, the Sparrow, Hen, the Nightingale, the Thrush, Pellican, Partridge, Ficedula, a little Bird Feeding on Grapes; the Wren, Eagles, the Swan, the Swallow, the Owsel or Black Bird, the Pye.
Fishes.	The Dolphin.
Places.	Gardens, Fountaines, Bride-chambers, faire lodgings, Beds, Hangings, Dancing-Schooles, Wardrobes.
Metals or Minerals, Stones.	Copper, especially the Corinthian and White; Brasse, all Lattenware. Cornelian, the sky-colour'd Saphyre, white and red Coral, Margasite, Alabaster, *Lapis Lazuli* because it expels Melancholy, the Berill, Chrisolite. /
Winds and Weather.	She governeth the South-winde being hot and moyst; in the temperament of the Ayre, she ruleth the *Etesia*; she foretelleth in Summer, Serenity or cleer weather; in Winter, rain or snow.
[Mecurial] *Sicknesse*	[Book I, Chap. XIII.] All Vertigoe's, Lethargies or giddinesse in the Head, Madnesse, either Lightnesse, or any Disease of the Brain; Ptisick, all / stammering and imperfection in the Tongue, vaine and fond Imaginations, all defects in the Memory, Hoarcenesse, dry Coughs, too much abundance of Spettle, all snaffling and snuffling in the Head or Nose; the Hand and Feet Gout, Dumnesse, Toungue-evil, all evils in the Fancy and intellectual parts.
Colours and Savours.	Mixed and new colours, the Gray mixed with Sky-colour, such as is on the Neck of the Stock-dove, Linsie-woolsie colours, or consisting of many colours mixed in one. Of Savours an hodge-podge of all things together, so that no one can give it any true name; yet usually such as doe quicken the Spirits, are subtill and penetrate, and in a manner insensible.
Hearbs and Plants.	Herbs attributed to ☿, are known by the various colour of the flower, and love sandy barren places, they bear their seed in husks or cobs, they smell rarely or subtilly, and have principall relation to the tongue, braine, lungs or memory; they dispell winde, and comfort the Annimal spirits, and open obstructions. Beanes, three

Beasts.	leaved-grasse, the Walnut and Walnut-tree; the Filbert-tree and Nut; the Elder-tree, Adders-tongue, Dragon-wort, Twopenny-grasse, Lungwort, Anniseeds, Cubebs, Marioran. What hearbs are used for the Muses and Divination, as Vervine, the Reed; of Drugs, Treacle, Hiera, Diambra.
Beasts.	The Hyaena, Ape, Fox, Squirrel, Weasel, the Spider, the Grayhound, the Hermophradite, being partaker of both sexes; all cunning creatures.
Birds.	The Lynnet, the Parrot, the Popinian, the Swallow, the Pye, the Beetle, Pismires, Locusts, Bees, Serpent, the Crane.
Fishes.	The Forke-fish, Mullet.
Places.	Tradesmens-shops, Markets, Fayres, Schooles, Common-Hals, Bowling-Allyes, Ordinaries, Tennis-Courts:
Minerals.	Quicksilver.
Stones.	The Milstone, Marchasite or fire-stone, the Achates, Topaz, Vitroil, all stones of divers colours.
Winds and Weather.	He delights in Windy, Stormy and Violent, Boistrous Weather, and stirs up that Wind which the Planet signifies to which he applyes; sometimes Rain, at other times Haile, Lightning, Thunder and Tempests, in hot Countries Earthquakes, but this / must be observed really from the Signe and Season of the yeere. (Lilly 1985: 59-80)

The information found in Lilly and other astrological manuals became available to the Cunning Folk through various small chapbooks and cheap "Books of Knowledge", as well as in almanacs and other popular sources – including even cookbooks. I will now include some sections from these classic resources of the Cunning Folk, as well as of local healers and housewives whose responsibilities included seeing to the health of their family members. The first example is the well-known "zodiacal man" included in all almanacs to indicate which parts of the human body were governed by what astrological sign. This example is taken from *The Original Book of Knowledge* (London, 1725) although it could also be found in any number of other sources.

The first is *Aries* ♈; The Sign governs the Head and Face, and is by Nature hot and dry.

The second is *Taurus* ♉; This Sign governs the Neck and Throat, and is by Nature cold and dry.

The third is *Gemini* ♊; This Sign governs the Arms and Shoulders, and is by Nature hot and moist.

The fourth is *Cancer* ♋; This Sign governs the Breast and Stomach, and is cold and moist.

The fifth is *Leo* ♌; This Sign governs the Heart and Back, and is hot and dry.

The sixth is *Virgo* ♍; This Sign governs the Bowels and Belly, and is cold and dry.

The seventh is *Libra* ♎; This Sign governs the Reins and Loins, and is hot and moist.

The eight is *Scorpio* ♏; This Sign govern the secret Members, and is cold and moist.

The ninth is *Sagitary* ♐; This Sign governs the Thighs and Hips, and is hot an[d] moist.

The tenth is *Capricorn* ♑; This Sign governs the Knees and Hams, and is hot and dry.

The eleventh is *Aquarius* ♒; This Sign governs the Legs, and is by Nature hot and moist.

The twelfth is *Pisces* ♓; This Sign governs the Feet, and is cold and moist. 16-17

The importance of the humours in astrological medicine is clear from this familiar list. Another central feature of the old humoural system, and one which Cunning Folk sometimes employed, if for no other reason than it was expected of them, was analysis of the patient's urine. Urine was supposed to reveal the state of the bodily humours and their balance or imbalance. This might appear almost scientific at first glance, but as the examination was by visual appearance alone – not the chemical analysis of today – it had quite a different significance from modern medicine. Some licensed physicians made their diagnosis of disease (as all disease involved an imbalance in the humours) by a urine sample alone, delivered to them in a distinctive round flask that became the symbol of traditional medicine. Paracelsian competitors might insult traditional Galenic physicians by calling them "piss-pot prophets", but the practice was firmly established in the profession, and Galenic medicine remained dominant into the 19th century. Even astrological healers might include this universal tool of diagnosis in addition to the chart they erected for the patient. The following simplified instructions are taken from *The Shepherd's Kalendar: or, the Citizen's and Country Man's Daily Companion*. From what is said, criticism of the uroscopy of Cunning Folk and quacks had become widespread, but the practice still flourished – and would shortly be revived to evolve into its modern chemical form.

> *The Urinal Doctor, or a Astrilogical and Physical Observation, on Casting Urine, Relating to Health and Sickness, with Cautions to prevent threatened Evils.*
>
> **C**Asting of Urine is now become a new Trade [outside of official practice], and many People much rely upon it, to know the Constitution of their Bodies, as to Sickness or Health, and although there is something in it, yet they many times go to ignorant pretenders, who will take their Money, and tell them a plausible Story, though they know nothing of the Matter; therefore among these several useful things, I shall give the Reader an Insight to know himself; and in this very one Thing, save him or her the Money, this whole Book fraught with so many Rarities will have cost them.
>
> *First,* Then if the Urine be Red, it signifies the Blood is fleated, and you must either Bleed or Allay that Heat with cooling Things to prevent sickness.
>
> *2d,* The Urine White, shows Rawness, and Phlegmatick Indigestions in the Stomach, which must be remedies by gentle Purges, to cleanse it, and restore lost Appetite.
>
> *3d,* Thick and Muddy Urine betokens the Body surfeited, by over heating in Labour, Walking, or other Exercise, or by excessive Drinking, and then to prevent a Fever, taking cooling cordials. /
>
> *4th,* A White and Red Setling, Gravelly, or sandy in the Urine, betokes the Stone, beginning to putrify in the Reigns or Bladder; Drink to prevent it the Juice of Parsley, in Rhenish or white Wine.
>
> *5th,* A clear Perspicuous or Transparent Urine, shows a good Concoction, and perfect Digestion, and withal a Healthful Constitution.
>
> *6th,* Bloody spots in the Urine denotes an Ulceration in the Reins, or Neck of the Bladder.
>
> *7th,* The Urine Blackish, shows much a Dull Melancholy, and fore-runs some violent Diseases that often brings Death or a Long Tedious Sickness.
>
> *8th,* The Urine Clammy and Sweet, denotes a Consumption of the Inner Parts, by bad Digestion.
>
> *9th,* Urine of a Lead Colour, signifies the Body to be in an ill Habit (and threatens Death) without speedy Remedies Applyed.

10*th*, Urine that has Yellow sparkles, or sediment in it, shews Choller has the Predominancy, and much Afflicts the Body, threatens Fevers, and other hot Diseases; and by these kinds you may perfectly learn the state of the Body, as to Health or Sickness: present or approaching, for the Urine passing thro' those parts where the Distempers are Generating, carry a Tincture along with it of the Humours predominant, that is Encreasing or propagating the Disease, or on the contrary shows a healthful Constitution, tho' few are Skilful to discern it ... (*The Shepherd's Kalendar* 1725: 83-84)

Every person had his or her own particular "temperament" or proper humoural mixture, whether sanguine, choleric, phlegmatic or melancholic, which marked their optimum state of health. There was also always one humour that predominated, giving the individual their particular internal constitution or "complexion", which was mirrored in their features. Mild signs of choler in a choleric person (whose complexion was supposed to be ruddy with blond or red hair) indicated good health, although there could also be too much, indicating something like high blood pressure. Those same signs of choler in a phlegmatic person, however, would indicate an imbalance, and suggest that cooling and moistening medicines be used to restore the natural balance. Too much or too little of a vital humour was bad, as was the case when one or more humour had become corrupted. The humours could be balanced by drugs, or by expelling the excess through bleeding, purging and so forth.

An example of how this concept was presented to a popular audience can be found in *The Book of Knowledge Treating of the Wisdom of the Ancients* by "Erra Pater". The older concept of a naturally predominant humour or complexion appears to have been simplified away, but otherwise the concept is the same:

Containing Prognostications for ever, necessary for
keeping the Body in Health, &c.

As I have found in the Astrological Science there are four different sorts of humours in the body of man, of which the four complexions are formed; and of these one is made of yellow choler, another of black choler, a third Phlegm, and a fourth of blood [sanguine]. And if any of these be wanting the body must perish, because they equally sustain it.

And all those ought be kept in an equality, or if one be predominant over the rest, it puts the body out of order and brings diseases, which many times end in death, for the blood [which carried the humours throughout the body] stagnated and gathering in clots, causeth shortness of breath, which by degrees growing less and less at last proves without remedy; but if a person be let blood in the beginning of those disordered humours, the danger may be easily prevented. To purge the blood.

R. [i.e., ℞] Of both sorts of scurvey grass, of each six handfuls, of ground-ivy eight handfuls, of sage six handfuls, of soapwort root four ounces, agrimony and cresses, of each four handfuls; of rosemary and balm, of each a handful, four orange peals, a / large nutmeg grated; put all into four gallons of new ale; and when it is done working stop the barrel close. Take a pint every morning, and at four in the afternoon.

Likewise the black choler, or melancholy, is extremely dangerous, and when it gains the ascendant over the other, do great prejudice to the body several ways, causing divers distempers; and sometimes prevails so much over the senses that a man may become a mere Idiot, and also raises a kind of scurf all over the body, which sometimes turns to the measles, and are besides very apt to make a man afraid even of his own shadow, and turn a stout man into a coward, and a well bred person into one that's unmannerly: But by the use of proper medicines, such as herbs, flowers, and the like, all this may be either prevented or cured: First, shave the head, then bleed plentifully; afterwards purge well with the extract of Hellebore; lastly; let them use the following diet drink.

R. Epithymum Dodder of Thyme, Wood Sorrel, of each a handful, Rosemary flowers, Lavender flowers, of each two drams, Primrose & Cowslip roots, of each an ounce, Dock root half a pound; slice the roots, and infuse all in a gallon of small Ale, and drink as common drink.

White Phlegm is also very hurtful, if it exceed in quantity and overpower the other humours, for then they cause the gout, and divers other diseases, and are prejudicial to the feet, legs, knees, hands and reins, causing an evil favor both front teeth, mouth, nose, and ears: but also this may be cured by medicines compounded of roots, herbs and flowers; likewise by physical drinks and taking a vomit.

R. Dried Rosemary tops, Rose leaves [petals], Lavender / flowers, red Sage and Mint, of each a handful, Roots Succory two ounces, Senna Hermoducts [rupturewort or *Hernaria glabra*] Turbinth, and Scammony, of each two drams, of Zedoary, Ginger, Cloves and Cubebs of each one dram, infuse them in three Quarts of good white Wine for two days; take a wine glass full three times a day. Yellow choler is likewise very bad when it predominates in the body, affecting the heart and troubling the brain and weakening all the members of the body, causing a general faintness, with such a loose [sic] of appetite that neither meat nor drink will go down: Besides which, it alters a man's colour, and is hurtful to the eyesight. This also may be helped by taking a vomit, and applying proper medicines, compounded of the roots and flowers of several herbs.

R. Of the roots of Tumerick half an ounce, [P]ods of Centaury the less, Roman Wormwood and Horehound, of each an handful, Roots of the greater Nettle two ounces, boil them in three pints of water to the half [i.e., reduce by half], then add two scruples of Saffron tied in a bag, and a pint of white Wine, give it a warm or two, and strain it for use; dose a small glass full night and morning.

Note. That the four humours are the four complexions, which have their several times of dominion or government in the body of man, according to the several seasons of the year. (*Erra Pater* 1799: 35-37)

Examples of medical astrology are also found in citations from Thomas Lupton's *A Thousand Notable Things*, although for most of the book's many medical recopies the influence is implicit rather than specific as it is in these examples. For the most part, the elemental qualities rather than the occult properties of herbs or stones were focused on.

Book 1/80: Planten is judged by *Hermes*, to bee the herbe of *Mars,* and therefore good against the diseases and paines of the head: because that ye signe *Aries* which is one of the houses of *Mars,* doth gouern the head. And also Planten is very good against the griefe & diseases of the stones, and the Vllcers of the bladder: and also *Gonorrha pasio,* and Hemerods, because *Scorpio* the other house of *Mars,* doth rule that parts of the body. Lyke iudgement maye be had of other herbes of the planets. *Myzaldus.*

Book 2/29: Knotgrasse is thought to be the herbe of the Sun, where vpon it helpes greatly all the diseases of the harte, and the mouth of the stomacke. Whereof *Leo*, the Lyon gouernour, which is the house of the Sunne. And it is very good against ye great griefes of the backe, the Stone and the Collicke, by drinking of it, or by infusion. It was affirmed to *Mizaldus,* that it was found true by experience.

Book 3/45: Fyve leaued grasse, through *Iupiters* force, doth resyst venym or poyson. Whereof , if one leafe twyse euery daye, morning and euning be drunken with wine: It is sayd to put away the Quotidian ague. Three leaves the Tertian ague. And fowre leaues the Quarten ague. *Marcilinus Ficinus.*

Book 5/52: A Lamen, or thyn plate of Gold, borne on the seame of the brayne, doth strengthen the brayne. The same hanged against the region or place of the harte: doth helpe the beating of the harte, and encreaseth gladnes. And if it be put vpon the reynes, and cooles the same, and easeth the paynes of the backe. But *Mizaldus* wysheth that the same plate be beaten and made of pure and fyne Golde, when the sunne is in Leo, called the Lion: And Iupeter & the Moone beholden each other happely. *Hermes. Arnold Villa nouanus, &c.* (Lupton 1586: 19, 32, 61, 121)

Lupton also gives a number of astrological precepts concerning illness for indications to observe in horary charts, such as this example from Book 3, number 67: "If the Lorde of the Ascendent or of the Moone, or the Lorde of ye syxt house, be Combust, or Retrograde, & the Lord of the Ascendent be in the eyght house conuinct to *Mars*, or *Saturne*: the sicke must dye of that disease. *Iohannes Ganiuetus.* (But God can restore health past all hope.)" (Lupton 1586: 69). The astrological chart was a primary means by which the diagnosis of disease was made, but the technical specifics of orthodox medical astrology lie outside of this survey.

Healing was a major – perhaps the primary – service asked of the Cunning Folk, and most of the traditional herbal cures of the country folk were based on each plant's ascribed "elemental virtue" rather than on highly structured therapies involving changing astrological conditions. These are usually expressed through simple assertions such as "object W is the appropriate treatment for affliction X", or "thing Y has a sympathy with or an antipathy towards thing Z". No explanatory theory is assumed – it is simply the fact of the matter. While some of these were presumably the result of empiric observation, a great many seem not only entirely random but also (to modern eyes) flatly absurd. Even so, they had been repeated over and over again for thousands of years, which testifies to the iron hand of classical authority, and though susceptible to refutation by trial and error, were never subjected to objective experiment. For example, even lists of supposed elemental sympathies in learned authorities such as Agrippa reflect this fixed reliance on tradition:

> They say that certain acts, and observations have a certain power of naturall things, that they believe diseases may be expelled, or brought thus, and thus. So they say that quartanes may be driven away if the parings of the nails of the sick be bound to the / neck of a live Eel in a linnen clout [rag], and she be let go into the water. And *Pliny* saith, that the paring of a sick mans nailes of his feet, and hands being mixed with wax, cure the quartan, tertian, and quotidian Ague [malaria or like disease], and if they be before Sun rising fastened to another mans gate, will cure such like diseases. In like manner let all the parings of the nailes be put into Pismires caves [anthills], and they say that that which begun to draw the nailes first must be taken, and bound to the neck, and by this means will the disease be removed. They say that by Wood stricken with lightning, and cast behind the back with ones hands, any disease may be cured, and in quartanes a piece of a naile from a Gibbet, wrapt up in Wooll, and hanged about the neck, cures them; also a Rope doth the like, that is taken from a Gallows, and hid under ground, that the Sun cannot reach it. Also the throat of him that hath a hard swelling, or imposthume [abscess], being touched with the hand of him that dyed by an immature death, is cured thereby. Also they say, that a woman is presently eased of her hard travel [birth labour], if any one shall put into the bed, where the woman in travel is, a stone, or dart, with which either of these Animals, *viz.* a Man, a Boar, or a Bear were at one blow killed. (Agrippa 1651: 102-103)

The same is true for antipathies:

> Origanum [oregano] is contrary to a certain poisonous fly, which cannot endure the Sun, and resists Salamanders, and loathes Cabbage with such a deadly hatred, that they destroy one the other; so Cucumbers hate oile, and will run themselves into a ring least they should touch it. And it is said that the Gall of a Crow makes men afraid, and drives them sway from where it is, as also certain other things; so a Diamond doth disagree with the Loadstone, that being set by it, it will not suffer Iron to be drawn to it; and sheep fly from Frog-parsley as from some deadly thing: and that which is more wonderfull, nature hath pictured the sign of this death in the livers of sheep, in which the very figure of Frog-parsley being described, doth naturally appear; So Goats do so hate garden basil, as if there were nothing more pernicious. And again, amongst Animals, Mice, and Weesels do disagree; whence it is said that Mice will not touch Cheese, if the brains of a Weesel be put in the rennet, and besides that the Cheese will not be corrupt with age. So a Lizard is so contrary to Scorpions, that it makes them afraid with its very sight, as also it puts them into a cold sweat; therefore they are killed with the oile of them, which oile also cures the wounds made by Scorpions. There is also an enmity betwixt Scorpions, and Mice: wherefore if a Mouse be applyed to a prick or wound made by a Scorpion, it cures it, as it is reported. There is also an enmity betwixt Scorpions, and Stalabors, Aspes, and Waspes. It is reported also that nothing is so much an enemy to Snakes as Crabs, and that if Swine be hurt therewith they eat them, and are cured. (Agrippa 1651: 41)

Country folk shared similar inherited bodies of knowledge concerning the plants available to them on a local or regional basis, specifying what each particular herb was good for. Simple herbal identifications of this sort are found in Culpeper's *The English Physitian* (1652) and in other period sources. Not only were the herbs classified by their qualities and uses, there were also rules for when and how they were to be gathered, which involved astrological times. Beyond this, there were directions for harvesting herbs in traditional sources that are solely magical. Oral knowledge of these charms is both scarce and scattered, so I've included a Scottish example as well as Scot's instance of what was once a widespread magical practice:

Another charme that witches use at the gathering of their medicinable hearbs.
Haile be thou holie hearbe
/ growing on the ground
All in the mount Calvarie
/ first wert thou found,
Thou art good for manie a sore,
/ And healest manie a wound,
In the name of sweete Jesus
/ I take thee from the ground. (Scot1973: 198)

AN EARNAID SHITH [162]   THE FAIRY WORT

The 'fairy wort' referred to here is a vague name which may be applied to 'fairy flax' (Linum catharticum), cowslip or possibly foxglove (Digitalis pupurea).

Fairy Flax *Linum catharticum*
Also called fairywort, and known as purging flax in Cheshire, fairy lint in Northumberland and mill mountain in Shropshire. Catharticum derives from its value as a purgative. Often combined with peppermint and white wine, it was considered powerful enough to 'evacuate viscid and watery humours from the most remote lodgements'. It was also used to procure abortions. An infusion of it was used to treat muscular rheumatism, bronchitis and liver complaints. It is seldom used in modern herbalism.

BUAINIDH mi an earnaid,	PLUCK will I the fairy wort,
Le earlaid a bruth,	With expectation from the fairy bower,
Chur barrlait air gach ainreit,	To overcome every oppression,
Fad 's is earnaid i.	As long as it be fairy wort.
Earnaid shith, earnaid shith,	Fairy wort, fairy wort,
Mo niarach an neach dh' am bi,	I envy the one who has thee,
Ni bheil ni mu iadhadh grein,	There is nothing the sun encircles,
Nach bheil di-se le buaidh reidh.	But is to her a sure victory.
Buainidh mi a chraobh urramach	Pluck will I mine honoured plant
Bhuain Moire mhor, Mathair chobhair an t-sluaigh,	Plucked by the great Mary, helpful Mother of the people,
Chur dhiom gach sgeula sguana, sgulanach,	To cast off me every tale of scandal and flippancy,
Dim-bith, dim-baigh, dim-buaidh,	Ill-life, ill-love, ill-luck,
Fuailisg, guailisg, duailisg, doilisg,	Hatred, falsity, fraud and vexation,
Gun teid mi dh' an fhuar lic fo'n talamh.	Till I go in the cold grave beneath the sod.
(Carmichael 1900: 92)	(Carmichael 1900: 93)

However, recorded remedies more commonly involved more than a single herb, involving complicated "receipts" (and there is a distinct correlation between the recipes for preparing food and those for preparing medicines) containing several ingredients with detailed directions for turning them into medicine. Perhaps it was assumed that, as with the basic instructions in cookery that were omitted in contemporary cookbooks, it was unnecessary to note down simpler remedies.

Cures found in early cookbooks illustrate the almost seamless connection between medicine and nutrition in traditional sources. They also show the complexity of many "home" remedies, as mentioned above. These examples are drawn from two quite popular publications, Gervase Markham's *The English Housewife* (1615) and *The Queen's Closet Opened* (1655), which was supposed to be the household book of Queen Henrietta Maria. Both were aimed at the "middling sort" (the middle classes) in contrast to earlier cookbooks intended for the wealthy. Note the instruction to distil herbs in the remedy for kidney-stones – skill in distilling essences for consumption and medicine was considered to be a standard achievement of better-off housewives, which suggests that still-room arts were a part of some Wise Women's repertoires as well.

Of her virtues in physick.

To begin then with one of the most principal virtues which doth belong to our English housewife: you shall understand that sith the preservation and care of the family touching their health and soundness of body consisteth most in her diligence, it is meet that she have a physical kind of knowledge; how to administer many wholesome receipts or medicines for the good of their health …

For infection of the plague.

But if you are infected with the plague, and feel the assured signs thereof, as pain in the head, drought, burning, weakness of stomach and such like, then you shall take a dram of the best mithridate*, and dissolve it in three or four spoonful of water, and immediately drink it off, and then with hot cloths or bricks made extreme hot, and laid to the soles of your feet after they have been wrapped in woollen cloths, compel the sick party to sweat, which if he do, keep him moderately therein till the sore begin to rise; then to the same apply a live pigeon cut in two parts, or else a plaster made of the yolk of an egg, honey, herb of grace chopped exceeding small, and wheat flour, which in a very short space will not only ripen, but also break the same without any other incision; then after it hath run a day or two you shall apply a plaster of melilot unto it until it be whole.

For the headache.

For the headache, you shall take of rose-water, of the juice of camomile, of woman's milk, and of strong vinegar, of each two spoonful; mix them together well upon a chafing-dish of coals, then take of a piece of a dry rose cake and steep it therein, and as soon as it hath drunk up the liquor and is thoroughly hot, take a couple of sound nutmegs grated to powder, and strew them upon the rose cake; then breaking it into two parts, bind it on each side upon the temples of the head, and so lie the party down to rest, and the pain in a short space will be taken from him.

For the toothache.

Take two or three dock roots, and as many daisy roots, and boil them in water till they be soft, then take them out of the water, and boil them well over again in olive oil, then strain them through a clean cloth, and anoint the pained teeth therewith, and keep your mouth close, and it will not only take away the pain, but also ease any megrim or grief in the head.

For costiveness.

For extreme costiveness [constipation], or binding in the body, so as a man cannot avoid [i.e., void or discharge] his excrements, take aniseeds, fenugreek, linseed, and the powder of peony, of each half an ounce, and boil them in a quart of white wine, then drink a good draught thereof, and it will make a man go to stool orderly and at great ease.

---

* 'Mithridatium contained 48 ingredients, the formula in the 1746 *London Pharmacopoeia* being: 'myrrh, saffron, agaric, ginger, cinnamon, spikenard, frankincense, treacle, mustard seed, of each ten drachms hartwort seed, balsam of Peru, camels' hay, French lavender flowers, costos root, galbanum, Cyprus turpentine, long pepper, castor, juice of the hypocistis, storax, opoponax, Indian leaves, of each one ounce, cassia lignea, mountain poly, white pepper, scordium leaves, Cretan carrot seeds, carpobabamum, troches of cyperus, bdellium, of each seven drachms, Celtic spikenard, gum arabic, Macedonian parsley seed, opium, lesser cardamom seed, fennel seed, gentian root, red roses, dittany of Crete, of each five drachms, aniseed, asarabacca, sweet flag, wild valerian root, fagapenum, of each three drachms, spignel root, acacia, skinks' [lizards] bellies, St Johnswort seed, of each two and a half drachms. Add purified honey thrice the weight of the above species, add Canary wine sufficient to dissolve the gums; mix them into an electuary.' J. M. Haigh, "The British Dispensatory", *S. A. Medical Journal* 5 Oct. 1974, p. 2044.

A water for the stone.

To make a water for the stone [gall or kidney stones], take a gallon of new milk of a red cow, and put therein a handful of pellitory of the wall, and a handful of wild thyme, and a handful of saxifrage and a handful of parsley, and two or three radish roots sliced and a quantity of filipendula [meadowsweet] roots; let them lie in the milk a night, and in the morning put the milk with the herbs into a still, and distil them with a moderate fire of charcoal or such like: then when you use the water, take a draught of Rhenish wine or white wine, and put into it five spoonful of the distilled water, and a little sugar and nutmeg sliced, and then drink of it; the next day meddle not with it, but the third day do as you did the first day, and so every other day for a week's space.

For the gout.

For the gout, take aristolochia rotunda [birthwort], althea, betony, and the roots of wild nep, and the root of the wild dock cut into thin pieces after the upper rind is taken away, of each a like quantity, boil them all in running water till they be soft and thick: then stamp them in a mortar as small as may be, and put thereto a little quantity of chimney soot, and a pint or better of new milk of a cow which in all of one entire colour, and as much of the urine of a man that is fasting, and having stirred them well together, boil them once again on the fire, then, as hot as the party can suffer it, apply it to the grieved place, and it will give him ease.

To take away pimples.

To take away either pimples from the face, or any other part of the body, take virgin wax, and spermacetti, of each a like quantity, and boil them together, and dip in a fine linen cloth, and as it cools dip it well of both sides, then lay it upon another fair cloth upon a table, and then fold up as much cloth in your hands, and all to sleight [rip or shred] it with the cloth, then take as much as will cover the grieved place.

Of oil of swallows.

To make the oil of swallows, take lavender cotton, spike, knotgrass, ribwort, balm, valerian, rosemary tops, woodbine tops, vine strings, French mallows, the tops of alecost, strawberry strings, tutsan, plantain, walnut tree leaves, the tops of young bays, hyssop, violet leaves, sage of virtue, fine Roman wormwood, of each of them a handful, camomile and red roses, of each two handful, twenty quick [live] swallows, and beat them altogether in a large mortar, and put to them a quart of neat's-foot oil, or May butter, and grind them all well together in an earthen pot, and stop it very close, that no air come into it, and set it nine days in a cellar or cold place, then open your pot and put into it half a pound of butter, then set your pot close stopped into a pan of water, and let it boil six or eight hours, and then strain it. This oil is exceeding sovereign for any broken bones, bones out of joint, or any pain or grief either in the bone or sinews.[85]

As is evident from the above, English popular medicine wasn't just about herbs from Granny's garden. Ingredients such as urine, soot, woman's milk or live pigeons and swallows cut and crushed to death, or that ever-popular omnibus remedy, mithridatium, are not what we might think of for traditional healing by Wise Women. Neither are cochineal, "Diamargaritum Frigidum"* or white dog shit, but all are found below in receipts from *The Queen's Closet Opened*. However, their inclusion in home remedies probably indicates that the Cunning Folk used similar formulas, as they reflected contemporary opinion of what medicine was supposed to be. Queen Henrietta's remedies do seem a bit more culinary that those of Markham.

---

[85] Gervase Markham. *The English Housewife* (1615), Michael R. Best, ed. Montreal: McGill-Queen's University Press, 1986, pp. 8,12,13,19,32,36,42,44,56.

* *Diamargaritum Frigidum* "Take of the four greater cold seeds, of Purslan, white Poppies, Endive, Sorrel, Citrons, the three Sanders, wood of Aloes, Ginger, red Roses exungulated, the flowers of Water-lillies, Buglos, Violets, the Berries of Myrtles, bone in a Stag's heart, Ivory, Contrayerva, Cinnamon, of each half a dram, Camphire six grams; make them into a pouder according to Art." Nicholas Culpeper. *Pharmacopœia Londinensis*. London: W. Churchill, 1718, p. 186. For Diambra, see page 187 (the type in my copy being too broken up to decipher).

Jim Baker

To comfort the Heart and the Spirits, and to suppress Melancholy.
Take the juyces of Borage and Buglosse, of each one point and a half, juyce of Pippins, or Queen Apples pone point, juyce of Balm half a point, clarifie them, then add Cochenel, made into powder, four drams, infuse it in the said juices being cold in an earthen pan for two days, stirring it often, then strain it, and with four pound of powder Sugar, (or two pound if you mean not to keep it long) boyl it to a syrup, then take it off, and when it is almost cold, put to it Diamargaritum Frigidum* one dram and a half, Diambra four scruples. Take thereof a spoonful or two for many mornings together, and when you awake in the / night, if therebe cause; you may also adde to some part of it Saffron to make it more cordial, by putting some powder of Saffron in a linen clowt tyed up, and so milking it out into the syrup, let the substance thereof remain in the cloth, and take thereof sometimes. *Approved.*

A Cordial Electuary for stuffing of the Stomach, or shortness of Breath.
Take a pinte of the best Honey, set it on the fire and scum it clean, then put to it a bundle of Hysop bruised small before you tie it up, let it boyl well, till the Honey taste of the Hysop, then strain out the Honey very hard, and put it to the powder of Angelica root the weight of six pence, powder of Eleicampane root the weight of 6 pence, Ginger and Pepper of each the weight of two pence, Liquorish and Aniseed of each the weight of eight pence, all beaten very small severally: put all these into the strained Honey, and let them boyl a little space, stirring them well together all the time, then take them from the fire, and pour all into a clean / Gally pot, stirring it always till it be through cold, and keep it close covered for your use. When any are troubled with stuffing at the Stomach or shortness of breath, let them take this Electuary with a bruised Liquorish stick, and they shall sensibly finde much good by it. This was Queen Elizabeths Electuary for these infirmities.

A very good clyster for the Winde.
Take Mallow leaves, Cammomil, Mercury [herb], Pellitory of the Wall, Mugwort and Pennyroyal, of each a small handful, Melilot and Camomil flowers, of each half a handful, of the seeds of Anise, Caroway, Cummin, and Fennel of each one quarter of an ounce, Bay berries and Juniper berries of each three drams; boyl all these in three pints of clear posset Ale to twelve ounces, and use it warm.

For an Ague.
Take a quantity of Plantain, shred it and double distil it, and take six or eight spoonfuls of the water, with as much Borage water with a little Sugar and one Nutmeg, and drink it warm in the cold fit, by Gods help it will cure you.

A special medicine for one that cannot swallow,
although no inward Medicine can be taken for it.
Take the soiling of a Dog that is hard and white, powder it, and mingle it well with English Honey, spread it thick upon a linnen cloth, and hold it to the fire, and lay it all over the Throat down to the Channel bone, use fresh morning and evening, binde it hard to, and by Gods grace it will help.

For heat or pimples in the Face.
Take the Liverwort that groweth in the Well, stamp it and strain it, and put the Juyce into Cream, and so anoynt your face as long as you will, and it will help you. Proved. Also the Juyce of Liverwort drunk in Beer warm, is good for the heat of the Liver.[86]

The recipes often require imported ingredients such as sugar for syrups or foreign herbs and spices sold by grocers and apothecaries, which might be a strain on the finances of many people, but then as now, illness often involved extraordinary expense. A lot of the basic "simpling" done by housewives for their family and husbandmen for their livestock didn't involve the advice of Cunning Folk, but they

---

[86] W. M. *The Queen's Closet Opened Incomparable Secrets in Physick, Chirugery, Preserving, Candying, and Cookery.* [London:] Printed for Nathaniel Brook, at the Angel in Cornhill, 1655, pp. 4-5,5-6,30,32,51,54.

were quick to ask for help if the home remedies didn't work. Did the Cunning Folk use the same sort of remedies as their neighbors or more "magical" ones when a show of uncommon knowledge and learned expertise was expected of someone who would be paid for their efforts? The likely answer is – both.

The interconnections between the stars, the elements, and human humours, activated through the elemental and occult virtues, was the foundation of astrological healing. In the same manner, material objects acted as receptors and re-transmitters of celestial *virtus* in magic, as discussed in the chapters on conjuration. Yet while occult properties had an inextricable association with the heavenly bodies and beings that sent the streams of astral *virtus*, elemental qualities *could* be postulated quite apart from any ostensible astral origin, just as chemical properties are today. Whether housewife or physician, anyone who learned or could reference traditional formulas could use elemental medicine. The astrological efficacy that in theory powered medicines as well as charms might be omitted from consideration and the effect thought of as wholly "natural", that is, material. You didn't need to know why something worked in order to use one of the recipes. In magic, on the other hand, not only did the theory need to be understood, but the magician also had to know which appropriate materials to select and calculate auspicious times to begin the work. This gave the Cunning Folk, who had the interest and motivation to learn some astrology, an advantage over their neighbors when home remedies failed, as they could dazzle their clientele with arcane patter and offer "professional" services.

Today we judge the effectiveness of medicines (herbal or chemical) by their physical properties. Things that have an active chemical influence on the body are deemed effective (or dangerous), while those for which an effect cannot be demonstrated, are considered false and irrelevant. In magic as well as traditional healing, however, it wasn't necessarily the chemical properties of an herb or mineral that were sought after, but rather the astral/elemental ones. This may help us to understand how remedies that did not involve ingestion were supposed to work. If a stone or a piece of an animal or a written charm had the assumed capacity to radiate the appropriate astral influence on the bodily humours, suspending it in a bag about the neck was logically as effective as anything taken internally. It should be kept in mind that our ancestors had no knowledge of germs or viruses, and believed that most disease was caused by an imbalance of the bodily humours. They did have theories about external sources of infection, but these were thought to be the result of "miasmas" or the pollution of "bad air", evil odors and such that negatively influenced the humours, rather than living bacteria.

I haven't attempted a chapter on simple herbal healing because the variety of elementary cures is both arbitrary and endless, and the basic herbal remedies can be found in easily available reprints of Culpeper's herbal. Instead I have chosen to cover traditional healing through its evident theoretical context, in which the most important components are humoural and astrological. I have also chosen to omit a broad area of medicine that was important to both the Cunning Folk and their clients dealing with animal husbandry, feeling that this now fairly obsolete area of healing would greatly expand the need for examples in an already extensive survey

Astrology's Cultural Role

How was astrological influence viewed in the wider culture? Before the Enlightenment, even astrology's severest critics (who basically said that while the stars might have a general influence, there wasn't anything people could do about it) expressed opinions that supported the overall concept. For example, even as leading Puritan theologian William Perkins denounced judicial astrology, he at the same time attested to the reality of astral influence. Although Perkins had renounced arcane studies by the time he wrote this, as a college student he had been very involved in the study of astrology and magic – he knew a lot more about this field than the average theologian.

> ... it is not possible for any man, truely and certainly to observe all particular events brought forth by the starres, whereupon he might ground his rules. And for proofe hereof; Suppose there was a heap of all kinds of herbs growing upon the earth gathered together, which should be all strained into one vessel, and the liquor brought to the most skilfull / Physitian that is, or ever was; can we think him able by tasting or smelling thereof, to distinguish the vertues of the hearbs, and to say which is which? To doe this when all are severed each from other, is a hard matter, yet possible,

considering they have their severall natures and operations; but in this confused mixture to discerne the severalls is a thing passing the skill of man. The like may be said of the particular vertue of every starre; for they all have their operation in the bodies of men, and other creatures; but their vertues beeing all mixed together in the subject whereon they work, can no more be knowne distinctly, then the vertues of a masse of hearbs of infinite sorts beaten together. For this is an undoubted truth in nature: that the vertues of Celestial bodies, in their operations are mingled with the qualities of the elements in the inferiour bodies, and the vertues of them all doe so concurre, that neither the heate or light of the starres, nor the vertue of the elements, can be severed one from another. And therefore though there be notable vertue in the starres, yet in regard of the mixture thereof in their operation, no man is able to say by observation, that this is the vertue of this star, and this of that. The seaven planets beeing more notable, then the other lights of the heaven, specially the Sunne and Moone, have their operations and effects plainely and perfectly knowne; as for the other, there was never any man that could either feele their heate, or certainely determine of any thing by them. There beeing then some starres, whose vertues are unknowne, how can their operations and effects be discerned in particular? Therefore no rules can be made by observation of the vertues of the starres in their operations, wherupon we may foretell particular events of things contingent, either concerning mens persons, families, or kingdomes. (Perkins 1615: 23-24)

The Cunning Man might reply by saying in the first case, the seven planets' influence was more important than all of the rest, and secondly, astrologers had long ago developed their art to account for the mixed interaction of all the major powers involved (they were not just "juiced" together), and in the case of magic or medicine, knowledge of which receptors to gather made the attraction and use of any particular impellations a simple matter. The other side of the argument was joined by almost every writer on astrology. When it came to medicine and astrology, Rev. Richard Napier (1559–1634) offered a more supportive view:

… But here question may bee moved, whether anie profitt might come to the Phisicion by the knowledge of the heavenlie bodies touching the cure of sicke persons; to this I answere that they knowledge of these thinges are soe necessarielie required to a Physitian, that hee cannott bee will reckoned an absolute & skilfull Physitian that is utterlie ignorant of this Astrologie, especiallie if that bee true, which that excellent Astrologer Guido Bonatus hath in his first part of Astronomie & 2: cap: where hee hath these wordes, I suppose saith Guido, That every one taketh this for a principle, and an undoubted trueth That the heavens with theer motion Compassing round about the elements with their perpetuall Turning round about do first alter and Chaunge the elementes of the fyre and ayer, and then thye thus Chaunged by their motion deeply imprinted in them do agayne alter and Chaunge the other elementes the water and earth and all livinge Creatures and vegetables and all other thinges that have their essence and being under the globe of the moone and whatsoever els is Capable of Chaunge and alteration Because (sayth he) / The Sunne and the eyer do worke upon every Individuall and severall thing and Creature in the earth and upon the very partes of every particuler Creature forasmuch as, no alteration can happen unto the earth except it hapen through the alteration of the Sunne And so further he sayth That the Astrologer knoweth What maner of motion the motion of every Cælestiall Body is Now (sayth he) if he knowe the qualityes of these motions Then must he needs knowe what impressions they do imprint and make, and so withall he must understand their significons and all thinges which are done upon the earth attending to the Course and order of nature. and also what other things are caused in the elements by Reason of the motions of the heavenly bodyes wherof no man can doubt nisi forte insipiens vel Idiota except he be a starke foole and an Ideott By which it plainly appeareth that in the opinion and Judgement of learned Guido the knowledge of Astrologie is verie requisite for an expert phisitian that would worke advisedlie in all his cares and indeavours. But to leave Guido because hee was an Astrologer, & therefore may bee thought partiall in this controversie; I will site such as had knowledg alsoe in phisicke, Ganivetus (noe doubt) had good knowledge in both faculties, yet hee in his booke entituled Amicus Medicorum, the physitians friend doth make Astrologie the Physitians right hand, & setteth him downe in that booke how hee may doe the dutie of a good physitian, & tell the cause of the disease, and the place & part affected, & whether or noe to bee cured, & the best & readiest waye how to cure it, & all this hee sheweth best to bee done by a diligent respect had to the celestiall bodies, & to their motions, aspects, radiations, & configurations, which they beare towardes themselves, & the earthlie bodies they aspect.[87]

While the principle of astral receptors is absolutely vital in any magical work, there aren't many explicit examples in published sources before the 19th century "occult revival". The reason for this is due to the strange reluctance that Owen Davies noted of English writers to publish the overtly magical formulas that are commonly found in continental sources, but it is frustrating, nonetheless. That such "receipts" existed is clear from the grimoires insistence on the observation of favourable astrological conditions, as well as the oral sources recorded by folklorists in the 19th century and after. One exceptional source for healing and astral magic that became available in English at the close of the 17th century was Israel Hiebner's *Mysterium sigillorum, herbarum & lapidum*, originally published in 1651. The English edition by "B. Clayton" was published in 1698 (after official censorship had ceased), and in addition to some very specific information on herbs and astral influence, it gives some very specific directions for creating planetary talismans for healing adapted from Agrippa's magical squares. His talisman for Jupiter will serve as an example:

The Description of the Second Metal of Copper Or Tin, or the Sigil of Jupiter, how it is to be prepared and used against all Jovial Sicknesses.

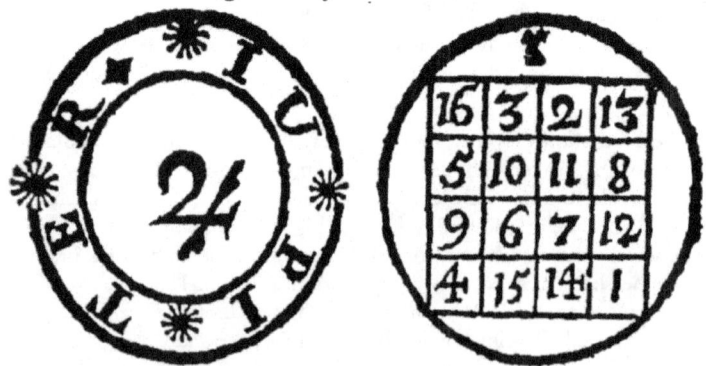

Purgatio Jovis.
Take Tin and melt it, and when it is very hot fling in a piece of Rosin; this do nine times. When it is all burnt away, cast into it the Juice of Rue, or its Water, and it is purged. This must be done in the Influence of Jupiter, as may be seen from page 126, to 139 [a list of times when Jupiter was in the ascendant for 1698 and 1699].

A short Preparation of Copper, *according to* Theophrastus.
Copper must be laid in *Vitriol-Water*. Or *Camphire-Water*, mix'd with *Vinegar*, for six or eight hours, take it out, wash it and dry it, and it is prepared. /

Configuration.
Cast of such *Copper* a *Sigil*, of the bigness of a Half-a-Crown; upon one side must be the Body of *Jupiter*, with the four Stars that are about him, as may be seen in the Heavens with a Telliscope, in the middle must be the Character of *Jupiter*, and round the Body the name JUPITER; on the other side

---

[87] Richard Napier. "A treatise touching the Defence of Astrology (Normalised Version)", *Casebooks Project* (http://www.magicandmedicine.hps.cam.ac.uk/view/text/normalised/TEXT3/), < f. 192 r, v> (Accessed 2012-06-18). Napier, the rector in Great Linford, Buckinghamshire, took up the practice of astrological medicine. His records survive in full, from 1598 to his death in 1634. They contain roughly 75,000 consultations.

must be these Numbers, 1, 2, 3, 4, 5, 6, 7, 8, 9, 10, 11, 12, 13, 14, 15, 16, in a square, so let that by Addition, they may make everyweays 34, on the top, this *Hebrew* Character א

Impressio.

The Stamp must be made as *Saturn's*, but upon both sides must be cut the Figure and Number of *Jupiter*, then stampe'd in the Influence of *Jupiter*.

The Vse.

When this *Sigil* is prepared in the influence of *Jupiter*, and put in a blue Silk bag, it cures all the *Sicknesses* of *Jupiter*, page 3. /

Of the Gem of JUPITER.

To *Jupiter* belong the *Smaragadine, Sapphire,* and *Amethist*: the Body of *Jupiter*, as is here noted, must be cutt in the Influence of *Jupiter*, in a *Jovial* Stone, and carried about the Neck, or on the Breast, or in the inward part of a Copper Ring, so as to touch the Skin. (Clayton 1698: 165-167)

The reference to cutting a stamp the same as for Saturn is to directions for preparing steel dies like those used in coining money to impress images in each side of the talisman. The Jovial diseases found on the third page are: "Pleurise and Swelling in the Sides, Convulsion and Cramp, Pains in the Back, Stubborness [!], Yearly Fever, Liver-grown, Lungs, Ribbs, Knee-pan, Pulse, Sinews and Grissels, and Sperm". This is followed by a list of three animals governed by Jupiter – sheep, cranes, and larks.

Astrology was therefore inextricably interwoven into the practice of healing and magic alike. It also served as the foundation in geomancy, which similarly made use of the concept of the four elements, and focused on the celestial houses (though it employed its own particular figures rather than the planets), and was central to chiromancy, or the interpretation of the lines of the hand, which all had astrological associations. It was not a factor in moleoscopy, or physiognomy, however, beyond the fact that these signs were imbedded in the human frame by the seminal reasons received at the time of birth. The following chapter on electional and horary astrology, which formed the backbone of practical judicial astrology, takes us into yet another significant area of popular "magic" that occupied an increasingly large number of Cunning Folk.

CHAPTER 12:

Judicial Astrology

Whereas astrology literally had to be rediscovered in France in the 1890s and in Germany during the early 1900s, the British astrological revival that took place in the 1890s merely represented a more vigorous continuation of a social phenomena that had already had an uninterrupted domestic history since the end of the seventeenth century. Indeed, during the period of close on two hundred years, from c. 1700 until 1890 or thereabouts, in the West astrology was remembered and practiced only in Great Britain. On the Continent it remained well underground or was almost completely forgotten.[88]

The true practice of astrology, as opposed to the derivative "non-computational" offshoots discussed earlier, is perhaps the most respectable of the arcane arts so far considered. "Astrology was probably the most ambitious attempt ever made to reduce the baffling diversity of human affairs to some sort of intelligible order…" (Thomas 1971: 287) and belief in the influence of the stars was shared by the Cunning Folk with their "betters" – until they inherited the art altogether after astrology lost its cultural legitimacy in the 18th century. While astrology is too important to overlook, there are difficulties in trying to deal with it through excerpts in the same manner as the other services offered by the Cunning Folk included in this book. The usual practice in any discussion of astrology, whether historical or instructional, is to include an overview on the technical directions involved in creating or "erecting" a horoscope. However, the technical terminology and instructions are too extensive to include in this survey so I must assume that the reader has or can obtain the basic instruction necessary to understand what follows. Those who do not should refer to one of the many practical manuals on astrological computation. It is not the practical construction of the astrological figure or chart that is important here, but rather the interpretation involved in answering the concerns and problems brought by the clients of the Cunning Folk.

There was so much to learn in mastering traditional astrology! Not only did the reader need instruction in the mathematical computations used in erecting and rectifying charts, but also the myriad rules, aphorisms and conditions separately applicable to nativities, elections and horary questions, with their illustrative examples. Added to this, the temptation to include spirited defences of the art or its history result in very extensive texts, running to hundreds of pages. Except for Joseph Blagrave's *Introduction to Astrology* (1650), comparatively succinct texts like *The New Astrology* (1786) by "C. Heydon, jun." or Raphael's *Manual of Astrology* (1828) were not available to simplify the learning curve in the earlier years. Most astrological authorities from William Lilly to Ebenezer Sibley, in trying to deal comprehensively with all these different functions, tended to be long-winded and their works are seldom amenable to excerption. Because of this, I have used just one lengthy example from Lilly's crucial *Christian Astrology* and none from Sibley's *Complete Illustration*, despite their historical importance.

Astral impellations played so central a role in the success or failure of both magical and ordinary events that investigation of those influences (i.e., *Apotelesma*, the influence of the stars on human destiny) was crucial to anyone who sought to understand what the future held, from court astrologers to village Cunning Folk. The practice spread slowly among the less-well educated, but it grew steadily from the 17th century on. A majority of the Cunning Folk may have lacked the technical skills needed for the proper application of astrology, depending instead on the general principles found in the *Erra Pater* and similar sources, but having some astrological knowledge greatly increased the credibility of a practitioner. Some *pretended* to make abstruse astrological calculations but as with bluffing about literacy, this was mere "window dressing" to impress the client rather than the real thing. Early on, only a minority of

---

[88] Ellic Howe. *Urania's Children: The Strange World of the Astrologers*. London: William Kimber and Co., 1967, p. 21.

practitioners serving the general public, such as Simon Forman, William Lilly or Richard Napier, could effectively employ the calculations and interpretive texts (most of which were in Latin) required for serious astrological analysis. From the 1640s on, however, an increasing number of those resources became available in English, which made it possible for many more persons to become competent consultants. By the turn of the 18th century, England was enjoying an impressive if brief flowering of the art – only to have the Enlightenment undermine astrology's reputation and force it underground.

As a result, the arcane art of astrology, once the monopoly of kings and clerics, came into the possession of the Cunning Folk. It was they who preserved and nurtured it during its century-long cultural exile, and saw to it that the tradition didn't die out as it did in continental Europe, making possible the 19th century revival. "In the post-Restoration world, seen through the window of contemporary astrology, a line was drawn – not between magic and reason, as is so often assumed, but through magic, dividing it into acceptable and unacceptable sorts. The force of this social and intellectual redefinition is clearly perceptible in the difference between Lilly and Ashmole and their heirs in the following decades. It is virtually impossible to find one [i.e., anyone "respectable"] who openly espoused a magical or divinatory astrology. That was simply no longer a viable option, beyond the ambit of the town cunning-man or -woman." (Curry 1989: 39)

Loss of respectability had another important influence on traditional astrology; one that still complicates our understanding of its pre-Enlightenment form. Once astrology lost its social standing and was dismissed by cultural authorities as spurious, the practice (always controversial) lost its influential patrons and protectors. With only the Cunning Folk and a few eccentric scholars involved in its practice, there was no restraining learned influence on those who had no compunction about ignoring tradition and introduced idiosyncratic notions and alien concepts into what had been a fairly stable body of knowledge. Traditional astrology for this reason is quite different from popular astrology today. Similarly, the loss of patronage allowed the full opprobrium of the law to be brought to bear on astrologers as cheats and frauds. This had little impact socially until the 19th century when astrology enjoyed a revival among the middle classes, and it resulted in the prosecution of otherwise respectable middle class individuals as illegal fortune-tellers.

By the end of the century, a shift was taking place in the focus of astrology from prediction and problem solving to the psychological analysis of the querent's nativity, and from the significance of planetary motion to the static influence of the "sun signs". This effect became even more pronounced at the end of the 20th century, as is clear from Benjamin Dykes patient explanation of the differences between the older tradition and the "New Age" character of contemporary practice in his *Traditional Astrology for Today* (2011) Although certainly not absolute (and recently, less so), this change resulted in the popular perception of astrology as fundamentally genethlial in nature and indeterminative in essence, which left the Cunning Folk's particular interests – elections and horary questions – out of the picture.

Of the four major divisions of traditional astrology – mundane (dealing in topics of national or international significance as well as the weather), genethlialogy (individual nativities), elections (identifying auspicious times) and horary (answering specific questions) – it was the last two that were most important for the practicing Cunning Man. Casting accurate nativities was always important, but these were often just the starting point for deeper investigations. The other astral services performed by both orthodox astrologers and Cunning Folk – astrological medicine and talismanic magic – are discussed in Chapters 10 and 11.

Electional and horary astrology are related approaches to prediction. As John Frawley has succinctly described them, "… while horary takes the moment and judges the likely consequence, in electional astrology we take the desired consequence and look for the moment most likely to produce that result." The basic idea behind electional astrology is to identify a future date on which the heavenly alignments promised the best possible indications for success in some project or undertaking, such as a wedding, a journey or other initiative. The astrologer surveyed the upcoming movements of the stars (usually within a narrow compass of time) to find a configuration of aspects that would advance rather than hinder the goals of the querent, and selected a date and time that best accomplishes this. Unlike the apparent "anything you want is possible" tendency today, it was quite possible that *no* suitable result would be forthcoming. Although the stars did not compel, neither could the querent ignore nor manipulate them to his own satisfaction.

The modern appeal to "free will" as an excuse for manipulation towards more positive worldly results is not what free will implied historically. Traditionally, it was accepted that the stars had a definite influence on *all* sub-lunar things, except for the ability to accept or reject God's grace; that is, to choose to live in accordance with the divine plan and thus achieve sanctification (salvation), or not. Although Calvinists denied that anyone had any choice in the matter (predestination alone accounted for grace and salvation so nothing a human did had any effect on the matter), traditional theology held that free will did allow the individual a choice – of God's giving. Jim Tester explains the problem: "What had to be preserved through all this [i.e., astrological science and magic] was the freedom of man's will, his responsibility to God. His physical make-up might be subject to the influences of the heavens, but never his personal being, his will. This was not always an easy distinction to preserve ..." (Tester 1987: 177). He also cites a letter of Berthold of Regensburg, ca. 1270, which maintained:

> 'As God gave their power to stones and to herbs and to words, so also he gave power to the stars, that they have power over all things, except over one thing. They have power over trees and over vines, over leaves and grasses, over vegetables, and herbs over corn and all such things; over the birds in the air, over the animals in the forests, and over the fishes in the water and over the worms in the earth; over all such things that are under heaven, over them our Lord gave power to the stars, except over one thing. Over that thing no man has any power nor any might, neither have stars nor herbs, nor word nor stones nor angel nor devil nor any man, but God alone. And he will not exercise his power, nor have any authority over that thing, it is man's free will (*friiu willekür* = *liberum arbitrium*, "free choice"): over that no man has any authority except thyself.'

> It is important to remember that no one questioned the validity of astrology. It could be criticized as too complicated and too difficult to be possible and parts of it, notably 'judicial' astrology – genethlialogy and the attendant judgments of the affairs of men – might be rejected as wrong. But that it was all possible, everyone accepted. In particular, what might be called scientific or natural astrology was more or less universally acceptable: that is, the uses of astrology in medicine and in meteorology and in alchemy. (Tester 1987: 178)

Electional Astrology

Two particular methods of electional astrology concern us here – radical and ephemeral. The former was the preferred approach but it was quite complex, involving a comparison of the natal or birth horoscope with the potential electional chart to see whether indications in the latter might conflict with the details of the former. What might at first appear to be a quite suitable set of future alignments for beginning some undertaking could have adverse effects if they were in an unfavourable aspect to the alignments in the progressed natal chart. The ephemeral chart, on the other hand, as in horary questions, focused on the details of a particular selected date, without reference to a natal chart. Historically, authorities such as William Ramesey declared that elections made without comparison to an accurate natal chart wouldn't work at all, but the simpler approach was apparently a popular one, especially in light of the fact that accurate natal charts were often impossible to acquire. Many people had no idea of their exact date and time of birth, and even regular nativities could require "rectification" for imperfect charts by various expedients.

In selecting favourable dates to do things, the first step was to "fortify" the crucial planets and significators by insuring that they were in favourable houses and aspects. William Lilly does not cover electional astrology to any extent in his magnum opus, *Christian Astrology* (1647), so William Ramesey's *Astrologia Restauratai, or Astrology Restored* (1654) is a better source for a general consideration of traditional electional astrology:

> Know then that in judging of the stars in Elections, special care must be had unto the business in hand; for according unto the nature thereof must your business be ordered, and the time chosen; as for earthy businesses, as planting and sowing and the like, an earthy sign is to be chosen or placed in

the ascendent; if appertaining to fire, a fiery sign; if to the water, a watry one, &c. As for example, if you would elect a time to plant, you must prefer *Virgo* before any other of the signs, because she is an earthy sign, and such a one as is participating more of the nature of the fruits of the earth then any other, *viz. Taurus* or *Capricorn*; and so understand of any business; be sure you still select a sign proper for your business, and agreeable to the nature thereof.

And for the speedy dispatch of any business, let a moveable sign be chosen; if the permanency you would elect any time, take a fixed sign; if you be indifferent, or desire your business shall neither be of long or short continuance, prefer a common sign, &c.

But still look to the fundamental grounds of Elections, *viz.* to fortify your chief significators, and cheifly the *Moon*, because she hath a general signification in all things, in journeys, times, places, and all businesses whatsoever; also the *Sun*, he being as it were cheif Ruler or King amongst all the other Planets; but more particularly the Planet signifying the business in hand: as if your Election be concerning war or fireworks, you must fortify *Mars*; if so to speak to the King, the *Sun*; to gain money, *Jupiter* if concerning marriage or love-matters, *Venus*; because these significations these Planets are generally of; and so understand of any business whatsoever; still have a care to fortify the Planet signifying your business, in general as well as particular, if you can.

In like manner you must choose and fortify the Sign signifying your business in generall (for as I have sayd, as is the nature of your business, such must the Sign be chosen and fortify) as if you were to go by water as to Sea, &c. you must fortify a watry Sign, and more especially *Cancer*, for she is the house of the *Moon*; if by land, as a journey &c. an earthy Sign, &c. *viz.* free from misfortune or affliction of the malevolent aspects of the Infortunes, and place in the ascendent of your Election, or the Lord of the Ascendent therein, or the *Moon*, or both, if possible; and this is necessary in all Elections and the Antients moreover have for men elected a masculine sign, for women a feminine; but this is needless, &c.

The sign also and house signifying your business in your *Radix* [natal chart] ought to be regarded and well dignified; also fortify the house and sign signifying the business in your Election; as if you would elect a time for profit, you must fortify (in the figure of your Election) the second house in the *Radix*, it sign and the Lord thereof, as well as the second in your Election, &c. in all Elections, remember to fortify the Ascendent, its Lord and Disposer of him, and the fourth, and the Lord of the fourth and also his Dispositor; for by fortifying the Ascendent, the Lord thereof and his Dispositor, the health and safety of the Parties body electing is promised: by fortifying the fourth, its Lord and his Dispositor, a good and safe conclusion and end of the business. ... /

Also in electing any work, have especial care to fortify the part of fortune, the Lord thereof and its Dispositor, so that they may be either in body or aspect helped by the fortunes, and free from the configurations of the Malevolents. Let not the Lord of your Ascendent by any means retrograde, for it will occasion tardity and hindrance in any thing, although all the other significators were essentially strong and promising the effecting of business ... in the beginning of any work also see that the Dragons tayl be not with either of the Luminaries when they are in conjunction of opposition, or in the Ascendent, or house of the business of the Election, or in the Angles of the Figure at the time of Election. But have a special care in all Elections you put not the Moon in the Ascendent; for she is an enemy thereunto; so also the Sun; for he therein dissolves and undoes what is accomplished and done. (Ramesey 1654: 123-124)

There are a few terms used in judicial astrology that may not be familiar to modern readers, such as "dispositor", which refers to a planet that is located in the sign that planet rules.

Ramsey is quite thorough in his *Liber III. De IVDICIIS ASTRORVM IN ELELECTIONIBVS, Or An Introduction to Elections*. He covers the basic rules for erecting electional charts, and the importance of the moon in this work, providing a table that indicates the effect of the moon's aspects with the other planets, and another that codifies the significance of the "lunar mansions" (Ramsey 1654: 130):

The Cunning Man's Handbook

A Table of the Mansions of the Moon.

Mansions	Sig.	D.	M.	Qualities.	Elections.
1	♈	20	6	Temperate.	Take thy journey and Physick, Laxatives.
2	♉	2	57	Dry.	Take thy Journey by water, buy Cattel, plant.
3	♉	15	49	Moist.	Chaffer, or buy and sell, but goe not to Sea.
4	☿	28	40	Moist and cold. More cold.	Plant and sowe, marry not, nor journey by water.
5	♊	11	12	Dry.	Use Merchandise, Voyage; joyn Wedlock, and take Physick.
6	♊	24	23	Temper.	War, sowe not, nor take in hand any good.
7	♋	7	5	Moist.	Plough, Sowe, Travell not either by Sea or Land.
8	♋	20	6	[unclear]	Journey, and take Physick.
9	♌	5	57	Dry.	Navigate.
10	♌	15	49	Moist.	Plant, Build, Marry, but make no voyage.
11	♌	28	40	Temperate and cold.	Sowe, Plant, Deliver prisoners, but take no Purgation.
12	♍	11	31	Moist.	Plant, Marry, but Navigate not.
13	♍	24	23	Temper.	Journey, Navigate, Sowe, Plough, Marry, and send messengers.
14	♎	7	15	Temper.	Sowe, Plant, take Physick, neither travel nor marry.
15	♎	20	6	Moist.	Delve and Dig, but neither marry nor travel.
16	♏	2	57	Cold and moist.	Unfortunate for any thing.
17	♏	15	49	Moist.	Buy cattel, but Navigate not.
18	♏	28	40	Dry.	Build, Sowe, Plant, Navigate, but Wed not.
19	♐	11	32	Moist.	War, Plant, Sowe, and Voyage.
20	♐	24	23	Temper.	Buy cattel, use hunting, but Wed not.
21	♑	7	25	Temper.	Build, Repair to a Magistrate for favour, but marry not.
22	♑	20	6	Moist	Take Physick, Navigate and put on new apparel.
23	♒	2	56	Temper.	Take Physick, Voyage, but neither Marry nor lend.
24	♒	25	49	Temper.	Lead an Army, Marry, Sowe, take Physick.
25	♒	28	40	Dry.	Build, Marry, seek friendship, take thy journey.
26	♓	11	32	Dry.	It is in all things unfortunate, save in taking Physick.
27	♓	24	23	Moist.	Plant, Sowe, Chaffer, Marry, but Navigate not.
28	♈	24	15	Temper.	Use Merchandise, Marry, take Physick, but lend not, neither enterprise any voyage.

Ramesey warns that there is no guarantee of success in electional work – the astrologer may try to find favourable indications in the times concerned, but he can't change the inexorability of the heavenly positions and movements, so it often turns out that the desire of the client is doomed to failure. "If the chief significator of any businesse be unfortunate in the radix, there can be no time Elected to prevent the mischief threatened; for whom the Lord hath ordained to destruction or punishment, either by inclination or casualty (according to Divine will and preordination the harmonious concordancy of Astrology with Divinity &c.)" (Ramesey 1654: 122).

He then considers the topics for which opportune times might be found according to the various houses of the chart. For some houses there are many "businesses" that can potentially be scheduled for successful outcome, while others have but few. A quick survey of the miscellaneous topics will indicate the concerns – trivial and otherwise – that his contemporaries would wish an astrologer to find the best time to do or begin:

First House	1.	Nursing (breastfeeding), weaning, schooling and trades for children.
	2.	Cutting hair.
	3.	Cutting nails and corns.
Second House	1.	Receiving and borrowing money.
	2.	Borrowing and lending money.
	3.	"Of buying to profit against the sale thereof"
	4.	Selling to advantage.
	5.	Further buying and selling.
	6.	Buying clothing, putting on of apparel.
	7.	"Flitting", removal from one place to another.
	8.	Distillation and alchemy.
Third House	1.	Short journeys.
	2.	Making friends or any two people at variance.
	3.	Divine study and contemplation.
Fourth House	1.	Building houses.
	2.	Building castles and cities.
	3.	Building churches.
	4.	Building mills.
	5.	Pulling down houses.
	6.	Buying land, houses &c.
	7.	Buying land for husbandry.
	8.	Bringing water to a property, digging wells.
	9.	Tillage and manuring grounds.
	10.	Renting or hiring all sorts of things.
	11.	Planting and grafting trees.
	12.	Sowing.
	13.	"Of ridding Houses or places from evil Spirits".

Fifth House	1.	Fit time for begetting boys or girls.
	2.	Delivering a dead child.
	3.	Christening or circumcising children.
	4.	Giving and receiving gifts and presents.
	5.	"Rules for electing a time for putting on apparel".
	6.	Feasting or eating meat.
	7.	Drinking wine &c.
	8.	Writing letters "or any thing else of Ingenuity".
	9.	"Making odoriferous smels and unguents."
	10.	Sending ambassadors or messengers.
Sixth House	1.	"Of the true Knowledge of the Crisis or Critical and Judicial Days, very useful to those that study Physick".
	2.	Applying medicines generally to the body.
	3.	Administration of remedies to diseases of the head.
	4.	Administration of remedies to the eyes.
	5.	Administration of remedies to the nose.
	6.	Injecting clysters, and stopping of rheums or fluxes.
	7.	Gargarisms, or sneezes and such like.
	8.	Giving vomits.
	9.	Purges and laxatives (long).
	10.	Baths.
	11.	"Chirurgery".
	12.	Phlebotomy.
	13.	Physicians going to patients.
	14.	Hiring servants.
	15.	Getting birds (for falconry &.)
	16.	Buying four-footed beasts.
	17.	Bringing up dogs and taming "small cattle".
Seventh House	1.	Marriage.
	2.	"Venereall Sports" [sex].
	3.	Partnerships and agreements.
	4.	War, duels, quarrels, lawsuits, controversies.
	5.	Making peace, suppressing rebels, storming castles & towns.
	6.	Buying arms, warships.
	7.	Seeking fugitives, thieves.
	8.	Knowing the subject of whisperings (gossip), win at chess.
	9.	Hunting, fowling and fishing.
Eighth House	1.	Making wills.
	2.	Heritage of the dead (inheritances?)
Ninth House	1.	"Returning of such as are absent", journeys, entering places.
	2.	Building ships, launchings, sea voyages.
	3.	Learning sciences, singing and music.
Tenth House	1.	Electing kings, installing them and their governments.
	2.	Obtaining favor of kings and great men, justice on enemies, pardons, going on royal progresses.
	3.	Learning any art or occupation.

Eleventh House	1.	Accomplishing things, gaining good repute, love of friends.
	2.	Obtaining promises and requests.
Twelfth House	1.	Freeing prisoners and captives.
	2.	Buying and riding horses. (Ramesey 1654: 130)

Each of these entries – some of which are pages long and others just a brief paragraph – include the particular aspects and planetary positions the astrologer should look for in specific cases to advise the client of a propitious date – or that his desire was doomed to "destruction" or failure. An example (one of the shorter) of the sort of advice Ramesey gives, for determining when take a short journey, is as follows:

Section IV.
Comprehending Rules, in Electing such matters as appertain
to the Signification of the third House.
Chap. I.
Of short Journeys, and their Elections.

Many men are not acquainted with this Language; wherefore I shall more plainly declare, that by short journeys we are to understand such as can be finished in a day or two, or less; wherefore then in such an Election, fortifie the Ascendant and its Lord, the *Moon* and its dispositor, *Part of Fortune* also, and its dispositor, and the Planet to whom the *Moon* is joyned or in configuration with; the sign of the third house and its Lord, the Lord of the hour, and the Lord of the thing, or the Planet signifying the thing or business for which the Party takes his journey (if it be related to you) as also its dispositor.

But if all these thou canst possibly observe, neither (your occasions being such) can you defer them until such a time; then I say fortify the *Moon* and the Lord of the hour; and if you cannot fortifie the *Moon*, yet be sure your Lord of the hour be no ways impeded or weak, and make the *Moon* fall from the Ascendent, and if possible from the Lord thereof; But more of this in the ninth house when wee come to treat of Elections concerning long journeys. (Ramesey 1645: 140)

A second example, from Chapter 13, on elections concerning the Fourth House.

Of ridding Houses or places from evil Spirits.

Evil spirits and the way of commanding them or ridding houses of them, is best known to such as practice and make use thereof, it being no part of the study of an Astrologian; however since often times mischief is done in such actions for want of understanding, I though it good here to set down a fit time for such businesses, it being otherwise very dangerous.

There have been several instructions for this matter given to us by the Antients; but most, and those most authentick too, say as followeth.

See that the Moon be not in the Ascendent, and that neither the Ascendent or the Moon be in Cancer, Leo, Scorpio, or Aquaries, but in some other signs, and let the Moon separate from the Malevolents, and apply to the Fortunes, &c. [Ramesey 1654: 151]

Although I have cited Ramesey because he best explains the historical practice of electional astrology, it might be objected that the possession of large and relatively expensive works such as Ramesey's or Lilly's were beyond the reach of the Cunning Folk. This is true to a certain extent (although it is not good to underestimate the acquisitive ability of even poor Wise Women, as the example of Ann Watts in Chapter 13 indicates), but they could be borrowed, copied and excerpted. Astrological information did descend into the lower ranks of Cunning Folk through channels we cannot now recreate. For example, I have a small (16 pp.) astrological notebook, ca. 1750, that belonged to a

"T. U. Coth" (or "Goth") which has two pages of aphorisms concerning electional astrology. Interestingly enough, this same list, in more modern spelling and with a few differences, was published by "Raphael" as *Some choice Aphorisms, and Rules for Elections relating to most undertakings. Communicated by Wm. Delamere Massy* ("Raphael" 1832: 173-175):

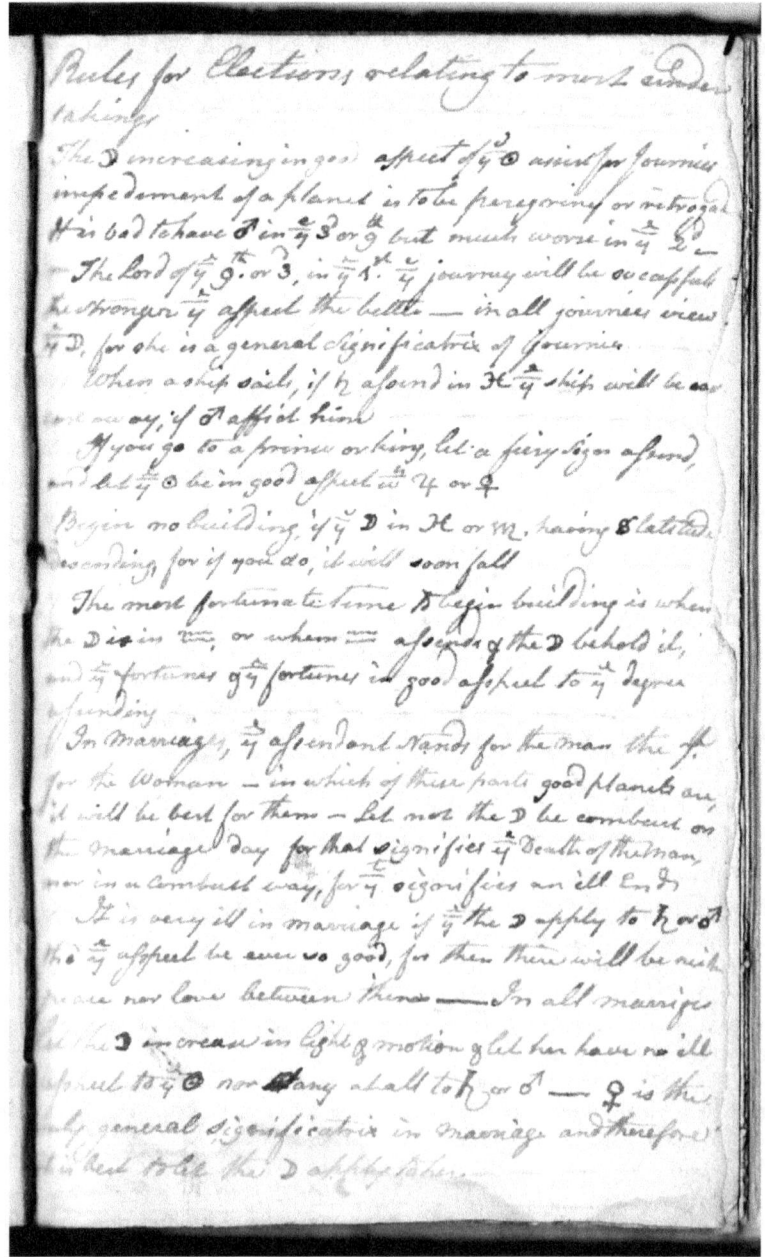

Rules for Elections relating to most undertakings

The ☽ increasing in good aspect of yᵉ ☉ assist for Journies impediment of a planet in to be peregrine or retrograd

It is bad to have ♂ in yᵉ 3ʳᵈ or 9ᵗʰ but much worse in ye 2ⁿᵈ.

The Lord of ye 9ᵗʰ or 3ᵈ, in ye 1ˢᵗ. ye journey will be successful, the stronger yᵗ aspect the better—in all journies view yᵉ ☽, for she is in a general Significator of Journies.

When a ship sails, if ♄ afound in ♋ ye ship will be so cast away, if ♂ afflict him

If you go to a prince or king, let a fiery Sign ascend, and let ye ☉ be in good aspect wh ♃ or ♀

Begin no building, if yᵉ ☽ in ♋ or ♏, having S latitude descending, for if you do, it will soon fall

The most fortunate time to begin building is when the ☽ is in ♒, or when ♒ ascends & the ☽ behold it, and ye fortunes if ye fortunes is good aspect to ye degree ascending

In Marriages, yᵉ ascendant stands for the Man the 7ᵗʰ for the Woman – in which of these parts good planets are, it will be best for them – let not the ☽ be combust on the Marriage day, for that signifies yᵉ Death of the Man, nor in a Combust way, for yᵗ signifies an ill End

It is very ill in marriage if yᵉ the [sic] ☽ apply to ♄ or ♂ tho' yᵉ aspect be ever so good, for then there will be neither peace nor love between them—In all marriages let the ☽ increase in light & motion & let her have no ill aspect to yᵉ ☉ nor any atall to ♄ or ♂ — ♀ is the truly general significatrix in Marriage and therefore it is best to let the ☽ apply to her, /

If the Lord of yᵉ ascendant is weak, & the Lord of the 7ᵗʰ Strong, in yᵉ 7ᵗʰ & he a command[in]g planet, & in good aspect of ♂, she will wear yᵉ breaches, & domineer over her husband

["I know one, who had ♏ ascending at the time of marriage, and ♂ and ♀ in ♏, and both combust, and in ☍ to the ☽, and it proved a very unhappy marriage." This entry is in Raphael but not Coth.]

Let not ♄ or ♂ be in the 7ᵗʰ for yᵗ always makes the Woman out of order

["Such as go to war, ought to consider of coming home safe again." Also in Raphael but not Coth.]

For this End, let yᵉ ☉, ♃, ♀, or ☊ be yᵉ ascendant, or else they may fail of it – if ♄ be in yᵉ ascendant he will [crossed out] come again a coward, surpres'd with fear and not fight

If ♂ be there, he will either die there, or be dangerously wounded – but if ♄ & ♂ be both there you may be confident he will never return, if in the tenth he will be taken prisoner, especially if the Lord of the ascendant be in yᵉ twelfth

Judge of the challenger by the ascendant and so vary the houses accordingly

But Judge of the opponent by yᵉ 7ᵗʰ & so vary yᵉ houses as before, the 10ᵗʰ being his 4ᵗʰ & 4ᵗʰ his tenth –

It is not good to fight when yᵉ lord of the ascendant is in the 8ᵗʰ for then there is danger of Death

The assailant always loses the battle, if the Lord of the ascendant be in an infortune, retrograde, or combust

But if the Lord of ye 7ᵗʰ be so, the opponent is beaten when ye ☽, ♄, and ♂ shall be join'd together then will be great effusion of blood

If you make application to a king, let the ☽ be in the ascendant, in ♋, or △ to yᵉ ☉ in yᵉ 10ᵗʰ house [Raphael's list stops here]

To a Bishop or judge, let ye ☽ be join'd to ♃ by body or good places of the figure, the angles have greatest force

Business with Women, let yᵉ ☽ apply to ♀, if to Matters as pertain as accomplants [?] to ☿ and so of the rest

This information, copied from some early authority, had made its way into the shadowy world of the Cunning Folk. Another example of the ability of a determined amateur to acquire the sources he wanted can be found in a letter sent to the astrologer and almanac publisher William Seed of Bradford while Seed was actually in jail for practicing his trade. It illustrates the problems facing amateur astrologers at the time concerning sources and instruction:

"RD. A., Newgate-street, Chester."

"SIR, *Stockton-on-Tees, June 3*, 1844.

"You will probably remember that, in 1842, you received a letter from me requesting a supply of your ephemeris (one for each year) since the commencement. These I received from your hand, together with a few copies over, which you gratuitously enclosed in the parcel to defray the expence of carriage. The almanacks, I must add, gave entire satisfaction; and for the gift I now embrace an opportunity of returning you my hearty thanks. The years 1843 and 1844 have been applied to for of the different booksellers at this town and also at Yarm—copies of which I have been unable to obtain. I shall therefore be extremely obliged to you, Sir, if you will interchange a few lines with me on the subject, being in hopes I can obtain them from you as heretofore. I want one copy for 1843 and two copies for the present year 1844; on the receipt of yours I will forward the required remittance, and you can send them so as to come by railway. I have a great inclination towards astrology, and have acquired some little knowledge thereof, solely by myself and attention to study. Some years ago I was favoured by a friend with a copy of 'Sibley's Illustration of Astrology,' and since that time I have got 'Raphael's Manual,' his 'Astrologer of the Nineteenth Century,' and some other of his publications, but having no one to direct me, I am frequently enveloped in difficulties, and make less progress in the science than I otherwise should do, a circumstance by no means uncommon in my situation.

"I was born in the year 1824, on the 1st August, about half-past eight o'clock in the morning, in Bilsdale, which lays half way between the market towns of Helmsley and Stokesley, in the county of York. As I have no ephemeris for that year, I am incapable of erecting a figure for the period of my birth; but by referring to 'Moore's Almanack' for that year, I find I had the luminaries in exact □ and ☿ in the medium coeli, consequently he would be in □ dance □ to the asc., &c. These, I am aware, are evil positions, but the benefices may be so placed in my nativity as to effect a great mitigation of this evil. I had ♃ in ♋, consequently he would be in the 10th, at the time of birth, and the ☽ in ✶ to ♅, which accounts for my inclination towards the 'celestial science.' I shall be obliged to you, Sir, if you will state in your letter what you can calculate my nativity for. At all events, I should like to know my general fate as pointed out by the 'celestial messengers.' An early answer will oblige yours truly,

"JOHN H., *an admirer of Astrology.*

"N.B.—Direct for John H., care of Mr. Wm. H., Thistle Green, Stockton-on-Tees.

"To Mr. Wm. Seeds, 21, Croft-street, Manchester-road, Bradford.'[89]

Seed was a country astrologer who enjoyed some local fame, as a later folklorist noted:

> Another local celebrity in his day was William Seed, the noted fortune-teller and almanack-maker, who in the estimation of more than his neighbours was a very Zadkiel of astrological lore. Old Seed was after all no common trickster. He was a good though self-taught mathematician and astronomer, and possessed qualifications which rightly directed might have brought him no mean reputation.[90]

Would-be astrologer "John H." was able to buy two out-of-print works to study astrology, even if he was unable to fully make sense of them. How available were these books at the time? Checking a few antiquarian book listings of the time (thanks to Google Books!), one finds that

Sibley's *Illustration of Astrology* (1784) was advertised in Thomas Oxley's *Celestial Planisphere* (1830) at £2 12s 6d; by William Brough (1853) at 16s 6d; by Willis and Sotheran (1862) at 16s; and George Redway (Hockley Library sale, 1887) at 32s. Raphael's *Manual of Astrology* (1828) in Oxley went for 10s 6d; by Brough at 4s.; by Willis and Sotheran for 4s 6d; and (the 1837 ed.) by Redway at 12s 6d. It originally sold for 10s 6d , although Oxley says 9s.

---

[89] *Tenth Report of the Inspectors to Visit the Different Prisons of Great Britain. II. Northern and Eastern District.* London: HMSO, 1845, p. 28.

[90] William Cudworth. *Round about Bradford: A Series of Sketches Bradford.* Bradford: Thomas Brear, 1876, p. 50.

Horary Astrology

Turning now to horary astrology, we come to the primary tool of the working astrologer by which he or she could address almost any concern or question for a client. Horary astrology is pure inductive divination – by capturing in a chart the astral configuration of the moment a question was asked, the astrologer was able in theory to discern the truth about the past or future by the clues that the indicated impellations revealed. This "snapshot of the instant" premise is what underlies many systems of divination. From Roman auguries of sacrificial entrails and the casting of an African to the intricate combinations of significations in the *I Ching*, the spirit of moment is held to embody the knowledge of all earthly things and events.

Horary queries might involve any subject, but they were not open ended. The query had to meet certain specifications, or else it could not be successfully dealt with. The question had to be simple and direct, not ambiguous nor asked more than once, and capable of a straightforward answer. The chart or figure itself, once drawn up, had to be inspected to see if it was "radical" or even capable of providing guidance at all. Sometimes the time was simply not opportune for asking a question. As William Lilly notes, "All the *Ancients* that have wrote of Questions, doe give warning to the *Astrologer*, that before he deliver judgement he well consider whether the Figure is radicall and capable of judgement; the Question then shall be taken for radicall, or fit to be judged, when as the Lord of the hour at the time proposing the Question, and erecting the figure, and the Lord of the Ascendant or first House, are of one Triplicity, or be one, or of the same nature." (Lilly 1985: 121). Then, too, the astrologer had be wary of insincere or mischievous questions – always a danger in fortune telling – and as "C. Heydon, jun." says under certain conditions, "…it will not be proper to give judgement; it denotes the question has been proposed merely out of ridicule."

I have used William Lilly's *Christian Astrology Modestly Treated in Three Books* (1647) as the primary source in this instance, as it was the best known and most widely celebrated example of the art from the time of its publication to the 19th century – and even today. His many informational lists and aphorisms have been used by generations of astrologers. Lilly prefaces his horary section with a general introduction about the process in the last two chapters of his first book, *An Introduction to Astrology*, and then moves on to book II, *The Resolution of all manner of Questions and Demands*, covering the twelve astrological houses (in 357 pages) for horary queries as Ramesey did for elections, with details on what to look for in specific queries or "questieds", and adding sample charts showing how the instructions were to be applied in practice.

CHAP. XX.
What Significator, Querent and Questied are; and an Introduction to the Judgment of a Question.

THE Querent is he or she that propounds the question, and desires resolution: the Quesited is he or she, or the thing sought and enquired after.

The significator is no more then that Planet which ruleth the house that signifies the thing demanded: as if ♈ is ascending, ♂ being the Lord of ♈, shal be *significator* of the Querent, *viz*, the Sign ascending shall in part signifie his corporature, body or stature, the Lord of the Ascendant, the ☽ and Planet in the Ascendant, or that the ☽ or Lord of the Ascendant are in aspect with, shall shew his quality or conditions equally mixed together; so that let any Sign ascend, what Planet is Lord of that Sign, shall be called Lord of the House, or Significator of the person enquiring, &c.

So that in the first place therefore, When any Question is propounded, the Sign ascending and his Lord are always given unto him or her that asks the question.

2ly. You must then consider the matter propounded, and see to which of the twelve houses it doth properly belong: when you have found the house, consider the Sign and Lord of that Sign, / how, and in what Signe and what part of Heaven he is placed, how dignified, what aspect he hath to the Lord of the Ascendant, who impedites your *Significator*, who is friend unto him, *viz*, what Planet it is, and what house he is Lord of, or in what house posited; from such a man or woman signified by that Planet, shall you be furthered or hindered; or of such relation unto you as that Planet signifies; if

Lord of such a house, such an enemy, if Lord of such a house as signifieth enemies, then an enemy verily; if of a friendly house, a friend: The whole naturall key to all Astrology reflect in the words preceding rightly understood:... [Lilly 1985: 123-124]

As in Ramesey, some houses have a great many things that can be asked about and others just a few. I have chosen the lengthy example of Chapter 50 (which is on Seventh House significations for theft; the house that also covered "Marriage, open Enemies, Law-suits, Controversies, Contracts, Warres, Bargaines, Fugitives, ... &c.") to illustrate fascinating complexity involved in the art. Lilly describes the scope of the seventh house thusly:

The SEVENTH House.

It giveth judgement of Marriage, and describes the person inquired after, whether it be Man or Woman, all manner of Love questions, our publique enemies; the Defendant in a Lawsuit; in Astrology the Artist himselfe; in Physicke the Physitian; Theeves and Thefts; the person stealing, whether Man or Woman, Wives, Sweethearts; their shape, description, condition, Nobly or ignobly borne: in an Annuall Ingresse, whether Warre or Peace maby be expected: of Victory, who overcomes, and who worsted; Fugitives or run-awayes; Bannished and Out-lawed-men.

It hath consignificator ♎ and ☽, ♄ or ♂ unfortunate herein, shew ill in Marriage.

Of colour, a dark Blacke colour.

It ruleth the Haunches, and the Navill to the Buttocks; and is called the Angle of the West; and is Masculine. (Lilly 1985: 54)

In an age before police and detectives (or insurance) were available, theft was a very serious problem for its victims and the Cunning Folk were a primary resource for resolving such cases. It is interesting to note that although astrologers might receive many more inquiries about sickness and health, the medical material in Lilly's coverage of the Sixth House is only slightly longer (50 pages versus 46) than that concerning theft. Ninety per cent of the 85,000 figures in Simon Forman's and Richard Napier's casebooks deal with health and disease, only 107 dealt with theft[91].

The very density of this single series of rules shows how important answers were to those concerned, and also how detailed horary investigations might be. It isn't necessary to read the full text – just looking at the potential questions and identifying details (the headings in italics) which Lilly provides directions for shows the impressive detail that a horary chart might provide. This isn't just prediction but a full investigation of how, when, and who (including the owner who might be guilty of fraud) committed the theft, the appearance of the guilty party, where the stolen items or strayed livestock might be, and whether they can be recovered. I have omitted most of the marginal notes as redundant in this instance.

CHAP. L.
Of Servants fled, Beasts strayed, and things lost.

The *Signifier* of the thing lost is the ☽, wherefore if you find the ☽ applying to the Lord of the Ascendant, or to the Lord of the twelfth from the Ascendant, or to the Lord of the house of the ☽, the thing missing shall be found againe; / but if the ☽ apply to none of these, nor abide in the ascendant nor in the second house, the thing lost or miscarried shall not be found: if the Lord of the house of the ☽ be in the third, or in a ✶ to the Ascendant, there is some hope of finding the thing againe, during that aspect with the degree ascending: And againe, if he separate himselfe from the Lord of the twelfth, eighth, or sixt house, and apply unto the degree of the house of Substance,

---

[91] www.magicandmedicine.hps.cam.ac.uk/the-manuscripts/introduction-to-the-casebooks (accessed 5/27/2012)

(what aspect soever it be) there is hope to find it again; or if the Lord of the house of the ☽ do behold ☽ ; but if you finde these Constellations contrary, judge the contrary; if the ☽ be fortunate by any of the two Fortunes, the thing that is lost chanced into the hands of some trusty body, which keepeth the same, and would fame restore it againe; or if that Fortune apply to the ascendant, or behold the same, or the ☽ behold the ascendant, that faithfull person will restore the same again to the owner.

The place where the thing is that is lost.

The Signifier of the place where the thing is at time of the Question, is the place of the Moon according to the nature of the Signe she is in, for if the Signe be Orientall, it is in the east part; if it be Occidentall, it is west, &c. Behold also the place of the Moon in the Figure, for if she be in the Ascendant, it is in the east, &c. if the Lord of the house of the Moon be in humane Signes, it is in a place where men use to be; if in Signes of small Beasts, as ♉ and ♑ it is where such kind of Beasts be: Also, look to the ☽, and see if she be in a fiery Signe, it is where fire is; if in a watry Signe, where water is &c. if the ☽ be with the Lord of the ascendant in one quarter, and there be not between them more then one Signe, the thing lost is in the house of him that lost it, or about it; but if there be between more then thirty degrees, and lesse then seventy degrees, the thing is in the Town where the owner is, but if they be not in one quarter, it is then farre from the owner. /

How the things or Goods was lost.

If you will know how in what manner they were lost, behold from whom the Lord of the Ascendant did last separate, and if he did separate from ♄, the cause of the lost thing was through forgetfulnesse of the owner, who knowes not where he laid it, or it is forgotten by reason of some cold or sicknesse which afflicted the loser, especially if ♄ be Retrograde, if he be separated from ♃, or in the house of ♃, then through fast or abstinency, or ordering of Lawes, or by his excesse of care of governing of things, or managing the affaires of the house, or else by some trust put upon him that carried it away or mislaid it.

If he be separated from ♂, or in the house of ♂, it was lost through fear, or by some hidden passion, provoking the loser to anger, fury, fire, or for emnity, or upon a quarrell. If from the ☉ or his house, then by the meanes of the King, study of hunting or pastime, or by meanes of the master of the Family, or a Gentleman. If from ♀ or in her house, then by drinking, Cards or Dice, or making merry in an Alehouse or Taverne, or by pastime, or singing and dallying with women, &c. If from ☿ by reason of writing, or sending, or dictating of Letters, or going on a Message: If from the ☽, or in the house of the ☽, it was lost by too frequent use, and shewing the Commodity of thing lost, or the party made it too common, or some Messenger, Widdow or Servant lost the same. If the thing lost or missing be a Beast, and not a thing moveable, the signification in knowing the place, and the state thereof, is as the said significations of things not having life, but that it is needful to seek whether it fled away of it selfe, or some other drove him away, whether it liveth or no? and to find the cause of the death of it, if it be dead.

Whether it be stolen or no.

If you would know if the Beast fled away by it selfe, or some body took it, behold if you find the Lord of the house of the ☽ / separating himselfe from any Planet, say then, that he fled away of his owne accord; but if the lord of the house of the ☽ be not separated from any Planet, but that another Planet is separating himselfe from him, say that some one or other took it and fled away; but if the lord of the house of the *Moon* be not in any of these two we speak of, behold what you see by the positure of the Lord of the second house, and judge by him as you judge by the Lord of the house of the *Moon*, and her separation; and if you find of these two no separation, say that the Beast is still in his place, or neer it, and that he fled not away.

Whether it be alive.

If you will know whether it be alive or not, behold the *Moon* and if you find her in application to the Lord of the eighth house from her, say it is dead; and if you find no such thing, behold her Lord, and if you find him applying to the Lord of the eighth house from the *Moon*, say likewise that it is dead, or it shall dye very shortly; but if in none of these you find application, take the signification from the Lord of the eighth house after the same manner.

Whether the thing missing be stolne, or fled of it selfe.

If the *Significator* of the Theef be in the ascendant, or giveth his vertue to the ☽, or the ☽ to him, it is stolen, or the Lord of the ascendant to the Significator of the Thiefe, or the *Signifier* of the Theef apply to the Lord of the Ascendant by □ or ☍, or the ☽ by ☌, □, or ☍, or the Lord of the house of the ☽, or her Terme, or the Lord of the second house, or ⊗ or his Lord, or if any Planet be in the Ascendant, and give his power to the *Signifier* of the Theef, or the *Signifier* to him by □ or ☍, if some of these constellations be not, it is not stolen, except there be an *Infortune* in the Ascendant or second, or the Lord of the house of the ☽, or her Terme be Infortunate, or the ⊗ or his Lord, or the Lord of the Ascendant, or the Lord of the second house be infortunate, these signifie losing.

Or of you find the Lord of the house of the ☽ separating / from any Planet, it is fled of its owne accord; if he separate not, but some other from him, it is driven away; the like in either by the Lord of the second, if he be in no such state or position, the thing abideth still, and it is not stolen.

For Beasts strayed, or Fugitives, or any thing lost.

The *Significator* is ☽, wherefore the ☽ applying to the Lord of the ascendant, or second house, or the Dispositor, it shall be found, otherwise not; ☽ in the Ascendant, or her Dispositor in a △ or ✶, gives hopes to find it; the Dispositor of the ☽ separating from the Lord of the sixt, eighth or twelfth, and applying to the Lord of the ascendant, or to the degree of the second house, good hopes also; ☽ in aspect to her Dispositor, good; ☽ infortunate of the Lord of the sixt, eighth, or twelfth house, it is in the hands of an ill person that will not depart from it, chiefly if the *Infortune* behold the Ascendant or his Lord.

☽ beholding ♃ or ♀, it is in the hands of an honest man that will restore it againe; if ♃ or ♀ have any aspect to the ascendant, or ☽ apply to the ascendant; ☽ in the ascendant, it is restored with trouble or paine; or the Lord of the twelfth in the twelfh house, the Lord of the seventh in the twelfth, the Fugitive is imprisoned.

The place: ☽ in the tenth, it is south; in the seventh, west; in the fourth, north; in the ascendant, east, &c. the Dispositor of the ☽ in a humane Signe, it is in a place where men use; in ♋, ♏, or ♓, a place of Water or Wels; ☽ in the last face of Capricorn, it is amongst Ships; this must be when things are lost neer a Harbour.

☽ In ♉ ♌, ♐, in a place of fire; ☽ or her Dispositor being in movable Signes, it is in a place newly broken up.

☽ Within thirty degrees of the Lord of the ascendant the thing is with the Loser, or neer him; ☽ more then 30 degrees from the Lord of the ascendant, it is farre off; the Dispositor of the ☽ separating from another Planet, it is strayed; another Planet separating from the Dispositor of the ☽, it is stolen. /

☽ Or her Dispositor applying to the Lord of the eighth, or eighth house from the ☽, it is dead or will dye shortly.

☽ In the ascendant, or △ to the Lord of the Ascendant; ☽ in △ to ☉, found.
The Lord of the second in the tenth or nineth, it is in the house of the Querent, or in the power of a familiar friend; ☉ in the Ascendant (unlesse in ♎ or ♒) found; the Lord of the second in the eleventh or twelfth, farre off.

Of Beasts or Strayes.

If the Lord of the sixth be in the sixt, the Beasts be small: if the Lord of the twelfth be in the twelfth, the Beasts be great: if the Lord of the sixt be in the sixt or twelfth, they be in a Pound; if the Lord of the sixt be in fiery Signes, they shal be under fetters and locks; if the Lord of the Ascendant and Lord of the hour be one Planet, then it is true they are in Pound; if the *Moon* be in common Signes, they are in rushy grounds; if in an angle, they be in Closes or Grounds, if in a succedant, they be within Closes, or about them, on the right hand of the owner; if the *Moon* be in a cadent house, they are in common Fields; if in ♋, where Dennes and water-beasts be, or some little Rivolet, if ♒ or ♓ in watry or fishing places, or neer Fish-ponds, in the last moity of ♑, in a place of Ships, or some Wood or Wood-yard.

Behold the Signe where the *Moon* is, if in fiery Signes, in a place where fire is, or about a fire, or where fire hath formerly been made; the *Moon* in watry Signes, where water is, or about waters; the *Moon* in ayery Signes, in a place of many windowes, or open places, as Garrets, and such like; * the *Moon* in earthly Signes, in an earthly place, where houses are made of earth, or neer mud wals or clay; the *Moon*, or the Lord of the house where she is, be in a movable Signe, in a place new peopled, or a house new built, or where are hils, and in other places levell grounds; the *Moon* in a fixed Signe, in a plaine Country or champion; the *Moon* in a common Signe in a place of much water, according to the nature of the place where the thing was lost or missing.

*This has relation to Beasts strayed. /

Another Judgment

Common Signs, as ♊, ♍, ♐ or ♓, do signifie within the house, if it be dead things, as rings &c. but if it be quick or living things, or Cattle, it signifieth watry grounds, Ditiches, Pits, Rushes, a Market-place; fixed Signes, the Goods are hid, or laid low by the earth, or neer it, in wals, or in hollow Trees; movable Signs, high places, Roofs, or Seeling of houses; watry Signes, in water, or under the earth, a Pavement, Foundation of houses, &c.

That the Beasts are lost.

The Lord of the sixt unfortunate by ♄ or ♂, the Beasts be lost, chiefly if the Lord of the sixt be cadent, or that the Cattle are drived away or stolen; if any Planet doe separate from the Lord of the house of the ☽, it is driven away or sold; if the Planet separate from the Lord of the second, *idem*; if you find none of these, the Beasts are not far off.

Dead or alive.

If the ☽ apply to the Lord of the eighth, it is dead, or to the eighth house; if the Lord of the house of the ☽ apply to eighth, *idem*; or if the *Significator* of the Beast be in the eighth, in □ to any infortunate in the fourth.

In Pound or not.

If the Lord of the sixt or twelfth be in the nineth or tenth, then are the Beasts with some Justice or Officer, as Baily or Constable, or under Lock, or are commanded to be safe kept; for the most part Lord of the twelfth or sixt in the twelfth or sixt, they are kept close.

That the Cattle shall be found againe.

If the Lord of the sixt be fortunate by ♃ or ♀, and if they be found in the second, fift or eleventh houses, the Beasts will be had again; if the Lord of the Terme of the *Moon*, or the Lord of the Cusp of the fourth house be with the Lord of the ascendant, *idem*; or if the Lord of the sixt or twelfth be in Δ of ☉ out of angles. /

How farre off a thing lost is from the owner.

The *Moon* in the same quarter with the Lord of the ascendant if there be but one Signe between them, the lost thing is in the house, or about his house that lost it; if there be more then thirty degrees unto seventy, the thing lost is in the Town, and in the same limits and bounds where the owner is; and if it be not within ninety degrees, the thing list is farre distant from the owner; for usually when the *Significator* of the thing lost is in the same Quadrant, or the *Moon*, the goods are in the same Town or Hundred where the *querent* liveth.

Beasts stolen or strayed.

If the Lord of the house of the *Moon*, or Lord of the second doe separate from their owne houses (if the goods be fixed) it is stolen; if moveable, fled of his owne accord.

In what place they are.

If the Lord of the sixt be in an angle, the Beasts be of small growth and in Pounds, Closes or houses; in cadent, in a Common, and are going way-ward; in succedant, in some Pasture neer hand.

Which way.

If the Lord of the sixt be in fiery Signes, east-ward in Woods or where Bushes, Brambles or Ferne have been burned; but in angles in fiery Signes, in Closes or Pound, or under Lock.

The Lord of the sixt in earthly Signes, South on dry lands, or grounds, but if in an angle, in a Pound, or close Pound with a thing that earth is about it, *viz.* a mud wall; if succedant, it is about Closes on the right hand of the *querent*.

The Lord of the sixt in an ayery Signe, they are most in plaine ground, if he be in an angle, they be in Pound or housed west from the place where they were lost; In succedant, on the right hand westward; on cadent, on the left and going away- / ward, *viz.* Straying further from their right Owner.

If the Lord of the sixt be in watry Signes, North, in a low place; if in an angle, in Close-ground, northward; in succedant, on the right hand northward; in cadent, in the Common on the left hand, where water is, or Medowes, going away-ward, or where people water their Cattle.

In what grounds they be.

If the Lord of the sixt be in movable Signes, they are in hilly grounds.

If the Lord of the sixt be in fixed Signes, in plaine ground where is new building, or some grounds new plowed or turned up.

Common Signes, where water is, rushy grounds, ditches.

If the Lord of the Terme of the *Moon* be in a fixed Signe they are in a plain ground newly taken in, or nigh a new building.

In movable, in new land, or ground full of hils.

In common Signes, in a watry place, rushy or a marshy ground, nigh ditches and pits.

The Cattle shall to Pound.

If the *Moon* be in the twelfth, they shall be had to Pound or be pounded, what signification soever, if the *Moon* be unfortunate, they shall toPound [sic]; if the Lord of the twelfth and principall *Significator* be unfortunate, they shall to pound, or be kept obscurely in some private or close place.

Long in Pound.

If ♄ be in the twelfth, or in the first (when the Querent comes to know of you what is become of the Cattle) or the *Moon* in the twelfth, any of them unfortunate, than shall they be long in pound; if

♂ aspect ♄ or the *Moon* in the twelfth, with ☌, □ or ☍, they will be killed in Pound, or dye there, or be very neer starving.

From hence the movable, fixed or common Signes may easily / be knowne, when Sheep be stolen, whether and where they are killed or not? if ♄ be in the ascendant, fourth, eighth or twelfth, long in pound.

Escape the Pound.

If the Lord of the ascendant be in a movable Signe, in the third, ninth or tenth, they shall escape Pound; if the Lord of the ascendant be in the twelfth, though good, yet sick and ill in Pound. If the Lord of the ascendant be in the eighth, it's probable they dye in pound.

If the principall *Significator* of the ascendant be Retrograde they dye in Pound.

If the Lord of the sixt behold the Lord of the ascendant with ✶ or △, they will be had againe; if he behold him with □ or ☍, then they will be stopped: if he behold the *Moon* or the Lord of the house of the *Moon*, with ✶ or △, had againe; with □ or ☍, stopt or staid in some Village or Towne.

Whether the Fugitive shall be taken.

Give the ascendant and his Lord and the ☉ unto the Querent, and the seventh and his Lord unto the Fugitive or thing asked for, and behold what aspect is between them, and so judge; for if the Lord of the ascendant apply unto the Lord of the seventh with Conjunction, ✶ or △, or that the Lord of the Ascendant be in the seventh, it betokeneth the Querent shall recover the things lost or Fugitive, gone away. Also, if the Lord of the seventh be in the Ascendant, or apply to the Lord thereof, or there be any translation of light betwixt them, it sheweth the same with more facility.

Of the Moon.

For Fugitives, have respect to the *Moon*, being naturall *Significatrix* of them, by reason of her quick motion, for if she be in the Ascendant, or apply to the Lord thereof with a good aspect, or that the lord of the seventh or the *Moon* separate from the *Fortunes*, and be immediately conjoyned to the *Infortunes*, all / these shew, that the Fugitive shall returne and be recovered, or shall be so hindered, that he shall come againe.

The ☽ encreasing in light and number, he shall be long in search; decreasing, soon found, and with lesse labour: also, the ☽ separating from the Lord of the seventh, and joyned with the Lord of the ascendant, the *Fugitive* is sorry he went, and will send some to entreat for him; the Lord of the seventh Combust, signifies the *Fugitive* will be taken, will he, nill he; behold in what quarter the Moon is, that way the *Fugitive* draweth, or intendeth to goe.

Whether he shall be taken.

The Lord of the seventh joyned to an Infortune in an angle, upon good search, the *Fugitive* will be taken; but if both be not in an angle, he shall be detained or staid by the way, but not imprisoned; if the Lord of the ascendant behold that Infortune who afflicts the Fugitive, the Querent shall find the *Fugitive* detained by some one, to whom he ought to give money, or who wil demand mony before he so restore the *Fugitive* unto him: if the *Infortune* be in the ninth, he shall be staid in his journey and taken; the Lord of the seventh with a Planet stationary, in his first or second station, in an angle or succedant, he knoweth not which way to fly but shall be taken.

If a Fugitive shall be found, or come againe.

If the Lord of the seventh be in the ascendant, the Fugitive will returne of his owne accord; ☽ separating from the Lord of the ascendant, and joyned immediately to the Lord of the seventh house, or to the seventh house, one will shortly bring newes of him; the Lord of the seventh combust, or entring combustion, the *Fugitive* shall be found (*volens, nolens;*) the ☽ separating from the Lord of the seventh, and joyned immediately to the ascendant, or Lord thereof, the *Fugitive* repenteth his departure, and will send some to entreat for him; ☽ joyned to *Infortunes*, viz. ♄, ♂ or ☋, or to a Planet Retrograde, he shall be found or come againe, and hath endured much misery since his departure; the Lord of the seventh beholding and *Infortune* / from the seventh, the Querent shall find him that is fled with some to whom he must give money before he can have him; ☽ separating from ♃ or ♀, he shall quickly come back againe, or, a thing lost shall suddenly be found; ☽ aspecting her owne house with ✶ or △, the *Fugitive* returneth within three dayes; for according to probability, the *querent* shall hear where he is within three dayes, if the distance be not too great.

Distance.

Behold the Lord of the seventh, and the Lord of the hour, and look how many degrees are between them, so many miles he is off from the place he went from.

The former rule I doe conceive not so perfect as this which followes; see what distance there is betwixt the ☽ and *Significator, viz.* their aspect and what Signes they are in; give for every degree in a movable Signe seventeen houses or Furlongs, at discretion; in common Signes, give for every degree five Furlongs or distance of five houses; in fixed Signes, for every degree give one Furlong, or one house, &c. having relation to the thing lost, and whether it be in a Town, or in the Fields.

Of a Woman flying from her Husband.

The ☉ under the earth, ♀ Occidentall and Retrograde, she will returne of her owne will; ♀ Orientall, she cometh, but not willingly; Lord of the ascendant, the ☽, and Lord of the seventh in △, she returneth, with a □ or ☍ without Reception, never; ♂ in an angle, and giving the ☽ strength, and the ascendant movable, they shall be contented to be separated for ever.

Of a Thief and Theft.

Haly saith, you must know that the ascendant is the *Significator* of the *querent*, the Lord of the second is *Significator* of the thing that is stolen or taken away, and the seventh house is the *Significator* of the *Thiefe*, if there be no Peregrine Planet in an angle or second house; the tenth house is the Signifier of the / King, and the Signe of the fourth the *Signifier* of the place where the thing is, that is, or was taken away; whose proper significations you must know from the Lords of those houses, whereby you may know the condition and state of what is missing, and if you find in the ascendant a Planet peregrine, put him as the *Significator* of the *Thiefe*, and especially if he be Lord of the seventh house; but if no Planet be in the ascendant, look if there be any in the other angles, and give him to be *Signifier* of the *Thief*.

Of the SIGNIFICATOR of the Thiefe.

The Lord of the seventh commonly signifies the *Thief*, but especially if he be peregrine in the ascendant, or in any other angle; but if he be not so, then behold if any other Planet be peregrine in any of the angles, call him the *Thief*; if none be peregrine in any of the angles, take the Lord of the Hour, and call him the Thief, and if it happen that the Lord of the Hour be Lord of the seventh, then it is more radicall; if the Lord of the seventh be in the ascendant, the *querent* is Thief; this will hold where just suspition is made of the *querent's* fidelity, or most cause above all others, whose complexion and condition is according to the Planet, Lord of the seventh, and Signe thereof.

The SIGNIFICATOR of the thing stolen.

*The *Significator* of the thing stolen is the Lord of the Term the ☽ is in; when thou hast found the *Significator* of the Thief, and understandest the nature of his disposition by the significant Planet and his aspects, know that the ascendant is *Signifier* of the *question*, or *Demandant*, and if thou see the Lord of the ascendant draw towards the Lord of the seventh, or to the Lord of the houre, or be in the seventh, it signifieth that the Thief shall be taken anon after, or it gives hopes of discovery of the thing lost.

*This rule is vulgar, and not of any credit.

Of THEFTS.

The first house, which is the ascendant, is for the *querent*, and / his Lord for him that hath lost the Goods, and signifieth the place from whence the Goods was taken; the seventh house and his Lord, and the peregrine Planet in an angle, and the Lord of the hour, signifieth the Thief, or party that took away the Goods.

The second house and the Lord of the second house and the ☽, shall signifie the Goods or thing that is lost, stolen or mist; the fourth house and his Lord shall signifie the place where it is laid, put or done, or conveyed unto, and is in at that instant of time.

The aspects of the ☉ and ☽, of the Lord of the ascendant, of the Lord of the second house, and of the Lord of the house of the ☽, to the Lord of the ascendant, and their application and aspects one to another, shall tell and shew whether the Goods shall be found and had againe or not: If the Lord of the second and the ☽ be in the seventh, in the Signe if the seventh, and the Lord of the seventh house behold them both by △ or ✶ aspect (though long out, viz. if the aspect be by many degrees distance) then is the Goods taken away by some body. viz. they are not simply lost: if the ☽ be *Lady* of the second and in the house of the Lord of the hour, going to Conjunction of the Lord of the seventh house, then hath the party lost the thing or Goods in some place where he was, and hath forgot it, and it is neither lost or stolen, but carelesly mislaid.

If the Moon be Lady of the ascendant, and in the fourth, and the Lord of the second in the seventh, or in the sign of the eighth house, in ☍ to the second house, at a ✶ or △ to the ☽, the thing is not stolen, but taken away in jest. If the ☽ be Lady of the ascendant, and in the ascendant, not farre remote, and the ☉ Lord of the second in the tenth with the Lord of the seventh house, and the Lord of the seventh oppresse the ☽ with a □, then is the Goods stolen and taken away; if the ☽ be in the third, opprest with the Lord of the seventh house by his □ aspect, and Lord of the second also being Lord of the ascendant, and in the seventh, in the Signe of the seventh, then it is stolen, but first it was taken in jest, and it will be hard to get it againe, except the ☉ and ☽ behold the ascendant. /

If ☽ be in the seventh in the Signe of the Lord of the hour, the Lord of the hour being Lord of the seventh, then is the Goods not stolen or taken away, but overlooked and mistaken. If ☽ be in the fifth house and in Capricorn, and be Lady of the hour, and ♀ Lady of the second in the tenth, in the Signe of the tenth, and ☽ in ☍ to the Lord of the seventh, then hath the party lost the Goods as he went by the way, or was in some place where he left them: If the ☽ be Lady of the hour, in ♋, in the eighth, and Lord of the second in the fifth, and neither of them behold the Lord of the seventh, but the Lord of the seventh be in the seventh, then is the Goods taken away in jest by the Master of the house, and he will deny it: If the ☽ be Lady of the hour in the fourth, in ☍ to the Lord of the seventh, and the Lord of the second in the twelfth, in a ✶ to the Lord of the seventh, then hath somebody taken the things away in jest: If ☽ be in the Signe of the Lord of the seventh, and not beholding the Lord of the seventh, but ☽ in the twelfth, and Lord of the second in the sixt, then is the Goods taken away in jest, if the Lord of the second did last separate from the Lord of the house of the Moon, then the Goods is stolen in jest, but will scant be had again. If the ☽ doe separate from the Lord of the second by □, the Goods is taken where she is, then it is stolen: If the Lord of the ascendant doe separate from ♃, or from the Lord of the second house, then did the *Querent* lay it downe and forget it, and so it was lost: but when the Lord of the Ascendant and Lord of the second doe separate from ♃, it is the surer: and sometimes it fals out, that the ☽ is *Lady* of the ascendant, and separates from ♃, and doth apply unto the Lord of the second house, which did also last separate from ♃, and sometimes the Lord of the Ascendant, as ☉ is also Lord of the second, and doth separate from ♃, yet if it be so, it giveth all one judgment as aforesaid: If the Lord of the second or ♃ doe separate from the Lord of the ascendant, then did the party lose the Goods by the way as he went, or in some secret place where he was, or else it tumbled out of his pocket privily into some secret place where it is not stolen or found: But if there be none of these separations / aforesaid, then see if the peregrine Planet or Lord of the seventh or ☿, who is also for the Thief, doe apply to ♃, or the Lord of the second; if they doe, then is the Goods absolutely stolen, and the Thief came with intent for to steale: If the Lord of the second or ♃ doe apply unto the peregrine Planet, or to the Lord of the seventh, or to ☿, who is for the Thief, then the Goods or the thing lost did offer it selfe to the Thiefe, or he came easily by them without trouble; for he that stole them, came not with intent for to have stolen it, but seeing the thing did lye so open, and so carelesly, he took it and carried it away. If the ☽ be Lady of the ascendant, and also lady of the second, and be in ♉, and apply by ☌ to the ☉, within one degree, and ☉ be the Lord of the third house, and ♂ be the peregrine Planet, and in the tenth, and ☿ apply to ♂, none of the abovesaid separations or applications impediting, or the Lord of the seventh in the 3rd, then the *Querent* did lose the thing by the way as he went, and it is not stolen from him.

Whether it be stolen or no.

For this, behold if the *Signifier* of the Thiefe be in the ascendant, or give his vertue to the ☽ or the ☽ to him, it is stolen; if the Lord of the ascendant give his vertue to the *Signifier* of the Thiefe, it is stolen; if the *Signifier* behold the Lord of the ascendant by □ or ☍, or the ☽ by ☌, □ or ☍, or the Lord of the house of the *Moon*, or the Lord of the Terme of the *Moon*, or the Lord of the second house, or the ⊗ or his Lord be unfortunate, or the Lord of the ascendant, or the Lord of the second house be infortunate, all these signifie losse of losing. /

That the Goods are stolen.

If any Planet be in the ascendant peregrine, it is stolen; or the peregrine Planet give vertue to the ☽, or the ☽ to him, it is stolen; the Lord of the ascendant peregrine, it is stolen; if the Thiefe be peregrine, that is, if he have no dignities where he is, it is stolen; if the *Significator* be with the Lord of the ascendant or in □ or ☍ to the Lord of the ascendant, it is stolen.

If any Planet doe separate from the Lord of the house of the ☽, it is stolen; if any Planet have respect to the Lord of the Terme of the ☽, with ☌ □ or ☍, it is stolen: if any Planet be separate from the Lord of the house of Substance, it is taken away: if the Thiefe have respect unto the Lord of the house of the ☽, with ☌, □ or ☍, it is taken away.

Not stolen.

If neither the Lord of the house of the *Moon* or Lord of the second separate not themselves from one another, or any other Planet from them, then what you look for is in his owne place; if the Moon give vertue to ♄ or ♂, or to any Planet in cadent houses, or to the Lord of the eighth, not stole, but missing, or else negligently throwne aside.

It will be (or is intended to be stolen.)

If the *Moon* be Lady of the seventh, and give her vertue to a Planet in the second, or in the eleventh or fifth, having her selfe neither ✶ or △ to the Cusps of the houses, or if any Planet in the seventh give vertue to a Planet in the second, fifth or eleventh, and have no ✶ or △ to the Planet in the seventh, it will be, or if the Lord of the tenth be in ☌, ☐ or ☍ with the Thiefe, it will be stolen.

It is Lost of Stolen.

If a Planet doe separate himselfe from the lord of the house of / the ☽, or from the Lord of the second, then it is taken away with hands and stolen: If the ☽ be Lady of the seventh, and give vertue to the Lord of the ascendant, it is stolen: if the Lord of the ascendant give vertue to the *Moon* in the seventh, it is stolen.

If any Planet in the ascendant give vertue to the *Signifier* of the Thiefe, it is stolen, or the Thief to the Lord of the ascendant, its stolen, but the Thief gives so much of the Goods to the owner againe, according to the vertue or light that the Thief giveth to the Lord of the ascendant; if any Planet in the ascendant be peregrine, it is stolen, and the Thief shall escape.

If the peregrine Planet give vertue to the *Moon*, or the *Moon* to him, if the Thief aspect the *Moon* with Conjunction, ☐ or ☍, or aspect the Lord of the Terme of the *Moon*, it is stolen.

If the ☽ give vertue to ♄ or ♂, or if she give vertue to any Planet in a cadent house, or if the *Moon* give vertue to the Lord of the eighth, and he in a movable Signe, the things are stolen, but in fixed Signes, taken away.

If the Lord of the house of the *Moon* separate from any Planet, or the Lord of the second doe separate from any Planet, stolen.

If the Lord of the house of the *Moon* or second be in his owne house, and have vertue of ♄ or ♂, gone away by it selfe, and not stolen.

Of the age of the Thief.

The age is taken from the Planet that is *Significator* of the Thiefe, if he be Orientall, he is young; in the midst of his Orientality, then of middle age; if he be in the end of his Orientallity, he is old, saith *Haly*.

To judge by the distance of the Planets from the ☉, for by the ☉ the Planets are Orientall and Occidentall, by which the signification of age is taken, after *Haly*, and other Writers.

If together with this, you consider in what degrees of the Signe the *Significator* is in, you shall doe better, for a Planet Orientall and in a few degrees, denotes youth, or younger; in more degrees, more age; frame the age according to an exact mixture. /

If ♄, ♃ or ♂ be significators, then behold the distance of them from the ☉; from their ☌ with the ☉ to the ☐ aspect, signifieth the age of 18. yeers, and the neerer the ☉ the lesser in age, and from the ☐ to the ☍ signifieth the age of 36. from the ☍ to the next ☐ signifies the age of 45. from that last ☐ to the ☌ signifieth the age of 72. and so to the end of life.

Guido Bonatus saith, the ☉ being *Significator*, and being between the ascendant and Mid-heaven or tenth house (which is all one) signifieth the thiefe to be young, and so increasing till he come to the angle of the earth.

And if ♀ or ☿ be significators, the age is taken by their distance or elongation from the ☉, from their ☌ with the ☉, being direct to the mid-way of their ☌ in their Retrogradation, signifies the age of the thiefe to be about 18. and the neerer the ☉ the younger, and from the mid-way to their ☌ in their Retrogradation, signifieth the age of 36. or neer that age, the neerer to the ☌ the elder, and from the ☌ in the Retrogradation, to the mid-way of their ☌ in direction, signifieth the age of 72. and so to the end of life; and if the ☽ be signifier judge as by Saturn, ♃ and ♂, as before is said.

The same *Guido* saith, ♀ signifieth the thiefe to be young, a woman or a Maid, ☿ of lesse age then ♀, ♂ signifieth full age, or in prime of his youth, ♃ more of yeers then ♂, and ♄ signifieth old age or decrepit, or well in yeers, the ☉ signifieth as before said; young; and if she be neer to the full ☽, it signifieth the middle age or perfect man; and if she be in the end of the Moneth, it signifieth the Thiefe to be aged, or of greater yeers.

The age of the Thiefe.

If the ☽ increases, he is young; if decrease he is old; if the significator be in the house of ♄, or aspected by him, or in the last degree of a Signe, it signifies old age; ♄ the same; ♂, ☉, ♀, ☿ from the Ascendant unto the tenth, signifie young / yeers, especially if they be in the beginning of Signes: from the tenth to the seventh, middle yeers; if the significator be a superiour Planet and direct, then he is of good yeers, if Retrograde elder or very old, and so judge of inferior Planets; for if they be Retrograde or joyned to Planets Retrograde, it augmenteth the age: thus is you mingle your signification, you may judge better. The ☉ between the Ascendant and mid heaven argueth a childe, between the *Meridian* and *Occident*, accuseth a young Man, between the *Occident* and *Septentrionall* angle, a Man growne; and from the *Septentrionall* to *Orientall*, accuseth a very old Man; Lord of the ascendant in the East quarter, or ☽ in the Ascendant, a young Man; ☿ always signifies a Childe or a young Man, especially being in the *Ascendant* and *Orientall*: any Planet, except ♄, Signifieth young Man; or if the signifier be joyned to ♀, ☽ increasing in light, or in the first ten degrees or middle of the Signe, or the significator in the beginning of the *Orientall* quarter, signifies a Childe, or a young Man, or a Woman, &c.

Whether the Thiefe be a Man or Woman.

Behold the Signe ascending and the Lord of the houre; if both be Masculine, the Thiefe is Masculine; and if the Lord of the houre and Ascendant be both Feminine, the Thiefe is Feminine; if the Signe Ascending be Masculine, and the Lord of the houre Feminine, it is both Masculine and Feminine, *viz*. there were two Theeves, both a Man and a Woman.

Also the Significator Masculine and ☽ in a Masculine Sign, signifieth a Man-kinde, *& e contra*. If the Lord of the Ascendant and the Lord of the houre be both in the Ascendant in Masculine Signes, it is a Man; in Feminine Signes, a Woman.

If the Lord of the Ascendant and the Lord of the houre be the one in a Masculine, and the other in a Feminine Sign, both a Man and a Woman had a hand in the Theft.

The Angles of the Figure Masculine, a Man; Feminine a Woman.

♀ Significatrix aspecting ♂ with □, notes impediment in hearing, principally in the left eare. /

♀, ☿, ☽ noteth Woman, Saturn, ♃, ♂ and ☉ Men; respecting the Signe and quarter wherein they be.

If one Thiefe or more.

Behold the Significator of the Thiefe; if he be in a fixed Signe, and of direct Ascensions, or a Signe of few Children, or of few shapes and likenesse; it signifies to be one and no more. If the Signe be of two bodies, *viz*. a common or bycorporeall Signe, it signifies more then one, and more likely if there be in the Signe many Planets peregrine: also when the ☉ and ☽ behold themselves by a □ in the Angles, it signifies more then one: Signes that signifie many Children are Cancer, Scorpio and Pisces; few Children are ♈ ♉ ♎ ♐ ♑ and ♒. Divers shapes or formes, ♊ ♋ ♐ ♒ : barren Signes are ♊ ♌ and ♍; Signes of direct Ascensions ♋ ♌ ♍ ♎ ♏ ♐; Signes of oblique Ascensions are ♑ ♒ ♓ ♈ ♉ ♊. If the ☽ in the houre of the Question be in the Angle of the Earth, in a common Sign, there is more then one; if she be in any of the other Angles, in a fixed Sign, there is but one Thiefe. Looke how many Planets are with the Thieves significator, so many

Theeves; the ☽ in a common Signe more then one. Lord of the Ascendant in a Male Signe, and Lord of the houre in a Female, Man and Woman (as aforesaid;) looke to which the ☽ doth agree, viz. to whom she applies, that person is the principall actor; the Angles moveable especially the 1st and seventh, or the Significator being in ♋, ♏ or ♓, more then one. The Sign wherein the significator of the Thiefe is in, if it be immoveable, or a double bodied Sign, more then one. Both the Luminaries beholding one another from Angles, more then one; ☽ in the Ascendant, and it a double bodied Signe, doth demonstrate there were more Thieves then one.

Of the Cloathes of the Thiefe.

You must know the colour of the Cloathing by the Planets, Signs and Degrees, and the House the Significator is in; and after the mixture the one with the other, accordingly judge the colour of / their Cloathes. If there be signification of many Theeves, judge them by the Lord of the triplicity the Significators are in. The Significators of the Colours of the Planets after *Alcabitius* are these, ♄ Blacke, ♃ Green, Spotted, or Ashy, or such like; ♂ Red; ☉ Tawny or Saffron, I rather conceive an high Sandy colour. The Colours by mixing the Planets one with another are these; ♄ and ♃, a darke Greene, or deepe spotted with Blacke; ♄ and ♂ a darke Tawney, ♄ and ☉ a Blacke— yellow and shining, ♄ and ♀ a White gray, ♄ and ☿ a Black Black or Blewish, ♄ and ☽ a deepe Tawney, or deep Gray or Russet. ♃ and ♂ a Tawney, somewhat light spotted, ♃ and ☉ much after the mixture of the *Sunne* and *Mars* but more shining, ♃ and ♀ a Greenish-gray, ♃ and ☿ a Spotted Green, ♃ and ☽ a somewhat high Greene. ♂ and ☉ a deepe Red shining, ♂ and ♀ a light Red or Crimson, ♂ and Mercury a Red or a red Tawney, ♂ and the ☽ a Tawny or light Red. You must mix the colour of the Signifier with the colour of the House he is in, and thereafter judge the colour of their Cloathes; or judge the Colour by the Signes and the Degrees the Signifier is in; as if he be in the Signe, or House, or Terme of ♄, judge after ♄ as before; and if he be in the House of ♄ and Terme of ♃, judge after the mixture of ♄ and ♃, and so of all other as before.

For Names.

♃, ☉ and ♂ in Angles signifie short Names and of few Sylables, and being neer the Mid-heaven doe begin with *A* or *E*: ♄ or ♀ Significator, the Name is of more Syllables, as *Richard* or *William*, for the most part if the Querents Names be short, so is also the Quesited.

Names of Theeves or Men, as Astrologers write.

To know the Names by the Lord of the seventh house; or the Planet in the seventh House, or the Planet joyned with them, as followeth: /

The principall Significator.

Mens names						**Womens names**
☿	♂	Matthew.	♂	☿		Katherine.
☽	☿	Simon.	☿	♂	☉	Christian.
☉	♃	Laurence.	♄	☽	♀	Joane.
☿	☉	Clement.	♀	♄		Isabel.

	The Planet joyned.		The *Significator.*	The Planets	Conjoyned.	
☿	♄	Edmund.	♄	☉		Elizabeth.
♃	☉	John.	♄	☉		Julian.
♄	♀	William.	☽	♂	☉	Mary.
♂	☉	Robert.	☽	♀		Ellin.
♂	☉	Peter.	♀	☿		Agnes.
♂		Anthony.	☉	☿		Margaret.
☉	☿	Benjamin.	☉	♀		Alice.
♃	♄	Thomas.	☉	☿		Edith.
☉		Roger.	☉	♃		Maud.
☉		Phillip.	☉			Lucy.
♄	☉	George.	♃			Anne.
☉	♄	Andrew.	☽			Rachel.
☽	☉	Henry.				Nell, Ellenor.
☽	♄	Nicholas.				
♃	☉	Richard.				
☉		James.				
☉		Stephen.				

Some moderne Professors, have endeavoured to give a probable conjecture what Christian name the Thiefe is of, or party enquired after, whether man or woman. First, they consider if the Planet who is principall *Significator* of the party enquired of, whether he be angular or no, and then whether he be in aspect (it matters not what aspect, good or ill) with any Planet or Planets: if he be in no aspect, then in whose Dignities he is, and from hence they make their mixture; for example; let us admit ☿ to be Lord of the seventh, and *Significator* / of a Maids Lover, and he in aspect, or in the dignities of ♂, I shall then have recourse on the Table before, and there I find in the first line over against ☿ and ♂ *Matthew*, I shall then say the man's name is *Matthew*, or of a name equivalent in length, or same number of letters: for my part I never use this way, nor yet have much credited it; yet I beleeve, were it well practiced we might find out very pretty conclusions, and goe neer to find the very name, or somewhat neer it.

Jim Baker

Whether the Thief be out of the house or not.

If both the Lights behold the ascendant, or he be in their owne houses, the Thief is one of the Family, the Lord of the seventh in the ascendant, *idem*; the Lord of the sixt in the second, it is a Servant; if either of the *Luminaries* behold the ascendant, it is no stranger; ☉ opposite to the ascendant, it is an overthwart Neighbour; the Lord of the seventh beholding the ascendant with a friendly aspect, *idem*.

A Stranger or Familiar.

☉ and ☽ beholding the ascendant or the Lord of the ascendant in the 1st, or joyned to the Lord of the seventh, it is one of the house, or one that frequents the house; the *Luminaries* in their proper houses, or in the house of the Lord of the ascendant, the same; in the Triplicity of the Lord of the ascendant, a Neighbor; in the Terms of him, a familiar; ☽ in the ninth in ☌, □ or ☍ to ♄ or ♂, brings back the Thief; without fail if they be Retrograde.

Another.

If the ☉ and ☽ aspect the Lord of the ascendant, and not the ascendant, the Thiefe is knowne to the owner; the *Significator* of the Thiefe strong in the ascendant, noteth a Brother or Kinsman; *Zael*, Lord of the seventh in the ninth from his owne house, it is a Stranger; ☉ and ☽ beholding each other, a Kinsman; the Lord of the ascendant in the third or fourth, accuseth thine owne household-Servant; this I have oft proved true by experience. /

Ruled by the Lord of the Seventh house.

The Lord of the seventh in the ascendant or fourth, noteth one of the house, or of the household, or frequenting the house, and is in the City or Towne, and is one whom the *querent* least mistrusteth, and one which will hardly confesse the fact.

The Lord of the seventh in the second, noteth one of the household, or an acquaintance (if is be in a Masculine Signe,) but if it be in a Feminine Signe, it is his Wife, perhaps a Sweetheart or Mayd of the house, and is within the power of the Loser, or some of his house, and may be recovered by money.

The Lord of the seventh in the third, one of the Kindred, Brother, Sisters, Cozens, or his onely Fellow by way of service, or some Neighbour often in his sight, or his Disciple, Messenger or Servant, &c.

The Lord of the seventh in the fourth, it is his Father, or some old Body, or of his Fathers Kin, or one dwelling in the Heritage or house of his Father, and the Thiefe hath given it to his Wife, or the Woman to her Husband, or it is the good man or good Wife of the house, or else he is a Tiller or Labourer of the Land for the *querent*.

The Lord of the seventh in the fifth, the Sonne or Daughter of him, or the Sonne or Daughter of his Cozen or Nephew, (if the Sign be a masculine) or of the household of his Father, or else his very Friend.

The Lord of the seventh in the sixt, A Servant, a Disciple or Labourer to the *querent*, or one conversant with some Churchman, a Brother or Sister of the Father, a sick body or unsteadfast, or grieved person.

The Lord of the seventh in the seventh, his Wife or Lady, or an Harlot, or a woman that useth to be suspected for such matters, or a Buyer or Seller in Markets; if it be a feminine Signe, the Taker is an utter enemy to the Loser, by some cause formerly happened between them, and dwels somewhat far from him, and the things are in his custody still, and hard to be recovered.

The Lord of the seventh in the eighth, a Stranger, yet seemeth to be one / of the household, or one of his open enemies, or of his neer Kinswoman, for some cause of offence done, or some evill disposed person (and of the Livery of the Man) and he useth to come to his House, and either is kept by him, or else doth some servile acts, as a Butcher or Labourer doth, otherwhiles to kill Cattell, and it seemeth the thing lost will not be had againe but by either faire words, or dread of death, or by reason of some threats, or else the thing is lost by some Man absent, the which is not now had in the minde at this time, but seems to be quite forgotten.

The Lord of the seventh in the ninth, an honest person, a Clarke, or a Church-man, and the Thiefe is out of the way or Country, a Disciple, or Governour to some Master of some priviledged Place, or a poore vagrant person, hard to be recovered but by some religious person as aforesaid.

The Lord of the seventh in the tenth, a Lord, or Master, or Governour in the Kings House, or of his Household; or some Lady or Gentlewoman, if the Figure be Feminine, *& e contra*; or some crafts-Master; usually its some person that lives handsomely, and is not necessitated to this course of life.

The Lord of the seventh in the eleventh, a Friend or one knowne by some service done; or of the household of some man of the Church, or Neighbour, or Servant in the place where the Querent hath some Lordship, and is put in trust, or is of the Household of the Querent his Mother, and by such a one or his meanes to be recovered againe.

The Lord of the seventh in the twelfth, a Stranger, envious a false person, and inthralled, incumbered or oppressed with poverty, and hath no riches; wherefore he hath visited many Regions, as some Enemy or Beggar doth, and he joyneth in it; judge his quality by the Signe and Place, and commix all these with the other testimonies of the Signes and Planets.

Whether the Thiefe be in the Towne or no.

Behold the Significator of the Thiefe, if thou find him in the end of the Signe direct, or separating from Combustion, or applying to a Planet in the third or ninth House; say, he is gone or / going out of the Towne, for the removing of the *Significator* out of one Signe into another, denoteth change of Lodging or removing; if it be a superiour Planet, the rule is infallible.

If the Lord of the ascendant and the Moon be not in one quarter but above 90 degrees asunder, it noteth departure, or a great distance betwixt the Goods and the Owner; but if they be in angles, and applying to Planets in angles, it noteth no farre distance, especially if the Moon and the Lord of the ascendant be in one quarter.

Distance betwixt the Owner and the Thief.

If the Thief, viz. his *Significator*, be in a fixed Signe, account for every house betwixt the Lord of the ascendant and him, three miles; in common Signes, every house betwixt the ascendant and Thief, one mile; in movable Signes, for every house betwixt the ascendant and the Thiefe, account that so many houses on the earth are betwixt the Loser and the Thiefe.

If the Signe ascending be a fixed Signe, for every house give three miles; if a common Signe, then for every house give one mile; if a movable Signe, for every house reckon one halfe mile.

If his *Significator* be in an angle, he is still in the Towne; in a succedant, not far off, in a cadent he is far gone.

Where the Thief is.

☽ in an angle, at home; succedant, about home; if in cadent, far from home,

The *Significator* of the Thief in an Angle, in a house; ☽ in an angle, in his owne house; in a succedant, he is in Closes; Moon in a succedant, in his owne Closes,

The *Significator* of the Thiefe in a cadent house, he is in a Common; Moon in a cadent, in his owne Common, or that which belongs to the Towne he lives in.

If the *Signifier* of the Thief be within thirty degrees of the Lord of the ascendant, then is the Thiefe neer him that lost the / Goods; if within seventy degrees, within the Towne or Parish of him that lost the Goods, the more degrees betwixt them, the farther off they are from each other.

If the *Significator* be in a □ aspect to the Lord of the ascendant, he is out of the Towne; if the Lord of the seventh be strong, & in an angle, the Thief is not yet gone out of the Town or Parish where the Theft was acted; if he be found weak in an angle, he is gone, or departing.

Another.

If the Lord of the seventh be in the ascendant, tell the Querent the Thiefe will be at home (before him) or before he get home, *probatum est*.

If the Lord of the seventh be in the seventh, he is hid at home and dare not be seen.

If the Lord of the sixt be in the first, or second with any of their Lords, the Thief is of the house of the *Querent*.

If the Lord of the ascendant and the Significator of the Thief be together, the Thief is with the *Querent*, probatum est; the very truth us, he cannot be far from him.

Towards what part the Thief is gone.

If you would know to what part he is fled, after he is gone out of Towne, behold the Planet that signifies his going out of Towne, and in what Sign he is; and if he be in a fiery Sign, say he is in the east part of the Towne or Country; if he be in a watry Signe, he is in the North; if in an Ayery Signe, he is in the west; if in an earthly Signe, he is in the south: Behold also in what quarter of Heaven he is in, and judge accordingly; if the *Signifier* be in the west, he is in the west; the east part or from the Mid-heaven to the ascendant, &c. mix the signification of the Signe with the signification of the quarter, and thereafter judge, preferring the Signe before the quarter, onely making use of the quarter to ballance your judgment when other testimonies are equall. /

Which way the Thief is gone.

Behold the significant Planet, in what Signe he is, and also the quarter, and accordingly judge; others judge by the place of the ☾ ; others behold the Lord of the seventh, and the Lord of the hour, what Signe and quarter they are in, and if they agree, then they judge thereafter; others regard the *Significator* to whom he doth apply, or render his power; others by the Lord of the fourth, I always judge by the strongest, either of the *Significator* or the ☾ .

If the *Significator* of the Thief be in a fiery Sign, he went east; earthly, south; ayery, west; watry, north; see what angle ☾ is in, there is the Thief; in no angle, look for the Lord of the house of the ☾ , to that part he went.

See what Signe the Lord of the seventh is in; if in ♈, eastward; in ♉, in the South against the east; and so of the rest.

Of the house of the Thiefe, and the mark thereof.

If you will know the quality of the house the thing lost is in, and the Signe and token thereof, and in what place the thing is, behold the Signe the *Significator* of the Thief is in, and in what part of heaven he is, and say in that part of the Towne the thing is; if it be in the ascendant, it is in the point of the east; in the seventh, just in the west; in the fourth, just in the north; in the tenth, it is south; and if it be between these angles, judge accordingly; as south-west or north-west; give the place of the ☉ to be the house the Thief is in, and the place of the ☾ to be the door of the house; if the ☉ be in an Orientall Signe, the house is in the east part from the Master, or from him that lost the Goods.

The Door of the house.

To know in what part of the house the Door is, behold the place the ☾ is in, whether in the angles, succedants or cadents, and judge as it is said in the parts of the house, the which part / is taken of or from the Signe the ☾ is in one way; if the ☾ be in a fixed Signe, say the house hath but one door; in a movable Signe, say the door is high above the earth, and it may be there is one other little one; and if ♄ have any aspect to that Signe, the door hath been broken and after mended againe, or else it is black or very old.

If ♂ have any aspect thereunto, the gate or door shall have some token of burning or fire; and if ♄ and ♂ have a friendly aspect to the same Signe, the gate is Iron, or most part of it, or a good strong one; and if the ☾ have small light, the house hath no door opening to the highway, but opens on the back part of the house.

Tokens of the Thiefe house.

If the ☽ be in □, ☌, or ☍ to ♂, the door is burned with iron, fire or candle, or hath been cut with some iron instrument; if the ☽ be in Δ or ✱ to ♂, say the door of the Thiefs house is mended with iron; if the ☽ be but newly encreased in light, his gate or door is part under the earth, or under a Bank-side, or they goe downe by a step, ☽ in a fixed or movable Signe, he hath but one door outwardly, in common Signs more then one.

☽ in a fixed Signe, the gate is under the earth, viz. if in ♉, or the house standeth on the Bank-side, if in ♒; ☽ in movable Signs, the gate or door is above the earth, and a step to go up in to it (*probatumn est.*) or one ascends somewhat in going into the house.

☽ Infortunate, the gate is broken, and note what part of heaven ☽ is in, that part of the house the door standeth in; if ♄ aspect the Moon with ☌, □ or ☍, the door or gate is broken downe, old or black; if with ✱ or Δ, the door is mended againe.

Of the house where the Thiefe remaineth or dwelleth.

Behold the Signe wherein the *Signifier* is in, and in what / part of heaven he is, & say the Goods so taken are in that quarter of the Town, as if in ascendant, east; the place of the ☽ sheweth in what part the gate is in; for if she be in an easterly quarter, the gate is on the east-side of the house; if in a westerly quarter, on the west; and if the ☽ be fixed, the house hath but one door, neer to the ground; if in a movable Signe, the gate is, or hath been broken, and is very ancient, or is black; if ♂ behold it, it doth encrease the signification, *viz.*, that it is rent or crackt, or torne, or needs repaire; if at such an aspect the ☽ hath but then small light, as there is no great appearance of iron work.

Are the Goods in the Owners hands.

Lord of the Ascendant in an Angle, the Goods are in his hands; the Lord of the houre in an Angle the same: if the Lord of the House of the ☽ be with the Lord of the houre in an Angle, the Goods are in his hands and are Goods moveable; if the Lord of the houre and the Lorde of the terme of the ☽ and the Lord of the second be in an Angle with the Lord of the Ascendant, they are in his hands and fixt Goods; if any of these Lords be in an Angle, with □ Δ or ✱ to the Lord of the Ascendant, the Owner shall have his Goods againe.

If the Lord of the Ascendant and Lord of the houre be in a succedant House, the Goods are about the Owner, ☽ or the Lord of the House of the ☽ in a moveable Signe, they are not farre from the Owner; if the Lord of the terme of the ☽, or the Lorde of the second be in a succedent House, then the things are about the Owner, and not much elongated.

The Planets last spoken of, or rehearsed, placed in cadent Houses, shew the Goods farre from the Owner.

Whether the Goods be in custody of the Thiefe.

Behold the signifier if the Thiefe or Theeves; and if he or they give their power to another Planet, the things stolen are not in the keeping of the Thiefe or Theeves; if he or they give not their power to another, it remaineth in his own power, custody or possession. /

Behold the Lord of the terme wherein the *Significator* of the Thiefe is, and by him judge the estate of the Thiefe; if an infortunate Planet be in a fortunate terme, he was of a wilde stocke, and now is in good state: If a fortune be in the terme of an infortune, say the contrary.

If he carried all with him.

Behold the Lord of the seventh and eighth, if the Lord of the seventh be in an Angle, he was willing to have carried all away, but could not; if in a succedent, and the Lord of the eighth with him strong, he had all; if both the Lord of the seventh and eighth be in cadent Houses, he neither carried it away or had it.

The distance of the thing from the Owner.

Behold how many Degrees are between the *Significator* and the Moon; and whether the Signes be fixed, movable or common; in fixed Signes account for every Degree a Mile; in common Signes so many tenths of Miles; in Movable Signes so many Rods. How many Degrees betwixt the Lord of the seventh and the Lord of the houre, so many thousand Paces betwixt the Querent and the Fugitive.

Looke what distance is betwixt the Ascendant and his Lord, such is the distance betwixt the place where the thing was lost and the thing it selfe.

Looke how many Degrees the *Signifier* is in his Signe, and so many Miles are the Cattle from the place where they went, and in that quarter or coast where the Lord of the fourth is.

How farre the thing is from the Querent.

Behold the Lord of the Ascendant and the Ascendant, and see how many Signes and Degrees are betwixt the Lord of the Ascendant and the Ascendant; and if the Lord of the Ascendant be in a fixed Signe, then give for every Signe (betwixt him and the Ascendant) foure Miles; and if he be in a common Signe, give for every Signe a Mile and a halfe; and if he be in / a moveable Signe, give for every Signe (bewtixt them) half a Mile, and the overplus of the Degrees, according to the Signe the Lord of the Ascendant is in: *As for Example*;

A Question was asked, and the seventh Degree of ♑ ascended, and ♄ in ♏ foure Degrees; so there is between the Ascendant and ♄ three Signes, and ♄ in a fixed Signe; therefore I must give for every Signe foure Miles, three times foure is twelve, and there is three Degrees more to the which belong halfe a Mile; so the whole sum is twelve Miles and a halfe.

The Place where the Goods stolne are.

If you will know the place where the thing stolne is in; take Signification of the Place from the Signe the *Significator* of the Thiefe is in, and from the place of the Lord of the fourth House; if they be both in one Signification it is well; if not, behold then what place is *Signified* by the Lord of the fourth House, and judge by that Signe the nature of the place where the thing stolne is. If he be in a moveable Signe, it is in a place high from the ground; if in a fixed Signe, it is in the Earth; and if in a common Signe, it is under some Eaves of a House; and helpe your judgment in these by the Terme of the Signes, as if the *Significator* be in ♈, it is in a place where Beasts doe use that be small, as Sheep, or Hogs &c. if he be in ♌, it is in a place of Beasts which bite as Dogs, &c. if he be in ♐, it is in a place of great Beasts that are ridden; as in a Stable of Horses, or such like: if in ♉, ♍ or ♑, it signifieth a House or place of great Beasts, as Oxen, Kine or such other Cattle: ♍ and ♑ Signifieth a place of Camels, Mules, Horses, Asses, and such like: ♍ hath the Signification of a Barn, or of such places as be under the Earth, or neer to the Earth, or Granaries, such as they put Corne in: ♑ signifieth a place of Goats, Sheepe, Hogs, and such like. If he be in ♊, ♎, ♒, it is in the House; in ♊ it is in the Wall of the House; ♎ neer a little House or Closet, ♒ it is neer a Doore that is above a Doore or Gate, in some place on high. If ♋, ♏ or ♓, the thing is in Water, or neer Water, and these doe Signifie a Pit or Cistern: ♏ it is neer a place of unclean Water, or where they use to / cast out filthy Water, as a Gutter: ♓ sheweth a place always moyst.

The place where the thing lost or stolne is hidden.

Behold the place of the *Significator* of the Thiefe, and the Lord of the fourth, if they be both in one *Signification* and wel agreeing, if not, behold the Lord of the fourth; if he be in a moveable Signe, it is in an high place; if in a fixed Signe, it is on the Earth; if in a common Signe, in a covered place. Herein behold what Signe the ☽ is, or whether in the Ascendant or Mid-heaven, or about it, behold the forme or Signe that Ascends with her, and say the thing is in that place which the forme thereof representeth.

Where the Goods are.

Looke to the Lord of the second and his *Almuten*, (*viz.* he that hath most dignities there) there are the Goods: if the Lord thereof and the Lord of the fourth be both in one Signe, judge the things to be where they are, and the Thiefe and Theft both together; if they be not together, judge by the fourth, &c.

If the Lord of the fourth be found in a fixed Sign, the Goods are in the Earth, or in a House having no Chamber.

If the Lord of the fourth be in a moveable Signe, the Goods are in a Chamber above another, or in an upper Loft or Room.

If in a common Signe, in a Chamber within another Chamber. If the Goods be found in a fiery Signe, they are East; in an Earthly South; in an Aery, West; in a Watry, North.

If the Lord of the Terme of the ☽ be in an Angle, and in a moveable Signe, the Goods are in Closes where are both Corne and Grasse.

If in a succedent and fixed Signe, in Woods, Parkes, or in closed Grounds that lyeth from the High-way-side: if in a cadent and common Signes, in a Common of divers Mens, or Pasture or Meddow of divers Mens.

Haly saith, it was asked him one time when Leo was Ascending / and ♀ therein; and he saith, the thing was under a Bed neer a Robe or Covering; because ♀ was in the Ascendant, the which is *Significatrix* of a Bed, and after these considerations judge.

Lost or stolen in what part of the house.

If the thing is lost or stolen be in the house, & you would know the place where it is, behold the Lord of the fourth. and the Planet which is therein; if it be ♄, it is hid in a dark place or part of the house, or in a desolate or stinking place and deep, be it a seige-house or Jakes [outhouse], where people seldome come.

If it be ♃, it signifies a place of Wood, Bushes or Bryers. If it be ♂, it is in some Kitchin, or in a place where fire is used, or in a Shop, &c.

If it be ☉, it signifieth the Cloyster or Hall of the House, or the Place or Seat of the Master of the House.

If it be ♀, it signifieth the place of the Seat of a Woman, or Bed or Cloathes, or where women are most conversant.

If it be ☿, it is in a place of Pictures, Carving or Books, or a place of Corne, and chiefly in ♍.

If it be ☽, it is in a Pit, Cisterne or Lavatory.

The forme or likenesse of the entring of the house.

Behold the place of the ☉, from him is knowne the forme and likenesse of the opening of the house; from ☽ is knowne the Sellar, and the place that holdeth the water, or a Pit; by ♀, the place of Mirth, Play and women &c. from the place of the ☊ is knowne the place of height, or highest Seat, Stool, Stairs or Ladder to climbe by; and from the place of the ☋ is knowne the place the Wood is in, or the house the Beasts be in, or a Pillar in the house; and if ☿ be in a common Signe it is in a little Cell within another Chamber; if he be in a movable Signe, it is within a little Cell that hath another Chamber about it; if in a fixed Signe, it is in a house that hath no Sellar nor other Chamber, as many Country-houses have not. /

And if ♃ or ♀, or both of them be in the tenth house, the door hath a faire opening; if ♄ be in the tenth, the opening of the door is neer some Ditch or Pit, or deep place; if ♂ be there, neer to the opening of the house is the place of making the fire, or killing of Beasts, or heading; if ☿ be in the tenth, say in the opening of the house, is a place where the Master of the house keeps his things in, *viz.* his instruments or Tools he uses about his Beasts; and if ☉ be in the tenth, in the opening is some Stoole or Seat to sit on, or a bed; if the ☽ be in the tenth house, say that in the entring of the house is a door under the ground, or some other necessary thing that a man hath much occasion to use in his house, as a Furnace or Quern, or such like.

What is stolne by the Lord of the second or tenth House.

♄ Lead, Iron, Azure, blacke or blew colour, Wooll, blacke Garments, Leather, heavy things, labouring tooles for the Earth: ♃ Oyle, Honey, Quinces, Silke, Silver: ♀ white Cloth, and white Wine, Green-colour.

♂ Pepper, Armour, Weapons, red Wine, red Cloathes, Brasse, Horses for Warre, hot things; ☿ Books, Pictures, implements; ☉ Gold, Oringes, Brasse, Carbuncles, yellow Cloathes: ☽ ordinary and common Commodities.

The quality of the Goods stolne.

Behold the Lord of the second; if he be ♄, it is Lead, Iron, or a Kettle, something with three feet; a Garment or some blacke thing, or a Hide or Beasts skin.

If ♃ be Lord of the second, some white thing; as Tyn, Silver, or mixed with vaines, as it were with yellow and white, or broad Cloath, &c.

☉ Signifies Gold and precious things, or things of good value. ♂ those which be fiery belong to the fire, Swords, Knives. ♀ Such things as belong to Women, Rings, faire Garments, Smocks, Wastecoats, Peticoats.

☽ Beasts, as the Horse, Mules, Cowes, or Poultry in the

Country / of all sorts; ☿ Money, Books, Paper, Pictures, Garments of divers colours.

A signe of recovery.

The ☽ in the seventh Aspecting the Lord of the Ascendant with a △, ♀ or the Lord of the second in the Ascendant, ♃ in the second direct, ♀ Lady of the second in the Ascendant, ☽ in the tenth in △ to a Planet in the second: ☽ in the second, with a △ to the Lord of the second: ☽ in the second, to a □ of ☉ in the twelfth: The Lord of the Ascendant in the second, ☉ and ☽ aspecting each other with a △, ☉ and ☽ aspecting the cuspe of the second with a △: Lord of the second in the fourth, or in the House of the Querent, *viz.* in the Ascendant.

If it shall be recovered.

To know if it shall be recovered or not: For resolution hereof, behold the Lord of the terme of the ☽, the which is *Signifier* of the substance stolne to be recovered. If the Lord of the terme of the ☽, and the Lord of the house of the ☽ be increasing both in motion and number, and free from infortunes; it shews it shall be recovered whole and found, and nothing diminished thereof.

Consider also the Lord of the houre, and take his testimony, as you did from the Lord of the terme of the ☽; behold also the application of the Lord of the Ascendant, unto the Lord of the terme of the ☽, or unto the Lord of the second House; or if that they apply unto him, for when he doth apply unto one of them, or to both, and the ☽ apply unto them both or to the Lord of the House, or if the ☉ doe apply unto the Lord of his House, and the ☽ be diminished in light; I meane if the

Lord of the House of the ☉, doe apply to the ☉; for the state of all these doe Signifie that the thing stole shall be found, and especially if the Planet *Signifier* be in an angle or succedant.

Also if the Lord of the terme of the ☽, or the Lord of the House of the ☽, or the Lord of the second house apply unto / the Lord of the Ascendant, the Master of the thing lost shall recover the same. Also if the ☽ or Lord of the Ascendant apply unto the Ascendant, or one of them apply unto the Lord of the second House, or unto the Lord of the terme of the ☽, the thing stolne shall be had againe through inquisition and diligent search.

And if the Lord of the House of the ☽, and the Lord of the Terme of the ☽ be both diminished in their motion or number, say the more part is lost and shall not be recovered.

If the Lord of the terme of the ☽, and the Lord of the house of the ☽ be increasing in number and motion, and safe from ill fortunes, the thing shall be restored whole and nothing diminished; for if those *Signifiers* be not Cadent from angles, it *Signifieth* the things shall be soon recovered; but is they be in angles, it *Signifieth* meanly, *viz.* neither very soone nor very late, *viz.* the recovery.

In what time it shall be recovered.

Behold the application of the two Planets that *Signifie* the recovery, and number the Degrees that are between them, or from the one to the other, and determine dayes, weekes, yeers, or houres, in this manner; Behold the place they are in, or the place of their application; for if they be in moveable Signes, the shorter time is required, or it shal be in weeks, or in months; in fixed Signes it *Signifies* Moneths or Yeers; in common Signs a meane betwixt both: helpe your selfe from these judgments: or if the *Significator* be quick in motion, they *Signifie* it shall be recovered quickly, or lightly: which *Significators*, if they be falling from angles, signifieth a time short, wherein the Goods shall be recovered: These Judgements are made properly for this Chapter; you must not judge in other things by these, or by this Method.

Aphorismes concerning Recovery.

The Lord of the eighth in the Ascendant, or with the Lord / thereof, signifies the recovery of the theft. The Lord of the second in the eighth, denieth recovery.

♄ also, or ♂, or ☋, signifieth dividing and losse of the thing, and that all shall not be recovered.

The Lord of the second in the Ascendant sheweth recovery.

The Lord of the Ascendant in the second, signifieth recovery after long search.

If the second House be hindered or the Lord thereof, it cannot be that all shall be found and recovered.

When the Lord of the Ascendant and the ☽; with the ☉, or the Lord of the tenth, or the Lord of the House of the ☽; or if the Lord of the seventh be with the Lord of the Ascendant, or have good aspect to him; or if the Lord of the seventh be in combustion; or at least the Lord of the tenth, and the Lord of the house of the ☽ agree well together, upon such a position it is probable the thing lost shall and may be recovered. When both the Luminaries are under the earth it cannot be recovered.

Whatsoever is lost, the ☉ together with the ☽, beholding the Ascendant cannot be lost but will, shortly be discovered.

Behold when the body of the ☽ and the body of the Lord of the Ascendant, *viz.* when one of them applyeth bodily to the Planet that signifieth recovery; the thing stolne shall then be recovered; and if the application of the Significators be by Retrogradation, the recovery shall bee sudden, if the application be by direction, the recovery shall be before it be looked for.

Behold also the Lord of the term of the ☽, if he do apply to the same term, and the Lord of the house of the ☽ applies to the same house, or when the Lord of the second applies to his own house: or when any of them apply to the Ascendant; all these do signify the time of recovery.

Look also if the ⊗ have any testimony with the Lord of the Ascendant, or with the ☽, because when any of them apply to each other, or the Lord of the house of the ☽ to the ☽, there is the time of the recovery in hope; and when the Lord of the ⊗ applyes to the Lord of the Ascendant, or to the second house, or unto the place in which the ⊗ is, or to the Moon; all these / signify recovery: Behold also how many degrees is from the planet which signifyeth recovery, unto the angle he goeth first to, and the number of those degrees is the time of recovery.

When both the lights behold themselves in angles, it signifies recovery of the thing at length, but with labour and pain; and it signifies more then one thief; if the aspect be a △, it signifyeth the lighter recovery.

The ☽ in the Ascendant with any Fortune, it signifies recovery: If the ☽ be in *sub radijs*, or combust, it signifieth the thing lost shall not be recovered, if it be, it shall be with much pain and labour; ☉ and ☽ in the tenth, sudden recovery.

If both ☉ and ☽ be nearer the Ascendant then any other angle, it signifyes recovery of the thing with much trouble, anxiety, strife, bloodshed, or quarrelling.

When ☉ is in the Ascendant, the thing stolen shall be recovered, except the Ascendant be ♎ or ♒; for therein the ☉ is weak. The ☽ in the Ascendant and ♃ with her, it shall be recovered.

Of the discovery of the thief, and recovery of the goods.

If the ☽ be in the Ascendant, or in a △ aspect to the Lord thereof, thou findest the thief.

If there be a △ aspect between ☉ and ☽, it signifies recovery. If ☉ and ☽ be joyned to the Lord of the seventh, or beholding him by aspect, he cannot hide himself.

If the Lord of the Ascendant apply to the second, or the Lord of the second to the Ascendant; if there be any application or translation of light between the Lord of the eighth, and the Lord of the second; or the Lord of the eighth be in the second, it signifyes recovery. ☽ in the second with one of the Fortunes, or applying with a good aspect to her own house, or the Lord of the sign wherein she is, sheweth recovery.

The chiefest signes of no recovery are if ♄, ♂ or ☋, be in the second, or the Lord of the second in the eighth, or combust, or when the Lord of the second applieth to the Lord of the eighth with any aspect, all or any of these are signes of no recovery. If the Lord of the second be in his exaltation, there is / a great hope of recovery, especially if there be any other testimony of the recovery.

Of Theft.

If the Lord of the seventh be in the Ascendant, the theft shall be restored againe; if the Lord of the Ascendant be in the seventh, it will be found after much enquiry; if ☽ be in the ascendant, or with the Lord of the ascendant, it will be found or may be found; if the ☽ be in the fift, with the Lord of the ascendant, it may be had; or if ☉ and ☽ be in the fift, and the Lord of the eighth be with the Lord of the ascendant in the ascendant, it will be found.

If the Lord of the second be in the eighth, it cannot be had; if Saturn or ♂ or ☋ be in the second, it will not be had; if the Lord of the second be in the ascendant, it will be had againe, and none shall know how; if the Lord of the ascendant be in the second, with great labour it may be had; if the Lord of the second be cadent, it will not be had; but if he be in his exaltation, it will be quickly restored; the sooner if ☽ apply unto him.

Other Judgments of Thefts.

Lord of the ascendant and Lord of the seventh joyned, it shall be got by searching of the *querent*.

Lord of the ascendant in the seventh, or the Lord of the ascendant joined to the Lord of the eighth, or Lord of the seventh in the ascendant, the Thief comes of his owne accord before he goes any farther; very many times I have found it so.

If ☽ be separated from the Lord of the ascendant, and be joyned to the Lord of the seventh, he shall be found, *viz.* the Thief.

The Lord of the seventh joyned to an *Infortune* in an angle, he shall be taken: the Lord of the seventh joyned to a Fortune, he shall not be taken, unlesse that Fortune be under the ☉ Beames, or impedited; if he goe to combustion, it signifies his death.

☽ joyned to an infortunate Planet, he shall be found; the ☽ joyned to a retrograde Planet, he returnes of his owne accord /, if he went; if the same Planet be stationary, he shall not remove from his owne place untill he be taken.

Whether the Thief shall be knowne or not.

Most Planets in cadents, he shall be knowne: ☉ Conjunct, □ or ☍ to the Significator of the Thief, knowne; ☉ in ✶ to him, he is suspected, but not openly knowne.

Whether the Thief be suspected of the Owner or not.

If the Thief be in □ or ☍ to the Lord of the ascendant he is suspected, a △ or ✶, not; if the Thieve's *Significator* be in ☌ with the ☽, the Owner suspecteth one with him, or using his owne company.

If the Moon be in □ or ☍ to any Planet in the tenth or seventh, say he suspecteth one far from him, except the *Almuten* of the tenth or seventh house be in □ or ☍ to the ☽.

If ☽ have ☌ □ or ☍ to a Planet in the seventh, or to the *Almuten* thereof, the Owner suspecteth him; but if ☽ aspecteth another Planet, he suspecteth another, and not the Thief: if the ☽ be joyned to, or received of an evill Planet, the suspected is the Thiefe; look to the Lord of the ascendant and the ☽, and take the strongest of them, who if he have received any vertue from evill Planets, *viz.* separated from them, he hath played the Thiefe; and so much the more being received of the Lord of the second: Lord of the ascendant in an angle, applying or separating to a Planet in a cadent house, truth is said of him; or ☽ conjoyned to a Planet in an angle, especially in the tenth, signifies the same.

Who did the Deed or Theft.

Lord of the ascendant in the second, or seventh, it is the Owner himselfe; or Lord of the second in the ascendant, the owner. If ☉ and ☽ be with the Lord of the 3ᵈ, it's Owner's Kinsman; ☉ and ☽ in the fourth, Father or Mother, or a Friend; ☉ or ☽ in the fift, a Sonne or Daughter of the Owner; ☉ or ☽ in the sixt, a Servant; ☉ or ☽ in the seventh his Wife or a Woman, /

☉ and ☽ together cojoyned, beholding the ascendant, the Owner's acquaintance; or if either of them behold the ascendant, *idem*.

☉ or ☽ in their proper houses, or in the ascendant, the Owner may be justly suspected.

If ☉ or ☽ be not together, but one of them behold the ascendant, it was one was borne, or formerly lived in the house where the robbery was done, If ☉ or ☽ be in their owne Triplicity, the Thief retaines him that lost the Goods; they having but a Face where they are, then he is not one of the house, but Kin unto him.

If ☉ or ☽ behold the ascendant, and not the Thief, the Thief entred not the house before he took it.

If the Thiefe have any great Dignities in the ascendant, the Thiefe is Kin to the *Querent*, or a very neer acquaintance.

♂ being *Significator* of the Thiefe, and placed in the tenth, the *querent* is the Thief, or very negligent.

The Lord of the seventh in the ascendant, he is suspected to be the Thiefe.

Whether it be the first fact the Thief hath committed.

If ☉ and ☽ doe behold the Lord of the house where the ☽ is from an angle, he hath plaid the Thiefe more then once. If ⊗ or Lord of the seventh be free from misfortunes, or ♃ *Significator* alone of the Thiefe, it is the first fact he hath committed.

♂ separating from the Lord of the seventh, or Saturn Orientall, it is not the first; ♂ *Significator*, he breaketh in*; ♀, under the cloak of love; Mercury, by subtilty and flattery.   **viz. by violence.*

Of Theft by Astrologie, or LILLIES best experienced Rules.

Many Thieves, if Peregrine Planets be in angles.

The Significator in a Signe of Fruitfulnesse, viz. ♋, ♏, ♓; or in a Bycoporeall, viz. Gemini, ♐, ♍, ♓; or beholding many peregrine Planets.

The angles fixed, or the ☽ or Significator in Signes of direct ascention which are ♋, ♌, ♌ ♍, ♎, ♏, ♐; or in Signes not fruitfull, viz. ♈, ♉, ♊, ♌, ♎, ♐, ♑ /.

The Sex.

Masculine, if the Lord of the hour, Lord of the seventh and his Dispositor be Masculine, or if the Dispositor of the Moon and the Planet to whom she applies be masculine; or if the *Significator* be in the part of Heaven, *viz.* in the first, twelfth, eleventh or seventh, sixt, fift, and Orientiall.

Feminine, if the contrary to this happen.

Age.

Old, or in yeers, the *Significator* being ♄.

A man, if ♃, ♂ or ☉.

Not so old, if ☿ or ♀ be *Significators*.

The ☽ for her age, *viz.* young, she in her first quarter; more man if in her second quarter; and so in her third quarter more aged; in her last quarter of greater yeers.

Where note, the ☽ or any Planet Orientall, denotes the Thief more young; Occidentall, more aged.

Or thus; observe in what house the *Significator* is in, give for every house five yeers from the ascendant.

Or observe the degree descending in the seventh house, and give for every degree two yeers.

Or see the age of the Planet to whom the ☽ applyes, or the *Significator* of the Thief, or consider the day of the moneth the Question is asked, give for every day elapsed to the day of the Question two yeers.

The best way, and most sure is, to consider most of these wayes, and pitch upon the greatest number.

Forme and Stature.

Proportion great, if the *Significator* have much Orientality, and be in ♌, ♏ or ♐.

Proportion little, if his Occidentality be much, or the *Significator* in ♋, ♏ or ♓.

The upper part of his body is thick and strong, if the *Significator* be in ♈, ♉, ♌; his lower parts if in ♐, ♊, ♏. /

Fat.

If the *significator* have much latitude from the *Ecliptick*, be Retrograde, or in his first station, or in the first part of ♈, ♉, ♌, or in the last part of ♊, ♏, ♐.

It's probable he inclines to talnesse, the ☽ in ♋ or ♐, ♎, ♍ or ♒ give fleshy bodies, and well proportioned.

Leane.

The *significator* having small latitude, or direct, or in his second station, or in the beginning of ♊, ♏, ♐, or in the summity of his Eccentricity.

☉ beholding the *Significator*, gives a handsome shape and fatnesse; the ☽ Beholding, gives temperature and moystnesse.

The Thiefs strength.

Significator in South Latitude, the party is nimble; in North latitude, slow in motion.

A Planet in his first station gives strong bodies; going out of one Signe into another, weak and feeble.

Where the Knave is.

He flyes, or is running out of one place into another, or removing his Lodging, if the *significators* be going out of one Signe into another; or if the *significator* be leaving combustion, or the Rayes of the ☉; or if the Thiefs Dispositor separate from the Lord of the first, and apply to a Planet in the sixt, eighth or twelft.

He flies, or is farre distant if the *significator* of the Thiefe and thing sought after be not in one quarter of heaven, or apply to the Lord of the third or ninth, or if the *significators* be in the third or ninth.

He remaines.

If the Lord of the first be joyned to a Planet in a cadent house, and behold the ascendant. /

Who the Thief is.

A Familiar if ☉ and ☽ at one time behold the ascendant, or if the Lord of the first be joyned to the Lord of the seventh in the ascendant.

Or if ☉ and ☽ be in ♌ or ♋, or in the ascendant it selfe, or in the house of the Lord of the ascendant, and beholding him, or the Lord of the seventh house in the twelft or eight, the ☉ or ☽ in their exaltation, note one well knowne, but not of the Family.

The *Luminaries* in their Termes or Faces, the party is known to some of the household, but not of the Family; Lord of the seventh in the seventh he is of the Household.

A Stranger.

If the Lord of the seventh be in the third or ninth from his house.

Lord of the ascendant and Lord of the seventh not if one Triplicity.

If you see the Thief is domesticall, then

☉ Signifies Father, or Master.

☽ The Mother, or Mistris.

♀ The Wife, or a Woman.

♄ A Servant, or a Stranger lying there by chance.

♂ A Son, or a Brother, or Kinsman.

☿ A Youth, Familiar or Friend.

Whither is the Thief gone, or Fugitive.

Where you are principally to observe, that the ascendant or a *significator* in the ascendant, signifieth the East; but this Table expresses the quarters of Heaven more fully.

First house East.
Second house Northeast by East.
Third house North Northeast.
Fourth house North.
Fift house Northwest by North.
Sixt house West, Northwest.

Seventh house West.
Eight house Southwest by South.
Ninth house South Southwest.
Tenth South.
Eleventh Southeast by South.
Twelft East, South-east.

The Signes.

Aries *East.*
Taurus *South and by East.*
Gemini *West and by South.*
Cancer *is full North.*
Leo *East and by North.*
Virgo *South and by West.*
Libra *full West.*
Scorpio *North and by East.*
Sagittarius *East and by South.*
Capricornus *full South.*
Aquarius *West and by North.*
Pisces *North and by West.*

♈ *East.*
♌ *Northeast by East.*
♋ *East Southeast.*
♎ *West.*
♊ *Southwest by West.*
♒ *West, Northwest.*
♋ *North.*
♏ *North, Northeast.*
♐ *Northwest by North.*
♑ *South.*
♉ *Southeast by South.*
♍ *South, Southeast.*

The flight of the Thiefe.

It's swift, if his *Significator* be swift in motion, or joyned to Planets swift in motion, or being himselfe in Signes movable or of short ascentions.

His flight is uncertaine.

If his or their *Significators* are in their second station, or joyned to stationary Planets in angles or succedants.

He makes slow haste.

If his *Significator* is slow in motion, or joyned to Planets of slow motion, or in Signes fixed or of long ascentions.

He shall be taken.

If the Lord of the ascendant be in the seventh, or in ☌ to the Lord of the seventh; or the Lord of the seventh in the first, or joyned to the Lord of the first, or a Retrograde Planet; or if the ☽ separate from the Lord of the seventh, to the ☌ of the Lord of the first; or from the ☌ of the Lord of the first to the Lord of the seventh; or if ☉ and ☽ be in ☌ with the Lord of the seventh, some day, if they behold him; or if the Lord of the seventh be going to ☌, *viz.* Combustion; or if the Lord of the ascendant be in ☌ in the ascendant, tenth or seventh, or an infortunate Planet in the seventh. /

Not Taken.

If the Lord of the seventh be in aspect with a *Fortune*, if in aspect to ♃ or ♀ in the eleventh, he escapes by friends; if in the third, by strangers.

The Goods restored.

If the Lord of the first and second are in ☌ with the Lord of the eight, or in any strong Reception:

Or if the Lord of the second depart from Combustion; or *Sol* or ☽ in the ascendant or tenth house, it notes recuperation; the most part, if they are strong; lesse, if they be weak.

There's hope of retribution when the Lights behold themselves with any aspect, chiefly in angles; or the Lord of the seventh or eighth.

No Restitution.

If the Lord of the second be Combust or the Lord of the seventh in ☌ with the Lord of the eight; or if the Lord of the second behold not the first house, or his Lord; or the *Sunne* and ☽ not aspecting themselves, or the ⊗, or when both are under the earth.

Other Rules that the Thiefe shall be taken.

☽ in the seventh, applying to the Lord of the eight.
Lord of the first in the ascendant.
☽ in the seventh applying to a □ of ♂.
☽ separating from a □ of Saturn or Mercury, applying to a □ of *Sol*.
☽ in the sixt, eighth or twelfth.
☽ Separating from a ☌ of ♄, applying to a □ of ☿, Lord of the seventh in the first.
☽ in the eight, in ☍ to ♂ in the second. [Lilly 1985: 319-366]

All this for one particular query – it shows why it was said that learning horary astrology first would prepare someone for any other use of the art. While Lilly's work was certainly a valuable encyclopedic reference, it presented an imposing learning curve to the novice. One of the earlier publications in the astrological revival by the anonymous "C. Heydon, jun. Astro-philo.", is a better example of the sort of primer that Cunning Folk would find useful. "C. Heydon's" *The New Astrology* (1786) is a small duodecimo book of 188 pages which offers a concise introduction to astrological computation and interpretation. His overview of horary astrology appears to be quite adequate and sensible, especially when compared to that of "Raphael's" *Manual of Astrology*, which will be considered later.

Of the Art of resolving Horary Questions.

ALL enquiries that are serious, and of some importance, that come under the name of Horary Questions, must necessarily relate either to things *past, present,* or *to come,* or to concerns that *once were, now are,* or *may be hereafter*; and the answer to such questions must be either *essential* or *accidental*: The essential answer is always one of the three following, concerning which the enquiry is made; 1st, *To be, or not to be?* 2dly, either good or evil; 3dly either true or false: Therefore, if the question is real, and the matter rightly stated, the true answer, which is always short, will be easily discovered by the following rules:

The Accidental Answer is that which appertains to the accidents of the business in hand, and is always defined by *where, when, how,* and *why*; and whoever attempts to extend his judgment beyond these limits, strains art beyond its bounds: by this /means many pretenders to Astrology fail shamefully in their undertakings. To avoid which, let the following Queries be attended to.

The consideration of the matter proposed is taken from that house which has relation to and signification of the same; and this signification is either *simple* or *compound*. The *simple* signification of the houses is that which hath relation singly to the person or the querent. *Compound* signification is that which hath relation to the matter, or quesited. The *Querent* is he or she that asks the question. The matter, or quesited, is that about which the question is proposed. The *simple* signification of the houses is as follows: —The 1st house signifies the querent's life and person; the 2d house his substance; the 3d his kindred, neighbors, and short journies; the 4th his grave, father, and the lands; the 5th his pleasures and offspring; the 6th his sickness, servants, and small cattle; the 7th his wife, public enemies, and lawsuits; the 8th his death and legacies; the 9th his religion, long voyages, and learning; the 10th his mother, trade, and honour; the 11th his friends and hopes; the 12th his private enemies, great cattle, imprisonment, and crosses. The *compound* signification is derived from the *simple*, by considering what house, that is, which signifies the / matter or quesited, and accounting that, be it whatsoever it may, the 1st house or Ascendant; and so ascribing the signification of the 1st house of the figure to it; doing in like manner to all the other houses in order: so that, if a question relate to a brother or relation, the 3d house is then his Ascendant or 1st house, and signifies his life and person; the 4th house (which in this case is his 2d) his substance or estate; the 5th house his 3d, his relations and short journies; the 6th his 4th house, his father; the 7th, his children; the 8th, his sickness; the 9th, his wife, &c. and the same of all others. These things being laid as a foundation, we come now to shew the perfection of the matter by the different affections of the Aspects.

QUERY 1. *Is the subject of enquiry,* To be or Not to be?

The first thing to be attended to, is the destruction or perfection of every matter under consideration. The completion or perfection of the subject of enquiry may be affected several ways, viz. by the *application, translation, reception,* and *position,* of the planets; and these are determined by the respective significators of the subject of enquiry; which are, 1st, the Lords of those Houses which / relate to the matter in hand; 2dly, planets near the cusps of those house; 3dly, planets exalted or dignified therein; and, 4thly, the consignificators of those houses; which we have described before, in the significators of the Twelve Houses. The Lords of the Houses are those planets which are Lords of the signs that happen to fall on the cusps of the houses, as shewn before, and may be seen in the Table of the Planets Houses. From hence it appears, that each house has a primary and second consignificator; the first whereof arises from the order of the planets, the other from the order of the signs; as the 1st house or ascendant, Saturn or Mars; that is, Saturn and Aries; and so on, &c.

The Ascendant, his Lord, and the Moon, are to signify the querent; and that house and his lord to which the question belongs, to signify the quesited: then consider what *application* is between the *significators:* if they apply to a conjunction, in angles, swift in motion in any of their essential dignities, it shews the matter enquired after will be brought to perfection speedily; if in succedent houses, not so soon; if in cadent houses, with much loss of time.

When the significators apply by sextile or trine, from good houses, and they in any of their essential / dignities, and free from the evil rays of the Infortunes, it is an argument the matter will soon be completed. If the significators apply by a quartile aspect, in good houses, and they be in their essential dignities, it shews the thing enquired after will be brought to perfection sometimes when the significators are in *opposition,* but this happens when the significators are in mutual *reception* by houses; but if it is completed, it is with much trouble and anxiety, and the querent will be sorry he sought after it. Matters are brought to *perfection* by *translation* of light and virtue, when the significators do not behold each other each other, but some lighter planet separateth himself from the one significator which he was in mutual *reception* with, and then applies to the other significator before he comes to the body or aspect of another planet; and you may judge the thing enquired after will be brought to perfection by such a planet as that planet signifies which thus translates the light and virtue of one significator to the other.

The subject of enquiry may be brought to perfection by *position;* that is, when the significator of the thing is posited in the Ascendant, or if the Lord of the Ascendant be posited in the house of the quesited; but this single testimony seldom perfect the business, without some of the aforesaid arguments happen, or the two significators cast their several aspects to some more weighty planet than themselves, whom they are both in reception with, and then the person signified by that planet who collects both their lights may bring it to perfection.

QUERY 2. *What shall be the destruction or hindrance of a matter enquired after?*

The thing enquired after is destroyed by Prohibition, Frustration, Refranation, Aspect, Separation, Translation, and Combustion; for which please refer to the technical terms used in Astrology, where a full definition is given of them. Any of these is sufficient to destroy the matter, more especially if some or all of these significators happen to be in fixed signs, and in a cadent or succedent house.

For instance: when you find the significators applying to conjunction or aspect, and before they come to their partile aspect some other planet comes to the conjunction or aspect of one of the significators, and that planet hinders the thing from being brought to perfection; consider the nature of that planet; also what house he is lord of; from hence you may know what person will / be the hindrance. If it be the Lord of the third, it shews some neighbour, brother, &c. if it be the Lord of the 4th, the querent's father, &c. will be the hindrance, or impediting planet. Also, when the significators apply by body or aspect, and before they come to their partile aspect one of the significators falls retrograde, and so prevents the completion of the thing enquired after, if the Lord of the Ascendant falls retrograde, the querent will hardly proceed any further.

Combustion, or the conjunction of the Sun, is the greatest affliction of all. Separation is when the significators of the querent have lately been in aspect, and are newly or just separated, though never so little; and this denotes the full and entire destruction of the matter; which we seldom or ever find to fail.

QUERY 3. *Is the matter* good *or* evil?

Consider the house to which the thing belongs, its Lord, and planets therein; and the house signifying the matter of the end, its Lord, and planets therein; and if the house signifying the thing be fortified by the presence or beams of good planets, or if the Dragon's-head be there, it shews good; but the contrary, evil. /

QUERY 4. *Is the report* true *or* false?

If any planet be in the house signifying the matter concerning which the report is, or the Dragon's-head be there, or the Lord of the same house be angular, or in conjunction or aspect of any planet, the matter or report is true: but if the report was good, and the said significator or planet posited in the said house be retrograde, slow, combust, or peregrine, or in evil aspect of a more weighty planet, or cadent, or in conjunction with the Dragon's-tail, or the Dragon's-tail posited in the said house, it certainly signifies the report is false; and so contrarywise. The Moon angular generally signifies the report to be true, if the report be evil, especially if she be in evil aspect; or if good, if she be in good aspect of the benevolent. The Moon in a fixed sign, and in conjunction with the Dragon's-head, shews truth; but moveable, void of course, and in conjunction with the Dragon's-tail, falsehood. Hitherto of the essential answer of a question; we now come to the accidental.

QUERY 5. *Where or which way?*

Wherever the significator is, there is the thing. The house where he is posited shews the quarter of Heaven, or the point of the compass, which way the thing may be. If the house and sign agree, this judgment is the more firm; if they disagree, / consider the position of the Moon, and with what she agrees most, and give judgement from her. If the Moon agrees neither with the sign nor house in which the significator is posited, then consider the Part of Fortune in the same manner as you considered the Moon, and judge accordingly. If this answer not, consider the Disposer of the Part of Fortune.

The distance is discovered from the proximity of the significators to body or aspect, considered as they may happen to be either *angular, succedent,* or *cadent*; respect being had to their latitude, whether little or great, North or South. Great latitude shews obscurity and great difficulty in finding what is sought for; if North latitude, difficulty only, not impossibility; but if South, then all the labour of seeking is in vain, unless the significators be angular, and in near aspect. *Angles* signify nearness; *succedents,* farther off; *cadents,* beyond all imagination. The signficator *angular* and without latitude, shews some paces; if North latitude, shews some furlongs; if South, some miles distant. The significator *succedent*, and without latitude, shews some furlongs; if it hath North latitude, some miles; if South, some leagues. If *cadent*, and without latitude, shews some miles; North latitude, some leagues; South, some / degreees. These rules are to be considered chiefly in things that have life. If it be required to know the number of paces, furlongs, miles, leagues or degrees distance, consider the number of degrees and minutes between the body or aspect of the significator; and according to the number of degrees which are between the conjunction, sextile, quartile, trine, or opposition, so many paces, furlongs, miles, leagues or degrees, is the thing sought after distant from the place from whence it was lost; or from the person making enquiry; and so many minutes as adhere to the degrees, so many 60th parts of the same denomination of the measure which one degree signifieth is to be accounted and added to the former number.

QUERY 6. *When or in what time?*

The limitation of time is taken either by house or sign, or by aspect. If the significator hath latitude, the measure of time hath its limitation from house and sign. Whether things are to be brought to pass or destroyed, the time, if it be signified by house and sign, must be considered, as the significator is angular, succedent, or cadent—having *moveable, fixed*, or common signs. Angles signify suddenly; succedents, long time, and with much difficulty; cadents, scarcely at all, or with vexation. Angles signify, if the have moveable / signs, some days; if common signs, long weeks; and if fixed signs, some months. Succedent signify, if moveable, some months; common signs, some years; and if fixed signs, when all hopes are past, if at all. If you desire to know the numbers of days, weeks, months, or years, consider the degrees and minutes between the body or aspect of the significator; and according to the number of degrees which are between their conjunction, sextile, quartile, trine or opposition, so many days, weeks, months, or years, shall it be before the matter is accomplished or destroyed. Great S. latitude often prolongs the time; N. latitude often cuts it off shorter; but if the significators have no latitude, the exact time is made simply by the aspects. The time significators meet is found in the Ephemeris.

QUERY 7. *How or why?*

The planets which make the prohibition or frustration are the hurting, impeding planets; that is, the planets that signify him or her, or that thing, which shall hinder the business; which we have treated of before: and observe, lastly, that whatsoever has been said of the impeding or hindering planet, the same holds good of the adjuvant or helping planet. /

General Rules to know if a Question is radical, or fit to be judged,

Before you give judgement upon your figure, you ought to consider whether the figure erected is radical or fit for judgement, lest the querent come purposely to abuse you, for the discovery of which the ancients have left us the following Rules:

1st. if you find the Lord of the House and Lord of the Ascendant of one and the same Triplicity, or when the Lord of the hour and the sign ascending shall be of one triplicity, the question is then radical, and fit to be judged.

If the sign and the planet in the ascendant describe the person of the querent, the question is radical, and fit to be judged; but if either the very beginning or extreme end only of a sign ascend, it will not be proper to give judgement; it denotes the question has been proposed merely out of ridicule. This rule I have often verified in practice. The same thing is indicated by the quartile or opposition of the Moon with the Lord of the 7th, or by the Moon being void of course, or combust; which position denotes the question improperly stated, Saturn in the / Ascendant, impeded or afflicted, shews the question proposed either false, or the subject past hope; and whenever the Lord of the Ascendant is combust, or retrograde, it implies the same thing. The Artist must always judge by the greater testimonies; but if the significators are found especially strong set and against the matter, it is better to defer judgement to a future time. ("C. Heydon" 1786: 106-118)

The revival of astrology resulted in a new factor in which the art was represented in magazines and journals. The first of these, the *Conjuror's Magazine*, ran from 1791 to 1793. Astrology became such a major theme of its articles that it changed its name in August 1793 to the *Astrologer's Magazine* and ran for six more issues. John Corfield published his self-produced *The Urania, or, the Philosophical and Scientific Magazine* in 1814. Another short-lived attempt was the *Spirit of Partridge* (Aug. 5, 1824-Jan 15, 1825), and of course, there were "Raphael's" weekly *The Straggling Astrologer* (1824) and the monthly *Urania; or, the Astrologer's Chronicle, and Mystical Magazine* (1825); the unsold sheets of which became the book *The Astrologer of the Nineteenth Century* (1825). In 1845, E. L. Blanchard published his *The Astrologer and Oracle of Destiny* in which he offered to respond to mailed horary inquiries for free (to avoid prosecution and secure readership). This example is the first in his series of replies, which had grown considerably in length by the time the paper folded.

The Oracle of Destiny.

In which all Questions from Correspondents are answered gratuitously in accordance with the true and unerring principles of Astrological Science.

To our Querists – this department of our work involves the solution of "horary questions," so called from a figure of the heavens being erected for the hour in which the question is asked, and from the indications manifest in which the corresponding answers are derived. It will, therefore, be absolutely necessary for all correspondents to *specify the exact hour and day* on which they commit the question to paper for our judgment, and the replies will then be given accordingly. As this important feature of the starry science will necessarily occupy considerable time which he is willing to devote without reward to benefit the public, THE ASTROLOGER hopes that the liberality of his offer will protect him from the correspondence of those who desire adjudication upon frivolous subjects, or who are merely actuated thereto by motives of idle and foolish curiosity. All subjects on which they may be *really serious*, can be solved with absolute certainty; and the election of favourable periods for marriage, speculation, or commencing any new undertaking with advantage, will be carefully and readily pointed out from week to week. All communications addressed to "THE ASTROLOGER" will be considered as strictly confidential, and the initials only given in the Oracle.

TO CORRESPONDENTS.

G. R. – The constellation *Ursa Major* is now on the meridian at midnight Any modern treatise on astronomy will give you the position of the stars, but a celestial globe is best adapted for the calculations he requires.

E. R. S. – Mars is now in his own sign of Scorpio. We would advise him to select the 26th day for the enterprise he mentions.

VINCENT. – An article on Palmistry, or the art of divining by the lines of the hand, will appear forthwith.

S. H. – We are open to the contributions of those who have proof to adduce of the influence of the stars, and shall be happy to afford room to the lucubration of our correspondents.

W. K. – Yes, there are professors of Astrology in the University of Cambridge, at this moment.

L. L. – We have erected a figure for the time mentioned by our correspondent, and find the querent is now environed by circumstances of doubt and difficulty, His genius appears decidedly adapted to mechanical pursuits, and moderate success is indicated. The party inquired after is deceptive, though with no evil intention; he will soon be embarrassed in pecuniary matters. The indications in the seventh house are very singular, and seem to show this is not the first time he has been engaged in adventures of this kind. There is one, however, who is endeavouring to supplant the querent, and who will eventually prove a dangerous rival. The crises will be in a fortnight—wait that time and then communicate again.

ROSE. – Your lover is not the faithless swain you imagine. Under the guise of friendship your confidence has been abused.

S. S., W. R., MASK, &c. – We cannot undertake private correspondence, except under circumstances of a peculiar nature. The time of committing the questions to paper should be exact to the minute, as the Astrologer has afterwards to correct it to astronomical time. It would trespass less upon our space if *one* question only were given us by each querent to answer in each number, as always preserving the figure we can make reference again.

GEORGIUS. – Let our correspondent extend the circulation of our work by recommendation to his friends, and he will best advance the interests of our publisher. The Astrologer reaps his reward in the continual proofs of that truth for the advancement of which he labours.

E. B. (Soho), who has forwarded the nativities of himself and family, must allow us a few days to give our judgments thereon. It is gratifying indeed to find the art studied by those who have perhaps less time for contemplation than the arrogant philosophers of the day, who refuse to examine aught that is not reducible to the elements of matter.

INQUIRENDO. – You will speedily, through a friend, inducted to a mechanical pursuit which will, with perseverance, extricate you from the presen[t] difficulties. There is, in this scheme we have erected, an indication of former extravagance, if not dissipation. Is this so?

A STUDENT. – The figure is not sufficiently perfected to enable us to give a decision. For back numbers of the Ephemeris write to Mr. John Lyon, 13, Humber Dock Street, Hull, who had, and doubtless still has, a complete set.

H. P. (Ely). – You have trafficked heretofore in the produce of the earth, do not hastily reject what has been profitable to your health, though it has not to your purse. Avoid dealing in metals. Should you desire further advice write again; we cannot spare time always for personal consultation.

J. C. S. – Your unhappy malady requires the judgment of a physician rather that of an astrologer. We can see no prospect of relief.

J. P. – You are too young, Read and learn.

J. C. (Somers Town). – Answered as wished.

E. W. H. (Kennington). – The Astrologer will give an outline of the judgment, if the time of birth be stated.

JOSEPHUF. – Fear not; you will speedily recover.

J. W. (Norwich). – You and your brother have not long to suffer. A termination is indicated shortly.

LA MERE. – Could we communicate privately with our correspondent? The scheme of the hour has unfolded some strange disclosures. When we see the fond, affectionate and romantic girl, still surrounded by the singular fatalities which have pursued her through life, we feel anxious to caution her against those to come. You have one link to bind you to your husband's heart, but the love of THE PAST is not yet extinct. You are still thought of at *midnight*.

"ANXIETY." – So courteous a querist need not fear trespassing. Your life, indeed, has been a chequered one. A gleam of good fortune appears upon the horizon of your destiny which should be manifest in a fortnight—Wait that time, and then write again. (*The Astrologer and The Oracle of Destiny*. No. 2, Vol. 1, (Feb. 22, 1845), p. 16.)

Other astrologers took advantage of the 1840 postal reform to answer questions by mail for the same reason, including Dr. William Simmonite, who published several astrological periodicals and also one of the few serious contemporary works on the horary art, *The Prognostic Astronomer: or, Horary Astrology* (1851).

I will end this chapter with three examples of horary charts or figures from William Lilly (on his stolen fish), "C. Heydon, jun." (on virginity), and "Raphael" on horary questions in general. Raphael's other horary examples were on the destiny of the then new London Bridge (it fails to predict the wholesale moving of the bridge to Lake Havasu City, *Arizona, in the 1960s*) and the success of the *Manual of Astrology* itself (!).

CHAP. LIV.
Fish stolen.

LIving in the Country 1637. I had bought at London some Fish for my provision in Lent, it came down by the Barge at *Walton*, on Saturday the 10. of *Febr.* one of [t]he Watermen, instead of bringing my Fish home, acquainted me, their warehouse was robbed last night, and my Fish stolen: I took the exact time when I first heard the report, and erected the Figure accordingly, endeavouring to give my selfe satisfaction what became of my goods, and, of possible, to recover part or all of them againe.

I first observed, there was no peregrine Planet in angle but ♃ whom I found upon the cusp of the seventh house, the thing I lost was Fish, therefore any Gentleman would scorne such a course Commodity: I considered the signification of ♃ in ♏, a moyst Signe, and the *Significator* of my Goods, *viz.* ☿ that he was in ♓, a moyst Signe, and that ⊗ was in ♋, a moyst Signe. Discretion, together with Art, assisted me to think he must be a man whose profession or calling was to live upon the Water, that had my Goods, and that they were in some moyst place, or in some low rooms, because ⊗ was in ♋, and the ☽ in ♉ an earthly Sign. /

I was confident I should heare of my Goods againe, because ☿ Lord of my house of Substance, was applyed unto by a ✳ of ☽, who was Lady of my ⊗; and yet without hopes of recovering them, but as he was in his own Termes, and had a △ aspect to ⊗, there was hopes of some of my Goods.

There being never a Waterman in that Town of *Walton* neer unto the description of ♃ in ♏, I examined what Fisherman there was of that complexion; and because ♂ Lord of the 7th was departing the Sign ♏, *viz.* his owne, and entring another Signe, I examined if never a Fisherman of ♂ and ♃ his nature had lately sold any Land, or was leaving his proper house, and going to another habitation; such a one I descovered, and that he was much suspected of theevery, who was a good fellow, lived neer the *Thames* side, and was a meer Fisherman, or man conversant in water; for all *Significators* in watry Signes, argued, he must needs live neer the water, or a watry place, that stole the Goods, or be much conversant in waters,

The man that was the Thiefe was a Fisherman, of good stature, thick, full bodied, faire of complexion, a red or yellowish haire.

I procured a Warrent from a Justice of Peace, and reserved it privately untill Sunday the eighteenth of February following, and then with a Constable and the Barge-man, I searched only that one house of this Fisherman suspected; I found part of my Fish in water, part eaten, part not consumed, all confessed. This jest happened in the search; a part of my Fish being in a bag, it happened the Thiefe stole the bag as well as the Fish; the Barge-man, whose sack it was, being in the same room where the bag was, and oft looking upon it (being clean washed) said to the woman of the house, Woman, so I may have my sack which I lost that night, I care not: the Woman answered; she had never a sack but that which her husband brought home the same night as the Fish. I am perswaded the Barge-man looked upon the sack twenty times before, and knew it not, for the woman had washed it cleane: I as heavily complained to the woman for seven *Portugall Onyons* which I lost; she not knowing what they were, made pottage with them, as she said. / The remainder of my Fish I freely remitted, though the hireling Priest of *Walton* affirmed I had satisfaction for it, but he never hurt himselfe with a lye.

So that you see the peregrine Planet in an angle describes the Thiefe, and that either the ☉ or ☽ in the ascendant, and in essentiall Dignities, gives assured hopes of discovering who it was; the application of ☽ to the Lord of the second, argues recovery; a full recovery, if both the ☽ and the Lord of the second be essentially dignified; part, if accidentally fortified; a discovery, but no recovery, if they apply and be both peregrine. (Lilly 1985: 397-399)

QUESTION 3. *Is she a Maid or Virgin that asks a Question?*

My Professional Friend had a desire to know, if the young woman that lately came to him about some business, was a maid or not. He erected the following figure for that purpose. I have inserted this, because it is a nice figure. In some we may see quite evidently if they are maids or debauched.

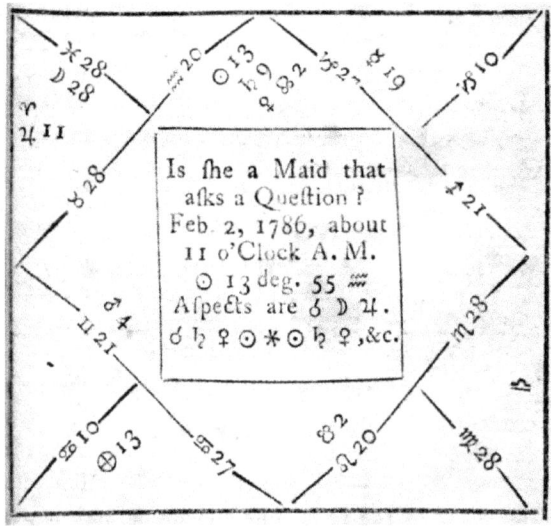

This figure was erected 10 min. before Eleven o'Clock, or 22h. 50 min. past Noon. /
I observe, that an astrological hour or day begins at noon, and ends the next day at noon.

First, I consider if ♀ Lord of the Ascendant in ♒ describes her, or the sign ascending. I find that Venus in Aquarius exactly represents the young woman; she being handsome, of a well-shaped body, an excellent complexion, good-natured, and full of vivacity. ♀ in a fixed sign, her 1st; Venus, Lord of Taurus, is fixed also; both these testimonies assure me she is chaste, she is ☌ with ♄ ☉ in the 10th; suppose her to be a servant belonging to a person of fashion; and ♀, her significator, is Lord of almost all the 6th House; ⊕ is cadent, disposed of by ☽, who is cadent also' which confirms me in it.

I find many planets angular, and her significator with that noble Monarch of Heaven, Sol; ☿ also in his own term, and ♃ both in his own House and Triplicity. These are all testimonies of virtue.

She has not had any child; ♌ occupies the cusp of her 5th House, but that she has had great trials for her honour, is indicated by ☋ being near the cusp of the 5th; and ♀ being in conjunction with ♄, Lord of the 10th, undoubtedly I think was with her master she lived with. After weighing the above I pronounced her an honourable and handsome virgin. /

Had the Lord of the Ascendant been with moveable or common signs, or a fruitful sign on the 5th, or ♀ in the 5th, in evil aspect to Infortunes, I should have deemed her lewd and unchaste. ☉ in the 7th is a certain proof of a woman's chastity or constancy to one man; because the Sun is sole Lord of the Heavenly Spheres. This reason always holds good. One great thing in this woman's favour, is, Mars, Lord of the 7th in the 1st: let her marry when she will, she will not defile her marriage bed. ("C. Heydon" 1786: 160-163)

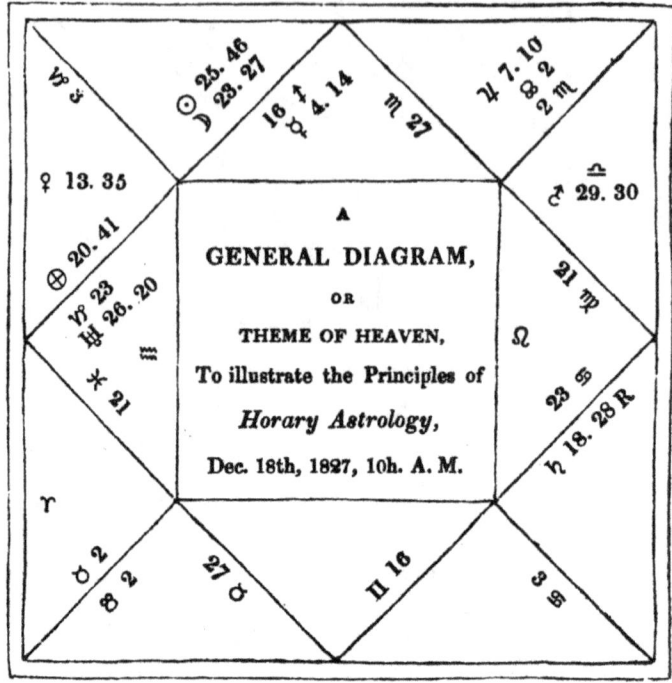

☽ ab quintilo ♃ ad ☌ ☉, and each to a ✶ ♂.

In the foregoing diagram, the sign ♃ ascending, is the sign given to the *querent* or enquirer, *and as* ♄ *rules that sign, he is under the influences of that planet at the time he proposes the question.* In a general way the lord of the ascendant being retrograde in ♋, the sign of his detriment in the sixth house, denotes indisposition, sickness, and great anxiety respecting servants; ♃ and ♂ denotes his *pecuniary* resources, as ruling the second / house; ♃, the former of these planets being in the ninth house free of any evil configuration, would denote a *respectable* person, and one whose resources were sufficient to meet his wants; but ♂, the latter significator, being in the eighth house opposite to the second, and disposed of by ♀ lady of the third house, who is found in the twelfth, portends anxiety and temporary vexation concerning the money, or well being of his kindred, with expenditure in short journeys, but gain in merchandise as ♃ ruler of the tenth house is found in the ninth, and bears rule in the house of wealth.—The ☌ of the ☉ and ☽ in the eleventh house denotes trouble and vexation by means of a public opponent, or a law-suit; wherein, as these planets are each disposed of by ♃ the lord of the eleventh house, and *he* in the ninth, it promises a fair stout person from a great distance (and a religious generous person) will be an active *friend*; while ♄ ruling the twelfth house, denotes his *private* enemies to be in his own power; and ♃ ruling the second, indicates the means *why*, namely by the means of his large pecuniary resources. — ☿, lord of the fourth house in the tenth, *separating* from a sesquiquadrate ray of ♄ and *applying* to his bi-quintile, indicates some transaction relating to the purchase of lands or houses, and a change of residence as naturally to be expected. ♀ in the twelfth house and ruling the eighth, denotes the death of a female relative as approaching, and by the measure of time already given, it may take place *in about five months*, accounting from the time for which the figure is calculated. (The same thing is shewn by the ☋ in the third house to those who believe in *its* efficacy.) In the *accidental* significations (see page 109) ♄ in the sixth house denotes the death of a friend; and the planet ♅ in the ascendant foreshows many strange unexpected occurrences, rather vexatious, as about speedily to happen.—In *particular* questions—

Were the query concerning money *generally*, it is favourable. Were it concerning the expected *receipt* of money, it is against it, as ♃ forms no aspects but in the △ of ♄; and before he meets the △, ♀ interposes her ☍ to ♄ and thereby *prohibits* the affair, or at least hinders it for a very long space of time. The ☍ of ♄ and ♀ also denotes a cessation of friendship between / a near relation and the party enquiring, with evil intelligence by letters; and spiteful neighbours.

Were the query respecting the obtaining *trade* or profession, c. ☿ angular, in semisextile to ♃ denotes money to be requisite in the affair, and by *such* means it might be obtained; as ☿ is bi-quintile to ♄, and ♃ rules the eleventh house.

Were the query concerning the probable success in a *law-suit*, the querent would lose the day, or have to *pay* money, as ♂ the lord of the second house is in the house of his opponent's wealth, and ♀ ruling the house is in *his* twelfth house.—But the adversary would also be near ruin, owing to the position of the luminaries in the eleventh house, and ♂ accidentally *in* the opponent's second.

Were it concerning a *duel*, the challenging party would be killed, as the ☌ of ☉ and ☽ would be fatal, added to ♄ in the sixth and ♂ in the eighth house, or house of mortality.

Were it concerning *marriage*, no marriage would take place, as sickness or death would prevent it.—♄ ruling the ascendant, being in the house of sickness and the ☽ *combust*, which signifies infinite vexation and defection of friends, from the houses these planets rule.

Were it concerning *children*, ☿ angular in ♊ a bi-coporeal sign and ♃ in ♏ a fruitful sign, denotes a large family of both sexes; several of whom would be great travellers, but deaths and sickness in such a family would be probable.

Were the question concerning *short* journeys, ♀ going to the ☍ of ♄, denotes all possible misfortune therein, and sickness to the wife (if married) while absent.

If of *long* journeys partial gain would acrue, as ♃ is in the ninth house, but *a* death would cause the querent to speedily return, as ♄ is retrograde and ♂ ruling the ninth house in the house of death.

Were the question of the general *state of life*, ♄ in the sixth house denotes sickness by violent colds, danger by water, but long life in the end; as ♃ and ♄ meet by △ aspect before they quite the sign—this is seen by the Ephemeris; yet ♀ meeting the ☍ an evil aspect *first*, denotes great and lasting troubles, and fear of imprisonment or great scandal though a female / neighbour; but ☿ angular, is a testimony of his being led to expect an active, public life, yet but few real friends.

In this symbolic system of judgement, where events are *indicated* (not caused strictly speaking,) *the lords of each house* being directed longitudinally, or by their motion in the zodiac, void of latitude and the arcs equated by the measure of time, … will also show the various events that will happen: thus for instance, ♂, lord of the second house, is going in the next sign to a ☌ of ♃, a fortunate star; this aspect being about 7 ¾ degrees distant, denotes some particular gainful event, (unexpected at the time of the figure being set) in about 7 ¾ weeks time, and partly by means of a friend.— ♄ approaching a retrograde △ of ♃ being nearly eleven degrees distant, denotes the same thing in about eleven months reckoned from the time of the figure was cast; but previous to this his ☍ to ♀ as before said, acts powerfully in evil.

In all cases, the student will bear this in mind; that the horary system of judicial Astrology presumes *the end or final issue of every contingency may be foreseen, either by a figure erected for the occasion by one whose mind is interested and anxious therein, or by casting a figure for the exact time of its commencement;* and this rule holds good in every undertaking; as a few examples which we will give will illustrate. (Raphael 1837: 210-212)

CHAPTER 13:

Conjuration, Part I

One image that stands out above all others in the depiction of magic is of the wizard or witch standing within a magic circle and brandishing a sword or wand, conjuring up spirits from the vasty deep. The ability to summon aid from the Invisible World was the acme of the magical art, promising direct access to preternatural power and knowledge. Difficult, dangerous, and potentially damnable as it was, traffic with spiritual beings and intelligences, whether angelic, demonic or "other" (nature spirits, fairies and the dead) was what set the conjuror apart from other mortals.

There were two primary reasons for such communication; theurgic quests for spiritual elevation, divine visions and higher knowledge, or, securing spiritual aid for more mundane purposes such as treasure hunting, sex, divination or revenge. The forbidden application of "addressive magic", i.e., the contact of intelligent angelic and demonic spiritual beings to realize personal desires rather than salvation and divine knowledge, resulted in the composition of texts of magical invocation we now know as "grimoires". Theurgic or ceremonial magic of the sort derived from Renaissance Hermeticism and Neo-Platonism, is not part of this survey – it was something few Cunning Men or Wise Women chose to engage in, not having a philosophical interest in such things. Similarly, the rituals of image magic such as the *Ars Notoria* that were used to directly impart knowledge and improve mental acuity are not likely to have been part of the Cunning Folks' repertoire. However, some did employ conjurations for pragmatic purposes, using the complex rituals, special tools and elaborate preparations of the medieval magus for their clients' benefit.

It could be argued that anyone who was skilled in the complex and demanding arcane arts, such as the invocation of spirits or professional astrology, shouldn't be classified as a folk magician at all. However, conjuring "Cunning Folk" such as William Lilly and Simon Forman – or Wise Woman Mary Parish[92] – differed from learned adepts such as John Dee, Elias Ashmole and Dr. Rudd not so much in ability and knowledge as that they worked for paying clients rather than for their own edification. The most accomplished Cunning Men came from humble origins and had irregular educations at best yet they still attained proficiency in magical arts equal to that of far more educated and wealthier hermeticists and magi.

Christian ritual magic, or the "necromancy" of the grimoires, developed in the 13th and 14th centuries out of a blending of astral magic and the rituals of exorcism. "The former is a foreign import, derived from Islamic culture; the latter is essentially a domestic product, long established within Christendom, though there is reason to suspect the influence of Jewish tradition in the development of this component." (Kieckhefer 1989: 165) There were obvious similarities with pre-Christian Greek and Egyptian or Coptic Christian magic as well, involving magical circles, wands and swords, sigils and "barbaric" names that appear to have been reintroduced into European magic during the "twelfth century renaissance" from Arabic and Jewish sources, although some may have been long preserved in the shadowy courtly and clerical *demimondes*. There is nothing involved in conjuration that did not have an equivalent in the magical practices of pagan antiquity, but by the 14th century all had been "Christianized", just as earlier sacred sites had been occupied by Christian churches. The magicians of the Middle Ages rationalized their activity by the promise Christ made, "And whatever you ask in My name, that I will do, that the Father may be glorified in the Son. If you ask anything in My name, I will do it." (*John* 14:13-14). It is for that reason that the key to understanding the late Medieval art of

---

[92] Mary Tomson Boucher Lawrence Parish (1630-1703) had a rather amazing career as a Wise Woman, which involved astrology, alchemy, conjuring for treasure, necromancy, healing and making talismans, plus conferring with angels and the Queen of the Fairies; all of which she confided to her influential "patron" Goodwin Wharton (1653-1704) during a magical relationship that survived for twenty years. See J. Kent Clark. *Goodwin Wharton*. New York: Oxford University Press, 1984, and Chapter 15 on Treasure Hunting, below.

conjuration is the Church's own rites for dealing with spirits, whereby the ritual of exorcism provided the precedent and rationale for illicit Christian magic.

Until the 12th century, banishing demons had been a fairly simple practice, requiring only a saintly relic, holy water (itself produced with a basic exorcist formula) and perhaps the simple exorcism included in the liturgy of baptism. Subsequently, however, cases of demonic attack seemed to have not only greatly increased in number and severity, but the demons had also apparently developed an immunity to simple prayers and relics. Stronger spiritual sanctions were sought that could coerce the most powerful and stubborn demon into submission. Exorcists began to experiment with longer and more elaborate rites, taking note which elements worked and which did not. Biblical extracts were multiplied, prayers heaped upon prayers and ever more imperious commands employed. The most successful versions of the rituals were compiled into manuals of exorcism, for although all exorcisms followed a similar formula, there was no single official Catholic version before 1614, while the Anglican Church omitted even baptismal exorcism from the liturgy in 1552.

In fact, it was not necessary to be an ordained priest to perform exorcisms. Christian doctrine technically allowed anyone to perform an exorcism provided they were sufficiently pure in spirit and conscience, and used appropriate prayers and exhortations. A 17th century theological author, François Humier, even cited a case of a child "of five or six years" acting successfully as an exorcist[93] ("even a child can do it"), which also speaks to the practice of employing virginal children to assist magicians in summoning visions in crystals or on polished thumbnails. The rituals of exorcism therefore enabled all sorts of people – laymen as well as clerics – to banish evil spirits from victims of demonic possession by commanding their obedience.

The exorcist prepared for the ordeal with a regimen of fasting, prayer, abstinence, attending Mass and receiving the sacrament. As Cotton Mather observed, "It seems that Long Fasting is not only Tolerable, but strangely Agreeable to such as have something more than Ordinary to do with the Invisible World."[94] The exorcist had to be clean in body as well as soul, with an untroubled conscience and strong sincere faith in God. Any taint of sin and earthly pollution could short circuit the whole operation.

First the afflicted person was examined to see if in fact there was a demon involved. The exorcist began the ritual began by reciting an extensive series of liturgical components of psalms, prayers, holy names and selections from the gospel. The occupying demon or demons were then summoned forth and interrogated to find out their names, rank and characteristics, as this knowledge was key to gaining mastery over them. They were then driven out and banished through further prayers and exhortations. Actual exorcisms were a lengthy and exhausting process for exorcist and demoniac alike, and too long to be included in full here, but to illustrate the similarities between exorcism and the conjurations that follow, I include an outline (in translation) of a 16th-century ritual by the Italian Franciscan exorcist, Girolamo Menghi.[95]

The rite is prefaced with an address to the potential exorcist that begins "Whoever you are—you who are about to exorcise, driven not by a frivolous spirit, but only by necessity or love—prepare yourself to take on this difficult task, first of all, by making a sacramental confession and a fast of three days. While humbling yourself in your heart and remembering that you are a sinner, trust in the power of God, and not in your own. ..." The exorcist began with a self-blessing with the sign of the cross on his forehead, mouth and breast, after which he did the same for the possessed person. He recites the Confiteor (a prayer of confession), absolves the possessed and others present (exorcisms were usually done before witnesses), and reads the initial "commandments" against the demons:

---

[93] Francois Humier. *Discours Theologique*. Niort: Phillippes Bureau, 1659, p. 39 (citation from Sarah Ferber, *Demonic Possession and Exorcism in Early Modern France*. London: Routledge, 2004).

[94] Cotton Mather . "A Brand Pluck'd From the Burning", in George Lincoln Burr, ed. *Narratives of the Witchcraft Cases, 1648-1706*. New York: Scribners, 1914, p. 266.

[95] Girolamo Menghi. *The Devil's Scourge*. Gaetano Paxia, ed. New York: Weiser Books, 2002, p. 41ff.

I command you, demons, who have come to help the other demons tormenting this creature of God, [name], on behalf of the Most Holy Trinity, Father, Son, and Holy Spirit. Subject to the punishment of being immersed in the pool of fire and sulphur by the hands of your enemies, subject to the punishment of surrendering to the hand of your enemies and being condemned to the pool of fire and sulphur for a thousand years, I command you to not give any help or favor to the demons tormenting the body of this creature of God, [name]; I order you to abandon this body and to go straight away to the places God has destined for you.

Here is the cross + of the Lord: flee, you enemy forces; the lion of the tribe of Judah has won, the root of David is victorious.

I also order you, demons who torment this creature of God, [name], to go out from him and leave him free and healthy, with no lesion of soul or body, so that he can serve God, his Creator. And I also command all your enemies, in the name of the Most Holy Trinity, Father, Son, and Holy Spirit, to force you to obey my orders and commandments. And subject to the same punishments, I order you not to say or do anything that might displease those present or absent, unless you are interrogated by me. In the name of the Fat+her, S+on, and Holy + Spirit. Amen.

The exorcist tied his stole around the possessed with three knots and an exhortation, then laid his hands on the victim's head and said,

May every power of the devil be extinguished in you, [name], by the imposition of our hands and by the invocation of all the holy angels and archangels, patriarchs and prophets, apostles, martyrs, confessors and virgins, and of all the saints in heaven. Amen.

He then recited a series of divine names, making the sign of the cross on the forehead of the possessed where indicated:

Eli +, Elohim +, Eloah +, Eheye +, Tetragram +, Adonai +, Shaddi +, Saboath +, Soter +. Emmanuele +, Alpha +, and Omega +, First and Last +, Beginning and End +, Hagios +, Ischyros +, ho Theos +, Anathantos +, Alga +, Jehova +, Homousion +, Yah +, Messiah +, Eserheie +, Christ conquers +, Christ reigns +, Christ rules +, Non-created the Father +, non-created the Son +, non-created the Holy Spirit +, By the sign of the holy cross, free us from our enemies, Oh Lord, our God.

This was followed with a reading of the beginning of the *Gospel of John* (a magical favourite, by the way), the Creed, more selections from the *Gospels, Psalm 51, Psalm 70,* the *Litanies of the Saints* with responses by those present, and three prayers. The exorcist then begins the work at hand with two exorcisms and two prayers for the possessed person before the first actual adjuration aimed at the demons directly:

EXORCISM

[Name], I exorcise you in the name of the Father + almighty, of his Son + Jesus Christ our Lord, and with the force of the Holy + Spirit, that you might become a clean body, holy and purified of every stain of iniquity and of all curses, incantations, bonds, evil spells, and sorcery that have been made on your body and around it.

I, [name], sinner and unworthy servant of God, with the authority that has been given me, in the name of God himself, almighty Father +, in the name of Jesus + Christ, his Son, our Lord, in the power of the Holy + Spirit, I destroy and want to see destroyed all aforementioned curses, incantations, bonds, evil spells, and sorcery. And I command you, cursed devil, and your companions, to possess no longer the power of remaining in this body, from the soles of the feet to the ends of the hair, but you must immediately go away with all your curses and enchantments. Through him who will come to judge with fire the living and the dead and the entire world. Amen.

PRAYER

God of mercy, clement God, who, according to the multitude of your mercies, corrects those you love and leads to penitence those whom you accept, we invoke you so that you will deign to grant your grace to your servant [name], who suffers in body for the weakness of its members. Rejoin to the unity of the body of the Church all that which out of human fraility has been corrupted or violated. Have mercy, oh Lord, on the moaning, have mercy on the tears of one who has no trust except in your mercy, and admit him to the sacrament of your reconciliation. Through Christ our Lord. Amen.

The possessed is sprinkled with holy water.

EXORCISM
I exorcise you, [name], who are infirm, but were regenerated with the water of baptism, by the living God +, by the true God +, by the holy God +, by the God who redeemed you with his precious blood, so that you will be free of the devil and so that any ghost and iniquity of diabolical deceit will flee from you, and any impure spirit be driven out. We ask you this through he who will come to judge with fire the living and the dead. Amen.

PRAYER
Oh God, who always rules over your creatures with merciful affection, hear our supplications and look with kindness upon your servant [name], who suffers in his body of a painful malady. Come to visit him and give him the comfort of salvation and heavenly grace. Through Christ our Lord. Amen.

More holy water, after which the demon is addressed directly:

EXORCISM
Hear me, filthy diabolical spirit; I warn you and exorcise + you and I command you—vain, senseless, false, heretical, vacuous, inimical, inebriated, foolish, ill-speaking tempter abandoned by the grace of God and Christ. I exorcise + you by means of he who came down to Earth for us, who received his name from the angel, who was made flesh through the working of the Holy Spirit, was born of the Virgin Mary, grew in age, wisdom, and grace; at twelve years of age, he came to the temple and, sitting amid the doctors, interrogated them with wisdom. I command you + through he who was baptised by John the Baptist in the Jordan River, who was tempted by the devil, was sold out and betrayed by his disciple Judas; was taken prisoner, derided, whipped, fed bile, made to drink vinegar, tied and crowned with thorns, stripped of his robes, which were gambled away. I command you + through he who was crucified, died, and was buried, and the third day rose from the dead, ascended to heaven, and sits at the right hand of the Father; from there he will come to judge with fire the living and the dead and the entire world. Immediately come out and flee this body, formed by God, and do not offend either me or those present, nor wound this person in any way. I exorcise you + through the same Christ whose future coming the angel Gabriel announced from the womb of the Virgin Mary and whom John greeted, while still in the womb of Elizabeth; through that same Christ, I order you to respond to me in everything I ask, and to tell me the truth as to the name of your master, your name, whether you are inside or outside this body, whether you are alone or whether you are joined by one or more legions.

Here the interrogation of the demon takes place for purposes of identification, followed by four further exorcisms of varying length and a second interrogation. If this was not enough, Menghi has six additional full exorcism rituals, three of which could be used against devils attacking the physical body, and three against evil and unclean spirits in general.

The test for possession is rather interesting in its own right, as it involved verses in a quasi-Latinate demonic language and supposedly was composed by Satan himself:

Si vis scire utrum homo sit obsessus an non, scribe ista versa {sic} in una carta vel littera: ALGA ✠ LAY ✠ ELEYTH ✠ et illos quatuor versus que vocantur versus dyaboli quia per se fecit illos versus:
Omimara chentazirim post hossita lossita lux
Ebulus lepolpes mala raphamius allilous
Helmo starius sed poli polisque
Lux capit horrontis latet vertice montis
Dissen prieff solman in sein hand lege. Recipit autem in manu, tunc non est obsessus; si autem non, tunc est obssesus.[96]

---

[96] "If you want to know whether a person is possessed or not, write these verses on a card or sheet: ALGA ✠ LAY ✠ ELEYTH ✠ Along with the four verses that are called 'the devil's verses,' because he composed those verses himself. Omimara chentazirim post hossita lossita lux / Ebulus lepolpes mala raphamius allilous / Helmo starius

Exorcism occupied a rather anomalous position in Christian doctrine. It wasn't a sacrament that could only be celebrated by an ordained priest. Neither did it work regardless of the spiritual and moral state of the presiding cleric *"ex opere operato"*, that is, as a "divinely ordained occasion for divine intervention" like the Eucharist through the power of God's enduring promise to the Church, as Kieckhefer notes. Instead, it was a "sacramental" that only worked *"ex opere operatis"*, that is, in a contingent manner depending on conditions. Exorcism – or conjuration – could only succeed if the person performing the rite was satisfactorily free from spiritual and physical pollution. What was needed was "charisma" in its theological sense; the "favor freely given" by God to those of sufficient virtue to work miracles. This was why conjurors undertook similar preparatory measures to those the exorcists underwent before their rituals. They couldn't do conjure spirits by ritual action alone – at a minimum they needed God's forbearance to get the invocations to function. Lacking the crucial charisma, it would be just words and gestures without efficacy, although they might very well attract (but not be able to control) some evil spirit, with disastrous results. Why the Deity should choose to abet the often sordid aims of conjurors is never made clear, but it was evidently assumed that charisma, plus Christ's unqualified promise to work when his name was invoked, could be made to ratify many purposes.

From Exorcism to Magic

It was no great jump in logic to believe that the ability to assert authority to banish a spirit could also be used to force demons into metaphysical slavery, commanding them to appear and do the bidding of the magician.

> Exorcism was in principle carried out on behalf of the demoniac; conjurations could be done as ways of afflicting enemies, and could be carried out on behalf of clients. In both cases, then, the ritual performer was acting as an authorized clergy, but while conjuring was forbidden to all, it was because of the one key difference: the exorcist's intent was to dispel the demons, while the conjuror's was to summon them, and mainstream opinion held that it was better to be rid of malign spirits than to invite them into one's life. Study of conjurations ... suggest that there is no essential difference between this form of magic and religious practices, and that it is better to perceive demonic magic as an illicit form of religion than as a cultural phenomenon distinct from religion. (Kieckheffer 1997: 14)

Ritual magic remained firmly embedded in the Christian system, but in a highly heterodox manner. The illegitimate use of spiritual authority involved in conjuration flourished despite imprecations from the pulpit and prosecution by authorities. By the 16th century, students were experimenting with illegal conjuration in the same way they do with drugs today. To the exorcist's preparatory attainment of charisma and *virtus* by the prayers, adjurations and holy names, magicians added the fumigations and observations of auspicious times and planetary aspects of astral magic. They also used sanctified garments (mimicking the vestments of the clergy), physical symbols of power and authority such as scepters, swords and rings, and a variety of consecrated tools. As a substitute for the holy sanctuary of churches where regular exorcisms took place, they used magic circles in special hidden locations and dedicated "oratories". The conjurors may have felt that by adapting the doctrinal practices of orthodox exorcists they had legitimized their activities to some extent, but to most observers they were simply usurping clerical authority for illicit purposes, a sort of "spiritual hacking" into the workings of the cosmos.

The Satanic Pact as an Alternative Basis for Magic

There was as well conflicting theological opinion about the basis of conjuration, in particular the theory of the demonic pact.

---

sed poli polisque / Lux capit horrontis latet vertice montis. {The following sentence is in German} This proof should be placed in his hand. {The Latin resumes} If he takes it in his hand, then he is not possessed; if he does not, then he is possessed." (Caciola 2003: 245)

> It is assumed ... that everything in the creation—the human beings who acted on it, as well as the things on which they acted—had been given its own attributes, virtues, and properties. Any effect lying beyond these various capacities could only be achieved, or even hoped for, if some agency with the ability to substitute alternative efficacies was also involved. In the case of an allowable effect, like a miracle, the agency was assumed to be religious and the intentions and expectations were said to be appropriate to true worship. Otherwise, the agency was demonic, and the intentions and expectations were in effect, idolatrous. (Clark 1997: 480)

In short, although the conjurors asserted that their rituals and expectations were allowed and empowered by divine law, religious authorities strongly disagreed and maintained that, despite the mimicking of religious action in conjuration, any unorthodox achievement of effect beyond the natural ability of ordinary humans had nothing to do with God's enabling or forbearance. Instead it depended solely on the connivance of the Devil and his demonic cohorts through an agreement or pact between the powers of evil and the magician or witch. In this view, God never enabled conjurors but only gave them enough rope to damn themselves by allowing the Devil to tempt and delude them into sin. The term "conjure" actually implied contractual agreement and religious authorities saw deals with the Devil as the basis for all magic, as well as a rationale for the tragic "black witch" persecutions in which the heretical practice of magic demanded severe punishment.

A contributing factor to the theory of the pact may have come from memory of the pre-Christian precedent for a contractual agreement between magicians and demonic helpers. In Hellenistic belief, for example, demons were not inevitably the evil spirits of Christian belief. Gods and good demons – the equivalent of Judeo-Christian angels – were sought out to act as *parhedroi*, or magical guides and mentors. A *parhedros* was not forced into subservience but entreated to become a collaborator with the magus – in fact the role was one of superior guidance rather like a Christian saint, or one of the "secret masters" of Freemasonry, Theosophy and the Golden Dawn, where an advanced being agreed to assist the human with powers beyond those of any mortal. The *parhedros* was not the "higher genius" or dedicated guardian of the theurgists, but an independent superior being who voluntarily agreed to help. To orthodox Christians, however, non-angelic spirits and pagan deities were all wicked demons by default, and any traffic with them a forbidden and damnable example of idolatry and an insult to God. The positive aspects of the earlier connection were recast as a contract with Hell.

The pact was a favorite trope of theologians for denouncing any sort of magic as heresy. For them magic inevitably involved a relationship with the Devil, whether explicitly as in the case of Faust involving a contract – written or oral – of satanic conditions in exchange for magical power, or unconscious and implicit simply by getting involved with magic in the first place. All of the magicians' impious attempts at charisma or achieving mastery over spirits were worthless and illusory, they asserted. The demons actually had the upper hand, and only pretended to be under control to inveigle the foolish mortal deeper into sin and damnation. The whole thing in orthodox opinion was no more than a divinely-sanctioned trap for the spiritually deluded. As the great English Calvinist divine William Perkins put it:

> [T]he league between the Devil and a Witch [i.e., any magician], is twofold: either expressed and open, or secret and close. The expresse and manifest compact is so tearmed, because it is made by solemne words on both parties. And it is not so expressly set downe in Scriptures, as in the writings of learned men, which have recorded the confessions of Witches: and they express it in this manner. First, the Witch for his part, as a slave of the devil, bindes himselfe unto him by solemn vow and promise to renounce the true God, his holy word, the covenant he made in Baptisms, and his redemption by Christ; and withall to believe in the Devil, to expect and receive aide and helpe from him, and at the ende of his life, to give him either body, or soule, or both: and for the ratifying hereof, he gives to the devil for the present, either his owne hand writing, or some part of his blood, as a pledge and earnest penny to bind the bargaine. The devil on the other side, for his part promiseth to be ready at his vassals command, to appeare at any time in the likeness of any creature, to consult with him, to aide and helpe him in any thing he shall take in hand, for the procuring of pleasures, honour, wealth, or preferment, to go for him, to carry him whether he will; in a word, to doe for him, whatsoever hee shall command. ... The secret and close league betweene the Witch and

Satan is that, wherein they mutually give consent each to other, but yet without a sworn covenant conceived in expresse words and conference. Of this there be two degrees. First, when a man useth superstitious formes of prayer, wherein hee expressely requireth the helpe of the devil, without any mention of solemne words or covenant going before. That this is a kinde of compact it is plaine, because herein there is a mutuall under-hand consent, betweene the party and the devil, though it be not manifest. For when a man is content to use superstitious formes of invocation, for help in time of neede; by the very using of them, his heart consenteth to Sathan, and he would gladly have the thing effected. ... The second degree is, when a man useth superstitious meanes to bring any thing to passe, which in his owne knowledge, hath no such vertue in themselves to effect it, without the especiall operation of the devil. (Perkins 1631: 17-18)

Perkins goes on to say that the Catholic practice of exorcism is similarly superstitious and magical, as the Apostles' unique ability to cast out demons had ceased over a millennium earlier, so that "for an ordinary man now to command the Devil in such sort, is meere presumption, and a practise of Sorcerie".

Despite the universal agreement within the religious establishment about the unavoidability of the pact and the spuriousness of ritual magic, there is little indication that members of the magical community were impressed with this blanket condemnation (although they recognized the legal danger of being tarred with the brush of idolatry), nor were they deterred from their illicit practices. In the case of the witch trials, the accused were generally coerced into admitting they had made such pacts, despite attempts at honest denial on their part. Alternately, testimony in the trials indicate that a certain proportion of those accused, being poor, desperate and aware of the popular claims for diabolic contracts, actually had tried to ally themselves with the Devil. If there are examples of ritual magicians actually seeking to make an explicit pact with the Devil after the manner of Faust (outside of fiction), it only shows that, as in later Satanism, some educated individuals were more susceptible to common cultural memes than others. Most magical practitioners evidently rejected the idea of an implicit pact and while aware of the danger of legal prosecution (civil or ecclesiastical), were not deterred by the alleged moral issues involved.

Angels, Demons and Fairies

The next areas to consider is who (or what) the conjurors were trying to exploit, and briefly survey the demographics of the Invisible World itself. The spiritual realm extended from God down through the angelic hierarchy, the heavenly spheres and the sub-lunar aerial realm of the demons, worldly spirits and fairy folk, to the infernal realm of Satan and his legions. The existence of an invisible hierarchy or chain of beings extending from God to Man, inherited with modifications from classical philosophy, was universally accepted. It was philosophically unacceptable to believe that the tremendous gulf between God and humanity could be a void empty of intermediary beings. The principle of plenitude held that God's creation was full and unbroken, and required that "every potential place be filled" and populated by descending orders of spiritual beings. The highest of these, and the model for lower series, was that of the angels. The nine orders, as delineated by the Neo-Platonist Pseudo-Dionysius the Areopagite (fl. 520 CE), were: Seraphim, Cherubim, Thrones, Dominations, Principalities, Powers, Virtues, Archangels, and plain Angels. In general, only the last few angelic species were supposed to have regular communication with humans, the higher orders being more gainfully employed singing God's praises. It was, however, an angelic mission to communicate God's message to His people and to act as guardians for individuals, thus insuring regular interaction between angels and humans. Mankind, by reason of its microcosmic status, could also initiate communication under certain conditions. Magicians who actively demanded angelic interaction instead of praying for its passive reception like saints acted irregularly, but not outside the bounds of theological reason.

Beneath the angelic realm there were planetary and astral intelligences (the specialised angels who caused the planetary spheres to revolve, and governed individual stars and constellations), and below the lunar sphere, additional demonic orders. These were not always well-defined, but in general they included fallen angels and a fluctuating number of lower demonic species. Michael Psellus (1018-ca.

1079), who composed the most influential demonic hierarchy (or as the prefix "hier-" denotes holiness, perhaps a "malum-archy"), divided them into six categories including those representing the four elements:

> This [first fiery] order of dæmons haunts the air above us, for the entire genus has been expelled from the regions adjacent to the moon, as a profane thing with us would be expelled from a temple, but the second occupies the air contiguous to us, and is called by the proper name Aërial; the third is the Earthly, the fourth the Aqueous and Marine, the fifth the Subterranean, and the last the Lucifugus [i.e., "flee the light"], which can scarcely be considered sentient beings. All these species of dæmons are haters of God, and enemies of man, and they say, that the Aqueous and Subterranean are worse than the merely bad, but that the Lucifugus are eminently malicious and mischievous, for these, said he, not merely impair men's intellects, by phantasies and illusions, but destroy them with the same alacrity as we would the most savage wild beast.[97]

Alternately, Agrippa in his third book of *Occult Philosophy*, chapter 18, describes nine orders of demons corresponding to the nine orders of angels: 1) False Gods led by Beelzebub, who seek to be worshiped as the pagan gods had been; 2) Spirits of Lies led by Pytho, who manipulate demonic divination; 3) Vessels of Wrath led by Belial, who invent and teach wicked arts; 4) Revengers of Evil led by Asmodeus, who punish sinners; 5) Deluders led by Satan, who produce the *mira* (wonders) and magical illusions sought by magicians; 6) Aerial Powers led by Meririm, being four fallen angels who control natural disasters and govern the four points of the compass; 7) Furies led by Apollyon, who stir up hatred, discord and wars; 8) Accusers led by Astaroth, who spread (false) accusations and denunciations, and 9) Tempters led by Mammon, who promote greed and covetousness. In addition, there was a grab-bag of supernatural entities left over from older systems of belief, such as genii, fairies, satyrs, goblins, nymphs, pixies and, on another level, ghosts. Many of these were credited with some sort of magical *virtus* or power that could help a conjuror, aid in divination, or locate hidden treasure (see the fuller discussion of *virtus* in Chapter 2, "How Magic Was Supposed to Work").

One result of the exploration of the Invisible World were directories of angels, planetary intelligences and demons that gave their names, attributes, correspondences, personal seals or "sigils" and supposed areas of expertise. Allegedly developed during previous invocations, these registers allowed conjurors to select the appropriate spirit to call up for any particular purpose. Although different lists were included in many of the grimoires, possibly the most influential example of a demonic directory was first published by Johann Weyer in his *Pseudomonarchia daemonum* (1563) to demonstrate the absurdity of such things. It was then copied in translation by Reginald Scot for the same purpose. Despite its intentional incompleteness – as Joseph H. Peterson tells us, "Weyer's text seems to be missing text from the beginning, that would have had information on Lucifer, Beelzebub, Satan, and the four demons of the cardinal points"[98] as well as their necessary seals – it was subsequently "détourned" by working magicians into the very thing Weyer hoped to avoid, a catalog of 68 demons (and their anonymous legions) available for conjuration. The various descriptions are instructive in showing how the demons were conceptualized and individualised. The magician could choose the spirit with the appropriate expertise or skills to meet his needs, and also know the appearance for proper identification and other idiosyncrasies of each of the available demons. The sigils here have been added from the Wilby edition of the *Lemegetton*:

> *An inventarie of the names, shapes, powers, governement, and effects of divels and spirits, of their severall segniories and degrees: a strange discourse woorth the reading.*

---

[97] Psellos, Michael. *Psellus' Dialogue on the Operation of Daemons.* Marcus Collisson, trans. and ed. Sydney: J. Tegg, and printed by D. L. Welch, 1843, p. 31. See Joseph H. Peterson's edition, www.esotericarchives.com/psellos/daemonibus.pdf (accessed 11/15/2011)
[98] www.esotericarchives.com/solomon/weyer.htm (accessed 12/30/2011)

Baell. THEIR first and principall king (which is of the power of the east) is called *Baëll* who when he is conjured up, appeareth with three heads; the first, like a tode; the second, like a man; the third, like a cat. He speaketh with a hoarse voice, he maketh a man go invisible, he hath under his obedience and rule sixtie and six legions of divels.

Agares. The first duke under the power of the east, is named *Agares*, he commeth up mildile in the likenes of a faire old man, riding upon a crocodile, and carrieng a hawke on his fist; hee teacheth presentlie all maner of toongs, he fetcheth backe all such as runne awaie, and maketh them runne that stand still; he overthroweth all dignities supernaturall and temporall, hee maketh earthquakes, and is of the order of vertues, having under his regiment thirtie one legions.

*Marbas, *alias Barbas* is a great president, and appeareth in the forme of a mightie lion; but at the commandement of a conjuror commeth up in the likenes of a man, and answereth fullie as touching anie thing which is hidden or secret: he bringeth diseases, and cureth them, he promoteth wisedome, and the knowledge of mechanicall arts, or handicrafts; he changeth men into other shapes, and under his presidencie or gouvernement are thirtie six legions of divels conteined.

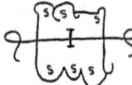

Amon, or *Aamon*, is a great and mightie marques, and commeth abroad in the likenes of a woolfe, having a serpents taile, spetting out and breathing flames of fier; when he putteth on the shape of a man, he sheweth out dogs teeth, and a great head like to a mightie raven; he is the strongest prince of all other, and understandeth of all things past and to come, he procureth favor, and reconcileth both freends and foes, and ruleth fourtie legions of divels.

Barbatos, a great countie or earle, and also a duke, he appeareth in *Signo sagittarii sylvestris*, with foure kings, which bring companies and great troopes. He understandeth the singing of birds, the barking of dogs, the lowings of bullocks, and the voice of all living creatures. He detecteth treasures hidden by magicians and inchanters, and is of the order of vertues, which in part beare rule: he knoweth all things past, and to come, and reconcileth freends / and powers; and governeth thirtie legions of divels by his authoritie.

Buer is a great president, and is seene in this signe; he absolutelie teacheth philosophie morall and naturall, and also logicke, and the vertue of herbes: he giveth the best familiars, he can heale all diseases, speciallie of men, and reigneth over fiftie legions.

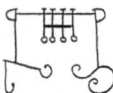

Gusoin is a great duke, and a strong, appearing in the forme of a *Xenophilus*, he answereth all things, present, past, and to come, expounding all questions. He reconcileth freendship, and distributeth honours and dignities, and ruleth over fourtie legions of divels.

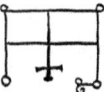

Botis, otherwise *Otis*, a great president and an earle he commeth foorth in the shape of an ouglie viper, and if he put on humane shape, he sheweth great teeth, and two hornes, carrieng a sharpe sword in his hand: he giveth answers of things present, past, and to come, and reconcileth friends, and foes, ruling sixtie legions.

Bathin, sometimes called *Mathim*, a great duke and a strong, he is seene in the shape of a verie strong man, with a serpents taile, sitting on a pale horsse, understanding the vertues of hearbs and pretious stones, transferring men suddenlie from countrie to countrie, and ruleth thirtie legions of divels.

Purson, *alias Curson*, a great king, he commeth foorth like a man with a lions face, carrieng a most cruell viper, and riding on a beare; and before him go alwaies trumpets, he knoweth things hidden, and can tell all things present, past, and to come: he bewraieth treasure, he can take a bodie either humane or aierie; he answereth truelie of all things earthlie and secret, of the divinitie and creation of the world, and bringeth foorth the best familiars; and there obeie him two and twentie legions of divels, partlie of the order of vertues, & partlie of the order of thrones.

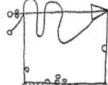

Eligor, *alias Abigor*, is a great duke, and appeereth as a goodlie knight, carrieng a lance, an ensigne, and a scepter: he answereth fullie of things hidden, and of warres, and how souldiers should meete: he knoweth things to come, and procureth the favour of lords and knights, governing sixtie legions of divels.

Leraie, *alias Oray*, a great marquesse, shewing himselfe in the likenesse of a galant archer, carrieng a bowe and a quiver, he is author of all battels, he dooth putrifie all such wounds as are made with arrowes by archers, *Quos optimos objicit tribus diebus*, and he hath regiment over thirtie legions.

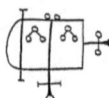

Valefar, * alias *Malephar*, is a strong duke, comming foorth in the shape of a lion, and the head of a theefe, he is verie familiar with them / to whom he maketh himself acquainted, till he hath brought them to the gallowes, and ruleth ten legions.

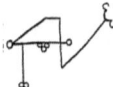

Morax, **alias* Foraii*, a great earle and a president, he is seene like a bull, and if he take unto him a mans face, he maketh men wonderfull cunning in astronomie, & in all the liberall sciences: he giveth good familiars and wise, knowing the power & vertue of hearbs and stones which are pretious, and ruleth thirtie six legions.

Ipos, **alias* Ayporos*, is a great earle and a prince, appeering in the shape of an angell, and yet indeed more obscure and filthie than a lion, with a lions head, a gooses feet, and a hares taile: he knoweth things to come and past, he maketh a man wittie, and bold, and hath under his jurisdiction thirtie six legions.

Naberius, **alias* Cerberus*, is a valiant marquesse, shewing himselfe in the forme of a crowe, when he speaketh with a hoarse voice: he maketh a man amiable and cunning in all arts, and speciallie in rhetorike, he procureth the losse of prelacies and dignities: nineteene legions heare and obeie him.

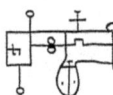

Glasya Labolas, **alias* Caacrinolaas*, or *Caassimolar*, is a great president, who commeth foorth like a dog, and hath wings like a griffen, he giveth the knowledge of arts, and is the captaine of all mansleiers: he understandeth things present and to come, he gaineth the minds and love of freends and foes, he maketh a man go invisible, and hath the rule of six and thirtie legions.

Zepar is a great duke, appearing as a souldier, inflaming women with the loove of men, and when he is bidden he changeth their shape, untill they maie enjoie their beloved, he also maketh them barren, and six and twentie legions are at his obeie and commandement.

Bileth is a great king and a terrible, riding on a pale horsse, before whome go trumpets, and all kind of melodious musicke. When he is called up by an exorcist, he appeareth rough and furious, to deceive him. Then let the exorcist or conjuror take heed to himself; and to allaje his courage, let him hold a *hazell bat* in his hand, wherewithall he must reach out toward the east and south, and make a *triangle* without besides the *circle*; but if he hold not out his hand unto him, and he bid him come in, and he still refuse the bond or chain of spirits; let the conjuror proceed to reading, and by and by he will submit himselfe, and come in, and doo whatsoever the exorcist commandeth him, and he shalbe safe. If *Bileth* the king be more stubborne, and refuse to enter into the circle at the first call, and the conjuror shew himselfe fearfull, or if he have not the chaine of spirits, certeinelie he will never feare nor regard him after. Also, if the place he unapt for a triangle to be made without the circle, then set / there a boll of wine, and the exorcist shall certeinlie knowe when he commeth out of his house, with his fellowes, and that the foresaid *Bileth* will be his helper, his friend, and obedient unto him when he commeth foorth. And when he commeth, let the exorcist receive him courteouslie, and glorifie him in his pride, and therfore he shall adore him as other kings doo, bicause he saith nothing without other princes. Also, if he be cited by an exorcist, alwaies a *silver ring* of the middle finger of the left hand must be held against the exorcists face, as they doo for *Amaimon*. And the dominion and power of so great a prince is not to be pretermitted; for there is none under the power & dominion of the conjuror, but he that deteineth both men and women in doting love, till the exorcist hath had his pleasure. He is of the orders of powers, hoping to returne to the seaventh throne, which is not altogether credible, and he ruleth eightie five legions.

*Sitri, *alias Bitru*, is a great prince, appeering with the face of a leopard, and having wings as a griffen: when he taketh humane shape, he is verie beautiful, he inflameth a man with a womans love, and also stirreth up women to love men, being commanded he willinglie *deteineth* secrets of women, laughing at them and mocking them, to make them luxuriouslie naked, and there obeie him sixtie legions.

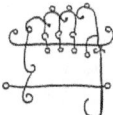

Paimon is more obedient in *Lucifer* than other kings are. *Lucifer* is heere to be understood he that was drowned in the depth of his knowledge: he would needs be like God, and for his arrogancie was throwne out into destruction, of whome it is said; Everie pretious stone is thy covering. *Paimon* is constrained by divine vertue to stand before the exorcist; where he putteth on the likenesse of a man: he sitteth on a beast called a dromedarie, which is a swift runner, and weareth a glorious crowne, and hath an effeminate countenance. There goeth before him an host of men with trumpets and well sounding cymbals, and all musicall instruments. At the first he appeereth with a great crie and roring, as in *Circulo Salomonis*, and in the art is declared. And if this *Paimon* speake sometime that the conjuror understand him not, let him not therefore be dismaied. But when he hath delivered him the first obligation to observe his desire, he must bid him also answer him distinctlie and plainelie to the questions he shall aske you, of all philosophie, wisedome, and science, and of all other secret things. And if you will knowe the disposition of the world, and what the earth is, or what holdeth it up in the water, or any other thing, or what is *Abyssus*, or where the wind is, or from whence it commeth, he will teach you aboundantlie. Consecrations also as well of sacrifices as otherwise may be reckoned. / He giveth dignities and confirmations; he bindeth them that resist him in his owne chaines, and subjecteth them to the conjuror; he prepareth good familiars, and hath the understanding of all arts. Note, that at the calling up of him, the exorcist must looke towards the northwest, bicause there is his house. When he is called up, let the exorcist receive him constantlie without feare, let him aske what questions or demands he list, and no doubt he shall obteine the same of him. And the exorcist must beware he forget not the creator, for those things, which have beene rehearsed before of *Paimon*, some saie he is of the order of dominations; others saie, of the order of cherubim. There follow him two hundred legions, partlie of the order of angels, and partlie of potestates. Note that if *Paimon* be cited alone by an offering or sacrifice, two kings followe him; to wit, *Beball & Abalam*, & other potentates: in his host are twentie five legions, bicause the spirits subject to them are not alwaies with them, except they be compelled to appeere by divine vertue.

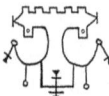

Some saie that the king *Beliall* was created immediatlie after *Lucifer*, and therefore they thinke that he was father and seducer of them which fell being of the orders. For he fell first among the worthier and wiser sort, which went before *Michael* and other heavenlie angels, which were lacking. Although *Beliall* went before all them that were throwne downe to the earth, yet he went not before them that tarried in heaven. This *Beliall* is constrained by divine venue, when he taketh sacrifices, gifts, and offerings, that he againe may give unto the offerers true answers. But he tarrieth not one houre in the truth, except he be constrained by the divine power, as is said. He taketh the forme of a beautifull angell, sitting in a firie chariot; he speaketh faire, he distributeth preferments of senatorship, and the favour of friends, and excellent familiars: he hath rule over eightie legions, partlie of the order of vertues, partlie of angels; he is found in the forme of an exorcist in the bonds of spirits. The exorcist must consider, that this *Beliall* doth in everie thing assist his subjects. If he will not submit himselfe, let the bond of spirits be read: the spirits chaine is sent for him, wherewith wise *Salomon* gathered them togither with their legions in a brasen vessell, where were inclosed among all the legions seventie two kings, of whome the cheefe was *Bileth*, the second was *Beliall*, the third *Asmoday*, and above a thousand thousand legions. Without doubt (I must confesse) I learned this of my maister *Salomon*; but he told me not why he gathered them together, and shut them up so: but I beleeve it was for the pride of this *Beliall*. Certeine nigromancers doo saie, that *Salomon*, being on a certeine daie seduced by the craft of a certeine woman, inclined himselfe to praie before the same idoll, / *Beliall* by name: which is not credible. And therefore we must rather thinke (as it is said) that they were gathered together in that great brasen vessell for pride and arrogancie, and throwne into a deepe lake or hole in *Babylon*. For wise *Salomon* did accomplish his workes by the divine power, which never forsooke him. And therefore we must thinke he worshipped not the image *Beliall*; for then he could not have constrained the spirits by divine vertue: for this *Beliall*, with three kings were in the lake. But the Babylonians woondering at the matter, supposed that they should find therein a great quantitie of treasure, and therefore with one consent went downe into the lake, and uncovered and brake the vessell, out of the which immediatlie flew the capteine divels, and were delivered to their former and proper places. But this Beliall entred into a certeine image, and there gave answer to them that offered and sacrificed unto him: as *Tocz.* in his sentences reporteth, and the Babylonians did worship and sacrifice thereunto.

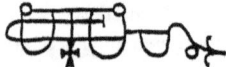

Bune is a great and a strong Duke, he appeareth as a dragon with three heads, the third whereof is like to a man; he speaketh with a divine voice, he maketh the dead to change their place, and divels to assemble upon the sepulchers of the dead: he greatlie inricheth a man, and maketh him eloquent and wise, answering trulie to all demands, and thirtie legions obeie him.

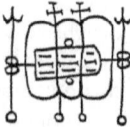

Forneus is a great marquesse, like unto a monster of the sea, he maketh men woondeffull in rhetorike, he adorneth a man with a good name, and the knowledge of toongs, and maketh one beloved as well of foes as freends: there are under him nine and twentie legions, of the order partlie of thrones, and partlie of angels.

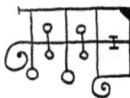

Ronove a marquesse and an earle, he is resembled to a monster, he bringeth singular understanding in rhetorike, faithfull servants, knowledge of toongs, favour of freends and foes; and nineteene legions obeie him.

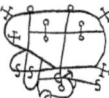

Berith is a great and a terrible duke, and hath three names. Of some he is called *Beall*; of the Jewes *Berithi*; of Nigromancers *Bolfry*: he commeth foorth as a red souldier, with red clothing, and upon a horsse of that colour, and a crowne on his head. He answereth trulie of things present, past, and to come. He is compelled at a certeine houre, through divine vertue, by a ring of art magicke. He is also a lier, he turneth all mettals into gold, he adorneth a man with dignities, and confirmeth them, he speaketh with a cleare and a subtill voice, and six and twentie legions are under him.

Astaroth is a great and a strong duke, comming foorth in the shape of a fowle angell, sitting upon an infernall dragon, and carrieng on his right hand a viper: he answereth trulie to matters present, past, / and to come, and also of all secrets. He talketh willinglie of the creator of spirits, and of their fall, and how they sinned and fell: he saith he fell not of his owne accord. He maketh a man woonderfull learned in the liberall sciences, he ruleth fourtie legions. Let everie exorcist take heed, that he admit him not too neere him, bicause of his stinking breath. And therefore let the conjuror hold neere to his face a magicall ring, and that shall defend him.

Foras, *alias *Forcas* is a great president, and is seene in the forme of a strong man, and in humane shape, he understandeth the vertue of hearbs and pretious stones: he teacheth fullie logicke, ethicke, and their parts: he maketh a man invisible, wittie, eloquent, and to live long; he recovereth things lost, and discovereth treasures, and is lord over nine and twentie legions.

Furfur is a great earle, appearing as an hart, with a firie taile, he lieth in everie thing, except he be brought up within a triangle; being bidden, he taketh angelicall forme, he speaketh with a hoarse voice, and willinglie maketh love betweene man and wife; he raiseth thunders and lightnings, and blasts. Where he is commanded, he answereth well, both of secret and also of divine things, and hath rule and dominion over six and twentie legions.

Marchosias is a great marquesse, he sheweth himselfe in the shape of a cruell shee woolfe, with a griphens wings, with a serpents taile, and spetting I cannot tell what out of his mouth. When he is in a mans shape, he is an excellent fighter, he answereth all questions trulie, he is faithfull in all the conjurors businesse, he was of the order of dominations, under him are thirtie legions: he hopeth after 1200. yeares to returne to the seventh throne, but he is deceived in that hope.

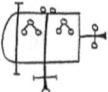

Malphas is a great president, he is seene like a crowe, but being cloathed with humane image, speaketh with a hoarse voice, be buildeth houses and high towres wonderfullie, and quicklie bringeth artificers togither, he throweth downe also the enimies edifications, he helpeth to good familiars, he receiveth sacrifices willinglie, but he deceiveth all the sacrificers, there obeie him fourtie legions.

*Vepar, *alias Separ*, a great duke and a strong, he is like a mermaid, he is the guide of the waters, and of ships laden with armour; he bringeth to passe (at the commandement of his master) that the sea shalbe rough and stormie, and shall appeare full of shippes; he killeth men in three daies, with putrifieng their wounds, and producing maggots into them; howbeit, they maie be all healed with diligence, he ruleth nine and twentie legions.

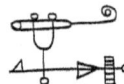

*Sabnacke, *alias Salmac*, is a great marquesse and a strong, he commeth foorth as an armed soldier with a lions head, sitting on a / pale horsse, he dooth marvelouslie change mans forme and favor, he buildeth high towres full of weapons, and also castels and cities; he inflicteth men thirtie daies with wounds both rotten and full of maggots, at the exorcists commandement, he provideth good familiars, and hath dominion over fiftie legions.

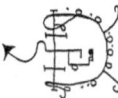

*Sidonay, *alias Asmoday*, a great king, strong and mightie, he is seene with three heads, whereof the first is like a bull, the second like a man, the third like a ram, he hath a serpents taile, he belcheth flames out of his mouth, he hath feete like a goose, he sitteth on an infernall dragon, he carrieth a lance and a flag in his hand, he goeth before others, which are under the power of *Amaymon*. When the conjuror exerciseth this office, let him be abroad, let him be warie and standing on his feete; if his cap be on his head, he will cause all his dooings to be bewraied, which if he doo not, the exorcist shalbe deceived by *Amaymon* in everie thing. But so soone as he seeth him in the forme aforesaid, he shall call him by his name, saieng; Thou art *Asmoday*; he will not denie it, and by and by he boweth downe to the ground; he giveth the ring of venues, he absolutelie teacheth geometrie, arythmetike, astronomie, and handicrafts. To all demands he answereth fullie and trulie, he maketh a man invisible, he sheweth the places where treasure lieth, and gardeth it, if it be among the legions of *Amaymon*, he hath under his power seventie two legions.

*Gaap, *alias Tap*, a great president and a prince, he appeareth in a meridionall signe, and when he taketh humane shape he is the guide of the foure principall kings, as mightie as *Bileth*. There were certeine necromancers that offered sacrifices and burnt offerings unto him; and to call him up, they exercised an art, saieng that *Salomon* the wise made it. Which is false: for it was rather *Cham*, the sonne of *Noah*, who after the floud began first to invocate wicked spirits. He invocated *Bileth*, and made an art in his name, and a booke which is knowne to manie mathematicians. There were burnt offerings and sacrifices made, and gifts given, and much wickednes wrought by the exorcists, who mingled therewithall the holie names of God, the which in that art are everie where expressed. Marie there is an epistle of those names written by *Salomon*, as also write *Helias Hierosolymitanus* and *Helisæus*. It is to be noted, that if anie exorcist have the art of *Bileth*, and cannot make him stand before him, nor see him, I may not bewraie how and declare the meanes to conteine him, bicause it is abhomination, and for that I have learned nothing from *Salomon* of his dignitie and office. But yet I will not hide this; to wit, that he maketh a man woonderfull in philosophie and all the liberall sciences: he maketh love, / hatred, insensibilitie, invisibilitie, consecration, and consecration [sic] of those things that are belonging unto the domination of *Amaymon*, and delivereth familiars out of the possession of other conjurors, answering truly and perfectly of things present, past, & to come, & transferreth men most speedilie into other nations, he ruleth sixtie six legions, & was of the order of potestats.

*Shax, *alias Scox*, is a darke and a great marquesse, like unto a storke, with a hoarse and subtill voice: he dooth marvellouslie take awaie the sight, hearing and understanding of anie man, at the commandement of the conjuror: he taketh awaie monie out of everie kings house, and carrieth it backe after 1200. yeares, if he be commanded, he is a horssestealer, he is thought to be faithfull in all commandements: and although he promise to be obedient to the conjuror in all things; yet is he not so, he is a lier, except he be brought into a triangle, and there he speaketh divinelie, and telleth of things which are hidden, and not kept of wicked spirits, he promiseth good familiars, which are accepted if they be not deceivers, he hath thirtie legions.

Procell is a great and a strong duke, appearing in the shape of an angell, but speaketh verie darklie of things hidden, he teacheth geometrie and all the liberall arts, he maketh great noises, and causeth the waters to rore, where are none, he warmeth waters, and distempereth bathes at certeine times, as the exorcist appointeth him, he was of the order of potestats, and hath fourtie eight legions under his power.

Furcas is a knight and commeth foorth in the similitude of a cruell man, with a long beard and a hoarie head, he sitteth on a pale horsse, carrieng in his hand a sharpe weapon, he perfectlie teacheth practike philosophie, rhetorike, logike, astronomie, chiromancie, pyromancie, and their parts: there obeie him twentie legions.

Murmur is a great duke and an earle, appearing in the shape of a souldier, riding on a griphen, with a dukes crowne on his head; there go before him two of his ministers, with great trumpets, he teacheth philosophie absolutelie, he constraineth soules to come before the exorcist, to answer what he shall aske them, he was of the order partlie of thrones, and partlie of angels, and ruleth thirtie legions.

Caim is a great president, taking the forme of a thrush, but when he putteth on man's shape, he answereth in burning ashes, carrieng in his hand a most sharpe sword, he maketh the best disputers, he giveth men the understanding of all birds, of the lowing of bullocks, and barking of dogs, and also of the sound and noise of waters, he answereth best of things to come, he was of the order of angels, and ruleth thirtie legions of divels. /

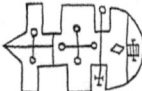

Raum, or *Raim* is a great earle, he is seene as a crowe, but when he putteth on humane shape, at the commandement of the exorcist, he stealeth woonderfullie out of the kings house, and carrieth it whether he is assigned, he destroieth cities, and hath great despite unto dignities, he knoweth things present, past, and to come, and reconcileth freends and foes, he was of the order of thrones, and governeth thirtie legions.

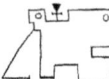

Halphas is a great earle, and commeth abroad like a storke, with a hoarse voice, he notablie buildeth up townes full of munition and weapons, he sendeth men of warre to places appointed, and hath under him six and twentie legions.

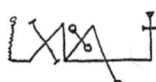

Focalor is a great duke comming foorth as a man, with wings like a griphen, he killeth men, and drowneth them in the waters, and overturneth ships of warre, commanding and ruling both winds and seas. And let the conjuror note, that if he bid him hurt no man, he willinglie consenteth thereto: he hopeth after 1000. yeares to returne to the seventh throne, but he is deceived, he hath three legions.

Vine is a great king and an earle, he showeth himselfe as a lion, riding on a blacke horsse, and carrieth a viper in his hand, he gladlie buildeth large towres, he throweth downe stone walles, and maketh waters rough. At the commandement of the exorcist he answereth of things hidden, of witches, and of things present, past, and to come.

Bifrons is seene in the similitude of a monster, when he taketh the image of a man, he maketh one woonderfull cunning in astrologie, absolutelie declaring the mansions of the planets, he dooth the like in geometrie, and other admesurements, he perfectlie understandeth the strength and vertue of hearbs, pretious stones, and woods, he changeth dead bodies from place to place, he seemeth to light candles upon the sepulchres of the dead, and hath under him six and twentie legions.

Gamigin is a great marquesse, and is seene in the forme of a little horsse, when he taketh humane shape he speaketh with a hoarse voice, disputing of all liberall sciences; he bringeth also to passe, that the soules, which are drowned in the sea, or which dwell in purgatorie (which is called *Cartagra*, that is, affliction of soules) shall take aierie bodies, and evidentlie appeare and answer to interrogatories at the conjurors commandement; he tarrieth with the exorcist, untill he have accomplished his desire, and hath thirtie legions under him.

Zagan is a great king and a president, he commeth abroad like a bull, with griphens wings, but when he taketh humane shape, he maketh men wittie, he turneth all mettals into the coine of that dominion, and turneth water into wine, and wine into water, he also / turneth bloud into wine, & wine into bloud, & a foole into a wise man, he is head of thirtie and three legions.

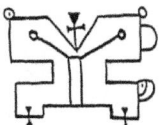

Orias is a great marquesse, and is seene as a lion riding on a strong horsse, with a serpents taile, and carrieth in his right hand two great serpents hissing, he knoweth the mansion of planets and perfectlie teacheth the vertues of the starres, he transformeth men, he giveth dignities, prelacies, and confirmations, and also the favour of freends and foes, and hath under him thirtie legions.

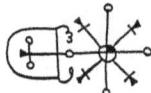

Valac is a great president, and commeth abroad with angels wings like a boie, riding on a twoheaded dragon, he perfectlie answereth of treasure hidden, and where serpents may be seene, which he delivereth into the conjurors hands, void of anie force or strength, and hath dominion over thirtie legions of divels.

Gomory a strong and a mightie duke, he appeareth like a faire woman, with a duchesse crownet about hir midle, riding on a camell, he answereth well and truelie of things present, past, and to come, and of treasure hid, and where it lieth: he procureth the love of women, especiallie of maids, and hath six and twentie legions.

Decarabia or *Carabia*, he commeth like a * [sic] and knoweth the force of herbes and pretious stones, and maketh all birds flie before the exorcist, and to tarrie with him, as though they were tame, and that they shall drinke and sing, as their maner is, and hath thirtie legions.

Amduscias a great and a strong duke, he commeth foorth as an unicorne, when he standeth before his maister in humane shape, being commanded, he easilie bringeth to passe, that trumpets and all musicall instruments may be heard and not seene, and also that trees shall bend and incline, according to the conjurors will, he is excellent among familiars, and hath nine and twentie legions.

Andras is a great marquesse, and is seene in an angels shape with a head like a blacke night raven, riding upon a blacke and a verie strong woolfe, flourishing with a sharpe sword in his hand, he can kill the maister, the servant, and all assistants, he is author of discords, and ruleth thirtie legions.

Andrealphus is a great marquesse, appearing as a pecocke, he raiseth great noises, and in humane shape perfectlie teacheth geometrie, and all things belonging to admeasurements, he maketh a man to be a subtill disputer, and cunning in astronomie, and transformeth a man into the likenes of a bird, and there are under him thirtie legions.

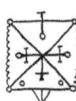

Ose is a great president, and commeth foorth like a leopard, and counterfeting to be a man, he maketh one cunning in the liberall sciences, he answereth truelie of divine and secret things, he transformeth / a mans shape, and bringeth a man to that madnes, that he thinketh himselfe to be that which he is not; as that he is a king or a pope, or that he weareth a crowne on his head, *Durátque id regnum ad horam.*

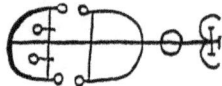

Aym or *Haborim* is a great duke and a strong, he commeth foorth with three heads, the first like a serpent, the second like a man having two * [sic] the third like a cat, he rideth on a viper, carrieng in his hand a light fier brand, with the flame whereof castels and cities are fiered, he maketh one wittie everie kind of waie, he answereth truelie of privie matters, and reigneth over twentie six legions.

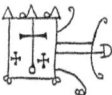

Orobas is a great prince, he commeth foorth like a horsse, but when he putteth on him a mans idol, he talketh of divine vertue, he giveth true answers of things present, past, and to come, and of the divinitie, and of the creation, he deceiveth none, nor suffereth anie to be tempted, he giveth dignities and prelacies, and the favour of freends and foes, and hath rule over twentie legions.

Vapula is a great duke and a strong, he is seene like a lion with griphens wings, he maketh a man subtill and wonderfull in handicrafts, philosophie, and in sciences conteined in bookes, and is ruler over thirtie six legions.

Cimeries is a great marquesse and a strong, ruling in the parts of *Aphrica*, he teacheth perfectue grammar, logicke, and rhetorike, he discovereth treasures and things hidden, he bringeth to passe, that a man shall seeme with expedition to be turned into a soldier, he rideth upon a great blacke horsse, and ruleth twentie legions.

Amy is a great president, and appeareth in a flame of fier, but having taken mans shape, he maketh one marvelous in astrologie, and in all the liberall sciences, he procureth excellent familiars, he bewraieth treasures preserved by spirits, he hath the governement of thirtie six legions, he is partlie of the order of angels, partlie of potestats, he hopeth after a thousand two hundreth yeares to returne to the seventh throne: which is not credible.

Flauros a strong duke, is seene in the forme of a terrible strong leopard, in humane shape, he sheweth a terrible countenance, and fierie eies, he answereth trulie and fullie of things present, past, and to come; if he be in a triangle, he lieth in all things and deceiveth in other things, and beguileth in other busines, he gladlie talketh of the divinitie, and of the creation of the world, and of the fall; he is constrained by divine vertue, and so are all divels or spirits, to burne and destroie all the conjurors adversaries. And if he be commanded, he suffereth the conjuror not to be tempted, and he hath twentie legions under him.

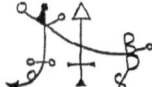

Balam is a great and a terrible king, he commeth foorth with three / heads, the first of a bull, the second of a man, the third of a ram, he hath a serpents taile, and flaming eies, riding upon a furious beare, and carrieng a hawke on his fist, he speaketh with a hoarse voice, answering perfectlie of things present, past, and to come, hee maketh a man invisible and wise, hee governeth fourtie legions, and was of the order of dominations.

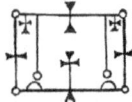

Allocer is a strong duke and a great, he commeth foorth like a soldier, riding on a great horsse, he hath a lions face, verie red, and with flaming eies, he speaketh with a big voice, he maketh a man woonderfull in astronomie, and in all the liberall sciences, he bringeth good familiars, and ruleth thirtie six legions.

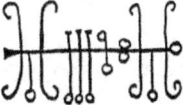

Saleos is a great earle, he appeareth as a gallant soldier, riding on a crocodile, and weareth a dukes crowne, peaceable, &c.

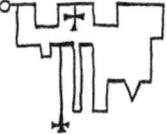

Vuall is a great duke and a strong, he is seene as a great and terrible dromedarie, but in humane forme, he soundeth out in a base voice the *Ægyptian* toong. This man above all other procureth the especiall love of women, and knoweth things present, past, and to come, procuring the love of freends and foes, he was of the order of potestats, and governeth thirtie seven legions.

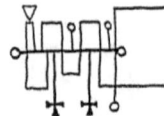

Haagenti is a great president, appearing like a great bull, having the wings of a griphen, but when he taketh humane shape, he maketh a man wise in everie thing, he changeth all mettals into gold, and changeth wine and water the one into the other, and commandeth as manie legions as *Zagan*.

Phoenix is a great marquesse, appearing like the bird *Phoenix*, having a childs voice: but before he standeth still before the conjuror, he singeth manie sweet notes. Then the exorcist with his companions must beware he give no eare to the melodie, but must by and by bid him put on humane shape; then will he speake marvellouslie of all woonderfull sciences. He is an excellent poet, and obedient, he hopeth to returne to the seventh throne after a thousand two hundreth yeares, and governeth twentie legions.

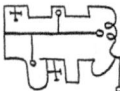

Stolas is a great prince, appearing in the forme of a nightraven, before the exorcist, he taketh the image and shape of a man, and teacheth astronomie, absolutelie understanding the vertues of herbes and pretious stones; there are under him twentie six legions.

Note that a legion is 6 6 6 6, and now by multiplication
count how manie legions doo arise out of
everie particular.
(Scot 1973: Book 15, chapter 2, pp. 314-326; Wilby 1985: pp. 6-24)

The grimoires added the necessary seals and magical characters Weyer omitted (see "Sigils and Pentacles," below), as well as specific directions for summoning. The demonic population appears to have been organized in a military pattern after the model of medieval chivalry, with titles of nobility (kings, dukes, marquises and the like) and the assumption of legions of innumerable "foot soldiers" ready to follow their leader's command in providing magical assistance.

This list and others like it established the cast of characters involved in demonic conjuration. The theoretical basis was actually quite simple. The conjuror was endowed with the ability to communicate with the Invisible World through his (suitably purified) soul on a spiritual level and his intellect and will on a practical level. He or she could employ rituals derived from and consistent with Christian rites of exorcism to assert authority over demons (or call for willing cooperation in the case of angels and beneficent spirits, or even God Himself) to assist in achieving his or her aims and desires through magic. As Kieckhefer observes, "Ceremonial magic is illicit religion, not something separate". The way in which this was accomplished was by invoking sufficient holy power or *virtus* through the use of divine and magical names, tools, seals, and sigils to coerce or convince the beings being invoked to cooperate with the demands of the operator.

As with exorcism, the work was experimental. Repeated "experiments" had developed a body of efficacious rituals derived in part from the forced revelations of the invoked spirits themselves. The demons were questioned not only to discover how they might be addressed, summoned and controlled, but what their "correspondences" or related sources of *virtus* were, and also to establish the authority of the conjuror, for if the demon answered the queries, then the operator was truly in charge:

> When the spiryt is apperyd: what is thy name? Under what state and what dynite (i.e., dignity) hast thow? What is thy power and thy offyse? Undyr what planet and sygn art thow? Of what parte arte thow of the world? Of which element art thow? Whych is thy month? What is thy day, and thyne [h]owyr? What is thyne howre, day or nyght? Whyche is thy winde? What be they caretes [characters] that thow obeyst to? Which is thy mansion and thy day? Which is thy sterre? Which is thy stone? What is thyne Aungellys name that thow moste obeyst to? And in what lyknes aperyst thou? How many commyst thow wythal?[99]

If the theory was straight forward enough, the actual practice was quite the opposite. Insuring success and averting danger – the threat to one's immortal soul being as significant as the physical destruction depicted in medieval *exempla* and modern horror stories – demanded a number of obsessively complex requirements on the operator, or the "exorcist", as the magician was often referred to. It was the same two-part process called for in regular exorcism. Firstly, the operator sought to attain the personal purity and charisma for obtaining authority through divine acquiescence to do the work, and secondly, by accumulating sufficient *virtus* to insure the ritual is effective. In keeping with the religious character of conjuration, the operator had to observe the same purifying regimen that mystics and saints observed to prepare themselves for interaction with divinity. "For it is not possible that a wicked and unclean man could truly work this art; for men are not bound unto spirits, but spirits are constrained against their will to answer clean men and fulfill their requests." (*Honourius* 1977: 2) Fasting, sexual abstinence, prayer, attendance at divine services, absolution, heavenly contemplation and avoidance of sinful thoughts and deeds purified the soul and loosened polluting ties to earthly things and concerns, as prescribed in *The Heptameron, or, Magical Elements of Peter de Abano*:

> The Operator ought to be clean and purified by the space of nine daies before the beginning of the work, and to be confessed, and receive the holy Communion. Let him have ready the perfume appropriated to the day wherein he would perform the work. He ought also to have holy water from a Priest, and a new earthen vessel with fire, a Vesture and a Pentacle; and let all these things be rightly and duly consecrated and prepared. Let one of the servants carry the earthen vessel full of fire, and the perfumes, and let another bear the book, another the Garment and Pentacle, and let the master carry the Sword; over which there must be said one mass of the Holy Ghost; and on the middle of the Sword, let there be written this name *Agla* +, and on the other side thereof, this name + *On* +. And as he goeth to the consecrated place, let him continually read Letanies, the servants answering. And when he cometh to the place where he will erect the Circle, let him draw the lines of the Circle, as we have before taught: and after he hath made it, let him sprinkle the Circle with holy water, saying, *Asperges me Domine,* &c. (Wash me O Lord, &c.)
>
> The Master therefore ought to be purified with fasting, chastity, and abstinency from all luxury the space of three whole dayes before the day of the operation. And on the day that he would do the work, being clothed with pure garments, and furnished with Pentacles, Perfumes, and other things necessary hereunto, let him enter the Circle, and call the Angels from the four parts of the world, which do govern the seven Planets the seven dayes of the week, Colours and Metals; whose name you shall see in their places. (*Agrippa's Fourth Book*, 1978: 81)

The attracting of the appropriate *virtus* followed the same pattern as natural or astral magic of bringing together words, symbols and material items, each with their own particular virtues. Like the magic involved in the rituals of the *Picatrix* or in Ficino's third book of the *De vita libri tres*, material objects that contained particular virtues relating to specific impellations of astral power contributed to the compound *virtus* needed for the task at hand. When combined with the prayers and invocations of the ritual, this battery of spiritual power achieved effects in a manner analogous to contact with the relics of a saint. The most important devices for this were the pentacles bearing the seals, characters and sigils that identified and channeled the *virtus* to control the particular spirits involved.

---

[99] Rawlinson D. 252, f65v (citation from Frank Klaassen, "Unstable and Modal Approaches to the Written Word in Medieval European Ritual Magic", in: Keith Thor Carlson, Kristina Fagan, and Natalia Khanenko-Friesen. *Orality and Literacy: Reflections Across Disciplines.* Toronto: University of Toronto, 2011, p. 227).

The preparations for the work, the acquisition of the various tools and equipment needed for the ritual, together with their consecration, could be famously exacting, although the prescribed manner of preparation differed from grimoire to grimoire. A pre-eminent requirement for increasing the holy *virtus* was by the use of pure materials unsullied through previous earthly employment. The paper and/or parchment of the book or magic circles and sigils had to be new, unused and thus "virgin", in contrast to the common re-use of parchment in palimpsests where the old text is more or less pumiced off and new lettering applied. Similarly, wands were to be made from freshly cut new-growth shoots, knives especially forged, earthenware censors expressly thrown for magical use, and so forth. As in every aspect of magical work, their variety and complexity ranged from the multifarious tools and special locations required by advanced grimoires such as the *Key of Solomon* to the simpler requirements of the workaday conjurations of Cunning Folk, as exemplified in Arthur Gauntlet's manuscript (see below). The perceived dangers of demonic magic called for more elaborate apparatus than the magic of angels and good astral spirits, which might not call for weapons or even protective circles. Also, measures for calling spirits into the relative safety of a crystal were less onerous than experiments involving tangible manifestation.

Magical Sources and Tools of Conjuration

The critical prerequisite for the practice of conjuration was a mastery of the magical texts or grimoires containing the directions for invoking spiritual beings. This was bookish magic *par excellence*. While it seems to be commonly assumed that the typical Cunning Folk were poor, illiterate peasants and labourers (and certainly there were those who fit this description), the average magical folk practitioner was in fact of a slightly higher status. He or she was more commonly of yeoman, artisan, or tradesman status, whose basic schooling (often including basic Latin) could be enough to allow an ambitious autodidact to achieve literacy sufficient for the secondary trade of folk magic – even conjuration for those so inclined. The Cunning Man or Wise Woman who aspired to ritual magic had to be literate and with sufficient resourses in time and wealth to carry out the demands made by the grimoires, which in theory would limit conjuration to a very small minority among folk practitioners. However, a number of actual conjurors, particularly those doing work for clients rather than their own satisfaction, presumably cut corners and did what they could with simpler preparations and less rigorously prepared tools, either taking a "no seatbelts" approach to dangerous work, or as Owen Davies observes, just putting on "a theatrical semblance" of conjuration, as the unfortunate Ann Bodenham did with her young confederates.

There was also the challenge of acquiring the necessary texts. From the example of Cunning Folk who did engage in conjuration, it appears that it was not that difficult to secure copies of publications such as Reginald Scot or the *Fourth Book of Occult Philosophy*, or even manuscript grimoires and related spells. Today we tend to see manuscripts and printed books as separate genres with the former leading only to the latter, but historically, scarce printed sources were as often copied back into manuscript form and the manuscripts themselves copied and changed by successive readers. Even in the 19th century, bookseller John Denley (d. 1842) was asked to loan books and manuscripts or send them on approval to country Cunning Men so that they could make handwritten excerpts or transcripts. For example, a correspondent, Peter Drinkwater, a farmer in Gloucestershire, wrote asking:

> Sandhurst near Gloucester Feb 3 1832
> Sir I received yours with the book last night. am sorry the Herbal was gone, as I wanted all of [William] Salmon's works – as to Barnaby Googes, that cannot be the book I mean. By Googe, or Black Googe, is a work on spirits, ghosts &c. quoted by Reginald Scot[100], as to the books that friend wanted, he would not wish to give more than 6s for bagino, and 8d or 1s for that number of

---

[100] Barnabe Googe's 1570 translation of Thomas Kirchmeyer's ("Naogeorgus") *Regnum Papisticum* as *The Popish Kingdom*, a idiosyncratic Protestant diatribe against Catholic "superstition". Denley may have offered Googe's translation of Conrad Heresbach's *The Whole Art and Trade of Husbandry* (1614), because of the herbal. Also see Owen Davies reference to Drinkwater from his 1839 obituary, in *Cunning Folk* (2003), pp 127-128.

benbow's with venus rising out of the sea. If you can send them at that well, along with agrippa for which I shall be very much obliged to you, and will safely return it. have you, sir, no works as will raise spirits? there are such books. It is a small voll. parsons have them. Anyone with the book may rise the spirit in 10 minutes. a friend is coming to London as will post this for you and am Sir yours &c.
Peter Drinkwater

It would appear that Denley also dealt in erotica; "bagino" (bath house or brothel) being suggestive, while William Benbow's picture "Mars, Venus and Vulcan" was prosecuted for obscenity in 1822. The following undated letter is possibly from Drinkwater as well, being embossed "Cumm Stationer Gloucester":

Sir, forgive my troubling you once more. will you send me the m.s. 2559 abraham the jew on talismans as marked [£]1.11.6 for the books I have of you. the 5 books 1.19.6 and will you be so kind as to look in 2788 blagraves cures for witchcraft. and write out the receipts. I dare say it is not much of it. you do not know how cattle &c. have suffered here lately to. If you would but send blagrave down with the m.s. it should come back with your books uninjured and if I approved of the worth, I would return you the 14s for it. I have seen some old books and gathered some receipts from them as have cured in some instance but not in all. I am afraid blagrave have none beyond my own or I should have ordered it before perhaps in 1561 history works may be done for cures for it. pardon me sir for troubling you and am sincerely yours
P [?]. D.
p.s. have you any work as will lay or raise spirits. there is a work in print called the whole art and science of supernatural divination magic. talismans &c. printed 100 years ago. I know not the author. I wanted it.

A rather cruder request shows that even less-educated Cunning Men knew to seek information on conjuration:

March 14 1838

Most Respected
Sir
I receved yourer Ansur I hop you give mee corect instructian to in vok the Angel Tarchael. The Rite ingredients for Feumigations & perticular govments if required. The Demetion of curcle of Defense For Safetey and place were to invok this Spirit Sir. I hop you will Inform mee so far as it lays in yourer power.
     Yourer Most Humble and
      Obedient Sarvant
       Thos. Thomas
  Place to Derect
    Thomas Price
    Bookseller
    Hy street Menthyn
(note: "a modest and very reasonable Request to [London astrologer John] Palmer given me by Mr. Palmer")[101]

Also, manuscripts are often considered to be more authentically magical than mechanically produced books, and were sometimes consecrated to add to their magical potency. Anyone who was connected in the esoteric underground could eventually come across what was needed if they were persistent enough.

The most influential printed sources were Reginald Scot's *Discoverie of Witchcraft* (especially the augmented 1665 edition), and the *Fourth Book of Occult Philosophy* (1655), which included the *Heptameron* of Peter de Abano and *Arbatel*), followed by Ebenezer Sibley, *A New and Complete Illustration of the Occult Sciences*, Book 4 (ca. 1795) and Francis Barrett's *The Magus* (1801). One would think Henry Cornelius Agrippa's predominantly scholarly and theoretical *Three Books Of Occult Philosophy* (1651) would have been

---

[101] The three letters are found in *The Wonderful Magical Scrapbook 1450-1850*, in the Harry Price Collection, University of London Library.

of less practical value to Cunning Folk than the *Fourth Book*, but a copy did turn up in the hands of a poor London Wise Woman named Ann Watts (who also had copies of the *Fourth Book* and Scot's *Discoverie*) when she was discovered sleeping rough in the Essex woods in 1687 and prosecuted by Justice Sir William Holcroft[102]. It was, however, the predominant source for *The Magus*, which included paraphrased material from both the original three books and the *Fourth Book*, as well as the *Heptameron* of de Abano and a translation of Trithemius' *Book of Secrets* with directions for conjuration. There were also conjurations included in "Raphael's" *The Astrologer of the Nineteenth Century* (1825) for "Egin, King of the North" and "Oberion", and the *Conjuror's Magazine* (1791-92) contained the *Arbatel* serialized in monthly numbers. Most of the examples below are from these books.

Following my editorial principals for the rest of the book that a) only published sources known to have been available for use by Cunning Folk before 1900 be used, and b) a division between the Cunning Folk and practitioners of learned magic be observed, I could pass over sources that only circulated in manuscript, but that would leave an incomplete sample to work with before the 19th century when authorities had lost interest in suppressing publications of a magical nature. For that reason I will include some extracts from manuscript sources, including the fundamentally influential *Key of Solomon* (which only appeared in print in English with S. L. Mathers' 1889 translation[103]) as a sort of base line for comparison, the wonderfully revealing magical notebook (Sloane MS 3851, British Library) of the known Cunning Man Arthur Gauntlet recently transcribed and published by David Rankine[104], an example from *The Wonderful Magical Scrapbook 1450-1850* in the Harry Price Collection, University of London Library, and another from Rawlinson MS D 253 in the Bodleian Library, of Moses Long of Gloucestershire (1683) that had been previously owned by three other Cunning Men: an "Allen" of Shifford near Bampton, and a "Cornelius" and a "Seckford" (who was a glover), both of Oxford.

Once the appropriate ritual sources were acquired and before the preliminarily purifying exercises were begun, the task was the construction of the tools and equipment need for the "experiment". There is an interesting example of a 17th-century magician's equipment that deserves quotation, both for the description and for the fact that its sale was evidently non-controversial. It is difficult to imagine a similar auction offering a century earlier. Thomas Britton (1644-1714), the deceased owner of the equipment, was not a Cunning Man, although as a dealer in "small coals", he came from the same social class as many of them. Famous for his skill as a musician and concert promoter, as well as being a "Rosicrucian" chemist and bibliophile, Britton was an unusual figure who straddled the social barrier between men who worked for their living and the wealthy and leisured "virtuosi", the learned dilettantes among whose ranks the hermeticists, ceremonial magicians and alchemists were usually found. Britton's magical apparatus were sold together with copy of the *Lemegeton* in 1694 for £10.15s.

> "a large Magical Circle, with the divine names of Gods, Angels, Spirits, etc., being 7 foot square, and fairly drawn on Vellum pasted to Cloth and rolled up, together with two Magical Tablets or / Leaves about a yard square each, the one containing abundance of Chaldy and Magical Characters or Letters with the several Names of God about Triangles ... the other Table contains the spirit Pamerfiels ... handsomely stained into [painted on] Cedar wood. Also two Cherubims Heads on Pedestals. There belongs also to this famous magical collection, a round solid Christal Glass, 3 inches and more diameter, and fixed on a solid Brass Stand. Four more globular and solid green Glasses about 3 and 4 inches diameter. Two oval hollow Glasses with holes at the top, all fixed in Tin Candlesticks. A very strange Lamp in Tin with 3 lights, in the fashion of a Semicircle. A magical Staff about 7 foot wreathed about with white and black. Five pair of holy Slippers all stained with several Red Crosses.

---

[102] Philip C. Almond. *England's First Demonologist: Reginald Scot and 'The Discoverie of Witchcraft' London*. I. B. Tauris, 2011, p. 7; also Owen Davies, *Cunning Folk* (2003), pp 126-127.

[103] A considerable portion of the *Key* omitting the experiments with named demons was published in the curious hectographic facsimile publication, the *Art of Talismanic Magic* by a "Raphael" – possibly Robert T. Cross (1850-1923) – in 1880, which was pirated by De Laurence in 1916.

[104] Guantlet's MS was later owned by a probable Wise Woman, one "Ann Savadage in Rosemary Lane". Rankine tentatively locates this in Mortlake, well outside of London, but I think the Rosemary Lane in question is more likely the one noted in Roque's *Plan of London* (1747) as being in the Minories near the Tower of London, between the northeast corner of the Tower and Cable Street.

> A magical Table with a Pyramidical Triangle, drawn on a Sheet of Parchment. The form of an Instrument to command by magical Invocations, Constraingations, etc., any Spirit ... to bring in an instant of time any hidden Treasures of what kind soever ... A brief Introduction explaining the Uses of the magical Tables. The practice of the East Table. The regal Invocation, together with the practice of the West, North and South Tables ..."[105]

Swords:

The most common tool called for in conjuration, with its connotations of superior status and authority, was the sword. In the *Key of Solomon*, swords are to be carried by each participant:

> Furthermore, each of the Companions should have a new Sword drawn in his hand (besides the consecrated Magical Sword of the Art), and he should keep his hand resting upon the hilt thereof ... (Mathers 1976: 18)

The text did not specify any particular use of the consecrated weapon, but it gave instructions for its sanctification:

> Swords are also frequently necessary for use in Magical Arts. Thou shalt therefore take a new Sword which thou shalt clean and polish on the day of Mercury, and at the first or the fifteenth hour, and after this thou shalt write on one side these divine names in Hebrew, YOD HE VAU HE, ADONAI, EHEIEH, YAYAI; and on the other side ELOHIM GIBOR; sprinkle and cense it and repeat over it the following conjuration: –
>
> **THE CONJURATION OF THE SWORD.**
> I conjure thee, O Sword, by these names, ABRAHACH, ABRACH, ABRACADABRA, YOD HE VAU HE, that thou serve me for a strength and defence in all Magical Operations, against all mine Enemies, visible and invisible.
> I conjure thee anew by the Holy and Indivisible name of EL, strong and wonderful, by the name SHADDAI Almighty; and by these names QADOSCH, QADOSCH, QADOSCH, ADONAI ELOHIM TZABAOTH, EMANUEL, the First and the Last, Wisdom, Way, Life, Truth, Chief, Speech, Word, Splendour, Light, Sun, Fountain, Glory, the Stone of the Wise, Virtue, Shepherd, Priest, Messiach Immortal; by these Names then, and by the other Names, I conjure thee, O Sword, that thou servest me for a protection in all adversities. Amen.
> This being finished thou shalt wrap it also in silk like all the other Instruments, being duly purified and consecrated by the Ceremonies requisite for the perfection of all Magical Arts and Operations. (Mathers 1976: 97-98)

Mathers also gave further specifications for three other swords used by the disciples. In contrast to the more demanding formulas for such things in later 19th century books on magic (see Ebenezer Sibley and Eliphas Levi, below) the only requirement here is that the swords be new and then appropriately inscribed. Personally forging a sword was understandably beyond the scope of even the expert magician. The drawing of the sword in Mathers' illustration that has a distinctive double-crescent/two-disk guard is most likely his own design based on Levi's ideas – those shown in the crude drawings of the grimoires are much more generic.

Reginald Scot. *The Discoverie of Witchcraft* only specifes that swords be new and inscribed:

> Book 15, Chapter 12:
> "...have in redines, five bright swords: and in some secret place make one circle, with one of the said swords. And then write this name, *Sitrael*: which doone, standing in the circle, thrust in thy sword into that name. And write againe *Malanthon*, with another sword; and *Thamaor*, with another; and *Falaur*, with another; and *Sitrami*, with another; and doo as ye did with the first. (Scot 1971: 344)
> Book 15, (additional material from the 1665 edition) Chapter "3":
> When the Candles are lighted, let the Magician being in the midst of the Circle, and supporting himself with two drawn Swords, (Scot 1971: 476)

---

[105] Ron Heisler. "Introduction to the Hermetic Adeptii", *The Hermetic Journal.* Issue 35, Spring 1987, pp. 34-35.

> When particular Instruments are to be sanctified, the Magitian must sprinkle the same with consecrated Water, and fumigate them with fumigations, anoint them with consecrated Oyl: And lastly, Seal them with holy Characters; after all which is performed, an Oration or Prayer must follow, relating the particulars of the Consecration with Petitions to that Power in whose Name and Authority the Ceremony is performed. (Scot 1971: *479*)
> Book 15, (1665 ed.) Chapter "9":
> …a new Sword with **Agla** on the one side, and **On** upon the other; … (Scot 1971: 488)

The Arthur Gauntlet MS (Sloane MS 3851):

From his translation of the *Heptameron*:

> And let the Master bear a Sword upon which let him say a Mass of the Holy Ghost And in the middle of the sword let this name **+ Agla +** be written And on the other side this name **+ On +** (Rankine 2010: 162)
> There is also a "Holy sword" in his version of the *Fourth Book of Agrippa* for use with evil spirits. (Rankine 2010: 206-7)

Ebenezer Sibley. *The Complete Illustration of the Celestial Art of Astrology* only casually mentions swords:

> … their swords are steel, without guards, the points being reversed [?]… (Sibley 1795: 1110)

Francis Barrett. *The Magus, or Celestial Intelligencer*:

Barrett's illustration of the sword is rather unusual in that it has no cross guard. He gives general instructions for its consecration, and its use in dealing with evil spirits:

> And, in the consecration of instruments, and every other thing that is used in this art, you must proceed after the same manner, by sprinkling with holy water the same, by fumigation, by anointing with holy oil, sealing it with some holy seal, and blessing it with prayer, and by commemorating holy things out of the sacred Scriptures, collecting divine names which are agreeable to the things to be consecrated; as for example, in the consecration of the sword we are to remember in the gospel, "he that hath two coats," &c. and that in the second of the Maccabees, it is said that a sword was divinely and miraculously sent to *Judas Maccabeus*; and if there is any thing of the like in the prophets, as "take unto you two-edged swords," &c. (Barrett 1967: 88)
> And after these courses are finished, cease; and if the spirit shall appear, let the invocant turn himself towards the spirit, and courteously receive him, and, earnestly entreating him, let him ask his name, which write down on your holy paper, and then proceed by asking him whatsoever you will; and if in any / thing the spirit shall appear to be obstinate, ambiguous, or lying, let him be bound by convenient conjurations; and if you doubt any thing, make, without the circle with the consecrated sword, the figure of a triangle or pentagon, and compel the spirit to enter into it; and if you receive any promise which you would have confirmed with an oath, stretch the sword out of the circle, and swear the spirit by laying his hand on the sword. (Barrett 1967: 100-101)

Wands and Rods:

The other common tool for conjuration was the wand (or staff, sceptre or rod). The various specifications for these traditional instruments of spiritual authority are as follows:

Key of Solomon I (Mathers edition):

> The Saff (*see Figure* 68) should be of elderwood, or cane, or rosewood; and the Wand (*Figure* 69) of hazel, in all cases the wood being virgin, that is of one year's growth only. They should each be cut from the tree at a single stroke, on the day of Mercury, at sunrise. The characters shown should be written or engraved thereon in the day and hour of Mercury. This being done, thou shalt say: –
> ADONAI, most holy, deign to bless and to consecrate this Wand, and this staff, that they may obtain the necessary virtue, through thee, O Most Holy ADONAI, whose kingdom endureth unto the Ages of the Ages. Amen."

There are rows of magical characters on each.

Fig. 68. The Staff.   Fig. 69. The Wand.

Elder has the useful quality of easily removable pith, which made the later practice of the insertion of magnetized cores easier. Hazel is a traditional coppice crop where the shoots from old stumps or "stools" are sprouted and cut every so often. One wonders whether a rod could be cut with a single blow with anything lighter than a hedger's bill-hook rather than the usual swords and knives involved. Also, while a useable length of 18" is standard for a year's growth, it doesn't seem like a 1-inch diameter shoot is predictable.

Key of Solomon II (Sibley/Peterson edition):

"Also you must have a Hazel stick of the length of the Box [note – "a foot and a half long", p. 287.], and about an inch thick, and a little green stick of the same wood, about the same length.", p. 336. The image of the two sticks indicate that on the wand, the characters are (roughly) "n (x (" (perhaps the Hebrew נאנה?) on each end (in reverse order to the left) and "TETRAGRAMMATON" in the middle, while the green stick has the letters "+ (n (", with "SADAY" towards the left and "ELOHIM" towards the right. There are no specific instructions for consecration beyond sprinkling the object with holy water and presumably fumigating it with the appropriate planetary incense, depending on the time of the operation.

Reginald Scot. *Discoverie of Witchcraft*:

Book 10, chapter 7: "There must be made upon a hazell wand three crosses, and certeine words both blasphemous and impious must be said over it, and hereunto must be added certeine characters, & barbarous names." Supplement, chapter 1 (1665): "Then with his Magical Wand, which must be a new hazel-stick, about two yards of length …", Chapter 2: "…the Exorcist must seek out for the straightest hazel wand that he can find, to the top whereof he must binde the head of an Owl, with a bundle of St. John's Wort, or Millies Perforatum…" [which was then consecrated]. This last was also included in Sibley (Sibley 1795: 1106).

The *Arthur Gauntlet MS (Sloane MS 3851)*:

The Consecration of a wand or Rod:
Take a hazel wand of a years growth And bathe it in the fire and consecrate it with these words **Purify me O God and I** shall be clean That no ill thing shall abide near me. Then write these names of God + Alpha + et + Omega + on both sides of the Rod and Jesus Christ at the end forward and in writing these names with the blood of a lamb of a Ewe Consecrate the wand as followeth /
Strengthen me O lord God Almighty Creator in all things As thou didst the Rod of Moses That parted the sea in sunder That the children of Israel passed through safe work in me the same virtue O God and I shall be so strong that no ill Spirit shall abide me Sanctify me O God of the Sabaoth And let thy name be Glorified in me that as the Rod of Moses did strike the hard stone and water gushed out So sanctify thy name that wheresoever it is writ or spoken all evil and unclean Spirits may be excluded + fiat + fiat + fiat + Amen +
Write these Words on a Hazel wand for a defensative
+ Tetragrammaton + Adonay + Secamon + Sadu ay + Sicamosey + Sepatate + Ambriell + Joell + Finis + (Rankine 2011: 252-253).

A wand is also mentioned in an experiment for sexual conquest with no details about its construction, although a possible set of characters to be inscribed is provided. (Rankine 2011: 150-151).

Francis Barrett. *The Magus*:

> A wand from Trithemius' *Book of Secrets*: "… take your black ebony wand, with the gilt characters on it …". The illustrative plate facing page 129 shows a straight rod with *Alga*, a hexagram, *On*, a second hexagram with a Hebrew yod (׳) in it, *Tetragrammaton*, and a cross (✠). The reverse side is to have *E go Alpha et Omega* on it. As the marks are not specified in the text, it is probably Barrett's own design. (Barrett 1975: 136)

I would also like to direct the reader to Joseph H. Peterson's history of wands, which can be found at http://www.esotericarchives.com/wands/index.html.

Knives:

In contrast to the central role knives play in modern Wiccan rituals, the knives of the grimoires were of lesser importance except in the *Key of Solomon*, and mainly used for the practical purpose of constructing other magical things. There is famously a great variety of knives in the *Key of Solomon*, but they are limited in number or absent altogether elsewhere. Presumably the use of knives was assumed in those sources that omit the details. As the array from the *Key* can be found in readily available sources, I will concentrate on the references more applicable to the Cunning Folk.

Reginald Scot. *Discoverie of Witchcraft*:

> Scot calls for a single knife – "You must have also a bright knife that was never occupied, and he must write on the one side of the blade of the knife ✠ *Agla* ✠ and on the other side of the knifes blade ✠ ☊ ♋ ♈ ♋ ✠ " (p. 347). He also provides an image of the knife, which looks like a typical 16th century blade (p. 351):

(Scot 1973)

The *Arthur Gauntlet MS (Sloane MS 3851)*:

> Gauntlet specifies the use of a white-handled knife to "write" characters on parchment in a sleep charm (p. 52); knives are also provided at a "spirits' meal" taken from the *Fourth Book of Agrippa*: "Lastly when thou art about to call these spirits though oughtest to prepare a table in the place of invocation, cornered with clean linen, on which thou shalt put new loaves of bread, And aquavit or milk in new earthen vessels, and new knives: …" (p. 210); and a circle to be drawn "with a knife with a black haft" for preparing a crystal for viewing (p. 213). There are no specifications for any of these outside of the "newness" of the second example. It might be that the requirements mentioned elsewhere in conjuring tradition are simply assumed, or that more specific preparations are simply unneccessary. (Rankine 2011)

Ebenezer Sibley. *The Complete Illustration of the Celestial Art of Astrology*:

The knife in Sibley (which he doesn't give instructions for the use of) is clearly drawn from Scot:

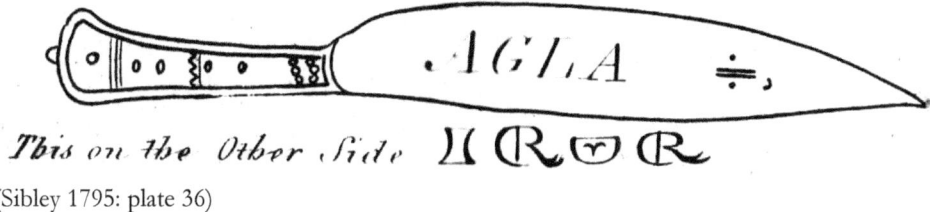

(Sibley 1795: plate 36)

Arthur Gauntlet's references include the *Heptameron* and the *Arbatel*. There is no knife mentioned or described in Barrett's *Magus*.

Sigils and Pentacles:

If the acts of faith and abstinence, and the adjurations and prayers represent the influence of exorcism on conjuration, magical characters and pentacles are a contribution from astral magic. The strange alphabets, characters, figures, seals and sigils in books, on pentacles, and in magic circles were as vital to the success of the conjuration as the verbal invocations and bindings. In the same way that knowledge of the personal name of a planetary intelligence, angel or demon that gave the operator power over that being, so their personal magical characters and seals provided the necessary means by which to invoke and control them. The abstractions embodied in written characters and signs channeled the *virtus* of spiritual beings from the astral realms (as both lacked a physical form) in the same way that a combination of tangible materials such as herbs, stones, and animal parts transmitted astral *virtus* in natural magic. Magical alphabets and figures were also formed by linking stars together, as in the mapping of the figures of the constellations. It should also be noted that some sigils very much resemble those found in Hellenistic magical papyri, charms and lead *defixiones* or curse tablets, as well as in Arabic magic (which was the source of Agrippa's numerical squares).

Seals or sigils were the spiritual equivalents of the signets of powerful men or the "merchant's marks" (which often resembled magical sigils) that identified medieval business men and their property. They provided a dependable link with a particular spirit (like an astral URL?). Pentacles with divine names, images and sigils also provided protection for the magician. These pentacles apparently intimidated evil spirits by reference to good spirits that would protect the magician and activate punishment by the good spirits of the demons for disobedience or aggression. As the *Key of Solomon* explains, "… the Seals, Characters, and Divine Names, serve only to fortify the work, to preserve from unforeseen accidents, and to attract the familiarity of the Angels and Spirits …" (Mathers 1976: 46)

The sigils needed to invoke the demons in Weyer's list in the *Pseudomonarchia daemonum* (1563) as reproduced from Scot's *Discoverie* in the previous chapter, are from Kevin Wilby's 1985 edition of the *Lemegeton*. I haven't included the *Lemegeton* itself as one of the illustrative sources because it was only available in manuscript and not *known* to have been widely circulated among the Cunning Folk – although it could have been.

Three other series of sigils that turn up repeatedly in successive magical sources are: 1) the magical squares and derivative sigils of the seven planetary intelligences as worked out by Agrippa; 2) similar symbols for the seven planetary angels that governed the days of the week, as found in the *Heptameron*; and 3) the seven oddly geometric characters of the demonic (or "Olympic") governors of the planets from the *Arbatel*. Agrippa's sigils have the attraction of being rationally derived from the planetary squares, whereas the others seem to have been more arbitrary in composition, and may be assumed to have been revealed to magicians through previous conjurations or through divine inspiration. There were innumerable other examples in the grimoires, but these will suffice to illustrate the genre.

Henry Cornelius Agrippa. *Three Books Of Occult Philosophy* (1651):

A scan of the first page from the 1651 English edition showing Agrippa's sigils, with additional clearer images from *The Magus*:

244   Of Occult Philosophy.   Book II

The Table of Saturn *in his compass.*   *In Hebrew notes.*

4	9	2
3	5	7
8	1	6

The Seales or Characters

Of Saturn.   *Of the Intelligence of* Saturn.   *Of the Spirit of* Saturn.

The Table of Jupiter *in his compass.*   *In Hebrew notes.*

4	14	15	1
9	7	6	12
5	11	10	8
16	2	3	13

The Seales or Characters

Of Jupiter.   *Of the Intelligence of* Jupiter.   *The Spirit of* Jupiter.

The

The Fourth Book of Occult Philosophy. From the *Heptameron: or, Magical Elements of Peter de Abano*:

These sigils were for the seven angels of the day of the week. Each was introduced as the full example of "the Lord's day" illustrates, with all of angels associated with Sunday, an appropriate conjuration and notes concerning the "Spirits of the Air" for that day. For the other accompanying texts, please consult http://www.esotericarchives.com/solomon/heptamer.htm

Considerations of the Lord's Day.

THe Angel of the Lord's day, his Sigil, Planet, Signe of the Planet, and the name of the fourth heaven.

                                    The Angels of the Lords day.

Michael, Dardiel, Huratapal.

                              The Angels of the Air ruling on the Lords day.

Varcan, King.

                                           His Ministers.

Tus, Andas, Cynabal.

The winde which the Angels of the Air abovesaid are under.

The North-winde.

The Angel of the fourth heaven, ruling on the Lords day, which ought to be called from the four parts of the world.

                                         At the East.

Samael.	*Baciel.*	*Atel.*
Gabriel.	*Vionairaba.*	

                                         At the West.

Anael.	*Pabel.*	*Ustael.*
Burchat.	*Suceratos.*	*Capabili.*

                                         At the North.

Aiel.	*Aniel, vel Aquiel.*	*Masgabriel.*
Sapiel.	*Matuyel.*	

                                         At the South.

Haludiel.	*Machasiel.*	*Charsiel.*
Uriel.	*Naromiel.*	

                                    The perfume of the Lords day.

Red Wheat.

The Conjuration of the Lords day.

COnjuro & confirmo super vos Angeli fortes Dei, & sancti, in nomine Adonay, Eye, Eye, Eya, qui est ille, qui fuit, est & erit, Eye, Abraye: & in nomine Saday, Cados, Cados, Cados, alte sendentis super Cherubin, & per nomen magnum ipsius Dei fortis & potentis, exaltatique super omnes coelos, Eye, Saraye, plasmatoris seculorum, qui creavit mundum, coelum, terram, mare, & omnia quæ in eis sunt in primo die, & sigillavit ea sancto nomine suo Phaa: & per nomina sanctorum Angelorum, qui dominantur in quarto exercitu, & serviunt coram potentissimo Salamia, Angelo magno & honorato: & per nomen stellæ, quæ est Sol, & per signum, & per immensum nomen Dei vivi, & per nomina omnia prædicta, conjuro te Michael angele magne, qui es præpositus Diei Dominicæ: & per nomen Adonay, Dei Israel, qui creavit mundum & quicquid in eo est, quod pro me labores, & ad moleas omnem meam petitionem, juxta meum velle & votum meum, in negotio & causa mea. And here thou shalt declare thy cause and business, and for what thing thou makest this Conjuration.

The Spirits of the Air of the Lords day, are under the North-winde; their nature is to procure Gold, Gemmes, Carbuncles, Riches; to cause one to obtain favour and benevolence; to dissolve the enmities of men; to raise men to honors; to carry or take away informities. But in what manner they appear, it's spoken already in the former book of Magical Ceremonies.

The Cunning Man's Handbook
Considerations of Munday.

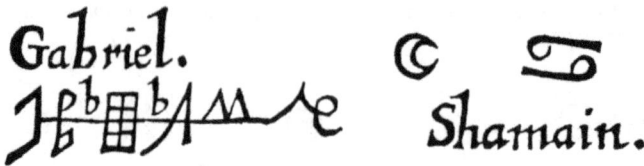

Considerations of Tuesday.

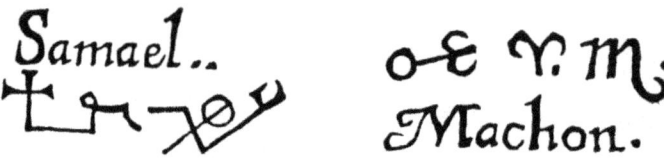

Considerations of Wednesday.

Considerations of Thursday.

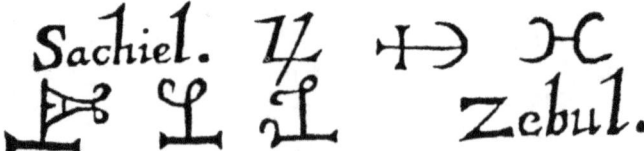

Considerations of Friday.

Considerations of Saturday, or the Sabbath day.

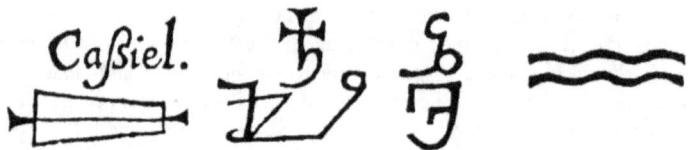

Jim Baker

The Fourth Book of Occult Philosophy. The Arbatel of Magick:

The characters of the seven "stars" that make up the "seven different governments of the Spirits of Olympus, by whom God hath appointed the whole frame and universe of this world to be governed:"

Aratron (Saturn)

His character.

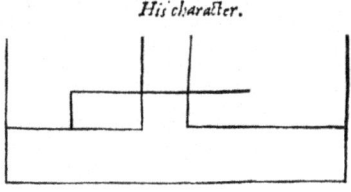

Bethor (Jupiter)

His character.

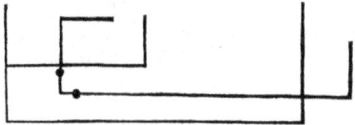

Phaleg (Mars)

His character

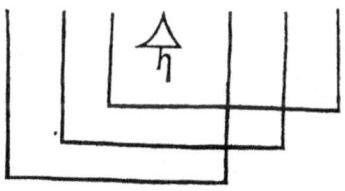

Och (the Sun)

The Character.

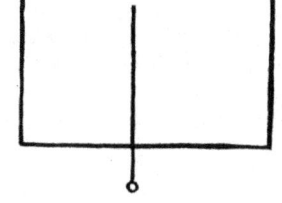

Hagith (Venus)

His Character.

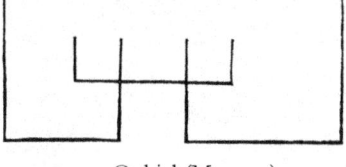

Ophiel (Mercury)

445

his Character is this.

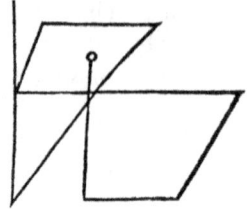

Phul (the Moon)

Phul hath this Character.

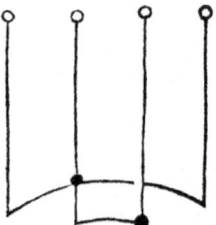

These examples (plus the others included elsewhere in this book) indicate what the scope of sigil creation encompassed.

Pentacles were more elaborate designs engraved on metal lamens or inscribed in coloured inks (and bird's or bat's blood) on parchment and worn (veiled) on the chest of the operator. They served as defences against dangerous spirits and sources of power to instill fear into the demons and command their obedience by providing connections to good spirits, angels and divine *virtus*. The *Key of Solomon* provides a series of 44 pentacles for various purposes representing the seven planets, while Arthur Gauntlet's MS has a series of four increasingly complex versions of a "Pentaculum of Solomon". Barrett's *Magus* depicts a lamen of the Archangel Michael and pentacles bearing the holy names of God and a protective example taken from Agrippa's third book, all with Hebrew characters, while Sibley depicts two examples taken from Scot's *Discoverie*. These graphic representations are more common in the illustrated manuscript grimoires than they are in published texts, where they may be just described verbally. The following examples are 1) two planetary pentacles from the *Key of Solomon* (Mathers 1974: plate 5), 2) the fourth "Pentaculum of Solomon" (Rankine 2010: 112), and the original pentacle with the names of God from *Three Books of Occult Philosophy* (Agrippa 1651: 376-377).

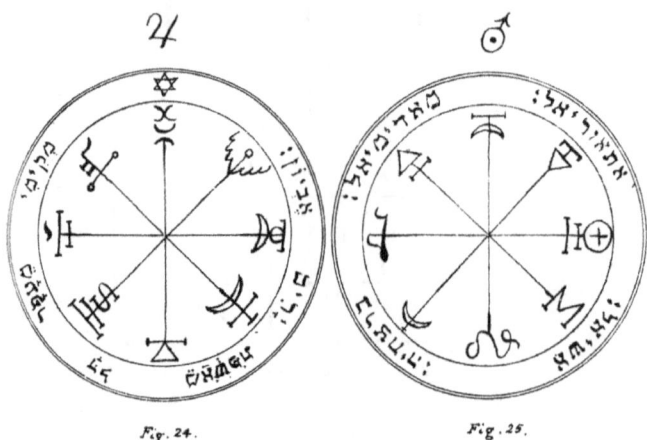

Fig. 24.   Fig. 25.

 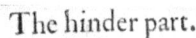

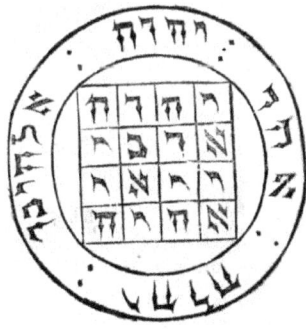 

Parchment and paper:

Although virgin paper is simple enough, the possibilities with parchment, as noted above, inspired some imaginative possibilities. However, most early texts apparently require only virgin, i.e., new parchment. In Book II, Chapter 17 of the *Key of Solomon*, it was prescribed that "virgin" parchment was not just pure and unused, but that the lamb from which the skin was required had to be virgin as well, even from one not yet born:

OF VIRGIN PARCHMENT, OR VIRGIN PAPER, AND
HOW IT SHOULD BE PREPARED

Virgin paper, or card, is that which is new, pure, clean, and exorcised, never having served for any other purpose.

Virgin parchment is necessary in many Magical Operations, and should be properly prepared and consecrated. There are two kinds, one called Virgin, the other Unborn. Virgin parchment is that which is taken from an Animal which hath not attained the age of generation, whether it be ram, or kid, or other animal.

Unborn parchment is taken from an animal which hath been taken before its time from the uterus of its mother. (Mathers 1976: 111)

Typically, this was "romanticized" to even more elaborate levels in Ebenezer Sibley's 19th century version:

> This then is the manner in which it must be prepared. It must be Virgin Parchment.—You must be ready on the Vigil of St. John the Baptist, with a little white Lamb, or Kid of 6 months { [correction] *weeks} old. You must lead {it} to a Fountain, the water of which is clear and flowing, and after having plunged it 7 times, to clear it of all sorts of Filth, you must cut its Throat with a new knife which should be devoted to the Operation of this Art, and which has never been applied to any other purpose. Then you must let all the Blood run out, with the Water of the Fountain, and having cut it, you shall place the Hide in running water, & fix it, while you are being employed in Burying the Body deep enough to prevent it being devoured by Beasts. Afterwards you shall draw the Hide from out of the Water, and prepare it in the same manner as the Manufacturers usually prepare Parchment, with the circumstance that everything made use of on this occasion shall never be applied to a Prophane use.[106]

The parchment or paper called for in the other sources is simply new and unused.

Fourth Book of Occult Philosophy (1655):

> There remains with those Magicians who use very much the ministry of the Devils, a certain rite for calling Spirits by a book consecrated before which is rightly called the book of Spirits, of that now there are a few things to be spoken: This book is consecrated, being the book of evil Spirits after its name and manner rightly composed. To which book the Spirits within written have vowed obedience at hand by their holy Oath Therefore this book is made of most pure paper, which not as yet is put to any use. Many call it virgin paper. (Rankine 2011: 198-199; and with slightly different wording, in *Agrippa's Fourth Book*, 1978: 57)

Incenses and perfumes:

The use of incense in magic, as in religious rituals, has been an important part of attracting (or on occasion, banishing) spiritual beings since time immemorial. Ficino stressed the importance of fumigations for his astral magic (in part borrowed from Arabic sources such as the *Picatrix*, as well as from newly rediscovered Neoplatonic texts), while Agrippa describes their use in natural magic: "Some Suffumigations also, or perfumings, that are proper to the Stars, are of great force for the opportune receiving of Celestiall gifts under the rayes of the Stars, in as much as they do strongly work upon the Aire, and breath", with details about which substances should be used for the particular planets (Agrippa 1651: 85, 88-89). Suffumigation was sometimes seen by critics as a marker for impious idolatry, as opposed to operations of natural magic.

Key of Solomon I (Mathers edition):

> For perfumes of good odour, take thou [frank]incense, aloes, nutmeg, gum benjamin, musk, and other fragrant spices ... (Mathers 1976: 101)

Reginald Scot. *Discoverie of Witchcraft*:

> ... and make suffumigations to thy selfe, and to thy fellowe or fellowes, with frankincense, mastike, lignum aloes: then put it in wine, and saie with good devotion, in the worship of the high God almightie, all together, that he may defend you from all evils. (Scot 1973: 348)
> I conjure thee most filthy and horrible spirit, and everie vision of our enimie, &c: that thou go and depart from out of this creature of frankincense, with all thy deceipt and wickednes, that this creature may be sanctified, and in the name of our Lord + Jesus + Christ + that all they that taste, touch, or smell the same, may receive the virtue and assistance of the Holie-ghost; so as wheresoever this incense or frankincense shall remain, that there thou in no wise be so bold as to approch or once presume or attempt to hurt: but what uncleane spirit so ever thou be, that thou with all thy

---

[106] Ebenezer Sibley, M. D. *The Clavis or Key to the Magic of Solomon the King*. Joseph Peterson, ed. Lake Worth, FL: Ibis Press, 2009, p. 334.

craft and subtiltie avoid and depart, being conjured by the name of God the father almightie, &c. And that wheresoever the fume or smoke thereof shall come, everie kind and sort of divels may be driven awaie, and expelled; as they were at the increase of the liver of fish, which the archangell Raphaell made, &c. (Scot 1973: 376)

… with a Chafing-dish of Charcole, perfume it with Frankincense and Cinamon, (Scot 1973: 476)

The *Arthur Gauntlet MS* (*Sloane MS 3851*):

(From the *Heptameron*) **The blessing of Fumigations:**
O God of Abraham God of Isaac God of Jacob bless these Creatures that they may hold in the force and virtue of their Odours, that the enemy nor Phantasms may not enter into them, Through our Lord Jesus Christ. Afterwards sprinkle them with Holy water.
An Exorcism of the Fire upon which the Fumigations are put.
The fire which we use in fumigations let it be put in a new earthen vessel and exorcise it as followeth.
I exorcise thee creature of fire by him by whom all things were made that presently thou cast off from thee (or out of thee) Every Phantasm that may hurt in any kind. Afterwards say.
Bless lord this Creature of fire and sanctify it That it may be blessed to the praise of thy holy name That it may not hurt the lookers-on, through our Lord Jesus Christ. (Rankine 2010: 159-160)
Let him have his fumigations assigned to that day in which he worketh. (Rankine 2010: 162)

Incenses for each day of the week:

Sunday Red Saunders (Turner's 1655 edition, "red wheat")
Moonday Aloes
Tuesday pepper
Wednesday Mastic
Thursday Saffron
Friday Costu (Turner's 1655 edition, "pepperwort")
Saturday Brimstone. (Rankine 2010: 169-179)

The following list is based on chapter 43 of the first book of Agrippa's *Three Books of Occult Philosophy*: "Of Perfumes, or Suffumigations, their manner, and power"

Of Perfumes ~:

A Perfume made of Hempseed and of the Seeds of Fleawort and violet roots and Parsley and (Smallage) maketh to see things to come **And** is available for Prophecy.

A Perfume made with Coriander, Saffron, Henbane and Parsley (Smallage) and White Poppy ana [i.e., "of equal quantity"] bruised and Pounded together If any shall dig Gold or Silver or any precious thing the ☾ being joined to the ☉ in the lower heaven let him perfume the place with this suffumigation. /

A Perfume of the Planets. Myrrh, Gostu [Rankine corrects this to "Costum"], Mastic, Camphor, Frankincense, Sanders, Opoponax, Lignum Aloes, Alum, Euphorbium, Storax or Thimyam [Rankine: "probably Thyme"] ana 1 oz.

A Perfume of ☉ yellow amber ½ oz Musk 12 grains Lignum Aloes 36 grains Lignum Balsam and the berries of Laurel ana 46 grains Of Gilleflowers Myrrh and Frankincense ana 1 oz with the blood of a white Cock make pills in the quantity of ½ dram.

A Perfume of ☾ Take of white Poppy seeds 1 oz of Male Frankincense ½ oz Of Camphor 1 oz with the blood of a Goose made in balls.

A perfume of ♄ Seeds of Black Poppies and the Seeds of Hoyseami [henbane] ana 2 oz The Root of Mandragoras 1 ½ oz The stone Lapis Lazuli ½ oz [Rankine notes the probable error as Agrippa has lodestone] Myrrh 3 grains with the Brains or blood of A Bat in balls the quantity of 1 oz

A Perfume of ♃ Seeds of Ash 20 oz Lignum Aloes 2 oz Storax, Benjamin 1 oz Lapis Lazuli 1 oz Of the very tips of the feathers of the Peacock Let them be incorporated with the blood of a Stork or of a / Swallow or the brain of a bat let there be made a troschisk [tablet] in the quantity of a Groat [the weight of an English four pence piece, about 2.1 grains].

A Perfume of ♂ Euphorbium Bedelum 1 oz Ammoniac roots of both sorts of Eleborus [Hellebores] and the lodestone 2 drams Brimstone 1 dram let it be incorporated with the brain of a Crow and with Mans blood of a black Cat make Trochisks in quantity ½ dram

A Perfume of ♀ Musk 38 grains Amber 21 grains lignum aloes 1 oz Red Roses 2 oz Red Coral 2 oz mingle it with the brain of a Sparrow and the blood of a Boar. Make a Trochisk in quantity ½ dram

A Perfume of ☿ Mastic 1 oz frankincense 2 oz Gilleflowers, pantaphile [Cinquefoil] 2 oz ac Lapidi Achate. (with Agate Stone) Incorporate it with the brain of a fox or a weasel and with the blood of a Pie [Magpie] make Trochisk in quantity ½ dram

A Perfume of every planet ♄ Costum ♃ Nucis Muscate [Nutmeg] ♂ Lignum aloes ☉ Mastic ♀ Crocum ☿ Cinnamomum ☾ Mirtum [Myrtle] ana 1 oz (Rankine 2010: 254-256)

A second series of planetary suffumigations in Latin follows this list.

Fourth Book of Occult Philosophy (1655):

There are no particular incenses called for, the choice being left up to the operator when "... odoriferous Suffumigations appertaining to holy Worship" (p. 53), "... holy Fumigations" (p. 55), "a precious perfume" (p. 59), "contrary fumigations" (for banishing, p. 67), and so forth are called for. (*Agrippa's Fourth Book*, 1978)

Ebenezer Sibley. *The Complete Illustration of the Celestial Art of Astrology:*

Sibley's list, like that of Gauntlet's, is based generally on Agrippa.

> Thus the fumigation for spirits under Saturn, are made of frankincense-tree, pepper-wort roots, storax, and galbanum; by these the spirits **Marbas, Corban, Stilkon, Idas,** &c. and all of the first order in the astringency, are appeased and provoked, when the *fumes* are put upon a tripod in the hour of Saturn according to the planetary division. For Spirits under Jupiter, they take lignum aloes, ashtree-keys, benjamin, storax, peacocks-feathers, and lapis lazuli, mixing the same with the blood of a stork, a swallow, or a hart; the brains being also added: the fumes are kindled in Jupiter's hour, and in a place appropriate to his nature. They make fumigations unto such spirits of the order of powers as are under Mars, in the planetary division, with aromatic gum, bdellium, euphorbium, load-stone, hellebore white and black, and an addition or sulphur to make them into an amalgama, with man's blood, and the blood of a black cat; which mixtures are said to be so exceeding magical, that, without any other addition, they say, this fumigation is able of itself to make spirits under Mars appear before the Exorcist. To the spirits under Sol, being of the order of thrones, they likewise suffumigate saffron, musk, laurel, cinnamon, ambergrise, cloves, myrrh, and frankincense, musk, and the balsamic tree mixed up together with the brains of an eagle, and the blood of a white cock, being made up like pills, or little balls, and put upon the tripod. The fumigations appropriate to spirits under Venus, are roses, coral, lignum aloes, and spermaceti, made up with sparrows brains, and blood / of pigeons. To those under Mercury, they fumigate frankincense, mastic, cinquefoil, incorporated with the brains of a fox and the blood of a magpye. To spirits under Luna, fumigations are offered of frogs dried, white poppy-seed, bull's eyes, camphire, and frankincense, incorporated with goose's blood and *fluxus muliebris* [menstrual blood]. (Sibley 1795: 1109-1110)

The first list in Barrett's *The Magus* (Book I, p. 92) follows Agrippa as well, although he adds a second list of planetary incenses as well. He also gives the "blessing of fumigations" (book II, p. 109) from the *Heptameron*.

"Raphael" *The Astrologer of the Nineteenth Century* (1825):

Some of the archaic names for plants are now a puzzle, although "canabus" (cannibis), "archangel" (angelica), "camphire" (camphor), "coriandrum" (coriander), and "petersilion" (parsley), "croco" (crocus or saffron) and hemlock are evident.

> The following extraordinary magical virtues of herbs, &. Are extracted from an ancient manuscript in the possession of *"Raphael:"*—
> "Anoint thee with the juice of *canabus* and *archangel*; and, before a mirror of steel, call spirits, and thou shalt see them, and have power to bind and to lose them.
> "The fume of *fleniculis* chaseth away *spirits*.
> "Take the herb *avisum*, and join it to *camphire*, and thou shalt see spirits, that shall dread thee. It helpeth much to the achieving of secret things.
> "*Coriandrum* gathereth spirits together; a fume being made therefore with *apia nisquio*, and *lazias cicuta*, urgeth spirits, and therefore it is said to be the herb of spirits.
> "*Petersilion* chaseth away all the spirits of riches.
> "Take *coriandrum* of the second kind, which maketh one to sleep; and join thereto *croco*, *insgreno*, and *apio*, and grind them together with the juice of *hemlock*; then make a suffumigation therewith, and suffume the place where thou will hide treasure in, which the ☽ is joined to the ☉, in the angle of the earth; and that treasure, so hidden, shall never be found.
> "*Saturia* is an herb which, being worn about one, giveth grace and good fortune. ("Raphael" 1825: 196n)
> If, at the third rehearsal of the above mystic ceremonial, the spirit refuses to appear, prepare a fume of sweet-smelling savours, such as frankincense, aloes, cinnamon, oil, olives, nutmegs, musk, cassia, roses, saffron, and white wax; which must be burnt, commixed together, on a fire consecrated for the purpose ... ("Raphael" 1825: 218)

Costume:

Here as in other things, the earlier examples of conjuration (excepting the highly detailed *Key of Solomon*) generally have fairly simple requirements. Here are some of the specifications for the proper garb for magic.

Key of Solomon I (Mathers edition):
> Let the Master now arise and place upon his head a Crown made of virgin paper, on the which there must be written (with the Colours and other necessary things which we shall describe hereafter), these four names AGLA, AGLAI, AGLATA, AGLATAI. The which Names are to be placed in the front, behind, and on either side of the head.
> Furthermore, the Master ought to have with him in the Circle, those Pentacles or Medals which are necessary to his purpose, which are described hereinafter, and which should be constructed according to the rules given in the Chapter on Pentacles. They should be described on virgin paper with a pen; and ink, blood, or colours, prepared according to the manner which we shall hereafter show in the Chapters on these subjects. It will be sufficient to take only those Pentacles which are actually required, they should be sewed to the front of the linen robe, on the chest, with the consecrated needle of the Art, and with a thread which has been woven by a young girl. (Mathers 1976:19)
> But for the safety both of soul and of body, the master and the companions should have the pentacles before their breasts, consecrated, and covered with a silken veil, and perfumed with the proper fumigations. (Mathers 1976: 87)

CHAPTER VI
OF THE GARMENTS AND SHOES OF THE ART

The exterior habiliments which the Master of the Art should wear ought to be of linen, as well as those which he weareth beneath them; and if he hath the means they should be of Silk. If they be of linen the thread of which they are made should have been spun by a young maiden.

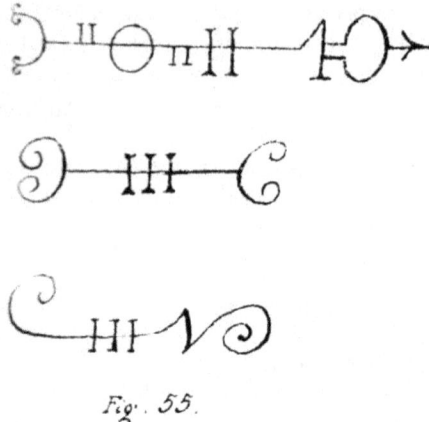

Fig. 55.

The characters shown in *Figure* 55 should be embroidered on the breast with the needle of Art in red silk.

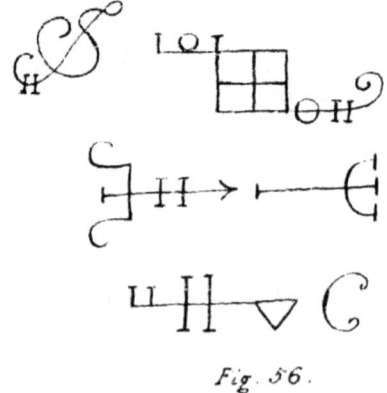

Fig. 56.

The shoes should also be White, upon the which the characters in *figure* 56 should be traced in the same way.
The shoes or boots should be made of white leather, on the which should be marked the Signs and Characters of Art. These shoes should be made during the days of fast and abstinence, namely, during the nine days set apart before the beginning of the Operation, during which the necessary instruments also should be prepared, polished, brightened, and cleaned.

Fig. 57

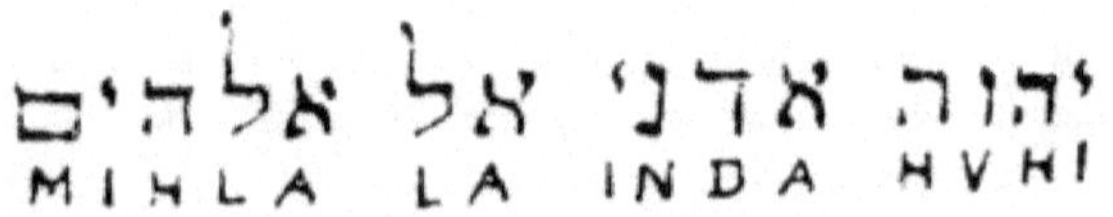

אלהים אל אדני יהוה
MIHLA   LA   INDA   HVHI

Besides this, the master of the art should have a Crown made of virgin paper, upon the which should be written these four Names:— YOD, HE, VAU, HE, in front; ADONAI behind; EL on the right; and ELOHIM on the left. (*See Figure* 57.) These Names should be written with the ink and pen of the art, whereof we shall speak in the proper Chapter. The Disciples should also each have a Crown of virgin paper whereon these Divine symbols should be marked in scarlet. (*See Figure* 58.)

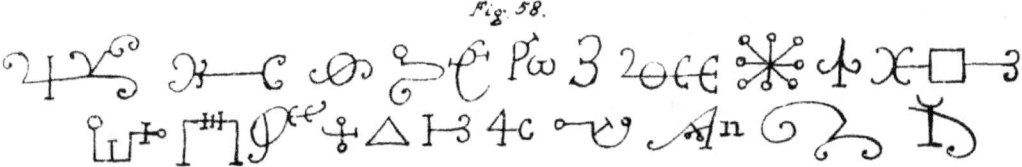

Fig. 58.

Take heed also that in clothing thyself with these aforesaid habiliments, that thou recite these Psalms:— Psalms xv.; cxxxi., cxxxvii.; cxvii.; lxvii.; lxviii.; and cxxii.

After this perfume the vestments with the perfumes and suffumigations of the Art, and sprinkle them with the water and hyssop of the Art.

But when the Master and His Disciples shall commence to robe themselves after the first Psalm, and before continuing with the others, he should pronounce these words:—

ANCOR, AMATOR, AMIDES, IDEODANIACH, PAMOR, PLIAOR, ANITOR; through the merits of these holy Angels will I robe and indue myself with the Vestments of Power, through which may I conduct unto the desired end those things which I ardently wish, through Thee, O Most Holy ADONAI, whose Kingdom and Empire endureth for ever. Amen. (Mathers 1976: 92-93)

Reginald Scot. *Discoverie of Witchcraft*:

The following example is from the enlarged version of Chapter 15 in the 1665 edition.

Let the Exorcist, being cloathed with a black Garment, reaching to his knee, and under that a white Robe of fine Linnen that falls unto his ankles, fix himself in the midst of that place where he intends to perform his Conjurations: And throwing his old Shooes about ten yards from the place, let him put on his consecrated shooes of russet Leather with a Cross cut on the top of each shooe. (Scot 1973: 471)

Fourth Book of Occult Philosophy (1655):

Three references from the *Fourth Book*: being clothed with a holy linen garment ... Thou shalt also have a long Garment of white linen shut before and behind which may cover the whole body and feet which thou shall bind with the Girdle. Thou shall also have a headpiece like a mitre made of fine linen You shall also have a veil of pure clean linen, and in the fore-part thereof let there be fixed golden or gilded Lamens, with the inscription of the name Tetragrammaton; all which things are to be sanctified and consecrated in order. But you must not enter into the holy place, unless it be first washed, and arayed with a holy garment; and then you shall enter into it with your feet naked. ... clothed with clean white garments ... (*Agrippa's Fourth Book*, 1978: 60-62)

The *Arthur Gauntlet MS (Sloane MS 3851)*:

Let it be a Priest's Garment If it may be had If not let it be clean linen. (Rankine 2010: 160)
(from Scot) Then he must be clothed in clean white clothes ... And he must have a dry thong of a lions or of a Harts skin And make therefore a Girdle And write the holy names of God all about An in the ends + A + and Ω +. (Rankine 2010: 223)

Ebenezer Sibley *The Complete Illustration of the Celestial Art of Astrology*:

The proper attire or *pontificalibus* of a magician, is an ephod made of fine white linen, over that a priestly robe of black bombazine, reaching to the ground, with the two seals of the earth, drawn correctly upon virgin parchment, and affixed to the breath of his outer vestment. Round his waste is tied a broad consecrated girdle, with the names Ya, Ya, ✠ Aie, Aaie, ✠ Elibra + Elohim + Sadai + Pah Adonai + tuo robore + Cinctus sum +. Upon his shoes must be written Tetragrammaton, with crosses round about; upon his head a high-crown cap of sable silk; and in his hands an holy Bible, printed or written (Sibley 1795: 1104)

Francis Barrett. *The Magus, or Celestial Intelligencer*.

> Now for your habit, you shall have a long garment of white linen, close before and behind, which may come down quite over the feet, and gird yourself about the loins with a girdle. You shall likewise have a veil made of pure white linen on which must be wrote in a gilt lamen, the name Tetragrammaton; all which things are to be consecrated and sanctfied in order. (Barrett 1801: book II, 93)
>
> ... let him enter into that place clothed in white linen ... (Barrett 1801: book II, 95)
>
> Of the HABIT of the EXORCIST.
>
> IT should be made, as we have before described, of fine white linen and clean, and to come round the body loose, but close before and behind. (Barrett 1801: book II, 109)

"Raphael" in *The Astrologer of the Nineteenth Century* has no specifications for costume in his several invocations.

In addition to these tools and objects, there were a variety of lesser articles (pens, ink, lamps and the like) specified in the *Key of Solomon* and other grimoires; some not seen elsewhere, such as a wooden trumpet sounded to begin the operation, which are not significant enough for the purposes of illustration here, but can be found in the sources indicated.

The requirements of tools grew more elaborate in the Romantic period, when writers on ceremonial magic such as Ebenezer Sibley, the composer of the *Grand Grimoire* or Eliphas Levi emulated the dramatic exaggerations in legends and fictional accounts of magical operations. In order to impress a more incredulous or spiritually jaded audience, they upped the ante considerably. Sibley's description of the tools of magic is considerably more "gothic" than even the elaborate but still practical armory from the *Key of Solomon*:

> And as by natural reason every magical charm or receipt had its first institution; in like manner have magicians disposed the matter and manner together with the times of their utensils and instruments, according to the principles of nature: as the hour wherein they compose their garments, must either be in the hour of Luna, or else of Saturn in the Moon's increase. Their garments they compose of white linen, black cloth, black cat-skins, wolves, bears, or swine's, skins. The linen, because of its abstracted quality for magic, delights not to have any utensils that are put to common uses. The skins of the aforesaid animals are by reason of the Saturnine and magical qualities in the particles of these beasts: their sowing thread is of silk, cat's gut, man's nerves, asses hair, thongs of skins from men, cats, bats, owls, and moles, all which are enjoined from the like magical cause. Their needles are made of hedge-hog prickles; or bones of any of the above-mentioned animals; their writing-pens are of owls or ravens, their ink of man's blood: their ointment is man's fat, blood, usnea [i.e., "moss" – actually lichen – grown on human skulls], hog's grease, or oil of whales. Their characters are ancient Hebrew or Samaritan: their speech is Hebrew or Latin. Their paper must be of the membranes of infants, which they call virgin parchment, or of the skins of cats or kids. They compose their fires of sweet wood, oil, or rosin: and their candles of the fat or marrow of men or children: their vessels are earthern, their candlesticks with three feet, of dead men's bones: their swords are steel, without guards, the points being reversed. These are their materials, which they particularly choose from the magical qualities whereof they are composed. Neither are the peculiar shapes without a natural cause. Their caps are oval, or like pyramids with lappets on each side, and fur within; their gowns reach to the ground, being furred with white fox-skins, under which they have a linen garment reaching to their knee. Their girdles are three inches broad, and have, according to its use, many caballistical names, with crosses, trines, and circles, inscribed thereon. Their knives are dagger-fashion: and the circles by which they defend themselves are commonly nine feet in breadth, though the eastern magicians allow but seven; for both of which a natural cause is pretended, in the force and sympathy of numbers. 1110-1111

In the *Great Grimoire*, a "blasting rod" (exhibiting the influence of Animal Magnetism) was created thusly:

On the eve of the great enterprise says this Ritual, you must go in search of a wand or rod of wild hazel which has never borne fruit; its length should be nineteen and a half inches. When you have met with a wand of the required form, touch it not otherwise than with your eyes; let it stay till the next morning, which is the day of the operation; then must you cut it absolutely at the moment when the sun rises; strip it of its leaves and lesser branches, if any there be, using the knife of sacrifice stained with the blood of the victim. Begin cutting it when the sun is first rising over this hemisphere, and pronouncing the following words:— *I beseech Thee, O Grand ADONAY, ELOIM, ARIEL and JEHOVAM, to be propitious unto me, and to endow this Wand which I am cutting with the power and virtue of the rods of Jacob, of Moses and of the mighty Joshua! I also beseech Thee, O Grand ADONAY, ELOIM, ARIEL and JEHOVAM, to infuse into this Rod the whole strength of Samson, the righteous wrath of EMANUEL and the thunders of mighty Zariatnatmik, who will avenge the crimes of men at the Day of Judgment! Amen.*

Having pronounced these sublime and terrific words, and still keeping your eyes turned towards the region of the rising sun, you may finish cutting your rod, and may then carry it to your abode. You must next go in search of a piece of ordinary wood, fashion the two ends like those of the genuine rod, and take it to an ironsmith, who shall weld the steel blade of the sacrificial knife into two pointed caps and shall affix them to the said ends. This done, you may again return home, and there, with your own hands, affix the steel caps to the joints of the genuine rod. Subsequently, you must obtain a piece of loadstone and magnetise the steel ends, pronouncing the following words:—*By the grand ADONAY, ELOIM, ARIEL and JEHOVAM, I bid thee join with and attract all substances which I desire, by the power of the sublime ADONAY, ELOIM, ARIEL and JEHOVAM. I command thee, by the opposition of fire and water, to separate all substances, as they were separated on the day of the world's creation. Amen.* Finally, you must rejoice in the honour and glory of the sublime Adonay, being convinced that you are in possession of a most priceless Treasure of the Light. (Waite 1969: 163-164)

As A. E. Waite noted, "The operator is overwhelmed with precautions concerning the secrecy which must be maintained in regard to it and might well be dejected by the difficulties of [the magic rod's] consecration. In view of such imputed importance, it is curious that De Abano and psuedo-Agrippa omit all mention of this tremendous instrument, while the *Key of Solomon* dismisses it in a few lines of easy instruction." (Waite 1969: 161).

Levi's material requirements can be equally fantastically demanding. For the magical sword, he requires a blade to be especially forged, where his medieval predecessors merely required a new sword to be written upon:

The sword—blade of steel should be forged in the hour of Mars, and new smith's tools should be used. The pommel should be of silver, made hollow, and containing a little quicksilver; the symbols of Mercury and Luna, with the monograms of Gabriel and Samael, should be engraved upon its surface. The hilt should be encased with tin, and should have the symbol of Jupiter and the monogram of Michael engraved upon it; see Cornelius Agrippa, *De occulta Philosophia*, liber iii., cap. 30. There should be a small triangular copper plate extending from the hilt up the blade of the sword a short distance on each side; on these should be engraved the symbols of Venus and Mercury.

The guard should end in two curved plates on each side; on these, the words Gedulah, Netzach upon one side, and Geburah, Hod upon the other, should be engraved; and in the middle between them engrave the Sephirotic name, Tiphereth. Upon the blade itself engrave upon one side Malkuth, and upon the other side the words *Quis ut Deus*.

The Consecration of the Magical Sword must be performed on a Sunday during the Solar hour and under the invoked power of Michael. Drape the Altar, prepare the Tripod, and burn therein the wood of laurel and cypress, consecrate the fire, and then thrust the blade of the sword into it, saying, "Elohim Tzabaoth, by the power of the Tetragrammaton, in the name of Adonai and of Mikael, may this sword become a weapon of might to scatter the beings of the unseen world, may its use in war bring peace, may it be brilliant as Tiphereth, terrible as Geburah, and merciful as Chesed." Withdraw the sword from the fire, and quench it in a liquid composed of the blood of a reptile mixed with sap to be obtained from a green laurel: then polish the blade with the ashes of vervain carefully burned.[107]

In another place, Levi has his own mesmeric wand in mind:

> The magical wand, which must not be confounded with the simple divining rod, with the fork of necromancers, or the trident of Paracelsus, the true and absolute magical wand must be one perfectly straight branch of almond or hazel cut at a single blow with the magical pruning-knife or golden sickle, before the rising of the sun, at the moment when the tree is ready to blossom. It must be pierced through its whole length without splitting or breaking it, and a long needle of magentized iron must occupy its entire length. To one of the extremidies must be fitted a polyhedral prism, cut in a triangular shape, and to the other a similar figure of black resin. Two rings, one of copper and one of zinc, must be placed at the centre of the wand; which afterwards must be gilt at the resin and silvered at the prisim end as far as the ringed centre; it must be covered with silk, the extremities not included. On the copper ring the characters must be engraved: דידושליסהקדשה and on the zinc ring: המולדשלמת. The consecration of the wand must last seven days, beginning at the new moon, and should be made by an adept possessing the great arcana, and having himself a consecrated wand.[108]

At the other extreme, other latter-day magicians tried to rationalize these painstaking preparations away, or even declare that all one really needs to do is use one's imagination to visualise things, which avoids the scrupulous production of the various items. Like Joseph Lisiewski, I consider this "wishful thinking" (pun intended) and an excuse to evade the labour and concentration involved in the practice of traditional magic. The scrupulosity involved in a "no effort spared" mentality towards securing the requisite *virtus* and purity strengthened the psychological focus needed to approach the ritual as seriously as possible, beyond the necessity of spiritual *virtus*. Strong faith was a requirement for magical success, which may have been easier to achieve in the age of faith before the Enlightenment. More rigorous preparations could alleviate this failing to some extent, while illegitimate shortcuts could shift the blame for failure of the rite on the careless operator, rather than the ritual itself.

Once all the tools and other preparations are taken care of, the actual conjuration could take place, examples of which will be presented in the following chapter. In addition, I include a few narratives of what took place in actual conjurations.

---

[107] Éliphaz Lévi. *The Magical Ritual of the Sanctum Regnum*. W. W. Westcott, trans. London: Crispin Press, 1970, pp. 29-30.
[108] Eliphas Levi. *Transcendental Magic*. A. E. Waite, trans. New York: Samuel Weiser, Inc., 1971, p 259.

CHAPTER 14:

Conjuration, Part II

Once the tools and materials had been acquired and the preparatory period of abstinence and worship for the ritual undertaken, the magician was ready to begin. The important astrologically appropriate times and planetary alignments for choosing *when* to carry out the ritual, as discussed by each of the sources, will be covered later in this chapter. First, the instructions for conjuration available to Cunning Folk in documented sources.

Proceeding to his secluded location or oratory, the magician prepared the magical circle(s) that would protect him and/or provide a locus for spiritual manifestation. It should be noted that although the protective purpose of such a circle was generally assumed, it was not always as simple as that. In some cases, the conjuror did stand with his partners (the need to have other people accompany the magician in his work, as in exorcism, is often stressed) within the classic circle, this was not always the case. Exceptions to the use of protective or focusing circles did occur, especially where the object of the operation was harmful or seductive magic where the operator worked alone and the rite was more similar to common sorcery than exorcism-like summoning: "... magic circles either are not used or are simple and relatively unimportant, and conjurations are less significant and elaborate here than in other forms of necromancy." (Kieckhefer 1997: 70). Also the invocation of spirits in crystals appears to have been far more popular in England than independent manifestations, and defensiveness was not as crucial in this case.

There were variations in the summoning of spirits, ranging from the full-blown conjurations as represented in the *De Nigromancia* attributed to Roger Bacon, the *Sworn Book of Honourius*, or the *Key of Solomon* to the fairly simple ones found in the Arthur Gauntlet MS or the Moses Long MS (Rawl. MS D 253). There are conjurations aimed at angels, planetary demons, infernal demons, fairies and even contractual agreements with men about to die to return as spirit guides, as was done by Mary Parish (1630-1703) with one George Whitmore. (Clark 1984: 27)[109] Also, some conjurations (apparently after the primary contact and binding made in a full summoning) were simple affairs commanding the bound spirit to activate a charm or similar service. Some conjurations dispensed with appearances altogether, and simply ordered the spirit to perform a stated task.

There are innumerable variations on the circle theme in the source works, as well as theoretical instructions for creating such barriers. In the *Key of Solomon* (omitting the footnotes), we find careful instructions for drawing a circle:

THE CONSTRUCTION OF THE CIRCLE.

Take thou the Knife, the Sickle, or the Sword of Magical Art consecrated after the manner and order which we shall deliver unto thee in the Second Book. With this knife or with the Sickle of Art thou shalt describe, beyond the inner Circle which thou shalt have already formed, a Second Circle, encompassing the other at the distance of one foot therefrom and having the same centre. Within this space of a foot in breadth between the first and the second circumferential line, thou shalt trace towards the Four Quarters of the Earth, the Sacred and Venerable symbols of the Holy letter Tau. And between the first and the second Circle, which thou shalt thyself have drawn with the Instrument of Magical Art, thou shalt make four hexagonal pentacles, and between these thou shalt write four terrible and tremendous Names of God, viz.:—

---

[109] It is odd that the well documented career of Mary Parish as a Wise Woman, involving angels, fairies and other activities, has seldom been mentioned except in Clark's excellent account.

Between the East and the South the supreme name IHVH, Tetragrammaton;—
Between the South and the West the essential Tetragrammatic name AHIH, Eheieh;—
Between the West and the North the name of power ALIVN, Elion;—
And between the North and the East the great name ALH, Eloah;—
Which names are of supreme importance in the list of the Sephiroth, and their sovereign equivalents. Furthermore, thou shalt circumscribe about these Circles two Squares, the Angles of which shall be turned towards the Four Quarters of the Earth; and the space between the Lines of the Outer and Inner Square shall be half-a-foot. The extreme Angles of the Outer Square shall be made the Centres of four Circles, the measure or diameter of which shall be one foot. All these are to be drawn with the Knife or consecrated Instrument of Art. And within these Four Circles thou must write these four Names of God the Most Holy One, in this order:—
At the East, AL, El;
At the West, IH, Yah;
At the South, AGLA, Agla;
And at the North ADNI, Adonaï
Between the two Squares the Name Tetragrammaton is to be written in the same way as is shown in the plate. *(See Figure 2.)*
While constructing the circle, the master should recite the following Psalms:—Psalm ii.; Psalm liv.; Psalm cxiii.; Psalm lxvii.; Psalm xlvii.; Psalm lxviii.
Or he may as well recite them before tracing the circle. (Mathers 1976: 17-18)

The relatively simple result is shown in "Figure 2":

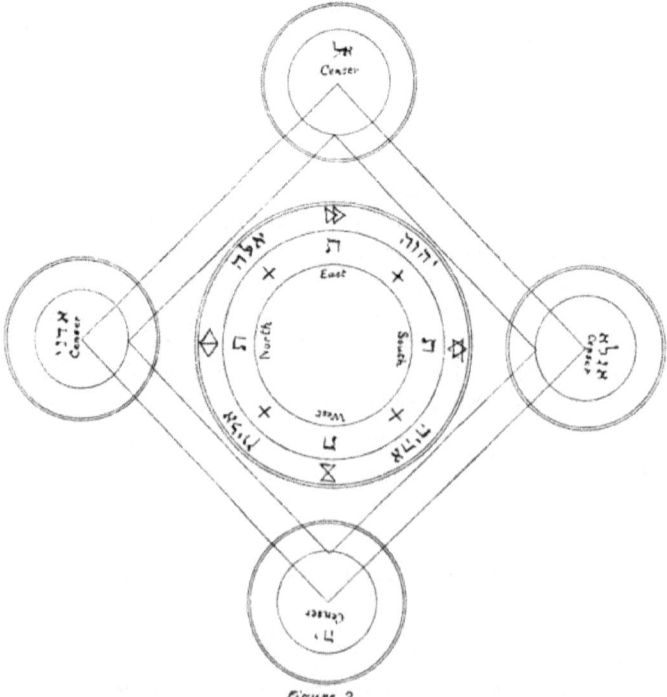

(Mathers 1976: Plate 1)

In Scot's *Discoverie*, his original instructions for magical circles are "… in some secret place make one circle, with one of the said swords And then write this name, *Sitrael*: which doone, standing in the circle, thrust in thy sword into that name. And write againe *Malanthon*, with another sword; and *Thamaor*, with another; and *Falaur*, with another; and *Sitrami*, with another; and doo as ye did with the first" (p. 344) which is accompanied with an often-reproduced illustration:

(Scot 1973: 346)

In other examples, he just says "make a circle" (p. 327) or if working on a floor, to "make a circle with chalke" (p. 338). His anonymous 1665 editor goes much further, however, and also offers the theory behind the use of circles. Except for the triangle for infernal spirits, no illustration is included:

Of Magical Circles, and the reason of their Institution.
Magitians, and the more learned sort of Conjurers, make use of Circles in various manners, and to various intentions. First, when convenience serves not, as to time or place that a real Circle should ne delineated, they frame an imaginary Circle, by means of Incantations and Consecrations, without either Knife, Pensil, or Compasses, circumscribing nine foot of ground round about them, which they pretend to sanctifie with words and Ceremonies, spattering their Holy Water all about so far as the said Limit extendeth; and with a form of Consecration following, do alter the property of the ground, that from common (as they say) it becomes sanctifi'd, and made fit for Magicall uses.

How to consecrate an imaginary Circle.
Let the Exorcist, being cloathed with a black Garment, reaching to his knee, and under that a white Robe of fine Linnen that falls unto his ankles, fix himself in the midst of that place where he intends to perform his Conjurations: And throwing his old Shooes about ten yards from the place, let him put on his consecrated shooes of russet Leather with a Cross cut on the top of each shooe. Then with his Magical Wand, which must be a new hazel-stick, about two yards of length, he must stretch forth his arm to all the four Windes thrice, turning himself round at every Winde, and saying all that while with fervency:
I who am the servant of the Highest, do by the vertue of his Holy Name Immanuel, sanctifie unto my self the circumference of nine foot / round about me, ✠ ✠ ✠. *from the East,* **Glaurah**; *from the West,* **Garron**; *from the North,* **Cabon**; *from the South,* **Berith**; *which ground I take for my proper defence from all malignant spirits, that they may have no power over my soul or body, nor come beyond these Limitations, but answer truely being summoned, without daring to transgress their bounds:* **Worrh. worrah. harcot. Gambalon.** ✠ ✠ ✠.
Which Ceremonies being performed, the place so sanctified is equivalent to any real Circle whatsoever. And in the composition of any Circle for Magical feats, the fittest time is the brightest Moon-light, or when storms of lightning, winde, or thunder, are raging through the air; because at such times the infernal Spirits are nearer unto the earth, and can more easily hear the Invocations of the Exorcist.
As for the places of Magical Circle, they are to be chosen melancholly, dolefull, dark and lonely; either in Woods or Deserts, or in a place where three wayes meet, or amongst ruines of Castles,

Abbies, Monasteries, &c. or upon the Sea-shore when the Moon shines clear, or else in some large Parlour hung with black, and the floor covered with the same, with doors and windowes closely shut, and Waxen Candles lighted. But if the Conjuration be for the Ghost of one deceased, the fittest places to that purpose are places of the slain, Woods where any have killed themselves, Church-yards, Burying-Vaults, &c. As also for all sorts of Spirits, the places of their abode ought to be chosen, when they are called; as, Pits, Caves, and hollow places, for Subterranean Spirits: The tops of Turrets, for Aerial Spirits: Ships and Rocks of the Sea, for Spirits of the Water: Woods and Mountains for Faries [sic], Nymphs, and Satyres; following the like order with all the rest.

And as the places where, so the manner how the Circles are to be drawn, ought to be perfectly known. First, for Infernal Spirits, let a Circle nine foot over be made with black, and within the same another Circle half a foor distant, leaving half a foot of both these Circles open for the Magitian and his assistant to enter in: And betwixt these Circles round about, write all the holy Names of God, with Crosses and Triangles at every Name; making also a larger triangle at one side of the Circle without on this manner with the names of the Trinity at the seven corners, *viz.* **Yehoway, Kuah Kedeth, Immanuel,** written in the little Circles.

The reason that Magitians give for Circles and their Institution, is, That so much ground being blest and consecrated by holy Words, hath a secret force to expel all evil Spirits from the bounds thereof; and being sprinkled with holy water, which hath been blessed by the Master, the ground is purified from all uncleanness; besides the holy Names of God written all about, whose force is very powerful; so that no wicked Spirit hath the ability to break through into the Circle after the Master and Scholler are entered, and have closed up the gap, by reason of the antipathy they possesse to these Mystical Names. And the reason of the Triangle is, that if the Spirit be not easily brought to speak the truth, they may by the Exorcist be conjured to enter the same, where by virtue of the names of the Sacred Trinity, they can speak nothing but what is true and right.

But if Astral Spirits as Faries, Nymphs, and Ghosts of men, be called upon, the Circle must be made with Chalk, without any Triangles; in the place whereof the Magical Character of that Element to which they belong, must be described at the end of every Name. (Scot 1973: 471-473)

The magical circle in Arthur Gauntlet's MS is taken from Scot, as shown here in the original from *The Discoverie of Witchcraft*, which is also found in Sibley's *A New and Complete Illustration of the Occult Sciences*, Book 4, plate 36:

(Scot 1973: 352)

Directions for drawing circles for the use on specific dates and times are found in the *Heptameron*:

Of the Circle, and the composition thereof.

The form of Circles is not alwaies one and the same; but useth to be changed, according to the order of the Spirits that are to be called, their places, times, daies and hours. For in making a Circle, it ought to be considered in what time of the year, what day, and what hour, that you make the Circle;

what Spirits you would call, to what Star and Region they do belong, and what functions they have. Therefore let there be made three Circles of the latitude of nine foot, and let them be distant one from another a hands breadth; and in the middle Circle, first, write the name of the hour wherein you do the work. In the second place, Write the name of the Angel of the hour. In the third place, The Sigil of the Angel of the hour. Fourthly, The name of the Angel that ruleth that day wherein you do the work, and the names of his ministers. In the fifth place, The name of the present time. Sixthly, The name of the Spirits ruling in that part of time, and their Presidents. Seventhly, The name of the head of the Signe ruling in that part of time wherein you work. Eighthly, The name of the earth, according to that part of time wherein you work. Ninthly, and for the compleating of the middle Circle, Write the name of the Sun and of the Moon, according to the said rule of time; for as the time is changed, so the names are to be altered. And in the outermost Circle, let there be drawn in the four Angles, the names of the presidential Angels of the Air, that day wherein you would do this work; to wit, the name of the King and his three Ministers. Without the Circle, in four Angles, let *Pentagones* be made. In the inner Circle let there be written four divine names with crosses interposed in the middle of the Circle; to wit, towards the East let there be written *Alpha*, and towards the West let there be written *Omega*, and let a cross divide the middle of the Circle. When the Circle is thus finished, according to the rule now before written, you shall proceed.

The example of such a circle:

(*Agrippa's Fourth Book*, 1978: 87)

In Barrett's *Magus*, this same circle is given on the plate facing p. 106. There is also a circle for use with a scrying crystal depicted on the final plate opposite p. 129:

The Cunning Man's Handbook

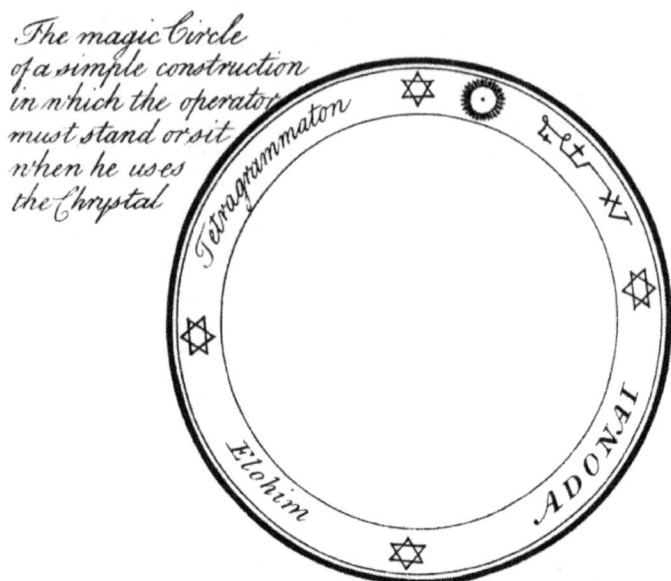

The Operation of Invocation:

Once the circle had been inscribed and the participants safely lodged within, all was ready for the ritual to begin. As noted earlier, the format of invocation was analogous to that of exorcism, but with different intent. The more complete ceremonies began with the recitation of several psalms before launching into the sequence of prayers and conjurations for the spirit being summoned. The *Key of Solomon*'s comprehensive formula for invocation (which is too long to include here, as well as being readily available[110]) includes six preliminary psalms (2, 54, 113, 67, 47, and 68), two prayers, a conjuration, the confession of the operator, two more prayers, the main conjuration, and then a stronger conjuration if the first yielded no results, another conjuration, an "address" to the defending angels, and an even stronger conjuration, upon which the invoked spirits were expected to arrive in view so that the operator could make his demands of them. The operator then recited a license for the spirits to depart. In the event that they wouldn't leave and were disobedient, there is a short ceremony for cursing them by burning their names on parchment, and a second license or command for them to depart.

Reginald Scot included several examples of invocations in his *Discoverie* that were readily used as a source for actual conjurations and drawn on for later books. Although these are both too long and too easily available to be fully included here, they were the first examples of conjurations in an English publication and important for their revelation of practices previously only available in manuscript form (such as the MS by one "T. R." dated 1570 in which they were made available to Scot). In particular, one complex series of invocations to call up and bind a dead person's spirit (as agreed upon before the death) in a crystal, who would then bring the fairy Sibylia – fairies and the dead being closely associated – for help in finding a hidden treasure. This series began with a general conjuration, followed by three more to bind the dead spirit. A subsequent ceremony involved the conjuration of the ghost to fulfill his task. Sibylia was then conjured with one or, if needed, two conjurations and then bound to help the magician, followed by a license for her to depart with the condition she come again when called. A separate ceremony for the same purpose involves three fairies; Sibylia and her two sisters, *Milia and Achilia*. Next a conjuration for angels to command the demon Citrael (or Sitrael) and four others to appear in a crystal was given in which the circle with five swords shown above was used:

---

[110] To see the entire text, please consult one of the many printed editions, or visit Joseph Peterson's *Esoteric Archives*. http://www.esotericarchives.com/solomon/ksol.htm#chap3 (accessed 2/23/2012).

Jim Baker

The eleventh Chapter.
An experiment following, of Citrael, &c: angeli diei dominici.
Saie first the praiers of the angels evrie daie, for the space of seaven daies.

Michael.	☉
Gabriel	☽
Samael	♂
Raphael	☿
Sachiel	♃
Anael	♀
Cassiel	♄

O Ye glorious angels written in this square, be you my O coadjutors, & helpers in all questions and demands, in all my busines, and other causes, by him which shall come to judge the quicke and the dead, and the world by fier. *O angeli gloriosi in hac quadra scripti, estote coadjutores & auxiliatores in omnibus quæstionibus & interrogationibus, in omnibus negotiis, cæterísque causis, per eum qui venturus est judicare vivos & mortuos, & mundum per ignem.*

Saie this praier fasting, called Regina linguæ.

☩ *Lemaac* ☩ *solmaac* ☩ *elmay* ☩ *gezagra* ☩ *raamaasin* ☩ *ezierego* ☩ *mial* ☩ *egziephiaz* ☩ *Josamin* ☩ *sabach* ☩ *ha* ☩ *aem* ☩ *re* ☩ *b* ☩ *e* ☩ *sepha* ☩ *sephar* ☩ *ramar* ☩ *semoit* ☩ *lemaio* ☩ *pheralon* ☩ *amic* ☩ *phin* ☩ *gergoin* ☩ *letos* ☩ *Amin* ☩ *amin* ☩ .

In the name of the most pitifullest and mercifullest God of Israel and of paradise, of heaven and of earth, of the seas and of the infernalles, by thine omnipotent helpe may performe this worke, which livest and reignest ever one God world without end, Amen.

O most strongest and mightiest God, without beginning or ending, by thy clemencie and knowledge I desire, that my questions, worke, and labour may be fullie and trulie accomplished, through thy worthines, good Lord, which livest and reignest, ever one God, world without end, Amen.

O holie, patient, and mercifull great God, and to be worshipped,
the Lord of all wisedome, cleare and just; I most hartilie
desire thy holines and clemencie, to fulfill, performe
and accomplish this my whole worke, thorough
thy worthines, and blessed power: which
livest and reignest, ever one God,
*Per omnia secula
seculorum,*
Amen. /

The twelfe Chapter.
How to enclose a spirit in a christall stone.

THIS operation following, is to have a spirit inclosed into a christall stone or berill glasse, or into anie other like instrument, &c. First thou in the new of the ☽ being clothed with all new, and fresh, & cleane araie, and shaven, and that day to fast with bread and water, and being cleane confessed, saie the seaven psalmes, and the letanie, for the space of two daies, with this praier following.

I desire thee O Lord God, my mercifull and most loving God, the giver of all graces, the giver of all sciences, grant that I thy welbeloved N. (although unworthie) may knowe thy grace and power, against all the deceipts and craftines of divels. And grant to me thy power, good Lord, to constraine them by this art: for thou art the true, and livelie, and eternall GOD, which livest and reignest ever one GOD through all worlds, Amen.

Thou must doo this five daies, and the sixt daie have in a redines, five bright swords: and in some secret place make one circle, with one of the said swords. And then write this name, *Sitrael*: which doone, standing in the circle, thrust in thy sword into that name. And write againe *Malanthon*, with another sword; and *Thamaor*, with another; and *Falaur*, with another; and *Sitrami*, with another; and doo as ye did with the first. All this done, turne thee to *Sitrael*, and kneeling saie thus, having the christall stone in thine hands.

O *Sitrael, Malantha, Thamaor, Falaur,* and *Sitrami*, written in these circles, appointed to this worke, I doo conjure and I doo exorcise you, by the father, by the sonne, and by the Holy-ghost, by him which did cast you out of paradise, and by him which spake the word and it was done, and by him which shall come to judge the quicke and the dead, and the world by fier, that all you five infernall maisters and princes doo come unto me, to accomplish and to fulfill all my desire and request, which I shall command you. Also I conjure you divels, and command you, I bid you, and appoint you, by the Lord Jesus Christ, the sonne of the most highest God, and by the blessed and glorious virgine Marie, and by all the saints, both of men and women of God, and by all the angels, archangels, patriarches, and prophets, apostles, evangelists, martyrs, and confessors, virgins, and widowes, and all the elect of God. Also I conjure you, and everie of you, ye infernall kings, by heaven, by the starres, by the ☉ and by the ☽ and by all the planets, by the earth, fier, aier, / and water, and by the terrestriall paradise, and by all things in them conteined, and by your hell, and by all the divels in it, and dwelling about it, and by your vertue and power, and by all whatsoever, and with whatsoever it be, which maie constreine and bind you. Therefore by all these foresaid vertues and powers, I doo bind you and constreine you into my will and power; that you being thus bound, may come unto me in great humilitie, and to appeare in your circles before me visiblie, in faire forme and shape of mankind kings, and to obeie unto me in all things, whatsoever I shall desire, and that you may not depart from me without my licence. And if you doo against my precepts, I will promise unto you that you shall descend into the profound deepenesse of the sea, except that you doo obeie unto me, in the part of the living sonne of God, which liveth and reigneth in the unitie of the Holie-ghost, by all world of worlds, Amen.

Saie this true conjuration five courses, and then shalt thou see come out of the northpart five kings, with a marvelous companie: which when they are come to the circle, they will allight downe off from their horsses, and will kneele downe before thee, saieng: Maister, command us what thou wilt, and we will out of hand be obedient unto thee. Unto whome thou shall saie; See that ye depart not from me, without my licence; and that which I will command you to doo, let it be done trulie, surelie, faithfullie and essentiallie. And then they all will sweare unto thee to doo all thy will. And after they have sworne, saie the conjuration immediatlie following.

I conjure, charge, and command you, and everie of you, *Sirrael, Malanthan, Thamaor, Falaur,* and *Sitrami*, you infernall kings, to put into this christall stone one spirit learned and expert in all arts and sciences, by the vertue of this name of God *Tetragrammaton*, and by the crosse of our Lord Jesu Christ, and by the bloud of the innocent lambe, which redeemed all the world, and by all their vertues & powers I charge you, ye noble kings, that the said spirit may teach, shew, and declare unto me, and to my freends, at all houres and minuts, both night and dale, the truth of all things, both bodilie and ghostlie, in this world, whatsoever I shall request or desire, declaring also to me my verie name. And this I command in your part to doo, and to obeie thereunto, as unto your owne lord and maister.

That done, they will call a certeine spirit, whom they will command to enter into the centre of the circled or round christall. Then put the christall betweene the two circles, and thou shalt see the christall made blacke.

Then command them to command the spirit in the christall, not / to depart out of the stone, till thou give him licence, & to fulfill thy will for ever. That done, thou shalt see them go upon the christall, both to answer your requests, & to tarrie your licence. That doone, the spirits will crave licence: and say; Go ye to your place appointed of almightie God, in the name of the father, &c. And then take up thy christall, and looke therein, asking what thou wilt, and it will shew it unto thee. Let all your circles be nine foote everie waie, & made as followeth. Worke this worke in ♋ ♏ or ♓ in the houre of the ☽ or ♃. And when the spirit is inclosed, if thou feare him, bind him with some bond, in such sort as is elsewhere expressed alreadie in this our treatise. (Scot 1973: 343-346)

Scot then includes a comprehensive ritual to invoke the spirit Bealphares in independent manifestation (rather than in a crystal) for finding treasure involved the 2nd, 20th and 51st psalms, a prayer, a conjuration, a binding, and the license to depart. There are also a simple crystal conjuration and binding, and a second ceremony for working with a ghost, including the preliminary agreement of the person about to die, and his later invocation.[111]

Besides Scot, the other most comprehensive printed source for conjuration was the *Fourth Book of Occult Philosophy* (1655), which includes the *Heptameron* of Peter de Abano and the *Arbatel*. Unlike Scot or the grimoires, the information is not presented as specific procedures to follow (which might have given the published book a taint of necromancy) but as theoretical explanations by which an astute magician could craft his own rituals. Working primarily with the safer planetary spirits rather than demons (although the *Fourth Book* itself discusses invoking evil spirits as well), these resources stress the astral nature of magic. The *Fourth Book* goes into some detail for discovering the names of the planetary spirits, suggests how to select appropriate biblical psalms and versicles and gives details for do-it-yourself composition of pentacles in addition to the examples of consecrations and bindings. The *Heptameron* includes examples of basic conjurations, astrological data, sigils, exorcisms, and prayers for each of the seven Intelligences. The *Arbatel* is divided into 49 "aphorisms". In Aphorism 15, the names, capabilities, sigils (like those of the *Heptameron*, these are included in the preceding chapter) and numerous "legions" of spirits commanded by each of seven "Olympic" spirits corresponding to the seven planets are given. Why they should be considered "olympian" is not explained, and again, there isn't any ritual structure provided for their summoning. This did not, however, deter magicians from successfully using these popular texts.

The best example of conjurations actually used by a Cunning Man can be found in the Arthur Gauntlet MS, which has over 30 conjurations (it is difficult on occasion to see where one ends and another begins) of various types, complete with the necessary psalms and other required elements. The first example, for summoning an angel into a crystal, is notable in that it does not employ threatening conjurations, but respectful adjurations. Angelic magic obviously was not of the same tenor as demonic conjurations:

> **How you shall work to have sight and conference with one Good Angel**
> **Say as followeth**. Our help is in the lord and in hid holy name O lord hear our prayers. The lord is with us **Amen**. So be it. +
> **We will not fear** nor be sorrowful because god is our father **Let us** fear the Lord our God and reverence him only + To whom be all honour virtue power and Glory both now and evermore **Amen** + For **Whosoever** calleth upon the name of the Lord shall be saved +. So be it **& then say** the Lord's Prayer **And** the Creed. **Then as followeth** ~
> **I call upon thee** and Invocate the O Omnipotent God which as King of all things Eternal Governor of all the world uncorrupt unspotted undefiled Invisible wonderful most faultless inreprehensible Almighty ruler Great and holy + Adonay + Eloy + Sabaoth + God of Gods and father of all Glories and most renowned virtues The truth itself High King father of our Lord and Saviour Jesus Christ Give thy benediction and blessing unto me thy humble servant AG And to all things I take in hand to bring to pass at this time Through thy most Holy and blessed name + Grant this O Heavenly father for Jesus Christ his sake thy only Son And our only saviour To whom with the Holy Ghost be all Honour Glory praise power might majesty Rule Dominion and Authority world without end. **Amen. Then say**
> Look upon me thy humble servant I beseech thee O my Lord God and Saviour Jesus Christ And have mercy upon me thy humble servant I humbly beseech thee. Thou art my helper and my refuge O Lord + Jesus + Christ + In thee only have I trusted and in no other neither will at any time hereafter trust in any other besides thee. Help me therefore O most mighty God which art + Alpha + et + ω + The first and the last whose virtue and aid I most humbly desire and heartily require Have mercy upon me O my God have mercy upon me and bless me with thy blessing everlasting. **Amen.**
> + In nomine Patris + Et filii + Et Spriritus Sanctus + Amen
> **Most Glorious God receive my Prayer. Amen.**

---

[111] For Scot's magical texts, see http://www.esotericarchives.com/solomon/scot16.htm (accessed 2/23/2012).

O Omnipotent and unresistable Jehovah who by the death of thy natural Son Our blessed Saviour Jesus Christ didst break the head of the Serpent and destroy the power of the Devil I humbly pray thy divine majesty to purge and free the place and Crystal stone (or Glass) from all infernal power To inhabit and discharge all apostate and descending Spirits from ever daring to approach near / my person) or near this place or presuming to appear in this Crystal stone (or Glass) To me AB thine unworthy servant for whom thy most blessed Son shed his most precious blood. To whom with thee and the Holy Ghost I yield all honour Laud praise Glory power might Majesty dominion rule and authority now and forever more world without end **Amen.**

The :51:Psalm
1. Have mercy upon me O God after thy great goodness According unto the multitude of thy mercies do away mine offenses.
2. Wash me thoroughly from my wickedness and cleanse me from my sin.
3. For I knowledge my faults and my sin is ever before me.
4. Against thee only have I sinned and done this evil in thy sight. That thou mightiest be justified in thy saying And clear when thou art judged.
5. Behold I was shapen in wickedness and in sin hath my mother conceived me.
6. But lo thou requires truth in the inward parts And shalt make me to understand wisdom secretly.
7. Thou shalt purge me with Hyssop and I shall be clean Thou shalt wash me and I shall be whiter than snow.
8. Thou shalt make me hear of joy and gladness That the bones which thou hast broken may rejoice.
9. Turn my face from my sins and put out all my misdeeds.
10. Make me a clean heart O God and renew a right Spirit within me.
11. Cast me not away from thy presence And take not thy holy spirit from me.
12. give me the comfort of thy help again and stablish me with thy free spirit.
13. Then shall I teach thy ways unto the wicked. And sinners shall be converted unto thee.
14. Deliver me from blood guiltiness O God thou that art the God of my health And my tongue shall sing of thy righteousness /
15. Thou shalt open my lips o lord and my mouth shall show thy praise.
16. For thou desirest no sacrifice else would I give it thee but thou delightest not in burnt offerings.
17. The sacrifice of God is a troubled spirit a broken and a contrite heart O God shalt thou not refuse.
18. be favourable and gracious unto Sion Build thou the walls of Jerusalem.
19. Then shalt thou be pleased with the sacrifice of righteousness; with the burnt offerings and oblations. Then shall they offer young bullocks up on thy altar. **Glory be to the father &c**

The :46:Psalm
1. **God is our hope** and strength a very present help in trouble.
2. Therefore will not we fear though the Earth be moved and though the hills be carried into the mids of the Sea.
3. Though the Waters thereof Rage and swell and though the mountains shake at the tempest of the same.
4. The rivers of the flood thereof shall make glad the city of God The holy place of the tabernacle of the most highest.
5. God is in the middest of her Therefore shall he not be removed. God shall help her and that right only.
6. The heathen make much ado and the kingdoms are moved But God hath showed his voice and the Earth shall melt away.
7. The Lord of Hosts is with us The God of Jacob is our refuge.
8. O come hither and behold the works of the lord what destruction he hath brought upon the Earth.
9. He maketh wars to cease in all the world ne breaketh the bow and snappeth the spear in sunder, and burneth the chariots in fire.

10. Be still then and know that I am God I will be exalted among the heathen and I will be exalted in the earth. /
11. The Lord of Hosts is with us The God of Jacob is our refuge. **Glory be** ~

The :91:Psalm:–:
1. **Whoso dwelleth** under the defense of the most high shall abide &c

You shall find this Psalm written in Page :35:
2. **The Lord is my Shepherd** Therefore can I lack nothing.
3. He shall feed me in a green pasture And lead me forth besides the waters of comfort.
4. He shall convert my soul and bring me forth in the parts of righteousness for his name's sake.
5. Yea though I walk through the valley of the shadow of death I will fear no evil for thou art with me Thy rod and thy staff comfort me.
6. Thou shalt prepare a table before me against them that trouble me Thou hast anointed my head with oil And my cup shall be ever full.
7. But thy loving kindness and mercy shall follow me all the days of my life And I will dwell in the house of the lord forever.

Glory be to the father and to the Son and to the Holy Ghost. As it was in the beginning is now and ever shall be world without end. **Amen.**

Then read this prayer following Three times with great devotion. If the angel appear not the first or second repetition.

O thou most glorious Sacred and invisible Trinity God the father God the Son and God the holy Ghost upon bended Knees of my soul and body I do most humbly and heartily implore thy Sacred Majesty at this present If it be thy holy will to give and grant unto me thy humble Servant **AB** The immediate visual vocal and audible presence and ministry of one of thy blessed persevering holy Angels In such an amiable peaceable constant and unchangeable form and manner as thy heavenly mercy and / wisdom towards me knoweth my frail nature most capable of without any hurt or astonishment offered or done to my mind or body to minister unto me and show and reveal unto me thy unworthy servant all such questions and things as I thy humble servant shall demand of him And I most humbly beseech thy Sacred Majesty to prepare and enable the faculties of my soul and body with sufficient Grace and power from thee to receive and use aright this thy so great a blessing for which I am an humble servant unto thee Grant this O heavenly father for Jesus Christ his sake thy clear and only Son And our Lord and only Saviour unto whom with the Holy Ghost I yield all honour laud praise Glory power might Majesty dominion rule and authority both now and evermore. **Amen.**

When he is appeared if his appearance be not perfect **Say**

If thou be that visible vocal and audible Angel which I have prayed for Show thyself apparently to the visible sight of me **AB** The servant of the everlasting God without all fraud guile deceit or delay as thou shalt answer to the contrary at the dreadful day of doom.

Being perfectly appeared demand his name the which being obtained Say **Art thou C** (naming his name) that blessed persevering holy Angel for whom I have prayed unto the Great God of Heaven and Earth. **If he answer** He is

Then say Blessed and welcome art thou C that comest to me in the name of the Lord. **Then say this Prayer following**

O Omnipotent and unsearchable Jehovah Lord and disposer of all holy Angels I give thy sacred Majesty most humble and hearty thank for thy great mercy and Special favour towards me thy unworthy servant In licensing and commending this thy blessed Angel **C** to appear to the sight of my thy humble servant **AB** In the form and in the manner and unto the end petitioned I most humbly beseech thy divine Majesty further to license and command this said most holy Angel So fully and perfectly to dilate and manifest himself To me thy humble Servant as out of thy mercy and wisdom thou art pleased shall at all times suffice for this blessed work which in thy name and fear I have begun and desire to continue

Then say to the Angel Thou holy and blessed Angel In the name of Jesus Christ by virtue whereof thou appearest I desire thee to give me plain and true answers of my questions doubts and demands to the plain understanding of me **AB** the servant of the ever living God. **Then say this prayer** /

+ O thou most Glorious infinite and Heavenly Lord God what is man that thou regardest him Or the Son of man that thou visitest him Man is a thing of nothing his time passeth away like a Shadow

In particular I confess myself to be but dust and ashes, a worm and no man the very matter and subject of thine eternal wrath and indignation yet thou feedest me with thy good things and givest me mercy instead of Judgment to drink Thou dost accumulate and multiply thy benefits upon me And in particular is thy special favour of the immediate visible vocal and audible presence and ministry of thy blessed Angel **C** A favour which thou has denied to the sons of men For those benefits and this what I shall say and render unto my lord but that Thou art my God and I will praise thee Thou art my God and I will exalt thee. I will take the cup of Salvation and call upon the name of the lord. I will pay my vows unto the lord in the presence of all his people The which that I may do I humbly crave thy assisting grace O heavenly father for thy Christ's sake to whom with thee and thy sacred spirit I give all honour and glory power praise majesty and dominion now and forever. **Amen.**

Then make your demands to the Angel Having what you desire give the Angel license to depart **Saying**

Thou good Angel C I thank thee And for this time I license thee to depart to the place appointed to thee of God. Go in peace ✚ In the name of the Father ✚ And of the Son ✚ And of the Holy Ghost ✚ Amen ✚ **Finis** (Rankine 2010: 127-132)

The securing of a familiar spirit helper (in this case a fairy) illustrates the common belief in familiars that was most often connected with witch's imps. There seems to be some confusion involved in the idea that Solomon enclosed the fairies in a glass vessel, a practice that is usually associated with demons rather than lesser spirits that C. S. Lewis classified as "Longaevi". The use of blood and the killing of animals – here they are all airborne, perhaps in recognition of the widespread belief of "spirits of the air" being the ones most actively associated with human interaction – was rejected by later magicians as inhumane and perhaps suggestive of blood sacrifice to spirits. However, this sort of use of animals and organic ingredients was not uncommon in traditional medical formulas in medieval and early modern times. It would not seem out of place among country folk who regularly trapped small birds (if not bats) for food and to whom the casual slaughter of living beasts in hunting, fowling and on the farm was a part of daily life.

To have Conference with familiar Spirits Do as followeth

In the day and hour of ☿ take a white howlet [young owl] and kill it under the right wing Saying these words

Fuua Handa Musdali faon dyiaga Samiel Rostalagath This fowl I do kill in the name of you all Commanding you by the name *Rufangoll* your Superior by whom you do all secrets in Earth amongst men, And by *Hemeolon* your prince I adjure you that you do your humble obedience unto me AB at all times henceforth and with your power unknown give virtue and strength to this my purpose constraining all inferiors under you to serve me at all times days hours and / minutes And at all times and in all places without hurting me my body or Soul or any living Creature.

Then reserve his blood in a Clean vessel, And of his fat In another clean vessel.

In the day of ♃ consequently following and in the hour of ☿ kill a lapwing as you did the Howlet under the right wing saying these words.

Dala Dangolath Emenguill Saluagan Arsdorth Sedmaon Pandolath, This fowl I kill in the name of you all Commanding you by this name *Rufangol* your superior by whom you do all secrets on Earth amongst men And by *Hemeolon* &c ut suya with his blood and fat.

In the day of ♀ in the hour of ☿ Kill a black Hen as you did the lapwing under the right wing against the Heart, Saying

Eloofe Pendagell Etheluill Enan Dirath Ruiaminta Edlodell, This fowl I kill in the name of you all &c Then reserve his blood and fat ut suya

In the day of ♄ in the hour of ☿ next following kill a black cat under the right side against the Heart saying

Felofell Gariguam Samion Eligamill Reumdath Fesoraell Hermadafin This beast I kill in the name &c. Reserve the blood and fat as before.

In the day of ☉ in the hour of ☿ kill a wart [i.e., "warp" or moldwarp] or mole under the right side saying
Odanan Opathan Deothan Hermiadall Fernola Gauiham Tlodalath This beast I kill &c.
Reserve his blood and fat &c.

In the day of ☾ in the hour of ☿ kill a bat under the right wing saying as followeth
Ramasael Kaeldath Riarnfa Fesaloell Reralath Dupanfalon This fowl I kill &c
Reserving his blood and fat &c

In the day of ♂ and in the hour of ☿ take a Raven and kill her under the right wing saying
Ohorma Sedelpha Oremaell Soquidaell Myiasalet Rendos Lymaxill This fowl I kill &c
Reserve the blood And fat in clean vessels /

Take the fat of all the aforesaid fowls and beasts of each of them 5ii {7} drams {7/8 oz.} mix well together with a slice of Bay tree upon the palm of thy hand washed clean with Rose water, Saying in the tempering of them these 5ii words *Julia Hodelsa Inafula Sedamylia Roauia Sagamex Delforia* Inferiors and servants to the Empress and Princess of all fairies Sybils and all amiable creatures delighting in the company of human people *Lady Delforia* as you be present amongst men invisible at all times as soon as I shall anoint my eyes with this ointment And that you be as familiar with me as you were with King Solomon the mighty prince And as you opened and showed to king Solomon the hidden natures and properties and virtues of Metals precious Stones Trees and Herbs and the secrets of all Sciences underneath Heaven Even so I command require and adjure you *Julia Hodelsa Inafula Sedamylia Roauia Sagamex* with the Empress *Delforia* to do the like to me at all times without disdainfulness by their names whereby I do bind you *Gath vasagath ulagar Jeramilia Roboracath Regath Segath* even as you fear the just judgment of *Readufan* upon pain of Hellfire and everlasting damnation.

This is done at the ☍ of the ☾ in the hour of ☿ put the ointment in a vessel into the midst of the Fairy Throne [centre of a mushroom circle]. But first take ii or iii drams {1/4 or 3/8 oz} of each blood And write these 5ii names in virgin parchment *Julia Hodelsa Inafula Sedamylia Roauia Sagamex* and *Delforia*. All these names must be written 5ii times, Three times with a pen made of the third feather of the lapwing on the left wing. And iiii times with the feather pen of a Raven made of the fourth feather of the Right wing with these Characters following

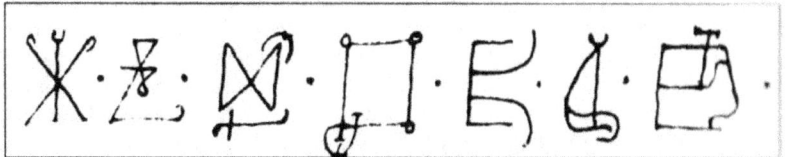

Characters of the Seven Fairy Sisters described in the preceding text. /

Then lap it about the vessel and seal it fast with virgin wax repeating these 5ii names *Julia Hodelsa Inafula Sedamylia Roauia Sagamex* and *Delforia* In sealing of it.

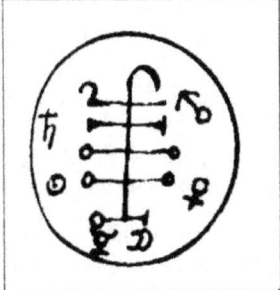

Seal for working with the Fairy, described in the following text.

The Seal must be made of Copper as this figure, But first before thou do put this into the Fairy Throne provided iiii Hazel rods of one years growth Cut them in the day and hour of ☿ the ☾ increasing shave them white Then write upon every one of them The 5ii names in the hour of ☿

Julia &c repeat these 5ii names iii times at every wand, First to the E{ast} then to the west then to the S{outh} last to the North, Saying the 5ii names *Julia Hodelsa Inafula Sedamylia Roauia Sagamex* with *Delforia* the Empress of all Fairies Sibils all other amiable creatures delighting in the company of Christian people Hear me I call you every each one by name, And the mighty names of Ligation wherewith Solomon did include you within a ball of Glass *Pannath Davion Segamilion Sugarnyell Darusa Jerasami Ariamilath* that you come at this present and make perfect this ointment That as often as I shall anoint mine eyes therewith I may see you perfect being without fraud or collusion truly showing to me all secrets of Herbs Trees Stones Metals privy talks of People Even as you fear the just Judgement of God upon pain of Hellfire and everlasting damnation whose names here included Sealed with the Seal of King Solomon the mighty prince with which he sealed the vessel wherein he bound you fiat fiat fiat.

Making this Pentaculum over the vessel upon the ground within the Throne with a Hazel Rod of one years growth /

Pentaculum described in the preceding text.

This do iii days iii times a day every day. This done or ended take it up and put in a secret dark place iii other days That ended put it into the Sun to rectify 6 other days Let it remain not moved.

But first before you anoint or presume to anoint your eyes therewith Be in clean life the space of 5ii days, Then anoint thine eyes therewith and look towards the East. Then shalt thou see diverse creatures most beautiful to behold in garments of diverse colours Then speak to one of them which thou likest best beckoning thy hand towards him [selecting one] with saying these words.

O thou beautiful creature and gentle virgin by what name soever thou art called By God the Father I call thee By God the Son I command thee By God the Holy Ghost I choose thee And by the obedience thou owest to thy Lord God, I adjure thee to be obedient unto me forever henceforth as thou dost hope to be saved at the dreadful day of Judgement In which he shall say Come ye Blessed and inherit my fathers Kingdom And go ye Cursed into everlasting Damnation In Hellfire to burn forever, Even as thou dost fear the Last Judgement of God upon pain of Hellfire and everlasting damnation Give me true answers of all such things as I ask or demand of thee. To this I swear thee by God the Father the Son and the Holy Ghost to be true to me at all times even as thou wilt avoid the heavy wrath of God Sitting in his high Throne to Judge everyone according to right And also I Command thee by all the power that God has over all Creatures, In Heaven, Earth and in Hell, Hereafter to meet me at all times thy Self alone quietly, whereupon depart at this time And the peace of God be between thee and me now and forever. Amen.

Then at all times she will meet with thee at what time thou anointest thine Eyes. Of this assure thy self to be most true, But when thou talkest with her Talk not long Neither yet demand her name Her Parentage nor yet her kindred or for what she is for fear of Indignation Nor yet whether she be Spirit or woman Let that talk go But demand things necessary for thy purpose. Beware you offer her no discourtesy at any time of polluting thyself, when thou hast / talked enough with her wash thine Eyes with Rose ♒ {water} or some other Sweet ♒ when she doth depart Say these words following.

Go in peace thou beautiful Creature of God to the place appointed of God Signing thy self with the sign of the Cross. Finis. (Rankine 2010: 290-295)

This invocation of "Sathan", which is the Hebrew spelling of "Satan" and had the meaning of "adversary", is curious in that William Bacon does not appear to have had any misgivings about contacting what certainly would suggest the Christian Devil, despite the ostensible "Roman" identification. As with the preceding conjuration involving blood, this sort of debatable rite was only found in the unexpurgated manuscripts of the Cunning Folk and were omitted by later authors such as S. L. Mathers as too dangerous or controversial to reveal in print.

The Roman Secret touching the Spirit called Sathan by which the Romans did understand of things present past and to come By W. Bacon

The Spirit of this invocation doth appear in a Basin and to be wrought every day except the Lords day and the double feast days.

First beware that thou be not defiled with luxury nor wrapped in any deadly sin but steadfast in faith belief and trusting in the lord. And be thou fasting And have a fair Chamber and take thee a fair and bright basin And have thou iiii wax Candles And make them fast on the brim of the Basin upon every candle write these names + Moses + Aaron + Jacob + Usion + Tetragrammaton + Moriaton + Then take the Sword and write upon it these words + Jesus Nazarenus rex iudeorum + Jesus of Nazareth King of the Jews the Son of the living God have mercy upon me + And make the Circle with the Sword And sitting in the midst of the / Circle Turning thee first towards the South putting the basin out of the Circle over against thee And perfuming the Basin with Mastic and Lignum Aloes Say the Gospel In the beginning was the word &c which done Sign thyself with the Cross Saing By the Sign of the Cross let everything that is evil be driven from hence. Then say this Conjuration.

I conjure thee Sathan by the Father + the Son + and the holy Ghost + By holy Mary mother of our lord Jesus Christ and by all the Martyrs And Confessors And by all the holy virgins and widows by the Crown of Christ on his head and by his teeth and ears and by the face and nose by his mouth and eyes by his tongue by his arms by his nails by his thumbs by his fingers Sinews and veins by his legs feet and the Soles of his feet by all his members in which he hath vouchsafed to suffer torments for the redemption of mankind by the wounds of Christ by all the torments of his passion and by all the torments of martyrs and Saints of God by the nativity of our lord Jesus Christ and by the circumcision of Christ by the death of Christ by the resurrection of Christ by the ascension of Christ by the coming of Christ in the day of Judgement by the dreadful day of Judgement in which every human and Christian Creature shall appear in the 30th year of his age by the 20 beasts sitting before the throne of God having eyes before and behind And by the wisdom of Solomon I Conjure thee Sathan by the virtue of all these and by the merits of the Saints and she Saints of God that thou appear in this basin in the likeness of a white Monk that thou tell and show me the whole truth and virtue of that thing whereof I shall examine thee without deceit or fraud faithfully + fiat + fiat + fiat + Amen +

Then put out the Candle that stands toward the South and turn thyself towards the west setting the Basin towards thee putting and performing the basin as aforesaid, then say

I Conjure thee Sathan by all these names of God + focnertu + forden + feon + fugorifedus + folo + diry + fumel + Mebon + Magon + Mesias + Alrararay + Adonay + Sabaoth + Sother + Sabn + Sponsus + And by all the names of them that be dead and their bodies And by the Seal of God By these names I Conjure thee Sathan that thou enter into this vessel In the likeness of a white monk and tell and show me the whole truth of what I shall demand of thee without deceit or falsity + fiat + fiat + fiat + /

Then extinguish the Candle and turn thy self towards the North having the Basin right before thee and Suffumigate the basin as before. Then say as followeth

I Conjure thee Sathan by the Rod of Moses And by the Tables of Moses and by the nine Celestial Candles and by the similitude or picture figure likeness of the 3 spirits by Daniel the prophet by holy Peter holy Paul and by these names of God + Agla + Aglay + Aray + Mara + Mandra + Mory + Motion + Motory + Matary + Matulia + Nata + Nazary + By the East and west by the South and by the North by the 4 plagues and the 4 Elements and by the 12 signs of the firmament that thou Sathan without any deceit tell me the truth without feigning counterfeiting or lying touching all my things matters that I shall require of thee + fiat + fiat + fiat +

Then put out the Candle that stands towards the north And then turn thyself towards the East with the Basin and suffumigate it as before and say

I Conjure thee Sathan by the bonds of Solomon and by the person of Solomon and by the seal (signet) of W. Bacon and by the seal of Raimond which is called Chath Malentes by holy Michael And by the holy salutation wherewith Holy Gabriel saluted the blessed virgin Mary saying Hail Mary full of Grace the lord is with thee blessed art thou among women and blessed is Jesus the fruit of thy womb + Amen + And by every good thing which may (can) be in heaven and in Earth And by all the Heavens and by the virtues in them and by the book of life and by the holy Spirit which God Jesus Christ sent upon the Earth And by these holy words which he spoke hanging upon the Cross

\+ Consumatum est + It is finished + And by all the words which I cannot utter speak or which I may not (or is not) lawful not to utter And by all these names and by their virtues (efficacy) I Conjure thee Satan that thou appear to me In the form or figure of a Monk in white without any hurt or without any fear or astonishment to me or us and that thou tell me the whole truth of things that I shall demand of thee omitting all impure (filthy) deceit and falsity + Amen + And if thou wilt not do my commandment and precept and obey my Statutes I loose thee from all thy office discharge, seeing that it is so into the depth of waters until the day of Judgement by the authority of him which shall come to judge the quick and the dead And the world by fire + fiat + fiat

Then put out the fourth Candle and suffumigate the Basin as aforesaid which done say /

By the virtue of all these And by the virtue of all the names of God + fiat + fiat + fiat + Amen +

Then the Spirit will appear to thee in manner as aforesaid And let him declare the truth of every thing that thou shalt inquire of him when thou wilt have him depart, Say,

Depart Sathan to the place predestined where the lord thy God hath appointed thee until I shall call upon thee another time (elsewhere) under pain of everlasting damnation and Curse of God the father almighty + The father + the Son + and the Holy Ghost + except thou depart and retire thee soon to the place appointed for thee by the lord and ordained thee without doing any hurt to me or my fellows And except thou come quickly when I call thee If by any means thou canst And make haste without delay and that thou appear without harm either without the House or in the fields when I call upon thee enjoying the benediction of thy prince + Amen + fiat + fiat + fiat + Amen (Rankine 2010: 248-251)

The two most common uses of conjuration were to acquire information and to discover hidden treasure, which was generally thought to have spirit guardians, as we will see in the following chapter. A conjuration in manuscript from the *The Wonderful Magical Scrapbook 1450-1850* in the Harry Price Collection, University of London Library illustrates the latter:

"From an old Welsh MS."

The Spirit of Tresuar

Your glass must be fixed upon a pedastal having a small hole at the top to bare it something like a candlestick – and 2 candles, one on either side, or [a] strong lamp at the back trimmed with fine oil. & your glass should have a gold + on the top, which is very easy with a small portion of gold leaf.

This way should be practiced by calling any spirit to appear in the glass, even was it required at noonday – you should put up your blinds or go to some dark room, & without magick lights, the spirit will not appear, unless he be very familiar, or great force be used. The first process according to the directions of the old magi. You must write your desire on clean paper, with the blood of a black cock, and put it on the back of the door of the room where you call the spirit. The black cock spoken of by them means the black grouse cock which in some places of Wales is very plentiful & were so in their days. The blood of a black bird mixed with water has answered the purpose but my opinion is that the blood of any bird or beast would answer, if not ink

You write the paper as this Satharn, Barampar, Barbarso come to me speedily to this place and tell me what treasure is secretly kept in – meaning the place you think at. They also require the room be cleaned and well scented with flowers or some sweet herbs. And upon a calm moonlit night, you begin to call at 11 o clock, saying I conjure and command the spirit Barbarson, the spirit of the treasure by the strength ~~of~~ [sic] and in the name of the Father, & of the Son & of the holy ghost, through the greatness of the true and living Jehova, who made Heaven & earth and the sea and all that is, in and through the most Noble and powerful + adla [sic] + Ellon + Tetragrammaton + adonay + Iscuros + ashanatus + paraclasus + Immortalus + alpha and omega, and in the secret of our Lord Jesus Christ, second person in everlasting trinity, who hath given Authority to them that believeth in his name, and to them that believeth in his name, hath given power over every spirit, of whatever order he be.

To do and obey to the man in all things that he shall ask or command and through the same authority, I command the spirit Barbarson to come speedily and arrear within this glass receiver and * in<u>strust</u> or instruct me in this my will & desire naming you wish in a plain voice. Then you say I charge and bind you to fulfill my before mentioned request – and that you will do no hurt or fright any man or Beast, but that you will make your appearance in the shape of a man, and your dress clean & decent then you speak your wish and say I desire the spirit Barbarson peaceably to instruct me in all my before mentioned request that I may use the same to my need and my good dayley – by this I conjure you in all the before mentioned desires, by the most High god & his Son Jesus Christ our mediator & advocate Judge of the living & the dead – I desire you to come speedily –

This Ends the Call

The time of calling is from the quarter to the full moon, choosing a calm light night and it is required to call nine times if the spirits do not familiarly appear sooner You are to wait between every call 8 or 10 minutes – keeping your eyes upon the glass, for sometimes – when they are very familiar, they make their appearance much sooner, wherefore it is required to keep your eye upon the glass, from the first calling – this is very correctly translated from ancient Welsh Mss – and it is very little different from the calls to the square[112] – I would have sent you the call to the square – but I did not know how to send them safe from being published.[113]

A dream conjuration from Rawlinson MS D 253 of Moses Long of Gloucestershire (1683), again involving the death of a bird:

FOR A VISION IN THE NIGHT

☞when ye wouldst know anything or *when* is best to doe anything of this world, Then According to ye Month of y^e ☾ be ye Clene & not poluted nor eate yn of any beast / or Creture wch have bloud in ·7· days before the first day of ye Month of ye ☾ viz. ·7· dayes before ye *Change*, nor in ye time touch no uncleane thing, nor Lye wth A woman & wash all y^e ·7· day *once*, wth cleane Runing water, befor ☉ *rise*, nor drinke noe wine, Then suffume thyselfe with Amber, frankensence, ligno Aloes, Croco [saffron], Costo [costmary, *Chrysanthemum balsamita*], Camphora, & Mastick mixed & made into *pills or Troches & fumigate thyself*. ☞Then ℞ two, live Turtles [turtledoves], or for want thereoff white Culvers [doves], & wth a red brassen knife with two edges, Cut of ye Necke. Cutting of one *Neck* of *Turtles* with one edge, & ye other wth ye other *Edge* & in likewise draw out ye Intrails, but keepe ye bloud in a glassen cup, & *cast it into ye fire, & wash ye intrails wth cleene water*, Then ·℞· Musk- three weights, & so much of croci, & cleere white francinsense, & cinnamon, black pep. Cornes ·12·, Cloves ·10·, Red Sander, & *Camphora*, white old wine, & *mustard*, & some *hony*, & put it all mixed into ye intrails & being filled divid them into ·7· ptes, & cast one pte upon coals of fire, in ye morrow before ye sun rise y^n [then] being covered with A white cloth, standing on thy feete, barefooted & barelegged & so doe all ye other ·7· Days till all ·7· ptes, & be burned into Ashes, Then gather all ye ashes of y^e ·7· ptes, & in A cleane privie place & house there strew ye Ashes *beforesayd* upon ye Earth, in ye midle of ye house, there having A bed to Sleepe, & when y^u [thou] enterest into ye Bed, Name y^e ·Ns· [names] / of ye Angells of y^e *Month*, & in ye night there will come one like A worshipfull man & Appe to thee in thy sleepe, & *shew thee all* w^{t}soever y^u hast desired *to know*, and shall not leave it as A Dreame but in truth & veryly *& also confirmed in thy memory*, ☞but y^u Aught to Say ye Ns· of ye Angells of ye month ·7· times each of the ·7· days y^u Sayd ·7· ptes are Aburning, & by this mayest y^u know w^{t}soever yu desirest & also ye Nature & vertue of all herbs plantes & beasts & w^t y^u wilt.

☞*Names of ye Angells of ye first Month*,

☞Niyssan, Oriel, Quiran, Acia, Yaziel, Paltisur, Yesmathia, Yariel, Avalon, Robica, Sephatya, Anaya, Gusesupale, Semquiel, Sereiel, Magua, Ancason, Pasite, Abdelram, Asdon, Casyel, Nastiafori, Sugin, Aszrq, Sovnadab, Admiel, Necamya, Caisdac, Benyt, ⁓qnor, Adzyriel.

These above sayd Angells off ·1· month are high & mighty but ye Angells of ye other months I have omitted supposing y^e *experiment* to difficult for this age to prove & also because I beleeve it may be don wth more ease by one of y^e ·7· planetary Angells, / or by some other Experiments written by *Ancient Magician*s &c — as by ye Ringe of planets, & their images made under their constellations, & also by holy divine Names & characters & taught by wise magitians &c. (Rawl. MS D253 1683: 120-123)

---

[112] Perhaps the *Almandal*?
[113] *The Wonderful Magical Scrapbook 1450-1850*, in the Harry Price Collection, University of London Library.

Ebenezer Sibley provided the first—if abridged and censored—instructions for conjuration in over a century in the fourth book of his *A New and Complete Illustration of the Occult Sciences* (first edition ca. 1784), derived from the additional chapters in the 1665 edition of Scot's *Discoverie of Witchcraft*. He excerpts and rearranges the original information into a very simple format that omits the psalms, prayers and lengthy conjurations of the classic grimoires:

> The circle therefore, according to this account of it, is the principal fort and shield of the magician, from which he is not, at the peril of his life, to depart, till he has completely dismissed the spirit, particularly if he be of a fiery or infernal nature. Instances are recorded of many who perished by this means; particularly Chiancungi, the famous Egyptian fortune-teller[114], who in the last century was so famous in England. He undertook for a wager, to raise up the spirit Bokim, and, having described the circle, he seated his sister Napala by him as his associate. After frequently repeating the forms of exorcism, and calling upon the spirit to appear, and nothing as yet answering his demand, they grew impatient of the business, and quitted the circle, but it cost them their lives; for they were instantaneously seized and crushed to death, by that internal spirit, who happened not to be sufficiently constrained till that moment, to manifest himself to human eyes. – The usual form of consecrating the circle is as follows: /
>
> *I, who am the servant of the Highest, do, by the virtue of his Holy Name Immanuel, sanctify unto myself the circumference of nine feet round about me,* ✠ ✠✠ *from the east, Glaurah; from the west, Garron; from the north, Cabon; from the south, Berith; which ground I take for my proper defence from all malignant spirits, that they may have no power over my soul or body, nor come beyond these limitations, but answer truly, being summoned, without daring to transgress their bounds. Worrh. worrah. harcot. Gambalon.* ✠ ✠ ✠
>
> The proper attire or *pontificalibus* of a magician, is an ephod made of fine white linen, over that a priestly robe of black bombazine, reaching to the ground, with the two seals of the earth, drawn correctly upon virgin parchment, and affixed to the breath of his outer vestment. Round his waste is tied a broad consecrated girdle, with the names *Ya, Ya,* ✠ *Aie, Aaie,* ✠ *Elibra* ✠ *Elohim* ✠ *Sadai* ✠ *Pah Adonai* ✠ *tuo robore* ✠ *Cinctus sum* ✠. Upon his shoes must be written **Tetragrammaton**, with crosses round about; upon his head a high-crown cap of sable silk; and in his hands an holy Bible, printed or written in pure Hebrew. When all these things are prepared, the circle drawn, the ground consecrated, and the exorcist securely placed within the circle, he proceeds to call up or conjure the spirit by his proper name, under a form somewhat similar to the following:
>
> *I exorcise and conjure thee, thou spirit of (here naming the spirit), by the holy and wonderful names of the Almighty Jehovah, Athanato* ✠ *Aionos* ✠ *Dominus sempiternus* ✠ *Aletheios* ✠ *Sadai* ✠ *Jehovah, Kedesh, El gabor* ✠ *Deus fortissimus* ✠ *Anapheraton, Amorule, Ameron* ✠ ✠✠ *Panthon* ✠ *Craton* ✠ *Muridon* ✠ *Jah, Jehovah, Elohim pentasseron* ✠ ✠ *trinus et unus* ✠ ✠ ✠ Θ *I exorcise and conjure, I invocate and command, thee, thou aforesaid spirit, by the power of angels and archangels, cherubim and seraphim, by the mighty Prince Coronzon, by the blood of Abel, by the righteousness of Seth, and the prayers of Noah, by the voices of thunder and dreadful day of judgment; by all these powerful and royal words abovesaid, that, without delay or malicious intent, thou do come before me here at the circumference of this consecrated circle to answer my proposals and desires, without any manner of terrible form, either of thyself or attendants; but only obediently, fairly, and with good intent, to present thyself before me, this circle being my defense, through his power who is Almighty, and hath sanctified the name of the Father, Son, and Holy Ghost. Amen.*
>
> After these forms of conjuration, and just before appearances are expected, the infernal spirits make strange and frightful noises, howlings, tremblings, flashes, and most dreadful shrieks and yells, as forerunners of / their presently becoming visible. Their first appearance is generally in the form of fierce and terrible lions or tygers, vomiting forth fire, and roaring hideously about the circle; all which time the Exorcist must not suffer any tremor or dismay; for, in that case, they will gain the ascendancy, and the consequences may touch his life. On the contrary, he must summon up a share of resolution, and continue repeating all the forms of constriction and confinement, until they are drawn nearer to the influence of the triangle, when their forms will change to appearances less

---

[114] Sibley gives examples of the fate of two earlier magicians as cautionary tales, a "Peters, the celebrated magician of Devonshire", and the Gypsy Chiancungi and his sister mentioned here. Regrettably they do not turn up in any other source, and were probably names remembered in the magical underground culture on the 18th century otherwise lost to history.

ferocious and frightful, and become more submissive and tractable. When the forms of conjuration have in this manner been sufficiently repeated, the spirits forsake their beastial shapes, and endow the human form, appearing like naked men of gentle countenance and behaviour. Yet is the magician to be warily on his guard that they deceive him not by such mild gestures; for they are exceedingly fraudulent and deceitful in their dealings with those who constrain them to appear without compact; having nothing in view but to suborn his mind, or accomplish his destruction. But with such as they have entered into agreement with they are frequent and officious; yet they more or less require certain oblations, which are frequently made to them, such as fumigations, odours, offerings or sacrifices of blood, fire, wine, ointments, incense, fruits, excrements, herbs, gums, minerals, and other ingredients; by which, from a magical cause, they have more influence and authority over the degenerated souls of men, and can insinuate into their inmost source and affection, piercing even through their bones and marrow, till they have so habituated them to their service, that it becomes their daily and sole delight to accomplish every villainy and abomination which the malicious and subtle instigations of Satan might purpose to lead them. So that the Exorcist must be greatly upon his guard, and when he has compleated the exorcism, and made such enquiries as he wished to obtain from the spirit, he must carefully discharge him by some form or ceremony like the following: *Because thou hast diligently answered my demands, and been ready to come at my first call, I do here licence thee to depart unto thy proper place, without injury or danger to man or beast; depart, I say, and be ever ready at my call, being duly exorcised and conjured by sacred rites of magic; I charge thee to withdraw with quiet and peace; and peace be continued betwixt me and thee, in the name of the Father, Son, and Holy Ghost.* Amen.

After this ceremony is finished, the spirit will begin to depart, resuming again the shrieks and noises, with flashes of fire, sulphur, and smoke, which the magician is to endure with patience, until it is entirely gone off, / and no signs whatever of such a procedure left. Then he may venture to withdraw from the circle, repeating the Lord's Prayer, after which he may take up the various utensils, and, having destroyed all traces of the circle, may return in safety to his proper home. (Sibley 1795: 1103-1107)

Sibley also gives a similarly basic necromantic conjuration which he illustrates with the now famous engraving of Edward Kelly and Paul Waring interrogating a resurrected corpse in St. Leonard's churchyard, Walton le Dale, Lancashire, as related in Weever's *Antient Funeral Monuments*.[115]

Francis Barrett, in *The Magus*, paraphrases and shortens information from "Agrippa's" *Fourth Book* (together with extensive charts and instructions for discerning the names of spirits from the *Three Books of Occult Philosophy*) and cribs much of the *Heptameron* in his coverage of conjuration. He also adds some material ostensibly from Johannes Trithemius for drawing a spirit into a crystal. As none of this is original – except in its paraphrasing – and as *The Magus* is widely available in reprint, excerpts from it can reasonably be omitted.

The most interesting and original later additions to the popular conjuration repertoire were made by Robert Cross Smith (1795-1832) who, writing as "Raphael" in *The Astrologer of the Nineteenth Century*, cited manuscripts once owned by the artist and magician, Richard Cosway. He tells us that "The late learned Mr. R. Cosway, R. A. hired a room, which he kept always consecrated for the purpose of raising spirits. On the floor, he had the magic circle drawn, and it was never entered by any idle or curious intruder. This we have been assured by a gentleman, who was an intimate friend of Mr. Cosway, was actually the case." ("Raphael" 1825: 210n). Cosway was a very successful artist, and his wife Maria was as well. In addition her artistic and musical skills, Maria Cosway is remembered for having Thomas Jefferson fall in love with her while the Cosways were in Paris in 1786. Our interest, however, is in Mr. Cosway's less well known fascination with magic.

Smith's examples of invocations are quite classic in form, although as in the case of Sibley and Barrett, the emphasis is on conjuration alone, omitting the psalms, prayers and versicles of a more pious age. The following extracts omit the chapter headings, but are otherwise as they appear in the 1825 text:

---

[115] John Weever. *Antient Funeral Monuments*. London: Printed by W. Tooke, 1767, pp. xlv-xlvi.

ILLUSTRATION, No. XVIII.
THE CIRCLE FOR RAISING THE SPIRIT EGIN.*

METHOD OF RAISING THE MIGHTY AND POWERFUL SPIRIT
Egin, King of the North.
EXTRACTED FROM AN ANCIENT MS.

"The Theurgist must call this spirit, in a fair chamber or quadrant, twenty or twenty-four feet at the most in breadth, in every part a window, a cubit wide, or a little more, east, west, north, and south. The floor of the chamber must be paved, boardered, or plastered, very plain and close, so that he may make his circle with chalk or [char]coal, that it may be perfectly seen. This house or chamber must / be in a void place, and not near the intercourse of men; for the opinion of some expert men in this art is, that spirits are more willing to appear in some waste place, as in woods, heaths, fens, moors, downs, or in any place where there is no resort, nor any of the sacraments have been administered; for otherwise thy purpose will not be effected. Therefore be warned.

"The weather must also be observed, for all weathers are not good for thy work; wherefore, when thou wilt begin thy work, see that the air is clear, and, if it be in the day, see that the sun shine; and, if it be in the night, let the moon be unobscured, or the sky full of stars; but take heed of foul or close weather, for in those the spirit will not be visible; and why? because it cannot receive bodily form or shape from the elements; wherefore select fine weather, for the spirit much delighteth therein.

"The spirit must also be invocated on even days of the moon, and in his proper hour, although some Theurgists say the have began in the new moon, and it hath been thirty days' labour before they could effect their entire purpose; therefore, let not this work seem tedious, nor think for one day being spent fruitlessly that thou wilt not effect thy purpose, seeing that expert clerks have spent several days before they obtain an appearance." This being performed, thy circle must be of the above form.

The Incantations.

[The editor adds a footnote here: "The MS. from which this is taken is valued at five hundred guineas, and was formerly in the possession of R[ichard] Cosway, Esq. R. A. but is now in the possession of the Mercurii." (i.e., an astrological society chaired by "Raphael")].

1. TO BIND THE GROUND, WHEREBY NEITHER MORTAL NOR SPIRITUAL BEINGS CAN HAVE POWER TO APPROACH WITHIN A LIMITED DISTANCE.

"Having made your necessary suffumigations and mystic preparations, describe a circle of a hundred feet or more in diameter, or as much or less as you may think fit; and, if you wish to keep all living creatures from within a quarter of a mile or more of your / experiment, make, at the four parts of the same, east, west, north, and south, proper crosses, and devoutly pronounce thrice the following incantation:—

"In the name of the **Father**, *and of the* **Son**, *and of the* **Holy Ghost**, *Amen. I bind all mortal and immortal, celestial and terrestrial, visible and invisible beings, except those spirits whom I have occasion to call, to avoid and quit this space of ground, which I now mark, and wherein I now stand, and that with all possible speed and dispatch. I bind you to avoid and no longer tarry, by the unspeakable power of* **Almighty God**, *by the most high and mighty name of* + **Tetragrammaton** + *by the all-powerful names* + **Agla** + **Saday** + **Jesu** + **Messias** + **Alpha** + *and* **Omega** +. *By all these most high and powerful names, I charge, adjure, bind, and constrain both mortal and immortal, celestial and terrestrial, visible and invisible beings to avoid, quit, and depart this ground, and do request that none of you, except those I have occasion to call at this time, be suffered to come within these sacred limits. These things I request in the in the name of the* **Father**, *and of the* **Son**, *and of the* **Holy Ghost**, *Amen.*

"Then dig a certain depth at the four parts of the compass, and bury the *seal* of the earth in each part, and no power, either visible or invisible, shall have power to come near thee, or to interrupt thy proceedings." /

[Editor's note: "These curious proceedings are copied from the MS before spoken of, and the Editor has thought proper to give the same orthography in the *Latin* and *Hebrew* words as in the original, and, notwithstanding some part may be found rather defective when compared with these languages as they are now used, yet the high antiquity of the MS. will be a sufficient excuse for the difference in point of *elegance*, should there be any.] /

217

ILLUSTRATION, No. XIX.

FORM IN WHICH THE SPIRIT USUALLY APPEARS.

INCANTATIONS FOR INVOKING THE SPIRIT TO VISIBLE APPEARANCE.

INCANTATIONS FOR INVOKING THE SPIRIT TO VISIBLE APPEARANCE.

I conjure thee, **Egin**, *Rex Borealis, and also charge thee that thou appear here before me, and before this circle, by the sufferance of Almighty God, and by the virtue of his passion and other sentences which shall be rehearsed, to bind and constrain thee.*

I conjure thee, **Egin**, *by the* **Father**, *the* **Son**, *and the* **Holy Ghost**, *and by the heavens, the air, the earth, and the sea, and by all that therein is contained, that thou come shortly, and appear to me and my fellows, not terrible nor fearful, but in mild and peaceable form, without hurt or envy to any of us.*

I conjure thee, **Egin**, *by all the holy words that* **God** *spake in the creation of the world, and by all creatures, [v]isible and invisible, and / by the four elements, and by the virtues of heaven, and by all the holy words that* **God** *spake unto Moses, and to all the other prophets, and by the incarnation, passion, death, and resurrection, of the mild and ineffable Saviour of all mankind.*

I conjure you, **Egin**, *by the general resurrection, and by the dreadful day of judgment; I conjure thee,* **Egin**, *by the coming of the* **Holy Ghost***; I conjure thee, also, by the virtue of all the spirits of the just, and by the most holy patriarchs, apostles, evangelists, and by the most holy saints of all ages.*

I conjure thee, **Egin***, by the mercy, grace, and power of God; I conjure thee, thou spirit* **Egin***, under the pain of condemnation, and thy fearful doom at the great day of judgment; I conjure thee,* **Egin***, by the great curse of God; by the high power and strength of our Lord Jesus Christ, the Son of God, the heavenly King of glory; and I conjure thee, by the whole of these, in what place of the world soever thou art, to appear instantly before me in the likeness of a child of three years old; and that, without fear, hurt, or envy, thou fulfil my request.*

Replicatory Incantations.

If, at the third rehearsal of the above mystic ceremonial, the spirit refuses to appear, prepare a fume of sweet-smelling savours, such as frankincense, aloes, cinnamon, oil, olives, nutmegs, musk, cassia, roses, saffron, and white wax; which must be burnt, commixed together, on a fire consecrated for the purpose; and, while the fume is forming, and the fire fiercely burning, repeat what follows:—

I conjure thee, **Egin***, and command thee instantly to appear before me, by the virtue of the sentences and words hereafter written, upon pain of the most awful and bitter maledictions of Almighty God.*

I conjure thee, O thou spirit **Egin***, that thou arise and appear to us, by the might, majesty, and power of the FIRST word that our Lord spake, in the creation of the world, when he made the light to shine, and said, "Lux et facta, est lux."*

I conjure thee, by the SECOND word that he spake when he made the firmament, and said, "Fiat firmamentum in medico aquas, et deinde aquas ab aquis." /

I conjure thee, by the THIRD word, when he gathered all the waters that were under heaven into one place, saying, "Congregentur aque que sub cœlo et apparia mida."

I conjure thee, by the FOURTH word, which he spake when he made to spring forth trees and herbs, "Germinant terram, herba vercli facientur semen cum semendi teipso sit super terram.["]

I conjure thee, by the virtue of the FIFTH word, when he made the ☉*,* ☽*, and * * *, saying, "Fiat luminaria magna in firmamento cœli ut illuminare terram."*

I conjure thee, by the SIXTH word, which he spake when he made birds, fishes, &c. "Producat aque reptile, aëre virentes et voluntate super terram sub firmamento cœlo."

I conjure thee, by the virtue of the SEVENTH word, which he spake when he blessed them, saying, "Crescite et multiplicamini et reptili aquas maris oves multiplicantur super terram."

I conjure thee, by the EIGHTH word, which he spake when he made beasts, worms, and serpents, "Ducat terram aliam in genero suo immenta et reptilia secundùm specias scias."

I conjure thee, by the NINTH word, which he spake when he made man in his own image, saying, "Faciamus homo ad imagine et similitudine nostra et per sit pissibus et volantibus que cœli et bestias terre et universe creature qui reptile que monentur in terrâ."

I conjure thee, O thou spirit **Egin***, instantly to appear, by virtue of the tenth word, which he spake when he placed Adam and Eve in Paradise, saying, "Crescite et multiplicamini et replete terra subjugate cam et semite vivi pissibus maris, et volantibus cœli et bestias terre, et universus animalibus que quem monentus super terra." Et per hac verba, conjuro te, spiritus* **Egin***."*

Lastly, I conjure, charge, bind, and command thee, O thou mighty and invincible spirit **Egin***, by these, most high, powerful, and ineffable names of the most highest—* + **Jesus** + **Fons** + **Salvator** + **Christus** + **Sabaoth** + **Adonay** + **Graton** + **Messias** + **Victor** + **Osanna** + **Nazarenus** + **Theas** + **Emmanuel** + **Unigenitus** + **Primogenitus** + **Alpha** + **Omega** + *and by the great, supreme, and all-powerful name* להלה*, which all creatures obey, at which the elements are moved, and the devils fear and tremble. By all these tremendous and awful names, I charge thee, finally, to appear before me. Fiat, fiat, fiat. Amen. /*

These things being rightly performed, with a rushing sound, "as of many waters," and a tremendous noise, will the spirit appear, and by powerful invocations thou shalt obtain what thou wishest. But let thy proceedings herein be secret, and beware of vain curiosity; for these mysteries are sacred.

ILLUSTRATION, No. XX.

FORM IN WHICH THE SPIRIT OBERION APPEARS.

CIRCLE III.—SECT. XIII.

TO INVOKE OR RAISE THE SPIRIT Oberion.

TO INVOKE OR RAISE THE SPIRIT Oberion.

[Editor's note: "From an ancient Ms. in the possession of 'Raphael.'"]

This almighty spirit is chiefly under the dominion of the sun and moon. He appears in great pomp and terror, generally in the form / of a scaly monster, the face of a woman, and a royal crown upon his head, attended by innumerable and countless legions.

The Theurgist who would raise or invocate this powerful spirit must, in the first place, draw out his seal and character, and the different offices subservient to him, in the first *Monday* after the full moon, and in the hour of the **Moon, Mars, Mercury,** or **Saturn:** and when these are made, he must repeat the following ceremonial words :—

O ye angels of the **sun** *and* **moon***, I now conjure and pray you, and exorcise you, that by the virtue and power of the most high God,* **Alpha** *and* **Omega***, and by the name that is marvellous* + **El** +*, and by him that made and formed you, and by these signs that be here, so drawn forth in these resemblances, and now in the most shining* **God***, and by the virtue of the* **Holy Ghost, that now, or whensoever that I shall call on Oberion,** *whose image is here pictured, made, or fashioned, and his name that is here written, and his signs here all drawn and graven, written, or made, that* **Oberion** *be compelled now to obey me, and here to appear openly before me, and fulfil my request.*

The next day, write or make the name of his first counsellor, **Taberyon,** and that on the right side of Oberion's character, saying, *I exorcise thee,* **Taberyon,** *by the power of God, and by the virtue of all heavenly things, earthly things, and infernal kings, and by king Solomon, who bound thee, and made thee subject unto him, and by all his signs and seals, and by the four elements, by which the world is sustained, and nourished, and by the serpent that was exalted in the wilderness,—that thou,* **Taberyon** *now help to give true council to thy Lord* **Oberion,** *that he do show himself instantly unto me, and fulfil my request.*

This must be said three times each day, and three times each night, over the writings.

The third day, in the third hour, write and make the name of his other counsellor **Teveyron,** with his signs and characters, and do say as before rehearsed.

This done, suffumigate your seals and writings with a suffumigation / of *saffron, aloes, mastic, olibanum, and orpient;* and note that the fire used for this purpose must be of *elder-wood* or *thorns.*

Then choose a secret and retired place, where no human footsteps may interrupt thee, and make the circle of the following form.

ILLUSTRATION, No. XXI.
THE CIRCLE FOR RAISING Oberion.

INCANTATIONS.

The circle being made, and consecrated according to the rules of ceremonial magic, enter therein, in the hour of Mercury, and begin thy invocations in this manner, on bended knees, and with great devotion,

I conjure, invocate, and call thee, **Oberion***, by the Father, the Son, / and the Holy Ghost, and by him who said, and it was done; who commanded, and it stood fast; who willed, and it was created; and by his Son JESUS CHRIST, in whose name, all heavenly, earthly, and infernal creatures do bend and obey; and by the unutterable name of ineffable majesty +* **Tetragrammaton** *+ O thou spirit Oberion, I command thee, wheresoever thou now art, whether in sea, fire, air, or flood, whether in the air above or in the region beneath, to appear instantly unto me, and my fellows, without hurting them or me, or any other living creatures which God has made. This I thrice command thee, in the name of the ineffable Adonai. Amen.*

If, at the third repetition of this invocation, the spirit gives no visible token of his appearance (for generally, previously to the actual appearance of the spirit, there are heard tremendous noises and frightful hisses, tumultuous yellings, and fearful shrieks); then begin to rehearse the following great bond or incantation, and if the spirit were bound in chains of darkness, in the lowest pit of the infernal regions, he must appear, when this great sentence is rehearsed."

THE GREAT AND POWERFUL INCANTATION,

For compelling Spirits to visible Appearance.

[Editor's note: "This great call is said to be equally powerful in raising any other spirit."]

O thou rebellious and fearful spirit, prince among the fallen angels, **Oberion***, I conjure and bind thee to visible appearance by the following most high, most terrible, and mighty invocation:—*

Hear, O ye heavens, and I will speak, saith the Lord, and let the sea, the earth—yea, hell, and all that is within them contained, mark the words of my mouth: Did not I, saith the Lord, fashion you, and make you? Did not I, as an eagle, who stirreth her nest, fluttereth over her young one with her wings, and carrieth them, on her shoulders? / Have I not so nourished you, that you were fat, and loaded with plenty? Why have you, then, so spurned with your heels against me, your Mother? Why have you seemed to coequal yourselves with me? What thereby have you reaped? Have you not purchased, instead of that heavenly felicity, hellish perplexity? Have you that fire kindled which doth and shall for ever, at my pleasure, burn you in the bottomless pit of perdition? Why are you so unfaithful and disobedient to my most holy names and words? Know you not that I am God alone, and there is none but me? Am I not the only חוה*. Is it not in my power to kill and make alive—to wound and to heal—to oppress and to deliver? If I whet the edge of my sword, and my hand take hold of it, to do justice against them who disobey my holy name, who are able to abide the same? To have their sword, eat their flesh, and my sharp arrows of hell fire to be drunk in their blood? Which of you that are disobedient to my name (saith the Lord) is able to withstand my anger? Am not I Lord of Lords, and omnipotent, and none but I? Who can command the heavens to smoke, the earth to fear, the waters to flow, and hell to* tremble? Are not the corners of them all in my hands? O thou obstinate and stubborn spirit, why hast thou dealt so froward with me (saith the Lord), to urge me to command my faithful servant **Michael**, my valiant champion, to expel and put thee out of the place where thou wast filled with wisdom and understanding, continually beholding my wondrous works? Didst not thou see my glory with thine eyes, and did not thy ears hear the majesty of my voice? Why art thou gone out of the way? Why art thou become an open sepulchre? With thy tongue dost thou deceive my servants, for poison is under thy lips, thy mouth is full of cursing and bitterness, and thy feet swift to shed innocent blood? Is this the obedience thou owest unto me, and the service thou offerest? Verily, for this thy obstinacy, disobedience, pride, and rebellion, thou shalt be bound, and most cruelly tormented with intolerable pains and endless and eternal perdition.

Then, if the spirit be still rebellious or refractory, make a fire of brimstone and stinking substances, thorns, and briars, &c. Then write the name of the spirit in virgin parchment, and burn it thrice, repeating the following adjuration:— /

I conjure thee, creature of God, FIRE, by him who commanded and all things were done, and by the LIVING God, and by the TRUE God, and by the HOLY God, and by him who made thee and all elements by his word, by him who appeared to Moses in a burning bush, and by him who led the children of Israel in a fiery pillar, through the wilderness, and by him who shall come to judge the world by fire and brimstone, that thou perform my will upon this refractory and disobedient spirit; till he come unto me, and show himself obedient in all things as I shall command him. O heavenly God, father and author of all virtues, and the invisible king of glory, most strong and mighty captain of the strong and triumphant arm of angels, God of gods, Lord of hosts, which holdest on thy hands the corners of the earth, which with the breath of thy mouth makest all things to shake and tremble, which maketh thy angels lightnings, and thy spirits flames of fire, vouchsafe I beseech the, O Lord, to send thy holy angels into this place of fire, to torment, vex, and persecute this disobedient spirit, Oberion, and overcome him, as Michael the archangel overcame Lucifer, the prince of darkness, till he come to me, and fulfil all my will and desire. Fiat, fiat, fiat. Amen.

O thou most puissant prince Radamanthus, which dost punish in thy prison of perpetual perplexity, the disobedient spirits, and also the grisly ghosts of men dying in dreadful despair, I conjure, bind, and charge thee, by Lucifer, Beelzebub, Satan, Tamanill, and by their power, and by the homage thou owest unto them; and also I charge thee, by the triple crown of Cerberus, by Styx, and Phlegethon, by the spirit Barantos, and his ministers, that you torment and punish this disobedient spirit Oberion, until you make him come corporeally to my sight, and obey my will and commandment in whatsoever I shall charge or command him to do. Fiat, fiat, fiat. Amen.

These things being rightly performed, the spirit will be constrained to visible appearance; but, after the above incantation, he will come in a very horrible and ghastly form, and attended by terrible convulsions of all the elements, raging furiously, and assuming every terrible appearance that is possible, to frighten the Invocator. And for which purpose, roaring lions, hissing serpents, and furious beasts with all the mighty horrors of the infernal regions, and every other / possible attempt, will be made to cause terror and alarm. At this juncture, if the magic circle be not well made and fortified, the Invocator will be in the utmost peril, and if he escape with his life may deem himself fortunate; but, if the circle be properly made, there is no fear from the assaults of this rebellious and wicked one, who must become obedient when thus exorcised.

After the spirit has appeared, and performed thy will and request, it is be well observed, that the utmost caution must be used in quitting the limits of the *magic circle*. For this end, the Theurgist must devoutly rehearse the following license.

A LICENSE FOR TO DISCHARGE SPIRITS.

I conjure thee (Oberion) by the visible and holy temple of Solomon, which he did prepare to the most holy God, by all the elements, and by that most holy name that was graven on Solomon's sceptre, that, for this time, thou do depart quickly, quietly, and peaceably, without lightnings, thunder, rain, wind, storm, or tempest, or any noise or terror whatsoever; and, whenever I shall call thee, I charge thee that thou do come to me and my fellows, without delay or tract of time, not molesting me or any other creature that God hath made in his glory and praise, and the use of man, or without disordering any thing, putting up or casting down any thing, or doing hurt any other way whatsoever, either in thy coming or going, not hurting, troubling, or molesting me, or any other creature, neither by thyself, nor any other spirit or spirits for thee, or at thy procurement, at any time or times, now or hereafter; by the virtue of our Lord Jesus Christ, the Father, and the Holy Ghost, go thy way in peace to the place where God hath appointed for thee, and peace be between thee and me. In nomine patris + et filii, + et spiritus sancti + Amen.

The Theurgist must repeat this license three times, and afterwards repeating the Lord's Prayer, must leave the circle, walking backwards. he must then destroy all traces of the circle, and remove all instruments / used for the purpose, keeping the whole as secret as possible; and must also return home by a different path to that by which he came. So shall no spirit have power to harm him, but let him upon no account neglect any of the foregoing rules, for they are essential to his safety. ("Raphael" 1825: 214-217)

"Raphael" also gives a long example of conjuration for crystal scrying from an illuminated manuscript on "celestial magic" owned by Cosway:

CELESTIAL MAGIC.
PART 1.
Copied verbatim from a beautifully illuminated magical Manuscript, formerly in the possession of the celebrated Mr. Richard Cosway, R. A.

Isagogical instructions how to know good Spirits from bad, when they appear.

Signs.

The Signs of appearance, both of GOOD ANGELS and EVIL SPIRITs are, and ought, *carefully* to be well observed by reason, they are foregoers of such appearances, and whereby are, known the differences thereof, which is a matter of material consequence, as hereafter shall be more plainly shewed forth.

Good Angels moved.

If *good Angels*, or elemental powers, or other wise dignified spirits, of a benevolent or symbolizing nature with celestial powers, and allied to the welfare and preservation of mankind, are moved and *called forth to visible appearance* in a CHRISTALL STONE, or glass receiver, as one usual way or *customary* form is among the learned Magicians, then the sign of their appearance seemeth most like *a vail, or curtain, or some beautiful colour hanging in or about the glass or stone*, as a bright cloud, or / other pretty kind of hierogliphical shew, both strange and very delightful to behold.

It is therefore to be remembered, that the Magical student ought to have for his purpose a christal stone, of a round globick form, very clear and transparent, or other of like diaphanity or ball of clear and solid glass, with a little hole on the top, of like form, of any convenient bigness or diameter, according as can reasonably be obtained or made, and the same to be set in a form; and also the Glasses, to be made with a stalk or shank fixed thereto, and so to be put into a socket with a foot or pedestal to stand upright; the stone being called by the name of a shew stone, and the glass by the name of a glass receptacle; or in practice or action upon invocation or motion, made for spiritual appearance, there shall either be a wax candle on each side thereof, or a lamp behind the same, burning *during the time of action*, set on a table apart, fitted and furnished for this purpose. But if appearance hereof aforesaid be moved for by invocation, *out* of the shewstone or christal glass; or if yet, notwithstanding appearance happen to shew themselves out of them, yet *the sign of their appearance will be very delectable and pleasant;* various, amazing the senses to behold, as a shining brightness or sudden flashes, or such like similitudes, very splended in shew, or in the place where action is made, or appearance moved.

Invocation.

When *Invocation* is made to any of the CELESTIAL POWERS, or dignified elemental spirits of light, and appearance accordingly is presented, and visibly / sheweth itself, either in the shew stone or christal glass, or otherwise out of them; then view the same very well, and also take notice of its corporature physiognomy, or features of the face, vestures or garments, deportment, language, and whatsoever else may be worthy of note, by reason of making a fine distinction between the appearance of good Angels or Spirits, and others that are evil, and of knowing the same without being deceived; for although evil powers or spirits of darkness may be invocated, moved, or called forth to visible appearance, and consulted withal and made use of, in such concerns or upon such actions, wherein by nature and office they may be commanded to serve in all such matters as thereupon are dependent, and as the necessity thereof shall be suitable and requisite; but then actions with them are different both in time, and place, and order, and also the manner of operation, which by them are diversly and severally else where, hereafter inserted and shewed forth in its proper place;

therefore do the magick philosophers give *this caution,* saying, beware that one action, operation, or secret in the art, be not mixed with another.

Action apart.

But let celestial, elemental, and infernal actions, operations, and invocations, be used and kept apart, according to the method and manner as are in particular ascribed, and properly referred unto each of them. Now then, *observe,* that the appearance of celestial and benevolent angels, and other dignified elemental spirits of powers of light, are to be *thus* known or distinguished from those that / are infernal, or evil powers, or spirits of darkness. *The good angels, or dignified powers of light as aforesaid, are in countenance very fair, beautiful, affable, smiling, amiable, and usually of a flaxen or golden coloured hair;* in behaviour or gesture, courteous and friendly; in speech, very gentle, mild, grave, and eloquent, using no vain, idle, or superfluous language in their discourse; in their corporature very handsome, straight, comely, well-favoured; and in every limb most exactly formall and well composed; their motions, sometimes to be plainly perceived, sometimes swift, and sometimes interceptable, both in their appearance, countenance, and departure; and their garments, of what fashion, form, and colour soever, are likewise very fair and beautiful, or Oriental; and if it be of many colours or strange fashion, yet they are also very splendid and rare, and lively to behold; and, in short, they are celestial and dignified in all their appearances, as they are in countenance and corporature, without the least deformity either in hairyness in the face or body, or a swarthy complexion, or any crookedness, or any ill shaped member of the body; so also their garments are clean and unsoiled, without spot or blemish, and untorn or ragged, or anywise dirty with any filthy soil, and always embrace the word **MERCY**!

Appearance.

When the appearance of any celestial angels, or angelic powers of light, or dignified elemental spirits, are visibly shewed forth, and by good testimony or diligent observation well known to be so, / then, with due reverence given thereto, may be said as followeth :—

Receive thus.

WELCOME be the Light of the Highest, and welcome be the Messengers of Divine Grace and Mercy unto us, the true servants and worshippers of the same, your God, whose name be glorified, both now and for evermore.

Good or Evil.

And if the appearance be *good,* then it will stay; but if not, then *it will immediately vanish* away, at the rehearsing of the word **MERCY**. But if any evil power shall appear in the place of that which is good, or instead, and impudently withstand and opposing, then vanish it as in this case. Evil spirits are to be dealt with in manner and form as hereafter is inserted in its place, by reason those powers or spirits, who are by nature evil, and so are contrary to those by nature good, *may not be dealt with* as in those actions or operations; nor those powers of light, by nature good, to be moved in reference to that otherwise, properly appertaineth, or belongeth by nature and office to the evil spirits or powers of darkness, more than as for their assistance, and so according for deliverance from any violent surprize, assaults, illusions, or other infernal temptations, or envious attempts.

Expected appearance.

Now then, if by those observations *the expected appearance* is understood, and found to be celestial and of good, or to be dignified elemental spirits, or / powers of light, and so likewise of good, as accordingly was invocated, moved, or called forth to visible appearance by name, order, and office, to such appearance say thus :—

Demand.

Are you the same whom we have moved and called forth to visible appearance, here before us at this time, the name (**N**) or who else are ye, and *of what order, and what else is your name,* that we may so note of you, either as you may be ranked in order amongst the blessed angels, or otherwise known or called by any of mortal man: if you be of celestial or elemental verity, and so of charity, you cannot mislike or deny these our sayings.

Answer.

Then if it maketh any answer, as peradventure it may, then make reply according as the nature of discourse requireth. But if it make *no* answer, then repeat the words aforesaid, Are you the same, &c. &c.; then it will shew forth or tell its name, order, and office; the which when it is known by hearing, then it will speak or otherwise shew forth; say then as followeth:

Who it is.

If you be (**N**) as you say, *In the name of Jesus, say that all wicked angels are justly condemned; and yet by the mercy of God in the merits of Christ, man kind elect are to be saved.*

Whereunto it will then return a satisfactory answer, or else it will depart and be gone away; then if the appearance be good, as may be known / by the answer and the reasons thereof, that was made or given to the aforesaid proposition, say as followeth:

Speak to the appearance.

O ye servants and messengers of Divine grace and mercy, and celestial angels, or angelic powers of light, or dignified elemental spirits, and mediums of benevolence to mankind, servants of God, you both now at this time, and always are and shall be unto truly and sincerely welcome, humbly desiring you to be friendly unto us, and to do for us in whatsoever it shall please God to give by your order and office unto you, for the better knowledge of mankind living on earth, and to make us partakers of true science and sapience, in the undefiled and secret wisdom of the Creator.

Answer made.

And if any answer shall be made hereunto, or any discourse from hence should arise or proceed hereupon, then both wisdom and reason must be the principle conduct in the management thereof; but if there be silence, and no discourse arise from thence, then begin to make humble request for answer to such desires and proposalls, as in a certain writing is contained, which ought to be in readiness with you, and then will the effects of all things be undoubtedly, and with good success be determined.

Intrusion.

The *sign of intrusion, or appearance of evil,* when action or invocation is otherwise made for moving or calling forth celestial angels or intelligences, or / their dignified powers, or elemental spirits of light, are not apparent or visible, to be any ways discernible than your shapes, forms, gestures, or other little principals in appearance, quite contrary in behaviour, language, cloathing, or vestures, to those above related, and to be observed of the good, &c.; neither are they herein otherwise to judge of them than as intruders, tempters, and illuders, on purpose, if possible, to deceive and also to destroy the perseverance and hopes of obtaining any benefit, by celestial and good mediums, by reason they are degraded and deprived of power to send or shew forth any foregoing sign of their appearance, in those such superior actions, invocations, or moving only celestial or dignified elemental powers, and to visible appearance, herein no ways to have farther notice of them, to be vanquished or sent away as before has been said. Observe then the corporative forms and shapes of evil powers, or spirits of darkness, in their appearances, by forcible intrusions of the kind *are easily discovered from the good powers* and spirits of light, as now shall be declared, as followeth:

Of Evil Powers.

EVIL POWERS, or *spirits of darkness, are ugly, ill favoured, and beastly in shape* and appearance; wherein observe, if they do appear in upright or human stature, then either body, face, or covering, are quite contrary to the other, before specified of good; for although an evil or infernal spirit may appear in the likeness of an angel of light, especially in the time and place when good angels or / spirits of light are moved, invocated, or called forth, forming themselves very nearly, so even almost imperceptibly to sight and appearance, except ingeniously discovered by any curious observation, and clearly may be discerned quickly by their ragedness, uncleanness of their garments, and difference of their countenance in beauty, features, and other decent composures of the body, language, and behaviour, and the corporal difference of the limbs, or bestial similitudes, who in times do usually and suddenly make their appearance, and as readily shew forth motions, gestures, and speakings unusually blasphemous, ridiculous or different language, altogether dissonant and contrary both in manner and matter, to that of the celestial angels, which also *may be soon discovered* by the diligence of a sober and curious speculator, which notable intrusions they make on this action, properly to destroy the reason, hope, and judgement of the invocation, and by great errors, and other ignorant mistakes, not only to deceive and confound the more solid and genuine knowledge and capacitys of man labouring therein, but also to distract the senses, and thereby lead the understanding into a meander, and therein to weary and tire us with verity of doubt and desperation, not knowing how to unravel the Gordian knot, or to be satisfied or delivered from the hopeless pilgrimage, but by the help of Icarian wings; from hence it may be understood, that *evil spirits and powers of darkness, sooner appear as impudent intruders in time of good action,* and in place where invocation is made for the moving and calling forth of any good angels, or dignified elemental spirits or powers of light, to / visible appearance, than at any other time and place, which as unto themselves they shall be indifferently by order, office, and name: invocated, moved, and called forth to visible appearance, for such their assistance, as by nature and office, wherein they are accordingly serviceable and suitable to the occasion, wherein they are commanded. Therefore, in such actions are to be only referred unto those of evil powers or spirits of darkness, those actions we say are differently set apart, and to be distinguished both in time, place, order, and method, and other aforesaid, &c. so they may be moved and called forth, commanded and constrained, and according so dealt withall, and used as the present action shall require, and the discretion of the invocant shall find agreeable to the nature and office: so then it is observable, that the evil spirits may be invocated and dealt withall, differently, or apart by themselves, according as aforesaid; but not in such place, or in such time, as when action or motion is made for the appearance of any celestial spirit of light, and other elemental powers or different spirits by nature good as well as evil, and other wandering spirits, none resident in orders certain of like nature, &c. may be constrained and commanded by invocation properly thereto referred, with several appurtenant rules and observations inserted therein, as ample and at large shewed forth; but celestial angels and other elemental powers, by nature and office benevolent or good, may not be commanded nor constrained by any invocant; they are only to be moved and called forth by humble entreaties, thereby acquiring favour and friendship. /

When wicked Intruders come.

KNOW THEN, if at any time and place, where action or motion is made, and humbly entreated, earnestly besought, for the appearance of any celestial power, &c., and wicked intruders shall impudently thrust themselves in place, and would enforce credulity into the speculator, and that it shall be plainly discovered, *then shall the magician dismiss, discharge, send away, and banish them from hence,* after the manner hereafter shewn, in the second Part of this magical formula.

CELESTIAL MAGIC.
PART 2.
Copied verbatim from a beautifully illuminated magical Manuscript, formerly in the possession of the celebrated Mr. Richard Cosway, R. A.

To banish the Evil Spirits.
SAY THIS ORATION.

The vengeance of God is a two-edged sword, cutting rebellious and wicked spirits of darkness, and all other usurping powers, in pieces; the hand of God is like a strong oak, which, when it falleth, breaketh in pieces many shrubs; the light of his eyes expelleth darkness, and the sweetness of his mouth keepeth from corruption. Blessed are all those to whom he sheweth mercy, and reserveth from temptation, and illusion of wicked intruders, defending them by his mighty power, under the covert of divine grace; not suffering his humble servants to be overcome or overthrown by any infernal assaults. Now therefore, because you have come hither, and entered without license, seeking to entrap and ensnare us, and secretly conspired by these your subtleties, to deceive and destroy us and our hopes, in the true meaning of these our sober, innocent, honourable, and celestial actions, we do, in the great mighty name, and by the power of the most high God, triumph imperially over you; and by the virtue, force, and efficacy whereof, be you and your powers vanished, overthrown, and utterly defeated; and behold, by virtue of that celestial power, by divine grace given unto us, and wherewith we are potently dignified; and as heirs of God's promise, through faith containing inherent with us, we do hereby wholly deface and overthrow you, and ye are totally vanquished: therefore we say depart, and immediately begone from hence in peace, without noise, turbulence, injury, harm, violence, or other damage to us, or this place, or any other place or person whatsoever; and as you are of darkness, and the places of darkness, and have without any charge or permission enviously intruded, seeking thereby to ensare, deceive, or overwhelm us, the divine judgement and vengeance of the most high God, for your wicked and malicious conspiracy and intrusion, be your deserved reward; and as it was delivered to you, so take it with you, that the malice which you have shewn us may heap your own destruction; be ye therefore dismissed, and immediately we say depart hence unto your orders, and there to continue in the bonds of confinement daring the divine pleasure of the Highest. /

If they are yet obstinate and impudent, and will not depart, but rather will withstand the commands of the Magician, let him say as followeth.

To Vanish[sic]

Do you thus impudently withstand, and obstinately refuse, to depart from our presence, and from the place, and perniciously attempt yet farther against us: in the name of Jesus, we say, depart ye wicked seducers, and be ye immediately gone away from hence; and so be it unto you, according to the word of God, which judgeth righteously, from evil unto worse, from worse unto confusion, from confusion unto desperation, from desperation unto damnation, from damnation unto eternal death. Depart therefore, we say, unto the last cry, and remain with the Prince of Darkness, in punishment justly due, as a fit reward unto your wicked, malicious deservings, and the God of mercy graciously deliver us from you.—**Jehovah Tertragrammaton Sadai**

And if no celestial angel, or other dignified spirit of light, appear in place to vanquish and send away, or seal up any wicked or infernal spirit or spirits of darkness, when appearance is presented, a notorious intruder in the time and place, when celestial or elementall actions, with dignified powers of light, are in agitation and operation.

Rules to be Observed.

Then let the discreet Magician, with prudent passion, have diligent regard to himself, and consult the foregoing rules, according to respective and serious observations; who, by the office of himself, will undoubtly, not only contract the sight and friendship of the celestial angels, and dignified, elemental, and other benevolent spirits of light, to his relief and comfort, and to vanquish and overcome all evil spirits and powers of darkness; but also he shall have power to command, call forth, and constrain all sublunary spirits and powers, of / natures, orders, and offices, both good and evil, light and darkness, or otherwise relating thereunto, and bring them to such obedience, as according to their severall and respective natures and offices, they may be so commanded and constrained to serve and obey.

A second Introduction.

When invocation, and replication thereunto, is amply made, according to time, method, and order, and the celestial angel or intelligence thereby moved, doth appear, or any other angel or intelligence of the same hierarchy, then mark and observe well the manner, shape and form, corporature, gesture, vestments, and foregoing sign thereof, and if in all symbolical likelyhood and probable symptoms, the apparition seemeth to be no less otherwise conjected, that which is from hence to be expected, although that very intelligence that was moved and called forth by name, doth not appear, by reason it is of the superior order of the hierarchy, who are not always sent, are usually go forth, neither are moved to visible appearance, but of especial grace and divine pleasure, more immediately unto choice and peculiar vessels of honour accordingly appointed immediately by the Holy Ghost, to fulfill the command of the Highest, but yet some or other or more of the celestial powers of the same order as aforesaid, more inferior in degree, may be moved hereby to descend and appear, at the earnest request of the Magician, and perform whatsoever shall be requested, according to its nature and office.

Good or Bad.

It cannot be unknown to any discreet Magician, that whensoever any good angel or celestial intelligence is moved, or called forth to visible appearance, but also that evil spirits, and infernal powers of darkness, are immediately ready to encroach and appear in the place of good angels; therefore, it behoveth to be very careful, and greatly observing thereof, both the method and manner how to know rightly and distinguish the appearance, and how to vanquish and banish evil spirits when they intrude, and enter into place and presence, to deceive and overwhelm us, we have sufficiently and at large inserted and shewed forth in our Isogogicall Preface, before annexed thereunto; therefore, we shall in this place only shew forth a method of our greeting the apparition of any celestial angel, or dignified power of light; and when, by all the prescript rules given, that apparition is truly known to be celestial, and of good, then humbly receive it with ample benevolence, saying as followeth.

To receive a good appearance.

Welcome be the light of the Highest, and welcome be the messenger of Divine Grace and Mercy unto us, the true servants and worshippers of the same your God, whose name be glorified, both now and for evermore.

When known to be good.

If the appearance is perfectly known and understood, and by all signs and tokens perfectly known to be celestial or angelical powers of light, then with due reverence, say as followeth.

Receiving good angels.

O thou servants and messengers of divine grace and mercy, and celestial angels or intelligence, powers of light, or dignified elemental spirits and / mediums of benevolence to mankind, servants of God, you, both now at this time, and always are, and shall be unto us, truly and sincerely welcome. Humbly desiring you also to be friendly, and to do for us in whatsoever it shall please God to give by your order and office unto you, for the better knowledge and benefit of mankind living here upon earth, and make us partakers of true science, in the undefiled and sincere sacred wisdom of your Creator.

Answer.

And if any answer shall be made thereunto, or any discourse from hence should arise or proceed thereupon, then both wisdom and reason must be the principal conduct of the management thereof; but if there be silence, that no discourse ariseth from hence, then begin to make humble request for answer to your desires and proposals; then will the effects of all things, undoubtedly, and with good success, be determined.

Fear or Mistrust.

But if there should any fear, doubt, or misprission, or just cause or jealousy be had or made of any expected apparition, or any angel or intelligence of celestial orders, or other elemental power of light, celestially dignified, or otherwise; if at any time there should appear a spirit which you do not think is of good, nor of the order you moved for, or have any mistrust of it, the which you may easily perceive by form, and also by its answering you in your question, and then you may say as followeth.

To know who it is.

In the name of Jesus, who art thou? then, perhaps, it will say, I am the servant of God; then you may say, art thou come from God? art thou sent from him with good tidings or messuage? then, perhaps, it / will say to you, or some such like words, what I am, he knoweth of whom I hear witness! Then you may ask its name, saying then, what is your name, either as it is notified among the blessed angels, or called by any mortal man? if you be of verity, and so of charity, you cannot dislike my speeches. Then it will tell you its name, or say nothing at all: but if it doth tell you its name, then you may say to it, if you be in the name of Jesus, say that all wicked angels are justly condemned, and that by the mercies of God in the merits of Christ, mankind elect is to be saved! Then it will give you a sufficient answer to satisfy you, or else it will be gone from you; and then, if it be of good, and hath answered your request, then, perhaps, it will say, thus much thou hast required; then you may say, I did so, for so is his judgement and justice against the impenitent, and his mercy to his elect, testify truth.

Then you may ask your desire.

We thought good to instance thus much, for better information and instruction, although a full narrative hereof is amply and at large shewed forth, in the foregoing Isogogicall Preface, both as to knowledge, and receiving of good angels, or celestial intelligences, or other elemental spirits or powers of light, angellically or celestially dignified; and for the knowledge, vanquishing, and driving away of all evil spirits and infernal powers of darkness, whensoever any such shall forcibly intrude, or make entrance or appearance, instead of celestial / and good angels, or other dignified elemental powers of light, in the time and place of these actions, purposely to deceive, confound, and, if possible, destroy the hopes, and expectations, and benefits of the philosophers, in their elaborate industry, and care, and earnest addresses unto the celestial angels and blessed intelligence, or dignified elemental powers, or other spiritual mediums or messengers of divine grace, for the true knowledge and finding out the use of all physical and metaphysical arcanums, or secrets in a superior profound mistery, which can not otherwise be known or found out, but by the divine light and conduct of angellical ministry, and other spiritual revelation and instruction by such mediums and benevolence to mankind; and through the divine grace, mercy, and goodness of the Highest, as are by nature, order, and office, thereunto pre-ordinately decreed and appointed. But as touching the insisting any farther of this matter, we think it needless; since it is more fully treated in the foregoing preface, which we advise to be well understood, by a due and serious consideration, before any progress or unadvisedly proceedings are made herein. Observe, also, whereas we have severally and particularly mentioned celestial angels, or blessed intelligences, and other dignified spirits of light, who are by nature and office good, and also friendly unto mankind, and generally inserts them together with material distinction; yet let grave and sober Magicians take notice what consideration be first had, of what angel or intelligence, of what spirits, and of what orders, office, he would move or call forth; and so in particular to make mention thereof according, and not otherwise, whereunto every thing ought by nature, degree, order, and office, properly to be referred.
Here endeth the Isogogicall Preface, or Second Introduction. ("Raphael" 1832: 542-552; 615-622).

The text continues with further prayers and states that it will present nine angelic calls, again in quite small type, but only offers the first of the calls.

Conjuration Narratives:

These examples illustrate the materials that could be used by Cunning Folk in the practice of conjuration. What exactly happened when the rituals were undertaken? Below are a few examples from the literature on what allegedly occurred when conjurations were actually undertaken. The first example is not from an English ritual, but as Cellini's experience is an interesting period example of conjuration, I include it here. Benvenuto Cellini (1500-1571) was an outstanding Renaissance sculptor, who like artist Richard Cosway, was curious about the practice of magic:

> It happened, through a variety of odd accidents, that I made acquaintance with a Sicilian priest, who was a man of genius, and well versed in the Latin and Greek authors. Happening one day to have some conversation with him upon the art / of necromancy, I, who had a great desire to know something of the matter, told him, that I had all my life felt a curiosity to be acquainted with the mysteries of this art. The priest made answer, "that the man must be of a resolute and steady temper who enters upon that study." I replied, "that I had fortitude and resolution enough, if I could but find an opportunity." The priest subjoined, "If you think you have the heart to venture, I will give you all the satisfaction you can desire." Thus we agreed to undertake this matter.
> The priest one evening prepared to satisfy me, and desired me to look out for a companion or two. I invited one Vicenzio Romoli, who was my intimate acquaintance: he brought with him a native of Pistoia, who cultivated the black art himself. We repaired to the [Colosseum], and the priest,

according to the custom of necromancers, began to draw circles upon the ground with the most impressive ceremonies imaginable: he likewise brought thither assafoetida, several precious perfumes, and fire, with some compositions which diffused noisome odours. As soon as he was in readiness, he made an opening in the circle, and having take us by the hand one by one, he placed us within it. Then having arranged the other parts and assumed his wand, he ordered the other necromancer, his partner, to throw the perfumes into the fire at a proper time, entrusting the care of the fire and the perfumes to the rest, and began his incantations. This ceremony lasted above an hour and a half, when there appeared several legions of devils, insomuch that the amphitheatre was quite filled with them.

I was busy about the perfumes, when the priest, perceiving there was a considerable number of infernal spirits, turned to me, and said, "Benvenuto, ask them something." I answered, "Let them bring me into the company of my Sicilian mistress, Angelica." That night we obtained no answer of any sort; but I had received great satisfaction in having my curiosity so far indulged. The necromancer told me it was requisite we should go a second time, assuring me, that I should be satisfied in whatever I asked, but that I must bring with me a pure and immaculate boy.

I took with me a youth who was in my service, of about / twelve years of age, together with the same Vincenzio Romoli, who had been my companion the first time, and one Agnolino Gaddi, an intimate acquaintance, whom I likewise prevailed on to assist at the ceremony. When we came to the place appointed, the priest having made his preparations as before, with the same and even more striking ceremonies, placed us within the circle, which he had likewise drawn with a more wonderful art, and in a more solemn manner than at our former meeting. Thus having committed the care of the perfumes and the fire to my friend Vincenzio, who was assisted by Agnolino Gaddi, he put into my hand a pintaculo [pentacle] or magical chart, and bid me turn it towards the places that he should direct me; and under the pintaculo I held my boy. The necromancer having begun to make his tremendous invocations, called by their names a multitude of demons, who were the leaders of the several legions, and invoked them by the virtue and power of the eternal uncreated God, who lives for ever, in the Hebrew language, as likewise in Latin and Greek; insomuch, that the amphitheatre was almost in an instant filled with demons a hundred times more numerous than at the former conjuration. Vincenzio Romoli was busied in making a fire with the assistance of Agnolino, and burning a great quantity of precious perfumes. I, by the direction of the necromancer, again desired to be in the company of my Angelica. The former thereupon turning to me said, "Know, they have declared that in the space of a month you shall be in her company." [This didn't happen.]

He then requested me to stand resolutely by him, because the legions were now above a thousand more in number than he had designed, and besides, these were the most dangerous, so that after they had answered my question it behooved him to be civil to them, and dismiss them quietly. At the same time, the boy under the pintaculo was in a terrible fright, saying, that there were in that place a million of fierce men, who threatened to destroy us; and that moreover four armed giants of an enormous stature were / endeavouring to break into our circle. During this time, whilst the necromancer, trembling with fear, endeavoured by mild and gentle methods to dismiss them in the best way he could, Vincenzio Romoli, who quivered like an aspen leaf, took care of the perfumes. Though I was as much terrified as any of them, I did my utmost to conceal the terror I felt, so that I greatly contributed to inspire the rest with resolution; but the truth is, I gave myself over for a dead man, seeing the horrid fright the necromancer was in. The boy placed his head between his knees, and said, "In this posture will I die; for we shall all surely perish." I told him that all those demons were under us, and what he saw was smoke and shadow; so bid him hold up his head and take courage. No sooner did he look up, but he cried out, "The whole amphitheatre is burning, and the fire is just falling upon us;" so covering his eyes with his hands, he again exclaimed, that destruction was inevitable, and he desired to see no more. The necromancer entreated me to have a good heart, and take care to burn proper perfumes; upon which I turned to Romoli, and bid him burn all the most precious perfumes he had. At the same time I cast my eye upon Agnolino Gaddi, who was terrified to such a degree, that he could scarce distinguish objects, and seemed to be half dead. Seeing him in this condition, I said, "Agnolo, upon these occasions a man should not yield to fear, but should stir about and give his assistance; so come directly and put on some more of these perfumes." Poor Agnolo, upon attempting to move, was so violently terrified, that the effects of his fear overpowered all the perfumes we were burning. The boy hearing a crepitation [crackling sound], ventured once more to raise his head, when seeing me laugh, he began to take courage, and said, that the devils were flying away with a vengeance.

In this condition we stayed till the bell rang for morning prayer. The boy again told us that there remained but few devils, and these were at a great distance. When the magician had performed the rest of his ceremonies, he / stripped off his gown, and took up a wallet full of books which he had brought with him. We all went out of the circle together, keeping as close to each other as we possibly could, especially the boy, who had placed himself in the middle, holding the necromancer by the coat and me by the cloak. As we were going to our houses, in the quarter of Banchi, the boy told us that two of the demons whom we had seen at the amphitheatre, went on before us leaping and skipping, sometimes running upon the roofs of the houses, and sometimes upon the ground.

The priest declared, that though he had often entered magic circles, nothing so extraordinary had ever happened to him. As we went along he would fain have persuaded me to assist with him at consecrating a book, from which he said we should derive immense riches: we should then ask the demons to discover to us the various treasures with which the earth abounds, which would raise us to opulence and power; but that those love affairs were mere follies, from whence no good could be expected. I answered, "That I would have readily accepted his proposal, if I had understood Latin." He redoubled his persuasions, assuring me that the knowledge of the Latin language was by no means material. He added, that he could have found Latin scholars enough, if he had thought it worth while to look out for them, but that he could never have met with a partner of resolution and intrepidity equal to mine, and that I should by all means follow his advice. Whilst we were engaged in this conversation, we arrived at our respective homes, and all that night dreamt of nothing but devils.

As I every day saw the priest, he did not fail to renew his solicitations to engage me to come into his proposal. I asked him what time it would take to carry his plan into execution, and where this scene was to be acted. He answered, "That in less than a month we might complete it, and that the place best calculated for our purpose was the mountains of Norcia: though a master of his had performed the ceremony of consecration hard by the mountains of the Abbey of Farfa, but that he had met with some difficulties which would not occur in those of Norcia." He added, "that the neighbouring peasants were men who might be confided in, and had some knowledge of necromancy, insomuch, that they were likely to give us great assistance upon occasion." Such an effect had the persuasions of this holy conjurer, that I readily agreed to all he desired, but told him, that I should be glad to finish the medals I was making for the Pope first: this secret I communicated to him, but to nobody else, and begged he would not divulge it. I constantly asked him whether he thought I should, at the time mentioned by the devil, have an interview with my mistress Angelica; and finding it approach, I was surprised to hear no tidings of her. The priest always assured me that I should without fail enjoy her company, as the demons never break their promise, when they make it in the solemn manner they had done to me. He bid me, therefore, wait patiently, and avoid giving room to any scandal upon that occasion, but make an effort to bear something against my nature, as he was aware of the great danger I was to encounter; adding, that it would be happy for me if I would go with him to consecrate the book, as it would be the way to obviate the danger, and could not fail to make both him and me happy.[116]

An English example recorded by William Lilly involved a search for treasure in Westminster Abbey in 1634. It shows how quite influential people were convinced that spiritual assistance in finding treasure was both a viable and "reputable" activity:

Davy Ramsey, his Majesty's Clock-maker, had been informed, that there was a Great quantity of Treasure buried in the Cloyster of *Westminster*-Abbey; he acquaints Dean *Williams* therewith, who was also then Bishop of *Lincoln*; the Dean gave him Liberty to search after it, with this *Proviso*, that if any was discovered, his Church should have a Share of it. *Davy Ramsey* finds out one *John Scott*, who pretended the use of the *Mosaical* Rods, to assist him herein: I was desired to join with him, unto which I consented. One Winter's Night, *Davy Ramsey*, with several Gentlemen, myself, and *Scott*, entered the Cloysters; we play'd the Hazel-rod round about the Cloyster; upon the West-side of the

---

[116] *Memoirs of Benvenuto Cellini*. Thomas Roscoe, trans. London: Henry. G. Bohn, 1850, pp. 143-148.

Cloysters the Rods turned one over another, an Argument that the Treasure was there. The labourers digged at least six Foot deep, and then we met with a Coffin; but in regard it was not heavy, we did not open, which we afterwards much repented. From the Cloysters we went into the Abbey Church, where, upon a sudden, (there being no Wind when we began) so fierce, so high, so blustering and loud a Wind did rise, that we verily believed the West-end of the Church would have fallen upon us; our Rods would not move at all; the Candles and Torches, all but one, were extinguished, or burned very dimly. *John Scott*, my Partner, was amazed, looked pale, knew not what to think or do, until I gave Directions and Command to dismiss the *Daemons*; which when done, all was quiet again, and each Man returned unto his Lodging late, about 12 a-Clock at Night; I could never since be induced to join with any in such like Actions.

The true Miscarriage of the Business, was by reason of so many People being present at the Operation; for there was about thirty, some laughing, others deriding us; so that if we had not dismissed the *Daemons*, I believe most part of the *Abbey*-Church had been blown down; Secrecy and intelligent Operators, with a strong Confidence and Knowledge of what they are doing, are best for this Work. (Lilly 1974: 32)

Lilly also has anecdotes about his old mentor, John Evans, and conjuration:

There was in *Staffordshire* a young Gentlewoman that had, for her Preferment, marry'd an aged rich Person, who being desirous to purchase some Lands for his wife's Maintenance; but this young Gentlewoman, his Wife, was desired to buy the Land in the Name of a Gentleman, her very dear Friend, but for her Use: After the aged Man was dead, the Widow could by no Means procure the Deed of Purchase from her Friend; whereupon she applies herself to *Evans*, who, for a Sum of Money, promises to have her Deed safely delivered into her own Hands; the Sum was Forty Pounds. *Evans* applies himself to the Invocation of the Angel *Salmon*, of the Nature of *Mars*, reads his Litany in the Common-Prayer-Book every Day, at select Hours, wears his Surplice, lives orderly all that Time; at the Fortnight's End *Salmon* appear'd, and having received his Commands what to do, in a small Time returns with the very Deed desired, lays it down gently upon a Table where a white Cloth was spread, and then, being dismiss'd, vanish'd. The Deed was, by the Gentleman who formerly kept it, placed among many other of his Evidences in a large wooden Chest, and in a Chamber at one End of the House; but upon *Salmon's* removing and bringing away the Deed, all that Bay of Building was quite blown down, and all his own proper Evidences torn all to pieces. The second Story followeth.

Some time before I became acquainted with him, he then living in the Minories, was desired by the Lord *Bothwell* and Sir *Kenelm Digby* to show them a Spirit, he promised so to do: the time came, and they were all in the Body of the Circle, when lo, upon a sudden, after some time of Invocation, *Evans* was taken from out the Room, and carried into the Field near *Battersea* Causeway, close to the *Thames*. Next Morning a Country-man going by to his Labour, and espying a Man in black Cloaths, came unto him and awaked him, and asked him how he came there; *Evans* by this understood his Condition, enquired where he was, how far from *London*, and in what Parish he was; which when he understood, he told the Labourer he had been late at *Battersea* the Night before, and by chance was left there by his Friends. Sir *Kenelm Digby* and the Lord *Bothwell* went home without any Harm, and came next Day to hear what was become of him; just as they, in the Afternoon, came into the House, a messenger came from *Evans* to his Wife, to come to him at *Battersea*: I enquired upon what Account the Spirit carry'd him away: who said, he had not, at the time of Invocation, made any Suffumigation, at which the Spirits were vexed. (Lilly 1974: 21-22)

A cautionary narrative about the dangers involved with conjuration included in Sibley's *Occult Sciences* involved a luckless student of the occult named Thomas Perks, which reads like one of M. R. James' ghost tales. "Raphael" includes an illustration of Perks' conjuration in *The Familiar Astrologer* (1832), as shown here. It should be remembered that mathematics was traditionally associated with magic and astrology in the past:

THOMAS PERKS, RAISING A SPIRIT, TO HIS OWN DESTRUCTION!
(Raphael 1832: opposite p. 213)

AUTHENTIC COPY *of a* LETTER *sent to the Bishop of Gloucester, by the Reverend Mr. Arthur Bedford, Minister of Temple Church, in Bristol.*
MY LORD, *Bristol, August 2, 1703.*
Being informed by Mr. Shute of your lordship's desire that I should communicate to you what I had known concerning a certain person, who was acquainted with spirits to his own destruction, I have made bold to give you the trouble of this letter, hoping my desire to gratify your lordship in every particular may be an apology for the length thereof. I had formerly given an account to the late Bishop of Hereford, in which there are probably some things contained, which I do not now remember, which, if your lordship could procure from his lady, (who now lives near Gloucester,) would be more authentic.

About thirteen years ago, whilst I was curate to Dr. Read, rector of St. Nicholas in this city, I began to be acquainted with one Thomas Perks, a man about twenty years of age, who lived with his father at Mongatsfield, a gunsmith; and contracted an intimacy with him, he being not only a very good-natured man, but extremely skilled in mathematical studies, which were his constant delight, viz. arithmetic, geometry, / gauging, surveying, astronomy, and algebra; he had a notion of the perpetual motion, much like that wheel in Archimedes's Mathematical Magic, in which he had made some improvements, and which he has held was demonstrable from mathematical principles, though I could never believe it. I have seen an iron wheel, to which he intended to add several things of his own invention, in order to finish the same; but, thinking it of no use, and being otherwise unfortunately engaged, it was never perfected. He gave himself so much to astronomy, that he could not only calculate the motions of the planets, but an eclipse also, and demonstrate any problem in spherical trigonometry from mathematical principles, in which he discovered a clear force of reason. When one Mr. Bailey, minister of St. James's in this city, endeavoured to set up a mathematical school, I advised him to this Thomas Perks, for an acquaintance, in whom, as he told me, he found a greater proficiency in those studies than he expected or could have imagined. After this he applied himself to astrology, and would sometimes calculate nativities and resolve horary questions. When by the providence of God I was settled in Temple-parish, and had not seen him for some time, he came to me, and, we being in private, he asked my opinion very seriously concerning the lawfulness of conversing with spirits; and, after I had given my thoughts in the negative, and confirmed them with the best reasons I could, he told me he had considered all these arguments, and believed they only related to conjurations, but there was an innocent society with them which a man might use, if he made no compacts with them, did no harm by their means, and were not curious in prying into hidden things; and that he himself had discoursed with them, and heard them sing to his great satisfaction; and gave an offer to me and Mr. Bayley at another time, that, if we would go with him one night to Kingswood, we should see them, and hear them both talk and sing, and talk with them whenever we had a mind, and we would return very safe; but neither of us had the courage to venture. I told him the subtilty of the devil to delude mankind, and to transform himself into an angel of light; but he would not believe it was the devil. I had several conferences with him upon this subject, but could never convince him, in all which I could never observe the least disorder of mind, his discourse being very rational; and I proposed (to try him) a question in astronomy relating to the projection, of the sphere, which he projected and resolved, and did afterwards demonstrate from the mathematics, so as to show at the same time that his brain was free from the least tincture of madness and distraction.—Having this opportunity of asking him several particulars, concerning the methods he used, and the discourses he had with them, he told me he had a book whose directions he followed, and accordingly /, in the dead time of the night, he went out to a cross way, with a lanthorn and candle consecrated for this purpose with several incantations. He had also consecrated chalk, consisting of several mixtures, with which he made a circle at what distance he thought fit, within which no spirit had power to enter. After this he invoked the spirit by several forms of words, (some of which he told me were taken out of the holy Scriptures, and therefore he thought them lawful, without considering how they might be wrested to his destruction;) accordingly the spirits appeared to him which he called for, in the shape of little maidens, about a foot and half high, and played about a circle. At first he was somewhat affrighted; but, after some small acquaintance, this antipathy in nature wore off, and he became pleased with their company. He told me they spoke with a very shrill voice, like an ancient woman. He asked them if there was a heaven or hell? they said there was. He asked them what place heaven was? which they described as a place of great glory and happiness; and he asked them what hell was? and they bade him ask no questions of that nature, for it was a dreadful thing to relate, and the devils believe and tremble. He further asked them what method or order they had among themselves? they told him they were divided into three orders; that they had a chief whose residence was in the air; that he had several counsellors which were placed by him in form of a globe, and he in the centre, which was the chiefest order; another order was employed in going to and from thence to the earth, to carry intelligence from those lower spirits; and their own order was on the earth, according to the directions they should receive from those in the air.

This description was very surprising, but, being contrary to the account we have in Scripture of the hierarchy of the blessed angels, made me conclude they were devils, but I could not convince him of it. He told me he had bade them sing, and they went to some distance behind a bush, from whence he could hear a perfect concert of such exquisite music as he never before heard; and in the upper part he heard something very harsh and shrill like a reed, but, as it was managed, did give a particular grace to the rest.

About a quarter of a year after he came again to me, and wished he had taken my advice, for he thought he had done that which would cost him his life, and which he did heartily repent of; and indeed his eyes and countenance showed a great alteration. I asked him what he had done. He told me that, being bewitched to his acquaintance, he resolved to proceed farther in this art, and to have some familiar spirit at his command, according to the directions of his book, which were as follows:—

He was to have a book made of virgin parchment consecrated with several incantations; likewise a particular ink-horn, ink, &c. for his purpose; with these he was to go out as usual to a cross way, and call up a spirit, and ask him his name, which he was to put in the first page of his book, and this was to be his familiar. Thus he was to do as many as he pleased, writing their names in distinct pages, only one in a leaf; and then, whenever he took the book and opened it, the spirit whose name appeared should appear also; and, putting this in practice, the familiar he had called Malchi, a word in Hebrew of an unknown signification. After this they appeared faster than he desired, and in most dismal shapes, like serpents, lions, bears, &c. hissing at him, and attempting to throw spears and balls of fire, which did very much affright him, and the more when he found it not in his power to stay them, insomuch that his hair (as he told us) stood upright, and he expected every moment to be torn in pieces; this happened in December about midnight, when he continued there in a sweat till break of day, and then they left him, and from that time he was never well as long as he lived. In his sickness he came frequently to Bristol, to consult with Mr. Jacob, an apothecary in Broad-street, concerning a cure, but I know not whether he told him the origin of his sickness or not; he also came to me at the same time, and owned every matter of fact until the last, and insisted that, when he did anything of this nature, he was deluded in his conscience to think it lawful, but he was since convinced to the contrary. He declared he made no compact with any of those spirits, and never did any harm by their means, nor ever pryed into the future fortune of himself or others, and expressed a hearty repentance and detestation of his sins; so that, though those methods cost him his life in this world, yet I have great reason to believe him happy in the other. I am not certain that he gave this account to any other person but myself, though he communicated something of it to Mr. Bayly, minister of St. James's, in this city; perhaps your lordship may be further informed by his relations and neighbors of Mangotsfield, which lies in Gloucestershire, not above a mile out of the road to Bath.

I have frequently told this story, but never mentioned his name before, and therefore, if your lordships hath any design of printing such accounts as these, I desire it may be with such tenderness to his memory, as he deserved, and so as may not be the least prejudice to his relations, who have the deserved character of honest and sober people, I am,
Your Lordship's dutiful
Son and Servant,
ARTHUR BEDFORD. (Sibley 1795: 1121-1124)

The final example, found in "Raphael's" *Familiar Astrologer*, has a ring of credibility about it:

Invocation of Spirits.

The following extraordinary Fragment is extracted verbatim from a curious and original Manuscript in the British Museum.

"*Wednesday, Oct. 16, 1585.*

"At eleven o'clock at night, I and my companions having began action, at the request and full consent of all the company, we did fully agree, that we should not desist till we had brought something to completion. And having began action, and all things for the same purpose ready and fitted, we give a brief account of what followed.

"After the first invocation, twice or thrice repeated, there appeared two men in the farthest glass, visible to some part of the company, and not to other some; but, proceeding on, and invocating highly, there came a great blow upon the floor, which made a very great noise; and, before it ceased, it did whirl about several times, to the great astonishment and admiration of all the company. And still proceeding on, and reading further, there came something which fell pat upon the table, and from the table upon the ground, which made a smaller noise on the floor, than the other did; and so vanished. And so much for that night only. When action was ended, we could find nothing that was the cause for that noise, for what it was we could not tell; but, be what it would, as it *came*, so it *went*, for we could not find any thing.

"*Thursday, October 17th.*

"At eleven at night we began action again; and, having performed several invocations and constraints, there appeared three spirits of fire, which broke, and were quickly gone. Next appeared a veil or curtain in the stone, of a very bright colour; which continued a great while, and so vanished. And after that appeared several black clouds, filling the glass with a dark dismal show: but, immediately proceding, and invocating higher, we had more remarkable matters; for there was thrown a great piece of tile with such a force upon the floor, that if it had hit upon the head of any of the company, / it would have split their skulls. And there it lay *visibly* upon the floor before us, during the whole action. Immediately after, came another great blow upon the floor, visible to all, which made a very great noise and rattling; which, after action, we perceived to be a great piece of earth tile, which did make the company very much to admire how it came there, it being very wet, as if it had newly come out of the earth. But proceeding yet higher, and invocating at large, there appeared a thing like unto a fly, which hovered and flew over the lamps and receptacles a great while. At last, it flew down upon the table, and run upon the *seal* of the spirit, and there, visibly to us all, did not leave one line nor scroll in the seal unsearched, but run over it all, and then whirled round several times together, and likewise run over every line of the *bond*, and likewise run over the petition, and thoroughly searched all our writings, and viewed our concerns, at large, as they lay.

Presently after, appeared *six* large flies, which hovered all around the other fly; and so all vanished at once, and were never seen after. After that, appeared several shapes of black, gleaming up and down the room, but quickly vanished. After this, something fell again, with a great noise, near the table, and there whirled up and down the room for a great while together, and also vanished, and was never seen again, nor ever could we find what it was.

"The time being spent, and our action almost over, we licensed the sprits to depart to their orders, at which time there was such a noise and such a rattling upon the top of the house, as if a cart and horses had run from one end of the house to the other; and so we gave over, for that action.

"Friday, October 18th.

"At eleven o'clock at night, we began action again; and, as before we were well seated in the circle, undoubtedly they were with us; for, from the fuming-pan, which stood upon the table, there came several flashes of fire, one after another, and a pretty long space between each flash; and between every flash a blaze of blue as steel, and such a strong and infernal stink of brimstone issued from thence as was ready to choke us all. Whereupon, falling upon high action, immediately appeared a great flint stone, which came upon / the floor with such a force, that the floor shaked; and immediately after, proceeding farther and constraining higher, there descended a pebble down, which broke our bottle of red ink all in pieces standing upon the table before us all, and, after a little space longer, there appeared two acorns upon the table, which, with the pebble, lay visibly before us, during the whole action. After this, appeared in the stone which stood in the midst, a thing like unto a crocodile, turning and twisting upon the table, around the glass, which, before action was done, turned to the shape of a perfect man, and so vanished. But, being resolute, and resolved to force them to appearance, moving something nearer the edge of the circle than I ought have done, I had like to be nipped out, for some part of my book, hanging over the circle, had such a blow which beat the book quite out of my hand, to the farthest part of the room, and almost beat me over; which all the company saw, and beheld with great wonder. After which pretty feat, there came to our hearing the sweetest harmony of music that we ever heard, which continued some time, but no louder than the humming of a humble bee; which we could not suppose to be any thing but for joy that they had hindered our proceedings, by beating the book out of my hand, and spoiling the height of our action for the time; which, in all likelihood was so, for, immediately after our book was gone, what we looked for before quickly came; for there were several gleams all around the room, and especially at one end of the room appeared something of a whitish colour, but did not continue long: but quickly after this there came a great black bowl, which swiftly ran quite round the circle, and so vanished; and so we gave over for the time.

"But take notice, that the next morning, after that action, I and my companions walking towards a wood, where we supposed the treasure to be laid and hidden, we were all amazed and astonished; for, by the side of an alder, near a well (which some of my companions, in searching and digging for the treasure, chanced to find a former time, but which at this time was a fine spring), there, afar off, before any of us came near the place, was brought and laid our glass ball, that stood in the middle of our other glasses upon the / table, the night before, with all the matter of appearance in it (and there left standing upon the table when we left the room from action), at the root of the alder, which we all knew to be our's; but coming home, we proved it to be so, for, entering the room, which was locked, we found our middle glass wanting. It was gone, but the pedestal whereon it stood left behind, to our great wonder and astonishment. This wood was a full mile from our place of action.

"Wednesday, October 23d.

"At eleven o'clock at night, we began our action again; and, after some time, we perceived at least *eleven* acorns come upon the table with great force, and made such a rattling and flying about the room, that we were all astonished; for, in short, some of our company did not know whether to stand or run; for afterwards descended a great stone, into the consecrated water, which made the water flash all our concerns."

The foregoing fragment is copied out of a transcript of "Dee's Conferences with Angels," but is no part of the Conferences, but written at the latter end thereof. The *whole* transcript was made by Elias Ashmole, Esq. from the original MSS. and is No. 3677 in the Sloanian Library of MSS. in the British Museum. ("Raphael" 1825: 82-85)

Conjuration could be as simple as a spell involving names of power or as complex and demanding as the invocation of angels, demons and fairies shown above. The necessary preparatory purification of the mage, his various tools and magic circles, the religious versicles and psalms, the secret names of God or the spirits, the mysterious words, sigils and magical characters, and the ceremonial circles are found throughout the genre, and absolutely central to the work. As can be seen from references in this chapter, the search for treasure was one of the most common applications of conjuration. The following chapter takes up this central component of magic and divination.

CHAPTER 15:

Treasure Hunting

It is obvious from the many examples found in grimoires and magician's workbooks that treasure-hunting was a perennial theme for conjuration. It was widely believed that hidden treasures were numerous, guarded by spirits and that astrology and proper rituals not only revealed the location of the hoards, but could also neutralize their protective spirits and secure the prize. Although it is evident that some treasure hoards were real – they have been continually discovered since ancient times and are still being uncovered today – faith in their existence outdistanced the actual evidence to the extent that people to expect to find them in the most unlikely places, such as rural New England or upstate New York.

The assumptions surrounding the search for treasure were various and seductive:

- Hidden treasure was generally and widely available, secreted away by earlier inhabitants or by magical beings such as fairies or leprechauns.
- It could be located and acquired through astrological and magical methods.
- Both treasure and mineral wealth were often guarded by spirits, who might harm the unwary searcher, or whisk the stuff away if not properly dealt with.
- Likely locations included mounds and barrows (hence the slang "hill digger"), monastic ruins, roadside crosses, and other places identified by rumor, dreams and divination.
- The locations could be tested astrologically or by "mosaical rods" to see if the suspicion of "treasure hid" was true.

"Treasure" could mean gold, silver, jewels and similar objects, but it could also be veins of ore, or even things as miscellaneous as women's ornaments, pictures, books and household stuff. Although the long-term human occupation of Britain had made the possibility of finding someone's long-lost wealth a reasonable assumption, the strength of the belief in "magical" treasures (plus the more reasonable search for mineral wealth) resulted in a veritable fad of treasure seeking in 18th and 19th century America. Some treasure hunters were self-taught amateurs, but more often than not, there was a Cunning Man or Wise Woman involved.

Unlike the furtive practice of conjuring spirits for private exploitation, treasure hunting was often a group project, occasionally even enjoying the public support of authorities, providing it was done under license by the Crown or other officials who were promised a percentage of the "treasure trove" (i.e., "treasure found"). Examples of this include the instance recorded by William Lilly of the sanctioned search in Westminster Abbey and a curious Norfolk case of 1521, in which three men – William Smith, one Amylyon and William Judy – who had been deputized to not only search for treasure but also prosecute unlicensed "hill diggers" under a "placard" or patent given to Robert Lord Curzon by Henry VIII. They accused one William Goodred of illegal treasure hunting, and threatened to bring him before the magistrates at Norwich Castle unless he paid them 20 shillings to be let go, only to be confronted by Goodred's friends, who in turn accused Smith of libeling the Duke of Buckingham and the Duke of Suffolk.[117]

John Dee, who was always trying to get Queen Elizabeth to finance his schemes, proposed to Lord Burghley in 1574 that he should be licensed to search for treasure on the principles of natural rather than demonic magic:

---

[117] Dawson Turner. "Remarks on Trial by Jury, Treasure-Trove and the Invocation of Spirits" *Norfolk Archaeology*, vol. I, (1847), pp. 47-57.

> But, if, (besides all bokes, dreames, visions, reports and *virgula divina*) by any other naturall meanes and likely demonstrations of *sympathia* and *antipathia rerum*, or by attraction and repulsion, the places may be discryed or discovered, where gold, silver, or better matter, doth lye hid, within a certayne distance: how great a / commodity shold it be for the Quenens Majestie, and the common weale of this Kingdome, by such a secret, not onely threasor hid may be deciphered in precise place: but, also, it may be disclosed where, in this land, any mynes, vaynes, or owre of gold or silver be naturally planted. ... uppon this comfortable consideration, that her Majesty do frely give unto me, by good warranty and assurance of her letters-patents, her right and propriety to all *thresor trouve*, and such things commodious, as (under that name and meaning comprised) by digging or search any where, in her graces kingdomes and dominions, I, or my assignes shall come to, or finde: and with all good warranty (for my indemnity) agayn all laws and persons, to make serch by digging, or otherwise. And this to dure the terme of my life. [118]

For the most part, however, treasure hunting was done privately and secretly, which made it illegal. Each of the "Witchcraft Acts" included a clause making treasure hunting a crime, and in fact concern about treasure hunting made up the greater part of the first Witchcraft act, as it was of far greater concern to the government than witchcraft itself:

> 1542: "...haue also made Crownes Septures Swordes rynges glasses and other things, and gyuing faithe & credit to suche fantasticall practices, have dygged up and pulled downe an infinite nombre of Crosses wtin [within] this Realme, and taken vpon them to declare and tell where thinges lost or stollen shulde be become; wiche things cannot be used and exersised but to the great offence of Godes lawe, hurt and damage of the Kinges subjects, and losse of the sowles of such Offenders, to the greate dishonor of God, Infamy and disquyetnes of the Realme ... to thentent to get or fynde money or treasure ... for lucre of money, digge vp or pull downe any Crosse or Crosses, or by suche invocacons or conjuracons of Sprites wichecraftes enchauntmentes or sorcerie or any of them take vpon them to declare where goodes stollen or lost shall become, That then all and evy suche Offence and Offences, from the saide first daye of Maye shalbe demyde [deemed] accepted and adjuged Fe-lonye...
>
> 1563: That yf any pson or psons shall from and after the sayd first daye of June nexte coming, take upon him or them, by Witchecrafte Enchantement Charme or Sorcerie, to tell or declare in what Place any Treasure of Golde or Sylver shoulde or might bee founde or had in the Earthe or other secret Places, or where Goodes or Thinges lost or stollen should bee founde or becume ...
>
> 1604: ... if any pson or psons shall from and after the saide Feaste of Saint Michaell the Archangell next cominge, take upon him or them by Witchcrafte Inchantment Charme or Sorcerie to tell or declare in what place any treasure of Golde or silver should or had in the earth or other secret places, or where Goodes or Thinges loste or stollen should be founde or become ...
>
> 1734: ... That if any Person shall, from and after the said Twenty-fourth Day of June, *pretend* [my emphasis], from his or her Skill or Knowledge in any occult or crafty Science, to discover where or in what manner any Goods or Chattels, supposed to have been stolen or lost, may be found ...

How then did people go about their search for "treasure hid"? Once the existence of a treasure was suspected or at least desired, the first step might be to enlist the aid of an astrologer who could ascertain the potential viability, and in some cases, even help pinpoint the location of the horde. For example, Nicholas Culpeper in his *Opus Astrologicum* gives these directions for treasure seeking:

ELECTIONS Concerning Hidden Treasures

> 1. Hidden Treasures belong to the fourth house, and to his Lord.
> 2. If the Lord of the Ascendent, and the Lord of the fourth house, be fortunate in the Nativity of any, and in good aspect the one to the other, and the Luminaries behold the Ascendent by good aspect; that native will be subject to, and fortunate in finding Hidden Treasures.
> 3. In Questions about such businesses, if the Lord of the fourth house be fortunate in the Ascendent, or the Lord of the Ascendent, or in the fourth house, the treasure may be found.

---

[118] James Orchard Halliwell. *Collection of Letters Illustrative of the Progress of Science in England.* London: Historical Society of Science, 1841, p.

4. If in the Question *Saturn, Mars*, or the Dragons tail, be in the Ascendent, the Querent will take labour in vain in searching for it, and in the act will be troubled with foolish phantasies and illusions.

5. If good Planets be in angles, let the game go which way it will, there is a possibility of finding it, if good courses be taken.

6. If you would know whether there be any treasure or no, consider the Angles of the heaven, especially the Ascendent, then the fourth, then the tenth: for the seventh is of little or no value, in such businesses as these.

7. If within the first degrees (to wit, five degrees from the Cusp) of these Angles, there be any good Planet, 'tis a good argument there is treasure hid.

8. If the Signe possessing the Cusp of the fourth house be a fiery Signe, it lies in the east part; if airy, the west; if watry, the north; if earthly, the fourth part of the house.

9. Fiery Signes signifie it to be neer chimneys; airy, on the top of the house, about the ceiling or rafters; watry Signes, neer water; earthly Signes, in the earth, or cellars.

10. For the Planets, the Sun signifies open places; the Moon, neer gates or doors; *Saturn*, stinking moist places, cellars, and where they lay dust and coles.

11. *Jupiter* signifies halls of entertainment; *Venus*, bed-chambers; Mercury, walls.

12. You must also consider other testimonies, *viz.* the nature of the Signes, and of the Planets, Whether Oriental, or Occidental; whether Septentrional, or Meridional; and in what part of the heavens they be.

13. If the Lord of the Ascendent be in his house or exaltation, the treasure is great; if in his detriment or fall, 'tis worth little.

14. If the Lord of the Ascendent be Oriental, 'tis newly laid there: if Occidental, it hath been there a long time.

15. If the Lord of the Ascendent be fortunate, it may be had all; if infortunate, you must be content with part, and glad you can get that too.

16. Fiery and Airy Signes shew things of greater value then Earthly and Watry Signes do.[119]

Similarly, John Gadbury's *Genethlialogia* has this useful advice:

SECT. 4
Of Treasure hid, if attainable?

1. Common is it for Persons to hide Treasure, and as common for those that hide a great deal, to forget where some part of it may be; therefore after erection of your Figure, consider what application, reception, translation, *&c.* there may be between the Lords of the Ascendant and fourth House.

2. If there be a friendly application and reception, the Person enquiring shall obtain the Treasure he looketh for. But if there be a □ or ☍ between the Significators, without reception, the Treasure hid will very hardly be found.

3. When the Signicators apply to each other Corporally in a fixed Sign, there is much hopes of finding and obtaining the same suddenly; chiefly, if the application be in a good House.

4. Both or either of the lights in the Ascendant no way unfortunated, or else friendly beholding the same, argues a speedy recovery of the Treasure hid; But if instead hereof they happen to be Cadent, or in □ or ☍ thereto, it denotes small hopes.

5. If the part of fortune be in the Ascendant, and there beheld / by the fortunate Planets, or the Luminaries, the Querent will then be in good hopes of acquiring the Treasure hid.

6. But if the ⊕ and the Luminaries be Cadent, chiefly the ☽ ; and neither of the lights cast a friendly Aspect to the ⊕, or the Ascendant; Nor the Lord of the Ascendant behold the Ascendant, it is an argument the Querent cannot obtain the Treasure hid.

---

[119] Nicholas Culpeper. *Opus Astrologicum Or, An Astrological Work Left to Posterity.* London,: Printed by J. Cottrel for Ri. Moone and Steph. Chatfield: 1654, sigs. F4ᵛ – F6ᵛ.

7. I always observe in Questions of this nature, if Fortunate Planets be in the Fourth, or govern the Fourth, that there is Treasure; and if the Lord of the Ascendent or ☽ be in good Aspect with those Planets, the Querent doth attain to it by search.
8. On the contrary, if Infortunes be in the fourth House, or the Luminaries weak there, it is an argument of irrecovery; or shews (sometimes) that it is taken away before. I remember about five or six years since, a Captain who had a Patent to search for hidden Treasure, asked my opinion concerning a business he was about in Chick-Lane London; I erected a Scheam upon his proposal, and found the ☽ in ♏ in the fourth in □ to ♄ : I told him I conceived there was no Treasure, or if there were, it was removed, and advised him to forbear his scruitinie, for fear of gaining prejudice instead of Treasure, in his going on. He enquired of me what prejudice? I answered (considering the Moons position in a moyst Sign, in □ to ♄ in the twelfth House) that either some malicious people would put some trick upon him; or else some Vault might break in upon him and his Company, &c. the later of which I most feared, and not the former. The Captain was perswaded at present to break off, and went from me so resolved: But an itch of covetousness over-prevailed with him, and caused him straight-way to change purpose, and to digging he goes again (the same night he had been with me) and reaped what he well deserved (for his mutability of minde) and was for all his pains, appayd with the breaking of a Jakes [a privy, or rather its cesspit] upon him and his Company.

SECT. 5.

Is there Treasure in the place supposed?

9. A Question being thus in a general way propounded, give the Lord of the Ascendent and the ☽ to the Querent for his Significators; the fourth House, and the Planet or Planets posited therein, shall signifie the Treasure enquired after.
10. When ♃, ♀, or ☊ is in the fourth House, they declare Treasure to be in the place supposed; and, if they be in their essential Dignities, it is very certain that there is a great deal there.
11. If you find any of the other Planets in their own Houses, in the fourth House without impediment, *&c.* you may conclude that there is Treasure in the place supposed; and it is of the Nature of the Planet signifying it.
12. If the Planet signifying the Treasure be ☉, you may say, there is Gold, or Jewels, *&c.* If it is the ☽, 'tis Silver. If ♄, Lead, Coles, or a quarry of Stone; according to the place supposed. If ♂, it is Brass or Iron, or such like. If ♃, Tin. If ♀, women's Ornaments. If ☿, Pictures, Medals, Books, or such like.
13. If the fourth House be unfortunated (*i.e.*, if the ☋, or ♄, or ♂, be there, and in no way essentially dignified; or, if ♄, or ♂, call a □ or ☍ thereunto) you may safely judge there is no Treasure at all.
14. The Lord of the fourth, or ☽ separated from good Planets, shews / that there hath been some Treasure in the place supposed, but it is gone; But if he or she separate ill, tell your Qurent there was never any Treasure in the place supposed.
15. Some conclude the Lord of the seventh ought to shew the Nature and Quality of the Treasure. Those who have a desire, may make tryal of that way: but for my part, I confess I understand no reason for it.[120]

Once the treasure had been "verified" by astrology or information from the spirit world, the next step might be to try to find the exact location by the use of a divining rod (*virgula divina*) or rods, also referred to as "Mosaical rods" as in William Lilly's example. The interesting thing here is that this device was a recent innovation that first turned up in 15th century Germany and quickly spread to Britain and

[120] John Gadbury. *Genethlialogia, or the Doctrine of Nativities, with The Doctrine of Horary Questions, Astrologically handled.* London: Printed by Ja. Cotterl, for Giles Calvert,1658, pp. 260-262.

elsewhere. The earliest examples appear to be the same as the traditional "dowsing rod" now used for finding water – a forked twig or stick – but the use of two straight unconnected rods was an early variation as well, and rods could be made of other materials besides wood. Because the divining rod was a new innovation, directions for its preparation and use do not turn up in some traditional books of magic. Reginald Scot gives a less than complete example for the rod, but includes a written charm that may have been like the one used by Mary Parish (see below).

The art and order to be used in digging for monie, revealed by dreames, how to procure pleasant dreames, of morning and midnight dreames.

There must be made upon a hazell wand three crosses, and certeine words both blasphemous and impious must be said over it, and hereunto must be added certeine characters, & barbarous names. And whilest the treasure is a digging, there must be read the psalmes, *De profundis, Missa, Misereatur nostri, Requiem, Pater noster, Ave Maria, Et ne nos inducas in tentationem, sed libera nos à malo, Amen. A porta inferi credo videre bona, &c. Expectate Dominum, Requiem æternam.* And then a certeine praier. And if the time of digging be neglected, the divell will carie all the treasure awaie. (Scot 1973: 147)

To know of treasure hidden in the earth.

WRITE in paper these characters following, on the saturdaie, in the hour of , and laie it where thou thinkest treasure to be: if there be anie, the paper will burne, else not. And these be the characters. (Scot 1973: 341)

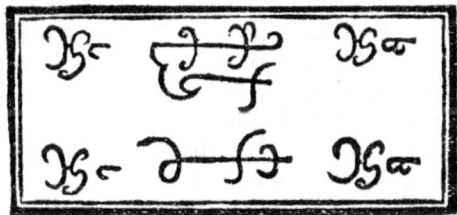

Perhaps in some cases the formula for the magical wand or rod was used, as the preferred wood was also hazel (or witch hazel). Some further examples from popular sources are as follows:

The Mosaic Wand to find hidden Treasure. — Cut a hazel wand forked at the upper end like a Y. Peel off the rhine, and dry it in a moderate heat; then steep it in the juice of wake-robin or nightshade, and cut the single lower end sharp, and where you suppose any rich mine or hidden treasure is near, place a piece of the same mettal you conceive is hid, or in the earthe, to the top of one of the forks by a hair, or very fine silk or thread, and do the like to the other end; pitch the sharp single end lightly to the ground, at the going down of the sun, the moone being in the encrease, and in the morning at sun-rise, by a natural sympathy, you will find the mettal inclining, as it were pointing to the places where the other is hid.[121]

To Cut Fortune Wand. Proceed in the forenoon before twelve o'clock to a hazelnut shrub, which grew within one year and has two twigs, then place yourself toward the rising sun, and take the twigs in both hands and speak: I conjure thee, one summer long, Hazel rod, by the power of God, by the obedience of Jesus Christ of Nazareth, God and Mary's own son, who died on the cross, and by the power of God, by the truth of God arose from the dead; God the Father, Son and Holy Ghost, who art the very truth thyself, that thou showest me where silver and gold is hidden. (*Albertus Magnus n. d.*: 98)

11. To make a Wand to seek Iron, Ore, Water and the like.

The first Christmas-night, between 1 and 12 o'clock, break a young branch, of one year's growth, towards the sunrising, in three highest names. When you use the rod to seek something, use it three times; i.e. – take the wand – it must be forked – take one part in each hand, so that the thick part stands up; if the third part strikes toward the earth, that is the place where the thing is which you seek. You are at the same time, to repeat these words: Thou Archangel, Gabriel, I beseech thee, in

---

[121] *The Shepherd's Kalendar, or the Citizen and Countryman's daily Companion*, 12mo., London ; p. 61.

the name of God, the Almighty, is water here or not? Say.╫ Or iron or ore, etc.; whichever you seek. (Brown 1904: 109)

62. To Consecrate a Divining Rod.

When one makes a divining rod, or luck rod, he breaks it as before said and says while making it and before he uses it: Luck-rod, retain thy strength, retain thy virtue, whereto God hath ordained thee. ╫╫╫ (Brown 1904: 116)

The other approach was through conjuration, especially because of the association of spirits and fairies as guardians of the treasure. The following examples come from the *Key of Solomon*, Arthur Gauntlet's magical notebook, Sloane MS 3824 (*The Book of Treasure Spirits*), with a commentary on the subject by Ebenezer Sibley. Other examples that have already been given in Chapter 13 include William Lilly's adventure in Westminster Abbey and the formula from the *The Wonderful Magical Scrapbook 1450-1850*.

The Key of Solomon:

HOW TO RENDER THYSELF MASTER OF A TREASURE POSSESSED BY THE SPIRITS

The Earth being inhabited, as I have before said unto thee, by a great number of Celestial Beings and Spirits, who by their subtilty and prevision know the places wherein treasures are hidden, and seeing that it often happeneth that those men who undertake a search for these said treasures are molested and sometimes put to death by the aforesaid Spirits, which are called Gnomes; which, however, is not done through the Avarice of these said Gnomes, a Spirit being incapable of possessing anything, having no material senses wherewith to bring it into use, but because these Spirits, who are enemies of the passions, are equally so of Avarice, unto which men are so much inclined; and foreseeing the evil ends for which these treasures will be employed have some interest and aim in maintaining the earth in its condition of price and value, seeing that they are its inhabitants, and when they slightly disturb the workers in such kind of treasures, it is a warning which they give them to cease from the work, and if it happen that the greedy importunity of the aforesaid workers oblige them to continue, notwithstanding the aforesaid warnings, the Spirits, irritated by their despising the same, frequently put the workmen to death. But know, O my Son, that from the time that thou shalt have the good fortune to be familiar with such kinds of Spirits, and that thou shalt be able by means of what I have taught thee to make them submit unto thine orders, they will be happy to give thee, and to make thee partaker in that which they uselessly possess, provided that thine object and end shall be to make a good use thereof.

THE MANNER OF PERFORMING THE OPERATION.

On a Sunday before sunrise, between the 10th of July and the 20th of August, when the moon is in the Sign of the Lion, thou shalt go unto the place where thou shalt know either by interrogation of the Intelligences, or otherwise, that there is a treasure; there thou shalt describe a Circle of sufficient size with the Sword of Magic Art wherein to open up the earth, as the nature of the ground will allow; thrice during the day shalt thou cense it with the incense proper for the day, after which being clothed in the raiment proper for the Operation thou shalt suspend in some way by a machine immediately above the opening a lamp, whose oil should be mingled with the fat of a man who has died in the month of July, and the wick being made from the cloth wherein he has been buried. Having kindled this with fresh fire, thou shalt fortify the workmen with a girdle of the skin of a goat newly slain, whereon shall be written with the blood of the dead man from whom thou shalt have taken the fat these words and characters:

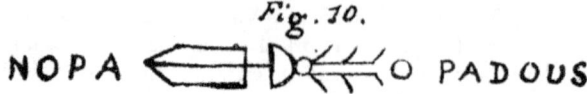

and thou shalt set them to work in safety, warning them not to be at all disturbed at the Spectres which they will see, but to work away boldly. In case they cannot finish the work in a single day, every time they shall have to leave it thou shalt cause them to put a covering of wood over the opening, and above the covering about six inches of earth; and thus shalt thou continue unto the end, being all the time present in the raiment of the Art, and with the Magic Sword, during the operation. After which thou shalt repeat this prayer:—

PRAYER

ADONAI, ELOHIM, EL, EHEIEH ASHER EHEIEH, Prince of Princes, Existence of Existences, have mercy upon me, and cast Thine eyes upon Thy Servant (N.), who invokes Thee most devotedly, and supplicates Thee by Thy Holy and tremendous Name Tetragrammaton to be propitious, and to order Thine Angels and Spirits to come and take up their abode in this place; O ye Angels and Spirits of the Stars, O all ye Angels and Elementary Spirits, O all ye Spirits present before the Face of God, I the Minister and faithful Servant of the Most High conjure ye, let God himself, the Existence of Existences, conjure ye to come and be present at this Operation, I, the Servant of God, most humbly entreat ye. Amen.

Having then caused the workmen to fill in the hole, thou shalt license the Spirits to depart, thanking them for the favour they have shown unto thee, and saying:—

THE LICENSE TO DEPART.

O ye good and happy Spirits, we thank ye for the benefits which we have just received from your liberal bounty; depart ye in peace to govern the Element which God hath destined for your habitation. Amen. (Mathers 1978: 57-58)

Arthur Gauntlet:

For Treasure hidden :~:

You must have A Turf or a piece of the Earth where you mistrust [suspect] Treasure to be hidden. Having the Turf or piece of earth in your Hand, **Say**

You Angels of God Tell us truly in the name of the most Holy Blessed and Glorious Trinity whether In the Ground (or Room) from whence this Turf (or piece of earth) was taken There be any treasure hidden or not Tell us truly in the name of Jesus. If they say there is, Then say **you Angels of God** Tell us truly what it is whether it be Gold Plate Jewels Books Household stuff or what it is They have told you say you Angels of God tell us truly whether it lie just under where this Turf was taken up or how far from that place a foot, 2, 3, 4, 5, 10, 20 foot or how far They have told you Say you Angels of God Show us the place and Open the Ground and show us in what fashion it lyeth and what it is All which they will show. Also how deep it lyeth &c.

In this manner you must work fore Coles, Lead, Tin, Iron, Copper mines &c. They will tell you how deep and how the colours of Earth will alter in every foot, 2 or 3, &c. For these and such like this will suffice. (Rankine 2011: 118 – the angels being conjured into a crystal)

The Book of Treasure Spirits:

CONJURATION OF TREASURE SPIRITS

He who would call upon, and speak with any spirit or spirits of this order, concerning treasure Trove, or any other mineral Treasures Enclosed in the Bowels of the Earth, or the Keepers thereof (if there be any) may Do It at such place or places, where they are Conversant & most frequent in, for it is most proper & significant So to do, Else a particular private place therefore be selected & and made choice of, where those spirits are either Seen or said to haunt or to frequent in, or where Treasures are supposed to be hidden, or as near it as possibly may be, and at a Convenient time, in the Evening, when the night is serene, Go there & solemnly Invocate &c:

At the Entering the Circle, Say thus: *In nomine Die Altisini Creatoris omnium Rerum in Coelo, & Terra, Glory be to God on high, on Earth Peace, Good will towards all*

Then Invocate as followeth: *O ye Spirit or Spirits, by whatsoever name, you are Called that haunteth inhabiteth this place, and frequenteth this house; Ground, or place, or that hath the Keeping of treasures hidden, Buried or otherwise concealed from and denied the Discovery and use of by the Sons of men, I do in the name of the Father & of the Son & of the holy Ghost, Exorcise, command, Constrain and most Earnestly Urge and require you, to appear visibly unto me, and my Brethren, in fair & Decent form, to show forth unto us, what we shall desire of you,* /

& I do by these powers, and in the Great And most powerful names of the Immense and Almighty Creator of heaven & Earth, And all that is therein Contained, both spiritual, animal, Vegetable and mineral, Even the Incomprehensible & Ever living God, **Sabaoth, Adonai, Dominus, Deus, Erarmus, Otheos, Iskyos, Athanatos, Paracletus, Elohim, Agla, El, On, Tetragrammaton,** and by & in the names of his Only Begotten Son Jesus Christ, the high King & Lord of all the world, Who shall come to Judge both you & us, at the dissolution of this Earthly Fabric, **Jesus Christus, Messias, Sother, Emanuel, Alpha & Omega,** and by his Birth, Passion, Most Glorious Resurrection, & Ascension, And by the Coming of the holy Ghost, the most Sacred Comforter, I do hereby powerfully and Earnestly command, urge, and constrain you, & in the name of the Prince, & by his Seal & Characters binding most Solidly, & by the Head of your Hierarchy, and the power thereof, I most urgently Require you, to appear visibly and formally unto me, before this Circle, to inform us Concerning the Treasures that are hidden, Buried, or by what way or means soever it is otherwise Kept, & Concealed from us,

I do therefore call upon, command, constrain and require you Spirit or spirits, of whatsoever Order you are of, or by whatsoever name as you are Called or Known by, though not Known to us, that hath the Keeping of Treasures hidden Buried in this house, Ground or Place, or near adjacent here abouts, to appear Visibly to us, and to detect & disclose the said hidden Treasures to us, and Either to Direct and instruct us, how to recover & take the Same away, for the Supply of our Necessities, or otherwise that you avoid and depart from the said Treasures, that are here or hereabouts adjacent, hidden, buried or otherwise concealed, and that you permit / the Same & Quietly, peaceably, meekly, gently and benevolently, in all friendship and love, to Quit the Same, and to Lay it openly bare & naked to us, Visibly to the Sight of our own Eyes, and Surrender & Deliver up the Said Treasures unto us, and that you permit and suffer us to bear the same away, & to enjoy It and convert It to our Necessary uses, without hindrance or delay,

And I do, Exorcise, bind and adjure you spirit or spirits, that have the Keeping of the treasures, that are hidden or Buried in this house, Ground or place, & All other spirits whatsoever, & of whatsoever nature or order they are of, whether Aerial, Terrestrial, or Infernal, that shall be here or where the said Treasures are; who by their Visible or invisible Craft or Subtleties, shall in anywise Oppose: or Strive to hinder, or thwart us from obtaining & bearing away the Said Treasure, I do in the name of the only Almighty and heavenly God, the Great **Jehovah,** & in the name of Jesus Christ our Lord, Command, bind and Constrain you all spirits whatsoever, As aforesaid, that shall in anywise by your Crafts or Subtleties, Seek to Let or hinder from the Obtaining and bearing away of the Said Treasures, that is here or hereabouts hidden or buried, Quietly, peaceably & Gently to avoid and depart from this place, where the Said treasures are hidden or buried, and that ye tarry not, neither continue or Remain one hour longer there or thereabouts,

But I command bind and Constrain You spirits as aforesaid of &c: that shall be here or hereabouts, to Let or hinder us, from Obtaining & bearing away of the Said hidden treasures, we are seeking for, In the Name of him, who sayeth but the word and it is done, that you haste away from thence, and forthwith repair in peace to your order or place of Residence, preordained, Decreed and appointed for you: and / now I do by those Princes, and in the name of almighty God the Father the Son & the holy Ghost, discharge you: from tarrying any Longer here or hereabouts, I do Command, Charge, bind, and Constrain you spirit or spirits, that shall be here or hereabouts, or where the treasures are hidden, to Let or hinder us from obtaining & bearing away the Same, for our Requisite uses, as aforesaid, to depart & hasten away to your Orders or place of Residence, preordained & decreed for you, & I potently adjure, and command you to haste away, & Immediately begone, to your orders as aforesaid, and tarry not one hour Longer go in peace be with you Amen.

And now I do once again in the name of the Eternal & our Everliving God, Exorcise, Call upon, and adjure you spirit or spirits, that haunteth & frequenteth this Ground, or house, or place, and that hath the Keeping of the treasures, that are hid, buried or otherwise Concealed here or hereabouts adjacent, to appear Visibly, & in fair & Decent form to us, to Instruct, Direct and verily to inform us, how to detect, discover, and obtain the treasures that are hidden or Buried In this place, or in any other place Elsewhere hereabouts; or that ye peaceably & quietly Demit & Depart from the Same, and leave it openly, bare and naked, visibly to the sight of our own Eyes, and Deliver the same to us in our possession freely, so that we may bear the Same away, and firmly without fraud, or later hindrance, or any other Crafty or Deceitful act, deed or thing to be Done, that we for Ever Enjoy the same, and Convert it to our necessary uses,

And further Know spirit or spirits aforesaid, that frequenteth and is conversant in this house, Ground or place, and that hath the Keeping of Treasures that are hidden or Buried herein or hereabouts, Know ye I say and understand, that though I call not upon you, neither by name, Knowledge / or any Signature, more or otherwise than by the name of spirit or spirits, as being at present altogether unknown to us, that I call upon you with the Tongue, Heart & Spirit of faith and Confidence, for we do eagerly & sincerely believe of you, and that you are, that which our forefathers have reported and Declared to us, of you, & in all things concerning you, And of all those noble services you have done for them, and of your worthy friendship And familiarity with them, & we also absolutely believe you to be as courteous, friendly & Benevolent, to whom you please, and have love to, and that Sympathies in faith Love and Friendship with you, as you are justly Displeased and adversely obstinate to such, who are Wilful, perverse and blind Ignorance, doth not only misbelieve, and are wholly incredible of you, but also much abuse you, in their most Gross & scurrilous Language, frequent Discourses, & most abominable mistakes; all which wilful obvious scurrility, abusiveness And incredulity, we do here in the presence of heaven And Earth, and of all the Good Angels and Spirits, utterly detest and abhor, and do Absolutely protest against It as most ridiculous, impertinent & heretical &c:

Therefore we verily, absolutely & clearly believe of you, & desire friendship with you, and the help, Council & instructions, and all Such personal and visible Assistances, as we shall Rationally Require of you, according to your orders and offices appointed you of Almighty God, be pleased readily to assist us in all Such of our Terrestrial Affairs, & more Especially Concerning all hidden treasures, and mines of Gold or Silver &c: that we shall at any time ask or seek for, accordingly to your Customs and, usual formalities or as shall please and be seen your Goodness & benevolence herein, any manner of wise and in all friendship and humanity, to accommodate, instruct, assist and Serve us. /

And now having thus far Declared, and in all fidelity and honest integrity without fear (as I humbly conceive) uncontrolled and unmasked our Selves, in our more Reasonable beliefs & confidence; both of you & in our affairs, & of your favourable Resolves and friendly Assistance therein, I do in the name, and by the power of the prince and head of your Hierarchies, and primarily by his, their, and your seals and Characters binding Most Solidly, Adjure, command and most Earnestly and confidently urge, request and importune you again, to move, & visibly show your Self or Selves unto us, and to Declare truly unto us, and instruct us, how we shall Discover and Recover the treasures that are hidden or Buried in this house or place, or wheresoever else it is hereabouts &c: or otherwise to bring it to this place to us, and here leave it openly bare & nakedly visible to us, & Deliver the Same Really without fraud, Deceit or any Crafty or Subtle Devices, tricks, Or other Delusions, whereby we may be as soon deprived again thereof, to us so freely And friendly, that we may certainly bear it away, for any proper uses & behoofs; And herein we Earnestly & urgently entreat you, to do for us, as for the Servants of the highest.

Let the master continue Invocating and calling upon those spirits, Every night, from Eleven of the Clock or somewhat past, until toward two; observing to give over at the break of Day, especially to follow it very Close all the Increase of the Moon, and not at all to Despair in the tediousness or prolixity thereof; And when any appearance or sign of any Appearance shall present itself, either to the master, or his Associate or Associates that are with him, And it should be moveable, and seem to float and shift itself to & fro, let the master continue his invocation until it seems to be more static, & stand before you; & by some kind of proof, or Kind of / Signature, showeth an offer of love & friendship, and a Kind of willingness to satisfy your desires, and then shall you bind him with the Bond of spirits, if you so desire; but if any offer, seem with a voluntary success to be perceived &c: then it may be needless: Then ask him his name, and bid him show his Seal or Character, to which he giveth obedience, & ask him to whence he belongeth, the which when he hath Declared, then propose your requests, showing them fairly written with you; when all is Done according to your desire, then Licence him to Depart &c: or &c:

We need not instance further to enlighten the understanding, or for any further, better or more Instructions to any Philosopher in this Art, touching this Subject, for if his more rational and Intelligible faculty be not genuine Enough to comprehend and improve, what is here hinted; all the instructions of men & Angels avail little, for it is a hard matter to make A silken purse of a swine's Ear, only thus far in a word we shall give to understand, that by how much the Greater the noises are heard, and visions Seen about the house or place, so much the Greater the Treasures may be judged to be, & nearer the Superficies of the Earth. (Rankine 2009: 101-107)

Another example, following Reginald Scot (as "Barbason", the chief demon here is also mentioned in *The Merry Wives of Windsor*):

Choice Experiment How to obtain Treasure Trove

Having a Chamber pretty free or private, from the passage of many people, in a place Indifferent: Airy, being Kept Clean, and Suffumigated with good Odours; write upon an Abortive or on fair Clean Paper, with the Blood of a black Cock as followeth:

Sathan, Baramper, Barbasan, come with Speed to this place, and bring to me the Treasure: &c: (have set down either the particular thing you invocate for, and the place from whence you would have It brought, or Else a sum certain from Such a place or places, where treasures Lyeth hidden, also Kept from the use of man, for whose Relief it was Originally Decreed and preordained, by the Goodness of the most High and Omnipotent Creator of Heaven & Earth, & all that is in them Contained, as the Sum of 300 &c)

Then have a Circle in readiness (made as is hereafter taught) and lay It down on the Chamber floor, and have a little pallet bed at the one End of the Chamber, that hath a full or good sight to the Door, and in a pretty fair starlight Evening, first fix the paper, or Abortive Parchment, whereon is written your Request, with the blood of the black Cock, & / then Enter and so Consequently the Circle, And say the following Conjuration 9 times,

I Exorcise, Conjure and Constrain thee Spirit **Barbasan**, *the spirit of Treasures, by the power and in the name of the Father, and of the Son, & of the Holy Ghost, and by the majesty and Potency of the Omnipotent & Everliving God,* **Jehovah**, *who made Heaven & Earth, the Sea, & Created all that in them is, and by these his great & Efficacious names,* **Agla, El, On, Tetragrammaton, Adonag, Iskgros, Athanatos, Paracletus, Immortalis, Alpha & Omega,** *and in the Sacred name of our Lord Jesus Christ the Second person in the Trinity, & in the Godhead and the saviour of the world, who hath given full power & Authority to all that believe, & Lay Hold on him by faith in his name, to adjure & command all spirits of all orders what so ever, whether Aerial, Terrestrial or Infernal, to serve & obey them, whatsoever they shall Command them to Do, in their Several & Respective offices, where they are ordained, and set, by almighty God, and therein to fulfil the Desires & Requests of us, as we are Children & Servants of the Highest,*

& by those inestimable & unparalleled Miracles, by our Saviour & only mediator, & advocate, Jesus Christ, the High King & Sovereign Lord of all the world, showered Down upon Earth, and by him left to his Apostles and Disciples, and by him to all posterity, that believe by the virtue, power, efficacy and remembrance whereof, I Exorcise, Conjure and powerfully Command the spirit **Barbasan** *And more Especially and particularly, by these Great & Sacred names of one god In three persons* **Almo, Glyas, Messias, Agios, Jesus Christus,** *who is was & is to come, & by the High Great & powerful name Egia, which wise Solomon heard in Gabaon, & obtained that Inestimable treasure of wisdom and Riches, By all that is / before Said, & the great Efficacious and inestimable power, and virtue thereof, thereby Command & Constrain thee* **Barbasan,** *the which if your Master shall Command you to Do Anything that you may Do, that you Bring to me this night (here nominate your Desires as aforesaid)*

And I further Charge & command thee, that in the performance hereof, As thou art bound according to thy orders & office to Do; that thou neither obstruct [?] nor affrighten me, nor any other person, whatsoever, but Quietly and in humility Come, appear & show in a Comely & Decent form and shape, & no ways terrible to me, your Self personally present before me, and Bring along with you the Treasure (rehearsing here again, what is written on the Schedule, Either the treasure from Such or Such a place, if you are certain with thy good Information or otherwise, that such a thing is there mentioning whether It be Gold, Silver, Plate, Jewels, or any matter Whatsoever, that was Ordained for the use of man, or Else so nominated to the sum of 300 pounds in Coin), And peaceably Leave It here with me, so that I may enjoy the same for necessary and worthy use, Benefit & Relief

All which I adjure & Command thee to Do & perform, in all things, particularly and fully, according as I have written & hereby specified, Requested and commanded of you, forthwith immediately without any fraud, loss, hindrance or tarrying, in the name of the Great & Immense **Jehovah** *the Almighty & Everliving God, & of his Son Jesus Christ the Great Messiah, & Ever to be glorified Second person in the holy trinity in the Godhead; our only Saviour, advocate and mediator, who shall Come to judge the Quick & the Dead, and the world by fire, In whose name therefore prepare ye & make haste. /*

Say this Conjuration nine times Manfully, and with Good faith and Courage & then Say as followeth, and be not Dismayed, for nothing can hurt you, then proceed viz

I Earnestly request you & Conjure you **Baramper,** *that you send your Servant* **Barbasan** *to me this night, with the Treasure in Such a place, or the Sum of £300 in current Coin &* (here also you must mention your Desires, as is before expressed) *in nomine Patris & filii & Spiritus Sanctus*

Then betake yourself to your Bed, and about midnight you may perceive the Spirit **Barbasan** will appear in the Chamber, probably in human Shape or form, as in the Similitude of man, or man Kind, and will bring with him that which was invocated for – now if you have a mind to speak to him, before you Licence him to Depart, you may say unto him thus – who are you – he will answer again & Say, I am the spirit **Barbasan**, or to the like purpose, bringing to you the treasure, or such a sum of money accordingly as you have So Earnestly Requested, Then shall you answer again and say unto him as followeth,

*I thank you master **Baramper** and you likewise, and I give you leave & adjure you to depart in peace to your orders, the place of your Residence originally Decreed, & by almighty God appointed for you, And I command you In the name of the Father, & of the Son, & of the Holy Ghost, that you without injuring me nor hurt me, nor anyone upon the face of the Earth whatsoever: wherefore Depart in peace, and let peace be and continue between you & me, in the name of Jesus Christ the high King & Lord of all the world, and I Request and adjure you to be ready to come again to me upon the Like occasion, whensoever & wheresoever I shall call upon you & so you may Depart, & the peace of God remain between us, in nomine Patris & filii & Spiritus Sanctus. /*

Then will he Depart, and leave with you that which was Required of him, then at your Leisure you may arise from Bed, and Return thanks to God for the benefits received.

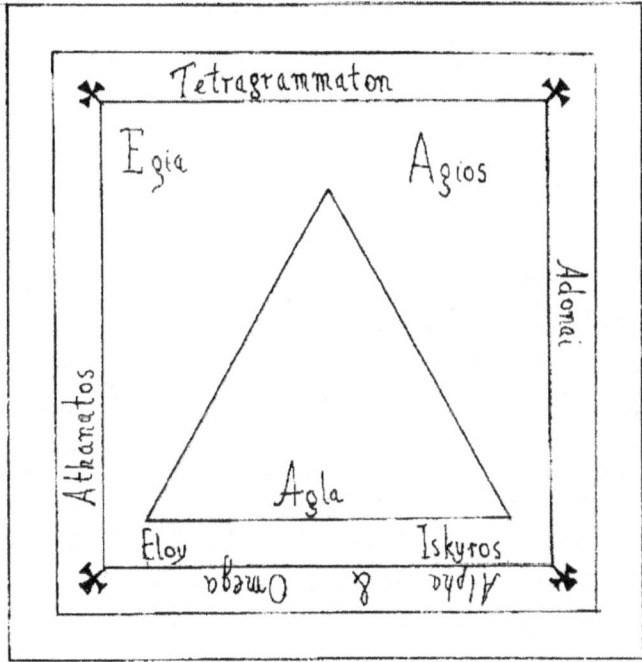

"MAGIC CIRCLE" FOR BARBASAN

Circles, Triangles, Quadrangles, Pentagonals, Hexagonals, Septagonals, Octagonals, &c: be they, or what form soever they are all Called, Circles of Art, And are all but one & the same In matter & signification, for they are a Fortress or Defence for the Invocant, against Malevolent assault of false appearances Or Evil Illuding spirits, who are many times at hand, to do some Malefices or so to put by the Invocant off his purpose, Which he may perceive if he be Learned Or any way Skillful in this Art, for Being Inviolate on Every Side, with some one or other of the great and Sacred Names of God, Is thereby Defended from any personal / Assault or prejudice, because all spirits, of what Orders Under the Celestial Angels & Intelligences &c: Do Obey them, fear them, & Even tremble At them, So that the Invocant having time & Courage to Speak to them, may be Earnest, Interrogating them to Know, whether the apparition be the Same he Called for, or any other Illusive show; the which his prudence must Direct him.

As for the making of those Circles, for any purpose Or Experiment in this Art, Do thus take your Large Calf Skin parchment, and paste or fasten them together, So that they may be Easily cut or made four squares, on the outside, when they are fastened Or fixed Together, first cutting the insides even where they meet together in the Inwards parts, to be pasted or otherwise fastened together, and then at what time, & in what place Soever, one is minded to invocate, it is but taking up the Circle, roll it up and carry it where occasion & place requires, & So Lay It Down without any trouble, having a loop at Each corner to fasten it to the Ground.

When the four Skins are fastened together and set four Square, then with a pencil {then meaning a small paint brush}& good Ink or Other painting or Colouring matter, Draw the Lines and write the names that are to be written; As in the Example, Then take the Juice of marigold, Vervain and Langue-de-boeuf, and wash the Names that are in the inside of the Circle therewith, And the names of art in the Outward Circle Wash with the Blood of the Black Cock, & then is all Done & made fit for Practice & Action. (Rankine 2009: 120-125)

Sibley on Treasure-hunting:

Distinct from fiery spirits are a species which properly belong to the metallic kingdom, abiding in mountains, caves, dens, deeps, hiatas or chasms of the earth, hovering over hidden gold, tombs, vaults, and sepulchres of the dead. These spirits are termed by the ancient philosophers "*protectors of hidden treasure*," from a principle or quality in their nature whence they exceedingly delight in mines of gold and silver, and places of hidden treasure; but are violently inimical to man, and envy his benefit or accommodation in the discovery thereof; ever haunting those places where money is concealed, and retaining malevolent and poisonous influences to blast the lives and limbs of those who attempt to make such discoveries; and therefore extremely dangerous for magicians to exorcise or call up. It is recorded in several of the ancient British authors, that Peters, the celebrated magician of Devonshire, together with his associates, having exorcised one of these malicious spirits to conduct them to a subterranean vault, where a considerable quantity of treasure was known to be hid, they had no sooner quitted the magic circle, than they were instantaneously crushed into atoms, as it were in the twinkling of an eye. And in this particular we have too many fatal examples / upon record, of the sudden destruction of those who by magical spells had called upon this description of spirits, for the purpose of discovering hidden gold; which examples seem to prove, that these spirits have more affinity with the infernal than with the astral hierarchy; and that they are the diabolical agents of Mammon bringing about all the evils of this world, which spring from an insatiable lust after gold; whence the saying in scripture, that "*we cannot serve God and Mammon*," and that "*it is easier for a camel to pass through the eye of a needle than for a rich man to enter into the kingdom of heaven;*" hyperbolically spoken, in reference to the innumerable sins and wickedness committed by mankind, for the sake of temporary wealth and riches! Hence too a reason offers, why, of all other subordinate spirits, these are the most pernicious to mortal men. The nature of them is so violent, that in the histories of the gold and silver mines abroad, it is recorded that whole companies of labourers have been destroyed by them at once; and that their delight is in tormenting, killing, and crushing to death, those who most greedily lust after and seek for such treasures. The richest and largest silver mine in Germany was haunted by one of these spirits, who sometimes used to appear in the shape of an he-goat, with golden horns, pushing down the workmen with uncommon violence; and at others in the shape of a horse, breathing fiery flames and pestilential vapours at his nostrils, till, by continual destruction, fear, and alarm, they were obliged to desist from working that mine any longer; and it continues shut to this day. (Sibley 1785: 1084-1085)

Guardian spirits were blamed for the difficulties in actually obtaining alleged treasures, but spirits could also be recruited to help locate and secure hoards. Certain demons were credited with a special skill in revealing the location of treasures (see Weyer/Scot's list in Chapter 12), including:

- *Barbatos*, a great countie or earle, and also a duke, ... He detecteth treasures hidden by magicians and inchanters ...
- *Purson, alias Curson*, a great king, ... he bewraieth [i.e., reveals] treasure ...
- *Valac* is a great president, ... he perfectlie answereth of treasure hidden, and where serpents may be seene ...
- *Gomory* a strong and a mightie duke, ... he answereth well and truelie of things present, past, and to come, and of treasure hid ...
- *Amy* is a great president, ... he bewraieth treasures preserved by spirits ...
-

Treasure Hunters in Action:

Examples of actual treasure hunts show how Cunning Folk were sought out to help discover (and neutralize spiritual guardians) of treasure hordes by wealthy and influential men. An extensive investigation into illicit treasure hunting in 1510 found in the records of the Archbishop of York's court provides insight into the preconceptions and procedures of English treasure hunters. Editor James Blaine's introduction is as follows:

> PROCEEDINGS CONNECTED WITH A REMARKABLE CHARGE OF SORCERY, BROUGHT AGAINST JAMES RICHARDSON AND OTHERS, IN THE DIOCESE OF YORK, A.D. 1510.
>
> THE following striking instance of the belief in divination, at one time so prevalent, has been extracted from one of the Archiepiscopal registers at York. It describes a singularly romantic scene which occurred in that wild country by which Halifax is surrounded. The evidence is highly curious, and that given by Steward, the chief offender, exhibits much shrewdness and ingenuity. The document is given without comment.
>
> As there were many persons concerned in the adventure, it soon made a stir in the county, and came to the ears of the authorities. On the 5th of May, 1510, the Vicar-general of the Archbishop of York requested John Shaw, the Lord Mayor of York, to surrender Jameson for examination. Two days after this, he desired Thomas Lord Darcy to give up Steward, who was a Knaresborough man. On the 12th he issued a commission to the suffragan, John, Bishop of Negropont, and Richard Newitt, bachelor of decrees, to commence the examination of Steward.
>
> The investigation being ended, on the 11th of June, 1510, the culprits submitted themselves for correction. Their punishment (Steward excepted) was as follows: on the Sunday ensuing, between ten and eleven in the morning, they were ordered to go in procession from the Minster at York, down Petergate, as far as the door of the Friars Carmelites, with bare feet and heads, and carrying three banners with certain characters and figures upon them. They were also to pass through the market at the Pavement, through Ousegate, Coney Street, and Stonegate, and to be chastised by the Dean of the Christianity of York at the gates of the Minster and of the House of the Carmelites, at the church of All Saints, Pavement, and before the house of the Augustines. Jameson was directed to carry a sceptre, Otewell at Hay a lighted torch, William Wilson a holy water fat, with "a strynkill," Wod a thurible with incense, and Laurence a torch with salt on it, *"super hastas."* [set on spears] On Thursday before the feast of the Nativity of St. John the Baptist, they were to submit to a like punishment at Bingley.
>
> On Thursday before the feast of St. Laurence, 1510, Steward, the chief offender, was released from excommunication with the following penance; he was to carry one of the above-mentioned banners on three several market-days around the markets at York and Knaresborough, and on two Saturdays around the churches of Knaresborough, Ripon, and Doncaster.
>
> Jameson, the chief offender, was one of the Sheriffs of York in 1497, and Lord Mayor in 1504. The citizens would not like to see him, only six years afterwards, doing penance with his sceptre in his hand. He died on the 20th of April, 1527, and was buried in Christ Church.[122]

As the full transcript of the investigation is quite long and partially in Latin, I will summarize the testimony in modernized spelling about the activities of the gentlemen, priests, and Cunning Man John Steward in the Mixindale hunt. The cast of characters included:

- James Richardson, priest and former Sheriff and Lord Mayor of York.
- Thomas Jameson, priest at Bingley.
- Henry Banke, priest at Bingley and Addingham.
- John Wilkinson, Canon of Drax Abbey.
- Richard Greenwood, priest at York.
- John Steward, school teacher at Knaresborough, 48 years of age.

---

[122] James Raine. "Proceedings Connected with a Remarkable Charge of Sorcery, Brought Against James Richardson and Others, in the Diocese of York, A.D. 1510." *Archaeological Journal*, vol 16, (1859). London: The Archaeological Institute of Great Britain and Ireland, pp. 71-81.

- Laurence Knolles of Harrowgate, 28 years of age.
- William Otwell At Hay of Bingley, 50 years of age.
- Thomas Wood of Bingley, 35 years of age.
- William Wilson of Bingley, Otwell's servant, 21 years of age.

The quest was instigated by Richardson, who heard from Richard Greenwod that there was a great stolen treasure near "Mixindale" [Mixenden?] at Halifax, Yorkshire, and was determined to uncover the hoard for himself and his partners. Apparently various people claimed to have seen this treasure guarded by a spirit, reporting that "there was a chist of gold in Myxindale, and every noble as thik as fyve, and opon the same chist a swerd [sword] of mayntenaunce, and a booke covered w^t blakke ledder..." A man named Robert Leventhorp, then deceased, even claimed that he had seen the end of the chest with the spirit sitting on it, and that he used a sword to remove it, slicing it in two as it had been a mere rush. He wasn't able to get the treasure, however.

Richardson's associate, Thomas Jameson, knew of a Cunning Man, John Steward of Knaresborough, and his success in locating a runaway servant of Christopher Scarsborough's, for which he got 6 shillings, eight pence. Steward, who was recruited to undertake the conjuration of the treasure spirits, had a considerable reputation as a magician. Sir Thomas Spurret of Pole, in the parish of Otteley, testified during the investigation that he had seen Steward with three "humble" (bumble) bees, or something like humble bees, which he kept under a stone, calling them out one by one to give each a drop of blood from his finger. The keeping of familiar spirits in the form of bees or flies was a common belief at the time. Steward denied this, and while admitted to baptizing a fowl or a cat as part of a ritual, denied using it as a sacrifice to the spirits. He admitted to his practice as a Cunning Man in helping people through prayers and good works, but denied being an actual sorcerer. He said that when people came to him to "have knowlege of thinges lost and stollen", he would show them a booke of astronomy (astrology) to have them believe that he was "cunning", but that he could do nothing except sometimes by accident he would hit upon the truth, like a blind man feeling about with his staff. Some clients paid him in cash and others in wax, with which he said he kept certain lights going in the church.

The nine principles met on the Monday after Candlemas in 1509 at Otwell's house at Bingely to plan their recovery of the treasure. At that time, Otwell's servant Wilson later testified that Sir John, Sir James[123], and Thomas Jameson went into a chamber, and opened 2 "bogettes" (purses or bags) on a bed, and he saw the 21-foot wide parchment circle and "a grete masse boke", from which they copied a necessary collect as well a formula for hallowing the incense. Directions for consecrating the holy water came from a magical notebook. He also saw two priests stoles, the gilt sceptre, and "a thing gilt of a fote long, like a holywatir strynkill [strinkle or aspergillum], and frankynnecense, w' dyverse bookes of their craft". Sir John then gave Wilson 18 "singing loves" ("singing loaves" or wafer hosts), not yet consecrated. Asking what they were for, he was told that if the spirit would not obey, he would consecrate the hosts and hold them up to overawe the spirit so that it would appear to him in the unthreatening likeness of a two-year old child and obey his commands. Jameson asked that Richard Greenwood's father show them where the treasure was supposed to be, but it was decided that it made no difference where the conjuration of the spirit Belphares[124] took place, as the demon would fetch the hoard from wherever it lay and bring it to them, anyhow.

Steward got a virgin parchment from another Cunning Man, Thomas Laton of Durham, and drew a magical circle on it with the appropriate characters and magical names, and also made a gilded sceptre or wand. On the Friday before the first of March, Richardson and Jameson met in York to make a lamen, a square plate of lead with the graven image of the spirit Oberion and four other names, including "Storax", according to directions found in a grimoire ("a booke of experience") borrowed from Canon Wilkinson. The lamen had to be made between "the change of the moon and the prime", so they chose

---

[123] Priests at this time were often alloted the title "Sir".
[124] See Scot 1985: Book 15; Chapter XIII. "An experiment of Bealphares", pp. 347-354, which also includes the holy water formula mentioned in this account. It should be noted that the Halifax case took place years before Scot's book was published.

to make their invocation on the following Thursday, at five o'clock in the morning. Wilkinson had been asked to travel to York for this, but he apparently got cold feet from fear of the rumors going around about the treasure and the Cunning Man, so he declined to join them in their special chamber (with a window on each of the four walls) where they would summon Oberion to find out if the treasure was in fact real. Wilkinson then asked them to send an hour glass, a magnetic compass and some sort of stone, perhaps a lodestone, to Bingley to help in the subsequent magical operation for the treasure. Among the other tools for magic, there were three additional thirty-foot magical circles, and there is mention of a ring and a crown. The conspirators were carefully cautioned to remain within the circles, but Steward said that he felt free to go in and out of them as he undertook the conjuration, because he believed himself safe from harm, being so steadfast in Christian faith that he feared nothing (and, one suspects, confidence in his magical prowess).

On the morning of the Bingley expedition, the men went to church in the morning and heard two masses, and were shriven so that the spirits would have no power over them. Sir James sang one mass and Sir Richard the other. They agreed to meet at a wayside cross at the west end of Solehill [Solehill End, Ovenden] in Halifax at sunset that day (Tuesday), which was about a mile away from Mixendale and the treasure, to do the conjuration. They left town separately to avoid suspicion, and while Thomas Wood and Richard Greenwood kept the appointment, the others got lost and the whole affair descended into farce. Seven men met on a moor called Wilston Lee, but a great mist suddenly rose up and caused them to go the wrong way, ending up at Cokkam, a mile from Solehill Cross. They then discovered that Richardson had lost the strinkle on the moor, but still had the thurifur with the incense. For some reason they then went to a different cross at Mykilmosse, which was still a mile from the original meeting place. Steward, Otwell, and Knolles volunteered to go and find Solehill Cross, and recruited a local guide whom they paid tuppence to help them, but in vain – they still couldn't locate the right cross. Returning to Mykilmosse, they gave up and returned to Cokkam for supper and then went back to Bingley. The next day, the group planned to meet on Arden Wood Moor to try again, but apparently got into an argument about how the treasure should be divided instead. Jameson said that every "yeoman" (i.e., excluding servants) should have £20, and he would take the rest to York. The others protested this, saying it should be evenly divided, at which Jameson angrily said he'd see them all in court first, which appears to have put paid to the whole venture. Afterward, Wilkinson and Greenwood said that they blamed the bad weather that thwarted their expedition as a side effect of the "heresy and conjuration" involved.

Possibly the oddest thing about this was that there *was* actually a large treasure hidden at Morton near Bingley: "In 1775 a treasure chest was found which contained a large hoard of Roman coins, reported at the time to be one of the most important finds ever made. It was reputed to have contained nearly a hundredweight of Roman denarii dating from 54 CE to 238 CE in a brass chest assumed to be of military origin." [125]

Three later instances illustrate the strong will to believe that would-be treasure finders had, despite strings of disappointments and failures. The first is the merry chase (for which I have depended on J. Kent Clark's account in *Goodwin Wharton*, 1984) Wise Woman Mary Parish led Goodwin Wharton on in pursuit of an ever elusive "treasure hid" reputed to be on Hounslow Heath, near where she said an entrance to the "lowlands" (i.e., fairyland) was located. This was just one of several treasure locations Wharton and Parish attempted to uncover (none of which yielded any practical result) but it is well worth describing because it involves several themes that animated the activities of the Cunning Folk, including dealings with fairies, spirits and conjuration.

Goodwin Wharton (1653-1704), son of Philip Lord Wharton and heiress Jane Goodwin, was a well-born member of the wealthy upper classes, and despite a series of expensive failed projects involving alchemical experiments, patented fire engines and diving machines – not to mention estrangement from his family – he was elected to Parliament several times, given a military commission as Lieutenant

---

[125] www.visitoruk.com/historydetail.php?id=51983&f=Bingley (accessed 7/12/2010).

Colonel of the Earl of Macclesfield's cavalry regiment and became a Lord Commissioner of the Admiralty. None of these worldly honors were as important to him, however, as his long intense involvement with the spiritual world and in treasure hunting.

It began in the spring of 1683 when Wharton, always desperate for funds, sought out a London Wise Woman named Mary Parish whom he found in a squalid room recovering from a broken leg. Despite her impressive previous career as alchemist, healer, treasure hunter and as a conjuror who possessed a familiar spirit named George Whitmore and visited the Queen of the Fairies (and then alienated both), what Wharton found was a rather blowsy 52-year old woman too fond of brandy, and obviously down on her luck. She was able to convince him, that despite appearances, she could in fact greatly improve his career, giving him a gambling charm and hinting of greater things. Thus began an unequal partnership that lasted until her death in 1703.

Mary's first success (having allegedly pawned and lost her book of magic) was reconciliation with her spirit assistant, George Whitmore. She had met Whitmore as a living man while they were in Ludgate prison together, she for debt and he as a felon about to be executed. She got him to agree to become her spirit aid after his death (for which there is a ceremony in Scot's *Discoverie*, pp. 356-362), which he apparently did. Wharton was unable to see Whitmore as Mary did, and was not allowed to remain in the room while Mary talked with him, although he could hear two voices while he waited in the corridor. The gambling charm having proved ineffectual, the other obvious solution to his financial problems was the recovery of hidden treasure. With George acting as a go-between, they were confident that the fairies that lived beneath Hounslow Heath could be convinced to help them.

The pursuit for the Hounslow treasure began on May 30, 1683, with Mary and Goodwin going to an inn near the western boundary of Hounslow, which was closest to where Mary had once entered the "lowlands" (as she termed the fairy settlement). However, it poured rain for days, so they returned to London until mid-June. Although a proposed meeting with the Fairy court was postponed (as always), the ghostly George made a great discovery – a hidden treasure site:

> Goodwin had been hoping for this ever since he had heard of George's ability to locate treasure. His first opportunity came when he was walking on a common just outside Hounslow. There he noticed 'four great mighty trees set by themselves all alone, with a mount of earth cast up between them'. This configuration struck him as unnatural and somehow significant; and when George investigated, he found that the site, significant indeed, concealed a 'vast treasure', buried during the reign of King John and attended by no less than thirteen guardian spirits—spirits of the people who had buried it. Of these, George reported, five were good (eager to part with their treasure) and eight were miserly and depraved. (Clark 1984: 49)

Because of the exposed location of the mound and the problem of the spirits, the partners didn't immediately begin digging. Instead Mary, who had been instructed in the art of treasure recovery and first introduced to fairies by her grandfather and her uncle John (who also had a spirit assistant and taught Mary the Cunning Craft), set about to do the job magically, using a parchment with astrological sigils and two witch hazel rods. Unfortunately, one of these had to be from a special *female* witch hazel. Such shrubs were hard to find, especially since unlike the holly, there isn't actually a separate female plant. It took a long time to discover this mysterious shrub, but eventually one was found and the two rods were prepared, but they didn't work when Mary tried them because they hadn't been consecrated. Mary contacted an ancient and learned fairy named Father Friar who explained the consecration problem and agreed to help them. Father Friar was able to get into the mound, only to find the spirit guardians opposed the removal of the treasure. Mary also prepared a love charm for Wharton. However, a continual series of misadventures in the fairy realm, involving illness, the death of the fairy King in July, political intrigues concerning Queen Penelope LaGard (the Portuguese fairy princess), and other problems prevented them from receiving the help they needed – and tediously prolonged the project.

In addition, Mary and Wharton had fights and reconciliations – including sexual relations that made it impossible to proceed for a while because of spiritual pollution, and which allegedly resulted in the birth of two sons, Peregrine and Charles, (the latter "dying" shortly afterward) whom Wharton was never allowed to see. In addition, Wharton had been promised a visit by the fairy queen, but despite carefully preparing for the visit by buying new candlesticks and candles, fine linens, and fresh herbs and flowers, he waited twice in vain. On the third try, he fell asleep, only to be told that he had indeed been visited but the fairies had been unwilling to wake him up. Eventually he would supposedly have sex (in his sleep) with the queen, resulting in her miscarriage and a promise that he should be her heir as King of the Fairies, a promise that came to naught like all the rest.

They were further interrupted in their efforts at Hounslow by a random cow herder, rain, the sudden appearance of a horseman, and very cold winter weather (the Thames froze over in the winter of 1683-1684). Mary then resorted to conjuration of the angel Uriel in a glass, and also a second angel named Ahab. They learned they had to banish the spirit guardians, which included three powerful demons named Gabetius, Hyadromicon and Belsacanom. This was eventually accomplished in August, 1684. They were then to exorcise eight uncooperative ghostly guardians from King John's time (Samuel Storton, Richard Barnely, Ralph Sharpe, Thomas Phelps, John and Ann Carmell, Thomas Ownes and Fandom Barwick Jacobs) on August 16, which left five well-disposed "good spirits" named William Spensely, John Abram Thevers, Robert Jackson and Ralph Clivens. By February 1685, the spirits had been cleared and they received £1,800 in gold in a magical purse – that couldn't be opened. By this time Wharton had begun to doubt this and the other treasure ventures, as well as the "voice of God" that he had heard when Mary was outside of his chamber. When he finally opened a chest supposedly containing the gold in 1696, he found it empty – but then he had been told that to open the chest before he had seen his alleged fairy subjects, the treasure would vanish away. Nevertheless, he admired and cherished Mary Parish to the end.

Another example of fruitless treasure hunting took place in Morristown, New Jersey, in 1788. Although most of my examples of magical activity are of English origin, with treasure hunting, American instances are almost as plentiful as those from the mother country. There appears to have been an extensive interest in hidden treasure in the northeastern part of the thirteen colonies and the new Republic. In New England, Silas Hamilton (1736-1816), a prominent citizen of Whitingham, Vermont, left a notebook (ca. 1786) which included over 40 reported instances of buried treasure and mineral wealth he had heard about, as well as a ritual for their discovery:

A Method to Tak up hid Treasure (viz.)
Tak Nine Steel Rods about ten or twelve Inches in Length Sharp or Piked to Perce in to the Erth, and let them be Besmeared with fresh blood from a hen mixed with hogdung. Then mak two Surkels Round the hid Treasure one of Sd Surkels a Littel Larger in surcumference than the hid Treasure lays in the Erth the other Surkel Sum Larger still, and as the hid treasure is wont to move to North or South East or west Place your Rods as is Discribed on the other sid of this leaf.

The manner of placing the rods in proper position is described by a diagram, of which the following is an exact copy both in form and size, as it appears in the notes made by the hand of Silas Hamilton, who appears to have been a leading spirit in all visionary schemes wherein gold, silver, or other precious metals were supposed to be the object of pursuit.[126]

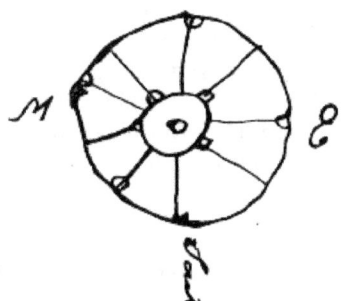

---

[126] Clark Jillson. *Green Leaves from Whitingham, Vermont: A History of the Town*. Worcester: By the Author, 1894. p. 120.

Other instances of treasure hunting turn up in Concord, Massachusetts, where Henry Thoreau found abandoned pits useful for berry picking[127], and in Maine as late as 1909:

> During most of his long life, as often as he has found opportunity, Uncle Ossian [Dustin] has hunted and dug along the ragged Lincoln [Maine] coast. He has toiled nights, for the most part, believing that in the night a treasure-seeker can best circumvent the enchantments laid on buried pirate spoils. He has kept vigil oftenest in the region of Cod Lead Nubble. He searches with a treasure-rod made with his own hands. He has the tip of a cow's horn, plugged with wood and containing various metals. In the wooden plug are stuck parallel strips of whale-bone, and he clutches these strips, one in each hand, and walks along, balancing the tip of horn. When he passes over the famous iron pot the tip, this is his belief, will turn down and point at the buried treasure. There is nothing remarkable in Uncle Ossian's quest, for other men in Maine have hunted for Kidd's treasure. But his radiant courage and his unfailing optimism are striking.[128]

It wasn't just a New England thing. Apparently local wealth-seekers in Morristown, New Jersey had long been convinced that there was some sort of treasure secreted on a local hillside which they had been unable to secure: "… a prevailing opinion, that there was money deposited in the bowels of the earth, at Schooler's mountain, with an enchantment upon it—that it could not be obtained without a peculiar art in legerdemain, or to dispel the hobgoblins & apparitions…" ("Philanthropist" 1876: 9) Two of these men happened to run into a school teacher name Rainsford Rogers in Smith's Clove (Munroe), NY) and in conversation discovered that he claimed the ability to raise spirits and find "treasure hid". They then got him a teaching position in Morristown in August, 1788. Rogers then returned to his native New England in September (he had been born in Connecticut and had lived in Massachusetts) and recruited another teacher to help him. Rogers "interrogated" the spirits by magical means and reported to forty interested citizens that "…there was an immense sum deposited at the abovementioned place; and there had been several persons murdered and buried with the money, in order to retain it in the earth. He likewise informed them, that those spirits must be raised and conversed with, before the money could be obtained." ("Philanthropist" 1876: 12) Thus began a succession of conjurations and ceremonies to raise the ghosts and get the treasure.

At 10:00 PM one stormy night in November, 1788, Rogers led his patrons to an isolated field where there was a tent supported on four posts protecting several magical circles lit by candlelight. The patrons, who had been told they had each to pay Rogers £12 (in gold or silver – not paper money) and obey him implicitly, were instructed that "…they must form certain angles and circles, and they must proceed in drawing their lines and forming their circles as Rogers directed, and then be careful to keep within the circles, or they would provoke the spirits to that degree, they would finally extirpate them from the place." ("Philanthropist" 1876: 14) As the cold, wet witnesses awaited the results of the conjuration, there was a sudden explosion off to one side with flames "ris[ing] to a considerable height", and a hideous groaning was heard from the nearby woods. Following this demonstration a great many meetings of the patrons were held over the winter, arguing about what this all portended and whether it was what it appeared to be. Another conjuration in March, 1789 revealed that the treasure could potentially be secured in May, so on May Eve, the group proceeded to Schooler's mountain to conjure up the treasure. Disappointingly, the conjuration proved a failure. "The [sheeted] ghosts appeared without the circle, with great choler [anger], and hedious groanings, wreathing themselves in various positions, that appeared most ghastly in the night" and scolded the assembly for revealing the secret of the hunt and that, by their "wicked dispositions and animosities", they had forfeited for the present any chance of getting the treasure. ("Philanthropist" 1876: 18)

---

[127] "On the sand thrown out by the money-diggers, I found the first ripe blackberries thereabouts. The heat reflected from the sand had ripened them earlier than elsewhere. It did not at first occur to me what sand it was, nor that I was indebted to the money-diggers or their Moll Pitcher who sent them hither for these blackberries. I am probably the only one who has got any fruit out of that hole." (July 19, 1856). *The Writings of Henry David Thoreau. Journal.* Bradford Torrey. Ed., vol. 8. Boston: Houghton Mifflin, 1906. p. 419.
[128] Holman Day. "The Queer Folk of the Maine Coast." *Harper's Magazine*, Sept. 1909, p. 178.

There followed a sequence of magical workings, including one where five men were required to take blank sheets of paper, pray on their knees, walk around a room and then go outside to where there was a twelve-foot circle. There they waited with eyes closed until ordered back into the house, where they found the blank papers now had messages on them – reiterating the need for every patron to pay Rogers his £12 before anything could proceed. In June, the ghostly requirement was for 37 people to attend a conjuration (but only 20 showed up) in a meadow, where further ghostly written messages were received while the participants lay blindfolded and face down on the ground within a 30-foot circle. The messages read, "O faithful man – what more need I exhibit to you! I am a spirit sent from Heaven to declare these things unto you: and I can have no rest until I have delivered great possessions into your hands; but look to GOD, there is greater treasure in Heaven for you! O faithless man. Press forward in faith and the prize is yours!" with some biblical chapters to read and psalms to sing. ("Philanthropist" 1876: 24) Unsurprisingly, the patrons preferred money in hand to salvation in the future, and further conjurations were done, including one where the stipulated deposit money enjoyed a discount – "not more than £12 and not less than £6", but again the requirement of 37 attendees was not met. Only 12 showed up and of them only 6 had any money to turn over (about £40 in all), which was left at the foot of a tree outside the circle.

However, the whole scheme fell apart soon after due to encouraging "hauntings" and window rappings at the men's houses when one wife found a mysterious packet of bone powder her husband had been give at one of the séances. She took it to the local priest to see if it was some sort of witchcraft, and an investigation traced the footprints of the "haunts" to Roger's house. Rainsford Rogers and Benjamin Freeman were arrested for fraud, and Freeman was fined £50, but Rogers escaped. While the details of this adventure are useful in demonstrating the continuity of magical traditions between England, Germany and the new Republic, it is even more revealing that a large number of citizens could maintain their faith in the process despite the Enlightenment and progress in manufacturing and education that was once supposed to have destroyed credulity in anyone above the lower levels of society.

These accounts would not be complete without a brief mention of America's most influential treasure-hunter – Joseph Smith, Jr., the founder of the Mormon faith. Smith and his father were involved in the Cunning Folk traditions that flourished in New England and upstate New York, and in treasure hunting in particular. Despite efforts by some Mormon apologists to minimize or refute such allegations, it is evident that the Smiths were indeed caught up in the treasure-hunting fad. The family had moved from Vermont where treasure hunting was rife to upstate New York in 1816, only to find the same sort of popular belief in their new location. The best documented instance is Joseph Smith Jr.'s employment by Joseiah Stowell, a well-to-do New York farmer who believed he had discovered the existence of a gold mine (and possibly a cache of ingots and coins) that Spanish explorers had allegedly worked at some time in the past. Under an agreement dated November 1, 1825, whereby each would get one-eleventh share of whatever was uncovered, Joseph Smith and his father went to Harmony, New York to help search for Stowell's mine. Despite considerable digging, nothing was found, and the Smiths returned to Palmyra, none the richer.

Other hearsay details about magical activity involved in the search may or may not be accurate, but they do reflect the accepted beliefs associated with treasure hunting:

> Joseph's neighbour's letter poured out tales of seer stones, ghosts, magic incantations, and nocturnal excavations. Joseph Capron swore that young Joseph had told him a chest of gold watches was buried on his property, and had given orders to his followers "to stick a parcel of large stakes in the ground, several rods around, in a circular form," directly over the spot. One of the group then marched around the circle with a drawn sword "to / guard any assault which his Satanic majesty might be disposed to make," and others dug furiously, but futilely, for the treasure.
> Another neighbour, William Stafford, swore that Joseph told him there was buried money on his property, but that it could not be secured until a black sheep was taken to the spot, and "led around a circle" bleeding, with its throat cut. This ritual was necessary to appease the evil spirit guarding the treasure. "To gratify my curiosity," Stafford admitted, "I let them have a large fat sheep. They afterwards informed me that the sheep was killed pursuant to commandment; but as there was some

mistake in the process, it did not have the desired effect. This, I believe, is the only time they ever made money-digging a profitable business." [129]

Stowell had recruited Smith because of his reputation as a scryer, and Smith was later arrested and tried on March 20, 1826 – perhaps under the new 1824 Poor Laws that updated New York's 1788 vagrancy act – as a "glass-looker". Smith had several "seerstones" (which seem not to have been classic translucent or reflective beryls and crystals, but rather coloured pebbles with holes in them) that he "used to help people find lost property and other hidden things,"[130] in traditional Cunning Man practice. He consulted a stone by putting it in his hat, and holding the hat over his face so as to exclude all light, received a vision that answered the question. Smith soon dropped this sort of treasure hunting and devoted himself to translating the "golden tablets" he had found by similar means, the translation from the original "Reformed Egyptian" script being accomplished by the use of seerstone and hat and resulting in the *Book of Mormon*. He denounced the former practice of locating lost things and similar magic as "peeping", which he asserted was quite different from his own seership.

In addition, the family had other magical interests. Smith valued astrology, and apparently owned a silver Jupiter talisman copied from the Agrippa/Barrett design, while several ceremonial items, including a knife with a sigil of Mars on it and some parchment lamens owned by his brother Hyrum survive in collections today. Their mother Lucy Mack Smith, in the first draft of her 1845 history of the family, went so far as to state: "let not my reader suppose that because I shall pursue another topic for a season that we stopt our labor and went at trying to win the faculty of Abrac drawing Magic circles our sooth saying to the neglect of all kinds of business we never during our lives suffered one important interest to swallow up every other obligation …"[131]; the "faculty of Abrac" being a pseudo-Masonic reference to the linking of magic with religion (although it was later explained as being derived from the "Abracadabra" charm), as was common among some pietistic and mystical sects in the 18th century.

The significance of the Smiths' interest in and practice of folk magic is not that they did these things, but that the evidence for it survived. Had not Joseph, Jr. been the founder of a major new religion and for that reason the details of his life (actual and spurious) diligently preserved by both the Mormons and their critics, these examples would have been lost and forgotten. Even if specific details from hostile sources may be argued against, the overall picture that arises is quite sufficient to prove historically that the Smiths were actively involved in folk magic. This just goes to show how much of the evidence for the workings of the Cunning Folk, done as far as possible in secret and below the historical radar, has been lost, resulting in a far smaller historical impression of what was being commonly done throughout the English speaking world.

---

[129] Faith Brodie. *No Man Knows My History: the Life of Joseph Smith.* New York: Vintage Books, 1995, pp. 19-20.
[130] Richard Bushman. *Joseph Smith Rough Stone Rolling.* New York: Vintage Books, 2007, p. 49. For a more in-depth survey of the Smith family and magic, see D. Michael Quinn. *Early Mormonism and the Magic World View.* Salt Lake City: Signature Books, 1987.
[131] Quinn, *op. cit.*, p. 54.

CHAPTER 16:

Conclusion

> "Wise-wo. Ay, I warrant you, I think I can see as far into a mill-stone as another. You have heard of Mother Nottingham, who for her time was prettily well skilled in casting of waters; and after her, Mother Bomby; and then there is one Hatfield in Pepper Alley, he doth pretty well for a thing that's lost. There's another in Coleharbour, that's skilled in the planets. Mother Sturton, in Golden Lane, is for fore-speaking; Mother Phillips, of the Bankside, for the weakness of the back; and then there's a very reverend matron on Clerkenwell Green, good at many things. Mistress Mary on the Bankside is for 'recting a figure; and one (what do you call her?) in Westminster, that practiseth the book and the key, and the sieve and the shears: and all do well, according to their talent. For myself, let the world speak. Hark you, my friend, you shall take— *(She whispers...)*."
> Thomas Heywood. *The Wise-Woman of Hogsdon*.[132]

We will never know what secret knowledge the Wise Woman may have imparted, as that was but one of the oracular whispers that have been lost in the mists of time. The thrust of this study has been on what the Cunning Folk, the magical professionals in English society, actually did during the period between 1550 and 1900 as far as that can be construed from surviving texts and records. Unlike the *virtus* theory of magical agency, which is my own interpretation of "how it was supposed to work", the methods of divination, charming, healing, conjuration and treasure seeking that I have excerpted represent the sum of known practices of generations of magical practitioners in English, and to a lesser extent, American culture. The reader is welcome to form his or her own opinion about the former, but there can be no serious objection to the latter. There has been a lot of loose speculation and romantic assertions made about what the village or neighborhood Cunning Folk were up to, much of it without historical basis. For example, it has been asserted that a sizeable number of Wise Women (and some of their male colleagues) were caught up in the witch trial panic and executed as a result, when in fact this doesn't appear to have been the case.[133] I trust this book will provide those who are interested in such things with the documentation they need to arrive at a more informed view of the matter.

It is only recently that the Cunning Folk have become a subject of interest, and the historical "white witches" separated from the mythical "black witches" of the great witchcraft persecution. Although innumerable accounts of their activities have survived, the Cunning Folk were of little interest to scholars and academics – except among folklorists, who were responsible for the greater part of the documentation we now rely on. Once the Cunning Folk's independent existence apart from the "witches" of the trials and Renaissance "high" magicians was brought to public attention by Eric Maple, Keith Thomas, Owen Davies and Ronald Hutton, this overlooked aspect of social history has received considerable attention. Possibly the most concise single survey of the Cunning Folk can be found in chapter 6, "Finding a Low Magic", of Hutton's *The Triumph of the Moon* (1999). However, the descriptions of Cunning Men's and Wise Women's activities are too brief to fully reveal just how they acted as healers, fortune tellers, thief hunters, astrologers, conjurors and general all-round magical problem-solvers. It has been my aim to expand upon the work of these excellent scholars to provide a fuller picture of the Cunning Folk's historical vocation, by reproducing the resources they used to show how they practiced the art of folk magic. The sources from which I have selected my often tediously long examples could have been excerpted at far greater length (it was always a temptation to do so), but although there is much more that could be included, the representative materials collected here will at least begin to clarify who the Cunning Folk were and what they did.

---

[132] Thomas Heywood. "The Wise-Woman of Hogsdon". *The Best Plays of the Old Dramatists: Thomas Heywood*. A. Wilson Verity, ed. London: Vizetelly & Co., 1888, p. 266.
[133] See: (Macfarlane 1970: 128); (de Blécourt 1994: 288ff); (Hutton 1999: 379).

As I have relied exclusively on documentary sources, there remains the problem of what was never written down and has been lost. Inevitably the oral traditions that informed the practices of the Cunning Folk, especially in the earlier years, cannot be discounted even if they are now beyond recall. It may be objected that by disregarding such traditions as are occasionally reported by contemporary claimants to the Cunning heritage I have misrepresented the overall picture. That there were beliefs, practices and activities for which no documentation survives is entirely possible, but having conducted as broad a survey as I have, I must say that I do not believe that any *significant* elements of folk magic *in the period covered* have been overlooked. I have purposefully abstained from speculating as to how magic was perceived and practiced in pre-Christian England and the early Middle Ages, or for the most part in regions where Celtic culture still had a measureable influence. I freely admit it is quite possible that some of the historical assertions by modern neopagans or Wiccans might be accurate concerning the earlier period, or as with shamanism, accurate for historical instances found outside the cultural and geographical territory I have been concerned with. All I can say to the sort of contentions and arguments that critics have raised concerning Professor Hutton's work, that it ignored or overlooked evidence from pre-Christian or continental sources, is that they are irrelevant in this case. I have reported from what evidence exists for the 1550-1900 period, and no more. Truthfully, I would have been overjoyed to find convincing evidence that challenged my hypothesis in this matter, as that would have made this book far more groundbreaking and appealing. However, that wasn't the case.

There are two factors, however, that need to be acknowledged concerning the criticisms referred to above. The first is the problem of historical continuity. Despite often fervent appeals to evidence from antiquity or the rest of Europe concerning paganism and magical activity, the mere citation of what occurred a thousand years before or in distant and alien cultures, is not admissible in proving claims about English circumstances – unless instances can be found in the historical record that testify to their presence and *continued* existence in the intervening years, or evidence presented that demonstrates communication between a foreign culture and the English people. To assert otherwise is to fall foul of a variety of the logical fallacy, *Post hoc ergo propter hoc*, Latin for "after this, therefore because of this". Simply finding historical precedents for some cultural concept, practice or belief does not prove that same intellectual artifact was influential or significant at a later period or in a different culture unless continuity (as opposed to revival) can be demonstrated. "*Post hoc* is a particularly tempting error because temporal sequence appears to be integral to causality [or historical influence]. The fallacy lies in coming to a conclusion based *solely* on the order of events, rather than taking into account other factors that might rule out the connection."[134]

The other factor is the anachronistic re-introduction of obsolete concepts into a culture that had thoroughly forgotten about them, or the adoption of appealing but previously unknown concepts from another culture, and surreptitiously introducing under false pretenses as having been significant – if hidden – all along. Appeals involving "invented traditions" are to be regretted as they frequently convince sincere if historically unsophisticated individuals that spurious claims are true in the face of less appealing but more reliable evidence. Historical roots are both important and desirable, but false ones are fragile and potentially damaging to belief, which explains the defensiveness of many historically dubious faiths. As to the damage historical illusions can cause, consider: "[o]ne classic example of a novel movement claiming spurious ancient roots is the rigid fundamentalism that has developed, over the past century or two, among the scripture-based religions."[135] My position is that I have not found any evidence to support certain claims concerning paganism and magic during the time period and in the areas I studied, and therefore I'm not inclined to accept that such practices did in fact exist in English culture then, and due to the question of continuity, their "survival" today must be suspect as well. We all have our biases, and I think I have made mine sufficiently clear.

Having said that, the survival of tradition still raises interesting points. As I mentioned in the introduction, shifts in the cultural *habitus*, or shared body of accepted opinion, can through "iconotropy"

---

[134] http://en.wikipedia.org/wiki/Post_hoc_ergo_propter_hoc (accessed 8/8/2012)
[135] Philip Jenkins. *Dream Catchers*. New York: Oxford University Press, 2004, p. 251.

("the accidental or deliberate misinterpretation by one culture of the icons or myths of an earlier one, especially so as to bring them into accord with those of the later one"[136]) effectively wipe out whole swaths of oral tradition when its heirs adopt what they unconsciously believe to be a better or more effective expression of what they had thought all along. The evolution of modern occultism appears to have accomplished this with regrettable efficiency, as old traditions were reworked out of recognition and new ideas replaced those that had survived for centuries. The closest we can get to the Cunning Folk's inner beliefs appears to be what the more discerning and scrupulous folklorists have recorded, even if that was filtered through their own perceptions and paraphrasing.

While we cannot recover the oral traditions that the Cunning Folk relied on, we could look at American hoodoo as a model for what this body of knowledge was once like, as noted in Chapter 13.[137] Henry Hyatt's sympathetic and meticulous recording of the oral traditions presents a wonderful snapshot of folk magic as a living culture, to which the work of Zora Neale Hurston can be added as well. What is most striking about the historical trajectory of hoodoo or obeah, however, is that, unlike the folk magic of England, they made a successful transition from oral tradition to modern commodification and as a result are flourishing today. Where the magic of the Cunning Folk in Britain was effectively supplanted by modern occultism, the practices and beliefs of the root doctors and hoodoo operators survived long enough to attract commercially-minded purveyors of the *materia magica* (aka "spiritual supplies") that had previously been personally gathered in the wild. These "curio-merchants" (items were labeled and sold as "alleged curios" to avoid prosecution under laws governing mail-order fraud and the Pure Food and Drug Act) sold people the materials they needed in certain shops and drugstores and, more significantly, by way of mail order catalogs. In addition, these same merchants offered a great many cheap publications such as almanacs, dream books and books of spells such as Hohman's *Pow-Wows, or the Long Lost Friend* and "de Claremont's" *Legends of Incense, Herb, and Oil Magic* that contained instructions about how their products could be used.

The premier supplier of magical and occult books and some *materia magica* was L. W. De Laurence of Chicago, who established his De Laurence, Scott & Co. about 1903 and published bulky catalogs touting his own ideas and "credentials", as well as a wide selection of occult source books. Although he was a shameless pirate of other men's work [138] (including A. E. Waite and S. L. Mathers), as well as reworking Barrett's *Magus* and adding some Hindu material to produce his self-styled *Great Book of Magical Art and Hindu Magic* (ca. 1908, and still in print as "The Obeah Bible" as well as under its original title), De Laurence effectively acted as the great popularizer of the occult, making hitherto scarce occult resources available to everyone. His catalog (with interminable essays on the occult) and books were eagerly seized upon by folk magicians around the English-speaking world, especially in Africa and the Caribbean. It is still a crime to import De Laurence titles into Jamaica, where they are still a treasured resource of obeah men. Hyatt found De Laurence's influence was widespread among the hoodoo practitioners, while the eminently successful root doctor Jim Jordan (1871-1962) ordered a number of titles from De Laurence's catalog:

> Brodge Wilson gave the doctor a catalogue sent out by a Chicago mail order house that sold conjure books and supplies. Son Isaac says his father ordered and studied / the 6th, 7th, 8th, 9th, and 10th Books of Moses, Lucky Star Dream Book, Palmistry, Secrets of the Psalms, and The Master Book of Candle Burning. (Johnson 1968: 56-57)

---

[136] http://en.wiktionary.org/wiki/iconotropy (accessed 8/15/2012)
[137] I use "hoodoo" as the general term for these traditions rather than the recently-popular and equally accurate label of "conjure", as that might be confused with the European conjuration traditions discussed elsewhere in this book.
[138] "I cannot begin to convey my contempt for L.W. de Laurence and his bootleg edition(s)." Joseph H. Peterson, www.esotericarchives.com/solomon/ksol.htm (accessed 10/12/11).

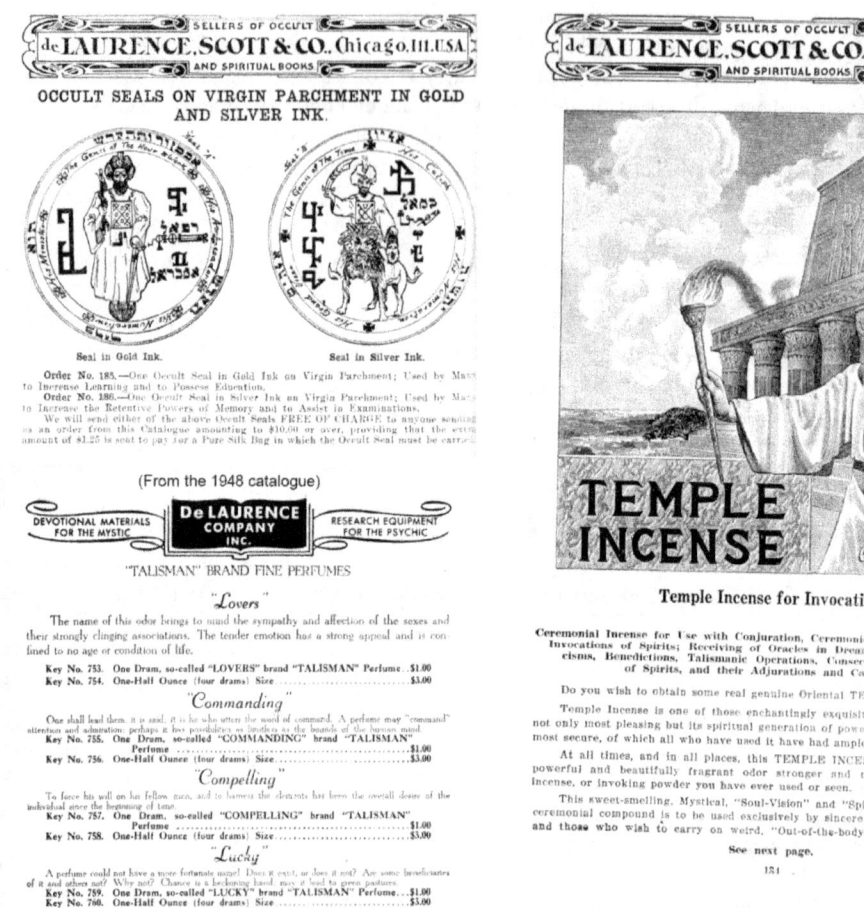

Although he did include books on traditional magic and conjuration in his offering, De Laurence represents an even better example of the shift from European folk magic to modern occultism. In his eagerness to exploit the occult, De Laurence was quick to adopt the contemporary fascination with Theosophy's "mystic orient" and Spiritualism's psychic offshoots, incorporating Hinduism, Buddhism, New Thought, mesmerism (his first book was on hypnosis) and related themes. The 1913 De Laurence, Scott & Co. catalog has only a few "spiritual" items (as well as rings and "Crystal Maize Antiseptic Tooth Powder") such as a curious Cabalistic talisman and "Temple Incense", (see image above) but twelve years after his death, the 1948 catalog was perceptibly catering to hoodoo and obeah. It offered a great many talismans from popular books such as the *Sixth and Seventh Books of Moses*, both the *Greater* and the *Lesser Key of Solomon* and "Raphael's" publications as well as perfumes and coloured candles. The shift in emphasis is also evident from the fact that De Laurence's portrait on the 1948 cover shows him without the turban he affected in 1913 (although the earlier portrait is shown inside). The turbaned portrait was also copied by his pseudonymous rival, "Lewis de Claremont".

If De Laurence, Scott and Co. was the largest purveyor of occult supplies, it was neither the first nor, over time, the most complete source of "spiritual supplies". Publishers of cheap books and reprints such as Dick & Fitzgerald (New York), I. & M. Ottenheimer (Baltimore), Wehman Bros. (New York), and Laird & Lee (Chicago) had been offering books on dreams, fortune telling, palmistry and the like from the 1860s to the turn of the 20th century, while specialist publishers in England such as George Redway and William Rider and Son issued the more serious books that De Laurence would pirate.

Although the basis of hoodoo came from its African roots, like most systems of folk magic it was avidly eclectic, borrowing whatever promising material it found attractive. The result was a vibrant synthesis of African and European traditions that was used by African-Americans and people of European heritage alike. Their practice had the same results-oriented focus as that of the Cunning Folk, as both dealt with a clientele seeking healing, love magic, divination, anti-witchery and curses. Like the English Cunning Folk, American hoodooers and root doctors, as well as Pennsylvania Dutch pow-wowers and Braucherei, were firmly entrenched in the Christian world view. This helped reassure their clients that what they did was in keeping with their preconceptions about how the world worked, and it was not even unusual for hoodoo doctors to double as Christian ministers or religious leaders in their communities.

"Occult—Spiritual and Religious Supplies" (*Marvel Book Company*, N. Y.: ca. 1950)

Rather than being overtaken by modern occultism, American folk magic demonstrated its viability by adopting anything it found promising, and was similarly successful in competing with popular astrology, medical quackery or patent medicine through advertising and mail-order services. If commercialization helped preserve American folk magic, it also led to "do-it-yourself" magic and fortune-telling, but in so doing, simply increased the public's exposure to a magical way of thinking. Once customers became familiar with the paraphernalia and concepts of hoodoo, they were all the more likely to seek out professional practitioners in their quest for results. In contrast with the English situation, the American tradition appears to have enhanced its capacity for survival in large part because of a readiness to publish its spells and rituals. As Owen Davies noted (Davies 2003: 133), there was an unexplained reluctance among British publishers to put the magical information found in oral tradition and in the manuscript notebooks of the Cunning Folk into print, which resulted in its eventual loss to popular culture. Had the English public been exposed to the same sort of magical information in cheap publications as were available in other countries, we might not be talking today about an extinct Cunning tradition. What I find most surprising, however, is that no descendant of one of these many Cunning Folk, who are only a couple generations away from us in time, has come forward with reliable information about their ancestor's activities.

There are now a two remaining questions that might be addressed. Firstly, did the magic actually *work*? That I leave up to the reader, as my own opinion here is irrelevant. You now have a body of evidence to work with, in which to arrive at your own conclusion. Seeing as it is so heavily invested in the Judaeo-Christian world view, we might equally ask, does the Christian religion *work*? Secondly, if not, were the Cunning Folk by in large pious frauds or were they sincere practitioners of their ancient traditions? Here the answer is clearer, if ambiguous. Some Cunning Folk were obviously out-and-out swindlers, using the arcane as a cover by which to extract the maximum amount of money from their dupes. Others, especially charmers and astrologers, were quite sincere in what they did, having as much faith in their art as their clients did – or even more – and provided their services without any intent to cheat or deceive. The most common situation, however, may have been that most were neither con-men nor true believers, but rather a little of both. Leaving aside the cynical cheats, it seems evident that while the average Cunning Man or Wise Woman may have genuinely believed that the arts they practiced were real, they were not above using a bit of trickery to help things along, such as using a bit of prestidigitation or some clandestine information concerning their clients. Folk magic is not the same thing as materialistic science, and its results have often been nudged into credibility by a little exaggeration concerning the results or a surreptitious manipulation of the "facts". This is certainly true of far more respectable sciences such as psychology or economics, so I think we can extend some "wiggle room" to our Cunning Folk, and acknowledge the very human way in which they acted to accommodate the very human desires they sought to fulfill.

APPENDICES

APPENDIX I: LAWS PERTAINING TO MAGIC AND WITCHCRAFT

Defining Illicit Magic (Faculty of Paris 1398)

"In September 1398 the theology faculty at the University of Paris approved a set of twenty-eight articles condemning the practice of ritual magic. The articles determined that various arguments magicians had been using to defend their practices were erroneous and in some cases blasphemous. In making this pronouncement, the Parisian faculty presented the argument, developed by scholastic theologians during the fourteenth century, that the practice of summoning up demons and commanding them to perform deeds was heretical because it gave to demons what was due only to God. ... This translation of the pronouncement is based on the Latin text included in the preface to Jean Bodin, *Démonomanie des sorciers* (Paris, 1580)"[139]

Determination made by the faculty of theology at Paris in the year of our lord 1398 regarding certain newly arisen superstitions

- The first article is this: that to seek intimacy, friendship, and help from demons by means of magical arts, harmful magical acts *[maleficia]*, and forbidden invocations is not idolatry. This is an error, because the demon is judged to be an undaunted and implacable adversary of God and man. He is incapable of ever receiving any truly divine honor or dominion by participation or by suitability, like other rational creatures that have not been condemned. Nor is God adored in these demons in a sign instituted at His pleasure, such as images and shrines.
- The second article: that to give, or to offer, or to promise demons any sort of thing so that they fulfill the desire of man – even to bear something valued by them in their honor - is not idolatry. This is an error.
- The third article: to enter an implicit or explicit pact with demons is neither idolatry nor a species of idolatry or apostasy. This is an error. And by "implicit pact" we mean every superstitious ritual, the effects of which cannot be reasonably traced to either God or nature.
- The fourth: that it is not idolatrous to use magical arts to try to enclose, to force, to restrain demons in stones, rings or images consecrated – better, execrated – to their names, or even to make these objects come to life [by demons]. This is an error.
- The fifth: that it is allowed to use magical arts or other kinds of superstition prohibited by God and the Church for any good moral purpose. This is an error because according to the Apostle, evil cannot be done that good may result from it.
- The sixth: that it is allowed and even to be permitted to repel *maleficia*.
- The seventh: that someone can dispense with something in a particular situation in order to use such [arts] licitly. This is an error.
- The eighth: the magical arts, similar superstitions, and their practice are unreasonably prohibited by the Church. This is an error.
- The ninth: that the magical arts and *malefecia* lead God to compel demons to obey his precations. This is an error.
- The tenth: that the offering of incense and smoke, performed in the exercise of such arts and *maleficia*, is in God's honor and pleases Him. This is an error and a blasphemy, since God would not otherwise punish or prohibit [it].
- The eleventh: that to use such and do so is not to sacrifice or to make immolations to demons and, therefore, it is not damnable idolatry. This is an error.
- The twelfth: that sacred words and certain kinds of devout prayers and fasts and cleansings and bodily self-control in boy's and others [and] the celebration of Mass and other types of good works which are [all] performed in order to do these arts, that these (good) works exculpate the evil in the arts and do not, rather, indict it. This is an error, for by means of such sacred acts, an attempt is made to sacrifice something – even God Himself in the Eucharist –

---

[139] Brian Levack. *The Witchcraft Sourcebook.* London: Routledge, 2003, pp. 46-50.

to demons. The demon makes these sacrifices either because he wishes to be honored like the Most High [Isaiah 14: 14], or because he wishes to conceal his frauds, or to trap the simple-minded more easily and destroy them more damnably.

- The thirteenth: that by such arts the holy prophets and other saints had the power of their prophecies and performed miracles or expelled demons. This is an error and blasphemy.
- The fourteenth: that God by Himself and with no intermediary or with the good angels revealed such *maleficia to* holy persons. This is an error and blasphemy.
- The fifteenth: that such arts can force the free will of a person to bend to the will or desire of another person. This is an error: and to try to do this is impious and nefarious.
- The sixteenth: that for that reason the aforesaid arts are good and from God, and that it is permissible to practice them. For through their observance sometimes or often come about that which the observers seek or say, because good sometimes comes from them. This is an error.
- The seventeenth: that such arts truly force and compel demons and not vice versa, i.e., that the demons pretend they are forced to seduce men. This is an error.
- The eighteenth: that such arts and irreligious rites, lots, charms and conjurings of demons, mockeries, and other malefices in the service of demons never produce any effect. This is an error. For God does sometimes permit such things to happen: as was obvious in the magicians of Pharaoh and several other places, either because the practitioners or devotees have been given over to reprobate understanding for their bad faith and other terrible sins and deserve to be deceived.
- The nineteenth: that good angels may be confined within stones and [that] they consecrate images or vestments or do other things included in these arts. This is an error.

The twentieth: that the blood of a little girl or of a goat or of another animal or a lamb's skin or pelt of a lion and other such things have the power to attract or repel demons by the exercise of such arts. This is an error.

- The twenty-first: that images made of bronze, lead or gold, of white or red wax or other material, when baptized and exorcized and consecrated rather, execrated! – as prescribed by these same arts, have tremendous powers on those days of the year described in the books of such arts. This is an error in the faith, in natural philosophy and in true astronomy.
- The twenty-second: that it is not idolatry and infidelity to practice such arts and believe in them. This is an error.
- The twenty-third: that some demons are good demons, others are omniscient, still others neither saved nor damned. This is an error.
- The twenty-fourth: that the offerings of smoke, performed in such activities, turn into spirits or that the smoke offerings are due to the same spirits. This is an error.
- The twenty-fifth: that one demon is King of the East and mainly by his merit, another of the West, another of the North, another of the South. This is an error.
- The twenty-sixth: that the Sphere of Intelligence that moves the heavens flows into the rational soul in the same manner that the body of the heavens flows into the human body. This is an error.
- The twenty-seventh: that the heavens, without any intermediary, produces our intellectual thoughts and our interior intentions, and that such [thoughts and intents] can be known through some magical tradition, and that it is permissible to certify the pronouncements made in this way. This is an error.
- The twenty-eighth article: that such magical arts of any kind can lead us to a vision of the Divine Essence or to the spirit of the Saints. This is an error.
- These determinations have been enacted by us and our deputies after prolonged and frequent examination; they have been agreed upon in our general congregation of Paris, called this morning and especially for this purpose at the church of St Mathurin, on the nineteenth day of the month of September in the year of our Lord 1398. We have witnessed the proceedings by the seal of the aforesaid faculty appended to these documents.

English Laws:
The Witchcraft Act of 1542. (33 Henry VIII. cap. 8.)
1542. Act *against* Witchcraft. 33 Henry VIII. cap. 8. Where dyvers and sundrie persones haue vnlawfully have deuised and practised invocacons and conjuracons of Sprites, ptendyng by such meanes to vnderstande and get Knowlede for their own lucre in what place treasure of golde and Silver shulde or mought be founde or had in the earthe or other secrete place, and also have vsed and occupied wichecraftes, inchauntment and sorceries, to the distruccon of their neighbours persons and goods. And for the execucon of the said falce deuices and practices haue made or caused to be made dyuers Images and pictures of men women childrene Angells or deuells beastes or fowls, and haue also made Crownes Septures Swordes rynges glasses and other things, and gyuing faithe & credit to suche fantasticall practices, have dygged up and pulled downe an infinite nombre of Crosses wtin [within] this Realme, and taken vpon them to declare and tell where thinges lost or stollen shulde be become; wiche thinges cannot be used and exersised but to the great offence of Godes lawe, hurt and damage of the Kinges subjects, and losse of the sowles of such Offenders, to the greate dishonor of God, Infamy and disquyetnes of the Realme: For Reformacon wherof be it enacted by the Kyng oure Soueraigne Lord wt thassent of the Lordes spuall [spiritual] and temporall and the Comons in this psent Parliament assembled and by autoritie of the same, that yf any persone or persones, after the first daye of Maye next comyng, vse devise practise or exercise, or cause to be vsed devysed practised or exercised, any Invocacons or conjuracons of Sprites wichecraftes enchauntmentes or sorceries, to thentent to get or fynde money or treasure, or to waste, consume, or destroy any persone in his bodie membres, or goodes, or to pvoke [provoke] any persone to unlawfull love, or for any other unlawfull intente or purpose, or by occacon or colour of suche thinges or any of them, or for dispite of Cryste [Christ], or for lucre of money, digge vp or pull downe any Crosse or Crosses, or by suche invocacons or conjuracons of Sprites wichecraftes enchauntmentes or sorcerie or any of them take vpon them to declare where goodes stollen or lost shall become, That then all and evy suche Offence and Offences, from the saide first daye of Maye shalbe demyde [deemed] accepted and adjuged Felonye; And that all and evy persone and persones offendyng as is abouesaide their Councellors Abettors and Procurors and evy of them from the saide first daye of Maye shalbe demyde accepted and adjuged a Felon and felones; And thoffender and offenders contrarie to this Acte, being therof lawfullie conuicte before suche as shall haue power and auctoritie to here and determyn felonyes, shall haue and and suffre such paynes of deathe losse and forfaytures of their lands tentes [tenements] goodes and Catalles [chattes] as in cases of felonie by the course of the Comon lawes of this Realme, And also shall lose priuilege of Clergie and Sayntuarie [sanctuary].

The Herbalists (Quack's) Charter of 1543. (34&35 Henry VIII. C8.)
"An Act that Persons, Being No Common Surgeons, May Administer Outward Medicines" 1542/3.
Where in the Parliament holden at Westminster in the third Year of the King's most gracious Reign, amongst other Things, for the avoiding of Sorceries, Witchcrafts and other Inconveniences, it was enacted, that no Person within the City of London, nor within Seven Miles of the same, should take upon him to exercise and occupy as Physician or Surgeon, except he be first examined, approved, and admitted by the Bishop of London and other, under and upon certain Pains and Penalties in the same Act mentioned;
Sithence the making of which said Act, the Company and Fellowship of Surgeons of London, minding only their own Lucres and nothing the Profit or ease of the Diseased or Patient, have sued, troubled and vexed divers honest Persons, as well as Men and Women, whom God hath endued with the Knowledge of the Nature, Kind and Operation of certain Herbs, Roots and Waters, and the using and ministring of them to such as been pained with customable Diseases, as Women's Breasts beings sore, a Pin and the Web in the Eye, Uncomis of Hands, Burnings, Scaldings, Sore Mouths, the Stone, Strangury, Saucelim and Morphew, and such other like Diseases; and yet the said Persons have not taken anything for their Pains or Cunning, but have ministered the same to poor People only for Neighborhood and God' sake, and of Pity and Charity:
And it is now well known that the Surgeons admitted will do no Cure to any Person but where they shall be rewarded with a greater Sum or Reward that the Cure extendeth unto; for in the case they would minister the Cunning unto sore People unrewarded, there should not so many rot and perish

to death for Lack or Help of Surgery as daily do; but the greatest part of Surgeons admitted been much more to be blamed than those Persons that they troubled, for although the most Part of the Persons of the said Craft of Surgeons have small Cunning yet they will take great sums of Money, and do little therefore, and by Reason thereof they do oftentimes impair and hurt their Patients, rather than do them good.

In consideration whereof, and for the Ease, Comfort, Succour, Help, Relief and Health of the King's poor Subjects, Inhabitants of this Realm, now pained or diseased:

Be it ordained, established and enacted, by Authority of this present Parliament, That at all Time from henceforth it shall be lawful to every Person being the King's subject, having Knowledge and Experience of the Nature of Herbs, Roots and Waters, or of the Operation of the same, by Speculation or Practice, within any part of the Realm of England, or within any other the King's Dominions, to practice, use and minister in and to any outward Sore, Uncome Wound, Aposelmations, outward Swelling or Disease, any Herb or Herbs, Ointments, Baths, Pultess, and Emplaisters, according to their Cunning, Experience and Knowledge in any of the Diseases, Sores and Maladies beforesaid, and all other like to the same, or Drinks for the Stone, Strangury or Agues, without suit, vexation, trouble, penalty or loss of their goods;

The foresaid Statute in the foresaid Third Year of the King's most gracious Reign, or any other Act, Ordinance or Statues the contrary heretofore made in anywise, not withstanding.

The Witchcraft Act of 1563 (5 Eliz I, c.16.)
An Act agaynst Conjuracons Inchantments and Witchecraftes.

Where at this present, there ys no ordinarye ne condigne Punishement provided agaynst the Practisers of the wicked Offences of Conjuracons and Invocacons of evill Spirites, and of Sorceries Enchauntmentes Charmes and Witchecraftes, the wch Offences by force of a Statute made in the xxxiij yere of the Reigne of the late King Henry the Eyghthe were made to bee Felonye, and so continued untill the sayd Statute was repealed by Thacte and Statute of Repeale made in the first yere of the Reigne of the late King Edwarde the vjth; sythens the Repeale wherof many fantasticall and devilishe psons have devised and practised Invocacons and Conjuracons of evill and wicked Spirites, and have used and practised Wytchecraftes Enchantementes Charms and Sorceries, to the Destruccoon of the Psons and Goodes of their Neighebours and other Subjectes of this Realme, and for other lewde Intentes and Purposes contrarye to the Lawes of Almighty God, to the Perill of theyr owne Soules, and to the great Infamye and Disquietnes of this Realme: For REFORMACON wherof bee it enacted by the Quenes Matie with thassent of the Lordes Spuall and Temporall and the Comons in this pnte Pliament assembled, and by thaaucthoritee of the same, That yf any pson or psons after the first daye of June nexte coming, use practise or exercise any Invocacons or Conjuracons of evill and wicked Spirites, to or for any Intent or Purpose; or els if any pson or psons after the said first daye of June shall use practise or exercise any Witchecrafte Enchantment Charme or Sorcerie, wherby any pson shall happen to bee killed or destroyed, that then aswell every suche offendor or offendors in Invocacons and Conjuracons as ys aforesayd, their Concellors & Aidours, as also every suche offendor or offendors in Witchecrafte Enchantement Charme or Sorcerie whereby the Deathe of anny pson dothe ensue, their Aidours and Concellors, being of either of the said Offences laufully convicted and attainted, shall suffer paynes of Deathe as a Felon or Felons, and shall lose the Priviledg and Benefite of Sanctuarie & Clergie: Saving to the Wief of such persone her Title of Dower, and also to the Heyre and Successour of suche pson his or theyr Tytles of Inheritaunce Succession and other Rightes, as thoughe nu suche Attayndour of the Auncestour or Predecessour had been hadd or made.

And further bee yt enacted by thaucthoritee aforesayd, That if any pson or psons, after the saide forst daye of June nexte comyng, shall use practise or exercyse any Wytchecrafte Enchauntement Charme or Sorcerie, wherby any pon shall happen to bee wasted consumed or lamed in his or her Bodye or Member, or wherby any Goodes or Cattles of any pson shalbee destroyed wasted or impayred, then every suche offendour or Offendours their Councelloures and Aydoures, being therof laufully caonvicted, shall for his or their first Offence or Offences, suffer Imprisonment by the Space of one whole Yere, without Bayle or Mayneprise, and once in every Quarter of the said Yere, shall in some Market towne, upon the Market Daye or at such tyme as any Fayer shalbee kepte there, stande openly upon the Pillorie by the Space of Syxe Houres, and there shall openly confesse his or her Erroure and Offence; and for the Seconde offence, being as ys aforesayd laufully convicted or attaynted shall suffer deathe as a Felon, and shall lose the Privilege of Clergie and Sanctuarye: Saving to the Wief [as above].

Provided alwaies, That yf the Offendour, in any of the Cases aforesayd for whiche the paynes of Deathe shall ensue, shall happen to bee a Peere of this Realme, then his Triall thereyn to be hadd by hys Peeres, as yt ys used in cases of Felonye or Treason and not otherwyse.

And further to thintent that all maner of practise use or exercise of Witchecrafte Enchantement Charme or Sorcerye shoulde bee from hensforthe utterly avoyded abolished and taken away; Bee it enacted by thaucthoritee of this pnte Pliament. That yf any pson or psons shall from and after the sayd first daye of June nexte coming, take upon him or them, by Witchecrafte Enchantement Charme or Sorcerie, to tell or declare in what Place any Treasure of Golde or Sylver shoulde or might bee founde or had in the Earthe or other secret Places, or where Goodes or Thinges lost or stollen should bee founde or becume, or shall use or practise anye Sorcerye Enchantement Charme or Witchcrafte, to thintent to provoke any pson to unlaufull love, or to hurte or destroye any pson in his or her Body, Member or Goodes; that then every suche pson or psons so offending, and being therof laufully convicted, shall for the said offence suffer Imprysonement by the space of One whole yere without Bayle or Mayneprise, and once in every Quarter of the said Yere, shall in some Market towne, upon the Marcket Daye or at such tyme as any Fayer shalbee kepte there, stande openly upon the Pillorie by the Space of Syxe Houres, and there shall openly confesse his or her Erroure and Offence; And yf anye pson or psons, beyng once convicted of the same Offences as ys aforesayd, doo eftesones ppetrate and comitt the lyke Offence, that then every suche Offendour beyng therof the seconde tyme convicted as ys aforesaid, shall forfaitee unto the Quenes Majestie her heires and successoures, all his Goodes and Cattelles and suffer Imprysonement during Lyef.

The Witchcraft Act of 1604 (1 Jas. I, c. 12)
An Acte against conjuration Witchcrafte and dealinge with evill and wicked Spirits.
BE it enacted by the King our Sovraigne Lorde the Lordes Spirituall and Temporall and the Comons in this p'sent Parliment assembled, and by the authoritie of the same, That the Statute made in the fifte yeere of the Raigne of our late Sov'aigne Ladie of the most famous and happy memorie Queene Elizabeth, intituled An Acte againste Conjurations Inchantments and witchcraftes, be from the Feaste of St. Michaell the Archangell nexte cominge, for and concerninge all Offences to be comitted after the same Feaste, utterlie repealed.

AND for the better restrayning of saide Offenses, and more severe punishinge the same, be it further enacted by the authoritie aforesaide, That if any pson or persons after the saide Feaste of Saint Michaell the Archangell next comeing, shall use practise or exercsise any Invocation or Conjuration of any evill and spirit, or shall consult covenant with entertaine employ feede or rewarde any evill and wicked Spirit to or for any intent or pupose; or take any dead man woman or child out of his her or theire grave or any other place where the dead body resteth, or the skin, bone or any other parte of any dead person, to be imployed or used in any manner of Witchecrafte, Sorcerie, Charme or Inchantment; or shall use practise or exercise any Witchcrafte Sorcerie, Charme or Incantment wherebie any pson shall be killed destroyed wasted consumed pined or lamed in his or her bodie, or any parte therof; then that everie such Offendor or Offendors theire Ayders Abettors and Counsellors, being of the saide Offences dulie and lawfullie convicted and attainted, shall suffer pains of deathe as a Felon or Felons, and shall loose the priviledge and benefit of Cleargie and Sanctuarie.

AND FURTHER, to the intent that all manner of practise use or exercise of declaring by Witchcrafte, Inchantment Charme or Sorcerie should be from henceforth utterlie avoyded abolished and taken away, Be it enacted by the authorite of this p'sent Parliament, that if any pson or psons shall from and after the saide Feaste of Saint Michaell the Archangell next cominge, take upon him or them by Witchcrafte Inchantment Charme or Sorcerie to tell or declare in what place any treasure of Golde or silver should or had in the earth or other secret places, or where Goodes or Thinges loste or stollen should be founde or become; or to the intent to Pvoke any person to unlawfull love, or wherebie and Cattell or Goods of any pson shall be destroyed wasted or impaired, or to hurte or destroy any Pson in his bodie, although the same be not effected and done: that then all and everie such pson or psons so offendinge, and beinge therof lawfullie convicted , shall for the said Offence suffer Imprisonment by the space of one whole yeere, without baile or maineprise, and once in everie quarter of the saide yeere, shall in some Markett Towne, upon the Markett Day, or at such tyme as any Faire shalbe kept there, stande openlie upon the Pillorie by the space of sixe houres, and there shall openlie confesse his or her error and offence; And if any pson or psons beinge once convicted of the same offences as is aforesaide, doe eftsones ppetrate and comit the like offence, that then everie such Offender, beinge of the saide offences the second tyme lawfullie and duelie convicted and attainted as is aforesaide, shall suffer paines of deathe as a Felon or Felons, and shall loose the benefitt and priviledge of Clergie and Sanctuarie: Saving to the wife of such person as shall offend in any thinge contrarie to this Acte; her title of dower; and also to the heire and successor of everie such person his or theire titles of Inheritance Succession and other Rights, as though no such Attaindor or the Ancestor or Predecessor had been made ; Provided alwaies that if the offender in any cases aforesaide shall happen to be a Peere of this Realme, then his Triall therein is to be had by his Peeres, as it is used in cases of Felonie or Treason and not otherwise.

NOTE:
According to the Journal of the House of Lords this Bill was read for the first time on 2th March 1604 and committed on 29th March. However, having been considered and found to be imperfect, a new Bill was brought in on 2nd April. On 7th May amendments were read and the Bill appointed to be engrossed. On 11th May it was read in the House of Commons for the first time. A month later it was passed and was returned to the Lords.

The Witchcraft Act of 1736 (9 Geo. 2 c. 5)
"An Act to repeal the Statute made in the First Year of the Reign of King James the First, intituled, An Act against Conjuration, Witchcraft, and dealing with evil and wicked Spirits, except so much thereof as repeals an *Act of the Fifth Year of the Reign of Queen Elizabeth, Against Conjurations, Inchantments, and Witchcrafts*, and to repeal an Act passed in the Parliament of Scotland in the Ninth Parliament of Queen Mary, intituled, *Anentis Witchcrafts*, and for punishing such Persons as pretend to exercise or use any kind of Witchcraft, Sorcery, Inchantment, or Conjuration.

Be it enacted by the King's most Excellent Majesty, by and with the Advice and Consent of the Lords Spiritual and Temporal, and Commons, in this present Parliament assembled, and by the Authority of the same, That the Statute made in the First Year of the Reign of King James the First, intituled, *An Act against Conjuration, Witchcraft, and dealing with evil and wicked Spirits*, shall, from the Twenty-fourth Day of June next, be repealed and utterly void, and of none effect (except so much thereof as repeals the Statute made in the Fifth Year of the Reign of Queen Elizabeth) intituled, *An Act against Conjurations, Inchantments, and Witchcrafts*.

And be it further enacted by the Authority aforesaid, That from and after the said Twenty-fourth Day of June, the Act passed in the Parliament of Scotland, in the Ninth Parliament of Queen Mary, intituled, *Anentis Witchcrafts*, shall be, and is hereby repealed.

And be it further enacted, That from and after the said Twenty-fourth Day of June, no Prosecution, Suit, or Proceeding, shall be commenced or carried on against any Person or Persons for Witchcraft, Sorcery, Inchantment, or Conjuration, or for charging another with any such Offence, in any Court whatsoever in Great Britain.

And for the more effectual preventing and punishing of any Pretences to such Arts or Powers as are before mentioned, whereby ignorant Persons are frequently deluded and defrauded; be it further enacted by the Authority aforesaid, That if any Person shall, from and after the said Twenty-fourth Day of June, pretend to exercise or use any kind of Witchcraft, Sorcery, Inchantment, or Conjuration, or undertake to tell Fortunes, or pretend, from his or her Skill or Knowledge in any occult or crafty Science, to discover where or in what manner any Goods or Chattels, supposed to have been stolen or lost, may be found, every Person, so offending, being thereof lawfully convicted on Indictment or Information in that part of Great Britain called England, or on Indictment or Libel in that part of Great Britain called Scotland, shall, for every such Offence, suffer Imprisonment by the Space of one whole Year without Bail or Mainprize, and once in every Quarter of the said Year, in some Market Town of the proper County, upon the Market Day, there stand openly on the Pillory by the Space of One Hour, and also shall (if the Court by which such Judgement shall be given shall think fit) be obliged to give Sureties for his or her good Behaviour, in such Sum, and for such Time, as the said Court shall judge proper according to the Circumstances of the Offence, and in such case shall be further imprisoned until such Sureties be given."

Idle and Disorderly Persons, and Rogues and Vagabonds. (5º GEORGII IV. Cap.83.)
An Act for the Punishment of idle and disorderly Persons, and Rogues and Vagabonds, in that Part of Great Britain called England, [21st June 1824]
WHEREAS an Act was passed in the Third Year of the Reign of His present Majesty, intituled An Act for consolidating *into One Act and amending the Laws relating to idle and disorderly Persons, Rogues and Vagabonds, incorrigible Rogues and other Vagrants* in England: And whereas the said Act was to continue in force until the First Day of *September* One thousand eight hundred and twenty-four, and no longer; and it is expedient to make further Provision for the Suppression of Vagrancy, and for the Punishment of idle and disorderly Persons, Rogues and Vagabonds, and incorrigible Rogues, in *England*: ... /

p. 699 IV. And be it further enacted, That every Person committing any of the Offences hereinbefore mentioned, after having been convicted as an idle and disorderly Person; every Person or pretending to tell Fortunes, or using any subtle Craft, Means, or Device, by Palmistry or otherwise, to deceive and impose on any of His Majesty's Subjects; every Person wandering abroad and lodging in any Barn or Outhouse, or in any deserted or unoccupied Building, or in the open Air, or under a Tent, or in any Cart or Waggon, not having any visible Means of Subsistence, and not giving a good Account of himself or herself; every Person wilfully exposing to view, in any Street, Road, Highway, or public Place, any obscene Print, Picture, or other indecent Exhibition; every Person wilfully, openly, lewdly, and obscenely exposing his Person in any Street, Road, or public Highway, or in the View thereof, or in any Place of public Resort, with Intent to insult any Female; every Person wandering abroad, and endeavouring by the Exposure of Wounds or Deformities to obtain or gather Alms; every Person going about as a Gatherer or Collector of Alms, or endeavouring to procure charitable Contributions of any Nature or Kind, under any false or fraudulent Pretence; every Person running away, and leaving his Wife or his or her Child or Children chargeable, or whereby she or they or any of them shall become chargeable to any Parish, Township, or Place; every Person playing or betting in any Street, Road, Highway, or other open and public Place, at or with any Table or Instrument of gaming, at any Game or pretended Game of Chance; every Person having in his or her Custody or Possession any Picklock Key, Crow, Jack, Bit, or other Implement, with Intent feloniously to break into any Dwelling House, Warehouse, Coach-house, Stable, or Outbuilding, or being armed with any Gun, Pistol, Hanger, Cutlass, Bludgeon, or other offensive Weapon, or having upon him or her any Instrument, with Intent to commit any felonious Act; every Person being found in or upon any Dwelling House, Warehouse, Coach-house, Stable, or Outhouse, or in any inclosed Yard, Garden, or Area, for any unlawful Purpose; every suspected Person or reputed Thief, frequenting any River, Canal, or navigable Stream, Dock, or Basin, or any Quay, Wharf, or Warehouse near or adjoining thereto, or any Street, Highway, or Avenue leading thereto, or any Place of public Resort or, any Avenue leading thereto, or any Street, Highway, or Place adjacent, with Intent to commit Felony; and every Person apprehended as an idle and disorderly Person, and violently resisting any Constable or other Peace Officer so apprehending him or her, and being subsequently convicted of the Offence for which he or she shall have been so apprehended, shall be deemed a Rogue and Vagabond, within the true Intent and Meaning of this Act; and it shall be lawful for any Justice of the Peace to commit such Offender (being thereof convicted before him by the Confession of such Offender, or by the Evidence on Oath of One or more credible Witness / or Witnesses,) to the House of Correction, there to be kept to Hard Labour for any Time not exceeding Three Calendar Months; and every such Picklock, Key, Crow, Jack, Bit, and other Implement, and every such Gun, Pistol, Hanger, Cutlass, Bludgeon, or other offensive Weapon, and every such Instrument as aforesaid, shall, by the Conviction of the Offender, become forfeited to the King's Majesty.

APPENDIX II:

"White Witches: An Apology to Louise Huebner"

Written January 1993; previously published in James Lewis, ed. *Magical Religion and Modern Witchcraft*. Albany: SUNY, 1996.

When I became interested in Wicca or modern witchcraft in the early 1960s, it was Gerald Gardner's *Witchcraft Today* and Margaret Murray's *The Witchcult in Western Europe* that formed my impression of the subject. The idea of the continuous survival in England of an ancient, universal cult to the time of the witch persecutions or even to the present seemed well demonstrated. By the time I was able to visit Gardner's witch museum at Castleton and meet Alex Sanders in 1970, I was fully convinced of the historical veracity of these claims.

It was at this time while characteristically buying up every book that might shed some light on the subject, I found *Power Through Witchcraft* (1969) by Louise Huebner, "The Official Witch of Los Angeles." It was a disappointment. A quick reading caused me to dismiss her as a ignorant practitioner of some sort of vulgar folk magic, who wasn't part of or even aware of the real witch tradition that I was so fascinated with. It was writers such as Gardner, Doreen Valiente, Justine Glass, Sybil Leek, June Johns, and Paul Huson (after a fashion) who had the real dope! Together, their books constructed what I came to call "the Witch Party Line;" the foundational myth and orthodoxy of Wiccan origins.

As a historian by temperament and profession, it was my ambition to discover all of the links between contemporary Wicca (or "Wica," as Gardner invariably spelled it) and its roots in the past. This was not a search for the proof of Wiccan claims but rather a desire to know more of what had been so coyly hinted at in Gardner and other books. Having a university library at my disposal, I diligently searched through every likely monograph and serial to find more about the early days of Witchcraft. I tracked down the majority of Gardner's references in *Witchcraft Today*, the bibliography in *The Meaning of Witchcraft*, and any other source that might shed some light on Wicca before Gardner. Anthropology and archaeology, theological history and Classical studies; everything was grist to the mill.

But the result was mostly chaff. It became clear after two years or so that there wasn't much out there to be found, if one was strictly interested in Wiccan history. All of the material quoted by Gardner and the others, with the exception of the *Book of Shadows* itself, was neither new nor directly relevant to British Wicca. There was a wealth of suggestive material from other times and other cultures, but there was no demonstrable pattern of white religious witchcraft, as exemplified by contemporary witchcraft. The ritual material in the *Book of Shadows* itself was skeletal in nature and quite inadequate as theology or exegesis. I searched for evidence and examples of a unified Horned God and Goddess cult, for the religious use of pentagrams, athames, cords and the sigils in the *Book of Shadows*, for casting Wiccan as opposed to Solomonic circles, for the application of Wiccan values, but all to no avail.

Alex was no help. He just suggested various books I already knew about or occult ones which, while tangentially related, represented quite different mindsets from Wicca as a religion. Robert Graves' *White Goddess* for example was evocative and inspirational, but its symbols didn't really accord with Gardner at all. In addition, the "poetical truth" that Graves invoked was obviously quite a different matter from historical veracity. I had become a bit impatient with "poetical truth" by this point. I had no quarrel with Wicca as a valid faith and religious practice, but the dawning realization that I had been deceived by its historical claims was galling.

The final revelation came from Francis King's excellent *Ritual Magic in England* (1970). As a schoolboy in 1953 he had interviewed novelist Louis Wilkinson ("Louis Marlow") about Aleister Crowley. Wilkinson had off-handedly mentioned that Crowley had known of a coven of witches "in his youth" but had declined to join[140]. Questioned about this, Wilkinson asserted that he himself had met such a coven, possibly the same one that Gardener knew, in the late 30s or early 40s. He described their use of protective ointments and, taken orally, the hallucinogenic fly agaric mushroom. It was his impression that "... there had been a fusion of an authentic surviving folk-tradition with a more middle-class occultism."[141] Here at last was independent testimony that there had actually been a quite different witch cult before Gardner.

Wilkinson's evidence indicated that something was there before, but what? As Francis said, Gardner apparently got bored with the simple ceremonies, and "... he consequently decided to found a more elaborate and romanticized witch-cult of his own."[142] The trick was to discern what might have been added by Gardner or some other middle-class occultist (a "proto-Gardner") and identify the residue as traditional. After talking with Francis at the Warlock Shop in Brooklyn, N.Y. in 1973, I decided to both fulfill my curiosity and assuage my annoyance at being bamboozled by tracing not only Wicca's past but the entire history of Western occultism. It seemed reasonable that this would make it possible to separate the occult introductions and inventions from the actual folk practices in Wicca.

There is a wealth of material on the practice of folk magic in English history. Even the earliest books on Wicca, such as Gardner's works or Doreen Valiente's *Where Witchcraft Lives* (1961), contain mostly historical folk magic unrelated to the rituals, practices and beliefs of Wicca. From the sources liberally referred to by Keith Thomas in *Religion and the Decline of Magic* (1971) or G. L. Kittredge in *Witchcraft in Old and New England* (1929) and the many county and local folklore studies, it is not difficult to observe a pattern of traditional magical belief and practice. What it demonstrates however is that almost all of the characteristic elements of modern witchcraft have an "occult" bookish rather than traditional origin. I came to the conclusion that there are in fact *two* separate "White Witchcraft" traditions in English history; one very old and fairly moribund, and another which is very active yet no older than the Twentieth Century. The latter is modern Wicca. The former is the tradition of the cunning men and wise women, the more or less beneficent practitioners of traditional English folk magic and popular sorcery.[143] Ironically, this was just what Louise Huebner was talking about!

I eventually found that many of my observations and conclusions had been paralleled by Aidan Kelly when *Crafting the Art of Magic* was published in 1991. Another invaluable source which separates the "religious" element from the magical one with consideration of modern paganism is Ronald Hutton, *The Pagan Religions of the Ancient British Isles* (1991). I trust that this short essay can serve as a useful adjunct to these books by casting some additional light on the sources of the *Book of Shadows* and by providing an outline of the actual white witches of English history.

White Witchcraft Then and Now

The criteria by which I hoped to separate the "middle-class occult" elements from the true folk traditions in Wicca was essentially the same as Kelly's. I divided the *Book of Shadows* material into three possible categories:

A) Those elements were characteristic of known English traditions of folk magic.

B) Those which were either clearly anachronistic in conception and/or representative of book-learning and intellectualised occultism. The latter would have to be easily available in published sources in the period when Gardner (or some other innovator) was working.

C) Any element which could not be found in either type of historical source might be assumed to be new or a part of an unknown tradition.

---

[140] This is supported by Bracelin, who notes that it was while Crowley was at Oxford, in Gerald Gardner: Witch (London: Octagon, 1960) p. 174.
[141] King, Francis. *Ritual Magic in England*. London: Neville Spearman, 1970, p. 179.
[142] *Ibid.* The erroneous statement in the same book that Gardner had hired Crowley to write "elaborate rituals" for his cult can be attributed to a remark by Crowley's patron Gerald Yorke, whom King had no reason to doubt.
[143] See Kelly, *Op. Cit.*, p.38.

Only segments of the rituals in the *Book of Shadows* can be said to belong to the third category, and we have no reason to doubt that they are modern compositions, thanks to Aiden Kelly. I have no reason to duplicate his excellent analysis of this material. However, some other sources for borrowed material which I investigated may be of interest. Omitting details of the more obvious borrowings from Freemasonry and ceremonial magic[144] in interest of space, I have chosen to show the probable sources for the following unique elements from the *Book of Shadows*: the worship of the Goddess, the more obscure chants (the "Eko, Eko" and "Bagabi lacha" passages) in the *Book of Shadows*, the use of the term "athame", "Drawing Down the Moon", the title "Book of Shadows" itself, and the term "wicca" or "wica".

The assertion of a continuous British tradition of self-conscious Goddess/Horned God worship would appear to be quite ahistorical, but I do not intend to develop that argument here. Suffice it to say that the generic goddess cult resembles the Christian notion of a single universalistic theism far more than the localized deities and "pluri-cultural" approach to religion in ancient times. Gardner is known to have been considerably interested in such a concept as his novels, *A Goddess Arrives* and *High Magic's Aid* demonstrates[145]. Other potential sources of contemporary witchcraft, from Margaret Murray *The Witch-cult in Western Europe* (1921) and Theda Kenyon *Witches Still Live* (1929)[146] to Jack Parson "The Witchcraft" (ca. 1950)[147] has the lack this distinctive goddess emphasis. Even "F.P.D." ("Foy pour Devoir" – Col. C.R.F Seymour) "The Old Religion – A Study in the Symbolism of the Moon Mysteries"[148] which was written in the 1930s and does centre on the evocative visualization of the Celtic feminine force bears little resemblance to the Wiccan theology.[149] Only Leland's *Aradia* (1899) approaches Wicca in tone, but it must be considered as a source rather than independent testimony. It should be noted that Leland was not blind to the possibility of *Aradia* being in part the invention of his informant Maddalena.[150]

The "Eko, Eko Azarak, Eko, Eko Zomelak" and "Bagabi Lacha bachabe" chants which appear in *High Magic's Aid* (p. 291), but not in the Cardell "Book of Shadows" in 1964, actually come from two

---

[144] Freemasonry contributed, either directly or through the various occult orders such as the Soc. Ros., the G∴D∴ & the O∴T∴O∴ (of which Gardner was a member) which were in form Masonic offshoots: the system of three initiatory degrees, the sharp point on the breast at entry, the form of the oath, "neither bound nor free," the hoodwink, the cabletow, and the terms "working tools", the "charge", the "Craft", and "the five[fold] points of fellowship". The "Oh, do not tell the Priest, &c." rhyme in the May Eve ritual is borrowed from Kipling's *Puck of Pook's Hill*, hence Gardner's odd defensive mention of Kipling in *Witchcraft Today* (p.47). There are a number of other borrowings from occult literature, such as Doreen Valiente's adaptation of the Charge from Leland's *Aradia*, the "Great God Karnayna [Pan], return to Earth again," from Dion Fortune's *Moon Magic* (1956, p. 176), or the selection beginning "Hail Aradia [Tyche] from the Amalthean Horn..." which is the reworked first stanza from Aleister Crowley's poem to Fortuna (Tyche) in his *Collected Works* (3 vol., 1905-07) and other assorted quotes from Crowley, as Kelly notes.

[145] Gardner, G. B. *A Goddess Arrives* London: Arthur S. Stockwell, Ltd., 29 Ludgate Hill, E.C.4, (1939). Red-headed Dayonis inadvertently inspires the triumph of a cult of Astoreth in Paphos which includes ritual nudity and bloodless sacrifice. Otherwise, however, there is nothing which would presage the creation of Wicca except an ambiguous mention of a "great rite" on p.197.

[146] Kenyon's *index* would appear to outline a Wiccan perspective (1 Witchcraft - the Universal Faith; 2 The Nature Cult; 3 The Gospel of the Witches [Aradia]; 4 The First Witch Doctrine: Transmutation; 5 The Initiation of a Witch, &c.) but it is still fixed on the older negative beliefs on the subject.

[147] Parsons, Jack. *Magick, Gnosticism & The Witchcraft*. Quebec: 93 Publishing, 1979.

[148] in *The New Dimensions Red Book*, Basil Wilby, ed., 1968, pp. 47 - 83.

[149] Aiden Kelly does offer some possible predecessors to the New Forest/Gardnerian pattern on pps. 21 - 25 of *Crafting the Art of Magic: Book 1*. St. Paul: Llewellyn, 1991. I agree with his opinion on the Victor Anderson group and the Gundella covens which could have been easily developed independently. The Randolph material points in quite a different, less benign direction, but would appear to be a real folk tradition (perhaps borrowing from the less savory aspects of hoodoo?) in which the witch myths inspired emulation, as in the case of Satanism where belief preceded practice. I must demur in the case of Rhea W., however. The parallels with Wicca are too great for my credulity, and the evidence too sparse.

[150] Leland, Charles G. *Etruscan Magic and Occult Remedies*. London: New York: University Books, 1963, p. xxiv.

separate sources. The first originally appeared in the art magazine *Form* in 1921 in an article "The Black Arts" by J.F.C. Fuller, apparently quoted from some Victorian source.[151] The full chant is as follows:

Eko! eko! Azarak. Eko! eko! Zomelak!

Zod-ru-kod e Zod-ru-koo

Zod-ru-koz e Goo-ru-mu!

Eo! Eo! Oo... Oo... Oo!

The "Bagabi Lacha" segment is found in Grillot de Givry, *Picture Museum of Sorcery* (first English edition 1931), as also noted by Doreen Valiente[152]. In the 1963 University Books reprint De Givry says that in "...*Le Miracle de Theophile*, by the celebrated thirteenth Trouvere, Rutebouef, ...we find the sorcerer Salatin conjuring the Devil in terms not belonging to any known language: Bagabi laca Lamac cahi achababe Karrelyos Lamac Lamec Bachalyas Cabahagy Sabalyos Barryolos Lagoz atha cabbyolas Samahac et famyolas Harrahya." Ray Buckland once speculated that this may originally have been Hebrew (or Greek?) garbled in the usual manner by the composers of grimoires, which is a better explanation than Valiente's hope that it was an indigenous French chant.

In the *Roots of Witchcraft* (1975), Michael Harrison goes to great lengths to prove that both of these passages are Basque and evidence of the antiquity of European witchcraft. He pointedly sidesteps considering Hebrew or Greek or even English, which is best shown by his discussion of the "witch words" mentioned by Gardner. "It is a pity that Dr. Gardner could not have let us know the meaning of 'Halch', 'Dwale', 'Warrick', 'Ganch', etc., for I could hardly begin to trace their origins in Basque unless I know the meanings these words bear among today's witches."[153] It did not stop him from tracing the other meaningless words, but there would have been no use trying to "find" these words in Basque when they are all good if obscure English words found in the *Oxford English Dictionary*.

The use of a black handled knife called an "athame" might be said to be a trademark of Gardnerian witchcraft. Knives have never played as central a role in British magic as wands or swords, so the presence of such a tool with its distinctive name would seem to be an important clue. There is no record in British folk tradition of such a knife before Gardner (who loved knives in general and wrote a book on the Malay kris), but there is in the grimoires. As Valiente notes, an "arthana" knife can be found in a 1572 *Clavicle of Solomon* in the British Museum. De Givry uses the term "arthame" as a generic name for a magical knife with the reference of a Solomonic manuscript *Le Secrets de Secrets*[154], which is where perhaps Clark Ashton Smith got the term which he used with this spelling in his story "The Master of the Crabs," as Kelly notes, in an issue of *Weird Tales* in 1947.

Using Valiente's clue, I would suggest that the most likely source is from C.J.S. Thompson, *The Mysteries and Secrets of Magic* (1927), which cites Sloane MS. 3847, "the Worke of Salomon the Wise called his clavicle revealed by King Ptolomeus the Egyptian, written by H.G. on April 18th, 1572." Although the symbols on the Gardnerian knives came from the Mathers edition of the *Key of Solomon*, Thompson discusses the "arthany" or "arthana" itself. On page 235 a row of knives is shown among which are a "cuttelus niger" or black handled knife, a "cuttelus alba" or white-handled knife, and the "arthany", which also has a white handle. The latter he notes on page 237 is used for "cutting herbs and making the pen of the Art". Apparently Gardner based his usage of the black, white and "boleen" knives on these, and switched the name "arthame" to the more witchy black handled knife. On the derivation of the name itself, a plausible source (rather than Harrison's Basque and Arkon Daraul's or Robert Graves

---

[151] *Form*, Nov./Dec. 1921, vol. I, no. 2, p.62; reprinted in *The Occult Review*, April 1926, p. 231. *Form* was edited by A.O. Spare, and had a number of occult articles in it.
[152] Valiente, Doreen. *An ABC of Witchcraft Past and Present*. New York: St. Martin's Press, 1973, p. 206.
[153] Harrison, Martin. *The Roots of Witchcraft*. London: Muller, 1973, p. 174; Gardner, Gerald. *The Meaning of Witchcraft*, London: Aquarian, 1959, p. 75.
[154] Arsenal Ms. No. 2350.

Arabic "Al-dhamme") might be the Old French "attame"; "to cut or to pierce", which also can be found in the *O.E.D.*

The other reason I have for choosing Thompson as the source is that it is here that "drawing down the moon" can be found. The often reproduced drawing of two women, with sword (not knife) and wand first appears in Thompson on page 79. This is very definitely not a British tradition but it is a well-known and rather sinister Greek tradition, as can be seen from the second of the *Idylls of Theocritus*, which has survived in modern Greek folk tradition.[155]

I would agree with Valiente that Gardner got the idea for the title "Book of Shadows" (which he never used in print) from Mir Bashir's account of a "Book of Shadows" found in Bombay in 1941, which he wrote about in an article in a magazine published by Gardner's own publisher Michael Houghton in 1949. "...The story ran that there was an ancient manuscript written on palm leaves, some thousands of years old in Sanskrit which tells you about your whole life by measuring your shadow."[156] It is interesting that the idea of the "measure" (which is also an old British practice) is not in the first degree rite in *High Magic's Aid* published that same year but can be found (without any information on how it is to be done) in subsequent versions of the degree.[157]

The final contribution by Gardner is the choice of term "Wica" to indicate religious witchcraft. While it is quite correct that "wicca" is the masculine form of the Anglo-Saxon term for "witch" (which is noted in *The Meaning of Witchcraft*), it had been out of popular usage for centuries before Gardner adopted this variant spelling to denote his sect. He apparently intended to make witchcraft mean "the craft of the wise" (as in "wise woman") as he dropped one "c" from the correct spelling to associate it with the root form "wis", and modified the pronunciation to a hard "c", as in "wicka". Later writers innocently corrected the spelling, but kept the hard "c" sound rather than adopting the correct "ch" sound, as "wicha".

Having discarded Gardner's attempted "wise" definition, Wiccans now tell us that a root meaning "to bend" is in some favourable way relevant to the use of the word when it was used to denote illicit practitioners of magic. This is philological nonsense. "Wicca", like "strega" or "hexe" was always pejorative. Also, as Edward Peters says, "... the modern word 'witch' comes from wicca, but in an etymological sense only. [The early 11th century] certainly had no conception of the future meaning of the feminine form of wicca."[158] It was only from the 15th century on that the word "witch" has meant the sort of individual that we associate with the Persecutions, Halloween and Walt Disney. Back when the terms "wicca" and "wicce" were in use, they simply meant a sorcerer or magician – a cunning man or wise woman, in fact.

Modern Wicca is not a survival of an ancient tradition, but rather the modern syncretization of a number of old and new elements that never ever co-existed, much less were united, before. A good example of this syncretic tendency is the eight yearly festivals. Far from being a single "traditional" pattern, they are a combination of the Celtic festivals of Samhain, Imbolc, Beltane and Lughnasadh; the Anglo-Saxon Yule and the Michaelmas-like September feast; the traditional Midsummers (not part of either system) and, as Hutton says, the vernal equinox (rather than Lady Day, 25 March) is added for

---

[155] Lang, Andrew, ed. *Theocritus, Bion and Moschus*. London: Macmillan, 1920, pp. 11-19; "There was an old Greek saying that 'the witch who draws down the moon finally draws it down on herself.'...It was generally held that of all charms one of the most dangerous was 'drawing down the moon' – so dangerous in fact that the magician deemed it wise to arm himself in advance with a protective counter-charm against the very power whom he was about to invoke." Kirby Flower Smith, "MAGIC (Greek and Roman)", Hastings, James. *Encyclopedia of Religion and Ethics*. New York: Scribner's, 1915, vol. VIII, p. 283.

[156] Bashir, Mir. "The Book of Shadows", *The Occult Observer*, vol. I, nos. 3 & 4, 1949-50, p. 154. Incidentally, the term "skyclad" Gardner himself credits to an Indian source; *Witchcraft Today*, p. 149.

[157] Cardell, *Op. Cit.*, Sec. II, p. 3; Kelly, *Op. Cit.*, pp. 56, 124.

[158] Peters, Edward. *The Magician, the Witch and the Law*. Philadelphia: Univ. of Pennsylvania, 1978, p. 168-169.

symmetry. There is no historic recognition of the vernal equinox, nor for the orderly eight part system itself.[159]

If Not Wicca, What?

The Wise Women and Cunningmen were the real "wicca", the white witches in British history. Hundreds of documented examples survive from between the Middle Ages and the end of the 19th century. Some were no more than local amateurs with a single spell or charm, while others were literate professional practitioners with a working knowledge of astrology and ceremonial magic who attracted clients from near and far. Although the witches shared a number of traditional practices and beliefs, true white witchcraft was never systematized. White witchcraft was never a self-conscious pagan faith opposed to Christianity but rather an accommodation of traditional magical practices within popular religion. The Cunningfolk's magic was practical not theoretical, "solitary" rather than group oriented (although often collegial), more a trade or calling than a faith, and simultaneously traditional and continuously mutable. A very similar situation can be found for example in the practice of Obeah in the Bahamas. There an amalgam of European and African magic has resulted in a practical profession or trade of magic. Although Obeah retains a number of religious elements, it is not an organized cult or sect, as in the case of Santeria or Candomble.[160]

Just as there is no reason to recapitulate Aidan Kelly's thorough work on Wicca in this short piece, it is unnecessary to try to reproduce the masterful picture of British folk magic in Keith Thomas' *Religion and the Decline of Magic* (1971). His chapters on "Magical Healing", "Cunning Men and Popular Magic" and the section on "Witchcraft" more than adequately demonstrate both the extent and practice of white witchcraft in early modern England. Eric Maple's discussion of the Cunningfolk in his *Dark World of Witches* (1961), the best popular account of the real British white witch in action, carries the story into the last century. Instead I would like to outline the most characteristic of these practices to create a composite picture of historic white witchcraft to set against the Gardnerian one.[161]

---

[159] Hutton, Ronald. *The Pagan Religions of the Ancient British Isles*. Oxford: Blackwell 1992, p. 337.

[160] McCartney, Timothy. "Obeah, Superstition and Folklore", *Insight Guides: Bahamas*. Singapore: APA Publications, 1988, p. 265.

[161] For further reading on the Cunningfolk in addition to those articles cited further on, the following are among the more useful.
Magical formulae: Simpson, W. Sparrow, "On a Seventeenth Century Roll Containing Prayers and Magical Signs..." *Jour. British Archaeological Assoc.*, vol. 40, 1884, pp. 297-332; Gaster, Moses. "English Charms of the Seventeenth Century" [Cod. Gaster, No. 1562] *Folklore* vol. 21, 1910, pp. 375-378; Wright, A.R. "Seventeenth Century Cures and Cures" [from John Durant, *Art and Nature Joyn Hand in Hand...*, 1697], *Ibid.*, vol. 23, 1912, pp. 230-236, 490-497.
British Cunningfolk: Lewes, Mary L. "The Wizards of Cwrt-Y-Cadno" [John and Henry Harries] *Occult Review*, vol. 40, July 1924, pp. 17-24; Marlowe, Christopher. "A White Wizard" [Fiddler Fynes, the Wiseman of Louth] *Legends of the Fenland People*. London: Cecil Palmer, 1926, pp. 213-221; Dawson, W. Harbutt. "Timothy Crowther of Skipton", *History of Skipton (West Riding, Yorks)*. London: Simpkin, Marshall, 1882, pp. 390-394 [also on Crowther, see John Wesley's *Journal*, Standard Ed, 1913 vol. 4, (July 1761) p. 472]; Pope, F. J. "A Conjuror or Cunning Man of the 17th Century", *British Archivist*, vol.1, no.18 (Aug. 1914), pp. 145-147; *The Severall Notorious and Lewd Cousinages of Iohn West and Alice West, Falsely Called the King and Queene of the Fayries*. London: Edward Marchant, 1613; Rawlence, E.A. "Folklore and Superstitions Still Obtaining in Dorset", *Proc. of the Dorset Natural History and Antiquarian Field Club*, vol. 35, 1914, pp. 81-87; *The Character of a Quack-Astrologer...* (London, 1673);
A treasure trove of primary documents concerning the Cunningfolk at the beginning of the 19th century can be found in "The Wonderful Magical Scrapbook 1450-1850" in the Harry Price Collection at Goldsmith's Library, Univ. of London.
The transference of the traditional practices of Cunningfolk to America include the German Pietist traditions in Pennsylvania Dutch country, the African-American traditions in Voodoo, and the traditional British practices in New England and elsewhere. David D. Hall and John P. Demos have early New England material. A good source for later New England Cunningfolk is Whittier, John G. *The Supernaturalism of New England*. Edward Wagenknecht, ed., Norman: Univ. of Oklahoma Press, 1969.

While the Cunningfolk used rituals, they were not the group-oriented circles of the legendary Medieval "Sabbat" or modern Wicca but the practical rites of the sorcerer or the priest. Some of their practices were survivals of what country people called "the old religion", i.e., the Catholic church; others came from the Solomonic grimoires or from various innovations of individual practitioners. The deities invoked were not pagan gods but the Christian Trinity and the Saints, the planets (occasionally visualised as spiritual beings rather than satellites of the Sun), the Fairies and assorted imps or devils.

Their dress was not a skyclad minimalism and seldom the quasi-monkish robes now associated with the occult. More often than not the Cunningfolk simply wore usual styles of the time, although it was not uncommon for some to adopt "scholars' robes" that denoted the professionalism of the cleric, doctor or lawyer, or some other distinctive articles of dress to impress their clients of their status. The setting for the consultation was often staged to impress as well. Charts, books, wands, dried crocodiles and so forth were arranged to give the impression of magical authority. There was no call for nudity (or flagellation), and the occasional use of sex was incidental rather than central to the work at hand. There is little or no indication of any "Golden Bough"-like seasonal fertility rites.

The tools of the trade were not a standard set of ritual tools but simply regional British variations of the paraphernalia of sorcerers the world over. Scrying crystals, the divinatory "Bible and Key", and the sieve and shears were characteristically British as were wax, cloth or clay poppets; charms written on vellum, paper or metal; divining or "Mosaical" rods; witch bottles and swords, wands and knives (not called athames). All sorts of animal (including human) parts, as well as vegetable, cloth, glass, pottery, metal or mineral fragments were employed in "receipts" for magical work.[162]

The Cunningfolk had no unifying Book of Shadows but they did use many books, even if only for effect when they themselves were illiterate. Manuscript grimoires, miscellaneous collections of charms, books of formulae, astrological and pseudo-astrological handbooks and works on occult subjects were a major means of transmitting magical knowledge among English white witches. These not only passed ideas between higher and lower culture, but provided a legitimating aura of learning in the shadowy underworld of the witch and wizard.

Ritual initiations after the Wiccan, Masonic or secret society pattern were unknown. Instead some acted as apprentices to established Cunningfolk while others were self-taught in the traditions of the countryside. In this way the independent folk tradition was successfully maintained until the end of the Nineteenth century. The real death of the old tradition was not the result of a bourgeois revolution in rationalism but rather the defection of the clientele to new and more modern, exotic forms of the same practices by Mesmerists, Spiritualists, quacks and occultists.

Astrological patterns and agricultural cycles governed traditional magic rather than a system of astronomical observances. Lucky days and propitious moments identified through traditional lists of "Egyptian Days" and astrological calculations determined the time for magic. The moon's cycles were more important than annual anniversaries, although May Eve, Midsummers' and All Hallows Eve retained their traditional importance.

Neither devotion to a god and goddess, nor the social cohesion of group activity inspired traditional magical practices. It was instead the needs and desires of clients for healing, detection of theft, treasure hunting, fortune telling, helping the "overlooked", removing curses or charms for luck which motivated the activities of the Cunningfolk.

Public opinion about the Cunningfolk was ambiguous, to say the least. The Puritans in fact deemed the white witches worse than the black satanic variety, as the latter were perceptibly evil while the white witches might easily fool a Christian into a damnable relationship by appearing beneficent and actually providing a useful service. Cunning women, wise men, blessers, conjurors, currens and all of the other names for the White Witches were regularly reviled from the pulpit and secretly supported by the populace – unless of course the white witch did something to earn the enmity of his or her neighbors.

---

[162] For example, "Kilnsey Nan" of Wharftdale, Yorks, who told the future with a pack of cards, a diving rod and a guinea pig (Lofthouse, Jessica. *North Country Folklore*. London: Robert Hale, 1976, p. 78).

While both sexes were represented in the trade, the most eminent of the white witches were usually men. The women nearly always laboured under a more mixed reputation and were more liable to be suspected of (and persecuted for) black as well as white magic.[163]

A good example of this dangerous ambiguity can be seen in the case of Ann Bodenham in 1653. She had been a servant and student of the notorious Dr. Lambe in the 1620s, and set up her own practice in Fisherton Anger (near Salisbury) after he was beaten to death by a London mob in 1628. Apparently she had acted as a wise woman for the district for years. Edmund Bower wrote of her that she taught divers young children to read, was much addicted to Popery (or the superstition of the "Old Religion") and lucky and unlucky days. "She was one that would undertake to cure almost any disease, which she did mostly by charms and spells." Her downfall occurred at age 80 when she was accused of witchcraft by Anne Styles, servant to Richard Goddard. Stiles had lost a silver spoon of her master's, and went to Bodenham to detect its whereabouts. Bodenham told Stiles that she knew why she came, but "as the wind didn't blow, nor the sun shine nor Jupiter appear, so she could not help her".[164]

Nevertheless, when Goddard lost some gold pieces Stiles went again. This time the wise woman demanded 7 shillings, and opened three books with pictures in them, laying a green glass on one of the pages and, holding the book up to the sun, asked the maid to look into it. She thereupon saw some people doing something in her master's house. Stiles accepted a charm made from a yellow powder made into a cross in a piece of paper for Mr. Goddard. It was on a third visit that Bodenham used the glass and book and some incense to conjure up some imps ("in the likeness of ragged boys") in a magical circle. This was too much for Stiles and the Goddards, who took her to the law, saying she had impelled the maid to sign a "Devil's book" (held by a Mr. Withers) and bewitched her. Bodenham was tried and hung for her magic, with which she had tried too hard to impress the credulous Stiles. It was a fine line obviously between acceptable and unacceptable magic and poor Bodenham was unfortunate enough to upset her nervous clients.[165]

Even so Wise women, such as Hannah Green, the "Ling Bob witch" of Yeadon, Yorkshire, might have quite successful careers. She inherited her mother's practice and flourished for 40 years, leaving an estate of a thousand pounds at her death on May 12, 1810. She was even able to threaten to call the law on the editor of the *Leeds Mercury*, who had prematurely announced her death on May 17, 1806, without triggering any difficulties.[166]

Three Cunningmen who flourished in or after the Age of Reason – "Auld" John Wrightson of Stokesly, Yorkshire; James ("Cunning") Murrrell of Hadleigh, Essex; and Big Johnnie Bracken of Barnton, Cheshire – typify the trade in both its traditional strength and its decline. There is only room for the barest outlines of their careers here, but I would encourage interested readers to search out the references for a fuller picture of these representative white witches. Their stories will provide a far more accurate impression of the real English magical tradition than any of the post-Gardnerian corpus.

The Wiseman of Stokesley (Yorkshire), John Wrightson, flourished in the second half of the eighteenth century. Rev. Atkinson quotes an anonymous writer in 1819 that the Wise man "... are believed to possess the most extraordinary power in remedying all diseases incidental to the brute creation, as well as the human race; to discover lost or stolen property, and to foretell future events." The writer was quite disparaging in the accepted rationalist manner of "Au'd Wreeghtson" as a greedy fraud but Atkinson characterises this as "gratuitous misrepresentation". Respected informants who had known Wrightson were impressed by his shrewd skill and honest judgment, and as frugal North Country

---

[163] Cf. Nanny Morgan, the Witch of Westwood Common, nr. Much Wenlock (Shropshire), who was murdered at age 69 on September 12, 1857. She learned her trade from Gypsies and had been consulted by both servant girls and respectable women for miles around. She was often paid in jewelry, when cash was not available, and a considerable hoard was discovered after her death. Burne, Charlotte, *Shropshire Folk-Lore*. London: Trubner, 1883, p. 161.

[164] Bower, Edmund. *Dr. Lambe Revived, or Witchcraft Condemned in Ann Bodenham....* London: Richard Best & John Place, 1653. p. 1, 2.

[165] *Ibid.*, p. 2-10.

[166] Smith, William. *Old Yorkshire*. London: Longmans, Green, 1889, p. 271.

men, the value of his services. When one John Unthank visited Wrightson about a suffering bullock, he found the Wise Man "seated in his consulting room, dressed in some sort of long robe or gown, girded round him with a noticeable girdle, and a strange-looking head covering on. These were some of the accustomed paraphernalia of the character assumed and its pretensions – a skull, a globe, some mysterious-looking preparations, dried herbs, etc., etc." Before the client could get his bearings, however, the wizard further astounded him by knowing exactly what his errand was, with great detail about the byre and situation of "Tommy Frank's black beast" and then told him that nothing could be done, that the animal would die anyways, and that if they "opened" the carcass, they would find a certain abnormality. Everything occurred as the Wise Man predicted.

All of this fits the traditional pattern of the Wise Man. His apparent prescience (or clairvoyance), his confident assessment of the situation and the uncanny aura around him and his trade are all part of the picture. Well-remembered successes which fit the pattern of belief overshadowed the failures until the whole trade fell into disrepute not only with the educated but with the general public, as we shall see in our last example. [167]

"Cunning" (James) Murrell (1780 - 1860), a shoemaker of Hadleigh, Essex, is a particularly good example of an accomplished Cunningman both because of the breadth of his expertise and for the relative wealth of surviving information about him. Murrell's practice ranged across the whole spectrum of white witchcraft, from healing and detection to defeating the alleged malice of black witchcraft and the evil eye. He was born in Rochford, Essex, and was fortunate enough to have some schooling which he put to good use in occult career. He also worked for a time as a chemist's stillman in London which was presumably useful in his work as a healer. Murrell was a competent astrologer, herbalist, charmer, restorer of lost property and antagonist of "black witches". He was particularly famous for his iron "witch bottles", which may have been considered a technological advance on the older earthenware or glass varieties. Stories surrounding his occult reputation such as his magical powers of flight or clairvoyance in the matter of theft recapitulate the lore of the Cunningfolk from centuries before. Years after his death, his trunk of books and manuscripts was examined by Arthur Morrison, who found works on conjuration, herbalism and astrology Murrell had copied or inherited dating back to the 17th century. There were as well letters from clients from as far away as London, nativities, charms, geomantic exercises and local intelligence that might be of use in consultations. This treasure trove of documentation was tragically destroyed in 1956.[168]

In 'Big Johnny' Bracken of Rose Hill, Barnton, Cheshire, we have an example of the sort of illiterate traditional country wizard that could serve as a portrait of his contemporary the now notorious George Pickingill (of which more later). Where Wrightson and Murrell were luminaries in their chosen profession, poor Johnnie was not only a more modest practitioner but outlived the cultural viability of his trade. Consequently in his old age he suffered the ridicule and jesting of a community no longer committed to the old ways. Big Johnnie and his wife "Tuffee" (toffee) Ann, who acted as the local shopkeeper and midwife, lived a precarious existence in the 1880s. Being illiterate, Johnnie had no use for the bookish arts of astrology or geomancy. Instead he relied on an egg-shaped crystal for his insight into the future husbands of inquiring girls, the whereabouts of wandering children (or husbands) for their mothers and the location of stolen objects. Because of the "witchcraft" laws concerning payment for alleged magical services, Johnnie was careful to say that he did not charge for his skill while making it perfectly clear that a suitable gratuity was unquestionably called for. Once when an ingenuous (or willfully dense) client accepted his "Aw mak no charge" at face value, Johnnie yelled after her "Dosto y'er, no luck follow thee, withersoiver thou gooas".

---

[167] Atkinson, Rev. J.C. *Forty Years in a Moorland Parish*. London: Macmillan, 1891, pp. 103 - 125; Brockie, William. *Legends and Superstitions of the County of Durham*. Sutherland, 1886 pp. 21 - 25; Blakeborough, Richard. *Wit, Character, Folklore & Customs of the North Riding of Yorkshire*. Saltburn by the Sea: W. Rapp & Sons, 1911, pp 180 - 185.
[168] Morrison, Arthur. "A Wizard of Yesterday", *The Strand Magazine*, vol. 20, Oct. 1900, pp. 433-442; Maple, Eric. "Cunning Murrell", *Folklore*, vol. 71, March 1960, pp. 37-43. Morrison also wrote an interesting novel using stories about Murrell, *Cunning Murrell* (1900) which was reprinted by the Boydell Press, PO Box 24, Ipswich, Essex IP1 1JJ, in 1977.

Towards the end of his life, he relied on the trade of those from outside Barnton for his livelihood. A six foot tall shabby eccentric with notoriously big feet, he became a figure of fun with the locals. His habit of wearing a bedraggled fur cap outdoors and a dirty red skull cap at home gave him the nickname of "Owd Redcap" among the local children, which he fiercely resented. He also suffered at the pranks of the local men, who on one occasion stole his watch and hid it in his lunch. When he was unable to discern its whereabouts, it greatly diminished his local reputation. Squalid and pinched as his career had become, Johnnie nevertheless retained the pride, independence and shrewdness of the old Cunningfolk to the last as he shuffled about leaning on a stick carved with twining serpents, like Aleister Crowley's. It was men and women like him, Bodenham, Wrightson, Green and Murrell who were the real white witches of history.[169]

Wicca: The New Religion.

When Gardner dropped his revelatory bombshell in *Witchcraft Today* with the implication that Wicca was or had been a pervasive secret sect in the English countryside, he was a member of the Folklore Society. I was able to ask Katherine Briggs, who remembered the event, about the impact of his book and his article in "Folklore".[170] The members of Folklore Society apparently quickly compared notes and came to the conclusion that as none of them had ever seen any indication of such a sect, their thorough knowledge of their own various regional areas led them to dismiss his assertions. Gardner, although recognized as possessing a wide if miscellaneous knowledge of anthropological literature, was notorious as a flamboyant crank who would bring imposing knives to meetings (which intimidated some people) and Miss Briggs was rather sharp about his influence on "young people". She was firm in her opinion that it was all "moonshine".

Here we come to the central paradox for the alleged "hereditary traditions". If religious witchcraft was as old and widespread as would be necessary for even a minority of the English and American claimants to have been connected with families with such initiatory practices, then it is inconceivable that their beliefs and symbols would have no echo in the historical record which contains so many other pagan and magical practices and symbols.[171] On the other hand, if traditional or "hereditary" Wicca was so small and secret as to escape *any* detection (and any professional historian will recognize how ephemeral, insignificant and localized a sect would have to be to escape all notice), then it is hardly possible that it could have been of any importance before Gardner and his successors blithely laid the whole thing open to the world. Hutton and Kelly show quite convincingly that this was the case.

I agree with Aidan Kelly that Gardner (or, less likely, an anonymous "proto-Gardner") was indirectly responsible for just about all modern witch activity. Some groups such as the Gardnerians and the Alexandrians are admittedly direct derivative from his work. Other groups, either discerning that the Old Man had (embarrassing) feet of clay or desiring to modify his teachings, chose to disavow him as soon as they could and build independent traditions while retaining what they liked. It is revealing for example that no "hereditary" rivals to Gardner (as opposed to jealous occultists such as Charles Cardell) publicly challenged Gardner in his lifetime.[172]

The most exotic of these attempts to depose Gerald Gardner was an extravagant hoax which first surfaced shortly after his death in February, 1964. The gist of the matter was that the real witch tradition could be traced not to Gardner but rather to an Essex cunningman named George Pickingill, who died in 1909. I first read about the Pickingill claim in the *Wiccan* #42 (a mimeographed newsletter) in 1975. It contained a preposterous ahistorical muddle purporting to connect Pickingill to practically every major 19th century occultist, and implied that Pickingill and Hargreave Jennings were responsible for forging

---

[169] Fox, Arthur W. "The Old Fortune Teller", *Papers of the Manchester Literary Club*, vol. 28, 1902, pp. 34-56.
[170] Private Communication, Amherst, MA, October 29, 1973.
[171] See Kelly, *Op. Cit.*, p. xix.
[172] Cardell published a mean-spirited expose of Gardner (and printed the entire *Book of Shadows*): "Rex Nemorensis". *Witch*. Clarkwood, Surrey: Dumblecott Magick Productions, 1964. He apparently had ambitions of creating his own witch organization.

the cipher MSS. that formed the basis for the Golden Dawn! On getting the preceding two issues of the *Wiccan*, I found that it had begun on a slightly more plausible note by questioning Crowley's connection with Gardner's rituals, but then spun off on a similar fantasy about Pickingill and his alleged control over nine hereditary covens that were apparently scattered over most of southern England. The writer had had a good idea for a plausible if fraudulent attribution of "hereditary" Wicca to an actual cunningman rather than Gardner, but had spoiled it by overreaching.

I had read of Pickingill (or Pickingale) in Eric Maple's *Dark World of Witches* (1962) and contacted him to see what he might know about this.[173] He told me about the earliest appearance of the claim was in *The News of the World* in 1963 or 1964, but interest soon subsided. It was his opinion that people associated with Doreen Valiente were behind it, though I would doubt that, as she is one of the most honest of commentators on the subject. He assured me that he had talked with old people who remembered Pickingill and knew his reputation at first hand, and that the whole idea was preposterous.[174] Pickingill was a real old cunning man, one of the last of the type, but quite illiterate and in his later years more interested in caging beer and getting a rise out of people than anything else. He was very much a practicing sorcerer, but the claim that he *governed* nine covens (Eric said the number in question was nine individual witches) was backwards. In traditional folk magic, it is one of the regular claims of the white witch that she or he knows of and can *constrain* a great number of black witches since it is a major part of their trade to repair or prevent evil witchcraft. The idea that Pickingill was either a witch king or a leading occultist with international connections was out of the question. Pickingill apparently received some local notoriety in the folklore boom at the end of the century. It was Eric's opinion that whoever invented all of this claptrap had gotten the idea from his book, and had expanded the theme considerably to make an old hedge wizard into some sort of occult übermensch.[175]

Shrewder independence movements were careful to excise those elements which would easily connect them with Gardner (such as scourging, the use of the titles "High Priest" and "High Priestess", the emphasis on nudity and so forth), and anything else they believed was anachronistic. Some became more bourgeois by adopting robes and downplaying the sexual element (at least publicly) while others swung in the opposite direction by increasing the orgiastic elements and adding initiations with severe whippings and wooden dildos, as is shown the Frost's School of Wicca or in Francis King's discoveries about a Midland group in *Sexuality, Magic and Perversion*.[176]

Still others, which had begun quite independently, were swept up by the sheer popular attraction of the new Goddess movement and adopted many of its practices and tenets while claiming independence. They seem to have made good use of the description of the North African Dhulqarneni cult in Arkon Daraul's *Secret Societies* (1962) with its forked staff (stang) and all. It is, as Valiente notes, a particularly suitable model for modern Wicca, even though there is no evidence that such a sect ever reached Britain. However, any "wiccan" group which employs the use of athames, tripartite ritual initiations, "draws down the moon", or any of the other paraphernalia of Gardnerian Wicca owes a debt to the Old Man.

Wicca is what Eric Hobsbawm calls "an invented tradition". It was formulated in response to the psychic needs of modern people cut off from older traditions by cultural repression, industrialization, education, loss of historic community (how many people still live where their great-grandparents did?)

---

[173] Private Communication, Brook Green (Hammersmith), London, December 29, 1975.
[174] Ronald Hutton made a similar survey; see *Op. Cit.*, p. 332.
[175] Claims such as "It is no exaggeration that George Pickingill's machinations materially influenced the founding of two 'Rosicrucian' orders – the Rosicrucian Society in England and the Hermetic Order of the Golden Dawn" or "Old George was acknowledged as the world's greatest living authority on Witchcraft, Satanism, and Black Magic. He was consulted by occultists of every hue and tradition [and never mentioned by any of these notoriously prolific sorts in print!]. They came by hundreds from all over England, Europe and even America." reveal the crank nature of the whole body of nonsense. The collected letters from the *Wiccan* and the *Cauldron* 'zines, attributed to someone calling himself "Lugh", have been reprinted in booklet form in England and America; the latter edition being by Taray Publications, Charlottesville, VA, 1984.
[176] King, Francis. *Sexuality, Magic and Perversion*, New York: Citadel, 1972, pps. 3-9; 163-168.

and separation from nature. It offers a constructive balance to our culture by giving the Feminine a more than equal role in its system. It also follows the Romantic and Celtic Revival movements in offering an alternative to both patriarchal Christianity and intellectual rationalism. While it borrows heavily from the past, it is an unprecedented synthesis of concepts particularly suited to our own times.

Wicca has no need of its past pious fictions such as "the Witch Party Line" as social legitimacy and acceptance will come from its own merits, rather than alleged historical genealogies. I find it very irritating that the old fiction asserted by so-called hereditary" or "traditional" or "Celtic" covens that they have been practicing Wicca or something very like it since time immemorial is still current. The implied independence from the more honest groups who recognize their debt to Gardner, as well as to the legitimate Dianic groups which owe their existence to Z. Budapest and others, is both divisive and, to a historian, dishonest. I realize that many people received the "Witch Party Line" from their original "teachers" at face value and are reluctant to let it go. Yet if Wicca is ever to achieve social acceptance, it must be prepared to relinquish myths which do little but offer Wicca's opponents an excuse by which to deny public recognition.

Bibliography

Albertus Magnus ... Egyptian Secrets, or White and Black Art for Man and Beast. (ca. 1880) n. p.

Arcandam's astrology, or book of destiny ... , Translated from the French of J. Fr. Neveau, London: J. Bew, 1774

Archaeologia Cambresis (1907) vol. 7, pt. 3, July.

The Book of Secrets of Albertus Magnus. (1974) Michael R. Best and Frank H. Brightman, eds. New York: Oxford University Press, 1974.

Choice Notes from "Notes and Queries" Folk Lore. (1859) London: Bell and Daldy.

The Compost of Ptolomeus Prince of Astronomy. Very necessary and profitable for all as desire the knowledge of the famous Art of Astronomy. Corrected and amended with new additions. (2007) Vancouver: Antiquus Astrologia.

The Connoisseur, (1755) No. LVI, Thursday, February 20, 1755, pp. 333-336.

The Folk-Lore Journal vol, 5, pt 1, Jan-Mar 1887.

Fontaine's Golden Wheel Dream Book. (1862) New York: Dick & Fitzgerald.

The Gypsy Dream Book and Fortune Teller. (1882) New York: M. J. Ivers & Co.

High German fortune-teller, with rules and directions, by which men and women may know their good and bad fortune ... S. and T. Martin, Printers, Birmingham, ca. 1810. (ECCO Print Edition, ca. 2009 - same pagination as earlier editions.)

Le Marchand's Fortune Teller and Dream Book. (1863) New York: Dick & Fitzgerald, 130-133.

Letters and Papers, Foreign and Domestic, of the Reign of Henry VIII, Vol 13. (1892) London: Her Majesty's Stationary Office.

Mother Bunch's Golden Fortune-Teller. (ca. 1850) Glasgow: Printed for the Booksellers.

Mother Shipton's Gypsy Fortune Teller and Dream Book with Napoleon's Oraculum. (1890) I. & M. Ottenheimer Publishers, Baltimore.

Notes and Queries for Somerset and Dorset, (1895) vol. 4, pp. 157-58

The Oracles: or, the secrets of fortune and wisdom laid open. Adapted to the four seasons of life. Translated from a Greek sage A New Edition. (ca. 1790) London: J. Barker.

The Original Book of Knowledge. (1725) London: Printed by D. Prat.

The Shepherd's Kalendar: or, the Citizen's and Country Man's Daily Companion...The Third Edition. (1725?) London: Printed for and by Thos. Norris.

The Sixth and Seventh Books of Moses, (ca. 1900) n. p.: Egyptian Publishing Co.

The Sworn Book of Honourius the Magician. (1977) Gillete, NJ: Heptangle Books.

Witchcraft Detected and Prevented; or, the School of the Black Art Newly Opened. (1824) Peterhead: P. Buchan.

Witch Doctor's Dream Book and Fortune Teller (1891) New York: Wehman Bros.

The Works of Aristotle, the Famous Philosopher, in Four Parts. (1801) London: Printed for the Booksellers.

Joseph Addison (1830). *The Spectator #487.* Philadephia: J. J. Woodward, vol. 2, pp. 242-243.

Henry Cornelius Agrippa. (1651) *Three Books of Occult Philosophy.* London: Gregory Moule.

Henry Cornelius Agrippa His Fourth Book of Occult Philosophy (1978). London: Askin Publishers.

Al Kindi. *De Radiis Stellicic: On the Stellar Rays.* (1975) Robert Zoller, trans. and ed. London: New Library Limited.

P. F. S. Amery. (1899) "Sixteenth Report of the Committee on Devonshire Folk-Lore", *Reports and Transactions of the Devonshire Association,* vol. 31, pp.110 -

St. Thomas Aquinas. (1920) *The "Summa Theologia"of St. Thomas Aquinas.* London: Burns Oates & Washbourne, vol. 9, Question 95, article 6, pp. 204-205.

Aristotle. (1927) *Problemata.* E. S. Foster, ed. Oxford: Oxford University Press.

John Aubrey. (1972) *Three Prose Works: Miscellanies, Remaines of Gentilisme and Judaisme, Observations.* John Buchannan-Brown, ed. Carbondale: Southern Illinois University Press.

W. A. Axton. (1907) "Divination by Books". *Manchester Quarterly,* Vol. 26.

W. Paley Baildon. (1901) "Sixteenth Century Leaden Charm (obverse and reverse) found at Lincoln's Inn", *Proceedings of the Society of Antiquaries of London,* Second Series, vol. 18, 1901, pp. 141-147.

Francis Barrett. (1967) *The Magus, or Celestial Intelligencer.* Timothy D'Arch Smith, ed. New York: University Books.

Richard Bernard. (1617) *A Guide to Grand Jury Men, Divided into Two Books.* London: Printed by Felix Kyngston for Edw. Blackmore.

Richard Blakeborough. (1898) *Wit, Character, Folklore & Customs of the North Riding of Yorkshire.* London: Henry Frowde, 1898.

Joseph Blagrave. (1689) *Blagrave's Astrological Practice of Physick*, London: Obediah Blagrave.

James J. Bono. (1984) "Medical Spirits and the Medieval Language of Life." *Traditio*, Vol. 40, pp. 91-130.

Edmund Bower. (1653) *Doctor Lamb Revived, Or, Anne Bodenham A Servant of his, who was Arraigned and Executed the Lent Assizes last at Salisbury, before the Right Honourable the Lord Chief Baron Wild, Judge of the Assise.* London, Printed by T. W. for Richard Best, and John Place.

John Brand. (1900) *Observations on Popular Antiquities.* London: Chatto & Windus.

Noel L. Brann. (1999) *Trithemius and Magical Theology.* Albany: State University of New York.

Jan N. Bremmer & Jan R. Veensta. (2002) *The Metamorphosis of Magic from Late Antiquity to the Early Modern Period.* Dudley, MA: Peeters.

Katherine M. Briggs. (1953) "Some Seventeenth-Century Books of Magic" *Folklore*, Vol. 64, No. 4, Dec.

Katherine M. Briggs. (1977) *Pale Hecate's Team.* New York: Arno Press.

Carleton F. Brown. (1904) "The Long Hidden Friend by John George Hohman", *The Journal of American Folklore*, Vol. 17, No. 65, pp. 89-152.

Charles Burnett. (1996) *Magic and Divination in the Middle Ages.* Aldershot, UK: Variorum.

Robert Burton (1850) . *The Anatomy of Melancholy.* Philadelphia: J. W. Moore.

Nancy Caciola. (2003) *Discerning Spirits.* Ithaca, NY: Cornell University Press.

Alexander Carmichael. (1900) *Carmina Gadelica: Hymns and Incantations. Volume II*, Edinburgh: T. and A. Constable.

Carolyn M. Carty. (1999) "The Role of Medieval Dream Images in Authenticating Ecclesiastical Construction" *Zeitschrift für Kunstgeschichte*, 62. Bd., H. 1, pp. 45-90

Christopher Cattan. (1591) *The Geomancie of Maister Christopher Cattan.* London: John Wolfe & Edward White.

Henry Chettle. (1841) *Kind-Heart's Dream, 1592.* Ed. Edward F. Rimbault, Esq. London: Reprinted for the Percy Society.

J. Kent Clark. (1984) *Goodwin Wharton.* Oxford: Oxford University Press.

Stuart Clark. (1997) *Thinking with Demons: The Idea of Witchcraft in Early Modern Europe.* Oxford: Oxford University Press.

B. Clayton. (1698) *Mysterium sigillorum, herbarum & lapidum…Written Originally in Saxon, by … Israel Hibner.* London: Printed by W. Downing …

Thomas O. Cockayne. (1864-1866) *Leechdoms, Wortcunning, and Starcraft of Early England.* London: Longman, Green; Longman, Roberts and Green, 3 vols.

William Coles. (1968) *The Art of Simpling.* (1656). St. Catherines, Ontario.

Jonathan Couch. (1871) *The History of Polperro.* London: Simpkin, Marshall.

Ioan P. Couliano. (1987) *Eros and Magic in the Renaissance.* Margaret Cook, trans. Chicago: University of Chicago Press.

Robert Darnton. (1968) *Mesmerism and the End of the Enlightenment in France.* Cambridge: Harvard University Press.

Owen Davies. (2003) *Cunning-Folk: Popular Magic in English History.* New York: Hambledon and London.

Owen Davies. (1996) "Healing Charms in Use in England and Wales 1700-1950". *Folklore*, Vol. 107 (1996), pp. 19-32 .

Owen Davies. (1998) "Charmers and Charming in England and Wales from the Eighteenth to the Twentieth Century" *Folklore*, Vol. 109, pp. 41-52.

Owen Davies. (1997) "Urbanization and the Decline of Witchcraft: An Examination of London". *Journal of Social History* Vol. 30, No. 3, pp. 597-617.

Owen Davies. (1999) *Witchcraft, Magic and Culture 1736-1951.* Manchester: Manchester University Press.

W. Harbutt Dawson. (1882) *History of Skipton.* London: Simpkin, Marshall and Co.

Willem de Blécourt. (1994) "Witch Doctors, Soothsayers and Priests. On Cunning Folk in European Historiography and Tradition". *Social History*, Vol. 19, No. 3 (Oct., 1994), pp. 285-303.

Daniel Defoe. (1973) *A System of Magick* (1728). East Ardsley, Yorks: E P Publishing.

Jean de Meun. *The dodechedron of fortune; or, The exercise of a quick wit .... Englished by Sr. W.B. Knight. The vse of the booke the preface annexed declareth.*, London : Printed by Iohn Pindley, for H. H[ooper] and S. M[an], 1613.

"Q. K. Philander Doesticks, P. B" (Mortimer Q. Thompson). (1859) *The Witches of New York.* New York: Rudd & Carleton.

John Durant. (1697) *Art and Nature Joyn Hand in Hand, or The Poor Man's Daily Companion.* London: Sam. Clark.

Cecil L'Estrange Ewen. (1970) *Witchcraft and Demonianism.* New York, Barnes & Noble.

Cecil L'Estrange Ewen. (1971) *Witch hunting and Witch Trials; the indictments for witchcraft from the records of 1373 assizes held for the Home Circuit A.D. 1559-1736.* New York, Barnes & Noble.

"Erra Pater". (1799) *The Book of Knowledge Treating of the Wisdom of the Ancients.*Suffield [CT]: Edward Gray.

Marsilio Ficino. (2002) *Three Books on Life.* Carol V. Kaske & John R. Clark, eds. Tempe, AZ: The Renaissance Society of America.

Fontaine's Golden Wheel Dream-Book and Fortune-Teller. (1862) New York: Dick & Fitzgerald.

J. S. Forsyth. (1827) *Demonologia; or, Natural knowledge revealed, by J.S.F.* London: John Bumpus.

Arthur W. Fox.(1902) "The Old Fortune Teller". *Papers of the Manchester Literary Club*, vol. 28.

John G. Gager. (1992) *Curse Tablets and Binding Spells from the Ancient World.* Oxford: Oxford University Press, p.195

Moses Gaster. (1910) "English Charms of the Seventeenth Century". *Folklore*, Vol. 21, No. 3, "from a manuscript (Cod. Gaster, No. 1562), written mostly by a certain Thomas Parker in the years 1693-5".

Marion Gibson, ed. (2003) *Witchcraft and Society in England and America 1550-1750.* London: Continuum.

Carlo Ginzburg. (1991) *Ecstasies: Deciphering the Witches' Sabbath.* New York: Pantheon Books.

John Glyde. (1872) *The Norfolk Garland.* London: Jarrold and Sons. (Glyde 1872:)

George Laurence Gomme, ed. (1885) *Mother Bunch's Closet Newly Broke Open,* [1685] *and the History of Mother Bunch of The West.* [1780] London: Villon Society.

Edward Grant.(1996) *Planets. Stars, & Orbs The Medieval Cosmos, 1200-1687.* New York: Cambridge University Press.

Lady Eveline Camilla Gurdon, ed. (1893) *County Folk-Lore. Printed Extracts II.* Suffolk. London: D. Nutt for the Folk-Lore Society.

Frederick Hancock. (1897) *The Parish of Selworthy in the County of Somerset.* Taunton: Barnicott and Pearce.

John Harland and T. T. Wilkinson. (1867) *Lancashire Folk-Lore.* London: Frederick Warne.

William Henderson. (1866) *Notes on the Folklore of the Northern Counties.* Sabine Baring-Gould, ed. London: Longmans, Green and Co.

Sarah Hewett. (1900) *Nummits and Crummits: Devonshire Customs, Characteristics, and Folk-lore.* London: Thomas Burleigh.

"C. Heydon, jun." (1786) *The new astrology : or, the art of predicting or foretelling future events, by the aspects, positions, and influences, of the heavenly bodies, &c.* London: G. Kearsley.

James John Hissey. (1898) *Over Fen and Wold.* London MacMillan and Co., 397-398.

Ronald Hutton. (1999) *The Triumph of the Moon.* New York: Oxford University Press.

Harry M. Hyatt. (1970) *Hoodoo – Conjuration – Witchcraft – Rootwork.* Hannibal, Mo: Printed for the Alma Egan Hyatt Foundation, Western Publishing Co., v. I.

Harry M. Hyatt. (1973) *Hoodoo – Conjuration – Witchcraft – Rootwork*. Cambridge, MD: Printed for the Alma Egan Hyatt Foundation, Western Publishing Co., v. III-V.

F. Roy Johnson. (1968) *The Fabled Doctor Jim Jordan*. Murfreesboro, N C: Johnson Publishing Company.

Michael Keffer. "Agrippa's Dilemma: Hermetic 'Rebirth' and the Ambivalences of De vanitate and De occulta philosophia." *Renaissance Quarterly*, Vol. 41, No. 4, p. 620.

Richard Kieckhefer. (1997) *Forbidden Rites: A Necromancer's Manual of the Fifteenth Century*. Stroud, Glouscestershire: Sutton Publishing.

"H[erman] Kirchenhoffer". (1835) *The Oracle or Book of Fate, formerly in the possession of Napoleon, late Emperor of France, and now first rendered into English, from a German translation, of an ancient Egyptian manuscript found in the year 1801 by M. Sonnini…* London: M. Arnold.

Frank Klaassen. (2011) "Three early modern magic rituals to spoil witches". *Opuscula: Short Texts of the Middle Ages and Renaissance*, Vol.1:1.

George Lyman Kitteredge. (1929) *Witchcraft in Old and New England*. Cambridge: Harvard University Press.

Charlotte Latham. (1878) *Some West Sussex Superstitions Lingering in 1868. Collected by …, at Fittleworth*. London: Folk-Lore Record, vol. 1.

Christopher I. Lehrich. (2003) *The Language of Demons and Angels: Cornelius Agrippa's Occult Philosophy*. Leiden: Brill.

C. S. Lewis. (1964) *The Discarded Image*. Cambridge: Cambridge University Press.

"Mr. Lilly". (1670) *A Groatsworth of Wit for a Penny, Or, the Interpretation of Dreams*. London: W.T.

William Lilly. (1985) *A facsimile edition of Christian Astrology W. Lilly*. (1647) London: Regulus Publishing Co.

William Lilly. (1974) *The Last of the Astrologers. Mr. William Lilly's History of his Life and Times from the year 1602 to 1681*. London: Folklore Society.

Carolyn Morrow Long. (2001) *Spiritual Merchants: Religion, Magic, and Commerce*. Knoxville, TN: University of Tennesee Press.

Edward Lovett. (1925) *Magic in Modern London*. Croydon: The "Advertiser" Offices.

Thomas Lupton. (1586) *A Thousand Notable Things*. London : printed for Edward White.

W. M. (1655) *The Queen's Closet Opened Incomparable Secrets in Physick, Chirugery, Preserving, Candying, and Cookery*. [London:] Printed for Nathaniel Brook, at the Angel in Cornhill.

Alan Macfarlane. (1970) *Witchcraft in Tudor and Stuart England*. New York: Harper and Row.

Cotton Mather. (1862) *Wonders of the Invisible World, Being an Account of the Tryals of Several Witches Lately Executed in New-England*. London: John Russell Smith.

S. Liddell MacGregor Mathers. (1976) *The Key of Solomon the King* (1888). New York: Samuel Weiser.

Charles Makie, ed.(1901) *Norfolk Annals vol. I, 1801-1850*. Norwich: Norfolk Chronicle.

John Melton. (1975) *Astrologaster, or the Figure-Caster* (1620) Los Angeles: Augustan Reprint Society.

Gervase Markham. (1986) *The English Housewife* (1615), Michael R. Best, ed. Montreal: McGill-Queen's University Press.

J. Fr. Neveau. (1774) *Arcandam's astrology, or book of destiny …, Translated from the French of J. Fr. Neveau*, London: J. Bew.

John Gough Nichols. (1859) *Narratives of the Days of the Reformation*. London: Camden Society.

G. F. Northall.(1892) *English Folk-Rhymes*. London: Kegan Paul, Trench, Trübner & Co.

John Walker Ord.(1846) *History and Antiquities of Cleveland*. London: Simpkin, Marshall.

Peter Padden. (2010) *A Grimoire for Modern Cunning Folk: A Practical Guide to Witchcraft on the Crooked Path*. Sunland, CA: Pendraig Publishing.

Paracelsus. (1975) *The Archidoxes of Magic by Paracelsus* (1656). London: Askin Publishers.

Joseph Frank Payne.(1904) *English Medicine in the Anglo-Saxon Times*, Oxford: Oxford University Press.

Edward Peacock. (1890) "A Welsh Conjuror – 1831" *Folklore* vol. I, pp. 131-133 .

William Perkins. (1615) *A Discourse of the Damned Art of Witchcraft*. Cambridge: Printed by Cantrell Legge.

"Philanthropist". *An account of the beginning, transactions, and discovery of Ransford Rogers, who seduced many by pretended hobgoblins and apparitions, and thereby extorted money from their pockets, in the county of Morris and state of New-Jersey in the year 1788.* (1876) Morristown, N.J. : L.A. Vogt.

William Ramesey. (1654) *An Introduction To The Judgement of the Stars. Wherein The Whole Art of Astrology Is plainly Taught.* London: Nathaniel Elkins.

David Rankine, ed. (2009) *The Book of Treasure Spirits.* London: Avelonia.

David Rankine, ed. (2011) *The Grimoire of Arthur Gauntlet.* London: Avelonia.

"Raphael". (1825) *The Astrologer of the Nineteenth Century.* London: Knight & Lacey.

"Raphael". (1832) *The Familiar Astrologer.* London: John Bennett.

"Raphael". (1837) *A Manual of Astrology or the Book of the Stars.* London: Thomas Tegg.

Dr. C.W. Roback. (1854) *The Mysteries of Astrology and Wonders of Magic.* Boston: Published by the Author.

Charles Roper. (1893) "On Witchcraft Superstition in Norfolk". *Harper's New Monthly Magazine*, vol. 87, issue 521, pp. 792-797.

Abraham Viktor Rydberg. (1879) *The Magic of the Middle Ages.* New York: Henry Holt.

Walter Rye. (1900) "A notebook of Sir Miles Branthwayt in 1605, *Norfolk Archaeology*, v. 14.

Reginal Scot. (1973) *The Discoverie of Witchcraft.* (1584/1651). Totowa, NJ: Rowman and Littlefield (reprint of 1886 edition).

Ebenezer Sibley. (1795) *The Complete Illustration of the Celestial Art of Astrology.* London: Champante and Whitrow, parts 1- 4 bound as one.

W. Sparrow Simpson. (1884) "On a Seventeenth Century Roll Containing Prayers and Magical Signs". *Journal of the British Archaeological Association*, London: For the Association, Vol. 40.

Godfrid Storms. *Anglo-Saxon Magic.* (1948) The Hague: M. Nijhoff.

Stanley J. Tambiah. (1968) "The Magical Power of Words", *Man, New Series*, Vol. 3, No. 2, pp. 175-208.

Jim Tester. (1987) *A History of Western Astrology.* Woodbridge, Suffolk: The Boydell Press.

Keith Thomas. (1971) *Religion and the Decline of Magic.* NY: Charles Scribner's Sons.

O. G. T. Treherne. (1907) "Notes on Eglwys Cymmyn, Parc-Y-Ceryg Sanctaidd, and Llandarwke", *Archaeologia Cambrensis* vol. 7 pt 3, pp. 267-276.

Wim van Binsbergen. (1996) "The astrological origin of Islamic geomancy" ('*Global and Multicultural Dimensions of Ancient and Medieval Philosophy and Social Thought: Africana, Christian, Greek, Islamic, Jewish, Indigenous and Asian Traditions*', Binghamton University, Department of Philosophy/ Centre for Medieval and Renaissance studies (CEMERS), October 1996)

Ernst von Dobschütz. (1913) "Charms and Amulets (Christian)." *Encylopedia of Religion and Ethics*, James Hastings, ed. Edinburgh: T. & T. Clark, vol. III, p. 425.

A. E. Waite. (1969) *The Book of Ceremonial Magic.* New York: Land's End Press.

D. P. Walker. (1958) *Spiritual and Demonic Magic from Ficino to Campanella.* London: Warburg Institute.

William Ward. (1592) *The Most Excellent and Profitable and pleasant book,, of the famous Doctor and expert Astrologian Aracandam or Aleandrin ... Now newly turned out of French into our vulgar tongue by William Warde.* London: Thomas Orwin.

Johann J. Wecker. (1661) *Eighteen Books of the Secrets of Art & Nature.* Dr. R. Read, ed. Printed for Simon Miller at the Starre in St. Pauls Church-yard.

W. Self Weeks. (1910) "Witch Stones and Charms in Clitheroe and District". *Transactions of the Lancashire and Cheshire Antiquarian Society*, vol. 27 (1909), Manchester: Richard Gill, pp. 105-06.

Johann Weyer. (1991) *Witches, Devils, and Doctors in the Renaissance [De Praestigiis Daemonum 1583].* Binghamton: Medieval & Renaissance Texts & Studies.

John White. (1859) *The Way to the True Church* (1624), cited in Choice Notes from "Notes and Queries": *Folklore.* London: Bell and Daldy

Kevin Wilby, ed. (1985) *The Lemegetton A Medieval Manual of Solomonic Magic.* Silian near Lampeter: Hermetic Research Series.

INDEX

A

A Collection of Highland Rites and Customs .158, See Bodleian Library MS Carte 269
A Discourse of the Subtill Practices of Deuilles by Witches 19
A Discovery of the Impostures of Witches and Astrologers 54
A Groatsworth of Wit for a Penny, Or, the Interpretation of Dreams 204
A Manual of the Chronicles of England 111
A New and Complete Illustration of the Celestial Science of Astrology 23
A New and Complete Illustration of the Occult Sciences 435, 460, 474
A Thousand Notable Things 203, 204, 309, 354
Abgarus V 291
Act against Conjuration, Witchcraft, and dealing with evil and wicked Spirits 1736 .... 22, 531
Additional MS 25311 235
Additional MS 36674 .... 238, 294
Aeneid 101
Agrippa, Cornelius 13, 15, 16, 21, 30, 31, 32, 33, 37, 38, 42, 46, 47, 55, 98, 161, 163, 171, 177, 178, 179, 180, 197, 200, 201, 272, 273, 339, 340, 342, 355, 362, 419, 433, 435, 438, 440, 441, 442, 446, 448, 449, 450, 453, 455, 461, 475, 516
Al Kindi 37, 38, 41, 42
Albertus Magnus .. 112, 201, 239, 242, 248, 250, 251, 252, 253, 255, 263, 281, 282, 288, 312, 313, 314, 315, 338, 340, 342, 501
Alcher of Clairvaux 44
Aldridge, L. Lloyd 112, 113
Alexander the Great 113, 336
All The Year Round Dream Books 204
Allen, Robert 283, 338
Anatomy of Melancholy 44
Antient Funeral Monuments 475
Aquinas, Thomas 38, 197
Arbatel 21, 435, 441, 445, 465
Arcandam 316, 326
Arcandum 14
Aristotle .. 27, 30, 35, 38, 44, 139, 165, 334, 335, 336
Aristotle's Experienced Midwife 335
Aristotle's Master-Piece 335
Ars Notoria 21, 33, 412
Art and Nature Joyn Hand in Hand ..245, 340, 538

Artemidorus Daldianus 196
Ashmole, Elias 412, 495
Astrampsychus 113, 200
Astrologaster, or the Figure-Caster 58
Astrologer's Magazine 405
Astrologia Restauratai, or Astrology Restored 366
Astrological Practice of Physick 245, 342
Astronomical Geomancy 21
Athenian Oracle 99
Aubrey, John 97, 302
Aunt Sally's Policy Players Dream Book 204, 205

B

Bacon, Roger 457
Bacon, William 470
Baker, Anne 316
Barrett, Francis .. 23, 48, 435, 438, 440, 454, 475
Bernard, Rev. Richard 95
Between the Living and the Dead 276
Blagrave, Joseph 24, 364
Blanchard, E. L. 405
Bodenham, Ann 62, 63, 434, 540
Bodin, Jean 44, 526
Bodleian Library MS Carte 269 158
Bodleian MS Canon, Misc 396 158
Bodleian MS D253 .... 338, 473
Bodleian MS Lat. liturg. e. 10 110
Bodleian. e Mus. 173 277
Boehme, Jacob 47
Book of Knowledge 103, 104, 109, 111, 125, 135, 146, 204, 319, 353
Books as Totems in Seventeenth-Century England and New England 101, 102
Bracken, 'Big Johnny' 74, 541
Brigg, Mabel 270
Briggs, Katherine ..231, 232, 238, 241, 248, 277, 282, 283, 294, 302, 311, 336, 542
Brinley, John 54
Britton, Thomas 436
Burchard of Worms 302
Burckhardt, Jacob 27
Burton, Robert 44

C

Calvin, John 19, 39, 95
Cambrensis, Giraldus 157
Campanella, Tommaso 15, 44, 342
Carmichael, Alexander 274, 291, 298, 356
Carmina Gadelica 274, 291

Catholic Encyclopedia 45
Celestial Planisphere 374
Cellini, Benvenuto 488, 490
Chaffer, Clayton 127
Charles I, King 101
Chettle, Henry 56
Chiero 144
Choice emblems, divine and moral, antient and modern 104
Christian Astrology ... 280, 342, 344, 364, 366, 375
Clark, Stuart 39, 41
Cockayne, Thomas O. 243
Cod. Gaster, No. 1562 .... 311, 538
Commiers, Claude 117
Complete Herbal 342
Compost of Ptolemeus 316, 320
Confessions 101
Conjuror's Magazine 405, 436
Corfield, John 405
Cressy, David 101, 102
Crowley, Aleister 32, 340, 533, 534, 535, 542, 543
Crowther, Timothy 24, 287, 538
Culpeper, Nicolas . 335, 342, 355, 358, 360, 498, 499
Cunning-Folk Popular Magic in English History 24

D

d'Este, Sorita 5, 13
Davies, Owen . 15, 22, 24, 25, 34, 43, 52, 54, 55, 203, 231, 232, 245, 255, 309, 362, 434, 436, 517, 522
De Arcanis Naturae 309
de Gebélin, Court 49
De Laurence, L. W. 519
De Nigromancia 457
De Occulta Philosophia .... See Three books of Occult Philosophy
De praestigiis daemonum 98
De Secretis Libri XVII 279
De Spiritu 44
De Vita Libri Tres 341
Decretum 302
Dee, John 13, 15, 16, 76, 96, 258, 309, 412, 495, 497
Defoe, Daniel 67
della Mirandola. Pico 13, 38
Della Porta, Giambattista 21
Démonomanie des sorciers 526
Denley, John 124, 434
Doesticks, Q. K. Philander 76

E

Egyptian Secrets 112, 239, 338, 340, 342
Eighteen Books of the Secrets of Art & Nature ... 201, 279, 340
Elizabeth I, Queen 258
Erra Pater ... 61, 94, 135, 204, 316, 319, 320, 333, 353, 354, 364
Evans, John 24, 73, 273, 491
Expositio Problematum 334

F

Ficino, Marsilio 13, 15, 16, 31, 33, 34, 37, 38, 40, 44, 340, 341, 342, 433, 448
Fludd, Robert 13, 164
Fontaine's Golden Wheel 100
Forman, Simon 24, 164, 338, 365, 376, 412
Fourth Book of Occult Philosophy . 21, 161, 232, 434, 435, 442, 445, 448, 450, 453, 465
Fox, Adam 43
Frazer, James 27

G

Gadbury, John 499, 500
Galen 27, 30, 44, 45, 62, 334
Gardner, Gerald 15, 533, 534, 542
Gauntlet, Arthur 5, 12, 88, 96, 201, 242, 279, 300, 310, 338, 434, 436, 438, 439, 440, 441, 446, 449, 453, 457, 460, 465, 502, 503
Genethlialogia 499, 500
Geomancie 161, 164, 165
George I, King 259
Gifford, George 19
Ginzburg, Carlo 13
Godwin, Jocelyn 49
Gospel of John 235, 414
Grafton, Richard 111
Graham, George W. 124
Grand Grimoire 454
Green, Hannah 540
Gypsy Dream Book 112
Gypsy's Witch Dream Book of Numbers 205

H

Harley MS.424 283
Harries, Henry 24, 538
Harries, John 24
Harvey, Gabriel 316
Henrietta Maria, Queen 356
Henry I, King 157
Henry VIII, King 270, 271, 497, 528

Heptameron 21, 433, 435, 438, 441, 442, 449, 450, 460, 465, 475
Herbarium of Apuleius 243
Heydon, C. 364, 375, 402, 405, 407, 409
Heydon, Thomas 164, 341
Hiebner, Israel 362
High German Fortune-teller 137, 144
Hill, Thomas 196, 197
Hohman, John George 49, 263, 280, 313, 519
Hoodoo – Conjuration – Witchcraft – Rootwork 84
Huebner, Louise 533, 534
Humier, François 413
Hutton, Ronald. 14, 15, 24, 25, 54, 56, 127, 517, 534, 543
Hyatt, Harry 55, 56, 84

I

Iliad 100
Illustration of Astrology 374
Introduction to Astrology 364, 375
Isagoge 21

K

Kelly, Edward 475
Keriomantia 135
Key of Solomon ... 98, 434, 436, 437, 438, 439, 440, 441, 446, 447, 448, 451, 454, 455, 457, 462, 502, 520, 536
Kieckhefer, Richard 412, 416, 432, 457
Kieckheffer, Richard 28, 416
Kind-Heart's Dream 56
King, Francis 15, 533, 543
Kirchenhoffer, H. 23, 120
Kircher, Athanasius 50
Kirk, Robert 157
Kirkwood, James 158
Kittredge, George Lyman 15, 24, 56, 97, 274, 534

L

Lacnunga 243
Lambe, John 24
Lansdowne MS 231 97
Latham, Charlotte 100
Le Marchand's Fortune Teller and Dream Book .. 130, 204, 301, 305
Le Marchand's Fortune Teller and Ladies' Love Oracle 144, 146
Le Marchand's Fortune-Teller and the Dreamer's Dictionary 130
Le Monde Primitif 49
Le Petit Albert 340

Leechbook of Bald 244
Leechdoms, Wortcunning, and Starcraft of Early England 243
Legends of Incense, Herb, and Oil Magic 519
Lemegeton 436, 441
Lemnius, Lævinus 335, 340
Lemoine, Henry 23
Levi, Eliphas 49, 98, 437, 454, 456
Lewis, C. S. 25, 31, 37, 41, 468
Liber III. De IVDICIIS ASTRORVM IN ELELECTIONIBVS, Or An Introduction to Elections 367
Lilly, William... 66, 135, 204, 280, 319, 342, 344, 346, 349, 350, 351, 364, 365, 366, 371, 375, 376, 402, 407, 408, 412, 490, 491, 497, 500, 502
Long Lost Friend 49, 280, 519
Long, Moses 436, 457, 473
Lovett, Edward 55
Lupton, Thomas 203, 309, 354

M

Macfarlane, Alan 24, 55
Macrobius 196, 197
Magic in Modern London 55
Magical Religion and Modern Witchcraft 15, 533
Magick and Astrology Vindicated 340
Maimonides 37
Manual of Astrology 364, 374, 402, 407
Maple, Eric 24, 517, 538, 543
Marie Laveau 55
Markham, Gervase 356, 358
Mather, Cotton 98, 413
Mathers, S. L. 436, 470, 519
McDonald, Sarah 203
Melanchthon 44
Melton, John 58
Menghi, Girolamo 413
Mesmer, Franz Anton 48, 49
Mizauld, Antonio 309
Mother Bombie 290
Mother Bunch's Closet Newly Broke Open .. 202, 301
Mother Bunch's Golden Fortune-Teller 131, 133, 301
Mother Shipton's Gipsy Fortune Teller and Dream Book 154
Mother Shipton's Gypsy Fortune Teller and Dream Book with Napoleon's Oraculum 204
MS. Bod. E Mus. 243 .... 248, 283, 302
Murray, Margaret 15, 533, 535
Mysteries of Magic 98
Mysterium sigillorum, herbarum & lapidum 362

N

Napier, Rev. Richard 361, 362, 365, 376
Napoleon's Book of Fate 124
Napoleon's Lucky Dream Book 126
Natural Magick 21
New Erra Pater 135
New Fortune-Book 127
Newton, Isaac 22
Notory Art .... 21, 94, *See* Ars Notoria

O

Old Aunt Dinah's Sure Guide to Lucky Numbers and Lucky Dreams 204
Old Gypsy Madge's Fortune Teller and the Witches Key to Lucky Dreams 204
On the Stellar Rays 38
Oneirocritica 196
Oneirocriticon 200
Urania 405
Original Book of Knowledge 102, 103, 104, 111, 154, 351
Oxley, Isabel 266

P

Paracelsus 24, 45, 47, 62, 196, 456
Parish, Mary 412, 457, 501, 511, 512, 513
Parker, Thomas 311
Parkins, John 23, 24
Parmenides 36
Perkins, William 96, 232, 360, 417
Perks, Thomas 491, 492
Peter of Abano 334
Peterson, Joseph H. ..5, 202, 237, 338, 419, 440, 519
Pettengill's Fortune Teller and Dream book 204
Plato 30, 36, 128
Power Through Witchcraft 533
Pratique Curieuse Ou Les Oracles Des Sibylles 117
Problems of Aristotle 335
Proclus 31
Psellus, Michael 418
Pseudo-Dionysius the Areopagite 418
Pseudo-Galen 28
Pseudomonarchia daemonum 419, 441
Ptolemy, Claudius 37, 113, 320
Pythagoras 96, 102, 109, 113, 139

R

Ramesey, William .. 366, 367, 369, 371, 375, 376
Rankine, David5, 12, 13, 97, 201, 242, 279, 280, 283, 284, 300, 301, 311, 436, 438, 439, 440, 446, 448, 449, 450, 453, 468, 470, 472, 503, 505, 508
Raphael
   Robert Cross Smith.... 23, 104, 108, 199, 202, 232, 236, 241, 287, 296, 312, 372, 407, 436, 450, 451, 454, 475, 476, 482, 488, 491, 495
Raphael's Witch 23, 124, 126, 127
Rawlinson MS D 253 .... 436, 457, 473
Religion and the Decline of Magic 15, 24, 47, 534, 538
Ritual Magic in England 15, 533, 534
Roback, C. W. 164, 180
Royal Book of Dreams 23, 199
Royal Book of Fate 23, 124
Rudd, Dr. 412

S

Saunders, Richard 146, 342
Savadage, Ann 436
Scot, Reginald19, 55, 97, 99, 238, 336, 340, 419, 434, 435, 436, 437, 439, 440, 448, 453, 462, 501, 505
Secret Miracles of Nature in Four Books 341
Secreta Secretorum 316, 334, 336
Seed, William 373, 374
Sepher Schimmush Tehillim 237
Shepherd's Kalendar....14, 103, 125, 319, 320, 352, 353, 501
Sibley, Ebenezer....... 23, 364, 435, 437, 438, 441, 447, 448, 450, 453, 454, 474, 502
Simmonite, William 407
Simon Magus 32
Sixth and Seventh Books of Moses .49, 55, 201, 202, 237, 520
Sloane MS 3824 502
Sloane MS 3850 311
Sloane MS 3851 .... 96, 201, 242, 300, 338, 436, 438, 439, 440, 449, 453
Smith, Jr., Joseph 515
Socrates 36, 128, 139
Somniale Danielis 200
Sortes Sanctorum 100, 101
South English Legendary 37
Spenser, Edmund 319
Spirit of Partridge 405
St. Adalbert 267
St. Anthony 253
St. Augustine 29, 38, 101, 267
St. Catherine 305
St. Elian 73, 273
St. Exuperus 253

St. Gabriel..288
St. George..294
St. Honorius...253
St. John . 236, 267, 284, 285, 287, 289, 298, 439, 448, 509
St. Michael...............................235, 267, 288
St. Paul...97, 98
St. Peter 97, 98, 250, 284, 288
St. Silvester..267
St. Stephen 267
St. Thomas 197, 202, 203
St. Trinian..270
Stapleton, William 336
Strangehopes, Sam 104
Swedenborg, Emanuel..............................47
Sworn Book of Honourius 457

T

Tamponelli, Tomaso...............................131
The Ancient Wheel of Fortune..................103
The Archidoxes of Magic.........................196
The Astrologer and Oracle of Destiny.......405
The Astrologer of the Nineteenth Century...... 23, 236, 405, 436, 450, 454, 475
The boke of secretes of Albertus Magnus................338
The Book of Fate 23, 120, 124, 127
The Book of Palmestry and Physiognomy..... 135, 143, 334
The Book of Secrets of Albertus Magnus................340
The Cabinet of Wealth 23
The Combination Fortune-Teller and Dictionary of Dreams...130
The Complete Illustration of the Celestial Art of Astrology 438, 441, 450, 453
The Complete Midwives's Practice 335
The Conjurors Magazine 23
The Connoisseur.............................. 301, 303
The Covntry-mans Covnsellor.................203
The Dark World of Witches.......................24
The Discoverie of Witchcraft.19, 232, 238, 336, 435, 436, 437, 439, 440, 448, 453, 460, 474
The Dodechedron of Fortune 114
The English Housewife 356, 358
The Examination of John Walsh or Welshe..........274
The Familiar Astrologer............... 23, 104, 111, 491
The Gipsy Dream Book and Fortune Teller..........126
The Golden Wheel Dream Book.............204
The High German Fortune-Teller........113, 129, 204
The History of Mother Bunch of The West............301
The Interpretation of Dreams Digested into Five Books by that Ancient and Excellent Philosopher, Artemidorus..204

The Knowledge of Things Unknown......................333
The Magus... 23, 48, 435, 438, 440, 442, 450, 454, 475
The Marriage of the Seven Arts...............................98
The Medicina De Quadrupedius of Sextus Placitus244
The Moste Pleasunte Arte of the Interpretacion of Dreames 196, 197
The Mysteries of Astrology and the Wonders of Magic 180
The New Astrology............................... 364, 402
The Philosophical Merlin..............................124
The Prognostic Astronomer or, Horary Astrology..............................407
The Pronostycacion for euer of Erra Pater 110
The Queen's Closet Opened 356, 358, 359
The Rise of Magic in Early Medieval Europe 34
The Secret Book of Black Arts.................... 112, 113
The Secret Commonwealth of Elves, Fauns, and Fairies... 157, 158
The Secret Miracle of Nature.........................335
The Straggling Astrologer 405
The Stripping of the Altars.............................17
The Temple of Cythnos.................................117
The Triumph of the Moon 24, 517
The Unerring Fortune-Teller 124
The Universal Fortune-Teller.........................23
The Urania, or, the Philosophical and Scientific Magazine 405
The Wide, Wide World and All The Year Round Dream Books 204
The Witches Dream Book and Fortune Teller.......126
The Witches of New York..........................76, 83
The Wonderful Magical Scrapbook 1450-1850...435, 436, 472, 473, 502, 538
Theocritus 97, 99, 537
Theomagia or the Temple of Wisdom 164
Thinking with Demons....................................39
Thomas, Keith . 24, 25, 47, 54, 55, 56, 161, 203, 233, 517, 534, 538
Thoreau, Henry..514
Three Books of Occult Philosophy .21, 197, 272, 342, 446, 449, 475
Trithemius.... 31, 33, 49, 106, 292, 436, 440, 475

U

Urania; or, the Astrologer's Chronicle, and Mystical Magazine 405
Urban VIII, Pope......................................342

W

Waite, A. E. 455, 456, 519
Walker, D. P. 44, 47, 342

Walton, Richard "Dick Spot" 24
Warren, Hardick 340
Watts, Ann 371, 436
Wecker, Johann Jacob 279
Weyer, Johann 98, 267, 419
Wharton, George 135
Wheel of Pythagoras 14, 104, 108, 124, 127
Whitmore, George 457, 512
Wicca Magical Beginnings 13
Wicherly, William 99
Wilson, Stephen 24
Witch Doctor's Dream Book and Fortune Teller .. 199, 204
Witchcraft Detected ... 232, 266, 279, 281, 285, 286, 287, 296, 304, 305, 309, 312, 340
Witchcraft in Old and New England 15, 24, 534
Witchcraft in Tudor and Stuart England 24
Witchcraft, Magic and Culture 1736-1951 24
Wonders of the Invisible World 98
Wrightson, John 540
Wyer, Robert 317, 319, 320, 333, 334

PUBLISHED BY AVALONIA
WWW.AVALONIABOOKS.CO.UK

www.ingramcontent.com/pod-product-compliance
Lightning Source LLC
Chambersburg PA
CBHW080720300426
44114CB00019B/2430